# PLA[...] FOOTBALL WHO'S WHO 1999

## JACK ROLLIN

HEADLINE

First published in 1998
by HEADLINE BOOK PUBLISHING

10 9 8 7 6 5 4 3 2 1



**Cover photographs** Left to right: Sol Campbell (Tottenham Hotspur), David Seaman (Arsenal), Paul Ince (Liverpool) (all *Allsport*), Brian Laudrup (Rangers) (*Action Images*)

ISBN 0 7472 6010 9

Typeset by Wearset, Boldon, Tyne and Wear

Printed and bound in Great Britain by
Mackays of Chatham PLC,
Chatham, Kent

HEADLINE BOOK PUBLISHING
A division of Hodder Headline PLC
338 Euston Road
London NW1 3BH

# THE AUTHOR

Jack Rollin was a soccer columnist for the *Sunday Telegraph* for twenty-one years, worked on BBC's *Match of the Day*, has written and compiled more than sixty books including twenty-six editions of *Rothmans Football Yearbook*. He is the soccer consultant to the *Encyclopaedia Britannica*.

The British Library's *A Football Compendium* said: 'Jack Rollin's classic *Soccer at War 1939–45* provides an extremely comprehensive account of one of the lesser known eras of soccer's rich history.'

In 1975 he won the Designers and Art Directors Association Silver Award for the outstanding specialist feature of the year, the *Radio Times World Cup Special*.

# PREFACE

The second edition of *Playfair Football Who's Who* contains career details of all players who appeared during the 1997–98 season in the FA Carling Premiership, Nationwide Football League and Bell's Scottish Premier Division, plus Dundee, the club promoted from the First Division. The book also includes players in England who were contracted to clubs in the four English divisions who did not make appearances. Players' information includes date and place of birth, height and weight where known, playing position, League appearances and goals scored, source and main honours achieved. Appearances include those made as a substitute. Players from foreign clubs with an asterisk * beside the team name indicates that club was outside its leading division that season.

The author would like to thank Glenda Rollin for her much valued contribution, Alan Elliott for Scottish League information and Gavin Willacy for England Schoolboy International details. The author also wishes to acknowledge the co-operation of Mike Foster and Mike Kelleher of the FA Premier League, and Sheila Andrew, Debbie Birch and Jonathan Hargreaves of the Football League. Once again a special mention for Lorraine Jerram of Headline Book Publishing, whose invaluable input was much appreciated.

The Football League welcome Halifax Town to the Third Division in 1998–99. The club's Vauxhall Conference appearances and goals can be found on page 442 and there is a Stop Press for summer transfers on the following two pages, 441 and 442.

# FOREWORD

The second edition of *Playfair Football Who's Who*, by Jack Rollin, maintains the long tradition of excellent football books produced by Headline, publishers of *Rothmans Football Yearbook*.

It is a difficult task these days to keep up to date with the changing face of personnel at clubs with the ever-increasing cosmopolitan nature of the game and Jack Rollin is to be congratulated on achieving this task successfully. There are precise details of professional players in England, Wales and Scotland which can be found by quick and easy alphabetical reference and the book provides all the information necessary for a football factfinder and devotees of fantasy football.

*Playfair Football Who's Who* will prove an invaluable help to all administrators, managers, soccer writers and supporters of football throughout the United Kingdom and will occupy a prominent place on my desk and I do not hesitate to recommend it.

Gordon Taylor

Gordon Taylor,

*Chief Executive, The Professional Footballers' Association*

## Out now . . .

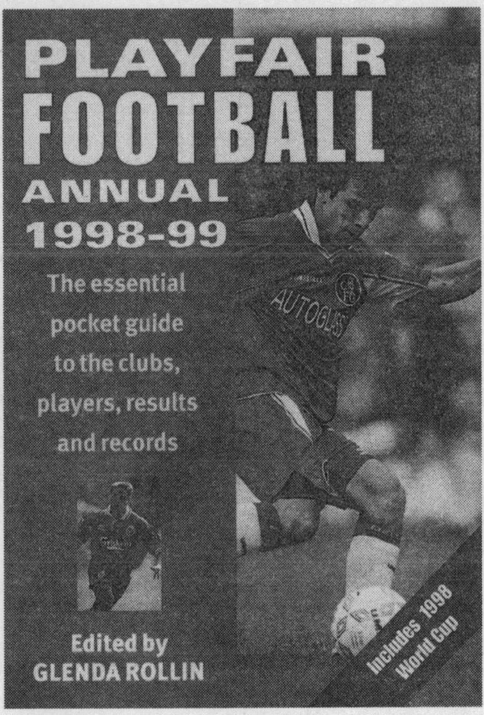


Published by Headline on 6 August 1998, price £4.99 (ISBN 0 7472 5917 8)

*All Headline books are available at your local bookshop or newsagent, or can be ordered direct from the publisher. Prices and availability subject to change without notice.*

## ABBEY, Nathan — Goalkeeper

H: 6 1 W: 11 13 b.Islington 11-7-78

*Source:* Trainee.

| Season | Club | Appearances | Goals |
|---|---|---|---|
| 1995–96 | Luton T | 0 | 0 |
| 1996–97 | Luton T | 0 | 0 |
| 1997–98 | Luton T | 0 | 0 |

## ABLETT, Gary — Defender

H: 6 0 W: 11 04 b.Liverpool 19-11-65

*Source:* Apprentice. *Honours:* England Under-21, B.

| Season | Club | Appearances | Goals |
|---|---|---|---|
| 1983–84 | Liverpool | 0 | 0 |
| 1984–85 | Liverpool | 0 | 0 |
| 1984–85 | Derby Co (loan) | 6 | 0 |
| 1985–86 | Liverpool | 0 | 0 |
| 1986–87 | Hull C (loan) | 5 | 0 |
| 1986–87 | Liverpool | 5 | 1 |
| 1987–88 | Liverpool | 17 | 0 |
| 1988–89 | Liverpool | 35 | 0 |
| 1989–90 | Liverpool | 15 | 0 |
| 1990–91 | Liverpool | 23 | 0 |
| 1991–92 | Liverpool | 14 | 0 |
| 1991–92 | Everton | 17 | 1 |
| 1992–93 | Everton | 40 | 0 |
| 1993–94 | Everton | 32 | 1 |
| 1994–95 | Everton | 26 | 3 |
| 1995–96 | Everton | 13 | 0 |
| 1995–96 | Sheffield U (loan) | 12 | 0 |
| 1996–97 | Birmingham C | 42 | 1 |
| 1997–98 | Birmingham C | 36 | 0 |
| **Total:** | | **338** | **7** |

## ABOU, Samassi — Forward

H: 6 0 W: 11 05 b.Gagnoa 4-8-73

*Honours:* Ivory Coast, full caps.

| Season | Club | Appearances | Goals |
|---|---|---|---|
| 1996–97 | Cannes | 27 | 4 |
| 1997–98 | Cannes | 10 | 1 |
| 1997–98 | West Ham U | 19 | 5 |
| **Total:** | | **56** | **10** |

## ABRAHAMS, Paul — Forward

H: 5 10 W: 11 00 b.Colchester 31-10-73

*Source:* Trainee.

| Season | Club | Appearances | Goals |
|---|---|---|---|
| 1991–92 | Colchester U | 0 | 0 |
| 1992–93 | Colchester U | 23 | 6 |
| 1993–94 | Colchester U | 4 | 0 |
| 1994–95 | Colchester U | 28 | 2 |
| 1994–95 | Brentford | 10 | 3 |
| 1995–96 | Brentford | 17 | 3 |
| 1995–96 | Colchester U (loan) | 8 | 2 |
| 1996–97 | Brentford | 8 | 2 |
| 1996–97 | Colchester U | 29 | 7 |
| 1997–98 | Colchester U | 25 | 7 |
| **Total:** | | **152** | **32** |

## ADAM, Stephane — Forward

H: 5 11 W: 12 00 b.Lille 15-5-69

*Source:* Creteil, Amiens.

| Season | Club | Appearances | Goals |
|---|---|---|---|
| 1995–96 | Metz | 19 | 1 |
| 1996–97 | Metz | 21 | 3 |
| 1997–98 | Hearts | 30 | 8 |
| **Total:** | | **70** | **12** |

## ADAMCZUK, Dariusz — Midfield

H: 5 10 W: 12 00 b.Stettin 20-10-69

*Source:* Eintracht Frankfurt.

| Season | Club | Appearances | Goals |
|---|---|---|---|
| 1993–94 | Dundee | 11 | 1 |
| From Pogon Stettin. | | | |
| 1995–96 | Dundee | 13 | 0 |
| 1996–97 | Dundee | 30 | 1 |
| 1997–98 | Dundee | 34 | 1 |
| **Total:** | | **88** | **3** |

## ADAMS, Kieran — Midfield

H: 5 11 W: 11 03 b.St Ives 20-10-77

*Source:* Trainee.

| Season | Club | Appearances | Goals |
|---|---|---|---|
| 1994–95 | Barnet | 4 | 0 |
| 1995–96 | Barnet | 1 | 0 |
| 1996–97 | Barnet | 3 | 0 |
| 1997–98 | Barnet | 11 | 1 |
| **Total:** | | **19** | **1** |

## ADAMS, Micky — Defender

H: 5 8 W: 11 11 b.Sheffield 8-11-61

*Source:* Apprentice. *Honours:* England Youth.

| Season | Club | Appearances | Goals |
|---|---|---|---|
| 1979–80 | Gillingham | 4 | 0 |
| 1980–81 | Gillingham | 13 | 0 |
| 1981–82 | Gillingham | 31 | 2 |
| 1982–83 | Gillingham | 44 | 3 |
| 1983–84 | Coventry C | 17 | 1 |
| 1984–85 | Coventry C | 31 | 3 |
| 1985–86 | Coventry C | 31 | 3 |
| 1986–87 | Coventry C | 11 | 2 |
| 1986–87 | Leeds U | 17 | 1 |
| 1987–88 | Leeds U | 40 | 0 |
| 1988–89 | Leeds U | 16 | 1 |
| 1988–89 | Southampton | 8 | 0 |
| 1989–90 | Southampton | 15 | 0 |
| 1990–91 | Southampton | 30 | 0 |
| 1991–92 | Southampton | 34 | 3 |
| 1992–93 | Southampton | 38 | 4 |

## Adams, Neil

| | | | |
|---|---|---|---|
| 1993–94 | Southampton | 19 | 0 |
| 1993–94 | Stoke C | 10 | 3 |
| 1994–95 | Fulham | 21 | 7 |
| 1995–96 | Fulham | 5 | 2 |
| 1996–97 | Fulham | 3 | 0 |
| 1997–98 | Fulham | 0 | 0 |
| 1997–98 | Swansea C | 0 | 0 |
| 1997–98 | Brentford | 0 | 0 |
| **Total:** | | **438** | **35** |

## ADAMS, Neil — Midfield

H: 5 8 W: 10 12 b.Stoke 23-11-65

*Source:* Local. *Honours:* England Under-21.

| | | | |
|---|---|---|---|
| 1985–86 | Stoke C | 32 | 4 |
| 1986–87 | Everton | 12 | 0 |
| 1987–88 | Everton | 8 | 0 |
| 1988–89 | Everton | 0 | 0 |
| 1988–89 | Oldham Ath (loan) | 9 | 0 |
| 1989–90 | Oldham Ath | 27 | 4 |
| 1990–91 | Oldham Ath | 31 | 6 |
| 1991–92 | Oldham Ath | 26 | 4 |
| 1992–93 | Oldham Ath | 32 | 9 |
| 1993–94 | Oldham Ath | 13 | 0 |
| 1993–94 | Norwich C | 14 | 0 |
| 1994–95 | Norwich C | 33 | 3 |
| 1995–96 | Norwich C | 42 | 2 |
| 1996–97 | Norwich C | 45 | 13 |
| 1997–98 | Norwich C | 30 | 4 |
| **Total:** | | **354** | **49** |

## ADAMS, Tony — Defender

H: 6 3 W: 13 11 b.London 10-10-66

*Source:* Apprentice. *Honours:* England Youth, Under-21, B, 55 full caps, 4 goals.

| | | | |
|---|---|---|---|
| 1983–84 | Arsenal | 3 | 0 |
| 1984–85 | Arsenal | 16 | 0 |
| 1985–86 | Arsenal | 10 | 0 |
| 1986–87 | Arsenal | 42 | 6 |
| 1987–88 | Arsenal | 39 | 2 |
| 1988–89 | Arsenal | 36 | 4 |
| 1989–90 | Arsenal | 38 | 5 |
| 1990–91 | Arsenal | 30 | 1 |
| 1991–92 | Arsenal | 35 | 2 |
| 1992–93 | Arsenal | 35 | 0 |
| 1993–94 | Arsenal | 35 | 0 |
| 1994–95 | Arsenal | 27 | 3 |
| 1995–96 | Arsenal | 21 | 1 |
| 1996–97 | Arsenal | 28 | 3 |
| 1997–98 | Arsenal | 26 | 3 |
| **Total:** | | **421** | **30** |

## ADAMSON, Christopher — Goalkeeper

H: 5 11 W: 11 00 b.Ashington 4-11-78

*Source:* Trainee.

| | | | |
|---|---|---|---|
| 1997–98 | WBA | 3 | 0 |
| **Total:** | | **3** | **0** |

## ADCOCK, Tony — Forward

H: 5 11 W: 11 05 b.Bethnal Green 27-3-63

*Source:* Apprentice.

| | | | |
|---|---|---|---|
| 1980–81 | Colchester U | 1 | 0 |
| 1981–82 | Colchester U | 40 | 5 |
| 1982–83 | Colchester U | 30 | 17 |
| 1983–84 | Colchester U | 43 | 26 |
| 1984–85 | Colchester U | 28 | 24 |
| 1985–86 | Colchester U | 33 | 15 |
| 1986–87 | Colchester U | 35 | 11 |
| 1987–88 | Manchester C | 15 | 5 |
| 1987–88 | Northampton T | 18 | 10 |
| 1988–89 | Northampton T | 46 | 17 |
| 1989–90 | Northampton T | 8 | 3 |
| 1989–90 | Bradford C | 28 | 5 |
| 1990–91 | Bradford C | 10 | 1 |
| 1990–91 | Northampton T | 21 | 3 |
| 1991–92 | Northampton T | 14 | 7 |
| 1991–92 | Peterborough U | 24 | 7 |
| 1992–93 | Peterborough U | 45 | 16 |
| 1993–94 | Peterborough U | 42 | 12 |
| 1994–95 | Luton T | 2 | 0 |
| 1995–96 | Colchester U | 41 | 12 |
| 1996–97 | Colchester U | 36 | 11 |
| 1997–98 | Colchester U | 25 | 5 |
| **Total:** | | **585** | **212** |

## ADEBOLA, Dele — Forward

H: 6 3 W: 12 08 b.Lagos 23-6-75

*Source:* Trainee.

| | | | |
|---|---|---|---|
| 1992–93 | Crewe Alex | 6 | 0 |
| 1993–94 | Crewe Alex | 0 | 0 |
| 1994–95 | Crewe Alex | 30 | 8 |
| 1995–96 | Crewe Alex | 29 | 8 |
| 1996–97 | Crewe Alex | 32 | 16 |
| 1997–98 | Crewe Alex | 27 | 7 |
| 1997–98 | Birmingham C | 17 | 7 |
| **Total:** | | **141** | **46** |

## AGGREY, Jimmy — Defender

H: 6 3 W: 13 06 b.London 26-10-78

*Source:* Chelsea Trainee.

| | | | |
|---|---|---|---|
| 1997–98 | Fulham | 0 | 0 |

## AGNEW, Paul — Defender

H: 5 9 W: 10 07 b.Lisburn 15-8-65

*Source:* Cliftonville. *Honours:* Northern Ireland Schools, Youth, Under-23.

| | | | |
|---|---|---|---|
| 1983–84 | Grimsby T | 1 | 0 |
| 1984–85 | Grimsby T | 12 | 0 |
| 1985–86 | Grimsby T | 16 | 0 |
| 1986–87 | Grimsby T | 29 | 0 |
| 1987–88 | Grimsby T | 38 | 1 |
| 1988–89 | Grimsby T | 34 | 0 |
| 1989–90 | Grimsby T | 24 | 2 |
| 1990–91 | Grimsby T | 7 | 0 |
| 1991–92 | Grimsby T | 24 | 0 |
| 1992–93 | Grimsby T | 23 | 0 |
| 1993–94 | Grimsby T | 23 | 0 |
| 1994–95 | Grimsby T | 10 | 0 |
| 1994–95 | WBA | 14 | 1 |
| 1995–96 | WBA | 3 | 0 |
| 1996–97 | WBA | 22 | 0 |
| 1997–98 | Swansea C | 7 | 0 |
| **Total:** | | **287** | **4** |

## AGNEW, Steve — Midfield

H: 5 9 W: 10 06 b.Shipley 9-11-65

*Source:* Apprentice.

| | | | |
|---|---|---|---|
| 1983–84 | Barnsley | 1 | 0 |
| 1984–85 | Barnsley | 10 | 1 |
| 1985–86 | Barnsley | 2 | 0 |
| 1986–87 | Barnsley | 33 | 0 |
| 1987–88 | Barnsley | 25 | 6 |
| 1988–89 | Barnsley | 39 | 6 |
| 1989–90 | Barnsley | 46 | 8 |
| 1990–91 | Barnsley | 38 | 8 |
| 1991–92 | Blackburn R | 2 | 0 |
| 1992–93 | Blackburn R | 0 | 0 |
| 1992–93 | Portsmouth (loan) | 5 | 0 |
| 1992–93 | Leicester C | 9 | 1 |
| 1993–94 | Leicester C | 36 | 3 |
| 1994–95 | Leicester C | 11 | 0 |
| 1994–95 | Sunderland | 16 | 2 |
| 1995–96 | Sunderland | 29 | 5 |
| 1996–97 | Sunderland | 15 | 2 |
| 1997–98 | Sunderland | 3 | 0 |
| **Total:** | | **320** | **42** |

## AGOGO, Manuel — Midfield

H: 5 9 W: 11 07 b.Accra 1-8-79

| | | | |
|---|---|---|---|
| 1996–97 | Sheffield W | 0 | 0 |
| 1997–98 | Sheffield W | 1 | 0 |
| **Total:** | | **1** | **0** |

## AINSWORTH, Gareth — Midfield

H: 5 8 W: 13 02 b.Blackburn 10-5-73

*Source:* Blackburn R Trainee.

| | | | |
|---|---|---|---|
| 1991–92 | Preston NE | 5 | 0 |
| 1992–93 | Cambridge U | 4 | 1 |
| 1992–93 | Preston NE | 26 | 0 |
| 1993–94 | Preston NE | 38 | 11 |
| 1994–95 | Preston NE | 16 | 1 |
| 1995–96 | Preston NE | 2 | 0 |
| 1995–96 | Lincoln C | 31 | 12 |
| 1996–97 | Lincoln C | 46 | 22 |
| 1997–98 | Lincoln C | 6 | 3 |
| 1997–98 | Port Vale | 40 | 5 |
| **Total:** | | **214** | **55** |

## AISTON, Sam — Midfield

H: 6 0 W: 12 01 b.Newcastle 21-11-76

*Source:* Newcastle U Trainee. *Honours:* England Schools.

| | | | |
|---|---|---|---|
| 1995–96 | Sunderland | 14 | 0 |
| 1996–97 | Sunderland | 2 | 0 |
| 1996–97 | Chester C (loan) | 14 | 0 |
| 1997–98 | Sunderland | 3 | 0 |
| **Total:** | | **33** | **0** |

## AKINBIYI, Ade — Forward

H: 6 0 W: 12 05 b.Greenwich 10-10-74

*Source:* Trainee.

| | | | |
|---|---|---|---|
| 1992–93 | Norwich C | 0 | 0 |
| 1993–94 | Norwich C | 2 | 0 |
| 1993–94 | Hereford U (loan) | 4 | 2 |
| 1994–95 | Norwich C | 13 | 0 |
| 1994–95 | Brighton & HA (loan) | 7 | 4 |
| 1995–96 | Norwich C | 22 | 3 |
| 1996–97 | Norwich C | 12 | 0 |
| 1996–97 | Gillingham | 19 | 7 |
| 1997–98 | Gillingham | 44 | 21 |
| **Total:** | | **123** | **37** |

## ALBERT, Philippe — Defender

H: 6 3 W: 12 04 b.Bouillon 10-8-67

*Honours:* Belgium 40 full caps, 5 goals.

| | | | |
|---|---|---|---|
| 1987–88 | Charleroi | 32 | 5 |
| 1988–89 | Charleroi | 33 | 2 |
| 1989–90 | Mechelen | 22 | 0 |
| 1990–91 | Mechelen | 32 | 3 |
| 1991–92 | Mechelen | 33 | 2 |
| 1992–93 | Anderlecht | 25 | 5 |
| 1993–94 | Anderlecht | 25 | 4 |
| 1994–95 | Newcastle U | 17 | 2 |
| 1995–96 | Newcastle U | 23 | 4 |

| | | | |
|---|---|---|---|
| 1996–97 | Newcastle U | 27 | 2 |
| 1997–98 | Newcastle U | 23 | 0 |
| **Total:** | | **292** | **29** |

## ALBERTZ, Jorg — Midfield

H: 6 2 W: 13 05 b.Moenchengladbach 29-1-71

*Honours:* Germany 2 full caps.

| | | | |
|---|---|---|---|
| 1990–91 | Fortuna Dusseldorf | 12 | 1 |
| 1991–92 | Fortuna Dusseldorf | 11 | 0 |
| 1992–93 | Fortuna Dusseldorf | 35 | 3 |
| 1993–94 | Hamburg | 31 | 4 |
| 1994–95 | Hamburg | 34 | 9 |
| 1995–96 | Hamburg | 34 | 9 |
| 1996–97 | Rangers | 32 | 10 |
| 1997–98 | Rangers | 31 | 10 |
| **Total:** | | **220** | **46** |

## ALCIDE, Colin — Midfield

H: 6 2 W: 13 11 b.Huddersfield 14-4-72

*Source:* Emley.

| | | | |
|---|---|---|---|
| 1995–96 | Lincoln C | 27 | 6 |
| 1996–97 | Lincoln C | 42 | 7 |
| 1997–98 | Lincoln C | 29 | 12 |
| **Total:** | | **98** | **25** |

## ALDERSON, Richard — Forward

H: 5 11 W: 12 00 b.Durham 27-1-75

*Source:* Spennymoor U.

| | | | |
|---|---|---|---|
| 1997–98 | York C | 1 | 0 |
| **Total:** | | **1** | **0** |

## ALDRIDGE, John — Forward

H: 5 11 W: 12 03 b.Liverpool 18-9-58

*Source:* South Liverpool. *Honours:* Eire 69 full caps, 19 goals.

| | | | |
|---|---|---|---|
| 1978–79 | Newport Co | 0 | 0 |
| 1979–80 | Newport Co | 38 | 14 |
| 1980–81 | Newport Co | 27 | 7 |
| 1981–82 | Newport Co | 36 | 11 |
| 1982–83 | Newport Co | 41 | 17 |
| 1983–84 | Newport Co | 28 | 20 |
| 1983–84 | Oxford U | 8 | 4 |
| 1984–85 | Oxford U | 42 | 30 |
| 1985–86 | Oxford U | 39 | 23 |
| 1986–87 | Oxford U | 25 | 15 |
| 1986–87 | Liverpool | 10 | 2 |
| 1987–88 | Liverpool | 36 | 26 |
| 1988–89 | Liverpool | 35 | 21 |
| 1989–90 | Liverpool | 2 | 1 |
| 1989–90 | Real Sociedad | 28 | 16 |
| 1990–91 | Real Sociedad | 35 | 17 |
| 1991–92 | Tranmere R | 43 | 22 |
| 1992–93 | Tranmere R | 30 | 21 |
| 1993–94 | Tranmere R | 34 | 21 |
| 1994–95 | Tranmere R | 33 | 24 |
| 1995–96 | Tranmere R | 45 | 27 |
| 1996–97 | Tranmere R | 43 | 18 |
| 1997–98 | Tranmere R | 14 | 5 |
| **Total:** | | **672** | **362** |

## ALDRIDGE, Martin — Forward

H: 5 11 W: 12 03 b.Northampton 6-12-74

*Source:* Trainee.

| | | | |
|---|---|---|---|
| 1991–92 | Northampton T | 5 | 0 |
| 1992–93 | Northampton T | 9 | 2 |
| 1993–94 | Northampton T | 29 | 8 |
| 1994–95 | Northampton T | 27 | 7 |
| 1995–96 | Northampton T | 0 | 0 |
| 1995–96 | Oxford U | 18 | 9 |
| 1996–97 | Oxford U | 30 | 8 |
| 1997–98 | Oxford U | 24 | 2 |
| 1997–98 | Southend U (loan) | 11 | 1 |
| **Total:** | | **153** | **37** |

## ALEXANDER, Graham — Midfield

H: 5 11 W: 12 02 b.Coventry 10-10-71

*Source:* Trainee.

| | | | |
|---|---|---|---|
| 1989–90 | Scunthorpe U | 0 | 0 |
| 1990–91 | Scunthorpe U | 1 | 0 |
| 1991–92 | Scunthorpe U | 36 | 5 |
| 1992–93 | Scunthorpe U | 41 | 5 |
| 1993–94 | Scunthorpe U | 41 | 4 |
| 1994–95 | Scunthorpe U | 40 | 4 |
| 1995–96 | Luton T | 37 | 1 |
| 1996–97 | Luton T | 45 | 2 |
| 1997–98 | Luton T | 39 | 8 |
| **Total:** | | **280** | **29** |

## ALEXANDERSSON, Niclas — Midfield

H: 6 2 W: 11 07 b.Halmstad 29-12-71

*Honours:* Sweden 21 full caps, 2 goals.

| | | | |
|---|---|---|---|
| 1990 | Halmstad | 22 | 2 |
| 1991 | Halmstad | 16 | 3 |
| 1992 | Halmstad* | 0 | 0 |
| 1993 | Halmstad | 25 | 4 |
| 1994 | Halmstad | 25 | 4 |
| 1995 | Halmstad | 26 | 5 |
| 1996 | IFK Gothenburg | 26 | 7 |
| 1997 | IFK Gothenburg | 26 | 6 |
| 1997–98 | Sheffield W | 6 | 0 |
| **Total:** | | **172** | **31** |

## ALJOFREE, Hasney — Defender

H: 6 0 W: 12 03 b.Manchester 11-7-78

*Source:* Trainee.

| | | | |
|---|---|---|---|
| 1996–97 | Bolton W | 0 | 0 |
| 1997–98 | Bolton W | 2 | 0 |
| **Total:** | | **2** | **0** |

## ALLAN, Derek — Defender

H: 5 11 W: 12 05 b.Irvine 24-12-74

*Source:* Ayr U BC.

| | | | |
|---|---|---|---|
| 1992–93 | Ayr U | 5 | 0 |
| 1992–93 | Southampton | 1 | 0 |
| 1993–94 | Southampton | 0 | 0 |
| 1994–95 | Southampton | 0 | 0 |
| 1995–96 | Southampton | 0 | 0 |
| 1995–96 | Brighton & HA (loan) | 8 | 0 |
| 1996–97 | Brighton & HA | 31 | 0 |
| 1997–98 | Brighton & HA | 19 | 1 |
| **Total:** | | **64** | **1** |

## ALLARDYCE, Craig — Defender

H: 6 2 W: 12 05 b.Bolton 9-6-75

*Source:* Trainee.

| | | | |
|---|---|---|---|
| 1992–93 | Preston NE | 1 | 0 |
| 1993–94 | Preston NE | 0 | 0 |
| 1994–95 | Blackpool | 0 | 0 |
| 1995–96 | Blackpool | 1 | 0 |
| From Chorley. | | | |
| 1997–98 | Chesterfield | 1 | 0 |
| **Total:** | | **3** | **0** |

## ALLEN, Alex — Defender

H: 6 1 W: 11 09 b.Mexborough 12-2-80

*Source:* Trainee.

| | | | |
|---|---|---|---|
| 1996–97 | Norwich C | 0 | 0 |
| 1997–98 | Norwich C | 0 | 0 |

## ALLEN, Bradley — Forward

H: 5 8 W: 11 00 b.Harold Wood 13-9-71

*Source:* School. *Honours:* England Youth, Under-21.

| | | | |
|---|---|---|---|
| 1988–89 | QPR | 1 | 0 |
| 1989–90 | QPR | 0 | 0 |
| 1990–91 | QPR | 10 | 2 |
| 1991–92 | QPR | 11 | 5 |
| 1992–93 | QPR | 25 | 10 |
| 1993–94 | QPR | 21 | 7 |
| 1994–95 | QPR | 5 | 2 |
| 1995–96 | QPR | 8 | 1 |
| 1995–96 | Charlton Ath | 10 | 3 |
| 1996–97 | Charlton Ath | 18 | 4 |
| 1997–98 | Charlton Ath | 12 | 2 |
| **Total:** | | **121** | **36** |

## ALLEN, Chris — Midfield

H: 5 11 W: 12 04 b.Oxford 18-11-72

*Source:* Trainee. *Honours:* England Under-21.

| | | | |
|---|---|---|---|
| 1990–91 | Oxford U | 0 | 0 |
| 1991–92 | Oxford U | 14 | 1 |
| 1992–93 | Oxford U | 31 | 3 |
| 1993–94 | Oxford U | 45 | 3 |
| 1994–95 | Oxford U | 36 | 2 |
| 1995–96 | Oxford U | 24 | 3 |
| 1995–96 | Nottingham F (loan) | 3 | 1 |
| 1996–97 | Nottingham F | 24 | 0 |
| 1997–98 | Nottingham F | 1 | 0 |
| 1997–98 | Luton T (loan) | 14 | 1 |
| **Total:** | | **192** | **14** |

## ALLEN, Graham — Defender

H: 6 1 W: 12 00 b.Bolton 8-4-77

*Source:* Trainee. *Honours:* England Youth.

| | | | |
|---|---|---|---|
| 1994–95 | Everton | 0 | 0 |
| 1995–96 | Everton | 0 | 0 |
| 1996–97 | Everton | 1 | 0 |
| 1997–98 | Everton | 5 | 0 |
| **Total:** | | **6** | **0** |

## ALLEN, Lee — Midfield

H: 5 10 W: 12 00 b.Islington 12-3-79

| | | | |
|---|---|---|---|
| 1997–98 | Leicester C | 0 | 0 |

## ALLEN, Martin — Midfield

H: 5 10 W: 11 00 b.Reading 14-8-65

*Source:* School. *Honours:* England Youth, Under-21, B, Football League.

| | | | |
|---|---|---|---|
| 1983–84 | QPR | 0 | 0 |
| 1984–85 | QPR | 5 | 0 |
| 1985–86 | QPR | 31 | 3 |
| 1986–87 | QPR | 32 | 5 |
| 1987–88 | QPR | 38 | 4 |
| 1988–89 | QPR | 28 | 4 |
| 1989–90 | QPR | 2 | 0 |
| 1989–90 | West Ham U | 39 | 9 |
| 1990–91 | West Ham U | 40 | 3 |
| 1991–92 | West Ham U | 19 | 0 |
| 1992–93 | West Ham U | 34 | 4 |
| 1993–94 | West Ham U | 26 | 6 |
| 1994–95 | West Ham U | 29 | 2 |

| | | | |
|---|---|---|---|
| 1995–96 | West Ham U | 3 | 1 |
| 1995–96 | Portsmouth | 27 | 4 |
| 1996–97 | Portsmouth | 4 | 0 |
| 1997–98 | Portsmouth | 14 | 0 |
| 1997–98 | Southend U (loan) | 5 | 0 |
| **Total:** | | **376** | **45** |

## ALLEN, Paul — Midfield

H: 5 7 W: 11 02 b.Aveley 28-6-62

*Source:* Apprentice. *Honours:* England Youth, Under-21.

| | | | |
|---|---|---|---|
| 1979–80 | West Ham U | 31 | 2 |
| 1980–81 | West Ham U | 3 | 1 |
| 1981–82 | West Ham U | 28 | 0 |
| 1982–83 | West Ham U | 33 | 0 |
| 1983–84 | West Ham U | 19 | 0 |
| 1984–85 | West Ham U | 38 | 3 |
| 1985–86 | Tottenham H | 33 | 1 |
| 1986–87 | Tottenham H | 37 | 3 |
| 1987–88 | Tottenham H | 39 | 3 |
| 1988–89 | Tottenham H | 37 | 1 |
| 1989–90 | Tottenham H | 32 | 6 |
| 1990–91 | Tottenham H | 36 | 3 |
| 1991–92 | Tottenham H | 39 | 3 |
| 1992–93 | Tottenham H | 38 | 3 |
| 1993–94 | Tottenham H | 1 | 0 |
| 1993–94 | Southampton | 32 | 1 |
| 1994–95 | Southampton | 11 | 0 |
| 1994–95 | Luton T (loan) | 4 | 0 |
| 1994–95 | Stoke C (loan) | 17 | 1 |
| 1995–96 | Southampton | 0 | 0 |
| 1995–96 | Swindon T | 27 | 0 |
| 1996–97 | Swindon T | 10 | 1 |
| 1996–97 | Bristol C | 14 | 0 |
| 1997–98 | Millwall | 28 | 0 |
| **Total:** | | **587** | **32** |

## ALLEN, Rory — Forward

H: 5 11 W: 11 02 b.Beckenham 17-10-77

*Source:* Trainee. *Honours:* England Under-21.

| | | | |
|---|---|---|---|
| 1995–96 | Tottenham H | 0 | 0 |
| 1996–97 | Tottenham H | 12 | 2 |
| 1997–98 | Tottenham H | 4 | 0 |
| 1997–98 | Luton T (loan) | 8 | 6 |
| **Total:** | | **24** | **8** |

## ALLISON, Wayne — Forward

H: 6 0 W: 14 00 b.Huddersfield 16-10-68

| | | | |
|---|---|---|---|
| 1986–87 | Halifax T | 8 | 4 |
| 1987–88 | Halifax T | 35 | 4 |
| 1988–89 | Halifax T | 41 | 15 |
| 1989–90 | Watford | 7 | 0 |
| 1990–91 | Bristol C | 37 | 6 |
| 1991–92 | Bristol C | 43 | 10 |
| 1992–93 | Bristol C | 39 | 4 |
| 1993–94 | Bristol C | 39 | 15 |
| 1994–95 | Bristol C | 37 | 13 |
| 1995–96 | Swindon T | 44 | 17 |
| 1996–97 | Swindon T | 41 | 11 |
| 1997–98 | Swindon T | 16 | 3 |
| 1997–98 | Huddersfield T | 27 | 6 |
| **Total:** | | **414** | **108** |

## ALLMAN, Anthony — Midfield

b.Sidcup 14-12-80

*Source:* Trainee. *Honours:* England Schools.

| | | | |
|---|---|---|---|
| 1997–98 | Charlton Ath | 0 | 0 |

## ALLON, Joe — Forward

H: 5 11 W: 13 00 b.Gateshead 12-11-66

*Source:* Trainee. *Honours:* England Youth.

| | | | |
|---|---|---|---|
| 1984–85 | Newcastle U | 1 | 0 |
| 1985–86 | Newcastle U | 3 | 1 |
| 1986–87 | Newcastle U | 5 | 1 |
| 1987–88 | Swansea C | 32 | 11 |
| 1988–89 | Swansea C | 2 | 0 |
| 1988–89 | Hartlepool U | 21 | 4 |
| 1989–90 | Hartlepool U | 45 | 18 |
| 1990–91 | Hartlepool U | 46 | 28 |
| 1991–92 | Chelsea | 11 | 2 |
| 1991–92 | Port Vale (loan) | 6 | 0 |
| 1992–93 | Chelsea | 3 | 0 |
| 1992–93 | Brentford | 24 | 6 |
| 1993–94 | Brentford | 21 | 13 |
| 1993–94 | Southend U (loan) | 3 | 0 |
| 1993–94 | Port Vale | 4 | 2 |
| 1994–95 | Port Vale | 19 | 7 |
| 1995–96 | Lincoln C | 4 | 0 |
| 1995–96 | Hartlepool U | 22 | 8 |
| 1996–97 | Hartlepool U | 30 | 9 |
| 1997–98 | Hartlepool U | 4 | 2 |
| **Total:** | | **306** | **112** |

## ALLOTT, Mark — Forward

H: 5 11 W: 12 05 b.Manchester 16-3-78

*Source:* Trainee.

| | | | |
|---|---|---|---|
| 1995–96 | Oldham Ath | 0 | 0 |
| 1996–97 | Oldham Ath | 5 | 1 |
| 1997–98 | Oldham Ath | 22 | 2 |
| **Total:** | | **27** | **3** |

## ALOISI, John — Forward

H: 6 0 W: 12 06 b.Australia 5-2-76

*Source:* Cremonese. *Honours:* Australia, 6 full caps, 1 goal.

| | | | |
|---|---|---|---|
| 1997–98 | Portsmouth | 38 | 12 |
| **Total:** | | **38** | **12** |

## ALSFORD, Julian — Defender

H: 6 2 W: 13 01 b.Poole 24-12-72

*Source:* Trainee.

| | | | |
|---|---|---|---|
| 1991–92 | Watford | 0 | 0 |
| 1992–93 | Watford | 5 | 0 |
| 1993–94 | Watford | 8 | 1 |
| 1994–95 | Chester C | 35 | 0 |
| 1995–96 | Chester C | 24 | 0 |
| 1996–97 | Chester C | 43 | 2 |
| 1997–98 | Chester C | 39 | 4 |
| 1997–98 | Dundee U | 3 | 0 |
| **Total:** | | **157** | **7** |

## ALSOP, Julian — Forward

H: 6 4 W: 14 03 b.Nuneaton 28-5-73

*Source:* Nuneaton, VS Rugby, RC Warwick, Tamworth, Halesowen T.

| | | | |
|---|---|---|---|
| 1996–97 | Bristol R | 16 | 3 |
| 1997–98 | Bristol R | 17 | 1 |
| 1997–98 | Swansea C (loan) | 12 | 3 |
| **Total:** | | **45** | **7** |

## ALVES, Paolo — Forward

H: 6 1 W: 11 07 b.Mateus Villareal 10-12-69

*Source:* Sporting Lisbon. *Honours:* Portugal 11 full caps, 7 goals.

| | | | |
|---|---|---|---|
| 1997–98 | West Ham U | 4 | 0 |
| **Total:** | | **4** | **0** |

## AMORUSO, Lorenzo — Defender

H: 6 2 W: 13 10 b.Bari 28-6-71

| | | | |
|---|---|---|---|
| 1988–89 | Bari | 3 | 0 |
| 1989–90 | Bari | 3 | 0 |
| 1990–91 | Bari | 5 | 1 |
| 1991–92 | Bari | 0 | 0 |
| 1991–92 | Mantova | 13 | 1 |
| 1992–93 | Bari | 0 | 0 |
| 1992–93 | Pescavo | 19 | 1 |
| 1993–94 | Bari | 37 | 3 |
| 1994–95 | Bari | 27 | 4 |
| 1995–96 | Fiorentina | 31 | 2 |
| 1996–97 | Fiorentina | 23 | 1 |
| 1997–98 | Rangers | 4 | 0 |
| **Total:** | | **165** | **13** |

## AMPADU, Kwame — Midfield

H: 5 10 W: 11 10 b.Bradford 20-12-70

*Source:* Belvedere, Trainee. *Honours:* Eire Youth, Under-21.

| | | | |
|---|---|---|---|
| 1988–89 | Arsenal | 0 | 0 |
| 1989–90 | Arsenal | 2 | 0 |
| 1990–91 | Arsenal | 0 | 0 |
| 1990–91 | Plymouth Arg (loan) | 6 | 1 |
| 1990–91 | WBA (loan) | 7 | 1 |
| 1991–92 | WBA | 21 | 3 |
| 1992–93 | WBA | 10 | 0 |
| 1993–94 | WBA | 11 | 0 |
| 1993–94 | Swansea C | 13 | 0 |
| 1994–95 | Swansea C | 44 | 6 |
| 1995–96 | Swansea C | 43 | 2 |
| 1996–97 | Swansea C | 29 | 4 |
| 1997–98 | Swansea C | 18 | 0 |
| **Total:** | | **204** | **17** |

## ANASTASIADIS, Konstantinos — Midfield

b.Sydney 4-8-78

*Source:* Univ NSW.

| | | | |
|---|---|---|---|
| 1997–98 | Scarborough | 0 | 0 |

## ANDERSON, Dale — Forward

H: 5 11 W: 11 12 b.Birmingham 10-11-79

*Source:* Trainee.

| | | | |
|---|---|---|---|
| 1996–97 | Nottingham F | 0 | 0 |
| 1997–98 | Nottingham F | 0 | 0 |

## ANDERSON, Derek — Defender

H: 6 0 W: 11 00 b.Paisley 15-5-72

*Source:* Kilwinning Rangers.

| | | | |
|---|---|---|---|
| 1993–94 | Kilmarnock | 0 | 0 |
| 1994–95 | Kilmarnock | 20 | 0 |
| 1995–96 | Kilmarnock | 28 | 0 |
| 1996–97 | Kilmarnock | 17 | 0 |
| 1997–98 | Kilmarnock | 1 | 0 |
| **Total:** | | **66** | **0** |

## ANDERSON, Iain — Forward

H: 5 8 W: 9 07 b.Glasgow 23-7-77

*Source:* X-Form. *Honours:* Scotland Under-21.

| | | | |
|---|---|---|---|
| 1994–95 | Dundee | 10 | 1 |

## Anderson, Ijah

| | | | |
|---|---|---|---|
| 1995–96 | Dundee | 17 | 0 |
| 1996–97 | Dundee | 35 | 5 |
| 1997–98 | Dundee | 36 | 6 |
| **Total:** | | **98** | **12** |

## ANDERSON, Ijah — Midfield

H: 5 8 W: 10 03 b.Hackney 30-12-75

*Source:* Tottenham H Trainee.

| | | | |
|---|---|---|---|
| 1994–95 | Southend U | 0 | 0 |
| 1995–96 | Brentford | 25 | 2 |
| 1996–97 | Brentford | 46 | 1 |
| 1997–98 | Brentford | 17 | 0 |
| **Total:** | | **88** | **3** |

## ANDERSON, Russell — Defender

H: 5 11 W: 10 09 b.Aberdeen 25-10-78

*Source:* Dyce Juniors. *Honours:* Scotland Under-21.

| | | | |
|---|---|---|---|
| 1996–97 | Aberdeen | 14 | 0 |
| 1997–98 | Aberdeen | 26 | 0 |
| **Total:** | | **40** | **0** |

## ANDERSSON, Anders — Midfield

H: 5 9 W: 11 09 b.Tomelilla 15-3-74

*Honours:* Sweden 9 full caps, 1 goal.

| | | | |
|---|---|---|---|
| 1991 | Malmo | 1 | 0 |
| 1992 | Malmo | 28 | 3 |
| 1993 | Malmo | 19 | 4 |
| 1994 | Malmo | 19 | 2 |
| 1995 | Malmo | 23 | 3 |
| 1996 | Malmo | 23 | 5 |
| 1997 | Malmo | 13 | 2 |
| 1997–98 | Blackburn R | 4 | 0 |
| **Total:** | | **130** | **19** |

## ANDERSSON, Andreas — Forward

H: 6 1 W: 12 01 b.Osterhoninge 10-4-74

*Source:* Hova. *Honours:* Sweden 17 full caps, 4 goals.

| | | | |
|---|---|---|---|
| 1993 | Tidaholm | 9 | 6 |
| 1994 | Degerfors | 14 | 3 |
| 1995 | Degerfors | 26 | 13 |
| 1996 | IFK Gothenburg | 26 | 19 |
| 1997 | IFK Gothenburg | 13 | 13 |
| 1997–98 | AC Milan | 13 | 1 |
| 1997–98 | Newcastle U | 12 | 2 |
| **Total:** | | **113** | **57** |

## ANDERSSON, Mikael — Forward

H: 5 8 W: 10 07 b.Orebro 21-3-71

| | | | |
|---|---|---|---|
| 1989 | Orebro | 1 | 0 |
| 1990 | Orebro | 0 | 0 |
| 1991 | Orebro | 10 | 1 |
| 1992 | Orebro | 15 | 1 |
| 1993 | Orebro | 18 | 0 |
| 1994 | Orebro | 26 | 2 |
| 1995 | Orebro | 18 | 4 |
| 1996 | Orebro | 25 | 1 |
| 1997 | Orebro | 24 | 0 |
| 1997–98 | Dundee U | 3 | 0 |
| **Total:** | | **140** | **9** |

## ANDERSSON, Thomas — Midfield

b.Koping 20-1-68

| | | | |
|---|---|---|---|
| 1997 | Vasteras | 25 | 6 |
| 1997–98 | St Johnstone | 3 | 0 |
| **Total:** | | **28** | **6** |

## ANDERTON, Darren — Forward

H: 6 1 W: 12 05 b.Southampton 3-3-72

*Source:* Trainee. *Honours:* England Youth, Under-21, B, 22 full caps, 6 goals.

| | | | |
|---|---|---|---|
| 1989–90 | Portsmouth | 0 | 0 |
| 1990–91 | Portsmouth | 20 | 0 |
| 1991–92 | Portsmouth | 42 | 7 |
| 1992–93 | Tottenham H | 34 | 6 |
| 1993–94 | Tottenham H | 37 | 6 |
| 1994–95 | Tottenham H | 37 | 5 |
| 1995–96 | Tottenham H | 8 | 2 |
| 1996–97 | Tottenham H | 16 | 3 |
| 1997–98 | Tottenham H | 15 | 0 |
| **Total:** | | **209** | **29** |

## ANDRADE, Jose — Forward

H: 5 11 W: 11 07 b.Gaboverde 1-6-70

*Source:* Academico.

| | | | |
|---|---|---|---|
| 1994–95 | Stoke C | 4 | 1 |
| 1995–96 | Stoke C | 0 | 0 |
| From Academico. | | | |
| 1997–98 | Stoke C | 12 | 1 |
| **Total:** | | **16** | **2** |

## ANDREWS, Ben — Defender

H: 6 0 W: 12 10 b.Burton-on-Trent 18-11-80

*Source:* Trainee.

| | | | |
|---|---|---|---|
| 1997–98 | Brighton & HA | 3 | 0 |
| **Total:** | | **3** | **0** |

## ANDREWS, Ian — Goalkeeper

H: 6 2 W: 14 01 b.Nottingham 1-12-64

*Source:* Apprentice. *Honours:* England Youth, Under-21.

| | | | |
|---|---|---|---|
| 1982–83 | Leicester C | 0 | 0 |
| 1983–84 | Leicester C | 2 | 0 |
| 1983–84 | Swindon T (loan) | 1 | 0 |
| 1984–85 | Leicester C | 31 | 0 |
| 1985–86 | Leicester C | 39 | 0 |
| 1986–87 | Leicester C | 42 | 0 |
| 1987–88 | Leicester C | 12 | 0 |
| 1988–89 | Celtic | 5 | 0 |
| 1988–89 | Leeds U (loan) | 1 | 0 |
| 1989–90 | Celtic | 0 | 0 |
| 1989–90 | Southampton | 3 | 0 |
| 1990–91 | Southampton | 1 | 0 |
| 1991–92 | Southampton | 1 | 0 |
| 1992–93 | Southampton | 0 | 0 |
| 1993–94 | Southampton | 5 | 0 |
| 1994–95 | Southampton | 0 | 0 |
| 1994–95 | Bournemouth | 38 | 0 |
| 1995–96 | Bournemouth | 26 | 0 |
| 1996–97 | Bournemouth | 0 | 0 |
| 1996–97 | Leicester C (loan) | 0 | 0 |
| 1997–98 | Leicester C | 0 | 0 |
| **Total:** | | **207** | **0** |

## ANDREWS, John — Defender

H: 6 1 W: 13 00 b.Cork 27-9-78

*Source:* Trainee.

| | | | |
|---|---|---|---|
| 1996–97 | Coventry C | 0 | 0 |
| 1997–98 | Coventry C | 0 | 0 |

## ANDREWS, Keith — Midfield

b.Dublin 13-9-80

*Source:* Trainee.

| | | | |
|---|---|---|---|
| 1997–98 | Wolverhampton W | 0 | 0 |

## ANDREWS, Wayne — Forward

H: 5 8 W: 11 07 b.Paddington 25-11-77

*Source:* Trainee.

| | | | |
|---|---|---|---|
| 1995–96 | Watford | 1 | 0 |
| 1996–97 | Watford | 25 | 4 |
| 1997–98 | Watford | 2 | 0 |
| **Total:** | | **28** | **4** |

## ANELKA, Nicolas — Forward

H: 5 11 W: 12 03 b.Versailles 14-3-79

*Honours:* France Youth, Under-21, 1 full cap.

| | | | |
|---|---|---|---|
| 1995–96 | Paris St Germain | 2 | 0 |
| 1996–97 | Paris St Germain | 8 | 1 |
| 1996–97 | Arsenal | 4 | 0 |
| 1997–98 | Arsenal | 26 | 6 |
| **Total:** | | **40** | **7** |

## ANGEL, Mark — Midfield

H: 5 10 W: 11 07 b.Newcastle 23-8-75

*Source:* Trainee.

| | | | |
|---|---|---|---|
| 1993–94 | Sunderland | 0 | 0 |
| 1994–95 | Sunderland | 0 | 0 |
| 1995–96 | Oxford U | 27 | 1 |
| 1996–97 | Oxford U | 24 | 2 |
| 1997–98 | Oxford U | 22 | 1 |
| **Total:** | | **73** | **4** |

## ANGELL, Brett — Forward

H: 6 2 W: 13 10 b.Marlborough 20-8-68

*Source:* Portsmouth, Cheltenham T.

| | | | |
|---|---|---|---|
| 1987–88 | Derby Co | 0 | 0 |
| 1988–89 | Stockport Co | 26 | 5 |
| 1989–90 | Stockport Co | 44 | 23 |
| 1990–91 | Southend U | 42 | 15 |
| 1991–92 | Southend U | 43 | 21 |
| 1992–93 | Southend U | 13 | 5 |
| 1993–94 | Southend U | 5 | 4 |
| 1993–94 | Everton (loan) | 1 | 0 |
| 1993–94 | Southend U | 12 | 2 |
| 1993–94 | Everton | 15 | 1 |
| 1994–95 | Everton | 4 | 0 |
| 1994–95 | Sunderland | 8 | 0 |
| 1995–96 | Sunderland | 2 | 0 |
| 1995–96 | Sheffield U (loan) | 6 | 2 |
| 1995–96 | WBA (loan) | 3 | 0 |
| 1996–97 | Sunderland | 0 | 0 |
| 1996–97 | Stockport Co | 34 | 15 |
| 1997–98 | Stockport Co | 45 | 18 |
| **Total:** | | **303** | **111** |

## ANNAND, Edward — Forward

H: 5 11 W: 11 01 b.Glasgow 24-3-73

*Source:* Sligo R.

| | | | |
|---|---|---|---|
| 1995–96 | Clyde | 35 | 21 |
| 1996–97 | Clyde | 29 | 21 |
| 1996–97 | Dundee | 5 | 2 |
| 1997–98 | Dundee | 34 | 12 |
| **Total:** | | **103** | **56** |

## ANNONI, Enrico — Defender

H: 5 10 W: 13 00 b.Gloussand 10-7-66

| | | | |
|---|---|---|---|
| 1982–83 | Seregno | 27 | 0 |
| 1983–84 | Como | 2 | 0 |
| 1984–85 | Como | 0 | 0 |
| 1985–86 | Sambened | 28 | 3 |
| 1986–87 | Sambened | 32 | 1 |
| 1987–88 | Como | 28 | 1 |
| 1988–89 | Como | 33 | 1 |
| 1989–90 | Como | 34 | 0 |
| 1990–91 | Torino | 22 | 1 |
| 1991–92 | Torino | 29 | 1 |
| 1992–93 | Torino | 25 | 0 |
| 1993–94 | Torino | 27 | 0 |
| 1994–95 | Torino | 24 | 0 |
| 1995–96 | Roma | 23 | 0 |
| 1996–97 | Roma | 12 | 0 |
| 1996–97 | Celtic | 3 | 0 |
| 1997–98 | Celtic | 20 | 0 |
| **Total:** | | **369** | **8** |

## ANSAH, Andy — Forward

H: 5 7 W: 10 07 b.Lewisham 19-3-69

*Source:* Crystal Palace.

| | | | |
|---|---|---|---|
| 1988–89 | Brentford | 7 | 2 |
| 1989–90 | Brentford | 1 | 0 |
| 1989–90 | Southend U | 7 | 1 |
| 1990–91 | Southend U | 40 | 9 |
| 1991–92 | Southend U | 40 | 9 |
| 1992–93 | Southend U | 30 | 7 |
| 1993–94 | Southend U | 27 | 7 |
| 1994–95 | Southend U | 9 | 0 |
| 1994–95 | Brentford (loan) | 3 | 1 |
| 1995–96 | Southend U | 4 | 0 |
| 1995–96 | Brentford (loan) | 6 | 1 |
| 1995–96 | Peterborough U | 2 | 1 |
| 1995–96 | Gillingham | 2 | 0 |
| 1996–97 | Leyton Orient | 2 | 0 |
| 1997–98 | Leyton Orient | 0 | 0 |
| 1997–98 | Brighton & HA | 14 | 3 |
| **Total:** | | **194** | **41** |

## ANSELL, Gary — Midfield

H: 5 10 W: 12 00 b.Redbridge 8-11-78

*Source:* Trainee.

| | | | |
|---|---|---|---|
| 1997–98 | Stockport Co | 0 | 0 |

## ANTHONY, Graham — Midfield

H: 5 7 W: 10 09 b.South Shields 9-8-75

*Source:* Trainee.

| | | | |
|---|---|---|---|
| 1993–94 | Sheffield U | 0 | 0 |
| 1994–95 | Sheffield U | 1 | 0 |
| 1995–96 | Sheffield U | 0 | 0 |
| 1995–96 | Scarborough (loan) | 2 | 0 |
| 1996–97 | Sheffield U | 2 | 0 |
| 1996–97 | Swindon T | 3 | 0 |
| 1997–98 | Plymouth Arg | 5 | 0 |
| 1997–98 | Carlisle U | 25 | 3 |
| **Total:** | | **38** | **3** |

## ANTHONY, Marc — Midfield

H: 5 6 W: 10 03 b.Edinburgh 28-3-78

*Source:* Celtic BC. *Honours:* Scotland Under-21, Under-18.

| | | | |
|---|---|---|---|
| 1995–96 | Celtic | 0 | 0 |
| 1996–97 | Celtic | 2 | 0 |
| 1997–98 | Celtic | 0 | 0 |
| 1997–98 | Tranmere R (loan) | 0 | 0 |
| **Total:** | | **2** | **0** |

## ANTHROBUS, Steve — Forward

H: 6 2 W: 12 06 b.Lewisham 10-11-68

| | | | |
|---|---|---|---|
| 1986–87 | Millwall | 0 | 0 |
| 1987–88 | Millwall | 3 | 0 |
| 1988–89 | Millwall | 3 | 0 |
| 1989–90 | Millwall | 15 | 4 |
| 1989–90 | Southend U (loan) | 0 | 0 |
| 1989–90 | Wimbledon | 10 | 0 |
| 1990–91 | Wimbledon | 3 | 0 |
| 1991–92 | Wimbledon | 10 | 0 |
| 1992–93 | Wimbledon | 5 | 0 |
| 1993–94 | Wimbledon | 0 | 0 |
| 1993–94 | Peterborough U (loan) | 2 | 0 |
| 1994–95 | Wimbledon | 0 | 0 |
| 1994–95 | Chester C (loan) | 7 | 0 |
| 1995–96 | Shrewsbury T | 39 | 10 |
| 1996–97 | Shrewsbury T | 33 | 6 |
| 1996–97 | Crewe Alex | 10 | 0 |
| 1997–98 | Crewe Alex | 30 | 6 |
| **Total:** | | **170** | **26** |

## APPLEBY, Matty — Defender

H: 5 7 W: 12 01 b.Middlesbrough 16-4-72

*Source:* Trainee.

| | | | |
|---|---|---|---|
| 1989–90 | Newcastle U | 0 | 0 |
| 1990–91 | Newcastle U | 1 | 0 |
| 1991–92 | Newcastle U | 18 | 0 |
| 1992–93 | Newcastle U | 0 | 0 |

| | | | |
|---|---|---|---|
| 1993–94 | Newcastle U | 1 | 0 |
| 1993–94 | Darlington (loan) | 10 | 1 |
| 1994–95 | Darlington | 36 | 1 |
| 1995–96 | Darlington | 43 | 6 |
| 1996–97 | Barnsley | 35 | 0 |
| 1997–98 | Barnsley | 15 | 0 |
| **Total:** | | **159** | **8** |

## APPLEBY, Ritchie — Forward

H: 5 9 W: 11 03 b.Stockton 18-9-75

*Source:* Trainee. *Honours:* England Youth.

| | | | |
|---|---|---|---|
| 1993–94 | Newcastle U | 0 | 0 |
| 1994–95 | Newcastle U | 0 | 0 |
| 1994–95 | Darlington (loan) | 0 | 0 |
| 1995–96 | Ipswich T | 3 | 0 |
| 1996–97 | Swansea C | 11 | 1 |
| 1997–98 | Swansea C | 35 | 3 |
| **Total:** | | **49** | **4** |

## APPLETON, Michael — Midfield

H: 5 8 W: 11 00 b.Salford 4-12-75

*Source:* Trainee.

| | | | |
|---|---|---|---|
| 1994–95 | Manchester U | 0 | 0 |
| 1995–96 | Manchester U | 0 | 0 |
| 1995–96 | Lincoln C (loan) | 4 | 0 |
| 1996–97 | Manchester U | 0 | 0 |
| 1996–97 | Grimsby T (loan) | 10 | 3 |
| 1997–98 | Preston NE | 38 | 2 |
| **Total:** | | **52** | **5** |

## ARBER, Mark — Defender

H: 6 1 W: 11 09 b.South Africa 9-10-77

*Source:* Trainee.

| | | | |
|---|---|---|---|
| 1995–96 | Tottenham H | 0 | 0 |
| 1996–97 | Tottenham H | 0 | 0 |
| 1997–98 | Tottenham H | 0 | 0 |

## ARCHDEACON, Owen — Defender

H: 5 7 W: 11 00 b.Greenock 4-3-66

*Source:* Gourock U. *Honours:* Scotland Youth, Under-21.

| | | | |
|---|---|---|---|
| 1982–83 | Celtic | 0 | 0 |
| 1983–84 | Celtic | 1 | 0 |
| 1984–85 | Celtic | 3 | 1 |
| 1985–86 | Celtic | 23 | 3 |
| 1986–87 | Celtic | 29 | 2 |
| 1987–88 | Celtic | 10 | 1 |
| 1988–89 | Celtic | 10 | 0 |
| 1989–90 | Barnsley | 21 | 3 |
| 1990–91 | Barnsley | 45 | 2 |
| 1991–92 | Barnsley | 40 | 6 |
| 1992–93 | Barnsley | 38 | 6 |
| 1993–94 | Barnsley | 42 | 2 |
| 1994–95 | Barnsley | 9 | 1 |
| 1995–96 | Barnsley | 38 | 3 |
| 1996–97 | Carlisle U | 46 | 6 |
| 1997–98 | Carlisle U | 18 | 4 |
| **Total:** | | **373** | **40** |

## ARCHER, Lee — Midfield

H: 5 6 W: 9 06 b.Bristol 6-11-72

*Source:* Trainee.

| | | | |
|---|---|---|---|
| 1991–92 | Bristol R | 5 | 0 |
| 1992–93 | Bristol R | 2 | 1 |
| 1993–94 | Bristol R | 37 | 5 |
| 1994–95 | Bristol R | 42 | 6 |
| 1995–96 | Bristol R | 19 | 1 |
| 1996–97 | Bristol R | 21 | 2 |
| 1997–98 | Bristol R | 0 | 0 |
| **Total:** | | **126** | **15** |

## ARCHER, Paul — Midfield

H: 5 8 W: 9 07 b.Leicester 25-4-78

*Source:* Trainee.

| | | | |
|---|---|---|---|
| 1994–95 | Nottingham F | 0 | 0 |
| 1995–96 | Nottingham F | 0 | 0 |
| 1996–97 | Nottingham F | 0 | 0 |
| 1997–98 | Nottingham F | 0 | 0 |

## ARCOS-DIAZ, Miguel — Forward

H: 5 6 W: 9 11 b.Loughborough 1-9-78

*Source:* Trainee.

| | | | |
|---|---|---|---|
| 1997–98 | Leicester C | 0 | 0 |

## ARDLEY, Neal — Midfield

H: 5 11 W: 11 09 b.Epsom 1-9-72

*Source:* Trainee. *Honours:* England Under-21.

| | | | |
|---|---|---|---|
| 1990–91 | Wimbledon | 1 | 0 |
| 1991–92 | Wimbledon | 8 | 0 |
| 1992–93 | Wimbledon | 26 | 4 |
| 1993–94 | Wimbledon | 16 | 1 |
| 1994–95 | Wimbledon | 14 | 1 |
| 1995–96 | Wimbledon | 6 | 0 |
| 1996–97 | Wimbledon | 34 | 2 |
| 1997–98 | Wimbledon | 34 | 2 |
| **Total:** | | **139** | **10** |

## ARENDSE, Andre — Goalkeeper

H: 6 4 W: 11 05 b.Cape Town 27-6-67

*Source:* Cape Town S. *Honours:* South Africa 27 full caps.

| | | | |
|---|---|---|---|
| 1997–98 | Fulham | 6 | 0 |
| **Total:** | | **6** | **0** |

## ARIS, Steve — Defender

H: 5 11 W: 11 06 b.London 27-7-79

| | | | |
|---|---|---|---|
| 1995–96 | Millwall | 0 | 0 |
| 1996–97 | Millwall | 0 | 0 |
| 1997–98 | Millwall | 0 | 0 |

## ARMITAGE, Gavin — Midfield

H: 5 10 W: 12 06 b.Maldon 2-9-78

*Source:* Trainee.

| | | | |
|---|---|---|---|
| 1997–98 | Colchester U | 0 | 0 |

## ARMSTRONG, Alun — Forward

H: 6 1 W: 12 02 b.Gateshead 22-2-75

*Source:* School.

| | | | |
|---|---|---|---|
| 1993–94 | Newcastle U | 0 | 0 |
| 1994–95 | Stockport Co | 45 | 14 |
| 1995–96 | Stockport Co | 46 | 13 |
| 1996–97 | Stockport Co | 39 | 9 |
| 1997–98 | Stockport Co | 29 | 12 |
| 1997–98 | Middlesbrough | 11 | 7 |
| **Total:** | | **170** | **55** |

## ARMSTRONG, Chris — Forward

H: 6 0 W: 12 10 b.Newcastle 19-6-71

*Source:* Llay Welfare. *Honours:* England B.

| | | | |
|---|---|---|---|
| 1988–89 | Wrexham | 0 | 0 |
| 1989–90 | Wrexham | 22 | 3 |
| 1990–91 | Wrexham | 38 | 10 |
| 1991–92 | Millwall | 25 | 4 |
| 1992–93 | Millwall | 3 | 1 |
| 1992–93 | Crystal Palace | 35 | 15 |
| 1993–94 | Crystal Palace | 43 | 22 |
| 1994–95 | Crystal Palace | 40 | 8 |
| 1995–96 | Tottenham H | 36 | 15 |
| 1996–97 | Tottenham H | 12 | 5 |
| 1997–98 | Tottenham H | 19 | 5 |
| **Total:** | | **273** | **88** |

## ARMSTRONG, Craig — Midfield

H: 5 11 W: 12 10 b.South Shields 23-5-75

*Source:* Trainee.

| | | | |
|---|---|---|---|
| 1992–93 | Nottingham F | 0 | 0 |
| 1993–94 | Nottingham F | 0 | 0 |
| 1994–95 | Nottingham F | 0 | 0 |
| 1994–95 | Burnley (loan) | 4 | 0 |
| 1995–96 | Nottingham F | 0 | 0 |
| 1995–96 | Bristol R (loan) | 14 | 0 |
| 1996–97 | Nottingham F | 0 | 0 |
| 1996–97 | Gillingham (loan) | 10 | 0 |
| 1996–97 | Watford (loan) | 15 | 0 |
| 1997–98 | Nottingham F | 18 | 0 |
| **Total:** | | **61** | **0** |

## ARMSTRONG, Dean — Midfield

b.Chiswick 7-9-79

*Source:* Trainee.

| | | | |
|---|---|---|---|
| 1997–98 | Cambridge U | 0 | 0 |

## ARMSTRONG, Gordon — Midfield

H: 6 0 W: 12 11 b.Newcastle 15-7-67

*Source:* Apprentice.

| | | | |
|---|---|---|---|
| 1984–85 | Sunderland | 4 | 0 |
| 1985–86 | Sunderland | 14 | 2 |
| 1986–87 | Sunderland | 41 | 5 |
| 1987–88 | Sunderland | 37 | 5 |
| 1988–89 | Sunderland | 45 | 8 |
| 1989–90 | Sunderland | 46 | 8 |
| 1990–91 | Sunderland | 35 | 6 |
| 1991–92 | Sunderland | 40 | 10 |
| 1992–93 | Sunderland | 45 | 3 |
| 1993–94 | Sunderland | 26 | 2 |
| 1994–95 | Sunderland | 15 | 1 |
| 1995–96 | Sunderland | 1 | 0 |
| 1995–96 | Bristol C (loan) | 6 | 0 |
| 1995–96 | Northampton T (loan) | 4 | 1 |
| 1996–97 | Bury | 32 | 2 |
| 1997–98 | Bury | 37 | 2 |
| **Total:** | | **428** | **55** |

## ARMSTRONG, Paul — Midfield

H: 5 10 W: 10 09 b.Dublin 5-10-78

*Source:* Trainee.

| | | | |
|---|---|---|---|
| 1997–98 | Brighton & HA | 20 | 0 |
| **Total:** | | **20** | **0** |

## ARMSTRONG, Simon — Midfield

H: 5 10 W: 11 02 b.Skegness 23-11-78

*Source:* Boston U.

| | | | |
|---|---|---|---|
| 1997–98 | Port Vale | 0 | 0 |

## ARNISON, Paul — Defender

H: 5 10 W: 10 12 b.Hartlepool 18-9-77

*Source:* Trainee.

| | | | |
|---|---|---|---|
| 1995–96 | Newcastle U | 0 | 0 |
| 1996–97 | Newcastle U | 0 | 0 |
| 1997–98 | Newcastle U | 0 | 0 |

## ARNOTT, Andy — Defender

H: 6 0 W: 13 03 b.Chatham 18-10-73

*Source:* Trainee.

| | | | |
|---|---|---|---|
| 1990–91 | Gillingham | 0 | 0 |
| 1991–92 | Gillingham | 19 | 2 |
| 1992–93 | Gillingham | 15 | 6 |
| 1992–93 | Manchester U (loan) | 0 | 0 |
| 1993–94 | Gillingham | 10 | 2 |
| 1994–95 | Gillingham | 28 | 2 |
| 1995–96 | Gillingham | 1 | 0 |
| 1995–96 | Leyton Orient | 19 | 3 |
| 1996–97 | Leyton Orient | 31 | 3 |
| 1997–98 | Fulham | 1 | 0 |
| **Total:** | | **124** | **18** |

## ARNOTT, Doug — Forward

H: 5 7 W: 10 07 b.Lanark 5-8-64

*Source:* Pollok Juniors.

| | | | |
|---|---|---|---|
| 1986–87 | Motherwell | 1 | 0 |
| 1987–88 | Motherwell | 2 | 0 |
| 1988–89 | Motherwell | 14 | 1 |
| 1989–90 | Motherwell | 30 | 5 |
| 1990–91 | Motherwell | 29 | 14 |
| 1991–92 | Motherwell | 26 | 8 |
| 1992–93 | Motherwell | 33 | 6 |
| 1993–94 | Motherwell | 29 | 8 |
| 1994–95 | Motherwell | 27 | 10 |
| 1995–96 | Motherwell | 27 | 3 |
| 1996–97 | Motherwell | 15 | 3 |
| 1997–98 | Motherwell | 7 | 1 |
| **Total:** | | **240** | **59** |

## ARPHEXAD, Pegguy — Goalkeeper

H: 6 2 W: 13 07 b.Abymes 18-5-73

*Source:* Brest.

| | | | |
|---|---|---|---|
| 1994–95 | Lens | 0 | 0 |
| 1995–96 | Lens | 3 | 0 |
| 1996–97 | Lens | 0 | 0 |
| 1997–98 | Leicester C | 6 | 0 |
| **Total:** | | **9** | **0** |

## ASABA, Carl — Forward

H: 6 1 W: 13 07 b.London 28-1-73

*Source:* Dulwich Hamlet.

| | | | |
|---|---|---|---|
| 1994–95 | Brentford | 0 | 0 |
| 1994–95 | Colchester U (loan) | 12 | 2 |
| 1995–96 | Brentford | 10 | 2 |
| 1996–97 | Brentford | 44 | 23 |
| 1997–98 | Reading | 32 | 8 |
| **Total:** | | **98** | **35** |

## ASANOVIC, Aljosa — Midfield

H: 6 1 W: 11 12 b.Split 14-12-65

*Honours:* Croatia 46 full caps, 3 goals.

| | | | |
|---|---|---|---|
| 1984–85 | Hajduk Split | 31 | 6 |
| 1985–86 | Hajduk Split | 29 | 3 |
| 1986–87 | Hajduk Split* | 0 | 0 |
| 1987–88 | Hajduk Split | 25 | 5 |
| 1988–89 | Hajduk Split | 31 | 14 |
| 1989–90 | Hajduk Split* | 0 | 0 |
| 1990–91 | Metz | 35 | 13 |
| 1991–92 | Cannes | 28 | 7 |
| 1992–93 | Montpellier | 13 | 2 |
| 1993–94 | Montpellier | 30 | 8 |
| 1994–95 | Hajduk Split | 21 | 5 |
| 1995–96 | Hajduk Split | 12 | 3 |
| 1996–97 | Derby Co | 34 | 6 |
| 1997–98 | Derby Co | 4 | 1 |
| **Total:** | | **293** | **73** |

## ASHBEE, Ian — Defender

H: 6 1 W: 13 04 b.Birmingham 6-9-76

*Source:* Trainee. *Honours:* England Youth.

| | | | |
|---|---|---|---|
| 1994–95 | Derby Co | 1 | 0 |
| 1995–96 | Derby Co | 0 | 0 |
| 1996–97 | Derby Co | 0 | 0 |
| 1996–97 | Cambridge U | 18 | 0 |
| 1997–98 | Cambridge U | 27 | 1 |
| **Total:** | | **46** | **1** |

## ASHBY, Barry — Defender

H: 6 1 W: 13 02 b.London 2-11-70

*Source:* Trainee.

| | | | |
|---|---|---|---|
| 1988–89 | Watford | 0 | 0 |
| 1989–90 | Watford | 18 | 1 |
| 1990–91 | Watford | 23 | 0 |

| | | | |
|---|---|---|---|
| 1991–92 | Watford | 21 | 0 |
| 1992–93 | Watford | 35 | 0 |
| 1993–94 | Watford | 17 | 2 |
| 1993–94 | Brentford | 8 | 1 |
| 1994–95 | Brentford | 40 | 1 |
| 1995–96 | Brentford | 33 | 1 |
| 1996–97 | Brentford | 40 | 1 |
| 1997–98 | Gillingham | 43 | 0 |
| **Total:** | | **278** | **7** |

## ASHCROFT, Lee — Forward

H: 5 10 W: 11 00 b.Preston 7-9-72

*Source:* Trainee. *Honours:* England Under-21.

| | | | |
|---|---|---|---|
| 1990–91 | Preston NE | 14 | 1 |
| 1991–92 | Preston NE | 38 | 5 |
| 1992–93 | Preston NE | 39 | 7 |
| 1993–94 | WBA | 21 | 3 |
| 1994–95 | WBA | 38 | 10 |
| 1995–96 | WBA | 26 | 4 |
| 1995–96 | Notts Co (loan) | 6 | 0 |
| 1996–97 | WBA | 5 | 0 |
| 1996–97 | Preston NE | 27 | 8 |
| 1997–98 | Preston NE | 37 | 14 |
| **Total:** | | **251** | **52** |

## ASHLEY, Neil — Midfield

H: 5 10 W: 10 10 b.Chesterfield 16-9-80

*Source:* Nottingham F Trainee.

| | | | |
|---|---|---|---|
| 1997–98 | Leicester C | 0 | 0 |

## ASHTON, Jon — Defender

H: 6 0 W: 12 00 b.Plymouth 4-8-79

*Source:* Trainee.

| | | | |
|---|---|---|---|
| 1997–98 | Plymouth Arg | 0 | 0 |

## ASKEY, John — Forward

H: 6 0 W: 12 02 b.Stoke 4-11-64

*Source:* Port Vale.

| | | | |
|---|---|---|---|
| 1997–98 | Macclesfield T | 39 | 6 |
| **Total:** | | **39** | **6** |

## ASPIN, Neil — Defender

H: 6 0 W: 13 12 b.Gateshead 12-4-65

*Source:* Apprentice.

| | | | |
|---|---|---|---|
| 1981–82 | Leeds U | 1 | 0 |
| 1982–83 | Leeds U | 15 | 0 |
| 1983–84 | Leeds U | 21 | 1 |
| 1984–85 | Leeds U | 32 | 1 |
| 1985–86 | Leeds U | 38 | 2 |
| 1986–87 | Leeds U | 41 | 1 |
| 1987–88 | Leeds U | 26 | 0 |
| 1988–89 | Leeds U | 33 | 0 |
| 1989–90 | Port Vale | 42 | 0 |
| 1990–91 | Port Vale | 41 | 1 |
| 1991–92 | Port Vale | 42 | 0 |
| 1992–93 | Port Vale | 35 | 0 |
| 1993–94 | Port Vale | 40 | 1 |
| 1994–95 | Port Vale | 37 | 0 |
| 1995–96 | Port Vale | 22 | 1 |
| 1996–97 | Port Vale | 33 | 0 |
| 1997–98 | Port Vale | 26 | 0 |
| **Total:** | | **525** | **8** |

## ASPINALL, Warren — Midfield

H: 5 9 W: 11 12 b.Wigan 13-9-67

*Source:* Apprentice. *Honours:* England Youth.

| | | | |
|---|---|---|---|
| 1984–85 | Wigan Ath | 10 | 1 |
| 1985–86 | Wigan Ath | 0 | 0 |
| 1985–86 | Everton | 1 | 0 |
| 1985–86 | Wigan Ath (loan) | 41 | 21 |
| 1986–87 | Everton | 6 | 0 |
| 1986–87 | Aston Villa | 12 | 3 |
| 1987–88 | Aston Villa | 32 | 11 |
| 1988–89 | Portsmouth | 40 | 11 |
| 1989–90 | Portsmouth | 3 | 0 |
| 1990–91 | Portsmouth | 33 | 4 |
| 1991–92 | Portsmouth | 24 | 4 |
| 1992–93 | Portsmouth | 27 | 2 |
| 1993–94 | Portsmouth | 5 | 0 |
| 1993–94 | Swansea C (loan) | 5 | 0 |
| 1993–94 | Bournemouth | 24 | 5 |
| 1994–95 | Bournemouth | 9 | 4 |
| 1994–95 | Carlisle U (loan) | 7 | 1 |
| 1995–96 | Carlisle U | 42 | 6 |
| 1996–97 | Carlisle U | 40 | 5 |
| 1997–98 | Carlisle U | 18 | 0 |
| 1997–98 | Brentford | 24 | 3 |
| **Total:** | | **403** | **81** |

## ASPRILLA, Faustino — Forward

H: 5 9 W: 11 03 b.Tulua 10-11-69

*Source:* Tulua, Nacional. *Honours:* Colombia 41 full caps, 16 goals.

| | | | |
|---|---|---|---|
| 1989 | Cucuta | 15 | 7 |
| 1990 | Nacional | 18 | 9 |
| 1991 | Nacional | 36 | 15 |
| 1992 | Nacional | 7 | 1 |
| 1992–93 | Parma | 26 | 7 |
| 1993–94 | Parma | 27 | 10 |
| 1994–95 | Parma | 25 | 6 |
| 1995–96 | Parma | 6 | 2 |

| | | | |
|---|---|---|---|
| 1995–96 | Newcastle U | 14 | 3 |
| 1996–97 | Newcastle U | 24 | 4 |
| 1997–98 | Newcastle U | 10 | 2 |
| **Total:** | | **208** | **66** |

## ATHERTON, Peter — Defender

H: 5 11 W: 13 13 b.Wigan 6-4-70

*Source:* Trainee. *Honours:* England Schools, Under-21.

| | | | |
|---|---|---|---|
| 1987–88 | Wigan Ath | 16 | 0 |
| 1988–89 | Wigan Ath | 40 | 1 |
| 1989–90 | Wigan Ath | 46 | 0 |
| 1990–91 | Wigan Ath | 46 | 0 |
| 1991–92 | Wigan Ath | 1 | 0 |
| 1991–92 | Coventry C | 35 | 0 |
| 1992–93 | Coventry C | 39 | 0 |
| 1993–94 | Coventry C | 40 | 0 |
| 1994–95 | Sheffield W | 41 | 1 |
| 1995–96 | Sheffield W | 36 | 0 |
| 1996–97 | Sheffield W | 37 | 2 |
| 1997–98 | Sheffield W | 27 | 3 |
| **Total:** | | **404** | **7** |

## ATKIN, Paul — Defender

H: 6 0 W: 13 00 b.Nottingham 3-9-69

*Source:* Trainee. *Honours:* England Schools, Youth.

| | | | |
|---|---|---|---|
| 1987–88 | Notts Co | 0 | 0 |
| 1988–89 | Notts Co | 0 | 0 |
| 1988–89 | Bury | 1 | 0 |
| 1989–90 | Bury | 9 | 1 |
| 1990–91 | Bury | 11 | 0 |
| 1991–92 | York C | 33 | 1 |
| 1992–93 | York C | 31 | 2 |
| 1993–94 | York C | 14 | 0 |
| 1994–95 | York C | 34 | 0 |
| 1995–96 | York C | 29 | 0 |
| 1996–97 | York C | 12 | 0 |
| 1996–97 | Leyton Orient (loan) | 5 | 0 |
| 1997–98 | Scarborough | 34 | 1 |
| **Total:** | | **213** | **5** |

## ATKINS, Mark — Midfield

H: 6 1 W: 12 00 b.Doncaster 14-8-68

*Honours:* England Schools.

| | | | |
|---|---|---|---|
| 1986–87 | Scunthorpe U | 26 | 0 |
| 1987–88 | Scunthorpe U | 22 | 2 |
| 1988–89 | Blackburn R | 46 | 6 |
| 1989–90 | Blackburn R | 41 | 7 |
| 1990–91 | Blackburn R | 42 | 4 |
| 1991–92 | Blackburn R | 44 | 6 |
| 1992–93 | Blackburn R | 31 | 5 |
| 1993–94 | Blackburn R | 15 | 1 |
| 1994–95 | Blackburn R | 34 | 6 |
| 1995–96 | Blackburn R | 4 | 0 |
| 1995–96 | Wolverhampton W | 32 | 3 |
| 1996–97 | Wolverhampton W | 45 | 4 |
| 1997–98 | Wolverhampton W | 34 | 2 |
| **Total:** | | **416** | **46** |

## ATKINSON, Brian — Midfield

H: 5 10 W: 12 10 b.Darlington 19-1-71

*Source:* Trainee. *Honours:* England Under-21.

| | | | |
|---|---|---|---|
| 1988–89 | Sunderland | 3 | 0 |
| 1989–90 | Sunderland | 13 | 0 |
| 1990–91 | Sunderland | 6 | 0 |
| 1991–92 | Sunderland | 30 | 2 |
| 1992–93 | Sunderland | 36 | 2 |
| 1993–94 | Sunderland | 29 | 0 |
| 1994–95 | Sunderland | 17 | 0 |
| 1995–96 | Sunderland | 7 | 0 |
| 1995–96 | Carlisle U (loan) | 2 | 0 |
| 1996–97 | Darlington | 30 | 3 |
| 1997–98 | Darlington | 32 | 1 |
| **Total:** | | **205** | **8** |

## ATKINSON, Graeme — Defender

H: 5 8 W: 11 05 b.Hull 11-11-71

*Source:* Trainee.

| | | | |
|---|---|---|---|
| 1989–90 | Hull C | 13 | 1 |
| 1990–91 | Hull C | 16 | 0 |
| 1991–92 | Hull C | 25 | 8 |
| 1992–93 | Hull C | 46 | 6 |
| 1993–94 | Hull C | 40 | 7 |
| 1994–95 | Hull C | 9 | 1 |
| 1994–95 | Preston NE | 15 | 1 |
| 1995–96 | Preston NE | 44 | 5 |
| 1996–97 | Preston NE | 17 | 0 |
| 1997–98 | Preston NE | 3 | 0 |
| 1997–98 | Rochdale (loan) | 6 | 0 |
| 1997–98 | Brighton & HA | 9 | 0 |
| **Total:** | | **243** | **29** |

## ATKINSON, Paddy — Defender

H: 5 9 W: 11 06 b.Singapore 22-5-70

*Source:* Sheffield U Trainee.

| | | | |
|---|---|---|---|
| 1988–89 | Hartlepool U | 13 | 3 |
| 1989–90 | Hartlepool U | 8 | 0 |
| From Workington. | | | |
| 1995–96 | York C | 22 | 0 |
| 1996–97 | York C | 14 | 0 |
| 1997–98 | York C | 5 | 0 |
| **Total:** | | **62** | **3** |

## AUGUSTINE, Steve — Midfield

H: 6 0 W: 13 07 b.Hammersmith 13-12-78

| | | | |
|---|---|---|---|
| 1997–98 | Luton T | 0 | 0 |

## AUNGER, Geoff — Midfield

H: 5 11 W: 11 09 b.Red Deer 4-2-68

*Source:* Ipswich Town, Vancouver 86ers. *Honours:* Canada full caps.

| | | | |
|---|---|---|---|
| 1993–94 | Luton T | 5 | 1 |
| 1994–95 | Chester C | 5 | 0 |
| From Seattle S. | | | |
| 1997–98 | Stockport Co | 1 | 0 |
| **Total:** | | **11** | **1** |

## AUSTIN, Dean — Defender

H: 6 0 W: 11 06 b.Hemel Hempstead 26-4-70

*Source:* St. *Honours:* Albans C.

| | | | |
|---|---|---|---|
| 1989–90 | Southend U | 7 | 0 |
| 1990–91 | Southend U | 44 | 0 |
| 1991–92 | Southend U | 45 | 2 |
| 1992–93 | Tottenham H | 34 | 0 |
| 1993–94 | Tottenham H | 23 | 0 |
| 1994–95 | Tottenham H | 24 | 0 |
| 1995–96 | Tottenham H | 28 | 0 |
| 1996–97 | Tottenham H | 15 | 0 |
| 1997–98 | Tottenham H | 0 | 0 |
| **Total:** | | **220** | **2** |

## AUSTIN, Kevin — Defender

H: 6 1 W: 14 00 b.Hackney 12-2-73

*Source:* Saffron Walden.

| | | | |
|---|---|---|---|
| 1993–94 | Leyton Orient | 30 | 0 |
| 1994–95 | Leyton Orient | 39 | 2 |
| 1995–96 | Leyton Orient | 40 | 1 |
| 1996–97 | Lincoln C | 44 | 1 |
| 1997–98 | Lincoln C | 46 | 0 |
| **Total:** | | **199** | **4** |

## AWFORD, Andy — Defender

H: 5 9 W: 11 09 b.Worcester 14-7-72

*Source:* Worcester C. *Honours:* England Schools, Youth, Under-21, Football League.

| | | | |
|---|---|---|---|
| 1988–89 | Portsmouth | 4 | 0 |
| 1989–90 | Portsmouth | 0 | 0 |
| 1990–91 | Portsmouth | 14 | 0 |
| 1991–92 | Portsmouth | 45 | 0 |
| 1992–93 | Portsmouth | 44 | 0 |
| 1993–94 | Portsmouth | 35 | 0 |
| 1994–95 | Portsmouth | 4 | 0 |
| 1995–96 | Portsmouth | 18 | 1 |
| 1996–97 | Portsmouth | 39 | 0 |
| 1997–98 | Portsmouth | 39 | 0 |
| **Total:** | | **242** | **1** |

## AYORINDE, Sam — Forward

H: 6 0 W: 12 07 b.Lagos 20-10-74

*Source:* Stade Tunisien, Sturm Graz.

| | | | |
|---|---|---|---|
| 1995–96 | Leyton Orient | 1 | 0 |
| 1996–97 | Leyton Orient | 12 | 2 |
| 1997–98 | Leyton Orient | 0 | 0 |
| **Total:** | | **13** | **2** |

## BAARDSEN, Espen — Goalkeeper

H: 6 5 W: 13 03 b.San Rafael 7-12-77

*Source:* San Francisco All Blacks. *Honours:* USA Youth, Norway Under-21, 1 full cap.

| | | | |
|---|---|---|---|
| 1996–97 | Tottenham H | 2 | 0 |
| 1997–98 | Tottenham H | 9 | 0 |
| **Total:** | | **11** | **0** |

## BABAYARO, Celestine — Defender

H: 5 9 W: 10 12 b.Kaduna 29-8-78

*Honours:* Nigeria 9 full caps.

| | | | |
|---|---|---|---|
| 1994–95 | Anderlecht | 22 | 0 |
| 1995–96 | Anderlecht | 28 | 5 |
| 1996–97 | Anderlecht | 25 | 3 |
| 1997–98 | Chelsea | 8 | 0 |
| **Total:** | | **83** | **8** |

## BABB, Phil — Defender

H: 6 0 W: 12 03 b.Lambeth 30-11-70

*Source:* Trainee. *Honours:* Eire B, 25 full caps.

| | | | |
|---|---|---|---|
| 1988–89 | Millwall | 0 | 0 |
| 1989–90 | Millwall | 0 | 0 |
| 1990–91 | Bradford C | 34 | 10 |
| 1991–92 | Bradford C | 46 | 4 |
| 1992–93 | Coventry C | 34 | 0 |
| 1993–94 | Coventry C | 40 | 3 |
| 1994–95 | Coventry C | 3 | 0 |
| 1994–95 | Liverpool | 34 | 0 |
| 1995–96 | Liverpool | 28 | 0 |
| 1996–97 | Liverpool | 22 | 1 |
| 1997–98 | Liverpool | 19 | 0 |
| **Total:** | | **260** | **18** |

## BADDELEY, Lee — Defender

H: 6 1 W: 12 07 b.Cardiff 2-7-74

*Source:* Trainee. *Honours:* Wales Under-21.

| | | | |
|---|---|---|---|
| 1990–91 | Cardiff C | 2 | 0 |
| 1991–92 | Cardiff C | 18 | 0 |
| 1992–93 | Cardiff C | 8 | 0 |
| 1993–94 | Cardiff C | 30 | 0 |
| 1994–95 | Cardiff C | 36 | 1 |
| 1995–96 | Cardiff C | 30 | 0 |
| 1996–97 | Cardiff C | 9 | 0 |
| 1996–97 | Exeter C | 11 | 0 |
| 1997–98 | Exeter C | 32 | 1 |
| **Total:** | | **176** | **2** |

## BAGAN, David — Midfield

H: 5 6 W: 9 07 b.Irvine 26-4-77

*Source:* Troon Juniors. *Honours:* Scotland Under-21.

| | | | |
|---|---|---|---|
| 1995–96 | Kilmarnock | 0 | 0 |
| 1996–97 | Kilmarnock | 17 | 0 |
| 1997–98 | Kilmarnock | 7 | 0 |
| **Total:** | | **24** | **0** |

## BAGSHAW, Paul — Forward

H: 5 7 W: 12 02 b.Sheffield 29-5-79

*Source:* Trainee.

| | | | |
|---|---|---|---|
| 1997–98 | Barnsley | 0 | 0 |

## BAIANO, Francesco — Forward

H: 5 6 W: 10 07 b.Naples 24-2-68

| | | | |
|---|---|---|---|
| 1985–86 | Napoli | 4 | 0 |
| 1986–87 | Empoli | 26 | 2 |
| 1987–88 | Napoli | 1 | 0 |
| 1987–88 | Parma | 25 | 4 |
| 1988–89 | Empoli | 38 | 14 |
| 1989–90 | Avellino | 32 | 6 |
| 1990–91 | Foggia | 36 | 22 |
| 1991–92 | Foggia | 33 | 16 |
| 1992–93 | Fiorentina | 31 | 10 |
| 1993–94 | Fiorentina | 11 | 4 |
| 1994–95 | Fiorentina | 27 | 2 |
| 1995–96 | Fiorentina | 28 | 11 |
| 1996–97 | Fiorentina | 21 | 2 |
| 1997–98 | Derby Co | 33 | 12 |
| **Total:** | | **346** | **105** |

## BAILEY, Alan — Forward

H: 5 9 W: 11 07 b.Macclesfield 1-11-78

*Source:* Trainee.

| | | | |
|---|---|---|---|
| 1997–98 | Manchester C | 0 | 0 |

## BAILEY, Danny — Midfield

H: 5 8 W: 12 11 b.Leyton 21-5-64

*Source:* Apprentice.

| | | | |
|---|---|---|---|
| 1980–81 | Bournemouth | 2 | 0 |
| Dagenham | | | |
| 1983–84 | Torquay U | 1 | 0 |
| From Wealdstone. | | | |
| 1989–90 | Exeter C | 46 | 1 |
| 1990–91 | Exeter C | 18 | 1 |
| 1990–91 | Reading | 26 | 2 |
| 1991–92 | Reading | 24 | 0 |
| 1992–93 | Reading | 0 | 0 |
| 1992–93 | Fulham (loan) | 3 | 0 |
| 1992–93 | Exeter C | 27 | 0 |
| 1993–94 | Exeter C | 34 | 0 |
| 1994–95 | Exeter C | 14 | 1 |
| 1995–96 | Exeter C | 42 | 1 |
| 1996–97 | Exeter C | 35 | 2 |
| 1997–98 | Exeter C | 0 | 0 |
| **Total:** | | **272** | **8** |

## BAILEY, Dennis — Forward

H: 5 10 W: 11 08 b.Lambeth 13-11-65

*Source:* Fulham, Farnborough T.

| | | | |
|---|---|---|---|
| 1987–88 | Crystal Palace | 5 | 1 |
| 1988–89 | Crystal Palace | 0 | 0 |
| 1988–89 | Bristol R (loan) | 17 | 9 |
| 1989–90 | Birmingham C | 43 | 18 |
| 1990–91 | Birmingham C | 32 | 5 |
| 1990–91 | Bristol R (loan) | 6 | 1 |
| 1991–92 | QPR | 24 | 9 |
| 1992–93 | QPR | 15 | 1 |
| 1993–94 | QPR | 0 | 0 |
| 1993–94 | Charlton Ath (loan) | 4 | 0 |
| 1993–94 | Watford (loan) | 8 | 4 |
| 1994–95 | QPR | 0 | 0 |
| 1994–95 | Brentford (loan) | 6 | 3 |
| 1995–96 | Gillingham | 45 | 8 |
| 1996–97 | Gillingham | 30 | 2 |
| 1997–98 | Gillingham | 13 | 1 |
| 1997–98 | Lincoln C | 5 | 1 |
| **Total:** | | **253** | **63** |

## BAILEY, John — Midfield

H: 5 8 W: 10 02 b.London 6-5-69

*Source:* Enfield.

| | | | |
|---|---|---|---|
| 1995–96 | Bournemouth | 44 | 4 |
| 1996–97 | Bournemouth | 40 | 1 |
| 1997–98 | Bournemouth | 32 | 1 |
| **Total:** | | **116** | **6** |

## BAILEY, Mark — Midfield

H: 5 7 W: 10 12 b.Stoke 12-8-76

*Source:* Trainee.

| | | | |
|---|---|---|---|
| 1994–95 | Stoke C | 0 | 0 |
| 1995–96 | Stoke C | 0 | 0 |
| 1996–97 | Stoke C | 0 | 0 |
| 1996–97 | Rochdale | 15 | 0 |
| 1997–98 | Rochdale | 33 | 0 |
| **Total:** | | **48** | **0** |

## BAIN, Kevin — Midfield

H: 5 11 W: 12 05 b.Kirkcaldy 19-9-72

| | | | |
|---|---|---|---|
| 1989–90 | Dundee | 1 | 0 |
| 1990–91 | Dundee | 0 | 0 |
| 1991–92 | Dundee | 0 | 0 |
| 1992–93 | Dundee | 24 | 0 |
| 1993–94 | Dundee | 7 | 0 |
| 1994–95 | Dundee | 20 | 1 |
| 1995–96 | Dundee | 10 | 1 |
| 1996–97 | Dundee | 12 | 0 |
| 1996–97 | Rotherham U | 12 | 0 |
| 1997–98 | Rotherham U | 0 | 0 |
| **Total:** | | **86** | **2** |

## BAIRD, Andrew — Defender

b.East Kilbride 18-1-79

*Source:* Trainee.

| | | | |
|---|---|---|---|
| 1997–98 | Wycombe W | 2 | 0 |
| **Total:** | | **2** | **0** |

## BAIRD, Ian — Forward

H: 6 0 W: 12 00 b.Rotherham 1-4-64

*Source:* Apprentice. *Honours:* England Schools.

| | | | |
|---|---|---|---|
| 1981–82 | Southampton | 0 | 0 |
| 1982–83 | Southampton | 11 | 2 |
| 1983–84 | Southampton | 6 | 1 |
| 1983–84 | Cardiff C (loan) | 12 | 6 |
| 1984–85 | Southampton | 5 | 2 |
| 1984–85 | Newcastle U (loan) | 5 | 1 |
| 1984–85 | Leeds U | 10 | 6 |
| 1985–86 | Leeds U | 35 | 12 |
| 1986–87 | Leeds U | 40 | 15 |
| 1987–88 | Portsmouth | 20 | 1 |
| 1987–88 | Leeds U | 10 | 3 |
| 1988–89 | Leeds U | 43 | 10 |
| 1989–90 | Leeds U | 24 | 4 |
| 1989–90 | Middlesbrough | 19 | 5 |
| 1990–91 | Middlesbrough | 44 | 14 |
| 1991–92 | Hearts | 30 | 6 |
| 1992–93 | Hearts | 34 | 9 |
| 1993–94 | Bristol C | 19 | 5 |
| 1994–95 | Bristol C | 37 | 6 |
| 1995–96 | Bristol C | 1 | 0 |
| 1995–96 | Plymouth Arg | 27 | 5 |
| 1996–97 | Brighton & HA | 35 | 13 |
| 1997–98 | Brighton & HA | 9 | 1 |
| **Total:** | | **476** | **127** |

## BAKER, Joe — Forward

H: 5 8 W: 10 07 b.London 9-4-77

*Source:* Charlton Ath Trainee.

| | | | |
|---|---|---|---|
| 1994–95 | Leyton Orient | 0 | 0 |
| 1995–96 | Leyton Orient | 20 | 0 |
| 1996–97 | Leyton Orient | 20 | 0 |
| 1997–98 | Leyton Orient | 31 | 3 |
| **Total:** | | **71** | **3** |

## BAKER, Martin — Defender

H: 6 0 W: 10 12 b.Govan 8-6-74

*Source:* St Mirren BC.

| | | | |
|---|---|---|---|
| 1992–93 | St Mirren | 29 | 0 |
| 1993–94 | St Mirren | 38 | 1 |
| 1994–95 | St Mirren | 26 | 2 |
| 1995–96 | St Mirren | 26 | 0 |
| 1996–97 | St Mirren | 31 | 0 |
| 1997–98 | Kilmarnock | 19 | 0 |
| **Total:** | | **169** | **3** |

## BAKER, Paul — Forward

H: 6 2 W: 14 07 b.Newcastle 5-1-63

*Source:* Bishop Auckland.

| | | | |
|---|---|---|---|
| 1984–85 | Southampton | 0 | 0 |
| 1985–86 | Carlisle U | 35 | 2 |
| 1986–87 | Carlisle U | 36 | 9 |
| 1987–88 | Hartlepool U | 39 | 19 |
| 1988–89 | Hartlepool U | 40 | 7 |
| 1989–90 | Hartlepool U | 43 | 16 |
| 1990–91 | Hartlepool U | 46 | 12 |
| 1991–92 | Hartlepool U | 29 | 13 |
| 1992–93 | Motherwell | 9 | 1 |
| 1992–93 | Gillingham | 21 | 6 |
| 1993–94 | Gillingham | 33 | 8 |
| 1994–95 | Gillingham | 8 | 2 |
| 1994–95 | York C | 30 | 13 |
| 1995–96 | York C | 18 | 5 |
| 1995–96 | Torquay U | 20 | 4 |
| 1996–97 | Torquay U | 10 | 4 |
| 1996–97 | Scunthorpe U | 21 | 9 |
| 1996–97 | Hartlepool U | 6 | 2 |
| 1997–98 | Hartlepool U | 16 | 5 |
| **Total:** | | **460** | **137** |

## BAKER, Steve — Defender

H: 5 10 W: 11 11 b.Pontefract 8-9-78

| | | | |
|---|---|---|---|
| 1997–98 | Middlesbrough | 6 | 0 |
| **Total:** | | **6** | **0** |

## BALDRY, Simon — Midfield

H: 5 9 W: 11 08 b.Huddersfield 12-2-76

*Source:* Trainee.

| | | | |
|---|---|---|---|
| 1993–94 | Huddersfield T | 10 | 2 |
| 1994–95 | Huddersfield T | 11 | 0 |
| 1995–96 | Huddersfield T | 14 | 0 |
| 1996–97 | Huddersfield T | 7 | 0 |
| 1997–98 | Huddersfield T | 11 | 1 |
| **Total:** | | **53** | **3** |

## BALL, Kevin — Midfield

H: 5 9 W: 11 06 b.Hastings 12-11-64

*Source:* Apprentice.

| | | | |
|---|---|---|---|
| 1983–84 | Portsmouth | 1 | 0 |
| 1984–85 | Portsmouth | 0 | 0 |
| 1985–86 | Portsmouth | 9 | 0 |
| 1986–87 | Portsmouth | 16 | 0 |
| 1987–88 | Portsmouth | 29 | 1 |
| 1988–89 | Portsmouth | 14 | 1 |
| 1989–90 | Portsmouth | 36 | 2 |
| 1990–91 | Sunderland | 33 | 3 |
| 1991–92 | Sunderland | 33 | 1 |
| 1992–93 | Sunderland | 43 | 3 |
| 1993–94 | Sunderland | 36 | 0 |
| 1994–95 | Sunderland | 42 | 2 |
| 1995–96 | Sunderland | 36 | 4 |
| 1996–97 | Sunderland | 32 | 3 |
| 1997–98 | Sunderland | 31 | 3 |
| **Total:** | | **391** | **23** |

## BALL, Michael — Midfield

b.Liverpool 2-10-79

*Source:* Trainee. *Honours:* England Schools, Youth.

| | | | |
|---|---|---|---|
| 1996–97 | Everton | 5 | 0 |
| 1997–98 | Everton | 25 | 1 |
| **Total:** | | **30** | **1** |

## BALMER, Stuart — Defender

H: 6 0 W: 12 11 b.Falkirk 20-9-69

*Source:* Celtic BC.

| | | | |
|---|---|---|---|
| 1987–88 | Celtic | 0 | 0 |
| 1988–89 | Celtic | 0 | 0 |
| 1989–90 | Celtic | 0 | 0 |
| 1990–91 | Charlton Ath | 24 | 0 |
| 1991–92 | Charlton Ath | 18 | 0 |
| 1992–93 | Charlton Ath | 45 | 2 |
| 1993–94 | Charlton Ath | 31 | 1 |
| 1994–95 | Charlton Ath | 29 | 2 |
| 1995–96 | Charlton Ath | 32 | 1 |
| 1996–97 | Charlton Ath | 32 | 2 |
| 1997–98 | Charlton Ath | 16 | 0 |
| **Total:** | | **227** | **8** |

## BANGER, Nicky — Forward

H: 5 8 W: 11 11 b.Southampton 25-2-71

*Source:* Trainee.

| | | | |
|---|---|---|---|
| 1988–89 | Southampton | 0 | 0 |
| 1989–90 | Southampton | 0 | 0 |
| 1990–91 | Southampton | 6 | 0 |
| 1991–92 | Southampton | 4 | 0 |
| 1992–93 | Southampton | 27 | 6 |
| 1993–94 | Southampton | 14 | 0 |
| 1994–95 | Southampton | 4 | 2 |
| 1994–95 | Oldham Ath | 28 | 3 |
| 1995–96 | Oldham Ath | 13 | 2 |
| 1996–97 | Oldham Ath | 23 | 5 |
| 1997–98 | Oxford U | 28 | 3 |
| **Total:** | | **147** | **21** |

## BANKOLE, Ademola — Goalkeeper

H: 6 3 W: 12 08 b.Lagos 9-9-69

*Source:* Leyton Orient.

| | | | |
|---|---|---|---|
| 1996–97 | Crewe Alex | 3 | 0 |
| 1997–98 | Crewe Alex | 3 | 0 |
| **Total:** | | **6** | **0** |

## BANKS, Steve — Goalkeeper

H: 6 0 W: 13 02 b.Hillingdon 9-2-72

*Source:* Trainee.

| | | | |
|---|---|---|---|
| 1991–92 | West Ham U | 0 | 0 |
| 1992–93 | West Ham U | 0 | 0 |
| 1993–94 | Gillingham | 29 | 0 |
| 1994–95 | Gillingham | 38 | 0 |
| 1995–96 | Blackpool | 24 | 0 |
| 1996–97 | Blackpool | 46 | 0 |
| 1997–98 | Blackpool | 45 | 0 |
| **Total:** | | **182** | **0** |

## BANNERMAN, Scott — Forward

H: 5 6 W: 10 04 b.Edinburgh 21-3-79

*Source:* Hutchison Vale BC.

| | | | |
|---|---|---|---|
| 1995–96 | Hibernian | 0 | 0 |

**Baraclough, Ian**

| | | | |
|---|---|---|---|
| 1996–97 | Hibernian | 0 | 0 |
| 1997–98 | Hibernian | 1 | 0 |
| **Total:** | | **1** | **0** |

## BARACLOUGH, Ian — Defender

H: 6 1 W: 12 02 b.Leicester 4-12-70

*Source:* Trainee.

| | | | |
|---|---|---|---|
| 1988–89 | Leicester C | 0 | 0 |
| 1989–90 | Leicester C | 0 | 0 |
| 1989–90 | Wigan Ath (loan) | 9 | 2 |
| 1990–91 | Leicester C | 0 | 0 |
| 1990–91 | Grimsby T (loan) | 4 | 0 |
| 1991–92 | Grimsby T | 0 | 0 |
| 1992–93 | Grimsby T | 1 | 0 |
| 1992–93 | Lincoln C | 36 | 5 |
| 1993–94 | Lincoln C | 37 | 5 |
| 1994–95 | Mansfield T | 36 | 3 |
| 1995–96 | Mansfield T | 11 | 2 |
| 1995–96 | Notts Co | 35 | 2 |
| 1996–97 | Notts Co | 38 | 2 |
| 1997–98 | Notts Co | 38 | 6 |
| 1997–98 | QPR | 8 | 0 |
| **Total:** | | **253** | **27** |

## BARCLAY, Dominic — Forward

H: 5 10 W: 11 07 b.Bristol 5-9-76

*Source:* Trainee.

| | | | |
|---|---|---|---|
| 1993–94 | Bristol C | 2 | 0 |
| 1994–95 | Bristol C | 0 | 0 |
| 1995–96 | Bristol C | 2 | 0 |
| 1996–97 | Bristol C | 0 | 0 |
| 1997–98 | Bristol C | 8 | 0 |
| **Total:** | | **12** | **0** |

## BARDSLEY, David — Defender

H: 5 10 W: 12 03 b.Manchester 11-9-64

*Source:* Apprentice. *Honours:* England Youth, 2 full caps.

| | | | |
|---|---|---|---|
| 1981–82 | Blackpool | 1 | 0 |
| 1982–83 | Blackpool | 28 | 0 |
| 1983–84 | Blackpool | 16 | 0 |
| 1983–84 | Watford | 25 | 0 |
| 1984–85 | Watford | 17 | 0 |
| 1985–86 | Watford | 13 | 2 |
| 1986–87 | Watford | 41 | 5 |
| 1987–88 | Watford | 4 | 0 |
| 1987–88 | Oxford U | 34 | 1 |
| 1988–89 | Oxford U | 37 | 6 |
| 1989–90 | Oxford U | 3 | 0 |
| 1989–90 | QPR | 31 | 1 |
| 1990–91 | QPR | 38 | 0 |
| 1991–92 | QPR | 41 | 0 |
| 1992–93 | QPR | 40 | 3 |
| 1993–94 | QPR | 32 | 0 |
| 1994–95 | QPR | 30 | 0 |
| 1995–96 | QPR | 29 | 0 |
| 1996–97 | QPR | 0 | 0 |
| 1997–98 | QPR | 12 | 0 |
| **Total:** | | **472** | **18** |

## BARKER, Richard — Forward

H: 6 0 W: 14 03 b.Sheffield 30-5-75

*Source:* Trainee. *Honours:* England Schools.

| | | | |
|---|---|---|---|
| 1993–94 | Sheffield W | 0 | 0 |
| 1994–95 | Sheffield W | 0 | 0 |
| 1995–96 | Sheffield W | 0 | 0 |
| 1995–96 | Doncaster R (loan) | 6 | 0 |
| 1996–97 | Sheffield W | 0 | 0 |
| From Linfield. | | | |
| 1997–98 | Brighton & HA | 17 | 2 |
| **Total:** | | **23** | **2** |

## BARKER, Simon — Midfield

H: 5 9 W: 11 07 b.Farnworth 4-11-64

*Source:* Apprentice. *Honours:* England Under-21.

| | | | |
|---|---|---|---|
| 1982–83 | Blackburn R | 0 | 0 |
| 1983–84 | Blackburn R | 28 | 3 |
| 1984–85 | Blackburn R | 38 | 2 |
| 1985–86 | Blackburn R | 41 | 10 |
| 1986–87 | Blackburn R | 42 | 11 |
| 1987–88 | Blackburn R | 33 | 9 |
| 1988–89 | QPR | 25 | 1 |
| 1989–90 | QPR | 28 | 3 |
| 1990–91 | QPR | 35 | 1 |
| 1991–92 | QPR | 34 | 6 |
| 1992–93 | QPR | 25 | 1 |
| 1993–94 | QPR | 37 | 5 |
| 1994–95 | QPR | 37 | 4 |
| 1995–96 | QPR | 33 | 5 |
| 1996–97 | QPR | 38 | 4 |
| 1997–98 | QPR | 23 | 3 |
| **Total:** | | **497** | **68** |

## BARLOW, Andy — Defender

H: 5 7 W: 11 01 b.Oldham 24-11-65

| | | | |
|---|---|---|---|
| 1984–85 | Oldham Ath | 33 | 0 |
| 1985–86 | Oldham Ath | 26 | 0 |
| 1986–87 | Oldham Ath | 29 | 2 |
| 1987–88 | Oldham Ath | 26 | 0 |
| 1988–89 | Oldham Ath | 15 | 0 |
| 1989–90 | Oldham Ath | 44 | 1 |
| 1990–91 | Oldham Ath | 46 | 0 |
| 1991–92 | Oldham Ath | 28 | 2 |
| 1992–93 | Oldham Ath | 6 | 0 |
| 1993–94 | Oldham Ath | 6 | 0 |

| | | | |
|---|---|---|---|
| 1993–94 | Bradford C (loan) | 2 | 0 |
| 1994–95 | Oldham Ath | 2 | 0 |
| 1995–96 | Blackpool | 34 | 1 |
| 1996–97 | Blackpool | 46 | 1 |
| 1997–98 | Rochdale | 38 | 0 |
| **Total:** | | **381** | **7** |

## BARLOW, Martin — Midfield

H: 5 7 W: 10 03 b.Barnstable 25-6-71

*Source:* Trainee.

| | | | |
|---|---|---|---|
| 1988–89 | Plymouth Arg | 1 | 0 |
| 1989–90 | Plymouth Arg | 1 | 0 |
| 1990–91 | Plymouth Arg | 30 | 1 |
| 1991–92 | Plymouth Arg | 28 | 3 |
| 1992–93 | Plymouth Arg | 24 | 1 |
| 1993–94 | Plymouth Arg | 26 | 2 |
| 1994–95 | Plymouth Arg | 42 | 2 |
| 1995–96 | Plymouth Arg | 28 | 5 |
| 1996–97 | Plymouth Arg | 40 | 1 |
| 1997–98 | Plymouth Arg | 42 | 4 |
| **Total:** | | **262** | **19** |

## BARLOW, Stuart — Forward

H: 5 10 W: 10 12 b.Liverpool 16-7-68

*Source:* School.

| | | | |
|---|---|---|---|
| 1990–91 | Everton | 2 | 0 |
| 1991–92 | Everton | 7 | 0 |
| 1991–92 | Rotherham U (loan) | 0 | 0 |
| 1992–93 | Everton | 26 | 5 |
| 1993–94 | Everton | 22 | 3 |
| 1994–95 | Everton | 11 | 2 |
| 1995–96 | Everton | 3 | 0 |
| 1995–96 | Oldham Ath | 26 | 7 |
| 1996–97 | Oldham Ath | 35 | 12 |
| 1997–98 | Oldham Ath | 32 | 12 |
| 1997–98 | Wigan Ath | 9 | 3 |
| **Total:** | | **173** | **44** |

## BARMBY, Nick — Forward

H: 5 6 W: 11 00 b.Hull 11-2-74

*Source:* Trainee. *Honours:* England Schools, Youth, Under-21, B, 10 full caps, 3 goals.

| | | | |
|---|---|---|---|
| 1991–92 | Tottenham H | 0 | 0 |
| 1992–93 | Tottenham H | 22 | 6 |
| 1993–94 | Tottenham H | 27 | 5 |
| 1994–95 | Tottenham H | 38 | 9 |
| 1995–96 | Middlesbrough | 32 | 7 |
| 1996–97 | Middlesbrough | 10 | 1 |
| 1996–97 | Everton | 25 | 4 |
| 1997–98 | Everton | 30 | 2 |
| **Total:** | | **184** | **34** |

## BARNARD, Darren — Defender

H: 5 6 W: 12 00 b.Rinteln 30-11-71

*Source:* Wokingham T. *Honours:* England Schools, Wales 1 full cap.

| | | | |
|---|---|---|---|
| 1990–91 | Chelsea | 0 | 0 |
| 1991–92 | Chelsea | 4 | 0 |
| 1992–93 | Chelsea | 13 | 1 |
| 1993–94 | Chelsea | 12 | 1 |
| 1994–95 | Chelsea | 0 | 0 |
| 1994–95 | Reading (loan) | 4 | 0 |
| 1995–96 | Chelsea | 0 | 0 |
| 1995–96 | Bristol C | 34 | 4 |
| 1996–97 | Bristol C | 44 | 11 |
| 1997–98 | Barnsley | 35 | 2 |
| **Total:** | | **146** | **19** |

## BARNARD, Mark — Defender

H: 5 11 W: 11 10 b.Sheffield 27-11-75

*Source:* Trainee.

| | | | |
|---|---|---|---|
| 1994–95 | Rotherham U | 0 | 0 |
| 1995–96 | Darlington | 37 | 3 |
| 1996–97 | Darlington | 37 | 0 |
| 1997–98 | Darlington | 36 | 0 |
| **Total:** | | **110** | **3** |

## BARNES, John — Midfield

H: 5 11 W: 12 07 b.Jamaica 7-11-63

*Source:* Sudbury Court. *Honours:* England Under-21, 79 full caps, 11 goals.

| | | | |
|---|---|---|---|
| 1981–82 | Watford | 36 | 13 |
| 1982–83 | Watford | 42 | 10 |
| 1983–84 | Watford | 39 | 11 |
| 1984–85 | Watford | 40 | 12 |
| 1985–86 | Watford | 39 | 9 |
| 1986–87 | Watford | 37 | 10 |
| 1987–88 | Liverpool | 38 | 15 |
| 1988–89 | Liverpool | 33 | 8 |
| 1989–90 | Liverpool | 34 | 22 |
| 1990–91 | Liverpool | 35 | 16 |
| 1991–92 | Liverpool | 12 | 1 |
| 1992–93 | Liverpool | 27 | 5 |
| 1993–94 | Liverpool | 26 | 3 |
| 1994–95 | Liverpool | 38 | 7 |
| 1995–96 | Liverpool | 36 | 3 |
| 1996–97 | Liverpool | 35 | 4 |
| 1997–98 | Newcastle U | 26 | 6 |
| **Total:** | | **573** | **155** |

## BARNES, Paul — Forward

H: 5 11 W: 13 05 b.Leicester 16-11-67

*Source:* Apprentice.

| Season | Club | Apps | Goals |
|---|---|---|---|
| 1985–86 | Notts Co | 14 | 4 |
| 1986–87 | Notts Co | 0 | 0 |
| 1987–88 | Notts Co | 11 | 2 |
| 1988–89 | Notts Co | 15 | 7 |
| 1989–90 | Notts Co | 13 | 1 |
| 1989–90 | Stoke C | 5 | 0 |
| 1990–91 | Stoke C | 6 | 0 |
| 1990–91 | Chesterfield (loan) | 1 | 0 |
| 1991–92 | Stoke C | 13 | 3 |
| 1992–93 | York C | 40 | 21 |
| 1993–94 | York C | 42 | 24 |
| 1994–95 | York C | 36 | 16 |
| 1995–96 | York C | 30 | 15 |
| 1995–96 | Birmingham C | 15 | 7 |
| 1996–97 | Birmingham C | 0 | 0 |
| 1996–97 | Burnley | 40 | 24 |
| 1997–98 | Burnley | 25 | 6 |
| 1997–98 | Huddersfield T | 15 | 1 |
| **Total:** | | **321** | **131** |

## BARNES, Phil — Goalkeeper

H: 6 1 W: 11 01 b.Rotherham 2-3-79

*Source:* Trainee.

| Season | Club | Apps | Goals |
|---|---|---|---|
| 1996–97 | Rotherham U | 2 | 0 |
| 1997–98 | Blackpool | 1 | 0 |
| **Total:** | | **3** | **0** |

## BARNES, Steve — Forward

H: 5 4 W: 10 05 b.Wembley 5-1-76

*Source:* Welling U.

| Season | Club | Apps | Goals |
|---|---|---|---|
| 1995–96 | Birmingham C | 3 | 0 |
| 1996–97 | Birmingham C | 0 | 0 |
| 1997–98 | Birmingham C | 0 | 0 |
| 1997–98 | Brighton & HA (loan) | 12 | 0 |
| **Total:** | | **15** | **0** |

## BARNESS, Anthony — Defender

H: 5 10 W: 11 11 b.Lewisham 25-2-73

*Source:* Trainee.

| Season | Club | Apps | Goals |
|---|---|---|---|
| 1990–91 | Charlton Ath | 0 | 0 |
| 1991–92 | Charlton Ath | 22 | 1 |
| 1992–93 | Charlton Ath | 5 | 0 |
| 1992–93 | Chelsea | 2 | 0 |
| 1993–94 | Chelsea | 0 | 0 |
| 1993–94 | Middlesbrough (loan) | 0 | 0 |
| 1994–95 | Chelsea | 12 | 0 |
| 1995–96 | Chelsea | 0 | 0 |
| 1995–96 | Southend U (loan) | 5 | 0 |
| 1996–97 | Charlton Ath | 45 | 2 |
| 1997–98 | Charlton Ath | 29 | 1 |
| **Total:** | | **120** | **4** |

## BARNETT, Christopher — Midfield

H: 5 11 W: 12 00 b.Derby 20-12-78

*Source:* Trainee.

| Season | Club | Apps | Goals |
|---|---|---|---|
| 1996–97 | Coventry C | 0 | 0 |
| 1997–98 | Coventry C | 0 | 0 |

## BARNETT, Dave — Defender

H: 6 1 W: 14 06 b.London 16-4-67

*Source:* Windsor & Eton.

| Season | Club | Apps | Goals |
|---|---|---|---|
| 1988–89 | Colchester U | 20 | 0 |
| 1989–90 | WBA | 0 | 0 |
| 1990–91 | Walsall | 5 | 0 |
| From Kidderminster H. | | | |
| 1991–92 | Barnet | 4 | 0 |
| 1992–93 | Barnet | 36 | 2 |
| 1993–94 | Barnet | 19 | 1 |
| 1993–94 | Birmingham C | 9 | 0 |
| 1994–95 | Birmingham C | 31 | 0 |
| 1995–96 | Birmingham C | 0 | 0 |
| 1996–97 | Birmingham C | 6 | 0 |
| 1997–98 | Dunfermline Ath | 21 | 1 |
| 1997–98 | Port Vale | 9 | 1 |
| **Total:** | | **160** | **5** |

## BARNETT, Jason — Defender

H: 5 9 W: 10 10 b.Shrewsbury 21-4-76

*Source:* Trainee.

| Season | Club | Apps | Goals |
|---|---|---|---|
| 1994–95 | Wolverhampton W | 0 | 0 |
| 1995–96 | Wolverhampton W | 0 | 0 |
| 1995–96 | Lincoln C | 32 | 2 |
| 1996–97 | Lincoln C | 36 | 0 |
| 1997–98 | Lincoln C | 33 | 0 |
| **Total:** | | **101** | **2** |

## BARNWELL-EDINBORO, Jamie — Forward

H: 5 11 W: 11 10 b.Hull 26-12-75

*Source:* Trainee.

| Season | Club | Apps | Goals |
|---|---|---|---|
| 1994–95 | Coventry C | 0 | 0 |
| 1995–96 | Coventry C | 1 | 0 |
| 1995–96 | Swansea C (loan) | 4 | 0 |
| 1995–96 | Wigan Ath (loan) | 10 | 1 |
| 1995–96 | Cambridge U | 7 | 2 |

| | | | |
|---|---|---|---|
| 1996–97 | Cambridge U | 40 | 6 |
| 1997–98 | Cambridge U | 16 | 4 |
| **Total:** | | **78** | **13** |

## BARR, Andrew — Forward

H: 5 11 W: 11 12 b.Solihull 21-6-79

*Source:* Trainee.

| | | | |
|---|---|---|---|
| 1997–98 | Luton T | 0 | 0 |

## BARR, Billy — Midfield

H: 5 11 W: 10 08 b.Halifax 21-1-69

*Source:* Trainee.

| | | | |
|---|---|---|---|
| 1987–88 | Halifax T | 30 | 0 |
| 1988–89 | Halifax T | 43 | 4 |
| 1989–90 | Halifax T | 23 | 2 |
| 1990–91 | Halifax T | 37 | 1 |
| 1991–92 | Halifax T | 35 | 3 |
| 1992–93 | Halifax T | 28 | 3 |
| From Halifax T. | | | |
| 1994–95 | Crewe Alex | 34 | 2 |
| 1995–96 | Crewe Alex | 17 | 0 |
| 1996–97 | Crewe Alex | 34 | 5 |
| 1997–98 | Carlisle U | 39 | 3 |
| **Total:** | | **320** | **23** |

## BARRAS, Tony — Defender

H: 6 0 W: 13 00 b.Stockton 29-3-71

*Source:* Trainee.

| | | | |
|---|---|---|---|
| 1988–89 | Hartlepool U | 3 | 0 |
| 1989–90 | Hartlepool U | 9 | 0 |
| 1990–91 | Stockport Co | 40 | 0 |
| 1991–92 | Stockport Co | 42 | 5 |
| 1992–93 | Stockport Co | 14 | 0 |
| 1993–94 | Stockport Co | 3 | 0 |
| 1993–94 | Rotherham U (loan) | 5 | 1 |
| 1994–95 | York C | 31 | 1 |
| 1995–96 | York C | 32 | 3 |
| 1996–97 | York C | 46 | 1 |
| 1997–98 | York C | 38 | 6 |
| **Total:** | | **263** | **17** |

## BARRETT, Earl — Defender

H: 5 10 W: 11 02 b.Rochdale 28-4-67

*Source:* Apprentice. *Honours:* England Under-21, B, 3 full caps.

| | | | |
|---|---|---|---|
| 1984–85 | Manchester C | 0 | 0 |
| 1985–86 | Manchester C | 1 | 0 |
| 1985–86 | Chester C (loan) | 12 | 0 |
| 1986–87 | Manchester C | 2 | 0 |
| 1987–88 | Manchester C | 0 | 0 |
| 1987–88 | Oldham Ath | 18 | 0 |
| 1988–89 | Oldham Ath | 44 | 0 |
| 1989–90 | Oldham Ath | 46 | 2 |
| 1990–91 | Oldham Ath | 46 | 3 |
| 1991–92 | Oldham Ath | 29 | 2 |
| 1991–92 | Aston Villa | 13 | 0 |
| 1992–93 | Aston Villa | 42 | 1 |
| 1993–94 | Aston Villa | 39 | 0 |
| 1994–95 | Aston Villa | 25 | 0 |
| 1994–95 | Everton | 17 | 0 |
| 1995–96 | Everton | 8 | 0 |
| 1996–97 | Everton | 36 | 0 |
| 1997–98 | Everton | 13 | 0 |
| 1997–98 | Sheffield U (loan) | 5 | 0 |
| 1997–98 | Sheffield W | 10 | 0 |
| **Total:** | | **406** | **8** |

## BARRETT, Paul — Midfield

H: 5 9 W: 10 11 b.Newcastle 13-4-78

*Source:* Trainee.

| | | | |
|---|---|---|---|
| 1996–97 | Newcastle U | 0 | 0 |
| 1997–98 | Newcastle U | 0 | 0 |

## BARRETT, Scott — Goalkeeper

H: 6 0 W: 14 05 b.Ilkeston 2-4-63

*Source:* Ilkeston T.

| | | | |
|---|---|---|---|
| 1984–85 | Wolverhampton W | 4 | 0 |
| 1985–86 | Wolverhampton W | 21 | 0 |
| 1986–87 | Wolverhampton W | 5 | 0 |
| 1987–88 | Stoke C | 27 | 0 |
| 1988–89 | Stoke C | 17 | 0 |
| 1989–90 | Stoke C | 7 | 0 |
| 1989–90 | Colchester U (loan) | 13 | 0 |
| 1989–90 | Stockport Co (loan) | 10 | 0 |
| 1990–91 | Colchester U | 0 | 0 |
| 1991–92 | Colchester U | 0 | 0 |
| 1992–93 | Gillingham | 34 | 0 |
| 1993–94 | Gillingham | 13 | 0 |
| 1994–95 | Gillingham | 4 | 0 |
| 1995–96 | Cambridge U | 31 | 0 |
| 1996–97 | Cambridge U | 45 | 0 |
| 1997–98 | Cambridge U | 43 | 0 |
| **Total:** | | **274** | **0** |

## BARRICK, Dean — Defender

H: 5 8 W: 12 00 b.Hemsworth 30-9-69

*Source:* Trainee.

| | | | |
|---|---|---|---|
| 1987–88 | Sheffield W | 0 | 0 |
| 1988–89 | Sheffield W | 8 | 2 |
| 1989–90 | Sheffield W | 3 | 0 |
| 1990–91 | Sheffield W | 0 | 0 |
| 1990–91 | Rotherham U | 19 | 2 |

## Barron, Michael

| | | | |
|---|---|---|---|
| 1991–92 | Rotherham U | 34 | 1 |
| 1992–93 | Rotherham U | 46 | 4 |
| 1993–94 | Cambridge U | 44 | 1 |
| 1994–95 | Cambridge U | 44 | 1 |
| 1995–96 | Cambridge U | 3 | 1 |
| 1995–96 | Preston NE | 40 | 0 |
| 1996–97 | Preston NE | 36 | 0 |
| 1997–98 | Preston NE | 33 | 1 |
| **Total:** | | **310** | **13** |

## BARRON, Michael — Defender

H: 5 11 W: 11 12 b.Lumley 22-12-74

*Source:* Trainee.

| | | | |
|---|---|---|---|
| 1992–93 | Middlesbrough | 0 | 0 |
| 1993–94 | Middlesbrough | 2 | 0 |
| 1994–95 | Middlesbrough | 0 | 0 |
| 1995–96 | Middlesbrough | 1 | 0 |
| 1996–97 | Middlesbrough | 0 | 0 |
| 1996–97 | Hartlepool U (loan) | 16 | 0 |
| 1997–98 | Hartlepool U | 33 | 0 |
| **Total:** | | **52** | **0** |

## BARROW, Lee — Defender

H: 5 11 W: 13 00 b.Belper 1-5-73

*Source:* Trainee.

| | | | |
|---|---|---|---|
| 1991–92 | Notts Co | 0 | 0 |
| 1992–93 | Scarborough | 11 | 0 |
| 1992–93 | Torquay U | 15 | 2 |
| 1993–94 | Torquay U | 20 | 0 |
| 1994–95 | Torquay U | 40 | 3 |
| 1995–96 | Torquay U | 41 | 0 |
| 1996–97 | Torquay U | 46 | 0 |
| 1997–98 | Torquay U | 2 | 0 |
| **Total:** | | **175** | **5** |

## BARROWCLIFF, Paul — Midfield

H: 5 7 W: 11 03 b.Hillingdon 15-6-69

*Source:* Stevenage Bor.

| | | | |
|---|---|---|---|
| 1997–98 | Brentford | 11 | 0 |
| **Total:** | | **11** | **0** |

## BARRY, Gareth — Defender

b.Hastings 23-2-81

*Source:* Trainee.

| | | | |
|---|---|---|---|
| 1997–98 | Aston Villa | 2 | 0 |
| **Total:** | | **2** | **0** |

## BART-WILLIAMS, Chris — Midfield

H: 5 11 W: 11 00 b.Freetown 16-6-74

*Source:* Trainee. *Honours:* England Youth, Under-21.

| | | | |
|---|---|---|---|
| 1990–91 | Leyton Orient | 21 | 2 |
| 1991–92 | Leyton Orient | 15 | 0 |
| 1991–92 | Sheffield W | 15 | 0 |
| 1992–93 | Sheffield W | 34 | 6 |
| 1993–94 | Sheffield W | 37 | 8 |
| 1994–95 | Sheffield W | 38 | 2 |
| 1995–96 | Nottingham F | 33 | 0 |
| 1996–97 | Nottingham F | 16 | 1 |
| 1997–98 | Nottingham F | 33 | 4 |
| **Total:** | | **242** | **23** |

## BARTON, Warren — Defender

H: 5 11 W: 12 00 b.Stoke Newington 19-3-69

*Source:* Leytonstone/Ilford. *Honours:* England B, 3 full caps.

| | | | |
|---|---|---|---|
| 1989–90 | Maidstone U | 42 | 0 |
| 1990–91 | Wimbledon | 37 | 3 |
| 1991–92 | Wimbledon | 42 | 1 |
| 1992–93 | Wimbledon | 23 | 2 |
| 1993–94 | Wimbledon | 39 | 2 |
| 1994–95 | Wimbledon | 39 | 2 |
| 1995–96 | Newcastle U | 31 | 0 |
| 1996–97 | Newcastle U | 18 | 1 |
| 1997–98 | Newcastle U | 23 | 3 |
| **Total:** | | **294** | **14** |

## BARTRAM, Vince — Goalkeeper

H: 6 2 W: 13 07 b.Birmingham 7-8-68

*Source:* Local.

| | | | |
|---|---|---|---|
| 1985–86 | Wolverhampton W | 0 | 0 |
| 1986–87 | Wolverhampton W | 1 | 0 |
| 1987–88 | Wolverhampton W | 0 | 0 |
| 1988–89 | Wolverhampton W | 0 | 0 |
| 1989–90 | Wolverhampton W | 0 | 0 |
| 1989–90 | Blackpool (loan) | 9 | 0 |
| 1990–91 | Wolverhampton W | 4 | 0 |
| 1990–91 | WBA (loan) | 0 | 0 |
| 1991–92 | Bournemouth | 46 | 0 |
| 1992–93 | Bournemouth | 45 | 0 |
| 1993–94 | Bournemouth | 41 | 0 |
| 1994–95 | Arsenal | 11 | 0 |
| 1995–96 | Arsenal | 0 | 0 |
| 1996–97 | Arsenal | 0 | 0 |
| 1996–97 | Wolverhampton W (loan) | 0 | 0 |
| 1997–98 | Arsenal | 0 | 0 |
| 1997–98 | Huddersfield T (loan) | 12 | 0 |
| 1997–98 | Gillingham | 9 | 0 |
| **Total:** | | **178** | **0** |

## BARWOOD, Danny — Forward

H: 5 9 W: 11 00 b.Caerphilly 25-2-81

*Source:* Trainee.

| | | | |
|---|---|---|---|
| 1997–98 | Swansea C | 3 | 1 |
| **Total:** | | **3** | **1** |

## BASFORD, Luke — Defender

H: 5 6 W: 8 07 b.Lambeth 6-1-80

*Source:* Trainee.

| | | | |
|---|---|---|---|
| 1997–98 | Bristol R | 7 | 0 |
| **Total:** | | **7** | **0** |

## BASHAM, Mike — Defender

H: 6 2 W: 13 02 b.Barking 27-9-73

*Source:* Trainee. *Honours:* England Schools.

| | | | |
|---|---|---|---|
| 1992–93 | West Ham U | 0 | 0 |
| 1993–94 | West Ham U | 0 | 0 |
| 1993–94 | Colchester U (loan) | 1 | 0 |
| 1993–94 | Swansea C | 5 | 0 |
| 1994–95 | Swansea C | 13 | 0 |
| 1995–96 | Swansea C | 11 | 1 |
| 1995–96 | Peterborough U | 14 | 1 |
| 1996–97 | Peterborough U | 5 | 0 |
| 1997–98 | Barnet | 20 | 1 |
| **Total:** | | **69** | **3** |

## BASHAM, Steve — Forward

H: 5 11 W: 11 11 b.Southampton 2-12-77

*Source:* Trainee.

| | | | |
|---|---|---|---|
| 1996–97 | Southampton | 6 | 0 |
| 1997–98 | Southampton | 9 | 0 |
| 1997–98 | Wrexham (loan) | 5 | 0 |
| **Total:** | | **20** | **0** |

## BASS, David — Midfield

H: 5 11 W: 12 03 b.Frimley 29-11-74

*Source:* Trainee.

| | | | |
|---|---|---|---|
| 1991–92 | Reading | 3 | 0 |
| 1992–93 | Reading | 5 | 0 |
| 1993–94 | Reading | 1 | 0 |
| 1994–95 | Reading | 0 | 0 |
| 1995–96 | Reading | 0 | 0 |
| 1996–97 | Reading | 2 | 0 |
| 1997–98 | Rotherham U | 18 | 0 |
| **Total:** | | **29** | **0** |

## BASS, Jonathan — Defender

H: 6 0 W: 12 02 b.Weston-Super-Mare 1-1-76

*Source:* Trainee. *Honours:* England Schools.

| | | | |
|---|---|---|---|
| 1994–95 | Birmingham C | 0 | 0 |
| 1995–96 | Birmingham C | 5 | 0 |
| 1996–97 | Birmingham C | 13 | 0 |
| 1996–97 | Carlisle U (loan) | 3 | 0 |
| 1997–98 | Birmingham C | 30 | 0 |
| **Total:** | | **51** | **0** |

## BASSINDER, Gavin — Defender

H: 6 0 W: 12 02 b.Mexborough 24-9-79

*Source:* Trainee.

| | | | |
|---|---|---|---|
| 1997–98 | Barnsley | 0 | 0 |

## BATES, Jamie — Defender

H: 6 1 W: 12 12 b.London 24-2-68

*Source:* Trainee.

| | | | |
|---|---|---|---|
| 1986–87 | Brentford | 24 | 1 |
| 1987–88 | Brentford | 23 | 1 |
| 1988–89 | Brentford | 36 | 1 |
| 1989–90 | Brentford | 15 | 0 |
| 1990–91 | Brentford | 32 | 2 |
| 1991–92 | Brentford | 42 | 1 |
| 1992–93 | Brentford | 24 | 0 |
| 1993–94 | Brentford | 45 | 2 |
| 1994–95 | Brentford | 38 | 2 |
| 1995–96 | Brentford | 36 | 4 |
| 1996–97 | Brentford | 37 | 2 |
| 1997–98 | Brentford | 40 | 1 |
| **Total:** | | **392** | **17** |

## BATES, Robert — Forward

H: 5 9 W: 12 00 b.Redbridge 27-2-78

*Source:* Trainee.

| | | | |
|---|---|---|---|
| 1997–98 | Colchester U | 0 | 0 |

## BATTERSBY, Tony — Forward

H: 6 0 W: 12 09 b.Doncaster 30-8-75

*Source:* Trainee.

| | | | |
|---|---|---|---|
| 1993–94 | Sheffield U | 0 | 0 |
| 1994–95 | Sheffield U | 0 | 0 |
| 1994–95 | Southend U (loan) | 8 | 1 |
| 1995–96 | Sheffield U | 10 | 1 |
| 1995–96 | Notts Co | 21 | 7 |

| | | | |
|---|---|---|---|
| 1996–97 | Notts Co | 18 | 1 |
| 1996–97 | Bury (loan) | 11 | 2 |
| 1997–98 | Bury | 37 | 6 |
| **Total:** | | **105** | **18** |

## BATTY, David — Midfield

H: 5 8 W: 11 10 b.Leeds 2-12-68

*Source:* Trainee. *Honours:* England Under-21, B, 35 full caps.

| | | | |
|---|---|---|---|
| 1987–88 | Leeds U | 23 | 1 |
| 1988–89 | Leeds U | 30 | 0 |
| 1989–90 | Leeds U | 42 | 0 |
| 1990–91 | Leeds U | 37 | 0 |
| 1991–92 | Leeds U | 40 | 2 |
| 1992–93 | Leeds U | 30 | 1 |
| 1993–94 | Leeds U | 9 | 0 |
| 1993–94 | Blackburn R | 26 | 0 |
| 1994–95 | Blackburn R | 5 | 0 |
| 1995–96 | Blackburn R | 23 | 1 |
| 1995–96 | Newcastle U | 11 | 1 |
| 1996–97 | Newcastle U | 32 | 1 |
| 1997–98 | Newcastle U | 32 | 1 |
| **Total:** | | **340** | **8** |

## BATTY, Mark — Forward

H: 5 9 W: 10 10 b.Nottingham 30-1-79

*Source:* Trainee.

| | | | |
|---|---|---|---|
| 1995–96 | Sheffield W | 0 | 0 |
| 1996–97 | Sheffield W | 0 | 0 |
| 1997–98 | Sheffield W | 0 | 0 |

## BAXTER, Craig — Defender

H: 6 0 W: 11 00 b.Glasgow 24-4-79

*Source:* Morrison YMcA.

| | | | |
|---|---|---|---|
| 1997–98 | Hull C | 0 | 0 |

## BAYES, Ashley — Goalkeeper

H: 6 1 W: 13 05 b.Lincoln 19-4-72

*Source:* Trainee.

| | | | |
|---|---|---|---|
| 1989–90 | Brentford | 1 | 0 |
| 1990–91 | Brentford | 0 | 0 |
| 1991–92 | Brentford | 1 | 0 |
| 1992–93 | Brentford | 2 | 0 |
| 1993–94 | Torquay U | 32 | 0 |
| 1994–95 | Torquay U | 37 | 0 |
| 1995–96 | Torquay U | 28 | 0 |
| 1996–97 | Exeter C | 41 | 0 |
| 1997–98 | Exeter C | 45 | 0 |
| **Total:** | | **187** | **0** |

## BAYLISS, Dave — Defender

H: 6 0 W: 11 02 b.Liverpool 8-6-76

*Source:* Trainee.

| | | | |
|---|---|---|---|
| 1994–95 | Rochdale | 1 | 0 |
| 1995–96 | Rochdale | 28 | 0 |
| 1996–97 | Rochdale | 24 | 0 |
| 1997–98 | Rochdale | 29 | 2 |
| **Total:** | | **82** | **2** |

## BAYNE, Graham — Forward

H: 6 1 W: 12 07 b.Kirkcaldy 22-8-79

*Source:* Newburgh.

| | | | |
|---|---|---|---|
| 1997–98 | Dundee | 2 | 0 |
| **Total:** | | **2** | **0** |

## BAZELEY, Darren — Defender

H: 5 10 W: 11 07 b.Northampton 5-10-72

*Source:* Trainee. *Honours:* England Under-21.

| | | | |
|---|---|---|---|
| 1989–90 | Watford | 1 | 0 |
| 1990–91 | Watford | 7 | 0 |
| 1991–92 | Watford | 34 | 6 |
| 1992–93 | Watford | 22 | 1 |
| 1993–94 | Watford | 10 | 1 |
| 1994–95 | Watford | 28 | 4 |
| 1995–96 | Watford | 41 | 1 |
| 1996–97 | Watford | 41 | 3 |
| 1997–98 | Watford | 16 | 3 |
| **Total:** | | **200** | **19** |

## BAZELYA, Eammon — Forward

H: 5 9 W: 11 00 b.London 25-10-78

*Source:* Trainee.

| | | | |
|---|---|---|---|
| 1996–97 | Scarborough | 0 | 0 |
| 1997–98 | Scarborough | 0 | 0 |

## BEADLE, Peter — Forward

H: 6 2 W: 13 07 b.London 13-5-72

*Source:* Trainee.

| | | | |
|---|---|---|---|
| 1988–89 | Gillingham | 2 | 0 |
| 1989–90 | Gillingham | 10 | 2 |
| 1990–91 | Gillingham | 22 | 7 |
| 1991–92 | Gillingham | 33 | 5 |
| 1992–93 | Tottenham H | 0 | 0 |
| 1992–93 | Bournemouth (loan) | 9 | 2 |
| 1993–94 | Tottenham H | 0 | 0 |
| 1993–94 | Southend U (loan) | 8 | 1 |
| 1994–95 | Tottenham H | 0 | 0 |
| 1994–95 | Watford | 20 | 1 |

| | | | |
|---|---|---|---|
| 1995–96 | Watford | 3 | 0 |
| 1995–96 | Bristol R | 27 | 12 |
| 1996–97 | Bristol R | 42 | 12 |
| 1997–98 | Bristol R | 40 | 15 |
| **Total:** | | **216** | **57** |

## BEAGRIE, Peter — Midfield

H: 5 8 W: 12 00 b.Middlesbrough 28-11-65

*Source:* Local. *Honours:* England Under-21, B.

| | | | |
|---|---|---|---|
| 1983–84 | Middlesbrough | 0 | 0 |
| 1984–85 | Middlesbrough | 7 | 1 |
| 1985–86 | Middlesbrough | 26 | 1 |
| 1986–87 | Sheffield U | 41 | 9 |
| 1987–88 | Sheffield U | 43 | 2 |
| 1988–89 | Stoke C | 41 | 7 |
| 1989–90 | Stoke C | 13 | 0 |
| 1989–90 | Everton | 19 | 0 |
| 1990–91 | Everton | 17 | 2 |
| 1991–92 | Everton | 27 | 3 |
| 1991–92 | Sunderland (loan) | 5 | 1 |
| 1992–93 | Everton | 22 | 3 |
| 1993–94 | Everton | 29 | 3 |
| 1993–94 | Manchester C | 9 | 1 |
| 1994–95 | Manchester C | 37 | 2 |
| 1995–96 | Manchester C | 5 | 0 |
| 1996–97 | Manchester C | 1 | 0 |
| 1997–98 | Bradford C | 34 | 0 |
| 1997–98 | Everton (loan) | 6 | 0 |
| **Total:** | | **382** | **35** |

## BEALL, Billy — Midfield

H: 5 8 W: 10 11 b.Enfield 4-12-77

*Source:* Trainee.

| | | | |
|---|---|---|---|
| 1995–96 | Cambridge U | 15 | 4 |
| 1996–97 | Cambridge U | 36 | 2 |
| 1997–98 | Cambridge U | 30 | 1 |
| **Total:** | | **81** | **7** |

## BEARD, Mark — Midfield

H: 5 10 W: 10 12 b.Roehampton 8-10-74

*Source:* Trainee.

| | | | |
|---|---|---|---|
| 1992–93 | Millwall | 0 | 0 |
| 1993–94 | Millwall | 14 | 1 |
| 1994–95 | Millwall | 31 | 1 |
| 1995–96 | Sheffield U | 20 | 0 |
| 1996–97 | Sheffield U | 16 | 0 |
| 1997–98 | Sheffield U | 2 | 0 |
| 1997–98 | Southend U (loan) | 8 | 0 |
| **Total:** | | **91** | **2** |

## BEARDSLEY, Peter — Forward

H: 5 8 W: 11 07 b.Newcastle 18-1-61

*Source:* Wallsend BC. *Honours:* England B, 59 full caps. Football League.

| | | | |
|---|---|---|---|
| 1979–80 | Carlisle U | 39 | 8 |
| 1980–81 | Carlisle U | 43 | 10 |
| 1981–82 | Carlisle U | 22 | 4 |
| From Vancouver Whitecaps. | | | |
| 1982–83 | Manchester U | 0 | 0 |
| From Vancouver Whitecaps. | | | |
| 1983–84 | Newcastle U | 35 | 20 |
| 1984–85 | Newcastle U | 38 | 17 |
| 1985–86 | Newcastle U | 42 | 19 |
| 1986–87 | Newcastle U | 32 | 5 |
| 1987–88 | Liverpool | 38 | 15 |
| 1988–89 | Liverpool | 37 | 10 |
| 1989–90 | Liverpool | 29 | 10 |
| 1990–91 | Liverpool | 27 | 11 |
| 1991–92 | Everton | 42 | 15 |
| 1992–93 | Everton | 39 | 10 |
| 1993–94 | Newcastle U | 35 | 21 |
| 1994–95 | Newcastle U | 34 | 12 |
| 1995–96 | Newcastle U | 35 | 8 |
| 1996–97 | Newcastle U | 25 | 5 |
| 1997–98 | Newcastle U | 0 | 0 |
| 1997–98 | Bolton W | 17 | 2 |
| 1997–98 | Manchester C (loan) | 6 | 0 |
| 1997–98 | Fulham (loan) | 8 | 1 |
| **Total:** | | **623** | **203** |

## BEARDSMORE, Russell — Midfield

H: 5 8 W: 10 04 b.Wigan 28-9-68

*Source:* Apprentice. *Honours:* England Under-21.

| | | | |
|---|---|---|---|
| 1986–87 | Manchester U | 0 | 0 |
| 1987–88 | Manchester U | 0 | 0 |
| 1988–89 | Manchester U | 23 | 2 |
| 1989–90 | Manchester U | 21 | 2 |
| 1990–91 | Manchester U | 12 | 0 |
| 1991–92 | Manchester U | 0 | 0 |
| 1991–92 | Blackburn R (loan) | 2 | 0 |
| 1992–93 | Manchester U | 0 | 0 |
| 1993–94 | Bournemouth | 24 | 0 |
| 1994–95 | Bournemouth | 43 | 3 |
| 1995–96 | Bournemouth | 44 | 0 |
| 1996–97 | Bournemouth | 38 | 0 |
| 1997–98 | Bournemouth | 29 | 1 |
| **Total:** | | **236** | **8** |

## BEASANT, Dave — Goalkeeper

H: 6 4 W: 13 12 b.Ealing 20-3-59

*Source:* Edgware T. *Honours:* England B, 2 full caps.

| | | | |
|---|---|---|---|
| 1979–80 | Wimbledon | 2 | 0 |

| | | | |
|---|---|---|---|
| 1980–81 | Wimbledon | 34 | 0 |
| 1981–82 | Wimbledon | 46 | 0 |
| 1982–83 | Wimbledon | 46 | 0 |
| 1983–84 | Wimbledon | 46 | 0 |
| 1984–85 | Wimbledon | 42 | 0 |
| 1985–86 | Wimbledon | 42 | 0 |
| 1986–87 | Wimbledon | 42 | 0 |
| 1987–88 | Wimbledon | 40 | 0 |
| 1988–89 | Newcastle U | 20 | 0 |
| 1988–89 | Chelsea | 22 | 0 |
| 1989–90 | Chelsea | 38 | 0 |
| 1990–91 | Chelsea | 35 | 0 |
| 1991–92 | Chelsea | 21 | 0 |
| 1992–93 | Chelsea | 17 | 0 |
| 1992–93 | Grimsby T (loan) | 6 | 0 |
| 1992–93 | Wolverhampton W (loan) | 4 | 0 |
| 1993–94 | Chelsea | 0 | 0 |
| 1993–94 | Southampton | 25 | 0 |
| 1994–95 | Southampton | 13 | 0 |
| 1995–96 | Southampton | 36 | 0 |
| 1996–97 | Southampton | 14 | 0 |
| 1997–98 | Southampton | 0 | 0 |
| 1997–98 | Nottingham F | 41 | 0 |
| **Total:** | | **632** | **0** |

## BEATTIE, James — Forward

H: 6 1 W: 12 00 b.Lancaster 27-2-78

*Source:* Trainee.

| | | | |
|---|---|---|---|
| 1994–95 | Blackburn R | 0 | 0 |
| 1995–96 | Blackburn R | 0 | 0 |
| 1996–97 | Blackburn R | 1 | 0 |
| 1997–98 | Blackburn R | 3 | 0 |
| **Total:** | | **4** | **0** |

## BEAUCHAMP, Joey — Midfield

H: 5 10 W: 12 11 b.Oxford 13-3-71

*Source:* Trainee.

| | | | |
|---|---|---|---|
| 1988–89 | Oxford U | 1 | 0 |
| 1989–90 | Oxford U | 3 | 0 |
| 1990–91 | Oxford U | 4 | 0 |
| 1991–92 | Oxford U | 27 | 7 |
| 1991–92 | Swansea C (loan) | 5 | 2 |
| 1992–93 | Oxford U | 44 | 7 |
| 1993–94 | Oxford U | 45 | 6 |
| 1994–95 | West Ham U | 0 | 0 |
| 1994–95 | Swindon T | 42 | 3 |
| 1995–96 | Swindon T | 3 | 0 |
| 1995–96 | Oxford U | 32 | 7 |
| 1996–97 | Oxford U | 45 | 7 |
| 1997–98 | Oxford U | 44 | 13 |
| **Total:** | | **295** | **52** |

## BEAUMONT, Chris — Midfield

H: 5 11 W: 11 12 b.Sheffield 5-12-65

*Source:* Denaby U.

| | | | |
|---|---|---|---|
| 1988–89 | Rochdale | 34 | 7 |
| 1989–90 | Stockport Co | 22 | 5 |
| 1990–91 | Stockport Co | 45 | 15 |
| 1991–92 | Stockport Co | 34 | 2 |
| 1992–93 | Stockport Co | 44 | 14 |
| 1993–94 | Stockport Co | 32 | 1 |
| 1994–95 | Stockport Co | 38 | 2 |
| 1995–96 | Stockport Co | 43 | 0 |
| 1996–97 | Chesterfield | 33 | 1 |
| 1997–98 | Chesterfield | 39 | 1 |
| **Total:** | | **364** | **48** |

## BEAVERS, Paul — Forward

H: 6 3 W: 13 05 b.Blackpool 2-10-78

*Source:* Trainee.

| | | | |
|---|---|---|---|
| 1996–97 | Sunderland | 0 | 0 |
| 1997–98 | Sunderland | 0 | 0 |

## BECK, Mikkel — Forward

H: 6 2 W: 12 09 b.Aarhus 12-5-73

*Source:* Kolding. *Honours:* Denmark 13 full caps, 3 goals.

| | | | |
|---|---|---|---|
| 1992–93 | B 1909 | 13 | 2 |
| 1993–94 | Fortuna Cologne | 32 | 8 |
| 1994–95 | Fortuna Cologne | 19 | 11 |
| 1995–96 | Fortuna Cologne | 28 | 7 |
| 1996–97 | Middlesbrough | 25 | 5 |
| 1997–98 | Middlesbrough | 39 | 14 |
| **Total:** | | **156** | **47** |

## BECKETT, Duane — Midfield

H: 5 8 W: 11 06 b.Sheffield 31-1-78

*Source:* Trainee.

| | | | |
|---|---|---|---|
| 1996–97 | Barnsley | 0 | 0 |
| 1997–98 | Barnsley | 0 | 0 |

## BECKETT, Luke — Forward

H: 5 11 W: 11 06 b.Sheffield 25-11-76

*Source:* Trainee.

| | | | |
|---|---|---|---|
| 1995–96 | Barnsley | 0 | 0 |
| 1996–97 | Barnsley | 0 | 0 |
| 1997–98 | Barnsley | 0 | 0 |

## BECKFORD, Darren — Forward

H: 6 1 W: 11 01 b.Manchester 12-5-67

*Source:* Apprentice. *Honours:* England Schools, Youth.

| | | | |
|---|---|---|---|
| 1984–85 | Manchester C | 4 | 0 |
| 1985–86 | Manchester C | 3 | 0 |
| 1985–86 | Bury (loan) | 12 | 5 |
| 1986–87 | Manchester C | 4 | 0 |
| 1986–87 | Port Vale (loan) | 11 | 4 |
| 1987–88 | Port Vale | 40 | 9 |
| 1988–89 | Port Vale | 42 | 20 |
| 1989–90 | Port Vale | 42 | 17 |
| 1990–91 | Port Vale | 43 | 22 |
| 1991–92 | Norwich C | 30 | 7 |
| 1992–93 | Norwich C | 8 | 1 |
| 1992–93 | Oldham Ath | 7 | 3 |
| 1993–94 | Oldham Ath | 22 | 6 |
| 1994–95 | Oldham Ath | 3 | 0 |
| 1995–96 | Oldham Ath | 20 | 2 |
| 1996–97 | Hearts | 8 | 0 |
| 1996–97 | Preston NE | 2 | 0 |
| 1996–97 | Fulham | 0 | 0 |
| 1996–97 | Walsall | 8 | 0 |
| 1997–98 | Walsall | 0 | 0 |
| **Total:** | | **309** | **96** |

## BECKHAM, David — Midfield

H: 6 0 W: 11 09 b.Leytonstone 2-5-75

*Source:* Trainee. *Honours:* England Youth, Under-21, 18 full caps, 1 goal.

| | | | |
|---|---|---|---|
| 1992–93 | Manchester U | 0 | 0 |
| 1993–94 | Manchester U | 0 | 0 |
| 1994–95 | Manchester U | 4 | 0 |
| 1994–95 | Preston NE (loan) | 5 | 2 |
| 1995–96 | Manchester U | 33 | 7 |
| 1996–97 | Manchester U | 36 | 7 |
| 1997–98 | Manchester U | 37 | 9 |
| **Total:** | | **115** | **25** |

## BEDEAU, Anthony — Forward

H: 5 10 W: 11 00 b.Hammersmith 24-3-79

*Source:* Trainee.

| | | | |
|---|---|---|---|
| 1995–96 | Torquay U | 4 | 0 |
| 1996–97 | Torquay U | 8 | 1 |
| 1997–98 | Torquay U | 34 | 5 |
| **Total:** | | **46** | **6** |

## BEECH, Chris — Midfield

H: 5 10 W: 11 13 b.Blackpool 16-9-74

*Source:* Trainee.

| | | | |
|---|---|---|---|
| 1992–93 | Blackpool | 1 | 0 |
| 1993–94 | Blackpool | 35 | 2 |
| 1994–95 | Blackpool | 28 | 2 |
| 1995–96 | Blackpool | 18 | 0 |
| 1996–97 | Hartlepool U | 42 | 7 |
| 1997–98 | Hartlepool U | 36 | 6 |
| **Total:** | | **160** | **17** |

## BEECH, Chris — Defender

H: 5 9 W: 11 06 b.Congleton 5-11-75

*Source:* Trainee. *Honours:* England Schools, Youth.

| | | | |
|---|---|---|---|
| 1992–93 | Manchester C | 0 | 0 |
| 1993–94 | Manchester C | 0 | 0 |
| 1994–95 | Manchester C | 0 | 0 |
| 1995–96 | Manchester C | 0 | 0 |
| 1996–97 | Manchester C | 0 | 0 |
| 1997–98 | Cardiff C | 46 | 1 |
| **Total:** | | **46** | **1** |

## BEENEY, Mark — Goalkeeper

H: 6 4 W: 14 07 b.Pembury 30-12-67

| | | | |
|---|---|---|---|
| 1986–87 | Gillingham | 2 | 0 |
| 1987–88 | Maidstone U | 0 | 0 |
| 1988–89 | Maidstone U | 0 | 0 |
| 1989–90 | Maidstone U | 33 | 0 |
| 1989–90 | Aldershot (loan) | 7 | 0 |
| 1990–91 | Maidstone U | 17 | 0 |
| 1990–91 | Brighton & HA | 2 | 0 |
| 1991–92 | Brighton & HA | 25 | 0 |
| 1992–93 | Brighton & HA | 42 | 0 |
| 1992–93 | Leeds U | 1 | 0 |
| 1993–94 | Leeds U | 22 | 0 |
| 1994–95 | Leeds U | 0 | 0 |
| 1995–96 | Leeds U | 10 | 0 |
| 1996–97 | Leeds U | 1 | 0 |
| 1997–98 | Leeds U | 1 | 0 |
| **Total:** | | **163** | **0** |

## BEESLEY, Paul — Defender

H: 6 1 W: 12 07 b.Wigan 21-9-65

*Source:* Marine.

| | | | |
|---|---|---|---|
| 1984–85 | Wigan Ath | 2 | 0 |
| 1985–86 | Wigan Ath | 17 | 0 |
| 1986–87 | Wigan Ath | 39 | 0 |
| 1987–88 | Wigan Ath | 42 | 1 |
| 1988–89 | Wigan Ath | 44 | 2 |
| 1989–90 | Wigan Ath | 11 | 0 |
| 1989–90 | Leyton Orient | 32 | 1 |
| 1990–91 | Sheffield U | 37 | 1 |
| 1991–92 | Sheffield U | 40 | 2 |
| 1992–93 | Sheffield U | 39 | 2 |
| 1993–94 | Sheffield U | 25 | 0 |
| 1994–95 | Sheffield U | 27 | 2 |

## Beeston, Carl

| | | | |
|---|---|---|---|
| 1995–96 | Leeds U | 10 | 0 |
| 1996–97 | Leeds U | 12 | 0 |
| 1996–97 | Manchester C | 6 | 0 |
| 1997–98 | Manchester C | 7 | 0 |
| 1997–98 | Port Vale (loan) | 5 | 0 |
| 1997–98 | WBA (loan) | 8 | 0 |
| **Total:** | | **403** | **11** |

## BEESTON, Carl — Midfield

H: 5 10 W: 12 08 b.Stoke 30-6-67

*Source:* Apprentice. *Honours:* England Under-21.

| | | | |
|---|---|---|---|
| 1984–85 | Stoke C | 1 | 0 |
| 1985–86 | Stoke C | 5 | 0 |
| 1986–87 | Stoke C | 0 | 0 |
| 1987–88 | Stoke C | 12 | 0 |
| 1988–89 | Stoke C | 23 | 2 |
| 1989–90 | Stoke C | 38 | 2 |
| 1990–91 | Stoke C | 37 | 2 |
| 1991–92 | Stoke C | 43 | 3 |
| 1992–93 | Stoke C | 27 | 3 |
| 1993–94 | Stoke C | 0 | 0 |
| 1994–95 | Stoke C | 16 | 1 |
| 1995–96 | Stoke C | 16 | 0 |
| 1996–97 | Stoke C | 18 | 0 |
| 1996–97 | Hereford U (loan) | 9 | 2 |
| 1997–98 | Southend U | 6 | 0 |
| **Total:** | | **251** | **15** |

## BEETON, Alan — Defender

H: 5 11 W: 11 13 b.Watford 4-10-78

*Source:* Trainee.

| | | | |
|---|---|---|---|
| 1997–98 | Wycombe W | 20 | 0 |
| **Total:** | | **20** | **0** |

## BEHARALL, David — Defender

H: 6 0 W: 11 07 b.Newcastle 8-3-79

*Source:* Trainee.

| | | | |
|---|---|---|---|
| 1997–98 | Newcastle U | 0 | 0 |

## BELL, Leon — Midfield

H: 5 8 W: 11 00 b.Ipswich 23-9-77

*Source:* Trainee. *Honours:* England Schools.

| | | | |
|---|---|---|---|
| 1995–96 | Ipswich T | 0 | 0 |
| 1996–97 | Ipswich T | 0 | 0 |
| 1997–98 | Ipswich T | 0 | 0 |

## BELL, Mickey — Defender

H: 5 8 W: 10 04 b.Newcastle 15-11-71

*Source:* Trainee.

| | | | |
|---|---|---|---|
| 1989–90 | Northampton T | 6 | 0 |
| 1990–91 | Northampton T | 28 | 0 |
| 1991–92 | Northampton T | 30 | 4 |
| 1992–93 | Northampton T | 39 | 5 |
| 1993–94 | Northampton T | 38 | 0 |
| 1994–95 | Northampton T | 12 | 1 |
| 1994–95 | Wycombe W | 31 | 3 |
| 1995–96 | Wycombe W | 41 | 1 |
| 1996–97 | Wycombe W | 46 | 2 |
| 1997–98 | Bristol C | 44 | 10 |
| **Total:** | | **315** | **26** |

## BELLAMY, Craig — Forward

H: 5 8 W: 10 10 b.Cardiff 13-1-79

*Source:* Trainee. *Honours:* Wales Under-21, 3 full caps, 1 goal.

| | | | |
|---|---|---|---|
| 1996–97 | Norwich C | 3 | 0 |
| 1997–98 | Norwich C | 36 | 13 |
| **Total:** | | **39** | **13** |

## BENALI, Francis — Midfield

H: 5 9 W: 11 02 b.Southampton 30-12-68

*Source:* Apprentice. *Honours:* England Schools.

| | | | |
|---|---|---|---|
| 1986–87 | Southampton | 0 | 0 |
| 1987–88 | Southampton | 0 | 0 |
| 1988–89 | Southampton | 7 | 0 |
| 1989–90 | Southampton | 27 | 0 |
| 1990–91 | Southampton | 12 | 0 |
| 1991–92 | Southampton | 22 | 0 |
| 1992–93 | Southampton | 33 | 0 |
| 1993–94 | Southampton | 37 | 0 |
| 1994–95 | Southampton | 35 | 0 |
| 1995–96 | Southampton | 29 | 0 |
| 1996–97 | Southampton | 18 | 0 |
| 1997–98 | Southampton | 33 | 1 |
| **Total:** | | **253** | **1** |

## BENJAMIN, Trevor — Midfield

H: 6 3 W: 13 05 b.Wellingborough 8-2-79

*Source:* Trainee.

| | | | |
|---|---|---|---|
| 1995–96 | Cambridge U | 5 | 0 |
| 1996–97 | Cambridge U | 7 | 1 |
| 1997–98 | Cambridge U | 25 | 4 |
| **Total:** | | **37** | **5** |

## BENNETT, Dean — Forward

H: 5 10 W: 11 00 b.Wolverhampton 13-12-77

| | | | |
|---|---|---|---|
| 1996–97 | WBA | 1 | 0 |
| 1997–98 | WBA | 0 | 0 |
| **Total:** | | **1** | **0** |

## BENNETT, Frankie — Forward

H: 5 7 W: 12 01 b.Birmingham 13-1-69

*Source:* Halesowen T.

| | | | |
|---|---|---|---|
| 1992–93 | Southampton | 0 | 0 |
| 1993–94 | Southampton | 8 | 1 |
| 1994–95 | Southampton | 0 | 0 |
| 1995–96 | Southampton | 11 | 0 |
| 1996–97 | Southampton | 0 | 0 |
| 1996–97 | Shrewsbury T (loan) | 4 | 3 |
| 1996–97 | Bristol R | 11 | 1 |
| 1997–98 | Bristol R | 19 | 2 |
| **Total:** | | **53** | **7** |

## BENNETT, Gary — Defender

H: 6 1 W: 12 01 b.Manchester 4-12-61

*Source:* Amateur.

| | | | |
|---|---|---|---|
| 1979–80 | Manchester C | 0 | 0 |
| 1980–81 | Manchester C | 0 | 0 |
| 1981–82 | Cardiff C | 19 | 1 |
| 1982–83 | Cardiff C | 36 | 8 |
| 1983–84 | Cardiff C | 32 | 2 |
| 1984–85 | Sunderland | 37 | 3 |
| 1985–86 | Sunderland | 28 | 3 |
| 1986–87 | Sunderland | 41 | 4 |
| 1987–88 | Sunderland | 38 | 2 |
| 1988–89 | Sunderland | 40 | 3 |
| 1989–90 | Sunderland | 36 | 3 |
| 1990–91 | Sunderland | 37 | 2 |
| 1991–92 | Sunderland | 39 | 3 |
| 1992–93 | Sunderland | 15 | 0 |
| 1993–94 | Sunderland | 38 | 0 |
| 1994–95 | Sunderland | 20 | 0 |
| 1995–96 | Sunderland | 0 | 0 |
| 1995–96 | Carlisle U | 26 | 5 |
| 1996–97 | Scarborough | 46 | 9 |
| 1997–98 | Scarborough | 42 | 9 |
| **Total:** | | **570** | **57** |

## BENNETT, Gary — Forward

H: 5 10 W: 12 00 b.Kirby 20-9-63

*Source:* Kirby T.

| | | | |
|---|---|---|---|
| 1984–85 | Wigan Ath | 20 | 3 |
| 1985–86 | Chester C | 43 | 13 |
| 1986–87 | Chester C | 33 | 13 |
| 1987–88 | Chester C | 43 | 10 |
| 1988–89 | Chester C | 7 | 0 |
| 1988–89 | Southend U | 17 | 2 |
| 1989–90 | Southend U | 25 | 4 |
| 1989–90 | Chester C | 8 | 1 |
| 1990–91 | Chester C | 30 | 3 |
| 1991–92 | Chester C | 42 | 11 |
| 1992–93 | Wrexham | 35 | 16 |
| 1993–94 | Wrexham | 41 | 32 |
| 1994–95 | Wrexham | 45 | 29 |
| 1995–96 | Tranmere R | 29 | 9 |
| 1995–96 | Preston NE | 8 | 1 |
| 1996–97 | Preston NE | 16 | 3 |
| 1996–97 | Wrexham | 15 | 5 |
| 1997–98 | Chester C | 41 | 12 |
| **Total:** | | **498** | **167** |

## BENNETT, Ian — Goalkeeper

H: 6 0 W: 12 10 b.Worksop 10-10-71

*Source:* Newcastle U Trainee.

| | | | |
|---|---|---|---|
| 1991–92 | Peterborough U | 7 | 0 |
| 1992–93 | Peterborough U | 46 | 0 |
| 1993–94 | Peterborough U | 19 | 0 |
| 1993–94 | Birmingham C | 22 | 0 |
| 1994–95 | Birmingham C | 46 | 0 |
| 1995–96 | Birmingham C | 24 | 0 |
| 1996–97 | Birmingham C | 40 | 0 |
| 1997–98 | Birmingham C | 45 | 0 |
| **Total:** | | **249** | **0** |

## BENNETT, Mickey — Midfield

H: 5 10 W: 11 11 b.Camberwell 22-7-69

*Source:* Apprentice. *Honours:* England Youth.

| | | | |
|---|---|---|---|
| 1986–87 | Charlton Ath | 2 | 0 |
| 1987–88 | Charlton Ath | 16 | 1 |
| 1988–89 | Charlton Ath | 11 | 0 |
| 1989–90 | Charlton Ath | 6 | 1 |
| 1989–90 | Wimbledon | 7 | 1 |
| 1990–91 | Wimbledon | 6 | 0 |
| 1991–92 | Wimbledon | 5 | 1 |
| 1992–93 | Brentford | 38 | 4 |
| 1993–94 | Brentford | 8 | 0 |
| 1993–94 | Charlton Ath | 10 | 1 |
| 1994–95 | Charlton Ath | 14 | 0 |
| 1994–95 | Millwall | 0 | 0 |
| 1995–96 | Millwall | 2 | 0 |
| 1996–97 | Cardiff C | 14 | 1 |
| From Cambridge C. | | | |
| 1997–98 | Leyton Orient | 2 | 0 |
| **Total:** | | **141** | **10** |

## BENNETT, Tom — Midfield

H: 5 11 W: 11 08 b.Falkirk 12-12-69

*Source:* Trainee.

| | | | |
|---|---|---|---|
| 1987–88 | Aston Villa | 0 | 0 |
| 1988–89 | Wolverhampton W | 2 | 0 |
| 1989–90 | Wolverhampton W | 30 | 0 |
| 1990–91 | Wolverhampton W | 26 | 0 |
| 1991–92 | Wolverhampton W | 38 | 2 |
| 1992–93 | Wolverhampton W | 1 | 0 |
| 1993–94 | Wolverhampton W | 10 | 0 |
| 1994–95 | Wolverhampton W | 8 | 0 |
| 1995–96 | Stockport Co | 24 | 1 |
| 1996–97 | Stockport Co | 43 | 3 |
| 1997–98 | Stockport Co | 27 | 1 |
| **Total:** | | **209** | **7** |

## BENNETT, Troy — Midfield

H: 6 1 W: 11 13 b.Barnsley 25-12-75

*Source:* Trainee. *Honours:* England Youth.

| | | | |
|---|---|---|---|
| 1992–93 | Barnsley | 2 | 0 |
| 1993–94 | Barnsley | 0 | 0 |
| 1994–95 | Barnsley | 0 | 0 |
| 1995–96 | Barnsley | 0 | 0 |
| 1996–97 | Barnsley | 0 | 0 |
| 1996–97 | Scarborough (loan) | 5 | 1 |
| 1997–98 | Scarborough | 34 | 2 |
| **Total:** | | **41** | **3** |

## BENSON, Mark — Defender

H: 5 5 W: 10 05 b.Dublin 7-8-78

*Source:* Trainee.

| | | | |
|---|---|---|---|
| 1995–96 | Blackburn R | 0 | 0 |
| 1996–97 | Blackburn R | 0 | 0 |
| 1997–98 | Blackburn R | 0 | 0 |

## BENSTEAD, Graham — Goalkeeper

H: 6 2 W: 14 00 b.Aldershot 20-8-63

*Source:* Apprentice. *Honours:* England Youth.

| | | | |
|---|---|---|---|
| 1981–82 | QPR | 0 | 0 |
| 1982–83 | QPR | 0 | 0 |
| 1983–84 | QPR | 0 | 0 |
| 1984–85 | QPR | 0 | 0 |
| 1984–85 | Norwich C (loan) | 1 | 0 |
| 1985–86 | Norwich C | 0 | 0 |
| 1986–87 | Norwich C | 13 | 0 |
| 1987–88 | Norwich C | 2 | 0 |
| 1987–88 | Colchester U (loan) | 18 | 0 |
| 1987–88 | Sheffield U (loan) | 8 | 0 |
| 1988–89 | Sheffield U | 39 | 0 |
| 1989–90 | Sheffield U | 0 | 0 |
| 1990–91 | Brentford | 45 | 0 |
| 1991–92 | Brentford | 37 | 0 |
| 1992–93 | Brentford | 25 | 0 |
| 1993–94 | Brentford | 5 | 0 |
| 1997–98 | Brentford | 1 | 0 |
| **Total:** | | **194** | **0** |

## BENT, Junior — Forward

H: 5 5 W: 10 06 b.Huddersfield 1-3-70

*Source:* Trainee.

| | | | |
|---|---|---|---|
| 1987–88 | Huddersfield T | 7 | 0 |
| 1988–89 | Huddersfield T | 22 | 5 |
| 1989–90 | Huddersfield T | 7 | 1 |
| 1989–90 | Burnley (loan) | 9 | 3 |
| 1989–90 | Bristol C | 1 | 0 |
| 1990–91 | Bristol C | 20 | 2 |
| 1991–92 | Bristol C | 17 | 2 |
| 1991–92 | Stoke C (loan) | 1 | 0 |
| 1992–93 | Bristol C | 20 | 3 |
| 1993–94 | Bristol C | 20 | 2 |
| 1994–95 | Bristol C | 41 | 6 |
| 1995–96 | Bristol C | 40 | 2 |
| 1996–97 | Bristol C | 22 | 3 |
| 1996–97 | Shrewsbury T (loan) | 6 | 0 |
| 1997–98 | Bristol C | 2 | 0 |
| 1997–98 | Blackpool | 36 | 3 |
| **Total:** | | **271** | **32** |

## BENT, Marcus — Forward

H: 6 3 W: 11 13 b.Hammersmith 19-5-78

*Source:* Trainee. *Honours:* England Under-21.

| | | | |
|---|---|---|---|
| 1995–96 | Brentford | 12 | 1 |
| 1996–97 | Brentford | 34 | 3 |
| 1997–98 | Brentford | 24 | 4 |
| 1997–98 | Crystal Palace | 16 | 5 |
| **Total:** | | **86** | **13** |

## BERESFORD, David — Forward

H: 5 6 W: 10 07 b.Manchester 11-11-76

*Source:* Trainee. *Honours:* England Schools, Youth.

| | | | |
|---|---|---|---|
| 1993–94 | Oldham Ath | 1 | 0 |
| 1994–95 | Oldham Ath | 2 | 0 |
| 1995–96 | Oldham Ath | 28 | 2 |
| 1995–96 | Swansea C (loan) | 6 | 0 |
| 1996–97 | Oldham Ath | 33 | 0 |
| 1996–97 | Huddersfield T | 6 | 1 |
| 1997–98 | Huddersfield T | 8 | 0 |
| **Total:** | | **84** | **3** |

## BERESFORD, John — Midfield

H: 5 7 W: 12 01 b.Sheffield 4-9-66

*Source:* Apprentice. *Honours:* England Schools, Youth, B.

| | | | |
|---|---|---|---|
| 1983–84 | Manchester C | 0 | 0 |
| 1984–85 | Manchester C | 0 | 0 |
| 1985–86 | Manchester C | 0 | 0 |
| 1986–87 | Barnsley | 27 | 1 |
| 1987–88 | Barnsley | 34 | 3 |
| 1988–89 | Barnsley | 27 | 1 |
| 1988–89 | Portsmouth | 2 | 0 |
| 1989–90 | Portsmouth | 28 | 0 |
| 1990–91 | Portsmouth | 42 | 2 |
| 1991–92 | Portsmouth | 35 | 6 |
| 1992–93 | Newcastle U | 42 | 1 |
| 1993–94 | Newcastle U | 34 | 0 |
| 1994–95 | Newcastle U | 33 | 0 |
| 1995–96 | Newcastle U | 33 | 0 |
| 1996–97 | Newcastle U | 19 | 0 |
| 1997–98 | Newcastle U | 18 | 2 |
| 1997–98 | Southampton | 10 | 0 |
| **Total:** | | **384** | **16** |

## BERESFORD, Marlon — Goalkeeper

H: 6 1 W: 13 05 b.Lincoln 2-6-69

*Source:* Trainee.

| | | | |
|---|---|---|---|
| 1987–88 | Sheffield W | 0 | 0 |
| 1988–89 | Sheffield W | 0 | 0 |
| 1989–90 | Sheffield W | 0 | 0 |
| 1989–90 | Bury (loan) | 1 | 0 |
| 1989–90 | Ipswich T (loan) | 0 | 0 |
| 1990–91 | Sheffield W | 0 | 0 |
| 1990–91 | Northampton T (loan) | 13 | 0 |
| 1990–91 | Crewe Alex (loan) | 3 | 0 |
| 1991–92 | Sheffield W | 0 | 0 |
| 1991–92 | Northampton T (loan) | 15 | 0 |
| 1992–93 | Burnley | 44 | 0 |
| 1993–94 | Burnley | 46 | 0 |
| 1994–95 | Burnley | 40 | 0 |
| 1995–96 | Burnley | 36 | 0 |
| 1996–97 | Burnley | 40 | 0 |
| 1997–98 | Burnley | 34 | 0 |
| 1997–98 | Middlesbrough | 3 | 0 |
| **Total:** | | **275** | **0** |

## BERG, Henning — Defender

H: 6 0 W: 12 01 b.Eidsvoll 1-9-69

*Source:* Lillestrom. *Honours:* Norway Under-21, 56 full caps, 5 goals.

| | | | |
|---|---|---|---|
| 1992–93 | Blackburn R | 4 | 0 |
| 1993–94 | Blackburn R | 41 | 1 |
| 1994–95 | Blackburn R | 40 | 1 |
| 1995–96 | Blackburn R | 38 | 0 |
| 1996–97 | Blackburn R | 36 | 2 |
| 1997–98 | Manchester U | 27 | 1 |
| **Total:** | | **186** | **5** |

## BERGER, Patrik — Midfield

H: 6 1 W: 12 06 b.Prague 10-11-73

*Honours:* Czech Republic 26 full caps, 12 goals.

| | | | |
|---|---|---|---|
| 1991–92 | Slavia Prague | 20 | 3 |
| 1992–93 | Slavia Prague | 29 | 10 |
| 1993–94 | Slavia Prague | 12 | 4 |
| 1994–95 | Slavia Prague | 28 | 7 |
| 1995–96 | Borussia Dortmund | 25 | 4 |
| 1996–97 | Liverpool | 23 | 6 |
| 1997–98 | Liverpool | 22 | 3 |
| **Total:** | | **159** | **37** |

## BERGKAMP, Dennis — Forward

H: 6 0 W: 12 05 b.Amsterdam 18-5-69

*Honours:* Holland 64 full caps, 36 goals.

| | | | |
|---|---|---|---|
| 1986–87 | Ajax | 14 | 2 |
| 1987–88 | Ajax | 25 | 5 |
| 1988–89 | Ajax | 30 | 13 |
| 1989–90 | Ajax | 25 | 8 |
| 1990–91 | Ajax | 33 | 25 |
| 1991–92 | Ajax | 30 | 24 |
| 1992–93 | Ajax | 28 | 26 |
| 1993–94 | Internazionale | 31 | 8 |
| 1994–95 | Internazionale | 21 | 3 |
| 1995–96 | Arsenal | 33 | 11 |
| 1996–97 | Arsenal | 29 | 12 |
| 1997–98 | Arsenal | 28 | 16 |
| **Total:** | | **327** | **153** |

## BERGSSON, Gudni — Defender

H: 6 1 W: 12 03 b.Reykjavik 21-7-65

*Source:* Valur. *Honours:* Iceland Youth, Under-21, 75 full caps, 1 goal.

| | | | |
|---|---|---|---|
| 1988–89 | Tottenham H | 8 | 0 |
| 1989–90 | Tottenham H | 18 | 0 |
| 1990–91 | Tottenham H | 12 | 1 |
| 1991–92 | Tottenham H | 28 | 1 |
| 1992–93 | Tottenham H | 5 | 0 |
| 1993–94 | Tottenham H | 0 | 0 |
| 1994–95 | Bolton W | 8 | 0 |
| 1995–96 | Bolton W | 34 | 4 |
| 1996–97 | Bolton W | 33 | 3 |
| 1997–98 | Bolton W | 35 | 2 |
| **Total:** | | **181** | **11** |

## BERKLEY, Austin — Forward

H: 5 9 W: 10 10 b.Gravesend 28-1-73

*Source:* Trainee.

| | | | |
|---|---|---|---|
| 1990–91 | Gillingham | 0 | 0 |
| 1991–92 | Gillingham | 3 | 0 |
| 1992–93 | Swindon T | 0 | 0 |
| 1993–94 | Swindon T | 0 | 0 |
| 1994–95 | Swindon T | 1 | 0 |
| 1995–96 | Shrewsbury T | 38 | 1 |
| 1996–97 | Shrewsbury T | 24 | 0 |
| 1997–98 | Shrewsbury T | 36 | 3 |
| **Total:** | | **102** | **4** |

## BERKOVIC, Eyal — Midfield

H: 5 7 W: 10 02 b.Haifa 2-4-72

*Honours:* Israel 45 full caps, 4 goals.

| | | | |
|---|---|---|---|
| 1992–93 | Maccabi Haifa | 32 | 7 |
| 1993–94 | Maccabi Haifa | 38 | 10 |
| 1994–95 | Maccabi Haifa | 29 | 5 |
| 1995–96 | Maccabi Haifa | 29 | 3 |
| 1996–97 | Southampton | 28 | 4 |
| 1997–98 | West Ham U | 35 | 7 |
| **Total:** | | **191** | **36** |

## BERNAL, Andy — Defender

H: 5 10 W: 12 05 b.Canberra 16-7-66

*Source:* Sporting Gijon. *Honours:* Australia 8 full caps.

| | | | |
|---|---|---|---|
| 1992–93 | Ipswich T | 9 | 0 |
| 1993–94 | Ipswich T | 0 | 0 |
| From Sydney Olympic. | | | |
| 1994–95 | Reading | 33 | 0 |
| 1995–96 | Reading | 34 | 2 |
| 1996–97 | Reading | 41 | 0 |
| 1997–98 | Reading | 34 | 0 |
| **Total:** | | **151** | **2** |

## BERNARD, Curtis — Forward

H: 5 7 W: 12 00 b.Leeds 3-7-80

*Source:* Trainee.

| | | | |
|---|---|---|---|
| 1997–98 | Barnsley | 0 | 0 |

## BERNARD, Paul — Midfield

H: 5 11 W: 11 08 b.Edinburgh 30-12-72

*Source:* Trainee. *Honours:* Scotland Under-21, 2 full caps.

| | | | |
|---|---|---|---|
| 1990–91 | Oldham Ath | 2 | 1 |
| 1991–92 | Oldham Ath | 21 | 5 |
| 1992–93 | Oldham Ath | 33 | 4 |
| 1993–94 | Oldham Ath | 32 | 5 |
| 1994–95 | Oldham Ath | 17 | 2 |
| 1995–96 | Oldham Ath | 7 | 1 |
| 1995–96 | Aberdeen | 31 | 1 |
| 1996–97 | Aberdeen | 14 | 0 |
| 1997–98 | Aberdeen | 17 | 0 |
| **Total:** | | **174** | **19** |

## BERRY, Trevor — Midfield

H: 5 6 W: 11 00 b.Haslemere 1-8-74

*Source:* Bournemouth.

| | | | |
|---|---|---|---|
| 1991–92 | Aston Villa | 0 | 0 |
| 1992–93 | Aston Villa | 0 | 0 |
| 1993–94 | Aston Villa | 0 | 0 |
| 1994–95 | Aston Villa | 0 | 0 |
| 1995–96 | Aston Villa | 0 | 0 |
| 1995–96 | Rotherham U | 36 | 7 |
| 1996–97 | Rotherham U | 30 | 4 |
| 1997–98 | Rotherham U | 42 | 3 |
| **Total:** | | **108** | **14** |

## BERTHE, Mohamed — Midfield

b.Guyana 12-9-72

*Source:* Gaz Ajaccio.

| | | | |
|---|---|---|---|
| 1997–98 | West Ham U | 0 | 0 |

## BERTI, Nicola — Midfield

H: 6 1 W: 12 02 b.Salsomaggiore Terme 14-4-67

*Honours:* Italy 39 full caps, 3 goals.

| | | | |
|---|---|---|---|
| 1982–83 | Parma | 1 | 0 |
| 1983–84 | Parma | 0 | 0 |
| 1984–85 | Parma | 27 | 0 |
| 1985–86 | Fiorentina | 28 | 3 |
| 1986–87 | Fiorentina | 27 | 4 |
| 1987–88 | Fiorentina | 25 | 1 |
| 1988–89 | Internazionale | 32 | 7 |
| 1989–90 | Internazionale | 29 | 5 |
| 1990–91 | Internazionale | 30 | 4 |
| 1991–92 | Internazionale | 30 | 1 |
| 1992–93 | Internazionale | 32 | 4 |
| 1993–94 | Internazionale | 9 | 2 |
| 1994–95 | Internazionale | 30 | 5 |
| 1995–96 | Internazionale | 10 | 0 |
| 1996–97 | Internazionale | 23 | 1 |
| 1997–98 | Internazionale | 4 | 0 |
| 1997–98 | Tottenham H | 17 | 3 |
| **Total:** | | **354** | **40** |

## BESWETHERICK, John — Defender

H: 5 11 W: 11 04 b.Liverpool 15-1-78

*Source:* Trainee.

| | | | |
|---|---|---|---|
| 1996–97 | Plymouth Arg | 0 | 0 |
| 1997–98 | Plymouth Arg | 2 | 0 |
| **Total:** | | **2** | **0** |

## BETTNEY, Chris — Forward

H: 5 10 W: 11 00 b.Chesterfield 27-10-77

*Source:* Trainee.

| | | | |
|---|---|---|---|
| 1995–96 | Sheffield U | 0 | 0 |
| 1996–97 | Sheffield U | 1 | 0 |
| 1997–98 | Sheffield U | 0 | 0 |
| 1997–98 | Hull C (loan) | 30 | 1 |
| **Total:** | | **31** | **1** |

## BETTS, Robert — Midfield

H: 5 10 W: 11 00 b.Doncaster 21-12-81

*Source:* School.

| | | | |
|---|---|---|---|
| 1997–98 | Doncaster R | 3 | 0 |
| **Total:** | | **3** | **0** |

## BETTS, Simon — Defender

H: 5 6 W: 11 06 b.Middlesbrough 3-5-73

*Source:* Trainee.

| | | | |
|---|---|---|---|
| 1991–92 | Ipswich T | 0 | 0 |
| 1992–93 | Scarborough | 0 | 0 |
| 1992–93 | Colchester U | 23 | 0 |
| 1993–94 | Colchester U | 33 | 1 |
| 1994–95 | Colchester U | 35 | 2 |
| 1995–96 | Colchester U | 45 | 5 |
| 1996–97 | Colchester U | 10 | 1 |
| 1997–98 | Colchester U | 17 | 0 |
| **Total:** | | **163** | **9** |

## BEVAN, Scott — Goalkeeper

H: 6 5 W: 16 01 b.Southampton 16-9-79

*Source:* Trainee.

| | | | |
|---|---|---|---|
| 1997–98 | Southampton | 0 | 0 |

## BIBBO, Sal — Goalkeeper

H: 6 2 W: 14 00 b.Basingstoke 24-8-74

*Source:* Bournemouth.

| | | | |
|---|---|---|---|
| 1993–94 | Sheffield U | 0 | 0 |
| 1994–95 | Sheffield U | 0 | 0 |
| 1994–95 | Chesterfield (loan) | 1 | 0 |
| 1995–96 | Sheffield U | 0 | 0 |
| 1996–97 | Reading | 5 | 0 |
| 1997–98 | Reading | 2 | 0 |
| **Total:** | | **8** | **0** |

## BIGNOT, Marcus — Defender

H: 5 9 W: 11 00 b.Birmingham 22-8-74

*Source:* Kidderminster H.

| | | | |
|---|---|---|---|
| 1997–98 | Crewe Alex | 42 | 0 |
| **Total:** | | **42** | **0** |

## BILIC, Slaven — Defender

H: 6 2 W: 13 02 b.Split 11-9-68

*Honours:* Croatia 43 full caps, 3 goals.

| | | | |
|---|---|---|---|
| 1988–89 | Hajduk Split | 3 | 2 |
| 1989–90 | Hajduk Split | 27 | 3 |
| 1990–91 | Hajduk Split | 32 | 2 |
| 1991–92 | Hajduk Split | 20 | 1 |
| 1992–93 | Hajduk Split | 27 | 5 |
| 1993–94 | Karlsruhe | 26 | 2 |
| 1994–95 | Karlsruhe | 28 | 3 |
| 1995–96 | West Ham U | 13 | 0 |
| 1996–97 | West Ham U | 35 | 2 |
| 1997–98 | Everton | 24 | 0 |
| **Total:** | | **235** | **20** |

## BILLINGTON, David — Defender

H: 5 7 W: 10 07 b.Oxford 15-10-80

*Source:* Trainee.

| | | | |
|---|---|---|---|
| 1996–97 | Peterborough U | 5 | 0 |
| 1996–97 | Sheffield W | 0 | 0 |
| 1997–98 | Sheffield W | 0 | 0 |
| **Total:** | | **5** | **0** |

## BILLIO, Patrizio — Midfield

H: 5 8 W: 11 00 b.Treviso 19-4-74

| | | | |
|---|---|---|---|
| 1997–98 | Crystal Palace | 3 | 0 |
| **Total:** | | **3** | **0** |

## BILLY, Chris — Defender

H: 5 11 W: 11 08 b.Huddersfield 2-1-73

*Source:* Trainee.

| | | | |
|---|---|---|---|
| 1991–92 | Huddersfield T | 10 | 2 |
| 1992–93 | Huddersfield T | 13 | 0 |
| 1993–94 | Huddersfield T | 34 | 0 |
| 1994–95 | Huddersfield T | 37 | 2 |
| 1995–96 | Plymouth Arg | 32 | 4 |
| 1996–97 | Plymouth Arg | 45 | 3 |
| 1997–98 | Plymouth Arg | 41 | 2 |
| **Total:** | | **212** | **13** |

## BIMSON, Stuart — Defender

H: 5 11 W: 11 08 b.Liverpool 29-9-69

*Source:* Macclesfield T.

| | | | |
|---|---|---|---|
| 1994–95 | Bury | 19 | 0 |
| 1995–96 | Bury | 16 | 0 |
| 1996–97 | Bury | 1 | 0 |
| 1996–97 | Lincoln C | 15 | 1 |
| 1997–98 | Lincoln C | 12 | 0 |
| **Total:** | | **63** | **1** |

## BINGHAM, David — Forward

H: 5 10 W: 10 07 b.Dunfermline 3-9-70

*Source:* Oakley Utd.

| | | | |
|---|---|---|---|
| 1989–90 | St Johnstone | 1 | 0 |
| 1990–91 | St Johnstone | 7 | 2 |
| 1991–92 | St Johnstone | 9 | 1 |
| 1992–93 | St Johnstone | 0 | 0 |
| 1992–93 | Forfar Ath | 20 | 6 |
| 1993–94 | Forfar Ath | 38 | 13 |
| 1994–95 | Forfar Ath | 36 | 22 |
| 1995–96 | Forfar Ath | 5 | 3 |
| 1995–96 | Dunfermline Ath | 15 | 3 |
| 1996–97 | Dunfermline Ath | 17 | 1 |
| 1997–98 | Dunfermline Ath | 30 | 5 |
| **Total:** | | **178** | **56** |

## BIRCH, Mark — Defender

H: 5 11 W: 12 02 b.Stoke 5-1-77

*Source:* Trainee.

| | | | |
|---|---|---|---|
| 1995–96 | Stoke C | 0 | 0 |
| 1996–97 | Stoke C | 0 | 0 |
| 1997–98 | Stoke C | 0 | 0 |

## BIRCH, Paul — Midfield

H: 5 6 W: 10 04 b.West Bromwich 20-11-62

*Source:* Apprentice.

| | | | |
|---|---|---|---|
| 1980–81 | Aston Villa | 0 | 0 |
| 1981–82 | Aston Villa | 0 | 0 |
| 1982–83 | Aston Villa | 0 | 0 |
| 1983–84 | Aston Villa | 22 | 2 |
| 1984–85 | Aston Villa | 25 | 3 |
| 1985–86 | Aston Villa | 27 | 2 |
| 1986–87 | Aston Villa | 29 | 3 |
| 1987–88 | Aston Villa | 38 | 6 |
| 1988–89 | Aston Villa | 12 | 0 |
| 1989–90 | Aston Villa | 12 | 0 |
| 1990–91 | Aston Villa | 8 | 0 |
| 1990–91 | Wolverhampton W | 20 | 2 |
| 1991–92 | Wolverhampton W | 45 | 8 |
| 1992–93 | Wolverhampton W | 28 | 3 |
| 1993–94 | Wolverhampton W | 32 | 1 |
| 1994–95 | Wolverhampton W | 10 | 1 |
| 1995–96 | Wolverhampton W | 7 | 0 |
| 1995–96 | Preston NE (loan) | 11 | 2 |
| 1996–97 | Doncaster R | 27 | 2 |
| 1996–97 | Exeter C | 2 | 0 |
| 1997–98 | Exeter C | 33 | 5 |
| **Total:** | | **388** | **40** |

## BIRCHAM, Marc — Defender

H: 5 10 W: 12 08 b.Brent 11-5-78

*Source:* Trainee.

| | | | |
|---|---|---|---|
| 1996–97 | Millwall | 6 | 0 |
| 1997–98 | Millwall | 4 | 0 |
| **Total:** | | **10** | **0** |

## BIRD, Tony — Forward

H: 5 11 W: 12 10 b.Cardiff 1-9-74

*Source:* Trainee. *Honours:* Wales Under-21.

| | | | |
|---|---|---|---|
| 1991–92 | Cardiff C | 0 | 0 |
| 1992–93 | Cardiff C | 9 | 1 |
| 1993–94 | Cardiff C | 35 | 5 |
| 1994–95 | Cardiff C | 19 | 4 |
| 1995–96 | Cardiff C | 12 | 3 |
| From Barry T. | | | |
| 1997–98 | Swansea C | 41 | 14 |
| **Total:** | | **116** | **27** |

## BISHOP, Charlie — Defender

H: 6 0 W: 12 11 b.Nottingham 16-2-68

*Source:* Stoke C Apprentice.

| | | | |
|---|---|---|---|
| 1986–87 | Watford | 0 | 0 |
| 1987–88 | Bury | 17 | 0 |
| 1988–89 | Bury | 38 | 3 |
| 1989–90 | Bury | 30 | 1 |
| 1990–91 | Bury | 29 | 2 |
| 1991–92 | Barnsley | 28 | 0 |
| 1992–93 | Barnsley | 43 | 0 |
| 1993–94 | Barnsley | 38 | 1 |
| 1994–95 | Barnsley | 8 | 0 |
| 1995–96 | Barnsley | 13 | 0 |
| 1995–96 | Preston NE (loan) | 4 | 0 |
| 1995–96 | Burnley (loan) | 9 | 0 |
| 1996–97 | Wigan Ath | 21 | 0 |
| 1997–98 | Wigan Ath | 7 | 0 |
| 1997–98 | Northampton T | 7 | 0 |
| **Total:** | | **292** | **7** |

## BISHOP, Ian — Midfield

H: 5 9 W: 10 12 b.Liverpool 29-5-65

*Source:* Apprentice. *Honours:* England B.

| | | | |
|---|---|---|---|
| 1983–84 | Everton | 1 | 0 |
| 1983–84 | Crewe Alex (loan) | 4 | 0 |
| 1984–85 | Everton | 0 | 0 |
| 1984–85 | Carlisle U | 30 | 2 |
| 1985–86 | Carlisle U | 36 | 6 |
| 1986–87 | Carlisle U | 42 | 3 |
| 1987–88 | Carlisle U | 24 | 3 |
| 1988–89 | Bournemouth | 44 | 2 |
| 1989–90 | Manchester C | 19 | 2 |
| 1989–90 | West Ham U | 17 | 2 |
| 1990–91 | West Ham U | 40 | 4 |
| 1991–92 | West Ham U | 41 | 1 |
| 1992–93 | West Ham U | 22 | 1 |
| 1993–94 | West Ham U | 36 | 1 |
| 1994–95 | West Ham U | 31 | 1 |
| 1995–96 | West Ham U | 35 | 1 |
| 1996–97 | West Ham U | 29 | 1 |
| 1997–98 | West Ham U | 3 | 0 |
| 1997–98 | Manchester C | 6 | 0 |
| **Total:** | | **460** | **30** |

## BJORKLUND, Joachim — Midfield

H: 5 11 W: 12 08 b.Vaxjo 15-3-71

*Honours:* Sweden 58 full caps.

| | | | |
|---|---|---|---|
| 1988 | Osters | 6 | 0 |
| 1989 | Osters | 0 | 0 |
| 1990 | Brann | 21 | 0 |
| 1991 | Brann | 22 | 0 |
| 1992 | Brann | 13 | 0 |
| 1993 | IFK Gothenburg | 19 | 0 |
| 1994 | IFK Gothenburg | 16 | 0 |
| 1995 | IFK Gothenburg | 11 | 0 |
| 1995–96 | Vicenza | 33 | 0 |
| 1996–97 | Rangers | 28 | 0 |
| 1997–98 | Rangers | 31 | 0 |
| **Total:** | | **200** | **0** |

## BJORNEBYE, Stig Inge — Defender

H: 5 10 W: 11 09 b.Elverum 11-12-69

*Honours:* Norway 66 full caps, 1 goal.

| | | | |
|---|---|---|---|
| 1988 | Strommen | 19 | 0 |
| 1989 | Kongsvinger | 21 | 2 |
| 1990 | Kongsvinger | 20 | 0 |
| 1991 | Kongsvinger | 21 | 1 |
| 1992 | Rosenborg | 21 | 3 |
| 1992–93 | Liverpool | 11 | 0 |
| 1993–94 | Liverpool | 9 | 0 |
| 1994–95 | Liverpool | 31 | 0 |
| 1995–96 | Liverpool | 2 | 0 |
| 1996–97 | Liverpool | 38 | 2 |
| 1997–98 | Liverpool | 25 | 0 |
| **Total:** | | **218** | **8** |

## BLACK, Kingsley — Midfield

H: 5 8 W: 12 03 b.Luton 22-6-68

*Source:* School. *Honours:* England Schools, Northern Ireland Under-21, 30 full caps, 1 goal.

| | | | |
|---|---|---|---|
| 1986–87 | Luton T | 0 | 0 |
| 1987–88 | Luton T | 13 | 0 |
| 1988–89 | Luton T | 37 | 8 |
| 1989–90 | Luton T | 36 | 11 |
| 1990–91 | Luton T | 37 | 7 |
| 1991–92 | Luton T | 4 | 0 |
| 1991–92 | Nottingham F | 25 | 4 |
| 1992–93 | Nottingham F | 24 | 5 |
| 1993–94 | Nottingham F | 37 | 3 |
| 1994–95 | Nottingham F | 10 | 2 |
| 1994–95 | Sheffield U (loan) | 11 | 2 |
| 1995–96 | Nottingham F | 2 | 0 |
| 1995–96 | Millwall (loan) | 3 | 1 |
| 1996–97 | Grimsby T | 24 | 0 |
| 1997–98 | Grimsby T | 39 | 2 |
| **Total:** | | **302** | **45** |

## BLACK, Michael — Midfield

H: 5 8 W: 11 08 b.Chigwell 6-10-76

*Source:* Trainee. *Honours:* England Schools.

| | | | |
|---|---|---|---|
| 1995–96 | Arsenal | 0 | 0 |
| 1996–97 | Arsenal | 0 | 0 |
| 1997–98 | Arsenal | 0 | 0 |
| 1997–98 | Millwall (loan) | 13 | 2 |
| **Total:** | | **13** | **2** |

## BLACK, Tony — Forward

H: 5 8 W: 11 01 b.Barrow 15-7-69

*Source:* Bamber Bridge.

| | | | |
|---|---|---|---|
| 1994–95 | Wigan Ath | 9 | 0 |
| 1995–96 | Wigan Ath | 21 | 2 |
| 1996–97 | Wigan Ath | 0 | 0 |
| 1997–98 | Wigan Ath | 1 | 0 |
| **Total:** | | **31** | **2** |

## BLACKMORE, Clayton — Midfield

H: 5 7 W: 11 13 b.Neath 23-9-64

*Source:* Apprentice. *Honours:* Wales Schools, Youth, Under-21, 39 full caps, 1 goal.

| | | | |
|---|---|---|---|
| 1982–83 | Manchester U | 0 | 0 |
| 1983–84 | Manchester U | 1 | 0 |
| 1984–85 | Manchester U | 1 | 0 |

| | | | |
|---|---|---|---|
| 1985–86 | Manchester U | 12 | 3 |
| 1986–87 | Manchester U | 12 | 1 |
| 1987–88 | Manchester U | 22 | 3 |
| 1988–89 | Manchester U | 28 | 3 |
| 1989–90 | Manchester U | 28 | 2 |
| 1990–91 | Manchester U | 35 | 4 |
| 1991–92 | Manchester U | 33 | 3 |
| 1992–93 | Manchester U | 14 | 0 |
| 1993–94 | Manchester U | 0 | 0 |
| 1994–95 | Middlesbrough | 30 | 2 |
| 1995–96 | Middlesbrough | 5 | 0 |
| 1996–97 | Middlesbrough | 16 | 2 |
| 1996–97 | Bristol C (loan) | 5 | 1 |
| 1997–98 | Middlesbrough | 2 | 0 |
| **Total:** | | **244** | **24** |

## BLACKWELL, Dean — Defender

H: 6 1 W: 12 10 b.Camden 5-12-69

*Source:* Trainee. *Honours:* England Under-21.

| | | | |
|---|---|---|---|
| 1988–89 | Wimbledon | 0 | 0 |
| 1989–90 | Wimbledon | 3 | 0 |
| 1989–90 | Plymouth Arg (loan) | 7 | 0 |
| 1990–91 | Wimbledon | 35 | 0 |
| 1991–92 | Wimbledon | 4 | 1 |
| 1992–93 | Wimbledon | 24 | 0 |
| 1993–94 | Wimbledon | 18 | 0 |
| 1994–95 | Wimbledon | 0 | 0 |
| 1995–96 | Wimbledon | 8 | 0 |
| 1996–97 | Wimbledon | 27 | 0 |
| 1997–98 | Wimbledon | 35 | 0 |
| **Total:** | | **161** | **1** |

## BLACKWELL, Kevin — Goalkeeper

H: 5 11 W: 12 10 b.Luton 21-12-58

*Source:* Boston U, Barnet. *Honours:*

| | | | |
|---|---|---|---|
| 1987–88 | Scarborough | 21 | 0 |
| 1988–89 | Scarborough | 15 | 0 |
| 1989–90 | Scarborough | 8 | 0 |
| 1989–90 | Notts Co | 0 | 0 |
| 1990–91 | Notts Co | 0 | 0 |
| 1991–92 | Notts Co | 0 | 0 |
| 1992–93 | Notts Co | 0 | 0 |
| 1992–93 | Torquay U | 18 | 0 |
| 1993–94 | Huddersfield T | 1 | 0 |
| 1994–95 | Huddersfield T | 4 | 0 |
| 1995–96 | Plymouth Arg | 20 | 0 |
| 1996–97 | Plymouth Arg | 4 | 0 |
| 1997–98 | Plymouth Arg | 0 | 0 |
| **Total:** | | **91** | **0** |

## BLACKWOOD, Michael — Forward

b.Birmingham 30-9-79

*Source:* Trainee.

| | | | |
|---|---|---|---|
| 1997–98 | Aston Villa | 0 | 0 |

## BLAKE, Aslam — Forward

H: 6 0 W: 11 12 b.Birmingham 19-10-79

*Source:* Trainee.

| | | | |
|---|---|---|---|
| 1996–97 | Coventry C | 0 | 0 |
| 1997–98 | Coventry C | 0 | 0 |

## BLAKE, Dean — Midfield

H: 5 8 W: 10 01 b.Southampton 20-2-80

*Source:* Trainee.

| | | | |
|---|---|---|---|
| 1997–98 | Southampton | 0 | 0 |

## BLAKE, Mark — Defender

H: 6 0 W: 12 06 b.Portsmouth 17-12-67

*Source:* Apprentice. *Honours:* England Youth.

| | | | |
|---|---|---|---|
| 1985–86 | Southampton | 1 | 0 |
| 1986–87 | Southampton | 8 | 1 |
| 1987–88 | Southampton | 6 | 1 |
| 1988–89 | Southampton | 3 | 0 |
| 1989–90 | Southampton | 0 | 0 |
| 1989–90 | Colchester U (loan) | 4 | 1 |
| 1989–90 | Shrewsbury T (loan) | 10 | 0 |
| 1990–91 | Shrewsbury T | 46 | 2 |
| 1991–92 | Shrewsbury T | 39 | 0 |
| 1992–93 | Shrewsbury T | 32 | 1 |
| 1993–94 | Shrewsbury T | 15 | 0 |
| 1994–95 | Fulham | 35 | 3 |
| 1995–96 | Fulham | 38 | 5 |
| 1996–97 | Fulham | 41 | 7 |
| 1997–98 | Fulham | 26 | 2 |
| **Total:** | | **304** | **23** |

## BLAKE, Mark — Midfield

H: 5 11 W: 12 10 b.Nottingham 16-12-70

*Source:* Trainee. *Honours:* England Schools, Youth, Under-21.

| | | | |
|---|---|---|---|
| 1989–90 | Aston Villa | 9 | 0 |
| 1990–91 | Aston Villa | 7 | 0 |
| 1990–91 | Wolverhampton W (loan) | 2 | 0 |
| 1991–92 | Aston Villa | 14 | 2 |
| 1992–93 | Aston Villa | 1 | 0 |
| 1993–94 | Portsmouth | 15 | 0 |
| 1993–94 | Leicester C | 11 | 1 |
| 1994–95 | Leicester C | 30 | 3 |

| | | | |
|---|---|---|---|
| 1995–96 | Leicester C | 8 | 0 |
| 1996–97 | Leicester C | 0 | 0 |
| 1996–97 | Walsall | 38 | 4 |
| 1997–98 | Walsall | 23 | 1 |
| **Total:** | | **158** | **11** |

## BLAKE, Nathan — Forward

H: 5 11 W: 12 08 b.Cardiff 27-1-72

*Source:* Chelsea Trainee. *Honours:* Wales B, Under-21, 7 full caps, 2 goals.

| | | | |
|---|---|---|---|
| 1989–90 | Cardiff C | 6 | 0 |
| 1990–91 | Cardiff C | 40 | 4 |
| 1991–92 | Cardiff C | 31 | 6 |
| 1992–93 | Cardiff C | 34 | 11 |
| 1993–94 | Cardiff C | 20 | 14 |
| 1993–94 | Sheffield U | 12 | 5 |
| 1994–95 | Sheffield U | 35 | 17 |
| 1995–96 | Sheffield U | 22 | 12 |
| 1995–96 | Bolton W | 18 | 1 |
| 1996–97 | Bolton W | 42 | 19 |
| 1997–98 | Bolton W | 35 | 12 |
| **Total:** | | **295** | **101** |

## BLAKE, Noel — Defender

H: 6 2 W: 14 02 b.Jamaica 12-1-62

*Source:* Walsall Amateur, Sutton Coldfield T.

| | | | |
|---|---|---|---|
| 1979–80 | Aston Villa | 3 | 0 |
| 1980–81 | Aston Villa | 0 | 0 |
| 1981–82 | Aston Villa | 1 | 0 |
| 1981–82 | Shrewsbury T (loan) | 6 | 0 |
| 1982–83 | Aston Villa | 0 | 0 |
| 1982–83 | Birmingham C | 37 | 3 |
| 1983–84 | Birmingham C | 39 | 2 |
| 1984–85 | Portsmouth | 42 | 3 |
| 1985–86 | Portsmouth | 42 | 4 |
| 1986–87 | Portsmouth | 41 | 3 |
| 1987–88 | Portsmouth | 19 | 0 |
| 1988–89 | Leeds U | 44 | 4 |
| 1989–90 | Leeds U | 7 | 0 |
| 1989–90 | Stoke C | 18 | 0 |
| 1990–91 | Stoke C | 44 | 3 |
| 1991–92 | Stoke C | 13 | 0 |
| 1991–92 | Bradford C (loan) | 6 | 0 |
| 1992–93 | Bradford C | 32 | 3 |
| 1993–94 | Bradford C | 7 | 0 |
| 1993–94 | Dundee | 23 | 2 |
| 1994–95 | Dundee | 31 | 0 |
| 1995–96 | Exeter C | 44 | 2 |
| 1996–97 | Exeter C | 46 | 6 |
| 1997–98 | Exeter C | 38 | 1 |
| **Total:** | | **583** | **36** |

## BLAKE, Robbie — Forward

H: 5 8 W: 11 00 b.Middlesbrough 4-3-76

*Source:* Trainee.

| | | | |
|---|---|---|---|
| 1994–95 | Darlington | 9 | 0 |
| 1995–96 | Darlington | 29 | 11 |
| 1996–97 | Darlington | 30 | 10 |
| 1996–97 | Bradford C | 5 | 0 |
| 1997–98 | Bradford C | 34 | 8 |
| **Total:** | | **107** | **29** |

## BLAMEY, Nathan — Defender

H: 5 10 W: 11 05 b.Plymouth 10-6-77

*Source:* Trainee.

| | | | |
|---|---|---|---|
| 1995–96 | Southampton | 0 | 0 |
| 1996–97 | Southampton | 0 | 0 |
| 1996–97 | Shrewsbury T | 6 | 0 |
| 1997–98 | Shrewsbury T | 9 | 1 |
| **Total:** | | **15** | **1** |

## BLANEY, Steven — Defender

H: 6 0 W: 13 00 b.Orsett 24-3-77

*Source:* Trainee. *Honours:* England Schools, Wales Under-21.

| | | | |
|---|---|---|---|
| 1995–96 | West Ham U | 0 | 0 |
| 1996–97 | West Ham U | 0 | 0 |
| 1997–98 | West Ham U | 0 | 0 |
| 1997–98 | Brentford | 5 | 0 |
| **Total:** | | **5** | **0** |

## BLATHERWICK, Steve — Defender

H: 6 1 W: 15 00 b.Nottingham 20-9-73

*Source:* Notts Co.

| | | | |
|---|---|---|---|
| 1992–93 | Nottingham F | 0 | 0 |
| 1993–94 | Nottingham F | 3 | 0 |
| 1993–94 | Wycombe W (loan) | 2 | 0 |
| 1994–95 | Nottingham F | 0 | 0 |
| 1995–96 | Nottingham F | 0 | 0 |
| 1995–96 | Hereford U (loan) | 10 | 1 |
| 1996–97 | Nottingham F | 7 | 0 |
| 1996–97 | Reading (loan) | 7 | 0 |
| 1997–98 | Burnley | 21 | 0 |
| **Total:** | | **50** | **1** |

## BLINKER, Regi — Forward

H: 5 8 W: 11 07 b.Surinam 2-6-69

*Honours:* Holland 3 full caps.

| | | | |
|---|---|---|---|
| 1986–87 | Feyenoord | 26 | 1 |
| 1987–88 | Feyenoord | 24 | 2 |

| | | | |
|---|---|---|---|
| 1988–89 | Feyenoord | 1 | 0 |
| 1988–89 | Den Bosch | 25 | 6 |
| 1989–90 | Feyenoord | 31 | 2 |
| 1990–91 | Feyenoord | 26 | 1 |
| 1991–92 | Feyenoord | 28 | 5 |
| 1992–93 | Feyenoord | 30 | 13 |
| 1993–94 | Feyenoord | 29 | 9 |
| 1994–95 | Feyenoord | 30 | 8 |
| 1995–96 | Feyenoord | 13 | 4 |
| 1995–96 | Sheffield W | 9 | 2 |
| 1996–97 | Sheffield W | 33 | 1 |
| 1997–98 | Celtic | 16 | 1 |
| **Total:** | | **321** | **55** |

## BLONDEAU, Patrick — Defender

H: 5 9 W: 11 13 b.Marseille 27-1-68

*Source:* Septemes, Martigues. *Honours:* France 2 full caps.

| | | | |
|---|---|---|---|
| 1989–90 | Monaco | 13 | 0 |
| 1990–91 | Monaco | 16 | 0 |
| 1991–92 | Monaco | 4 | 0 |
| 1992–93 | Monaco | 15 | 0 |
| 1993–94 | Monaco | 14 | 0 |
| 1994–95 | Monaco | 30 | 1 |
| 1995–96 | Monaco | 25 | 1 |
| 1996–97 | Monaco | 31 | 0 |
| 1997–98 | Sheffield W | 6 | 0 |
| **Total:** | | **154** | **2** |

## BLOOMER, Matthew — Defender

H: 6 1 W: 13 00 b.Grimsby 3-11-78

*Source:* Trainee.

| | | | |
|---|---|---|---|
| 1997–98 | Grimsby T | 0 | 0 |

## BLUNT, Jason — Midfield

H: 5 9 W: 10 10 b.Penzance 16-8-77

*Source:* Trainee. *Honours:* England Youth.

| | | | |
|---|---|---|---|
| 1994–95 | Leeds U | 0 | 0 |
| 1995–96 | Leeds U | 3 | 0 |
| 1996–97 | Leeds U | 1 | 0 |
| 1997–98 | Leeds U | 0 | 0 |
| **Total:** | | **4** | **0** |

## BOA MORTE, Luis — Forward

H: 5 10 W: 11 05 b.Lisbon 4-8-77

*Source:* Sporting Lisbon, Lourihanense (loan). *Honours:* Portugal Under-21.

| | | | |
|---|---|---|---|
| 1997–98 | Arsenal | 15 | 0 |
| **Total:** | | **15** | **0** |

## BOATENG, George — Midfield

H: 5 9 W: 10 12 b.Nkawkaw 5-9-75

| | | | |
|---|---|---|---|
| 1994–95 | Excelsior | 9 | 0 |
| 1995–96 | Feyenoord | 24 | 1 |
| 1996–97 | Feyenoord | 26 | 0 |
| 1997–98 | Feyenoord | 18 | 0 |
| 1997–98 | Coventry C | 14 | 1 |
| **Total:** | | **91** | **2** |

## BOCHENSKI, Simon — Forward

H: 5 11 W: 11 13 b.Worksop 6-12-75

*Source:* Trainee.

| | | | |
|---|---|---|---|
| 1994–95 | Barnsley | 0 | 0 |
| 1995–96 | Barnsley | 1 | 0 |
| 1996–97 | Barnsley | 0 | 0 |
| 1996–97 | Scarborough | 19 | 1 |
| 1997–98 | Scarborough | 0 | 0 |
| **Total:** | | **20** | **1** |

## BOCO, Jean-Marc — Defender

H: 5 11 W: 12 10 b.Cotonou 22-12-63

*Source:* Creil, Amiens, Rouen, Tours.

| | | | |
|---|---|---|---|
| 1991–92 | Lens | 32 | 0 |
| 1992–93 | Lens | 33 | 0 |
| 1993–94 | Lens | 38 | 0 |
| 1994–95 | Lens | 32 | 0 |
| 1995–96 | Lens | 28 | 0 |
| 1996–97 | Lens | 32 | 0 |
| 1997–98 | Hibernian | 30 | 0 |
| **Total:** | | **225** | **0** |

## BODEN, Chris — Defender

H: 5 9 W: 11 12 b.Wolverhampton 13-10-73

*Source:* Trainee.

| | | | |
|---|---|---|---|
| 1991–92 | Aston Villa | 0 | 0 |
| 1992–93 | Aston Villa | 0 | 0 |
| 1993–94 | Aston Villa | 0 | 0 |
| 1993–94 | Barnsley (loan) | 4 | 0 |
| 1994–95 | Aston Villa | 1 | 0 |
| 1994–95 | Derby Co | 6 | 0 |
| 1995–96 | Derby Co | 4 | 0 |
| 1995–96 | Shrewsbury T (loan) | 5 | 0 |
| 1996–97 | Derby Co | 0 | 0 |
| 1997–98 | Derby Co | 0 | 0 |
| **Total:** | | **20** | **0** |

## BODIN, Paul — Defender

H: 6 0 W: 12 06 b.Cardiff 13-9-64

*Source:* Chelsea Amateur. *Honours:* Wales Youth, Under-21, 23 full caps, 3 goals.

| | | | |
|---|---|---|---|
| 1981–82 | Newport Co | 0 | 0 |
| 1982–83 | Cardiff C | 31 | 0 |
| 1983–84 | Cardiff C | 26 | 3 |
| From Bath C. | | | |
| 1987–88 | Newport Co | 6 | 1 |
| 1987–88 | Swindon T | 5 | 1 |
| 1988–89 | Swindon T | 16 | 1 |
| 1989–90 | Swindon T | 41 | 5 |
| 1990–91 | Swindon T | 31 | 2 |
| 1990–91 | Crystal Palace | 5 | 0 |
| 1991–92 | Crystal Palace | 4 | 0 |
| 1991–92 | Newcastle U (loan) | 6 | 0 |
| 1991–92 | Swindon T | 21 | 2 |
| 1992–93 | Swindon T | 35 | 11 |
| 1993–94 | Swindon T | 32 | 7 |
| 1994–95 | Swindon T | 25 | 6 |
| 1995–96 | Swindon T | 33 | 2 |
| 1996–97 | Reading | 37 | 1 |
| 1997–98 | Reading | 4 | 0 |
| 1997–98 | Wycombe W (loan) | 5 | 0 |
| **Total:** | | **363** | **42** |

## BODLEY, Mike — Defender

H: 6 1 W: 13 01 b.Hayes 14-9-67

*Source:* Apprentice.

| | | | |
|---|---|---|---|
| 1985–86 | Chelsea | 0 | 0 |
| 1986–87 | Chelsea | 0 | 0 |
| 1987–88 | Chelsea | 6 | 1 |
| 1988–89 | Chelsea | 0 | 0 |
| 1988–89 | Northampton T | 20 | 0 |
| 1989–90 | Northampton T | 0 | 0 |
| 1990–91 | Barnet | 0 | 0 |
| 1991–92 | Barnet | 36 | 1 |
| 1992–93 | Barnet | 33 | 2 |
| 1993–94 | Southend U | 16 | 1 |
| 1994–95 | Southend U | 12 | 0 |
| 1994–95 | Gillingham (loan) | 7 | 0 |
| 1994–95 | Birmingham C (loan) | 3 | 0 |
| 1995–96 | Southend U | 39 | 1 |
| 1996–97 | Peterborough U | 31 | 0 |
| 1997–98 | Peterborough U | 31 | 1 |
| **Total:** | | **234** | **7** |

## BOERE, Jeroen — Forward

H: 6 3 W: 13 02 b.Arnheim 18-11-67

*Source:* Go Ahead.

| | | | |
|---|---|---|---|
| 1993–94 | West Ham U | 4 | 0 |
| 1993–94 | Portsmouth (loan) | 5 | 0 |
| 1994–95 | West Ham U | 20 | 6 |
| 1994–95 | WBA (loan) | 5 | 0 |
| 1995–96 | West Ham U | 1 | 0 |
| 1995–96 | Crystal Palace | 8 | 1 |
| 1995–96 | Southend U | 6 | 2 |
| 1996–97 | Southend U | 36 | 9 |
| 1997–98 | Southend U | 31 | 14 |
| **Total:** | | **116** | **32** |

## BOERTIEN, Paul — Defender

H: 5 10 W: 11 00 b.Haltwhistle 20-1-79

*Source:* Trainee.

| | | | |
|---|---|---|---|
| 1996–97 | Carlisle U | 0 | 0 |
| 1997–98 | Carlisle U | 9 | 0 |
| **Total:** | | **9** | **0** |

## BOGIE, Ian — Midfield

H: 5 9 W: 11 10 b.Newcastle 6-12-67

*Source:* Apprentice. *Honours:* England Schools.

| | | | |
|---|---|---|---|
| 1985–86 | Newcastle U | 0 | 0 |
| 1986–87 | Newcastle U | 1 | 0 |
| 1987–88 | Newcastle U | 7 | 0 |
| 1988–89 | Newcastle U | 6 | 0 |
| 1988–89 | Preston NE | 13 | 1 |
| 1989–90 | Preston NE | 35 | 3 |
| 1990–91 | Preston NE | 31 | 8 |
| 1991–92 | Millwall | 25 | 0 |
| 1992–93 | Millwall | 22 | 0 |
| 1993–94 | Millwall | 4 | 1 |
| 1993–94 | Leyton Orient | 34 | 3 |
| 1994–95 | Leyton Orient | 31 | 2 |
| 1994–95 | Port Vale | 9 | 2 |
| 1995–96 | Port Vale | 32 | 3 |
| 1996–97 | Port Vale | 31 | 1 |
| 1997–98 | Port Vale | 38 | 1 |
| **Total:** | | **319** | **25** |

## BOHINEN, Lars — Midfield

H: 6 1 W: 13 00 b.Vadso 8-9-69

*Source:* Young Boys. *Honours:* Norway 48 full caps, 10 goals.

| | | | |
|---|---|---|---|
| 1988 | Valerengen | 15 | 2 |
| 1989 | Valerengen | 18 | 3 |
| 1990 | Viking | 10 | 0 |
| 1990–91 | Young Boys | 22 | 4 |
| 1991–92 | Young Boys | 34 | 2 |
| 1992–93 | Young Boys | 2 | 0 |
| 1993–94 | Nottingham F | 23 | 1 |
| 1994–95 | Nottingham F | 34 | 6 |
| 1995–96 | Nottingham F | 7 | 0 |
| 1995–96 | Blackburn R | 19 | 4 |
| 1996–97 | Blackburn R | 23 | 2 |

| | | | |
|---|---|---|---|
| 1997–98 | Blackburn R | 16 | 1 |
| 1997–98 | Derby Co | 9 | 1 |
| **Total:** | | **232** | **26** |

## BOKOTO, Mommainais — Forward

H: 5 11 W: 11 13 b.France 20-10-74

*Source:* Maria Aalter.

| | | | |
|---|---|---|---|
| 1996–97 | Bristol C | 0 | 0 |
| 1997–98 | Bristol C | 0 | 0 |

## BOLAND, Willie — Midfield

H: 5 9 W: 11 02 b.Ennis 6-8-75

*Source:* Trainee. *Honours:* Eire Youth, Under-21.

| | | | |
|---|---|---|---|
| 1992–93 | Coventry C | 1 | 0 |
| 1993–94 | Coventry C | 27 | 0 |
| 1994–95 | Coventry C | 12 | 0 |
| 1995–96 | Coventry C | 3 | 0 |
| 1996–97 | Coventry C | 1 | 0 |
| 1997–98 | Coventry C | 19 | 0 |
| **Total:** | | **63** | **0** |

## BOLI, Roger — Forward

H: 5 8 W: 10 12 b.Adjame 26-9-65

*Source:* Romainville, Auxerre, Lille.

| | | | |
|---|---|---|---|
| 1991–92 | Lens | 33 | 4 |
| 1992–93 | Lens | 30 | 3 |
| 1993–94 | Lens | 35 | 20 |
| 1994–95 | Lens | 38 | 9 |
| 1995–96 | Lens | 28 | 4 |
| 1996–97 | Le Havre | 26 | 4 |
| 1997–98 | Walsall | 41 | 12 |
| **Total:** | | **231** | **56** |

## BOLLAN, Gary — Midfield

H: 5 11 W: 12 12 b.Dundee 24-3-73

*Source:* Celtic BC. *Honours:* Scotland Under-21.

| | | | |
|---|---|---|---|
| 1987–88 | Celtic | 0 | 0 |
| 1988–89 | Celtic | 0 | 0 |
| 1989–90 | Celtic | 0 | 0 |
| 1990–91 | Dundee U | 2 | 0 |
| 1991–92 | Dundee U | 10 | 1 |
| 1992–93 | Dundee U | 15 | 3 |
| 1993–94 | Dundee U | 12 | 0 |
| 1994–95 | Dundee U | 7 | 0 |
| 1994–95 | Rangers | 6 | 0 |
| 1995–96 | Rangers | 4 | 0 |
| 1996–97 | Rangers | 0 | 0 |
| 1997–98 | Rangers | 1 | 0 |
| **Total:** | | **57** | **4** |

## BOLLAND, Paul — Midfield

H: 5 10 W: 10 12 b.Bradford 23-12-79

*Source:* Trainee.

| | | | |
|---|---|---|---|
| 1997–98 | Bradford C | 10 | 0 |
| **Total:** | | **10** | **0** |

## BONALAIR, Thierry — Midfield

H: 5 8 W: 10 05 b.Paris 14-6-66

| | | | |
|---|---|---|---|
| 1987–88 | Nantes | 13 | 0 |
| 1988–89 | Nantes | 35 | 1 |
| 1989–90 | Nantes | 31 | 0 |
| 1990–91 | Nantes | 35 | 0 |
| 1991–92 | Nantes | 31 | 1 |
| 1992–93 | Auxerre | 25 | 1 |
| 1993–94 | Lille | 34 | 3 |
| 1994–95 | Lille | 35 | 2 |
| 1995–96 | Neuchatel Xamax | 34 | 3 |
| 1996–97 | Neuchatel Xamax | 34 | 6 |
| 1997–98 | Nottingham F | 31 | 2 |
| **Total:** | | **338** | **19** |

## BONETTI, Ivano — Midfield

H: 5 9 W: 11 05 b.Brescia 1-8-64

*Source:* Torino.

| | | | |
|---|---|---|---|
| 1995–96 | Grimsby T | 19 | 3 |
| 1996–97 | Tranmere R | 13 | 1 |
| 1997–98 | Crystal Palace | 2 | 0 |
| **Total:** | | **34** | **4** |

## BONNER, Mark — Midfield

H: 5 10 W: 11 00 b.Ormskirk 7-6-74

*Source:* Trainee.

| | | | |
|---|---|---|---|
| 1991–92 | Blackpool | 3 | 0 |
| 1992–93 | Blackpool | 15 | 0 |
| 1993–94 | Blackpool | 40 | 7 |
| 1994–95 | Blackpool | 17 | 0 |
| 1995–96 | Blackpool | 42 | 3 |
| 1996–97 | Blackpool | 29 | 1 |
| 1997–98 | Blackpool | 32 | 3 |
| **Total:** | | **178** | **14** |

## BOOGERS, Marco — Midfield

H: 6 1 W: 12 00 b.Dordrecht 12-1-67

| | | | |
|---|---|---|---|
| 1986–87 | DS 79 | 31 | 13 |
| 1987–88 | DS 79 | 29 | 5 |
| 1988–89 | Utrecht | 33 | 11 |
| 1989–90 | Utrecht | 27 | 4 |
| 1990–91 | RKC | 33 | 14 |
| 1991–92 | Fortuna Sittard | 29 | 13 |

| | | | |
|---|---|---|---|
| 1992–93 | RKC | 32 | 17 |
| 1993–94 | RKC | 32 | 11 |
| 1994–95 | RKC | 7 | 4 |
| 1994–95 | Sparta | 25 | 11 |
| 1995–96 | West Ham U | 4 | 0 |
| 1996–97 | West Ham U | 0 | 0 |
| 1997–98 | West Ham U | 0 | 0 |
| **Total:** | | **282** | **103** |

## BOOTH, Andy — Forward

H: 6 1 W: 13 00 b.Huddersfield 6-12-73

*Source:* Trainee. *Honours:* England Under-21.

| | | | |
|---|---|---|---|
| 1991–92 | Huddersfield T | 3 | 0 |
| 1992–93 | Huddersfield T | 5 | 2 |
| 1993–94 | Huddersfield T | 26 | 10 |
| 1994–95 | Huddersfield T | 46 | 26 |
| 1995–96 | Huddersfield T | 43 | 16 |
| 1996–97 | Sheffield W | 35 | 10 |
| 1997–98 | Sheffield W | 23 | 7 |
| **Total:** | | **181** | **71** |

## BOOTHROYD, Aidy — Defender

H: 5 9 W: 11 07 b.Bradford 8-2-71

*Source:* Trainee.

| | | | |
|---|---|---|---|
| 1989–90 | Huddersfield T | 10 | 0 |
| 1990–91 | Bristol R | 3 | 0 |
| 1991–92 | Bristol R | 13 | 0 |
| 1992–93 | Hearts | 4 | 0 |
| 1993–94 | Hearts | 0 | 0 |
| 1993–94 | Mansfield T | 23 | 1 |
| 1994–95 | Mansfield T | 36 | 0 |
| 1995–96 | Mansfield T | 43 | 2 |
| 1996–97 | Peterborough U | 26 | 1 |
| 1997–98 | Peterborough U | 0 | 0 |
| **Total:** | | **158** | **4** |

## BOOTY, Martyn — Defender

H: 5 8 W: 11 02 b.Kirby Muxloe 30-5-71

*Source:* Trainee.

| | | | |
|---|---|---|---|
| 1991–92 | Coventry C | 3 | 0 |
| 1992–93 | Coventry C | 0 | 0 |
| 1993–94 | Coventry C | 2 | 0 |
| 1993–94 | Crewe Alex | 31 | 1 |
| 1994–95 | Crewe Alex | 44 | 2 |
| 1995–96 | Crewe Alex | 21 | 2 |
| 1995–96 | Reading | 17 | 1 |
| 1996–97 | Reading | 14 | 0 |
| 1997–98 | Reading | 25 | 0 |
| **Total:** | | **157** | **6** |

## BORBOKIS, Vassilis — Defender

H: 5 11 W: 12 00 b.Serres 10-2-69

| | | | |
|---|---|---|---|
| 1992–93 | Apollon | 29 | 2 |
| 1993–94 | AEK Athens | 24 | 2 |
| 1994–95 | AEK Athens | 11 | 1 |
| 1995–96 | AEK Athens | 24 | 2 |
| 1996–97 | AEK Athens | 27 | 4 |
| 1997–98 | Sheffield U | 36 | 2 |
| **Total:** | | **151** | **13** |

## BORG, John — Midfield

H: 5 7 W: 10 07 b.Salford 22-2-80

*Source:* Trainee.

| | | | |
|---|---|---|---|
| 1997–98 | Doncaster R | 1 | 0 |
| **Total:** | | **1** | **0** |

## BORROWS, Brian — Defender

H: 5 10 W: 11 12 b.Liverpool 20-12-60

*Source:* Amateur. *Honours:* England B.

| | | | |
|---|---|---|---|
| 1979–80 | Everton | 0 | 0 |
| 1980–81 | Everton | 0 | 0 |
| 1981–82 | Everton | 15 | 0 |
| 1982–83 | Everton | 12 | 0 |
| 1982–83 | Bolton W | 9 | 0 |
| 1983–84 | Bolton W | 44 | 0 |
| 1984–85 | Bolton W | 42 | 0 |
| 1985–86 | Coventry C | 41 | 0 |
| 1986–87 | Coventry C | 41 | 1 |
| 1987–88 | Coventry C | 33 | 0 |
| 1988–89 | Coventry C | 38 | 1 |
| 1989–90 | Coventry C | 37 | 1 |
| 1990–91 | Coventry C | 38 | 6 |
| 1991–92 | Coventry C | 35 | 0 |
| 1992–93 | Coventry C | 38 | 2 |
| 1993–94 | Coventry C | 29 | 0 |
| 1993–94 | Bristol C (loan) | 6 | 0 |
| 1994–95 | Coventry C | 35 | 0 |
| 1995–96 | Coventry C | 21 | 0 |
| 1996–97 | Coventry C | 23 | 0 |
| 1997–98 | Coventry C | 0 | 0 |
| 1997–98 | Swindon T | 40 | 0 |
| **Total:** | | **577** | **11** |

## BOS, Gijsbert — Forward

H: 6 4 W: 12 09 b.Spakenburg 22-2-73

*Source:* Ijsselmeervogels. *Honours:*

| | | | |
|---|---|---|---|
| 1995–96 | Lincoln C | 11 | 5 |
| 1996–97 | Lincoln C | 23 | 1 |

| | | | |
|---|---|---|---|
| 1997–98 | Rotherham U | 16 | 4 |
| 1997–98 | Walsall (loan) | 0 | 0 |
| **Total:** | | **50** | **10** |

## BOSANCIC, Jovo — Midfield

H: 5 11 W: 13 00 b.Novi Sad 7-8-70

*Source:* Uniao Madeira.

| | | | |
|---|---|---|---|
| 1996–97 | Barnsley | 25 | 1 |
| 1997–98 | Barnsley | 17 | 2 |
| **Total:** | | **42** | **3** |

## BOSNICH, Mark — Goalkeeper

H: 6 1 W: 14 07 b.Fairfield 13-1-72

*Source:* Croatia Sydney. *Honours:* Australia 17 full caps, 1 goal.

| | | | |
|---|---|---|---|
| 1989–90 | Manchester U | 1 | 0 |
| 1990–91 | Manchester U | 2 | 0 |
| 1991–92 | Aston Villa | 1 | 0 |
| 1992–93 | Aston Villa | 17 | 0 |
| 1993–94 | Aston Villa | 28 | 0 |
| 1994–95 | Aston Villa | 30 | 0 |
| 1995–96 | Aston Villa | 38 | 1 |
| 1996–97 | Aston Villa | 20 | 0 |
| 1997–98 | Aston Villa | 30 | 0 |
| **Total:** | | **167** | **1** |

## BOSWELL, Matthew — Goalkeeper

H: 6 2 W: 13 08 b.Shrewsbury 19-8-77

| | | | |
|---|---|---|---|
| 1996–97 | Port Vale | 0 | 0 |
| 1997–98 | Port Vale | 0 | 0 |
| 1997–98 | Barnet (loan) | 0 | 0 |

## BOULD, Steve — Defender

H: 6 4 W: 14 02 b.Stoke 16-11-62

*Source:* Apprentice. *Honours:* England 2 full caps.

| | | | |
|---|---|---|---|
| 1980–81 | Stoke C | 0 | 0 |
| 1981–82 | Stoke C | 2 | 0 |
| 1982–83 | Stoke C | 14 | 0 |
| 1982–83 | Torquay U (loan) | 9 | 0 |
| 1983–84 | Stoke C | 38 | 2 |
| 1984–85 | Stoke C | 38 | 3 |
| 1985–86 | Stoke C | 33 | 0 |
| 1986–87 | Stoke C | 28 | 1 |
| 1987–88 | Stoke C | 30 | 0 |
| 1988–89 | Arsenal | 30 | 2 |
| 1989–90 | Arsenal | 19 | 0 |
| 1990–91 | Arsenal | 38 | 0 |
| 1991–92 | Arsenal | 25 | 1 |
| 1992–93 | Arsenal | 24 | 1 |
| 1993–94 | Arsenal | 25 | 1 |
| 1994–95 | Arsenal | 31 | 0 |
| 1995–96 | Arsenal | 19 | 0 |
| 1996–97 | Arsenal | 33 | 0 |
| 1997–98 | Arsenal | 24 | 0 |
| **Total:** | | **460** | **11** |

## BOUND, Matthew — Defender

H: 6 2 W: 14 00 b.Bradford-on-Avon 9-11-72

*Source:* Trainee.

| | | | |
|---|---|---|---|
| 1990–91 | Southampton | 1 | 0 |
| 1991–92 | Southampton | 0 | 0 |
| 1992–93 | Southampton | 3 | 0 |
| 1993–94 | Southampton | 1 | 0 |
| 1993–94 | Hull C (loan) | 7 | 1 |
| 1994–95 | Southampton | 0 | 0 |
| 1994–95 | Stockport Co | 14 | 0 |
| 1995–96 | Stockport Co | 26 | 5 |
| 1995–96 | Lincoln C (loan) | 4 | 0 |
| 1996–97 | Stockport Co | 4 | 0 |
| 1997–98 | Stockport Co | 0 | 0 |
| 1997–98 | Swansea C | 28 | 0 |
| **Total:** | | **88** | **6** |

## BOWEN, Jason — Midfield

H: 5 7 W: 11 00 b.Merthyr 24-8-72

*Source:* Trainee. *Honours:* Wales Youth, Under-21, 2 full caps.

| | | | |
|---|---|---|---|
| 1990–91 | Swansea C | 3 | 0 |
| 1991–92 | Swansea C | 11 | 0 |
| 1992–93 | Swansea C | 38 | 10 |
| 1993–94 | Swansea C | 41 | 11 |
| 1994–95 | Swansea C | 31 | 5 |
| 1995–96 | Birmingham C | 23 | 4 |
| 1996–97 | Birmingham C | 25 | 3 |
| 1997–98 | Birmingham C | 0 | 0 |
| 1997–98 | Southampton (loan) | 3 | 0 |
| 1997–98 | Reading | 14 | 1 |
| **Total:** | | **189** | **34** |

## BOWEN, Mark — Defender

H: 5 8 W: 11 07 b.Neath 7-12-63

*Source:* Apprentice. *Honours:* Wales Schools, Youth, Under-21, 41 full caps, 3 goals.

| | | | |
|---|---|---|---|
| 1981–82 | Tottenham H | 0 | 0 |
| 1982–83 | Tottenham H | 0 | 0 |
| 1983–84 | Tottenham H | 7 | 0 |
| 1984–85 | Tottenham H | 6 | 0 |
| 1985–86 | Tottenham H | 2 | 1 |
| 1986–87 | Tottenham H | 2 | 1 |
| 1987–88 | Norwich C | 24 | 1 |
| 1988–89 | Norwich C | 35 | 2 |
| 1989–90 | Norwich C | 38 | 7 |

| | | | |
|---|---|---|---|
| 1990–91 | Norwich C | 37 | 1 |
| 1991–92 | Norwich C | 36 | 3 |
| 1992–93 | Norwich C | 42 | 1 |
| 1993–94 | Norwich C | 41 | 5 |
| 1994–95 | Norwich C | 36 | 2 |
| 1995–96 | Norwich C | 31 | 2 |
| 1996–97 | West Ham U | 17 | 1 |

From Shimizu.

| | | | |
|---|---|---|---|
| 1997–98 | Charlton Ath | 36 | 0 |
| **Total:** | | **390** | **27** |

## BOWER, Mark — Defender

H: 5 10 W: 10 11 b.Bradford 23-1-80

*Source:* Trainee.

| | | | |
|---|---|---|---|
| 1997–98 | Bradford C | 3 | 0 |
| **Total:** | | **3** | **0** |

## BOWLING, Ian — Goalkeeper

H: 6 3 W: 13 11 b.Sheffield 27-7-65

*Source:* Gainsborough T.

| | | | |
|---|---|---|---|
| 1988–89 | Lincoln C | 8 | 0 |
| 1989–90 | Lincoln C | 0 | 0 |
| 1989–90 | Hartlepool U (loan) | 1 | 0 |
| 1990–91 | Lincoln C | 16 | 0 |
| 1991–92 | Lincoln C | 20 | 0 |
| 1992–93 | Lincoln C | 15 | 0 |
| 1992–93 | Bradford C (loan) | 7 | 0 |
| 1993–94 | Bradford C | 23 | 0 |
| 1994–95 | Bradford C | 6 | 0 |
| 1995–96 | Mansfield T | 44 | 0 |
| 1996–97 | Mansfield T | 46 | 0 |
| 1997–98 | Mansfield T | 33 | 0 |
| **Total:** | | **219** | **0** |

## BOWMAN, Darren — Midfield

b.Abergavenny 4-11-78

*Source:* Trainee.

| | | | |
|---|---|---|---|
| 1997–98 | WBA | 0 | 0 |

## BOWMAN, David — Midfield

H: 5 10 W: 11 02 b.Tunbridge Wells 10-3-64

*Source:* Salvesen BC. *Honours:* Scotland Under-21, 6 full caps.

| | | | |
|---|---|---|---|
| 1980–81 | Hearts | 17 | 1 |
| 1981–82 | Hearts | 16 | 1 |
| 1982–83 | Hearts | 39 | 5 |
| 1983–84 | Hearts | 33 | 0 |
| 1984–85 | Hearts | 11 | 1 |
| 1984–85 | Coventry C | 10 | 0 |
| 1985–86 | Coventry C | 30 | 2 |
| 1986–87 | Dundee U | 29 | 0 |
| 1987–88 | Dundee U | 39 | 1 |
| 1988–89 | Dundee U | 29 | 1 |
| 1989–90 | Dundee U | 24 | 1 |
| 1990–91 | Dundee U | 20 | 1 |
| 1991–92 | Dundee U | 41 | 3 |
| 1992–93 | Dundee U | 24 | 0 |
| 1993–94 | Dundee U | 35 | 2 |
| 1994–95 | Dundee U | 31 | 0 |
| 1995–96 | Dundee U | 17 | 0 |
| 1996–97 | Dundee U | 28 | 0 |
| 1997–98 | Dundee U | 19 | 0 |
| **Total:** | | **492** | **19** |

## BOWMAN, Gary — Forward

H: 5 11 W: 11 04 b.Glasgow 12-8-74

*Source:* Knightswood Juv.

| | | | |
|---|---|---|---|
| 1993–94 | Clydebank | 1 | 0 |
| 1994–95 | Clydebank | 32 | 0 |
| 1995–96 | Clydebank | 33 | 2 |
| 1996–97 | Clydebank | 22 | 0 |
| 1996–97 | St Johnstone | 4 | 0 |
| 1997–98 | St Johnstone | 1 | 0 |
| **Total:** | | **93** | **2** |

## BOWMAN, Rob — Defender

H: 6 0 W: 12 10 b.Durham 21-11-75

*Source:* Trainee. *Honours:* England Youth.

| | | | |
|---|---|---|---|
| 1992–93 | Leeds U | 4 | 0 |
| 1993–94 | Leeds U | 0 | 0 |
| 1994–95 | Leeds U | 0 | 0 |
| 1995–96 | Leeds U | 3 | 0 |
| 1996–97 | Leeds U | 0 | 0 |
| 1996–97 | Rotherham U | 13 | 0 |
| 1997–98 | Carlisle U | 7 | 1 |
| **Total:** | | **27** | **1** |

## BOWRY, Bobby — Midfield

H: 5 8 W: 10 08 b.Croydon 19-5-71

| | | | |
|---|---|---|---|
| 1991–92 | Crystal Palace | 0 | 0 |
| 1992–93 | Crystal Palace | 11 | 1 |
| 1993–94 | Crystal Palace | 21 | 0 |
| 1994–95 | Crystal Palace | 18 | 0 |
| 1995–96 | Millwall | 38 | 2 |
| 1996–97 | Millwall | 28 | 1 |
| 1997–98 | Millwall | 43 | 2 |
| **Total:** | | **159** | **6** |

## BOWYER, Lee — Midfield

H: 5 9 W: 9 09 b.London 3-1-77

*Source:* Trainee. *Honours:* England Youth, Under-21.

| | | | |
|---|---|---|---|
| 1993–94 | Charlton Ath | 0 | 0 |
| 1994–95 | Charlton Ath | 5 | 0 |
| 1995–96 | Charlton Ath | 41 | 8 |
| 1996–97 | Leeds U | 32 | 4 |
| 1997–98 | Leeds U | 25 | 3 |
| **Total:** | | **103** | **15** |

## BOXALL, Danny — Defender

H: 5 8 W: 10 05 b.Croydon 24-8-77

*Source:* Trainee.

| | | | |
|---|---|---|---|
| 1994–95 | Crystal Palace | 0 | 0 |
| 1995–96 | Crystal Palace | 1 | 0 |
| 1996–97 | Crystal Palace | 6 | 0 |
| 1997–98 | Crystal Palace | 1 | 0 |
| 1997–98 | Oldham Ath (loan) | 18 | 0 |
| **Total:** | | **26** | **0** |

## BOYACK, Steven — Midfield

H: 5 10 W: 10 07 b.Edinburgh 4-9-76

*Source:* Rangers BC. *Honours:* Scotland Under-21.

| | | | |
|---|---|---|---|
| 1996–97 | Rangers | 1 | 0 |
| 1997–98 | Rangers | 0 | 0 |
| 1997–98 | Hull C (loan) | 12 | 3 |
| **Total:** | | **13** | **3** |

## BOYCE, Emmerson — Defender

H: 5 11 W: 11 07 b.Aylesbury 24-9-79

*Source:* Trainee.

| | | | |
|---|---|---|---|
| 1997–98 | Luton T | 0 | 0 |

## BOYD, Tom — Defender

H: 5 11 W: 11 04 b.Glasgow 24-11-65

*Source:* 'S' Form. *Honours:* Scotland Youth, Under-21 B, 58 full caps, 1 goal.

| | | | |
|---|---|---|---|
| 1983–84 | Motherwell | 13 | 0 |
| 1984–85 | Motherwell | 36 | 0 |
| 1985–86 | Motherwell | 31 | 0 |
| 1986–87 | Motherwell | 31 | 0 |
| 1987–88 | Motherwell | 42 | 2 |
| 1988–89 | Motherwell | 36 | 1 |
| 1989–90 | Motherwell | 33 | 1 |
| 1990–91 | Motherwell | 30 | 2 |
| 1991–92 | Chelsea | 23 | 0 |
| 1991–92 | Celtic | 13 | 1 |
| 1992–93 | Celtic | 42 | 0 |
| 1993–94 | Celtic | 38 | 0 |
| 1994–95 | Celtic | 35 | 1 |
| 1995–96 | Celtic | 34 | 0 |
| 1996–97 | Celtic | 31 | 0 |
| 1997–98 | Celtic | 33 | 0 |
| **Total:** | | **501** | **8** |

## BOYES, Scott — Defender

H: 5 10 W: 11 06 b.Guisborough 7-1-79

*Source:* York C Trainee.

| | | | |
|---|---|---|---|
| 1997–98 | Scarborough | 0 | 0 |

## BOYLAN, Lee — Forward

b.Chelmsford 2-9-78

*Source:* Trainee.

| | | | |
|---|---|---|---|
| 1996–97 | West Ham U | 1 | 0 |
| 1997–98 | West Ham U | 0 | 0 |
| **Total:** | | **1** | **0** |

## BOYLE, Wesley — Midfield

b.Portadown 30-3-79

*Source:* Trainee. *Honours:* Northern Ireland Under-21.

| | | | |
|---|---|---|---|
| 1995–96 | Leeds U | 0 | 0 |
| 1996–97 | Leeds U | 1 | 0 |
| 1997–98 | Leeds U | 0 | 0 |
| **Total:** | | **1** | **0** |

## BRABIN, Gary — Midfield

H: 5 11 W: 14 08 b.Liverpool 9-2-70

*Source:* Trainee.

| | | | |
|---|---|---|---|
| 1989–90 | Stockport Co | 1 | 0 |
| 1990–91 | Stockport Co | 1 | 0 |
| From Runcorn. | | | |
| 1994–95 | Doncaster R | 28 | 8 |
| 1995–96 | Doncaster R | 31 | 3 |
| 1995–96 | Bury | 5 | 0 |
| 1996–97 | Blackpool | 32 | 2 |
| 1997–98 | Blackpool | 24 | 3 |
| **Total:** | | **122** | **16** |

## BRACE, Deryn — Defender

H: 5 7 W: 10 12 b.Haverfordwest 15-3-75

*Source:* Trainee. *Honours:* Wales Under-21.

| | | | |
|---|---|---|---|
| 1993–94 | Norwich C | 0 | 0 |
| 1993–94 | Wrexham | 1 | 0 |
| 1994–95 | Wrexham | 14 | 0 |

| | | | |
|---|---|---|---|
| 1995–96 | Wrexham | 16 | 1 |
| 1996–97 | Wrexham | 26 | 1 |
| 1997–98 | Wrexham | 8 | 0 |
| **Total:** | | **65** | **2** |

## BRACEWELL, Paul — Midfield

H: 5 9 W: 12 03 b.Heswall 19-7-62

*Source:* Apprentice. *Honours:* England Under-21, 3 full caps.

| | | | |
|---|---|---|---|
| 1979–80 | Stoke C | 6 | 0 |
| 1980–81 | Stoke C | 40 | 2 |
| 1981–82 | Stoke C | 42 | 1 |
| 1982–83 | Stoke C | 41 | 2 |
| 1983–84 | Sunderland | 38 | 4 |
| 1984–85 | Everton | 37 | 2 |
| 1985–86 | Everton | 38 | 3 |
| 1986–87 | Everton | 0 | 0 |
| 1987–88 | Everton | 0 | 0 |
| 1988–89 | Everton | 20 | 2 |
| 1989–90 | Everton | 0 | 0 |
| 1989–90 | Sunderland | 37 | 2 |
| 1990–91 | Sunderland | 37 | 0 |
| 1991–92 | Sunderland | 39 | 0 |
| 1992–93 | Newcastle U | 25 | 2 |
| 1993–94 | Newcastle U | 32 | 1 |
| 1994–95 | Newcastle U | 16 | 0 |
| 1995–96 | Sunderland | 38 | 0 |
| 1996–97 | Sunderland | 38 | 0 |
| 1997–98 | Sunderland | 1 | 0 |
| 1997–98 | Fulham | 36 | 0 |
| **Total:** | | **561** | **21** |

## BRACEY, Lee — Goalkeeper

H: 6 2 W: 13 02 b.Barking 11-9-68

*Source:* Trainee.

| | | | |
|---|---|---|---|
| 1987–88 | West Ham U | 0 | 0 |
| 1988–89 | Swansea C | 30 | 0 |
| 1989–90 | Swansea C | 31 | 0 |
| 1990–91 | Swansea C | 35 | 0 |
| 1991–92 | Swansea C | 3 | 0 |
| 1991–92 | Halifax T | 32 | 0 |
| 1992–93 | Halifax T | 41 | 0 |
| 1993–94 | Bury | 40 | 0 |
| 1994–95 | Bury | 6 | 0 |
| 1995–96 | Bury | 21 | 0 |
| 1996–97 | Bury | 0 | 0 |
| 1996–97 | Ipswich T (loan) | 0 | 0 |
| 1997–98 | Ipswich T | 0 | 0 |
| **Total:** | | **239** | **0** |

## BRADBURY, Lee — Forward

H: 6 2 W: 13 10 b.Isle of Wight 3-7-75

*Source:* Cowes. *Honours:* England Under-21.

| | | | |
|---|---|---|---|
| 1995–96 | Portsmouth | 12 | 0 |
| 1995–96 | Exeter C (loan) | 14 | 5 |
| 1996–97 | Portsmouth | 42 | 15 |
| 1997–98 | Manchester C | 27 | 7 |
| **Total:** | | **95** | **27** |

## BRADLEY, Mark — Midfield

H: 5 6 W: 9 07 b.Glasgow 10-8-76

*Source:* Ashfield J.

| | | | |
|---|---|---|---|
| 1997–98 | Hearts | 1 | 0 |
| **Total:** | | **1** | **0** |

## BRADLEY, Russell — Defender

H: 6 2 W: 13 02 b.Birmingham 28-3-66

*Source:* Dudley T.

| | | | |
|---|---|---|---|
| 1987–88 | Nottingham F | 0 | 0 |
| 1988–89 | Nottingham F | 0 | 0 |
| 1988–89 | Hereford U (loan) | 12 | 1 |
| 1989–90 | Hereford U | 33 | 1 |
| 1990–91 | Hereford U | 41 | 2 |
| 1991–92 | Hereford U | 3 | 0 |
| 1991–92 | Halifax T | 26 | 2 |
| 1992–93 | Halifax T | 30 | 1 |
| 1993–94 | Scunthorpe U | 34 | 1 |
| 1994–95 | Scunthorpe U | 25 | 2 |
| 1995–96 | Scunthorpe U | 38 | 1 |
| 1996–97 | Scunthorpe U | 22 | 1 |
| 1996–97 | Hartlepool U (loan) | 12 | 1 |
| 1997–98 | Hartlepool U | 43 | 1 |
| **Total:** | | **319** | **14** |

## BRADLEY, Shayne — Forward

H: 5 11 W: 13 02 b.Gloucester 8-12-79

*Source:* Trainee. *Honours:* England Schools.

| | | | |
|---|---|---|---|
| 1997–98 | Southampton | 0 | 0 |

## BRADSHAW, Carl — Defender

H: 5 10 W: 11 11 b.Sheffield 2-10-68

*Source:* Apprentice. *Honours:* England Youth.

| | | | |
|---|---|---|---|
| 1986–87 | Sheffield W | 9 | 2 |
| 1986–87 | Barnsley (loan) | 6 | 1 |
| 1987–88 | Sheffield W | 20 | 2 |
| 1988–89 | Sheffield W | 3 | 0 |
| 1988–89 | Manchester C | 5 | 0 |
| 1989–90 | Manchester C | 0 | 0 |

| | | | |
|---|---|---|---|
| 1989–90 | Sheffield U | 30 | 3 |
| 1990–91 | Sheffield U | 27 | 1 |
| 1991–92 | Sheffield U | 18 | 2 |
| 1992–93 | Sheffield U | 32 | 1 |
| 1993–94 | Sheffield U | 40 | 1 |
| 1994–95 | Norwich C | 26 | 1 |
| 1995–96 | Norwich C | 21 | 1 |
| 1996–97 | Norwich C | 17 | 0 |
| 1997–98 | Norwich C | 1 | 0 |
| 1997–98 | Wigan Ath | 28 | 1 |
| **Total:** | | **283** | **16** |

## BRADSHAW, Darren — Defender

H: 5 11 W: 11 03 b.Sheffield 19-3-67

*Source:* Matlock T.

| | | | |
|---|---|---|---|
| 1987–88 | Chesterfield | 18 | 0 |
| 1987–88 | York C | 25 | 1 |
| 1988–89 | York C | 34 | 2 |
| 1989–90 | York C | 0 | 0 |
| 1989–90 | Newcastle U | 12 | 0 |
| 1990–91 | Newcastle U | 7 | 0 |
| 1991–92 | Newcastle U | 19 | 0 |
| 1992–93 | Peterborough U | 34 | 0 |
| 1993–94 | Peterborough U | 39 | 1 |
| 1994–95 | Peterborough U | 0 | 0 |
| 1994–95 | Plymouth Arg (loan) | 6 | 1 |
| 1994–95 | Blackpool | 26 | 1 |
| 1995–96 | Blackpool | 25 | 0 |
| 1996–97 | Blackpool | 10 | 0 |
| 1997–98 | Blackpool | 6 | 0 |
| **Total:** | | **261** | **6** |

## BRADY, Garry — Midfield

H: 5 10 W: 10 95 b.Glasgow 7-9-76

*Source:* Trainee.

| | | | |
|---|---|---|---|
| 1993–94 | Tottenham H | 0 | 0 |
| 1994–95 | Tottenham H | 0 | 0 |
| 1995–96 | Tottenham H | 0 | 0 |
| 1996–97 | Tottenham H | 0 | 0 |
| 1997–98 | Tottenham H | 9 | 0 |
| **Total:** | | **9** | **0** |

## BRADY, Matthew — Midfield

H: 5 11 W: 11 01 b.London 27-10-77

*Source:* Trainee.

| | | | |
|---|---|---|---|
| 1994–95 | Barnet | 1 | 0 |
| 1995–96 | Barnet | 2 | 0 |
| 1996–97 | Barnet | 7 | 0 |
| 1997–98 | Barnet | 0 | 0 |
| **Total:** | | **10** | **0** |

## BRAITHWAITE, Leon — Forward

H: 6 0 W: 12 00 b.Hackney 17-12-72

*Source:* Bishops Stortford.

| | | | |
|---|---|---|---|
| 1995–96 | Exeter C | 23 | 3 |
| 1996–97 | Exeter C | 38 | 5 |
| 1997–98 | Exeter C | 5 | 1 |
| **Total:** | | **66** | **9** |

## BRAMMER, David — Midfield

H: 5 9 W: 12 00 b.Bromborough 28-2-75

*Source:* Trainee.

| | | | |
|---|---|---|---|
| 1992–93 | Wrexham | 2 | 0 |
| 1993–94 | Wrexham | 22 | 2 |
| 1994–95 | Wrexham | 14 | 1 |
| 1995–96 | Wrexham | 11 | 2 |
| 1996–97 | Wrexham | 21 | 1 |
| 1997–98 | Wrexham | 33 | 4 |
| **Total:** | | **103** | **10** |

## BRANAGAN, Keith — Goalkeeper

H: 6 0 W: 13 02 b.Fulham 10-7-66

*Honours:* Eire B. 1 full cap.

| | | | |
|---|---|---|---|
| 1983–84 | Cambridge U | 1 | 0 |
| 1984–85 | Cambridge U | 19 | 0 |
| 1985–86 | Cambridge U | 9 | 0 |
| 1986–87 | Cambridge U | 46 | 0 |
| 1987–88 | Cambridge U | 35 | 0 |
| 1987–88 | Millwall | 0 | 0 |
| 1988–89 | Millwall | 0 | 0 |
| 1989–90 | Millwall | 16 | 0 |
| 1989–90 | Brentford (loan) | 2 | 0 |
| 1990–91 | Millwall | 18 | 0 |
| 1991–92 | Millwall | 12 | 0 |
| 1991–92 | Gillingham (loan) | 1 | 0 |
| 1991–92 | Fulham (loan) | 0 | 0 |
| 1992–93 | Bolton W | 46 | 0 |
| 1993–94 | Bolton W | 10 | 0 |
| 1994–95 | Bolton W | 43 | 0 |
| 1995–96 | Bolton W | 31 | 0 |
| 1996–97 | Bolton W | 36 | 0 |
| 1997–98 | Bolton W | 34 | 0 |
| **Total:** | | **359** | **0** |

## BRANCA, Marco — Forward

H: 6 0 W: 11 07 b.Grosseto 6-1-65

| | | | |
|---|---|---|---|
| 1981–82 | Grosseto | 0 | 0 |
| 1982–83 | Cagliari | 0 | 0 |
| 1983–84 | Cagliari | 0 | 0 |
| 1984–85 | Cagliari | 25 | 2 |
| 1985–86 | Cagliari | 27 | 2 |

| | | | |
|---|---|---|---|
| 1986–87 | Udinese | 18 | 2 |
| 1987–88 | Sampdoria | 9 | 1 |
| 1988–89 | Udinese | 28 | 4 |
| 1989–90 | Udinese | 27 | 9 |
| 1990–91 | Sampdoria | 20 | 5 |
| 1991–92 | Fiorentina | 23 | 5 |
| 1992–93 | Udinese | 29 | 8 |
| 1993–94 | Udinese | 29 | 14 |
| 1994–95 | Parma | 25 | 7 |
| 1995–96 | Roma | 7 | 2 |
| 1995–96 | Internazionale | 24 | 17 |
| 1996–97 | Internazionale | 21 | 5 |
| 1997–98 | Internazionale | 7 | 1 |
| 1997–98 | Middlesbrough | 11 | 9 |
| **Total:** | | **330** | **93** |

## BRANCH, Graham — Forward

H: 6 2 W: 12 02 b.Liverpool 12-2-72

*Source:* Heswall.

| | | | |
|---|---|---|---|
| 1991–92 | Tranmere R | 4 | 0 |
| 1992–93 | Tranmere R | 3 | 0 |
| 1992–93 | Bury (loan) | 4 | 1 |
| 1993–94 | Tranmere R | 13 | 0 |
| 1994–95 | Tranmere R | 1 | 0 |
| 1995–96 | Tranmere R | 21 | 2 |
| 1996–97 | Tranmere R | 35 | 5 |
| 1997–98 | Tranmere R | 25 | 3 |
| 1997–98 | Wigan Ath (loan) | 3 | 0 |
| **Total:** | | **109** | **11** |

## BRANCH, Michael — Forward

H: 5 10 W: 11 00 b.Liverpool 18-10-78

*Source:* Trainee. *Honours:* England Schools, Youth, Under-21.

| | | | |
|---|---|---|---|
| 1995–96 | Everton | 3 | 0 |
| 1996–97 | Everton | 25 | 3 |
| 1997–98 | Everton | 6 | 0 |
| **Total:** | | **34** | **3** |

## BRANNAN, Ged — Defender

H: 6 0 W: 12 05 b.Liverpool 15-1-72

*Source:* Trainee.

| | | | |
|---|---|---|---|
| 1990–91 | Tranmere R | 18 | 1 |
| 1991–92 | Tranmere R | 18 | 1 |
| 1992–93 | Tranmere R | 38 | 1 |
| 1993–94 | Tranmere R | 45 | 9 |
| 1994–95 | Tranmere R | 41 | 2 |
| 1995–96 | Tranmere R | 44 | 0 |
| 1996–97 | Tranmere R | 34 | 6 |
| 1996–97 | Manchester C | 11 | 1 |
| 1997–98 | Manchester C | 32 | 3 |
| **Total:** | | **281** | **24** |

## BRANSTON, Guy — Defender

H: 6 1 W: 14 00 b.Leicester 9-1-79

*Source:* Trainee.

| | | | |
|---|---|---|---|
| 1997–98 | Leicester C | 0 | 0 |
| 1997–98 | Colchester U (loan) | 12 | 1 |
| **Total:** | | **12** | **1** |

## BRASS, Chris — Defender

H: 5 9 W: 12 06 b.Easington 24-7-75

*Source:* Trainee.

| | | | |
|---|---|---|---|
| 1993–94 | Burnley | 0 | 0 |
| 1994–95 | Burnley | 5 | 0 |
| 1994–95 | Torquay U (loan) | 7 | 0 |
| 1995–96 | Burnley | 9 | 0 |
| 1996–97 | Burnley | 39 | 0 |
| 1997–98 | Burnley | 40 | 1 |
| **Total:** | | **100** | **1** |

## BRATTBAKK, Harald — Forward

b.Norway 1-2-71

| | | | |
|---|---|---|---|
| 1990 | Rosenborg | 3 | 1 |
| 1991 | Rosenborg | 11 | 1 |
| 1992 | Bodo Glimt* | 0 | 0 |
| 1993 | Bodo Glimt | 22 | 9 |
| 1994 | Rosenborg | 22 | 17 |
| 1995 | Rosenborg | 26 | 26 |
| 1996 | Rosenborg | 26 | 28 |
| 1997 | Rosenborg | 26 | 23 |
| 1997–98 | Celtic | 18 | 7 |
| **Total:** | | **154** | **112** |

## BRAY, Justin — Goalkeeper

b.Great Yarmouth 1-11-79

*Source:* Trainee.

| | | | |
|---|---|---|---|
| 1997–98 | Wolverhampton W | 0 | 0 |

## BRAYSON, Paul — Forward

H: 5 4 W: 10 10 b.Newcastle 16-9-77

*Source:* Trainee. *Honours:* England Youth.

| | | | |
|---|---|---|---|
| 1995–96 | Newcastle U | 0 | 0 |
| 1996–97 | Newcastle U | 0 | 0 |
| 1996–97 | Swansea C (loan) | 11 | 5 |
| 1997–98 | Newcastle U | 0 | 0 |
| 1997–98 | Reading | 6 | 1 |
| **Total:** | | **17** | **6** |

## BRAZIER, Jeffrey — Midfield

b.Ascot 27-5-79

| | | | |
|---|---|---|---|
| 1997–98 | Leyton Orient | 0 | 0 |

## BRAZIER, Matthew — Midfield

H: 5 8 W: 11 08 b.Whipps Cross 2-7-76

*Source:* Trainee.

| | | | |
|---|---|---|---|
| 1994–95 | QPR | 0 | 0 |
| 1995–96 | QPR | 11 | 0 |
| 1996–97 | QPR | 27 | 2 |
| 1997–98 | QPR | 11 | 0 |
| 1997–98 | Fulham | 7 | 1 |
| **Total:** | | **56** | **3** |

## BRAZIER, Phil — Defender

H: 6 0 W: 13 00 b.Liverpool 3-9-77

*Source:* Trainee.

| | | | |
|---|---|---|---|
| 1995–96 | Liverpool | 0 | 0 |
| 1996–97 | Liverpool | 0 | 0 |
| 1997–98 | Liverpool | 0 | 0 |

## BREACKER, Tim — Defender

H: 5 11 W: 13 00 b.Bicester 2-7-65

*Source:* Apprentice. *Honours:* England Under-21.

| | | | |
|---|---|---|---|
| 1983–84 | Luton T | 2 | 0 |
| 1984–85 | Luton T | 35 | 0 |
| 1985–86 | Luton T | 36 | 0 |
| 1986–87 | Luton T | 29 | 1 |
| 1987–88 | Luton T | 40 | 1 |
| 1988–89 | Luton T | 22 | 0 |
| 1989–90 | Luton T | 38 | 1 |
| 1990–91 | Luton T | 8 | 0 |
| 1990–91 | West Ham U | 24 | 1 |
| 1991–92 | West Ham U | 34 | 2 |
| 1992–93 | West Ham U | 39 | 2 |
| 1993–94 | West Ham U | 40 | 3 |
| 1994–95 | West Ham U | 33 | 0 |
| 1995–96 | West Ham U | 22 | 0 |
| 1996–97 | West Ham U | 26 | 0 |
| 1997–98 | West Ham U | 19 | 0 |
| **Total:** | | **447** | **11** |

## BREBNER, Grant — Midfield

H: 5 10 W: 11 11 b.Edinburgh 6-12-77

*Source:* Trainee. *Honours:* Scotland Under-21.

| | | | |
|---|---|---|---|
| 1994–95 | Manchester U | 0 | 0 |
| 1995–96 | Manchester U | 0 | 0 |
| 1996–97 | Manchester U | 0 | 0 |
| 1997–98 | Manchester U | 0 | 0 |
| 1997–98 | Cambridge U (loan) | 6 | 1 |
| 1997–98 | Hibernian (loan) | 9 | 1 |
| **Total:** | | **15** | **2** |

## BRECKIN, Ian — Defender

H: 5 11 W: 11 07 b.Rotherham 24-2-75

*Source:* Trainee.

| | | | |
|---|---|---|---|
| 1993–94 | Rotherham U | 10 | 0 |
| 1994–95 | Rotherham U | 41 | 2 |
| 1995–96 | Rotherham U | 39 | 1 |
| 1996–97 | Rotherham U | 42 | 3 |
| 1997–98 | Chesterfield | 43 | 1 |
| **Total:** | | **175** | **7** |

## BREEN, Gary — Defender

H: 6 1 W: 11 12 b.London 12-12-73

*Source:* Charlton Ath. *Honours:* Eire Under-21, 15 full caps, 2 goals.

| | | | |
|---|---|---|---|
| 1991–92 | Maidstone U | 19 | 0 |
| 1992–93 | Gillingham | 29 | 0 |
| 1993–94 | Gillingham | 22 | 0 |
| 1994–95 | Peterborough U | 44 | 1 |
| 1995–96 | Peterborough U | 25 | 0 |
| 1995–96 | Birmingham C | 18 | 1 |
| 1996–97 | Birmingham C | 22 | 1 |
| 1996–97 | Coventry C | 9 | 0 |
| 1997–98 | Coventry C | 30 | 1 |
| **Total:** | | **218** | **4** |

## BRENNAN, Damien — Defender

b.Dublin 30-8-80

*Source:* Belvedere.

| | | | |
|---|---|---|---|
| 1997–98 | Huddersfield T | 0 | 0 |

## BRENNAN, Dean — Midfield

b.Dublin 17-6-80

| | | | |
|---|---|---|---|
| 1997–98 | Sheffield W | 0 | 0 |

## BRENNAN, Jim — Defender

H: 5 9 W: 11 06 b.Toronto 8-5-77

*Source:* Sora Lazio.

| | | | |
|---|---|---|---|
| 1994–95 | Bristol C | 0 | 0 |
| 1995–96 | Bristol C | 0 | 0 |
| 1996–97 | Bristol C | 8 | 0 |
| 1997–98 | Bristol C | 6 | 0 |
| **Total:** | | **14** | **0** |

## BRENNAN, Karl — Midfield

b.Leicester 19-3-81

*Source:* Trainee.

| | | | |
|---|---|---|---|
| 1997–98 | Leicester C | 0 | 0 |

## BRESLAN, Geoff — Forward

b.Torbay 4-6-80

*Source:* Trainee.

| | | | |
|---|---|---|---|
| 1997–98 | Exeter C | 1 | 0 |
| **Total:** | | **1** | **0** |

## BREVETT, Rufus — Defender

H: 5 8 W: 11 08 b.Derby 24-9-69

*Source:* Trainee.

| | | | |
|---|---|---|---|
| 1987–88 | Doncaster R | 17 | 0 |
| 1988–89 | Doncaster R | 23 | 0 |
| 1989–90 | Doncaster R | 42 | 0 |
| 1990–91 | Doncaster R | 27 | 3 |
| 1990–91 | QPR | 10 | 0 |
| 1991–92 | QPR | 7 | 0 |
| 1992–93 | QPR | 15 | 0 |
| 1993–94 | QPR | 7 | 0 |
| 1994–95 | QPR | 19 | 0 |
| 1995–96 | QPR | 27 | 1 |
| 1996–97 | QPR | 44 | 0 |
| 1997–98 | QPR | 23 | 0 |
| 1997–98 | Fulham | 11 | 0 |
| **Total:** | | **272** | **4** |

## BREWER, Ben — Defender

b.Pontypool 6-10-78

*Source:* Trainee.

| | | | |
|---|---|---|---|
| 1996–97 | Blackburn R | 0 | 0 |
| 1997–98 | Blackburn R | 0 | 0 |

## BRIDGE, Wayne — Forward

H: 5 10 W: 11 11 b.Southampton 5-8-80

*Source:* Trainee.

| | | | |
|---|---|---|---|
| 1997–98 | Southampton | 0 | 0 |

## BRIDGES, Michael — Forward

H: 6 1 W: 10 11 b.North Shields 5-8-78

*Source:* Trainee. *Honours:* England Schools, Youth, Under-21.

| | | | |
|---|---|---|---|
| 1995–96 | Sunderland | 15 | 4 |
| 1996–97 | Sunderland | 25 | 3 |
| 1997–98 | Sunderland | 9 | 1 |
| **Total:** | | **49** | **8** |

## BRIEN, Tony — Defender

H: 6 0 W: 13 02 b.Dublin 10-2-69

*Source:* Apprentice.

| | | | |
|---|---|---|---|
| 1986–87 | Leicester C | 0 | 0 |
| 1987–88 | Leicester C | 15 | 1 |
| 1988–89 | Leicester C | 1 | 0 |
| 1988–89 | Chesterfield | 29 | 1 |
| 1989–90 | Chesterfield | 43 | 3 |
| 1990–91 | Chesterfield | 43 | 3 |
| 1991–92 | Chesterfield | 41 | 0 |
| 1992–93 | Chesterfield | 39 | 1 |
| 1993–94 | Chesterfield | 9 | 0 |
| 1993–94 | Rotherham U | 26 | 2 |
| 1994–95 | Rotherham U | 17 | 0 |
| 1995–96 | WBA | 2 | 0 |
| 1995–96 | Mansfield T (loan) | 4 | 0 |
| 1995–96 | Chester C (loan) | 8 | 0 |
| 1996–97 | Hull C | 32 | 1 |
| 1997–98 | Hull C | 15 | 0 |
| **Total:** | | **324** | **12** |

## BRIGGS, Simon — Goalkeeper

b.Sheffield 14-10-78

| | | | |
|---|---|---|---|
| 1997–98 | Leeds U | 0 | 0 |

## BRIGHT, Mark — Forward

H: 6 0 W: 13 04 b.Stoke 6-6-62

*Source:* Leek T.

| | | | |
|---|---|---|---|
| 1981–82 | Port Vale | 2 | 0 |
| 1982–83 | Port Vale | 1 | 1 |
| 1983–84 | Port Vale | 26 | 9 |
| 1984–85 | Leicester C | 16 | 0 |
| 1985–86 | Leicester C | 24 | 6 |
| 1986–87 | Leicester C | 2 | 0 |
| 1986–87 | Crystal Palace | 28 | 8 |
| 1987–88 | Crystal Palace | 38 | 25 |
| 1988–89 | Crystal Palace | 46 | 20 |
| 1989–90 | Crystal Palace | 36 | 12 |
| 1990–91 | Crystal Palace | 32 | 9 |
| 1991–92 | Crystal Palace | 42 | 17 |
| 1992–93 | Crystal Palace | 5 | 1 |
| 1992–93 | Sheffield W | 30 | 11 |
| 1993–94 | Sheffield W | 40 | 19 |
| 1994–95 | Sheffield W | 37 | 11 |
| 1995–96 | Sheffield W | 25 | 7 |
| 1996–97 | Sheffield W | 1 | 0 |
| 1996–97 | Millwall (loan) | 3 | 1 |
| 1996–97 | Sion | 0 | 0 |

| | | | |
|---|---|---|---|
| 1996–97 | Charlton Ath | 6 | 2 |
| From Sion. | | | |
| 1997–98 | Charlton Ath | 16 | 7 |
| **Total:** | | **456** | **166** |

## BRIGHTWELL, David — Defender

H: 6 2 W: 13 05 b.Lutterworth 7-1-71

*Source:* Trainee.

| | | | |
|---|---|---|---|
| 1987–88 | Manchester C | 0 | 0 |
| 1988–89 | Manchester C | 0 | 0 |
| 1989–90 | Manchester C | 0 | 0 |
| 1990–91 | Manchester C | 0 | 0 |
| 1990–91 | Chester C (loan) | 6 | 0 |
| 1991–92 | Manchester C | 4 | 0 |
| 1992–93 | Manchester C | 8 | 0 |
| 1993–94 | Manchester C | 22 | 1 |
| 1994–95 | Manchester C | 9 | 0 |
| 1995–96 | Manchester C | 0 | 0 |
| 1995–96 | Lincoln C (loan) | 5 | 0 |
| 1995–96 | Stoke C (loan) | 1 | 0 |
| 1995–96 | Bradford C | 22 | 0 |
| 1996–97 | Bradford C | 2 | 0 |
| 1996–97 | Blackpool (loan) | 2 | 0 |
| 1997–98 | Northampton T | 35 | 1 |
| **Total:** | | **116** | **2** |

## BRIGHTWELL, Ian — Defender

H: 5 10 W: 12 05 b.Lutterworth 9-4-68

*Source:* Congleton T. *Honours:* England Schools, Youth, Under-21.

| | | | |
|---|---|---|---|
| 1986–87 | Manchester C | 16 | 1 |
| 1987–88 | Manchester C | 33 | 5 |
| 1988–89 | Manchester C | 26 | 6 |
| 1989–90 | Manchester C | 28 | 2 |
| 1990–91 | Manchester C | 33 | 0 |
| 1991–92 | Manchester C | 40 | 1 |
| 1992–93 | Manchester C | 21 | 1 |
| 1993–94 | Manchester C | 7 | 0 |
| 1994–95 | Manchester C | 30 | 0 |
| 1995–96 | Manchester C | 29 | 0 |
| 1996–97 | Manchester C | 37 | 2 |
| 1997–98 | Manchester C | 21 | 0 |
| **Total:** | | **321** | **18** |

## BRIGHTWELL, Stuart — Midfield

H: 5 6 W: 10 11 b.Easington 31-1-79

*Source:* Trainee. *Honours:* England Schools, Youth.

| | | | |
|---|---|---|---|
| 1995–96 | Manchester U | 0 | 0 |
| 1996–97 | Manchester U | 0 | 0 |
| 1997–98 | Manchester U | 0 | 0 |

## BRISCO, Neil — Midfield

H: 6 0 W: 11 05 b.Wigan 26-1-78

*Source:* Trainee.

| | | | |
|---|---|---|---|
| 1996–97 | Manchester C | 0 | 0 |
| 1997–98 | Manchester C | 0 | 0 |

## BRISCOE, Anthony — Forward

b.Birmingham 16-8-78

*Source:* Trainee.

| | | | |
|---|---|---|---|
| 1996–97 | Shrewsbury T | 1 | 0 |
| 1997–98 | Shrewsbury T | 0 | 0 |
| **Total:** | | **1** | **0** |

## BRISCOE, Lee — Forward

H: 5 11 W: 11 13 b.Pontefract 30-9-75

*Source:* Trainee. *Honours:* England Under-21.

| | | | |
|---|---|---|---|
| 1993–94 | Sheffield W | 1 | 0 |
| 1994–95 | Sheffield W | 6 | 0 |
| 1995–96 | Sheffield W | 26 | 0 |
| 1996–97 | Sheffield W | 6 | 0 |
| 1997–98 | Sheffield W | 7 | 0 |
| 1997–98 | Manchester C (loan) | 5 | 1 |
| **Total:** | | **51** | **1** |

## BRISSETT, Jason — Midfield

H: 5 9 W: 12 00 b.Redbridge 7-9-74

*Source:* Arsenal Trainee.

| | | | |
|---|---|---|---|
| 1993–94 | Peterborough U | 30 | 0 |
| 1994–95 | Peterborough U | 5 | 0 |
| 1994–95 | Bournemouth | 25 | 0 |
| 1995–96 | Bournemouth | 43 | 3 |
| 1996–97 | Bournemouth | 25 | 4 |
| 1997–98 | Bournemouth | 31 | 1 |
| **Total:** | | **159** | **8** |

## BRISTOW, Jason — Defender

b.Basingstoke 23-4-80

*Source:* Trainee.

| | | | |
|---|---|---|---|
| 1997–98 | Reading | 0 | 0 |

## BRITTON, Gerard — Forward

H: 6 0 W: 11 00 b.Glasgow 20-10-70

*Source:* Celtic BC.

| | | | |
|---|---|---|---|
| 1987–88 | Celtic | 0 | 0 |
| 1988–89 | Celtic | 0 | 0 |
| 1989–90 | Celtic | 0 | 0 |
| 1990–91 | Celtic | 2 | 0 |

| | | | |
|---|---|---|---|
| 1991–92 | Celtic | 0 | 0 |
| 1991–92 | Reading (loan) | 2 | 0 |
| 1992–93 | Partick Th | 40 | 12 |
| 1993–94 | Partick Th | 22 | 3 |
| 1993–94 | Dundee | 17 | 1 |
| 1994–95 | Dundee | 26 | 12 |
| 1995–96 | Dundee | 25 | 2 |
| 1996–97 | Dunfermline Ath | 33 | 13 |
| 1997–98 | Dunfermline Ath | 16 | 3 |
| **Total:** | | **183** | **46** |

## BROAD, Stephen — Defender

b.Epsom 10-6-80

*Source:* Trainee.

| | | | |
|---|---|---|---|
| 1997–98 | Chelsea | 0 | 0 |

## BROADBENT, David — Forward

H: 5 9 W: 10 06 b.Pembury 26-9-79

*Source:* Trainee.

| | | | |
|---|---|---|---|
| 1997–98 | Newcastle U | 0 | 0 |

## BRODIE, Steve — Forward

H: 5 7 W: 10 08 b.Sunderland 14-1-73

*Source:* Trainee.

| | | | |
|---|---|---|---|
| 1991–92 | Sunderland | 0 | 0 |
| 1992–93 | Sunderland | 0 | 0 |
| 1993–94 | Sunderland | 4 | 0 |
| 1994–95 | Sunderland | 8 | 0 |
| 1995–96 | Sunderland | 0 | 0 |
| 1995–96 | Doncaster R (loan) | 5 | 1 |
| 1996–97 | Sunderland | 0 | 0 |
| 1996–97 | Scarborough | 24 | 5 |
| 1997–98 | Scarborough | 44 | 10 |
| **Total:** | | **85** | **16** |

## BROLIN, Tomas — Midfield

H: 5 8 W: 13 00 b.Hudiksvall 29-11-69

*Honours:* Sweden 47 full caps, 26 goals.

| | | | |
|---|---|---|---|
| 1987 | Sundsvall | 12 | 3 |
| 1988 | Sundsvall | 21 | 6 |
| 1989 | Sundsvall | 21 | 4 |
| 1990 | Norrkoping | 11 | 7 |
| 1990–91 | Parma | 33 | 7 |
| 1991–92 | Parma | 34 | 4 |
| 1992–93 | Parma | 22 | 4 |
| 1993–94 | Parma | 29 | 5 |
| 1994–95 | Parma | 11 | 0 |
| 1995–96 | Parma | 4 | 0 |
| 1995–96 | Leeds U | 19 | 4 |
| 1996–97 | Leeds U | 0 | 0 |
| 1996–97 | Zurich (loan) | 3 | 0 |
| 1996–97 | Parma (loan) | 11 | 0 |
| 1997–98 | Leeds U | 0 | 0 |
| 1997–98 | Crystal Palace | 13 | 0 |
| **Total:** | | **244** | **44** |

## BROOKER, Paul — Forward

H: 5 8 W: 10 01 b.Hammersmith 25-11-76

*Source:* Trainee.

| | | | |
|---|---|---|---|
| 1995–96 | Fulham | 20 | 2 |
| 1996–97 | Fulham | 26 | 2 |
| 1997–98 | Fulham | 9 | 0 |
| **Total:** | | **55** | **4** |

## BROOKES, Darren — Defender

H: 6 3 W: 14 00 b.Sheffield 7-7-78

*Source:* Worksop T.

| | | | |
|---|---|---|---|
| 1997–98 | Doncaster R | 11 | 0 |
| **Total:** | | **11** | **0** |

## BROOMES, Marlon — Defender

H: 6 0 W: 12 12 b.Birmingham 28-11-77

*Source:* Trainee. *Honours:* England Schools, Youth, Under-21.

| | | | |
|---|---|---|---|
| 1994–95 | Blackburn R | 0 | 0 |
| 1995–96 | Blackburn R | 0 | 0 |
| 1996–97 | Blackburn R | 0 | 0 |
| 1996–97 | Swindon T (loan) | 12 | 1 |
| 1997–98 | Blackburn R | 4 | 0 |
| **Total:** | | **16** | **1** |

## BROUGHTON, Drewe — Forward

H: 6 3 W: 12 01 b.Hitchin 25-10-78

*Source:* Trainee.

| | | | |
|---|---|---|---|
| 1996–97 | Norwich C | 8 | 1 |
| 1997–98 | Norwich C | 1 | 0 |
| 1997–98 | Wigan Ath (loan) | 4 | 0 |
| **Total:** | | **13** | **1** |

## BROWN, Aaron — Forward

b.Bristol 14-3-80

*Source:* Trainee. *Honours:* England Schools.

| | | | |
|---|---|---|---|
| 1997–98 | Bristol C | 0 | 0 |

## BROWN, Andrew — Forward

H: 6 3 W: 13 10 b.Edinburgh 11-10-76

*Source:* Trainee.

| | | | |
|---|---|---|---|
| 1994–95 | Leeds U | 0 | 0 |
| 1995–96 | Leeds U | 0 | 0 |
| 1995–96 | Hull C | 0 | 0 |
| 1996–97 | Hull C | 26 | 1 |
| 1997–98 | Hull C | 3 | 0 |
| **Total:** | | **29** | **1** |

## BROWN, Daniel — Midfield

b.London 12-9-80

*Source:* Trainee.

| | | | |
|---|---|---|---|
| 1997–98 | Leyton Orient | 0 | 0 |

## BROWN, David — Forward

H: 5 10 W: 12 07 b.Bolton 2-10-78

*Source:* Trainee.

| | | | |
|---|---|---|---|
| 1995–96 | Manchester U | 0 | 0 |
| 1996–97 | Manchester U | 0 | 0 |
| 1997–98 | Manchester U | 0 | 0 |
| 1997–98 | Hull C (loan) | 7 | 2 |
| **Total:** | | **7** | **2** |

## BROWN, Grant — Defender

H: 6 0 W: 11 12 b.Sunderland 19-11-69

*Source:* Trainee.

| | | | |
|---|---|---|---|
| 1987–88 | Leicester C | 2 | 0 |
| 1988–89 | Leicester C | 12 | 0 |
| 1989–90 | Lincoln C | 34 | 2 |
| 1990–91 | Lincoln C | 32 | 1 |
| 1991–92 | Lincoln C | 37 | 1 |
| 1992–93 | Lincoln C | 40 | 1 |
| 1993–94 | Lincoln C | 38 | 3 |
| 1994–95 | Lincoln C | 39 | 3 |
| 1995–96 | Lincoln C | 34 | 0 |
| 1996–97 | Lincoln C | 34 | 1 |
| 1997–98 | Lincoln C | 15 | 0 |
| **Total:** | | **317** | **12** |

## BROWN, Greg — Defender

H: 5 10 W: 12 04 b.Wythenshawe 31-7-78

*Source:* Trainee.

| | | | |
|---|---|---|---|
| 1995–96 | Chester C | 3 | 0 |
| 1996–97 | Chester C | 1 | 0 |
| 1997–98 | Chester C | 0 | 0 |
| 1997–98 | Macclesfield T | 2 | 0 |
| **Total:** | | **6** | **0** |

## BROWN, James — Midfield

H: 5 10 W: 11 00 b.Grantham 13-9-78

*Source:* Trainee.

| | | | |
|---|---|---|---|
| 1997–98 | Grimsby T | 0 | 0 |

## BROWN, Justin — Midfield

H: 5 11 W: 10 06 b.Leeds 9-11-78

*Source:* Trainee.

| | | | |
|---|---|---|---|
| 1997–98 | Bristol R | 0 | 0 |

## BROWN, Keith — Defender

H: 6 0 W: 11 00 b.Edinburgh 24-12-79

| | | | |
|---|---|---|---|
| 1996–97 | Blackburn R | 0 | 0 |
| 1997–98 | Blackburn R | 0 | 0 |

## BROWN, Kenny — Defender

H: 5 8 W: 11 06 b.Upminster 11-7-67

*Source:* Apprentice.

| | | | |
|---|---|---|---|
| 1984–85 | Norwich C | 0 | 0 |
| 1985–86 | Norwich C | 0 | 0 |
| 1986–87 | Norwich C | 18 | 0 |
| 1987–88 | Norwich C | 7 | 0 |
| 1988–89 | Plymouth Arg | 39 | 1 |
| 1989–90 | Plymouth Arg | 44 | 0 |
| 1990–91 | Plymouth Arg | 43 | 3 |
| 1991–92 | West Ham U | 27 | 3 |
| 1992–93 | West Ham U | 15 | 2 |
| 1993–94 | West Ham U | 9 | 0 |
| 1994–95 | West Ham U | 9 | 0 |
| 1995–96 | West Ham U | 3 | 0 |
| 1995–96 | Huddersfield T (loan) | 5 | 0 |
| 1995–96 | Reading (loan) | 12 | 1 |
| 1995–96 | Southend U (loan) | 6 | 0 |
| 1995–96 | Crystal Palace (loan) | 6 | 2 |
| 1996–97 | West Ham U | 0 | 0 |
| 1996–97 | Reading (loan) | 5 | 0 |
| 1996–97 | Birmingham C | 11 | 0 |
| 1997–98 | Millwall | 45 | 0 |
| **Total:** | | **304** | **12** |

## BROWN, Linton — Forward

H: 5 10 W: 12 07 b.Driffield 12-4-68

*Source:* Guiseley.

| | | | |
|---|---|---|---|
| 1992–93 | Halifax T | 3 | 0 |
| 1992–93 | Hull C | 23 | 1 |
| 1993–94 | Hull C | 42 | 9 |
| 1994–95 | Hull C | 33 | 12 |
| 1995–96 | Hull C | 23 | 1 |
| 1995–96 | Swansea C | 4 | 0 |

| | | | |
|---|---|---|---|
| 1996–97 | Swansea C | 21 | 3 |
| 1997–98 | Swansea C | 2 | 0 |
| 1997–98 | Scarborough (loan) | 4 | 1 |
| **Total:** | | **155** | **27** |

## BROWN, Michael — Goalkeeper

H: 5 9 W: 10 07 b.Stranraer 6-11-79

*Source:* Trainee.

| | | | |
|---|---|---|---|
| 1996–97 | Manchester C | 0 | 0 |
| 1997–98 | Manchester C | 0 | 0 |

## BROWN, Michael R — Midfield

H: 5 10 W: 11 08 b.Hartlepool 25-1-77

*Source:* Trainee. *Honours:* England Under-21.

| | | | |
|---|---|---|---|
| 1994–95 | Manchester C | 0 | 0 |
| 1995–96 | Manchester C | 21 | 0 |
| 1996–97 | Manchester C | 11 | 0 |
| 1996–97 | Hartlepool U (loan) | 6 | 1 |
| 1997–98 | Manchester C | 26 | 0 |
| **Total:** | | **64** | **1** |

## BROWN, Mickey — Forward

H: 5 9 W: 10 12 b.Birmingham 8-2-68

*Source:* Apprentice.

| | | | |
|---|---|---|---|
| 1985–86 | Shrewsbury T | 0 | 0 |
| 1986–87 | Shrewsbury T | 22 | 2 |
| 1987–88 | Shrewsbury T | 41 | 5 |
| 1988–89 | Shrewsbury T | 41 | 0 |
| 1989–90 | Shrewsbury T | 43 | 1 |
| 1990–91 | Shrewsbury T | 43 | 1 |
| 1991–92 | Bolton W | 27 | 3 |
| 1992–93 | Bolton W | 6 | 0 |
| 1992–93 | Shrewsbury T | 17 | 1 |
| 1993–94 | Shrewsbury T | 41 | 7 |
| 1994–95 | Shrewsbury T | 9 | 3 |
| 1994–95 | Preston NE | 0 | 0 |
| 1995–96 | Preston NE | 10 | 1 |
| 1996–97 | Preston NE | 6 | 0 |
| 1996–97 | Rochdale (loan) | 5 | 0 |
| 1996–97 | Shrewsbury T | 19 | 1 |
| 1997–98 | Shrewsbury T | 30 | 2 |
| **Total:** | | **360** | **27** |

## BROWN, Simon — Goalkeeper

H: 6 2 W: 15 01 b.Chelmsford 3-12-76

*Source:* Trainee.

| | | | |
|---|---|---|---|
| 1995–96 | Tottenham H | 0 | 0 |
| 1996–97 | Tottenham H | 0 | 0 |
| 1997–98 | Tottenham H | 0 | 0 |
| 1997–98 | Lincoln C (loan) | 1 | 0 |
| **Total:** | | **1** | **0** |

## BROWN, Steve — Defender

H: 6 1 W: 14 03 b.Brighton 13-5-72

*Source:* Trainee.

| | | | |
|---|---|---|---|
| 1990–91 | Charlton Ath | 0 | 0 |
| 1991–92 | Charlton Ath | 1 | 0 |
| 1992–93 | Charlton Ath | 0 | 0 |
| 1993–94 | Charlton Ath | 19 | 0 |
| 1994–95 | Charlton Ath | 42 | 3 |
| 1995–96 | Charlton Ath | 19 | 0 |
| 1996–97 | Charlton Ath | 27 | 0 |
| 1997–98 | Charlton Ath | 34 | 2 |
| **Total:** | | **142** | **5** |

## BROWN, Steve — Forward

H: 6 0 W: 11 06 b.Southend 6-12-73

*Source:* Trainee.

| | | | |
|---|---|---|---|
| 1992–93 | Southend U | 10 | 2 |
| 1993–94 | Scunthorpe U | 0 | 0 |
| 1993–94 | Colchester U | 34 | 11 |
| 1994–95 | Colchester U | 28 | 6 |
| 1994–95 | Gillingham | 8 | 2 |
| 1995–96 | Gillingham | 1 | 0 |
| 1995–96 | Lincoln C | 26 | 3 |
| 1996–97 | Lincoln C | 15 | 2 |
| 1997–98 | Lincoln C | 31 | 3 |
| **Total:** | | **153** | **29** |

## BROWN, Steve — Midfield

H: 5 11 W: 11 12 b.Northampton 6-7-66

| | | | |
|---|---|---|---|
| 1985–86 | Northampton T | 0 | 0 |
| From Irthlingborough D. | | | |
| 1989–90 | Northampton T | 21 | 1 |
| 1990–91 | Northampton T | 40 | 2 |
| 1991–92 | Northampton T | 35 | 3 |
| 1992–93 | Northampton T | 38 | 9 |
| 1993–94 | Northampton T | 24 | 4 |
| 1993–94 | Wycombe W | 9 | 2 |
| 1994–95 | Wycombe W | 40 | 1 |
| 1995–96 | Wycombe W | 38 | 0 |
| 1996–97 | Wycombe W | 34 | 5 |
| 1997–98 | Wycombe W | 40 | 3 |
| **Total:** | | **319** | **30** |

## BROWN, Wayne — Goalkeeper

H: 6 0 W: 11 12 b.Southampton 14-1-77

*Source:* Trainee.

| | | | |
|---|---|---|---|
| 1993–94 | Bristol C | 1 | 0 |
| 1994–95 | Bristol C | 0 | 0 |
| 1995–96 | Bristol C | 0 | 0 |
| From Weston-S-Mare. | | | |
| 1996–97 | Chester C | 2 | 0 |
| 1997–98 | Chester C | 13 | 0 |
| **Total:** | | **16** | **0** |

## BROWN, Wayne — Defender

H: 6 0 W: 12 06 b.Barking 20-8-77

*Source:* Trainee.

| | | | |
|---|---|---|---|
| 1995–96 | Ipswich T | 0 | 0 |
| 1996–97 | Ipswich T | 0 | 0 |
| 1997–98 | Ipswich T | 1 | 0 |
| 1997–98 | Colchester U (loan) | 2 | 0 |
| **Total:** | | **3** | **0** |

## BROWN, Wes — Defender

H: 6 1 W: 11 11 b.Manchester 16-3-79

*Source:* Trainee. *Honours:* England Schools, Youth.

| | | | |
|---|---|---|---|
| 1996–97 | Manchester U | 0 | 0 |
| 1997–98 | Manchester U | 2 | 0 |
| **Total:** | | **2** | **0** |

## BROWNING, Marcus — Midfield

H: 6 0 W: 12 08 b.Bristol 22-4-71

*Source:* Trainee. *Honours:* Wales 5 full caps.

| | | | |
|---|---|---|---|
| 1989–90 | Bristol R | 1 | 0 |
| 1990–91 | Bristol R | 0 | 0 |
| 1991–92 | Bristol R | 11 | 0 |
| 1992–93 | Bristol R | 19 | 1 |
| 1992–93 | Hereford U (loan) | 7 | 5 |
| 1993–94 | Bristol R | 31 | 4 |
| 1994–95 | Bristol R | 41 | 2 |
| 1995–96 | Bristol R | 45 | 4 |
| 1996–97 | Bristol R | 26 | 2 |
| 1996–97 | Huddersfield T | 13 | 0 |
| 1997–98 | Huddersfield T | 14 | 0 |
| **Total:** | | **208** | **18** |

## BROWNRIGG, Andrew — Defender

H: 6 0 W: 11 11 b.Sheffield 2-8-76

*Source:* Trainee.

| | | | |
|---|---|---|---|
| 1994–95 | Hereford U | 8 | 0 |
| 1994–95 | Norwich C | 0 | 0 |
| 1995–96 | Norwich C | 0 | 0 |
| 1996–97 | Norwich C | 0 | 0 |
| 1997–98 | Rotherham U | 0 | 0 |
| **Total:** | | **8** | **0** |

## BRUCE, Paul — Midfield

H: 5 10 W: 12 01 b.London 18-2-78

*Source:* Trainee.

| | | | |
|---|---|---|---|
| 1996–97 | QPR | 0 | 0 |
| 1997–98 | QPR | 5 | 1 |
| **Total:** | | **5** | **1** |

## BRUCE, Steve — Defender

H: 6 0 W: 12 06 b.Corbridge 31-12-60

*Source:* Apprentice. *Honours:* England Youth.

| | | | |
|---|---|---|---|
| 1978–79 | Gillingham | 0 | 0 |
| 1979–80 | Gillingham | 40 | 6 |
| 1980–81 | Gillingham | 41 | 4 |
| 1981–82 | Gillingham | 45 | 6 |
| 1982–83 | Gillingham | 39 | 7 |
| 1983–84 | Gillingham | 40 | 6 |
| 1984–85 | Norwich C | 39 | 1 |
| 1985–86 | Norwich C | 42 | 8 |
| 1986–87 | Norwich C | 41 | 3 |
| 1987–88 | Norwich C | 19 | 2 |
| 1987–88 | Manchester U | 21 | 2 |
| 1988–89 | Manchester U | 38 | 2 |
| 1989–90 | Manchester U | 34 | 3 |
| 1990–91 | Manchester U | 31 | 13 |
| 1991–92 | Manchester U | 37 | 5 |
| 1992–93 | Manchester U | 42 | 5 |
| 1993–94 | Manchester U | 41 | 3 |
| 1994–95 | Manchester U | 35 | 2 |
| 1995–96 | Manchester U | 30 | 1 |
| 1996–97 | Birmingham C | 32 | 0 |
| 1997–98 | Birmingham C | 40 | 2 |
| **Total:** | | **727** | **81** |

## BRUMWELL, Phil — Midfield

H: 5 8 W: 11 00 b.Darlington 8-8-75

*Source:* Trainee.

| | | | |
|---|---|---|---|
| 1994–95 | Sunderland | 0 | 0 |
| 1995–96 | Darlington | 28 | 0 |
| 1996–97 | Darlington | 38 | 1 |
| 1997–98 | Darlington | 35 | 0 |
| **Total:** | | **101** | **1** |

## BRUNO, Pasquale — Defender

H: 6 0 W: 11 07 b.Lecce 19-6-62

*Source:* Fiorentina.

| | | | |
|---|---|---|---|
| 1995–96 | Hearts | 22 | 1 |
| 1996–97 | Hearts | 13 | 0 |
| 1997–98 | Hearts | 0 | 0 |
| 1997–98 | Wigan Ath (loan) | 1 | 0 |
| **Total:** | | **36** | **1** |

## BRYAN, Derek — Forward

H: 5 10 W: 11 05 b.London 11-11-74

*Source:* Hampton.

| | | | |
|---|---|---|---|
| 1997–98 | Brentford | 11 | 2 |
| **Total:** | | **11** | **2** |

## BRYAN, Marvin — Defender

H: 6 0 W: 12 02 b.Paddington 2-8-75

*Source:* Trainee.

| | | | |
|---|---|---|---|
| 1992–93 | QPR | 0 | 0 |
| 1993–94 | QPR | 0 | 0 |
| 1994–95 | QPR | 0 | 0 |
| 1994–95 | Doncaster R (loan) | 5 | 1 |
| 1995–96 | Blackpool | 46 | 1 |
| 1996–97 | Blackpool | 34 | 1 |
| 1997–98 | Blackpool | 43 | 1 |
| **Total:** | | **128** | **4** |

## BRYANT, Matthew — Defender

H: 6 0 W: 12 06 b.Bristol 21-9-70

*Source:* Trainee.

| | | | |
|---|---|---|---|
| 1989–90 | Bristol C | 0 | 0 |
| 1990–91 | Bristol C | 22 | 1 |
| 1990–91 | Walsall (loan) | 13 | 0 |
| 1991–92 | Bristol C | 43 | 2 |
| 1992–93 | Bristol C | 41 | 1 |
| 1993–94 | Bristol C | 28 | 0 |
| 1994–95 | Bristol C | 37 | 3 |
| 1995–96 | Bristol C | 32 | 0 |
| 1996–97 | Gillingham | 39 | 0 |
| 1997–98 | Gillingham | 35 | 0 |
| **Total:** | | **290** | **7** |

## BRYDON, Lee — Defender

H: 5 11 W: 13 00 b.Stockton 15-11-74

*Source:* Trainee. *Honours:* England Schools.

| | | | |
|---|---|---|---|
| 1992–93 | Liverpool | 0 | 0 |
| 1993–94 | Liverpool | 0 | 0 |
| 1994–95 | Liverpool | 0 | 0 |
| 1995–96 | Liverpool | 0 | 0 |
| 1996–97 | Darlington | 25 | 0 |
| 1997–98 | Darlington | 15 | 0 |
| **Total:** | | **40** | **0** |

## BRYSON, Ian — Defender

H: 5 11 W: 12 05 b.Kilmarnock 26-11-62

| | | | |
|---|---|---|---|
| 1981–82 | Kilmarnock | 14 | 3 |
| 1982–83 | Kilmarnock | 28 | 1 |
| 1983–84 | Kilmarnock | 25 | 4 |
| 1984–85 | Kilmarnock | 36 | 3 |
| 1985–86 | Kilmarnock | 38 | 14 |
| 1986–87 | Kilmarnock | 32 | 10 |
| 1987–88 | Kilmarnock | 42 | 5 |
| 1988–89 | Sheffield U | 37 | 8 |
| 1989–90 | Sheffield U | 39 | 9 |
| 1990–91 | Sheffield U | 29 | 7 |
| 1991–92 | Sheffield U | 34 | 9 |
| 1992–93 | Sheffield U | 16 | 3 |
| 1993–94 | Barnsley | 16 | 3 |
| 1993–94 | Preston NE | 25 | 2 |
| 1994–95 | Preston NE | 41 | 5 |
| 1995–96 | Preston NE | 44 | 9 |
| 1996–97 | Preston NE | 41 | 3 |
| 1997–98 | Rochdale | 15 | 1 |
| **Total:** | | **552** | **99** |

## BUCHAN, James — Midfield

H: 5 10 W: 10 10 b.Manchester 3-4-77

*Source:* Stonehaven. *Honours:* Scotland Under-21.

| | | | |
|---|---|---|---|
| 1995–96 | Aberdeen | 4 | 1 |
| 1996–97 | Aberdeen | 14 | 0 |
| 1997–98 | Aberdeen | 10 | 0 |
| **Total:** | | **28** | **1** |

## BUCKLE, Paul — Midfield

H: 5 9 W: 11 07 b.Welwyn 16-12-70

*Source:* Trainee.

| | | | |
|---|---|---|---|
| 1987–88 | Brentford | 1 | 0 |
| 1988–89 | Brentford | 0 | 0 |
| 1989–90 | Brentford | 10 | 0 |
| 1990–91 | Brentford | 26 | 0 |
| 1991–92 | Brentford | 15 | 1 |
| 1992–93 | Brentford | 5 | 0 |
| 1993–94 | Brentford | 0 | 0 |
| 1993–94 | Torquay U | 16 | 2 |
| 1994–95 | Torquay U | 32 | 3 |
| 1995–96 | Torquay U | 11 | 4 |
| 1995–96 | Exeter C | 22 | 2 |
| 1996–97 | Northampton T | 0 | 0 |
| 1996–97 | Wycombe W | 0 | 0 |

| | | | |
|---|---|---|---|
| 1996–97 | Colchester U | 24 | 0 |
| 1997–98 | Colchester U | 38 | 5 |
| **Total:** | | **200** | **17** |

## BUCKLEY, Adam — Midfield

b.Nottingham 2-8-79

| | | | |
|---|---|---|---|
| 1997–98 | Grimsby T | 0 | 0 |

## BUGGIE, Lee — Forward

b.Bury 11-2-81

*Source:* Trainee.

| | | | |
|---|---|---|---|
| 1997–98 | Bolton W | 0 | 0 |

## BULL, Gary — Forward

H: 5 10 W: 12 02 b.West Bromwich 12-6-66

*Source:* Swindon T Apprentice.

| | | | |
|---|---|---|---|
| 1986–87 | Southampton | 0 | 0 |
| 1987–88 | Southampton | 0 | 0 |
| 1987–88 | Cambridge U | 9 | 3 |
| 1988–89 | Cambridge U | 10 | 1 |
| From Barnet. | | | |
| 1991–92 | Barnet | 42 | 20 |
| 1992–93 | Barnet | 41 | 17 |
| 1993–94 | Nottingham F | 11 | 0 |
| 1994–95 | Nottingham F | 1 | 1 |
| 1994–95 | Birmingham C (loan) | 10 | 6 |
| 1995–96 | Nottingham F | 0 | 0 |
| 1995–96 | Brighton & HA (loan) | 10 | 2 |
| 1995–96 | Birmingham C (loan) | 6 | 0 |
| 1995–96 | York C | 15 | 8 |
| 1996–97 | York C | 41 | 2 |
| 1997–98 | York C | 27 | 1 |
| **Total:** | | **223** | **61** |

## BULL, Steve — Forward

H: 5 11 W: 11 04 b.Tipton 28-3-65

*Source:* Apprentice. *Honours:* England Under-21, B, 13 full caps, 4 goals.

| | | | |
|---|---|---|---|
| 1985–86 | WBA | 1 | 0 |
| 1986–87 | WBA | 3 | 2 |
| 1986–87 | Wolverhampton W | 30 | 15 |
| 1987–88 | Wolverhampton W | 44 | 34 |
| 1988–89 | Wolverhampton W | 45 | 37 |
| 1989–90 | Wolverhampton W | 42 | 24 |
| 1990–91 | Wolverhampton W | 43 | 26 |
| 1991–92 | Wolverhampton W | 43 | 20 |
| 1992–93 | Wolverhampton W | 36 | 16 |
| 1993–94 | Wolverhampton W | 27 | 14 |
| 1994–95 | Wolverhampton W | 31 | 16 |
| 1995–96 | Wolverhampton W | 44 | 15 |
| 1996–97 | Wolverhampton W | 43 | 23 |
| 1997–98 | Wolverhampton W | 31 | 7 |
| **Total:** | | **463** | **249** |

## BULLIMORE, Wayne — Midfield

H: 5 9 W: 12 01 b.Mansfield 12-9-70

*Source:* Trainee. *Honours:* FA Schools.

| | | | |
|---|---|---|---|
| 1988–89 | Manchester U | 0 | 0 |
| 1989–90 | Manchester U | 0 | 0 |
| 1990–91 | Manchester U | 0 | 0 |
| 1990–91 | Barnsley | 0 | 0 |
| 1991–92 | Barnsley | 18 | 1 |
| 1992–93 | Barnsley | 17 | 0 |
| 1993–94 | Barnsley | 0 | 0 |
| 1993–94 | Stockport Co | 0 | 0 |
| 1993–94 | Scunthorpe U | 18 | 3 |
| 1994–95 | Scunthorpe U | 35 | 6 |
| 1995–96 | Scunthorpe U | 14 | 2 |
| 1995–96 | Bradford C | 2 | 0 |
| 1996–97 | Bradford C | 0 | 0 |
| 1996–97 | Doncaster R (loan) | 4 | 0 |
| 1996–97 | Peterborough U | 6 | 0 |
| 1997–98 | Peterborough U | 15 | 1 |
| **Total:** | | **129** | **13** |

## BULLOCK, Darren — Midfield

H: 5 9 W: 13 04 b.Worcester 12-2-69

*Source:* Nuneaton Bor.

| | | | |
|---|---|---|---|
| 1993–94 | Huddersfield T | 20 | 3 |
| 1994–95 | Huddersfield T | 39 | 6 |
| 1995–96 | Huddersfield T | 42 | 6 |
| 1996–97 | Huddersfield T | 27 | 1 |
| 1996–97 | Swindon T | 13 | 1 |
| 1997–98 | Swindon T | 31 | 0 |
| **Total:** | | **172** | **17** |

## BULLOCK, Martin — Midfield

H: 5 4 W: 10 00 b.Derby 5-3-75

*Source:* Eastwood T. *Honours:* England Under-21.

| | | | |
|---|---|---|---|
| 1993–94 | Barnsley | 0 | 0 |
| 1994–95 | Barnsley | 29 | 0 |
| 1995–96 | Barnsley | 41 | 1 |
| 1996–97 | Barnsley | 28 | 0 |
| 1997–98 | Barnsley | 33 | 0 |
| **Total:** | | **131** | **1** |

## BULLOCK, Matthew — Midfield

H: 5 8 W: 11 00 b.Stoke 1-11-80

*Source:* Trainee.

| | | | |
|---|---|---|---|
| 1997–98 | Stoke C | 0 | 0 |

## BULLOCK, Tony — Goalkeeper

H: 6 1 W: 12 13 b.Warrington 18-2-72

*Source:* Northwich V, Leek T.

| | | | |
|---|---|---|---|
| 1996–97 | Barnsley | 0 | 0 |
| 1997–98 | Barnsley | 0 | 0 |

## BUNDY, Scott — Forward

H: 6 3 W: 12 00 b.Southampton 20-10-77

*Source:* Trainee.

| | | | |
|---|---|---|---|
| 1996–97 | Portsmouth | 0 | 0 |
| 1997–98 | Portsmouth | 0 | 0 |

## BUNN, James — Forward

b.Tottenham 12-1-78

*Source:* Trainee. *Honours:* England Schools.

| | | | |
|---|---|---|---|
| 1996–97 | Tottenham H | 0 | 0 |
| 1997–98 | Tottenham H | 0 | 0 |

## BURDOCK, Gary — Forward

b.Dublin 9-3-80

*Source:* Trainee.

| | | | |
|---|---|---|---|
| 1997–98 | Middlesbrough | 0 | 0 |

## BURGESS, Daryl — Defender

H: 5 11 W: 12 04 b.Birmingham 20-4-71

*Source:* Trainee.

| | | | |
|---|---|---|---|
| 1989–90 | WBA | 34 | 0 |
| 1990–91 | WBA | 25 | 0 |
| 1991–92 | WBA | 36 | 2 |
| 1992–93 | WBA | 18 | 1 |
| 1993–94 | WBA | 43 | 2 |
| 1994–95 | WBA | 22 | 0 |
| 1995–96 | WBA | 45 | 2 |
| 1996–97 | WBA | 33 | 1 |
| 1997–98 | WBA | 27 | 1 |
| **Total:** | | **283** | **9** |

## BURGESS, Mark — Defender

H: 5 10 W: 11 09 b.Ipswich 3-2-79

*Source:* Trainee.

| | | | |
|---|---|---|---|
| 1997–98 | Ipswich T | 0 | 0 |

## BURGESS, Richard — Forward

H: 5 8 W: 11 00 b.Bromsgrove 18-8-78

*Source:* Trainee.

| | | | |
|---|---|---|---|
| 1996–97 | Aston Villa | 0 | 0 |
| 1997–98 | Stoke C | 0 | 0 |

## BURGHALL, Terry — Forward

H: 6 0 W: 11 06 b.Liverpool 25-9-78

*Source:* Liverpool Trainee.

| | | | |
|---|---|---|---|
| 1996–97 | Newcastle U | 0 | 0 |
| 1997–98 | Newcastle U | 0 | 0 |

## BURKE, Alexander — Midfield

H: 5 7 W: 9 11 b.Glasgow 11-11-77

*Source:* Kilmarnock BC. *Honours:* Scotland Under-21.

| | | | |
|---|---|---|---|
| 1995–96 | Kilmarnock | 0 | 0 |
| 1996–97 | Kilmarnock | 17 | 3 |
| 1997–98 | Kilmarnock | 19 | 3 |
| **Total:** | | **36** | **6** |

## BURLEY, Craig — Midfield

H: 6 1 W: 12 13 b.Ayr 24-9-71

*Source:* Trainee. *Honours:* Scotland Schools, Youth, Under-21, 28 full caps, 2 goals.

| | | | |
|---|---|---|---|
| 1989–90 | Chelsea | 0 | 0 |
| 1990–91 | Chelsea | 1 | 0 |
| 1991–92 | Chelsea | 8 | 0 |
| 1992–93 | Chelsea | 3 | 0 |
| 1993–94 | Chelsea | 23 | 3 |
| 1994–95 | Chelsea | 25 | 2 |
| 1995–96 | Chelsea | 22 | 0 |
| 1996–97 | Chelsea | 31 | 2 |
| 1997–98 | Celtic | 35 | 10 |
| **Total:** | | **148** | **17** |

## BURNETT, Wayne — Midfield

H: 5 10 W: 12 00 b.Lambeth 4-9-71

*Source:* Trainee.

| | | | |
|---|---|---|---|
| 1989–90 | Leyton Orient | 3 | 0 |
| 1990–91 | Leyton Orient | 1 | 0 |
| 1991–92 | Leyton Orient | 36 | 0 |
| 1992–93 | Blackburn R | 0 | 0 |

## Burns, John

| | | | |
|---|---|---|---|
| 1993–94 | Plymouth Arg | 32 | 2 |
| 1994–95 | Plymouth Arg | 32 | 1 |
| 1995–96 | Plymouth Arg | 6 | 0 |
| 1995–96 | Bolton W | 1 | 0 |
| 1996–97 | Bolton W | 1 | 0 |
| 1996–97 | Huddersfield T | 35 | 0 |
| 1997–98 | Huddersfield T | 15 | 0 |
| 1997–98 | Grimsby T | 21 | 1 |
| **Total:** | | **183** | **4** |

## BURNS, John — Midfield

H: 5 10 W: 11 00 b.Dublin 4-12-77

*Source:* Belvedere, Trainee.

| | | | |
|---|---|---|---|
| 1994–95 | Nottingham F | 0 | 0 |
| 1995–96 | Nottingham F | 0 | 0 |
| 1996–97 | Nottingham F | 0 | 0 |
| 1997–98 | Nottingham F | 0 | 0 |

## BURNS, Liam — Defender

H: 6 1 W: 12 09 b.Belfast 30-10-78

*Source:* Trainee. *Honours:* Northern Ireland Under-21.

| | | | |
|---|---|---|---|
| 1997–98 | Port Vale | 1 | 0 |
| **Total:** | | **1** | **0** |

## BURROWS, David — Defender

H: 5 8 W: 11 08 b.Dudley 25-10-68

*Source:* Apprentice. *Honours:* England Under-21, B.

| | | | |
|---|---|---|---|
| 1985–86 | WBA | 1 | 0 |
| 1986–87 | WBA | 15 | 1 |
| 1987–88 | WBA | 21 | 0 |
| 1988–89 | WBA | 9 | 0 |
| 1988–89 | Liverpool | 21 | 0 |
| 1989–90 | Liverpool | 26 | 0 |
| 1990–91 | Liverpool | 35 | 0 |
| 1991–92 | Liverpool | 30 | 1 |
| 1992–93 | Liverpool | 30 | 2 |
| 1993–94 | Liverpool | 4 | 0 |
| 1993–94 | West Ham U | 25 | 1 |
| 1994–95 | West Ham U | 4 | 0 |
| 1994–95 | Everton | 19 | 0 |
| 1994–95 | Coventry C | 11 | 0 |
| 1995–96 | Coventry C | 11 | 0 |
| 1996–97 | Coventry C | 18 | 0 |
| 1997–98 | Coventry C | 33 | 0 |
| **Total:** | | **313** | **5** |

## BURROWS, Mark — Defender

H: 6 3 W: 12 08 b.Kettering 14-8-80

*Source:* Trainee.

| | | | |
|---|---|---|---|
| 1997–98 | Coventry C | 0 | 0 |

## BURT, David — Midfield

H: 5 9 W: 10 11 b.Newcastle 5-2-78

*Source:* Trainee.

| | | | |
|---|---|---|---|
| 1997–98 | Newcastle U | 0 | 0 |

## BURTON, Deon — Forward

H: 5 9 W: 11 10 b.Reading 25-10-76

*Source:* Trainee. *Honours:* Jamaica 18 full caps, 4 goals.

| | | | |
|---|---|---|---|
| 1993–94 | Portsmouth | 2 | 0 |
| 1994–95 | Portsmouth | 7 | 2 |
| 1995–96 | Portsmouth | 32 | 7 |
| 1996–97 | Portsmouth | 21 | 1 |
| 1996–97 | Cardiff C (loan) | 5 | 2 |
| 1997–98 | Derby Co | 29 | 3 |
| **Total:** | | **96** | **15** |

## BURTON, Sagi — Defender

H: 6 2 W: 13 06 b.Birmingham 25-11-77

*Source:* Trainee.

| | | | |
|---|---|---|---|
| 1995–96 | Crystal Palace | 0 | 0 |
| 1996–97 | Crystal Palace | 0 | 0 |
| 1997–98 | Crystal Palace | 2 | 0 |
| **Total:** | | **2** | **0** |

## BUSHELL, Steve — Midfield

H: 5 9 W: 11 05 b.Manchester 28-12-72

*Source:* Trainee.

| | | | |
|---|---|---|---|
| 1990–91 | York C | 15 | 0 |
| 1991–92 | York C | 16 | 0 |
| 1992–93 | York C | 8 | 0 |
| 1993–94 | York C | 31 | 4 |
| 1994–95 | York C | 10 | 1 |
| 1995–96 | York C | 23 | 0 |
| 1996–97 | York C | 31 | 3 |
| 1997–98 | York C | 40 | 2 |
| **Total:** | | **174** | **10** |

## BUTLER, Ian — Defender

H: 5 8 W: 11 05 b.Barnsley 9-11-79

*Source:* Trainee.

| | | | |
|---|---|---|---|
| 1997–98 | Barnsley | 0 | 0 |

## BUTLER, John — Defender

b.Dublin 28-10-79

*Source:* Belvedere.

| | | | |
|---|---|---|---|
| 1996–97 | Leeds U | 0 | 0 |
| 1997–98 | Leeds U | 0 | 0 |

## BUTLER, Lee — Goalkeeper

H: 6 2 W: 13 00 b.Sheffield 30-5-66

*Source:* Haworth Colliery. *Honours:*

| | | | |
|---|---|---|---|
| 1986–87 | Lincoln C | 30 | 0 |
| 1987–88 | Aston Villa | 0 | 0 |
| 1988–89 | Aston Villa | 4 | 0 |
| 1989–90 | Aston Villa | 0 | 0 |
| 1990–91 | Aston Villa | 4 | 0 |
| 1990–91 | Hull C (loan) | 4 | 0 |
| 1991–92 | Barnsley | 43 | 0 |
| 1992–93 | Barnsley | 28 | 0 |
| 1993–94 | Barnsley | 37 | 0 |
| 1994–95 | Barnsley | 9 | 0 |
| 1995–96 | Barnsley | 3 | 0 |
| 1995–96 | Scunthorpe U (loan) | 2 | 0 |
| 1996–97 | Wigan Ath | 46 | 0 |
| 1997–98 | Wigan Ath | 17 | 0 |
| **Total:** | | **227** | **0** |

## BUTLER, Martin — Forward

H: 5 11 W: 12 00 b.Wordsley 15-9-74

*Source:* Trainee.

| | | | |
|---|---|---|---|
| 1993–94 | Walsall | 15 | 3 |
| 1994–95 | Walsall | 8 | 0 |
| 1995–96 | Walsall | 28 | 4 |
| 1996–97 | Walsall | 23 | 1 |
| 1997–98 | Cambridge U | 31 | 10 |
| **Total:** | | **105** | **18** |

## BUTLER, Paul — Defender

H: 6 2 W: 13 00 b.Manchester 2-11-72

*Source:* Trainee.

| | | | |
|---|---|---|---|
| 1990–91 | Rochdale | 2 | 0 |
| 1991–92 | Rochdale | 25 | 0 |
| 1992–93 | Rochdale | 16 | 2 |
| 1993–94 | Rochdale | 38 | 2 |
| 1994–95 | Rochdale | 39 | 3 |
| 1995–96 | Rochdale | 38 | 3 |
| 1996–97 | Bury | 41 | 2 |
| 1997–98 | Bury | 43 | 2 |
| **Total:** | | **242** | **14** |

## BUTLER, Peter — Midfield

H: 5 9 W: 11 02 b.Halifax 27-8-66

*Source:* Apprentice.

| | | | |
|---|---|---|---|
| 1984–85 | Huddersfield T | 4 | 0 |
| 1985–86 | Huddersfield T | 1 | 0 |
| 1985–86 | Cambridge U (loan) | 14 | 1 |
| 1986–87 | Bury | 11 | 0 |
| 1986–87 | Cambridge U | 29 | 4 |
| 1987–88 | Cambridge U | 26 | 5 |
| 1987–88 | Southend U | 15 | 3 |
| 1988–89 | Southend U | 35 | 2 |
| 1989–90 | Southend U | 41 | 2 |
| 1990–91 | Southend U | 42 | 2 |
| 1991–92 | Southend U | 9 | 0 |
| 1991–92 | Huddersfield T (loan) | 7 | 0 |
| 1992–93 | West Ham U | 39 | 2 |
| 1993–94 | West Ham U | 26 | 1 |
| 1994–95 | West Ham U | 5 | 0 |
| 1994–95 | Notts Co | 20 | 0 |
| 1995–96 | Notts Co | 0 | 0 |
| 1995–96 | Grimsby T (loan) | 3 | 0 |
| 1995–96 | WBA (loan) | 9 | 0 |
| 1996–97 | WBA | 17 | 0 |
| 1997–98 | WBA | 34 | 0 |
| **Total:** | | **387** | **22** |

## BUTLER, Steve — Forward

H: 6 1 W: 12 02 b.Birmingham 27-1-62

*Source:* Windsor & Eton, Wokingham T.

| | | | |
|---|---|---|---|
| 1984–85 | Brentford | 3 | 1 |
| 1985–86 | Brentford | 18 | 2 |
| To Maidstone U (1986) | | | |
| 1989–90 | Maidstone U | 44 | 21 |
| 1990–91 | Maidstone U | 32 | 20 |
| 1990–91 | Watford | 10 | 1 |
| 1991–92 | Watford | 43 | 8 |
| 1992–93 | Watford | 9 | 0 |
| 1992–93 | Bournemouth (loan) | 1 | 0 |
| 1992–93 | Cambridge U | 23 | 6 |
| 1993–94 | Cambridge U | 33 | 21 |
| 1994–95 | Cambridge U | 37 | 14 |
| 1995–96 | Cambridge U | 16 | 10 |
| 1995–96 | Gillingham | 20 | 5 |
| 1996–97 | Gillingham | 38 | 9 |
| 1997–98 | Gillingham | 43 | 6 |
| **Total:** | | **370** | **124** |

## BUTLER, Tony — Defender

H: 6 2 W: 12 00 b.Stockport 28-9-72

*Source:* Trainee.

| | | | |
|---|---|---|---|
| 1990–91 | Gillingham | 6 | 0 |
| 1991–92 | Gillingham | 5 | 0 |
| 1992–93 | Gillingham | 41 | 0 |
| 1993–94 | Gillingham | 27 | 1 |
| 1994–95 | Gillingham | 33 | 2 |
| 1995–96 | Gillingham | 36 | 2 |
| 1996–97 | Blackpool | 42 | 0 |
| 1997–98 | Blackpool | 37 | 0 |
| **Total:** | | **227** | **5** |

## BUTT, Nicky — Midfield

H: 5 10 W: 11 05 b.Manchester 21-1-75

*Source:* Trainee. *Honours:* England Schools, Youth, Under-21, 6 full caps.

| | | | |
|---|---|---|---|
| 1992–93 | Manchester U | 1 | 0 |
| 1993–94 | Manchester U | 1 | 0 |
| 1994–95 | Manchester U | 22 | 1 |
| 1995–96 | Manchester U | 32 | 2 |
| 1996–97 | Manchester U | 26 | 5 |
| 1997–98 | Manchester U | 33 | 3 |
| **Total:** | | **115** | **11** |

## BUTTERFIELD, Danny — Defender

H: 5 9 W: 11 08 b.Boston 21-11-79

*Source:* Trainee. *Honours:* England Youth.

| | | | |
|---|---|---|---|
| 1997–98 | Grimsby T | 7 | 0 |
| **Total:** | | **7** | **0** |

## BUTTERS, Guy — Defender

H: 6 2 W: 14 01 b.Hillingdon 30-10-69

*Source:* Trainee. *Honours:* England Under-21.

| | | | |
|---|---|---|---|
| 1988–89 | Tottenham H | 28 | 1 |
| 1989–90 | Tottenham H | 7 | 0 |
| 1989–90 | Southend U (loan) | 16 | 3 |
| 1990–91 | Portsmouth | 23 | 0 |
| 1991–92 | Portsmouth | 33 | 2 |
| 1992–93 | Portsmouth | 15 | 1 |
| 1993–94 | Portsmouth | 15 | 1 |
| 1994–95 | Portsmouth | 24 | 0 |
| 1994–95 | Oxford U (loan) | 3 | 1 |
| 1995–96 | Portsmouth | 37 | 2 |
| 1996–97 | Portsmouth | 7 | 0 |
| 1996–97 | Gillingham | 30 | 0 |
| 1997–98 | Gillingham | 31 | 7 |
| **Total:** | | **269** | **18** |

## BUXTON, Nick — Goalkeeper

H: 6 0 W: 13 00 b.Doncaster 6-9-76

| | | | |
|---|---|---|---|
| 1996–97 | Bury | 0 | 0 |
| From Goole T. | | | |
| 1997–98 | Scarborough | 3 | 0 |
| **Total:** | | **3** | **0** |

## BYFIELD, Darren — Forward

H: 5 11 W: 11 11 b.Sutton Coldfield 29-9-76

*Source:* Trainee.

| | | | |
|---|---|---|---|
| 1993–94 | Aston Villa | 0 | 0 |
| 1994–95 | Aston Villa | 0 | 0 |
| 1995–96 | Aston Villa | 0 | 0 |
| 1996–97 | Aston Villa | 0 | 0 |
| 1997–98 | Aston Villa | 7 | 0 |
| **Total:** | | **7** | **0** |

## BYRNE, Chris — Midfield

H: 5 9 W: 10 02 b.Hulme 9-2-75

*Source:* Crewe Alex, Macclesfield T.

| | | | |
|---|---|---|---|
| 1997–98 | Sunderland | 8 | 0 |
| 1997–98 | Stockport Co | 26 | 7 |
| **Total:** | | **34** | **7** |

## BYRNE, Niall — Forward

H: 5 8 W: 11 00 b.Dublin 3-9-79

*Source:* Trainee.

| | | | |
|---|---|---|---|
| 1996–97 | Liverpool | 0 | 0 |
| 1997–98 | Liverpool | 0 | 0 |

## BYRNE, Paul — Midfield

H: 5 11 W: 13 00 b.Dublin 30-6-72

*Source:* Trainee. *Honours:* Eire Youth.

| | | | |
|---|---|---|---|
| 1989–90 | Oxford U | 3 | 0 |
| 1990–91 | Oxford U | 2 | 0 |
| 1991–92 | Oxford U | 1 | 0 |
| From Bangor. | | | |
| 1993–94 | Celtic | 22 | 2 |
| 1994–95 | Celtic | 6 | 2 |
| 1994–95 | Brighton & HA (loan) | 8 | 1 |
| 1995–96 | Southend U | 41 | 5 |
| 1996–97 | Southend U | 32 | 1 |
| 1997–98 | Southend U | 10 | 0 |
| **Total:** | | **125** | **11** |

## BYWATER, Steve — Goalkeeper

b.Manchester 7-6-81

*Source:* Trainee.

| | | | |
|---|---|---|---|
| 1997–98 | Rochdale | 0 | 0 |

## CADAMARTERI, Danny — Forward

b.Bradford 12-10-79

*Source:* Trainee. *Honours:* England Youth.

| | | | |
|---|---|---|---|
| 1996–97 | Everton | 1 | 0 |
| 1997–98 | Everton | 26 | 4 |
| **Total:** | | **27** | **4** |

## CADETTE, Nathan — Midfield

b.Cardiff 6-1-80

*Source:* Trainee.

| | | | |
|---|---|---|---|
| 1997–98 | Cardiff C | 4 | 0 |
| **Total:** | | **4** | **0** |

## CAHILL, Tim — Midfield

H: 5 10 W: 10 11 b.Sydney 6-12-79

*Source:* Sydney U.

| | | | |
|---|---|---|---|
| 1997–98 | Millwall | 1 | 0 |
| **Total:** | | **1** | **0** |

## CAIG, Tony — Goalkeeper

H: 6 1 W: 12 00 b.Whitehaven 11-4-74

*Source:* Trainee.

| | | | |
|---|---|---|---|
| 1992–93 | Carlisle U | 1 | 0 |
| 1993–94 | Carlisle U | 20 | 0 |
| 1994–95 | Carlisle U | 40 | 0 |
| 1995–96 | Carlisle U | 33 | 0 |
| 1996–97 | Carlisle U | 46 | 0 |
| 1997–98 | Carlisle U | 46 | 0 |
| **Total:** | | **186** | **0** |

## CAIRNS, Kwesi — Midfield

H: 5 5 W: 10 00 b.Westminster 5-8-79

| | | | |
|---|---|---|---|
| 1996–97 | Stoke C | 0 | 0 |
| 1997–98 | Stoke C | 0 | 0 |

## CALDERWOOD, Colin — Defender

H: 6 0 W: 13 00 b.Glasgow 20-1-65

*Source:* Amateur. *Honours:* Scotland 30 full caps, 1 goal. Football League.

| | | | |
|---|---|---|---|
| 1981–82 | Mansfield T | 1 | 0 |
| 1982–83 | Mansfield T | 28 | 0 |
| 1983–84 | Mansfield T | 30 | 1 |
| 1984–85 | Mansfield T | 41 | 0 |
| 1985–86 | Swindon T | 46 | 2 |
| 1986–87 | Swindon T | 46 | 1 |
| 1987–88 | Swindon T | 34 | 1 |
| 1988–89 | Swindon T | 43 | 4 |
| 1989–90 | Swindon T | 46 | 3 |
| 1990–91 | Swindon T | 23 | 2 |
| 1991–92 | Swindon T | 46 | 5 |
| 1992–93 | Swindon T | 46 | 2 |
| 1993–94 | Tottenham H | 26 | 0 |
| 1994–95 | Tottenham H | 36 | 2 |
| 1995–96 | Tottenham H | 29 | 0 |
| 1996–97 | Tottenham H | 34 | 0 |
| 1997–98 | Tottenham H | 26 | 4 |
| **Total:** | | **581** | **27** |

## CALDWELL, Garrett — Goalkeeper

H: 6 1 W: 13 00 b.Princeton 6-11-73

| | | | |
|---|---|---|---|
| 1995–96 | Colchester U | 0 | 0 |
| 1996–97 | Colchester U | 6 | 0 |
| 1997–98 | Colchester U | 0 | 0 |
| **Total:** | | **6** | **0** |

## CALDWELL, Stephen — Defender

H: 6 0 W: 11 05 b.Stirling 12-9-80

*Source:* Trainee.

| | | | |
|---|---|---|---|
| 1997–98 | Newcastle U | 0 | 0 |

## CALLAGHAN, Anthony — Defender

H: 5 7 W: 10 00 b.Manchester 11-1-78

*Source:* Trainee.

| | | | |
|---|---|---|---|
| 1995–96 | Manchester C | 0 | 0 |
| 1996–97 | Manchester C | 0 | 0 |
| 1997–98 | Manchester C | 0 | 0 |

## CALLAGHAN, Stuart — Midfield

H: 5 8 W: 10 03 b.Calderbank 20-7-76

*Source:* Blantyre BC.

| | | | |
|---|---|---|---|
| 1994–95 | Hearts | 0 | 0 |
| 1995–96 | Hearts | 1 | 0 |
| 1996–97 | Hearts | 4 | 0 |
| 1997–98 | Hearts | 1 | 0 |
| **Total:** | | **6** | **0** |

## CALVO-GARCIA, Alexander — Midfield

H: 5 11 W: 11 10 b.Ordizia 1-1-72

*Source:* Eibar.

| | | | |
|---|---|---|---|
| 1996–97 | Scunthorpe U | 13 | 1 |
| 1997–98 | Scunthorpe U | 44 | 6 |
| **Total:** | | **57** | **7** |

## CAMERON, Colin — Forward

H: 5 6 W: 9 06 b.Kirkcaldy 23-10-72

*Source:* Lochore Welfare. *Honours:* Scotland B.

| | | | |
|---|---|---|---|
| 1990–91 | Raith R | 0 | 0 |
| 1991–92 | Sligo R (loan) | 0 | 0 |
| 1992–93 | Raith R | 16 | 1 |
| 1993–94 | Raith R | 41 | 6 |
| 1994–95 | Raith R | 35 | 7 |

| | | | |
|---|---|---|---|
| 1995–96 | Raith R | 30 | 9 |
| 1995–96 | Hearts | 4 | 2 |
| 1996–97 | Hearts | 36 | 7 |
| 1997–98 | Hearts | 31 | 8 |
| **Total:** | | **193** | **40** |

## CAMPBELL, Andy — Forward

H: 6 0 W: 10 10 b.Middlesbrough 18-4-79

*Source:* Trainee. *Honours:* England Youth.

| | | | |
|---|---|---|---|
| 1995–96 | Middlesbrough | 2 | 0 |
| 1996–97 | Middlesbrough | 3 | 0 |
| 1997–98 | Middlesbrough | 7 | 0 |
| **Total:** | | **12** | **0** |

## CAMPBELL, Jamie — Midfield

H: 6 1 W: 12 06 b.Birmingham 21-10-72

*Source:* Trainee.

| | | | |
|---|---|---|---|
| 1991–92 | Luton T | 11 | 0 |
| 1992–93 | Luton T | 9 | 1 |
| 1993–94 | Luton T | 16 | 0 |
| 1994–95 | Luton T | 0 | 0 |
| 1994–95 | Mansfield T (loan) | 3 | 1 |
| 1994–95 | Cambridge U (loan) | 12 | 0 |
| 1995–96 | Barnet | 24 | 1 |
| 1996–97 | Barnet | 43 | 4 |
| 1997–98 | Cambridge U | 46 | 2 |
| **Total:** | | **164** | **9** |

## CAMPBELL, Kevin — Forward

H: 6 1 W: 13 08 b.Lambeth 4-2-70

*Source:* Trainee. *Honours:* England Under-21, B.

| | | | |
|---|---|---|---|
| 1987–88 | Arsenal | 1 | 0 |
| 1988–89 | Arsenal | 0 | 0 |
| 1988–89 | Leyton Orient (loan) | 16 | 9 |
| 1989–90 | Arsenal | 15 | 2 |
| 1989–90 | Leicester C (loan) | 11 | 5 |
| 1990–91 | Arsenal | 22 | 9 |
| 1991–92 | Arsenal | 31 | 13 |
| 1992–93 | Arsenal | 37 | 4 |
| 1993–94 | Arsenal | 37 | 14 |
| 1994–95 | Arsenal | 23 | 4 |
| 1995–96 | Nottingham F | 21 | 3 |
| 1996–97 | Nottingham F | 17 | 6 |
| 1997–98 | Nottingham F | 42 | 23 |
| **Total:** | | **273** | **92** |

## CAMPBELL, Neil — Forward

H: 6 2 W: 13 00 b.Middlesbrough 26-1-77

*Source:* Trainee.

| | | | |
|---|---|---|---|
| 1995–96 | York C | 0 | 0 |
| 1996–97 | York C | 11 | 1 |
| 1997–98 | York C | 1 | 0 |
| 1997–98 | Scarborough | 34 | 7 |
| **Total:** | | **46** | **8** |

## CAMPBELL, Paul — Midfield

H: 6 1 W: 11 00 b.Middlesbrough 29-1-80

*Source:* Trainee.

| | | | |
|---|---|---|---|
| 1997–98 | Darlington | 6 | 1 |
| **Total:** | | **6** | **1** |

## CAMPBELL, Sean — Midfield

b.Bristol 31-12-74

| | | | |
|---|---|---|---|
| 1997–98 | Peterborough U | 0 | 0 |

## CAMPBELL, Sol — Defender

H: 6 2 1 W: 14 04 b.Newham 18-9-74

*Source:* Trainee. *Honours:* England Youth, Under-21, 20 full caps.

| | | | |
|---|---|---|---|
| 1992–93 | Tottenham H | 1 | 1 |
| 1993–94 | Tottenham H | 34 | 0 |
| 1994–95 | Tottenham H | 30 | 0 |
| 1995–96 | Tottenham H | 31 | 1 |
| 1996–97 | Tottenham H | 38 | 0 |
| 1997–98 | Tottenham H | 34 | 0 |
| **Total:** | | **168** | **2** |

## CAMPBELL, Stuart — Midfield

H: 5 10 W: 10 08 b.Corby 9-12-77

*Source:* Trainee. *Honours:* Scotland Under-21.

| | | | |
|---|---|---|---|
| 1996–97 | Leicester C | 10 | 0 |
| 1997–98 | Leicester C | 11 | 0 |
| **Total:** | | **21** | **0** |

## CANHAM, Scott — Midfield

H: 5 10 W: 11 08 b.London 5-11-74

*Source:* Trainee.

| | | | |
|---|---|---|---|
| 1993–94 | West Ham U | 0 | 0 |
| 1994–95 | West Ham U | 0 | 0 |
| 1995–96 | West Ham U | 0 | 0 |
| 1995–96 | Torquay U (loan) | 3 | 0 |
| 1995–96 | Brentford (loan) | 14 | 0 |
| 1996–97 | Brentford | 13 | 1 |
| 1997–98 | Brentford | 22 | 0 |
| **Total:** | | **52** | **1** |

## CANOVILLE, Dean — Midfield

H: 5 10 W: 11 10 b.Perivale 30-11-78

*Source:* Trainee.

| | | | |
|---|---|---|---|
| 1995–96 | Millwall | 0 | 0 |
| 1996–97 | Millwall | 2 | 0 |
| 1997–98 | Millwall | 0 | 0 |
| **Total:** | | **2** | **0** |

## CAPPER, David — Defender

H: 6 0 W: 12 00 b.Stoke 8-9-78

*Source:* Trainee.

| | | | |
|---|---|---|---|
| 1997–98 | Sheffield U | 0 | 0 |

## CARBON, Matt — Defender

H: 6 2 W: 12 05 b.Nottingham 8-6-75

*Source:* Trainee. *Honours:* England Under-21.

| | | | |
|---|---|---|---|
| 1992–93 | Lincoln C | 1 | 0 |
| 1993–94 | Lincoln C | 9 | 0 |
| 1994–95 | Lincoln C | 33 | 7 |
| 1995–96 | Lincoln C | 26 | 3 |
| 1995–96 | Derby Co | 6 | 0 |
| 1996–97 | Derby Co | 10 | 0 |
| 1997–98 | Derby Co | 4 | 0 |
| 1997–98 | WBA | 16 | 1 |
| **Total:** | | **105** | **11** |

## CARBONE, Benito — Forward

H: 5 6 W: 10 09 b.Begnara 14-8-71

| | | | |
|---|---|---|---|
| 1988–89 | Torino | 3 | 0 |
| 1989–90 | Torino | 5 | 0 |
| 1990–91 | Reggina | 31 | 5 |
| 1991–92 | Casert | 31 | 4 |
| 1992–93 | Ascoli | 28 | 6 |
| 1993–94 | Torino | 28 | 3 |
| 1994–95 | Napoli | 29 | 5 |
| 1995–96 | Internazionale | 31 | 2 |
| 1996–97 | Internazionale | 1 | 0 |
| 1996–97 | Sheffield W | 25 | 6 |
| 1997–98 | Sheffield W | 33 | 9 |
| **Total:** | | **245** | **40** |

## CARDEN, Paul — Defender

H: 5 8 W: 11 02 b.Liverpool 29-3-79

*Source:* Trainee.

| | | | |
|---|---|---|---|
| 1996–97 | Blackpool | 1 | 0 |
| 1997–98 | Blackpool | 0 | 0 |
| 1997–98 | Rochdale | 7 | 0 |
| **Total:** | | **8** | **0** |

## CARDEN, Simon — Forward

H: 5 9 W: 11 06 b.Urmston 26-10-78

*Source:* Trainee.

| | | | |
|---|---|---|---|
| 1997–98 | Stockport Co | 0 | 0 |

## CAREY, Brian — Defender

H: 6 3 W: 13 12 b.Cork 31-5-68

*Source:* Cork C. *Honours:* Eire 3 full caps.

| | | | |
|---|---|---|---|
| 1989–90 | Manchester U | 0 | 0 |
| 1990–91 | Manchester U | 0 | 0 |
| 1990–91 | Wrexham (loan) | 3 | 0 |
| 1991–92 | Manchester U | 0 | 0 |
| 1991–92 | Wrexham (loan) | 13 | 1 |
| 1992–93 | Manchester U | 0 | 0 |
| 1993–94 | Leicester C | 27 | 0 |
| 1994–95 | Leicester C | 12 | 0 |
| 1995–96 | Leicester C | 19 | 1 |
| 1996–97 | Wrexham | 38 | 0 |
| 1997–98 | Wrexham | 43 | 1 |
| **Total:** | | **155** | **3** |

## CAREY, Louis — Midfield

H: 5 10 W: 11 10 b.Bristol 22-1-77

*Source:* Trainee. *Honours:* Scotland Under-21.

| | | | |
|---|---|---|---|
| 1995–96 | Bristol C | 23 | 0 |
| 1996–97 | Bristol C | 42 | 0 |
| 1997–98 | Bristol C | 38 | 0 |
| **Total:** | | **103** | **0** |

## CAREY, Shaun — Midfield

H: 5 9 W: 10 10 b.Rushden 13-5-76

*Source:* Trainee.

| | | | |
|---|---|---|---|
| 1994–95 | Norwich C | 0 | 0 |
| 1995–96 | Norwich C | 9 | 0 |
| 1996–97 | Norwich C | 14 | 0 |
| 1997–98 | Norwich C | 14 | 0 |
| **Total:** | | **37** | **0** |

## CARLISLE, Clarke — Defender

H: 6 1 W: 12 07 b.Preston 14-10-79

*Source:* Trainee.

| | | | |
|---|---|---|---|
| 1997–98 | Blackpool | 11 | 2 |
| **Total:** | | **11** | **2** |

## CARLISLE, Wayne — Midfield

H: 6 0 W: 11 06 b.Lisburn 9-9-79

*Source:* Trainee.

| | | | |
|---|---|---|---|
| 1996–97 | Crystal Palace | 0 | 0 |
| 1997–98 | Crystal Palace | 0 | 0 |

## CARLSTRAND, Lars-Gunnar — Forward

H: 6 1 W: 12 12 b.Gothenburg 29-8-73

| | | | |
|---|---|---|---|
| 1992 | Vastra Frolunda | 9 | 2 |
| 1993 | Vastra Frolunda | 20 | 5 |
| 1994 | Vastra Frolunda | 15 | 2 |
| 1995 | Vastra Frolunda | 13 | 5 |
| 1996 | Vastra Frolunda* | 0 | 0 |
| 1997 | Vastra Frolunda | 21 | 8 |
| 1997–98 | Leicester C | 0 | 0 |
| **Total:** | | **78** | **22** |

## CARPENTER, Richard — Midfield

H: 5 11 W: 13 00 b.Sheppey 30-9-72

*Source:* Trainee.

| | | | |
|---|---|---|---|
| 1990–91 | Gillingham | 9 | 1 |
| 1991–92 | Gillingham | 3 | 0 |
| 1992–93 | Gillingham | 28 | 0 |
| 1993–94 | Gillingham | 40 | 3 |
| 1994–95 | Gillingham | 29 | 0 |
| 1995–96 | Gillingham | 12 | 0 |
| 1996–97 | Gillingham | 1 | 0 |
| 1996–97 | Fulham | 34 | 5 |
| 1997–98 | Fulham | 24 | 2 |
| **Total:** | | **180** | **11** |

## CARR-LAWTON, Colin — Forward

b.South Shields 5-9-78

*Source:* Trainee.

| | | | |
|---|---|---|---|
| 1996–97 | Burnley | 0 | 0 |
| 1997–98 | Burnley | 1 | 0 |
| **Total:** | | **1** | **0** |

## CARR, Darren — Defender

H: 6 2 W: 13 07 b.Bristol 4-9-68

*Source:* Trainee.

| | | | |
|---|---|---|---|
| 1985–86 | Bristol R | 1 | 0 |
| 1986–87 | Bristol R | 20 | 0 |
| 1987–88 | Bristol R | 9 | 0 |
| 1987–88 | Newport Co | 9 | 0 |
| 1987–88 | Sheffield U | 3 | 0 |
| 1988–89 | Sheffield U | 10 | 1 |
| 1989–90 | Sheffield U | 0 | 0 |
| 1990–91 | Sheffield U | 0 | 0 |
| 1990–91 | Crewe Alex | 36 | 0 |
| 1991–92 | Crewe Alex | 36 | 3 |
| 1992–93 | Crewe Alex | 32 | 2 |
| 1993–94 | Chesterfield | 28 | 1 |
| 1994–95 | Chesterfield | 35 | 2 |
| 1995–96 | Chesterfield | 1 | 0 |
| 1996–97 | Chesterfield | 12 | 0 |
| 1997–98 | Chesterfield | 10 | 1 |
| **Total:** | | **242** | **10** |

## CARR, Franz — Forward

H: 5 6 W: 11 10 b.Preston 24-9-66

*Source:* Apprentice. *Honours:* England Youth, Under-21.

| | | | |
|---|---|---|---|
| 1984–85 | Blackburn R | 0 | 0 |
| 1985–86 | Nottingham F | 23 | 3 |
| 1986–87 | Nottingham F | 36 | 4 |
| 1987–88 | Nottingham F | 22 | 4 |
| 1988–89 | Nottingham F | 23 | 3 |
| 1989–90 | Nottingham F | 14 | 1 |
| 1989–90 | Sheffield W (loan) | 12 | 0 |
| 1990–91 | Nottingham F | 13 | 2 |
| 1990–91 | West Ham U (loan) | 3 | 0 |
| 1991–92 | Newcastle U | 15 | 2 |
| 1992–93 | Newcastle U | 10 | 1 |
| 1992–93 | Sheffield U | 8 | 3 |
| 1993–94 | Sheffield U | 10 | 1 |
| 1994–95 | Sheffield U | 0 | 0 |
| 1994–95 | Leicester C (loan) | 13 | 1 |
| 1994–95 | Aston Villa | 2 | 0 |
| 1995–96 | Aston Villa | 1 | 0 |
| 1996–97 | Reggiana | 6 | 0 |
| 1997–98 | Bolton W | 5 | 0 |
| 1997–98 | WBA | 4 | 0 |
| **Total:** | | **220** | **25** |

## CARR, Graeme — Defender

H: 5 9 W: 11 00 b.Chester-le-Street 28-10-78

*Source:* Trainee.

| | | | |
|---|---|---|---|
| 1997–98 | Scarborough | 0 | 0 |

## CARR, Stephen — Defender

H: 5 9 W: 12 04 b.Dublin 29-8-76

*Source:* Trainee. *Honours:* Eire Under-21.

| | | | |
|---|---|---|---|
| 1993–94 | Tottenham H | 1 | 0 |
| 1994–95 | Tottenham H | 0 | 0 |
| 1995–96 | Tottenham H | 0 | 0 |
| 1996–97 | Tottenham H | 26 | 0 |
| 1997–98 | Tottenham H | 38 | 0 |
| **Total:** | | **65** | **0** |

## CARRAGHER, Jamie — Midfield

H: 6 1 W: 13 00 b.Liverpool 28-1-78

*Source:* Trainee. *Honours:* England Youth, Under-21, B.

| | | | |
|---|---|---|---|
| 1995–96 | Liverpool | 0 | 0 |
| 1996–97 | Liverpool | 2 | 1 |
| 1997–98 | Liverpool | 20 | 0 |
| **Total:** | | **22** | **1** |

## CARRAGHER, Matthew — Defender

H: 5 10 W: 11 02 b.Liverpool 14-1-76

*Source:* Trainee.

| | | | |
|---|---|---|---|
| 1993–94 | Wigan Ath | 32 | 0 |
| 1994–95 | Wigan Ath | 41 | 0 |
| 1995–96 | Wigan Ath | 28 | 0 |
| 1996–97 | Wigan Ath | 18 | 0 |
| 1997–98 | Port Vale | 26 | 0 |
| **Total:** | | **145** | **0** |

## CARROLL, Dave — Midfield

H: 6 0 W: 12 01 b.Paisley 20-9-66

*Source:* Ruislip Manor. *Honours:* England Schools.

| | | | |
|---|---|---|---|
| 1993–94 | Wycombe W | 41 | 6 |
| 1994–95 | Wycombe W | 41 | 6 |
| 1995–96 | Wycombe W | 46 | 9 |
| 1996–97 | Wycombe W | 43 | 9 |
| 1997–98 | Wycombe W | 39 | 1 |
| **Total:** | | **210** | **31** |

## CARROLL, Roy — Goalkeeper

H: 6 2 W: 11 09 b.Enniskillen 30-9-77

*Source:* Trainee. *Honours:* Northern Ireland Under-21, 1 full cap.

| | | | |
|---|---|---|---|
| 1995–96 | Hull C | 23 | 0 |
| 1996–97 | Hull C | 23 | 0 |
| 1996–97 | Wigan Ath | 0 | 0 |
| 1997–98 | Wigan Ath | 29 | 0 |
| **Total:** | | **75** | **0** |

## CARRUTHERS, Martin — Forward

H: 5 11 W: 11 07 b.Nottingham 7-8-72

*Source:* Trainee.

| | | | |
|---|---|---|---|
| 1990–91 | Aston Villa | 0 | 0 |
| 1991–92 | Aston Villa | 3 | 0 |
| 1992–93 | Aston Villa | 1 | 0 |
| 1992–93 | Hull C (loan) | 13 | 6 |
| 1993–94 | Stoke C | 34 | 5 |
| 1994–95 | Stoke C | 32 | 5 |
| 1995–96 | Stoke C | 24 | 3 |
| 1996–97 | Stoke C | 1 | 0 |
| 1996–97 | Peterborough U | 14 | 4 |
| 1997–98 | Peterborough U | 39 | 15 |
| **Total:** | | **161** | **38** |

## CARSLEY, Lee — Defender

H: 5 9 W: 12 00 b.Birmingham 28-2-74

*Source:* Trainee. *Honours:* Eire 6 full caps.

| | | | |
|---|---|---|---|
| 1992–93 | Derby Co | 0 | 0 |
| 1993–94 | Derby Co | 0 | 0 |
| 1994–95 | Derby Co | 23 | 2 |
| 1995–96 | Derby Co | 35 | 1 |
| 1996–97 | Derby Co | 24 | 0 |
| 1997–98 | Derby Co | 34 | 1 |
| **Total:** | | **116** | **4** |

## CARSS, Anthony — Midfield

H: 5 10 W: 11 08 b.Alnwick 31-3-76

*Source:* Bradford C Trainee.

| | | | |
|---|---|---|---|
| 1994–95 | Blackburn R | 0 | 0 |
| 1995–96 | Darlington | 28 | 2 |
| 1996–97 | Darlington | 29 | 0 |
| 1997–98 | Cardiff C | 42 | 1 |
| **Total:** | | **99** | **3** |

## CARTER, Graeme — Defender

b.Middlesbrough 21-2-79

*Source:* Trainee.

| | | | |
|---|---|---|---|
| 1997–98 | Middlesbrough | 0 | 0 |

## CARTER, Jimmy — Forward

H: 5 10 W: 11 02 b.Belgrade 9-11-65

*Source:* Apprentice.

| | | | |
|---|---|---|---|
| 1983–84 | Crystal Palace | 0 | 0 |
| 1984–85 | Crystal Palace | 0 | 0 |
| 1985–86 | QPR | 0 | 0 |
| 1986–87 | Millwall | 12 | 1 |
| 1987–88 | Millwall | 26 | 0 |
| 1988–89 | Millwall | 20 | 5 |
| 1989–90 | Millwall | 28 | 2 |
| 1990–91 | Millwall | 24 | 2 |
| 1990–91 | Liverpool | 5 | 0 |
| 1991–92 | Liverpool | 0 | 0 |
| 1991–92 | Arsenal | 6 | 0 |
| 1992–93 | Arsenal | 16 | 2 |
| 1993–94 | Arsenal | 0 | 0 |
| 1993–94 | Oxford U (loan) | 5 | 0 |
| 1994–95 | Arsenal | 3 | 0 |
| 1994–95 | Oxford U (loan) | 4 | 0 |
| 1995–96 | Portsmouth | 35 | 4 |

| | | | |
|---|---|---|---|
| 1996–97 | Portsmouth | 27 | 1 |
| 1997–98 | Portsmouth | 10 | 0 |
| **Total:** | | **221** | **17** |

## CARTER, Mark — Forward

H: 5 8 W: 12 05 b.Liverpool 17-12-60

*Source:* S Liverpool, Bangor C, Runcorn.

| | | | |
|---|---|---|---|
| 1991–92 | Barnet | 36 | 19 |
| 1992–93 | Barnet | 41 | 11 |
| 1993–94 | Barnet | 5 | 0 |
| 1993–94 | Bury | 36 | 20 |
| 1994–95 | Bury | 26 | 14 |
| 1995–96 | Bury | 32 | 16 |
| 1996–97 | Bury | 40 | 12 |
| 1997–98 | Rochdale | 11 | 2 |
| **Total:** | | **227** | **94** |

## CARTER, Tim — Goalkeeper

H: 6 2 W: 13 00 b.Bristol 5-10-67

*Source:* Apprentice. *Honours:* England Youth.

| | | | |
|---|---|---|---|
| 1985–86 | Bristol R | 2 | 0 |
| 1986–87 | Bristol R | 38 | 0 |
| 1987–88 | Bristol R | 7 | 0 |
| 1987–88 | Newport Co (loan) | 1 | 0 |
| 1987–88 | Carlisle U (loan) | 4 | 0 |
| 1987–88 | Sunderland | 1 | 0 |
| 1988–89 | Sunderland | 2 | 0 |
| 1988–89 | Bristol C (loan) | 3 | 0 |
| 1989–90 | Sunderland | 18 | 0 |
| 1990–91 | Sunderland | 1 | 0 |
| 1991–92 | Sunderland | 2 | 0 |
| 1991–92 | Birmingham C (loan) | 2 | 0 |
| 1992–93 | Sunderland | 13 | 0 |
| 1993–94 | Hartlepool U | 18 | 0 |
| 1993–94 | Millwall | 2 | 0 |
| 1994–95 | Millwall | 2 | 0 |
| 1995–96 | Oxford U | 12 | 0 |
| 1995–96 | Millwall | 4 | 0 |
| 1996–97 | Millwall | 46 | 0 |
| 1997–98 | Millwall | 12 | 0 |
| **Total:** | | **190** | **0** |

## CARTWRIGHT, Jamie — Midfield

H: 5 7 W: 9 06 b.Lichfield 11-10-79

*Source:* Trainee.

| | | | |
|---|---|---|---|
| 1996–97 | Stoke C | 0 | 0 |
| 1997–98 | Stoke C | 0 | 0 |

## CARTWRIGHT, Lee — Forward

H: 5 8 W: 10 06 b.Rossendale 19-9-72

*Source:* Trainee.

| | | | |
|---|---|---|---|
| 1990–91 | Preston NE | 14 | 1 |
| 1991–92 | Preston NE | 33 | 4 |
| 1992–93 | Preston NE | 34 | 3 |
| 1993–94 | Preston NE | 39 | 1 |
| 1994–95 | Preston NE | 36 | 1 |
| 1995–96 | Preston NE | 26 | 3 |
| 1996–97 | Preston NE | 14 | 1 |
| 1997–98 | Preston NE | 36 | 2 |
| **Total:** | | **232** | **16** |

## CARTWRIGHT, Mark — Goalkeeper

H: 6 2 W: 13 06 b.Chester 13-1-73

*Source:* York C.

| | | | |
|---|---|---|---|
| 1994–95 | Wrexham | 0 | 0 |
| 1995–96 | Wrexham | 0 | 0 |
| 1996–97 | Wrexham | 3 | 0 |
| 1997–98 | Wrexham | 4 | 0 |
| **Total:** | | **7** | **0** |

## CASEY, Ryan — Forward

H: 6 0 W: 10 12 b.Coventry 3-1-79

*Source:* Trainee.

| | | | |
|---|---|---|---|
| 1996–97 | Swansea C | 10 | 0 |
| 1997–98 | Swansea C | 6 | 0 |
| **Total:** | | **16** | **0** |

## CASKEY, Darren — Midfield

H: 5 8 W: 11 09 b.Basildon 21-8-74

*Source:* Trainee. *Honours:* England Schools, Youth.

| | | | |
|---|---|---|---|
| 1991–92 | Tottenham H | 0 | 0 |
| 1992–93 | Tottenham H | 0 | 0 |
| 1993–94 | Tottenham H | 25 | 4 |
| 1994–95 | Tottenham H | 4 | 0 |
| 1995–96 | Tottenham H | 3 | 0 |
| 1995–96 | Watford (loan) | 6 | 1 |
| 1995–96 | Reading | 15 | 2 |
| 1996–97 | Reading | 35 | 0 |
| 1997–98 | Reading | 23 | 0 |
| **Total:** | | **111** | **7** |

## CASPER, Chris — Defender

H: 6 0 W: 12 02 b.Burnley 28-4-75

*Source:* Trainee. *Honours:* England Youth, Under-21.

| | | | |
|---|---|---|---|
| 1992–93 | Manchester U | 0 | 0 |
| 1993–94 | Manchester U | 0 | 0 |

| | | | |
|---|---|---|---|
| 1994–95 | Manchester U | 0 | 0 |
| 1995–96 | Manchester U | 0 | 0 |
| 1995–96 | Bournemouth (loan) | 16 | 1 |
| 1996–97 | Manchester U | 2 | 0 |
| 1997–98 | Manchester U | 0 | 0 |
| 1997–98 | Swindon T (loan) | 9 | 1 |
| **Total:** | | **27** | **2** |

## CASSIDY, Jamie — Midfield

H: 5 9 W: 10 08 b.Liverpool 21-11-77

*Source:* Trainee. *Honours:* England Schools, Youth.

| | | | |
|---|---|---|---|
| 1994–95 | Liverpool | 0 | 0 |
| 1995–96 | Liverpool | 0 | 0 |
| 1996–97 | Liverpool | 0 | 0 |
| 1997–98 | Liverpool | 0 | 0 |

## CASSIN, Graham — Forward

H: 5 10 W: 11 07 b.Dublin 24-3-78

*Source:* Belvedere, Trainee.

| | | | |
|---|---|---|---|
| 1994–95 | Blackburn R | 0 | 0 |
| 1995–96 | Blackburn R | 0 | 0 |
| 1996–97 | Blackburn R | 0 | 0 |
| 1997–98 | Blackburn R | 0 | 0 |

## CASTLE, Steve — Midfield

H: 5 10 W: 12 07 b.Ilford 17-5-66

*Source:* Apprentice.

| | | | |
|---|---|---|---|
| 1984–85 | Orient | 21 | 1 |
| 1985–86 | Orient | 23 | 4 |
| 1986–87 | Orient | 24 | 5 |
| 1987–88 | Orient | 42 | 10 |
| 1988–89 | Orient | 24 | 6 |
| 1989–90 | Orient | 27 | 7 |
| 1990–91 | Orient | 45 | 12 |
| 1991–92 | Orient | 37 | 10 |
| 1992–93 | Plymouth Arg | 31 | 11 |
| 1993–94 | Plymouth Arg | 44 | 21 |
| 1994–95 | Plymouth Arg | 26 | 3 |
| 1995–96 | Birmingham C | 15 | 1 |
| 1995–96 | Gillingham (loan) | 6 | 1 |
| 1996–97 | Birmingham C | 8 | 0 |
| 1996–97 | Leyton Orient (loan) | 4 | 1 |
| 1996–97 | Peterborough U | 0 | 0 |
| 1997–98 | Peterborough U | 37 | 3 |
| **Total:** | | **414** | **96** |

## CASTLEDINE, Stewart — Midfield

H: 6 1 W: 12 00 b.Wandsworth 22-1-73

*Source:* Trainee.

| | | | |
|---|---|---|---|
| 1991–92 | Wimbledon | 2 | 0 |
| 1992–93 | Wimbledon | 0 | 0 |
| 1993–94 | Wimbledon | 3 | 1 |
| 1994–95 | Wimbledon | 6 | 1 |
| 1995–96 | Wimbledon | 4 | 1 |
| 1995–96 | Wycombe W (loan) | 7 | 3 |
| 1996–97 | Wimbledon | 6 | 1 |
| 1997–98 | Wimbledon | 6 | 0 |
| **Total:** | | **34** | **7** |

## CATAROCHE, David — Midfield

H: 5 7 W: 11 07 b.Leeds 13-12-80

*Source:* Trainee.

| | | | |
|---|---|---|---|
| 1997–98 | Barnsley | 0 | 0 |

## CAVACO, Luis — Forward

H: 5 9 W: 11 06 b.Portugal 1-3-72

*Source:* Estoril.

| | | | |
|---|---|---|---|
| 1996–97 | Stockport Co | 27 | 5 |
| 1997–98 | Stockport Co | 2 | 0 |
| **Total:** | | **29** | **5** |

## CAWLEY, Peter — Defender

H: 6 4 W: 15 10 b.London 15-9-65

*Source:* Chertsey T.

| | | | |
|---|---|---|---|
| 1986–87 | Wimbledon | 0 | 0 |
| 1986–87 | Bristol R (loan) | 10 | 0 |
| 1987–88 | Wimbledon | 0 | 0 |
| 1988–89 | Wimbledon | 1 | 0 |
| 1988–89 | Fulham (loan) | 5 | 0 |
| 1989–90 | Bristol R | 3 | 0 |
| 1990–91 | Southend U | 7 | 1 |
| 1990–91 | Exeter C | 7 | 0 |
| 1991–92 | Barnet | 3 | 0 |
| 1992–93 | Barnet | 0 | 0 |
| 1992–93 | Colchester U | 24 | 3 |
| 1993–94 | Colchester U | 36 | 1 |
| 1994–95 | Colchester U | 23 | 2 |
| 1995–96 | Colchester U | 42 | 1 |
| 1996–97 | Colchester U | 28 | 1 |
| 1997–98 | Colchester U | 27 | 0 |
| **Total:** | | **216** | **9** |

## CHALK, Martyn — Midfield

H: 5 6 W: 10 00 b.Swindon 30-8-69

*Source:* Louth U.

| | | | |
|---|---|---|---|
| 1990–91 | Derby Co | 0 | 0 |
| 1991–92 | Derby Co | 7 | 1 |
| 1992–93 | Derby Co | 0 | 0 |
| 1993–94 | Derby Co | 0 | 0 |
| 1994–95 | Stockport Co | 33 | 6 |

| 1995–96 | Stockport Co | 10 | 0 |
|---|---|---|---|
| 1995–96 | Wrexham | 19 | 4 |
| 1996–97 | Wrexham | 43 | 1 |
| 1997–98 | Wrexham | 26 | 1 |
| **Total:** | | **138** | **13** |

## CHALLINOR, Dave — Defender

H: 6 1 W: 12 00 b.Chester 2-10-75

*Source:* Bromborough Pool. *Honours:* England Schools.

| 1994–95 | Tranmere R | 0 | 0 |
|---|---|---|---|
| 1995–96 | Tranmere R | 0 | 0 |
| 1996–97 | Tranmere R | 5 | 0 |
| 1997–98 | Tranmere R | 32 | 1 |
| **Total:** | | **37** | **1** |

## CHALLIS, Trevor — Defender

H: 5 8 W: 11 04 b.Paddington 23-10-75

*Source:* Trainee. *Honours:* England Youth, Under-21.

| 1994–95 | QPR | 0 | 0 |
|---|---|---|---|
| 1995–96 | QPR | 11 | 0 |
| 1996–97 | QPR | 2 | 0 |
| 1997–98 | QPR | 0 | 0 |
| **Total:** | | **13** | **0** |

## CHAMBERLAIN, Alec — Goalkeeper

H: 6 2 W: 13 10 b.March 20-6-64

*Source:* Ramsey T.

| 1981–82 | Ipswich T | 0 | 0 |
|---|---|---|---|
| 1982–83 | Colchester U | 0 | 0 |
| 1983–84 | Colchester U | 46 | 0 |
| 1984–85 | Colchester U | 46 | 0 |
| 1985–86 | Colchester U | 46 | 0 |
| 1986–87 | Colchester U | 46 | 0 |
| 1987–88 | Everton | 0 | 0 |
| 1987–88 | Tranmere R (loan) | 15 | 0 |
| 1988–89 | Luton T | 6 | 0 |
| 1989–90 | Luton T | 38 | 0 |
| 1990–91 | Luton T | 38 | 0 |
| 1991–92 | Luton T | 24 | 0 |
| 1992–93 | Luton T | 32 | 0 |
| 1992–93 | Chelsea (loan) | 0 | 0 |
| 1993–94 | Sunderland | 43 | 0 |
| 1994–95 | Sunderland | 18 | 0 |
| 1994–95 | Liverpool (loan) | 0 | 0 |
| 1995–96 | Sunderland | 29 | 0 |
| 1996–97 | Watford | 4 | 0 |
| 1997–98 | Watford | 46 | 0 |
| **Total:** | | **477** | **0** |

## CHAMBERS, Leroy — Forward

H: 5 11 W: 11 08 b.Sheffield 25-10-72

*Source:* Trainee.

| 1991–92 | Sheffield W | 0 | 0 |
|---|---|---|---|
| 1992–93 | Sheffield W | 0 | 0 |
| 1993–94 | Sheffield W | 0 | 0 |
| 1994–95 | Chester C | 13 | 0 |
| 1995–96 | Chester C | 8 | 1 |
| 1996–97 | Chesterfield | 0 | 0 |
| From Boston U. | | | |
| 1997–98 | Macclesfield T | 21 | 4 |
| **Total:** | | **42** | **5** |

## CHANDLER, Dean — Defender

H: 6 1 W: 11 02 b.Ilford 6-5-76

*Source:* Trainee.

| 1993–94 | Charlton Ath | 0 | 0 |
|---|---|---|---|
| 1994–95 | Charlton Ath | 1 | 1 |
| 1995–96 | Charlton Ath | 1 | 0 |
| 1996–97 | Charlton Ath | 0 | 0 |
| 1996–97 | Torquay U (loan) | 4 | 0 |
| 1997–98 | Lincoln C | 0 | 0 |
| **Total:** | | **6** | **1** |

## CHANNING, Justin — Defender

H: 5 11 W: 11 07 b.Reading 19-11-68

*Source:* Apprentice. *Honours:* England Youth.

| 1986–87 | QPR | 2 | 0 |
|---|---|---|---|
| 1987–88 | QPR | 14 | 1 |
| 1988–89 | QPR | 9 | 1 |
| 1989–90 | QPR | 23 | 2 |
| 1990–91 | QPR | 5 | 0 |
| 1991–92 | QPR | 0 | 0 |
| 1992–93 | QPR | 2 | 1 |
| 1992–93 | Bristol R | 25 | 3 |
| 1993–94 | Bristol R | 29 | 5 |
| 1994–95 | Bristol R | 40 | 2 |
| 1995–96 | Bristol R | 36 | 0 |
| 1996–97 | Leyton Orient | 40 | 5 |
| 1997–98 | Leyton Orient | 34 | 0 |
| **Total:** | | **259** | **20** |

## CHAPMAN, Ben — Defender

H: 5 7 W: 10 12 b.Scunthorpe 2-3-79

*Source:* Trainee.

| 1997–98 | Grimsby T | 0 | 0 |
|---|---|---|---|

## CHAPMAN, Ian — Defender

H: 5 8 W: 12 07 b.Brighton 31-5-70

*Source:* FA Schools, Trainee.

| | | | |
|---|---|---|---|
| 1986–87 | Brighton & HA | 5 | 0 |
| 1987–88 | Brighton & HA | 0 | 0 |
| 1988–89 | Brighton & HA | 19 | 0 |
| 1989–90 | Brighton & HA | 42 | 1 |
| 1990–91 | Brighton & HA | 23 | 0 |
| 1991–92 | Brighton & HA | 37 | 2 |
| 1992–93 | Brighton & HA | 34 | 1 |
| 1993–94 | Brighton & HA | 45 | 3 |
| 1994–95 | Brighton & HA | 40 | 4 |
| 1995–96 | Brighton & HA | 36 | 3 |
| 1996–97 | Gillingham | 23 | 1 |
| 1997–98 | Gillingham | 0 | 0 |
| **Total:** | | **304** | **15** |

## CHAPPLE, Phil — Defender

H: 6 2 W: 13 01 b.Norwich 26-11-66

*Source:* Apprentice.

| | | | |
|---|---|---|---|
| 1984–85 | Norwich C | 0 | 0 |
| 1985–86 | Norwich C | 0 | 0 |
| 1986–87 | Norwich C | 0 | 0 |
| 1987–88 | Norwich C | 0 | 0 |
| 1987–88 | Cambridge U | 6 | 1 |
| 1988–89 | Cambridge U | 46 | 3 |
| 1989–90 | Cambridge U | 45 | 5 |
| 1990–91 | Cambridge U | 43 | 5 |
| 1991–92 | Cambridge U | 29 | 3 |
| 1992–93 | Cambridge U | 18 | 2 |
| 1993–94 | Charlton Ath | 44 | 5 |
| 1994–95 | Charlton Ath | 21 | 2 |
| 1995–96 | Charlton Ath | 16 | 2 |
| 1996–97 | Charlton Ath | 26 | 2 |
| 1997–98 | Charlton Ath | 35 | 4 |
| **Total:** | | **329** | **34** |

## CHAPPLE, Shaun — Midfield

H: 5 11 W: 12 03 b.Swansea 14-2-73

*Source:* Trainee. *Honours:* Wales Under-21.

| | | | |
|---|---|---|---|
| 1991–92 | Swansea C | 21 | 2 |
| 1992–93 | Swansea C | 4 | 0 |
| 1993–94 | Swansea C | 29 | 3 |
| 1994–95 | Swansea C | 9 | 2 |
| 1995–96 | Swansea C | 22 | 2 |
| 1996–97 | Swansea C | 18 | 0 |
| 1997–98 | Swansea C | 4 | 0 |
| **Total:** | | **107** | **9** |

## CHARLERY, Ken — Forward

H: 6 0 W: 12 00 b.Stepney 28-11-64

*Source:* Fisher Ath, Basildon U, Beckton U.

| | | | |
|---|---|---|---|
| 1989–90 | Maidstone U | 30 | 2 |
| 1990–91 | Maidstone U | 29 | 9 |
| 1990–91 | Peterborough U | 4 | 0 |
| 1991–92 | Peterborough U | 37 | 16 |
| 1992–93 | Peterborough U | 10 | 3 |
| 1992–93 | Watford | 32 | 11 |
| 1993–94 | Watford | 16 | 2 |
| 1993–94 | Peterborough U | 26 | 8 |
| 1994–95 | Peterborough U | 44 | 16 |
| 1995–96 | Birmingham C | 17 | 4 |
| 1995–96 | Southend U (loan) | 3 | 0 |
| 1995–96 | Peterborough U | 19 | 7 |
| 1996–97 | Peterborough U | 37 | 5 |
| 1996–97 | Stockport Co | 10 | 0 |
| 1997–98 | Barnet | 32 | 5 |
| **Total:** | | **346** | **88** |

## CHARLES, Gary — Defender

H: 5 9 W: 11 03 b.London 13-4-70

*Source:* Trainee. *Honours:* England Under-21, 2 full caps.

| | | | |
|---|---|---|---|
| 1987–88 | Nottingham F | 0 | 0 |
| 1988–89 | Nottingham F | 1 | 0 |
| 1988–89 | Leicester C (loan) | 8 | 0 |
| 1989–90 | Nottingham F | 1 | 0 |
| 1990–91 | Nottingham F | 10 | 0 |
| 1991–92 | Nottingham F | 30 | 1 |
| 1992–93 | Nottingham F | 14 | 0 |
| 1993–94 | Derby Co | 43 | 1 |
| 1994–95 | Derby Co | 18 | 2 |
| 1994–95 | Aston Villa | 16 | 0 |
| 1995–96 | Aston Villa | 34 | 1 |
| 1996–97 | Aston Villa | 0 | 0 |
| 1997–98 | Aston Villa | 18 | 1 |
| **Total:** | | **193** | **6** |

## CHARLES, Lee — Forward

H: 5 11 W: 11 03 b.Hillingdon 20-8-71

*Source:* Chertsey T.

| | | | |
|---|---|---|---|
| 1995–96 | QPR | 4 | 0 |
| 1995–96 | Barnet (loan) | 5 | 0 |
| 1996–97 | QPR | 12 | 1 |
| 1997–98 | QPR | 0 | 0 |
| 1997–98 | Cambridge U (loan) | 7 | 1 |
| **Total:** | | **28** | **2** |

## CHARLTON, Simon — Defender

H: 5 8 W: 11 10 b.Huddersfield 25-10-71

*Source:* Trainee. *Honours:* FA Schools.

| | | | |
|---|---|---|---|
| 1989–90 | Huddersfield T | 3 | 0 |
| 1990–91 | Huddersfield T | 30 | 0 |
| 1991–92 | Huddersfield T | 45 | 0 |
| 1992–93 | Huddersfield T | 46 | 1 |
| 1993–94 | Southampton | 33 | 1 |
| 1994–95 | Southampton | 25 | 1 |
| 1995–96 | Southampton | 26 | 0 |
| 1996–97 | Southampton | 27 | 0 |
| 1997–98 | Southampton | 3 | 0 |
| 1997–98 | Birmingham C | 24 | 0 |
| **Total:** | | **262** | **3** |

## CHARNLEY, Chic — Midfield

H: 5 10 W: 11 12 b.Glasgow 11-6-63

*Source:* Pollok Juniors.

| | | | |
|---|---|---|---|
| 1987–88 | Clydebank | 28 | 10 |
| 1988–89 | Clydebank | 3 | 1 |
| 1988–89 | Hamilton A | 14 | 0 |
| 1988–89 | Partick Th | 14 | 4 |
| 1989–90 | Partick Th | 29 | 11 |
| 1990–91 | Partick Th | 30 | 7 |
| 1991–92 | St Mirren | 26 | 4 |
| 1991–92 | Bolton W (loan) | 3 | 0 |
| From Djurgaarden. | | | |
| 1993–94 | Partick Th | 26 | 1 |
| 1994–95 | Partick Th | 20 | 1 |
| 1995–96 | Dumbarton | 18 | 1 |
| 1995–96 | Dundee | 12 | 3 |
| 1996–97 | Dundee | 15 | 3 |
| 1996–97 | Hibernian | 9 | 1 |
| 1997–98 | Hibernian | 20 | 3 |
| **Total:** | | **267** | **50** |

## CHARNOCK, Phil — Midfield

H: 5 10 W: 11 03 b.Southport 14-2-75

*Source:* Trainee.

| | | | |
|---|---|---|---|
| 1992–93 | Liverpool | 0 | 0 |
| 1993–94 | Liverpool | 0 | 0 |
| 1994–95 | Liverpool | 0 | 0 |
| 1995–96 | Liverpool | 0 | 0 |
| 1995–96 | Blackpool (loan) | 4 | 0 |
| 1996–97 | Liverpool | 0 | 0 |
| 1996–97 | Crewe Alex | 32 | 1 |
| 1997–98 | Crewe Alex | 33 | 3 |
| **Total:** | | **69** | **4** |

## CHARVET, Laurent — Midfield

b.Beziers 8-5-73

| | | | |
|---|---|---|---|
| 1994–95 | Cannes | 19 | 4 |
| 1995–96 | Cannes | 31 | 8 |
| 1996–97 | Cannes | 38 | 6 |
| 1997–98 | Cannes | 11 | 1 |
| 1997–98 | Chelsea | 11 | 2 |
| **Total:** | | **110** | **21** |

## CHENERY, Ben — Defender

H: 5 11 W: 11 10 b.Ipswich 28-1-77

*Source:* Trainee.

| | | | |
|---|---|---|---|
| 1994–95 | Luton T | 0 | 0 |
| 1995–96 | Luton T | 2 | 0 |
| 1996–97 | Luton T | 0 | 0 |
| 1997–98 | Cambridge U | 36 | 2 |
| **Total:** | | **38** | **2** |

## CHERRY, Steve — Goalkeeper

H: 6 1 W: 13 00 b.Nottingham 5-8-60

*Source:* Apprentice. *Honours:* England Youth.

| | | | |
|---|---|---|---|
| 1977–78 | Derby Co | 0 | 0 |
| 1978–79 | Derby Co | 0 | 0 |
| 1979–80 | Derby Co | 4 | 0 |
| 1980–81 | Port Vale (loan) | 4 | 0 |
| 1981–82 | Derby Co | 4 | 0 |
| 1982–83 | Derby Co | 31 | 0 |
| 1983–84 | Derby Co | 38 | 0 |
| 1984–85 | Walsall | 41 | 0 |
| 1985–86 | Walsall | 30 | 0 |
| 1986–87 | Walsall | 0 | 0 |
| 1986–87 | Plymouth Arg | 21 | 0 |
| 1987–88 | Plymouth Arg | 37 | 0 |
| 1988–89 | Plymouth Arg | 15 | 0 |
| 1988–89 | Chesterfield (loan) | 10 | 0 |
| 1988–89 | Notts Co | 18 | 0 |
| 1989–90 | Notts Co | 46 | 0 |
| 1990–91 | Notts Co | 46 | 0 |
| 1991–92 | Notts Co | 42 | 0 |
| 1992–93 | Notts Co | 44 | 0 |
| 1993–94 | Notts Co | 45 | 0 |
| 1994–95 | Notts Co | 25 | 0 |
| 1995–96 | Watford | 4 | 0 |
| 1995–96 | Plymouth Arg (loan) | 16 | 0 |
| 1996–97 | Rotherham U | 20 | 0 |
| 1997–98 | Notts Co | 0 | 0 |
| **Total:** | | **541** | **0** |

## CHETTLE, Steve — Defender

H: 6 1 W: 13 01 b.Nottingham 27-9-68

*Source:* Apprentice. *Honours:* England Under-21.

| | | | |
|---|---|---|---|
| 1986–87 | Nottingham F | 0 | 0 |
| 1987–88 | Nottingham F | 30 | 0 |
| 1988–89 | Nottingham F | 28 | 2 |
| 1989–90 | Nottingham F | 22 | 1 |
| 1990–91 | Nottingham F | 37 | 2 |
| 1991–92 | Nottingham F | 22 | 1 |
| 1992–93 | Nottingham F | 30 | 0 |
| 1993–94 | Nottingham F | 46 | 1 |
| 1994–95 | Nottingham F | 41 | 0 |
| 1995–96 | Nottingham F | 37 | 0 |
| 1996–97 | Nottingham F | 32 | 0 |
| 1997–98 | Nottingham F | 45 | 1 |
| **Total:** | | **370** | **8** |

## CHRISTIE, Iyseden — Forward

H: 6 0 W: 12 02 b.Coventry 14-11-76

*Source:* Trainee.

| | | | |
|---|---|---|---|
| 1994–95 | Coventry C | 0 | 0 |
| 1995–96 | Coventry C | 1 | 0 |
| 1996–97 | Coventry C | 0 | 0 |
| 1996–97 | Bournemouth (loan) | 4 | 0 |
| 1996–97 | Mansfield T (loan) | 8 | 0 |
| 1997–98 | Mansfield T | 39 | 10 |
| **Total:** | | **52** | **10** |

## CHRISTIE, Kevin — Midfield

H: 6 1 W: 12 03 b.Aberdeen 1-4-76

*Source:* Lewis Utd.

| | | | |
|---|---|---|---|
| 1994–95 | Aberdeen | 0 | 0 |
| 1995–96 | Aberdeen | 2 | 0 |
| 1996–97 | East Fife | 9 | 1 |
| 1996–97 | Motherwell | 4 | 0 |
| 1997–98 | Motherwell | 21 | 0 |
| **Total:** | | **36** | **1** |

## CLAPHAM, Jamie — Midfield

H: 5 9 W: 10 11 b.Lincoln 7-12-75

*Source:* Trainee.

| | | | |
|---|---|---|---|
| 1994–95 | Tottenham H | 0 | 0 |
| 1995–96 | Tottenham H | 0 | 0 |
| 1996–97 | Tottenham H | 1 | 0 |
| 1996–97 | Leyton Orient (loan) | 6 | 0 |
| 1996–97 | Bristol R (loan) | 5 | 0 |
| 1997–98 | Tottenham H | 0 | 0 |
| 1997–98 | Ipswich T | 22 | 0 |
| **Total:** | | **34** | **0** |

## CLARE, Daryl — Forward

H: 5 9 W: 12 00 b.Jersey 1-8-78

*Source:* Trainee.

| | | | |
|---|---|---|---|
| 1995–96 | Grimsby T | 1 | 0 |
| 1996–97 | Grimsby T | 0 | 0 |
| 1997–98 | Grimsby T | 22 | 3 |
| **Total:** | | **23** | **3** |

## CLARIDGE, Steve — Forward

H: 5 11 W: 11 08 b.Portsmouth 10-4-66

*Source:* Portsmouth, Fareham T.

| | | | |
|---|---|---|---|
| 1984–85 | Bournemouth | 6 | 1 |
| 1985–86 | Bournemouth | 1 | 0 |
| From Weymouth. | | | |
| 1988–89 | Crystal Palace | 0 | 0 |
| 1988–89 | Aldershot | 37 | 9 |
| 1989–90 | Aldershot | 25 | 10 |
| 1989–90 | Cambridge U | 20 | 4 |
| 1990–91 | Cambridge U | 30 | 12 |
| 1991–92 | Cambridge U | 29 | 12 |
| 1992–93 | Luton T | 16 | 2 |
| 1992–93 | Cambridge U | 29 | 7 |
| 1993–94 | Cambridge U | 24 | 11 |
| 1993–94 | Birmingham C | 18 | 7 |
| 1994–95 | Birmingham C | 42 | 20 |
| 1995–96 | Birmingham C | 28 | 8 |
| 1995–96 | Leicester C | 14 | 5 |
| 1996–97 | Leicester C | 32 | 11 |
| 1997–98 | Leicester C | 17 | 0 |
| 1997–98 | Portsmouth (loan) | 10 | 2 |
| 1997–98 | Wolverhampton W | 5 | 0 |
| **Total:** | | **383** | **121** |

## CLARK, Billy — Defender

H: 6 0 W: 12 03 b.Christchurch 19-5-67

*Source:* Trainee.

| | | | |
|---|---|---|---|
| 1984–85 | Bournemouth | 1 | 0 |
| 1985–86 | Bournemouth | 1 | 0 |
| 1986–87 | Bournemouth | 0 | 0 |
| 1987–88 | Bournemouth | 2 | 0 |
| 1987–88 | Bristol R | 31 | 1 |
| 1988–89 | Bristol R | 11 | 0 |
| 1989–90 | Bristol R | 0 | 0 |
| 1990–91 | Bristol R | 14 | 1 |
| 1991–92 | Bristol R | 24 | 1 |
| 1992–93 | Bristol R | 24 | 1 |
| 1993–94 | Bristol R | 36 | 1 |
| 1994–95 | Bristol R | 42 | 6 |
| 1995–96 | Bristol R | 39 | 2 |
| 1996–97 | Bristol R | 27 | 1 |

## Clark, Dean

| | | | |
|---|---|---|---|
| 1997–98 | Bristol R | 0 | 0 |
| 1997–98 | Exeter C | 31 | 3 |
| **Total:** | | **283** | **17** |

## CLARK, Dean — Midfield

b.Hillingdon 31-3-80

*Source:* Trainee.

| | | | |
|---|---|---|---|
| 1997–98 | Brentford | 4 | 0 |
| **Total:** | | **4** | **0** |

## CLARK, Ian — Midfield

H: 5 10 W: 11 05 b.Stockton 23-10-74

*Source:* Stockton.

| | | | |
|---|---|---|---|
| 1995–96 | Doncaster R | 23 | 1 |
| 1996–97 | Doncaster R | 20 | 2 |
| 1997–98 | Doncaster R | 2 | 0 |
| 1997–98 | Hartlepool U | 24 | 7 |
| **Total:** | | **69** | **10** |

## CLARK, Lee — Midfield

H: 5 8 W: 11 07 b.Wallsend 27-10-72

*Source:* Trainee. *Honours:* England Schools, Youth, Under-21.

| | | | |
|---|---|---|---|
| 1989–90 | Newcastle U | 0 | 0 |
| 1990–91 | Newcastle U | 19 | 2 |
| 1991–92 | Newcastle U | 29 | 5 |
| 1992–93 | Newcastle U | 46 | 9 |
| 1993–94 | Newcastle U | 29 | 2 |
| 1994–95 | Newcastle U | 19 | 1 |
| 1995–96 | Newcastle U | 28 | 2 |
| 1996–97 | Newcastle U | 25 | 2 |
| 1997–98 | Sunderland | 46 | 13 |
| **Total:** | | **241** | **36** |

## CLARK, Martin — Defender

H: 5 9 W: 10 12 b.Accrington 12-9-70

*Source:* Accrington S.

| | | | |
|---|---|---|---|
| 1992–93 | Crewe Alex | 0 | 0 |
| 1993–94 | Crewe Alex | 0 | 0 |
| From Southport. | | | |
| 1997–98 | Rotherham U | 28 | 0 |
| **Total:** | | **28** | **0** |

## CLARK, Simon — Defender

H: 6 0 W: 12 12 b.Boston 12-3-67

*Source:* Boston U, Holbeach, Kings Lynn, Hendon, Stevenage Borough.

| | | | |
|---|---|---|---|
| 1993–94 | Peterborough U | 1 | 0 |
| 1994–95 | Peterborough U | 32 | 0 |
| 1995–96 | Peterborough U | 40 | 1 |
| 1996–97 | Peterborough U | 34 | 3 |
| 1997–98 | Leyton Orient | 39 | 4 |
| **Total:** | | **146** | **8** |

## CLARKE, Adrian — Midfield

H: 5 9 W: 11 00 b.Cambridge 28-9-74

*Source:* Trainee. *Honours:* England Schools.

| | | | |
|---|---|---|---|
| 1993–94 | Arsenal | 0 | 0 |
| 1994–95 | Arsenal | 1 | 0 |
| 1995–96 | Arsenal | 6 | 0 |
| 1996–97 | Arsenal | 0 | 0 |
| 1996–97 | Rotherham U (loan) | 2 | 0 |
| 1996–97 | Southend U (loan) | 7 | 0 |
| 1997–98 | Southend U | 45 | 5 |
| **Total:** | | **61** | **5** |

## CLARKE, Andy — Forward

H: 5 10 W: 11 07 b.Islington 22-7-67

*Source:* Barnet.

| | | | |
|---|---|---|---|
| 1990–91 | Wimbledon | 12 | 3 |
| 1991–92 | Wimbledon | 34 | 3 |
| 1992–93 | Wimbledon | 33 | 5 |
| 1993–94 | Wimbledon | 23 | 2 |
| 1994–95 | Wimbledon | 25 | 1 |
| 1995–96 | Wimbledon | 18 | 2 |
| 1996–97 | Wimbledon | 11 | 1 |
| 1997–98 | Wimbledon | 14 | 0 |
| **Total:** | | **170** | **17** |

## CLARKE, Clive — Defender

H: 6 1 W: 12 03 b.Dublin 14-1-80

*Source:* Trainee.

| | | | |
|---|---|---|---|
| 1996–97 | Stoke C | 0 | 0 |
| 1997–98 | Stoke C | 0 | 0 |

## CLARKE, Darrell — Midfield

H: 5 10 W: 10 11 b.Mansfield 16-12-77

*Source:* Trainee.

| | | | |
|---|---|---|---|
| 1995–96 | Mansfield T | 3 | 0 |
| 1996–97 | Mansfield T | 19 | 2 |
| 1997–98 | Mansfield T | 35 | 4 |
| **Total:** | | **57** | **6** |

## CLARKE, Jonathan — Midfield

b.Drogheda 4-9-78

*Source:* Trainee.

| | | | |
|---|---|---|---|
| 1997–98 | Crystal Palace | 0 | 0 |

## CLARKE, Matthew — Goalkeeper

H: 6 4 W: 13 10 b.Sheffield 3-11-73

*Source:* Trainee.

| | | | |
|---|---|---|---|
| 1992–93 | Rotherham U | 9 | 0 |
| 1993–94 | Rotherham U | 30 | 0 |
| 1994–95 | Rotherham U | 45 | 0 |
| 1995–96 | Rotherham U | 40 | 0 |
| 1996–97 | Sheffield W | 1 | 0 |
| 1997–98 | Sheffield W | 3 | 0 |
| **Total:** | | **128** | **0** |

## CLARKE, Steve — Defender

H: 5 10 W: 12 07 b.Saltcoats 29-8-63

*Source:* Beith Jun. *Honours:* Scotland Youth, Under-21, B, 6 full caps. Football League.

| | | | |
|---|---|---|---|
| 1981–82 | St Mirren | 0 | 0 |
| 1982–83 | St Mirren | 31 | 0 |
| 1983–84 | St Mirren | 33 | 2 |
| 1984–85 | St Mirren | 33 | 0 |
| 1985–86 | St Mirren | 31 | 3 |
| 1986–87 | St Mirren | 23 | 1 |
| 1986–87 | Chelsea | 16 | 0 |
| 1987–88 | Chelsea | 38 | 1 |
| 1988–89 | Chelsea | 36 | 0 |
| 1989–90 | Chelsea | 24 | 3 |
| 1990–91 | Chelsea | 18 | 1 |
| 1991–92 | Chelsea | 31 | 1 |
| 1992–93 | Chelsea | 20 | 0 |
| 1993–94 | Chelsea | 39 | 0 |
| 1994–95 | Chelsea | 29 | 0 |
| 1995–96 | Chelsea | 22 | 0 |
| 1996–97 | Chelsea | 31 | 0 |
| 1997–98 | Chelsea | 26 | 1 |
| **Total:** | | **481** | **13** |

## CLARKE, Tim — Goalkeeper

H: 6 3 W: 15 12 b.Stourbridge 19-9-68

*Source:* Halesowen T.

| | | | |
|---|---|---|---|
| 1990–91 | Coventry C | 0 | 0 |
| 1991–92 | Huddersfield T | 39 | 0 |
| 1992–93 | Huddersfield T | 31 | 0 |
| 1992–93 | Rochdale (loan) | 2 | 0 |
| 1993–94 | Shrewsbury T | 0 | 0 |
| 1994–95 | Shrewsbury T | 16 | 0 |
| 1995–96 | Shrewsbury T | 15 | 0 |

From Witton Alb.

| | | | |
|---|---|---|---|
| 1996–97 | York C | 17 | 0 |
| 1996–97 | Scunthorpe U | 15 | 0 |
| 1997–98 | Scunthorpe U | 41 | 0 |
| **Total:** | | **176** | **0** |

## CLARKSON, Ian — Defender

H: 5 11 W: 12 00 b.Solihull 4-12-70

*Source:* Trainee.

| | | | |
|---|---|---|---|
| 1988–89 | Birmingham C | 9 | 0 |
| 1989–90 | Birmingham C | 20 | 0 |
| 1990–91 | Birmingham C | 37 | 0 |
| 1991–92 | Birmingham C | 42 | 0 |
| 1992–93 | Birmingham C | 28 | 0 |
| 1993–94 | Birmingham C | 0 | 0 |
| 1993–94 | Stoke C | 14 | 0 |
| 1994–95 | Stoke C | 18 | 0 |
| 1995–96 | Stoke C | 43 | 0 |
| 1996–97 | Northampton T | 45 | 0 |
| 1997–98 | Northampton T | 42 | 1 |
| **Total:** | | **298** | **1** |

## CLARKSON, Phil — Midfield

H: 5 10 W: 12 05 b.Garstang 13-11-68

*Source:* Fleetwood T.

| | | | |
|---|---|---|---|
| 1991–92 | Crewe Alex | 28 | 6 |
| 1992–93 | Crewe Alex | 35 | 13 |
| 1993–94 | Crewe Alex | 7 | 2 |
| 1994–95 | Crewe Alex | 23 | 6 |
| 1995–96 | Crewe Alex | 5 | 0 |
| 1995–96 | Scunthorpe U | 24 | 6 |
| 1996–97 | Scunthorpe U | 28 | 13 |
| 1996–97 | Blackpool | 17 | 5 |
| 1997–98 | Blackpool | 45 | 13 |
| **Total:** | | **212** | **64** |

## CLAYTON, Gary — Midfield

H: 5 10 W: 12 08 b.Sheffield 2-3-63

*Source:* Rotherham U Apprentice, Burton Alb.

| | | | |
|---|---|---|---|
| 1986–87 | Doncaster R | 35 | 5 |
| 1987–88 | Cambridge U | 45 | 5 |
| 1988–89 | Cambridge U | 46 | 1 |
| 1989–90 | Cambridge U | 10 | 1 |
| 1990–91 | Cambridge U | 6 | 0 |
| 1990–91 | Peterborough U (loan) | 4 | 0 |
| 1991–92 | Cambridge U | 11 | 3 |
| 1992–93 | Cambridge U | 36 | 3 |
| 1993–94 | Cambridge U | 25 | 4 |
| 1993–94 | Huddersfield T | 17 | 1 |
| 1994–95 | Huddersfield T | 2 | 0 |
| 1995–96 | Plymouth Arg | 36 | 2 |
| 1996–97 | Plymouth Arg | 1 | 0 |

| | | | |
|---|---|---|---|
| 1997–98 | Plymouth Arg | 1 | 0 |
| 1997–98 | Torquay U | 41 | 2 |
| **Total:** | | **316** | **27** |

## CLEAVER, Christopher — Forward

H: 5 9 W: 11 07 b.Hitchin 24-3-79

*Source:* Trainee.

| | | | |
|---|---|---|---|
| 1996–97 | Peterborough U | 13 | 1 |
| 1997–98 | Peterborough U | 14 | 2 |
| **Total:** | | **27** | **3** |

## CLEGG, Michael — Defender

H: 5 8 W: 11 10 b.Ashton-under-Lyne 3-7-77

*Source:* Trainee. *Honours:* England Under-21.

| | | | |
|---|---|---|---|
| 1995–96 | Manchester U | 0 | 0 |
| 1996–97 | Manchester U | 4 | 0 |
| 1997–98 | Manchester U | 3 | 0 |
| **Total:** | | **7** | **0** |

## CLELAND, Alec — Defender

H: 5 8 W: 10 00 b.Glasgow 10-12-70

*Source:* 'S' Form. *Honours:* Scotland Under-21, B.

| | | | |
|---|---|---|---|
| 1987–88 | Dundee U | 1 | 0 |
| 1988–89 | Dundee U | 9 | 0 |
| 1989–90 | Dundee U | 15 | 0 |
| 1990–91 | Dundee U | 20 | 2 |
| 1991–92 | Dundee U | 31 | 4 |
| 1992–93 | Dundee U | 24 | 0 |
| 1993–94 | Dundee U | 33 | 1 |
| 1994–95 | Dundee U | 18 | 1 |
| 1994–95 | Rangers | 10 | 0 |
| 1995–96 | Rangers | 25 | 1 |
| 1996–97 | Rangers | 32 | 0 |
| 1997–98 | Rangers | 29 | 3 |
| **Total:** | | **247** | **12** |

## CLEMENCE, Stephen — Midfield

H: 5 11 W: 11 07 b.Liverpool 31-3-78

*Source:* Trainee. *Honours:* England Schools, Youth.

| | | | |
|---|---|---|---|
| 1994–95 | Tottenham H | 0 | 0 |
| 1995–96 | Tottenham H | 0 | 0 |
| 1996–97 | Tottenham H | 0 | 0 |
| 1997–98 | Tottenham H | 17 | 0 |
| **Total:** | | **17** | **0** |

## CLEMENT, Neil — Defender

H: 6 0 W: 12 03 b.Reading 3-10-78

*Source:* Trainee. *Honours:* England Schools, Youth.

| | | | |
|---|---|---|---|
| 1995–96 | Chelsea | 0 | 0 |
| 1996–97 | Chelsea | 1 | 0 |
| 1997–98 | Chelsea | 0 | 0 |
| **Total:** | | **1** | **0** |

## CLENCH, Philip — Midfield

b.Chester 23-3-79

*Source:* Trainee.

| | | | |
|---|---|---|---|
| 1997–98 | Chester C | 0 | 0 |

## CLITHEROE, Lee — Forward

H: 5 10 W: 10 04 b.Chorley 18-11-78

*Source:* Trainee.

| | | | |
|---|---|---|---|
| 1997–98 | Oldham Ath | 3 | 0 |
| **Total:** | | **3** | **0** |

## CLODE, Mark — Defender

H: 5 10 W: 10 10 b.Plymouth 24-2-73

*Source:* Trainee.

| | | | |
|---|---|---|---|
| 1991–92 | Plymouth Arg | 0 | 0 |
| 1992–93 | Plymouth Arg | 0 | 0 |
| 1993–94 | Swansea C | 28 | 1 |
| 1994–95 | Swansea C | 33 | 1 |
| 1995–96 | Swansea C | 30 | 0 |
| 1996–97 | Swansea C | 18 | 1 |
| 1997–98 | Swansea C | 8 | 0 |
| **Total:** | | **117** | **3** |

## CLOUGH, Nigel — Midfield

H: 5 10 W: 12 03 b.Sunderland 19-3-66

*Source:* AC Hunters. *Honours:* England Under-21, B, 14 full caps.

| | | | |
|---|---|---|---|
| 1984–85 | Nottingham F | 9 | 1 |
| 1985–86 | Nottingham F | 39 | 15 |
| 1986–87 | Nottingham F | 42 | 14 |
| 1987–88 | Nottingham F | 34 | 19 |
| 1988–89 | Nottingham F | 36 | 14 |
| 1989–90 | Nottingham F | 38 | 9 |
| 1990–91 | Nottingham F | 37 | 14 |
| 1991–92 | Nottingham F | 34 | 5 |
| 1992–93 | Nottingham F | 42 | 10 |
| 1993–94 | Liverpool | 27 | 7 |
| 1994–95 | Liverpool | 10 | 0 |
| 1995–96 | Liverpool | 2 | 0 |
| 1995–96 | Manchester C | 15 | 2 |

| | | | |
|---|---|---|---|
| 1996–97 | Manchester C | 23 | 2 |
| 1996–97 | Nottingham F (loan) | 13 | 1 |
| 1997–98 | Manchester C | 0 | 0 |
| 1997–98 | Sheffield W (loan) | 1 | 0 |
| **Total:** | | **402** | **113** |

## CLYDE, Glynn — Goalkeeper

H: 6 2 W: 11 07 b.Derry 16-1-79

*Source:* Barnsley Trainee. *Honours:*

| | | | |
|---|---|---|---|
| 1997–98 | Macclesfield T | 0 | 0 |

## COATES, Jonathan — Forward

H: 5 8 W: 10 04 b.Swansea 27-5-75

*Source:* Trainee. *Honours:* Wales Under-21.

| | | | |
|---|---|---|---|
| 1993–94 | Swansea C | 4 | 1 |
| 1994–95 | Swansea C | 5 | 0 |
| 1995–96 | Swansea C | 18 | 0 |
| 1996–97 | Swansea C | 40 | 3 |
| 1997–98 | Swansea C | 44 | 7 |
| **Total:** | | **111** | **11** |

## COCKERILL, Glenn — Midfield

H: 5 10 W: 12 08 b.Grimsby 25-8-59

*Source:* Louth U.

| | | | |
|---|---|---|---|
| 1976–77 | Lincoln C | 4 | 0 |
| 1977–78 | Lincoln C | 13 | 1 |
| 1978–79 | Lincoln C | 35 | 6 |
| 1979–80 | Lincoln C | 19 | 3 |
| 1979–80 | Swindon T | 10 | 1 |
| 1980–81 | Swindon T | 16 | 0 |
| 1981–82 | Lincoln C | 44 | 11 |
| 1982–83 | Lincoln C | 38 | 8 |
| 1983–84 | Lincoln C | 33 | 6 |
| 1983–84 | Sheffield U | 10 | 1 |
| 1984–85 | Sheffield U | 40 | 7 |
| 1985–86 | Sheffield U | 12 | 2 |
| 1985–86 | Southampton | 30 | 7 |
| 1986–87 | Southampton | 42 | 7 |
| 1987–88 | Southampton | 39 | 2 |
| 1988–89 | Southampton | 34 | 6 |
| 1989–90 | Southampton | 36 | 4 |
| 1990–91 | Southampton | 32 | 2 |
| 1991–92 | Southampton | 37 | 4 |
| 1992–93 | Southampton | 23 | 0 |
| 1993–94 | Southampton | 14 | 0 |
| 1993–94 | Leyton Orient | 19 | 2 |
| 1994–95 | Leyton Orient | 33 | 4 |
| 1995–96 | Leyton Orient | 38 | 1 |
| 1996–97 | Fulham | 32 | 1 |
| 1997–98 | Fulham | 8 | 0 |
| 1997–98 | Brentford | 23 | 0 |
| **Total:** | | **714** | **86** |

## COCKRILL, Darren — Forward

b.Great Yarmouth 28-2-80

*Source:* Trainee.

| | | | |
|---|---|---|---|
| 1997–98 | Cambridge U | 0 | 0 |

## COLDICOTT, Stacy — Midfield

H: 5 8 W: 11 04 b.Redditch 29-4-74

*Source:* Trainee.

| | | | |
|---|---|---|---|
| 1991–92 | WBA | 0 | 0 |
| 1992–93 | WBA | 14 | 0 |
| 1993–94 | WBA | 5 | 0 |
| 1994–95 | WBA | 11 | 0 |
| 1995–96 | WBA | 33 | 0 |
| 1996–97 | WBA | 19 | 3 |
| 1996–97 | Cardiff C (loan) | 6 | 0 |
| 1997–98 | WBA | 22 | 0 |
| **Total:** | | **110** | **3** |

## COLE, Andy — Forward

H: 5 10 W: 12 04 b.Nottingham 15-10-71

*Source:* Trainee. *Honours:* England Schools, Youth, Under-21, B, 2 full caps. Football League.

| | | | |
|---|---|---|---|
| 1989–90 | Arsenal | 0 | 0 |
| 1990–91 | Arsenal | 1 | 0 |
| 1991–92 | Arsenal | 0 | 0 |
| 1991–92 | Fulham (loan) | 13 | 3 |
| 1991–92 | Bristol C (loan) | 12 | 8 |
| 1992–93 | Bristol C | 29 | 12 |
| 1992–93 | Newcastle U | 12 | 12 |
| 1993–94 | Newcastle U | 40 | 34 |
| 1994–95 | Newcastle U | 18 | 9 |
| 1994–95 | Manchester U | 18 | 12 |
| 1995–96 | Manchester U | 34 | 11 |
| 1996–97 | Manchester U | 20 | 7 |
| 1997–98 | Manchester U | 33 | 16 |
| **Total:** | | **230** | **124** |

## COLEANO, Rudi — Goalkeeper

H: 5 8 W: 13 02 b.Leeds 27-5-79

*Source:* Trainee.

| | | | |
|---|---|---|---|
| 1997–98 | Barnsley | 0 | 0 |

## COLEMAN, Chris — Defender

H: 6 2 W: 14 04 b.Swansea 10-6-70

*Source:* Apprentice. *Honours:* Wales Under-21, 19 full caps, 3 goals.

| | | | |
|---|---|---|---|
| 1987–88 | Swansea C | 30 | 0 |
| 1988–89 | Swansea C | 43 | 0 |
| 1989–90 | Swansea C | 46 | 2 |
| 1990–91 | Swansea C | 41 | 0 |
| 1991–92 | Crystal Palace | 18 | 4 |
| 1992–93 | Crystal Palace | 38 | 5 |
| 1993–94 | Crystal Palace | 46 | 3 |
| 1994–95 | Crystal Palace | 35 | 1 |
| 1995–96 | Crystal Palace | 17 | 0 |
| 1995–96 | Blackburn R | 20 | 0 |
| 1996–97 | Blackburn R | 8 | 0 |
| 1997–98 | Blackburn R | 0 | 0 |
| 1997–98 | Fulham | 26 | 1 |
| **Total:** | | **368** | **16** |

## COLEMAN, Simon — Defender

H: 6 0 W: 10 08 b.Worksop 13-6-68

*Source:* Apprentice.

| | | | |
|---|---|---|---|
| 1985–86 | Mansfield T | 0 | 0 |
| 1986–87 | Mansfield T | 2 | 0 |
| 1987–88 | Mansfield T | 44 | 2 |
| 1988–89 | Mansfield T | 45 | 5 |
| 1989–90 | Mansfield T | 5 | 0 |
| 1989–90 | Middlesbrough | 36 | 1 |
| 1990–91 | Middlesbrough | 19 | 1 |
| 1991–92 | Derby Co | 43 | 2 |
| 1992–93 | Derby Co | 25 | 0 |
| 1993–94 | Derby Co | 2 | 0 |
| 1993–94 | Sheffield W | 15 | 1 |
| 1994–95 | Sheffield W | 1 | 0 |
| 1994–95 | Bolton W | 22 | 4 |
| 1995–96 | Bolton W | 12 | 1 |
| 1996–97 | Bolton W | 0 | 0 |
| 1997–98 | Bolton W | 0 | 0 |
| 1997–98 | Wolverhampton W (loan) | 4 | 0 |
| 1997–98 | Southend U | 14 | 0 |
| **Total:** | | **289** | **17** |

## COLGAN, Nick — Goalkeeper

H: 6 1 W: 13 06 b.Eire 19-9-73

*Source:* Drogheda. *Honours:* Eire Under-21.

| | | | |
|---|---|---|---|
| 1992–93 | Chelsea | 0 | 0 |
| 1993–94 | Chelsea | 0 | 0 |
| 1993–94 | Crewe Alex (loan) | 0 | 0 |
| 1994–95 | Chelsea | 0 | 0 |
| 1994–95 | Grimsby T (loan) | 0 | 0 |
| 1995–96 | Chelsea | 0 | 0 |
| 1995–96 | Millwall (loan) | 0 | 0 |
| 1996–97 | Chelsea | 1 | 0 |
| 1997–98 | Chelsea | 0 | 0 |
| 1997–98 | Brentford (loan) | 5 | 0 |
| 1997–98 | Reading (loan) | 5 | 0 |
| **Total:** | | **11** | **0** |

## COLKIN, Lee — Defender

H: 5 11 W: 12 04 b.Nuneaton 15-7-74

*Source:* Trainee.

| | | | |
|---|---|---|---|
| 1991–92 | Northampton T | 3 | 0 |
| 1992–93 | Northampton T | 13 | 0 |
| 1993–94 | Northampton T | 20 | 1 |
| 1994–95 | Northampton T | 33 | 1 |
| 1995–96 | Northampton T | 24 | 1 |
| 1996–97 | Northampton T | 6 | 0 |
| 1997–98 | Northampton T | 0 | 0 |
| 1997–98 | Leyton Orient (loan) | 11 | 0 |
| **Total:** | | **110** | **3** |

## COLL, Owen — Defender

H: 6 0 W: 11 07 b.Donegal 9-4-76

*Source:* Amateur.

| | | | |
|---|---|---|---|
| 1994–95 | Tottenham H | 0 | 0 |
| 1995–96 | Tottenham H | 0 | 0 |
| 1995–96 | Bournemouth | 8 | 0 |
| 1996–97 | Bournemouth | 16 | 0 |
| 1997–98 | Bournemouth | 0 | 0 |
| **Total:** | | **24** | **0** |

## COLLETT, Andy — Goalkeeper

H: 6 0 W: 12 10 b.Middlesbrough 28-10-73

*Source:* Trainee.

| | | | |
|---|---|---|---|
| 1991–92 | Middlesbrough | 0 | 0 |
| 1992–93 | Middlesbrough | 2 | 0 |
| 1993–94 | Middlesbrough | 0 | 0 |
| 1994–95 | Middlesbrough | 0 | 0 |
| 1994–95 | Bristol R | 4 | 0 |
| 1995–96 | Bristol R | 26 | 0 |
| 1996–97 | Bristol R | 44 | 0 |
| 1997–98 | Bristol R | 30 | 0 |
| **Total:** | | **106** | **0** |

## COLLINS, Chris — Defender

H: 6 0 W: 12 07 b.Chatham 26-9-79

*Source:* Trainee.

| | | | |
|---|---|---|---|
| 1997–98 | Southampton | 0 | 0 |

## COLLINS, James — Midfield

H: 5 8 W: 10 00 b.Liverpool 28-5-78

*Source:* Trainee.

| | | | |
|---|---|---|---|
| 1996–97 | Crewe Alex | 0 | 0 |
| 1997–98 | Crewe Alex | 1 | 0 |
| **Total:** | | **1** | **0** |

## COLLINS, Lee — Midfield

H: 5 9 W: 11 02 b.Bellshill 3-2-74

*Source:* Possil U.

| | | | |
|---|---|---|---|
| 1993–94 | Albion R | 20 | 0 |
| 1994–95 | Albion R | 17 | 0 |
| 1995–96 | Albion R | 8 | 1 |
| 1995–96 | Swindon T | 5 | 0 |
| 1996–97 | Swindon T | 4 | 0 |
| 1997–98 | Swindon T | 26 | 1 |
| **Total:** | | **80** | **2** |

## COLLINS, Lee — Defender

H: 6 1 W: 12 06 b.Birmingham 10-9-77

*Source:* Trainee.

| | | | |
|---|---|---|---|
| 1996–97 | Aston Villa | 0 | 0 |
| 1997–98 | Aston Villa | 0 | 0 |

## COLLINS, Sam — Defender

H: 6 1 W: 14 03 b.Pontefract 5-6-77

*Source:* Trainee.

| | | | |
|---|---|---|---|
| 1994–95 | Huddersfield T | 0 | 0 |
| 1995–96 | Huddersfield T | 0 | 0 |
| 1996–97 | Huddersfield T | 4 | 0 |
| 1997–98 | Huddersfield T | 10 | 0 |
| **Total:** | | **14** | **0** |

## COLLINS, Simon — Midfield

H: 6 0 W: 12 05 b.Pontefract 16-12-73

*Source:* Trainee.

| | | | |
|---|---|---|---|
| 1992–93 | Huddersfield T | 1 | 0 |
| 1993–94 | Huddersfield T | 1 | 0 |
| 1994–95 | Huddersfield T | 4 | 0 |
| 1995–96 | Huddersfield T | 30 | 3 |
| 1996–97 | Huddersfield T | 16 | 0 |
| 1996–97 | Plymouth Arg | 12 | 1 |
| 1997–98 | Plymouth Arg | 32 | 2 |
| **Total:** | | **96** | **6** |

## COLLINS, Wayne — Midfield

H: 6 0 W: 11 07 b.Manchester 4-3-69

*Source:* Winsford U.

| | | | |
|---|---|---|---|
| 1993–94 | Crewe Alex | 35 | 2 |
| 1994–95 | Crewe Alex | 40 | 11 |
| 1995–96 | Crewe Alex | 42 | 1 |
| 1996–97 | Sheffield W | 12 | 1 |
| 1997–98 | Sheffield W | 19 | 5 |
| 1997–98 | Fulham | 13 | 1 |
| **Total:** | | **161** | **21** |

## COLLYMORE, Stan — Forward

H: 6 2 W: 12 02 b.Stone 22-1-71

*Source:* Stafford R. *Honours:* England 3 full caps.

| | | | |
|---|---|---|---|
| 1990–91 | Crystal Palace | 6 | 0 |
| 1991–92 | Crystal Palace | 12 | 1 |
| 1992–93 | Crystal Palace | 2 | 0 |
| 1992–93 | Southend U | 30 | 15 |
| 1993–94 | Nottingham F | 28 | 19 |
| 1994–95 | Nottingham F | 37 | 22 |
| 1995–96 | Liverpool | 31 | 14 |
| 1996–97 | Liverpool | 30 | 12 |
| 1996–97 | Aston Villa | 0 | 0 |
| 1997–98 | Aston Villa | 25 | 6 |
| **Total:** | | **201** | **89** |

## COLWELL, Richard — Defender

H: 5 9 W: 11 02 b.Wordsley 2-9-79

*Source:* Trainee.

| | | | |
|---|---|---|---|
| 1997–98 | Coventry C | 0 | 0 |

## CONLON, Barry — Forward

H: 6 3 W: 14 00 b.Dublin 1-10-78

*Source:* QPR Trainee.

| | | | |
|---|---|---|---|
| 1997–98 | Manchester C | 7 | 0 |
| 1997–98 | Plymouth Arg (loan) | 13 | 2 |
| **Total:** | | **20** | **2** |

## CONLON, Paul — Forward

H: 5 8 W: 12 00 b.Sunderland 5-1-78

*Source:* Trainee.

| | | | |
|---|---|---|---|
| 1995–96 | Hartlepool U | 15 | 4 |
| 1996–97 | Sunderland | 0 | 0 |
| 1997–98 | Doncaster R | 14 | 1 |
| **Total:** | | **29** | **5** |

## CONNELLY, Sean — Defender

H: 5 10 W: 11 10 b.Sheffield 26-6-70

*Source:* Hallam.

| | | | |
|---|---|---|---|
| 1991–92 | Stockport Co | 0 | 0 |
| 1992–93 | Stockport Co | 7 | 0 |
| 1993–94 | Stockport Co | 32 | 0 |
| 1994–95 | Stockport Co | 39 | 0 |
| 1995–96 | Stockport Co | 43 | 0 |
| 1996–97 | Stockport Co | 45 | 0 |
| 1997–98 | Stockport Co | 45 | 2 |
| **Total:** | | **211** | **2** |

## CONNOLLY, Karl — Forward

H: 5 9 W: 11 00 b.Prescot 9-2-70

*Source:* Napoli (Liverpool Sunday League).

| | | | |
|---|---|---|---|
| 1990–91 | Wrexham | 0 | 0 |
| 1991–92 | Wrexham | 36 | 8 |
| 1992–93 | Wrexham | 42 | 9 |
| 1993–94 | Wrexham | 39 | 2 |
| 1994–95 | Wrexham | 45 | 10 |
| 1995–96 | Wrexham | 46 | 18 |
| 1996–97 | Wrexham | 30 | 14 |
| 1997–98 | Wrexham | 35 | 7 |
| **Total:** | | **273** | **68** |

## CONNOLLY, Patrick — Forward

H: 5 9 W: 11 00 b.Glasgow 25-6-70

*Honours:* 'S' Form. Scotland Under-21.

| | | | |
|---|---|---|---|
| 1986–87 | Dundee U | 0 | 0 |
| 1987–88 | Dundee U | 0 | 0 |
| 1988–89 | Dundee U | 2 | 0 |
| 1989–90 | Dundee U | 15 | 5 |
| 1990–91 | Dundee U | 10 | 2 |
| 1991–92 | Dundee U | 5 | 0 |
| 1992–93 | Dundee U | 42 | 16 |
| 1993–94 | Dundee U | 28 | 5 |
| 1994–95 | Dundee U | 6 | 0 |
| 1995–96 | Dundee U | 6 | 1 |
| 1995–96 | Airdrieonians | 6 | 3 |
| 1996–97 | Airdrieonians | 35 | 8 |
| 1997–98 | Airdrieonians | 23 | 8 |
| 1997–98 | St Johnstone | 4 | 0 |
| **Total:** | | **182** | **48** |

## CONNOLLY, Patrick — Midfield

b.Preston 3-3-80

*Source:* Trainee.

| | | | |
|---|---|---|---|
| 1997–98 | Blackburn R | 0 | 0 |

## CONNOLLY, Stuart — Midfield

H: 5 8 W: 10 09 b.Dublin 8-12-77

*Source:* Stella Maris.

| | | | |
|---|---|---|---|
| 1996–97 | Tranmere R | 0 | 0 |
| 1997–98 | Tranmere R | 0 | 0 |

## CONNOR, Daniel — Goalkeeper

H: 6 2 W: 12 09 b.Dublin 31-1-81

*Source:* Trainee.

| | | | |
|---|---|---|---|
| 1997–98 | Peterborough U | 0 | 0 |

## CONNOR, James — Midfield

H: 6 0 W: 13 00 b.Middlesbrough 22-8-74

*Source:* Trainee.

| | | | |
|---|---|---|---|
| 1992–93 | Millwall | 0 | 0 |
| 1993–94 | Millwall | 0 | 0 |
| 1994–95 | Millwall | 1 | 0 |
| 1995–96 | Millwall | 8 | 0 |
| 1996–97 | Millwall | 0 | 0 |
| 1997–98 | Millwall | 0 | 0 |
| **Total:** | | **9** | **0** |

## CONNOR, Paul — Forward

H: 6 2 W: 11 08 b.Bishop Auckland 12-1-79

*Source:* Trainee.

| | | | |
|---|---|---|---|
| 1996–97 | Middlesbrough | 0 | 0 |
| 1997–98 | Middlesbrough | 0 | 0 |
| 1997–98 | Hartlepool U (loan) | 5 | 0 |
| **Total:** | | **5** | **0** |

## CONROY, Mike — Forward

H: 6 0 W: 13 04 b.Glasgow 31-12-65

*Source:* Apprentice.

| | | | |
|---|---|---|---|
| 1983–84 | Coventry C | 0 | 0 |
| 1983–84 | Clydebank | 2 | 0 |
| 1984–85 | Clydebank | 26 | 11 |
| 1985–86 | Clydebank | 28 | 7 |
| 1986–87 | Clydebank | 36 | 9 |
| 1987–88 | Clydebank | 22 | 11 |
| 1987–88 | St Mirren | 10 | 1 |
| 1988–89 | Reading | 13 | 4 |
| 1989–90 | Reading | 34 | 2 |
| 1990–91 | Reading | 33 | 1 |
| 1991–92 | Burnley | 38 | 24 |
| 1992–93 | Burnley | 39 | 6 |
| 1993–94 | Preston NE | 32 | 12 |
| 1994–95 | Preston NE | 25 | 10 |
| 1995–96 | Fulham | 40 | 9 |

| | | | |
|---|---|---|---|
| 1996–97 | Fulham | 43 | 21 |
| 1997–98 | Fulham | 11 | 2 |
| 1997–98 | Blackpool | 6 | 0 |
| **Total:** | | **438** | **130** |

## CONWAY, Paul — Midfield

H: 6 1 W: 12 10 b.Wandsworth 17-4-70

*Source:* Oldham Ath.

| | | | |
|---|---|---|---|
| 1993–94 | Carlisle U | 18 | 4 |
| 1994–95 | Carlisle U | 24 | 6 |
| 1995–96 | Carlisle U | 22 | 3 |
| 1996–97 | Carlisle U | 25 | 9 |
| 1997–98 | Northampton T | 3 | 0 |
| 1997–98 | Scarborough (loan) | 13 | 2 |
| **Total:** | | **105** | **24** |

## COOK, Aaron — Defender

b.Caerphilly 6-12-79

*Source:* Trainee.

| | | | |
|---|---|---|---|
| 1997–98 | Portsmouth | 1 | 0 |
| **Total:** | | **1** | **0** |

## COOK, Andy — Midfield

H: 5 9 W: 12 00 b.Romsey 10-8-69

*Source:* Apprentice.

| | | | |
|---|---|---|---|
| 1987–88 | Southampton | 2 | 0 |
| 1988–89 | Southampton | 3 | 0 |
| 1989–90 | Southampton | 4 | 1 |
| 1990–91 | Southampton | 7 | 0 |
| 1991–92 | Southampton | 0 | 0 |
| 1991–92 | Exeter C | 38 | 0 |
| 1992–93 | Exeter C | 32 | 1 |
| 1993–94 | Swansea C | 28 | 0 |
| 1994–95 | Swansea C | 1 | 0 |
| 1995–96 | Swansea C | 33 | 0 |
| 1996–97 | Swansea C | 0 | 0 |
| 1996–97 | Portsmouth | 8 | 0 |
| 1997–98 | Portsmouth | 1 | 0 |
| 1997–98 | Millwall | 3 | 0 |
| **Total:** | | **160** | **2** |

## COOK, Jamie — Forward

H: 5 10 W: 10 09 b.Oxford 2-8-79

*Source:* Trainee.

| | | | |
|---|---|---|---|
| 1997–98 | Oxford U | 20 | 2 |
| **Total:** | | **20** | **2** |

## COOK, Paul — Midfield

H: 5 11 W: 11 00 b.Liverpool 22-6-67

*Source:* Marine.

| | | | |
|---|---|---|---|
| 1984–85 | Wigan Ath | 2 | 0 |
| 1985–86 | Wigan Ath | 13 | 2 |
| 1986–87 | Wigan Ath | 27 | 4 |
| 1987–88 | Wigan Ath | 41 | 8 |
| 1988–89 | Norwich C | 4 | 0 |
| 1989–90 | Norwich C | 2 | 0 |
| 1989–90 | Wolverhampton W | 28 | 2 |
| 1990–91 | Wolverhampton W | 42 | 6 |
| 1991–92 | Wolverhampton W | 43 | 8 |
| 1992–93 | Wolverhampton W | 44 | 1 |
| 1993–94 | Wolverhampton W | 36 | 2 |
| 1994–95 | Coventry C | 34 | 3 |
| 1995–96 | Coventry C | 3 | 0 |
| 1995–96 | Tranmere R | 15 | 1 |
| 1996–97 | Tranmere R | 36 | 3 |
| 1997–98 | Tranmere R | 9 | 0 |
| 1997–98 | Stockport Co | 25 | 3 |
| **Total:** | | **404** | **43** |

## COOKE, Andy — Forward

H: 5 11 W: 12 08 b.Stoke 20-1-74

*Source:* Newtown.

| | | | |
|---|---|---|---|
| 1994–95 | Burnley | 0 | 0 |
| 1995–96 | Burnley | 23 | 5 |
| 1996–97 | Burnley | 31 | 13 |
| 1997–98 | Burnley | 34 | 16 |
| **Total:** | | **88** | **34** |

## COOKE, Terry — Forward

H: 5 7 W: 11 00 b.Marston Green 5-8-76

*Source:* Trainee. *Honours:* England Youth, Under-21.

| | | | |
|---|---|---|---|
| 1994–95 | Manchester U | 0 | 0 |
| 1995–96 | Manchester U | 4 | 0 |
| 1995–96 | Sunderland (loan) | 6 | 0 |
| 1996–97 | Manchester U | 0 | 0 |
| 1996–97 | Birmingham C (loan) | 4 | 0 |
| 1997–98 | Manchester U | 0 | 0 |
| **Total:** | | **14** | **0** |

## COOPER, Colin — Defender

H: 5 9 W: 11 09 b.Sedgfield 28-2-67

*Honours:* England Under-21, 2 full caps.

| | | | |
|---|---|---|---|
| 1984–85 | Middlesbrough | 0 | 0 |
| 1985–86 | Middlesbrough | 11 | 0 |
| 1986–87 | Middlesbrough | 46 | 0 |
| 1987–88 | Middlesbrough | 43 | 2 |
| 1988–89 | Middlesbrough | 35 | 2 |

| | | | |
|---|---|---|---|
| 1989–90 | Middlesbrough | 21 | 2 |
| 1990–91 | Middlesbrough | 32 | 0 |
| 1991–92 | Millwall | 36 | 2 |
| 1992–93 | Millwall | 41 | 4 |
| 1993–94 | Nottingham F | 37 | 7 |
| 1994–95 | Nottingham F | 35 | 1 |
| 1995–96 | Nottingham F | 37 | 5 |
| 1996–97 | Nottingham F | 36 | 2 |
| 1997–98 | Nottingham F | 35 | 5 |
| **Total:** | | **445** | **32** |

## COOPER, Kevin — Midfield

H: 5 7 W: 10 07 b.Derby 8-2-75

*Source:* Trainee.

| | | | |
|---|---|---|---|
| 1993–94 | Derby Co | 0 | 0 |
| 1994–95 | Derby Co | 1 | 0 |
| 1995–96 | Derby Co | 1 | 0 |
| 1996–97 | Derby Co | 0 | 0 |
| 1996–97 | Stockport Co (loan) | 12 | 3 |
| 1997–98 | Stockport Co | 38 | 8 |
| **Total:** | | **52** | **11** |

## COOPER, Mark — Midfield

H: 5 10 W: 12 10 b.Wakefield 18-12-68

*Source:* Trainee.

| | | | |
|---|---|---|---|
| 1987–88 | Bristol C | 0 | 0 |
| 1988–89 | Bristol C | 0 | 0 |
| 1989–90 | Exeter C | 5 | 0 |
| 1989–90 | Southend U (loan) | 5 | 0 |
| 1990–91 | Exeter C | 42 | 11 |
| 1991–92 | Exeter C | 3 | 1 |
| 1991–92 | Birmingham C | 33 | 4 |
| 1992–93 | Birmingham C | 6 | 0 |
| 1992–93 | Fulham | 9 | 0 |
| 1992–93 | Huddersfield T (loan) | 10 | 4 |
| 1993–94 | Fulham | 5 | 0 |
| 1993–94 | Wycombe W | 2 | 1 |
| 1993–94 | Exeter C | 21 | 8 |
| 1994–95 | Exeter C | 40 | 6 |
| 1995–96 | Exeter C | 27 | 6 |
| 1996–97 | Hartlepool U | 33 | 9 |
| 1997–98 | Hartlepool U | 0 | 0 |
| 1997–98 | Macclesfield T (loan) | 8 | 2 |
| 1997–98 | Leyton Orient | 1 | 0 |
| **Total:** | | **250** | **52** |

## COOPER, Richard — Defender

H: 5 9 W: 11 00 b.Nottingham 27-9-79

*Source:* Trainee. *Honours:* England Schools, Youth.

| | | | |
|---|---|---|---|
| 1996–97 | Nottingham F | 0 | 0 |
| 1997–98 | Nottingham F | 0 | 0 |

## COOTE, Adrian — Forward

H: 6 3 W: 12 00 b.Gt Yarmouth 3-9-78

*Source:* Trainee. *Honours:* Northern Ireland Under-21.

| | | | |
|---|---|---|---|
| 1997–98 | Norwich C | 23 | 2 |
| **Total:** | | **23** | **2** |

## COPE, James — Midfield

H: 6 1 W: 11 01 b.Birmingham 4-10-77

*Source:* Trainee.

| | | | |
|---|---|---|---|
| 1995–96 | Shrewsbury T | 1 | 0 |
| 1996–97 | Shrewsbury T | 3 | 0 |
| 1997–98 | Shrewsbury T | 0 | 0 |
| **Total:** | | **4** | **0** |

## COPPINGER, James — Midfield

H: 5 7 W: 10 03 b.Middlesbrough 10-1-81

*Source:* Darlington Trainee.

| | | | |
|---|---|---|---|
| 1997–98 | Newcastle U | 0 | 0 |

## CORAZZIN, Carlo — Forward

H: 5 9 W: 12 05 b.Canada 25-12-71

*Source:* Vancouver 86ers. *Honours:* Canada full caps.

| | | | |
|---|---|---|---|
| 1993–94 | Cambridge U | 28 | 10 |
| 1994–95 | Cambridge U | 46 | 19 |
| 1995–96 | Cambridge U | 31 | 10 |
| 1995–96 | Plymouth Arg | 6 | 1 |
| 1996–97 | Plymouth Arg | 30 | 5 |
| 1997–98 | Plymouth Arg | 38 | 16 |
| **Total:** | | **179** | **61** |

## CORBETT, James — Forward

H: 5 9 W: 10 12 b.London 6-7-80

*Source:* Trainee.

| | | | |
|---|---|---|---|
| 1997–98 | Gillingham | 16 | 2 |
| **Total:** | | **16** | **2** |

## CORDEN, Wayne — Midfield

H: 5 10 W: 11 03 b.Leek 1-11-75

*Source:* Trainee.

| | | | |
|---|---|---|---|
| 1994–95 | Port Vale | 1 | 0 |
| 1995–96 | Port Vale | 2 | 0 |
| 1996–97 | Port Vale | 12 | 0 |
| 1997–98 | Port Vale | 33 | 1 |
| **Total:** | | **48** | **1** |

## CORICA, Steve — Midfield

H: 5 8 W: 10 10 b.Cairns 24-3-73

*Source:* Marconi. *Honours:* Australia 12 full caps.

| | | | |
|---|---|---|---|
| 1995–96 | Leicester C | 16 | 2 |
| 1995–96 | Wolverhampton W | 17 | 0 |
| 1996–97 | Wolverhampton W | 36 | 2 |
| 1997–98 | Wolverhampton W | 1 | 0 |
| **Total:** | | **70** | **4** |

## CORNFORTH, John — Midfield

H: 6 1 W: 14 07 b.Whitley Bay 7-10-67

*Source:* Apprentice. *Honours:* Wales 2 full caps.

| | | | |
|---|---|---|---|
| 1984–85 | Sunderland | 1 | 0 |
| 1985–86 | Sunderland | 0 | 0 |
| 1986–87 | Sunderland | 0 | 0 |
| 1986–87 | Doncaster R (loan) | 7 | 3 |
| 1987–88 | Sunderland | 12 | 2 |
| 1988–89 | Sunderland | 15 | 0 |
| 1989–90 | Sunderland | 2 | 0 |
| 1989–90 | Shrewsbury T (loan) | 3 | 0 |
| 1989–90 | Lincoln C (loan) | 9 | 1 |
| 1990–91 | Sunderland | 2 | 0 |
| 1991–92 | Swansea C | 17 | 0 |
| 1992–93 | Swansea C | 44 | 5 |
| 1993–94 | Swansea C | 38 | 6 |
| 1994–95 | Swansea C | 33 | 3 |
| 1995–96 | Swansea C | 17 | 2 |
| 1995–96 | Birmingham C | 8 | 0 |
| 1996–97 | Birmingham C | 0 | 0 |
| 1996–97 | Wycombe W | 10 | 0 |
| 1997–98 | Wycombe W | 24 | 5 |
| 1997–98 | Peterborough U (loan) | 4 | 0 |
| **Total:** | | **246** | **27** |

## CORT, Carl — Forward

H: 6 4 W: 12 07 b.Southwark 1-11-77

*Source:* Trainee.

| | | | |
|---|---|---|---|
| 1996–97 | Wimbledon | 1 | 0 |
| 1996–97 | Lincoln C (loan) | 6 | 1 |
| 1997–98 | Wimbledon | 22 | 4 |
| **Total:** | | **29** | **5** |

## CORT, Leon — Defender

b.Southwark 11-9-79

*Source:* Dulwich H.

| | | | |
|---|---|---|---|
| 1997–98 | Millwall | 0 | 0 |

## COTON, Tony — Goalkeeper

H: 6 2 W: 13 07 b.Tamworth 19-5-61

*Source:* Mile Oak R. *Honours:* England B.

| | | | |
|---|---|---|---|
| 1978–79 | Birmingham C | 0 | 0 |
| 1979–80 | Birmingham C | 0 | 0 |
| 1979–80 | Hereford U (loan) | 0 | 0 |
| 1980–81 | Birmingham C | 3 | 0 |
| 1981–82 | Birmingham C | 15 | 0 |
| 1982–83 | Birmingham C | 28 | 0 |
| 1983–84 | Birmingham C | 41 | 0 |
| 1984–85 | Birmingham C | 7 | 0 |
| 1984–85 | Watford | 33 | 0 |
| 1985–86 | Watford | 40 | 0 |
| 1986–87 | Watford | 31 | 0 |
| 1987–88 | Watford | 37 | 0 |
| 1988–89 | Watford | 46 | 0 |
| 1989–90 | Watford | 46 | 0 |
| 1990–91 | Manchester C | 33 | 0 |
| 1991–92 | Manchester C | 37 | 0 |
| 1992–93 | Manchester C | 40 | 0 |
| 1993–94 | Manchester C | 31 | 0 |
| 1994–95 | Manchester C | 23 | 0 |
| 1995–96 | Manchester C | 0 | 0 |
| 1995–96 | Manchester U | 0 | 0 |
| 1996–97 | Sunderland | 10 | 0 |
| 1997–98 | Sunderland | 0 | 0 |
| **Total:** | | **501** | **0** |

## COTTEE, Tony — Forward

H: 5 10 W: 12 06 b.West Ham 11-7-65

*Source:* Apprentice. *Honours:* England Youth, Under-21, 7 full caps.

| | | | |
|---|---|---|---|
| 1982–83 | West Ham U | 8 | 5 |
| 1983–84 | West Ham U | 39 | 15 |
| 1984–85 | West Ham U | 41 | 17 |
| 1985–86 | West Ham U | 42 | 20 |
| 1986–87 | West Ham U | 42 | 22 |
| 1987–88 | West Ham U | 40 | 13 |
| 1988–89 | Everton | 36 | 13 |
| 1989–90 | Everton | 27 | 13 |
| 1990–91 | Everton | 29 | 10 |
| 1991–92 | Everton | 24 | 8 |
| 1992–93 | Everton | 26 | 12 |
| 1993–94 | Everton | 39 | 16 |
| 1994–95 | Everton | 3 | 0 |
| 1994–95 | West Ham U | 31 | 13 |
| 1995–96 | West Ham U | 33 | 10 |
| 1996–97 | West Ham U | 3 | 0 |
| From Selangor. | | | |
| 1997–98 | Leicester C | 19 | 4 |
| 1997–98 | Birmingham C (loan) | 5 | 1 |
| **Total:** | | **487** | **192** |

## COTTERELL, Leo — Defender

H: 5 9 W: 10 00 b.Cambridge 2-9-74

*Source:* Trainee. *Honours:* England Schools.

| | | | |
|---|---|---|---|
| 1993–94 | Ipswich T | 0 | 0 |
| 1994–95 | Ipswich T | 2 | 0 |
| 1995–96 | Ipswich T | 0 | 0 |
| 1996–97 | Bournemouth | 9 | 0 |
| 1997–98 | Bournemouth | 0 | 0 |
| **Total:** | | **11** | **0** |

## COUGHLAN, Graham — Defender

H: 6 3 W: 14 00 b.Dublin 18-11-74

*Source:* Bray Wanderers.

| | | | |
|---|---|---|---|
| 1995–96 | Blackburn R | 0 | 0 |
| 1996–97 | Blackburn R | 0 | 0 |
| 1996–97 | Swindon T (loan) | 3 | 0 |
| 1997–98 | Blackburn R | 0 | 0 |
| **Total:** | | **3** | **0** |

## COULBAULT, Regis — Midfield

H: 5 9 W: 11 03 b.Brignoles 12-8-72

*Source:* Toulon.

| | | | |
|---|---|---|---|
| 1997–98 | Southend U | 34 | 4 |
| **Total:** | | **34** | **4** |

## COUSINS, Jason — Defender

H: 5 10 W: 12 01 b.Hayes 4-10-70

*Source:* Trainee.

| | | | |
|---|---|---|---|
| 1989–90 | Brentford | 13 | 0 |
| 1990–91 | Brentford | 8 | 0 |
| From Wycombe W. | | | |
| 1993–94 | Wycombe W | 37 | 1 |
| 1994–95 | Wycombe W | 41 | 2 |
| 1995–96 | Wycombe W | 30 | 0 |
| 1996–97 | Wycombe W | 37 | 0 |
| 1997–98 | Wycombe W | 29 | 0 |
| **Total:** | | **195** | **3** |

## COUZENS, Andy — Midfield

H: 5 10 W: 11 11 b.Shipley 4-6-75

*Source:* Trainee. *Honours:* England Under-21.

| | | | |
|---|---|---|---|
| 1992–93 | Leeds U | 0 | 0 |
| 1993–94 | Leeds U | 0 | 0 |
| 1994–95 | Leeds U | 4 | 0 |
| 1995–96 | Leeds U | 14 | 0 |
| 1996–97 | Leeds U | 10 | 1 |
| 1997–98 | Carlisle U | 27 | 2 |
| **Total:** | | **55** | **3** |

## COWAN, Tom — Defender

H: 5 8 W: 11 08 b.Bellshill 28-8-69

*Source:* Netherdale BC.

| | | | |
|---|---|---|---|
| 1988–89 | Clyde | 16 | 2 |
| 1988–89 | Rangers | 4 | 0 |
| 1989–90 | Rangers | 3 | 0 |
| 1990–91 | Rangers | 5 | 0 |
| 1991–92 | Sheffield U | 20 | 0 |
| 1992–93 | Sheffield U | 21 | 0 |
| 1993–94 | Sheffield U | 4 | 0 |
| 1993–94 | Stoke C (loan) | 14 | 0 |
| 1993–94 | Huddersfield T (loan) | 10 | 0 |
| 1994–95 | Huddersfield T | 37 | 2 |
| 1995–96 | Huddersfield T | 43 | 2 |
| 1996–97 | Huddersfield T | 42 | 4 |
| 1997–98 | Huddersfield T | 0 | 0 |
| **Total:** | | **219** | **10** |

## COWANS, Gordon — Midfield

H: 5 7 W: 9 07 b.Durham 27-10-58

*Source:* Apprentice. *Honours:* England Youth, Under-21, B, 10 full caps, 2 goals.

| | | | |
|---|---|---|---|
| 1975–76 | Aston Villa | 1 | 0 |
| 1976–77 | Aston Villa | 18 | 3 |
| 1977–78 | Aston Villa | 35 | 7 |
| 1978–79 | Aston Villa | 34 | 4 |
| 1979–80 | Aston Villa | 42 | 6 |
| 1980–81 | Aston Villa | 42 | 5 |
| 1981–82 | Aston Villa | 42 | 6 |
| 1982–83 | Aston Villa | 42 | 10 |
| 1983–84 | Aston Villa | 0 | 0 |
| 1984–85 | Aston Villa | 30 | 1 |
| 1985–86 | Bari | 20 | 0 |
| 1986–87 | Bari | 38 | 3 |
| 1987–88 | Bari | 36 | 0 |
| 1988–89 | Aston Villa | 33 | 2 |
| 1989–90 | Aston Villa | 34 | 4 |
| 1990–91 | Aston Villa | 38 | 1 |
| 1991–92 | Aston Villa | 12 | 0 |
| 1991–92 | Blackburn R | 26 | 1 |
| 1992–93 | Blackburn R | 24 | 1 |
| 1993–94 | Aston Villa | 11 | 0 |
| 1993–94 | Derby Co | 19 | 0 |
| 1994–95 | Derby Co | 17 | 0 |
| 1994–95 | Wolverhampton W | 21 | 0 |
| 1995–96 | Wolverhampton W | 16 | 0 |
| 1995–96 | Sheffield U | 20 | 0 |
| 1996–97 | Bradford C | 24 | 0 |
| 1996–97 | Stockport Co | 7 | 0 |
| 1997–98 | Burnley | 6 | 0 |
| **Total:** | | **688** | **54** |

## COWE, Steve — Forward

H: 5 7 W: 10 02 b.Gloucester 29-9-74

*Source:* Trainee.

| | | | |
|---|---|---|---|
| 1993–94 | Aston Villa | 0 | 0 |
| 1994–95 | Aston Villa | 0 | 0 |
| 1995–96 | Aston Villa | 0 | 0 |
| 1995–96 | Swindon T | 11 | 1 |
| 1996–97 | Swindon T | 38 | 6 |
| 1997–98 | Swindon T | 17 | 2 |
| **Total:** | | **66** | **9** |

## COWLING, Lee — Midfield

H: 5 9 W: 10 03 b.Doncaster 22-9-77

*Source:* Trainee.

| | | | |
|---|---|---|---|
| 1994–95 | Nottingham F | 0 | 0 |
| 1995–96 | Nottingham F | 0 | 0 |
| 1996–97 | Nottingham F | 0 | 0 |
| 1997–98 | Nottingham F | 0 | 0 |

## COX, Christopher — Midfield

H: 5 7 W: 10 01 b.Sunderland 17-9-79

*Source:* Trainee.

| | | | |
|---|---|---|---|
| 1996–97 | Nottingham F | 0 | 0 |
| 1997–98 | Nottingham F | 0 | 0 |

## COX, Ian — Midfield

H: 6 0 W: 12 00 b.Croydon 25-3-71

*Source:* Carshalton Ath.

| | | | |
|---|---|---|---|
| 1993–94 | Crystal Palace | 0 | 0 |
| 1994–95 | Crystal Palace | 11 | 0 |
| 1995–96 | Crystal Palace | 4 | 0 |
| 1995–96 | Bournemouth | 8 | 0 |
| 1996–97 | Bournemouth | 44 | 8 |
| 1997–98 | Bournemouth | 46 | 3 |
| **Total:** | | **113** | **11** |

## COX, Jimmy — Forward

H: 5 6 W: 10 07 b.Gloucester 11-4-80

*Source:* Trainee.

| | | | |
|---|---|---|---|
| 1997–98 | Luton T | 0 | 0 |

## COX, Lee — Midfield

b.Liverpool 16-10-78

*Source:* Trainee.

| | | | |
|---|---|---|---|
| 1997–98 | Crewe Alex | 0 | 0 |

## COX, Neil — Defender

H: 6 0 W: 13 07 b.Scunthorpe 8-10-71

*Source:* Trainee. *Honours:* England Under-21.

| | | | |
|---|---|---|---|
| 1989–90 | Scunthorpe U | 0 | 0 |
| 1990–91 | Scunthorpe U | 17 | 1 |
| 1990–91 | Aston Villa | 0 | 0 |
| 1991–92 | Aston Villa | 7 | 0 |
| 1992–93 | Aston Villa | 15 | 1 |
| 1993–94 | Aston Villa | 20 | 2 |
| 1994–95 | Middlesbrough | 40 | 1 |
| 1995–96 | Middlesbrough | 35 | 2 |
| 1996–97 | Middlesbrough | 31 | 0 |
| 1997–98 | Bolton W | 21 | 1 |
| **Total:** | | **186** | **8** |

## COYLE, Owen — Forward

H: 5 9 W: 9 12 b.Paisley 14-7-66

*Source:* Renfrew YM. *Honours:* Eire Under-21, B, 1 full cap.

| | | | |
|---|---|---|---|
| 1984–85 | Dumbarton | 0 | 0 |
| 1985–86 | Dumbarton | 16 | 5 |
| 1986–87 | Dumbarton | 43 | 17 |
| 1987–88 | Dumbarton | 41 | 14 |
| 1988–89 | Dumbarton | 3 | 0 |
| 1988–89 | Clydebank | 36 | 16 |
| 1989–90 | Clydebank | 27 | 17 |
| 1989–90 | Airdrieonians | 10 | 10 |
| 1990–91 | Airdrieonians | 28 | 20 |
| 1991–92 | Airdrieonians | 43 | 11 |
| 1992–93 | Airdrieonians | 42 | 9 |
| 1993–94 | Bolton W | 30 | 7 |
| 1994–95 | Bolton W | 19 | 5 |
| 1995–96 | Bolton W | 5 | 0 |
| 1995–96 | Dundee U | 28 | 5 |
| 1996–97 | Dundee U | 10 | 0 |
| 1996–97 | Motherwell | 15 | 7 |
| 1997–98 | Motherwell | 36 | 10 |
| **Total:** | | **432** | **153** |

## COYNE, Chris — Defender

H: 6 1 W: 13 10 b.Brisbane 20-12-78

*Source:* Perth SC.

| | | | |
|---|---|---|---|
| 1995–96 | West Ham U | 0 | 0 |
| 1996–97 | West Ham U | 0 | 0 |
| 1997–98 | West Ham U | 0 | 0 |

## COYNE, Danny — Goalkeeper

H: 5 11 W: 12 05 b.Prestatyn 27-8-73

*Source:* Trainee. *Honours:* Wales Under-21, 1 full cap.

| | | | |
|---|---|---|---|
| 1991–92 | Tranmere R | 0 | 0 |

| | | | |
|---|---|---|---|
| 1992–93 | Tranmere R | 1 | 0 |
| 1993–94 | Tranmere R | 5 | 0 |
| 1994–95 | Tranmere R | 5 | 0 |
| 1995–96 | Tranmere R | 46 | 0 |
| 1996–97 | Tranmere R | 21 | 0 |
| 1997–98 | Tranmere R | 16 | 0 |
| **Total:** | | **94** | **0** |

## COYNE, Tommy — Forward

H: 5 11 W: 12 00 b.Glasgow 14-11-62

*Source:* Hillwood BC. *Honours:* Eire B, 22 full caps, 6 goals.

| | | | |
|---|---|---|---|
| 1981–82 | Clydebank | 31 | 9 |
| 1982–83 | Clydebank | 38 | 18 |
| 1983–84 | Clydebank | 11 | 10 |
| 1983–84 | Dundee U | 18 | 3 |
| 1984–85 | Dundee U | 21 | 3 |
| 1985–86 | Dundee U | 13 | 2 |
| 1986–87 | Dundee | 20 | 9 |
| 1987–88 | Dundee | 43 | 33 |
| 1988–89 | Dundee | 26 | 9 |
| 1988–89 | Celtic | 7 | 0 |
| 1989–90 | Celtic | 23 | 7 |
| 1990–91 | Celtic | 26 | 18 |
| 1991–92 | Celtic | 39 | 15 |
| 1992–93 | Celtic | 10 | 3 |
| 1992–93 | Tranmere R | 12 | 1 |
| 1993–94 | Motherwell | 26 | 12 |
| 1994–95 | Motherwell | 31 | 16 |
| 1995–96 | Motherwell | 14 | 4 |
| 1996–97 | Motherwell | 27 | 11 |
| 1997–98 | Motherwell | 34 | 15 |
| **Total:** | | **470** | **198** |

## CRADDOCK, Jody — Defender

H: 6 0 W: 11 01 b.Bromsgrove 25-7-75

*Source:* Christchurch.

| | | | |
|---|---|---|---|
| 1993–94 | Cambridge U | 20 | 0 |
| 1994–95 | Cambridge U | 38 | 0 |
| 1995–96 | Cambridge U | 46 | 3 |
| 1996–97 | Cambridge U | 41 | 1 |
| 1997–98 | Sunderland | 32 | 0 |
| **Total:** | | **177** | **4** |

## CRAIGAN, Stephen — Defender

H: 5 10 W: 10 09 b.Newtonards 29-10-76

*Source:* Blantyre Vics.

| | | | |
|---|---|---|---|
| 1995–96 | Motherwell | 0 | 0 |
| 1996–97 | Motherwell | 0 | 0 |
| 1997–98 | Motherwell | 14 | 0 |
| **Total:** | | **14** | **0** |

## CRAMB, Colin — Forward

H: 6 0 W: 11 09 b.Lanark 23-6-74

*Source:* Hamilton A BC.

| | | | |
|---|---|---|---|
| 1990–91 | Hamilton A | 3 | 2 |
| 1991–92 | Hamilton A | 12 | 1 |
| 1992–93 | Hamilton A | 33 | 7 |
| 1993–94 | Southampton | 1 | 0 |
| 1994–95 | Falkirk | 8 | 1 |
| 1994–95 | Hearts | 6 | 1 |
| 1995–96 | Doncaster R | 21 | 7 |
| 1996–97 | Doncaster R | 41 | 18 |
| 1997–98 | Bristol C | 40 | 9 |
| **Total:** | | **165** | **46** |

## CRAVEN, Dean — Forward

H: 5 6 W: 10 10 b.Shrewsbury 17-2-79

*Source:* WBA Trainee.

| | | | |
|---|---|---|---|
| 1997–98 | Shrewsbury T | 1 | 0 |
| **Total:** | | **1** | **0** |

## CRAWFORD, Jimmy — Midfield

H: 5 11 W: 11 06 b.Chicago 1-5-73

*Source:* Bohemians.

| | | | |
|---|---|---|---|
| 1994–95 | Newcastle U | 0 | 0 |
| 1995–96 | Newcastle U | 0 | 0 |
| 1996–97 | Newcastle U | 2 | 0 |
| 1996–97 | Rotherham U (loan) | 11 | 0 |
| 1997–98 | Newcastle U | 0 | 0 |
| 1997–98 | Dundee U (loan) | 2 | 0 |
| 1997–98 | Reading | 6 | 0 |
| **Total:** | | **21** | **0** |

## CRAWFORD, Steve — Forward

H: 5 10 W: 10 07 b.Dunfermline 9-1-74

*Source:* Rosyth Recreation. *Honours:* Scotland Under-21, B, 1 full cap.

| | | | |
|---|---|---|---|
| 1992–93 | Raith R | 20 | 3 |
| 1993–94 | Raith R | 36 | 5 |
| 1994–95 | Raith R | 31 | 11 |
| 1995–96 | Raith R | 28 | 3 |
| 1996–97 | Millwall | 42 | 11 |
| 1997–98 | Hibernian | 35 | 9 |
| **Total:** | | **192** | **42** |

## CREANEY, Gerry — Forward

H: 5 10 W: 13 06 b.Coatbridge 13-4-70

*Source:* Celtic BC. *Honours:* Scotland Under-21.

| | | | |
|---|---|---|---|
| 1987–88 | Celtic | 0 | 0 |

| | | | |
|---|---|---|---|
| 1988–89 | Celtic | 0 | 0 |
| 1989–90 | Celtic | 6 | 1 |
| 1990–91 | Celtic | 31 | 7 |
| 1991–92 | Celtic | 32 | 14 |
| 1992–93 | Celtic | 26 | 9 |
| 1993–94 | Celtic | 18 | 5 |
| 1993–94 | Portsmouth | 18 | 11 |
| 1994–95 | Portsmouth | 39 | 18 |
| 1995–96 | Portsmouth | 3 | 3 |
| 1995–96 | Manchester C | 15 | 3 |
| 1995–96 | Oldham Ath (loan) | 9 | 2 |
| 1996–97 | Manchester C | 5 | 1 |
| 1996–97 | Ipswich T (loan) | 6 | 1 |
| 1997–98 | Manchester C | 1 | 0 |
| 1997–98 | Burnley (loan) | 10 | 8 |
| 1997–98 | Chesterfield (loan) | 4 | 0 |
| **Total:** | | **223** | **83** |

## CRESSWELL, Richard — Forward

H: 5 11 W: 11 07 b.Bridlington 20-9-77

*Source:* Trainee.

| | | | |
|---|---|---|---|
| 1995–96 | York C | 16 | 1 |
| 1996–97 | York C | 17 | 0 |
| 1996–97 | Mansfield T (loan) | 5 | 1 |
| 1997–98 | York C | 26 | 4 |
| **Total:** | | **64** | **6** |

## CRICHTON, Paul — Goalkeeper

H: 6 1 W: 12 02 b.Pontefract 3-10-68

*Source:* Apprentice.

| | | | |
|---|---|---|---|
| 1986–87 | Nottingham F | 0 | 0 |
| 1986–87 | Notts Co (loan) | 5 | 0 |
| 1986–87 | Darlington (loan) | 5 | 0 |
| 1986–87 | Peterborough U (loan) | 4 | 0 |
| 1987–88 | Nottingham F | 0 | 0 |
| 1987–88 | Darlington (loan) | 3 | 0 |
| 1987–88 | Swindon T (loan) | 4 | 0 |
| 1987–88 | Rotherham U (loan) | 6 | 0 |
| 1988–89 | Nottingham F | 0 | 0 |
| 1988–89 | Torquay U (loan) | 13 | 0 |
| 1988–89 | Peterborough U | 31 | 0 |
| 1989–90 | Peterborough U | 16 | 0 |
| 1990–91 | Doncaster R | 20 | 0 |
| 1991–92 | Doncaster R | 16 | 0 |
| 1992–93 | Doncaster R | 41 | 0 |
| 1993–94 | Grimsby T | 46 | 0 |
| 1994–95 | Grimsby T | 43 | 0 |
| 1995–96 | Grimsby T | 44 | 0 |
| 1996–97 | Grimsby T | 0 | 0 |
| 1996–97 | WBA | 30 | 0 |
| 1997–98 | WBA | 2 | 0 |
| 1997–98 | Aston Villa (loan) | 0 | 0 |
| **Total:** | | **329** | **0** |

## CRITCHLEY, Neil — Midfield

b.Crewe 18-10-78

*Source:* Trainee.

| | | | |
|---|---|---|---|
| 1997–98 | Crewe Alex | 0 | 0 |

## CRITTENDEN, Nick — Midfield

H: 5 8 W: 10 07 b.Bracknell 11-11-78

*Source:* Trainee.

| | | | |
|---|---|---|---|
| 1997–98 | Chelsea | 2 | 0 |
| **Total:** | | **2** | **0** |

## CROCI, Laurent — Midfield

b.Montbeliard 8-12-64

*Source:* Sochaux, Bordeaux, Sochaux, Bordeaux.

| | | | |
|---|---|---|---|
| 1997–98 | Carlisle U | 1 | 0 |
| **Total:** | | **1** | **0** |

## CROFT, Gary — Defender

H: 5 8 W: 10 08 b.Burton 17-2-74

*Source:* Trainee. *Honours:* England Under-21.

| | | | |
|---|---|---|---|
| 1990–91 | Grimsby T | 1 | 0 |
| 1991–92 | Grimsby T | 0 | 0 |
| 1992–93 | Grimsby T | 32 | 0 |
| 1993–94 | Grimsby T | 36 | 1 |
| 1994–95 | Grimsby T | 44 | 1 |
| 1995–96 | Grimsby T | 36 | 1 |
| 1995–96 | Blackburn R | 0 | 0 |
| 1996–97 | Blackburn R | 5 | 0 |
| 1997–98 | Blackburn R | 23 | 1 |
| **Total:** | | **177** | **4** |

## CRONIN, Gary — Midfield

b.Dublin 16-3-79

*Source:* Stella Maris.

| | | | |
|---|---|---|---|
| 1997–98 | Middlesbrough | 0 | 0 |

## CROOKES, Dale — Midfield

H: 5 7 W: 12 03 b.Sheffield 10-3-80

*Source:* Trainee.

| | | | |
|---|---|---|---|
| 1997–98 | Barnsley | 0 | 0 |

## CROOKS, Lee — Midfield

H: 6 1 W: 12 01 b.Wakefield 14-1-78

*Source:* Trainee. *Honours:* England Youth.

| | | | |
|---|---|---|---|
| 1994–95 | Manchester C | 0 | 0 |

## Crosby, Andy

| | | | |
|---|---|---|---|
| 1995–96 | Manchester C | 0 | 0 |
| 1996–97 | Manchester C | 15 | 0 |
| 1997–98 | Manchester C | 5 | 0 |
| **Total:** | | **20** | **0** |

## CROSBY, Andy — Defender

H: 6 2 W: 13 06 b.Rotherham 3-3-73

*Source:* Leeds U Trainee.

| | | | |
|---|---|---|---|
| 1991–92 | Doncaster R | 22 | 0 |
| 1992–93 | Doncaster R | 29 | 0 |
| 1993–94 | Doncaster R | 0 | 0 |
| 1993–94 | Darlington | 25 | 0 |
| 1994–95 | Darlington | 35 | 0 |
| 1995–96 | Darlington | 45 | 1 |
| 1996–97 | Darlington | 42 | 1 |
| 1997–98 | Darlington | 34 | 1 |
| **Total:** | | **232** | **3** |

## CROSS, Jamie — Defender

H: 5 10 W: 12 02 b.Blackpool 29-8-79

*Source:* Trainee.

| | | | |
|---|---|---|---|
| 1997–98 | Blackpool | 0 | 0 |

## CROSS, John — Midfield

H: 5 9 W: 13 00 b.Barking 6-4-76

*Source:* Trainee.

| | | | |
|---|---|---|---|
| 1994–95 | QPR | 0 | 0 |
| 1995–96 | QPR | 0 | 0 |
| 1996–97 | Cardiff C | 0 | 0 |
| 1997–98 | Cardiff C | 0 | 0 |

## CROSS, Jonathan — Midfield

H: 5 10 W: 11 07 b.Wallasey 2-3-75

*Source:* Trainee.

| | | | |
|---|---|---|---|
| 1991–92 | Wrexham | 6 | 0 |
| 1992–93 | Wrexham | 37 | 7 |
| 1993–94 | Wrexham | 25 | 2 |
| 1994–95 | Wrexham | 24 | 1 |
| 1995–96 | Wrexham | 7 | 0 |
| 1996–97 | Wrexham | 18 | 2 |
| 1996–97 | Hereford U (loan) | 5 | 1 |
| 1997–98 | Wrexham | 2 | 0 |
| 1997–98 | Tranmere R (loan) | 0 | 0 |
| **Total:** | | **124** | **13** |

## CROSS, Matthew — Defender

H: 5 6 W: 12 03 b.Bury 25-3-80

*Source:* Trainee.

| | | | |
|---|---|---|---|
| 1997–98 | Barnsley | 0 | 0 |

## CROSSLAND, Mark — Midfield

H: 5 11 W: 12 02 b.Ashton-under-Lyne 14-12-78

*Source:* Lincoln C Trainee.

| | | | |
|---|---|---|---|
| 1996–97 | Bury | 0 | 0 |
| 1997–98 | Bury | 0 | 0 |

## CROSSLEY, Mark — Goalkeeper

H: 6 0 W: 16 00 b.Barnsley 16-6-69

*Source:* Trainee. *Honours:* England Under-21, Wales B, 1 full cap.

| | | | |
|---|---|---|---|
| 1987–88 | Nottingham F | 0 | 0 |
| 1988–89 | Nottingham F | 2 | 0 |
| 1989–90 | Nottingham F | 8 | 0 |
| 1989–90 | Manchester U (loan) | 0 | 0 |
| 1990–91 | Nottingham F | 38 | 0 |
| 1991–92 | Nottingham F | 36 | 0 |
| 1992–93 | Nottingham F | 37 | 0 |
| 1993–94 | Nottingham F | 37 | 0 |
| 1994–95 | Nottingham F | 42 | 0 |
| 1995–96 | Nottingham F | 38 | 0 |
| 1996–97 | Nottingham F | 33 | 0 |
| 1997–98 | Nottingham F | 0 | 0 |
| 1997–98 | Millwall (loan) | 13 | 0 |
| **Total:** | | **284** | **0** |

## CROWE, Dean — Forward

H: 5 5 W: 11 02 b.Stockport 6-6-79

*Source:* Trainee.

| | | | |
|---|---|---|---|
| 1996–97 | Stoke C | 0 | 0 |
| 1997–98 | Stoke C | 16 | 4 |
| **Total:** | | **16** | **4** |

## CROWE, Glen — Forward

H: 5 10 W: 13 01 b.Dublin 25-12-77

*Source:* Trainee.

| | | | |
|---|---|---|---|
| 1995–96 | Wolverhampton W | 2 | 1 |
| 1996–97 | Exeter C (loan) | 10 | 5 |
| 1996–97 | Wolverhampton W | 6 | 0 |
| 1997–98 | Wolverhampton W | 2 | 0 |
| 1997–98 | Cardiff C (loan) | 8 | 1 |
| **Total:** | | **28** | **7** |

## CROWE, Jason — Defender

H: 5 9 W: 10 09 b.Sidcup 30-9-78

*Source:* Trainee. *Honours:* England Schools, Youth.

| | | | |
|---|---|---|---|
| 1995–96 | Arsenal | 0 | 0 |
| 1996–97 | Arsenal | 0 | 0 |
| 1997–98 | Arsenal | 0 | 0 |

## CROWE, Seamie — Midfield

b.Galway 18-11-80

*Source:* Trainee.

| | | | |
|---|---|---|---|
| 1997–98 | Wolverhampton W | 0 | 0 |

## CRUYFF, Jordi — Forward

H: 6 1 W: 10 12 b.Amsterdam 9-2-74

*Source:* Ajax. *Honours:* Holland 9 full caps, 1 goal.

| | | | |
|---|---|---|---|
| 1992–93 | Barcelona | 0 | 0 |
| 1993–94 | Barcelona | 0 | 0 |
| 1994–95 | Barcelona | 28 | 9 |
| 1995–96 | Barcelona | 13 | 2 |
| 1996–97 | Manchester U | 16 | 2 |
| 1997–98 | Manchester U | 5 | 0 |
| **Total:** | | **62** | **13** |

## CUERVO, Philippe — Midfield

H: 5 11 W: 11 03 b.France 13-8-69

| | | | |
|---|---|---|---|
| 1996–97 | St Etienne | 21 | 0 |
| 1997–98 | Swindon T | 23 | 0 |
| **Total:** | | **44** | **0** |

## CULKIN, Nick — Goalkeeper

H: 6 2 W: 13 05 b.York 6-7-78

*Source:* York C.

| | | | |
|---|---|---|---|
| 1995–96 | Manchester U | 0 | 0 |
| 1996–97 | Manchester U | 0 | 0 |
| 1997–98 | Manchester U | 0 | 0 |

## CULLEN, Jon — Midfield

H: 6 0 W: 11 10 b.Durham 10-1-73

*Source:* Trainee.

| | | | |
|---|---|---|---|
| 1990–91 | Doncaster R | 1 | 0 |
| 1991–92 | Doncaster R | 8 | 0 |
| 1992–93 | Doncaster R | 0 | 0 |
| 1993–94 | Doncaster R | 0 | 0 |
| From Morpeth T. | | | |
| 1996–97 | Hartlepool U | 6 | 0 |
| 1997–98 | Hartlepool U | 28 | 12 |
| 1997–98 | Sheffield U | 2 | 0 |
| **Total:** | | **45** | **12** |

## CULLIP, Danny — Defender

H: 6 0 W: 12 07 b.Bracknell 17-9-76

*Source:* Trainee.

| | | | |
|---|---|---|---|
| 1995–96 | Oxford U | 0 | 0 |
| 1996–97 | Fulham | 29 | 1 |
| 1997–98 | Fulham | 21 | 1 |
| 1997–98 | Brentford | 13 | 0 |
| **Total:** | | **63** | **2** |

## CULSHAW, Thomas — Defender

H: 5 10 W: 12 02 b.Liverpool 10-10-78

*Source:* Trainee. *Honours:* England Schools.

| | | | |
|---|---|---|---|
| 1995–96 | Liverpool | 0 | 0 |
| 1996–97 | Liverpool | 0 | 0 |
| 1997–98 | Liverpool | 0 | 0 |

## CULVERHOUSE, Ian — Defender

H: 5 10 W: 11 02 b.Bishop's Stortford 22-9-64

*Source:* Apprentice. *Honours:* England Youth.

| | | | |
|---|---|---|---|
| 1982–83 | Tottenham H | 0 | 0 |
| 1983–84 | Tottenham H | 2 | 0 |
| 1984–85 | Tottenham H | 0 | 0 |
| 1985–86 | Tottenham H | 0 | 0 |
| 1985–86 | Norwich C | 30 | 0 |
| 1986–87 | Norwich C | 25 | 0 |
| 1987–88 | Norwich C | 33 | 0 |
| 1988–89 | Norwich C | 38 | 0 |
| 1989–90 | Norwich C | 32 | 0 |
| 1990–91 | Norwich C | 34 | 0 |
| 1991–92 | Norwich C | 21 | 0 |
| 1992–93 | Norwich C | 41 | 0 |
| 1993–94 | Norwich C | 42 | 0 |
| 1994–95 | Norwich C | 0 | 0 |
| 1994–95 | Swindon T | 9 | 0 |
| 1995–96 | Swindon T | 46 | 0 |
| 1996–97 | Swindon T | 31 | 0 |
| 1997–98 | Swindon T | 11 | 0 |
| **Total:** | | **395** | **0** |

## CUMMINS, Michael — Midfield

H: 6 0 W: 11 11 b.Dublin 1-6-78

*Source:* Trainee. *Honours:* Eire Youth.

| | | | |
|---|---|---|---|
| 1995–96 | Middlesbrough | 0 | 0 |
| 1996–97 | Middlesbrough | 0 | 0 |
| 1997–98 | Middlesbrough | 0 | 0 |

## CUNDY, Jason — Defender

H: 6 0 W: 13 10 b.Wimbledon 12-11-69

*Source:* Trainee. *Honours:* England Under-21.

| | | | |
|---|---|---|---|
| 1988–89 | Chelsea | 0 | 0 |
| 1989–90 | Chelsea | 0 | 0 |
| 1990–91 | Chelsea | 29 | 0 |
| 1991–92 | Chelsea | 12 | 1 |
| 1991–92 | Tottenham H (loan) | 10 | 0 |
| 1992–93 | Tottenham H | 15 | 1 |
| 1993–94 | Tottenham H | 0 | 0 |
| 1994–95 | Tottenham H | 0 | 0 |
| 1995–96 | Tottenham H | 1 | 0 |
| 1995–96 | Crystal Palace (loan) | 4 | 0 |
| 1996–97 | Tottenham H | 0 | 0 |
| 1996–97 | Bristol C (loan) | 6 | 1 |
| 1996–97 | Ipswich T | 13 | 2 |
| 1997–98 | Ipswich T | 41 | 3 |
| **Total:** | | **131** | **8** |

## CUNNINGHAM, Harvey — Defender

H: 5 9 W: 11 05 b.Manchester 11-9-68

*Source:* Trafford Barons.

| | | | |
|---|---|---|---|
| 1996–97 | Doncaster R | 11 | 0 |
| 1997–98 | Doncaster R | 33 | 1 |
| **Total:** | | **44** | **1** |

## CUNNINGHAM, Kenny — Defender

H: 5 11 W: 11 02 b.Dublin 28-6-71

*Source:* Tolka R. *Honours:* Eire Under-21, B, 16 full caps.

| | | | |
|---|---|---|---|
| 1989–90 | Millwall | 5 | 0 |
| 1990–91 | Millwall | 23 | 0 |
| 1991–92 | Millwall | 17 | 0 |
| 1992–93 | Millwall | 37 | 0 |
| 1993–94 | Millwall | 39 | 1 |
| 1994–95 | Millwall | 15 | 0 |
| 1994–95 | Wimbledon | 28 | 0 |
| 1995–96 | Wimbledon | 33 | 0 |
| 1996–97 | Wimbledon | 36 | 0 |
| 1997–98 | Wimbledon | 32 | 0 |
| **Total:** | | **265** | **1** |

## CUNNINGTON, Shaun — Midfield

H: 5 11 W: 11 08 b.Bourne 4-1-66

*Source:* Bourne T.

| | | | |
|---|---|---|---|
| 1982–83 | Wrexham | 4 | 0 |
| 1983–84 | Wrexham | 42 | 0 |
| 1984–85 | Wrexham | 41 | 6 |
| 1985–86 | Wrexham | 42 | 2 |
| 1986–87 | Wrexham | 46 | 1 |
| 1987–88 | Wrexham | 24 | 3 |
| 1987–88 | Grimsby T | 15 | 2 |
| 1988–89 | Grimsby T | 44 | 1 |
| 1989–90 | Grimsby T | 44 | 3 |
| 1990–91 | Grimsby T | 46 | 2 |
| 1991–92 | Grimsby T | 33 | 5 |
| 1992–93 | Sunderland | 39 | 7 |
| 1993–94 | Sunderland | 11 | 1 |
| 1994–95 | Sunderland | 8 | 0 |
| 1995–96 | WBA | 9 | 0 |
| 1996–97 | WBA | 4 | 0 |
| 1996–97 | Notts Co | 8 | 0 |
| 1997–98 | Notts Co | 9 | 0 |
| **Total:** | | **469** | **33** |

## CURBISHLEY, Alan — Midfield

H: 5 10 W: 11 07 b.Forest Gate 8-11-57

*Source:* Apprentice. *Honours:* England Schools, Youth, Under-21.

| | | | |
|---|---|---|---|
| 1974–75 | West Ham U | 2 | 0 |
| 1975–76 | West Ham U | 14 | 2 |
| 1976–77 | West Ham U | 10 | 1 |
| 1977–78 | West Ham U | 32 | 1 |
| 1978–79 | West Ham U | 27 | 1 |
| 1979–80 | Birmingham C | 42 | 3 |
| 1980–81 | Birmingham C | 29 | 6 |
| 1981–82 | Birmingham C | 29 | 1 |
| 1982–83 | Birmingham C | 30 | 1 |
| 1982–83 | Aston Villa | 7 | 0 |
| 1983–84 | Aston Villa | 26 | 1 |
| 1984–85 | Aston Villa | 3 | 0 |
| 1984–85 | Charlton Ath | 23 | 2 |
| 1985–86 | Charlton Ath | 30 | 4 |
| 1986–87 | Charlton Ath | 10 | 0 |
| 1987–88 | Brighton & HA | 34 | 6 |
| 1988–89 | Brighton & HA | 37 | 6 |
| 1989–90 | Brighton & HA | 45 | 1 |
| 1990–91 | Charlton Ath | 25 | 0 |
| 1991–92 | Charlton Ath | 1 | 0 |
| 1992–93 | Charlton Ath | 1 | 0 |
| 1993–94 | Charlton Ath | 1 | 0 |
| 1994–95 | Charlton Ath | 0 | 0 |
| 1995–96 | Charlton Ath | 0 | 0 |
| 1996–97 | Charlton Ath | 0 | 0 |
| 1997–98 | Charlton Ath | 0 | 0 |
| **Total:** | | **458** | **36** |

## CURCIC, Sasa — Midfield

H: 5 9 W: 11 00 b.Belgrade 14-2-72

*Honours:* Yugoslavia 13 full caps, 1 goal.

| | | | |
|---|---|---|---|
| 1991–92 | OFK Belgrade | 17 | 2 |
| 1992–93 | OFK Belgrade | 32 | 3 |
| 1993–94 | Partizan Belgrade | 33 | 8 |
| 1994–95 | Partizan Belgrade | 31 | 6 |

| | | | |
|---|---|---|---|
| 1995–96 | Partizan Belgrade | 10 | 2 |
| 1995–96 | Bolton W | 28 | 4 |
| 1996–97 | Aston Villa | 22 | 0 |
| 1997–98 | Aston Villa | 7 | 0 |
| 1997–98 | Crystal Palace | 8 | 1 |
| **Total:** | | **188** | **26** |

## CURETON, Jamie — Forward

H: 5 7 W: 10 07 b.Bristol 28-8-75

*Source:* Trainee. *Honours:* England Youth.

| | | | |
|---|---|---|---|
| 1992–93 | Norwich C | 0 | 0 |
| 1993–94 | Norwich C | 0 | 0 |
| 1994–95 | Norwich C | 17 | 4 |
| 1995–96 | Norwich C | 12 | 2 |
| 1995–96 | Bournemouth (loan) | 5 | 0 |
| 1996–97 | Norwich C | 0 | 0 |
| 1996–97 | Bristol R | 38 | 11 |
| 1997–98 | Bristol R | 43 | 13 |
| **Total:** | | **115** | **30** |

## CURLE, Keith — Defender

H: 6 0 W: 12 07 b.Bristol 14-11-63

*Source:* Apprentice. *Honours:* England B, 3 full caps.

| | | | |
|---|---|---|---|
| 1981–82 | Bristol R | 20 | 2 |
| 1982–83 | Bristol R | 12 | 2 |
| 1983–84 | Bristol R | 0 | 0 |
| 1983–84 | Torquay U | 16 | 5 |
| 1983–84 | Bristol C | 6 | 0 |
| 1984–85 | Bristol C | 40 | 0 |
| 1985–86 | Bristol C | 44 | 1 |
| 1986–87 | Bristol C | 28 | 0 |
| 1987–88 | Bristol C | 3 | 0 |
| 1987–88 | Reading | 30 | 0 |
| 1988–89 | Reading | 10 | 0 |
| 1988–89 | Wimbledon | 18 | 0 |
| 1989–90 | Wimbledon | 38 | 2 |
| 1990–91 | Wimbledon | 37 | 1 |
| 1991–92 | Manchester C | 40 | 5 |
| 1992–93 | Manchester C | 39 | 3 |
| 1993–94 | Manchester C | 29 | 1 |
| 1994–95 | Manchester C | 31 | 2 |
| 1995–96 | Manchester C | 32 | 0 |
| 1996–97 | Wolverhampton W | 21 | 2 |
| 1997–98 | Wolverhampton W | 40 | 1 |
| **Total:** | | **534** | **27** |

## CURRAN, Chris — Defender

H: 5 11 W: 11 09 b.Birmingham 17-9-71

*Source:* Trainee.

| | | | |
|---|---|---|---|
| 1989–90 | Torquay U | 1 | 0 |
| 1990–91 | Torquay U | 13 | 0 |
| 1991–92 | Torquay U | 17 | 0 |
| 1992–93 | Torquay U | 34 | 0 |
| 1993–94 | Torquay U | 41 | 1 |
| 1994–95 | Torquay U | 27 | 2 |
| 1995–96 | Torquay U | 19 | 1 |
| 1995–96 | Plymouth Arg | 8 | 0 |
| 1996–97 | Plymouth Arg | 22 | 0 |
| 1997–98 | Exeter C | 9 | 0 |
| **Total:** | | **191** | **4** |

## CURRAN, Henry — Midfield

H: 5 8 W: 11 08 b.Glasgow 9-10-66

*Source:* Eastercraigs.

| | | | |
|---|---|---|---|
| 1984–85 | Dumbarton | 0 | 0 |
| 1985–86 | Dumbarton | 6 | 0 |
| 1986–87 | Dumbarton | 8 | 0 |
| 1987–88 | Dundee U | 5 | 0 |
| 1988–89 | Dundee U | 6 | 0 |
| 1989–90 | St Johnstone | 31 | 3 |
| 1990–91 | St Johnstone | 35 | 9 |
| 1991–92 | St Johnstone | 39 | 8 |
| 1992–93 | St Johnstone | 34 | 8 |
| 1993–94 | St Johnstone | 39 | 3 |
| 1994–95 | St Johnstone | 26 | 4 |
| 1995–96 | Partick T | 8 | 0 |
| 1996–97 | Dunfermline Ath | 20 | 1 |
| 1997–98 | Dunfermline Ath | 17 | 1 |
| **Total:** | | **274** | **37** |

## CURRIE, Darren — Midfield

H: 5 11 W: 12 07 b.Hampstead 29-11-74

*Source:* Trainee.

| | | | |
|---|---|---|---|
| 1993–94 | West Ham U | 0 | 0 |
| 1994–95 | West Ham U | 0 | 0 |
| 1994–95 | Shrewsbury T (loan) | 17 | 2 |
| 1995–96 | West Ham U | 0 | 0 |
| 1995–96 | Leyton Orient (loan) | 10 | 0 |
| 1995–96 | Shrewsbury T | 13 | 2 |
| 1996–97 | Shrewsbury T | 37 | 2 |
| 1997–98 | Shrewsbury T | 16 | 4 |
| 1997–98 | Plymouth Arg | 7 | 0 |
| **Total:** | | **100** | **10** |

## CURRIE, Michael — Midfield

b.Westminster 19-10-79

*Source:* Trainee.

| | | | |
|---|---|---|---|
| 1997–98 | QPR | 0 | 0 |

## CURTIS, John — Defender

H: 5 10 W: 11 07 b.Nuneaton 3-9-78

*Source:* Trainee. *Honours:* England Schools, Youth, Under-21, B.

| | | | |
|---|---|---|---|
| 1995–96 | Manchester U | 0 | 0 |
| 1996–97 | Manchester U | 0 | 0 |
| 1997–98 | Manchester U | 8 | 0 |
| **Total:** | | **8** | **0** |

## CURTIS, Tom — Midfield

H: 5 8 W: 10 08 b.Exeter 1-3-73

*Source:* School.

| | | | |
|---|---|---|---|
| 1991–92 | Derby Co | 0 | 0 |
| 1992–93 | Derby Co | 0 | 0 |
| 1993–94 | Chesterfield | 36 | 3 |
| 1994–95 | Chesterfield | 40 | 2 |
| 1995–96 | Chesterfield | 46 | 0 |
| 1996–97 | Chesterfield | 40 | 3 |
| 1997–98 | Chesterfield | 36 | 1 |
| **Total:** | | **198** | **9** |

## CURTOLO, David — Midfield

b.Stockholm 30-9-80

| | | | |
|---|---|---|---|
| 1997–98 | Aston Villa | 0 | 0 |

## CUSACK, Nick — Midfield

H: 6 0 W: 12 05 b.Rotherham 24-12-65

*Source:* Alvechurch.

| | | | |
|---|---|---|---|
| 1987–88 | Leicester C | 16 | 1 |
| 1988–89 | Peterborough U | 44 | 10 |
| 1989–90 | Motherwell | 31 | 11 |
| 1990–91 | Motherwell | 29 | 4 |
| 1991–92 | Motherwell | 17 | 2 |
| 1991–92 | Darlington | 21 | 6 |
| 1992–93 | Oxford U | 39 | 4 |
| 1993–94 | Oxford U | 20 | 6 |
| 1993–94 | Wycombe W (loan) | 4 | 0 |
| 1994–95 | Oxford U | 2 | 0 |
| 1994–95 | Fulham | 27 | 7 |
| 1995–96 | Fulham | 42 | 5 |
| 1996–97 | Fulham | 45 | 2 |
| 1997–98 | Fulham | 2 | 0 |
| 1997–98 | Swansea C | 32 | 0 |
| **Total:** | | **371** | **58** |

## CUSS, Paul — Goalkeeper

H: 6 1 W: 13 05 b.Hanover 19-4-79

*Source:* Trainee.

| | | | |
|---|---|---|---|
| 1997–98 | Huddersfield T | 0 | 0 |

## CUTLER, Neil — Goalkeeper

H: 6 1 W: 12 00 b.Birmingham 3-9-76

*Source:* Trainee. *Honours:* England Schools, Youth.

| | | | |
|---|---|---|---|
| 1993–94 | WBA | 0 | 0 |
| 1994–95 | WBA | 0 | 0 |
| 1995–96 | WBA | 0 | 0 |
| 1995–96 | Coventry C (loan) | 0 | 0 |
| 1995–96 | Chester C (loan) | 1 | 0 |
| 1996–97 | Crewe Alex | 0 | 0 |
| 1996–97 | Chester C (loan) | 5 | 0 |
| 1997–98 | Crewe Alex | 0 | 0 |
| **Total:** | | **6** | **0** |

## CYRUS, Andy — Defender

H: 5 8 W: 9 03 b.Lambeth 30-9-76

*Source:* Trainee.

| | | | |
|---|---|---|---|
| 1995–96 | Crystal Palace | 0 | 0 |
| 1996–97 | Crystal Palace | 1 | 0 |
| 1997–98 | Exeter C | 21 | 0 |
| **Total:** | | **22** | **0** |

## D'AURIA, David — Midfield

H: 5 10 W: 12 05 b.Swansea 26-3-70

*Source:* Trainee.

| | | | |
|---|---|---|---|
| 1987–88 | Swansea C | 4 | 0 |
| 1988–89 | Swansea C | 14 | 2 |
| 1989–90 | Swansea C | 7 | 0 |
| 1990–91 | Swansea C | 20 | 4 |
| From Barry T. | | | |
| 1994–95 | Scarborough | 34 | 7 |
| 1995–96 | Scarborough | 18 | 1 |
| 1995–96 | Scunthorpe U | 27 | 5 |
| 1996–97 | Scunthorpe U | 39 | 3 |
| 1997–98 | Scunthorpe U | 41 | 10 |
| **Total:** | | **204** | **32** |

## DA COSTA, Nelson — Defender

H: 5 10 W: 12 03 b.Angola 8-12-78

*Source:* Belenenses.

| | | | |
|---|---|---|---|
| 1996–97 | Stockport Co | 0 | 0 |
| 1997–98 | Macclesfield T | 0 | 0 |

## DABIZAS, Nikos — Defender

H: 6 0 W: 11 11 b.Amypeo 3-8-73

*Honours:* Greece 23 full caps.

| | | | |
|---|---|---|---|
| 1994–95 | Olympiakos | 26 | 2 |
| 1995–96 | Olympiakos | 27 | 1 |
| 1996–97 | Olympiakos | 31 | 0 |

| | | | |
|---|---|---|---|
| 1997–98 | Olympiakos | 20 | 5 |
| 1997–98 | Newcastle U | 11 | 1 |
| **Total:** | | **115** | **9** |

## DAHLIN, Martin — Forward

H: 6 1 W: 13 03 b.Lund 16-4-68

*Source:* Lund BK. *Honours:* Sweden 58 full caps, 28 goals.

| | | | |
|---|---|---|---|
| 1988 | Malmo | 21 | 17 |
| 1989 | Malmo | 17 | 4 |
| 1990 | Malmo | 19 | 7 |
| 1991 | Malmo | 22 | 11 |
| 1991–92 | Moenchengladbach | 12 | 2 |
| 1992–93 | Moenchengladbach | 20 | 10 |
| 1993–94 | Moenchengladbach | 27 | 12 |
| 1994–95 | Moenchengladbach | 24 | 11 |
| 1995–96 | Moenchengladbach | 23 | 15 |
| 1996–97 | Roma | 3 | 0 |
| 1997–98 | Blackburn R | 21 | 4 |
| **Total:** | | **209** | **93** |

## DAILLY, Christian — Defender

H: 6 0 W: 12 05 b.Dundee 23-10-73

*Source:* 'S' Form. *Honours:* Scotland B, Under-21, 13 full caps, 1 goal.

| | | | |
|---|---|---|---|
| 1990–91 | Dundee U | 18 | 5 |
| 1991–92 | Dundee U | 8 | 0 |
| 1992–93 | Dundee U | 14 | 4 |
| 1993–94 | Dundee U | 38 | 4 |
| 1994–95 | Dundee U | 33 | 4 |
| 1995–96 | Dundee U | 30 | 1 |
| 1996–97 | Derby Co | 36 | 3 |
| 1997–98 | Derby Co | 30 | 1 |
| **Total:** | | **207** | **22** |

## DAIR, Jason — Midfield

H: 5 11 W: 10 08 b.Dunfermline 15-6-74

*Source:* Castlebridge. *Honours:* Scotland Under-21.

| | | | |
|---|---|---|---|
| 1991–92 | Raith R | 4 | 0 |
| 1992–93 | Raith R | 15 | 1 |
| 1993–94 | Raith R | 38 | 6 |
| 1994–95 | Raith R | 18 | 1 |
| 1995–96 | Raith R | 19 | 3 |
| 1996–97 | Millwall | 24 | 1 |
| 1997–98 | Millwall | 0 | 0 |
| **Total:** | | **118** | **12** |

## DAISH, Liam — Defender

H: 6 2 W: 13 05 b.Portsmouth 23-9-68

*Source:* Apprentice. *Honours:* Eire Under-21, B, 5 full caps.

| | | | |
|---|---|---|---|
| 1986–87 | Portsmouth | 1 | 0 |
| 1987–88 | Portsmouth | 0 | 0 |
| 1988–89 | Cambridge U | 28 | 0 |
| 1989–90 | Cambridge U | 42 | 1 |
| 1990–91 | Cambridge U | 13 | 1 |
| 1991–92 | Cambridge U | 22 | 0 |
| 1992–93 | Cambridge U | 16 | 0 |
| 1993–94 | Cambridge U | 18 | 2 |
| 1993–94 | Birmingham C | 19 | 0 |
| 1994–95 | Birmingham C | 37 | 3 |
| 1995–96 | Birmingham C | 17 | 0 |
| 1995–96 | Coventry C | 11 | 1 |
| 1996–97 | Coventry C | 20 | 1 |
| 1997–98 | Coventry C | 0 | 0 |
| **Total:** | | **244** | **9** |

## DALE, Carl — Forward

H: 5 7 W: 12 01 b.Colwyn Bay 29-4-66

*Source:* Bangor C.

| | | | |
|---|---|---|---|
| 1987–88 | Chester C | 0 | 0 |
| 1988–89 | Chester C | 41 | 22 |
| 1989–90 | Chester C | 31 | 9 |
| 1990–91 | Chester C | 44 | 10 |
| 1991–92 | Cardiff C | 41 | 22 |
| 1992–93 | Cardiff C | 20 | 8 |
| 1993–94 | Cardiff C | 15 | 3 |
| 1994–95 | Cardiff C | 35 | 5 |
| 1995–96 | Cardiff C | 44 | 21 |
| 1996–97 | Cardiff C | 33 | 8 |
| 1997–98 | Cardiff C | 25 | 4 |
| **Total:** | | **329** | **112** |

## DALEY, Tony — Midfield

H: 5 9 W: 11 00 b.Birmingham 18-11-67

*Source:* Apprentice. *Honours:* England Youth, 7 full caps.

| | | | |
|---|---|---|---|
| 1984–85 | Aston Villa | 5 | 0 |
| 1985–86 | Aston Villa | 23 | 2 |
| 1986–87 | Aston Villa | 33 | 3 |
| 1987–88 | Aston Villa | 14 | 3 |
| 1988–89 | Aston Villa | 29 | 5 |
| 1989–90 | Aston Villa | 32 | 6 |
| 1990–91 | Aston Villa | 23 | 2 |
| 1991–92 | Aston Villa | 34 | 7 |
| 1992–93 | Aston Villa | 13 | 2 |
| 1993–94 | Aston Villa | 27 | 1 |
| 1994–95 | Wolverhampton W | 1 | 0 |
| 1995–96 | Wolverhampton W | 18 | 3 |
| 1996–97 | Wolverhampton W | 0 | 0 |
| 1997–98 | Wolverhampton W | 2 | 0 |
| **Total:** | | **254** | **34** |

## DALGLISH, Paul — Midfield

H: 5 9 W: 10 00 b.Glasgow 18-2-77

| | | | |
|---|---|---|---|
| 1995–96 | Celtic | 0 | 0 |
| 1996–97 | Liverpool | 0 | 0 |
| 1997–98 | Liverpool | 0 | 0 |
| 1997–98 | Newcastle U | 0 | 0 |
| 1997–98 | Bury (loan) | 12 | 0 |
| **Total:** | | **12** | **0** |

## DALTON, Paul — Midfield

H: 6 0 W: 12 07 b.Middlesbrough 25-4-67

*Source:* Brandon U.

| | | | |
|---|---|---|---|
| 1987–88 | Manchester U | 0 | 0 |
| 1988–89 | Manchester U | 0 | 0 |
| 1988–89 | Hartlepool U | 17 | 2 |
| 1989–90 | Hartlepool U | 45 | 11 |
| 1990–91 | Hartlepool U | 46 | 11 |
| 1991–92 | Hartlepool U | 43 | 13 |
| 1992–93 | Plymouth Arg | 32 | 9 |
| 1993–94 | Plymouth Arg | 40 | 12 |
| 1994–95 | Plymouth Arg | 26 | 4 |
| 1995–96 | Huddersfield T | 29 | 5 |
| 1996–97 | Huddersfield T | 29 | 4 |
| 1997–98 | Huddersfield T | 31 | 13 |
| **Total:** | | **338** | **84** |

## DARBY, Duane — Forward

H: 5 11 W: 12 06 b.Birmingham 17-10-73

*Source:* Trainee.

| | | | |
|---|---|---|---|
| 1991–92 | Torquay U | 14 | 2 |
| 1992–93 | Torquay U | 34 | 12 |
| 1993–94 | Torquay U | 36 | 8 |
| 1994–95 | Torquay U | 24 | 4 |
| 1995–96 | Doncaster R | 17 | 4 |
| 1995–96 | Hull C | 8 | 1 |
| 1996–97 | Hull C | 41 | 13 |
| 1997–98 | Hull C | 29 | 13 |
| **Total:** | | **203** | **57** |

## DARBY, Julian — Midfield

H: 6 0 W: 11 04 b.Bolton 3-10-67

*Source:* Trainee. *Honours:* England Schools.

| | | | |
|---|---|---|---|
| 1984–85 | Bolton W | 0 | 0 |
| 1985–86 | Bolton W | 2 | 0 |
| 1986–87 | Bolton W | 28 | 0 |
| 1987–88 | Bolton W | 35 | 2 |
| 1988–89 | Bolton W | 44 | 5 |
| 1989–90 | Bolton W | 46 | 10 |
| 1990–91 | Bolton W | 45 | 9 |
| 1991–92 | Bolton W | 44 | 6 |
| 1992–93 | Bolton W | 21 | 4 |
| 1993–94 | Bolton W | 5 | 0 |
| 1993–94 | Coventry C | 26 | 5 |
| 1994–95 | Coventry C | 29 | 0 |
| 1995–96 | Coventry C | 0 | 0 |
| 1995–96 | WBA | 22 | 1 |
| 1996–97 | WBA | 17 | 0 |
| 1997–98 | Preston NE | 12 | 0 |
| 1997–98 | Rotherham U (loan) | 3 | 0 |
| **Total:** | | **379** | **42** |

## DARCY, Ross — Defender

H: 6 0 W: 12 02 b.Balbriggan 21-3-78

*Source:* Trainee.

| | | | |
|---|---|---|---|
| 1995–96 | Tottenham H | 0 | 0 |
| 1996–97 | Tottenham H | 0 | 0 |
| 1997–98 | Tottenham H | 0 | 0 |

## DARRAS, Frederic — Defender

H: 5 11 W: 11 03 b.Calais 19-8-66

| | | | |
|---|---|---|---|
| 1990–91 | Auxerre | 11 | 0 |
| 1991–92 | Auxerre | 16 | 0 |
| 1992–93 | Sochaux | 26 | 0 |
| 1993–94 | Sochaux | 28 | 0 |
| 1994–95 | Bastia | 16 | 0 |
| 1995–96 | Bastia | 23 | 0 |
| 1996–97 | Swindon T | 35 | 0 |
| 1997–98 | Swindon T | 14 | 0 |
| **Total:** | | **169** | **0** |

## DASOVIC, Nick — Midfield

H: 6 1 W: 12 04 b.Vancouver 5-12-68

*Source:* Trelleborg.

| | | | |
|---|---|---|---|
| 1996–97 | St Johnstone | 14 | 0 |
| 1997–98 | St Johnstone | 19 | 0 |
| **Total:** | | **33** | **0** |

## DAVENPORT, Peter — Midfield

H: 5 11 W: 12 10 b.Birkenhead 24-3-61

*Source:* Everton, Cammell Laird. *Honours:* England B, 1 full cap.

| | | | |
|---|---|---|---|
| 1981–82 | Nottingham F | 5 | 4 |
| 1982–83 | Nottingham F | 18 | 6 |
| 1983–84 | Nottingham F | 33 | 15 |
| 1984–85 | Nottingham F | 35 | 16 |
| 1985–86 | Nottingham F | 27 | 13 |
| 1985–86 | Manchester U | 11 | 1 |
| 1986–87 | Manchester U | 39 | 14 |

| | | | |
|---|---|---|---|
| 1987–88 | Manchester U | 34 | 5 |
| 1988–89 | Manchester U | 8 | 2 |
| 1988–89 | Middlesbrough | 24 | 4 |
| 1989–90 | Middlesbrough | 35 | 3 |
| 1990–91 | Sunderland | 29 | 7 |
| 1991–92 | Sunderland | 36 | 4 |
| 1992–93 | Sunderland | 34 | 4 |
| 1993–94 | Airdrie | 38 | 9 |
| 1994–95 | St Johnstone | 22 | 4 |
| 1994–95 | Stockport Co | 6 | 1 |
| From Southport. | | | |
| 1997–98 | Macclesfield T | 4 | 1 |
| **Total:** | | **438** | **113** |

## DAVEY, Simon — Midfield

H: 5 10 W: 11 02 b.Swansea 1-10-70

*Source:* Trainee.

| | | | |
|---|---|---|---|
| 1986–87 | Swansea C | 1 | 0 |
| 1987–88 | Swansea C | 4 | 0 |
| 1988–89 | Swansea C | 3 | 0 |
| 1989–90 | Swansea C | 18 | 2 |
| 1990–91 | Swansea C | 18 | 2 |
| 1991–92 | Swansea C | 5 | 0 |
| 1992–93 | Carlisle U | 38 | 5 |
| 1993–94 | Carlisle U | 42 | 9 |
| 1994–95 | Carlisle U | 25 | 4 |
| 1994–95 | Preston NE | 13 | 3 |
| 1995–96 | Preston NE | 38 | 10 |
| 1996–97 | Preston NE | 37 | 6 |
| 1997–98 | Preston NE | 18 | 2 |
| 1997–98 | Darlington (loan) | 11 | 0 |
| **Total:** | | **271** | **43** |

## DAVIDSON, Callum — Defender

H: 5 10 W: 11 00 b.Stirling 25-6-76

*Source:* 'S' Form. *Honours:* Scotland Under-21.

| | | | |
|---|---|---|---|
| 1994–95 | St Johnstone | 7 | 1 |
| 1995–96 | St Johnstone | 2 | 0 |
| 1996–97 | St Johnstone | 20 | 2 |
| 1997–98 | St Johnstone | 15 | 1 |
| 1997–98 | Blackburn R | 1 | 0 |
| **Total:** | | **45** | **4** |

## DAVIDSON, Ross — Defender

H: 5 9 W: 11 06 b.Chertsey 13-11-73

*Source:* Walton & Hersham. *Honours:*

| | | | |
|---|---|---|---|
| 1993–94 | Sheffield U | 0 | 0 |
| 1994–95 | Sheffield U | 1 | 0 |
| 1995–96 | Sheffield U | 1 | 0 |
| 1995–96 | Chester C | 19 | 1 |
| 1996–97 | Chester C | 40 | 2 |
| 1997–98 | Chester C | 24 | 1 |
| **Total:** | | **85** | **4** |

## DAVIES, Billy — Midfield

H: 5 6 W: 10 09 b.Glasgow 31-5-64

*Source:* School.

| | | | |
|---|---|---|---|
| 1980–81 | Rangers | 0 | 0 |
| 1981–82 | Rangers | 4 | 0 |
| 1982–83 | Rangers | 4 | 0 |
| 1983–84 | Rangers | 3 | 1 |
| 1984–85 | Rangers | 0 | 0 |
| 1985–86 | Rangers | 0 | 0 |
| From IF Elfsborg. | | | |
| 1987–88 | St Mirren | 18 | 0 |
| 1988–89 | St Mirren | 27 | 4 |
| 1989–90 | St Mirren | 29 | 1 |
| 1990–91 | Lincoln C | 6 | 0 |
| 1990–91 | Dunfermline Ath | 26 | 0 |
| 1991–92 | Dunfermline Ath | 33 | 0 |
| 1992–93 | Dunfermline Ath | 41 | 10 |
| 1993–94 | Dunfermline Ath | 4 | 0 |
| 1993–94 | Motherwell | 10 | 0 |
| 1994–95 | Motherwell | 31 | 4 |
| 1995–96 | Motherwell | 33 | 2 |
| 1996–97 | Motherwell | 25 | 1 |
| 1997–98 | Motherwell | 17 | 2 |
| **Total:** | | **311** | **25** |

## DAVIES, Darren — Defender

H: 5 8 W: 11 07 b.Port Talbot 13-8-78

*Source:* Trainee.

| | | | |
|---|---|---|---|
| 1995–96 | Tottenham H | 0 | 0 |
| 1996–97 | Tottenham H | 0 | 0 |
| 1997–98 | Tottenham H | 0 | 0 |

## DAVIES, Gareth — Defender

H: 6 1 W: 11 03 b.Hereford 11-12-73

*Source:* Trainee. *Honours:* Wales Under-21.

| | | | |
|---|---|---|---|
| 1991–92 | Hereford U | 4 | 0 |
| 1992–93 | Hereford U | 32 | 1 |
| 1993–94 | Hereford U | 31 | 0 |
| 1994–95 | Hereford U | 28 | 0 |
| 1995–96 | Crystal Palace | 20 | 2 |
| 1996–97 | Crystal Palace | 6 | 0 |
| 1996–97 | Cardiff C (loan) | 6 | 2 |
| 1997–98 | Crystal Palace | 1 | 0 |
| 1997–98 | Reading | 18 | 0 |
| **Total:** | | **146** | **5** |

## DAVIES, Glen — Defender

H: 6 2 W: 13 08 b.Brighton 20-7-76

*Source:* Trainee.

| | | | |
|---|---|---|---|
| 1994–95 | Burnley | 0 | 0 |
| 1995–96 | Burnley | 0 | 0 |
| 1996–97 | Hartlepool U | 32 | 1 |
| 1997–98 | Hartlepool U | 20 | 0 |
| **Total:** | | **52** | **1** |

## DAVIES, Kevin — Forward

H: 6 0 W: 13 11 b.Sheffield 26-3-77

*Source:* Trainee. *Honours:* England Youth, Under-21.

| | | | |
|---|---|---|---|
| 1993–94 | Chesterfield | 24 | 4 |
| 1994–95 | Chesterfield | 41 | 11 |
| 1995–96 | Chesterfield | 30 | 4 |
| 1996–97 | Chesterfield | 34 | 3 |
| 1996–97 | Southampton | 0 | 0 |
| 1997–98 | Southampton | 25 | 9 |
| **Total:** | | **154** | **31** |

## DAVIES, Kevin — Midfield

H: 5 11 W: 12 00 b.Sheffield 15-11-78

*Source:* Trainee.

| | | | |
|---|---|---|---|
| 1997–98 | Sheffield U | 0 | 0 |

## DAVIES, Lawrence — Forward

H: 6 1 W: 11 11 b.Abergavenny 3-9-77

*Source:* Trainee.

| | | | |
|---|---|---|---|
| 1996–97 | Leeds U | 0 | 0 |
| 1997–98 | Bradford C | 4 | 0 |
| 1997–98 | Darlington (loan) | 2 | 0 |
| **Total:** | | **6** | **0** |

## DAVIES, Simon — Midfield

H: 6 0 W: 12 03 b.Winsford 23-4-74

*Source:* Trainee. *Honours:* Wales 1 full cap.

| | | | |
|---|---|---|---|
| 1992–93 | Manchester U | 0 | 0 |
| 1993–94 | Manchester U | 0 | 0 |
| 1993–94 | Exeter C (loan) | 6 | 1 |
| 1994–95 | Manchester U | 5 | 0 |
| 1995–96 | Manchester U | 6 | 0 |
| 1996–97 | Manchester U | 0 | 0 |
| 1996–97 | Huddersfield T (loan) | 3 | 0 |
| 1997–98 | Luton T | 20 | 1 |
| **Total:** | | **40** | **2** |

## DAVIES, Simon — Midfield

H: 5 10 W: 11 04 b.Haverfordwest 23-10-79

*Source:* Trainee.

| | | | |
|---|---|---|---|
| 1997–98 | Peterborough U | 6 | 0 |
| **Total:** | | **6** | **0** |

## DAVIS, Craig — Goalkeeper

H: 6 2 W: 12 00 b.Rotherham 12-10-77

*Source:* Trainee.

| | | | |
|---|---|---|---|
| 1996–97 | Rotherham U | 0 | 0 |
| 1997–98 | Rotherham U | 0 | 0 |
| 1997–98 | Doncaster R | 15 | 0 |
| **Total:** | | **15** | **0** |

## DAVIS, Kelvin — Goalkeeper

H: 6 1 W: 14 00 b.Bedford 29-9-76

*Source:* Trainee. *Honours:* England Youth, Under-21.

| | | | |
|---|---|---|---|
| 1993–94 | Luton T | 1 | 0 |
| 1994–95 | Luton T | 9 | 0 |
| 1994–95 | Torquay U (loan) | 2 | 0 |
| 1995–96 | Luton T | 6 | 0 |
| 1996–97 | Luton T | 0 | 0 |
| 1997–98 | Luton T | 32 | 0 |
| 1997–98 | Hartlepool U (loan) | 2 | 0 |
| **Total:** | | **52** | **0** |

## DAVIS, Kori — Defender

H: 6 0 W: 11 11 b.Wegburg 19-2-79

*Source:* Trainee.

| | | | |
|---|---|---|---|
| 1997–98 | Norwich C | 0 | 0 |

## DAVIS, Neil — Forward

H: 5 10 W: 11 07 b.Bloxwich 15-8-73

*Source:* Redditch U.

| | | | |
|---|---|---|---|
| 1991–92 | Aston Villa | 0 | 0 |
| 1992–93 | Aston Villa | 0 | 0 |
| 1993–94 | Aston Villa | 0 | 0 |
| 1994–95 | Aston Villa | 0 | 0 |
| 1995–96 | Aston Villa | 2 | 0 |
| 1996–97 | Aston Villa | 0 | 0 |
| 1996–97 | Wycombe W (loan) | 13 | 0 |
| 1997–98 | Aston Villa | 0 | 0 |
| **Total:** | | **15** | **0** |

## DAVIS, Sol — Defender

H: 5 7 W: 11 00 b.Cheltenham 4-9-79

*Source:* Trainee.

| | | | |
|---|---|---|---|
| 1997–98 | Swindon T | 6 | 0 |
| **Total:** | | **6** | **0** |

## DAVIS, Steve — Defender

H: 6 1 W: 13 06 b.Birmingham 26-7-65

*Source:* Stoke C Apprentice. *Honours:* England Youth.

| | | | |
|---|---|---|---|
| 1983–84 | Crewe Alex | 24 | 0 |
| 1984–85 | Crewe Alex | 40 | 0 |
| 1985–86 | Crewe Alex | 45 | 1 |
| 1986–87 | Crewe Alex | 33 | 0 |
| 1987–88 | Crewe Alex | 3 | 0 |
| 1987–88 | Burnley | 33 | 5 |
| 1988–89 | Burnley | 37 | 0 |
| 1989–90 | Burnley | 31 | 1 |
| 1990–91 | Burnley | 46 | 5 |
| 1991–92 | Barnsley | 9 | 0 |
| 1992–93 | Barnsley | 11 | 0 |
| 1993–94 | Barnsley | 0 | 0 |
| 1994–95 | Barnsley | 36 | 2 |
| 1995–96 | Barnsley | 27 | 5 |
| 1996–97 | Barnsley | 24 | 3 |
| 1997–98 | Barnsley | 0 | 0 |
| 1997–98 | York C (loan) | 2 | 1 |
| 1997–98 | Oxford U | 15 | 2 |
| **Total:** | | **416** | **25** |

## DAVIS, Steve — Defender

H: 6 2 W: 14 07 b.Hexham 30-10-68

*Source:* Trainee.

| | | | |
|---|---|---|---|
| 1987–88 | Southampton | 0 | 0 |
| 1988–89 | Southampton | 0 | 0 |
| 1989–90 | Southampton | 4 | 0 |
| 1989–90 | Burnley (loan) | 9 | 0 |
| 1990–91 | Southampton | 3 | 0 |
| 1990–91 | Notts Co (loan) | 2 | 0 |
| 1991–92 | Burnley | 40 | 6 |
| 1992–93 | Burnley | 37 | 2 |
| 1993–94 | Burnley | 42 | 7 |
| 1994–95 | Burnley | 43 | 7 |
| 1995–96 | Luton T | 36 | 2 |
| 1996–97 | Luton T | 44 | 8 |
| 1997–98 | Luton T | 38 | 5 |
| **Total:** | | **298** | **37** |

## DAVISON, Aidan — Goalkeeper

H: 6 1 W: 13 12 b.Sedgefield 11-5-68

*Source:* Billingham Synthonia. *Honours:* Northern Ireland 3 full caps.

| | | | |
|---|---|---|---|
| 1987–88 | Notts Co | 0 | 0 |
| 1988–89 | Notts Co | 1 | 0 |
| 1989–90 | Notts Co | 0 | 0 |
| 1989–90 | Leyton Orient (loan) | 0 | 0 |
| 1989–90 | Bury | 0 | 0 |
| 1989–90 | Chester C (loan) | 0 | 0 |
| 1990–91 | Bury | 0 | 0 |
| 1990–91 | Blackpool (loan) | 0 | 0 |
| 1991–92 | Millwall | 33 | 0 |
| 1992–93 | Millwall | 1 | 0 |
| 1993–94 | Bolton W | 31 | 0 |
| 1994–95 | Bolton W | 4 | 0 |
| 1995–96 | Bolton W | 2 | 0 |
| 1996–97 | Bolton W | 0 | 0 |
| 1996–97 | Ipswich T (loan) | 0 | 0 |
| 1996–97 | Hull C (loan) | 9 | 0 |
| 1996–97 | Bradford C | 10 | 0 |
| 1997–98 | Grimsby T | 42 | 0 |
| **Total:** | | **133** | **0** |

## DAWS, Nick — Midfield

H: 5 11 W: 13 06 b.Salford 15-3-70

*Source:* Altrincham.

| | | | |
|---|---|---|---|
| 1992–93 | Bury | 36 | 1 |
| 1993–94 | Bury | 37 | 1 |
| 1994–95 | Bury | 34 | 2 |
| 1995–96 | Bury | 37 | 1 |
| 1996–97 | Bury | 46 | 2 |
| 1997–98 | Bury | 46 | 2 |
| **Total:** | | **236** | **9** |

## DAWSON, Andrew — Midfield

H: 5 9 W: 10 02 b.Northallerton 20-10-78

*Source:* Trainee.

| | | | |
|---|---|---|---|
| 1995–96 | Nottingham F | 0 | 0 |
| 1996–97 | Nottingham F | 0 | 0 |
| 1997–98 | Nottingham F | 0 | 0 |

## DAY, Chris — Goalkeeper

H: 6 2 W: 13 06 b.Whipps Cross 28-7-75

*Source:* Trainee. *Honours:* England Under-21.

| | | | |
|---|---|---|---|
| 1992–93 | Tottenham H | 0 | 0 |
| 1993–94 | Tottenham H | 0 | 0 |
| 1994–95 | Tottenham H | 0 | 0 |
| 1995–96 | Tottenham H | 0 | 0 |

## Day, Jamie

| | | | |
|---|---|---|---|
| 1996–97 | Crystal Palace | 24 | 0 |
| 1997–98 | Watford | 0 | 0 |
| **Total:** | | **24** | **0** |

## DAY, Jamie — Midfield

H: 5 7 W: 10 09 b.Bexley 13-9-79

*Source:* Trainee. *Honours:* England Schools.

| | | | |
|---|---|---|---|
| 1997–98 | Arsenal | 0 | 0 |

## DAY, Richard — Goalkeeper

H: 6 2 W: 13 10 b.Chelmsford 25-1-79

*Source:* Trainee.

| | | | |
|---|---|---|---|
| 1996–97 | Carlisle U | 0 | 0 |
| 1997–98 | Carlisle U | 0 | 0 |

## DE GOEY, Ed — Goalkeeper

H: 6 6 W: 15 04 b.Gouda 20-12-66

*Honours:* Holland 31 full caps.

| | | | |
|---|---|---|---|
| 1985–86 | Sparta | 12 | 0 |
| 1986–87 | Sparta | 34 | 0 |
| 1987–88 | Sparta | 34 | 0 |
| 1988–89 | Sparta | 31 | 0 |
| 1989–90 | Sparta | 34 | 0 |
| 1990–91 | Feyenoord | 34 | 0 |
| 1991–92 | Feyenoord | 34 | 0 |
| 1992–93 | Feyenoord | 33 | 0 |
| 1993–94 | Feyenoord | 34 | 0 |
| 1994–95 | Feyenoord | 32 | 0 |
| 1995–96 | Feyenoord | 34 | 0 |
| 1997–98 | Chelsea | 28 | 0 |
| **Total:** | | **374** | **0** |

## DE SOUZA, Miguel — Forward

H: 5 11 W: 13 08 b.Newham 11-2-70

*Source:* Dagenham & Redbridge.

| | | | |
|---|---|---|---|
| 1993–94 | Birmingham C | 7 | 0 |
| 1994–95 | Birmingham C | 8 | 0 |
| 1994–95 | Bury (loan) | 3 | 0 |
| 1994–95 | Wycombe W | 7 | 6 |
| 1995–96 | Wycombe W | 43 | 18 |
| 1996–97 | Wycombe W | 33 | 6 |
| 1996–97 | Peterborough U | 8 | 2 |
| 1997–98 | Peterborough U | 24 | 3 |
| **Total:** | | **133** | **35** |

## DE ZEEUW, Arjan — Defender

H: 6 1 W: 13 04 b.Castricum 16-4-70

*Source:* Vitesse 22.

| | | | |
|---|---|---|---|
| 1992–93 | Telstar | 30 | 1 |
| 1993–94 | Telstar | 31 | 2 |
| 1994–95 | Telstar | 29 | 1 |
| 1995–96 | Telstar | 12 | 1 |
| 1995–96 | Barnsley | 31 | 1 |
| 1996–97 | Barnsley | 43 | 2 |
| 1997–98 | Barnsley | 26 | 0 |
| **Total:** | | **202** | **8** |

## DEAN, Michael — Midfield

H: 5 9 W: 11 10 b.Weymouth 9-3-78

*Source:* Trainee.

| | | | |
|---|---|---|---|
| 1995–96 | Bournemouth | 5 | 0 |
| 1996–97 | Bournemouth | 12 | 0 |
| 1997–98 | Bournemouth | 8 | 0 |
| **Total:** | | **25** | **0** |

## DEANE, Brian — Forward

H: 6 3 W: 12 07 b.Leeds 7-2-68

*Source:* Apprentice. *Honours:* England B, 3 full caps.

| | | | |
|---|---|---|---|
| 1985–86 | Doncaster R | 3 | 0 |
| 1986–87 | Doncaster R | 20 | 2 |
| 1987–88 | Doncaster R | 43 | 10 |
| 1988–89 | Sheffield U | 43 | 22 |
| 1989–90 | Sheffield U | 45 | 21 |
| 1990–91 | Sheffield U | 38 | 13 |
| 1991–92 | Sheffield U | 30 | 12 |
| 1992–93 | Sheffield U | 41 | 14 |
| 1993–94 | Leeds U | 41 | 11 |
| 1994–95 | Leeds U | 35 | 9 |
| 1995–96 | Leeds U | 34 | 7 |
| 1996–97 | Leeds U | 28 | 5 |
| 1997–98 | Sheffield U | 24 | 11 |
| **Total:** | | **425** | **137** |

## DEARDEN, Kevin — Goalkeeper

H: 5 11 W: 12 06 b.Luton 8-3-70

*Source:* Trainee.

| | | | |
|---|---|---|---|
| 1988–89 | Tottenham H | 0 | 0 |
| 1988–89 | Cambridge U (loan) | 15 | 0 |
| 1989–90 | Tottenham H | 0 | 0 |
| 1989–90 | Hartlepool U (loan) | 10 | 0 |
| 1989–90 | Oxford U (loan) | 0 | 0 |
| 1989–90 | Swindon T (loan) | 1 | 0 |
| 1990–91 | Tottenham H | 0 | 0 |
| 1990–91 | Peterborough U (loan) | 7 | 0 |
| 1990–91 | Hull C (loan) | 3 | 0 |

| | | | |
|---|---|---|---|
| 1991–92 | Tottenham H | 0 | 0 |
| 1991–92 | Rochdale (loan) | 2 | 0 |
| 1991–92 | Birmingham C (loan) | 12 | 0 |
| 1992–93 | Tottenham H | 1 | 0 |
| 1992–93 | Portsmouth (loan) | 0 | 0 |
| 1993–94 | Tottenham H | 0 | 0 |
| 1993–94 | Brentford | 35 | 0 |
| 1994–95 | Brentford | 43 | 0 |
| 1995–96 | Brentford | 41 | 0 |
| 1996–97 | Brentford | 44 | 0 |
| 1997–98 | Brentford | 35 | 0 |
| **Total:** | | **249** | **0** |

## DEBENHAM, Rob — Defender

H: 5 8 W: 10 09 b.Doncaster 28-11-79

*Source:* Trainee.

| | | | |
|---|---|---|---|
| 1997–98 | Doncaster R | 6 | 0 |
| **Total:** | | **6** | **0** |

## DELANY, Dean — Goalkeeper

b.Dublin 15-9-80

| | | | |
|---|---|---|---|
| 1997–98 | Everton | 0 | 0 |

## DELAP, Rory — Midfield

H: 6 0 W: 13 00 b.Sutton Coldfield 6-7-76

*Source:* Trainee. *Honours:* Eire 3 full caps.

| | | | |
|---|---|---|---|
| 1992–93 | Carlisle U | 1 | 0 |
| 1993–94 | Carlisle U | 1 | 0 |
| 1994–95 | Carlisle U | 3 | 0 |
| 1995–96 | Carlisle U | 19 | 3 |
| 1996–97 | Carlisle U | 32 | 4 |
| 1997–98 | Carlisle U | 9 | 0 |
| 1997–98 | Derby Co | 13 | 0 |
| **Total:** | | **78** | **7** |

## DELLAS, Traianos — Defender

H: 6 4 W: 15 00 b.Salonika 31-1-76

*Source:* Aris Salonika.

| | | | |
|---|---|---|---|
| 1997–98 | Sheffield U | 9 | 0 |
| **Total:** | | **9** | **0** |

## DEMPSEY, Gary — Midfield

b.Wexford 15-1-81

*Source:* Trainee.

| | | | |
|---|---|---|---|
| 1997–98 | Everton | 0 | 0 |

## DEMPSEY, Mark — Defender

H: 5 8 W: 11 02 b.Dublin 10-12-72

*Source:* Trainee. *Honours:* Eire Under-21.

| | | | |
|---|---|---|---|
| 1990–91 | Gillingham | 2 | 0 |
| 1991–92 | Gillingham | 30 | 2 |
| 1992–93 | Gillingham | 16 | 0 |
| 1993–94 | Gillingham | 0 | 0 |
| 1994–95 | Leyton Orient | 43 | 1 |
| 1995–96 | Shrewsbury T | 28 | 2 |
| 1996–97 | Shrewsbury T | 40 | 0 |
| 1997–98 | Shrewsbury T | 12 | 1 |
| **Total:** | | **171** | **6** |

## DEN BIEMAN, Ivo — Midfield

H: 6 2 W: 12 10 b.Wamel 4-2-67

*Source:* SV Leones.

| | | | |
|---|---|---|---|
| 1990–91 | Montrose | 36 | 5 |
| 1991–92 | Montrose | 42 | 6 |
| 1992–93 | Dundee | 24 | 3 |
| 1993–94 | Dunfermline Ath | 41 | 3 |
| 1994–95 | Dunfermline Ath | 31 | 5 |
| 1995–96 | Dunfermline Ath | 26 | 1 |
| 1996–97 | Dunfermline Ath | 28 | 1 |
| 1997–98 | Dunfermline Ath | 25 | 0 |
| **Total:** | | **253** | **24** |

## DENHAM, Greig — Defender

H: 6 0 W: 12 02 b.Glasgow 5-10-76

*Source:* Cumbernauld Utd.

| | | | |
|---|---|---|---|
| 1994–95 | Motherwell | 0 | 0 |
| 1995–96 | Motherwell | 13 | 0 |
| 1996–97 | Motherwell | 9 | 0 |
| 1997–98 | Motherwell | 18 | 0 |
| **Total:** | | **40** | **0** |

## DENNIS, Kevin — Midfield

H: 5 10 W: 12 00 b.Islington 14-12-76

*Source:* Arsenal Trainee.

| | | | |
|---|---|---|---|
| 1996–97 | Brentford | 12 | 0 |
| 1997–98 | Brentford | 5 | 0 |
| **Total:** | | **17** | **0** |

## DENNIS, Shaun — Defender

H: 6 1 W: 13 07 b.Kirkcaldy 20-12-69

*Source:* Lochgelly Albert. *Honours:* Scotland Under-21.

| | | | |
|---|---|---|---|
| 1988–89 | Raith R | 10 | 0 |
| 1989–90 | Raith R | 18 | 0 |
| 1990–91 | Raith R | 35 | 1 |

| | | | |
|---|---|---|---|
| 1991–92 | Raith R | 42 | 0 |
| 1992–93 | Raith R | 31 | 1 |
| 1993–94 | Raith R | 43 | 3 |
| 1994–95 | Raith R | 26 | 1 |
| 1995–96 | Raith R | 25 | 0 |
| 1996–97 | Raith R | 16 | 0 |
| 1996–97 | Hibernian | 4 | 1 |
| 1997–98 | Hibernian | 5 | 0 |
| **Total:** | | **255** | **7** |

## DENYS, Ryan — Forward

b.Brentford 16-8-78

*Source:* Trainee.

| | | | |
|---|---|---|---|
| 1997–98 | Brentford | 19 | 1 |
| **Total:** | | **19** | **1** |

## DERRY, Shaun — Midfield

H: 5 10 W: 10 13 b.Nottingham 6-12-77

*Source:* Trainee.

| | | | |
|---|---|---|---|
| 1995–96 | Notts Co | 12 | 0 |
| 1996–97 | Notts Co | 39 | 2 |
| 1997–98 | Notts Co | 28 | 2 |
| 1997–98 | Sheffield U | 12 | 0 |
| **Total:** | | **91** | **4** |

## DEVANEY, Martin — Midfield

H: 5 10 W: 11 12 b.Cheltenham 1-6-80

*Source:* Trainee.

| | | | |
|---|---|---|---|
| 1997–98 | Coventry C | 0 | 0 |

## DEVINE, Sean — Forward

H: 6 0 W: 13 08 b.Lewisham 6-9-72

*Source:* Omonia.

| | | | |
|---|---|---|---|
| 1995–96 | Barnet | 35 | 19 |
| 1996–97 | Barnet | 31 | 11 |
| 1997–98 | Barnet | 40 | 16 |
| **Total:** | | **106** | **46** |

## DEVITO, Claudio — Forward

H: 6 1 W: 12 02 b.Peterborough 21-7-78

*Source:* Trainee.

| | | | |
|---|---|---|---|
| 1996–97 | Northampton T | 0 | 0 |
| 1997–98 | Northampton T | 0 | 0 |
| 1997–98 | Barnet | 1 | 0 |
| **Total:** | | **1** | **0** |

## DEVLIN, Mark — Midfield

H: 5 10 W: 11 13 b.Irvine 8-1-73

*Source:* Trainee.

| | | | |
|---|---|---|---|
| 1990–91 | Stoke C | 21 | 2 |
| 1991–92 | Stoke C | 0 | 0 |
| 1992–93 | Stoke C | 3 | 0 |
| 1993–94 | Stoke C | 0 | 0 |
| 1994–95 | Stoke C | 0 | 0 |
| 1995–96 | Stoke C | 10 | 0 |
| 1996–97 | Stoke C | 21 | 0 |
| 1997–98 | Stoke C | 0 | 0 |
| 1997–98 | Exeter C (loan) | 33 | 2 |
| **Total:** | | **88** | **4** |

## DEVLIN, Paul — Midfield

H: 5 8 W: 11 05 b.Birmingham 14-4-72

*Source:* Stafford R.

| | | | |
|---|---|---|---|
| 1991–92 | Notts Co | 2 | 0 |
| 1992–93 | Notts Co | 32 | 3 |
| 1993–94 | Notts Co | 41 | 7 |
| 1994–95 | Notts Co | 40 | 9 |
| 1995–96 | Notts Co | 26 | 6 |
| 1995–96 | Birmingham C | 16 | 7 |
| 1996–97 | Birmingham C | 38 | 16 |
| 1997–98 | Birmingham C | 22 | 5 |
| 1997–98 | Sheffield U | 10 | 1 |
| **Total:** | | **227** | **54** |

## DEVOS, Jason — Defender

H: 6 4 W: 13 07 b.Ontario 2-1-74

*Source:* Montreal Impact. *Honours:* Canada 30 full caps.

| | | | |
|---|---|---|---|
| 1996–97 | Darlington | 8 | 0 |
| 1997–98 | Darlington | 24 | 3 |
| **Total:** | | **32** | **3** |

## DEWHURST, Rob — Defender

H: 6 3 W: 14 00 b.Keighley 10-9-71

*Source:* Trainee.

| | | | |
|---|---|---|---|
| 1990–91 | Blackburn R | 13 | 0 |
| 1991–92 | Blackburn R | 0 | 0 |
| 1991–92 | Darlington (loan) | 11 | 1 |
| 1992–93 | Blackburn R | 0 | 0 |
| 1992–93 | Huddersfield T (loan) | 7 | 0 |
| 1993–94 | Blackburn R | 0 | 0 |
| 1993–94 | Hull C | 27 | 2 |
| 1994–95 | Hull C | 41 | 8 |
| 1995–96 | Hull C | 16 | 0 |
| 1996–97 | Hull C | 22 | 0 |
| 1997–98 | Hull C | 24 | 3 |
| **Total:** | | **161** | **14** |

## DI CANIO, Paolo — Midfield

H: 5 9 W: 11 09 b.Rome 9-7-68

*Source:* Milan AC.

| | | | |
|---|---|---|---|
| 1985–86 | Lazio | 0 | 0 |
| 1986–87 | Ternana | 27 | 2 |
| 1987–88 | Lazio | 0 | 0 |
| 1988–89 | Lazio | 30 | 1 |
| 1989–90 | Lazio | 24 | 3 |
| 1990–91 | Juventus | 23 | 3 |
| 1991–92 | Juventus | 24 | 0 |
| 1992–93 | Juventus | 31 | 3 |
| 1993–94 | Napoli | 26 | 5 |
| 1994–95 | Juventus | 0 | 0 |
| 1994–95 | AC Milan | 15 | 1 |
| 1995–96 | AC Milan | 22 | 5 |
| 1996–97 | Celtic | 26 | 12 |
| 1997–98 | Sheffield W | 35 | 12 |
| **Total:** | | **283** | **47** |

## DI LELLA, Gustavo — Midfield

b.Buenos Aires 6-10-73

| | | | |
|---|---|---|---|
| 1997–98 | Darlington | 5 | 0 |
| From Blyth S. | | | |
| 1997–98 | Hartlepool U | 5 | 2 |
| **Total:** | | **10** | **2** |

## DI MATTEO, Roberto — Midfield

H: 5 10 W: 12 00 b.Schaffhausen 29-5-70

*Honours:* Italy 33 full caps, 1 goal.

| | | | |
|---|---|---|---|
| 1988–89 | Schaffhausen | 18 | 0 |
| 1989–90 | Schaffhausen | 31 | 2 |
| 1990–91 | Schaffhausen | 1 | 0 |
| 1991–92 | Zurich | 34 | 6 |
| 1992–93 | Aarau | 32 | 1 |
| 1993–94 | Lazio | 29 | 4 |
| 1994–95 | Lazio | 28 | 1 |
| 1995–96 | Lazio | 31 | 2 |
| 1996–97 | Chelsea | 34 | 7 |
| 1997–98 | Chelsea | 30 | 4 |
| **Total:** | | **268** | **27** |

## DIAZ, Isidro — Midfield

H: 5 7 W: 9 04 b.Valencia 15-5-72

*Source:* Balaguer.

| | | | |
|---|---|---|---|
| 1995–96 | Wigan Ath | 37 | 10 |
| 1996–97 | Wigan Ath | 39 | 6 |
| 1997–98 | Wolverhampton W | 1 | 0 |
| 1997–98 | Wigan Ath | 2 | 0 |
| **Total:** | | **79** | **16** |

## DIBBLE, Andy — Goalkeeper

H: 6 2 W: 16 02 b.Cwmbran 8-5-65

*Source:* Apprentice. *Honours:* Wales Schools, Youth, Under-21, 3 full caps.

| | | | |
|---|---|---|---|
| 1981–82 | Cardiff C | 1 | 0 |
| 1982–83 | Cardiff C | 20 | 0 |
| 1983–84 | Cardiff C | 41 | 0 |
| 1984–85 | Luton T | 13 | 0 |
| 1985–86 | Luton T | 7 | 0 |
| 1985–86 | Sunderland (loan) | 12 | 0 |
| 1986–87 | Luton T | 1 | 0 |
| 1986–87 | Huddersfield T (loan) | 5 | 0 |
| 1987–88 | Luton T | 9 | 0 |
| 1988–89 | Manchester C | 38 | 0 |
| 1989–90 | Manchester C | 31 | 0 |
| 1990–91 | Manchester C | 3 | 0 |
| 1990–91 | Aberdeen (loan) | 5 | 0 |
| 1990–91 | Middlesbrough (loan) | 19 | 0 |
| 1991–92 | Manchester C | 2 | 0 |
| 1991–92 | Bolton W (loan) | 13 | 0 |
| 1991–92 | WBA (loan) | 9 | 0 |
| 1992–93 | Manchester C | 2 | 0 |
| 1992–93 | Oldham Ath (loan) | 0 | 0 |
| 1993–94 | Manchester C | 11 | 0 |
| 1994–95 | Manchester C | 15 | 0 |
| 1995–96 | Manchester C | 0 | 0 |
| 1996–97 | Manchester C | 13 | 0 |
| 1996–97 | Rangers | 7 | 0 |
| 1997–98 | Luton T | 1 | 0 |
| 1997–98 | Middlesbrough | 2 | 0 |
| **Total:** | | **280** | **0** |

## DICHIO, Daniele — Forward

H: 6 3 W: 12 03 b.Hammersmith 19-10-74

*Source:* Trainee. *Honours:* England Schools, Under-21.

| | | | |
|---|---|---|---|
| 1993–94 | QPR | 0 | 0 |
| 1993–94 | Barnet (loan) | 9 | 2 |
| 1994–95 | QPR | 9 | 3 |
| 1995–96 | QPR | 29 | 10 |
| 1996–97 | QPR | 37 | 7 |
| 1997–98 | Sampdoria | 0 | 0 |
| 1997–98 | Lecce | 4 | 1 |
| 1997–98 | Sunderland | 13 | 0 |
| **Total:** | | **101** | **23** |

## DICKINSON, Patrick — Midfield

H: 5 10 W: 10 08 b.Vancouver 6-5-78

*Source:* Trainee.

| | | | |
|---|---|---|---|
| 1996–97 | Hull C | 1 | 0 |
| 1997–98 | Hull C | 3 | 0 |
| **Total:** | | **4** | **0** |

## DICKMAN, Elliot — Defender

H: 5 8 W: 9 08 b.Hexham 11-10-78

*Source:* Trainee. *Honours:* England Schools, Youth.

| | | | |
|---|---|---|---|
| 1996–97 | Sunderland | 0 | 0 |
| 1997–98 | Sunderland | 0 | 0 |

## DICKOV, Paul — Forward

H: 5 5 W: 11 09 b.Glasgow 1-11-72

*Source:* Trainee. *Honours:* Scotland Under-21.

| | | | |
|---|---|---|---|
| 1992–93 | Arsenal | 3 | 2 |
| 1993–94 | Arsenal | 1 | 0 |
| 1993–94 | Luton T (loan) | 15 | 1 |
| 1993–94 | Brighton & HA (loan) | 8 | 5 |
| 1994–95 | Arsenal | 9 | 0 |
| 1995–96 | Arsenal | 7 | 1 |
| 1996–97 | Arsenal | 1 | 0 |
| 1996–97 | Manchester C | 29 | 5 |
| 1997–98 | Manchester C | 30 | 9 |
| **Total:** | | **103** | **23** |

## DICKS, Julian — Defender

H: 5 10 W: 13 00 b.Bristol 8-8-68

*Source:* Apprentice. *Honours:* England Under-21, B.

| | | | |
|---|---|---|---|
| 1985–86 | Birmingham C | 23 | 0 |
| 1986–87 | Birmingham C | 34 | 0 |
| 1987–88 | Birmingham C | 32 | 1 |
| 1987–88 | West Ham U | 8 | 0 |
| 1988–89 | West Ham U | 34 | 2 |
| 1989–90 | West Ham U | 40 | 9 |
| 1990–91 | West Ham U | 13 | 4 |
| 1991–92 | West Ham U | 23 | 3 |
| 1992–93 | West Ham U | 34 | 11 |
| 1993–94 | West Ham U | 7 | 0 |
| 1993–94 | Liverpool | 24 | 3 |
| 1994–95 | Liverpool | 0 | 0 |
| 1994–95 | West Ham U | 29 | 5 |
| 1995–96 | West Ham U | 34 | 10 |
| 1996–97 | West Ham U | 31 | 6 |
| 1997–98 | West Ham U | 0 | 0 |
| **Total:** | | **366** | **54** |

## DIGBY, Fraser — Goalkeeper

H: 6 1 W: 12 12 b.Sheffield 23-4-67

*Source:* Apprentice. *Honours:* England Schools, Youth, Under-21.

| | | | |
|---|---|---|---|
| 1984–85 | Manchester U | 0 | 0 |
| 1985–86 | Manchester U | 0 | 0 |
| 1985–86 | Oldham Ath (loan) | 0 | 0 |
| 1985–86 | Swindon T (loan) | 0 | 0 |
| 1986–87 | Manchester U | 0 | 0 |
| 1986–87 | Swindon T | 39 | 0 |
| 1987–88 | Swindon T | 31 | 0 |
| 1988–89 | Swindon T | 46 | 0 |
| 1989–90 | Swindon T | 45 | 0 |
| 1990–91 | Swindon T | 41 | 0 |
| 1991–92 | Swindon T | 21 | 0 |
| 1992–93 | Swindon T | 33 | 0 |
| 1992–93 | Manchester U (loan) | 0 | 0 |
| 1993–94 | Swindon T | 28 | 0 |
| 1994–95 | Swindon T | 39 | 0 |
| 1995–96 | Swindon T | 25 | 0 |
| 1996–97 | Swindon T | 31 | 0 |
| 1997–98 | Swindon T | 38 | 0 |
| **Total:** | | **417** | **0** |

## DIJKSTRA, Sieb — Goalkeeper

H: 6 5 W: 14 10 b.Kerkrade 20-10-66

*Source:* Roda JC.

| | | | |
|---|---|---|---|
| 1991–92 | Motherwell | 1 | 0 |
| 1992–93 | Motherwell | 35 | 0 |
| 1993–94 | Motherwell | 44 | 0 |
| 1994–95 | QPR | 11 | 0 |
| 1995–96 | QPR | 0 | 0 |
| 1995–96 | Bristol C (loan) | 8 | 0 |
| 1995–96 | Wycombe W (loan) | 13 | 0 |
| 1996–97 | Dundee U | 22 | 0 |
| 1997–98 | Dundee U | 36 | 0 |
| **Total:** | | **170** | **0** |

## DILLON, Paul — Defender

H: 5 9 W: 10 11 b.Limerick 22-10-78

*Source:* Trainee.

| | | | |
|---|---|---|---|
| 1996–97 | Rotherham U | 13 | 1 |
| 1997–98 | Rotherham U | 16 | 0 |
| **Total:** | | **29** | **1** |

## DINNING, Tony — Defender

H: 6 0 W: 12 00 b.Wallsend 12-4-75

*Source:* Trainee.

| | | | |
|---|---|---|---|
| 1993–94 | Newcastle U | 0 | 0 |
| 1994–95 | Stockport Co | 40 | 1 |
| 1995–96 | Stockport Co | 10 | 1 |
| 1996–97 | Stockport Co | 20 | 2 |
| 1997–98 | Stockport Co | 30 | 4 |
| **Total:** | | **100** | **8** |

## DIUK, Wayne — Midfield

H: 5 9 W: 11 00 b.Nottingham 26-5-80

*Source:* Trainee.

| | | | |
|---|---|---|---|
| 1996–97 | Notts Co | 1 | 0 |

| | | | |
|---|---|---|---|
| 1997–98 | Notts Co | 1 | 0 |
| **Total:** | | **2** | **0** |

## DIXON, Alan — Midfield

b.Dublin 9-10-79

*Source:* Trainee.

| | | | |
|---|---|---|---|
| 1996–97 | Wolverhampton W | 0 | 0 |
| 1997–98 | Wolverhampton W | 0 | 0 |

## DIXON, Ben — Defender

H: 6 1 W: 11 00 b.Lincoln 16-9-74

*Source:* Trainee.

| | | | |
|---|---|---|---|
| 1991–92 | Lincoln C | 3 | 0 |
| 1992–93 | Lincoln C | 2 | 0 |
| 1993–94 | Lincoln C | 8 | 0 |
| 1994–95 | Lincoln C | 18 | 0 |
| 1995–96 | Lincoln C | 12 | 0 |
| 1996–97 | Blackpool | 11 | 0 |
| 1997–98 | Blackpool | 7 | 0 |
| **Total:** | | **61** | **0** |

## DIXON, George — Goalkeeper

H: 6 0 W: 14 02 b.Whitehaven 24-10-78

*Source:* Trainee.

| | | | |
|---|---|---|---|
| 1996–97 | Carlisle U | 0 | 0 |
| 1997–98 | Carlisle U | 0 | 0 |

## DIXON, Kerry — Forward

H: 6 1 W: 13 10 b.Luton 24-7-61

*Source:* Tottenham H Apprentice, Dunstable. *Honours:* England Under-21, 8 full caps, 4 goals.

| | | | |
|---|---|---|---|
| 1980–81 | Reading | 39 | 13 |
| 1981–82 | Reading | 42 | 12 |
| 1982–83 | Reading | 35 | 26 |
| 1983–84 | Chelsea | 42 | 28 |
| 1984–85 | Chelsea | 41 | 24 |
| 1985–86 | Chelsea | 38 | 14 |
| 1986–87 | Chelsea | 36 | 10 |
| 1987–88 | Chelsea | 33 | 11 |
| 1988–89 | Chelsea | 39 | 25 |
| 1989–90 | Chelsea | 38 | 20 |
| 1990–91 | Chelsea | 33 | 10 |
| 1991–92 | Chelsea | 35 | 5 |
| 1992–93 | Southampton | 9 | 2 |
| 1992–93 | Luton T (loan) | 17 | 3 |
| 1993–94 | Luton T | 29 | 9 |
| 1994–95 | Luton T | 29 | 7 |
| 1994–95 | Millwall | 9 | 4 |
| 1995–96 | Millwall | 22 | 5 |
| 1995–96 | Watford | 11 | 0 |
| 1996–97 | Doncaster R | 16 | 3 |
| 1997–98 | Doncaster R | 0 | 0 |
| **Total:** | | **593** | **231** |

## DIXON, Kevin — Midfield

H: 5 10 W: 12 11 b.Easington 27-6-80

*Source:* Trainee. *Honours:* England Youth.

| | | | |
|---|---|---|---|
| 1997–98 | Leeds U | 0 | 0 |

## DIXON, Lee — Defender

H: 5 8 W: 11 08 b.Manchester 17-3-64

*Source:* Local. *Honours:* England B, 21 full caps, 1 goal.

| | | | |
|---|---|---|---|
| 1982–83 | Burnley | 3 | 0 |
| 1983–84 | Burnley | 1 | 0 |
| 1983–84 | Chester C | 16 | 1 |
| 1984–85 | Chester | 41 | 0 |
| 1985–86 | Bury | 45 | 5 |
| 1986–87 | Stoke C | 42 | 3 |
| 1987–88 | Stoke C | 29 | 2 |
| 1987–88 | Arsenal | 6 | 0 |
| 1988–89 | Arsenal | 33 | 1 |
| 1989–90 | Arsenal | 38 | 5 |
| 1990–91 | Arsenal | 38 | 5 |
| 1991–92 | Arsenal | 38 | 4 |
| 1992–93 | Arsenal | 29 | 0 |
| 1993–94 | Arsenal | 33 | 0 |
| 1994–95 | Arsenal | 39 | 1 |
| 1995–96 | Arsenal | 38 | 2 |
| 1996–97 | Arsenal | 32 | 2 |
| 1997–98 | Arsenal | 28 | 0 |
| **Total:** | | **529** | **31** |

## DOBBIN, Jim — Midfield

H: 5 9 W: 10 07 b.Dunfermline 17-9-63

*Source:* Whitburn BC. *Honours:* Scotland Youth.

| | | | |
|---|---|---|---|
| 1980–81 | Celtic | 0 | 0 |
| 1981–82 | Celtic | 0 | 0 |
| 1982–83 | Celtic | 0 | 0 |
| 1983–84 | Celtic | 2 | 0 |
| 1983–84 | Motherwell (loan) | 2 | 0 |
| 1983–84 | Doncaster R | 11 | 2 |
| 1984–85 | Doncaster R | 17 | 1 |
| 1985–86 | Doncaster R | 31 | 6 |
| 1986–87 | Doncaster R | 5 | 4 |
| 1986–87 | Barnsley | 30 | 4 |
| 1987–88 | Barnsley | 16 | 2 |
| 1988–89 | Barnsley | 41 | 5 |
| 1989–90 | Barnsley | 28 | 1 |
| 1990–91 | Barnsley | 14 | 0 |
| 1991–92 | Grimsby T | 32 | 6 |
| 1992–93 | Grimsby T | 39 | 6 |
| 1993–94 | Grimsby T | 29 | 4 |

## Dobie, Scott

| | | | |
|---|---|---|---|
| 1994–95 | Grimsby T | 38 | 2 |
| 1995–96 | Grimsby T | 26 | 3 |
| 1996–97 | Rotherham U | 19 | 0 |
| 1997–98 | Doncaster R | 31 | 0 |
| 1997–98 | Scarborough | 1 | 0 |
| 1997–98 | Grimsby T | 2 | 0 |
| **Total:** | | **414** | **46** |

### DOBIE, Scott — Forward

H: 6 1 W: 12 12 b.Workington 10-10-78

*Source:* Trainee.

| | | | |
|---|---|---|---|
| 1996–97 | Carlisle U | 2 | 1 |
| 1997–98 | Carlisle U | 23 | 0 |
| **Total:** | | **25** | **1** |

### DOBSON, Ryan — Defender

b.Wellington 24-9-78

*Source:* Trainee.

| | | | |
|---|---|---|---|
| 1997–98 | Chester C | 6 | 0 |
| **Total:** | | **6** | **0** |

### DOBSON, Tony — Defender

H: 6 1 W: 13 07 b.Coventry 5-2-69

*Source:* Apprentice. *Honours:* England Under-21.

| | | | |
|---|---|---|---|
| 1986–87 | Coventry C | 1 | 0 |
| 1987–88 | Coventry C | 1 | 0 |
| 1988–89 | Coventry C | 16 | 0 |
| 1989–90 | Coventry C | 30 | 0 |
| 1990–91 | Coventry C | 6 | 1 |
| 1990–91 | Blackburn R | 17 | 0 |
| 1991–92 | Blackburn R | 5 | 0 |
| 1992–93 | Blackburn R | 19 | 0 |
| 1993–94 | Blackburn R | 0 | 0 |
| 1993–94 | Portsmouth | 24 | 2 |
| 1994–95 | Portsmouth | 14 | 0 |
| 1994–95 | Oxford U (loan) | 5 | 0 |
| 1995–96 | Portsmouth | 9 | 0 |
| 1995–96 | Peterborough U (loan) | 4 | 0 |
| 1996–97 | Portsmouth | 6 | 0 |
| 1997–98 | WBA | 11 | 0 |
| **Total:** | | **168** | **3** |

### DOBSON, Warren — Goalkeeper

H: 6 1 W: 13 08 b.North Shields 5-11-78

*Source:* QPR Trainee.

| | | | |
|---|---|---|---|
| 1997–98 | Hartlepool U | 1 | 0 |
| **Total:** | | **1** | **0** |

### DODD, Jason — Defender

H: 5 10 W: 12 06 b.Bath 2-11-70

*Source:* Bath C. *Honours:* England Under-21.

| | | | |
|---|---|---|---|
| 1988–89 | Southampton | 0 | 0 |
| 1989–90 | Southampton | 22 | 0 |
| 1990–91 | Southampton | 19 | 0 |
| 1991–92 | Southampton | 28 | 0 |
| 1992–93 | Southampton | 30 | 1 |
| 1993–94 | Southampton | 10 | 0 |
| 1994–95 | Southampton | 26 | 2 |
| 1995–96 | Southampton | 37 | 2 |
| 1996–97 | Southampton | 23 | 1 |
| 1997–98 | Southampton | 36 | 1 |
| **Total:** | | **231** | **7** |

### DODDS, Billy — Forward

H: 5 8 W: 10 10 b.New Cumnock 5-2-69

*Source:* Apprentice. *Honours:* Scotland B, 4 full caps.

| | | | |
|---|---|---|---|
| 1986–87 | Chelsea | 1 | 0 |
| 1987–88 | Chelsea | 0 | 0 |
| 1987–88 | Partick T (loan) | 30 | 9 |
| 1988–89 | Chelsea | 2 | 0 |
| 1989–90 | Dundee | 30 | 13 |
| 1990–91 | Dundee | 37 | 15 |
| 1991–92 | Dundee | 42 | 19 |
| 1992–93 | Dundee | 41 | 16 |
| 1993–94 | Dundee | 24 | 5 |
| 1993–94 | St Johnstone | 20 | 6 |
| 1994–95 | Aberdeen | 35 | 15 |
| 1995–96 | Aberdeen | 31 | 7 |
| 1996–97 | Aberdeen | 31 | 15 |
| 1997–98 | Aberdeeen | 34 | 10 |
| **Total:** | | **358** | **130** |

### DODS, Darren — Defender

H: 6 1 W: 12 13 b.Edinburgh 7-6-75

*Source:* Hutchison Vale BC. *Honours:* Scotland Under-21.

| | | | |
|---|---|---|---|
| 1994–95 | Hibernian | 1 | 0 |
| 1995–96 | Hibernian | 15 | 0 |
| 1996–97 | Hibernian | 20 | 0 |
| 1997–98 | Hibernian | 28 | 1 |
| **Total:** | | **64** | **1** |

### DOHERTY, Gary — Forward

H: 6 1 W: 13 00 b.Donegal 31-1-80

*Source:* Trainee.

| | | | |
|---|---|---|---|
| 1997–98 | Luton T | 10 | 0 |
| **Total:** | | **10** | **0** |

## DOHERTY, George — Forward

b.Derry 20-2-80

*Source:* Trainee.

| | | | |
|---|---|---|---|
| 1997–98 | Manchester C | 0 | 0 |

## DOHERTY, Kevin — Midfield

b.Dublin 18-4-80

| | | | |
|---|---|---|---|
| 1997–98 | Liverpool | 0 | 0 |

## DOHERTY, Martin — Midfield

H: 6 1 W: 12 02 b.Urmston 17-10-78

*Source:* Trainee.

| | | | |
|---|---|---|---|
| 1997–98 | Bolton W | 0 | 0 |

## DOHERTY, Tom — Midfield

H: 5 8 W: 9 13 b.Bristol 17-3-79

*Source:* Trainee.

| | | | |
|---|---|---|---|
| 1997–98 | Bristol C | 30 | 2 |
| **Total:** | | **30** | **2** |

## DOIG, Christopher — Defender

H: 6 2 W: 12 06 b.Dumfries 13-2-81

*Source:* Trainee.

| | | | |
|---|---|---|---|
| 1997–98 | Nottingham F | 0 | 0 |

## DOIG, Kevin — Defender

H: 6 0 W: 12 05 b.Glasgow 6-11-75

*Source:* Troon J.

| | | | |
|---|---|---|---|
| 1995–96 | Kilmarnock | 0 | 0 |
| 1996–97 | Kilmarnock | 0 | 0 |
| 1997–98 | Kilmarnock | 1 | 0 |
| **Total:** | | **1** | **0** |

## DOLAN, Jim — Forward

H: 5 10 W: 10 07 b.Salsburgh 22-2-69

*Source:* Motherwell BC.

| | | | |
|---|---|---|---|
| 1987–88 | Motherwell | 0 | 0 |
| 1988–89 | Motherwell | 5 | 0 |
| 1989–90 | Motherwell | 12 | 0 |
| 1990–91 | Motherwell | 8 | 1 |
| 1991–92 | Motherwell | 32 | 2 |
| 1992–93 | Motherwell | 25 | 2 |
| 1993–94 | Motherwell | 36 | 0 |
| 1994–95 | Motherwell | 31 | 0 |
| 1995–96 | Motherwell | 27 | 0 |
| 1996–97 | Motherwell | 18 | 0 |
| 1996–97 | Dundee U | 13 | 0 |
| 1997–98 | Dundee U | 26 | 0 |
| **Total:** | | **233** | **5** |

## DOMINGUEZ, Jose — Forward

H: 5 3 W: 10 00 b.Lisbon 16-2-74

*Source:* Benfica. *Honours:* Portugal 3 full caps.

| | | | |
|---|---|---|---|
| 1993–94 | Birmingham C | 5 | 0 |
| 1994–95 | Birmingham C | 30 | 3 |
| 1995–96 | Sporting Lisbon | 30 | 1 |
| 1996–97 | Birmingham C | 0 | 0 |
| 1997–98 | Tottenham H | 18 | 2 |
| **Total:** | | **83** | **6** |

## DONALD, Graeme — Forward

H: 6 0 W: 12 01 b.Stirling 14-4-74

*Source:* Gairdoch Utd. *Honours:* Scotland Under-21.

| | | | |
|---|---|---|---|
| 1991–92 | Hibernian | 5 | 3 |
| 1992–93 | Hibernian | 4 | 0 |
| 1993–94 | Hibernian | 6 | 0 |
| 1994–95 | Hibernian | 0 | 0 |
| 1995–96 | Hibernian | 13 | 1 |
| 1996–97 | Hibernian | 11 | 1 |
| 1997–98 | Hibernian | 4 | 0 |
| **Total:** | | **43** | **5** |

## DONALDSON, David — Midfield

H: 5 7 W: 9 08 b.Gravesend 17-12-78

*Source:* Arsenal Trainee.

| | | | |
|---|---|---|---|
| 1997–98 | Bradford C | 0 | 0 |

## DONALDSON, O'Neill — Forward

H: 5 11 W: 12 02 b.Birmingham 24-11-69

*Source:* Hinckley.

| | | | |
|---|---|---|---|
| 1991–92 | Shrewsbury T | 19 | 2 |
| 1992–93 | Shrewsbury T | 0 | 0 |
| 1993–94 | Shrewsbury T | 9 | 2 |
| 1994–95 | Doncaster R | 9 | 2 |
| 1994–95 | Mansfield T (loan) | 4 | 6 |
| 1994–95 | Sheffield W | 1 | 0 |
| 1995–96 | Sheffield W | 3 | 1 |
| 1996–97 | Sheffield W | 5 | 2 |
| 1997–98 | Sheffield W | 5 | 0 |
| 1997–98 | Oxford U (loan) | 6 | 2 |
| 1997–98 | Stoke C | 2 | 0 |
| **Total:** | | **63** | **17** |

## DONCEL, Antonio — Defender

H: 6 0 W: 12 01 b.Lugo 31-1-67

*Source:* Ferrol.

| | | | |
|---|---|---|---|
| 1996–97 | Hull C | 26 | 2 |
| 1997–98 | Hull C | 12 | 0 |
| **Total:** | | **38** | **2** |

## DONIS, George — Midfield

H: 6 0 W: 12 00 b.Greece 29-10-69

*Source:* Panaryiakos. *Honours:* Greece 22 full caps, 4 goals.

| | | | |
|---|---|---|---|
| 1990–91 | Yannina | 22 | 3 |
| 1991–92 | Panathinaikos | 30 | 4 |
| 1992–93 | Panathinaikos | 25 | 7 |
| 1993–94 | Panathinaikos | 24 | 7 |
| 1994–95 | Panathinaikos | 28 | 9 |
| 1995–96 | Panathinaikos | 29 | 7 |
| 1996–97 | Blackburn R | 22 | 2 |
| 1997–98 | Blackburn R | 0 | 0 |
| **Total:** | | **180** | **39** |

## DONLEVY, Andrew — Defender

H: 5 11 W: 10 12 b.Hong Kong 13-4-81

*Source:* Trainee.

| | | | |
|---|---|---|---|
| 1997–98 | Coventry C | 0 | 0 |

## DONNELLY, Mark — Midfield

H: 6 0 W: 11 02 b.Leeds 22-12-79

*Source:* Trainee.

| | | | |
|---|---|---|---|
| 1996–97 | Doncaster R | 2 | 0 |
| 1997–98 | Doncaster R | 9 | 1 |
| **Total:** | | **11** | **1** |

## DONNELLY, Paul — Midfield

b.Dublin 31-8-79

*Source:* Trainee.

| | | | |
|---|---|---|---|
| 1996–97 | Leeds U | 0 | 0 |
| 1997–98 | Leeds U | 0 | 0 |

## DONNELLY, Simon — Forward

H: 5 9 W: 10 12 b.Glasgow 1-12-74

*Source:* Celtic BC. *Honours:* Scotland Under-21, 8 full caps.

| | | | |
|---|---|---|---|
| 1993–94 | Celtic | 12 | 5 |
| 1994–95 | Celtic | 17 | 0 |
| 1995–96 | Celtic | 35 | 6 |
| 1996–97 | Celtic | 29 | 4 |
| 1997–98 | Celtic | 30 | 10 |
| **Total:** | | **123** | **25** |

## DONOVAN, Kevin — Forward

H: 5 8 W: 11 02 b.Halifax 17-12-71

*Source:* Trainee.

| | | | |
|---|---|---|---|
| 1989–90 | Huddersfield T | 1 | 0 |
| 1990–91 | Huddersfield T | 6 | 1 |
| 1991–92 | Huddersfield T | 10 | 0 |
| 1991–92 | Halifax T (loan) | 6 | 0 |
| 1992–93 | Huddersfield T | 3 | 0 |
| 1992–93 | WBA | 32 | 6 |
| 1993–94 | WBA | 37 | 8 |
| 1994–95 | WBA | 33 | 5 |
| 1995–96 | WBA | 34 | 0 |
| 1996–97 | WBA | 32 | 0 |
| 1997–98 | Grimsby T | 46 | 16 |
| **Total:** | | **240** | **36** |

## DONOWA, Lou — Midfield

H: 5 9 W: 11 00 b.Ipswich 24-9-64

*Source:* Apprentice. *Honours:* England Under-21.

| | | | |
|---|---|---|---|
| 1982–83 | Norwich C | 1 | 0 |
| 1983–84 | Norwich C | 25 | 4 |
| 1984–85 | Norwich C | 34 | 7 |
| 1985–86 | Norwich C | 2 | 0 |
| 1985–86 | Stoke C (loan) | 4 | 1 |
| From Coruna, Willem II. | | | |
| 1989–90 | Ipswich T | 23 | 1 |
| 1990–91 | Bristol C | 24 | 3 |
| 1991–92 | Birmingham C | 26 | 2 |
| 1992–93 | Birmingham C | 21 | 2 |
| 1992–93 | Crystal Palace (loan) | 0 | 0 |
| 1992–93 | Burnley (loan) | 4 | 0 |
| 1993–94 | Birmingham C | 21 | 5 |
| 1993–94 | Shrewsbury T (loan) | 4 | 0 |
| 1994–95 | Birmingham C | 31 | 9 |
| 1995–96 | Birmingham C | 13 | 0 |
| 1996–97 | Birmingham C | 4 | 0 |
| 1996–97 | Walsall (loan) | 6 | 1 |
| 1996–97 | Peterborough U | 22 | 1 |
| 1997–98 | Walsall | 6 | 0 |
| **Total:** | | **271** | **36** |

## DOOLAN, John — Midfield

H: 6 1 W: 13 01 b.Liverpool 7-5-74

*Source:* Trainee.

| | | | |
|---|---|---|---|
| 1992–93 | Everton | 0 | 0 |
| 1993–94 | Everton | 0 | 0 |
| 1994–95 | Mansfield T | 24 | 1 |

| | | | |
|---|---|---|---|
| 1995–96 | Mansfield T | 42 | 2 |
| 1996–97 | Mansfield T | 41 | 6 |
| 1997–98 | Mansfield T | 24 | 1 |
| 1997–98 | Barnet | 17 | 0 |
| **Total:** | | **148** | **10** |

## DORIGO, Tony — Defender

H: 5 10 W: 10 10 b.Melbourne 31-12-65

*Source:* Apprentice. *Honours:* England Under-21, B, 15 full caps.

| | | | |
|---|---|---|---|
| 1983–84 | Aston Villa | 1 | 0 |
| 1984–85 | Aston Villa | 31 | 0 |
| 1985–86 | Aston Villa | 38 | 1 |
| 1986–87 | Aston Villa | 41 | 0 |
| 1987–88 | Chelsea | 40 | 0 |
| 1988–89 | Chelsea | 40 | 6 |
| 1989–90 | Chelsea | 35 | 3 |
| 1990–91 | Chelsea | 31 | 2 |
| 1991–92 | Leeds U | 38 | 3 |
| 1992–93 | Leeds U | 33 | 1 |
| 1993–94 | Leeds U | 37 | 0 |
| 1994–95 | Leeds U | 28 | 0 |
| 1995–96 | Leeds U | 17 | 1 |
| 1996–97 | Leeds U | 18 | 0 |
| 1997–98 | Leeds U | 0 | 0 |
| **Total:** | | **428** | **17** |

## DORNER, Mario — Forward

H: 5 10 W: 13 02 b.Baden 21-3-70

*Source:* Susome Dorner, Wustef, Modling. *Honours:* Austria Under-21.

| | | | |
|---|---|---|---|
| 1997–98 | Motherwell | 2 | 0 |
| 1997–98 | Darlington | 27 | 10 |
| **Total:** | | **29** | **10** |

## DOUGLAS, Robert — Goalkeeper

H: 6 3 W: 14 12 b.Lanark 24-4-72

*Source:* Forth Wanderers. *Honours:* Scotland B.

| | | | |
|---|---|---|---|
| 1992–93 | Meadowbank T | 0 | 0 |
| 1993–94 | Meadowbank T | 4 | 0 |
| 1994–95 | Meadowbank T | 8 | 0 |
| 1995–96 | Livingston | 24 | 0 |
| 1996–97 | Livingston | 36 | 0 |
| 1997–98 | Dundee | 36 | 0 |
| **Total:** | | **108** | **0** |

## DOUGLAS, Stuart — Forward

H: 5 8 W: 11 05 b.London 9-4-78

*Source:* Trainee.

| | | | |
|---|---|---|---|
| 1995–96 | Luton T | 8 | 1 |
| 1996–97 | Luton T | 9 | 0 |
| 1997–98 | Luton T | 17 | 1 |
| **Total:** | | **34** | **2** |

## DOW, Andrew — Midfield

H: 5 9 W: 11 00 b.Dundee 7-2-73

*Source:* Sporting Club 85. *Honours:* Scotland Under-21.

| | | | |
|---|---|---|---|
| 1990–91 | Dundee | 0 | 0 |
| 1991–92 | Dundee | 4 | 0 |
| 1992–93 | Dundee | 14 | 1 |
| 1993–94 | Chelsea | 14 | 0 |
| 1994–95 | Chelsea | 0 | 0 |
| 1994–95 | Bradford C (loan) | 5 | 0 |
| 1995–96 | Chelsea | 1 | 0 |
| 1995–96 | Hibernian | 8 | 1 |
| 1996–97 | Hibernian | 22 | 2 |
| 1997–98 | Hibernian | 32 | 0 |
| **Total:** | | **100** | **4** |

## DOWELL, Wayne — Defender

H: 5 10 W: 11 13 b.Co Durham 28-12-73

*Source:* Trainee.

| | | | |
|---|---|---|---|
| 1992–93 | Burnley | 0 | 0 |
| 1993–94 | Burnley | 0 | 0 |
| 1994–95 | Burnley | 5 | 0 |
| 1995–96 | Burnley | 1 | 0 |
| 1995–96 | Carlisle U (loan) | 7 | 0 |
| 1996–97 | Rochdale | 7 | 0 |
| 1997–98 | Doncaster R | 1 | 0 |
| **Total:** | | **21** | **0** |

## DOWIE, Iain — Forward

H: 6 1 W: 13 07 b.Hatfield 9-1-65

*Source:* Hendon. *Honours:* Northern Ireland Under-21, 49 full caps, 11 goals.

| | | | |
|---|---|---|---|
| 1988–89 | Luton T | 8 | 0 |
| 1989–90 | Luton T | 29 | 9 |
| 1989–90 | Fulham (loan) | 5 | 1 |
| 1990–91 | Luton T | 29 | 7 |
| 1990–91 | West Ham U | 12 | 4 |
| 1991–92 | West Ham U | 0 | 0 |
| 1991–92 | Southampton | 30 | 9 |
| 1992–93 | Southampton | 36 | 11 |
| 1993–94 | Southampton | 39 | 5 |
| 1994–95 | Southampton | 17 | 5 |
| 1994–95 | Crystal Palace | 15 | 4 |
| 1995–96 | Crystal Palace | 4 | 2 |
| 1995–96 | West Ham U | 33 | 8 |
| 1996–97 | West Ham U | 23 | 0 |

| | | | |
|---|---|---|---|
| 1997–98 | West Ham U | 12 | 0 |
| 1997–98 | QPR | 11 | 1 |
| **Total:** | | **303** | **66** |

## DOWNEY, Glen — Defender

H: 6 1 W: 11 13 b.Newcastle 20-9-78

| | | | |
|---|---|---|---|
| 1997–98 | Hartlepool U | 0 | 0 |

## DOYLE, Kevin — Defender

H: 5 11 W: 11 10 b.Wexford 13-10-80

*Source:* Trainee.

| | | | |
|---|---|---|---|
| 1997–98 | Leeds U | 0 | 0 |

## DOYLE, Maurice — Midfield

H: 5 8 W: 10 07 b.Ellesmere Port 17-10-69

*Source:* Trainee.

| | | | |
|---|---|---|---|
| 1987–88 | Crewe Alex | 4 | 0 |
| 1988–89 | Crewe Alex | 4 | 2 |
| 1989–90 | QPR | 0 | 0 |
| 1990–91 | Crewe Alex (loan) | 7 | 2 |
| 1990–91 | Wolverhampton W (loan) | 0 | 0 |
| 1991–92 | QPR | 0 | 0 |
| 1992–93 | QPR | 5 | 0 |
| 1993–94 | QPR | 1 | 0 |
| 1994–95 | QPR | 0 | 0 |
| 1994–95 | Millwall | 0 | 0 |
| 1995–96 | Millwall | 18 | 0 |
| 1996–97 | Millwall | 28 | 1 |
| 1997–98 | Millwall | 20 | 0 |
| **Total:** | | **87** | **5** |

## DOZZELL, Jason — Midfield

H: 6 1 W: 13 08 b.Ipswich 9-12-67

*Source:* School. *Honours:* England Youth, Under-21.

| | | | |
|---|---|---|---|
| 1983–84 | Ipswich T | 5 | 1 |
| 1984–85 | Ipswich T | 14 | 2 |
| 1985–86 | Ipswich T | 41 | 3 |
| 1986–87 | Ipswich T | 42 | 2 |
| 1987–88 | Ipswich T | 39 | 1 |
| 1988–89 | Ipswich T | 29 | 11 |
| 1989–90 | Ipswich T | 46 | 8 |
| 1990–91 | Ipswich T | 30 | 6 |
| 1991–92 | Ipswich T | 45 | 11 |
| 1992–93 | Ipswich T | 41 | 7 |
| 1993–94 | Tottenham H | 32 | 8 |
| 1994–95 | Tottenham H | 7 | 0 |
| 1995–96 | Tottenham H | 28 | 3 |
| 1996–97 | Tottenham H | 17 | 2 |
| 1997–98 | Ipswich T | 8 | 1 |
| 1997–98 | Northampton T | 21 | 4 |
| **Total:** | | **445** | **70** |

## DRAPER, Mark — Midfield

H: 5 10 W: 12 04 b.Long Eaton 11-11-70

*Source:* Trainee. *Honours:* England Under-21.

| | | | |
|---|---|---|---|
| 1988–89 | Notts Co | 20 | 3 |
| 1989–90 | Notts Co | 34 | 3 |
| 1990–91 | Notts Co | 45 | 9 |
| 1991–92 | Notts Co | 35 | 1 |
| 1992–93 | Notts Co | 44 | 11 |
| 1993–94 | Notts Co | 44 | 13 |
| 1994–95 | Leicester C | 39 | 5 |
| 1995–96 | Aston Villa | 36 | 2 |
| 1996–97 | Aston Villa | 29 | 0 |
| 1997–98 | Aston Villa | 31 | 3 |
| **Total:** | | **357** | **50** |

## DREW, Padraig — Forward

b.Dublin 7-6-80

*Source:* Trainee.

| | | | |
|---|---|---|---|
| 1997–98 | Everton | 0 | 0 |

## DREYER, John — Defender

H: 6 1 W: 13 02 b.Alnwick 11-6-63

*Source:* Wallingford T.

| | | | |
|---|---|---|---|
| 1984–85 | Oxford U | 0 | 0 |
| 1985–86 | Oxford U | 0 | 0 |
| 1985–86 | Torquay U (loan) | 5 | 0 |
| 1985–86 | Fulham (loan) | 12 | 2 |
| 1986–87 | Oxford U | 25 | 2 |
| 1987–88 | Oxford U | 35 | 0 |
| 1988–89 | Luton T | 18 | 1 |
| 1989–90 | Luton T | 38 | 2 |
| 1990–91 | Luton T | 38 | 3 |
| 1991–92 | Luton T | 42 | 2 |
| 1992–93 | Luton T | 38 | 2 |
| 1993–94 | Luton T | 40 | 3 |
| 1994–95 | Stoke C | 18 | 2 |
| 1994–95 | Bolton W (loan) | 2 | 0 |
| 1995–96 | Stoke C | 19 | 0 |
| 1996–97 | Stoke C | 12 | 1 |
| 1996–97 | Bradford C | 28 | 1 |
| 1997–98 | Bradford C | 17 | 0 |
| **Total:** | | **387** | **21** |

## DRUCE, Mark — Forward

H: 6 0 W: 12 07 b.Oxford 3-3-74

*Source:* Trainee.

| | | | |
|---|---|---|---|
| 1991–92 | Oxford U | 2 | 0 |
| 1992–93 | Oxford U | 4 | 1 |
| 1993–94 | Oxford U | 19 | 0 |
| 1994–95 | Oxford U | 19 | 3 |
| 1995–96 | Oxford U | 8 | 0 |
| 1996–97 | Oxford U | 0 | 0 |
| 1996–97 | Rotherham U | 20 | 4 |
| 1997–98 | Rotherham U | 14 | 0 |
| **Total:** | | **86** | **8** |

## DRURY, Adam — Defender

H: 5 10 W: 11 06 b.Cottenham 29-8-78

*Source:* Trainee.

| | | | |
|---|---|---|---|
| 1995–96 | Peterborough U | 1 | 0 |
| 1996–97 | Peterborough U | 5 | 1 |
| 1997–98 | Peterborough U | 31 | 0 |
| **Total:** | | **37** | **1** |

## DRYDEN, Richard — Defender

H: 6 0 W: 13 11 b.Stroud 14-6-69

*Source:* Trainee.

| | | | |
|---|---|---|---|
| 1986–87 | Bristol R | 6 | 0 |
| 1987–88 | Bristol R | 6 | 0 |
| 1988–89 | Bristol R | 1 | 0 |
| 1988–89 | Exeter C | 21 | 0 |
| 1989–90 | Exeter C | 30 | 7 |
| 1990–91 | Manchester C (loan) | 0 | 0 |
| 1991–92 | Notts Co | 29 | 1 |
| 1992–93 | Notts Co | 2 | 0 |
| 1992–93 | Plymouth Arg (loan) | 5 | 0 |
| 1992–93 | Birmingham C | 11 | 0 |
| 1993–94 | Birmingham C | 34 | 0 |
| 1994–95 | Birmingham C | 3 | 0 |
| 1994–95 | Bristol C | 19 | 1 |
| 1995–96 | Bristol C | 18 | 1 |
| 1996–97 | Southampton | 29 | 1 |
| 1997–98 | Southampton | 13 | 0 |
| **Total:** | | **227** | **11** |

## DRYSDALE, Jason — Defender

H: 5 10 W: 12 00 b.Bristol 17-11-70

*Source:* Trainee. *Honours:* England Youth. Football League.

| | | | |
|---|---|---|---|
| 1988–89 | Watford | 0 | 0 |
| 1989–90 | Watford | 20 | 0 |
| 1990–91 | Watford | 30 | 0 |
| 1991–92 | Watford | 37 | 5 |
| 1992–93 | Watford | 39 | 6 |
| 1993–94 | Watford | 19 | 0 |
| 1994–95 | Newcastle U | 0 | 0 |
| 1994–95 | Swindon T | 1 | 0 |
| 1995–96 | Swindon T | 13 | 0 |
| 1996–97 | Swindon T | 14 | 0 |
| 1997–98 | Swindon T | 14 | 0 |
| 1997–98 | Northampton T | 1 | 0 |
| **Total:** | | **188** | **11** |

## D'JARTE, Sergio — Midfield

b.Brazil 20-1-66

*Source:* Boavista.

| | | | |
|---|---|---|---|
| 1997–98 | Dunfermline Ath | 16 | 0 |
| **Total:** | | **16** | **0** |

## DUBERRY, Michael — Defender

H: 6 1 W: 14 00 b.Enfield 14-10-75

*Source:* Trainee. *Honours:* England Under-21.

| | | | |
|---|---|---|---|
| 1993–94 | Chelsea | 1 | 0 |
| 1994–95 | Chelsea | 0 | 0 |
| 1995–96 | Chelsea | 22 | 0 |
| 1995–96 | Bournemouth (loan) | 7 | 0 |
| 1996–97 | Chelsea | 15 | 1 |
| 1997–98 | Chelsea | 23 | 0 |
| **Total:** | | **68** | **1** |

## DUBLIN, Dion — Forward

H: 6 0 W: 12 04 b.Leicester 22-4-69

*Honours:* England 3 full caps.

| | | | |
|---|---|---|---|
| 1987–88 | Norwich C | 0 | 0 |
| 1988–89 | Cambridge U | 21 | 6 |
| 1989–90 | Cambridge U | 46 | 15 |
| 1990–91 | Cambridge U | 46 | 16 |
| 1991–92 | Cambridge U | 43 | 15 |
| 1992–93 | Manchester U | 7 | 1 |
| 1993–94 | Manchester U | 5 | 1 |
| 1994–95 | Coventry C | 31 | 13 |
| 1995–96 | Coventry C | 34 | 14 |
| 1996–97 | Coventry C | 34 | 13 |
| 1997–98 | Coventry C | 36 | 18 |
| **Total:** | | **303** | **112** |

## DUBLIN, Keith — Defender

H: 6 0 W: 12 10 b.Brent 29-1-66

*Source:* Apprentice. *Honours:* England Youth.

| | | | |
|---|---|---|---|
| 1983–84 | Chelsea | 1 | 0 |
| 1984–85 | Chelsea | 11 | 0 |
| 1985–86 | Chelsea | 11 | 0 |
| 1986–87 | Chelsea | 28 | 0 |

| | | | |
|---|---|---|---|
| 1987–88 | Brighton & HA | 46 | 5 |
| 1988–89 | Brighton & HA | 43 | 0 |
| 1989–90 | Brighton & HA | 43 | 0 |
| 1990–91 | Watford | 43 | 0 |
| 1991–92 | Watford | 46 | 0 |
| 1992–93 | Watford | 46 | 1 |
| 1993–94 | Watford | 33 | 1 |
| 1994–95 | Southend U | 40 | 2 |
| 1995–96 | Southend U | 43 | 3 |
| 1996–97 | Southend U | 46 | 0 |
| 1997–98 | Southend U | 41 | 4 |
| **Total:** | | **521** | **16** |

## DUCROS, Andrew — Forward

H: 5 6 W: 9 08 b.Evesham 16-9-77

*Source:* Trainee. *Honours:* England Schools, Youth.

| | | | |
|---|---|---|---|
| 1994–95 | Coventry C | 0 | 0 |
| 1995–96 | Coventry C | 0 | 0 |
| 1996–97 | Coventry C | 5 | 0 |
| 1997–98 | Coventry C | 3 | 0 |
| **Total:** | | **8** | **0** |

## DUDFIELD, Lawrie — Forward

H: 6 0 W: 12 04 b.London 7-5-80

*Source:* Kettering T.

| | | | |
|---|---|---|---|
| 1997–98 | Leicester C | 0 | 0 |

## DUDLEY, Craig — Forward

H: 5 10 W: 11 04 b.Ollerton 12-9-79

*Source:* Trainee. *Honours:* England Youth.

| | | | |
|---|---|---|---|
| 1996–97 | Notts Co | 10 | 2 |
| 1997–98 | Notts Co | 17 | 1 |
| 1997–98 | Shrewsbury T (loan) | 4 | 0 |
| **Total:** | | **31** | **3** |

## DUERDEN, Ian — Forward

H: 5 10 W: 12 07 b.Burnley 27-3-78

*Source:* Trainee.

| | | | |
|---|---|---|---|
| 1996–97 | Burnley | 0 | 0 |
| 1997–98 | Burnley | 1 | 0 |
| **Total:** | | **1** | **0** |

## DUFF, Damien — Forward

H: 5 10 W: 9 07 b.Ballyboden 2-3-79

*Honours:* Eire Youth, 2 full caps.

| | | | |
|---|---|---|---|
| 1995–96 | Blackburn R | 0 | 0 |
| 1996–97 | Blackburn R | 1 | 0 |
| 1997–98 | Blackburn R | 26 | 4 |
| **Total:** | | **27** | **4** |

## DUFFY, Gary — Midfield

b.Kingston 10-2-79

*Source:* Trainee.

| | | | |
|---|---|---|---|
| 1997–98 | Brentford | 0 | 0 |

## DUFFY, Neil Cornelius — Midfield

H: 6 1 W: 11 13 b.Glasgow 5-6-67

*Source:* Shamrock SA.

| | | | |
|---|---|---|---|
| 1989–90 | Dundee U | 0 | 0 |
| 1990–91 | Falkirk | 25 | 2 |
| 1991–92 | Falkirk | 39 | 2 |
| 1992–93 | Falkirk | 34 | 5 |
| 1993–94 | Falkirk | 23 | 9 |
| 1993–94 | Dundee | 9 | 2 |
| 1994–95 | Dundee | 24 | 3 |
| 1995–96 | Dundee | 31 | 3 |
| 1996–97 | Dundee U | 13 | 1 |
| 1997–98 | Dundee U | 7 | 0 |
| **Total:** | | **205** | **27** |

## DUGUID, Karl — Midfield

H: 5 11 W: 11 00 b.Hitchin 21-3-78

*Source:* Trainee.

| | | | |
|---|---|---|---|
| 1995–96 | Colchester U | 16 | 1 |
| 1996–97 | Colchester U | 20 | 3 |
| 1997–98 | Colchester U | 21 | 3 |
| **Total:** | | **57** | **7** |

## DUKE, David — Midfield

b.Inverness 7-11-78

*Source:* Redby CA.

| | | | |
|---|---|---|---|
| 1997–98 | Sunderland | 0 | 0 |

## DUKES, Lee — Defender

H: 5 9 W: 11 06 b.Walsall 24-10-79

*Source:* Trainee.

| | | | |
|---|---|---|---|
| 1996–97 | Birmingham C | 0 | 0 |
| 1997–98 | Birmingham C | 0 | 0 |

## DUNCAN, Andrew — Defender

H: 5 11 W: 13 04 b.Hexham 20-10-77

*Source:* Trainee. *Honours:* England Schools.

| | | | |
|---|---|---|---|
| 1996–97 | Manchester U | 0 | 0 |

| | | | |
|---|---|---|---|
| 1997–98 | Manchester U | 0 | 0 |
| 1997–98 | Cambridge U | 19 | 0 |
| **Total:** | | **19** | **0** |

## DUNGEY, James — Goalkeeper

H: 5 9 W: 11 08 b.Plymouth 7-2-78

*Source:* Trainee. *Honours:* England Schools, Youth.

| | | | |
|---|---|---|---|
| 1994–95 | Plymouth Arg | 4 | 0 |
| 1995–96 | Plymouth Arg | 0 | 0 |
| 1996–97 | Plymouth Arg | 6 | 0 |
| 1997–98 | Plymouth Arg | 0 | 0 |
| 1997–98 | Exeter C | 1 | 0 |
| **Total:** | | **11** | **0** |

## DUNN, David — Midfield

b.Blackburn 27-12-79

*Source:* Trainee. *Honours:* England Youth.

| | | | |
|---|---|---|---|
| 1997–98 | Blackburn R | 0 | 0 |

## DUNN, Iain — Midfield

H: 5 10 W: 10 07 b.Derwent 1-4-70

*Source:* School. *Honours:* England Schools, Youth.

| | | | |
|---|---|---|---|
| 1988–89 | York C | 26 | 6 |
| 1989–90 | York C | 18 | 2 |
| 1990–91 | York C | 33 | 3 |
| 1991–92 | Chesterfield | 13 | 1 |
| From Goole T. | | | |
| 1992–93 | Huddersfield T | 28 | 3 |
| 1993–94 | Huddersfield T | 34 | 6 |
| 1994–95 | Huddersfield T | 39 | 5 |
| 1995–96 | Huddersfield T | 14 | 0 |
| 1996–97 | Huddersfield T | 5 | 0 |
| 1996–97 | Scunthorpe U (loan) | 3 | 0 |
| 1996–97 | Chesterfield | 11 | 0 |
| 1997–98 | Chesterfield | 7 | 0 |
| **Total:** | | **231** | **26** |

## DUNNE, Joe — Defender

H: 5 9 W: 11 06 b.Dublin 25-5-73

*Source:* Trainee. *Honours:* Eire Youth, Under-21.

| | | | |
|---|---|---|---|
| 1990–91 | Gillingham | 26 | 0 |
| 1991–92 | Gillingham | 11 | 0 |
| 1992–93 | Gillingham | 4 | 0 |
| 1993–94 | Gillingham | 37 | 0 |
| 1994–95 | Gillingham | 35 | 1 |
| 1995–96 | Gillingham | 2 | 0 |
| 1995–96 | Colchester U | 5 | 1 |
| 1996–97 | Colchester U | 35 | 0 |
| 1997–98 | Colchester U | 25 | 2 |
| **Total:** | | **180** | **4** |

## DUNNE, Richard — Defender

H: 6 0 W: 13 00 b.Dublin 21-9-79

*Source:* Trainee.

| | | | |
|---|---|---|---|
| 1996–97 | Everton | 7 | 0 |
| 1997–98 | Everton | 3 | 0 |
| **Total:** | | **10** | **0** |

## DURIE, Gordon — Forward

H: 6 0 W: 12 00 b.Paisley 6-12-65

*Source:* Hill of Beath Hawthorn. *Honours:* Scotland B, Under-21, 43 full caps, 7 goals.

| | | | |
|---|---|---|---|
| 1981–82 | East Fife | 13 | 1 |
| 1982–83 | East Fife | 25 | 2 |
| 1983–84 | East Fife | 34 | 16 |
| 1984–85 | East Fife | 9 | 7 |
| 1984–85 | Hibernian | 22 | 8 |
| 1985–86 | Hibernian | 25 | 6 |
| 1985–86 | Chelsea | 1 | 0 |
| 1986–87 | Chelsea | 25 | 5 |
| 1987–88 | Chelsea | 26 | 12 |
| 1988–89 | Chelsea | 32 | 17 |
| 1989–90 | Chelsea | 15 | 5 |
| 1990–91 | Chelsea | 24 | 12 |
| 1991–92 | Tottenham H | 31 | 7 |
| 1992–93 | Tottenham H | 17 | 3 |
| 1993–94 | Tottenham H | 10 | 1 |
| 1993–94 | Rangers | 24 | 12 |
| 1994–95 | Rangers | 21 | 6 |
| 1995–96 | Rangers | 27 | 17 |
| 1996–97 | Rangers | 16 | 5 |
| 1997–98 | Rangers | 26 | 4 |
| **Total:** | | **423** | **146** |

## DURKAN, Kieron — Midfield

H: 5 10 W: 12 09 b.Chester 1-12-73

*Source:* Trainee. *Honours:* Eire Under-21.

| | | | |
|---|---|---|---|
| 1991–92 | Wrexham | 1 | 0 |
| 1992–93 | Wrexham | 1 | 0 |
| 1993–94 | Wrexham | 10 | 1 |
| 1994–95 | Wrexham | 30 | 2 |
| 1995–96 | Wrexham | 8 | 0 |
| 1995–96 | Stockport Co | 16 | 0 |
| 1996–97 | Stockport Co | 41 | 3 |
| 1997–98 | Stockport Co | 7 | 1 |
| 1997–98 | Macclesfield T | 4 | 0 |
| **Total:** | | **118** | **7** |

## DURNIN, John — Midfield

H: 5 10 W: 11 10 b.Bootle 18-8-65

*Source:* Waterloo Dock.

| | | | |
|---|---|---|---|
| 1985–86 | Liverpool | 0 | 0 |
| 1986–87 | Liverpool | 0 | 0 |
| 1987–88 | Liverpool | 0 | 0 |
| 1988–89 | Liverpool | 0 | 0 |
| 1988–89 | WBA (loan) | 5 | 2 |
| 1988–89 | Oxford U | 19 | 3 |
| 1989–90 | Oxford U | 42 | 13 |
| 1990–91 | Oxford U | 26 | 9 |
| 1991–92 | Oxford U | 37 | 8 |
| 1992–93 | Oxford U | 37 | 11 |
| 1993–94 | Portsmouth | 28 | 6 |
| 1994–95 | Portsmouth | 16 | 2 |
| 1995–96 | Portsmouth | 41 | 3 |
| 1996–97 | Portsmouth | 34 | 3 |
| 1997–98 | Portsmouth | 34 | 10 |
| **Total:** | | **319** | **70** |

## DURRANT, Iain — Midfield

H: 5 8 W: 9 07 b.Glasgow 29-10-66

*Source:* Glasgow United. *Honours:* Scotland Youth, Under-21, 11 full caps.

| | | | |
|---|---|---|---|
| 1984–85 | Rangers | 5 | 0 |
| 1985–86 | Rangers | 30 | 2 |
| 1986–87 | Rangers | 39 | 4 |
| 1987–88 | Rangers | 40 | 10 |
| 1988–89 | Rangers | 8 | 2 |
| 1989–90 | Rangers | 0 | 0 |
| 1990–91 | Rangers | 4 | 1 |
| 1991–92 | Rangers | 13 | 0 |
| 1992–93 | Rangers | 30 | 3 |
| 1993–94 | Rangers | 23 | 0 |
| 1994–95 | Rangers | 25 | 4 |
| 1994–95 | Everton (loan) | 5 | 0 |
| 1995–96 | Rangers | 15 | 0 |
| 1996–97 | Rangers | 8 | 0 |
| 1997–98 | Rangers | 8 | 0 |
| **Total:** | | **253** | **26** |

## DUXBURY, Lee — Midfield

H: 5 10 W: 11 08 b.Keighley 7-10-69

*Source:* Trainee.

| | | | |
|---|---|---|---|
| 1988–89 | Bradford C | 1 | 0 |
| 1989–90 | Bradford C | 12 | 1 |
| 1989–90 | Rochdale (loan) | 10 | 0 |
| 1990–91 | Bradford C | 45 | 5 |
| 1991–92 | Bradford C | 46 | 5 |
| 1992–93 | Bradford C | 42 | 5 |
| 1993–94 | Bradford C | 43 | 9 |
| 1994–95 | Bradford C | 20 | 0 |
| 1994–95 | Huddersfield T | 26 | 2 |
| 1995–96 | Huddersfield T | 3 | 0 |
| 1995–96 | Bradford C | 30 | 4 |
| 1996–97 | Bradford C | 33 | 3 |
| 1996–97 | Oldham Ath | 12 | 1 |
| 1997–98 | Oldham Ath | 38 | 5 |
| **Total:** | | **361** | **40** |

## DYCHE, Sean — Defender

H: 6 0 W: 13 07 b.Kettering 28-6-71

*Source:* Trainee.

| | | | |
|---|---|---|---|
| 1988–89 | Nottingham F | 0 | 0 |
| 1989–90 | Nottingham F | 0 | 0 |
| 1989–90 | Chesterfield | 22 | 2 |
| 1990–91 | Chesterfield | 28 | 2 |
| 1991–92 | Chesterfield | 42 | 3 |
| 1992–93 | Chesterfield | 20 | 1 |
| 1993–94 | Chesterfield | 20 | 0 |
| 1994–95 | Chesterfield | 22 | 0 |
| 1995–96 | Chesterfield | 41 | 0 |
| 1996–97 | Chesterfield | 36 | 0 |
| 1997–98 | Bristol C | 11 | 0 |
| **Total:** | | **242** | **8** |

## DYER, Alex — Defender

H: 6 1 W: 12 00 b.West Ham 14-11-65

*Source:* Watford Apprentice.

| | | | |
|---|---|---|---|
| 1983–84 | Blackpool | 9 | 0 |
| 1984–85 | Blackpool | 36 | 8 |
| 1985–86 | Blackpool | 39 | 8 |
| 1986–87 | Blackpool | 24 | 3 |
| 1986–87 | Hull C | 17 | 4 |
| 1987–88 | Hull C | 28 | 8 |
| 1988–89 | Hull C | 15 | 2 |
| 1988–89 | Crystal Palace | 7 | 2 |
| 1989–90 | Crystal Palace | 10 | 0 |
| 1990–91 | Charlton Ath | 35 | 7 |
| 1991–92 | Charlton Ath | 13 | 0 |
| 1992–93 | Charlton Ath | 30 | 6 |
| 1993–94 | Oxford U | 38 | 5 |
| 1994–95 | Oxford U | 38 | 1 |
| 1995–96 | Oxford U | 0 | 0 |
| 1995–96 | Lincoln C | 1 | 0 |
| 1995–96 | Barnet | 35 | 2 |
| 1996–97 | Barnet | 0 | 0 |
| 1997–98 | Huddersfield T | 12 | 1 |
| 1997–98 | Notts Co | 10 | 0 |
| **Total:** | | **397** | **57** |

## DYER, Bruce — Forward

H: 5 11 W: 11 03 b.Ilford 13-4-75

*Source:* Trainee. *Honours:* England Under-21.

| | | | |
|---|---|---|---|
| 1992–93 | Watford | 2 | 0 |
| 1993–94 | Watford | 29 | 6 |
| 1993–94 | Crystal Palace | 11 | 0 |
| 1994–95 | Crystal Palace | 16 | 1 |
| 1995–96 | Crystal Palace | 35 | 13 |
| 1996–97 | Crystal Palace | 43 | 17 |
| 1997–98 | Crystal Palace | 24 | 4 |
| **Total:** | | **160** | **41** |

## DYER, Kieron — Midfield

H: 5 7 W: 9 07 b.Ipswich 29-12-78

*Source:* Trainee. *Honours:* England Youth, Under-21, B.

| | | | |
|---|---|---|---|
| 1996–97 | Ipswich T | 13 | 0 |
| 1997–98 | Ipswich T | 41 | 4 |
| **Total:** | | **54** | **4** |

## DYER, Wayne — Midfield

H: 6 0 W: 10 00 b.Birmingham 24-11-77

*Source:* Trainee.

| | | | |
|---|---|---|---|
| 1996–97 | Birmingham C | 0 | 0 |
| 1997–98 | Oxford U | 0 | 0 |

## DYSON, James — Defender

H: 6 2 W: 12 00 b.Wordsley 20-4-79

*Source:* Trainee.

| | | | |
|---|---|---|---|
| 1997–98 | Birmingham C | 0 | 0 |

## DYSON, Jon — Defender

H: 6 0 W: 12 07 b.Mirfield 18-12-71

*Source:* School.

| | | | |
|---|---|---|---|
| 1991–92 | Huddersfield T | 0 | 0 |
| 1992–93 | Huddersfield T | 15 | 0 |
| 1993–94 | Huddersfield T | 22 | 0 |
| 1994–95 | Huddersfield T | 28 | 2 |
| 1995–96 | Huddersfield T | 17 | 0 |
| 1996–97 | Huddersfield T | 23 | 0 |
| 1997–98 | Huddersfield T | 36 | 1 |
| **Total:** | | **141** | **3** |

## EADEN, Nicky — Defender

H: 5 8 W: 12 08 b.Sheffield 12-12-72

*Source:* Trainee.

| | | | |
|---|---|---|---|
| 1991–92 | Barnsley | 0 | 0 |
| 1992–93 | Barnsley | 2 | 0 |
| 1993–94 | Barnsley | 37 | 2 |
| 1994–95 | Barnsley | 45 | 1 |
| 1995–96 | Barnsley | 46 | 2 |
| 1996–97 | Barnsley | 46 | 3 |
| 1997–98 | Barnsley | 35 | 0 |
| **Total:** | | **211** | **8** |

## EADIE, Darren — Forward

H: 5 8 W: 11 00 b.Chippenham 10-6-75

*Source:* Trainee. *Honours:* England Youth, Under-21.

| | | | |
|---|---|---|---|
| 1992–93 | Norwich C | 0 | 0 |
| 1993–94 | Norwich C | 15 | 3 |
| 1994–95 | Norwich C | 26 | 2 |
| 1995–96 | Norwich C | 31 | 6 |
| 1996–97 | Norwich C | 42 | 17 |
| 1997–98 | Norwich C | 19 | 3 |
| **Total:** | | **133** | **31** |

## EARLE, Robbie — Midfield

H: 5 9 W: 10 10 b.Newcastle-under-Lyme 27-1-65

*Source:* Stoke C. *Honours:* Jamaica 10 full caps, 1 goal.

| | | | |
|---|---|---|---|
| 1981–82 | Port Vale | 0 | 0 |
| 1982–83 | Port Vale | 8 | 1 |
| 1983–84 | Port Vale | 12 | 0 |
| 1984–85 | Port Vale | 46 | 15 |
| 1985–86 | Port Vale | 46 | 15 |
| 1986–87 | Port Vale | 35 | 6 |
| 1987–88 | Port Vale | 25 | 4 |
| 1988–89 | Port Vale | 44 | 13 |
| 1989–90 | Port Vale | 43 | 12 |
| 1990–91 | Port Vale | 35 | 11 |
| 1991–92 | Wimbledon | 40 | 14 |
| 1992–93 | Wimbledon | 42 | 7 |
| 1993–94 | Wimbledon | 42 | 9 |
| 1994–95 | Wimbledon | 9 | 0 |
| 1995–96 | Wimbledon | 37 | 11 |
| 1996–97 | Wimbledon | 32 | 7 |
| 1997–98 | Wimbledon | 22 | 3 |
| **Total:** | | **518** | **128** |

## EARNSHAW, Mark — Defender

b.Leeds 11-11-78

*Source:* Trainee.

| | | | |
|---|---|---|---|
| 1997–98 | Oldham Ath | 0 | 0 |

## EARNSHAW, Robert — Forward

b.Zambia 6-4-81

*Source:* Trainee.

| | | | |
|---|---|---|---|
| 1997–98 | Cardiff C | 5 | 0 |
| **Total:** | | **5** | **0** |

## EASTON, Clint — Midfield

H: 6 0 W: 10 04 b.Barking 1-10-77

*Source:* Trainee. *Honours:* England Youth.

| | | | |
|---|---|---|---|
| 1996–97 | Watford | 17 | 1 |
| 1997–98 | Watford | 12 | 0 |
| **Total:** | | **29** | **1** |

## EASTON, Craig — Midfield

H: 5 9 W: 9 08 b.Bellshill 26-2-79

*Source:* Dundee U BC. *Honours:* Scotland Under-21, Under-18.

| | | | |
|---|---|---|---|
| 1995–96 | Dundee U | 0 | 0 |
| 1996–97 | Dundee U | 2 | 0 |
| 1997–98 | Dundee U | 29 | 1 |
| **Total:** | | **31** | **1** |

## EASTWOOD, Philip — Forward

H: 5 10 W: 12 02 b.Blackburn 6-4-78

*Source:* Trainee.

| | | | |
|---|---|---|---|
| 1996–97 | Burnley | 0 | 0 |
| 1997–98 | Burnley | 3 | 0 |
| **Total:** | | **3** | **0** |

## EATOCK, David — Forward

H: 5 4 W: 10 05 b.Wigan 11-11-76

*Source:* Chorley.

| | | | |
|---|---|---|---|
| 1995–96 | Newcastle U | 0 | 0 |
| 1996–97 | Newcastle U | 0 | 0 |
| 1997–98 | Newcastle U | 0 | 0 |

## EATON, Adam — Defender

b.Wigan 2-5-80

*Source:* Trainee.

| | | | |
|---|---|---|---|
| 1997–98 | Everton | 0 | 0 |

## EBBRELL, John — Midfield

H: 5 10 W: 11 11 b.Bromborough 1-10-69

*Honours:* FA Schools, England Schools, Youth, Under-21, B.

| | | | |
|---|---|---|---|
| 1986–87 | Everton | 0 | 0 |
| 1987–88 | Everton | 0 | 0 |
| 1988–89 | Everton | 4 | 0 |
| 1989–90 | Everton | 17 | 0 |
| 1990–91 | Everton | 36 | 3 |
| 1991–92 | Everton | 39 | 1 |
| 1992–93 | Everton | 24 | 1 |
| 1993–94 | Everton | 39 | 4 |
| 1994–95 | Everton | 26 | 0 |
| 1995–96 | Everton | 25 | 4 |
| 1996–97 | Everton | 7 | 0 |
| 1996–97 | Sheffield U | 1 | 0 |
| 1997–98 | Sheffield U | 0 | 0 |
| **Total:** | | **218** | **13** |

## EBDON, Marcus — Midfield

H: 5 10 W: 11 02 b.Pontypool 17-10-70

*Source:* Trainee. *Honours:* Wales Under-21.

| | | | |
|---|---|---|---|
| 1988–89 | Everton | 0 | 0 |
| 1989–90 | Everton | 0 | 0 |
| 1990–91 | Everton | 0 | 0 |
| 1991–92 | Peterborough U | 15 | 2 |
| 1992–93 | Peterborough U | 28 | 4 |
| 1993–94 | Peterborough U | 10 | 0 |
| 1994–95 | Peterborough U | 35 | 6 |
| 1995–96 | Peterborough U | 39 | 2 |
| 1996–97 | Peterborough U | 20 | 1 |
| 1996–97 | Chesterfield | 12 | 1 |
| 1997–98 | Chesterfield | 33 | 2 |
| **Total:** | | **192** | **18** |

## ECKHARDT, Jeff — Defender

H: 5 11 W: 12 00 b.Sheffield 7-10-65

| | | | |
|---|---|---|---|
| 1984–85 | Sheffield U | 7 | 0 |
| 1985–86 | Sheffield U | 33 | 2 |
| 1986–87 | Sheffield U | 22 | 0 |
| 1987–88 | Sheffield U | 12 | 0 |
| 1987–88 | Fulham | 29 | 1 |
| 1988–89 | Fulham | 43 | 2 |
| 1989–90 | Fulham | 40 | 2 |
| 1990–91 | Fulham | 29 | 2 |
| 1991–92 | Fulham | 43 | 7 |
| 1992–93 | Fulham | 30 | 6 |
| 1993–94 | Fulham | 35 | 5 |
| 1994–95 | Stockport Co | 27 | 1 |
| 1995–96 | Stockport Co | 35 | 6 |
| 1996–97 | Cardiff C | 35 | 5 |
| 1997–98 | Cardiff C | 21 | 3 |
| **Total:** | | **441** | **42** |

## EDDS, Gareth — Midfield

H: 5 11 W: 10 12 b.Sydney 3-2-81

*Source:* Trainee.

| | | | |
|---|---|---|---|
| 1997–98 | Nottingham F | 0 | 0 |

## EDEY, Cec — Defender

H: 6 1 W: 12 00 b.Manchester 12-3-65

*Source:* Witton A.

| | | | |
|---|---|---|---|
| 1997–98 | Macclesfield T | 13 | 0 |
| **Total:** | | **13** | **0** |

## EDGE, Roland — Defender

H: 5 9 W: 11 06 b.Gillingham 25-11-78

*Source:* Trainee.

| | | | |
|---|---|---|---|
| 1997–98 | Gillingham | 0 | 0 |

## EDGHILL, Richard — Defender

H: 5 9 W: 11 03 b.Oldham 23-9-74

*Source:* Trainee. *Honours:* England Under-21.

| | | | |
|---|---|---|---|
| 1992–93 | Manchester C | 0 | 0 |
| 1993–94 | Manchester C | 22 | 0 |
| 1994–95 | Manchester C | 14 | 0 |
| 1995–96 | Manchester C | 13 | 0 |
| 1996–97 | Manchester C | 0 | 0 |
| 1997–98 | Manchester C | 36 | 0 |
| **Total:** | | **85** | **0** |

## EDINBURGH, Justin — Defender

H: 5 10 W: 12 01 b.Basildon 18-12-69

*Source:* Trainee.

| | | | |
|---|---|---|---|
| 1988–89 | Southend U | 15 | 0 |
| 1989–90 | Southend U | 22 | 0 |
| 1989–90 | Tottenham H (loan) | 0 | 0 |
| 1990–91 | Tottenham H | 16 | 1 |
| 1991–92 | Tottenham H | 23 | 0 |
| 1992–93 | Tottenham H | 32 | 0 |
| 1993–94 | Tottenham H | 25 | 0 |
| 1994–95 | Tottenham H | 31 | 0 |
| 1995–96 | Tottenham H | 22 | 0 |
| 1996–97 | Tottenham H | 24 | 0 |
| 1997–98 | Tottenham H | 16 | 0 |
| **Total:** | | **226** | **1** |

## EDINHO — Forward

H: 5 8 W: 12 12 b.Brazil 21-2-67

| | | | |
|---|---|---|---|
| 1994–95 | Chaves | 32 | 14 |
| 1995–96 | Guimaraes | 32 | 15 |
| 1996–97 | Bradford C | 15 | 5 |
| 1997–98 | Bradford C | 41 | 10 |
| **Total:** | | **120** | **44** |

## EDMONDSON, Darren — Defender

H: 6 0 W: 12 04 b.Coniston 4-11-71

*Source:* Trainee.

| | | | |
|---|---|---|---|
| 1990–91 | Carlisle U | 31 | 0 |
| 1991–92 | Carlisle U | 27 | 2 |
| 1992–93 | Carlisle U | 34 | 0 |
| 1993–94 | Carlisle U | 22 | 3 |
| 1994–95 | Carlisle U | 38 | 2 |
| 1995–96 | Carlisle U | 42 | 1 |
| 1996–97 | Carlisle U | 20 | 1 |
| 1996–97 | Huddersfield T | 10 | 0 |
| 1997–98 | Huddersfield T | 19 | 0 |
| **Total:** | | **243** | **9** |

## EDWARDS, Andy — Defender

H: 6 2 W: 12 00 b.Epping 17-9-71

*Source:* Trainee.

| | | | |
|---|---|---|---|
| 1988–89 | Southend U | 1 | 0 |
| 1989–90 | Southend U | 8 | 0 |
| 1990–91 | Southend U | 2 | 1 |
| 1991–92 | Southend U | 9 | 0 |
| 1992–93 | Southend U | 41 | 0 |
| 1993–94 | Southend U | 42 | 1 |
| 1994–95 | Southend U | 44 | 3 |
| 1995–96 | Birmingham C | 37 | 1 |
| 1996–97 | Birmingham C | 3 | 0 |
| 1996–97 | Peterborough U | 25 | 0 |
| 1997–98 | Peterborough U | 46 | 2 |
| **Total:** | | **258** | **8** |

## EDWARDS, Christian — Defender

H: 6 2 W: 12 11 b.Caerphilly 23-11-75

*Source:* Trainee. *Honours:* Wales Under-21, B, 1 full cap.

| | | | |
|---|---|---|---|
| 1994–95 | Swansea C | 9 | 0 |
| 1995–96 | Swansea C | 38 | 2 |
| 1996–97 | Swansea C | 36 | 0 |
| 1997–98 | Swansea C | 32 | 2 |
| 1997–98 | Nottingham F | 0 | 0 |
| **Total:** | | **115** | **4** |

## EDWARDS, Daniel — Midfield

b.Greenwich 20-12-79

*Source:* Trainee.

| | | | |
|---|---|---|---|
| 1996–97 | Millwall | 0 | 0 |
| 1997–98 | Millwall | 0 | 0 |

## EDWARDS, Leigh — Goalkeeper

H: 6 1 W: 12 00 b.Wrexham 19-9-78

*Source:* Trainee.

| | | | |
|---|---|---|---|
| 1997–98 | Wrexham | 0 | 0 |

## EDWARDS, Michael

b.Beverley 25-4-80

*Source:* Trainee.

| | | | |
|---|---|---|---|
| 1997–98 | Hull C | 21 | 0 |
| **Total:** | | **21** | **0** |

## EDWARDS, Neil — Goalkeeper

H: 5 8 W: 11 02 b.Aberdare 5-12-70

*Source:* Trainee.

| | | | |
|---|---|---|---|
| 1988–89 | Leeds U | 0 | 0 |
| 1989–90 | Leeds U | 0 | 0 |
| 1990–91 | Leeds U | 0 | 0 |
| 1990–91 | Huddersfield T (loan) | 0 | 0 |
| 1991–92 | Stockport Co | 39 | 0 |
| 1992–93 | Stockport Co | 35 | 0 |
| 1993–94 | Stockport Co | 26 | 0 |
| 1994–95 | Stockport Co | 19 | 0 |
| 1995–96 | Stockport Co | 45 | 0 |
| 1996–97 | Stockport Co | 0 | 0 |
| 1997–98 | Stockport Co | 0 | 0 |
| 1997–98 | Rochdale | 27 | 0 |
| **Total:** | | **191** | **0** |

## EDWARDS, Paul — Goalkeeper

H: 5 11 W: 11 05 b.Liverpool 22-2-65

*Source:* St Helens T.

| | | | |
|---|---|---|---|
| 1988–89 | Crewe Alex | 10 | 0 |
| 1989–90 | Crewe Alex | 8 | 0 |
| 1990–91 | Crewe Alex | 9 | 0 |
| 1991–92 | Crewe Alex | 2 | 0 |
| 1992–93 | Shrewsbury T | 42 | 0 |
| 1993–94 | Shrewsbury T | 42 | 0 |
| 1994–95 | Shrewsbury T | 31 | 0 |
| 1995–96 | Shrewsbury T | 31 | 0 |
| 1996–97 | Shrewsbury T | 23 | 0 |
| 1997–98 | Shrewsbury T | 34 | 0 |
| **Total:** | | **232** | **0** |

## EDWARDS, Paul — Defender

H: 5 10 W: 11 08 b.Manchester 1-1-80

*Source:* Ashton U.

| | | | |
|---|---|---|---|
| 1997–98 | Doncaster R | 9 | 0 |
| **Total:** | | **9** | **0** |

## EDWARDS, Rob — Forward

H: 5 8 W: 11 11 b.Manchester 23-2-70

*Source:* Trainee.

| | | | |
|---|---|---|---|
| 1987–88 | Crewe Alex | 6 | 1 |
| 1988–89 | Crewe Alex | 4 | 0 |
| 1989–90 | Crewe Alex | 4 | 0 |
| 1990–91 | Crewe Alex | 29 | 11 |
| 1991–92 | Crewe Alex | 28 | 6 |
| 1992–93 | Crewe Alex | 23 | 7 |
| 1993–94 | Crewe Alex | 12 | 2 |
| 1994–95 | Crewe Alex | 17 | 2 |
| 1995–96 | Crewe Alex | 32 | 15 |
| 1995–96 | Huddersfield T | 13 | 7 |
| 1996–97 | Huddersfield T | 33 | 3 |
| 1997–98 | Huddersfield T | 38 | 1 |
| **Total:** | | **239** | **55** |

## EDWARDS, Robert — Defender

H: 6 0 W: 11 01 b.Kendal 1-7-73

*Source:* Trainee. *Honours:* Wales Youth, Under-21, 4 full caps.

| | | | |
|---|---|---|---|
| 1989–90 | Carlisle U | 12 | 0 |
| 1990–91 | Carlisle U | 36 | 5 |
| 1990–91 | Bristol C | 0 | 0 |
| 1991–92 | Bristol C | 20 | 1 |
| 1992–93 | Bristol C | 18 | 0 |
| 1993–94 | Bristol C | 38 | 2 |
| 1994–95 | Bristol C | 30 | 0 |
| 1995–96 | Bristol C | 19 | 0 |
| 1996–97 | Bristol C | 31 | 0 |
| 1997–98 | Bristol C | 37 | 2 |
| **Total:** | | **241** | **10** |

## EDWORTHY, Marc — Defender

H: 5 8 W: 10 03 b.Barnstaple 24-12-72

*Source:* Trainee.

| | | | |
|---|---|---|---|
| 1990–91 | Plymouth Arg | 0 | 0 |
| 1991–92 | Plymouth Arg | 15 | 0 |
| 1992–93 | Plymouth Arg | 15 | 0 |
| 1993–94 | Plymouth Arg | 12 | 0 |
| 1994–95 | Plymouth Arg | 27 | 1 |
| 1995–96 | Crystal Palace | 44 | 0 |
| 1996–97 | Crystal Palace | 45 | 0 |
| 1997–98 | Crystal Palace | 34 | 0 |
| **Total:** | | **192** | **1** |

## EHIOGU, Ugo — Defender

H: 6 2 W: 14 10 b.Hackney 3-11-72

*Source:* Trainee. *Honours:* England Under-21, B, 1 full cap.

| | | | |
|---|---|---|---|
| 1990–91 | WBA | 2 | 0 |

| | | | |
|---|---|---|---|
| 1991–92 | Aston Villa | 8 | 0 |
| 1992–93 | Aston Villa | 4 | 0 |
| 1993–94 | Aston Villa | 17 | 0 |
| 1994–95 | Aston Villa | 39 | 3 |
| 1995–96 | Aston Villa | 36 | 1 |
| 1996–97 | Aston Villa | 38 | 3 |
| 1997–98 | Aston Villa | 37 | 2 |
| **Total:** | | **181** | **9** |

## EKOKU, Efan — Forward

H: 6 2 W: 12 00 b.Manchester 8-6-67

*Source:* Sutton U. *Honours:* Nigeria 4 full caps.

| | | | |
|---|---|---|---|
| 1990–91 | Bournemouth | 20 | 3 |
| 1991–92 | Bournemouth | 28 | 11 |
| 1992–93 | Bournemouth | 14 | 7 |
| 1992–93 | Norwich C | 4 | 3 |
| 1993–94 | Norwich C | 27 | 12 |
| 1994–95 | Norwich C | 6 | 0 |
| 1994–95 | Wimbledon | 24 | 9 |
| 1995–96 | Wimbledon | 31 | 7 |
| 1996–97 | Wimbledon | 30 | 11 |
| 1997–98 | Wimbledon | 16 | 4 |
| **Total:** | | **200** | **67** |

## ELKINS, Gary — Defender

H: 5 9 W: 13 04 b.Wallingford 4-5-66

*Source:* Apprentice. *Honours:* England Youth.

| | | | |
|---|---|---|---|
| 1983–84 | Fulham | 0 | 0 |
| 1984–85 | Fulham | 21 | 0 |
| 1985–86 | Fulham | 13 | 0 |
| 1986–87 | Fulham | 9 | 0 |
| 1987–88 | Fulham | 29 | 0 |
| 1988–89 | Fulham | 22 | 1 |
| 1989–90 | Fulham | 10 | 1 |
| 1989–90 | Exeter C (loan) | 5 | 0 |
| 1990–91 | Wimbledon | 10 | 0 |
| 1991–92 | Wimbledon | 18 | 1 |
| 1992–93 | Wimbledon | 18 | 0 |
| 1993–94 | Wimbledon | 18 | 1 |
| 1994–95 | Wimbledon | 36 | 1 |
| 1995–96 | Wimbledon | 10 | 0 |
| 1996–97 | Wimbledon | 0 | 0 |
| 1996–97 | Swindon T | 23 | 1 |
| 1997–98 | Swindon T | 0 | 0 |
| **Total:** | | **242** | **6** |

## ELLINGTON, Lee — Defender

b.Bradford 3-7-80

*Source:* Trainee.

| | | | |
|---|---|---|---|
| 1996–97 | Hull C | 2 | 0 |
| 1997–98 | Hull C | 7 | 2 |
| **Total:** | | **9** | **2** |

## ELLIOT, David — Forward

H: 5 9 W: 11 00 b.Glasgow 13-11-69

*Source:* Celtic BC.

| | | | |
|---|---|---|---|
| 1987–88 | Celtic | 0 | 0 |
| 1988–89 | Celtic | 4 | 0 |
| 1989–90 | Celtic | 2 | 0 |
| 1990–91 | Partick T | 37 | 13 |
| 1991–92 | St Mirren | 28 | 1 |
| 1992–93 | St Mirren | 40 | 5 |
| 1993–94 | St Mirren | 36 | 8 |
| 1994–95 | St Mirren | 28 | 3 |
| 1995–96 | Falkirk | 32 | 0 |
| 1996–97 | Falkirk | 17 | 1 |
| 1996–97 | Hibernian | 7 | 0 |
| 1997–98 | Hibernian | 4 | 0 |
| **Total:** | | **235** | **31** |

## ELLIOTT, Andy — Forward

H: 5 9 W: 11 07 b.Newcastle 2-5-74

| | | | |
|---|---|---|---|
| 1996–97 | Hartlepool U | 4 | 0 |
| 1997–98 | Hartlepool U | 4 | 0 |
| **Total:** | | **8** | **0** |

## ELLIOTT, John — Forward

H: 5 9 W: 10 00 b.Edinburgh 4-7-80

*Source:* Whitehill Welfare.

| | | | |
|---|---|---|---|
| 1997–98 | Dundee | 17 | 2 |
| **Total:** | | **17** | **2** |

## ELLIOTT, Matt — Defender

H: 6 3 W: 14 05 b.Wandsworth 1-11-68

*Source:* Epsom & Ewell. *Honours:* Scotland 3 full caps.

| | | | |
|---|---|---|---|
| 1988–89 | Charlton Ath | 0 | 0 |
| 1988–89 | Torquay U | 13 | 2 |
| 1989–90 | Torquay U | 33 | 2 |
| 1990–91 | Torquay U | 45 | 6 |
| 1991–92 | Torquay U | 33 | 5 |
| 1991–92 | Scunthorpe U (loan) | 8 | 1 |
| 1992–93 | Scunthorpe U | 39 | 6 |
| 1993–94 | Scunthorpe U | 14 | 1 |
| 1993–94 | Oxford U | 32 | 5 |
| 1994–95 | Oxford U | 45 | 4 |
| 1995–96 | Oxford U | 45 | 8 |
| 1996–97 | Oxford U | 26 | 4 |
| 1996–97 | Leicester C | 16 | 4 |
| 1997–98 | Leicester C | 37 | 7 |
| **Total:** | | **386** | **55** |

## ELLIOTT, Robbie — Defender

H: 5 10 W: 10 13 b.Gosforth 25-12-73

*Source:* Trainee. *Honours:* England Under-21.

| | | | |
|---|---|---|---|
| 1990–91 | Newcastle U | 6 | 0 |
| 1991–92 | Newcastle U | 9 | 0 |
| 1992–93 | Newcastle U | 0 | 0 |
| 1993–94 | Newcastle U | 15 | 0 |
| 1994–95 | Newcastle U | 14 | 2 |
| 1995–96 | Newcastle U | 6 | 0 |
| 1996–97 | Newcastle U | 29 | 7 |
| 1997–98 | Bolton W | 4 | 0 |
| **Total:** | | **83** | **9** |

## ELLIOTT, Steve — Defender

H: 6 1 W: 13 12 b.Swadlincote 29-10-78

*Source:* Trainee.

| | | | |
|---|---|---|---|
| 1996–97 | Derby Co | 0 | 0 |
| 1997–98 | Derby Co | 3 | 0 |
| **Total:** | | **3** | **0** |

## ELLIOTT, Stuart — Defender

H: 5 8 W: 11 05 b.London 27-8-77

*Source:* Trainee.

| | | | |
|---|---|---|---|
| 1995–96 | Newcastle U | 0 | 0 |
| 1996–97 | Newcastle U | 0 | 0 |
| 1996–97 | Hull C (loan) | 3 | 0 |
| 1997–98 | Newcastle U | 0 | 0 |
| 1997–98 | Swindon T (loan) | 2 | 0 |
| **Total:** | | **5** | **0** |

## ELLIOTT, Tony — Goalkeeper

H: 6 0 W: 13 09 b.Nuneaton 13-11-69

*Honours:* England Schools, Youth.

| | | | |
|---|---|---|---|
| 1986–87 | Birmingham C | 0 | 0 |
| 1987–88 | Birmingham C | 0 | 0 |
| 1988–89 | Birmingham C | 0 | 0 |
| 1988–89 | Hereford U | 23 | 0 |
| 1989–90 | Hereford U | 29 | 0 |
| 1990–91 | Hereford U | 5 | 0 |
| 1991–92 | Hereford U | 18 | 0 |
| 1992–93 | Huddersfield T | 15 | 0 |
| 1993–94 | Carlisle U | 6 | 0 |
| 1994–95 | Carlisle U | 3 | 0 |
| 1995–96 | Carlisle U | 13 | 0 |
| 1996–97 | Cardiff C | 36 | 0 |
| 1997–98 | Cardiff C | 3 | 0 |
| 1997–98 | Scarborough | 15 | 0 |
| **Total:** | | **166** | **0** |

## ELLIS, Kevin — Defender

H: 6 2 W: 12 07 b.Gt Yarmouth 12-5-77

*Source:* Trainee.

| | | | |
|---|---|---|---|
| 1994–95 | Ipswich T | 1 | 0 |
| 1995–96 | Ipswich T | 0 | 0 |
| 1996–97 | Ipswich T | 0 | 0 |
| 1997–98 | Ipswich T | 0 | 0 |
| **Total:** | | **1** | **0** |

## ELLIS, Tony — Forward

H: 5 11 W: 11 00 b.Salford 20-10-64

*Source:* Horwich RMI, Northwich Vic.

| | | | |
|---|---|---|---|
| 1986–87 | Oldham Ath | 5 | 0 |
| 1987–88 | Oldham Ath | 3 | 0 |
| 1987–88 | Preston NE | 24 | 4 |
| 1988–89 | Preston NE | 45 | 19 |
| 1989–90 | Preston NE | 17 | 3 |
| 1989–90 | Stoke C | 24 | 6 |
| 1990–91 | Stoke C | 38 | 9 |
| 1991–92 | Stoke C | 15 | 4 |
| 1992–93 | Preston NE | 35 | 22 |
| 1993–94 | Preston NE | 37 | 26 |
| 1994–95 | Blackpool | 40 | 17 |
| 1995–96 | Blackpool | 43 | 14 |
| 1996–97 | Blackpool | 45 | 15 |
| 1997–98 | Blackpool | 18 | 8 |
| 1997–98 | Bury | 22 | 6 |
| **Total:** | | **411** | **153** |

## ELLISON, Lee — Forward

H: 5 11 W: 12 06 b.Darlington 13-1-73

*Source:* Trainee.

| | | | |
|---|---|---|---|
| 1990–91 | Darlington | 13 | 3 |
| 1991–92 | Darlington | 27 | 10 |
| 1992–93 | Darlington | 3 | 0 |
| 1992–93 | Hartlepool U (loan) | 4 | 1 |
| 1993–94 | Darlington | 29 | 4 |
| 1994–95 | Leicester C | 0 | 0 |
| 1995–96 | Crewe Alex | 1 | 0 |
| 1996–97 | Crewe Alex | 3 | 2 |
| 1996–97 | Hereford U | 1 | 0 |
| 1996–97 | Mansfield T | 0 | 0 |
| From Bishop Auckland. | | | |
| 1997–98 | Darlington | 8 | 3 |
| **Total:** | | **89** | **23** |

## EMBERSON, Carl — Goalkeeper

H: 6 2 W: 14 05 b.Epsom 13-7-73

*Source:* Trainee.

| | | | |
|---|---|---|---|
| 1991–92 | Millwall | 0 | 0 |

| | | | |
|---|---|---|---|
| 1992–93 | Millwall | 0 | 0 |
| 1992–93 | Colchester U (loan) | 13 | 0 |
| 1993–94 | Millwall | 0 | 0 |
| 1994–95 | Colchester U | 20 | 0 |
| 1995–96 | Colchester U | 41 | 0 |
| 1996–97 | Colchester U | 35 | 0 |
| 1997–98 | Colchester U | 46 | 0 |
| **Total:** | | **155** | **0** |

## EMBLEN, Neil — Defender

H: 6 1 W: 13 03 b.Bromley 19-6-71

*Source:* Tonbridge, Sittingbourne.

| | | | |
|---|---|---|---|
| 1993–94 | Millwall | 12 | 0 |
| 1994–95 | Wolverhampton W | 27 | 7 |
| 1995–96 | Wolverhampton W | 33 | 2 |
| 1996–97 | Wolverhampton W | 28 | 0 |
| 1997–98 | Wolverhampton W | 7 | 0 |
| 1997–98 | Crystal Palace | 13 | 0 |
| **Total:** | | **120** | **9** |

## EMBLEN, Paul — Forward

H: 5 11 W: 12 05 b.Bromley 3-4-76

*Source:* Tonbridge A.

| | | | |
|---|---|---|---|
| 1996–97 | Charlton Ath | 0 | 0 |
| 1997–98 | Charlton Ath | 4 | 0 |
| 1997–98 | Brighton & HA (loan) | 15 | 4 |
| **Total:** | | **19** | **4** |

## EMERSON — Midfield

H: 6 0 W: 14 05 b.Rio 12-4-72

*Source:* Flamengo, Curitiba. *Honours:* Brazil full caps.

| | | | |
|---|---|---|---|
| 1992–93 | Belenenses | 32 | 1 |
| 1993–94 | Belenenses | 23 | 0 |
| 1994–95 | Porto | 31 | 5 |
| 1995–96 | Porto | 29 | 4 |
| 1996–97 | Middlesbrough | 32 | 4 |
| 1997–98 | Middlesbrough | 21 | 5 |
| **Total:** | | **168** | **19** |

## EMERSON — Defender

b.Porto Alegre 30-3-72

*Source:* Benfica.

| | | | |
|---|---|---|---|
| 1997–98 | Sheffield W | 6 | 0 |
| **Total:** | | **6** | **0** |

## EMERSON, Paul — Defender

H: 6 1 W: 12 00 b.Newtonards 29-8-78

*Source:* Trainee.

| | | | |
|---|---|---|---|
| 1997–98 | Leicester C | 0 | 0 |

## EMSDEN, Nigel — Midfield

b.Oxford 15-8-78

*Source:* Trainee.

| | | | |
|---|---|---|---|
| 1997–98 | Oxford U | 0 | 0 |

## ENES, Robbie — Midfield

H: 5 8 W: 11 11 b.Australia 22-8-75

*Source:* Sydney U.

| | | | |
|---|---|---|---|
| 1997–98 | Portsmouth | 5 | 0 |
| **Total:** | | **5** | **0** |

## ERANIO, Stefano — Midfield

H: 5 10 W: 12 00 b.Genoa 29-12-68

*Honours:* Italy 20 full caps, 3 goals.

| | | | |
|---|---|---|---|
| 1984–85 | Genoa | 9 | 0 |
| 1985–86 | Genoa | 13 | 0 |
| 1986–87 | Genoa | 36 | 3 |
| 1987–88 | Genoa | 34 | 0 |
| 1988–89 | Genoa | 35 | 4 |
| 1989–90 | Genoa | 25 | 0 |
| 1990–91 | Genoa | 32 | 4 |
| 1991–92 | Genoa | 29 | 2 |
| 1992–93 | AC Milan | 21 | 2 |
| 1993–94 | AC Milan | 21 | 1 |
| 1994–95 | AC Milan | 11 | 0 |
| 1995–96 | AC Milan | 24 | 1 |
| 1996–97 | AC Milan | 21 | 2 |
| 1997–98 | Derby Co | 23 | 5 |
| **Total:** | | **334** | **24** |

## ERIBENNE, Chukkie — Forward

H: 5 10 W: 11 12 b.London 2-11-80

*Source:* Trainee.

| | | | |
|---|---|---|---|
| 1997–98 | Coventry C | 0 | 0 |

## ERIKSSON, Jan — Defender

H: 6 0 W: 12 04 b.Sundsvall 24-8-67

*Honours:* Sweden 36 full caps, 4 goals.

| | | | |
|---|---|---|---|
| 1987 | AIK | 9 | 0 |
| 1988 | AIK | 21 | 0 |
| 1989 | AIK | 22 | 0 |
| 1990 | AIK | 21 | 2 |

| | | | |
|---|---|---|---|
| 1991 | Norrkoping | 26 | 2 |
| 1992 | Norrkoping | 13 | 1 |
| 1992–93 | Kaiserslautern | 20 | 1 |
| 1993–94 | Kaiserslautern | 17 | 3 |
| 1994–95 | Kaiserslautern | 0 | 0 |
| 1995 | AIK | 7 | 0 |
| 1995–96 | Servette | 6 | 0 |
| 1996 | Helsingborg | 23 | 2 |
| 1996–97 | Sunderland | 1 | 0 |
| 1997–98 | Sunderland | 0 | 0 |
| **Total:** | | **186** | **11** |

## ESDAILLE, Darren — Defender

H: 5 8 W: 10 07 b.Manchester 4-11-74

*Source:* Knowsley U, Hyde U.

| | | | |
|---|---|---|---|
| 1996–97 | Doncaster R | 18 | 1 |
| 1997–98 | Doncaster R | 22 | 0 |
| **Total:** | | **40** | **1** |

## ESDAILLE, David — Midfield

H: 5 9 W: 12 01 b.Manchester 22-7-63

*Source:* Droylsden.

| | | | |
|---|---|---|---|
| 1997–98 | Doncaster R | 13 | 0 |
| **Total:** | | **13** | **0** |

## ETHERINGTON, Craig — Midfield

b.Essex 16-9-79

*Source:* Trainee.

| | | | |
|---|---|---|---|
| 1997–98 | West Ham U | 0 | 0 |

## ETHERINGTON, Matthew — Forward

H: 5 10 W: 10 07 b.Truro 14-8-81

*Source:* School.

| | | | |
|---|---|---|---|
| 1996–97 | Peterborough U | 1 | 0 |
| 1997–98 | Peterborough U | 2 | 0 |
| **Total:** | | **3** | **0** |

## EUELL, Jason — Forward

H: 5 11 W: 11 02 b.Lambeth 6-2-77

*Source:* Trainee. *Honours:* England Youth, Under-21.

| | | | |
|---|---|---|---|
| 1995–96 | Wimbledon | 9 | 2 |
| 1996–97 | Wimbledon | 7 | 2 |
| 1997–98 | Wimbledon | 19 | 4 |
| **Total:** | | **35** | **8** |

## EUSTACE, John — Midfield

H: 5 11 W: 11 12 b.Solihull 3-11-79

*Source:* Trainee.

| | | | |
|---|---|---|---|
| 1996–97 | Coventry C | 0 | 0 |
| 1997–98 | Coventry C | 0 | 0 |

## EUSTACE, Scott — Defender

H: 6 0 W: 13 06 b.Leicester 13-6-75

*Source:* Trainee.

| | | | |
|---|---|---|---|
| 1993–94 | Leicester C | 1 | 0 |
| 1994–95 | Leicester C | 0 | 0 |
| 1995–96 | Mansfield T | 27 | 1 |
| 1996–97 | Mansfield T | 42 | 4 |
| 1997–98 | Mansfield T | 29 | 1 |
| **Total:** | | **99** | **6** |

## EVANS, Gareth — Defender

H: 6 0 W: 11 07 b.Leeds 15-2-81

*Source:* Trainee. *Honours:* England Youth.

| | | | |
|---|---|---|---|
| 1997–98 | Leeds U | 0 | 0 |

## EVANS, James — Midfield

b.Epsom 3-10-78

*Source:* Trainee.

| | | | |
|---|---|---|---|
| 1997–98 | Tottenham H | 0 | 0 |

## EVANS, Kevin — Defender

H: 6 2 W: 12 09 b.Carmarthen 16-12-80

*Source:* Trainee.

| | | | |
|---|---|---|---|
| 1997–98 | Leeds U | 0 | 0 |

## EVANS, Michael — Forward

H: 6 0 W: 13 05 b.Plymouth 1-1-73

*Source:* Trainee. *Honours:* Eire 1 full cap.

| | | | |
|---|---|---|---|
| 1990–91 | Plymouth Arg | 4 | 0 |
| 1991–92 | Plymouth Arg | 13 | 0 |
| 1992–93 | Plymouth Arg | 23 | 1 |
| 1992–93 | Blackburn R (loan) | 0 | 0 |
| 1993–94 | Plymouth Arg | 22 | 9 |
| 1994–95 | Plymouth Arg | 23 | 4 |
| 1995–96 | Plymouth Arg | 45 | 12 |
| 1996–97 | Plymouth Arg | 33 | 12 |
| 1996–97 | Southampton | 12 | 4 |
| 1997–98 | Southampton | 10 | 0 |
| 1997–98 | WBA | 10 | 1 |
| **Total:** | | **195** | **43** |

## EVANS, Paul — Midfield

H: 5 8 W: 10 08 b.Oswestry 1-9-74

*Source:* Trainee. *Honours:* Wales Under-21.

| | | | |
|---|---|---|---|
| 1991–92 | Shrewsbury T | 2 | 0 |
| 1992–93 | Shrewsbury T | 4 | 0 |
| 1993–94 | Shrewsbury T | 13 | 0 |
| 1994–95 | Shrewsbury T | 32 | 5 |
| 1995–96 | Shrewsbury T | 34 | 3 |
| 1996–97 | Shrewsbury T | 42 | 6 |
| 1997–98 | Shrewsbury T | 39 | 6 |
| **Total:** | | **166** | **20** |

## EVANS, Tom — Goalkeeper

H: 6 1 W: 13 02 b.Doncaster 31-12-76

*Source:* Trainee.

| | | | |
|---|---|---|---|
| 1995–96 | Sheffield U | 0 | 0 |
| 1996–97 | Crystal Palace | 0 | 0 |
| 1996–97 | Coventry C (loan) | 0 | 0 |
| 1997–98 | Scunthorpe U | 5 | 0 |
| **Total:** | | **5** | **0** |

## EVANS, Wayne — Defender

H: 5 10 W: 12 00 b.Welshpool 25-8-71

*Source:* Welshpool.

| | | | |
|---|---|---|---|
| 1993–94 | Walsall | 41 | 0 |
| 1994–95 | Walsall | 36 | 0 |
| 1995–96 | Walsall | 24 | 0 |
| 1996–97 | Walsall | 28 | 0 |
| 1997–98 | Walsall | 43 | 1 |
| **Total:** | | **172** | **1** |

## EVANS, Wayne — Midfield

H: 5 9 W: 9 12 b.Carmarthen 23-10-80

*Source:* Trainee.

| | | | |
|---|---|---|---|
| 1997–98 | Manchester U | 0 | 0 |

## EVERS, Sean — Midfield

H: 5 9 W: 9 11 b.Hitchin 10-10-77

*Source:* Trainee.

| | | | |
|---|---|---|---|
| 1995–96 | Luton T | 1 | 0 |
| 1996–97 | Luton T | 1 | 0 |
| 1997–98 | Luton T | 23 | 3 |
| **Total:** | | **25** | **3** |

## EYDELIE, Jean-Jacques — Midfield

b.Angouleme 3-2-66

*Source:* Angouleme, Laval, Tours, Nantes, Marseille, Benfica, Bastia, Sion.

| | | | |
|---|---|---|---|
| 1997–98 | Walsall | 11 | 0 |
| **Total:** | | **11** | **0** |

## EYRE, John — Forward

H: 5 11 W: 13 00 b.Hull 9-10-74

*Source:* Trainee.

| | | | |
|---|---|---|---|
| 1993–94 | Oldham Ath | 2 | 0 |
| 1994–95 | Oldham Ath | 8 | 1 |
| 1994–95 | Scunthorpe U (loan) | 9 | 8 |
| 1995–96 | Scunthorpe U | 39 | 10 |
| 1996–97 | Scunthorpe U | 42 | 8 |
| 1997–98 | Scunthorpe U | 42 | 10 |
| **Total:** | | **142** | **37** |

## EYRE, Richard — Midfield

H: 5 11 W: 11 06 b.Poynton 15-9-76

*Source:* Trainee.

| | | | |
|---|---|---|---|
| 1995–96 | Port Vale | 0 | 0 |
| 1996–97 | Port Vale | 0 | 0 |
| 1997–98 | Port Vale | 1 | 0 |
| **Total:** | | **1** | **0** |

## EYRES, David — Forward

H: 6 0 W: 11 04 b.Liverpool 26-2-64

*Source:* Rhyl.

| | | | |
|---|---|---|---|
| 1989–90 | Blackpool | 35 | 7 |
| 1990–91 | Blackpool | 36 | 6 |
| 1991–92 | Blackpool | 41 | 9 |
| 1992–93 | Blackpool | 46 | 16 |
| 1993–94 | Burnley | 45 | 19 |
| 1994–95 | Burnley | 39 | 8 |
| 1995–96 | Burnley | 42 | 6 |
| 1996–97 | Burnley | 36 | 3 |
| 1997–98 | Burnley | 13 | 1 |
| 1997–98 | Preston NE | 28 | 4 |
| **Total:** | | **361** | **79** |

## FACEY, Delroy — Forward

H: 5 11 W: 13 07 b.Huddersfield 22-4-80

*Source:* Trainee.

| | | | |
|---|---|---|---|
| 1996–97 | Huddersfield T | 3 | 0 |
| 1997–98 | Huddersfield T | 3 | 0 |
| **Total:** | | **6** | **0** |

## FAIRCLOUGH, Chris — Defender

H: 5 11 W: 11 00 b.Nottingham 12-4-64

*Source:* Apprentice. *Honours:* England Under-21, B.

| | | | |
|---|---|---|---|
| 1981–82 | Nottingham F | 0 | 0 |
| 1982–83 | Nottingham F | 15 | 0 |
| 1983–84 | Nottingham F | 31 | 0 |
| 1984–85 | Nottingham F | 35 | 0 |
| 1985–86 | Nottingham F | 0 | 0 |
| 1986–87 | Nottingham F | 26 | 1 |
| 1987–88 | Tottenham H | 40 | 4 |
| 1988–89 | Tottenham H | 20 | 1 |
| 1988–89 | Leeds U | 11 | 0 |
| 1989–90 | Leeds U | 42 | 8 |
| 1990–91 | Leeds U | 34 | 4 |
| 1991–92 | Leeds U | 31 | 2 |
| 1992–93 | Leeds U | 30 | 3 |
| 1993–94 | Leeds U | 40 | 4 |
| 1994–95 | Leeds U | 5 | 0 |
| 1995–96 | Bolton W | 33 | 0 |
| 1996–97 | Bolton W | 46 | 8 |
| 1997–98 | Bolton W | 11 | 0 |
| **Total:** | | **450** | **35** |

## FALCONER, Willie — Midfield

H: 6 1 W: 11 09 b.Aberdeen 5-4-66

*Source:* Lewis United. *Honours:* Scotland Schools, Youth.

| | | | |
|---|---|---|---|
| 1982–83 | Aberdeen | 1 | 0 |
| 1983–84 | Aberdeen | 8 | 1 |
| 1984–85 | Aberdeen | 16 | 4 |
| 1985–86 | Aberdeen | 8 | 0 |
| 1986–87 | Aberdeen | 8 | 0 |
| 1987–88 | Aberdeen | 36 | 8 |
| 1988–89 | Watford | 33 | 5 |
| 1989–90 | Watford | 30 | 3 |
| 1990–91 | Watford | 35 | 4 |
| 1991–92 | Middlesbrough | 25 | 5 |
| 1992–93 | Middlesbrough | 28 | 5 |
| 1993–94 | Sheffield U | 23 | 3 |
| 1993–94 | Celtic | 14 | 1 |
| 1994–95 | Celtic | 26 | 4 |
| 1995–96 | Celtic | 2 | 0 |
| 1995–96 | Motherwell | 15 | 5 |
| 1996–97 | Motherwell | 21 | 2 |
| 1997–98 | Motherwell | 22 | 3 |
| **Total:** | | **351** | **53** |

## FARLEY, Adam — Defender

b.Liverpool 12-1-80

*Source:* Trainee.

| | | | |
|---|---|---|---|
| 1997–98 | Everton | 0 | 0 |

## FARNINGHAM, Ray — Midfield

H: 5 8 W: 11 05 b.Dundee 10-4-61

*Source:* Celtic BC.

| | | | |
|---|---|---|---|
| 1978–79 | Forfar Ath | 1 | 0 |
| 1979–80 | Forfar Ath | 38 | 5 |
| 1980–81 | Forfar Ath | 34 | 4 |
| 1981–82 | Forfar Ath | 39 | 5 |
| 1982–83 | Forfar Ath | 21 | 3 |
| 1983–84 | Forfar Ath | 37 | 6 |
| 1984–85 | Forfar Ath | 31 | 4 |
| 1985–86 | Forfar Ath | 37 | 2 |
| 1986–87 | Forfar Ath | 2 | 0 |
| 1986–87 | Motherwell | 29 | 3 |
| 1987–88 | Motherwell | 29 | 6 |
| 1988–89 | Motherwell | 18 | 3 |
| 1989–90 | Dunfermline Ath | 17 | 0 |
| 1990–91 | Dunfermline Ath | 10 | 0 |
| 1991–92 | Dunfermline Ath | 4 | 1 |
| 1991–92 | Partick T | 33 | 7 |
| 1992–93 | Partick T | 37 | 8 |
| 1993–94 | Partick T | 2 | 0 |
| 1993–94 | Dundee | 24 | 2 |
| 1994–95 | Dundee | 27 | 3 |
| 1995–96 | Dundee | 18 | 3 |
| 1996–97 | Dundee | 8 | 0 |
| 1997–98 | Dundee | 1 | 0 |
| 1997–98 | Forfar Ath (loan) | 9 | 1 |
| **Total:** | | **506** | **66** |

## FARNWORTH, Simon — Goalkeeper

H: 5 11 W: 13 04 b.Chorley 28-10-63

*Source:* Apprentice. *Honours:* England Schools.

| | | | |
|---|---|---|---|
| 1981–82 | Bolton W | 0 | 0 |
| 1982–83 | Bolton W | 0 | 0 |
| 1983–84 | Bolton W | 36 | 0 |
| 1984–85 | Bolton W | 46 | 0 |
| 1985–86 | Bolton W | 31 | 0 |
| 1986–87 | Bolton W | 0 | 0 |
| 1986–87 | Stockport Co (loan) | 10 | 0 |
| 1986–87 | Tranmere R (loan) | 7 | 0 |
| 1986–87 | Bury | 14 | 0 |
| 1987–88 | Bury | 39 | 0 |
| 1988–89 | Bury | 45 | 0 |
| 1989–90 | Bury | 7 | 0 |
| 1990–91 | Preston NE | 23 | 0 |
| 1991–92 | Preston NE | 23 | 0 |
| 1992–93 | Preston NE | 35 | 0 |
| 1993–94 | Wigan Ath | 42 | 0 |
| 1994–95 | Wigan Ath | 41 | 0 |
| 1995–96 | Wigan Ath | 43 | 0 |
| 1996–97 | Wigan Ath | 0 | 0 |
| 1997–98 | Wigan Ath | 0 | 0 |
| **Total:** | | **442** | **0** |

## FARQUHAR, Gary — Midfield

H: 5 7 W: 11 04 b.Wick 23-2-71

*Source:* Brora Rangers.

| | | | |
|---|---|---|---|
| 1994–95 | St Johnstone | 17 | 2 |
| 1995–96 | St Johnstone | 15 | 1 |
| 1996–97 | St Johnstone | 5 | 0 |
| 1997–98 | St Johnstone | 4 | 1 |
| **Total:** | | **41** | **4** |

## FARRELL, Andy — Defender

H: 5 11 W: 12 00 b.Colchester 7-10-65

*Source:* School.

| | | | |
|---|---|---|---|
| 1983–84 | Colchester U | 15 | 0 |
| 1984–85 | Colchester U | 38 | 0 |
| 1985–86 | Colchester U | 24 | 1 |
| 1986–87 | Colchester U | 28 | 4 |
| 1987–88 | Burnley | 45 | 3 |
| 1988–89 | Burnley | 36 | 4 |
| 1989–90 | Burnley | 36 | 2 |
| 1990–91 | Burnley | 37 | 2 |
| 1991–92 | Burnley | 39 | 3 |
| 1992–93 | Burnley | 42 | 3 |
| 1993–94 | Burnley | 22 | 2 |
| 1994–95 | Burnley | 0 | 0 |
| 1994–95 | Wigan Ath | 31 | 0 |
| 1995–96 | Wigan Ath | 23 | 1 |
| 1996–97 | Rochdale | 40 | 2 |
| 1997–98 | Rochdale | 40 | 4 |
| **Total:** | | **496** | **31** |

## FARRELL, Dave — Forward

H: 5 9 W: 11 07 b.Birmingham 11-11-71

*Source:* Redditch U.

| | | | |
|---|---|---|---|
| 1992–93 | Aston Villa | 2 | 0 |
| 1992–93 | Scunthorpe U (loan) | 5 | 1 |
| 1993–94 | Aston Villa | 4 | 0 |
| 1994–95 | Aston Villa | 0 | 0 |
| 1995–96 | Aston Villa | 0 | 0 |
| 1995–96 | Wycombe W | 33 | 7 |
| 1996–97 | Wycombe W | 27 | 1 |
| 1997–98 | Peterborough U | 42 | 6 |
| **Total:** | | **113** | **15** |

## FARRELL, Sean — Forward

H: 6 1 W: 13 03 b.Watford 28-2-69

*Source:* Apprentice.

| | | | |
|---|---|---|---|
| 1986–87 | Luton T | 0 | 0 |
| 1987–88 | Luton T | 0 | 0 |
| 1987–88 | Colchester U (loan) | 9 | 1 |
| 1988–89 | Luton T | 0 | 0 |
| 1989–90 | Luton T | 1 | 0 |
| 1990–91 | Luton T | 20 | 1 |
| 1991–92 | Luton T | 4 | 0 |
| 1991–92 | Northampton T (loan) | 4 | 1 |
| 1991–92 | Fulham | 25 | 10 |
| 1992–93 | Fulham | 35 | 12 |
| 1993–94 | Fulham | 34 | 9 |
| 1994–95 | Peterborough U | 33 | 8 |
| 1995–96 | Peterborough U | 26 | 9 |
| 1996–97 | Peterborough U | 7 | 3 |
| 1996–97 | Notts Co | 14 | 1 |
| 1997–98 | Notts Co | 35 | 15 |
| **Total:** | | **247** | **70** |

## FARRELLY, Gareth — Midfield

H: 6 0 W: 12 13 b.Dublin 28-8-75

*Source:* Home Farm. *Honours:* Eire Under-21, 5 full caps.

| | | | |
|---|---|---|---|
| 1992–93 | Aston Villa | 0 | 0 |
| 1993–94 | Aston Villa | 0 | 0 |
| 1994–95 | Aston Villa | 0 | 0 |
| 1994–95 | Rotherham U (loan) | 10 | 2 |
| 1995–96 | Aston Villa | 5 | 0 |
| 1996–97 | Aston Villa | 3 | 0 |
| 1997–98 | Everton | 26 | 1 |
| **Total:** | | **44** | **3** |

## FAULCONBRIDGE, Craig — Forward

H: 6 1 W: 13 00 b.Nuneaton 20-4-78

*Source:* Trainee.

| | | | |
|---|---|---|---|
| 1996–97 | Coventry C | 0 | 0 |
| 1997–98 | Coventry C | 0 | 0 |
| 1997–98 | Dunfermline Ath | 7 | 1 |
| **Total:** | | **7** | **1** |

## FEAR, Peter — Midfield

H: 5 10 W: 11 07 b.Sutton 10-9-73

*Source:* Trainee. *Honours:* England Under-21.

| | | | |
|---|---|---|---|
| 1992–93 | Wimbledon | 4 | 0 |
| 1993–94 | Wimbledon | 23 | 1 |
| 1994–95 | Wimbledon | 14 | 1 |
| 1995–96 | Wimbledon | 4 | 0 |
| 1996–97 | Wimbledon | 18 | 0 |
| 1997–98 | Wimbledon | 8 | 2 |
| **Total:** | | **71** | **4** |

## FEATHERSTONE, James — Forward

H: 6 0 W: 12 12 b.Wharfedale 12-11-79

*Source:* Blackburn R Trainee.

| | | | |
|---|---|---|---|
| 1997–98 | Scunthorpe U | 1 | 0 |
| **Total:** | | **1** | **0** |

## FEENEY, Warren — Forward

H: 5 9  W: 10 06  b.Belfast 17-1-81

*Source:* Trainee.

| | | | |
|---|---|---|---|
| 1997–98 | Leeds U | 0 | 0 |

## FENN, Neale — Forward

H: 5 10  W: 12 08  b.Edmonton 18-1-77

*Source:* Trainee. *Honours:* Eire Youth.

| | | | |
|---|---|---|---|
| 1995–96 | Tottenham H | 0 | 0 |
| 1996–97 | Tottenham H | 4 | 0 |
| 1997–98 | Tottenham H | 4 | 0 |
| 1997–98 | Leyton Orient (loan) | 3 | 0 |
| 1997–98 | Norwich C (loan) | 7 | 1 |
| **Total:** | | **18** | **1** |

## FENSOME, Andy — Defender

H: 5 8  W: 11 09  b.Northampton 18-2-69

*Source:* Trainee.

| | | | |
|---|---|---|---|
| 1986–87 | Norwich C | 0 | 0 |
| 1987–88 | Norwich C | 0 | 0 |
| 1988–89 | Norwich C | 0 | 0 |
| 1988–89 | Newcastle U (loan) | 0 | 0 |
| 1989–90 | Cambridge U | 24 | 0 |
| 1990–91 | Cambridge U | 36 | 0 |
| 1991–92 | Cambridge U | 34 | 1 |
| 1992–93 | Cambridge U | 30 | 0 |
| 1993–94 | Cambridge U | 2 | 0 |
| 1993–94 | Preston NE | 31 | 1 |
| 1994–95 | Preston NE | 42 | 0 |
| 1995–96 | Preston NE | 20 | 0 |
| 1996–97 | Rochdale | 40 | 0 |
| 1997–98 | Rochdale | 42 | 0 |
| **Total:** | | **301** | **2** |

## FENTON, Anthony — Defender

H: 5 10  W: 10 02  b.Preston 23-11-79

*Source:* Trainee.

| | | | |
|---|---|---|---|
| 1996–97 | Manchester C | 0 | 0 |
| 1997–98 | Manchester C | 0 | 0 |

## FENTON, Graham — Forward

H: 5 11  W: 12 10  b.Wallsend 22-5-74

*Source:* Trainee. *Honours:* England Under-21.

| | | | |
|---|---|---|---|
| 1991–92 | Aston Villa | 0 | 0 |
| 1992–93 | Aston Villa | 0 | 0 |
| 1993–94 | Aston Villa | 12 | 1 |
| 1993–94 | WBA (loan) | 7 | 3 |
| 1994–95 | Aston Villa | 17 | 2 |
| 1995–96 | Aston Villa | 3 | 0 |
| 1995–96 | Blackburn R | 14 | 6 |
| 1996–97 | Blackburn R | 13 | 1 |
| 1997–98 | Leicester C | 23 | 3 |
| **Total:** | | **89** | **16** |

## FENTON, Nicholas — Defender

H: 5 10  W: 10 04  b.Preston 23-11-79

*Source:* Trainee. *Honours:* England Youth.

| | | | |
|---|---|---|---|
| 1996–97 | Manchester C | 0 | 0 |
| 1997–98 | Manchester C | 0 | 0 |

## FERDINAND, Les — Forward

H: 5 11  W: 13 05  b.Acton 18-12-66

*Source:* Hayes. *Honours:* England B, 17 full caps, 5 goals.

| | | | |
|---|---|---|---|
| 1986–87 | QPR | 2 | 0 |
| 1987–88 | QPR | 1 | 0 |
| 1987–88 | Brentford (loan) | 3 | 0 |
| 1988–89 | QPR | 0 | 0 |
| 1988–89 | Besiktas (loan) | 24 | 14 |
| 1989–90 | QPR | 9 | 2 |
| 1990–91 | QPR | 18 | 8 |
| 1991–92 | QPR | 23 | 10 |
| 1992–93 | QPR | 37 | 20 |
| 1993–94 | QPR | 36 | 16 |
| 1994–95 | QPR | 37 | 24 |
| 1995–96 | Newcastle U | 37 | 25 |
| 1996–97 | Newcastle U | 31 | 16 |
| 1997–98 | Tottenham H | 21 | 5 |
| **Total:** | | **279** | **140** |

## FERDINAND, Rio — Defender

H: 6 2  W: 12 00  b.Peckham 7-11-78

*Source:* Trainee. *Honours:* England Youth, Under-21, 3 full caps.

| | | | |
|---|---|---|---|
| 1995–96 | West Ham U | 1 | 0 |
| 1996–97 | West Ham U | 15 | 2 |
| 1996–97 | Bournemouth (loan) | 10 | 0 |
| 1997–98 | West Ham U | 35 | 0 |
| **Total:** | | **61** | **2** |

## FERGUSON, Barry — Midfield

H: 5 11  W: 11 01  b.Glasgow 2-2-78

*Source:* Rangers SABC. *Honours:* Scotland Under-21.

| | | | |
|---|---|---|---|
| 1994–95 | Rangers | 0 | 0 |
| 1995–96 | Rangers | 0 | 0 |
| 1996–97 | Rangers | 1 | 0 |
| 1997–98 | Rangers | 7 | 0 |
| **Total:** | | **8** | **0** |

## FERGUSON, Darren — Midfield

H: 5 10 W: 10 04 b.Glasgow 9-2-72

*Source:* Trainee. *Honours:* Scotland Under-21.

| | | | |
|---|---|---|---|
| 1990–91 | Manchester U | 5 | 0 |
| 1991–92 | Manchester U | 4 | 0 |
| 1992–93 | Manchester U | 15 | 0 |
| 1993–94 | Manchester U | 3 | 0 |
| 1993–94 | Wolverhampton W | 14 | 0 |
| 1994–95 | Wolverhampton W | 24 | 0 |
| 1995–96 | Wolverhampton W | 33 | 1 |
| 1996–97 | Wolverhampton W | 16 | 3 |
| 1997–98 | Wolverhampton W | 26 | 0 |
| **Total:** | | **140** | **4** |

## FERGUSON, Duncan — Forward

H: 6 4 W: 14 06 b.Stirling 27-12-71

*Source:* Carse T. *Honours:* Scotland Under-21, 7 full caps.

| | | | |
|---|---|---|---|
| 1990–91 | Dundee U | 9 | 1 |
| 1991–92 | Dundee U | 38 | 15 |
| 1992–93 | Dundee U | 30 | 12 |
| 1993–94 | Rangers | 10 | 1 |
| 1994–95 | Rangers | 4 | 1 |
| 1994–95 | Everton | 23 | 7 |
| 1995–96 | Everton | 18 | 5 |
| 1996–97 | Everton | 33 | 10 |
| 1997–98 | Everton | 29 | 11 |
| **Total:** | | **194** | **63** |

## FERGUSON, Ian — Midfield

H: 5 10 W: 10 11 b.Glasgow 15-3-67

*Source:* Clyde BC. *Honours:* Scotland B, Under-21, 9 full caps.

| | | | |
|---|---|---|---|
| 1984–85 | Clyde | 2 | 0 |
| 1985–86 | Clyde | 19 | 4 |
| 1986–87 | Clyde | 5 | 0 |
| 1986–87 | St Mirren | 35 | 4 |
| 1987–88 | St Mirren | 22 | 6 |
| 1987–88 | Rangers | 8 | 1 |
| 1988–89 | Rangers | 30 | 6 |
| 1989–90 | Rangers | 24 | 0 |
| 1990–91 | Rangers | 11 | 1 |
| 1991–92 | Rangers | 16 | 1 |
| 1992–93 | Rangers | 30 | 4 |
| 1993–94 | Rangers | 35 | 5 |
| 1994–95 | Rangers | 16 | 1 |
| 1995–96 | Rangers | 18 | 2 |
| 1996–97 | Rangers | 24 | 1 |
| 1997–98 | Rangers | 11 | 0 |
| **Total:** | | **306** | **36** |

## FERGUSON, Ian — Forward

H: 6 1 W: 13 12 b.Dunfermline 5-8-68

*Source:* Lochgelly Albert.

| | | | |
|---|---|---|---|
| 1987–88 | Raith R | 9 | 4 |
| 1988–89 | Raith R | 28 | 4 |
| 1989–90 | Raith R | 32 | 6 |
| 1990–91 | Raith R | 33 | 8 |
| 1991–92 | Raith R | 9 | 1 |
| 1991–92 | Hearts | 30 | 4 |
| 1992–93 | Hearts | 24 | 4 |
| 1993–94 | Hearts | 6 | 1 |
| 1993–94 | St Johnstone | 22 | 3 |
| 1994–95 | St Johnstone | 0 | 0 |
| 1995–96 | St Johnstone | 10 | 1 |
| 1996–97 | St Johnstone | 8 | 2 |
| 1997–98 | St Johnstone | 2 | 0 |
| 1997–98 | Ayr U | 33 | 8 |
| **Total:** | | **246** | **46** |

## FERNANDES, Tamer — Goalkeeper

H: 6 2 W: 13 08 b.London 7-12-74

*Source:* Trainee.

| | | | |
|---|---|---|---|
| 1993–94 | Brentford | 1 | 0 |
| 1994–95 | Brentford | 4 | 0 |
| 1995–96 | Brentford | 5 | 0 |
| 1996–97 | Brentford | 2 | 0 |
| 1997–98 | Brentford | 0 | 0 |
| 1997–98 | Peterborough U (loan) | 0 | 0 |
| 1997–98 | Colchester U | 0 | 0 |
| **Total:** | | **12** | **0** |

## FESTA, Gianluca — Defender

H: 6 0 W: 13 02 b.Cagliari 15-3-69

| | | | |
|---|---|---|---|
| 1986–87 | Cagliari | 3 | 0 |
| 1987–88 | Fersuicis (loan) | 26 | 2 |
| 1988–89 | Cagliari | 27 | 0 |
| 1989–90 | Cagliari | 36 | 0 |
| 1990–91 | Cagliari | 28 | 0 |
| 1991–92 | Cagliari | 31 | 0 |
| 1992–93 | Cagliari | 31 | 0 |
| 1993–94 | Internazionale | 4 | 0 |
| 1993–94 | Roma (loan) | 21 | 1 |
| 1994–95 | Internazionale | 26 | 2 |
| 1995–96 | Internazionale | 31 | 1 |
| 1996–97 | Internazionale | 5 | 0 |
| 1996–97 | Middlesbrough | 13 | 1 |
| 1997–98 | Middlesbrough | 38 | 2 |
| **Total:** | | **320** | **9** |

## FETTIS, Alan — Goalkeeper

H: 6 2 W: 13 00 b.Belfast 1-2-71

*Source:* Ards. *Honours:* Northern Ireland 22 full caps.

| | | | |
|---|---|---|---|
| 1991–92 | Hull C | 43 | 0 |
| 1992–93 | Hull C | 20 | 0 |
| 1993–94 | Hull C | 37 | 0 |
| 1994–95 | Hull C | 28 | 2 |
| 1995–96 | Hull C | 7 | 0 |
| 1995–96 | WBA (loan) | 3 | 0 |
| 1996–97 | Nottingham F | 4 | 0 |
| 1997–98 | Nottingham F | 0 | 0 |
| 1997–98 | Blackburn R | 8 | 0 |
| **Total:** | | **150** | **2** |

## FEUER, Ian — Goalkeeper

H: 6 7 W: 15 06 b.Las Vegas 20-5-71

*Source:* Los Angeles Salsa. *Honours:* USA full caps.

| | | | |
|---|---|---|---|
| 1993–94 | West Ham U | 0 | 0 |
| 1994–95 | West Ham U | 0 | 0 |
| 1994–95 | Peterborough U (loan) | 16 | 0 |
| 1995–96 | West Ham U | 0 | 0 |
| 1995–96 | Luton T | 38 | 0 |
| 1996–97 | Luton T | 46 | 0 |
| 1997–98 | Luton T | 13 | 0 |
| **Total:** | | **113** | **0** |

## FEWINGS, Paul — Forward

H: 6 0 W: 12 06 b.Hull 18-2-78

*Source:* Trainee.

| | | | |
|---|---|---|---|
| 1994–95 | Hull C | 2 | 0 |
| 1995–96 | Hull C | 25 | 2 |
| 1996–97 | Hull C | 12 | 0 |
| 1997–98 | Hull C | 18 | 0 |
| **Total:** | | **57** | **2** |

## FICKLING, Ashley — Defender

H: 5 10 W: 11 08 b.Sheffield 15-11-72

*Source:* Trainee. *Honours:* England Schools.

| | | | |
|---|---|---|---|
| 1991–92 | Sheffield U | 0 | 0 |
| 1992–93 | Sheffield U | 0 | 0 |
| 1992–93 | Darlington (loan) | 14 | 0 |
| 1993–94 | Darlington (loan) | 1 | 0 |
| 1994–95 | Sheffield U | 0 | 0 |
| 1994–95 | Grimsby T | 1 | 0 |
| 1995–96 | Grimsby T | 11 | 0 |
| 1996–97 | Grimsby T | 27 | 2 |
| 1997–98 | Grimsby T | 0 | 0 |
| 1997–98 | Darlington (loan) | 8 | 0 |
| **Total:** | | **62** | **2** |

## FILAN, John — Goalkeeper

H: 5 11 W: 13 02 b.Sydney 8-2-70

*Source:* Budapest St George. *Honours:* Australia 2 full caps.

| | | | |
|---|---|---|---|
| 1992–93 | Cambridge U | 6 | 0 |
| 1993–94 | Cambridge U | 46 | 0 |
| 1994–95 | Cambridge U | 16 | 0 |
| 1994–95 | Nottingham F (loan) | 0 | 0 |
| 1994–95 | Coventry C | 2 | 0 |
| 1995–96 | Coventry C | 13 | 0 |
| 1996–97 | Coventry C | 1 | 0 |
| 1997–98 | Blackburn R | 7 | 0 |
| **Total:** | | **91** | **0** |

## FINDLAY, William — Midfield

H: 5 10 W: 10 13 b.Kilmarnock 29-8-70

*Source:* Kilmarnock BC. *Honours:* Scotland Under-21.

| | | | |
|---|---|---|---|
| 1987–88 | Hibernian | 0 | 0 |
| 1988–89 | Hibernian | 3 | 1 |
| 1989–90 | Hibernian | 10 | 0 |
| 1990–91 | Hibernian | 26 | 2 |
| 1991–92 | Hibernian | 9 | 0 |
| 1992–93 | Hibernian | 7 | 0 |
| 1993–94 | Hibernian | 20 | 3 |
| 1994–95 | Hibernian | 18 | 1 |
| 1994–95 | Kilmarnock | 9 | 0 |
| 1995–96 | Kilmarnock | 3 | 0 |
| 1996–97 | Kilmarnock | 20 | 1 |
| 1997–98 | Kilmarnock | 5 | 0 |
| 1997–98 | Ayr U | 6 | 1 |
| **Total:** | | **136** | **9** |

## FINLAYSON, Alex — Forward

H: 6 0 W: 12 02 b.Edinburgh 30-1-79

*Source:* Trainee.

| | | | |
|---|---|---|---|
| 1997–98 | Swindon T | 0 | 0 |
| 1997–98 | Cambridge U | 0 | 0 |

## FINLEY, Gary — Defender

H: 6 0 W: 12 12 b.Liverpool 14-11-70

*Source:* Netherfield.

| | | | |
|---|---|---|---|
| 1997–98 | Doncaster R | 7 | 0 |
| **Total:** | | **7** | **0** |

## FINN, Neil — Goalkeeper

b.London 29-12-78

*Source:* Trainee.

| | | | |
|---|---|---|---|
| 1995–96 | West Ham U | 1 | 0 |

| | | | |
|---|---|---|---|
| 1996–97 | West Ham U | 0 | 0 |
| 1997–98 | West Ham U | 0 | 0 |
| **Total:** | | **1** | **0** |

## FINNAN, Steve — Forward

H: 5 9 W: 10 09 b.Chelmsford 20-4-76

*Source:* Welling U.

| | | | |
|---|---|---|---|
| 1995–96 | Birmingham C | 12 | 1 |
| 1995–96 | Notts Co (loan) | 17 | 2 |
| 1996–97 | Birmingham C | 3 | 0 |
| 1996–97 | Notts Co | 23 | 0 |
| 1997–98 | Notts Co | 44 | 5 |
| **Total:** | | **99** | **8** |

## FINNEY, Steve — Forward

H: 5 10 W: 12 00 b.Hexham 31-10-73

*Source:* Trainee.

| | | | |
|---|---|---|---|
| 1991–92 | Preston NE | 2 | 1 |
| 1992–93 | Preston NE | 4 | 0 |
| 1993–94 | Manchester C | 0 | 0 |
| 1994–95 | Manchester C | 0 | 0 |
| 1995–96 | Swindon T | 30 | 12 |
| 1996–97 | Swindon T | 20 | 2 |
| 1997–98 | Swindon T | 23 | 4 |
| 1997–98 | Cambridge U (loan) | 7 | 2 |
| **Total:** | | **86** | **21** |

## FINNIGAN, John — Midfield

H: 5 8 W: 10 11 b.Wakefield 28-3-76

*Source:* Trainee.

| | | | |
|---|---|---|---|
| 1992–93 | Nottingham F | 0 | 0 |
| 1993–94 | Nottingham F | 0 | 0 |
| 1994–95 | Nottingham F | 0 | 0 |
| 1995–96 | Nottingham F | 0 | 0 |
| 1996–97 | Nottingham F | 0 | 0 |
| 1997–98 | Nottingham F | 0 | 0 |
| 1997–98 | Lincoln C (loan) | 6 | 0 |
| **Total:** | | **6** | **0** |

## FISH, Mark — Defender

H: 6 4 W: 12 11 b.Cape Town 14-3-74

*Source:* Orlando Pirates. *Honours:* South Africa 42 full caps, 2 goals.

| | | | |
|---|---|---|---|
| 1996–97 | Lazio | 15 | 1 |
| 1997–98 | Bolton W | 22 | 2 |
| **Total:** | | **37** | **3** |

## FISHER, Neil — Midfield

H: 5 10 W: 10 09 b.St Helens 7-11-70

*Source:* Trainee.

| | | | |
|---|---|---|---|
| 1990–91 | Bolton W | 0 | 0 |
| 1991–92 | Bolton W | 7 | 1 |
| 1992–93 | Bolton W | 4 | 0 |
| 1993–94 | Bolton W | 2 | 0 |
| 1994–95 | Bolton W | 11 | 0 |
| 1995–96 | Chester C | 44 | 2 |
| 1996–97 | Chester C | 29 | 1 |
| 1997–98 | Chester C | 35 | 1 |
| **Total:** | | **132** | **5** |

## FITCHETT, Scott — Midfield

H: 5 8 W: 9 06 b.Manchester 20-1-79

*Source:* Trainee.

| | | | |
|---|---|---|---|
| 1995–96 | Nottingham F | 0 | 0 |
| 1996–97 | Nottingham F | 0 | 0 |
| 1997–98 | Nottingham F | 0 | 0 |

## FITZGERALD, Scott — Defender

H: 6 0 W: 12 02 b.London 13-8-69

*Source:* Trainee. *Honours:* Eire Under-21, B.

| | | | |
|---|---|---|---|
| 1988–89 | Wimbledon | 0 | 0 |
| 1989–90 | Wimbledon | 1 | 0 |
| 1990–91 | Wimbledon | 0 | 0 |
| 1991–92 | Wimbledon | 36 | 1 |
| 1992–93 | Wimbledon | 20 | 0 |
| 1993–94 | Wimbledon | 28 | 0 |
| 1994–95 | Wimbledon | 17 | 0 |
| 1995–96 | Wimbledon | 4 | 0 |
| 1995–96 | Sheffield U (loan) | 6 | 0 |
| 1996–97 | Wimbledon | 0 | 0 |
| 1996–97 | Millwall (loan) | 7 | 0 |
| 1997–98 | Millwall | 18 | 0 |
| **Total:** | | **137** | **1** |

## FITZHENRY, Neil — Defender

H: 6 0 W: 12 00 b.Billinge 24-9-78

*Source:* Trainee.

| | | | |
|---|---|---|---|
| 1997–98 | Wigan Ath | 3 | 0 |
| **Total:** | | **3** | **0** |

## FITZPATRICK, Lee — Midfield

H: 5 10 W: 11 07 b.Manchester 31-10-78

*Source:* Trainee.

| | | | |
|---|---|---|---|
| 1996–97 | Blackburn R | 0 | 0 |
| 1997–98 | Blackburn R | 0 | 0 |

## FITZPATRICK, Trevor — Forward

H: 6 1 W: 12 10 b.Surrey 19-2-80

*Source:* Trainee.

| | | | |
|---|---|---|---|
| 1997–98 | Southend U | 3 | 0 |
| **Total:** | | **3** | **0** |

## FJORTOFT, Jan-Aage — Forward

H: 6 2 W: 14 00 b.Aalesund 10-1-67

*Honours:* Norway 71 full caps, 20 goals.

| | | | |
|---|---|---|---|
| 1987 | Hamar | 22 | 10 |
| 1988 | Lillestrom | 24 | 14 |
| 1989 | Lillestrom | 11 | 6 |
| 1989–90 | Rapid Vienna | 33 | 17 |
| 1990–91 | Rapid Vienna | 33 | 16 |
| 1991–92 | Rapid Vienna | 34 | 16 |
| 1992–93 | Rapid Vienna | 28 | 13 |
| 1993–94 | Swindon T | 36 | 12 |
| 1994–95 | Swindon T | 36 | 16 |
| 1994–95 | Middlesbrough | 8 | 3 |
| 1995–96 | Middlesbrough | 28 | 6 |
| 1996–97 | Middlesbrough | 5 | 0 |
| 1996–97 | Sheffield U | 17 | 10 |
| 1997–98 | Sheffield U | 17 | 9 |
| 1997–98 | Barnsley | 15 | 6 |
| **Total:** | | **347** | **154** |

## FLACK, Steve — Forward

H: 6 1 W: 11 04 b.Cambridge 29-5-71

*Source:* Cambridge C.

| | | | |
|---|---|---|---|
| 1995–96 | Cardiff C | 10 | 1 |
| 1996–97 | Cardiff C | 1 | 0 |
| 1996–97 | Exeter C | 27 | 4 |
| 1997–98 | Exeter C | 41 | 14 |
| **Total:** | | **79** | **19** |

## FLAHAVAN, Aaron — Goalkeeper

H: 6 1 W: 11 12 b.Southampton 15-12-75

*Source:* Trainee.

| | | | |
|---|---|---|---|
| 1993–94 | Portsmouth | 0 | 0 |
| 1994–95 | Portsmouth | 0 | 0 |
| 1995–96 | Portsmouth | 0 | 0 |
| 1996–97 | Portsmouth | 24 | 0 |
| 1997–98 | Portsmouth | 26 | 0 |
| **Total:** | | **50** | **0** |

## FLAHAVAN, Darryl — Goalkeeper

H: 5 10 W: 12 01 b.Southampton 28-11-78

*Source:* Trainee.

| | | | |
|---|---|---|---|
| 1996–97 | Southampton | 0 | 0 |
| 1997–98 | Southampton | 0 | 0 |

## FLASH, Richard — Midfield

H: 5 9 W: 11 08 b.Birmingham 8-4-76

*Source:* Trainee.

| | | | |
|---|---|---|---|
| 1994–95 | Manchester U | 0 | 0 |
| 1995–96 | Manchester U | 0 | 0 |
| 1995–96 | Wolverhampton W | 0 | 0 |
| 1996–97 | Watford | 1 | 0 |
| 1997–98 | Watford | 0 | 0 |
| 1997–98 | Lincoln C (loan) | 5 | 0 |
| **Total:** | | **6** | **0** |

## FLECK, Robert — Forward

H: 5 7 W: 11 09 b.Glasgow 11-8-65

*Source:* Possil YM. *Honours:* Scotland Youth, Under-21, 4 full caps.

| | | | |
|---|---|---|---|
| 1983–84 | Partick T | 2 | 1 |
| 1983–84 | Rangers | 1 | 0 |
| 1984–85 | Rangers | 8 | 0 |
| 1985–86 | Rangers | 15 | 3 |
| 1986–87 | Rangers | 40 | 19 |
| 1987–88 | Rangers | 21 | 7 |
| 1987–88 | Norwich C | 18 | 7 |
| 1988–89 | Norwich C | 33 | 10 |
| 1989–90 | Norwich C | 27 | 7 |
| 1990–91 | Norwich C | 29 | 5 |
| 1991–92 | Norwich C | 36 | 11 |
| 1992–93 | Chelsea | 31 | 2 |
| 1993–94 | Chelsea | 9 | 1 |
| 1993–94 | Bolton W (loan) | 7 | 1 |
| 1994–95 | Chelsea | 0 | 0 |
| 1994–95 | Bristol C (loan) | 10 | 1 |
| 1995–96 | Chelsea | 0 | 0 |
| 1995–96 | Norwich C | 41 | 10 |
| 1996–97 | Norwich C | 36 | 4 |
| 1997–98 | Norwich C | 27 | 2 |
| 1997–98 | Reading | 5 | 0 |
| **Total:** | | **396** | **91** |

## FLEMING, Craig — Defender

H: 6 0 W: 12 09 b.Calder 6-10-71

*Source:* Trainee.

| | | | |
|---|---|---|---|
| 1988–89 | Halifax T | 1 | 0 |
| 1989–90 | Halifax T | 10 | 0 |
| 1990–91 | Halifax T | 46 | 0 |

| | | | |
|---|---|---|---|
| 1991–92 | Oldham Ath | 32 | 1 |
| 1992–93 | Oldham Ath | 24 | 0 |
| 1993–94 | Oldham Ath | 37 | 0 |
| 1994–95 | Oldham Ath | 5 | 0 |
| 1995–96 | Oldham Ath | 22 | 0 |
| 1996–97 | Oldham Ath | 44 | 0 |
| 1997–98 | Norwich C | 22 | 1 |
| **Total:** | | **243** | **2** |

## FLEMING, Curtis — Defender

H: 5 10 W: 12 08 b.Manchester 8-10-68

*Source:* St Patrick's Ath. *Honours:* Eire Youth, Under-21, B, 10 full caps.

| | | | |
|---|---|---|---|
| 1991–92 | Middlesbrough | 28 | 0 |
| 1992–93 | Middlesbrough | 24 | 0 |
| 1993–94 | Middlesbrough | 40 | 0 |
| 1994–95 | Middlesbrough | 21 | 0 |
| 1995–96 | Middlesbrough | 13 | 1 |
| 1996–97 | Middlesbrough | 30 | 0 |
| 1997–98 | Middlesbrough | 31 | 1 |
| **Total:** | | **187** | **2** |

## FLEMING, Derek — Defender

H: 5 7 W: 10 02 b.Falkirk 5-12-73

*Source:* Broxburn Ath.

| | | | |
|---|---|---|---|
| 1992–93 | Meadowbank T | 4 | 0 |
| 1993–94 | Meadowbank T | 38 | 2 |
| 1994–95 | Meadowbank T | 7 | 1 |
| 1994–95 | Dunfermline Ath | 29 | 1 |
| 1995–96 | Dunfermline Ath | 33 | 3 |
| 1996–97 | Dunfermline Ath | 26 | 2 |
| 1997–98 | Dunfermline Ath | 2 | 0 |
| 1997–98 | Dundee | 17 | 0 |
| **Total:** | | **156** | **9** |

## FLEMING, Terry — Midfield

H: 5 9 W: 10 01 b.Marston Green 5-1-73

*Source:* Trainee.

| | | | |
|---|---|---|---|
| 1990–91 | Coventry C | 2 | 0 |
| 1991–92 | Coventry C | 0 | 0 |
| 1992–93 | Coventry C | 11 | 0 |
| 1993–94 | Northampton T | 31 | 1 |
| 1994–95 | Preston NE | 27 | 2 |
| 1995–96 | Preston NE | 5 | 0 |
| 1995–96 | Lincoln C | 22 | 0 |
| 1996–97 | Lincoln C | 37 | 0 |
| 1997–98 | Lincoln C | 40 | 3 |
| **Total:** | | **175** | **6** |

## FLETCHER, Carl

b.Surrey Heath 7-4-80

*Source:* Trainee.

| | | | |
|---|---|---|---|
| 1997–98 | Bournemouth | 1 | 0 |
| **Total:** | | **1** | **0** |

## FLETCHER, Steve — Forward

H: 6 2 W: 14 09 b.Hartlepool 26-6-72

*Source:* Trainee.

| | | | |
|---|---|---|---|
| 1990–91 | Hartlepool U | 14 | 2 |
| 1991–92 | Hartlepool U | 18 | 2 |
| 1992–93 | Bournemouth | 31 | 4 |
| 1993–94 | Bournemouth | 36 | 6 |
| 1994–95 | Bournemouth | 40 | 6 |
| 1995–96 | Bournemouth | 7 | 1 |
| 1996–97 | Bournemouth | 35 | 7 |
| 1997–98 | Bournemouth | 42 | 12 |
| **Total:** | | **223** | **40** |

## FLITCROFT, David — Midfield

H: 5 10 W: 13 05 b.Bolton 14-1-74

*Source:* Trainee.

| | | | |
|---|---|---|---|
| 1991–92 | Preston NE | 0 | 0 |
| 1992–93 | Preston NE | 8 | 2 |
| 1993–94 | Preston NE | 0 | 0 |
| 1993–94 | Lincoln C (loan) | 2 | 0 |
| 1993–94 | Chester C | 8 | 1 |
| 1994–95 | Chester C | 32 | 0 |
| 1995–96 | Chester C | 9 | 1 |
| 1996–97 | Chester C | 32 | 6 |
| 1997–98 | Chester C | 44 | 4 |
| **Total:** | | **135** | **14** |

## FLITCROFT, Garry — Midfield

H: 6 0 W: 11 08 b.Bolton 6-11-72

*Source:* Trainee. *Honours:* England Schools, Under-21.

| | | | |
|---|---|---|---|
| 1991–92 | Manchester C | 0 | 0 |
| 1991–92 | Bury (loan) | 12 | 0 |
| 1992–93 | Manchester C | 32 | 5 |
| 1993–94 | Manchester C | 21 | 3 |
| 1994–95 | Manchester C | 37 | 5 |
| 1995–96 | Manchester C | 25 | 0 |
| 1995–96 | Blackburn R | 3 | 0 |
| 1996–97 | Blackburn R | 28 | 3 |
| 1997–98 | Blackburn R | 33 | 0 |
| **Total:** | | **191** | **16** |

## FLO, Tor Andre — Forward

H: 6 4  W: 13 08  b.Strin 15-6-73

*Honours:* Norway 29 full caps, 13 goals.

| | | | |
|---|---|---|---|
| 1994 | Sogndal | 22 | 5 |
| 1995 | Tromso | 26 | 18 |
| 1996 | Brann | 24 | 19 |
| 1997 | Brann | 16 | 9 |
| 1997–98 | Chelsea | 34 | 11 |
| **Total:** | | **122** | **62** |

## FLOGEL, Thomas — Midfield

H: 5 9  W: 11 02  b.Vienna 7-6-71

*Source:* FK Austria. *Honours:* Austria 9 full caps.

| | | | |
|---|---|---|---|
| 1989–90 | FK Austria | 16 | 1 |
| 1990–91 | FK Austria | 28 | 5 |
| 1991–92 | FK Austria | 35 | 6 |
| 1992–93 | FK Austria | 35 | 10 |
| 1993–94 | FK Austria | 35 | 5 |
| 1994–95 | FK Austria | 36 | 7 |
| 1995–96 | FK Austria | 29 | 4 |
| 1996–97 | FK Austria | 34 | 4 |
| 1997–98 | Hearts | 29 | 5 |
| **Total:** | | **277** | **47** |

## FLOOD, Colin — Midfield

b.Liverpool 29-10-79

*Source:* Stantondale.

| | | | |
|---|---|---|---|
| 1997–98 | Crewe Alex | 0 | 0 |

## FLOWERS, Tim — Goalkeeper

H: 6 3  W: 14 04  b.Kenilworth 3-2-67

*Source:* Apprentice. *Honours:* England Youth, Under-21, 10 full caps.

| | | | |
|---|---|---|---|
| 1984–85 | Wolverhampton W | 38 | 0 |
| 1985–86 | Wolverhampton W | 25 | 0 |
| 1985–86 | Southampton (loan) | 0 | 0 |
| 1986–87 | Southampton | 9 | 0 |
| 1986–87 | Swindon T (loan) | 2 | 0 |
| 1987–88 | Southampton | 9 | 0 |
| 1987–88 | Swindon T (loan) | 5 | 0 |
| 1988–89 | Southampton | 7 | 0 |
| 1989–90 | Southampton | 35 | 0 |
| 1990–91 | Southampton | 37 | 0 |
| 1991–92 | Southampton | 41 | 0 |
| 1992–93 | Southampton | 42 | 0 |
| 1993–94 | Southampton | 12 | 0 |
| 1993–94 | Blackburn R | 29 | 0 |
| 1994–95 | Blackburn R | 39 | 0 |
| 1995–96 | Blackburn R | 37 | 0 |
| 1996–97 | Blackburn R | 36 | 0 |
| 1997–98 | Blackburn R | 25 | 0 |
| **Total:** | | **428** | **0** |

## FLYNN, Mike — Defender

H: 6 0  W: 11 02  b.Oldham 23-2-69

*Source:* Trainee.

| | | | |
|---|---|---|---|
| 1986–87 | Oldham Ath | 0 | 0 |
| 1987–88 | Oldham Ath | 31 | 1 |
| 1988–89 | Oldham Ath | 9 | 0 |
| 1988–89 | Norwich C | 0 | 0 |
| 1989–90 | Norwich C | 0 | 0 |
| 1989–90 | Preston NE | 23 | 1 |
| 1990–91 | Preston NE | 35 | 1 |
| 1991–92 | Preston NE | 43 | 3 |
| 1992–93 | Preston NE | 35 | 2 |
| 1992–93 | Stockport Co | 10 | 0 |
| 1993–94 | Stockport Co | 46 | 1 |
| 1994–95 | Stockport Co | 43 | 2 |
| 1995–96 | Stockport Co | 46 | 6 |
| 1996–97 | Stockport Co | 46 | 2 |
| 1997–98 | Stockport Co | 34 | 1 |
| **Total:** | | **401** | **20** |

## FLYNN, Sean — Midfield

H: 5 8  W: 11 08  b.Birmingham 13-3-68

*Source:* Halesowen T.

| | | | |
|---|---|---|---|
| 1991–92 | Coventry C | 22 | 2 |
| 1992–93 | Coventry C | 7 | 0 |
| 1993–94 | Coventry C | 36 | 3 |
| 1994–95 | Coventry C | 32 | 4 |
| 1995–96 | Derby Co | 42 | 2 |
| 1996–97 | Derby Co | 17 | 1 |
| 1996–97 | Stoke C (loan) | 5 | 0 |
| 1997–98 | WBA | 35 | 2 |
| **Total:** | | **196** | **14** |

## FOLAN, Tony — Defender

H: 5 10  W: 10 08  b.Lewisham 18-9-78

*Source:* Trainee.

| | | | |
|---|---|---|---|
| 1995–96 | Crystal Palace | 0 | 0 |
| 1996–97 | Crystal Palace | 0 | 0 |
| 1997–98 | Crystal Palace | 1 | 0 |
| **Total:** | | **1** | **0** |

## FOLEY, Dominic — Forward

H: 6 1  W: 12 08  b.Cork 7-7-76

*Source:* St James Gate.

| | | | |
|---|---|---|---|
| 1995–96 | Wolverhampton W | 5 | 0 |
| 1996–97 | Wolverhampton W | 5 | 1 |

| | | | |
|---|---|---|---|
| 1997–98 | Wolverhampton W | 5 | 0 |
| 1997–98 | Watford (loan) | 8 | 1 |
| **Total:** | | **23** | **2** |

## FOLLAND, Robert — Forward

H: 5 9 W: 10 13 b.Swansea 16-9-79

*Source:* Trainee.

| | | | |
|---|---|---|---|
| 1997–98 | Oxford U | 2 | 0 |
| **Total:** | | **2** | **0** |

## FOLLETT, Richard — Defender

H: 5 9 W: 10 02 b.Leamington Spa 29-8-79

*Source:* Trainee.

| | | | |
|---|---|---|---|
| 1996–97 | Nottingham F | 0 | 0 |
| 1997–98 | Nottingham F | 0 | 0 |

## FORAN, Mark — Defender

H: 6 3 W: 13 04 b.Aldershot 30-10-73

*Source:* Trainee.

| | | | |
|---|---|---|---|
| 1991–92 | Millwall | 0 | 0 |
| 1992–93 | Millwall | 0 | 0 |
| 1993–94 | Millwall | 0 | 0 |
| 1993–94 | Sheffield U | 0 | 0 |
| 1994–95 | Sheffield U | 4 | 1 |
| 1994–95 | Rotherham U (loan) | 3 | 0 |
| 1995–96 | Sheffield U | 7 | 0 |
| 1995–96 | Wycombe W (loan) | 5 | 0 |
| 1995–96 | Peterborough U | 17 | 1 |
| 1996–97 | Peterborough U | 4 | 0 |
| 1996–97 | Lincoln C (loan) | 2 | 0 |
| 1996–97 | Oldham Ath (loan) | 1 | 0 |
| 1997–98 | Peterborough U | 4 | 0 |
| 1997–98 | Crewe Alex | 12 | 1 |
| **Total:** | | **59** | **3** |

## FORBES, Adrian — Forward

H: 5 8 W: 11 04 b.Greenford 23-1-79

*Source:* Trainee. *Honours:* England Youth.

| | | | |
|---|---|---|---|
| 1996–97 | Norwich C | 10 | 0 |
| 1997–98 | Norwich C | 33 | 4 |
| **Total:** | | **43** | **4** |

## FORBES, Steve — Midfield

H: 6 1 W: 13 03 b.Hackney 24-12-75

*Source:* Sittingbourne.

| | | | |
|---|---|---|---|
| 1994–95 | Millwall | 1 | 0 |
| 1995–96 | Millwall | 4 | 0 |
| 1996–97 | Millwall | 0 | 0 |
| 1996–97 | Colchester U | 1 | 1 |
| 1997–98 | Colchester U | 35 | 1 |
| **Total:** | | **41** | **2** |

## FORD, Bobby — Midfield

H: 5 8 W: 11 00 b.Bristol 22-9-74

*Source:* Trainee.

| | | | |
|---|---|---|---|
| 1992–93 | Oxford U | 0 | 0 |
| 1993–94 | Oxford U | 14 | 0 |
| 1994–95 | Oxford U | 23 | 2 |
| 1995–96 | Oxford U | 28 | 3 |
| 1996–97 | Oxford U | 33 | 0 |
| 1997–98 | Oxford U | 18 | 2 |
| 1997–98 | Sheffield U | 23 | 1 |
| **Total:** | | **139** | **8** |

## FORD, John — Defender

H: 6 0 W: 13 12 b.Birmingham 12-4-68

*Source:* Cradley T.

| | | | |
|---|---|---|---|
| 1991–92 | Swansea C | 44 | 0 |
| 1992–93 | Swansea C | 43 | 3 |
| 1993–94 | Swansea C | 27 | 1 |
| 1994–95 | Swansea C | 46 | 3 |
| 1995–96 | Bradford C | 19 | 0 |
| 1996–97 | Gillingham | 4 | 0 |
| 1996–97 | Barnet | 13 | 1 |
| 1997–98 | Barnet | 19 | 0 |
| **Total:** | | **215** | **8** |

## FORD, Mark — Midfield

H: 5 7 W: 10 08 b.Pontefract 10-10-75

*Source:* Trainee. *Honours:* England Youth, Under-21.

| | | | |
|---|---|---|---|
| 1992–93 | Leeds U | 0 | 0 |
| 1993–94 | Leeds U | 1 | 0 |
| 1994–95 | Leeds U | 0 | 0 |
| 1995–96 | Leeds U | 12 | 0 |
| 1996–97 | Leeds U | 16 | 1 |
| 1997–98 | Burnley | 36 | 1 |
| **Total:** | | **65** | **2** |

## FORD, Mike — Defender

H: 6 0 W: 12 07 b.Bristol 9-2-66

*Source:* Apprentice.

| | | | |
|---|---|---|---|
| 1983–84 | Leicester C | 0 | 0 |
| From Devizes T. | | | |
| 1984–85 | Cardiff C | 20 | 1 |
| 1985–86 | Cardiff C | 44 | 4 |
| 1986–87 | Cardiff C | 36 | 1 |
| 1987–88 | Cardiff C | 45 | 7 |
| 1988–89 | Oxford U | 10 | 1 |

| | | | |
|---|---|---|---|
| 1989–90 | Oxford U | 31 | 2 |
| 1990–91 | Oxford U | 28 | 1 |
| 1991–92 | Oxford U | 9 | 1 |
| 1992–93 | Oxford U | 44 | 4 |
| 1993–94 | Oxford U | 41 | 1 |
| 1994–95 | Oxford U | 18 | 0 |
| 1995–96 | Oxford U | 44 | 2 |
| 1996–97 | Oxford U | 42 | 4 |
| 1997–98 | Oxford U | 22 | 2 |
| **Total:** | | **434** | **31** |

## FORD, Ryan — Midfield

H: 5 9 W: 10 04 b.Worksop 3-9-78

*Source:* Trainee.

| | | | |
|---|---|---|---|
| 1997–98 | Manchester U | 0 | 0 |

## FORD, Tony — Midfield

H: 5 9 W: 13 00 b.Grimsby 14-5-59

*Source:* Apprentice. *Honours:* England B.

| | | | |
|---|---|---|---|
| 1975–76 | Grimsby T | 15 | 0 |
| 1976–77 | Grimsby T | 6 | 0 |
| 1977–78 | Grimsby T | 34 | 2 |
| 1978–79 | Grimsby T | 45 | 16 |
| 1979–80 | Grimsby T | 37 | 5 |
| 1980–81 | Grimsby T | 28 | 4 |
| 1981–82 | Grimsby T | 35 | 7 |
| 1982–83 | Grimsby T | 37 | 4 |
| 1983–84 | Grimsby T | 42 | 8 |
| 1984–85 | Grimsby T | 42 | 6 |
| 1985–86 | Grimsby T | 34 | 3 |
| 1985–86 | Sunderland (loan) | 9 | 1 |
| 1986–87 | Stoke C | 41 | 6 |
| 1987–88 | Stoke C | 44 | 7 |
| 1988–89 | Stoke C | 27 | 0 |
| 1988–89 | WBA | 11 | 1 |
| 1989–90 | WBA | 42 | 8 |
| 1990–91 | WBA | 46 | 5 |
| 1991–92 | WBA | 15 | 0 |
| 1991–92 | Grimsby T | 22 | 1 |
| 1992–93 | Grimsby T | 17 | 2 |
| 1993–94 | Grimsby T | 29 | 0 |
| 1993–94 | Bradford C (loan) | 5 | 0 |
| 1994–95 | Scunthorpe U | 38 | 2 |
| 1995–96 | Scunthorpe U | 38 | 7 |
| From Barrow. | | | |
| 1996–97 | Mansfield T | 27 | 2 |
| 1997–98 | Mansfield T | 34 | 3 |
| **Total:** | | **800** | **100** |

## FORINTON, Howard — Forward

H: 5 11 W: 11 00 b.Boston 18-9-75

*Source:* Yeovil T.

| | | | |
|---|---|---|---|
| 1997–98 | Birmingham C | 1 | 0 |
| **Total:** | | **1** | **0** |

## FORREST, Craig — Goalkeeper

H: 6 5 W: 14 00 b.Vancouver 20-9-67

*Source:* Apprentice. *Honours:* Canada 37 full caps.

| | | | |
|---|---|---|---|
| 1985–86 | Ipswich T | 0 | 0 |
| 1986–87 | Ipswich T | 0 | 0 |
| 1987–88 | Ipswich T | 0 | 0 |
| 1987–88 | Colchester U (loan) | 11 | 0 |
| 1988–89 | Ipswich T | 28 | 0 |
| 1989–90 | Ipswich T | 45 | 0 |
| 1990–91 | Ipswich T | 43 | 0 |
| 1991–92 | Ipswich T | 46 | 0 |
| 1992–93 | Ipswich T | 11 | 0 |
| 1993–94 | Ipswich T | 27 | 0 |
| 1994–95 | Ipswich T | 36 | 0 |
| 1995–96 | Ipswich T | 21 | 0 |
| 1996–97 | Ipswich T | 6 | 0 |
| 1996–97 | Chelsea (loan) | 3 | 0 |
| 1997–98 | West Ham U | 13 | 0 |
| **Total:** | | **290** | **0** |

## FORREST, Martyn — Midfield

H: 5 10 W: 12 02 b.Bury 2-1-79

| | | | |
|---|---|---|---|
| 1997–98 | Bury | 0 | 0 |

## FORRESTER, Jamie — Forward

H: 5 6 W: 10 12 b.Bradford 1-11-74

*Source:* Auxerre. *Honours:* England Schools, Youth.

| | | | |
|---|---|---|---|
| 1992–93 | Leeds U | 6 | 0 |
| 1993–94 | Leeds U | 3 | 0 |
| 1994–95 | Leeds U | 0 | 0 |
| 1994–95 | Southend U (loan) | 5 | 0 |
| 1994–95 | Grimsby T (loan) | 9 | 1 |
| 1995–96 | Leeds U | 0 | 0 |
| 1995–96 | Grimsby T | 28 | 5 |
| 1996–97 | Grimsby T | 13 | 1 |
| 1996–97 | Scunthorpe U | 10 | 6 |
| 1997–98 | Scunthorpe U | 45 | 11 |
| **Total:** | | **119** | **24** |

## FORSTER, Nicky — Forward

H: 5 9 W: 11 05 b.Caterham 8-9-73

*Source:* Horley T. *Honours:* England Under-21.

| | | | |
|---|---|---|---|
| 1992–93 | Gillingham | 26 | 6 |

| | | | |
|---|---|---|---|
| 1993–94 | Gillingham | 41 | 18 |
| 1994–95 | Brentford | 46 | 24 |
| 1995–96 | Brentford | 38 | 5 |
| 1996–97 | Brentford | 25 | 10 |
| 1996–97 | Birmingham C | 7 | 3 |
| 1997–98 | Birmingham C | 28 | 3 |
| **Total:** | | **211** | **69** |

## FORSYTH, Mike — Defender

H: 5 11 W: 12 04 b.Liverpool 20-3-66

*Source:* Apprentice. *Honours:* England Youth, Under-21, B.

| | | | |
|---|---|---|---|
| 1983–84 | WBA | 8 | 0 |
| 1984–85 | WBA | 10 | 0 |
| 1985–86 | WBA | 11 | 0 |
| 1985–86 | Northampton T (loan) | 0 | 0 |
| 1985–86 | Derby Co | 0 | 0 |
| 1986–87 | Derby Co | 41 | 1 |
| 1987–88 | Derby Co | 39 | 3 |
| 1988–89 | Derby Co | 38 | 0 |
| 1989–90 | Derby Co | 38 | 0 |
| 1990–91 | Derby Co | 35 | 0 |
| 1991–92 | Derby Co | 43 | 1 |
| 1992–93 | Derby Co | 41 | 1 |
| 1993–94 | Derby Co | 28 | 2 |
| 1994–95 | Derby Co | 22 | 0 |
| 1994–95 | Notts Co | 7 | 0 |
| 1995–96 | Notts Co | 0 | 0 |
| 1996–97 | Notts Co | 0 | 0 |
| 1996–97 | Hereford U (loan) | 12 | 0 |
| 1996–97 | Wycombe W | 23 | 2 |
| 1997–98 | Wycombe W | 25 | 0 |
| **Total:** | | **421** | **10** |

## FORSYTH, Richard — Midfield

H: 5 11 W: 12 12 b.Dudley 3-10-70

*Source:* Kidderminster H.

| | | | |
|---|---|---|---|
| 1995–96 | Birmingham C | 26 | 2 |
| 1996–97 | Stoke C | 40 | 8 |
| 1997–98 | Stoke C | 37 | 7 |
| **Total:** | | **103** | **17** |

## FORTUNE-WEST, Leo — Forward

H: 6 4 W: 13 11 b.Stratford 9-4-71

*Source:* Tiptree, Dagenham, Dartford, Bishops Stortford, Stevenage Bor.

| | | | |
|---|---|---|---|
| 1995–96 | Gillingham | 40 | 12 |
| 1996–97 | Gillingham | 7 | 2 |
| 1996–97 | Leyton Orient (loan) | 5 | 0 |
| 1997–98 | Gillingham | 20 | 4 |
| **Total:** | | **72** | **18** |

## FOSTER, Colin — Defender

H: 6 4 W: 15 02 b.Chislehurst 16-7-64

*Source:* Apprentice.

| | | | |
|---|---|---|---|
| 1981–82 | Orient | 23 | 2 |
| 1982–83 | Orient | 43 | 2 |
| 1983–84 | Orient | 11 | 1 |
| 1984–85 | Orient | 42 | 1 |
| 1985–86 | Orient | 36 | 2 |
| 1986–87 | Orient | 19 | 2 |
| 1986–87 | Nottingham F | 9 | 1 |
| 1987–88 | Nottingham F | 39 | 2 |
| 1988–89 | Nottingham F | 18 | 2 |
| 1989–90 | Nottingham F | 6 | 0 |
| 1989–90 | West Ham U | 22 | 1 |
| 1990–91 | West Ham U | 36 | 3 |
| 1991–92 | West Ham U | 24 | 0 |
| 1992–93 | West Ham U | 6 | 1 |
| 1993–94 | West Ham U | 5 | 0 |
| 1993–94 | Notts Co (loan) | 9 | 0 |
| 1993–94 | Watford | 6 | 1 |
| 1994–95 | Watford | 34 | 2 |
| 1995–96 | Watford | 26 | 5 |
| 1996–97 | Watford | 0 | 0 |
| 1996–97 | Cambridge U (loan) | 7 | 0 |
| 1997–98 | Cambridge U | 26 | 1 |
| **Total:** | | **447** | **29** |

## FOSTER, Craig — Midfield

H: 5 11 W: 12 00 b.Australia 15-4-69

*Source:* Marconi.

| | | | |
|---|---|---|---|
| 1997–98 | Portsmouth | 16 | 2 |
| **Total:** | | **16** | **2** |

## FOSTER, John — Defender

H: 5 11 W: 13 02 b.Blackley 19-9-73

*Source:* Trainee. *Honours:* England Schools.

| | | | |
|---|---|---|---|
| 1992–93 | Manchester C | 0 | 0 |
| 1993–94 | Manchester C | 1 | 0 |
| 1994–95 | Manchester C | 11 | 0 |
| 1995–96 | Manchester C | 4 | 0 |
| 1996–97 | Manchester C | 3 | 0 |
| 1997–98 | Manchester C | 0 | 0 |
| 1997–98 | Carlisle U | 7 | 0 |
| **Total:** | | **26** | **0** |

## FOSTER, Martin — Midfield

H: 5 5 W: 9 10 b.Sheffield 29-10-77

*Source:* Trainee.

| | | | |
|---|---|---|---|
| 1994–95 | Leeds U | 0 | 0 |
| 1995–96 | Leeds U | 0 | 0 |

| | | | |
|---|---|---|---|
| 1996–97 | Leeds U | 0 | 0 |
| 1997–98 | Leeds U | 0 | 0 |
| 1997–98 | Blackpool (loan) | 1 | 0 |
| **Total:** | | **1** | **0** |

## FOSTER, Stephen — Defender

H: 6 1 W: 12 00 b.Mansfield 3-12-74

*Source:* Trainee.

| | | | |
|---|---|---|---|
| 1993–94 | Mansfield T | 5 | 0 |
| From Woking. | | | |
| 1997–98 | Bristol R | 34 | 0 |
| **Total:** | | **39** | **0** |

## FOTIADIS, Andrew — Forward

H: 5 11 W: 11 00 b.Hitchin 6-9-77

*Source:* School. *Honours:* England Schools.

| | | | |
|---|---|---|---|
| 1996–97 | Luton T | 17 | 3 |
| 1997–98 | Luton T | 15 | 1 |
| **Total:** | | **32** | **4** |

## FOWLER, Jason — Midfield

H: 6 2 W: 11 11 b.Bristol 20-8-74

*Source:* Trainee.

| | | | |
|---|---|---|---|
| 1992–93 | Bristol C | 1 | 0 |
| 1993–94 | Bristol C | 1 | 0 |
| 1994–95 | Bristol C | 13 | 0 |
| 1995–96 | Bristol C | 10 | 0 |
| 1996–97 | Cardiff C | 37 | 5 |
| 1997–98 | Cardiff C | 38 | 5 |
| **Total:** | | **100** | **10** |

## FOWLER, Robbie — Forward

H: 5 11 W: 11 10 b.Liverpool 9-4-75

*Source:* Trainee. *Honours:* England Youth, B, Under-21, 8 full caps, 2 goals.

| | | | |
|---|---|---|---|
| 1991–92 | Liverpool | 0 | 0 |
| 1992–93 | Liverpool | 0 | 0 |
| 1993–94 | Liverpool | 28 | 12 |
| 1994–95 | Liverpool | 42 | 25 |
| 1995–96 | Liverpool | 38 | 28 |
| 1996–97 | Liverpool | 32 | 18 |
| 1997–98 | Liverpool | 20 | 9 |
| **Total:** | | **160** | **92** |

## FOX, Martin — Defender

H: 5 8 W: 11 00 b.Sutton-in-Ashfield 21-4-79

*Source:* Trainee.

| | | | |
|---|---|---|---|
| 1997–98 | Leicester C | 0 | 0 |

## FOX, Peter — Goalkeeper

H: 5 11 W: 13 10 b.Scunthorpe 5-7-57

*Source:* Apprentice.

| | | | |
|---|---|---|---|
| 1972–73 | Sheffield W | 1 | 0 |
| 1973–74 | Sheffield W | 0 | 0 |
| 1974–75 | Sheffield W | 20 | 0 |
| 1975–76 | Sheffield W | 27 | 0 |
| 1976–77 | Sheffield W | 1 | 0 |
| 1976–77 | West Ham U (loan) | 0 | 0 |
| 1977–78 | Sheffield W | 0 | 0 |
| 1977–78 | Barnsley (loan) | 1 | 0 |
| 1977–78 | Stoke C | 0 | 0 |
| 1978–79 | Stoke C | 1 | 0 |
| 1979–80 | Stoke C | 23 | 0 |
| 1980–81 | Stoke C | 42 | 0 |
| 1981–82 | Stoke C | 38 | 0 |
| 1982–83 | Stoke C | 35 | 0 |
| 1983–84 | Stoke C | 42 | 0 |
| 1984–85 | Stoke C | 14 | 0 |
| 1985–86 | Stoke C | 37 | 0 |
| 1986–87 | Stoke C | 39 | 0 |
| 1987–88 | Stoke C | 17 | 0 |
| 1988–89 | Stoke C | 29 | 0 |
| 1989–90 | Stoke C | 38 | 0 |
| 1990–91 | Stoke C | 44 | 0 |
| 1991–92 | Stoke C | 0 | 0 |
| 1992–93 | Stoke C | 10 | 0 |
| 1992–93 | Wrexham (loan) | 0 | 0 |
| 1993–94 | Exeter C | 26 | 0 |
| 1994–95 | Exeter C | 31 | 0 |
| 1995–96 | Exeter C | 46 | 0 |
| 1996–97 | Exeter C | 5 | 0 |
| 1997–98 | Exeter C | 0 | 0 |
| **Total:** | | **567** | **0** |

## FOX, Ruel — Forward

H: 5 6 W: 10 05 b.Ipswich 14-1-68

*Source:* Apprentice. *Honours:* England B.

| | | | |
|---|---|---|---|
| 1985–86 | Norwich C | 0 | 0 |
| 1986–87 | Norwich C | 3 | 0 |
| 1987–88 | Norwich C | 34 | 2 |
| 1988–89 | Norwich C | 4 | 0 |
| 1989–90 | Norwich C | 7 | 3 |
| 1990–91 | Norwich C | 28 | 4 |
| 1991–92 | Norwich C | 37 | 2 |
| 1992–93 | Norwich C | 34 | 4 |
| 1993–94 | Norwich C | 25 | 7 |
| 1993–94 | Newcastle U | 14 | 2 |
| 1994–95 | Newcastle U | 40 | 10 |
| 1995–96 | Newcastle U | 4 | 0 |
| 1995–96 | Tottenham H | 26 | 6 |
| 1996–97 | Tottenham H | 25 | 1 |

| | | | |
|---|---|---|---|
| 1997–98 | Tottenham H | 32 | 3 |
| **Total:** | | **313** | **44** |

## FOYLE, Martin — Forward

H: 5 11 W: 12 01 b.Salisbury 2-5-63

*Source:* Amateur.

| | | | |
|---|---|---|---|
| 1980–81 | Southampton | 0 | 0 |
| 1981–82 | Southampton | 0 | 0 |
| 1982–83 | Southampton | 7 | 1 |
| 1983–84 | Southampton | 5 | 0 |
| 1983–84 | Blackburn R (loan) | 0 | 0 |
| 1984–85 | Aldershot | 44 | 15 |
| 1985–86 | Aldershot | 20 | 9 |
| 1986–87 | Aldershot | 34 | 11 |
| 1986–87 | Oxford U | 4 | 0 |
| 1987–88 | Oxford U | 33 | 10 |
| 1988–89 | Oxford U | 40 | 14 |
| 1989–90 | Oxford U | 13 | 2 |
| 1990–91 | Oxford U | 36 | 10 |
| 1991–92 | Port Vale | 43 | 11 |
| 1992–93 | Port Vale | 16 | 4 |
| 1993–94 | Port Vale | 37 | 18 |
| 1994–95 | Port Vale | 42 | 16 |
| 1995–96 | Port Vale | 25 | 8 |
| 1996–97 | Port Vale | 37 | 3 |
| 1997–98 | Port Vale | 39 | 8 |
| **Total:** | | **475** | **140** |

## FRAIL, Stephen — Defender

H: 5 11 W: 12 03 b.Glasgow 10-8-69

*Source:* Possilpark YM.

| | | | |
|---|---|---|---|
| 1985–86 | Dundee | 0 | 0 |
| 1986–87 | Dundee | 0 | 0 |
| 1987–88 | Dundee | 4 | 0 |
| 1988–89 | Dundee | 23 | 1 |
| 1989–90 | Dundee | 6 | 0 |
| 1990–91 | Dundee | 26 | 0 |
| 1991–92 | Dundee | 3 | 0 |
| 1992–93 | Dundee | 7 | 0 |
| 1993–94 | Dundee | 32 | 0 |
| 1993–94 | Hearts | 9 | 2 |
| 1994–95 | Hearts | 25 | 2 |
| 1995–96 | Hearts | 0 | 0 |
| 1996–97 | Hearts | 9 | 0 |
| 1997–98 | Hearts | 11 | 0 |
| 1997–98 | Tranmere R | 6 | 0 |
| **Total:** | | **161** | **5** |

## FRAIN, John — Defender

H: 5 8 W: 11 09 b.Birmingham 8-10-68

*Source:* Apprentice.

| | | | |
|---|---|---|---|
| 1985–86 | Birmingham C | 3 | 0 |
| 1986–87 | Birmingham C | 3 | 1 |
| 1987–88 | Birmingham C | 14 | 2 |
| 1988–89 | Birmingham C | 28 | 3 |
| 1989–90 | Birmingham C | 38 | 1 |
| 1990–91 | Birmingham C | 42 | 3 |
| 1991–92 | Birmingham C | 44 | 5 |
| 1992–93 | Birmingham C | 45 | 6 |
| 1993–94 | Birmingham C | 26 | 2 |
| 1994–95 | Birmingham C | 7 | 0 |
| 1995–96 | Birmingham C | 23 | 0 |
| 1996–97 | Birmingham C | 1 | 0 |
| 1996–97 | Northampton T | 13 | 0 |
| 1997–98 | Northampton T | 45 | 1 |
| **Total:** | | **332** | **24** |

## FRAMPTON, Andrew — Midfield

b.Wimbledon 3-9-79

*Source:* Trainee.

| | | | |
|---|---|---|---|
| 1997–98 | Crystal Palace | 0 | 0 |

## FRANCIS, Damien — Midfield

H: 6 0 W: 10 10 b.Wandsworth 27-2-79

*Source:* Trainee.

| | | | |
|---|---|---|---|
| 1996–97 | Wimbledon | 0 | 0 |
| 1997–98 | Wimbledon | 2 | 0 |
| **Total:** | | **2** | **0** |

## FRANCIS, Kevin — Forward

H: 6 7 W: 16 09 b.Moseley 6-12-67

*Source:* Mile Oak R.

| | | | |
|---|---|---|---|
| 1988–89 | Derby Co | 0 | 0 |
| 1989–90 | Derby Co | 8 | 0 |
| 1990–91 | Derby Co | 2 | 0 |
| 1990–91 | Stockport Co | 13 | 5 |
| 1991–92 | Stockport Co | 35 | 15 |
| 1992–93 | Stockport Co | 42 | 28 |
| 1993–94 | Stockport Co | 45 | 28 |
| 1994–95 | Stockport Co | 17 | 12 |
| 1994–95 | Birmingham C | 15 | 8 |
| 1995–96 | Birmingham C | 19 | 3 |
| 1996–97 | Birmingham C | 19 | 1 |
| 1997–98 | Birmingham C | 20 | 1 |
| 1997–98 | Oxford U | 15 | 7 |
| **Total:** | | **250** | **108** |

## FRANCIS, Steve — Goalkeeper

H: 6 0 W: 13 12 b.Billericay 29-5-64

*Source:* Apprentice. *Honours:* England Youth.

| | | | |
|---|---|---|---|
| 1981–82 | Chelsea | 29 | 0 |
| 1982–83 | Chelsea | 37 | 0 |

| | | | |
|---|---|---|---|
| 1983–84 | Chelsea | 0 | 0 |
| 1984–85 | Chelsea | 2 | 0 |
| 1985–86 | Chelsea | 3 | 0 |
| 1986–87 | Chelsea | 0 | 0 |
| 1986–87 | Reading | 14 | 0 |
| 1987–88 | Reading | 34 | 0 |
| 1988–89 | Reading | 22 | 0 |
| 1989–90 | Reading | 46 | 0 |
| 1990–91 | Reading | 34 | 0 |
| 1991–92 | Reading | 32 | 0 |
| 1992–93 | Reading | 34 | 0 |
| 1993–94 | Huddersfield T | 46 | 0 |
| 1994–95 | Huddersfield T | 43 | 0 |
| 1995–96 | Huddersfield T | 43 | 0 |
| 1996–97 | Huddersfield T | 42 | 0 |
| 1997–98 | Huddersfield T | 9 | 0 |
| **Total:** | | **470** | **0** |

## FRANDSEN, Per — Midfield

H: 6 1 W: 12 06 b.Copenhagen 6-2-70

*Source:* B 1903. *Honours:* Denmark 13 full caps.

| | | | |
|---|---|---|---|
| 1990–91 | Lille | 19 | 4 |
| 1991–92 | Lille | 27 | 8 |
| 1992–93 | Lille | 32 | 3 |
| 1993–94 | Lille | 31 | 4 |
| 1994–95 | FC Copenhagen | 29 | 12 |
| 1995–96 | FC Copenhagen | 26 | 7 |
| 1996–97 | Bolton W | 41 | 5 |
| 1997–98 | Bolton W | 38 | 2 |
| **Total:** | | **243** | **45** |

## FRASER, John — Midfield

H: 5 10 W: 11 01 b.Dunfermline 17-1-78

*Source:* Oakley Utd.

| | | | |
|---|---|---|---|
| 1995–96 | Dunfermline Ath | 0 | 0 |
| 1996–97 | Dunfermline Ath | 2 | 0 |
| 1997–98 | Dunfermline Ath | 7 | 0 |
| **Total:** | | **9** | **0** |

## FRASER, Stuart — Goalkeeper

H: 6 0 W: 12 00 b.Cheltenham 1-8-78

| | | | |
|---|---|---|---|
| 1996–97 | Stoke C | 0 | 0 |
| 1997–98 | Stoke C | 0 | 0 |

## FRASER, Stuart — Defender

H: 5 9 W: 11 00 b.Edinburgh 9-1-80

*Source:* Trainee.

| | | | |
|---|---|---|---|
| 1997–98 | Luton T | 1 | 0 |
| **Total:** | | **1** | **0** |

## FREEDMAN, Dougie — Forward

H: 5 9 W: 11 02 b.Glasgow 21-1-74

*Source:* Trainee. *Honours:* Scotland Under-21, B.

| | | | |
|---|---|---|---|
| 1991–92 | QPR | 0 | 0 |
| 1992–93 | QPR | 0 | 0 |
| 1993–94 | QPR | 0 | 0 |
| 1994–95 | Barnet | 42 | 24 |
| 1995–96 | Barnet | 5 | 3 |
| 1995–96 | Crystal Palace | 39 | 20 |
| 1996–97 | Crystal Palace | 44 | 11 |
| 1997–98 | Crystal Palace | 7 | 0 |
| 1997–98 | Wolverhampton W | 29 | 10 |
| **Total:** | | **166** | **68** |

## FREEMAN, Andy — Forward

H: 5 7 W: 9 06 b.Reading 8-9-77

*Source:* Crystal Palace Trainee.

| | | | |
|---|---|---|---|
| 1995–96 | Reading | 1 | 0 |
| 1996–97 | Reading | 0 | 0 |
| 1997–98 | Reading | 0 | 0 |
| **Total:** | | **1** | **0** |

## FREEMAN, Darren — Forward

H: 5 11 W: 13 00 b.Brighton 22-8-73

*Source:* Horsham T.

| | | | |
|---|---|---|---|
| 1994–95 | Gillingham | 2 | 0 |
| 1995–96 | Gillingham | 10 | 0 |
| 1996–97 | Fulham | 39 | 9 |
| 1997–98 | Fulham | 7 | 0 |
| **Total:** | | **58** | **9** |

## FREEMAN, David — Forward

H: 5 10 W: 10 13 b.Dublin 25-11-79

*Source:* Cherry Orchard.

| | | | |
|---|---|---|---|
| 1996–97 | Nottingham F | 0 | 0 |
| 1997–98 | Nottingham F | 0 | 0 |

## FREESTONE, Chris — Forward

H: 5 11 W: 11 07 b.Nottingham 4-9-71

*Source:* Arnold T.

| | | | |
|---|---|---|---|
| 1994–95 | Middlesbrough | 1 | 0 |
| 1995–96 | Middlesbrough | 3 | 1 |
| 1996–97 | Middlesbrough | 3 | 0 |
| 1996–97 | Carlisle U (loan) | 5 | 2 |
| 1997–98 | Middlesbrough | 2 | 0 |
| 1997–98 | Northampton T (loan) | 25 | 11 |
| **Total:** | | **39** | **14** |

## FREESTONE, Roger — Goalkeeper

H: 6 3 W: 14 06 b.Newport 19-8-68

*Source:* Trainee. *Honours:* Wales Under-21.

| | | | |
|---|---|---|---|
| 1986–87 | Newport Co | 13 | 0 |
| 1986–87 | Chelsea | 6 | 0 |
| 1987–88 | Chelsea | 15 | 0 |
| 1988–89 | Chelsea | 21 | 0 |
| 1989–90 | Chelsea | 0 | 0 |
| 1989–90 | Swansea C (loan) | 14 | 0 |
| 1989–90 | Hereford U (loan) | 8 | 0 |
| 1990–91 | Chelsea | 0 | 0 |
| 1991–92 | Swansea C | 42 | 0 |
| 1992–93 | Swansea C | 46 | 0 |
| 1993–94 | Swansea C | 46 | 0 |
| 1994–95 | Swansea C | 45 | 1 |
| 1995–96 | Swansea C | 45 | 2 |
| 1996–97 | Swansea C | 45 | 0 |
| 1997–98 | Swansea C | 43 | 0 |
| **Total:** | | **389** | **3** |

## FRENCH, Hamish — Midfield

H: 5 10 W: 11 07 b.Aberdeen 7-2-64

*Source:* Keith.

| | | | |
|---|---|---|---|
| 1987–88 | Dundee U | 20 | 2 |
| 1988–89 | Dundee U | 18 | 3 |
| 1989–90 | Dundee U | 12 | 2 |
| 1990–91 | Dundee U | 19 | 3 |
| 1991–92 | Dundee U | 6 | 1 |
| 1991–92 | Dunfermline Ath | 31 | 2 |
| 1992–93 | Dunfermline Ath | 38 | 12 |
| 1993–94 | Dunfermline Ath | 36 | 15 |
| 1994–95 | Dunfermline Ath | 25 | 12 |
| 1995–96 | Dunfermline Ath | 23 | 4 |
| 1996–97 | Dunfermline Ath | 35 | 3 |
| 1997–98 | Dunfermline Ath | 34 | 2 |
| **Total:** | | **297** | **61** |

## FRENCH, Jon — Midfield

H: 5 10 W: 10 10 b.Bristol 25-9-76

*Source:* Trainee.

| | | | |
|---|---|---|---|
| 1995–96 | Bristol R | 10 | 1 |
| 1996–97 | Bristol R | 4 | 0 |
| 1997–98 | Bristol R | 3 | 0 |
| **Total:** | | **17** | **1** |

## FRIARS, Sean — Midfield

H: 5 9 W: 11 00 b.Derry 15-5-79

*Source:* Trainee. *Honours:* Northern Ireland Under-21.

| | | | |
|---|---|---|---|
| 1995–96 | Liverpool | 0 | 0 |
| 1996–97 | Liverpool | 0 | 0 |
| 1997–98 | Liverpool | 0 | 0 |

## FRIEDEL, Brad — Goalkeeper

H: 6 3 W: 14 00 b.Lakewood 18-5-71

*Honours:* USA 59 full caps.

| | | | |
|---|---|---|---|
| 1997–98 | Liverpool | 11 | 0 |
| **Total:** | | **11** | **0** |

## FROGGATT, Steve — Midfield

H: 5 10 W: 11 00 b.Lincoln 9-3-73

*Source:* Trainee. *Honours:* England Under-21.

| | | | |
|---|---|---|---|
| 1990–91 | Aston Villa | 0 | 0 |
| 1991–92 | Aston Villa | 9 | 0 |
| 1992–93 | Aston Villa | 17 | 1 |
| 1993–94 | Aston Villa | 9 | 1 |
| 1994–95 | Wolverhampton W | 20 | 2 |
| 1995–96 | Wolverhampton W | 18 | 1 |
| 1996–97 | Wolverhampton W | 27 | 2 |
| 1997–98 | Wolverhampton W | 33 | 2 |
| **Total:** | | **133** | **9** |

## FRY, Chris — Forward

H: 5 10 W: 10 07 b.Cardiff 23-10-69

*Source:* Trainee.

| | | | |
|---|---|---|---|
| 1988–89 | Cardiff C | 9 | 0 |
| 1989–90 | Cardiff C | 23 | 1 |
| 1990–91 | Cardiff C | 23 | 0 |
| 1991–92 | Hereford U | 37 | 3 |
| 1992–93 | Hereford U | 37 | 4 |
| 1993–94 | Hereford U | 16 | 3 |
| 1993–94 | Colchester U | 17 | 0 |
| 1994–95 | Colchester U | 33 | 8 |
| 1995–96 | Colchester U | 38 | 2 |
| 1996–97 | Colchester U | 42 | 6 |
| 1997–98 | Exeter C | 28 | 1 |
| **Total:** | | **303** | **28** |

## FUGLESTAD, Erik — Defender

H: 5 11 W: 11 03 b.Randaberg 13-8-74

*Source:* Trainee.

| | | | |
|---|---|---|---|
| 1994 | Viking | 1 | 0 |
| 1995 | Viking | 25 | 2 |
| 1996 | Viking | 23 | 1 |
| 1997 | Viking | 25 | 1 |
| 1997–98 | Norwich C | 24 | 2 |
| **Total:** | | **98** | **6** |

## FULLARTON, Jamie — Midfield

H: 5 9 W: 10 09 b.Bellshill 20-7-74

| | | | |
|---|---|---|---|
| 1991–92 | St Mirren | 1 | 0 |
| 1992–93 | St Mirren | 25 | 0 |
| 1993–94 | St Mirren | 37 | 0 |
| 1994–95 | St Mirren | 17 | 1 |
| 1995–96 | St Mirren | 22 | 2 |
| 1996–97 | Bastia | 17 | 0 |
| 1997–98 | Crystal Palace | 25 | 1 |
| **Total:** | | **144** | **4** |

## FULTON, Stephen — Midfield

H: 5 10 W: 11 00 b.Greenock 10-8-70

*Source:* Celtic BC. *Honours:* Scotland Under-21, B.

| | | | |
|---|---|---|---|
| 1986–87 | Celtic | 0 | 0 |
| 1987–88 | Celtic | 0 | 0 |
| 1988–89 | Celtic | 3 | 0 |
| 1989–90 | Celtic | 16 | 0 |
| 1990–91 | Celtic | 21 | 0 |
| 1991–92 | Celtic | 30 | 2 |
| 1992–93 | Celtic | 6 | 0 |
| 1993–94 | Bolton W | 4 | 0 |
| 1993–94 | Peterborough U (loan) | 3 | 0 |
| 1994–95 | Falkirk | 28 | 3 |
| 1995–96 | Falkirk | 5 | 0 |
| 1995–96 | Hearts | 26 | 2 |
| 1996–97 | Hearts | 29 | 1 |
| 1997–98 | Hearts | 36 | 5 |
| **Total:** | | **207** | **13** |

## FURLONG, Paul — Forward

H: 6 0 W: 11 00 b.London 1-10-68

*Source:* Enfield.

| | | | |
|---|---|---|---|
| 1991–92 | Coventry C | 37 | 4 |
| 1992–93 | Watford | 41 | 19 |
| 1993–94 | Watford | 38 | 18 |
| 1994–95 | Chelsea | 36 | 10 |
| 1995–96 | Chelsea | 28 | 3 |
| 1996–97 | Birmingham C | 43 | 10 |
| 1997–98 | Birmingham C | 25 | 15 |
| **Total:** | | **248** | **79** |

## FUTCHER, Andy — Defender

H: 5 7 W: 10 07 b.Enfield 10-2-78

*Source:* Trainee. *Honours:* England Schools, Youth.

| | | | |
|---|---|---|---|
| 1994–95 | Wimbledon | 0 | 0 |
| 1995–96 | Wimbledon | 0 | 0 |
| 1996–97 | Wimbledon | 0 | 0 |
| 1997–98 | Wimbledon | 0 | 0 |

## GABBIADINI, Marco — Forward

H: 5 10 W: 13 04 b.Nottingham 20-1-68

*Source:* Apprentice. *Honours:* England Under-21, B.

| | | | |
|---|---|---|---|
| 1984–85 | York C | 1 | 0 |
| 1985–86 | York C | 22 | 4 |
| 1986–87 | York C | 29 | 9 |
| 1987–88 | York C | 8 | 1 |
| 1987–88 | Sunderland | 35 | 21 |
| 1988–89 | Sunderland | 36 | 18 |
| 1989–90 | Sunderland | 46 | 21 |
| 1990–91 | Sunderland | 31 | 9 |
| 1991–92 | Sunderland | 9 | 5 |
| 1991–92 | Crystal Palace | 15 | 5 |
| 1991–92 | Derby Co | 20 | 6 |
| 1992–93 | Derby Co | 44 | 9 |
| 1993–94 | Derby Co | 39 | 13 |
| 1994–95 | Derby Co | 32 | 11 |
| 1995–96 | Derby Co | 39 | 11 |
| 1996–97 | Derby Co | 14 | 0 |
| 1996–97 | Birmingham C (loan) | 2 | 0 |
| 1996–97 | Oxford U (loan) | 5 | 1 |
| 1997–98 | Stoke C | 8 | 0 |
| 1997–98 | York C | 7 | 1 |
| **Total:** | | **442** | **145** |

## GADSBY, Matthew — Defender

H: 6 0 W: 11 03 b.Sutton Coldfield 6-9-79

*Source:* Trainee.

| | | | |
|---|---|---|---|
| 1997–98 | Walsall | 1 | 0 |
| **Total:** | | **1** | **0** |

## GAGE, Kevin — Defender

H: 5 10 W: 12 05 b.Chiswick 21-4-64

*Source:* Apprentice. *Honours:* England Youth.

| | | | |
|---|---|---|---|
| 1980–81 | Wimbledon | 1 | 0 |
| 1981–82 | Wimbledon | 21 | 1 |
| 1982–83 | Wimbledon | 26 | 4 |
| 1983–84 | Wimbledon | 24 | 4 |
| 1984–85 | Wimbledon | 37 | 2 |
| 1985–86 | Wimbledon | 29 | 1 |
| 1986–87 | Wimbledon | 30 | 3 |
| 1987–88 | Aston Villa | 44 | 2 |
| 1988–89 | Aston Villa | 28 | 3 |
| 1989–90 | Aston Villa | 22 | 3 |
| 1990–91 | Aston Villa | 21 | 0 |
| 1991–92 | Aston Villa | 0 | 0 |
| 1991–92 | Sheffield U | 22 | 2 |
| 1992–93 | Sheffield U | 27 | 0 |
| 1993–94 | Sheffield U | 21 | 0 |
| 1994–95 | Sheffield U | 40 | 5 |
| 1995–96 | Sheffield U | 2 | 0 |
| 1995–96 | Preston NE | 7 | 0 |

| | | | |
|---|---|---|---|
| 1996–97 | Preston NE | 16 | 0 |
| 1997–98 | Preston NE | 0 | 0 |
| 1997–98 | Hull C | 10 | 0 |
| **Total:** | | **428** | **30** |

## GAIN, Peter — Midfield

H: 6 1 W: 11 00 b.Hammersmith 11-11-76

*Source:* Trainee.

| | | | |
|---|---|---|---|
| 1995–96 | Tottenham H | 0 | 0 |
| 1996–97 | Tottenham H | 0 | 0 |
| 1997–98 | Tottenham H | 0 | 0 |

## GALE, Shaun — Defender

H: 6 1 W: 12 02 b.Reading 8-10-69

*Source:* Trainee.

| | | | |
|---|---|---|---|
| 1989–90 | Portsmouth | 0 | 0 |
| 1990–91 | Portsmouth | 3 | 0 |
| 1991–92 | Portsmouth | 0 | 0 |
| 1992–93 | Portsmouth | 0 | 0 |
| 1993–94 | Portsmouth | 0 | 0 |
| 1994–95 | Barnet | 27 | 2 |
| 1995–96 | Barnet | 44 | 1 |
| 1996–97 | Barnet | 43 | 2 |
| 1997–98 | Exeter C | 43 | 4 |
| **Total:** | | **160** | **9** |

## GALL, Benny — Goalkeeper

H: 6 2 W: 14 04 b.Copenhagen 14-3-71

*Source:* KB Copenhagen, FC Copenhagen, Herfolge.

| | | | |
|---|---|---|---|
| 1994–95 | Dordrecht | 33 | 0 |
| 1995–96 | De Graafschap | 0 | 0 |
| 1996–97 | Shrewsbury T | 23 | 0 |
| 1997–98 | Shrewsbury T | 11 | 0 |
| **Total:** | | **67** | **0** |

## GALLACHER, Kevin — Forward

H: 5 8 W: 11 03 b.Clydebank 23-11-66

*Source:* Duntocher BC. *Honours:* Scotland Youth, Under-21, B, 39 full caps, 8 goals.

| | | | |
|---|---|---|---|
| 1983–84 | Dundee U | 0 | 0 |
| 1984–85 | Dundee U | 0 | 0 |
| 1985–86 | Dundee U | 20 | 3 |
| 1986–87 | Dundee U | 37 | 10 |
| 1987–88 | Dundee U | 26 | 4 |
| 1988–89 | Dundee U | 31 | 9 |
| 1989–90 | Dundee U | 17 | 1 |
| 1989–90 | Coventry C | 15 | 3 |
| 1990–91 | Coventry C | 32 | 11 |
| 1991–92 | Coventry C | 33 | 8 |
| 1992–93 | Coventry C | 20 | 6 |
| 1992–93 | Blackburn R | 9 | 5 |
| 1993–94 | Blackburn R | 30 | 7 |
| 1994–95 | Blackburn R | 1 | 1 |
| 1995–96 | Blackburn R | 16 | 2 |
| 1996–97 | Blackburn R | 34 | 10 |
| 1997–98 | Blackburn R | 33 | 16 |
| **Total:** | | **354** | **96** |

## GALLAGHER, Benn — Defender

H: 5 8 W: 11 00 b.Rugby 12-10-78

*Source:* Trainee.

| | | | |
|---|---|---|---|
| 1997–98 | Manchester C | 0 | 0 |

## GALLAGHER, Ian — Midfield

H: 5 10 W: 11 07 b.Hartlepool 13-5-78

*Source:* Trainee.

| | | | |
|---|---|---|---|
| 1995–96 | Hartlepool U | 1 | 0 |
| 1996–97 | Hartlepool U | 0 | 0 |
| 1997–98 | Hartlepool U | 0 | 0 |
| **Total:** | | **1** | **0** |

## GALLEN, Kevin — Forward

H: 5 11 W: 12 10 b.Hammersmith 21-9-75

*Source:* Trainee. *Honours:* England Schools, Youth, Under-21.

| | | | |
|---|---|---|---|
| 1992–93 | QPR | 0 | 0 |
| 1993–94 | QPR | 0 | 0 |
| 1994–95 | QPR | 37 | 10 |
| 1995–96 | QPR | 30 | 8 |
| 1996–97 | QPR | 2 | 3 |
| 1997–98 | QPR | 27 | 3 |
| **Total:** | | **96** | **24** |

## GALLIMORE, Tony — Defender

H: 5 11 W: 12 05 b.Crewe 21-2-72

*Source:* Trainee.

| | | | |
|---|---|---|---|
| 1989–90 | Stoke C | 1 | 0 |
| 1990–91 | Stoke C | 7 | 0 |
| 1991–92 | Stoke C | 3 | 0 |
| 1991–92 | Carlisle U (loan) | 16 | 0 |
| 1992–93 | Stoke C | 0 | 0 |
| 1992–93 | Carlisle U (loan) | 8 | 1 |
| 1993–94 | Carlisle U | 40 | 1 |
| 1994–95 | Carlisle U | 40 | 5 |
| 1995–96 | Carlisle U | 36 | 2 |
| 1995–96 | Grimsby T | 10 | 1 |
| 1996–97 | Grimsby T | 42 | 1 |
| 1997–98 | Grimsby T | 35 | 2 |
| **Total:** | | **238** | **13** |

## GALLOWAY, Mick — Midfield

H: 5 10 W: 12 05 b.Nottingham 13-10-74

*Source:* Trainee.

| | | | |
|---|---|---|---|
| 1993–94 | Notts Co | 0 | 0 |
| 1994–95 | Notts Co | 7 | 0 |
| 1995–96 | Notts Co | 9 | 0 |
| 1996–97 | Notts Co | 5 | 0 |
| 1996–97 | Gillingham (loan) | 9 | 1 |
| 1997–98 | Gillingham | 39 | 1 |
| **Total:** | | **69** | **2** |

## GANNON, Jim — Defender

H: 6 2 W: 13 00 b.Southwark 7-9-68

*Source:* Dundalk.

| | | | |
|---|---|---|---|
| 1988–89 | Sheffield U | 0 | 0 |
| 1989–90 | Sheffield U | 0 | 0 |
| 1989–90 | Halifax T (loan) | 2 | 0 |
| 1989–90 | Stockport Co | 7 | 1 |
| 1990–91 | Stockport Co | 41 | 6 |
| 1991–92 | Stockport Co | 43 | 16 |
| 1992–93 | Stockport Co | 46 | 12 |
| 1993–94 | Stockport Co | 35 | 4 |
| 1993–94 | Notts Co (loan) | 2 | 0 |
| 1994–95 | Stockport Co | 45 | 7 |
| 1995–96 | Stockport Co | 23 | 1 |
| 1996–97 | Stockport Co | 40 | 4 |
| 1997–98 | Stockport Co | 36 | 1 |
| **Total:** | | **320** | **52** |

## GARCIA SANJUAN, Jesus — Midfield

H: 5 10 W: 12 07 b.Zaragoza 22-8-71

*Source:* Zaragoza.

| | | | |
|---|---|---|---|
| 1997–98 | Wolverhampton W | 4 | 0 |
| **Total:** | | **4** | **0** |

## GARCIN, Eric — Midfield

H: 6 0 W: 12 05 b.Lille 6-12-65

*Source:* Toulouse.

| | | | |
|---|---|---|---|
| 1997–98 | Motherwell | 11 | 1 |
| **Total:** | | **11** | **1** |

## GARDE, Remi — Midfield

H: 5 9 W: 11 07 b.L'Arbresle 3-4-66

*Honours:* France 6 full caps.

| | | | |
|---|---|---|---|
| 1990–91 | Lyon | 24 | 3 |
| 1991–92 | Lyon | 24 | 1 |
| 1992–93 | Lyon | 33 | 9 |
| 1993–94 | Strasbourg | 21 | 1 |
| 1994–95 | Strasbourg | 31 | 2 |
| 1995–96 | Strasbourg | 16 | 0 |
| 1996–97 | Arsenal | 11 | 0 |
| 1997–98 | Arsenal | 10 | 0 |
| **Total:** | | **170** | **16** |

## GARDINER, Mark — Midfield

H: 5 10 W: 11 07 b.Cirencester 25-12-66

*Source:* Apprentice.

| | | | |
|---|---|---|---|
| 1983–84 | Swindon T | 1 | 0 |
| 1984–85 | Swindon T | 4 | 0 |
| 1985–86 | Swindon T | 1 | 0 |
| 1986–87 | Swindon T | 4 | 0 |
| 1986–87 | Torquay U | 22 | 3 |
| 1987–88 | Torquay U | 27 | 1 |
| 1988–89 | Crewe Alex | 38 | 10 |
| 1989–90 | Crewe Alex | 26 | 6 |
| 1990–91 | Crewe Alex | 33 | 10 |
| 1991–92 | Crewe Alex | 38 | 5 |
| 1992–93 | Crewe Alex | 13 | 1 |
| 1993–94 | Crewe Alex | 34 | 1 |
| 1994–95 | Crewe Alex | 11 | 0 |
| 1994–95 | Chester C (loan) | 3 | 0 |
| From Fredrikstad. | | | |
| 1997–98 | Macclesfield T | 7 | 2 |
| **Total:** | | **262** | **39** |

## GARDNER, James — Defender

H: 5 11 W: 10 06 b.Beckenham 26-10-78

*Source:* Trainee.

| | | | |
|---|---|---|---|
| 1996–97 | Wimbledon | 0 | 0 |
| 1997–98 | Wimbledon | 0 | 0 |

## GARDNER, Jimmy — Forward

H: 5 11 W: 11 08 b.Dunfermline 27-9-67

*Source:* Ayresome North.

| | | | |
|---|---|---|---|
| 1986–87 | Queen's Park | 1 | 0 |
| 1987–88 | Queen's Park | 1 | 0 |
| 1988–89 | Motherwell | 0 | 0 |
| 1989–90 | Motherwell | 1 | 0 |
| 1990–91 | Motherwell | 0 | 0 |
| 1991–92 | Motherwell | 12 | 0 |
| 1992–93 | Motherwell | 3 | 0 |
| 1993–94 | St Mirren | 21 | 1 |
| 1994–95 | St Mirren | 20 | 0 |
| 1995–96 | Scarborough | 6 | 1 |
| 1995–96 | Cardiff C | 35 | 4 |
| 1996–97 | Cardiff C | 28 | 1 |
| 1997–98 | Exeter C | 23 | 1 |
| **Total:** | | **151** | **8** |

## GARDNER, Lee — Defender

b.Doncaster 18-5-78

| | | | |
|---|---|---|---|
| 1997–98 | Birmingham C | 0 | 0 |

## GARNER, Darren — Midfield

H: 5 9 W: 12 07 b.Plymouth 10-12-71

*Source:* Trainee.

| | | | |
|---|---|---|---|
| 1988–89 | Plymouth Arg | 1 | 0 |
| 1989–90 | Plymouth Arg | 1 | 0 |
| 1990–91 | Plymouth Arg | 5 | 1 |
| 1991–92 | Plymouth Arg | 10 | 0 |
| 1992–93 | Plymouth Arg | 10 | 0 |
| 1993–94 | Plymouth Arg | 0 | 0 |
| From Dorchester T. | | | |
| 1995–96 | Rotherham U | 31 | 1 |
| 1996–97 | Rotherham U | 30 | 2 |
| 1997–98 | Rotherham U | 40 | 3 |
| **Total:** | | **128** | **7** |

## GARNETT, Shaun — Defender

H: 6 2 W: 13 05 b.Wallasey 22-11-69

*Source:* Trainee.

| | | | |
|---|---|---|---|
| 1987–88 | Tranmere R | 1 | 0 |
| 1988–89 | Tranmere R | 0 | 0 |
| 1989–90 | Tranmere R | 4 | 0 |
| 1990–91 | Tranmere R | 16 | 1 |
| 1991–92 | Tranmere R | 8 | 0 |
| 1992–93 | Tranmere R | 5 | 1 |
| 1992–93 | Chester C (loan) | 9 | 0 |
| 1992–93 | Preston NE (loan) | 10 | 2 |
| 1992–93 | Wigan Ath (loan) | 13 | 1 |
| 1993–94 | Tranmere R | 26 | 2 |
| 1994–95 | Tranmere R | 34 | 1 |
| 1995–96 | Tranmere R | 18 | 0 |
| 1995–96 | Swansea C | 9 | 0 |
| 1996–97 | Swansea C | 6 | 0 |
| 1996–97 | Oldham Ath | 23 | 1 |
| 1997–98 | Oldham Ath | 34 | 3 |
| **Total:** | | **216** | **12** |

## GARVEY, Steve — Forward

H: 5 9 W: 10 09 b.Stalybridge 22-11-73

*Source:* Trainee.

| | | | |
|---|---|---|---|
| 1990–91 | Crewe Alex | 1 | 0 |
| 1991–92 | Crewe Alex | 11 | 0 |
| 1992–93 | Crewe Alex | 10 | 1 |
| 1993–94 | Crewe Alex | 0 | 0 |
| 1994–95 | Crewe Alex | 28 | 3 |
| 1995–96 | Crewe Alex | 29 | 2 |
| 1996–97 | Crewe Alex | 16 | 0 |
| 1997–98 | Crewe Alex | 13 | 2 |
| 1997–98 | Chesterfield (loan) | 3 | 0 |
| **Total:** | | **111** | **8** |

## GASCOIGNE, Paul — Midfield

H: 5 10 W: 11 10 b.Gateshead 27-5-67

*Source:* Apprentice. *Honours:* England, Under-21 B, 57 full caps, 10 goals.

| | | | |
|---|---|---|---|
| 1984–85 | Newcastle U | 2 | 0 |
| 1985–86 | Newcastle U | 31 | 9 |
| 1986–87 | Newcastle U | 24 | 5 |
| 1987–88 | Newcastle U | 35 | 7 |
| 1988–89 | Tottenham H | 32 | 6 |
| 1989–90 | Tottenham H | 34 | 6 |
| 1990–91 | Tottenham H | 26 | 7 |
| 1991–92 | Tottenham H | 0 | 0 |
| 1992–93 | Lazio | 22 | 4 |
| 1993–94 | Lazio | 17 | 2 |
| 1994–95 | Lazio | 2 | 0 |
| 1995–96 | Rangers | 28 | 14 |
| 1996–97 | Rangers | 26 | 13 |
| 1997–98 | Rangers | 20 | 3 |
| 1997–98 | Middlesbrough | 7 | 0 |
| **Total:** | | **306** | **76** |

## GATTUSO, Gennaro — Forward

H: 5 9 W: 12 01 b.Corigliano Calabro 9-1-78

*Source:* Perugia

| | | | |
|---|---|---|---|
| 1995–96 | Perugia | 2 | 0 |
| 1996–97 | Perugia | 8 | 0 |
| 1997–98 | Rangers | 29 | 3 |
| **Total:** | | **39** | **3** |

## GAUGHAN, Steve — Midfield

H: 5 11 W: 11 04 b.Doncaster 14-4-70

*Source:* Hatfield Main.

| | | | |
|---|---|---|---|
| 1987–88 | Doncaster R | 4 | 0 |
| 1988–89 | Doncaster R | 34 | 2 |
| 1989–90 | Doncaster R | 29 | 1 |
| 1990–91 | Sunderland | 0 | 0 |
| 1991–92 | Sunderland | 0 | 0 |
| 1991–92 | Darlington | 20 | 0 |
| 1992–93 | Darlington | 37 | 1 |
| 1993–94 | Darlington | 32 | 3 |
| 1994–95 | Darlington | 41 | 8 |
| 1995–96 | Darlington | 41 | 3 |
| 1996–97 | Chesterfield | 18 | 0 |
| 1997–98 | Chesterfield | 2 | 0 |
| 1997–98 | Darlington | 24 | 1 |
| **Total:** | | **282** | **19** |

## GAVIN, Jason — Defender

b.Dublin 14-3-80

*Source:* Trainee.

| | | | |
|---|---|---|---|
| 1996–97 | Middlesbrough | 0 | 0 |
| 1997–98 | Middlesbrough | 0 | 0 |

## GAVIN, Mark — Forward

H: 5 7 W: 11 02 b.Holytown 10-2-63

*Source:* Apprentice.

| | | | |
|---|---|---|---|
| 1981–82 | Leeds U | 0 | 0 |
| 1982–83 | Leeds U | 7 | 1 |
| 1983–84 | Leeds U | 12 | 1 |
| 1984–85 | Leeds U | 11 | 1 |
| 1984–85 | Hartlepool U (loan) | 7 | 0 |
| 1985–86 | Carlisle U | 13 | 1 |
| 1985–86 | Bolton W | 8 | 1 |
| 1986–87 | Bolton W | 41 | 2 |
| 1987–88 | Rochdale | 23 | 6 |
| 1987–88 | Hearts | 7 | 0 |
| 1988–89 | Hearts | 2 | 0 |
| 1988–89 | Bristol C | 29 | 3 |
| 1989–90 | Bristol C | 40 | 3 |
| 1990–91 | Watford | 13 | 0 |
| 1991–92 | Watford | 0 | 0 |
| 1991–92 | Bristol C | 14 | 1 |
| 1992–93 | Bristol C | 19 | 1 |
| 1993–94 | Bristol C | 8 | 0 |
| 1993–94 | Exeter C | 12 | 0 |
| 1994–95 | Exeter C | 37 | 2 |
| 1995–96 | Exeter C | 28 | 2 |
| 1996–97 | Scunthorpe U | 11 | 0 |
| 1997–98 | Scunthorpe U | 0 | 0 |
| 1997–98 | Hartlepool U | 3 | 0 |
| **Total:** | | **345** | **25** |

## GAYLE, Brian — Defender

H: 6 2 W: 13 12 b.Kingston 6-3-65

| | | | |
|---|---|---|---|
| 1984–85 | Wimbledon | 12 | 1 |
| 1985–86 | Wimbledon | 13 | 0 |
| 1986–87 | Wimbledon | 32 | 1 |
| 1987–88 | Wimbledon | 26 | 1 |
| 1988–89 | Manchester C | 41 | 3 |
| 1989–90 | Manchester C | 14 | 0 |
| 1989–90 | Ipswich T | 20 | 0 |
| 1990–91 | Ipswich T | 33 | 4 |
| 1991–92 | Ipswich T | 5 | 0 |
| 1991–92 | Sheffield U | 33 | 3 |
| 1992–93 | Sheffield U | 31 | 2 |
| 1993–94 | Sheffield U | 13 | 3 |
| 1994–95 | Sheffield U | 35 | 1 |
| 1995–96 | Sheffield U | 5 | 0 |
| 1996–97 | Exeter C | 10 | 0 |
| 1996–97 | Rotherham U | 20 | 0 |
| 1996–97 | Bristol R (loan) | 7 | 0 |
| 1997–98 | Bristol R | 16 | 0 |
| 1997–98 | Shrewsbury T | 23 | 0 |
| **Total:** | | **389** | **19** |

## GAYLE, John — Forward

H: 6 2 W: 15 04 b.Bromsgrove 30-7-64

*Source:* Burton Alb.

| | | | |
|---|---|---|---|
| 1988–89 | Wimbledon | 2 | 0 |
| 1989–90 | Wimbledon | 11 | 1 |
| 1990–91 | Wimbledon | 7 | 1 |
| 1990–91 | Birmingham C | 22 | 6 |
| 1991–92 | Birmingham C | 3 | 1 |
| 1992–93 | Birmingham C | 19 | 3 |
| 1993–94 | Birmingham C | 0 | 0 |
| 1993–94 | Walsall (loan) | 4 | 1 |
| 1993–94 | Coventry C | 3 | 0 |
| 1994–95 | Coventry C | 0 | 0 |
| 1994–95 | Burnley | 14 | 3 |
| 1994–95 | Stoke C | 4 | 0 |
| 1995–96 | Stoke C | 10 | 3 |
| 1995–96 | Gillingham (loan) | 9 | 3 |
| 1996–97 | Stoke C | 12 | 1 |
| 1996–97 | Northampton T | 13 | 1 |
| 1997–98 | Northampton T | 35 | 6 |
| **Total:** | | **168** | **30** |

## GAYLE, Marcus — Forward

H: 6 1 W: 12 09 b.Hammersmith 27-9-70

*Source:* Trainee. *Honours:* England Youth. Jamaica 7 full caps, 1 goal.

| | | | |
|---|---|---|---|
| 1988–89 | Brentford | 3 | 0 |
| 1989–90 | Brentford | 9 | 0 |
| 1990–91 | Brentford | 33 | 6 |
| 1991–92 | Brentford | 38 | 6 |
| 1992–93 | Brentford | 38 | 4 |
| 1993–94 | Brentford | 35 | 6 |
| 1993–94 | Wimbledon | 10 | 0 |
| 1994–95 | Wimbledon | 23 | 2 |
| 1995–96 | Wimbledon | 34 | 5 |
| 1996–97 | Wimbledon | 36 | 8 |
| 1997–98 | Wimbledon | 30 | 2 |
| **Total:** | | **289** | **39** |

## GAYLE, Mark — Goalkeeper

H: 6 2 W: 12 03 b.Bromsgrove 21-10-69

*Source:* Trainee.

| | | | |
|---|---|---|---|
| 1988–89 | Leicester C | 0 | 0 |
| 1989–90 | Blackpool | 0 | 0 |
| From Worcester C. | | | |
| 1991–92 | Walsall | 24 | 0 |

| | | | |
|---|---|---|---|
| 1992–93 | Walsall | 41 | 0 |
| 1993–94 | Walsall | 10 | 0 |
| 1993–94 | Crewe Alex | 8 | 0 |
| 1993–94 | Liverpool (loan) | 0 | 0 |
| 1994–95 | Crewe Alex | 25 | 0 |
| 1995–96 | Crewe Alex | 46 | 0 |
| 1996–97 | Crewe Alex | 4 | 0 |
| 1996–97 | Birmingham C (loan) | 0 | 0 |
| 1997–98 | Crewe Alex | 0 | 0 |
| 1997–98 | Chesterfield (loan) | 5 | 0 |
| 1997–98 | Luton T (loan) | 0 | 0 |
| **Total:** | | **163** | **0** |

## GEARY, Derek — Defender

b.Dublin 19-6-80

| | | | |
|---|---|---|---|
| 1997–98 | Sheffield W | 0 | 0 |

## GEMMILL, Scot — Midfield

H: 5 11 W: 11 06 b.Paisley 2-1-71

*Source:* School. *Honours:* Scotland Under-21, 13 full caps.

| | | | |
|---|---|---|---|
| 1989–90 | Nottingham F | 0 | 0 |
| 1990–91 | Nottingham F | 4 | 0 |
| 1991–92 | Nottingham F | 39 | 8 |
| 1992–93 | Nottingham F | 33 | 1 |
| 1993–94 | Nottingham F | 31 | 8 |
| 1994–95 | Nottingham F | 19 | 1 |
| 1995–96 | Nottingham F | 31 | 1 |
| 1996–97 | Nottingham F | 24 | 0 |
| 1997–98 | Nottingham F | 44 | 2 |
| **Total:** | | **225** | **21** |

## GENAUX, Regis — Defender

H: 5 11 W: 12 06 b.Belgium 31-8-73

*Honours:* Belgium 14 full caps.

| | | | |
|---|---|---|---|
| 1990–91 | Standard Liege | 4 | 0 |
| 1991–92 | Standard Liege | 31 | 1 |
| 1992–93 | Standard Liege | 30 | 0 |
| 1993–94 | Standard Liege | 28 | 0 |
| 1994–95 | Standard Liege | 29 | 0 |
| 1995–96 | Standard Liege | 29 | 0 |
| 1996–97 | Coventry C | 4 | 0 |
| 1997–98 | Coventry C | 0 | 0 |
| **Total:** | | **155** | **1** |

## GENTILE, Marco — Midfield

b.Den Haag 24-8-68

*Source:* MVV.

| | | | |
|---|---|---|---|
| 1997–98 | Burnley | 0 | 0 |

## GEORGE, Danny — Defender

H: 6 1 W: 12 01 b.Lincoln 22-10-78

*Source:* Trainee.

| | | | |
|---|---|---|---|
| 1995–96 | Nottingham F | 0 | 0 |
| 1996–97 | Nottingham F | 0 | 0 |
| 1997–98 | Nottingham F | 0 | 0 |
| 1997–98 | Doncaster R | 18 | 1 |
| **Total:** | | **18** | **1** |

## GEORGE, Liam — Forward

H: 5 9 W: 11 04 b.Luton 2-2-79

*Source:* Trainee.

| | | | |
|---|---|---|---|
| 1996–97 | Luton T | 0 | 0 |
| 1997–98 | Luton T | 1 | 0 |
| **Total:** | | **1** | **0** |

## GEORGE, Matthew — Goalkeeper

b.Melton Mowbray 24-4-79

*Source:* Aston Villa Trainee.

| | | | |
|---|---|---|---|
| 1997–98 | Sheffield U | 0 | 0 |

## GERMAINE, Gary — Goalkeeper

H: 6 0 W: 11 07 b.Birmingham 2-8-76

*Source:* Trainee. *Honours:* Scotland Under-21.

| | | | |
|---|---|---|---|
| 1994–95 | WBA | 0 | 0 |
| 1995–96 | WBA | 0 | 0 |
| 1995–96 | Scunthorpe U (loan) | 11 | 0 |
| 1996–97 | WBA | 0 | 0 |
| 1997–98 | WBA | 0 | 0 |
| 1997–98 | Shrewsbury T (loan) | 1 | 0 |
| **Total:** | | **12** | **0** |

## GERRARD, Paul — Goalkeeper

H: 6 2 W: 13 01 b.Heywood 22-1-73

*Source:* Trainee. *Honours:* England Under-21.

| | | | |
|---|---|---|---|
| 1991–92 | Oldham Ath | 0 | 0 |
| 1992–93 | Oldham Ath | 25 | 0 |
| 1993–94 | Oldham Ath | 16 | 0 |
| 1994–95 | Oldham Ath | 42 | 0 |
| 1995–96 | Oldham Ath | 36 | 1 |
| 1996–97 | Everton | 5 | 0 |
| 1997–98 | Everton | 4 | 0 |
| **Total:** | | **128** | **1** |

## GERRARD, Steven — Midfield

b.Whiston 30-5-80

*Source:* Trainee.

| | | | |
|---|---|---|---|
| 1997–98 | Liverpool | 0 | 0 |

## GHAZGHAZI, Sufyan — Forward

H: 5 7  W: 11 00  b.Honiton 24-8-77

*Source:* Trainee. *Honours:* England Schools.

| | | | |
|---|---|---|---|
| 1996–97 | Exeter C | 6 | 0 |
| 1997–98 | Exeter C | 9 | 0 |
| **Total:** | | **15** | **0** |

## GHENT, Matthew — Goalkeeper

b.Burton 5-10-80

*Source:* Trainee. *Honours:* England Schools.

| | | | |
|---|---|---|---|
| 1997–98 | Aston Villa | 0 | 0 |

## GIALLANZA, Gaetano — Forward

H: 6 0  W: 11 03  b.Dornach 6-6-74

| | | | |
|---|---|---|---|
| 1996–97 | Basle | 32 | 19 |
| 1997–98 | Nantes | 12 | 2 |
| 1997–98 | Bolton W | 3 | 0 |
| **Total:** | | **47** | **21** |

## GIBB, Ali — Midfield

H: 5 9  W: 11 07  b.Salisbury 17-2-76

*Source:* Trainee.

| | | | |
|---|---|---|---|
| 1994–95 | Norwich C | 0 | 0 |
| 1995–96 | Norwich C | 0 | 0 |
| 1995–96 | Northampton T | 23 | 2 |
| 1996–97 | Northampton T | 18 | 1 |
| 1997–98 | Northampton T | 35 | 1 |
| **Total:** | | **76** | **4** |

## GIBBENS, Kevin — Midfield

H: 5 10  W: 12 13  b.Southampton 4-11-79

*Source:* Trainee.

| | | | |
|---|---|---|---|
| 1997–98 | Southampton | 2 | 0 |
| **Total:** | | **2** | **0** |

## GIBBS, Nigel — Defender

H: 5 6  W: 11 06  b.St Albans 20-11-65

*Source:* Apprentice. *Honours:* England Youth, Under-21.

| | | | |
|---|---|---|---|
| 1983–84 | Watford | 3 | 0 |
| 1984–85 | Watford | 12 | 0 |
| 1985–86 | Watford | 40 | 1 |
| 1986–87 | Watford | 15 | 0 |
| 1987–88 | Watford | 30 | 0 |
| 1988–89 | Watford | 46 | 1 |
| 1989–90 | Watford | 41 | 0 |
| 1990–91 | Watford | 34 | 0 |
| 1991–92 | Watford | 43 | 1 |
| 1992–93 | Watford | 7 | 0 |
| 1993–94 | Watford | 0 | 0 |
| 1994–95 | Watford | 11 | 0 |
| 1995–96 | Watford | 9 | 0 |
| 1996–97 | Watford | 45 | 1 |
| 1997–98 | Watford | 38 | 1 |
| **Total:** | | **374** | **5** |

## GIBBS, Paul — Defender

H: 5 10  W: 11 03  b.Gorleston 26-10-72

*Source:* Diss T.

| | | | |
|---|---|---|---|
| 1994–95 | Colchester U | 9 | 0 |
| 1995–96 | Colchester U | 24 | 3 |
| 1996–97 | Colchester U | 20 | 0 |
| 1997–98 | Torquay U | 41 | 7 |
| **Total:** | | **94** | **10** |

## GIBSON, Barry — Forward

H: 5 10  W: 10 12  b.Newcastle 30-3-79

*Source:* Trainee.

| | | | |
|---|---|---|---|
| 1997–98 | Newcastle U | 0 | 0 |

## GIBSON, Mark — Midfield

b.Hitchin 24-8-81

*Source:* Trainee.

| | | | |
|---|---|---|---|
| 1997–98 | Cambridge U | 0 | 0 |

## GIBSON, Neil — Midfield

H: 5 11  W: 10 08  b.St Asaph 11-10-79

*Source:* Trainee.

| | | | |
|---|---|---|---|
| 1997–98 | Tranmere R | 0 | 0 |

## GIBSON, Paul — Goalkeeper

H: 6 2  W: 13 06  b.Sheffield 1-11-76

*Source:* Trainee.

| | | | |
|---|---|---|---|
| 1995–96 | Manchester U | 0 | 0 |
| 1996–97 | Manchester U | 0 | 0 |
| 1997–98 | Manchester U | 0 | 0 |
| 1997–98 | Mansfield T (loan) | 13 | 0 |
| **Total:** | | **13** | **0** |

## GIGGS, Ryan — Forward

H: 5 11 W: 10 10 b.Cardiff 29-11-73

*Source:* School. *Honours:* England Schools, Wales Youth, Under-21, 21 full caps, 5 goals.

| | | | |
|---|---|---|---|
| 1990–91 | Manchester U | 2 | 1 |
| 1991–92 | Manchester U | 38 | 4 |
| 1992–93 | Manchester U | 41 | 9 |
| 1993–94 | Manchester U | 38 | 13 |
| 1994–95 | Manchester U | 29 | 1 |
| 1995–96 | Manchester U | 33 | 11 |
| 1996–97 | Manchester U | 26 | 3 |
| 1997–98 | Manchester U | 29 | 8 |
| **Total:** | | **236** | **50** |

## GILBERT, Dave — Midfield

H: 5 4 W: 10 08 b.Lincoln 22-6-63

*Source:* Apprentice.

| | | | |
|---|---|---|---|
| 1980–81 | Lincoln C | 1 | 0 |
| 1981–82 | Lincoln C | 29 | 1 |
| 1982–83 | Scunthorpe U | 1 | 0 |
| From Boston U. | | | |
| 1986–87 | Northampton T | 45 | 8 |
| 1987–88 | Northampton T | 41 | 6 |
| 1988–89 | Northampton T | 34 | 7 |
| 1988–89 | Grimsby T | 11 | 3 |
| 1989–90 | Grimsby T | 45 | 10 |
| 1990–91 | Grimsby T | 44 | 12 |
| 1991–92 | Grimsby T | 41 | 2 |
| 1992–93 | Grimsby T | 41 | 4 |
| 1993–94 | Grimsby T | 37 | 4 |
| 1994–95 | Grimsby T | 40 | 6 |
| 1995–96 | WBA | 40 | 5 |
| 1996–97 | WBA | 18 | 1 |
| 1996–97 | York C (loan) | 9 | 1 |
| 1997–98 | WBA | 4 | 0 |
| 1997–98 | Grimsby T (loan) | 5 | 0 |
| **Total:** | | **486** | **70** |

## GILCHRIST, Phil — Defender

H: 6 0 W: 13 03 b.Stockton 25-8-73

*Source:* Trainee.

| | | | |
|---|---|---|---|
| 1990–91 | Nottingham F | 0 | 0 |
| 1991–92 | Middlesbrough | 0 | 0 |
| 1992–93 | Hartlepool U | 24 | 0 |
| 1993–94 | Hartlepool U | 35 | 0 |
| 1994–95 | Hartlepool U | 23 | 0 |
| 1994–95 | Oxford U | 18 | 1 |
| 1995–96 | Oxford U | 42 | 3 |
| 1996–97 | Oxford U | 38 | 2 |
| 1997–98 | Oxford U | 39 | 2 |
| **Total:** | | **219** | **8** |

## GILES, Martin — Defender

b.Shrewsbury 1-1-79

*Source:* Trainee.

| | | | |
|---|---|---|---|
| 1997–98 | Chester C | 10 | 0 |
| **Total:** | | **10** | **0** |

## GILKES, Michael — Midfield

H: 5 8 W: 10 10 b.Hackney 20-7-65

*Source:* Leicester C.

| | | | |
|---|---|---|---|
| 1984–85 | Reading | 16 | 2 |
| 1985–86 | Reading | 9 | 2 |
| 1986–87 | Reading | 7 | 0 |
| 1987–88 | Reading | 39 | 4 |
| 1988–89 | Reading | 46 | 9 |
| 1989–90 | Reading | 42 | 2 |
| 1990–91 | Reading | 21 | 1 |
| 1991–92 | Reading | 20 | 0 |
| 1991–92 | Chelsea (loan) | 1 | 0 |
| 1991–92 | Southampton (loan) | 6 | 0 |
| 1992–93 | Reading | 38 | 12 |
| 1993–94 | Reading | 39 | 2 |
| 1994–95 | Reading | 40 | 8 |
| 1995–96 | Reading | 44 | 0 |
| 1996–97 | Reading | 32 | 1 |
| 1996–97 | Wolverhampton W | 5 | 1 |
| 1997–98 | Wolverhampton W | 3 | 0 |
| **Total:** | | **408** | **44** |

## GILL, Jeremy — Defender

H: 5 8 W: 11 00 b.Clevedon 8-9-70

*Source:* Yeovil T.

| | | | |
|---|---|---|---|
| 1997–98 | Birmingham C | 3 | 0 |
| **Total:** | | **3** | **0** |

## GILL, Matthew — Midfield

H: 5 11 W: 12 10 b.Cambridge 8-11-80

*Source:* Trainee.

| | | | |
|---|---|---|---|
| 1997–98 | Peterborough U | 2 | 0 |
| **Total:** | | **2** | **0** |

## GILL, Wayne — Midfield

H: 5 9 W: 11 00 b.Chorley 28-11-75

*Source:* Trainee.

| | | | |
|---|---|---|---|
| 1994–95 | Blackburn R | 0 | 0 |
| 1995–96 | Blackburn R | 0 | 0 |

| | | | |
|---|---|---|---|
| 1996–97 | Blackburn R | 0 | 0 |
| 1997–98 | Blackburn R | 0 | 0 |
| 1997–98 | Dundee U | 2 | 0 |
| **Total:** | | **2** | **0** |

## GILLESPIE, Keith — Forward

H: 5 9 W: 11 05 b.Larne 18-2-75

*Source:* Trainee. *Honours:* Northern Ireland Youth, Under-21, 21 full caps, 1 goal.

| | | | |
|---|---|---|---|
| 1992–93 | Manchester U | 0 | 0 |
| 1993–94 | Manchester U | 0 | 0 |
| 1993–94 | Wigan Ath (loan) | 8 | 4 |
| 1994–95 | Manchester U | 9 | 1 |
| 1994–95 | Newcastle U | 17 | 2 |
| 1995–96 | Newcastle U | 28 | 4 |
| 1996–97 | Newcastle U | 32 | 1 |
| 1997–98 | Newcastle U | 29 | 4 |
| **Total:** | | **123** | **16** |

## GILLIES, Richard — Forward

H: 5 10 W: 11 00 b.Glasgow 24-8-76

*Source:* St Mirren BC.

| | | | |
|---|---|---|---|
| 1992–93 | St Mirren | 8 | 1 |
| 1993–94 | St Mirren | 22 | 2 |
| 1994–95 | St Mirren | 24 | 3 |
| 1995–96 | St Mirren | 33 | 3 |
| 1996–97 | St Mirren | 29 | 6 |
| 1997–98 | Aberdeen | 21 | 0 |
| **Total:** | | **137** | **15** |

## GINOLA, David — Forward

H: 5 11 W: 11 10 b.Gassin 25-1-67

*Honours:* France 17 full caps, 3 goals.

| | | | |
|---|---|---|---|
| 1985–86 | Toulon | 14 | 0 |
| 1986–87 | Toulon | 34 | 0 |
| 1987–88 | Toulon | 33 | 4 |
| 1988–89 | Racing Paris | 29 | 7 |
| 1989–90 | Racing Paris | 32 | 1 |
| 1990–91 | Brest | 33 | 1 |
| 1991–92 | Brest | 17 | 9 |
| 1991–92 | Paris St Germain | 15 | 2 |
| 1992–93 | Paris St Germain | 34 | 6 |
| 1993–94 | Paris St Germain | 38 | 13 |
| 1994–95 | Paris St Germain | 28 | 11 |
| 1995–96 | Newcastle U | 34 | 5 |
| 1996–97 | Newcastle U | 24 | 1 |
| 1997–98 | Tottenham H | 34 | 6 |
| **Total:** | | **399** | **66** |

## GINTY, Rory — Midfield

H: 5 9 W: 11 00 b.Galway 23-1-77

*Source:* Trainee.

| | | | |
|---|---|---|---|
| 1994–95 | Crystal Palace | 0 | 0 |
| 1995–96 | Crystal Palace | 0 | 0 |
| 1996–97 | Crystal Palace | 0 | 0 |
| 1997–98 | Crystal Palace | 5 | 0 |
| **Total:** | | **5** | **0** |

## GISLASON, Valur — Midfield

H: 6 1 W: 11 12 b.Reykjavik 8-9-77

*Source:* Trainee. *Honours:* Iceland Schools, Youth.

| | | | |
|---|---|---|---|
| 1994 | Fram | 15 | 0 |
| 1995 | Fram | 15 | 2 |
| 1996–97 | Arsenal | 0 | 0 |
| 1997–98 | Arsenal | 0 | 0 |
| 1997–98 | Brighton & HA (loan) | 7 | 0 |
| **Total:** | | **37** | **2** |

## GITTENS, Jon — Defender

H: 5 11 W: 12 10 b.Moseley 22-1-64

*Source:* Paget R.

| | | | |
|---|---|---|---|
| 1985–86 | Southampton | 4 | 0 |
| 1986–87 | Southampton | 14 | 0 |
| 1987–88 | Swindon T | 29 | 0 |
| 1988–89 | Swindon T | 29 | 1 |
| 1989–90 | Swindon T | 40 | 4 |
| 1990–91 | Swindon T | 28 | 1 |
| 1990–91 | Southampton | 8 | 0 |
| 1991–92 | Southampton | 11 | 0 |
| 1991–92 | Middlesbrough (loan) | 12 | 1 |
| 1992–93 | Middlesbrough | 13 | 0 |
| 1993–94 | Portsmouth | 30 | 1 |
| 1994–95 | Portsmouth | 38 | 0 |
| 1995–96 | Portsmouth | 15 | 1 |
| 1996–97 | Torquay U | 33 | 3 |
| 1997–98 | Torquay U | 45 | 6 |
| **Total:** | | **349** | **18** |

## GIVEN, Shay — Goalkeeper

H: 6 0 W: 11 08 b.Lifford 24-4-76

*Source:* Celtic. *Honours:* Eire Under-21, 17 full caps.

| | | | |
|---|---|---|---|
| 1994–95 | Blackburn R | 0 | 0 |
| 1994–95 | Swindon T (loan) | 0 | 0 |
| 1995–96 | Blackburn R | 0 | 0 |
| 1995–96 | Swindon T (loan) | 5 | 0 |
| 1995–96 | Sunderland (loan) | 17 | 0 |
| 1996–97 | Blackburn R | 2 | 0 |
| 1997–98 | Newcastle U | 24 | 0 |
| **Total:** | | **48** | **0** |

## GLASGOW, Byron — Midfield

H: 5 6 W: 10 11 b.London 18-2-79

*Source:* Bognor Regis T.

| | | | |
|---|---|---|---|
| 1996–97 | Reading | 4 | 0 |
| 1997–98 | Reading | 3 | 0 |
| **Total:** | | **7** | **0** |

## GLASS, Jimmy — Goalkeeper

H: 6 1 W: 13 04 b.Epsom 1-8-73

*Source:* Trainee.

| | | | |
|---|---|---|---|
| 1991–92 | Crystal Palace | 0 | 0 |
| 1992–93 | Crystal Palace | 0 | 0 |
| 1993–94 | Crystal Palace | 0 | 0 |
| 1994–95 | Crystal Palace | 0 | 0 |
| 1994–95 | Portsmouth (loan) | 3 | 0 |
| 1995–96 | Crystal Palace | 0 | 0 |
| 1995–96 | Bournemouth | 13 | 0 |
| 1996–97 | Bournemouth | 35 | 0 |
| 1997–98 | Bournemouth | 46 | 0 |
| **Total:** | | **97** | **0** |

## GLASS, Stephen — Midfield

H: 5 9 W: 10 11 b.Dundee 25-5-76

*Source:* Crombie Sports. *Honours:* Scotland Under-21, B.

| | | | |
|---|---|---|---|
| 1994–95 | Aberdeen | 19 | 1 |
| 1995–96 | Aberdeen | 32 | 3 |
| 1996–97 | Aberdeen | 24 | 1 |
| 1997–98 | Aberdeen | 31 | 2 |
| **Total:** | | **106** | **7** |

## GLEGHORN, Nigel — Midfield

H: 6 0 W: 13 07 b.Seaham 12-8-62

*Source:* Seaham Red Star.

| | | | |
|---|---|---|---|
| 1985–86 | Ipswich T | 21 | 2 |
| 1986–87 | Ipswich T | 29 | 7 |
| 1987–88 | Ipswich T | 16 | 2 |
| 1988–89 | Manchester C | 32 | 6 |
| 1989–90 | Manchester C | 2 | 1 |
| 1989–90 | Birmingham C | 43 | 9 |
| 1990–91 | Birmingham C | 42 | 6 |
| 1991–92 | Birmingham C | 46 | 17 |
| 1992–93 | Birmingham C | 11 | 1 |
| 1992–93 | Stoke C | 34 | 7 |
| 1993–94 | Stoke C | 40 | 3 |
| 1994–95 | Stoke C | 46 | 7 |
| 1995–96 | Stoke C | 46 | 9 |
| 1996–97 | Burnley | 33 | 4 |
| 1997–98 | Burnley | 1 | 0 |
| 1997–98 | Brentford (loan) | 11 | 1 |
| 1997–98 | Northampton T (loan) | 8 | 1 |
| **Total:** | | **461** | **83** |

## GLENNON, Matthew — Goalkeeper

H: 6 2 W: 13 11 b.Stockport 8-10-78

*Source:* Trainee.

| | | | |
|---|---|---|---|
| 1997–98 | Bolton W | 0 | 0 |

## GLOVER, Dean — Defender

H: 5 11 W: 12 02 b.West Bromwich 29-12-63

*Source:* Apprentice.

| | | | |
|---|---|---|---|
| 1981–82 | Aston Villa | 0 | 0 |
| 1982–83 | Aston Villa | 0 | 0 |
| 1983–84 | Aston Villa | 0 | 0 |
| 1984–85 | Aston Villa | 5 | 0 |
| 1985–86 | Aston Villa | 18 | 0 |
| 1986–87 | Aston Villa | 0 | 0 |
| 1986–87 | Sheffield U (loan) | 5 | 0 |
| 1987–88 | Aston Villa | 5 | 0 |
| 1987–88 | Middlesbrough | 38 | 4 |
| 1988–89 | Middlesbrough | 12 | 1 |
| 1988–89 | Port Vale | 22 | 0 |
| 1989–90 | Port Vale | 44 | 4 |
| 1990–91 | Port Vale | 41 | 1 |
| 1991–92 | Port Vale | 46 | 1 |
| 1992–93 | Port Vale | 39 | 3 |
| 1993–94 | Port Vale | 46 | 3 |
| 1994–95 | Port Vale | 29 | 0 |
| 1995–96 | Port Vale | 29 | 0 |
| 1996–97 | Port Vale | 42 | 2 |
| 1997–98 | Port Vale | 25 | 1 |
| **Total:** | | **446** | **20** |

## GLOVER, Lee — Forward

H: 5 11 W: 11 09 b.Kettering 24-4-70

*Source:* Trainee. *Honours:* Scotland Under-21.

| | | | |
|---|---|---|---|
| 1986–87 | Nottingham F | 0 | 0 |
| 1987–88 | Nottingham F | 20 | 3 |
| 1988–89 | Nottingham F | 0 | 0 |
| 1989–90 | Nottingham F | 0 | 0 |
| 1989–90 | Leicester C (loan) | 5 | 1 |
| 1989–90 | Barnsley (loan) | 8 | 0 |
| 1990–91 | Nottingham F | 8 | 1 |
| 1991–92 | Nottingham F | 16 | 0 |
| 1991–92 | Luton T (loan) | 1 | 0 |
| 1992–93 | Nottingham F | 14 | 0 |
| 1993–94 | Nottingham F | 18 | 5 |
| 1994–95 | Port Vale | 28 | 4 |
| 1995–96 | Port Vale | 24 | 3 |

| | | | |
|---|---|---|---|
| 1996–97 | Rotherham U | 22 | 1 |
| 1996–97 | Huddersfield T (loan) | 11 | 0 |
| 1997–98 | Rotherham U | 37 | 17 |
| **Total:** | | **212** | **35** |

## GOATER, Shaun — Forward

H: 6 1 W: 11 10 b.Bermuda 25-2-70

*Honours:* Bermuda full caps.

| | | | |
|---|---|---|---|
| 1988–89 | Manchester U | 0 | 0 |
| 1989–90 | Manchester U | 0 | 0 |
| 1989–90 | Rotherham U | 12 | 2 |
| 1990–91 | Rotherham U | 22 | 2 |
| 1991–92 | Rotherham U | 24 | 9 |
| 1992–93 | Rotherham U | 23 | 7 |
| 1993–94 | Rotherham U | 39 | 13 |
| 1993–94 | Notts Co (loan) | 1 | 0 |
| 1994–95 | Rotherham U | 45 | 19 |
| 1995–96 | Rotherham U | 44 | 18 |
| 1996–97 | Bristol C | 42 | 23 |
| 1997–98 | Bristol C | 33 | 17 |
| 1997–98 | Manchester C | 7 | 3 |
| **Total:** | | **292** | **113** |

## GODBOLD, Jamie — Midfield

H: 5 4 W: 9 0 b.Great Yarmouth 10-1-80

*Source:* Trainee.

| | | | |
|---|---|---|---|
| 1996–97 | Stoke C | 0 | 0 |
| 1997–98 | Stoke C | 0 | 0 |

## GODDARD-CRAWLEY, Richard — Midfield

H: 6 3 W: 14 00 b.Burnt Oak 31-3-78

*Source:* Arsenal Trainee.

| | | | |
|---|---|---|---|
| 1996–97 | Brentford | 1 | 0 |
| 1997–98 | Brentford | 0 | 0 |
| **Total:** | | **1** | **0** |

## GOODEN, Ty — Midfield

H: 5 8 W: 12 06 b.Canvey Island 23-10-72

*Source:* Arsenal, Wycombe W.

| | | | |
|---|---|---|---|
| 1993–94 | Swindon T | 4 | 0 |
| 1994–95 | Swindon T | 16 | 2 |
| 1995–96 | Swindon T | 26 | 3 |
| 1996–97 | Swindon T | 13 | 1 |
| 1997–98 | Swindon T | 39 | 2 |
| **Total:** | | **98** | **8** |

## GOODHIND, Warren — Defender

H: 5 11 W: 11 02 b.Johannesburg 16-8-77

*Source:* Trainee.

| | | | |
|---|---|---|---|
| 1996–97 | Barnet | 3 | 0 |
| 1997–98 | Barnet | 35 | 1 |
| **Total:** | | **38** | **1** |

## GOODLAD, Mark — Goalkeeper

H: 6 0 W: 13 02 b.Barnsley 9-9-79

*Source:* Trainee.

| | | | |
|---|---|---|---|
| 1996–97 | Nottingham F | 0 | 0 |
| 1997–98 | Nottingham F | 0 | 0 |

## GOODMAN, Don — Forward

H: 5 10 W: 12 12 b.Leeds 9-5-66

*Source:* School.

| | | | |
|---|---|---|---|
| 1983–84 | Bradford C | 2 | 0 |
| 1984–85 | Bradford C | 25 | 5 |
| 1985–86 | Bradford C | 20 | 4 |
| 1986–87 | Bradford C | 23 | 5 |
| 1986–87 | WBA | 10 | 2 |
| 1987–88 | WBA | 40 | 7 |
| 1988–89 | WBA | 36 | 15 |
| 1989–90 | WBA | 39 | 21 |
| 1990–91 | WBA | 22 | 8 |
| 1991–92 | WBA | 11 | 7 |
| 1991–92 | Sunderland | 22 | 11 |
| 1992–93 | Sunderland | 41 | 16 |
| 1993–94 | Sunderland | 35 | 10 |
| 1994–95 | Sunderland | 18 | 3 |
| 1994–95 | Wolverhampton W | 24 | 3 |
| 1995–96 | Wolverhampton W | 44 | 16 |
| 1996–97 | Wolverhampton W | 27 | 6 |
| 1997–98 | Wolverhampton W | 30 | 8 |
| **Total:** | | **469** | **147** |

## GOODMAN, Jon — Forward

H: 6 0 W: 12 03 b.Walthamstow 2-6-71

*Source:* Bromley. *Honours:* Eire 4 full caps. Football League.

| | | | |
|---|---|---|---|
| 1990–91 | Millwall | 23 | 5 |
| 1991–92 | Millwall | 17 | 3 |
| 1992–93 | Millwall | 35 | 12 |
| 1993–94 | Millwall | 19 | 7 |
| 1994–95 | Millwall | 15 | 8 |
| 1994–95 | Wimbledon | 19 | 4 |
| 1995–96 | Wimbledon | 27 | 6 |
| 1996–97 | Wimbledon | 13 | 1 |
| 1997–98 | Wimbledon | 0 | 0 |
| **Total:** | | **168** | **46** |

## GOODRIDGE, Greg — Forward

H: 5 6 W: 10 00 b.Barbados 10-2-75

*Source:* Lambada. *Honours:* Barbados full caps.

| | | | |
|---|---|---|---|
| 1993–94 | Torquay U | 8 | 1 |
| 1994–95 | Torquay U | 30 | 3 |
| 1995–96 | QPR | 7 | 1 |
| 1996–97 | Bristol C | 28 | 6 |
| 1997–98 | Bristol C | 31 | 6 |
| **Total:** | | **104** | **17** |

## GOODWIN, Lee — Midfield

b.Stepney 5-9-78

*Source:* Trainee.

| | | | |
|---|---|---|---|
| 1997–98 | West Ham U | 0 | 0 |

## GOODWIN, Scott — Defender

H: 5 9 W: 11 08 b.Hull 13-9-78

*Source:* Trainee.

| | | | |
|---|---|---|---|
| 1995–96 | Coventry C | 0 | 0 |
| 1996–97 | Coventry C | 0 | 0 |
| 1997–98 | Coventry C | 0 | 0 |

## GOODWIN, Shaun — Midfield

H: 5 8 W: 11 04 b.Rotherham 14-4-69

*Source:* Trainee.

| | | | |
|---|---|---|---|
| 1987–88 | Rotherham U | 3 | 0 |
| 1988–89 | Rotherham U | 41 | 4 |
| 1989–90 | Rotherham U | 38 | 6 |
| 1990–91 | Rotherham U | 34 | 3 |
| 1991–92 | Rotherham U | 39 | 5 |
| 1992–93 | Rotherham U | 30 | 1 |
| 1993–94 | Rotherham U | 38 | 8 |
| 1994–95 | Rotherham U | 10 | 3 |
| 1995–96 | Rotherham U | 26 | 4 |
| 1996–97 | Rotherham U | 8 | 3 |
| 1997–98 | Rotherham U | 13 | 2 |
| **Total:** | | **280** | **39** |

## GOODYEAR, Craig — Midfield

H: 5 7 W: 12 01 b.Barnsley 7-11-80

*Source:* Trainee.

| | | | |
|---|---|---|---|
| 1997–98 | Barnsley | 0 | 0 |

## GORAM, Andy — Goalkeeper

H: 5 11 W: 11 06 b.Bury 13-4-64

*Source:* West Bromwich Apprentice, Scotland Under-21, 43 full caps.

| | | | |
|---|---|---|---|
| 1981–82 | Oldham Ath | 3 | 0 |
| 1982–83 | Oldham Ath | 38 | 0 |
| 1983–84 | Oldham Ath | 22 | 0 |
| 1984–85 | Oldham Ath | 41 | 0 |
| 1985–86 | Oldham Ath | 41 | 0 |
| 1986–87 | Oldham Ath | 41 | 0 |
| 1987–88 | Oldham Ath | 9 | 0 |
| 1987–88 | Hibernian | 33 | 1 |
| 1988–89 | Hibernian | 36 | 0 |
| 1989–90 | Hibernian | 34 | 0 |
| 1990–91 | Hibernian | 35 | 0 |
| 1991–92 | Rangers | 44 | 0 |
| 1992–93 | Rangers | 34 | 0 |
| 1993–94 | Rangers | 8 | 0 |
| 1994–95 | Rangers | 19 | 0 |
| 1995–96 | Rangers | 30 | 0 |
| 1996–97 | Rangers | 25 | 0 |
| 1997–98 | Rangers | 24 | 0 |
| **Total:** | | **517** | **1** |

## GORDON, Dean — Defender

H: 6 0 W: 13 04 b.Thornton Heath 10-2-73

*Source:* Trainee. *Honours:* England Under-21.

| | | | |
|---|---|---|---|
| 1991–92 | Crystal Palace | 4 | 0 |
| 1992–93 | Crystal Palace | 10 | 0 |
| 1993–94 | Crystal Palace | 45 | 5 |
| 1994–95 | Crystal Palace | 41 | 2 |
| 1995–96 | Crystal Palace | 34 | 8 |
| 1996–97 | Crystal Palace | 30 | 3 |
| 1997–98 | Crystal Palace | 37 | 2 |
| **Total:** | | **201** | **20** |

## GORDON, Gavin — Forward

H: 6 1 W: 12 00 b.Manchester 24-6-79

*Source:* Trainee.

| | | | |
|---|---|---|---|
| 1995–96 | Hull C | 13 | 3 |
| 1996–97 | Hull C | 20 | 4 |
| 1997–98 | Hull C | 5 | 2 |
| 1997–98 | Lincoln C | 13 | 3 |
| **Total:** | | **51** | **12** |

## GORE, Ian — Defender

H: 6 0 W: 12 07 b.Liverpool 10-1-68

| | | | |
|---|---|---|---|
| 1986–87 | Birmingham C | 0 | 0 |
| From Southport. | | | |
| 1987–88 | Blackpool | 0 | 0 |

| | | | |
|---|---|---|---|
| 1988–89 | Blackpool | 21 | 0 |
| 1989–90 | Blackpool | 34 | 0 |
| 1990–91 | Blackpool | 41 | 0 |
| 1991–92 | Blackpool | 41 | 0 |
| 1992–93 | Blackpool | 30 | 0 |
| 1993–94 | Blackpool | 29 | 0 |
| 1994–95 | Blackpool | 4 | 0 |
| 1995–96 | Torquay U | 25 | 2 |
| 1995–96 | Doncaster R | 5 | 0 |
| 1996–97 | Doncaster R | 36 | 1 |
| 1997–98 | Doncaster R | 25 | 0 |
| **Total:** | | **291** | **3** |

## GOSS, Jeremy — Midfield

H: 5 9 W: 11 08 b.Oekolia 11-5-65

*Source:* Amateur. *Honours:* England Youth, Wales 9 full caps.

| | | | |
|---|---|---|---|
| 1982–83 | Norwich C | 0 | 0 |
| 1983–84 | Norwich C | 1 | 0 |
| 1984–85 | Norwich C | 5 | 0 |
| 1985–86 | Norwich C | 0 | 0 |
| 1986–87 | Norwich C | 1 | 0 |
| 1987–88 | Norwich C | 22 | 2 |
| 1988–89 | Norwich C | 0 | 0 |
| 1989–90 | Norwich C | 7 | 0 |
| 1990–91 | Norwich C | 19 | 1 |
| 1991–92 | Norwich C | 33 | 1 |
| 1992–93 | Norwich C | 25 | 1 |
| 1993–94 | Norwich C | 34 | 6 |
| 1994–95 | Norwich C | 25 | 2 |
| 1995–96 | Norwich C | 16 | 1 |
| 1996–97 | Hearts | 10 | 0 |
| 1997–98 | Colchester U | 0 | 0 |
| **Total:** | | **198** | **14** |

## GOTTSKALKSSON, Olafur — Goalkeeper

H: 6 3 W: 13 12 b.Keflavik 12-3-68

*Honours:* Iceland 7 full caps.

| | | | |
|---|---|---|---|
| 1988 | IA Akranes | 18 | 0 |
| 1989 | IA Akranes | 15 | 0 |
| 1990 | KR | 18 | 0 |
| 1991 | KR | 18 | 0 |
| 1992 | KR | 18 | 0 |
| 1993 | KR | 17 | 0 |
| 1994 | Keflavik | 18 | 0 |
| 1995 | Keflavik | 17 | 0 |
| 1996 | Keflavik | 18 | 0 |
| 1997 | Keflavik | 10 | 0 |
| 1997–98 | Hibernian | 16 | 0 |
| **Total:** | | **183** | **0** |

## GOUCK, Andy — Midfield

H: 5 10 W: 12 00 b.Blackpool 8-6-72

*Source:* Trainee.

| | | | |
|---|---|---|---|
| 1989–90 | Blackpool | 8 | 1 |
| 1990–91 | Blackpool | 5 | 0 |
| 1991–92 | Blackpool | 24 | 2 |
| 1992–93 | Blackpool | 29 | 4 |
| 1993–94 | Blackpool | 27 | 2 |
| 1994–95 | Blackpool | 39 | 2 |
| 1995–96 | Blackpool | 16 | 1 |
| 1996–97 | Rochdale | 28 | 3 |
| 1997–98 | Rochdale | 38 | 5 |
| **Total:** | | **214** | **20** |

## GOUGH, Richard — Defender

H: 6 0 W: 12 00 b.Stockholm 5-4-62

*Source:* Wits University. *Honours:* Scotland Under-21, 61 full caps, 6 goals.

| | | | |
|---|---|---|---|
| 1980–81 | Dundee U | 4 | 0 |
| 1981–82 | Dundee U | 30 | 1 |
| 1982–83 | Dundee U | 34 | 8 |
| 1983–84 | Dundee U | 33 | 3 |
| 1984–85 | Dundee U | 33 | 6 |
| 1985–86 | Dundee U | 31 | 5 |
| 1986–87 | Tottenham H | 40 | 2 |
| 1987–88 | Tottenham H | 9 | 0 |
| 1987–88 | Rangers | 31 | 5 |
| 1988–89 | Rangers | 35 | 4 |
| 1989–90 | Rangers | 26 | 0 |
| 1990–91 | Rangers | 26 | 0 |
| 1991–92 | Rangers | 33 | 2 |
| 1992–93 | Rangers | 25 | 2 |
| 1993–94 | Rangers | 37 | 3 |
| 1994–95 | Rangers | 25 | 1 |
| 1995–96 | Rangers | 29 | 3 |
| 1996–97 | Rangers | 27 | 5 |
| 1997–98 | Rangers | 24 | 1 |
| **Total:** | | **532** | **51** |

## GOUGH, Steven — Midfield

H: 5 11 W: 11 10 b.Burton 16-9-80

*Source:* Trainee.

| | | | |
|---|---|---|---|
| 1997–98 | Nottingham F | 0 | 0 |

## GOULD, Jonathan — Goalkeeper

H: 6 1 W: 12 07 b.Paddington 18-7-68

*Source:* Clevedon T. *Honours:* Scotland B.

| | | | |
|---|---|---|---|
| 1990–91 | Halifax T | 23 | 0 |
| 1991–92 | Halifax T | 9 | 0 |
| 1991–92 | WBA | 0 | 0 |

| | | | |
|---|---|---|---|
| 1992–93 | Coventry C | 9 | 0 |
| 1993–94 | Coventry C | 9 | 0 |
| 1994–95 | Coventry C | 7 | 0 |
| 1995–96 | Coventry C | 0 | 0 |
| 1995–96 | Bradford C (loan) | 9 | 0 |
| 1996–97 | Bradford C | 9 | 0 |
| 1996–97 | Gillingham (loan) | 3 | 0 |
| 1997–98 | Celtic | 35 | 0 |
| **Total:** | | **113** | **0** |

## GOWER, Mark — Midfield

b.Edmonton 5-10-78

*Source:* Trainee. *Honours:* England Schools, Youth.

| | | | |
|---|---|---|---|
| 1996–97 | Tottenham H | 0 | 0 |
| 1997–98 | Tottenham H | 0 | 0 |

## GOWSHALL, Joby — Defender

H: 5 10 W: 13 00 b.Louth 7-8-75

*Source:* Trainee.

| | | | |
|---|---|---|---|
| 1993–94 | Grimsby T | 0 | 0 |
| 1994–95 | Grimsby T | 0 | 0 |
| 1995–96 | Grimsby T | 0 | 0 |
| 1996–97 | Grimsby T | 0 | 0 |
| 1997–98 | Lincoln C | 0 | 0 |

## GRADY, James — Forward

H: 5 7 W: 10 00 b.Paisley 14-3-71

*Source:* Arthurlie J.

| | | | |
|---|---|---|---|
| 1994–95 | Clydebank | 36 | 7 |
| 1995–96 | Clydebank | 36 | 10 |
| 1996–97 | Clydebank | 36 | 8 |
| 1997–98 | Dundee | 36 | 15 |
| **Total:** | | **144** | **40** |

## GRAHAM, Gareth — Midfield

H: 5 7 W: 10 02 b.Belfast 6-12-78

*Source:* Trainee.

| | | | |
|---|---|---|---|
| 1996–97 | Crystal Palace | 0 | 0 |
| 1997–98 | Crystal Palace | 0 | 0 |

## GRAHAM, Mark — Midfield

H: 5 7 W: 10 08 b.Newry 24-10-74

*Source:* Trainee.

| | | | |
|---|---|---|---|
| 1993–94 | QPR | 0 | 0 |
| 1994–95 | QPR | 0 | 0 |
| 1995–96 | QPR | 0 | 0 |
| 1996–97 | QPR | 18 | 0 |
| 1997–98 | QPR | 0 | 0 |
| **Total:** | | **18** | **0** |

## GRAHAM, Richard — Defender

H: 6 2 W: 12 08 b.Dewsbury 28-11-74

*Source:* Trainee.

| | | | |
|---|---|---|---|
| 1993–94 | Oldham Ath | 5 | 0 |
| 1994–95 | Oldham Ath | 32 | 3 |
| 1995–96 | Oldham Ath | 32 | 1 |
| 1996–97 | Oldham Ath | 19 | 1 |
| 1997–98 | Oldham Ath | 34 | 4 |
| **Total:** | | **122** | **9** |

## GRAHAM, Richard — Midfield

H: 5 8 W: 10 06 b.Newry 5-8-79

*Source:* Trainee. *Honours:* Northern Ireland Youth.

| | | | |
|---|---|---|---|
| 1996–97 | QPR | 0 | 0 |
| 1997–98 | QPR | 0 | 0 |

## GRAINGER, Martin — Defender

H: 5 10 W: 11 07 b.Enfield 23-8-72

*Source:* Trainee.

| | | | |
|---|---|---|---|
| 1989–90 | Colchester U | 7 | 2 |
| 1990–91 | Colchester U | 0 | 0 |
| 1991–92 | Colchester U | 0 | 0 |
| 1992–93 | Colchester U | 31 | 3 |
| 1993–94 | Colchester U | 8 | 2 |
| 1993–94 | Brentford | 31 | 2 |
| 1994–95 | Brentford | 37 | 7 |
| 1995–96 | Brentford | 33 | 3 |
| 1995–96 | Birmingham C | 8 | 0 |
| 1996–97 | Birmingham C | 23 | 3 |
| 1997–98 | Birmingham C | 33 | 2 |
| **Total:** | | **211** | **24** |

## GRANT, Brian — Midfield

H: 5 9 W: 10 07 b.Bannockburn 19-6-64

*Source:* Fallin Violet.

| | | | |
|---|---|---|---|
| 1981–82 | Stirling Albion | 1 | 0 |
| 1982–83 | Stirling Alb | 1 | 0 |
| 1983–84 | Stirling Alb | 24 | 3 |
| 1984–85 | Aberdeen | 0 | 0 |
| 1985–86 | Aberdeen | 0 | 0 |
| 1986–87 | Aberdeen | 15 | 4 |
| 1987–88 | Aberdeen | 7 | 1 |
| 1988–89 | Aberdeen | 26 | 1 |
| 1989–90 | Aberdeen | 31 | 6 |
| 1990–91 | Aberdeen | 32 | 2 |
| 1991–92 | Aberdeen | 33 | 6 |

| | | | |
|---|---|---|---|
| 1992–93 | Aberdeen | 29 | 3 |
| 1993–94 | Aberdeen | 30 | 2 |
| 1994–95 | Aberdeen | 32 | 2 |
| 1995–96 | Aberdeen | 25 | 0 |
| 1996–97 | Aberdeen | 2 | 0 |
| 1996–97 | Hibernian | 12 | 0 |
| 1997–98 | Hibernian | 5 | 0 |
| 1997–98 | Dundee | 8 | 0 |
| **Total:** | | **313** | **30** |

## GRANT, Gareth — Forward

b.Leeds 6-9-80

*Source:* Trainee.

| | | | |
|---|---|---|---|
| 1997–98 | Bradford C | 3 | 0 |
| **Total:** | | **3** | **0** |

## GRANT, Kim — Forward

H: 5 10 W: 11 05 b.Ghana 25-7-72

*Source:* Trainee. *Honours:* Ghana full caps.

| | | | |
|---|---|---|---|
| 1990–91 | Charlton Ath | 12 | 2 |
| 1991–92 | Charlton Ath | 4 | 0 |
| 1992–93 | Charlton Ath | 21 | 2 |
| 1993–94 | Charlton Ath | 30 | 1 |
| 1994–95 | Charlton Ath | 26 | 6 |
| 1995–96 | Charlton Ath | 30 | 7 |
| 1995–96 | Luton T | 10 | 3 |
| 1996–97 | Luton T | 25 | 2 |
| 1997–98 | Luton T | 0 | 0 |
| 1997–98 | Millwall | 39 | 8 |
| **Total:** | | **197** | **31** |

## GRANT, Peter — Midfield

H: 5 8 W: 11 07 b.Bellshill 30-8-65

*Source:* Celtic BC. *Honours:* Scotland Schools, Youth B, Under-21, 2 full caps.

| | | | |
|---|---|---|---|
| 1982–83 | Celtic | 0 | 0 |
| 1983–84 | Celtic | 3 | 0 |
| 1984–85 | Celtic | 20 | 4 |
| 1985–86 | Celtic | 30 | 1 |
| 1986–87 | Celtic | 37 | 1 |
| 1987–88 | Celtic | 37 | 2 |
| 1988–89 | Celtic | 21 | 0 |
| 1989–90 | Celtic | 26 | 0 |
| 1990–91 | Celtic | 27 | 0 |
| 1991–92 | Celtic | 22 | 0 |
| 1992–93 | Celtic | 31 | 2 |
| 1993–94 | Celtic | 28 | 0 |
| 1994–95 | Celtic | 28 | 2 |
| 1995–96 | Celtic | 30 | 3 |
| 1996–97 | Celtic | 23 | 0 |
| 1997–98 | Norwich C | 35 | 3 |
| **Total:** | | **398** | **18** |

## GRANT, Roderick — Forward

H: 5 11 W: 11 00 b.Gloucester 16-9-66

*Source:* Strathbrock Juniors.

| | | | |
|---|---|---|---|
| 1986–87 | Cowdenbeath | 24 | 14 |
| 1987–88 | Cowdenbeath | 32 | 11 |
| 1988–89 | Cowdenbeath | 8 | 2 |
| 1988–89 | St Johnstone | 28 | 5 |
| 1989–90 | St Johnstone | 37 | 19 |
| 1990–91 | St Johnstone | 30 | 7 |
| 1991–92 | St Johnstone | 25 | 2 |
| 1992–93 | Dunfermline Ath | 32 | 4 |
| 1993–94 | Partick Th | 37 | 13 |
| 1994–95 | Partick Th | 23 | 5 |
| 1995–96 | St Johnstone | 27 | 5 |
| 1996–97 | St Johnstone | 33 | 19 |
| 1997–98 | St Johnstone | 34 | 6 |
| **Total:** | | **370** | **112** |

## GRANT, Stephen — Forward

H: 6 1 W: 12 00 b.Birr 14-4-77

*Source:* Athlone T. *Honours:* Eire Schools.

| | | | |
|---|---|---|---|
| 1995–96 | Sunderland | 0 | 0 |
| 1996–97 | Sunderland | 0 | 0 |
| From Shamrock R. | | | |
| 1997–98 | Stockport Co | 16 | 3 |
| **Total:** | | **16** | **3** |

## GRANT, Tony — Midfield

H: 5 10 W: 10 02 b.Liverpool 14-11-74

*Source:* Trainee. *Honours:* England Under-21.

| | | | |
|---|---|---|---|
| 1993–94 | Everton | 0 | 0 |
| 1994–95 | Everton | 5 | 0 |
| 1995–96 | Everton | 13 | 1 |
| 1995–96 | Swindon T (loan) | 3 | 1 |
| 1996–97 | Everton | 18 | 0 |
| 1997–98 | Everton | 7 | 1 |
| **Total:** | | **46** | **3** |

## GRANVILLE, Danny — Defender

H: 5 11 W: 12 01 b.Islington 19-1-75

*Source:* Trainee. *Honours:* England Under-21.

| | | | |
|---|---|---|---|
| 1993–94 | Cambridge U | 11 | 5 |
| 1994–95 | Cambridge U | 16 | 2 |
| 1995–96 | Cambridge U | 35 | 0 |

| | | | |
|---|---|---|---|
| 1996–97 | Cambridge U | 37 | 0 |
| 1996–97 | Chelsea | 5 | 0 |
| 1997–98 | Chelsea | 13 | 0 |
| **Total:** | | **117** | **7** |

## GRAVES, Wayne — Midfield

b.Scunthorpe 18-9-80

*Source:* Trainee.

| | | | |
|---|---|---|---|
| 1997–98 | Scunthorpe U | 3 | 0 |
| **Total:** | | **3** | **0** |

## GRAY, Alan — Defender

H: 5 10 W: 12 04 b.Carlisle 2-5-74

*Source:* US Colleges.

| | | | |
|---|---|---|---|
| 1996–97 | Doncaster R | 1 | 0 |
| 1997–98 | Darlington | 6 | 0 |
| 1997–98 | Carlisle U | 1 | 0 |
| **Total:** | | **8** | **0** |

## GRAY, Andrew — Midfield

H: 6 0 W: 13 00 b.Harrogate 15-11-77

*Source:* Trainee.

| | | | |
|---|---|---|---|
| 1995–96 | Leeds U | 15 | 0 |
| 1996–97 | Leeds U | 7 | 0 |
| 1997–98 | Leeds U | 0 | 0 |
| 1997–98 | Bury (loan) | 6 | 1 |
| **Total:** | | **28** | **1** |

## GRAY, Andy — Midfield

H: 5 11 W: 14 04 b.Lambeth 22-2-64

*Source:* Corinthian C, Dulwich H. *Honours:* England Under-21, 1 full cap.

| | | | |
|---|---|---|---|
| 1984–85 | Crystal Palace | 21 | 5 |
| 1985–86 | Crystal Palace | 30 | 10 |
| 1986–87 | Crystal Palace | 30 | 6 |
| 1987–88 | Crystal Palace | 17 | 6 |
| 1987–88 | Aston Villa | 19 | 1 |
| 1988–89 | Aston Villa | 18 | 3 |
| 1988–89 | QPR | 11 | 2 |
| 1989–90 | Crystal Palace | 35 | 6 |
| 1990–91 | Crystal Palace | 30 | 4 |
| 1991–92 | Crystal Palace | 25 | 2 |
| 1991–92 | Tottenham H (loan) | 14 | 1 |
| 1992–93 | Tottenham H | 17 | 1 |
| 1992–93 | Swindon T (loan) | 3 | 0 |
| 1993–94 | Tottenham H | 2 | 1 |
| From Marbella. | | | |
| 1995–96 | Falkirk | 16 | 0 |
| 1996–97 | Falkirk | 0 | 0 |
| 1997–98 | Bury | 21 | 1 |
| 1997–98 | Millwall | 12 | 1 |
| **Total:** | | **321** | **50** |

## GRAY, Ian — Goalkeeper

H: 6 2 W: 12 00 b.Manchester 25-2-75

*Source:* Trainee.

| | | | |
|---|---|---|---|
| 1993–94 | Oldham Ath | 0 | 0 |
| 1994–95 | Oldham Ath | 0 | 0 |
| 1994–95 | Rochdale (loan) | 12 | 0 |
| 1995–96 | Rochdale | 20 | 0 |
| 1996–97 | Rochdale | 46 | 0 |
| 1997–98 | Stockport Co | 3 | 0 |
| **Total:** | | **81** | **0** |

## GRAY, Kevin — Defender

H: 5 11 W: 13 12 b.Sheffield 7-1-72

*Source:* Trainee.

| | | | |
|---|---|---|---|
| 1988–89 | Mansfield T | 1 | 0 |
| 1989–90 | Mansfield T | 16 | 0 |
| 1990–91 | Mansfield T | 31 | 1 |
| 1991–92 | Mansfield T | 18 | 0 |
| 1992–93 | Mansfield T | 33 | 0 |
| 1993–94 | Mansfield T | 42 | 2 |
| 1994–95 | Huddersfield T | 5 | 0 |
| 1995–96 | Huddersfield T | 38 | 0 |
| 1996–97 | Huddersfield T | 39 | 1 |
| 1997–98 | Huddersfield T | 35 | 1 |
| **Total:** | | **258** | **5** |

## GRAY, Martin — Midfield

H: 5 9 W: 11 05 b.Stockton 17-8-71

*Source:* Trainee.

| | | | |
|---|---|---|---|
| 1989–90 | Sunderland | 0 | 0 |
| 1990–91 | Sunderland | 0 | 0 |
| 1990–91 | Aldershot (loan) | 5 | 0 |
| 1991–92 | Sunderland | 1 | 0 |
| 1992–93 | Sunderland | 12 | 1 |
| 1993–94 | Sunderland | 22 | 0 |
| 1994–95 | Sunderland | 22 | 0 |
| 1995–96 | Sunderland | 7 | 0 |
| 1995–96 | Fulham (loan) | 6 | 0 |
| 1995–96 | Oxford U | 7 | 0 |
| 1996–97 | Oxford U | 43 | 2 |
| 1997–98 | Oxford U | 31 | 2 |
| **Total:** | | **156** | **5** |

## GRAY, Michael — Defender

H: 5 7 W: 10 08 b.Sunderland 3-8-74

*Source:* Trainee.

| | | | |
|---|---|---|---|
| 1992–93 | Sunderland | 27 | 2 |
| 1993–94 | Sunderland | 22 | 1 |
| 1994–95 | Sunderland | 16 | 0 |
| 1995–96 | Sunderland | 46 | 4 |
| 1996–97 | Sunderland | 34 | 3 |
| 1997–98 | Sunderland | 44 | 2 |
| **Total:** | | **189** | **12** |

## GRAY, Phil — Forward

H: 5 9 W: 12 09 b.Belfast 2-10-68

*Source:* Apprentice. *Honours:* Northern Ireland Schools, Youth, Under-23, 20 full caps, 5 goals.

| | | | |
|---|---|---|---|
| 1986–87 | Tottenham H | 1 | 0 |
| 1987–88 | Tottenham H | 1 | 0 |
| 1988–89 | Tottenham H | 1 | 0 |
| 1989–90 | Tottenham H | 0 | 0 |
| 1989–90 | Barnsley (loan) | 3 | 0 |
| 1990–91 | Tottenham H | 6 | 0 |
| 1990–91 | Fulham (loan) | 3 | 0 |
| 1991–92 | Luton T | 14 | 3 |
| 1992–93 | Luton T | 45 | 19 |
| 1993–94 | Sunderland | 41 | 14 |
| 1994–95 | Sunderland | 42 | 12 |
| 1995–96 | Sunderland | 32 | 8 |
| 1996–97 | Sunderland | 0 | 0 |
| 1997–98 | Luton T | 17 | 2 |
| **Total:** | | **206** | **58** |

## GRAY, Stuart — Defender

H: 5 11 W: 11 00 b.Harrogate 18-12-73

*Source:* Giffnock N. *Honours:* Scotland Under-21.

| | | | |
|---|---|---|---|
| 1992–93 | Celtic | 1 | 0 |
| 1993–94 | Celtic | 0 | 0 |
| 1994–95 | Celtic | 11 | 0 |
| 1995–96 | Celtic | 5 | 1 |
| 1996–97 | Celtic | 11 | 0 |
| 1997–98 | Celtic | 0 | 0 |
| 1997–98 | Reading | 7 | 0 |
| **Total:** | | **35** | **1** |

## GRAYSON, Simon — Defender

H: 6 0 W: 13 07 b.Ripon 16-12-69

*Source:* Trainee.

| | | | |
|---|---|---|---|
| 1987–88 | Leeds U | 2 | 0 |
| 1988–89 | Leeds U | 0 | 0 |
| 1989–90 | Leeds U | 0 | 0 |
| 1990–91 | Leeds U | 0 | 0 |
| 1991–92 | Leeds U | 0 | 0 |
| 1991–92 | Leicester C | 13 | 0 |
| 1992–93 | Leicester C | 24 | 1 |
| 1993–94 | Leicester C | 40 | 1 |
| 1994–95 | Leicester C | 34 | 0 |
| 1995–96 | Leicester C | 41 | 2 |
| 1996–97 | Leicester C | 36 | 0 |
| 1997–98 | Aston Villa | 33 | 0 |
| **Total:** | | **223** | **4** |

## GRAZIOLI, Guiliano — Forward

H: 5 11 W: 12 00 b.London 23-3-75

*Source:* Wembley.

| | | | |
|---|---|---|---|
| 1995–96 | Peterborough U | 3 | 1 |
| 1996–97 | Peterborough U | 4 | 0 |
| 1997–98 | Peterborough U | 0 | 0 |
| **Total:** | | **7** | **1** |

## GREAVES, Mark — Defender

H: 6 1 W: 13 00 b.Hull 22-1-75

*Source:* Brigg Town.

| | | | |
|---|---|---|---|
| 1996–97 | Hull C | 30 | 2 |
| 1997–98 | Hull C | 25 | 2 |
| **Total:** | | **55** | **4** |

## GREEN, Francis — Forward

H: 5 9 W: 11 04 b.Derby 23-4-80

*Source:* Ilkeston T.

| | | | |
|---|---|---|---|
| 1997–98 | Peterborough U | 4 | 1 |
| **Total:** | | **4** | **1** |

## GREEN, Joe — Defender

H: 6 3 W: 12 02 b.Wisbech 2-11-78

*Source:* Trainee. *Honours:* England Youth.

| | | | |
|---|---|---|---|
| 1997–98 | Norwich C | 0 | 0 |

## GREEN, Richard — Defender

H: 6 0 W: 12 00 b.Wolverhampton 22-11-67

*Source:* Apprentice.

| | | | |
|---|---|---|---|
| 1986–87 | Shrewsbury T | 15 | 0 |
| 1987–88 | Shrewsbury T | 31 | 2 |
| 1988–89 | Shrewsbury T | 39 | 3 |
| 1989–90 | Shrewsbury T | 40 | 0 |
| 1990–91 | Shrewsbury T | 0 | 0 |
| 1990–91 | Swindon T | 0 | 0 |
| 1991–92 | Swindon T | 0 | 0 |
| 1991–92 | Gillingham | 12 | 4 |
| 1992–93 | Gillingham | 39 | 3 |

| | | | |
|---|---|---|---|
| 1993–94 | Gillingham | 39 | 4 |
| 1994–95 | Gillingham | 37 | 1 |
| 1995–96 | Gillingham | 35 | 2 |
| 1996–97 | Gillingham | 29 | 2 |
| 1997–98 | Gillingham | 25 | 0 |
| **Total:** | | **341** | **21** |

## GREEN, Robert — Goalkeeper

H: 6 2 W: 12 02 b.Chertsey 19-1-80

*Source:* Trainee.

| | | | |
|---|---|---|---|
| 1997–98 | Norwich C | 0 | 0 |

## GREEN, Ryan — Defender

b.Cardiff 20-10-80

*Source:* Danes Court. *Honours:* Wales Under-21, 2 full caps.

| | | | |
|---|---|---|---|
| 1997–98 | Wolverhampton W | 0 | 0 |

## GREEN, Scott — Defender

H: 5 10 W: 12 05 b.Walsall 15-1-70

*Source:* Trainee.

| | | | |
|---|---|---|---|
| 1988–89 | Derby Co | 0 | 0 |
| 1989–90 | Derby Co | 0 | 0 |
| 1989–90 | Bolton W | 5 | 2 |
| 1990–91 | Bolton W | 41 | 6 |
| 1991–92 | Bolton W | 37 | 2 |
| 1992–93 | Bolton W | 41 | 6 |
| 1993–94 | Bolton W | 22 | 4 |
| 1994–95 | Bolton W | 31 | 1 |
| 1995–96 | Bolton W | 31 | 3 |
| 1996–97 | Bolton W | 12 | 1 |
| 1997–98 | Wigan Ath | 38 | 1 |
| **Total:** | | **258** | **26** |

## GREENACRE, Chris — Forward

H: 5 11 W: 12 08 b.Halifax 23-12-77

*Source:* Trainee.

| | | | |
|---|---|---|---|
| 1995–96 | Manchester C | 0 | 0 |
| 1996–97 | Manchester C | 4 | 0 |
| 1997–98 | Manchester C | 3 | 1 |
| 1997–98 | Cardiff C (loan) | 11 | 2 |
| 1997–98 | Blackpool (loan) | 4 | 0 |
| **Total:** | | **22** | **3** |

## GREENALL, Colin — Defender

H: 5 11 W: 12 12 b.Billinge 30-12-63

*Source:* Apprentice.

| | | | |
|---|---|---|---|
| 1980–81 | Blackpool | 12 | 0 |
| 1981–82 | Blackpool | 18 | 0 |
| 1982–83 | Blackpool | 24 | 1 |
| 1983–84 | Blackpool | 39 | 4 |
| 1984–85 | Blackpool | 44 | 3 |
| 1985–86 | Blackpool | 43 | 1 |
| 1986–87 | Blackpool | 3 | 0 |
| 1986–87 | Gillingham | 37 | 2 |
| 1987–88 | Gillingham | 25 | 2 |
| 1987–88 | Oxford U | 12 | 0 |
| 1988–89 | Oxford U | 40 | 2 |
| 1989–90 | Oxford U | 15 | 0 |
| 1989–90 | Bury (loan) | 3 | 0 |
| 1990–91 | Bury | 31 | 0 |
| 1991–92 | Bury | 37 | 5 |
| 1991–92 | Preston NE | 9 | 1 |
| 1992–93 | Preston NE | 20 | 0 |
| 1993–94 | Chester C | 42 | 1 |
| 1994–95 | Lincoln C | 39 | 3 |
| 1995–96 | Lincoln C | 4 | 0 |
| 1995–96 | Wigan Ath | 37 | 2 |
| 1996–97 | Wigan Ath | 46 | 2 |
| 1997–98 | Wigan Ath | 39 | 4 |
| **Total:** | | **619** | **33** |

## GREENE, David — Midfield

H: 6 3 W: 14 02 b.Luton 26-10-73

*Source:* Trainee. *Honours:* Eire Under-21.

| | | | |
|---|---|---|---|
| 1991–92 | Luton T | 0 | 0 |
| 1992–93 | Luton T | 1 | 0 |
| 1993–94 | Luton T | 10 | 0 |
| 1994–95 | Luton T | 8 | 0 |
| 1995–96 | Luton T | 0 | 0 |
| 1995–96 | Colchester U (loan) | 14 | 1 |
| 1995–96 | Brentford (loan) | 11 | 0 |
| 1996–97 | Colchester U | 44 | 2 |
| 1997–98 | Colchester U | 38 | 4 |
| **Total:** | | **126** | **7** |

## GREENING, Jonathan — Forward

H: 6 0 W: 11 03 b.Scarborough 2-1-79

*Source:* Trainee. *Honours:* England Youth.

| | | | |
|---|---|---|---|
| 1996–97 | York C | 5 | 0 |
| 1997–98 | York C | 20 | 2 |
| 1997–98 | Manchester U | 0 | 0 |
| **Total:** | | **25** | **2** |

## GREGAN, Sean — Midfield

H: 6 2 W: 12 03 b.Stockton 29-3-74

*Source:* Trainee.

| | | | |
|---|---|---|---|
| 1991–92 | Darlington | 17 | 0 |
| 1992–93 | Darlington | 17 | 1 |
| 1993–94 | Darlington | 23 | 1 |
| 1994–95 | Darlington | 25 | 2 |

| | | | |
|---|---|---|---|
| 1995–96 | Darlington | 38 | 0 |
| 1996–97 | Darlington | 16 | 0 |
| 1996–97 | Preston NE | 21 | 1 |
| 1997–98 | Preston NE | 35 | 2 |
| **Total:** | | **192** | **7** |

## GREGG, Matt — Goalkeeper

H: 5 11 W: 12 00 b.Cheltenham 30-11-78

*Source:* Trainee.

| | | | |
|---|---|---|---|
| 1995–96 | Torquay U | 1 | 0 |
| 1996–97 | Torquay U | 1 | 0 |
| 1997–98 | Torquay U | 19 | 0 |
| **Total:** | | **21** | **0** |

## GREGORY, Andrew — Midfield

H: 5 8 W: 11 06 b.Barnsley 8-10-76

*Source:* Trainee.

| | | | |
|---|---|---|---|
| 1995–96 | Barnsley | 0 | 0 |
| 1996–97 | Barnsley | 0 | 0 |
| 1997–98 | Barnsley | 0 | 0 |

## GREGORY, David — Midfield

H: 5 11 W: 12 03 b.Polstead 23-1-70

*Source:* Trainee.

| | | | |
|---|---|---|---|
| 1987–88 | Ipswich T | 0 | 0 |
| 1988–89 | Ipswich T | 2 | 0 |
| 1989–90 | Ipswich T | 4 | 0 |
| 1990–91 | Ipswich T | 21 | 1 |
| 1991–92 | Ipswich T | 1 | 0 |
| 1992–93 | Ipswich T | 3 | 1 |
| 1993–94 | Ipswich T | 0 | 0 |
| 1994–95 | Ipswich T | 1 | 0 |
| 1994–95 | Hereford U (loan) | 2 | 0 |
| 1995–96 | Peterborough U | 3 | 0 |
| 1995–96 | Colchester U | 10 | 0 |
| 1996–97 | Colchester U | 38 | 1 |
| 1997–98 | Colchester U | 44 | 5 |
| **Total:** | | **129** | **8** |

## GREGORY, Neil — Forward

H: 6 0 W: 12 03 b.Zambia 7-10-72

*Source:* Trainee.

| | | | |
|---|---|---|---|
| 1992–93 | Ipswich T | 0 | 0 |
| 1993–94 | Ipswich T | 0 | 0 |
| 1993–94 | Chesterfield (loan) | 3 | 1 |
| 1994–95 | Ipswich T | 3 | 0 |
| 1994–95 | Scunthorpe U (loan) | 10 | 7 |
| 1995–96 | Ipswich T | 17 | 2 |
| 1996–97 | Ipswich T | 17 | 6 |
| 1996–97 | Torquay U (loan) | 5 | 0 |
| 1997–98 | Ipswich T | 8 | 1 |
| 1997–98 | Peterborough U (loan) | 3 | 1 |
| 1997–98 | Colchester U | 15 | 7 |
| **Total:** | | **81** | **25** |

## GRIDELET, Phil — Midfield

H: 5 11 W: 13 00 b.Edgware 30-4-67

*Source:* Watford, Hendon, Barnet.

| | | | |
|---|---|---|---|
| 1990–91 | Barnsley | 4 | 0 |
| 1991–92 | Barnsley | 0 | 0 |
| 1992–93 | Barnsley | 2 | 0 |
| 1992–93 | Rotherham U (loan) | 9 | 0 |
| 1993–94 | Barnsley | 0 | 0 |
| 1993–94 | Southend U | 29 | 0 |
| 1994–95 | Southend U | 29 | 5 |
| 1995–96 | Southend U | 40 | 2 |
| 1996–97 | Southend U | 41 | 1 |
| 1997–98 | Southend U | 37 | 2 |
| **Total:** | | **191** | **10** |

## GRIEMINK, Bart — Goalkeeper

H: 6 3 W: 15 04 b.Holland 29-3-72

*Source:* WKE.

| | | | |
|---|---|---|---|
| 1995–96 | Birmingham C | 20 | 0 |
| 1996–97 | Birmingham C | 0 | 0 |
| 1996–97 | Barnsley (loan) | 0 | 0 |
| 1996–97 | Peterborough U | 27 | 0 |
| 1997–98 | Peterborough U | 0 | 0 |
| **Total:** | | **47** | **0** |

## GRIEVES, Daniel — Forward

H: 5 9 W: 10 07 b.Watford 21-9-78

*Source:* Trainee.

| | | | |
|---|---|---|---|
| 1996–97 | Watford | 0 | 0 |
| 1997–98 | Watford | 0 | 0 |

## GRIFFIN, Andrew — Defender

H: 5 8 W: 10 10 b.Wigan 17-3-79

*Source:* Trainee. *Honours:* England Youth.

| | | | |
|---|---|---|---|
| 1996–97 | Stoke C | 34 | 1 |
| 1997–98 | Stoke C | 23 | 1 |
| 1997–98 | Newcastle U | 4 | 0 |
| **Total:** | | **61** | **2** |

## GRIFFIN, Anthony — Defender

H: 5 11 W: 11 02 b.Bournemouth 22-3-79

*Source:* Trainee.

| | | | |
|---|---|---|---|
| 1997–98 | Bournemouth | 0 | 0 |

## GRIFFIN, Daniel — Defender

H: 5 10 W: 10 05 b.Belfast 10-8-77

*Source:* St Andrews, Belfast. *Honours:* Northern Ireland Under-21, 7 full caps.

| | | | |
|---|---|---|---|
| 1993–94 | St Johnstone | 0 | 0 |
| 1994–95 | St Johnstone | 3 | 0 |
| 1995–96 | St Johnstone | 31 | 1 |
| 1996–97 | St Johnstone | 29 | 1 |
| 1997–98 | St Johnstone | 13 | 0 |
| **Total:** | | **76** | **2** |

## GRIFFITHS, Andy — Midfield

H: 5 11 W: 12 00 b.Wirral 21-11-78

*Source:* Trainee.

| | | | |
|---|---|---|---|
| 1997–98 | Wrexham | 0 | 0 |

## GRIFFITHS, Carl — Forward

H: 5 10 W: 11 05 b.Oswestry 15-7-71

*Source:* Trainee. *Honours:* Wales Youth, Under-21.

| | | | |
|---|---|---|---|
| 1988–89 | Shrewsbury T | 28 | 6 |
| 1989–90 | Shrewsbury T | 18 | 4 |
| 1990–91 | Shrewsbury T | 19 | 4 |
| 1991–92 | Shrewsbury T | 27 | 8 |
| 1992–93 | Shrewsbury T | 42 | 27 |
| 1993–94 | Shrewsbury T | 9 | 5 |
| 1993–94 | Manchester C | 16 | 4 |
| 1994–95 | Manchester C | 2 | 0 |
| 1995–96 | Manchester C | 0 | 0 |
| 1995–96 | Portsmouth | 14 | 2 |
| 1995–96 | Peterborough U | 4 | 1 |
| 1996–97 | Peterborough U | 12 | 1 |
| 1996–97 | Leyton Orient | 13 | 6 |
| 1997–98 | Leyton Orient | 33 | 18 |
| **Total:** | | **237** | **86** |

## GRIFFITHS, Gareth — Defender

H: 6 4 W: 14 04 b.Winsford 10-4-70

*Source:* Rhyl.

| | | | |
|---|---|---|---|
| 1992–93 | Port Vale | 0 | 0 |
| 1993–94 | Port Vale | 4 | 2 |
| 1994–95 | Port Vale | 20 | 0 |
| 1995–96 | Port Vale | 41 | 2 |
| 1996–97 | Port Vale | 26 | 0 |
| 1997–98 | Port Vale | 3 | 0 |
| 1997–98 | Shrewsbury T (loan) | 6 | 0 |
| **Total:** | | **100** | **4** |

## GRIM, Robert — Midfield

H: 5 11 W: 11 08 b.London 10-9-78

*Source:* Trainee.

| | | | |
|---|---|---|---|
| 1995–96 | Nottingham F | 0 | 0 |
| 1996–97 | Nottingham F | 0 | 0 |
| 1997–98 | Nottingham F | 0 | 0 |

## GRIMANDI, Gilles — Defender

H: 6 0 W: 12 07 b.Gap 11-11-70

*Source:* FC Gap.

| | | | |
|---|---|---|---|
| 1991–92 | Monaco | 5 | 0 |
| 1992–93 | Monaco | 8 | 0 |
| 1993–94 | Monaco | 19 | 1 |
| 1994–95 | Monaco | 9 | 0 |
| 1995–96 | Monaco | 25 | 1 |
| 1996–97 | Monaco | 24 | 1 |
| 1997–98 | Arsenal | 22 | 1 |
| **Total:** | | **112** | **4** |

## GROBBELAAR, Bruce — Goalkeeper

H: 6 1 W: 12 08 b.Durban 6-10-57

*Source:* Vancouver Whitecaps. *Honours:* Zimbabwe full caps.

| | | | |
|---|---|---|---|
| 1979–80 | Crewe Alex | 24 | 1 |
| 1980–81 | Liverpool | 0 | 0 |
| 1981–82 | Liverpool | 42 | 0 |
| 1982–83 | Liverpool | 42 | 0 |
| 1983–84 | Liverpool | 42 | 0 |
| 1984–85 | Liverpool | 42 | 0 |
| 1985–86 | Liverpool | 42 | 0 |
| 1986–87 | Liverpool | 31 | 0 |
| 1987–88 | Liverpool | 38 | 0 |
| 1988–89 | Liverpool | 21 | 0 |
| 1989–90 | Liverpool | 38 | 0 |
| 1990–91 | Liverpool | 31 | 0 |
| 1991–92 | Liverpool | 37 | 0 |
| 1992–93 | Liverpool | 5 | 0 |
| 1992–93 | Stoke C (loan) | 4 | 0 |
| 1993–94 | Liverpool | 29 | 0 |
| 1994–95 | Southampton | 30 | 0 |
| 1995–96 | Southampton | 2 | 0 |
| 1996–97 | Plymouth Arg | 36 | 0 |
| 1997–98 | Oxford U | 0 | 0 |
| 1997–98 | Oldham Ath | 4 | 0 |
| **Total:** | | **540** | **1** |

## GRODAS, Frode — Goalkeeper

H: 6 2 W: 14 07 b.Volda 24-10-64

*Honours:* Norway 43 full caps.

| | | | |
|---|---|---|---|
| 1988 | Lillestrom | 22 | 0 |

| | | | |
|---|---|---|---|
| 1989 | Lillestrom | 22 | 0 |
| 1990 | Lillestrom | 7 | 0 |
| 1991 | Lillestrom | 22 | 1 |
| 1992 | Lillestrom | 22 | 0 |
| 1993 | Lillestrom | 19 | 0 |
| 1994 | Lillestrom | 22 | 0 |
| 1995 | Lillestrom | 25 | 0 |
| 1996 | Lillestrom | 21 | 0 |
| 1996–97 | Chelsea | 21 | 0 |
| 1997–98 | Chelsea | 0 | 0 |
| 1997–98 | Tottenham H | 0 | 0 |
| **Total:** | | **203** | **1** |

## GROVES, Paul — Midfield

H: 5 11 W: 11 05 b.Derby 28-2-66

*Source:* Burton Alb.

| | | | |
|---|---|---|---|
| 1987–88 | Leicester C | 1 | 1 |
| 1988–89 | Leicester C | 15 | 0 |
| 1989–90 | Leicester C | 0 | 0 |
| 1989–90 | Lincoln C (loan) | 8 | 1 |
| 1989–90 | Blackpool | 19 | 1 |
| 1990–91 | Blackpool | 46 | 11 |
| 1991–92 | Blackpool | 42 | 9 |
| 1992–93 | Grimsby T | 46 | 12 |
| 1993–94 | Grimsby T | 46 | 11 |
| 1994–95 | Grimsby T | 46 | 5 |
| 1995–96 | Grimsby T | 46 | 10 |
| 1996–97 | WBA | 29 | 4 |
| 1997–98 | Grimsby T | 46 | 7 |
| **Total:** | | **390** | **72** |

## GUDJONSSON, Bjarni — Forward

H: 5 8 W: 10 10 b.Akranes 26-2-79

*Honours:* Iceland Under-21, 1 full cap.

| | | | |
|---|---|---|---|
| 1995 | IA Akranes | 2 | 0 |
| 1996 | IA Akranes | 17 | 13 |
| 1997 | IA Akranes | 6 | 2 |
| 1997–98 | Newcastle U | 0 | 0 |
| **Total:** | | **25** | **15** |

## GUDMUNDSSON, Johann — Midfield

H: 5 9 W: 13 00 b.Reykjavik 7-12-77

| | | | |
|---|---|---|---|
| 1994 | Keflavik | 1 | 0 |
| 1995 | Keflavik | 14 | 4 |
| 1996 | Keflavik | 17 | 4 |
| 1997 | Keflavik | 17 | 5 |
| 1997–98 | Watford | 0 | 0 |
| **Total:** | | **49** | **13** |

## GUDNASON, Haukar — Forward

b.Keflavik 8-9-78

| | | | |
|---|---|---|---|
| 1995 | Keflavik | 3 | 1 |
| 1996 | Keflavik | 15 | 4 |
| 1997 | Keflavik | 16 | [illegible] |
| 1997–98 | Liverpool | 0 | [illegible] |
| **Total:** | | **34** | **11** |

## GUIMARRA, Willy

b.Ontario 26-8-71

*Source:* Montreal Impact.

| | | | |
|---|---|---|---|
| 1997–98 | Darlington | 4 | [illegible] |
| **Total:** | | **4** | **0** |

## GUINAN, Stephen — Forward

H: 6 1 W: 13 07 b.Birmingham 24-12-75

*Source:* Trainee.

| | | | |
|---|---|---|---|
| 1992–93 | Nottingham F | 0 | [illegible] |
| 1993–94 | Nottingham F | 0 | 0 |
| 1994–95 | Nottingham F | 0 | [illegible] |
| 1995–96 | Nottingham F | 2 | [illegible] |
| 1995–96 | Darlington (loan) | 3 | 1 |
| 1996–97 | Nottingham F | 2 | [illegible] |
| 1996–97 | Burnley (loan) | 6 | [illegible] |
| 1997–98 | Nottingham F | 2 | 0 |
| 1997–98 | Crewe Alex (loan) | 3 | [illegible] |
| **Total:** | | **18** | [illegible] |

## GULLIT, Ruud — Forward

H: 6 3 W: 13 12 b.Surinam 1-9-62

*Source:* DWS Amsterdam. *Honours:* Holland Youth, Under-21, 65 full caps, 16 goals.

| | | | |
|---|---|---|---|
| 1979–80 | Haarlem | 24 | 4 |
| 1980–81 | Haarlem | 36 | 14 |
| 1981–82 | Haarlem | 31 | 14 |
| 1982–83 | Feyenoord | 33 | 8 |
| 1983–84 | Feyenoord | 33 | 15 |
| 1984–85 | Feyenoord | 19 | [illegible] |
| 1985–86 | PSV Eindhoven | 34 | 24 |
| 1986–87 | PSV Eindhoven | 34 | 22 |
| 1987–88 | AC Milan | 29 | 9 |
| 1988–89 | AC Milan | 19 | 5 |
| 1989–90 | AC Milan | 2 | 0 |
| 1990–91 | AC Milan | 26 | [illegible] |
| 1991–92 | AC Milan | 26 | [illegible] |
| 1992–93 | AC Milan | 15 | [illegible] |
| 1993–94 | Sampdoria | 31 | 15 |
| 1994–95 | AC Milan | 8 | [illegible] |
| 1994–95 | Sampdoria | 22 | 9 |
| 1995–96 | Chelsea | 31 | [illegible] |

| | | | |
|---|---|---|---|
| 1996–97 | Chelsea | 12 | 1 |
| 1997–98 | Chelsea | 6 | 0 |
| **Total:** | | **471** | **174** |

## GUNN, Bryan — Goalkeeper

H: 6 2 W: 13 08 b.Thurso 22-12-63

*Source:* Invergordon BC. *Honours:* Scotland Schools, Youth, Under-21, B, 6 full caps.

| | | | |
|---|---|---|---|
| 1980–81 | Aberdeen | 0 | 0 |
| 1981–82 | Aberdeen | 0 | 0 |
| 1982–83 | Aberdeen | 1 | 0 |
| 1983–84 | Aberdeen | 0 | 0 |
| 1984–85 | Aberdeen | 2 | 0 |
| 1985–86 | Aberdeen | 10 | 0 |
| 1986–87 | Aberdeen | 2 | 0 |
| 1986–87 | Norwich C | 29 | 0 |
| 1987–88 | Norwich C | 38 | 0 |
| 1988–89 | Norwich C | 37 | 0 |
| 1989–90 | Norwich C | 37 | 0 |
| 1990–91 | Norwich C | 34 | 0 |
| 1991–92 | Norwich C | 25 | 0 |
| 1992–93 | Norwich C | 42 | 0 |
| 1993–94 | Norwich C | 41 | 0 |
| 1994–95 | Norwich C | 21 | 0 |
| 1995–96 | Norwich C | 43 | 0 |
| 1996–97 | Norwich C | 39 | 0 |
| 1997–98 | Norwich C | 4 | 0 |
| 1997–98 | Hibernian | 12 | 0 |
| **Total:** | | **417** | **0** |

## GUNNLAUGSSON, Arnar — Forward

H: 5 11 W: 11 04 b.Akranes 6-3-73

*Honours:* Iceland 23 full caps, 2 goals.

| | | | |
|---|---|---|---|
| 1992 | IA Akranes | 18 | 15 |
| 1992–93 | Feyenoord | 4 | 0 |
| 1993–94 | Feyenoord | 5 | 0 |
| 1994–95 | Nuremberg | 28 | 8 |
| 1995 | IA Akranes | 7 | 15 |
| From Sochaux. | | | |
| 1997 | IA Akranes | 2 | 1 |
| 1997–98 | Bolton W | 15 | 0 |
| **Total:** | | **79** | **39** |

## GUPPY, Steve — Midfield

H: 5 11 W: 12 00 b.Winchester 29-3-69

*Source:* Southampton. *Honours:* England Under-21, B.

| | | | |
|---|---|---|---|
| 1993–94 | Wycombe W | 41 | 8 |
| 1994–95 | Newcastle U | 0 | 0 |
| 1994–95 | Port Vale | 27 | 2 |
| 1995–96 | Port Vale | 44 | 4 |
| 1996–97 | Port Vale | 34 | 6 |
| 1996–97 | Leicester C | 13 | 0 |
| 1997–98 | Leicester C | 37 | 2 |
| **Total:** | | **196** | **22** |

## GURNEY, Andy — Defender

H: 5 11 W: 12 02 b.Bristol 25-1-74

*Source:* Trainee.

| | | | |
|---|---|---|---|
| 1992–93 | Bristol R | 0 | 0 |
| 1993–94 | Bristol R | 3 | 0 |
| 1994–95 | Bristol R | 38 | 1 |
| 1995–96 | Bristol R | 43 | 6 |
| 1996–97 | Bristol R | 24 | 2 |
| 1997–98 | Torquay U | 44 | 9 |
| **Total:** | | **152** | **18** |

## HAALAND, Alf-Inge — Midfield

H: 5 10 W: 12 12 b.Stavanger 23-11-72

*Source:* Bryne. *Honours:* Norway 28 full caps.

| | | | |
|---|---|---|---|
| 1993–94 | Nottingham F | 3 | 0 |
| 1994–95 | Nottingham F | 20 | 1 |
| 1995–96 | Nottingham F | 17 | 0 |
| 1996–97 | Nottingham F | 35 | 6 |
| 1997–98 | Leeds U | 32 | 7 |
| **Total:** | | **107** | **14** |

## HACKETT, Stephen — Defender

b.Dublin 17-9-80

*Source:* Trainee.

| | | | |
|---|---|---|---|
| 1997–98 | Wolverhampton W | 0 | 0 |

## HACKETT, Warren — Defender

H: 6 0 W: 12 05 b.Plaistow 16-12-71

*Source:* Tottenham H Trainee.

| | | | |
|---|---|---|---|
| 1990–91 | Leyton Orient | 0 | 0 |
| 1991–92 | Leyton Orient | 22 | 0 |
| 1992–93 | Leyton Orient | 17 | 0 |
| 1993–94 | Leyton Orient | 33 | 3 |
| 1994–95 | Doncaster R | 39 | 2 |
| 1995–96 | Doncaster R | 7 | 0 |
| 1995–96 | Mansfield T | 32 | 3 |
| 1996–97 | Mansfield T | 36 | 1 |
| 1997–98 | Mansfield T | 23 | 1 |
| **Total:** | | **209** | **10** |

## HACKWORTH, Tony — Forward

H: 6 2 W: 13 03 b.Durham 19-5-80

*Source:* Trainee. *Honours:* England Youth.

| | | | |
|---|---|---|---|
| 1997–98 | Leeds U | 0 | 0 |

## HADDOW, Paul — Midfield

H: 5 8 W: 10 10 b.Fleetwood 11-10-78

*Source:* Trainee.

| | | | |
|---|---|---|---|
| 1997–98 | Blackpool | 1 | 0 |
| **Total:** | | **1** | **0** |

## HADLAND, Guy — Defender

H: 6 1 W: 12 11 b.Nuneaton 23-1-79

*Source:* Trainee.

| | | | |
|---|---|---|---|
| 1997–98 | Aston Villa | 0 | 0 |

## HADLEY, Stewart — Forward

H: 5 11 W: 13 05 b.Stourbridge 30-12-73

*Source:* Halesowen T.

| | | | |
|---|---|---|---|
| 1992–93 | Derby Co | 0 | 0 |
| 1993–94 | Derby Co | 0 | 0 |
| 1993–94 | Mansfield T | 14 | 5 |
| 1994–95 | Mansfield T | 39 | 14 |
| 1995–96 | Mansfield T | 33 | 8 |
| 1996–97 | Mansfield T | 36 | 4 |
| 1997–98 | Mansfield T | 2 | 0 |
| **Total:** | | **124** | **31** |

## HAILS, Julian — Midfield

H: 5 10 W: 11 02 b.Lincoln 20-11-67

*Source:* Hemel Hempstead.

| | | | |
|---|---|---|---|
| 1989–90 | Fulham | 0 | 0 |
| 1990–91 | Fulham | 0 | 0 |
| 1991–92 | Fulham | 18 | 1 |
| 1992–93 | Fulham | 46 | 6 |
| 1993–94 | Fulham | 37 | 4 |
| 1994–95 | Fulham | 8 | 1 |
| 1994–95 | Southend U | 26 | 2 |
| 1995–96 | Southend U | 42 | 4 |
| 1996–97 | Southend U | 37 | 0 |
| 1997–98 | Southend U | 44 | 0 |
| **Total:** | | **258** | **18** |

## HALE, Matthew — Midfield

H: 5 6 W: 10 00 b.Bristol 2-2-79

*Source:* Trainee.

| | | | |
|---|---|---|---|
| 1997–98 | Bristol C | 0 | 0 |

## HALL, Gareth — Defender

H: 5 8 W: 12 00 b.Croydon 12-3-69

*Source:* Apprentice. *Honours:* England Schools, Wales Under-21, 9 full caps.

| | | | |
|---|---|---|---|
| 1986–87 | Chelsea | 1 | 0 |
| 1987–88 | Chelsea | 13 | 0 |
| 1988–89 | Chelsea | 22 | 0 |
| 1989–90 | Chelsea | 13 | 1 |
| 1990–91 | Chelsea | 24 | 0 |
| 1991–92 | Chelsea | 10 | 0 |
| 1992–93 | Chelsea | 37 | 2 |
| 1993–94 | Chelsea | 7 | 0 |
| 1994–95 | Chelsea | 6 | 0 |
| 1995–96 | Chelsea | 5 | 1 |
| 1995–96 | Sunderland | 14 | 0 |
| 1996–97 | Sunderland | 32 | 0 |
| 1997–98 | Sunderland | 2 | 0 |
| 1997–98 | Brentford (loan) | 6 | 0 |
| **Total:** | | **192** | **4** |

## HALL, Marcus — Defender

H: 6 1 W: 12 02 b.Coventry 24-3-76

*Source:* Trainee. *Honours:* England Under-21, B.

| | | | |
|---|---|---|---|
| 1994–95 | Coventry C | 5 | 0 |
| 1995–96 | Coventry C | 25 | 0 |
| 1996–97 | Coventry C | 13 | 0 |
| 1997–98 | Coventry C | 25 | 1 |
| **Total:** | | **68** | **1** |

## HALL, Paul — Forward

H: 5 9 W: 10 02 b.Manchester 3-7-72

*Source:* Trainee. *Honours:* Jamaica 26 full caps, 9 goals.

| | | | |
|---|---|---|---|
| 1989–90 | Torquay U | 10 | 0 |
| 1990–91 | Torquay U | 17 | 0 |
| 1991–92 | Torquay U | 38 | 1 |
| 1992–93 | Torquay U | 28 | 0 |
| 1992–93 | Portsmouth | 0 | 0 |
| 1993–94 | Portsmouth | 28 | 4 |
| 1994–95 | Portsmouth | 43 | 5 |
| 1995–96 | Portsmouth | 46 | 10 |
| 1996–97 | Portsmouth | 42 | 13 |
| 1997–98 | Portsmouth | 29 | 5 |
| **Total:** | | **281** | **38** |

## HALL, Richard — Defender

H: 6 2 W: 13 11 b.Ipswich 14-3-72

*Source:* Trainee. *Honours:* England Under-21.

| | | | |
|---|---|---|---|
| 1989–90 | Scunthorpe U | 1 | 0 |
| 1990–91 | Scunthorpe U | 21 | 3 |
| 1990–91 | Southampton | 1 | 0 |

| | | | |
|---|---|---|---|
| 1991–92 | Southampton | 26 | 3 |
| 1992–93 | Southampton | 28 | 4 |
| 1993–94 | Southampton | 4 | 0 |
| 1994–95 | Southampton | 37 | 4 |
| 1995–96 | Southampton | 30 | 1 |
| 1996–97 | West Ham U | 7 | 0 |
| 1997–98 | West Ham U | 0 | 0 |
| **Total:** | | **155** | **15** |

## HALL, Wayne — Defender

H: 5 9 W: 10 06 b.Rotherham 25-10-68

*Source:* Darlington.

| | | | |
|---|---|---|---|
| 1988–89 | York C | 2 | 0 |
| 1989–90 | York C | 27 | 3 |
| 1990–91 | York C | 46 | 1 |
| 1991–92 | York C | 37 | 3 |
| 1992–93 | York C | 42 | 1 |
| 1993–94 | York C | 45 | 0 |
| 1994–95 | York C | 37 | 0 |
| 1995–96 | York C | 23 | 0 |
| 1996–97 | York C | 13 | 0 |
| 1997–98 | York C | 32 | 0 |
| **Total:** | | **304** | **8** |

## HALLE, Gunnar — Defender

H: 5 11 W: 11 00 b.Larvik 11-8-65

*Source:* Lillestrom. *Honours:* Norway 61 full caps, 5 goals.

| | | | |
|---|---|---|---|
| 1990–91 | Oldham Ath | 17 | 0 |
| 1991–92 | Oldham Ath | 10 | 0 |
| 1992–93 | Oldham Ath | 41 | 5 |
| 1993–94 | Oldham Ath | 23 | 1 |
| 1994–95 | Oldham Ath | 40 | 5 |
| 1995–96 | Oldham Ath | 37 | 3 |
| 1996–97 | Oldham Ath | 20 | 3 |
| 1996–97 | Leeds U | 20 | 0 |
| 1997–98 | Leeds U | 33 | 2 |
| **Total:** | | **241** | **19** |

## HALLIDAY, Stephen — Forward

H: 5 10 W: 12 07 b.Sunderland 3-5-76

*Source:* Charlton Ath.

| | | | |
|---|---|---|---|
| 1993–94 | Hartlepool U | 11 | 0 |
| 1994–95 | Hartlepool U | 28 | 5 |
| 1995–96 | Hartlepool U | 39 | 7 |
| 1996–97 | Hartlepool U | 31 | 8 |
| 1997–98 | Hartlepool U | 31 | 5 |
| **Total:** | | **140** | **25** |

## HALLWORTH, Jon — Goalkeeper

H: 6 2 W: 14 09 b.Stockport 26-10-65

*Source:* School.

| | | | |
|---|---|---|---|
| 1983–84 | Ipswich T | 0 | 0 |
| 1984–85 | Ipswich T | 0 | 0 |
| 1984–85 | Swindon T (loan) | 0 | 0 |
| 1984–85 | Fulham (loan) | 0 | 0 |
| 1984–85 | Bristol R (loan) | 2 | 0 |
| 1985–86 | Ipswich T | 6 | 0 |
| 1986–87 | Ipswich T | 6 | 0 |
| 1987–88 | Ipswich T | 33 | 0 |
| 1988–89 | Ipswich T | 0 | 0 |
| 1988–89 | Oldham Ath | 16 | 0 |
| 1989–90 | Oldham Ath | 15 | 0 |
| 1990–91 | Oldham Ath | 46 | 0 |
| 1991–92 | Oldham Ath | 41 | 0 |
| 1992–93 | Oldham Ath | 16 | 0 |
| 1993–94 | Oldham Ath | 19 | 0 |
| 1994–95 | Oldham Ath | 6 | 0 |
| 1995–96 | Oldham Ath | 11 | 0 |
| 1996–97 | Oldham Ath | 4 | 0 |
| 1997–98 | Cardiff C | 43 | 0 |
| **Total:** | | **264** | **0** |

## HAMILTON, Des — Defender

H: 5 10 W: 12 13 b.Bradford 15-8-76

*Source:* Trainee. *Honours:* England Under-21.

| | | | |
|---|---|---|---|
| 1993–94 | Bradford C | 2 | 1 |
| 1994–95 | Bradford C | 30 | 1 |
| 1995–96 | Bradford C | 24 | 3 |
| 1996–97 | Bradford C | 32 | 0 |
| 1996–97 | Newcastle U | 0 | 0 |
| 1997–98 | Newcastle U | 12 | 0 |
| **Total:** | | **100** | **5** |

## HAMILTON, Gary — Forward

b.Bambridge 6-10-80

*Source:* Trainee.

| | | | |
|---|---|---|---|
| 1997–98 | Blackburn R | 0 | 0 |

## HAMILTON, Ian — Midfield

H: 5 10 W: 11 03 b.Stevenage 14-12-67

*Source:* Apprentice.

| | | | |
|---|---|---|---|
| 1985–86 | Southampton | 0 | 0 |
| 1986–87 | Southampton | 0 | 0 |
| 1987–88 | Southampton | 0 | 0 |
| 1987–88 | Cambridge U | 9 | 1 |
| 1988–89 | Cambridge U | 15 | 0 |
| 1988–89 | Scunthorpe U | 27 | 1 |
| 1989–90 | Scunthorpe U | 43 | 6 |

| | | | |
|---|---|---|---|
| 1990–91 | Scunthorpe U | 34 | 2 |
| 1991–92 | Scunthorpe U | 41 | 9 |
| 1992–93 | WBA | 46 | 7 |
| 1993–94 | WBA | 42 | 3 |
| 1994–95 | WBA | 35 | 4 |
| 1995–96 | WBA | 41 | 3 |
| 1996–97 | WBA | 39 | 5 |
| 1997–98 | WBA | 37 | 1 |
| 1997–98 | Sheffield U | 8 | 1 |
| **Total:** | | **417** | **43** |

## HAMILTON, James — Midfield

H: 6 0 W: 10 10 b.Aberdeen 9-2-76

*Source:* Keith. *Honours:* Scotland Under-21.

| | | | |
|---|---|---|---|
| 1993–94 | Dundee | 1 | 0 |
| 1994–95 | Dundee | 28 | 12 |
| 1995–96 | Dundee | 33 | 14 |
| 1996–97 | Dundee | 12 | 1 |
| 1996–97 | Hearts | 18 | 4 |
| 1997–98 | Hearts | 32 | 14 |
| **Total:** | | **124** | **45** |

## HAMILTON, Steven — Defender

H: 5 9 W: 12 10 b.Baillieston 19-3-75

*Source:* Troon Juniors.

| | | | |
|---|---|---|---|
| 1994–95 | Kilmarnock | 0 | 0 |
| 1995–96 | Kilmarnock | 0 | 0 |
| 1996–97 | Kilmarnock | 6 | 0 |
| 1997–98 | Kilmarnock | 6 | 0 |
| **Total:** | | **12** | **0** |

## HAMMOND, Andy — Forward

H: 6 0 W: 12 00 b.Rotherham 21-11-78

*Source:* Trainee.

| | | | |
|---|---|---|---|
| 1997–98 | Doncaster R | 1 | 0 |
| **Total:** | | **1** | **0** |

## HAMMOND, Nicky — Goalkeeper

H: 6 0 W: 11 13 b.Hornchurch 7-9-67

*Source:* Apprentice.

| | | | |
|---|---|---|---|
| 1985–86 | Arsenal | 0 | 0 |
| 1986–87 | Arsenal | 0 | 0 |
| 1986–87 | Bristol R (loan) | 3 | 0 |
| 1986–87 | Peterborough U (loan) | 0 | 0 |
| 1986–87 | Aberdeen (loan) | 0 | 0 |
| 1987–88 | Swindon T | 4 | 0 |
| 1988–89 | Swindon T | 0 | 0 |
| 1989–90 | Swindon T | 0 | 0 |
| 1990–91 | Swindon T | 5 | 0 |
| 1991–92 | Swindon T | 25 | 0 |
| 1992–93 | Swindon T | 13 | [illegible] |
| 1993–94 | Swindon T | 13 | [illegible] |
| 1994–95 | Swindon T | 7 | [illegible] |
| 1995–96 | Plymouth Arg | 4 | [illegible] |
| 1995–96 | Reading | 5 | [illegible] |
| 1996–97 | Reading | 1 | [illegible] |
| 1997–98 | Reading | 18 | [illegible] |
| **Total:** | | **98** | [illegible] |

## HAMPSHIRE, Steve — Forwar

H: 5 10 W: 10 10 b.Edinburgh 17-10-79

*Source:* Trainee.

| | | | |
|---|---|---|---|
| 1997–98 | Chelsea | 0 | [illegible] |

## HANDYSIDE, Peter — Defende

H: 6 1 W: 13 07 b.Dumfries 31-7-74

*Source:* Trainee. *Honours:* Scotland Under-21.

| | | | |
|---|---|---|---|
| 1992–93 | Grimsby T | 11 | [illegible] |
| 1993–94 | Grimsby T | 13 | [illegible] |
| 1994–95 | Grimsby T | 35 | [illegible] |
| 1995–96 | Grimsby T | 30 | [illegible] |
| 1996–97 | Grimsby T | 9 | [illegible] |
| 1997–98 | Grimsby T | 42 | [illegible] |
| **Total:** | | **140** | [illegible] |

## HANMER, Gary — Defende

H: 5 6 W: 10 02 b.Shrewsbury 12-10-73

*Source:* Newtown.

| | | | |
|---|---|---|---|
| 1996–97 | WBA | 0 | [illegible] |
| 1997–98 | Shrewsbury T | 39 | [illegible] |
| **Total:** | | **39** | [illegible] |

## HANNAH, David — Midfiel

H: 5 11 W: 11 01 b.Coatbridge 4-8-74

*Source:* Hamilton Th. *Honours:* Scotland Under-21.

| | | | |
|---|---|---|---|
| 1991–92 | Dundee U | 0 | [illegible] |
| 1992–93 | Dundee U | 5 | [illegible] |
| 1993–94 | Dundee U | 10 | [illegible] |
| 1994–95 | Dundee U | 32 | [illegible] |
| 1995–96 | Dundee U | 7 | [illegible] |
| 1996–97 | Dundee U | 12 | [illegible] |
| 1996–97 | Celtic | 18 | [illegible] |
| 1997–98 | Celtic | 15 | [illegible] |
| **Total:** | | **99** | [illegible] |

## HANSON, Dave — Forward

H: 6 1 W: 13 01 b.Huddersfield 19-11-68

*Source:* Manchester U, Farsley Celtic.

| | | | |
|---|---|---|---|
| 1993–94 | Bury | 1 | 0 |
| From Halifax T, Hednesford T. | | | |
| 1995–96 | Leyton Orient | 11 | 1 |
| 1996–97 | Leyton Orient | 25 | 3 |
| 1996–97 | Chesterfield (loan) | 3 | 1 |
| 1997–98 | Leyton Orient | 12 | 1 |
| **Total:** | | **52** | **6** |

## HAPGOOD, Leon — Midfield

H: 5 6 W: 10 00 b.Torbay 7-8-79

*Source:* Trainee.

| | | | |
|---|---|---|---|
| 1996–97 | Torquay U | 1 | 0 |
| 1997–98 | Torquay U | 22 | 3 |
| **Total:** | | **23** | **3** |

## HARDY, Phil — Defender

H: 5 7 W: 11 08 b.Chester 9-4-73

*Source:* Trainee. *Honours:* Eire Under-21.

| | | | |
|---|---|---|---|
| 1989–90 | Wrexham | 1 | 0 |
| 1990–91 | Wrexham | 32 | 0 |
| 1991–92 | Wrexham | 42 | 0 |
| 1992–93 | Wrexham | 32 | 0 |
| 1993–94 | Wrexham | 25 | 0 |
| 1994–95 | Wrexham | 44 | 0 |
| 1995–96 | Wrexham | 42 | 0 |
| 1996–97 | Wrexham | 13 | 0 |
| 1997–98 | Wrexham | 34 | 0 |
| **Total:** | | **265** | **0** |

## HARE, Matthew — Defender

H: 6 2 W: 13 00 b.Barnstaple 26-12-76

*Source:* Trainee.

| | | | |
|---|---|---|---|
| 1995–96 | Exeter C | 13 | 0 |
| 1996–97 | Exeter C | 25 | 1 |
| 1997–98 | Exeter C | 7 | 0 |
| **Total:** | | **45** | **1** |

## HAREWOOD, Marlon — Defender

H: 6 1 W: 10 00 b.Hampstead 25-8-79

*Source:* Trainee.

| | | | |
|---|---|---|---|
| 1996–97 | Nottingham F | 0 | 0 |
| 1997–98 | Nottingham F | 1 | 0 |
| **Total:** | | **1** | **0** |

## HARFORD, Mick — Forward

H: 6 3 W: 14 05 b.Sunderland 12-2-59

*Source:* Lambton St BC. *Honours:* England B, 2 full caps.

| | | | |
|---|---|---|---|
| 1977–78 | Lincoln C | 27 | 9 |
| 1978–79 | Lincoln C | 31 | 6 |
| 1979–80 | Lincoln C | 36 | 16 |
| 1980–81 | Lincoln C | 21 | 10 |
| 1980–81 | Newcastle U | 19 | 4 |
| 1981–82 | Bristol C | 30 | 11 |
| 1981–82 | Birmingham C | 12 | 9 |
| 1982–83 | Birmingham C | 29 | 6 |
| 1983–84 | Birmingham C | 39 | 8 |
| 1984–85 | Birmingham C | 12 | 2 |
| 1984–85 | Luton T | 22 | 15 |
| 1985–86 | Luton T | 37 | 22 |
| 1986–87 | Luton T | 18 | 4 |
| 1987–88 | Luton T | 25 | 9 |
| 1988–89 | Luton T | 33 | 7 |
| 1989–90 | Luton T | 4 | 0 |
| 1989–90 | Derby Co | 16 | 4 |
| 1990–91 | Derby Co | 36 | 8 |
| 1991–92 | Derby Co | 6 | 3 |
| 1991–92 | Luton T | 29 | 12 |
| 1992–93 | Chelsea | 28 | 9 |
| 1992–93 | Sunderland | 11 | 2 |
| 1993–94 | Coventry C | 1 | 1 |
| 1994–95 | Wimbledon | 27 | 6 |
| 1995–96 | Wimbledon | 21 | 2 |
| 1996–97 | Wimbledon | 13 | 1 |
| 1997–98 | Wimbledon | 0 | 0 |
| **Total:** | | **583** | **186** |

## HARKIN, Fergal — Midfield

H: 5 11 W: 11 08 b.Derry 26-11-76

*Source:* Loughborough Univ.

| | | | |
|---|---|---|---|
| 1997–98 | Leicester C | 0 | 0 |

## HARKIN, Maurice — Forward

H: 5 8 W: 11 07 b.Derry 16-8-79

*Source:* Trainee.

| | | | |
|---|---|---|---|
| 1996–97 | Wycombe W | 4 | 0 |
| 1997–98 | Wycombe W | 35 | 2 |
| **Total:** | | **39** | **2** |

## HARKNESS, Steve — Defender

H: 5 10 W: 11 02 b.Carlisle 27-8-71

*Source:* Trainee. *Honours:* England Youth.

| | | | |
|---|---|---|---|
| 1988–89 | Carlisle U | 13 | 0 |
| 1989–90 | Liverpool | 0 | 0 |
| 1990–91 | Liverpool | 0 | 0 |

| | | | |
|---|---|---|---|
| 1991–92 | Liverpool | 11 | 0 |
| 1992–93 | Liverpool | 10 | 0 |
| 1993–94 | Liverpool | 11 | 0 |
| 1993–94 | Huddersfield T (loan) | 5 | 0 |
| 1994–95 | Liverpool | 8 | 1 |
| 1994–95 | Southend U (loan) | 6 | 0 |
| 1995–96 | Liverpool | 24 | 1 |
| 1996–97 | Liverpool | 7 | 0 |
| 1997–98 | Liverpool | 25 | 0 |
| **Total:** | | **120** | **2** |

## HARLE, Mike — Defender

H: 6 0 W: 12 06 b.Lewisham 31-10-72

*Source:* Sittingbourne.

| | | | |
|---|---|---|---|
| 1993–94 | Millwall | 0 | 0 |
| 1994–95 | Millwall | 0 | 0 |
| 1995–96 | Millwall | 0 | 0 |
| 1995–96 | Bury (loan) | 1 | 0 |
| 1996–97 | Millwall | 21 | 1 |
| 1997–98 | Barnet | 43 | 2 |
| **Total:** | | **65** | **3** |

## HARLEY, Jon — Midfield

H: 5 8 W: 10 03 b.Maidstone 26-9-79

*Source:* Trainee.

| | | | |
|---|---|---|---|
| 1996–97 | Chelsea | 0 | 0 |
| 1997–98 | Chelsea | 3 | 0 |
| **Total:** | | **3** | **0** |

## HARPER, Kevin — Midfield

H: 5 6 W: 10 09 b.Oldham 15-1-76

*Source:* Hutcheson Vale BC. *Honours:* Scotland Under-21.

| | | | |
|---|---|---|---|
| 1993–94 | Hibernian | 2 | 0 |
| 1994–95 | Hibernian | 23 | 5 |
| 1995–96 | Hibernian | 16 | 3 |
| 1996–97 | Hibernian | 26 | 5 |
| 1997–98 | Hibernian | 27 | 1 |
| **Total:** | | **94** | **14** |

## HARPER, Lee — Goalkeeper

H: 6 1 W: 13 11 b.Chelsea 30-10-71

*Source:* Sittingbourne.

| | | | |
|---|---|---|---|
| 1994–95 | Arsenal | 0 | 0 |
| 1995–96 | Arsenal | 0 | 0 |
| 1996–97 | Arsenal | 1 | 0 |
| 1997–98 | QPR | 36 | 0 |
| **Total:** | | **37** | **0** |

## HARPER, Steve — Midfield

H: 5 10 W: 11 12 b.Newcastle-under-Lyne 3-2-69

*Source:* Trainee.

| | | | |
|---|---|---|---|
| 1987–88 | Port Vale | 21 | 2 |
| 1988–89 | Port Vale | 7 | 0 |
| 1988–89 | Preston NE | 5 | 0 |
| 1989–90 | Preston NE | 36 | 10 |
| 1990–91 | Preston NE | 36 | 0 |
| 1991–92 | Burnley | 35 | 3 |
| 1992–93 | Burnley | 34 | 5 |
| 1993–94 | Burnley | 0 | 0 |
| 1993–94 | Doncaster R | 31 | 2 |
| 1994–95 | Doncaster R | 33 | 9 |
| 1995–96 | Doncaster R | 1 | 0 |
| 1995–96 | Mansfield T | 29 | 5 |
| 1996–97 | Mansfield T | 40 | 2 |
| 1997–98 | Mansfield T | 46 | 5 |
| **Total:** | | **354** | **43** |

## HARPER, Steve — Goalkeeper

H: 6 1 W: 13 09 b.Easington 3-2-74

*Source:* Seaham Red Star.

| | | | |
|---|---|---|---|
| 1993–94 | Newcastle U | 0 | 0 |
| 1994–95 | Newcastle U | 0 | 0 |
| 1995–96 | Newcastle U | 0 | 0 |
| 1995–96 | Bradford C (loan) | 1 | 0 |
| 1996–97 | Newcastle U | 0 | 0 |
| 1996–97 | Stockport Co (loan) | 0 | 0 |
| 1997–98 | Newcastle U | 0 | 0 |
| 1997–98 | Hartlepool U (loan) | 15 | 0 |
| 1997–98 | Huddersfield T (loan) | 24 | 0 |
| **Total:** | | **40** | **0** |

## HARRIES, Paul — Forward

H: 6 1 W: 13 00 b.Australia 20-10-77

*Source:* NSWSF.

| | | | |
|---|---|---|---|
| 1997–98 | Portsmouth | 1 | 0 |
| **Total:** | | **1** | **0** |

## HARRINGTON, Justin — Forward

H: 5 9 W: 10 09 b.Truro 18-6-75

*Source:* Trainee.

| | | | |
|---|---|---|---|
| 1994–95 | Norwich C | 0 | 0 |
| 1995–96 | Norwich C | 0 | 0 |
| 1996–97 | Leicester C | 0 | 0 |
| 1997–98 | Bournemouth | 8 | 0 |
| **Total:** | | **8** | **0** |

## HARRIS, Andrew — Defender

H: 5 10 W: 12 02 b.Springs 26-2-77

*Source:* Trainee.

| | | | |
|---|---|---|---|
| 1993–94 | Liverpool | 0 | 0 |
| 1994–95 | Liverpool | 0 | 0 |
| 1995–96 | Liverpool | 0 | 0 |
| 1996–97 | Southend U | 44 | 0 |
| 1997–98 | Southend U | 27 | 0 |
| **Total:** | | **71** | **0** |

## HARRIS, Jamie — Forward

H: 6 2 W: 13 07 b.Swansea 28-6-79

*Source:* Mumbles R.

| | | | |
|---|---|---|---|
| 1997–98 | Swansea C | 6 | 0 |
| **Total:** | | **6** | **0** |

## HARRIS, Jason — Forward

H: 6 1 W: 11 10 b.Sutton 24-11-76

*Source:* Trainee.

| | | | |
|---|---|---|---|
| 1995–96 | Crystal Palace | 0 | 0 |
| 1996–97 | Crystal Palace | 2 | 0 |
| 1996–97 | Bristol R (loan) | 6 | 2 |
| 1997–98 | Crystal Palace | 0 | 0 |
| 1997–98 | Lincoln C (loan) | 1 | 0 |
| 1997–98 | Leyton Orient | 35 | 6 |
| **Total:** | | **44** | **8** |

## HARRIS, Mark — Defender

H: 6 3 W: 14 08 b.Reading 15-7-63

*Source:* Wokingham T.

| | | | |
|---|---|---|---|
| 1987–88 | Crystal Palace | 0 | 0 |
| 1988–89 | Crystal Palace | 2 | 0 |
| 1989–90 | Crystal Palace | 0 | 0 |
| 1989–90 | Burnley (loan) | 4 | 0 |
| 1989–90 | Swansea C | 41 | 2 |
| 1990–91 | Swansea C | 41 | 1 |
| 1991–92 | Swansea C | 44 | 3 |
| 1992–93 | Swansea C | 42 | 5 |
| 1993–94 | Swansea C | 46 | 3 |
| 1994–95 | Swansea C | 14 | 0 |
| 1995–96 | Swansea C | 0 | 0 |
| 1995–96 | Gillingham | 44 | 2 |
| 1996–97 | Gillingham | 21 | 1 |
| 1997–98 | Cardiff C | 38 | 1 |
| **Total:** | | **337** | **18** |

## HARRIS, Neil — Forward

H: 5 11 W: 12 08 b.Orsett 12-7-77

*Source:* Chelmsford C.

| | | | |
|---|---|---|---|
| 1997–98 | Millwall | 3 | 0 |
| **Total:** | | **3** | **0** |

## HARRIS, Richard — Midfield

b.Croydon 23-10-80

*Source:* Trainee.

| | | | |
|---|---|---|---|
| 1997–98 | Crystal Palace | 0 | 0 |

## HARRISON, Craig — Defender

H: 6 0 W: 11 13 b.Gateshead 10-11-77

*Source:* Trainee.

| | | | |
|---|---|---|---|
| 1996–97 | Middlesbrough | 0 | 0 |
| 1997–98 | Middlesbrough | 20 | 0 |
| **Total:** | | **20** | **0** |

## HARRISON, Edward — Midfield

b.Carlisle 14-2-80

*Source:* Trainee.

| | | | |
|---|---|---|---|
| 1997–98 | Carlisle U | 10 | 0 |
| **Total:** | | **10** | **0** |

## HARRISON, Gerry — Midfield

H: 5 9 W: 12 03 b.Lambeth 15-4-72

*Source:* Trainee. *Honours:* England Schools.

| | | | |
|---|---|---|---|
| 1989–90 | Watford | 3 | 0 |
| 1990–91 | Watford | 6 | 0 |
| 1991–92 | Bristol C | 4 | 0 |
| 1991–92 | Cardiff C (loan) | 10 | 1 |
| 1992–93 | Bristol C | 33 | 1 |
| 1993–94 | Bristol C | 1 | 0 |
| 1993–94 | Hereford U (loan) | 6 | 0 |
| 1993–94 | Huddersfield T | 0 | 0 |
| 1994–95 | Burnley | 19 | 2 |
| 1995–96 | Burnley | 35 | 1 |
| 1996–97 | Burnley | 35 | 0 |
| 1997–98 | Burnley | 35 | 0 |
| **Total:** | | **187** | **5** |

## HARRISON, Lee — Goalkeeper

H: 6 2 W: 12 08 b.Billericay 12-9-71

*Source:* Trainee.

| | | | |
|---|---|---|---|
| 1990–91 | Charlton Ath | 0 | 0 |
| 1991–92 | Charlton Ath | 0 | 0 |
| 1991–92 | Fulham (loan) | 0 | 0 |

## Harrison, Mark

| | | | |
|---|---|---|---|
| 1991–92 | Gillingham (loan) | 2 | 0 |
| 1992–93 | Charlton Ath | 0 | 0 |
| 1992–93 | Fulham (loan) | 0 | 0 |
| 1993–94 | Fulham | 0 | 0 |
| 1994–95 | Fulham | 7 | 0 |
| 1995–96 | Fulham | 5 | 0 |
| 1996–97 | Barnet | 21 | 0 |
| 1997–98 | Barnet | 46 | 0 |
| **Total:** | | **81** | **0** |

## HARRISON, Mark — Midfield

b.Sheffield 7-8-79

*Source:* Trainee.

| | | | |
|---|---|---|---|
| 1997–98 | Sheffield W | 0 | 0 |

## HARRISON, Ross — Forward

b.Leamington Spa 28-12-79

*Source:* From Trainee.

| | | | |
|---|---|---|---|
| 1997–98 | Reading | 0 | 0 |

## HARSLEY, Paul — Midfield

H: 5 10 W: 11 03 b.Scunthorpe 29-5-78

*Source:* Trainee.

| | | | |
|---|---|---|---|
| 1996–97 | Grimsby T | 0 | 0 |
| 1997–98 | Scunthorpe U | 15 | 1 |
| **Total:** | | **15** | **1** |

## HART, Barrie — Defender

H: 6 2 W: 12 12 b.Oldham 17-7-77

*Source:* Trainee.

| | | | |
|---|---|---|---|
| 1996–97 | Oldham Ath | 0 | 0 |
| 1997–98 | Oldham Ath | 0 | 0 |

## HART, Paul — Goalkeeper

H: 5 11 W: 11 07 b.Lewisham 16-11-78

*Source:* Trainee.

| | | | |
|---|---|---|---|
| 1996–97 | QPR | 0 | 0 |
| 1997–98 | QPR | 0 | 0 |

## HARTE, Ian — Defender

H: 5 9 W: 11 00 b.Drogheda 31-8-77

*Source:* Trainee. *Honours:* Eire 18 full caps, 2 goals.

| | | | |
|---|---|---|---|
| 1995–96 | Leeds U | 4 | 0 |
| 1996–97 | Leeds U | 14 | 2 |
| 1997–98 | Leeds U | 12 | 0 |
| **Total:** | | **30** | **2** |

## HARTFIELD, Charlie — Midfield

H: 6 0 W: 13 08 b.London 4-9-71

*Source:* Trainee.

| | | | |
|---|---|---|---|
| 1989–90 | Arsenal | 0 | 0 |
| 1990–91 | Arsenal | 0 | 0 |
| 1991–92 | Sheffield U | 7 | 0 |
| 1992–93 | Sheffield U | 17 | 0 |
| 1993–94 | Sheffield U | 5 | 0 |
| 1994–95 | Sheffield U | 25 | 1 |
| 1995–96 | Sheffield U | 0 | 0 |
| 1996–97 | Sheffield U | 2 | 0 |
| 1996–97 | Fulham (loan) | 2 | 0 |
| 1997–98 | Sheffield U | 0 | 0 |
| 1997–98 | Swansea C | 22 | 2 |
| **Total:** | | **80** | **3** |

## HARTSON, John — Forward

H: 6 1 W: 14 06 b.Swansea 5-4-75

*Source:* Trainee. *Honours:* Wales Under-21, 14 full caps, 2 goals.

| | | | |
|---|---|---|---|
| 1992–93 | Luton T | 0 | 0 |
| 1993–94 | Luton T | 34 | 6 |
| 1994–95 | Luton T | 20 | 5 |
| 1994–95 | Arsenal | 15 | 7 |
| 1995–96 | Arsenal | 19 | 4 |
| 1996–97 | Arsenal | 19 | 3 |
| 1996–97 | West Ham U | 11 | 5 |
| 1997–98 | West Ham U | 32 | 15 |
| **Total:** | | **150** | **45** |

## HARVEY, Richard — Defender

H: 5 10 W: 11 12 b.Letchworth 17-4-69

*Source:* Apprentice. *Honours:* England Schools, Youth.

| | | | |
|---|---|---|---|
| 1986–87 | Luton T | 5 | 0 |
| 1987–88 | Luton T | 0 | 0 |
| 1988–89 | Luton T | 12 | 0 |
| 1989–90 | Luton T | 26 | 0 |
| 1990–91 | Luton T | 29 | 0 |
| 1991–92 | Luton T | 32 | 2 |
| 1992–93 | Luton T | 1 | 0 |
| 1992–93 | Blackpool (loan) | 5 | 0 |
| 1993–94 | Luton T | 0 | 0 |
| 1994–95 | Luton T | 12 | 1 |
| 1995–96 | Luton T | 36 | 1 |
| 1996–97 | Luton T | 2 | 0 |
| 1997–98 | Luton T | 6 | 0 |
| **Total:** | | **166** | **4** |

## HASLAM, Steven — Midfield

b.Sheffield 6-9-79

*Source:* Trainee. *Honours:* England Schools, Youth.

| | | | |
|---|---|---|---|
| 1996–97 | Sheffield W | 0 | 0 |
| 1997–98 | Sheffield W | 0 | 0 |

## HASSELBAINK, Jimmy Floyd — Forward

H: 6 2 W: 13 05 b.Paramaribo 27-3-72

*Honours:* Holland 5 full caps, 2 goals.

| | | | |
|---|---|---|---|
| 1995–96 | Campomairorense | 31 | 12 |
| 1996–97 | Boavista | 29 | 20 |
| 1997–98 | Leeds U | 33 | 16 |
| **Total:** | | **93** | **48** |

## HASSELL, Bobby — Defender

H: 5 8 W: 12 02 b.Derby 4-6-80

*Source:* Trainee.

| | | | |
|---|---|---|---|
| 1997–98 | Mansfield T | 9 | 0 |
| **Total:** | | **9** | **0** |

## HATELEY, Mark — Forward

H: 6 2 W: 13 00 b.Liverpool 7-11-61

*Source:* Apprentice. *Honours:* England Youth, Under-21, 32 full caps, 9 goals.

| | | | |
|---|---|---|---|
| 1978–79 | Coventry C | 1 | 0 |
| 1979–80 | Coventry C | 4 | 0 |
| 1980–81 | Coventry C | 19 | 3 |
| 1981–82 | Coventry C | 34 | 13 |
| 1982–83 | Coventry C | 35 | 9 |
| 1983–84 | Portsmouth | 38 | 22 |
| 1984–85 | AC Milan | 21 | 7 |
| 1985–86 | AC Milan | 22 | 8 |
| 1986–87 | AC Milan | 23 | 2 |
| 1987–88 | Monaco | 28 | 14 |
| 1988–89 | Monaco | 18 | 6 |
| 1989–90 | Monaco | 13 | 2 |
| 1990–91 | Rangers | 33 | 10 |
| 1991–92 | Rangers | 30 | 21 |
| 1992–93 | Rangers | 37 | 19 |
| 1993–94 | Rangers | 42 | 22 |
| 1994–95 | Rangers | 23 | 13 |
| 1995–96 | QPR | 14 | 2 |
| 1996–97 | QPR | 13 | 1 |
| 1996–97 | Leeds U (loan) | 6 | 0 |
| 1996–97 | Rangers | 4 | 1 |
| 1997–98 | Hull C | 9 | 0 |
| **Total:** | | **467** | **175** |

## HATHAWAY, Ian — Midfield

H: 5 4 W: 10 12 b.Wordsley 22-8-68

*Source:* WBA Apprentice, Bedworth U.

| | | | |
|---|---|---|---|
| 1988–89 | Mansfield T | 12 | 1 |
| 1989–90 | Mansfield T | 22 | 1 |
| 1990–91 | Mansfield T | 10 | 0 |
| 1990–91 | Rotherham U | 5 | 1 |
| 1991–92 | Rotherham U | 8 | 0 |
| 1992–93 | Rotherham U | 0 | 0 |
| 1993–94 | Torquay U | 41 | 7 |
| 1994–95 | Torquay U | 38 | 5 |
| 1995–96 | Torquay U | 26 | 1 |
| 1996–97 | Torquay U | 35 | 1 |
| 1997–98 | Colchester U | 12 | 0 |
| **Total:** | | **209** | **17** |

## HATTON, Paul — Forward

H: 6 0 W: 11 00 b.Kidderminster 2-11-78

*Source:* Trainee. *Honours:* England Schools.

| | | | |
|---|---|---|---|
| 1995–96 | Birmingham C | 0 | 0 |
| 1996–97 | Birmingham C | 0 | 0 |
| 1997–98 | Birmingham C | 0 | 0 |

## HAWE, Steven — Forward

b.Machbrafelt 23-12-80

*Source:* Trainee.

| | | | |
|---|---|---|---|
| 1997–98 | Blackburn R | 0 | 0 |

## HAWES, Steve — Midfield

H: 5 8 W: 10 12 b.High Wycombe 17-7-78

*Source:* Trainee.

| | | | |
|---|---|---|---|
| 1995–96 | Sheffield U | 2 | 0 |
| 1996–97 | Sheffield U | 2 | 0 |
| 1997–98 | Sheffield U | 0 | 0 |
| 1997–98 | Doncaster R (loan) | 11 | 0 |
| **Total:** | | **15** | **0** |

## HAWKINS, Peter — Defender

H: 6 0 W: 11 04 b.Maidstone 19-9-78

*Source:* Trainee.

| | | | |
|---|---|---|---|
| 1996–97 | Wimbledon | 0 | 0 |
| 1997–98 | Wimbledon | 0 | 0 |

## HAWLEY, Jon — Defender

H: 6 1 W: 12 08 b.Lincoln 23-1-78

*Source:* Trainee.

| | | | |
|---|---|---|---|
| 1996–97 | Portsmouth | 0 | 0 |
| 1997–98 | Portsmouth | 0 | 0 |

## HAWORTH, Simon — Forward

H: 6 1 W: 13 01 b.Cardiff 30-3-77

*Source:* Trainee. *Honours:* Wales Under-21, 5 full caps.

| | | | |
|---|---|---|---|
| 1995–96 | Cardiff C | 13 | 0 |
| 1996–97 | Cardiff C | 24 | 9 |
| 1997–98 | Coventry C | 10 | 0 |
| **Total:** | | **47** | **9** |

## HAWTHORNE, Mark — Defender

H: 6 0 W: 12 10 b.Sunderland 21-8-79

*Source:* Trainee.

| | | | |
|---|---|---|---|
| 1996–97 | Doncaster R | 0 | 0 |
| 1997–98 | Doncaster R | 8 | 0 |
| **Total:** | | **8** | **0** |

## HAY, Chris — Forward

H: 6 0 W: 12 05 b.Glasgow 28-8-74

*Source:* Giffnock N.

| | | | |
|---|---|---|---|
| 1993–94 | Celtic | 2 | 0 |
| 1994–95 | Celtic | 5 | 0 |
| 1995–96 | Celtic | 4 | 0 |
| 1996–97 | Celtic | 14 | 4 |
| 1997–98 | Swindon T | 36 | 14 |
| **Total:** | | **61** | **18** |

## HAYDON, Nicky — Midfield

H: 5 9 W: 11 07 b.Barking 10-8-78

*Source:* Trainee.

| | | | |
|---|---|---|---|
| 1995–96 | Colchester U | 0 | 0 |
| 1996–97 | Colchester U | 1 | 1 |
| 1997–98 | Colchester U | 17 | 0 |
| **Total:** | | **18** | **1** |

## HAYES, Adie — Midfield

H: 6 0 W: 11 09 b.Norwich 22-5-78

*Source:* Trainee.

| | | | |
|---|---|---|---|
| 1995–96 | Cambridge U | 1 | 0 |
| 1996–97 | Cambridge U | 25 | 0 |
| 1997–98 | Cambridge U | 8 | 0 |
| **Total:** | | **34** | **0** |

## HAYFIELD, Matt — Midfield

H: 5 10 W: 11 07 b.Bristol 8-8-75

*Source:* Trainee.

| | | | |
|---|---|---|---|
| 1995–96 | Bristol R | 6 | 0 |
| 1996–97 | Bristol R | 17 | 0 |
| 1997–98 | Bristol R | 18 | 0 |
| **Total:** | | **41** | **0** |

## HAYLES, Barry — Forward

H: 5 9 W: 13 00 b.London 17-4-72

*Source:* Stevenage Bor.

| | | | |
|---|---|---|---|
| 1997–98 | Bristol R | 45 | 23 |
| **Total:** | | **45** | **23** |

## HAYTER, James — Forward

H: 5 9 W: 10 13 b.Newport (IW) 9-4-79

*Source:* Trainee.

| | | | |
|---|---|---|---|
| 1996–97 | Bournemouth | 2 | 0 |
| 1997–98 | Bournemouth | 5 | 0 |
| **Total:** | | **7** | **0** |

## HAYWARD, Andy — Midfield

H: 6 0 W: 11 00 b.Barnsley 21-6-70

*Source:* Frickley Ath.

| | | | |
|---|---|---|---|
| 1994–95 | Rotherham U | 37 | 6 |
| 1995–96 | Rotherham U | 36 | 2 |
| 1996–97 | Rotherham U | 34 | 4 |
| 1997–98 | Rotherham U | 13 | 3 |
| **Total:** | | **120** | **15** |

## HAYWARD, Steve — Midfield

H: 5 11 W: 12 07 b.Walsall 8-9-71

*Source:* Trainee. *Honours:* England Youth.

| | | | |
|---|---|---|---|
| 1988–89 | Derby Co | 0 | 0 |
| 1989–90 | Derby Co | 3 | 0 |
| 1990–91 | Derby Co | 1 | 0 |
| 1991–92 | Derby Co | 7 | 0 |
| 1992–93 | Derby Co | 7 | 1 |
| 1993–94 | Derby Co | 5 | 0 |
| 1994–95 | Derby Co | 3 | 0 |
| 1994–95 | Carlisle U | 9 | 2 |
| 1995–96 | Carlisle U | 38 | 4 |
| 1996–97 | Carlisle U | 43 | 7 |
| 1997–98 | Fulham | 35 | 4 |
| **Total:** | | **151** | **18** |

## HAZAN, Alon — Midfield

H: 6 0 W: 13 08 b.Ashdod 14-9-67

*Source:* Ironi Ashdod. *Honours:* Israel 62 full caps, 3 goals.

| | | | |
|---|---|---|---|
| 1997–98 | Watford | 10 | 0 |
| **Total:** | | **10** | **0** |

## HAZELL, Reuben — Defender

H: 5 11 W: 11 12 b.Birmingham 24-4-79

*Source:* Trainee.

| | | | |
|---|---|---|---|
| 1996–97 | Aston Villa | 0 | 0 |
| 1997–98 | Aston Villa | 0 | 0 |

## HEALD, Greg — Defender

H: 6 2 W: 13 01 b.Enfield 26-9-71

*Source:* Enfield. *Honours:* England Schools.

| | | | |
|---|---|---|---|
| 1994–95 | Peterborough U | 29 | 0 |
| 1995–96 | Peterborough U | 40 | 4 |
| 1996–97 | Peterborough U | 36 | 2 |
| 1997–98 | Barnet | 43 | 3 |
| **Total:** | | **148** | **9** |

## HEALD, Paul — Goalkeeper

H: 6 2 W: 12 05 b.Wath-on-Dearne 20-9-68

*Source:* Trainee.

| | | | |
|---|---|---|---|
| 1987–88 | Sheffield U | 0 | 0 |
| 1988–89 | Sheffield U | 0 | 0 |
| 1988–89 | Leyton Orient | 28 | 0 |
| 1989–90 | Leyton Orient | 37 | 0 |
| 1990–91 | Leyton Orient | 38 | 0 |
| 1991–92 | Leyton Orient | 2 | 0 |
| 1991–92 | Coventry C (loan) | 2 | 0 |
| 1992–93 | Leyton Orient | 26 | 0 |
| 1992–93 | Crystal Palace (loan) | 0 | 0 |
| 1993–94 | Leyton Orient | 0 | 0 |
| 1993–94 | Swindon T (loan) | 2 | 0 |
| 1994–95 | Leyton Orient | 45 | 0 |
| 1995–96 | Wimbledon | 18 | 0 |
| 1996–97 | Wimbledon | 2 | 0 |
| 1997–98 | Wimbledon | 0 | 0 |
| **Total:** | | **200** | **0** |

## HEALY, David — Forward

H: 5 8 W: 10 09 b.Downpatrick 5-8-79

*Source:* Trainee.

| | | | |
|---|---|---|---|
| 1997–98 | Manchester U | 0 | 0 |

## HEANEY, Neil — Forward

H: 5 9 W: 11 07 b.Middlesbrough 3-11-71

*Source:* Trainee. *Honours:* England Youth, Under-21.

| | | | |
|---|---|---|---|
| 1989–90 | Arsenal | 0 | 0 |
| 1990–91 | Arsenal | 0 | 0 |
| 1990–91 | Hartlepool U (loan) | 3 | 0 |
| 1991–92 | Arsenal | 1 | 0 |
| 1991–92 | Cambridge U (loan) | 13 | 4 |
| 1992–93 | Arsenal | 5 | 0 |
| 1993–94 | Arsenal | 1 | 0 |
| 1993–94 | Southampton | 2 | 0 |
| 1994–95 | Southampton | 34 | 2 |
| 1995–96 | Southampton | 17 | 2 |
| 1996–97 | Southampton | 8 | 1 |
| 1996–97 | Manchester C | 15 | 1 |
| 1997–98 | Manchester C | 3 | 0 |
| 1997–98 | Charlton Ath (loan) | 6 | 0 |
| **Total:** | | **108** | **10** |

## HEARY, Thomas — Midfield

H: 5 9 W: 12 03 b.Dublin 14-2-79

*Source:* Trainee.

| | | | |
|---|---|---|---|
| 1995–96 | Huddersfield T | 0 | 0 |
| 1996–97 | Huddersfield T | 5 | 0 |
| 1997–98 | Huddersfield T | 3 | 0 |
| **Total:** | | **8** | **0** |

## HEATH, Robert — Midfield

H: 5 9 W: 10 00 b.Stoke 31-8-78

| | | | |
|---|---|---|---|
| 1996–97 | Stoke C | 0 | 0 |
| 1997–98 | Stoke C | 6 | 0 |
| **Total:** | | **6** | **0** |

## HEATH, Stephen — Defender

H: 6 0 W: 11 08 b.Hull 15-11-77

*Source:* Trainee. *Honours:* England Youth.

| | | | |
|---|---|---|---|
| 1994–95 | Leeds U | 0 | 0 |
| 1995–96 | Leeds U | 0 | 0 |
| 1996–97 | Carlisle U | 1 | 0 |
| 1997–98 | Rotherham U | 0 | 0 |
| **Total:** | | **1** | **0** |

## HEATHCOTE, Mike — Defender

H: 6 2 W: 12 08 b.Durham 10-9-65

*Source:* Middlesbrough, Spennymoor U.

| | | | |
|---|---|---|---|
| 1987–88 | Sunderland | 1 | 0 |
| 1987–88 | Halifax T (loan) | 7 | 1 |
| 1988–89 | Sunderland | 0 | 0 |
| 1989–90 | Sunderland | 8 | 0 |

| | | | |
|---|---|---|---|
| 1989–90 | York C (loan) | 3 | 0 |
| 1990–91 | Shrewsbury T | 39 | 6 |
| 1991–92 | Shrewsbury T | 5 | 0 |
| 1991–92 | Cambridge U | 22 | 5 |
| 1992–93 | Cambridge U | 42 | 2 |
| 1993–94 | Cambridge U | 40 | 5 |
| 1994–95 | Cambridge U | 24 | 1 |
| 1995–96 | Plymouth Arg | 44 | 4 |
| 1996–97 | Plymouth Arg | 42 | 1 |
| 1997–98 | Plymouth Arg | 36 | 4 |
| **Total:** | | **313** | **29** |

## HEBEL, Dirk — Midfield

H: 5 10 W: 12 01 b.Cologne 24-11-72

*Source:* Cologne.

| | | | |
|---|---|---|---|
| 1997–98 | Tranmere R | 0 | 0 |

## HECKINGBOTTOM, Paul — Defender

H: 5 11 W: 12 00 b.Barnsley 17-7-77

*Source:* Manchester U Trainee.

| | | | |
|---|---|---|---|
| 1995–96 | Sunderland | 0 | 0 |
| 1996–97 | Sunderland | 0 | 0 |
| 1997–98 | Sunderland | 0 | 0 |
| 1997–98 | Scarborough (loan) | 29 | 0 |
| **Total:** | | **29** | **0** |

## HEDMAN, Magnus — Goalkeeper

H: 6 3 W: 14 00 b.Stockholm 19-3-73

*Honours:* Sweden 5 full caps.

| | | | |
|---|---|---|---|
| 1990 | AIK Stockholm | 2 | 0 |
| 1991 | AIK Stockholm | 2 | 0 |
| 1992 | AIK Stockholm | 7 | 0 |
| 1993 | AIK Stockholm | 26 | 0 |
| 1994 | AIK Stockholm | 26 | 0 |
| 1995 | AIK Stockholm | 25 | 0 |
| 1996 | AIK Stockholm | 26 | 0 |
| 1997 | AIK Stockholm | 13 | 0 |
| 1997–98 | Coventry C | 14 | 0 |
| **Total:** | | **141** | **0** |

## HEFFERNAN, Jason — Defender

b.Burnley 1-6-79

*Source:* Trainee.

| | | | |
|---|---|---|---|
| 1997–98 | Burnley | 0 | 0 |

## HEGGS, Carl — Forward

H: 6 1 W: 12 10 b.Leicester 11-10-70

*Source:* Doncaster R Trainee, Paget R.

| | | | |
|---|---|---|---|
| 1991–92 | WBA | 3 | 0 |
| 1992–93 | WBA | 17 | 2 |
| 1993–94 | WBA | 6 | 0 |
| 1994–95 | WBA | 14 | 1 |
| 1994–95 | Bristol R (loan) | 5 | 1 |
| 1995–96 | Swansea C | 32 | 5 |
| 1996–97 | Swansea C | 14 | 2 |
| 1997–98 | Northampton T | 33 | 4 |
| **Total:** | | **124** | **15** |

## HEIGHTON, Henry — Goalkeeper

H: 6 0 W: 13 02 b.Sunderland 27-11-78

*Source:* Trainee.

| | | | |
|---|---|---|---|
| 1997–98 | Blackpool | 0 | 0 |

## HEINOLA, Antti — Defender

H: 5 7 W: 10 05 b.Helsinki 20-3-73

*Honours:* Finland 5 full caps.

| | | | |
|---|---|---|---|
| 1991–92 | HJK Helsinki | 18 | 0 |
| 1992–93 | HJK Helsinki | 20 | 0 |
| 1993–94 | HJK Helsinki | 19 | 2 |
| 1994–95 | HJK Helsinki | 23 | 3 |
| 1995–96 | Emmen | 10 | 0 |
| 1996–97 | Emmen | 9 | 0 |
| 1996–97 | Heracles | 13 | 0 |
| 1997–98 | Heracles | 18 | 3 |
| 1997–98 | QPR | 10 | 0 |
| **Total:** | | **140** | **8** |

## HEISELBERG, Kim — Midfield

b.Tarm 21-9-77

*Source:* Esbjerg.

| | | | |
|---|---|---|---|
| 1996–97 | Sunderland | 0 | 0 |
| 1997–98 | Sunderland | 0 | 0 |

## HELDER, Glenn — Forward

H: 5 11 W: 11 07 b.Leiden 28-10-68

*Honours:* Holland 4 full caps.

| | | | |
|---|---|---|---|
| 1989–90 | Sparta | 22 | 2 |
| 1990–91 | Sparta | 29 | 4 |
| 1991–92 | Sparta | 24 | 2 |
| 1992–93 | Sparta | 18 | 1 |
| 1993–94 | Vitesse | 34 | 5 |
| 1994–95 | Vitesse | 18 | 7 |
| 1994–95 | Arsenal | 13 | 0 |

| | | | |
|---|---|---|---|
| 1995–96 | Arsenal | 24 | 1 |
| 1996–97 | Arsenal | 2 | 0 |
| 1997–98 | Arsenal | 0 | 0 |
| **Total:** | | **184** | **22** |

## HELLIWELL, Ian — Forward

H: 6 4 W: 14 08 b.Rotherham 7-11-62

*Source:* Matlock T.

| | | | |
|---|---|---|---|
| 1987–88 | York C | 32 | 8 |
| 1988–89 | York C | 41 | 11 |
| 1989–90 | York C | 46 | 14 |
| 1990–91 | York C | 41 | 7 |
| 1991–92 | Scunthorpe U | 39 | 9 |
| 1992–93 | Scunthorpe U | 41 | 13 |
| 1993–94 | Rotherham U | 40 | 3 |
| 1994–95 | Rotherham U | 12 | 1 |
| 1994–95 | Stockport Co | 17 | 4 |
| 1995–96 | Stockport Co | 22 | 9 |
| 1995–96 | Burnley | 4 | 0 |
| 1996–97 | Burnley | 0 | 0 |
| 1996–97 | Mansfield T (loan) | 5 | 1 |
| 1996–97 | Chester C (loan) | 9 | 1 |
| 1997–98 | Burnley | 0 | 0 |
| 1997–98 | Doncaster R (loan) | 8 | 1 |
| **Total:** | | **357** | **82** |

## HENCHOZ, Stephane — Defender

H: 6 1 W: 12 08 b.Billens 7-9-74

*Source:* Bulle. *Honours:* Switzerland 28 full caps.

| | | | |
|---|---|---|---|
| 1992–93 | Neuchatel Xamax | 35 | 0 |
| 1993–94 | Neuchatel Xamax | 21 | 1 |
| 1994–95 | Neuchatel Xamax | 35 | 0 |
| 1995–96 | Hamburg | 31 | 2 |
| 1996–97 | Hamburg | 18 | 0 |
| 1997–98 | Blackburn R | 36 | 0 |
| **Total:** | | **176** | **3** |

## HENDERSON, Kevin — Forward

b.Ashington 8-6-74

*Source:* Morpeth Town.

| | | | |
|---|---|---|---|
| 1997–98 | Burnley | 7 | 0 |
| **Total:** | | **7** | **0** |

## HENDON, Ian — Defender

H: 5 11 W: 11 05 b.Ilford 5-12-71

*Source:* Trainee. *Honours:* England Youth, Under-21.

| | | | |
|---|---|---|---|
| 1989–90 | Tottenham H | 0 | 0 |
| 1990–91 | Tottenham H | 2 | 0 |
| 1991–92 | Tottenham H | 2 | 0 |
| 1991–92 | Portsmouth (loan) | 4 | 0 |
| 1991–92 | Leyton Orient (loan) | 6 | 0 |
| 1992–93 | Tottenham H | 0 | 0 |
| 1992–93 | Barnsley (loan) | 6 | 0 |
| 1993–94 | Leyton Orient | 36 | 2 |
| 1994–95 | Leyton Orient | 29 | 0 |
| 1994–95 | Birmingham C (loan) | 4 | 0 |
| 1995–96 | Leyton Orient | 38 | 2 |
| 1996–97 | Leyton Orient | 28 | 1 |
| 1996–97 | Notts Co | 12 | 0 |
| 1997–98 | Notts Co | 38 | 0 |
| **Total:** | | **205** | **5** |

## HENDRIE, John — Forward

H: 5 7 W: 12 08 b.Lennoxtown 24-10-63

*Source:* Apprentice. *Honours:* Scotland Youth.

| | | | |
|---|---|---|---|
| 1981–82 | Coventry C | 6 | 0 |
| 1982–83 | Coventry C | 12 | 2 |
| 1983–84 | Coventry C | 3 | 0 |
| 1983–84 | Hereford U (loan) | 6 | 0 |
| 1984–85 | Bradford C | 46 | 9 |
| 1985–86 | Bradford C | 42 | 10 |
| 1986–87 | Bradford C | 42 | 14 |
| 1987–88 | Bradford C | 43 | 13 |
| 1988–89 | Newcastle U | 34 | 4 |
| 1989–90 | Leeds U | 27 | 5 |
| 1990–91 | Middlesbrough | 41 | 3 |
| 1991–92 | Middlesbrough | 38 | 3 |
| 1992–93 | Middlesbrough | 32 | 9 |
| 1993–94 | Middlesbrough | 29 | 13 |
| 1994–95 | Middlesbrough | 39 | 15 |
| 1995–96 | Middlesbrough | 13 | 1 |
| 1996–97 | Middlesbrough | 0 | 0 |
| 1996–97 | Barnsley | 36 | 15 |
| 1997–98 | Barnsley | 20 | 1 |
| **Total:** | | **509** | **117** |

## HENDRIE, Lee — Forward

H: 5 10 W: 10 02 b.Birmingham 18-5-77

*Source:* Trainee. *Honours:* England Youth, Under-21, B.

| | | | |
|---|---|---|---|
| 1993–94 | Aston Villa | 0 | 0 |
| 1994–95 | Aston Villa | 0 | 0 |
| 1995–96 | Aston Villa | 3 | 0 |
| 1996–97 | Aston Villa | 4 | 0 |
| 1997–98 | Aston Villa | 17 | 3 |
| **Total:** | | **24** | **3** |

## HENDRY, Colin — Defender

H: 6 1 W: 12 07 b.Keith 7-12-65

*Source:* Islavale. *Honours:* Scotland B, 35 full caps, 1 goal.

| | | | |
|---|---|---|---|
| 1983–84 | Dundee | 4 | 0 |
| 1984–85 | Dundee | 4 | 0 |

| | | | |
|---|---|---|---|
| 1985–86 | Dundee | 20 | 0 |
| 1986–87 | Dundee | 13 | 2 |
| 1986–87 | Blackburn R | 13 | 3 |
| 1987–88 | Blackburn R | 44 | 12 |
| 1988–89 | Blackburn R | 38 | 7 |
| 1989–90 | Blackburn R | 7 | 0 |
| 1989–90 | Manchester C | 25 | 3 |
| 1990–91 | Manchester C | 32 | 1 |
| 1991–92 | Manchester C | 6 | 1 |
| 1991–92 | Blackburn R | 30 | 4 |
| 1992–93 | Blackburn R | 41 | 1 |
| 1993–94 | Blackburn R | 23 | 0 |
| 1994–95 | Blackburn R | 38 | 4 |
| 1995–96 | Blackburn R | 33 | 1 |
| 1996–97 | Blackburn R | 35 | 1 |
| 1997–98 | Blackburn R | 34 | 1 |
| **Total:** | | **440** | **41** |

## HENDRY, John — Forward

H: 5 11 W: 10 12 b.Glasgow 6-1-70

*Source:* Hillington YC. *Honours:* Scotland Under-21.

| | | | |
|---|---|---|---|
| 1988–89 | Dundee | 2 | 0 |
| 1989–90 | Dundee | 0 | 0 |
| 1989–90 | Forfar Ath (loan) | 10 | 6 |
| 1990–91 | Tottenham H | 4 | 2 |
| 1991–92 | Tottenham H | 5 | 1 |
| 1991–92 | Charlton Ath (loan) | 5 | 1 |
| 1992–93 | Tottenham H | 5 | 2 |
| 1993–94 | Tottenham H | 3 | 0 |
| 1994–95 | Tottenham H | 0 | 0 |
| 1994–95 | Swansea C (loan) | 8 | 2 |
| 1995–96 | Motherwell | 16 | 2 |
| 1996–97 | Motherwell | 6 | 0 |
| 1997–98 | Motherwell | 13 | 1 |
| **Total:** | | **77** | **17** |

## HENRIKSEN, Tony — Goalkeeper

H: 6 3 W: 13 09 b.Hammel 25-4-73

*Source:* Randers Freja.

| | | | |
|---|---|---|---|
| 1996–97 | Southend U | 0 | 0 |
| 1997–98 | Southend U | 0 | 0 |

## HENRY, Anthony — Defender

b.London 13-9-79

*Source:* Trainee.

| | | | |
|---|---|---|---|
| 1997–98 | West Ham U | 0 | 0 |

## HENRY, David — Goalkeeper

H: 6 3 W: 14 09 b.Belfast 12-11-77

*Source:* Crusaders.

| | | | |
|---|---|---|---|
| 1995–96 | Nottingham F | 0 | 0 |
| 1996–97 | Nottingham F | 0 | 0 |
| 1997–98 | Nottingham F | 0 | 0 |

## HENRY, John — Forward

H: 5 9 W: 10 00 b.Vale of Leven 31-12-71

*Source:* Clydebank BC.

| | | | |
|---|---|---|---|
| 1990–91 | Clydebank | 3 | 1 |
| 1991–92 | Clydebank | 35 | 8 |
| 1992–93 | Clydebank | 32 | 12 |
| 1993–94 | Clydebank | 44 | 7 |
| 1994–95 | Kilmarnock | 30 | 4 |
| 1995–96 | Kilmarnock | 28 | 3 |
| 1996–97 | Kilmarnock | 22 | 2 |
| 1997–98 | Kilmarnock | 26 | 1 |
| **Total:** | | **220** | **38** |

## HENRY, Nick — Midfield

H: 5 6 W: 10 12 b.Liverpool 21-2-69

*Source:* Trainee.

| | | | |
|---|---|---|---|
| 1987–88 | Oldham Ath | 5 | 0 |
| 1988–89 | Oldham Ath | 18 | 0 |
| 1989–90 | Oldham Ath | 41 | 0 |
| 1990–91 | Oldham Ath | 43 | 4 |
| 1991–92 | Oldham Ath | 42 | 6 |
| 1992–93 | Oldham Ath | 32 | 6 |
| 1993–94 | Oldham Ath | 22 | 0 |
| 1994–95 | Oldham Ath | 34 | 2 |
| 1995–96 | Oldham Ath | 14 | 0 |
| 1996–97 | Oldham Ath | 22 | 1 |
| 1996–97 | Sheffield U | 9 | 0 |
| 1997–98 | Sheffield U | 1 | 0 |
| **Total:** | | **283** | **19** |

## HERBERT, Craig — Defender

H: 5 10 W: 11 00 b.Coventry 9-11-75

*Source:* Torquay U.

| | | | |
|---|---|---|---|
| 1993–94 | WBA | 0 | 0 |
| 1994–95 | WBA | 8 | 0 |
| 1995–96 | WBA | 0 | 0 |
| 1996–97 | WBA | 0 | 0 |
| 1997–98 | Shrewsbury T | 24 | 0 |
| **Total:** | | **32** | **0** |

## HERITAGE, Paul — Goalkeeper

H: 6 2 W: 12 11 b.Sheffield 17-4-79

*Source:* Trainee.

| | | | |
|---|---|---|---|
| 1996–97 | Sheffield U | 0 | 0 |
| 1997–98 | Sheffield U | 0 | 0 |
| 1997–98 | Barnsley | 0 | 0 |

## HERRERA, Robbie — Defender

H: 5 6 W: 10 08 b.Torbay 12-6-70

*Source:* Trainee.

| | | | |
|---|---|---|---|
| 1987–88 | QPR | 0 | 0 |
| 1988–89 | QPR | 2 | 0 |
| 1989–90 | QPR | 1 | 0 |
| 1990–91 | QPR | 3 | 0 |
| 1991–92 | QPR | 0 | 0 |
| 1991–92 | Torquay U (loan) | 11 | 0 |
| 1992–93 | QPR | 0 | 0 |
| 1992–93 | Torquay U (loan) | 5 | 0 |
| 1993–94 | QPR | 0 | 0 |
| 1993–94 | Fulham | 23 | 1 |
| 1994–95 | Fulham | 27 | 0 |
| 1995–96 | Fulham | 43 | 0 |
| 1996–97 | Fulham | 26 | 0 |
| 1997–98 | Fulham | 26 | 0 |
| **Total:** | | **167** | **1** |

## HESKEY, Emile — Forward

H: 6 2 W: 13 12 b.Leicester 11-1-78

*Source:* Trainee. *Honours:* England Youth, Under-21, B.

| | | | |
|---|---|---|---|
| 1994–95 | Leicester C | 1 | 0 |
| 1995–96 | Leicester C | 30 | 7 |
| 1996–97 | Leicester C | 35 | 10 |
| 1997–98 | Leicester C | 35 | 10 |
| **Total:** | | **101** | **27** |

## HESSENTHALER, Andy — Midfield

H: 5 7 W: 11 06 b.Gravesend 17-6-65

*Source:* Dartford, Redbridge Forest.

| | | | |
|---|---|---|---|
| 1991–92 | Watford | 35 | 1 |
| 1992–93 | Watford | 45 | 3 |
| 1993–94 | Watford | 42 | 5 |
| 1994–95 | Watford | 43 | 2 |
| 1995–96 | Watford | 30 | 0 |
| 1996–97 | Gillingham | 38 | 2 |
| 1997–98 | Gillingham | 42 | 0 |
| **Total:** | | **275** | **13** |

## HESSEY, Sean — Defender

H: 5 10 W: 12 06 b.Whiston 19-9-78

*Source:* Liverpool Trainee.

| | | | |
|---|---|---|---|
| 1997–98 | Wigan Ath | 0 | 0 |
| 1997–98 | Leeds U | 0 | 0 |
| 1997–98 | Huddersfield T | 1 | 0 |
| **Total:** | | **1** | **0** |

## HEWITT, Jamie — Midfield

H: 5 10 W: 10 08 b.Chesterfield 17-5-68

*Source:* School.

| | | | |
|---|---|---|---|
| 1984–85 | Chesterfield | 0 | 0 |
| 1985–86 | Chesterfield | 17 | 0 |
| 1986–87 | Chesterfield | 42 | 2 |
| 1987–88 | Chesterfield | 28 | 2 |
| 1988–89 | Chesterfield | 40 | 1 |
| 1989–90 | Chesterfield | 42 | 6 |
| 1990–91 | Chesterfield | 43 | 0 |
| 1991–92 | Chesterfield | 37 | 3 |
| 1992–93 | Doncaster R | 27 | 0 |
| 1993–94 | Doncaster R | 6 | 0 |
| 1993–94 | Chesterfield | 29 | 3 |
| 1994–95 | Chesterfield | 38 | 3 |
| 1995–96 | Chesterfield | 28 | 2 |
| 1996–97 | Chesterfield | 37 | 1 |
| 1997–98 | Chesterfield | 44 | 1 |
| **Total:** | | **458** | **24** |

## HEWLETT, Matthew — Midfield

H: 6 2 W: 10 11 b.Bristol 25-2-76

*Source:* Trainee. *Honours:* England Youth.

| | | | |
|---|---|---|---|
| 1993–94 | Bristol C | 12 | 0 |
| 1994–95 | Bristol C | 1 | 0 |
| 1995–96 | Bristol C | 27 | 2 |
| 1996–97 | Bristol C | 36 | 2 |
| 1997–98 | Bristol C | 34 | 4 |
| **Total:** | | **110** | **8** |

## HEY, Tony — Midfield

H: 5 9 W: 11 07 b.Berlin 19-9-70

| | | | |
|---|---|---|---|
| 1996–97 | Fortuna Cologne | 32 | 9 |
| 1997–98 | Birmingham C | 9 | 0 |
| **Total:** | | **41** | **9** |

## HIBBURT, James — Defender

H: 6 0 W: 12 08 b.Ashford 30-10-79

*Source:* Trainee. *Honours:* England Schools.

| | | | |
|---|---|---|---|
| 1996–97 | Crystal Palace | 0 | 0 |
| 1997–98 | Crystal Palace | 0 | 0 |

## HICKS, Stuart — Defender

H: 6 1 W: 13 03 b.Peterborough 30-5-67

*Source:* Peterborough U Apprentice, Wisbech T.

| | | | |
|---|---|---|---|
| 1987–88 | Colchester U | 7 | 0 |
| 1988–89 | Colchester U | 37 | 0 |
| 1989–90 | Colchester U | 20 | 0 |
| 1990–91 | Scunthorpe U | 46 | 1 |
| 1991–92 | Scunthorpe U | 21 | 0 |
| 1992–93 | Doncaster R | 36 | 0 |
| 1993–94 | Doncaster R | 0 | 0 |
| 1993–94 | Huddersfield T | 22 | 1 |
| 1993–94 | Preston NE | 4 | 0 |
| 1994–95 | Preston NE | 8 | 0 |
| 1994–95 | Scarborough | 6 | 0 |
| 1995–96 | Scarborough | 41 | 1 |
| 1996–97 | Scarborough | 38 | 1 |
| 1997–98 | Leyton Orient | 35 | 1 |
| **Total:** | | **321** | **5** |

## HIDEN, Martin — Defender

H: 6 1 W: 11 06 b.Stainz 11-3-73

*Source:* Sturm Graz, Rapid Vienna. *Honours:* Austria 3 full caps.

| | | | |
|---|---|---|---|
| 1997–98 | Leeds U | 11 | 0 |
| **Total:** | | **11** | **0** |

## HIGGINBOTHAM, Danny — Defender

H: 6 1 W: 12 03 b.Manchester 29-12-78

*Source:* Trainee.

| | | | |
|---|---|---|---|
| 1997–98 | Manchester U | 1 | 0 |
| **Total:** | | **1** | **0** |

## HIGGINS, Paul — Defender

H: 5 7 W: 10 02 b.Ilkeston 6-1-81

*Source:* Trainee.

| | | | |
|---|---|---|---|
| 1997–98 | Nottingham F | 0 | 0 |

## HIGGS, Shane — Goalkeeper

H: 6 2 W: 12 12 b.Oxford 13-5-77

*Source:* Trainee.

| | | | |
|---|---|---|---|
| 1994–95 | Bristol R | 0 | 0 |
| 1995–96 | Bristol R | 0 | 0 |
| 1996–97 | Bristol R | 2 | 0 |
| 1997–98 | Bristol R | 8 | 0 |
| **Total:** | | **10** | **0** |

## HIGNETT, Craig — Midfield

H: 5 8 W: 11 00 b.Whiston 12-1-70

*Source:* Liverpool Trainee.

| | | | |
|---|---|---|---|
| 1987–88 | Crewe Alex | 0 | 0 |
| 1988–89 | Crewe Alex | 1 | 0 |
| 1989–90 | Crewe Alex | 35 | 8 |
| 1990–91 | Crewe Alex | 38 | 13 |
| 1991–92 | Crewe Alex | 33 | 13 |
| 1992–93 | Crewe Alex | 14 | 8 |
| 1992–93 | Middlesbrough | 21 | 4 |
| 1993–94 | Middlesbrough | 29 | 5 |
| 1994–95 | Middlesbrough | 26 | 8 |
| 1995–96 | Middlesbrough | 22 | 5 |
| 1996–97 | Middlesbrough | 22 | 4 |
| 1997–98 | Middlesbrough | 36 | 7 |
| **Total:** | | **277** | **75** |

## HILEY, Scott — Defender

H: 5 9 W: 11 05 b.Plymouth 27-9-68

*Source:* Trainee.

| | | | |
|---|---|---|---|
| 1986–87 | Exeter C | 0 | 0 |
| 1987–88 | Exeter C | 15 | 1 |
| 1988–89 | Exeter C | 37 | 5 |
| 1989–90 | Exeter C | 46 | 0 |
| 1990–91 | Exeter C | 46 | 2 |
| 1991–92 | Exeter C | 33 | 1 |
| 1992–93 | Exeter C | 33 | 3 |
| 1992–93 | Birmingham C | 7 | 0 |
| 1993–94 | Birmingham C | 28 | 0 |
| 1994–95 | Birmingham C | 9 | 0 |
| 1995–96 | Birmingham C | 5 | 0 |
| 1995–96 | Manchester C | 6 | 0 |
| 1996–97 | Manchester C | 3 | 0 |
| 1997–98 | Manchester C | 0 | 0 |
| **Total:** | | **268** | **12** |

## HILL, Andy — Defender

H: 6 0 W: 13 08 b.Maltby 21-1-65

*Source:* Apprentice. *Honours:* England Youth.

| | | | |
|---|---|---|---|
| 1982–83 | Manchester U | 0 | 0 |
| 1983–84 | Manchester U | 0 | 0 |
| 1984–85 | Bury | 43 | 3 |
| 1985–86 | Bury | 35 | 2 |
| 1986–87 | Bury | 42 | 1 |
| 1987–88 | Bury | 43 | 2 |
| 1988–89 | Bury | 43 | 0 |
| 1989–90 | Bury | 46 | 2 |
| 1990–91 | Bury | 12 | 0 |
| 1990–91 | Manchester C | 8 | 1 |
| 1991–92 | Manchester C | 36 | 4 |
| 1992–93 | Manchester C | 24 | 1 |
| 1993–94 | Manchester C | 17 | 0 |

| | | | |
|---|---|---|---|
| 1994–95 | Manchester C | 13 | 0 |
| 1995–96 | Port Vale | 35 | 0 |
| 1996–97 | Port Vale | 38 | 1 |
| 1997–98 | Port Vale | 27 | 0 |
| **Total:** | | **462** | **17** |

## HILL, Clint — Defender

H: 6 0 W: 11 06 b.Liverpool 19-10-78

*Source:* Trainee.

| | | | |
|---|---|---|---|
| 1997–98 | Tranmere R | 14 | 0 |
| **Total:** | | **14** | **0** |

## HILL, Colin — Defender

H: 6 0 W: 12 11 b.Uxbridge 12-11-63

*Source:* Apprentice. *Honours:* Northern Ireland 26 full caps, 1 goal.

| | | | |
|---|---|---|---|
| 1981–82 | Arsenal | 0 | 0 |
| 1982–83 | Arsenal | 7 | 0 |
| 1983–84 | Arsenal | 37 | 1 |
| 1984–85 | Arsenal | 2 | 0 |
| 1985–86 | Arsenal | 0 | 0 |
| 1985–86 | Brighton & HA (loan) | 0 | 0 |
| From Maritimo. | | | |
| 1987–88 | Colchester U | 25 | 0 |
| 1988–89 | Colchester U | 44 | 0 |
| 1989–90 | Sheffield U | 43 | 0 |
| 1990–91 | Sheffield U | 24 | 0 |
| 1991–92 | Sheffield U | 15 | 1 |
| 1991–92 | Leicester C (loan) | 10 | 0 |
| 1992–93 | Leicester C | 46 | 0 |
| 1993–94 | Leicester C | 31 | 0 |
| 1994–95 | Leicester C | 24 | 0 |
| 1995–96 | Leicester C | 27 | 0 |
| 1996–97 | Leicester C | 7 | 0 |
| 1997 | Trelleborg | 11 | 0 |
| 1997–98 | Northampton T | 27 | 0 |
| **Total:** | | **380** | **2** |

## HILL, Danny — Midfield

H: 5 9 W: 11 12 b.Edmonton 1-10-74

*Source:* Trainee. *Honours:* England Under-21.

| | | | |
|---|---|---|---|
| 1992–93 | Tottenham H | 4 | 0 |
| 1993–94 | Tottenham H | 3 | 0 |
| 1994–95 | Tottenham H | 3 | 0 |
| 1995–96 | Tottenham H | 0 | 0 |
| 1995–96 | Birmingham C (loan) | 5 | 0 |
| 1995–96 | Watford (loan) | 1 | 0 |
| 1996–97 | Tottenham H | 0 | 0 |
| 1997–98 | Tottenham H | 0 | 0 |
| 1997–98 | Cardiff C (loan) | 7 | 0 |
| **Total:** | | **23** | **0** |

## HILL, Keith — Defender

H: 6 0 W: 12 04 b.Bolton 17-5-69

*Source:* Apprentice.

| | | | |
|---|---|---|---|
| 1986–87 | Blackburn R | 0 | 0 |
| 1987–88 | Blackburn R | 1 | 0 |
| 1988–89 | Blackburn R | 15 | 1 |
| 1989–90 | Blackburn R | 25 | 0 |
| 1990–91 | Blackburn R | 22 | 2 |
| 1991–92 | Blackburn R | 32 | 0 |
| 1992–93 | Blackburn R | 1 | 0 |
| 1992–93 | Plymouth Arg | 36 | 0 |
| 1993–94 | Plymouth Arg | 29 | 1 |
| 1994–95 | Plymouth Arg | 34 | 1 |
| 1995–96 | Plymouth Arg | 24 | 0 |
| 1996–97 | Rochdale | 43 | 3 |
| 1997–98 | Rochdale | 37 | 2 |
| **Total:** | | **299** | **10** |

## HILL, Kevin — Forward

H: 5 8 W: 9 12 b.Exeter 6-3-76

*Source:* Torrington.

| | | | |
|---|---|---|---|
| 1997–98 | Torquay U | 37 | 7 |
| **Total:** | | **37** | **7** |

## HILLIER, David — Midfield

H: 5 10 W: 12 00 b.Blackheath 19-12-69

*Source:* Trainee. *Honours:* England Under-21.

| | | | |
|---|---|---|---|
| 1987–88 | Arsenal | 0 | 0 |
| 1988–89 | Arsenal | 0 | 0 |
| 1989–90 | Arsenal | 0 | 0 |
| 1990–91 | Arsenal | 16 | 0 |
| 1991–92 | Arsenal | 27 | 1 |
| 1992–93 | Arsenal | 30 | 1 |
| 1993–94 | Arsenal | 15 | 0 |
| 1994–95 | Arsenal | 9 | 0 |
| 1995–96 | Arsenal | 5 | 0 |
| 1996–97 | Arsenal | 2 | 0 |
| 1996–97 | Portsmouth | 21 | 2 |
| 1997–98 | Portsmouth | 30 | 2 |
| **Total:** | | **155** | **6** |

## HILLS, John — Defender

H: 5 9 W: 10 08 b.St Annes-on-Sea 21-4-78

*Source:* Trainee.

| | | | |
|---|---|---|---|
| 1995–96 | Blackpool | 0 | 0 |
| 1995–96 | Everton | 0 | 0 |
| 1996–97 | Everton | 3 | 0 |
| 1996–97 | Swansea C (loan) | 11 | 0 |
| 1997–98 | Everton | 0 | 0 |

## Hilton, Damien

| | | | |
|---|---|---|---|
| 1997–98 | Swansea C (loan) | 7 | 1 |
| 1997–98 | Blackpool | 19 | 1 |
| **Total:** | | **40** | **2** |

## HILTON, Damien — Forward

H: 6 2 W: 12 06 b.Norwich 6-9-77

*Source:* Trainee.

| | | | |
|---|---|---|---|
| 1996–97 | Norwich C | 0 | 0 |
| 1997–98 | Norwich C | 0 | 0 |
| 1997–98 | Brighton & HA | 5 | 0 |
| **Total:** | | **5** | **0** |

## HILTON, David — Defender

H: 5 11 W: 10 10 b.Barnsley 10-11-77

*Source:* Trainee. *Honours:* England Schools, Youth.

| | | | |
|---|---|---|---|
| 1994–95 | Manchester U | 0 | 0 |
| 1995–96 | Manchester U | 0 | 0 |
| 1996–97 | Manchester U | 0 | 0 |
| 1997–98 | Darlington | 1 | 0 |
| **Total:** | | **1** | **0** |

## HILTON, Maurice — Defender

H: 5 11 W: 11 10 b.Sunderland 14-3-79

*Source:* Trainee.

| | | | |
|---|---|---|---|
| 1997–98 | Doncaster R | 10 | 0 |
| **Total:** | | **10** | **0** |

## HIMSWORTH, Gary — Forward

H: 5 7 W: 9 10 b.Appleton 19-12-69

*Source:* Trainee.

| | | | |
|---|---|---|---|
| 1987–88 | York C | 31 | 2 |
| 1988–89 | York C | 32 | 2 |
| 1989–90 | York C | 23 | 4 |
| 1990–91 | York C | 2 | 0 |
| 1990–91 | Scarborough | 23 | 1 |
| 1991–92 | Scarborough | 36 | 4 |
| 1992–93 | Scarborough | 33 | 1 |
| 1993–94 | Darlington | 28 | 3 |
| 1994–95 | Darlington | 38 | 2 |
| 1995–96 | Darlington | 28 | 3 |
| 1995–96 | York C | 8 | 1 |
| 1996–97 | York C | 33 | 2 |
| 1997–98 | York C | 15 | 0 |
| **Total:** | | **330** | **25** |

## HINCHCLIFFE, Andy — Defender

H: 5 10 W: 12 10 b.Manchester 5-2-69

*Source:* Apprentice. *Honours:* England Youth, Under-21, 6 full caps.

| | | | |
|---|---|---|---|
| 1986–87 | Manchester C | 0 | 0 |
| 1987–88 | Manchester C | 42 | 1 |
| 1988–89 | Manchester C | 39 | 5 |
| 1989–90 | Manchester C | 31 | 2 |
| 1990–91 | Everton | 21 | 1 |
| 1991–92 | Everton | 18 | 0 |
| 1992–93 | Everton | 25 | 1 |
| 1993–94 | Everton | 26 | 0 |
| 1994–95 | Everton | 29 | 2 |
| 1995–96 | Everton | 28 | 2 |
| 1996–97 | Everton | 18 | 1 |
| 1997–98 | Everton | 17 | 0 |
| 1997–98 | Sheffield W | 15 | 1 |
| **Total:** | | **309** | **16** |

## HINDS, Leigh — Forward

H: 5 8 W: 10 10 b.Beckenham 17-8-78

*Source:* Trainee.

| | | | |
|---|---|---|---|
| 1996–97 | Wimbledon | 0 | 0 |
| 1997–98 | Wimbledon | 0 | 0 |

## HINES, Leslie — Defender

H: 5 7 W: 9 10 b.Iserlohn 7-1-77

*Source:* Trainee.

| | | | |
|---|---|---|---|
| 1994–95 | Aston Villa | 0 | 0 |
| 1995–96 | Aston Villa | 0 | 0 |
| 1996–97 | Aston Villa | 0 | 0 |
| 1997–98 | Aston Villa | 0 | 0 |

## HINSHELWOOD, Danny — Defender

H: 5 9 W: 11 00 b.Bromley 12-12-75

*Source:* Trainee. *Honours:* England Youth.

| | | | |
|---|---|---|---|
| 1992–93 | Nottingham F | 0 | 0 |
| 1993–94 | Nottingham F | 0 | 0 |
| 1994–95 | Nottingham F | 0 | 0 |
| 1995–96 | Nottingham F | 0 | 0 |
| 1995–96 | Portsmouth | 5 | 0 |
| 1996–97 | Portsmouth | 0 | 0 |
| 1996–97 | Torquay U (loan) | 9 | 0 |
| 1997–98 | Portsmouth | 0 | 0 |
| **Total:** | | **14** | **0** |

## HINTON, Craig
Defender

H: 5 11 W: 11 00 b.Wolverhampton 26-11-77

*Source:* Trainee.

| | | | |
|---|---|---|---|
| 1996–97 | Birmingham C | 0 | 0 |
| 1997–98 | Birmingham C | 0 | 0 |

## HIRST, David
Forward

H: 6 0 W: 13 11 b.Barnsley 7-12-67

*Source:* Apprentice. *Honours:* England Youth, Under-21, B, 3 full caps, 1 goal.

| | | | |
|---|---|---|---|
| 1985–86 | Barnsley | 28 | 9 |
| 1986–87 | Sheffield W | 21 | 6 |
| 1987–88 | Sheffield W | 24 | 3 |
| 1988–89 | Sheffield W | 32 | 7 |
| 1989–90 | Sheffield W | 38 | 14 |
| 1990–91 | Sheffield W | 41 | 24 |
| 1991–92 | Sheffield W | 33 | 18 |
| 1992–93 | Sheffield W | 22 | 11 |
| 1993–94 | Sheffield W | 7 | 1 |
| 1994–95 | Sheffield W | 15 | 3 |
| 1995–96 | Sheffield W | 30 | 13 |
| 1996–97 | Sheffield W | 25 | 6 |
| 1997–98 | Sheffield W | 6 | 0 |
| 1997–98 | Southampton | 28 | 9 |
| **Total:** | | **350** | **124** |

## HIRST, Matthew
Defender

H: 6 4 W: 12 05 b.St Albans 14-11-77

*Source:* Millwall Trainee. *Honours:*

| | | | |
|---|---|---|---|
| 1996–97 | Bury | 0 | 0 |
| 1997–98 | Bury | 0 | 0 |

## HISLOP, Shaka
Goalkeeper

H: 6 3 W: 15 00 b.Hackney 22-2-69

*Source:* Howard Univ, USA. *Honours:* England Under-21.

| | | | |
|---|---|---|---|
| 1992–93 | Reading | 12 | 0 |
| 1993–94 | Reading | 46 | 0 |
| 1994–95 | Reading | 46 | 0 |
| 1995–96 | Newcastle U | 24 | 0 |
| 1996–97 | Newcastle U | 16 | 0 |
| 1997–98 | Newcastle U | 13 | 0 |
| **Total:** | | **157** | **0** |

## HITCHCOCK, Kevin
Goalkeeper

H: 6 1 W: 13 00 b.Custom House 5-10-62

*Source:* Barking.

| | | | |
|---|---|---|---|
| 1983–84 | Nottingham F | 0 | 0 |
| 1983–84 | Mansfield T (loan) | 14 | 0 |
| 1984–85 | Mansfield T | 43 | 0 |
| 1985–86 | Mansfield T | 46 | 0 |
| 1986–87 | Mansfield T | 46 | 0 |
| 1987–88 | Mansfield T | 33 | 0 |
| 1987–88 | Chelsea | 8 | 0 |
| 1988–89 | Chelsea | 3 | 0 |
| 1989–90 | Chelsea | 0 | 0 |
| 1990–91 | Chelsea | 3 | 0 |
| 1990–91 | Northampton T (loan) | 17 | 0 |
| 1991–92 | Chelsea | 21 | 0 |
| 1992–93 | Chelsea | 20 | 0 |
| 1992–93 | West Ham U (loan) | 0 | 0 |
| 1993–94 | Chelsea | 2 | 0 |
| 1994–95 | Chelsea | 12 | 0 |
| 1995–96 | Chelsea | 12 | 0 |
| 1996–97 | Chelsea | 12 | 0 |
| 1997–98 | Chelsea | 0 | 0 |
| **Total:** | | **292** | **0** |

## HITCHEN, Steve
Defender

H: 5 8 W: 11 07 b.Salford 28-11-76

*Source:* Trainee.

| | | | |
|---|---|---|---|
| 1995–96 | Blackburn R | 0 | 0 |
| 1996–97 | Blackburn R | 0 | 0 |
| 1997–98 | Macclesfield T | 2 | 0 |
| **Total:** | | **2** | **0** |

## HJELDE, Jon Olav
Defender

H: 6 0 W: 13 07 b.Levanger 30-7-72

| | | | |
|---|---|---|---|
| 1994 | Rosenborg | 1 | 0 |
| 1995 | Rosenborg | 7 | 0 |
| 1996 | Rosenborg | 16 | 1 |
| 1997 | Rosenborg | 3 | 0 |
| 1997–98 | Nottingham F | 28 | 1 |
| **Total:** | | **55** | **2** |

## HOBBS, Darren
Defender

H: 6 2 W: 13 00 b.Bristol 18-1-79

*Source:* Trainee.

| | | | |
|---|---|---|---|
| 1997–98 | Bristol C | 0 | 0 |

## HOBSON, Gary
Defender

H: 6 1 W: 13 05 b.North Ferriby 12-11-72

*Source:* Trainee.

| | | | |
|---|---|---|---|
| 1990–91 | Hull C | 4 | 0 |
| 1991–92 | Hull C | 16 | 0 |
| 1992–93 | Hull C | 21 | 0 |
| 1993–94 | Hull C | 36 | 0 |
| 1994–95 | Hull C | 36 | 0 |
| 1995–96 | Hull C | 29 | 0 |

| | | | |
|---|---|---|---|
| 1995–96 | Brighton & HA | 9 | 0 |
| 1996–97 | Brighton & HA | 37 | 1 |
| 1997–98 | Brighton & HA | 33 | 0 |
| **Total:** | | **221** | **1** |

## HOCKING, Matthew — Defender

H: 5 11 W: 12 00 b.Boston 30-1-78

*Source:* Trainee.

| | | | |
|---|---|---|---|
| 1995–96 | Sheffield U | 0 | 0 |
| 1996–97 | Sheffield U | 0 | 0 |
| 1997–98 | Sheffield U | 0 | 0 |
| 1997–98 | Hull C | 31 | 1 |
| **Total:** | | **31** | **1** |

## HOCKTON, Danny — Forward

H: 6 0 W: 11 11 b.Barking 7-2-79

*Source:* Trainee.

| | | | |
|---|---|---|---|
| 1996–97 | Millwall | 2 | 0 |
| 1997–98 | Millwall | 26 | 3 |
| **Total:** | | **28** | **3** |

## HODGE, John — Forward

H: 5 7 W: 11 13 b.Ormskirk 1-4-69

*Source:* Exmouth.

| | | | |
|---|---|---|---|
| 1991–92 | Exeter C | 23 | 1 |
| 1992–93 | Exeter C | 42 | 9 |
| 1993–94 | Swansea C | 27 | 2 |
| 1994–95 | Swansea C | 44 | 7 |
| 1995–96 | Swansea C | 41 | 1 |
| 1996–97 | Swansea C | 0 | 0 |
| 1996–97 | Walsall | 37 | 4 |
| 1997–98 | Walsall | 39 | 8 |
| **Total:** | | **253** | **32** |

## HODGE, Steve — Midfield

H: 5 8 W: 11 03 b.Nottingham 25-10-62

*Source:* Apprentice. *Honours:* England Under-21, B, 24 full caps.

| | | | |
|---|---|---|---|
| 1980–81 | Nottingham F | 0 | 0 |
| 1981–82 | Nottingham F | 1 | 0 |
| 1982–83 | Nottingham F | 39 | 8 |
| 1983–84 | Nottingham F | 39 | 10 |
| 1984–85 | Nottingham F | 42 | 12 |
| 1985–86 | Nottingham F | 2 | 0 |
| 1985–86 | Aston Villa | 36 | 8 |
| 1986–87 | Aston Villa | 17 | 4 |
| 1986–87 | Tottenham H | 19 | 4 |
| 1987–88 | Tottenham H | 26 | 3 |
| 1988–89 | Nottingham F | 34 | 7 |
| 1989–90 | Nottingham F | 34 | 10 |
| 1990–91 | Nottingham F | 14 | 3 |
| 1991–92 | Leeds U | 23 | 7 |
| 1992–93 | Leeds U | 23 | 2 |
| 1993–94 | Leeds U | 8 | 1 |
| 1994–95 | Leeds U | 0 | 0 |
| 1994–95 | Derby Co (loan) | 10 | 2 |
| 1994–95 | QPR | 15 | 0 |
| 1995–96 | QPR | 0 | 0 |
| 1995–96 | Watford | 2 | 0 |
| 1996–97 | Watford | 0 | 0 |
| 1997–98 | Leyton Orient | 1 | 0 |
| **Total:** | | **385** | **81** |

## HODGES, Danny — Defender

H: 6 0 W: 12 07 b.Greenwich 14-9-76

*Source:* Trainee. *Honours:* England Youth.

| | | | |
|---|---|---|---|
| 1995–96 | Wimbledon | 0 | 0 |
| 1996–97 | Wimbledon | 0 | 0 |
| 1997–98 | Wimbledon | 0 | 0 |

## HODGES, Glyn — Midfield

H: 6 0 W: 12 10 b.Streatham 30-4-63

*Source:* Apprentice. *Honours:* Wales Youth, Under-21, B, 18 full caps.

| | | | |
|---|---|---|---|
| 1980–81 | Wimbledon | 30 | 5 |
| 1981–82 | Wimbledon | 34 | 2 |
| 1982–83 | Wimbledon | 37 | 9 |
| 1983–84 | Wimbledon | 42 | 15 |
| 1984–85 | Wimbledon | 22 | 3 |
| 1985–86 | Wimbledon | 30 | 6 |
| 1986–87 | Wimbledon | 37 | 9 |
| 1987–88 | Newcastle U | 7 | 0 |
| 1987–88 | Watford | 24 | 3 |
| 1988–89 | Watford | 27 | 5 |
| 1989–90 | Watford | 35 | 7 |
| 1990–91 | Crystal Palace | 7 | 0 |
| 1990–91 | Sheffield U | 12 | 4 |
| 1991–92 | Sheffield U | 26 | 2 |
| 1992–93 | Sheffield U | 31 | 4 |
| 1993–94 | Sheffield U | 31 | 2 |
| 1994–95 | Sheffield U | 25 | 4 |
| 1995–96 | Sheffield U | 22 | 3 |
| 1995–96 | Derby Co | 9 | 0 |
| From Sin Tao. | | | |
| 1996–97 | Derby Co | 0 | 0 |
| From Sin Tao. | | | |
| 1997–98 | Hull C | 18 | 4 |
| 1997–98 | Nottingham F | 0 | 0 |
| **Total:** | | **506** | **87** |

## HODGES, Kevin
Midfield

H: 5 8 W: 11 02 b.Bridport 12-6-60

*Source:* Apprentice.

| | | | |
|---|---|---|---|
| 1977–78 | Plymouth Arg | 0 | 0 |
| 1978–79 | Plymouth Arg | 12 | 0 |
| 1979–80 | Plymouth Arg | 44 | 5 |
| 1980–81 | Plymouth Arg | 41 | 5 |
| 1981–82 | Plymouth Arg | 46 | 11 |
| 1982–83 | Plymouth Arg | 46 | 11 |
| 1983–84 | Plymouth Arg | 43 | 4 |
| 1984–85 | Plymouth Arg | 45 | 10 |
| 1985–86 | Plymouth Arg | 46 | 16 |
| 1986–87 | Plymouth Arg | 35 | 5 |
| 1987–88 | Plymouth Arg | 37 | 6 |
| 1988–89 | Plymouth Arg | 31 | 1 |
| 1989–90 | Plymouth Arg | 44 | 4 |
| 1990–91 | Plymouth Arg | 42 | 3 |
| 1991–92 | Plymouth Arg | 14 | 0 |
| 1991–92 | Torquay U (loan) | 3 | 0 |
| 1992–93 | Plymouth Arg | 4 | 0 |
| 1992–93 | Torquay U | 8 | 1 |
| 1993–94 | Torquay U | 29 | 2 |
| 1994–95 | Torquay U | 28 | 1 |
| 1995–96 | Torquay U | 2 | 0 |
| 1996–97 | Torquay U | 1 | 0 |
| 1997–98 | Torquay U | 0 | 0 |
| **Total:** | | **601** | **85** |

## HODGES, Lee
Forward

H: 6 0 W: 12 00 b.Epping 4-9-73

*Source:* Trainee.

| | | | |
|---|---|---|---|
| 1991–92 | Tottenham H | 0 | 0 |
| 1992–93 | Tottenham H | 4 | 0 |
| 1992–93 | Plymouth Arg (loan) | 7 | 2 |
| 1993–94 | Tottenham H | 0 | 0 |
| 1993–94 | Wycombe W (loan) | 4 | 0 |
| 1994–95 | Barnet | 34 | 4 |
| 1995–96 | Barnet | 40 | 17 |
| 1996–97 | Barnet | 31 | 5 |
| 1997–98 | Reading | 24 | 6 |
| **Total:** | | **144** | **34** |

## HODGES, Lee
Forward

H: 5 5 W: 10 02 b.Newham 2-3-78

*Source:* Trainee. *Honours:* England Schools.

| | | | |
|---|---|---|---|
| 1994–95 | West Ham U | 0 | 0 |
| 1995–96 | West Ham U | 0 | 0 |
| 1996–97 | West Ham U | 0 | 0 |
| 1996–97 | Exeter C (loan) | 17 | 0 |
| 1996–97 | Leyton Orient (loan) | 3 | 0 |
| 1997–98 | West Ham U | 2 | 0 |
| 1997–98 | Plymouth Arg (loan) | 9 | 0 |
| **Total:** | | **31** | **0** |

## HODGSON, Doug
Defender

H: 6 1 W: 12 07 b.Frankston 27-2-69

*Source:* Heidelberg.

| | | | |
|---|---|---|---|
| 1994–95 | Sheffield U | 1 | 0 |
| 1995–96 | Sheffield U | 16 | 0 |
| 1995–96 | Plymouth Arg (loan) | 5 | 0 |
| 1996–97 | Sheffield U | 13 | 0 |
| 1996–97 | Burnley (loan) | 1 | 0 |
| 1996–97 | Oldham Ath | 12 | 0 |
| 1997–98 | Oldham Ath | 28 | 4 |
| **Total:** | | **76** | **4** |

## HODGSON, Richard
Forward

H: 5 10 W: 10 11 b.Sunderland 1-10-79

*Source:* Trainee.

| | | | |
|---|---|---|---|
| 1996–97 | Nottingham F | 0 | 0 |
| 1997–98 | Nottingham F | 0 | 0 |

## HODSON, Ben
Forward

H: 6 2 W: 13 08 b.Nottingham 25-1-76

*Source:* Yeading.

| | | | |
|---|---|---|---|
| 1997–98 | Wycombe W | 0 | 0 |

## HODSON, Matthew
Midfield

b.Derby 20-9-79

*Source:* Trainee.

| | | | |
|---|---|---|---|
| 1997–98 | Wycombe W | 0 | 0 |

## HOGG, Graeme
Defender

H: 6 1 W: 12 04 b.Aberdeen 17-6-64

*Source:* Apprentice. *Honours:* Scotland Under-21.

| | | | |
|---|---|---|---|
| 1982–83 | Manchester U | 0 | 0 |
| 1983–84 | Manchester U | 16 | 1 |
| 1984–85 | Manchester U | 29 | 0 |
| 1985–86 | Manchester U | 17 | 0 |
| 1986–87 | Manchester U | 11 | 0 |
| 1987–88 | Manchester U | 10 | 0 |
| 1987–88 | WBA (loan) | 7 | 0 |
| 1988–89 | Portsmouth | 41 | 1 |
| 1989–90 | Portsmouth | 39 | 1 |
| 1990–91 | Portsmouth | 20 | 0 |
| 1991–92 | Hearts | 18 | 1 |
| 1992–93 | Hearts | 22 | 2 |
| 1993–94 | Hearts | 17 | 0 |

| | | | |
|---|---|---|---|
| 1994–95 | Hearts | 1 | 0 |
| 1994–95 | Notts Co | 17 | 0 |
| 1995–96 | Notts Co | 10 | 0 |
| 1996–97 | Notts Co | 35 | 0 |
| 1997–98 | Notts Co | 4 | 0 |
| 1997–98 | Brentford | 17 | 2 |
| **Total:** | | **331** | **8** |

## HOGGETH, Gary — Goalkeeper

H: 6 1 W: 12 07 b.South Shields 7-10-79

*Source:* Trainee.

| | | | |
|---|---|---|---|
| 1997–98 | Doncaster R | 8 | 0 |
| **Total:** | | **8** | **0** |

## HOLCROFT, Peter — Midfield

H: 5 9 W: 11 07 b.Liverpool 3-1-76

*Source:* Trainee.

| | | | |
|---|---|---|---|
| 1994–95 | Everton | 0 | 0 |
| 1995–96 | Everton | 0 | 0 |
| 1996–97 | Everton | 0 | 0 |
| 1996–97 | Swindon T | 3 | 0 |
| 1997–98 | Swindon T | 0 | 0 |
| 1997–98 | Exeter C (loan) | 6 | 0 |
| **Total:** | | **9** | **0** |

## HOLDEN, Dean — Defender

b.Salford 15-9-79

*Source:* Trainee. *Honours:* England Youth.

| | | | |
|---|---|---|---|
| 1997–98 | Bolton W | 0 | 0 |

## HOLDSWORTH, David — Defender

H: 6 0 W: 12 10 b.Walthamstow 8-11-68

*Source:* Trainee. *Honours:* England Youth, Under-21.

| | | | |
|---|---|---|---|
| 1986–87 | Watford | 0 | 0 |
| 1987–88 | Watford | 0 | 0 |
| 1988–89 | Watford | 33 | 1 |
| 1989–90 | Watford | 44 | 3 |
| 1990–91 | Watford | 15 | 2 |
| 1991–92 | Watford | 33 | 2 |
| 1992–93 | Watford | 39 | 0 |
| 1993–94 | Watford | 28 | 0 |
| 1994–95 | Watford | 39 | 1 |
| 1995–96 | Watford | 27 | 1 |
| 1996–97 | Watford | 0 | 0 |
| 1996–97 | Sheffield U | 37 | 1 |
| 1997–98 | Sheffield U | 40 | 2 |
| **Total:** | | **335** | **13** |

## HOLDSWORTH, Dean — Forward

H: 5 11 W: 11 13 b.Walthamstow 8-11-68

*Source:* Trainee.

| | | | |
|---|---|---|---|
| 1986–87 | Watford | 2 | 0 |
| 1987–88 | Carlisle U (loan) | 4 | 1 |
| 1987–88 | Port Vale (loan) | 6 | 2 |
| 1988–89 | Watford | 10 | 2 |
| 1988–89 | Swansea C (loan) | 5 | 1 |
| 1988–89 | Brentford (loan) | 7 | 1 |
| 1989–90 | Watford | 4 | 1 |
| 1989–90 | Brentford | 39 | 24 |
| 1990–91 | Brentford | 30 | 5 |
| 1991–92 | Brentford | 41 | 24 |
| 1992–93 | Wimbledon | 36 | 19 |
| 1993–94 | Wimbledon | 42 | 17 |
| 1994–95 | Wimbledon | 28 | 7 |
| 1995–96 | Wimbledon | 33 | 10 |
| 1996–97 | Wimbledon | 25 | 5 |
| 1997–98 | Wimbledon | 5 | 0 |
| 1997–98 | Bolton W | 20 | 3 |
| **Total:** | | **337** | **122** |

## HOLLAND, Chris — Midfield

H: 5 9 W: 11 05 b.Whalley 11-9-75

*Source:* Trainee. *Honours:* England Youth, Under-21.

| | | | |
|---|---|---|---|
| 1993–94 | Preston NE | 1 | 0 |
| 1993–94 | Newcastle U | 3 | 0 |
| 1994–95 | Newcastle U | 0 | 0 |
| 1995–96 | Newcastle U | 0 | 0 |
| 1996–97 | Newcastle U | 0 | 0 |
| 1996–97 | Birmingham C | 32 | 0 |
| 1997–98 | Birmingham C | 10 | 0 |
| **Total:** | | **46** | **0** |

## HOLLAND, Matt — Midfield

H: 5 10 W: 11 10 b.Bury 11-4-74

*Source:* Trainee.

| | | | |
|---|---|---|---|
| 1992–93 | West Ham U | 0 | 0 |
| 1993–94 | West Ham U | 0 | 0 |
| 1994–95 | West Ham U | 0 | 0 |
| 1994–95 | Bournemouth | 16 | 1 |
| 1995–96 | Bournemouth | 43 | 10 |
| 1996–97 | Bournemouth | 45 | 7 |
| 1997–98 | Ipswich T | 46 | 10 |
| **Total:** | | **150** | **28** |

## HOLLAND, Paul — Midfield

H: 5 11 W: 12 10 b.Lincoln 8-7-73

*Source:* School. *Honours:* England Schools, Under-21.

| | | | |
|---|---|---|---|
| 1990–91 | Mansfield T | 1 | 0 |

| | | | |
|---|---|---|---|
| 1991–92 | Mansfield T | 38 | 6 |
| 1992–93 | Mansfield T | 39 | 3 |
| 1993–94 | Mansfield T | 38 | 7 |
| 1994–95 | Mansfield T | 33 | 9 |
| 1995–96 | Sheffield U | 18 | 1 |
| 1995–96 | Chesterfield | 17 | 2 |
| 1996–97 | Chesterfield | 25 | 3 |
| 1997–98 | Chesterfield | 35 | 3 |
| **Total:** | | **244** | **34** |

## HOLLOWAY, Christopher — Midfield

b.Swansea 5-2-80

*Source:* Trainee.

| | | | |
|---|---|---|---|
| 1997–98 | Exeter C | 6 | 0 |
| **Total:** | | **6** | **0** |

## HOLLOWAY, Darren — Defender

H: 5 10 W: 12 06 b.Bishop Auckland 3-10-77

*Source:* Trainee. *Honours:* England Under-21.

| | | | |
|---|---|---|---|
| 1995–96 | Sunderland | 0 | 0 |
| 1996–97 | Sunderland | 0 | 0 |
| 1997–98 | Sunderland | 32 | 0 |
| 1997–98 | Carlisle U (loan) | 5 | 0 |
| **Total:** | | **37** | **0** |

## HOLLOWAY, Ian — Midfield

H: 5 7 W: 10 10 b.Kingswood 12-3-63

*Source:* Apprentice.

| | | | |
|---|---|---|---|
| 1980–81 | Bristol R | 1 | 0 |
| 1981–82 | Bristol R | 1 | 0 |
| 1982–83 | Bristol R | 31 | 7 |
| 1983–84 | Bristol R | 36 | 1 |
| 1984–85 | Bristol R | 42 | 6 |
| 1985–86 | Wimbledon | 19 | 2 |
| 1985–86 | Brentford (loan) | 13 | 2 |
| 1986–87 | Brentford | 16 | 0 |
| 1986–87 | Torquay U (loan) | 5 | 0 |
| 1987–88 | Brentford | 1 | 0 |
| 1987–88 | Bristol R | 43 | 5 |
| 1988–89 | Bristol R | 44 | 6 |
| 1989–90 | Bristol R | 46 | 8 |
| 1990–91 | Bristol R | 46 | 7 |
| 1991–92 | QPR | 40 | 0 |
| 1992–93 | QPR | 24 | 2 |
| 1993–94 | QPR | 25 | 0 |
| 1994–95 | QPR | 31 | 1 |
| 1995–96 | QPR | 27 | 1 |
| 1996–97 | Bristol R | 31 | 1 |
| 1997–98 | Bristol R | 39 | 0 |
| **Total:** | | **561** | **49** |

## HOLLUND, Martin — Goalkeeper

H: 6 0 W: 12 13 b.Stord 11-8-74

| | | | |
|---|---|---|---|
| 1994 | Brann | 3 | 0 |
| 1995 | Brann | 15 | 0 |
| 1996 | Brann | 0 | 0 |
| 1997 | Brann | 6 | 0 |
| 1997–98 | Hartlepool U | 28 | 0 |
| **Total:** | | **52** | **0** |

## HOLMES, Derek — Midfield

H: 6 0 W: 12 02 b.Lanark 18-10-78

*Source:* Royal Albert.

| | | | |
|---|---|---|---|
| 1995–96 | Hearts | 0 | 0 |
| 1996–97 | Hearts | 1 | 0 |
| 1997–98 | Hearts | 1 | 1 |
| 1997–98 | Cowdenbeath | 13 | 5 |
| **Total:** | | **15** | **6** |

## HOLMES, Matt — Midfield

H: 5 7 W: 11 00 b.Luton 1-8-69

*Source:* Trainee.

| | | | |
|---|---|---|---|
| 1988–89 | Bournemouth | 4 | 1 |
| 1988–89 | Cardiff C (loan) | 1 | 0 |
| 1989–90 | Bournemouth | 22 | 2 |
| 1990–91 | Bournemouth | 42 | 2 |
| 1991–92 | Bournemouth | 46 | 3 |
| 1992–93 | West Ham U | 18 | 0 |
| 1993–94 | West Ham U | 34 | 3 |
| 1994–95 | West Ham U | 24 | 1 |
| 1995–96 | Blackburn R | 9 | 1 |
| 1996–97 | Blackburn R | 0 | 0 |
| 1997–98 | Charlton Ath | 16 | 1 |
| **Total:** | | **216** | **14** |

## HOLMES, Paul — Defender

H: 5 10 W: 11 00 b.Stocksbridge 18-2-68

*Source:* Apprentice.

| | | | |
|---|---|---|---|
| 1985–86 | Doncaster R | 5 | 1 |
| 1986–87 | Doncaster R | 16 | 0 |
| 1987–88 | Doncaster R | 26 | 0 |
| 1988–89 | Torquay U | 25 | 0 |
| 1989–90 | Torquay U | 44 | 2 |
| 1990–91 | Torquay U | 33 | 1 |
| 1991–92 | Torquay U | 36 | 1 |
| 1992–93 | Birmingham C | 12 | 0 |
| 1992–93 | Everton | 4 | 0 |
| 1993–94 | Everton | 15 | 0 |
| 1994–95 | Everton | 1 | 0 |
| 1995–96 | Everton | 1 | 0 |
| 1995–96 | WBA | 18 | 0 |

## Holmes, Peter

| | | | |
|---|---|---|---|
| 1996–97 | WBA | 38 | 1 |
| 1997–98 | WBA | 30 | 0 |
| **Total:** | | **304** | **6** |

## HOLMES, Peter — Midfield

b.Bishop Auckland 18-11-80

*Source:* Trainee. *Honours:* England Schools.

| | | | |
|---|---|---|---|
| 1997–98 | Sheffield W | 0 | 0 |

## HOLMES, Shaun — Defender

b.Derry 27-12-80

*Source:* Trainee.

| | | | |
|---|---|---|---|
| 1997–98 | Manchester C | 0 | 0 |

## HOLMES, Steve — Defender

H: 6 2 W: 13 00 b.Middlesbrough 13-1-71

*Source:* Guisborough T.

| | | | |
|---|---|---|---|
| 1993–94 | Preston NE | 0 | 0 |
| 1994–95 | Preston NE | 5 | 1 |
| 1994–95 | Hartlepool U (loan) | 5 | 2 |
| From Guisborough T. | | | |
| 1995–96 | Preston NE | 8 | 0 |
| 1995–96 | Lincoln C | 23 | 2 |
| 1996–97 | Lincoln C | 28 | 4 |
| 1997–98 | Lincoln C | 46 | 4 |
| **Total:** | | **115** | **13** |

## HOLMES, Tommy — Defender

H: 6 0 W: 12 08 b.Bevington 1-9-79

*Source:* Trainee.

| | | | |
|---|---|---|---|
| 1997–98 | Tranmere R | 0 | 0 |

## HOLSGROVE, Lee — Defender

H: 6 2 W: 12 05 b.Wendover 13-12-79

*Source:* Trainee.

| | | | |
|---|---|---|---|
| 1996–97 | Millwall | 0 | 0 |
| 1997–98 | Millwall | 0 | 0 |
| 1997–98 | Wycombe W | 0 | 0 |

## HOLSGROVE, Paul — Midfield

H: 6 2 W: 13 03 b.Wellington 26-8-69

*Source:* Trainee.

| | | | |
|---|---|---|---|
| 1986–87 | Aldershot | 0 | 0 |
| 1987–88 | Aldershot | 2 | 0 |
| 1988–89 | Aldershot | 1 | 0 |
| 1988–89 | Wimbledon (loan) | 0 | 0 |
| 1989–90 | Aldershot | 0 | 0 |
| 1989–90 | WBA (loan) | 0 | 0 |
| From Wokingham T. | | | |
| 1990–91 | Luton T | 1 | 0 |
| 1991–92 | Luton T | 1 | 0 |
| From Heracles. | | | |
| 1992–93 | Millwall | 11 | 0 |
| 1993–94 | Millwall | 0 | 0 |
| 1994–95 | Reading | 24 | 3 |
| 1995–96 | Reading | 30 | 1 |
| 1996–97 | Reading | 14 | 2 |
| 1997–98 | Reading | 2 | 0 |
| 1997–98 | Grimsby T (loan) | 10 | 0 |
| 1997–98 | Crewe Alex | 8 | 1 |
| 1997–98 | Stoke C | 12 | 1 |
| **Total:** | | **116** | **8** |

## HOLT, Andy — Defender

H: 6 1 W: 12 09 b.Manchester 21-5-78

*Source:* Trainee.

| | | | |
|---|---|---|---|
| 1996–97 | Oldham Ath | 1 | 0 |
| 1997–98 | Oldham Ath | 14 | 1 |
| **Total:** | | **15** | **1** |

## HOLT, Gary — Midfield

H: 6 1 W: 11 11 b.Irvine 9-3-73

*Source:* Celtic.

| | | | |
|---|---|---|---|
| 1994–95 | Stoke C | 0 | 0 |
| 1995–96 | Kilmarnock | 26 | 0 |
| 1996–97 | Kilmarnock | 12 | 1 |
| 1997–98 | Kilmarnock | 27 | 2 |
| **Total:** | | **65** | **3** |

## HOLT, Michael — Forward

H: 5 10 W: 11 03 b.Barnoldswick 28-7-77

*Source:* Trainee.

| | | | |
|---|---|---|---|
| 1995–96 | Blackburn R | 0 | 0 |
| 1996–97 | Preston NE | 19 | 3 |
| 1997–98 | Preston NE | 14 | 2 |
| **Total:** | | **33** | **5** |

## HOLWYN, Jermaine — Defender

H: 6 2 W: 13 01 b.Amsterdam 16-4-73

*Source:* Ajax.

| | | | |
|---|---|---|---|
| 1995–96 | Port Vale | 0 | 0 |
| 1996–97 | Port Vale | 7 | 0 |
| 1997–98 | Port Vale | 0 | 0 |
| **Total:** | | **7** | **0** |

## HONE, Mark — Midfield

H: 6 1 W: 12 00 b.Croydon 31-3-68

*Source:* Trainee.

| | | | |
|---|---|---|---|
| 1985–86 | Crystal Palace | 0 | 0 |
| 1986–87 | Crystal Palace | 0 | 0 |
| 1987–88 | Crystal Palace | 3 | 0 |
| 1988–89 | Crystal Palace | 1 | 0 |
| 1989–90 | Crystal Palace | 0 | 0 |
| From Welling U. | | | |
| 1994–95 | Southend U | 40 | 0 |
| 1995–96 | Southend U | 16 | 0 |
| 1996–97 | Lincoln C | 29 | 0 |
| 1997–98 | Lincoln C | 24 | 2 |
| **Total:** | | **113** | **2** |

## HONEYBALL, Scott — Defender

b.London 9-3-79

| | | | |
|---|---|---|---|
| 1997–98 | Leyton Orient | 0 | 0 |

## HOPE, Chris — Defender

H: 6 1 W: 12 08 b.Sheffield 14-11-73

*Source:* Darlington.

| | | | |
|---|---|---|---|
| 1991–92 | Nottingham F | 0 | 0 |
| 1992–93 | Nottingham F | 0 | 0 |
| 1993–94 | Scunthorpe U | 41 | 0 |
| 1994–95 | Scunthorpe U | 24 | 0 |
| 1995–96 | Scunthorpe U | 40 | 3 |
| 1996–97 | Scunthorpe U | 46 | 3 |
| 1997–98 | Scunthorpe U | 46 | 5 |
| **Total:** | | **197** | **11** |

## HOPE, Richard — Defender

H: 6 2 W: 12 06 b.Stockton 28-8-78

*Source:* Trainee.

| | | | |
|---|---|---|---|
| 1995–96 | Blackburn R | 0 | 0 |
| 1996–97 | Blackburn R | 0 | 0 |
| 1996–97 | Darlington | 20 | 0 |
| 1997–98 | Darlington | 35 | 1 |
| **Total:** | | **55** | **1** |

## HOPKIN, David — Midfield

H: 5 9 W: 10 03 b.Greenock 21-8-70

*Source:* Pt Glasgow R BC. *Honours:* Scotland B, 4 full caps, 2 goals.

| | | | |
|---|---|---|---|
| 1989–90 | Morton | 8 | 0 |
| 1990–91 | Morton | 10 | 0 |
| 1991–92 | Morton | 0 | 0 |
| 1992–93 | Chelsea | 4 | 0 |
| 1993–94 | Chelsea | 21 | 0 |
| 1994–95 | Chelsea | 15 | 1 |
| 1995–96 | Crystal Palace | 42 | 8 |
| 1996–97 | Crystal Palace | 41 | 13 |
| 1997–98 | Leeds U | 25 | 1 |
| **Total:** | | **166** | **23** |

## HOPPER, Tony — Defender

H: 5 10 W: 12 08 b.Carlisle 31-5-76

*Source:* Trainee.

| | | | |
|---|---|---|---|
| 1992–93 | Carlisle U | 1 | 0 |
| 1993–94 | Carlisle U | 0 | 0 |
| 1994–95 | Carlisle U | 5 | 0 |
| 1995–96 | Carlisle U | 5 | 0 |
| 1996–97 | Carlisle U | 20 | 1 |
| 1997–98 | Carlisle U | 19 | 0 |
| **Total:** | | **50** | **1** |

## HORLOCK, Kevin — Midfield

H: 6 0 W: 12 00 b.Erith 1-11-72

*Source:* Trainee. *Honours:* Northern Ireland 12 full caps.

| | | | |
|---|---|---|---|
| 1991–92 | West Ham U | 0 | 0 |
| 1992–93 | West Ham U | 0 | 0 |
| 1992–93 | Swindon T | 14 | 1 |
| 1993–94 | Swindon T | 38 | 0 |
| 1994–95 | Swindon T | 38 | 1 |
| 1995–96 | Swindon T | 45 | 12 |
| 1996–97 | Swindon T | 28 | 8 |
| 1996–97 | Manchester C | 18 | 4 |
| 1997–98 | Manchester C | 25 | 5 |
| **Total:** | | **206** | **31** |

## HORNE, Barry — Midfield

H: 5 8 W: 12 00 b.St Asaph 18-5-62

*Source:* Rhyl. *Honours:* Wales 59 full caps, 2 goals.

| | | | |
|---|---|---|---|
| 1984–85 | Wrexham | 44 | 6 |
| 1985–86 | Wrexham | 46 | 3 |
| 1986–87 | Wrexham | 46 | 8 |
| 1987–88 | Portsmouth | 39 | 3 |
| 1988–89 | Portsmouth | 31 | 4 |
| 1988–89 | Southampton | 11 | 0 |
| 1989–90 | Southampton | 29 | 4 |
| 1990–91 | Southampton | 38 | 1 |
| 1991–92 | Southampton | 34 | 1 |
| 1992–93 | Everton | 34 | 1 |
| 1993–94 | Everton | 32 | 1 |
| 1994–95 | Everton | 31 | 0 |
| 1995–96 | Everton | 26 | 1 |
| 1996–97 | Birmingham C | 33 | 0 |
| 1997–98 | Birmingham C | 0 | 0 |
| 1997–98 | Huddersfield T | 30 | 0 |
| **Total:** | | **504** | **33** |

## HOTTE, Mark — Midfield

H: 5 11 W: 11 01 b.Bradford 27-9-78

*Source:* Trainee.

| | | | |
|---|---|---|---|
| 1997–98 | Oldham Ath | 1 | 0 |
| **Total:** | | **1** | **0** |

## HOUGHTON, Ray — Midfield

H: 5 7 W: 10 10 b.Glasgow 9-1-62

*Source:* Amateur. *Honours:* Eire 73 full caps, 6 goals.

| | | | |
|---|---|---|---|
| 1979–80 | West Ham U | 0 | 0 |
| 1980–81 | West Ham U | 0 | 0 |
| 1981–82 | West Ham U | 1 | 0 |
| 1982–83 | Fulham | 42 | 5 |
| 1983–84 | Fulham | 40 | 3 |
| 1984–85 | Fulham | 42 | 8 |
| 1985–86 | Fulham | 5 | 0 |
| 1985–86 | Oxford U | 35 | 4 |
| 1986–87 | Oxford U | 37 | 5 |
| 1987–88 | Oxford U | 11 | 1 |
| 1987–88 | Liverpool | 28 | 5 |
| 1988–89 | Liverpool | 38 | 7 |
| 1989–90 | Liverpool | 19 | 1 |
| 1990–91 | Liverpool | 32 | 7 |
| 1991–92 | Liverpool | 36 | 8 |
| 1992–93 | Aston Villa | 39 | 3 |
| 1993–94 | Aston Villa | 30 | 2 |
| 1994–95 | Aston Villa | 26 | 1 |
| 1994–95 | Crystal Palace | 10 | 2 |
| 1995–96 | Crystal Palace | 41 | 4 |
| 1996–97 | Crystal Palace | 21 | 1 |
| 1997–98 | Reading | 25 | 1 |
| **Total:** | | **558** | **68** |

## HOUGHTON, Scott — Forward

H: 5 6 W: 12 01 b.Hitchin 22-10-71

*Source:* Trainee. *Honours:* England Schools, Youth.

| | | | |
|---|---|---|---|
| 1990–91 | Tottenham H | 0 | 0 |
| 1990–91 | Ipswich T (loan) | 8 | 1 |
| 1991–92 | Tottenham H | 10 | 2 |
| 1992–93 | Tottenham H | 0 | 0 |
| 1992–93 | Cambridge U (loan) | 0 | 0 |
| 1992–93 | Gillingham (loan) | 3 | 0 |
| 1992–93 | Charlton Ath (loan) | 6 | 0 |
| 1993–94 | Luton T | 15 | 1 |
| 1994–95 | Luton T | 1 | 0 |
| 1994–95 | Walsall | 38 | 8 |
| 1995–96 | Walsall | 40 | 6 |
| 1996–97 | Peterborough U | 32 | 8 |
| 1997–98 | Peterborough U | 30 | 4 |
| **Total:** | | **183** | **30** |

## HOULT, Russell — Goalkeeper

H: 6 4 W: 14 07 b.Ashby 22-11-72

*Source:* Trainee.

| | | | |
|---|---|---|---|
| 1990–91 | Leicester C | 0 | 0 |
| 1991–92 | Leicester C | 0 | 0 |
| 1991–92 | Lincoln C (loan) | 2 | 0 |
| 1991–92 | Blackpool (loan) | 0 | 0 |
| 1992–93 | Leicester C | 10 | 0 |
| 1993–94 | Leicester C | 0 | 0 |
| 1993–94 | Bolton W (loan) | 4 | 0 |
| 1994–95 | Leicester C | 0 | 0 |
| 1994–95 | Lincoln C (loan) | 15 | 0 |
| 1994–95 | Derby Co (loan) | 15 | 0 |
| 1995–96 | Derby Co | 41 | 0 |
| 1996–97 | Derby Co | 32 | 0 |
| 1997–98 | Derby Co | 2 | 0 |
| **Total:** | | **121** | **0** |

## HOUSHAM, Steven — Midfield

H: 5 10 W: 12 03 b.Gainsborough T 24-2-76

*Source:* Trainee.

| | | | |
|---|---|---|---|
| 1993–94 | Scunthorpe U | 0 | 0 |
| 1994–95 | Scunthorpe U | 4 | 0 |
| 1995–96 | Scunthorpe U | 28 | 0 |
| 1996–97 | Scunthorpe U | 34 | 3 |
| 1997–98 | Scunthorpe U | 24 | 1 |
| **Total:** | | **90** | **4** |

## HOWARD, Jonathan — Forward

H: 5 11 W: 11 07 b.Sheffield 7-10-71

*Source:* Trainee.

| | | | |
|---|---|---|---|
| 1990–91 | Rotherham U | 1 | 0 |
| 1991–92 | Rotherham U | 10 | 3 |
| 1992–93 | Rotherham U | 17 | 2 |
| 1993–94 | Rotherham U | 8 | 0 |
| 1994–95 | Rotherham U | 0 | 0 |
| 1994–95 | Chesterfield | 12 | 1 |
| 1995–96 | Chesterfield | 30 | 2 |
| 1996–97 | Chesterfield | 35 | 9 |
| 1997–98 | Chesterfield | 35 | 6 |
| **Total:** | | **148** | **23** |

## HOWARD, Mike — Defender

H: 5 9 W: 11 13 b.Birkenhead 2-12-78

*Source:* Tranmere R Trainee.

| | | | |
|---|---|---|---|
| 1997–98 | Swansea C | 3 | 0 |
| **Total:** | | **3** | **0** |

## HOWARD, Steve — Midfield

H: 6 2 W: 14 12 b.Durham 10-5-76

*Source:* Tow Law T.

| | | | |
|---|---|---|---|
| 1995–96 | Hartlepool U | 39 | 7 |
| 1996–97 | Hartlepool U | 32 | 8 |
| 1997–98 | Hartlepool U | 43 | 7 |
| **Total:** | | **114** | **22** |

## HOWARTH, Lee — Defender

H: 6 3 W: 13 09 b.Bolton 3-1-68

*Source:* Chorley.

| | | | |
|---|---|---|---|
| 1991–92 | Peterborough U | 7 | 0 |
| 1992–93 | Peterborough U | 30 | 0 |
| 1993–94 | Peterborough U | 25 | 0 |
| 1994–95 | Mansfield T | 40 | 2 |
| 1995–96 | Mansfield T | 17 | 0 |
| 1995–96 | Barnet | 19 | 0 |
| 1996–97 | Barnet | 38 | 1 |
| 1997–98 | Barnet | 45 | 4 |
| **Total:** | | **221** | **7** |

## HOWARTH, Neil — Defender

H: 6 3 W: 13 07 b.Bolton 15-11-71

*Source:* Trainee.

| | | | |
|---|---|---|---|
| 1989–90 | Burnley | 1 | 0 |
| From Macclesfield T. | | | |
| 1997–98 | Macclesfield T | 41 | 3 |
| **Total:** | | **42** | **3** |

## HOWARTH, Paul — Defender

H: 5 6 W: 10 01 b.Nottingham 21-11-80

*Source:* Trainee.

| | | | |
|---|---|---|---|
| 1997–98 | Nottingham F | 0 | 0 |

## HOWE, Eddie — Defender

H: 5 9 W: 11 02 b.Amersham 29-11-77

*Source:* Trainee.

| | | | |
|---|---|---|---|
| 1995–96 | Bournemouth | 5 | 0 |
| 1996–97 | Bournemouth | 13 | 0 |
| 1997–98 | Bournemouth | 40 | 1 |
| **Total:** | | **58** | **1** |

## HOWE, Stephen — Midfield

H: 5 7 W: 10 06 b.Annitsford 6-1-73

*Source:* Trainee.

| | | | |
|---|---|---|---|
| 1991–92 | Nottingham F | 0 | 0 |
| 1992–93 | Nottingham F | 0 | 0 |
| 1993–94 | Nottingham F | 4 | 0 |
| 1994–95 | Nottingham F | 0 | 0 |
| 1995–96 | Nottingham F | 9 | 2 |
| 1996–97 | Nottingham F | 1 | 0 |
| 1996–97 | Ipswich T (loan) | 3 | 0 |
| 1997–98 | Nottingham F | 0 | 0 |
| 1997–98 | Swindon T | 10 | 0 |
| **Total:** | | **27** | **2** |

## HOWELLS, David — Midfield

H: 6 0 W: 12 07 b.Guildford 15-12-67

*Source:* Trainee. *Honours:* England Youth.

| | | | |
|---|---|---|---|
| 1984–85 | Tottenham H | 0 | 0 |
| 1985–86 | Tottenham H | 1 | 1 |
| 1986–87 | Tottenham H | 1 | 0 |
| 1987–88 | Tottenham H | 11 | 0 |
| 1988–89 | Tottenham H | 27 | 3 |
| 1989–90 | Tottenham H | 34 | 5 |
| 1990–91 | Tottenham H | 29 | 4 |
| 1991–92 | Tottenham H | 31 | 1 |
| 1992–93 | Tottenham H | 18 | 1 |
| 1993–94 | Tottenham H | 18 | 1 |
| 1994–95 | Tottenham H | 26 | 1 |
| 1995–96 | Tottenham H | 29 | 3 |
| 1996–97 | Tottenham H | 32 | 2 |
| 1997–98 | Tottenham H | 20 | 0 |
| **Total:** | | **277** | **22** |

## HOWES, Shaun — Midfield

H: 5 10 W: 11 07 b.Norwich 7-11-77

*Source:* Trainee.

| | | | |
|---|---|---|---|
| 1995–96 | Cambridge U | 1 | 0 |
| 1996–97 | Cambridge U | 0 | 0 |
| 1996–97 | Leyton Orient | 5 | 0 |
| 1997–98 | Leyton Orient | 0 | 0 |
| **Total:** | | **6** | **0** |

## HOWEY, Lee — Forward

H: 6 3 W: 14 05 b.Sunderland 1-4-69

*Source:* AC Hemptinne Eghezee.

| | | | |
|---|---|---|---|
| 1992–93 | Sunderland | 1 | 0 |
| 1993–94 | Sunderland | 14 | 3 |
| 1994–95 | Sunderland | 15 | 2 |
| 1995–96 | Sunderland | 27 | 3 |
| 1996–97 | Sunderland | 12 | 0 |
| 1997–98 | Burnley | 23 | 0 |
| **Total:** | | **92** | **8** |

## HOWEY, Steve — Defender

H: 6 1 W: 11 12 b.Sunderland 26-10-71

*Source:* Trainee. *Honours:* England 4 full caps.

| | | | |
|---|---|---|---|
| 1988–89 | Newcastle U | 1 | 0 |
| 1989–90 | Newcastle U | 0 | 0 |
| 1990–91 | Newcastle U | 11 | 0 |
| 1991–92 | Newcastle U | 21 | 1 |
| 1992–93 | Newcastle U | 41 | 2 |
| 1993–94 | Newcastle U | 14 | 0 |
| 1994–95 | Newcastle U | 30 | 1 |
| 1995–96 | Newcastle U | 28 | 1 |
| 1996–97 | Newcastle U | 8 | 1 |
| 1997–98 | Newcastle U | 14 | 0 |
| **Total:** | | **168** | **6** |

## HOWIE, Scott — Goalkeeper

H: 6 3 W: 13 07 b.Motherwell 4-1-72

*Source:* Ferguslie U. *Honours:* Scotland Under-21.

| | | | |
|---|---|---|---|
| 1991–92 | Clyde | 15 | 0 |
| 1992–93 | Clyde | 39 | 0 |
| 1993–94 | Clyde | 1 | 0 |
| 1993–94 | Norwich C | 2 | 0 |
| 1994–95 | Motherwell | 3 | 0 |
| 1995–96 | Motherwell | 36 | 0 |
| 1996–97 | Motherwell | 30 | 0 |
| 1997–98 | Motherwell | 0 | 0 |
| 1997–98 | Reading | 7 | 0 |
| **Total:** | | **133** | **0** |

## HOYLAND, Jamie — Defender

H: 6 0 W: 12 08 b.Sheffield 23-1-66

*Source:* Apprentice. *Honours:* England Youth.

| | | | |
|---|---|---|---|
| 1983–84 | Manchester C | 1 | 0 |
| 1984–85 | Manchester C | 1 | 0 |
| 1985–86 | Manchester C | 0 | 0 |
| 1986–87 | Bury | 36 | 2 |
| 1987–88 | Bury | 44 | 8 |
| 1988–89 | Bury | 46 | 9 |
| 1989–90 | Bury | 46 | 16 |
| 1990–91 | Sheffield U | 21 | 0 |
| 1991–92 | Sheffield U | 26 | 4 |
| 1992–93 | Sheffield U | 22 | 2 |
| 1993–94 | Sheffield U | 18 | 0 |
| 1993–94 | Bristol C (loan) | 6 | 0 |
| 1994–95 | Sheffield U | 2 | 0 |
| 1994–95 | Burnley | 30 | 2 |
| 1995–96 | Burnley | 23 | 0 |
| 1996–97 | Burnley | 25 | 1 |
| 1997–98 | Burnley | 9 | 0 |
| 1997–98 | Carlisle U (loan) | 5 | 0 |
| **Total:** | | **361** | **44** |

## HREIDARSSON, Hermann — Defender

H: 6 1 W: 12 12 b.Iceland 11-7-74

*Honours:* Iceland 6 full caps.

| | | | |
|---|---|---|---|
| 1993 | IBV | 2 | 0 |
| 1994 | IBV | 18 | 2 |
| 1995 | IBV | 18 | 1 |
| 1996 | IBV | 17 | 2 |
| 1997 | IBV | 11 | 0 |
| 1997–98 | Crystal Palace | 30 | 2 |
| **Total:** | | **96** | **7** |

## HRISTOV, Georgi — Forward

H: 6 0 W: 12 03 b.Bitola 30-1-76

*Honours:* Macedonia 15 full caps, 4 goals.

| | | | |
|---|---|---|---|
| 1994–95 | Partizan Belgrade | 12 | 3 |
| 1995–96 | Partizan Belgrade | 25 | 9 |
| 1997–98 | Barnsley | 23 | 4 |
| **Total:** | | **60** | **16** |

## HUCKERBY, Darren — Forward

H: 5 11 W: 11 04 b.Nottingham 23-4-76

*Source:* Trainee. *Honours:* England Under-21, B.

| | | | |
|---|---|---|---|
| 1993–94 | Lincoln C | 6 | 1 |
| 1994–95 | Lincoln C | 6 | 2 |
| 1995–96 | Lincoln C | 16 | 2 |
| 1995–96 | Newcastle U | 1 | 0 |
| 1996–97 | Newcastle U | 0 | 0 |
| 1996–97 | Millwall (loan) | 6 | 3 |
| 1996–97 | Coventry C | 25 | 5 |
| 1997–98 | Coventry C | 34 | 14 |
| **Total:** | | **94** | **27** |

## HUDSON, Danny — Midfield

H: 5 8 W: 10 03 b.Mexborough 25-6-79

*Source:* Trainee.

| | | | |
|---|---|---|---|
| 1997–98 | Rotherham U | 10 | 0 |
| **Total:** | | **10** | **0** |

## HUGHES, Aaron — Defender

H: 6 0 W: 11 02 b.Magherafelt 8-11-79

*Source:* Trainee. *Honours:* Northern Ireland 3 full caps.

| | | | |
|---|---|---|---|
| 1996–97 | Newcastle U | 0 | 0 |
| 1997–98 | Newcastle U | 4 | 0 |
| **Total:** | | **4** | **0** |

## HUGHES, Andy — Midfield

H: 6 0 W: 11 00 b.Manchester 2-1-78

*Source:* Trainee.

| | | | |
|---|---|---|---|
| 1995–96 | Oldham Ath | 15 | 1 |
| 1996–97 | Oldham Ath | 8 | 0 |
| 1997–98 | Oldham Ath | 10 | 0 |
| 1997–98 | Notts Co | 15 | 2 |
| **Total:** | | **48** | **3** |

## HUGHES, Bryan — Midfield

H: 5 9 W: 10 00 b.Liverpool 19-6-76

*Source:* Trainee.

| | | | |
|---|---|---|---|
| 1993–94 | Wrexham | 11 | 0 |
| 1994–95 | Wrexham | 38 | 9 |
| 1995–96 | Wrexham | 22 | 0 |
| 1996–97 | Wrexham | 23 | 3 |
| 1996–97 | Birmingham C | 11 | 0 |
| 1997–98 | Birmingham C | 40 | 5 |
| **Total:** | | **145** | **17** |

## HUGHES, Ceri — Midfield

H: 5 10 W: 12 07 b.Pontypridd 26-2-71

*Source:* Trainee. *Honours:* Wales Youth, Under-21, 8 full caps.

| | | | |
|---|---|---|---|
| 1989–90 | Luton T | 1 | 0 |
| 1990–91 | Luton T | 17 | 1 |
| 1991–92 | Luton T | 18 | 0 |
| 1992–93 | Luton T | 29 | 2 |
| 1993–94 | Luton T | 42 | 7 |
| 1994–95 | Luton T | 9 | 2 |
| 1995–96 | Luton T | 23 | 1 |
| 1996–97 | Luton T | 36 | 4 |
| 1997–98 | Wimbledon | 17 | 1 |
| **Total:** | | **192** | **18** |

## HUGHES, Darren — Defender

H: 5 11 W: 13 01 b.Prescot 6-10-65

*Source:* Apprentice.

| | | | |
|---|---|---|---|
| 1983–84 | Everton | 1 | 0 |
| 1984–85 | Everton | 2 | 0 |
| 1985–86 | Shrewsbury T | 31 | 1 |
| 1986–87 | Shrewsbury T | 6 | 0 |
| 1986–87 | Brighton & HA | 26 | 2 |
| 1987–88 | Brighton & HA | 0 | 0 |
| 1987–88 | Port Vale | 43 | 1 |
| 1988–89 | Port Vale | 44 | 0 |
| 1989–90 | Port Vale | 38 | 1 |
| 1990–91 | Port Vale | 17 | 0 |
| 1991–92 | Port Vale | 42 | 2 |
| 1992–93 | Port Vale | 0 | 0 |
| 1993–94 | Port Vale | 0 | 0 |
| 1994–95 | Northampton T | 13 | 0 |
| 1995–96 | Northampton T | 8 | 0 |
| 1995–96 | Exeter C | 26 | 0 |
| 1996–97 | Exeter C | 36 | 1 |
| 1997–98 | Exeter C | 0 | 0 |
| **Total:** | | **333** | **8** |

## HUGHES, David — Midfield

H: 5 10 W: 11 05 b.St Albans 30-12-72

*Source:* Trainee. *Honours:* England Schools.

| | | | |
|---|---|---|---|
| 1991–92 | Southampton | 0 | 0 |
| 1992–93 | Southampton | 0 | 0 |
| 1993–94 | Southampton | 2 | 0 |
| 1994–95 | Southampton | 12 | 2 |
| 1995–96 | Southampton | 11 | 1 |
| 1996–97 | Southampton | 6 | 0 |
| 1997–98 | Southampton | 14 | 0 |
| **Total:** | | **45** | **3** |

## HUGHES, David — Defender

H: 6 4 W: 13 06 b.Wrexham 1-2-78

*Source:* Trainee. *Honours:* Wales Under-21, B.

| | | | |
|---|---|---|---|
| 1996–97 | Aston Villa | 7 | 0 |
| 1997–98 | Aston Villa | 0 | 0 |
| 1997–98 | Carlisle U (loan) | 1 | 0 |
| **Total:** | | **8** | **0** |

## HUGHES, Ian — Defender

H: 5 11 W: 12 00 b.Bangor 2-8-74

*Source:* Trainee. *Honours:* Wales Under-21.

| | | | |
|---|---|---|---|
| 1991–92 | Bury | 17 | 0 |
| 1992–93 | Bury | 15 | 0 |
| 1993–94 | Bury | 38 | 0 |
| 1994–95 | Bury | 23 | 1 |
| 1995–96 | Bury | 32 | 0 |
| 1996–97 | Bury | 22 | 0 |
| 1997–98 | Bury | 13 | 0 |
| 1997–98 | Blackpool | 21 | 0 |
| **Total:** | | **196** | **1** |

## HUGHES, John — Defender

H: 6 0 W: 13 07 b.Edinburgh 9-9-64

*Source:* Newtongrange Star.

| | | | |
|---|---|---|---|
| 1988–89 | Berwick R | 27 | 10 |
| 1989–90 | Berwick R | 14 | 4 |
| 1989–90 | Swansea C | 24 | 4 |
| 1990–91 | Falkirk | 32 | 2 |
| 1991–92 | Falkirk | 38 | 2 |
| 1992–93 | Falkirk | 15 | 0 |

| | | | |
|---|---|---|---|
| 1993–94 | Falkirk | 29 | 3 |
| 1994–95 | Falkirk | 20 | 0 |
| 1995–96 | Celtic | 26 | 2 |
| 1996–97 | Celtic | 6 | 0 |
| 1996–97 | Hibernian | 4 | 0 |
| 1997–98 | Hibernian | 25 | 1 |
| **Total:** | | **260** | **28** |

## HUGHES, Lee — Forward

H: 5 10 W: 11 06 b.Birmingham 22-5-76

*Source:* Kidderminster H.

| | | | |
|---|---|---|---|
| 1997–98 | WBA | 37 | 14 |
| **Total:** | | **37** | **14** |

## HUGHES, Mark — Forward

H: 5 10 W: 13 03 b.Wrexham 1-11-63

*Source:* Apprentice. *Honours:* Wales Youth, Under-21, 66 full caps, 16 goals.

| | | | |
|---|---|---|---|
| 1980–81 | Manchester U | 0 | 0 |
| 1981–82 | Manchester U | 0 | 0 |
| 1982–83 | Manchester U | 0 | 0 |
| 1983–84 | Manchester U | 11 | 4 |
| 1984–85 | Manchester U | 38 | 16 |
| 1985–86 | Manchester U | 40 | 17 |
| 1986–87 | Barcelona | 28 | 4 |
| 1987–88 | Bayern Munich (loan) | 18 | 6 |
| 1988–89 | Manchester U | 38 | 14 |
| 1989–90 | Manchester U | 37 | 13 |
| 1990–91 | Manchester U | 31 | 10 |
| 1991–92 | Manchester U | 39 | 11 |
| 1992–93 | Manchester U | 41 | 15 |
| 1993–94 | Manchester U | 36 | 11 |
| 1994–95 | Manchester U | 34 | 8 |
| 1995–96 | Chelsea | 31 | 8 |
| 1996–97 | Chelsea | 35 | 8 |
| 1997–98 | Chelsea | 29 | 9 |
| **Total:** | | **486** | **154** |

## HUGHES, Michael — Midfield

H: 5 6 W: 10 08 b.Larne 2-8-71

*Source:* Carrick R. *Honours:* Northern Ireland Under-21, 42 full caps, 3 goals.

| | | | |
|---|---|---|---|
| 1988–89 | Manchester C | 1 | 0 |
| 1989–90 | Manchester C | 0 | 0 |
| 1990–91 | Manchester C | 1 | 0 |
| 1991–92 | Manchester C | 24 | 1 |
| 1992–93 | Strasbourg | 36 | 2 |
| 1993–94 | Strasbourg | 34 | 7 |
| 1994–95 | Strasbourg | 13 | 0 |
| 1994–95 | West Ham U (loan) | 17 | 2 |
| 1995–96 | West Ham U (loan) | 28 | 0 |
| 1996–97 | West Ham U | 33 | 3 |
| 1997–98 | West Ham U | 5 | 0 |
| 1997–98 | Wimbledon | 29 | 4 |
| **Total:** | | **221** | **19** |

## HUGHES, Paul — Midfield

H: 6 0 W: 12 06 b.Hammersmith 19-4-76

*Source:* Trainee. *Honours:* England Schools.

| | | | |
|---|---|---|---|
| 1994–95 | Chelsea | 0 | 0 |
| 1995–96 | Chelsea | 0 | 0 |
| 1996–97 | Chelsea | 12 | 2 |
| 1997–98 | Chelsea | 9 | 0 |
| **Total:** | | **21** | **2** |

## HUGHES, Richard — Defender

H: 5 9 W: 9 12 b.Glasgow 25-6-79

*Source:* Atalanta. *Honours:* Scotland Youth.

| | | | |
|---|---|---|---|
| 1997–98 | Arsenal | 0 | 0 |

## HUGHES, Stephen — Midfield

H: 6 0 W: 12 05 b.Wokingham 18-9-76

*Source:* Trainee. *Honours:* England Schools, Youth, Under-21.

| | | | |
|---|---|---|---|
| 1994–95 | Arsenal | 1 | 0 |
| 1995–96 | Arsenal | 1 | 0 |
| 1996–97 | Arsenal | 14 | 1 |
| 1997–98 | Arsenal | 17 | 2 |
| **Total:** | | **33** | **3** |

## HULBERT, Robin — Midfield

b.Plymouth 14-3-80

*Source:* Trainee. *Honours:* England Youth.

| | | | |
|---|---|---|---|
| 1997–98 | Swindon T | 1 | 0 |
| 1997–98 | Newcastle U (loan) | 0 | 0 |
| **Total:** | | **1** | **0** |

## HULSON, Shane — Defender

H: 5 9 W: 11 06 b.Barnsley 17-12-78

*Source:* Trainee.

| | | | |
|---|---|---|---|
| 1997–98 | Barnsley | 0 | 0 |

## HUME, Mark — Defender

H: 6 2 W: 13 04 b.Barnsley 21-5-78

*Source:* Trainee.

| | | | |
|---|---|---|---|
| 1996–97 | Barnsley | 0 | 0 |
| 1997–98 | Barnsley | 0 | 0 |

## HUMES, Tony — Defender

H: 6 0 W: 12 00 b.Blyth 19-3-66

*Source:* Apprentice.

| | | | |
|---|---|---|---|
| 1983–84 | Ipswich T | 0 | 0 |
| 1984–85 | Ipswich T | 0 | 0 |
| 1985–86 | Ipswich T | 0 | 0 |
| 1986–87 | Ipswich T | 22 | 2 |
| 1987–88 | Ipswich T | 27 | 0 |
| 1988–89 | Ipswich T | 26 | 3 |
| 1989–90 | Ipswich T | 24 | 3 |
| 1990–91 | Ipswich T | 16 | 2 |
| 1991–92 | Ipswich T | 5 | 0 |
| 1991–92 | Wrexham | 8 | 0 |
| 1992–93 | Wrexham | 38 | 0 |
| 1993–94 | Wrexham | 27 | 1 |
| 1994–95 | Wrexham | 29 | 0 |
| 1995–96 | Wrexham | 27 | 3 |
| 1996–97 | Wrexham | 34 | 4 |
| 1997–98 | Wrexham | 24 | 0 |
| **Total:** | | **307** | **18** |

## HUMPHREY, John — Defender

H: 5 10 W: 11 11 b.Paddington 31-1-61

*Source:* Apprentice.

| | | | |
|---|---|---|---|
| 1978–79 | Wolverhampton W | 0 | 0 |
| 1979–80 | Wolverhampton W | 2 | 0 |
| 1980–81 | Wolverhampton W | 12 | 0 |
| 1981–82 | Wolverhampton W | 23 | 0 |
| 1982–83 | Wolverhampton W | 42 | 3 |
| 1983–84 | Wolverhampton W | 28 | 0 |
| 1984–85 | Wolverhampton W | 42 | 0 |
| 1985–86 | Charlton Ath | 39 | 2 |
| 1986–87 | Charlton Ath | 39 | 0 |
| 1987–88 | Charlton Ath | 40 | 0 |
| 1988–89 | Charlton Ath | 38 | 1 |
| 1989–90 | Charlton Ath | 38 | 0 |
| 1990–91 | Crystal Palace | 38 | 1 |
| 1991–92 | Crystal Palace | 37 | 0 |
| 1992–93 | Crystal Palace | 32 | 0 |
| 1993–94 | Crystal Palace | 32 | 1 |
| 1993–94 | Reading (loan) | 8 | 0 |
| 1994–95 | Crystal Palace | 21 | 0 |
| 1995–96 | Charlton Ath | 28 | 0 |
| 1996–97 | Gillingham | 9 | 0 |
| 1996–97 | Brighton & HA | 11 | 0 |
| 1997–98 | Brighton & HA | 11 | 0 |
| **Total:** | | **570** | **8** |

## HUMPHREYS, Richie — Forward

H: 5 11 W: 14 07 b.Sheffield 30-11-77

*Source:* Trainee. *Honours:* England Youth, Under-21.

| | | | |
|---|---|---|---|
| 1995–96 | Sheffield W | 5 | 0 |
| 1996–97 | Sheffield W | 29 | 3 |
| 1997–98 | Sheffield W | 7 | 0 |
| **Total:** | | **41** | **3** |

## HUNT, Andy — Forward

H: 6 0 W: 11 02 b.Thurrock 9-6-70

*Source:* Kettering T.

| | | | |
|---|---|---|---|
| 1990–91 | Newcastle U | 16 | 2 |
| 1991–92 | Newcastle U | 27 | 9 |
| 1992–93 | Newcastle U | 0 | 0 |
| 1992–93 | WBA (loan) | 10 | 9 |
| 1993–94 | WBA | 35 | 12 |
| 1994–95 | WBA | 39 | 13 |
| 1995–96 | WBA | 45 | 14 |
| 1996–97 | WBA | 45 | 15 |
| 1997–98 | WBA | 38 | 13 |
| **Total:** | | **255** | **87** |

## HUNT, David — Defender

b.Durham 5-3-80

*Source:* Trainee.

| | | | |
|---|---|---|---|
| 1996–97 | Darlington | 1 | 0 |
| 1997–98 | Darlington | 0 | 0 |
| **Total:** | | **1** | **0** |

## HUNT, James — Midfield

H: 5 8 W: 10 03 b.Derby 17-12-76

*Source:* Trainee.

| | | | |
|---|---|---|---|
| 1994–95 | Notts Co | 0 | 0 |
| 1995–96 | Notts Co | 10 | 1 |
| 1996–97 | Notts Co | 9 | 0 |
| 1997–98 | Northampton T | 21 | 0 |
| **Total:** | | **40** | **1** |

## HUNT, Jonathan — Forward

H: 5 10 W: 11 13 b.London 2-11-71

*Source:* Barnet, Slough T. *Honours:*

| | | | |
|---|---|---|---|
| 1991–92 | Barnet | 14 | 0 |
| 1992–93 | Barnet | 19 | 0 |
| 1993–94 | Southend U | 42 | 6 |
| 1994–95 | Southend U | 7 | 0 |
| 1994–95 | Birmingham C | 20 | 5 |
| 1995–96 | Birmingham C | 45 | 11 |
| 1996–97 | Birmingham C | 12 | 2 |
| 1997–98 | Derby Co | 19 | 1 |
| **Total:** | | **178** | **25** |

## HUNTER, Barry — Defender

H: 6 3 W: 13 02 b.Coleraine 18-11-68

*Source:* Crusaders. *Honours:* Northern Ireland 11 full caps, 1 goal.

| | | | |
|---|---|---|---|
| 1993–94 | Wrexham | 23 | 1 |
| 1994–95 | Wrexham | 37 | 0 |
| 1995–96 | Wrexham | 31 | 3 |
| 1996–97 | Reading | 27 | 2 |
| 1997–98 | Reading | 0 | 0 |
| **Total:** | | **118** | **6** |

## HUNTER, Roy — Midfield

H: 5 10 W: 12 08 b.Middlesbrough 29-10-73

*Source:* Trainee.

| | | | |
|---|---|---|---|
| 1991–92 | WBA | 6 | 1 |
| 1992–93 | WBA | 1 | 0 |
| 1993–94 | WBA | 2 | 0 |
| 1994–95 | WBA | 0 | 0 |
| 1995–96 | Northampton T | 34 | 0 |
| 1996–97 | Northampton T | 36 | 6 |
| 1997–98 | Northampton T | 28 | 3 |
| **Total:** | | **107** | **10** |

## HURDLE, Gus — Defender

H: 6 0 W: 11 04 b.London 14-10-73

*Source:* Fulham.

| | | | |
|---|---|---|---|
| 1994–95 | Brentford | 9 | 0 |
| 1995–96 | Brentford | 14 | 0 |
| 1996–97 | Brentford | 31 | 0 |
| 1997–98 | Brentford | 17 | 0 |
| **Total:** | | **71** | **0** |

## HURST, Chris — Midfield

H: 5 11 W: 11 06 b.Barnsley 3-10-73

*Source:* Emley.

| | | | |
|---|---|---|---|
| 1997–98 | Huddersfield T | 3 | 0 |
| **Total:** | | **3** | **0** |

## HURST, Paul — Defender

H: 5 4 W: 9 0 b.Sheffield 25-9-74

*Source:* Trainee.

| | | | |
|---|---|---|---|
| 1993–94 | Rotherham U | 4 | 0 |
| 1994–95 | Rotherham U | 13 | 0 |
| 1995–96 | Rotherham U | 40 | 1 |
| 1996–97 | Rotherham U | 30 | 3 |
| 1997–98 | Rotherham U | 30 | 0 |
| **Total:** | | **117** | **4** |

## HURST, Richard — Goalkeeper

H: 6 0 W: 13 01 b.Hammersmith 23-12-76

*Source:* Trainee.

| | | | |
|---|---|---|---|
| 1994–95 | QPR | 0 | 0 |
| 1995–96 | QPR | 0 | 0 |
| 1996–97 | QPR | 0 | 0 |
| 1997–98 | QPR | 0 | 0 |

## HUTCHINGS, Carl — Midfield

H: 5 11 W: 11 00 b.London 24-9-74

*Source:* Trainee.

| | | | |
|---|---|---|---|
| 1993–94 | Brentford | 29 | 0 |
| 1994–95 | Brentford | 39 | 0 |
| 1995–96 | Brentford | 23 | 0 |
| 1996–97 | Brentford | 28 | 2 |
| 1997–98 | Brentford | 43 | 5 |
| **Total:** | | **162** | **7** |

## HUTCHINSON, Sean — Midfield

b.Bradford 14-4-79

*Source:* Trainee.

| | | | |
|---|---|---|---|
| 1997–98 | Sheffield W | 0 | 0 |

## HUTCHISON, Don — Midfield

H: 6 1 W: 11 11 b.Gateshead 9-5-71

*Source:* Trainee.

| | | | |
|---|---|---|---|
| 1989–90 | Hartlepool U | 13 | 2 |
| 1990–91 | Hartlepool U | 11 | 0 |
| 1990–91 | Liverpool | 0 | 0 |
| 1991–92 | Liverpool | 3 | 0 |
| 1992–93 | Liverpool | 31 | 7 |
| 1993–94 | Liverpool | 11 | 0 |
| 1994–95 | West Ham U | 23 | 9 |
| 1995–96 | West Ham U | 12 | 2 |
| 1995–96 | Sheffield U | 19 | 2 |
| 1996–97 | Sheffield U | 41 | 3 |
| 1997–98 | Sheffield U | 18 | 0 |
| 1997–98 | Everton | 11 | 1 |
| **Total:** | | **193** | **26** |

## HUTT, Stephen — Midfield

H: 6 2 W: 11 07 b.Middlesbrough 19-2-79

*Source:* Trainee.

| | | | |
|---|---|---|---|
| 1995–96 | Hartlepool U | 1 | 0 |
| 1996–97 | Hartlepool U | 0 | 0 |
| 1997–98 | Hartlepool U | 4 | 0 |
| **Total:** | | **5** | **0** |

## HUXFORD, Richard — Defender

H: 5 10 W: 11 06 b.Scunthorpe 25-7-69

*Source:* Kettering T.

| | | | |
|---|---|---|---|
| 1992–93 | Barnet | 33 | 1 |
| 1993–94 | Millwall | 31 | 0 |
| 1993–94 | Birmingham C (loan) | 5 | 0 |
| 1994–95 | Millwall | 1 | 0 |
| 1994–95 | Bradford C | 33 | 1 |
| 1995–96 | Bradford C | 26 | 1 |
| 1996–97 | Bradford C | 2 | 0 |
| 1996–97 | Peterborough U (loan) | 7 | 0 |
| 1996–97 | Burnley | 9 | 0 |
| 1997–98 | Burnley | 4 | 0 |
| 1997–98 | Dunfermline Ath (loan) | 10 | 0 |
| **Total:** | | **161** | **3** |

## HYDE, Graham — Midfield

H: 5 8 W: 12 04 b.Doncaster 10-11-70

*Source:* Trainee.

| | | | |
|---|---|---|---|
| 1988–89 | Sheffield W | 0 | 0 |
| 1989–90 | Sheffield W | 0 | 0 |
| 1990–91 | Sheffield W | 0 | 0 |
| 1991–92 | Sheffield W | 13 | 0 |
| 1992–93 | Sheffield W | 20 | 1 |
| 1993–94 | Sheffield W | 36 | 1 |
| 1994–95 | Sheffield W | 35 | 5 |
| 1995–96 | Sheffield W | 26 | 1 |
| 1996–97 | Sheffield W | 19 | 2 |
| 1997–98 | Sheffield W | 22 | 1 |
| **Total:** | | **171** | **11** |

## HYDE, Micah — Midfield

H: 5 9 W: 11 07 b.Newham 10-11-74

*Source:* Trainee.

| | | | |
|---|---|---|---|
| 1993–94 | Cambridge U | 18 | 2 |
| 1994–95 | Cambridge U | 27 | 0 |
| 1995–96 | Cambridge U | 24 | 4 |
| 1996–97 | Cambridge U | 38 | 7 |
| 1997–98 | Watford | 40 | 4 |
| **Total:** | | **147** | **17** |

## HYDE, Paul — Goalkeeper

H: 6 1 W: 14 09 b.Hayes 7-4-63

*Source:* Hayes.

| | | | |
|---|---|---|---|
| 1993–94 | Wycombe W | 42 | 0 |
| 1994–95 | Wycombe W | 46 | 0 |
| 1995–96 | Wycombe W | 17 | 0 |
| 1995–96 | Leicester C | 0 | 0 |
| 1996–97 | Leicester C | 0 | 0 |
| 1996–97 | Leyton Orient | 13 | 0 |
| 1997–98 | Leyton Orient | 28 | 0 |
| **Total:** | | **146** | **0** |

## IGA, Andrew — Goalkeeper

b.Kampala 9-12-77

*Source:* Trainee.

| | | | |
|---|---|---|---|
| 1995–96 | Millwall | 0 | 0 |
| 1996–97 | Millwall | 1 | 0 |
| 1996–97 | Gillingham | 0 | 0 |
| 1997–98 | Watford | 0 | 0 |
| **Total:** | | **1** | **0** |

## IGOE, Sammy — Midfield

H: 5 6 W: 9 07 b.Spelthorne 30-9-75

*Source:* Trainee.

| | | | |
|---|---|---|---|
| 1993–94 | Portsmouth | 0 | 0 |
| 1994–95 | Portsmouth | 1 | 0 |
| 1995–96 | Portsmouth | 22 | 0 |
| 1996–97 | Portsmouth | 40 | 2 |
| 1997–98 | Portsmouth | 31 | 3 |
| **Total:** | | **94** | **5** |

## ILIC, Sasa — Goalkeeper

H: 6 4 W: 14 00 b.Melbourne 18-7-72

*Source:* Daewoo Royals, St Leonards Stamcroft. *Honours:* Macedonia 2 full caps.

| | | | |
|---|---|---|---|
| 1997–98 | Charlton Ath | 14 | 0 |
| **Total:** | | **14** | **0** |

## ILLINGWORTH, Jeremy — Midfield

H: 5 10 W: 12 01 b.Huddersfield 20-5-77

*Source:* Trainee.

| | | | |
|---|---|---|---|
| 1995–96 | Huddersfield T | 0 | 0 |
| 1996–97 | Huddersfield T | 3 | 0 |
| 1997–98 | Huddersfield T | 0 | 0 |
| **Total:** | | **3** | **0** |

## ILLMAN, Neil — Forward

H: 5 7 W: 10 07 b.Doncaster 29-9-75

*Source:* Trainee.

| | | | |
|---|---|---|---|
| 1992–93 | Middlesbrough | 0 | 0 |
| 1993–94 | Middlesbrough | 1 | 0 |
| From Eastwood T. | | | |
| 1995–96 | Plymouth Arg | 0 | 0 |
| 1995–96 | Cambridge U (loan) | 5 | 0 |

| | | | |
|---|---|---|---|
| 1996–97 | Plymouth Arg | 25 | 4 |
| 1997–98 | Plymouth Arg | 6 | 0 |
| 1997–98 | Exeter C | 8 | 2 |
| **Total:** | | **45** | **6** |

## IMPEY, Andrew — Defender

H: 5 8 W: 11 02 b.Hammersmith 13-9-71

*Source:* Yeading. *Honours:* England Under-21.

| | | | |
|---|---|---|---|
| 1990–91 | QPR | 0 | 0 |
| 1991–92 | QPR | 13 | 0 |
| 1992–93 | QPR | 40 | 2 |
| 1993–94 | QPR | 33 | 3 |
| 1994–95 | QPR | 40 | 3 |
| 1995–96 | QPR | 29 | 3 |
| 1996–97 | QPR | 32 | 2 |
| 1997–98 | West Ham U | 19 | 0 |
| **Total:** | | **206** | **13** |

## INCE, Paul — Midfield

H: 5 10 W: 12 02 b.Ilford 21-10-67

*Source:* Trainee. *Honours:* England Youth, Under-21, B, 43 full caps, 2 goals.

| | | | |
|---|---|---|---|
| 1985–86 | West Ham U | 0 | 0 |
| 1986–87 | West Ham U | 10 | 1 |
| 1987–88 | West Ham U | 28 | 3 |
| 1988–89 | West Ham U | 33 | 3 |
| 1989–90 | West Ham U | 1 | 0 |
| 1989–90 | Manchester U | 26 | 0 |
| 1990–91 | Manchester U | 31 | 3 |
| 1991–92 | Manchester U | 33 | 3 |
| 1992–93 | Manchester U | 41 | 5 |
| 1993–94 | Manchester U | 39 | 8 |
| 1994–95 | Manchester U | 36 | 5 |
| 1995–96 | Internazionale | 30 | 3 |
| 1996–97 | Internazionale | 24 | 6 |
| 1997–98 | Liverpool | 31 | 8 |
| **Total:** | | **363** | **48** |

## INGHAM, Andrew — Midfield

b.Leeds 21-8-81

*Source:* Trainee.

| | | | |
|---|---|---|---|
| 1997–98 | Cambridge U | 0 | 0 |

## INGHAM, Gary — Goalkeeper

H: 6 1 W: 12 10 b.Rotherham 9-10-64

*Source:* Rotherham U.

| | | | |
|---|---|---|---|
| 1993–94 | Doncaster R | 1 | 0 |
| From Gainsborough T. | | | |
| 1997–98 | Doncaster R | 10 | 0 |
| **Total:** | | **11** | **0** |

## INGLETHORPE, Alex — Forward

H: 5 11 W: 11 04 b.Epsom 14-11-71

*Source:* School.

| | | | |
|---|---|---|---|
| 1990–91 | Watford | 1 | 0 |
| 1991–92 | Watford | 2 | 0 |
| 1992–93 | Watford | 0 | 0 |
| 1993–94 | Watford | 9 | 2 |
| 1994–95 | Watford | 0 | 0 |
| 1994–95 | Barnet (loan) | 6 | 3 |
| 1994–95 | Leyton Orient | 0 | 0 |
| 1995–96 | Leyton Orient | 30 | 9 |
| 1996–97 | Leyton Orient | 16 | 8 |
| 1997–98 | Leyton Orient | 38 | 9 |
| **Total:** | | **102** | **31** |

## INGLIS, John — Defender

H: 6 0 W: 13 00 b.Edinburgh 16-10-66

*Source:* Hutchison Vale.

| | | | |
|---|---|---|---|
| 1983–84 | East Fife | 4 | 1 |
| 1984–85 | East Fife | 9 | 0 |
| 1985–86 | East Fife | 30 | 0 |
| 1986–87 | East Fife | 13 | 0 |
| 1986–87 | Brechin C | 15 | 0 |
| 1987–88 | Brechin C | 26 | 3 |
| 1988–89 | Brechin C | 12 | 1 |
| 1988–89 | Meadowbank T | 12 | 1 |
| 1989–90 | Meadowbank T | 38 | 3 |
| 1990–91 | St Johnstone | 31 | 1 |
| 1991–92 | St Johnstone | 40 | 0 |
| 1992–93 | St Johnstone | 39 | 0 |
| 1993–94 | St Johnstone | 25 | 1 |
| 1994–95 | St Johnstone | 5 | 0 |
| 1994–95 | Aberdeen | 17 | 1 |
| 1995–96 | Aberdeen | 24 | 1 |
| 1996–97 | Aberdeen | 15 | 0 |
| 1997–98 | Aberdeen | 25 | 1 |
| **Total:** | | **380** | **14** |

## INGRAM, Denny — Defender

H: 5 11 W: 12 01 b.Sunderland 27-6-76

*Source:* Trainee.

| | | | |
|---|---|---|---|
| 1993–94 | Hartlepool U | 13 | 0 |
| 1994–95 | Hartlepool U | 35 | 0 |
| 1995–96 | Hartlepool U | 33 | 2 |
| 1996–97 | Hartlepool U | 37 | 1 |
| 1997–98 | Hartlepool U | 36 | 3 |
| **Total:** | | **154** | **6** |

## INGRAM, Rae — Defender

H: 5 11 W: 12 02 b.Manchester 6-12-74

*Source:* Trainee.

| | | | |
|---|---|---|---|
| 1993–94 | Manchester C | 0 | 0 |
| 1994–95 | Manchester C | 0 | 0 |
| 1995–96 | Manchester C | 5 | 0 |
| 1996–97 | Manchester C | 18 | 0 |
| 1997–98 | Manchester C | 0 | 0 |
| 1997–98 | Macclesfield T (loan) | 5 | 0 |
| **Total:** | | **28** | **0** |

## INMAN, Niall — Midfield

H: 5 9 W: 11 06 b.Wakefield 6-2-78

*Source:* Trainee. *Honours:* Eire Youth.

| | | | |
|---|---|---|---|
| 1995–96 | Peterborough U | 1 | 0 |
| 1996–97 | Peterborough U | 3 | 0 |
| 1997–98 | Peterborough U | 4 | 1 |
| **Total:** | | **8** | **1** |

## INNES, Mark — Defender

H: 5 10 W: 12 01 b.Bellshill 27-9-78

*Source:* Trainee.

| | | | |
|---|---|---|---|
| 1995–96 | Oldham Ath | 0 | 0 |
| 1996–97 | Oldham Ath | 0 | 0 |
| 1997–98 | Oldham Ath | 4 | 0 |
| **Total:** | | **4** | **0** |

## IRELAND, Craig — Defender

H: 6 3 W: 13 09 b.Dundee 29-11-75

*Source:* Aberdeen Lads.

| | | | |
|---|---|---|---|
| 1994–95 | Aberdeen | 0 | 0 |
| 1995–96 | Aberdeen | 0 | 0 |
| 1995–96 | Dunfermline Ath | 10 | 0 |
| 1996–97 | Dunfermline Ath | 9 | 1 |
| 1997–98 | Dunfermline Ath | 12 | 1 |
| **Total:** | | **31** | **2** |

## IRELAND, Simon — Midfield

H: 5 10 W: 11 10 b.Halifax 23-11-71

*Source:* School. *Honours:* England Schools.

| | | | |
|---|---|---|---|
| 1990–91 | Huddersfield T | 6 | 0 |
| 1991–92 | Huddersfield T | 9 | 0 |
| 1991–92 | Wrexham (loan) | 5 | 0 |
| 1992–93 | Huddersfield T | 4 | 0 |
| 1992–93 | Blackburn R | 1 | 0 |
| 1993–94 | Blackburn R | 0 | 0 |
| 1993–94 | Mansfield T (loan) | 9 | 1 |
| 1994–95 | Mansfield T | 40 | 5 |
| 1995–96 | Mansfield T | 39 | 5 |
| 1996–97 | Mansfield T | 6 | 0 |
| 1996–97 | Doncaster R | 27 | 2 |
| 1997–98 | Doncaster R | 34 | 0 |
| **Total:** | | **180** | **13** |

## IRONS, Kenny — Midfield

H: 5 10 W: 11 02 b.Liverpool 4-11-70

*Source:* Trainee.

| | | | |
|---|---|---|---|
| 1989–90 | Tranmere R | 3 | 0 |
| 1990–91 | Tranmere R | 32 | 6 |
| 1991–92 | Tranmere R | 43 | 7 |
| 1992–93 | Tranmere R | 42 | 7 |
| 1993–94 | Tranmere R | 34 | 3 |
| 1994–95 | Tranmere R | 38 | 4 |
| 1995–96 | Tranmere R | 32 | 3 |
| 1996–97 | Tranmere R | 41 | 5 |
| 1997–98 | Tranmere R | 43 | 4 |
| **Total:** | | **308** | **39** |

## IRONSIDE, Ian — Goalkeeper

H: 6 2 W: 12 10 b.Sheffield 8-3-64

*Source:* Barnsley Apprentice, N Ferriby U.

| | | | |
|---|---|---|---|
| 1987–88 | Scarborough | 6 | 0 |
| 1988–89 | Scarborough | 28 | 0 |
| 1989–90 | Scarborough | 14 | 0 |
| 1990–91 | Scarborough | 40 | 0 |
| 1991–92 | Middlesbrough | 1 | 0 |
| 1991–92 | Scarborough (loan) | 7 | 0 |
| 1992–93 | Middlesbrough | 12 | 0 |
| 1993–94 | Middlesbrough | 0 | 0 |
| 1993–94 | Stockport Co | 11 | 0 |
| 1994–95 | Stockport Co | 8 | 0 |
| 1994–95 | Scarborough | 9 | 0 |
| 1995–96 | Scarborough | 40 | 0 |
| 1996–97 | Scarborough | 39 | 0 |
| 1997–98 | Oldham Ath | 0 | 0 |
| **Total:** | | **215** | **0** |

## IRVINE, Brian — Defender

H: 6 2 W: 13 00 b.Bellshill 24-5-65

*Source:* Victoria Park. *Honours:* Scotland 9 full caps.

| | | | |
|---|---|---|---|
| 1983–84 | Falkirk | 3 | 0 |
| 1984–85 | Falkirk | 35 | 0 |
| 1985–86 | Aberdeen | 1 | 0 |
| 1986–87 | Aberdeen | 20 | 1 |
| 1987–88 | Aberdeen | 16 | 1 |
| 1988–89 | Aberdeen | 27 | 2 |
| 1989–90 | Aberdeen | 31 | 1 |
| 1990–91 | Aberdeen | 29 | 2 |
| 1991–92 | Aberdeen | 41 | 4 |
| 1992–93 | Aberdeen | 39 | 5 |

| | | | |
|---|---|---|---|
| 1993–94 | Aberdeen | 42 | 7 |
| 1994–95 | Aberdeen | 17 | 1 |
| 1995–96 | Aberdeen | 18 | 3 |
| 1996–97 | Aberdeen | 25 | 1 |
| 1997–98 | Dundee | 36 | 1 |
| **Total:** | | **380** | **29** |

## IRVINE, Stuart — Forward

H: 5 9 W: 11 06 b.Hartlepool 1-3-79

*Source:* Trainee.

| | | | |
|---|---|---|---|
| 1996–97 | Hartlepool U | 4 | 1 |
| 1997–98 | Hartlepool U | 9 | 0 |
| **Total:** | | **13** | **1** |

## IRVING, Richard — Forward

H: 5 7 W: 12 02 b.Halifax 10-9-75

*Source:* Trainee. *Honours:* England Schools, Youth.

| | | | |
|---|---|---|---|
| 1992–93 | Manchester U | 0 | 0 |
| 1993–94 | Manchester U | 0 | 0 |
| 1994–95 | Manchester U | 0 | 0 |
| 1995–96 | Nottingham F | 1 | 0 |
| 1996–97 | Nottingham F | 0 | 0 |
| 1997–98 | Macclesfield T | 9 | 0 |
| **Total:** | | **10** | **0** |

## IRWIN, Denis — Defender

H: 5 8 W: 10 10 b.Cork 31-10-65

*Source:* Apprentice. *Honours:* Eire Schools, Youth, Under-21, B, 48 full caps, 2 goals.

| | | | |
|---|---|---|---|
| 1983–84 | Leeds U | 12 | 0 |
| 1984–85 | Leeds U | 41 | 1 |
| 1985–86 | Leeds U | 19 | 0 |
| 1986–87 | Oldham Ath | 41 | 1 |
| 1987–88 | Oldham Ath | 43 | 0 |
| 1988–89 | Oldham Ath | 41 | 2 |
| 1989–90 | Oldham Ath | 42 | 1 |
| 1990–91 | Manchester U | 34 | 0 |
| 1991–92 | Manchester U | 38 | 4 |
| 1992–93 | Manchester U | 40 | 5 |
| 1993–94 | Manchester U | 42 | 2 |
| 1994–95 | Manchester U | 40 | 2 |
| 1995–96 | Manchester U | 31 | 1 |
| 1996–97 | Manchester U | 31 | 1 |
| 1997–98 | Manchester U | 25 | 2 |
| **Total:** | | **520** | **22** |

## IRWIN, Nick — Defender

H: 5 10 W: 12 00 b.Salford 25-12-78

| | | | |
|---|---|---|---|
| 1997–98 | Rochdale | 0 | 0 |

## ISMAEL, Valerien — Defender

H: 6 2 W: 13 01 b.Strasbourg 28-9-75

| | | | |
|---|---|---|---|
| 1993–94 | Strasbourg | 4 | 0 |
| 1994–95 | Strasbourg | 13 | 0 |
| 1995–96 | Strasbourg | 19 | 0 |
| 1996–97 | Strasbourg | 31 | 1 |
| 1997–98 | Strasbourg | 18 | 0 |
| 1997–98 | Crystal Palace | 13 | 0 |
| **Total:** | | **98** | **1** |

## IVERSEN, Steffen — Forward

H: 6 1 W: 11 08 b.Oslo 10-11-76

| | | | |
|---|---|---|---|
| 1996 | Rosenborg | 25 | 10 |
| 1996–97 | Tottenham H | 16 | 6 |
| 1997–98 | Tottenham H | 13 | 0 |
| **Total:** | | **54** | **16** |

## IZZET, Muzzy — Midfield

H: 5 10 W: 10 12 b.Mile End 31-10-74

*Source:* Trainee.

| | | | |
|---|---|---|---|
| 1993–94 | Chelsea | 0 | 0 |
| 1994–95 | Chelsea | 0 | 0 |
| 1995–96 | Chelsea | 0 | 0 |
| 1995–96 | Leicester C (loan) | 9 | 1 |
| 1996–97 | Leicester C | 35 | 3 |
| 1997–98 | Leicester C | 36 | 4 |
| **Total:** | | **80** | **8** |

## JAASKELAINEN, Jussi — Goalkeeper

H: 6 4 W: 12 10 b.Vaasa 17-4-75

| | | | |
|---|---|---|---|
| 1992 | MP | 6 | 0 |
| 1993 | MP | 6 | 0 |
| 1994 | MP | 26 | 0 |
| 1995 | MP | 26 | 0 |
| 1996 | VPS | 27 | 0 |
| 1997 | VPS | 27 | 0 |
| 1997–98 | Bolton W | 0 | 0 |
| **Total:** | | **118** | **0** |

## JABLONSKI, Mark — Defender

b.Oldham 9-1-79

*Source:* Trainee.

| | | | |
|---|---|---|---|
| 1997–98 | Oldham Ath | 0 | 0 |

## JACK, Rodney — Forward

H: 5 7 W: 10 09 b.Kingston, Jamaica 28-9-72

*Source:* Lambada. *Honours:* St Vincent full caps.

| | | | |
|---|---|---|---|
| 1995–96 | Torquay U | 14 | 2 |

| | | | |
|---|---|---|---|
| 1996–97 | Torquay U | 33 | 10 |
| 1997–98 | Torquay U | 40 | 12 |
| **Total:** | | **87** | **24** |

## JACKSON, Chris — Forward

H: 5 9 W: 11 06 b.Barnsley 16-1-76

*Source:* Trainee. *Honours:* England Schools, Youth.

| | | | |
|---|---|---|---|
| 1992–93 | Barnsley | 3 | 0 |
| 1993–94 | Barnsley | 4 | 1 |
| 1994–95 | Barnsley | 8 | 1 |
| 1995–96 | Barnsley | 8 | 0 |
| 1996–97 | Barnsley | 0 | 0 |
| 1997–98 | Barnsley | 0 | 0 |
| **Total:** | | **23** | **2** |

## JACKSON, Christopher — Midfield

H: 5 7 W: 10 11 b.Edinburgh 29-10-73

*Source:* Salvesen BC.

| | | | |
|---|---|---|---|
| 1992–93 | Hibernian | 1 | 0 |
| 1993–94 | Hibernian | 11 | 0 |
| 1994–95 | Hibernian | 0 | 0 |
| 1995–96 | Hibernian | 23 | 2 |
| 1996–97 | Hibernian | 19 | 0 |
| 1997–98 | Hibernian | 15 | 0 |
| **Total:** | | **69** | **2** |

## JACKSON, Darren — Forward

H: 5 10 W: 10 10 b.Edinburgh 25-7-66

*Source:* Broxburn Am. *Honours:* Scotland 26 full caps, 4 goals.

| | | | |
|---|---|---|---|
| 1985–86 | Meadowbank T | 39 | 17 |
| 1986–87 | Meadowbank T | 9 | 5 |
| 1986–87 | Newcastle U | 23 | 3 |
| 1987–88 | Newcastle U | 31 | 2 |
| 1988–89 | Newcastle U | 15 | 2 |
| 1988–89 | Dundee U | 1 | 0 |
| 1989–90 | Dundee U | 25 | 7 |
| 1990–91 | Dundee U | 33 | 12 |
| 1991–92 | Dundee U | 28 | 11 |
| 1992–93 | Hibernian | 36 | 13 |
| 1993–94 | Hibernian | 40 | 7 |
| 1994–95 | Hibernian | 31 | 10 |
| 1995–96 | Hibernian | 36 | 9 |
| 1996–97 | Hibernian | 30 | 11 |
| 1997–98 | Celtic | 23 | 3 |
| **Total:** | | **400** | **112** |

## JACKSON, Elliott — Goalkeeper

H: 6 2 W: 15 02 b.Swindon 27-8-77

*Source:* Trainee.

| | | | |
|---|---|---|---|
| 1996–97 | Oxford U | 3 | 0 |
| 1997–98 | Oxford U | 3 | 0 |
| **Total:** | | **6** | **0** |

## JACKSON, Justin — Forward

H: 5 11 W: 11 02 b.Nottingham 10-12-74

*Source:* Woking.

| | | | |
|---|---|---|---|
| 1997–98 | Notts Co | 15 | 1 |
| **Total:** | | **15** | **1** |

## JACKSON, Kirk — Forward

H: 5 10 W: 11 07 b.Barnsley 16-10-76

*Source:* Trainee.

| | | | |
|---|---|---|---|
| 1994–95 | Sheffield W | 0 | 0 |
| 1995–96 | Sheffield W | 0 | 0 |
| 1996–97 | Scunthorpe U | 4 | 1 |
| 1997–98 | Chesterfield | 3 | 0 |
| **Total:** | | **7** | **1** |

## JACKSON, Mark — Defender

H: 5 11 W: 12 00 b.Barnsley 30-9-77

*Source:* Trainee. *Honours:* England Youth.

| | | | |
|---|---|---|---|
| 1995–96 | Leeds U | 1 | 0 |
| 1996–97 | Leeds U | 17 | 0 |
| 1997–98 | Leeds U | 1 | 0 |
| **Total:** | | **19** | **0** |

## JACKSON, Matt — Defender

H: 6 1 W: 12 07 b.Leeds 19-10-71

*Source:* School. *Honours:* England Schools, Under-21.

| | | | |
|---|---|---|---|
| 1990–91 | Luton T | 0 | 0 |
| 1990–91 | Preston NE (loan) | 4 | 0 |
| 1991–92 | Luton T | 9 | 0 |
| 1991–92 | Everton | 30 | 1 |
| 1992–93 | Everton | 27 | 3 |
| 1993–94 | Everton | 38 | 0 |
| 1994–95 | Everton | 29 | 0 |
| 1995–96 | Everton | 14 | 0 |
| 1995–96 | Charlton Ath (loan) | 8 | 0 |
| 1996–97 | Everton | 0 | 0 |
| 1996–97 | QPR (loan) | 7 | 0 |
| 1996–97 | Birmingham C (loan) | 10 | 0 |
| 1996–97 | Norwich C | 19 | 2 |
| 1997–98 | Norwich C | 41 | 3 |
| **Total:** | | **236** | **9** |

## JACKSON, Michael — Defender

H: 5 11 W: 11 09 b.Chester 4-12-73

*Source:* Trainee.

| | | | |
|---|---|---|---|
| 1991–92 | Crewe Alex | 1 | 0 |
| 1992–93 | Crewe Alex | 4 | 0 |
| 1993–94 | Bury | 39 | 0 |
| 1994–95 | Bury | 24 | 2 |
| 1995–96 | Bury | 31 | 4 |
| 1996–97 | Bury | 31 | 3 |
| 1996–97 | Preston NE | 7 | 0 |
| 1997–98 | Preston NE | 40 | 2 |
| **Total:** | | **177** | **11** |

## JACKSON, Richard — Defender

H: 5 8 W: 10 12 b.Whitby 18-4-80

*Source:* Trainee.

| | | | |
|---|---|---|---|
| 1997–98 | Scarborough | 2 | 0 |
| **Total:** | | **2** | **0** |

## JACOBS, Wayne — Defender

H: 5 8 W: 11 02 b.Sheffield 3-2-69

*Source:* Apprentice.

| | | | |
|---|---|---|---|
| 1986–87 | Sheffield W | 0 | 0 |
| 1987–88 | Sheffield W | 6 | 0 |
| 1987–88 | Hull C | 6 | 0 |
| 1988–89 | Hull C | 33 | 0 |
| 1989–90 | Hull C | 46 | 3 |
| 1990–91 | Hull C | 19 | 1 |
| 1991–92 | Hull C | 25 | 0 |
| 1992–93 | Hull C | 0 | 0 |
| 1993–94 | Rotherham U | 42 | 2 |
| 1994–95 | Bradford C | 38 | 1 |
| 1995–96 | Bradford C | 28 | 0 |
| 1996–97 | Bradford C | 39 | 3 |
| 1997–98 | Bradford C | 36 | 2 |
| **Total:** | | **318** | **12** |

## JAFFA, Graeme — Forward

H: 5 6 W: 9 08 b.Falkirk 8-5-79

*Source:* Trainee.

| | | | |
|---|---|---|---|
| 1997–98 | Leicester C | 0 | 0 |

## JAGIELKA, Steve — Forward

H: 5 8 W: 11 03 b.Manchester 10-3-78

*Source:* Trainee.

| | | | |
|---|---|---|---|
| 1996–97 | Stoke C | 0 | 0 |
| 1997–98 | Shrewsbury T | 16 | 1 |
| **Total:** | | **16** | **1** |

## JAMES, Anthony — Midfield

b.Pontypool 9-10-78

| | | | |
|---|---|---|---|
| 1997–98 | WBA | 0 | 0 |

## JAMES, David — Goalkeeper

H: 6 5 W: 14 02 b.Welwyn 1-8-70

*Source:* Trainee. *Honours:* England Youth, Under-21, B, 1 full cap.

| | | | |
|---|---|---|---|
| 1988–89 | Watford | 0 | 0 |
| 1989–90 | Watford | 0 | 0 |
| 1990–91 | Watford | 46 | 0 |
| 1991–92 | Watford | 43 | 0 |
| 1992–93 | Liverpool | 29 | 0 |
| 1993–94 | Liverpool | 14 | 0 |
| 1994–95 | Liverpool | 42 | 0 |
| 1995–96 | Liverpool | 38 | 0 |
| 1996–97 | Liverpool | 38 | 0 |
| 1997–98 | Liverpool | 27 | 0 |
| **Total:** | | **277** | **0** |

## JAMES, Julian — Defender

H: 5 10 W: 12 04 b.Tring 22-3-70

*Source:* Trainee. *Honours:* England Under-21.

| | | | |
|---|---|---|---|
| 1987–88 | Luton T | 3 | 0 |
| 1988–89 | Luton T | 1 | 0 |
| 1989–90 | Luton T | 20 | 1 |
| 1990–91 | Luton T | 17 | 1 |
| 1991–92 | Luton T | 28 | 2 |
| 1991–92 | Preston NE (loan) | 6 | 0 |
| 1992–93 | Luton T | 43 | 2 |
| 1993–94 | Luton T | 33 | 3 |
| 1994–95 | Luton T | 42 | 3 |
| 1995–96 | Luton T | 27 | 0 |
| 1996–97 | Luton T | 44 | 1 |
| 1997–98 | Luton T | 24 | 0 |
| **Total:** | | **288** | **13** |

## JAMES, Kevin — Forward

H: 5 8 W: 10 05 b.Merthyr 26-3-80

*Source:* Trainee.

| | | | |
|---|---|---|---|
| 1997–98 | Southampton | 0 | 0 |

## JAMES, Tony — Defender

H: 6 3 W: 13 08 b.Sheffield 27-6-67

*Source:* Gainsborough T.

| | | | |
|---|---|---|---|
| 1988–89 | Lincoln C | 28 | 0 |
| 1989–90 | Lincoln C | 1 | 0 |
| 1989–90 | Leicester C | 31 | 2 |
| 1990–91 | Leicester C | 38 | 8 |

| | | | |
|---|---|---|---|
| 1991–92 | Leicester C | 13 | 0 |
| 1992–93 | Leicester C | 16 | 0 |
| 1993–94 | Leicester C | 9 | 1 |
| 1994–95 | Hereford U | 18 | 2 |
| 1995–96 | Hereford U | 17 | 2 |
| 1996–97 | Plymouth Arg | 34 | 1 |
| 1997–98 | Plymouth Arg | 0 | 0 |
| **Total:** | | **205** | **16** |

## JANSEN, Matt — Forward

H: 5 11 W: 11 03 b.Carlisle 20-10-77

*Source:* Trainee.

| | | | |
|---|---|---|---|
| 1995–96 | Carlisle U | 0 | 0 |
| 1996–97 | Carlisle U | 19 | 1 |
| 1997–98 | Carlisle U | 23 | 9 |
| 1997–98 | Crystal Palace | 8 | 3 |
| **Total:** | | **50** | **13** |

## JANSSON, Jan — Midfield

H: 5 11 W: 11 11 b.Kalmar 26-1-68

*Honours:* Sweden Under-21, 7 full caps.

| | | | |
|---|---|---|---|
| 1993 | Norrkoping | 23 | 8 |
| 1994 | Norrkoping | 19 | 0 |
| 1995 | Norrkoping | 25 | 0 |
| 1996 | Norrkoping | 6 | 1 |
| 1996–97 | Port Vale | 11 | 1 |
| 1997–98 | Port Vale | 33 | 5 |
| **Total:** | | **117** | **15** |

## JARMAN, Lee — Defender

H: 6 3 W: 13 05 b.Cardiff 16-12-77

*Source:* Trainee. *Honours:* Wales Under-21.

| | | | |
|---|---|---|---|
| 1995–96 | Cardiff C | 32 | 0 |
| 1996–97 | Cardiff C | 32 | 0 |
| 1997–98 | Cardiff C | 23 | 0 |
| **Total:** | | **87** | **0** |

## JASZCZUN, Tommy — Defender

H: 5 10 W: 10 10 b.Kettering 16-9-77

*Source:* Trainee.

| | | | |
|---|---|---|---|
| 1996–97 | Aston Villa | 0 | 0 |
| 1997–98 | Aston Villa | 0 | 0 |

## JEAN, Earl — Forward

H: 5 7 W: 11 00 b.St Lucia 9-10-71

*Source:* Oliveirense, Union Coimbra, Leca, Felgueiras.
*Honours:* St Lucia full caps.

| | | | |
|---|---|---|---|
| 1996–97 | Ipswich T | 1 | 0 |
| 1996–97 | Rotherham U | 18 | 6 |
| 1997–98 | Plymouth Arg | 36 | 4 |
| **Total:** | | **55** | **10** |

## JEANNE, Leon — Midfield

b.Cardiff 17-11-80

*Source:* Trainee.

| | | | |
|---|---|---|---|
| 1997–98 | QPR | 0 | 0 |

## JEFFERS, Francis — Forward

b.Merseyside 25-1-81

*Source:* Trainee. *Honours:* England Schools.

| | | | |
|---|---|---|---|
| 1997–98 | Everton | 1 | 0 |
| **Total:** | | **1** | **0** |

## JEFFERS, John — Forward

H: 5 10 W: 11 10 b.Liverpool 5-10-68

*Source:* Trainee. *Honours:* England Schools.

| | | | |
|---|---|---|---|
| 1986–87 | Liverpool | 0 | 0 |
| 1987–88 | Liverpool | 0 | 0 |
| 1988–89 | Liverpool | 0 | 0 |
| 1988–89 | Port Vale | 15 | 0 |
| 1989–90 | Port Vale | 40 | 1 |
| 1990–91 | Port Vale | 31 | 2 |
| 1991–92 | Port Vale | 33 | 3 |
| 1992–93 | Port Vale | 26 | 2 |
| 1993–94 | Port Vale | 25 | 1 |
| 1994–95 | Port Vale | 10 | 1 |
| 1994–95 | Shrewsbury T (loan) | 3 | 1 |
| 1995–96 | Port Vale | 0 | 0 |
| 1995–96 | Stockport Co | 23 | 3 |
| 1996–97 | Stockport Co | 34 | 3 |
| 1997–98 | Stockport Co | 0 | 0 |
| **Total:** | | **240** | **17** |

## JEMSON, Nigel — Forward

H: 5 11 W: 13 03 b.Preston 10-8-69

*Source:* Trainee. *Honours:* England Under-21.

| | | | |
|---|---|---|---|
| 1985–86 | Preston NE | 1 | 0 |
| 1986–87 | Preston NE | 4 | 3 |
| 1987–88 | Preston NE | 27 | 5 |
| 1987–88 | Nottingham F | 0 | 0 |
| 1988–89 | Nottingham F | 0 | 0 |
| 1988–89 | Bolton W (loan) | 5 | 0 |
| 1988–89 | Preston NE (loan) | 9 | 2 |
| 1989–90 | Nottingham F | 18 | 4 |
| 1990–91 | Nottingham F | 23 | 8 |
| 1991–92 | Nottingham F | 6 | 1 |
| 1991–92 | Sheffield W | 20 | 4 |
| 1992–93 | Sheffield W | 13 | 0 |

| | | | |
|---|---|---|---|
| 1993–94 | Sheffield W | 18 | 5 |
| 1993–94 | Grimsby T (loan) | 6 | 2 |
| 1994–95 | Notts Co | 11 | 1 |
| 1994–95 | Watford (loan) | 4 | 0 |
| 1994–95 | Coventry C (loan) | 0 | 0 |
| 1995–96 | Notts Co | 3 | 0 |
| 1995–96 | Rotherham U (loan) | 16 | 5 |
| 1996–97 | Oxford U | 44 | 18 |
| 1997–98 | Oxford U | 24 | 9 |
| 1997–98 | Bury | 15 | 1 |
| **Total:** | | **267** | **68** |

## JENKINS, Iain — Defender

H: 5 9 W: 11 10 b.Whiston 24-12-72

*Source:* Trainee. *Honours:* Northern Ireland 5 full caps.

| | | | |
|---|---|---|---|
| 1990–91 | Everton | 1 | 0 |
| 1991–92 | Everton | 3 | 0 |
| 1992–93 | Everton | 1 | 0 |
| 1992–93 | Bradford C (loan) | 6 | 0 |
| 1993–94 | Chester C | 34 | 0 |
| 1994–95 | Chester C | 40 | 0 |
| 1995–96 | Chester C | 13 | 0 |
| 1996–97 | Chester C | 39 | 0 |
| 1997–98 | Chester C | 34 | 1 |
| 1997–98 | Dundee U | 7 | 0 |
| **Total:** | | **178** | **1** |

## JENKINS, Jamie — Defender

H: 5 8 W: 10 07 b.Pontypool 1-1-79

*Source:* Trainee.

| | | | |
|---|---|---|---|
| 1997–98 | Bournemouth | 0 | 0 |

## JENKINS, Lee — Midfield

H: 5 9 W: 10 00 b.Pontypool 28-6-79

*Source:* Trainee. *Honours:* Wales Under-21.

| | | | |
|---|---|---|---|
| 1996–97 | Swansea C | 23 | 2 |
| 1997–98 | Swansea C | 21 | 0 |
| **Total:** | | **44** | **2** |

## JENKINS, Steve — Defender

H: 5 11 W: 12 04 b.Merthyr 16-7-72

*Source:* Trainee. *Honours:* Wales Under-21, 10 full caps.

| | | | |
|---|---|---|---|
| 1990–91 | Swansea C | 1 | 0 |
| 1991–92 | Swansea C | 34 | 0 |
| 1992–93 | Swansea C | 33 | 0 |
| 1993–94 | Swansea C | 40 | 1 |
| 1994–95 | Swansea C | 42 | 0 |
| 1995–96 | Swansea C | 15 | 0 |
| 1995–96 | Huddersfield T | 31 | 1 |
| 1996–97 | Huddersfield T | 33 | 0 |
| 1997–98 | Huddersfield T | 29 | 1 |
| **Total:** | | **258** | **3** |

## JENKINS, Steve — Defender

H: 6 1 W: 13 00 b.Bristol 2-1-80

*Source:* Trainee.

| | | | |
|---|---|---|---|
| 1997–98 | Southampton | 0 | 0 |

## JENKINSON, Leigh — Forward

H: 6 0 W: 12 02 b.Thorne 9-7-69

*Source:* Trainee. *Honours:* Wales B.

| | | | |
|---|---|---|---|
| 1987–88 | Hull C | 3 | 1 |
| 1988–89 | Hull C | 11 | 0 |
| 1989–90 | Hull C | 22 | 0 |
| 1990–91 | Hull C | 26 | 0 |
| 1990–91 | Rotherham U (loan) | 7 | 0 |
| 1991–92 | Hull C | 42 | 8 |
| 1992–93 | Hull C | 26 | 4 |
| 1992–93 | Coventry C | 5 | 0 |
| 1993–94 | Coventry C | 16 | 0 |
| 1993–94 | Birmingham C (loan) | 3 | 0 |
| 1994–95 | Coventry C | 11 | 1 |
| 1995–96 | St Johnstone | 18 | 2 |
| 1996–97 | St Johnstone | 25 | 5 |
| 1997–98 | St Johnstone | 24 | 3 |
| **Total:** | | **239** | **24** |

## JENNINGS, Patrick — Goalkeeper

H: 5 9 W: 11 00 b.Herts 24-9-79

| | | | |
|---|---|---|---|
| 1996–97 | Wimbledon | 0 | 0 |
| 1997–98 | Wimbledon | 0 | 0 |

## JEPSON, Ronnie — Forward

H: 6 1 W: 13 05 b.Audley 12-5-63

*Source:* Nantwich T.

| | | | |
|---|---|---|---|
| 1988–89 | Port Vale | 2 | 0 |
| 1989–90 | Port Vale | 5 | 0 |
| 1989–90 | Peterborough U (loan) | 18 | 5 |
| 1990–91 | Port Vale | 15 | 0 |
| 1990–91 | Preston NE | 14 | 3 |
| 1991–92 | Preston NE | 24 | 5 |
| 1992–93 | Exeter C | 38 | 8 |
| 1993–94 | Exeter C | 16 | 13 |
| 1993–94 | Huddersfield T | 23 | 5 |
| 1994–95 | Huddersfield T | 41 | 19 |
| 1995–96 | Huddersfield T | 43 | 12 |
| 1996–97 | Bury | 31 | 9 |

| | | | |
|---|---|---|---|
| 1997–98 | Bury | 16 | 0 |
| 1997–98 | Oldham Ath | 9 | 4 |
| **Total:** | | **295** | **83** |

## JERKAN, Nikola — Defender

H: 6 2 W: 12 07 b.Sinj 8-12-64

*Source:* Zagreb, Cibalia Vinkovci, Hajduk Split. *Honours:* Croatia 30 full caps, 1 goal.

| | | | |
|---|---|---|---|
| 1990–91 | Oviedo | 34 | 0 |
| 1991–92 | Oviedo | 33 | 0 |
| 1992–93 | Oviedo | 38 | 0 |
| 1993–94 | Oviedo | 32 | 0 |
| 1994–95 | Oviedo | 31 | 0 |
| 1995–96 | Oviedo | 35 | 1 |
| 1996–97 | Nottingham F | 14 | 0 |
| 1997–98 | Nottingham F | 0 | 0 |
| **Total:** | | **217** | **1** |

## JESS, Eoin — Forward

H: 5 10 W: 11 07 b.Aberdeen 13-12-70

*Source:* Rangers 'S' Form. *Honours:* Scotland Under-21, 14 full caps, 1 goal.

| | | | |
|---|---|---|---|
| 1987–88 | Aberdeen | 0 | 0 |
| 1988–89 | Aberdeen | 2 | 0 |
| 1989–90 | Aberdeen | 11 | 3 |
| 1990–91 | Aberdeen | 27 | 13 |
| 1991–92 | Aberdeen | 39 | 12 |
| 1992–93 | Aberdeen | 31 | 12 |
| 1993–94 | Aberdeen | 41 | 6 |
| 1994–95 | Aberdeen | 25 | 1 |
| 1995–96 | Aberdeen | 25 | 3 |
| 1995–96 | Coventry C | 12 | 1 |
| 1996–97 | Coventry C | 27 | 0 |
| 1997–98 | Aberdeen | 34 | 9 |
| **Total:** | | **274** | **60** |

## JEVONS, Phillip — Midfield

b.Liverpool 1-8-79

*Source:* Trainee.

| | | | |
|---|---|---|---|
| 1996–97 | Everton | 0 | 0 |
| 1997–98 | Everton | 0 | 0 |

## JEWELL, Paul — Forward

H: 5 8 W: 12 01 b.Liverpool 28-9-64

*Source:* Apprentice.

| | | | |
|---|---|---|---|
| 1982–83 | Liverpool | 0 | 0 |
| 1983–84 | Liverpool | 0 | 0 |
| 1984–85 | Wigan Ath | 26 | 9 |
| 1985–86 | Wigan Ath | 29 | 6 |
| 1986–87 | Wigan Ath | 39 | 9 |
| 1987–88 | Wigan Ath | 43 | 11 |
| 1988–89 | Bradford C | 39 | 4 |
| 1989–90 | Bradford C | 30 | 4 |
| 1990–91 | Bradford C | 38 | 4 |
| 1991–92 | Bradford C | 30 | 6 |
| 1992–93 | Bradford C | 46 | 16 |
| 1993–94 | Bradford C | 30 | 5 |
| 1994–95 | Bradford C | 38 | 14 |
| 1995–96 | Bradford C | 18 | 3 |
| 1995–96 | Grimsby T (loan) | 5 | 1 |
| 1996–97 | Bradford C | 0 | 0 |
| 1997–98 | Bradford C | 0 | 0 |
| **Total:** | | **411** | **92** |

## JOACHIM, Julian — Forward

H: 5 6 W: 12 00 b.Boston 20-9-74

*Source:* Trainee. *Honours:* England Youth, Under-21.

| | | | |
|---|---|---|---|
| 1992–93 | Leicester C | 26 | 10 |
| 1993–94 | Leicester C | 36 | 11 |
| 1994–95 | Leicester C | 15 | 3 |
| 1995–96 | Leicester C | 22 | 1 |
| 1995–96 | Aston Villa | 11 | 1 |
| 1996–97 | Aston Villa | 15 | 3 |
| 1997–98 | Aston Villa | 26 | 8 |
| **Total:** | | **151** | **37** |

## JOBLING, Kevin — Defender

H: 5 9 W: 12 02 b.Sunderland 1-1-68

*Source:* Apprentice.

| | | | |
|---|---|---|---|
| 1985–86 | Leicester C | 0 | 0 |
| 1986–87 | Leicester C | 3 | 0 |
| 1987–88 | Leicester C | 6 | 0 |
| 1987–88 | Grimsby T | 15 | 1 |
| 1988–89 | Grimsby T | 32 | 4 |
| 1989–90 | Grimsby T | 33 | 1 |
| 1990–91 | Grimsby T | 45 | 0 |
| 1991–92 | Grimsby T | 36 | 2 |
| 1992–93 | Grimsby T | 14 | 0 |
| 1993–94 | Grimsby T | 11 | 0 |
| 1993–94 | Scunthorpe U (loan) | 0 | 0 |
| 1994–95 | Grimsby T | 38 | 1 |
| 1995–96 | Grimsby T | 3 | 0 |
| 1996–97 | Grimsby T | 28 | 0 |
| 1997–98 | Grimsby T | 30 | 1 |
| **Total:** | | **294** | **10** |

## JOBSON, Richard — Defender

H: 6 1 W: 13 05 b.Holderness 9-5-63

*Source:* Burton Alb. *Honours:* England B.

| | | | |
|---|---|---|---|
| 1982–83 | Watford | 13 | 1 |
| 1983–84 | Watford | 13 | 2 |
| 1984–85 | Watford | 2 | 1 |

## Johansen, Martin

| | | | |
|---|---|---|---|
| 1984–85 | Hull C | 8 | 0 |
| 1985–86 | Hull C | 36 | 7 |
| 1986–87 | Hull C | 40 | 5 |
| 1987–88 | Hull C | 44 | 2 |
| 1988–89 | Hull C | 46 | 1 |
| 1989–90 | Hull C | 45 | 2 |
| 1990–91 | Hull C | 2 | 0 |
| 1990–91 | Oldham Ath | 44 | 1 |
| 1991–92 | Oldham Ath | 36 | 2 |
| 1992–93 | Oldham Ath | 40 | 2 |
| 1993–94 | Oldham Ath | 37 | 5 |
| 1994–95 | Oldham Ath | 20 | 0 |
| 1995–96 | Oldham Ath | 12 | 0 |
| 1995–96 | Leeds U | 12 | 1 |
| 1996–97 | Leeds U | 10 | 0 |
| 1997–98 | Leeds U | 0 | 0 |
| 1997–98 | Southend U (loan) | 8 | 1 |
| 1997–98 | Manchester C | 6 | 1 |
| **Total:** | | **474** | **34** |

## JOHANSEN, Martin — Midfield

H: 5 8 W: 11 01 b.Glostrup 22-7-72

| | | | |
|---|---|---|---|
| 1990 | KB Copenhagen | 20 | 4 |
| 1991 | KB Copenhagen | 0 | 0 |
| 1991–92 | B1903 | 25 | 8 |
| 1992–93 | FC Copenhagen | 21 | 12 |
| 1993–94 | FC Copenhagen | 22 | 11 |
| 1994–95 | FC Copenhagen | 25 | 4 |
| 1995–96 | FC Copenhagen | 24 | 2 |
| 1996–97 | FC Copenhagen | 24 | 2 |
| 1997–98 | Coventry C | 2 | 0 |
| **Total:** | | **163** | **43** |

## JOHANSEN, Michael — Midfield

H: 5 6 W: 10 05 b.Glostrup 22-7-72

| | | | |
|---|---|---|---|
| 1990 | KB Copenhagen | 15 | 1 |
| 1991–92 | B 1903 | 26 | 1 |
| 1992–93 | FC Copenhagen | 28 | 1 |
| 1993–94 | FC Copenhagen | 28 | 4 |
| 1994–95 | FC Copenhagen | 27 | 4 |
| 1995–96 | FC Copenhagen | 31 | 8 |
| 1996–97 | Bolton W | 33 | 5 |
| 1997–98 | Bolton W | 16 | 1 |
| **Total:** | | **204** | **25** |

## JOHANSEN, Stig — Forward

H: 5 9 W: 12 05 b.Norway 13-6-72

*Honours:* Norway 3 full caps.

| | | | |
|---|---|---|---|
| 1995 | Bodo Glimt | 26 | 19 |
| 1996 | Bodo Glimt | 26 | 14 |
| 1997 | Bodo Glimt | 18 | 12 |
| 1997–98 | Southampton | 6 | 0 |
| 1997–98 | Bristol C (loan) | 3 | 0 |
| **Total:** | | **79** | **45** |

## JOHANSSON, Jonatan — Midfield

H: 6 1 W: 12 08 b.Stockholm 16-8-75

*Source:* Flora Tallinn. *Honours:* Finland 8 full caps, 2 goals.

| | | | |
|---|---|---|---|
| 1997–98 | Rangers | 6 | 0 |
| **Total:** | | **6** | **0** |

## JOHNROSE, Lenny — Midfield

H: 5 11 W: 12 06 b.Preston 27-11-69

*Source:* Trainee.

| | | | |
|---|---|---|---|
| 1987–88 | Blackburn R | 1 | 0 |
| 1988–89 | Blackburn R | 0 | 0 |
| 1989–90 | Blackburn R | 8 | 3 |
| 1990–91 | Blackburn R | 26 | 7 |
| 1991–92 | Blackburn R | 7 | 1 |
| 1991–92 | Preston NE (loan) | 3 | 1 |
| 1991–92 | Hartlepool U | 15 | 2 |
| 1992–93 | Hartlepool U | 38 | 6 |
| 1993–94 | Hartlepool U | 13 | 3 |
| 1993–94 | Bury | 14 | 0 |
| 1994–95 | Bury | 26 | 4 |
| 1995–96 | Bury | 34 | 6 |
| 1996–97 | Bury | 43 | 4 |
| 1997–98 | Bury | 44 | 3 |
| **Total:** | | **272** | **40** |

## JOHNSEN, Ronny — Defender

H: 6 3 W: 13 02 b.Sandefjord 10-6-69

*Honours:* Norway 37 full caps, 2 goals.

| | | | |
|---|---|---|---|
| 1992 | Lyn | 12 | 1 |
| 1993 | Lyn | 19 | 6 |
| 1994 | Lillestrom | 10 | 3 |
| 1995 | Lillestrom | 13 | 1 |
| 1995–96 | Besiktas | 22 | 1 |
| 1996–97 | Manchester U | 31 | 0 |
| 1997–98 | Manchester U | 22 | 2 |
| **Total:** | | **129** | **14** |

## JOHNSON, Alan — Defender

H: 6 0 W: 14 00 b.Ince 19-2-71

*Source:* Trainee.

| | | | |
|---|---|---|---|
| 1988–89 | Wigan Ath | 8 | 1 |
| 1989–90 | Wigan Ath | 33 | 1 |
| 1990–91 | Wigan Ath | 43 | 5 |
| 1991–92 | Wigan Ath | 44 | 4 |
| 1992–93 | Wigan Ath | 36 | 1 |

| | | | |
|---|---|---|---|
| 1993–94 | Wigan Ath | 16 | 1 |
| 1993–94 | Lincoln C | 16 | 0 |
| 1994–95 | Lincoln C | 25 | 0 |
| 1995–96 | Lincoln C | 22 | 0 |
| 1995–96 | Preston NE (loan) | 2 | 0 |
| 1996–97 | Rochdale | 46 | 4 |
| 1997–98 | Rochdale | 0 | 0 |
| **Total:** | | **291** | **17** |

## JOHNSON, Alan — Goalkeeper

b.Manchester 10-11-78

*Source:* Trainee.

| | | | |
|---|---|---|---|
| 1997–98 | Oldham Ath | 0 | 0 |

## JOHNSON, Andrew — Forward

b.Bedford 10-2-81

*Source:* Trainee.

| | | | |
|---|---|---|---|
| 1997–98 | Birmingham C | 0 | 0 |

## JOHNSON, Andy — Midfield

H: 5 11 W: 13 03 b.Bristol 2-5-74

*Source:* Trainee.

| | | | |
|---|---|---|---|
| 1991–92 | Norwich C | 2 | 0 |
| 1992–93 | Norwich C | 2 | 1 |
| 1993–94 | Norwich C | 2 | 0 |
| 1994–95 | Norwich C | 7 | 0 |
| 1995–96 | Norwich C | 26 | 7 |
| 1996–97 | Norwich C | 27 | 5 |
| 1997–98 | Nottingham F | 34 | 4 |
| **Total:** | | **100** | **17** |

## JOHNSON, Andy — Forward

H: 5 9 W: 12 01 b.Brighton 25-1-79

*Source:* Trainee.

| | | | |
|---|---|---|---|
| 1996–97 | Watford | 0 | 0 |
| 1997–98 | Watford | 0 | 0 |

## JOHNSON, Chris — Midfield

H: 5 9 W: 12 03 b.Brighton 25-1-79

*Source:* Trainee. *Honours:* England Schools.

| | | | |
|---|---|---|---|
| 1996–97 | Watford | 1 | 0 |
| 1997–98 | Watford | 0 | 0 |
| **Total:** | | **1** | **0** |

## JOHNSON, Damien — Midfield

H: 5 8 W: 11 02 b.Blackburn 18-11-78

*Source:* Trainee. *Honours:* Northern Ireland Under-21.

| | | | |
|---|---|---|---|
| 1995–96 | Blackburn R | 0 | 0 |
| 1996–97 | Blackburn R | 0 | 0 |
| 1997–98 | Blackburn R | 0 | 0 |
| 1997–98 | Nottingham F (loan) | 6 | 0 |
| **Total:** | | **6** | **0** |

## JOHNSON, David — Forward

H: 5 6 W: 12 00 b.Kingston, Jam 15-8-76

*Source:* Trainee. *Honours:* England Schools, B.

| | | | |
|---|---|---|---|
| 1994–95 | Manchester U | 0 | 0 |
| 1995–96 | Bury | 36 | 5 |
| 1996–97 | Bury | 44 | 8 |
| 1997–98 | Bury | 17 | 5 |
| 1997–98 | Ipswich T | 31 | 20 |
| **Total:** | | **128** | **38** |

## JOHNSON, Gavin — Defender

H: 5 11 W: 11 07 b.Eye 10-10-70

*Source:* Trainee.

| | | | |
|---|---|---|---|
| 1988–89 | Ipswich T | 4 | 0 |
| 1989–90 | Ipswich T | 6 | 0 |
| 1990–91 | Ipswich T | 7 | 0 |
| 1991–92 | Ipswich T | 42 | 5 |
| 1992–93 | Ipswich T | 40 | 5 |
| 1993–94 | Ipswich T | 16 | 1 |
| 1994–95 | Ipswich T | 17 | 0 |
| 1995–96 | Luton T | 5 | 0 |
| 1995–96 | Wigan Ath | 27 | 3 |
| 1996–97 | Wigan Ath | 37 | 3 |
| 1997–98 | Wigan Ath | 20 | 2 |
| **Total:** | | **221** | **19** |

## JOHNSON, Grant — Midfield

H: 5 8 W: 10 09 b.Dundee 24-3-72

*Source:* Broughty Ferry. *Honours:* Scotland Under-21.

| | | | |
|---|---|---|---|
| 1990–91 | Dundee U | 0 | 0 |
| 1991–92 | Dundee U | 10 | 1 |
| 1992–93 | Dundee U | 17 | 1 |
| 1993–94 | Dundee U | 10 | 0 |
| 1994–95 | Dundee U | 13 | 1 |
| 1995–96 | Dundee U | 28 | 4 |
| 1996–97 | Dundee U | 7 | 0 |
| 1997–98 | Dundee U | 0 | 0 |
| 1997–98 | Huddersfield T | 29 | 1 |
| **Total:** | | **114** | **8** |

## JOHNSON, Marvin — Defender

H: 6 1 W: 13 06 b.Wembley 29-10-68

*Source:* Apprentice.

| | | | |
|---|---|---|---|
| 1986–87 | Luton T | 0 | 0 |
| 1987–88 | Luton T | 9 | 0 |
| 1988–89 | Luton T | 16 | 0 |
| 1989–90 | Luton T | 12 | 0 |
| 1990–91 | Luton T | 26 | 0 |
| 1991–92 | Luton T | 0 | 0 |
| 1992–93 | Luton T | 40 | 3 |
| 1993–94 | Luton T | 17 | 0 |
| 1994–95 | Luton T | 46 | 1 |
| 1995–96 | Luton T | 36 | 0 |
| 1996–97 | Luton T | 44 | 0 |
| 1997–98 | Luton T | 14 | 2 |
| **Total:** | | **260** | **6** |

## JOHNSON, Michael — Defender

H: 5 11 W: 11 00 b.Nottingham 4-7-73

*Source:* Trainee.

| | | | |
|---|---|---|---|
| 1991–92 | Notts Co | 5 | 0 |
| 1992–93 | Notts Co | 37 | 0 |
| 1993–94 | Notts Co | 34 | 0 |
| 1994–95 | Notts Co | 31 | 0 |
| 1995–96 | Notts Co | 0 | 0 |
| 1995–96 | Birmingham C | 33 | 0 |
| 1996–97 | Birmingham C | 35 | 0 |
| 1997–98 | Birmingham C | 38 | 3 |
| **Total:** | | **213** | **3** |

## JOHNSON, Richard — Midfield

H: 6 0 W: 11 13 b.Kurri Kurri 27-4-74

*Source:* Trainee.

| | | | |
|---|---|---|---|
| 1991–92 | Watford | 2 | 0 |
| 1992–93 | Watford | 1 | 0 |
| 1993–94 | Watford | 27 | 0 |
| 1994–95 | Watford | 35 | 3 |
| 1995–96 | Watford | 20 | 1 |
| 1996–97 | Watford | 37 | 2 |
| 1997–98 | Watford | 42 | 7 |
| **Total:** | | **164** | **13** |

## JOHNSON, Ross — Defender

H: 6 0 W: 13 00 b.Brighton 2-1-76

*Source:* Trainee.

| | | | |
|---|---|---|---|
| 1993–94 | Brighton & HA | 2 | 0 |
| 1994–95 | Brighton & HA | 0 | 0 |
| 1995–96 | Brighton & HA | 20 | 0 |
| 1996–97 | Brighton & HA | 29 | 0 |
| 1997–98 | Brighton & HA | 38 | 0 |
| **Total:** | | **89** | **0** |

## JOHNSON, Seth — Midfield

H: 5 10 W: 11 00 b.Birmingham 12-3-79

*Source:* Trainee. *Honours:* England Youth.

| | | | |
|---|---|---|---|
| 1996–97 | Crewe Alex | 11 | 1 |
| 1997–98 | Crewe Alex | 40 | 1 |
| **Total:** | | **51** | **2** |

## JOHNSON, Tommy — Forward

H: 5 11 W: 12 07 b.Newcastle 15-1-71

*Source:* Trainee. *Honours:* England Under-21.

| | | | |
|---|---|---|---|
| 1988–89 | Notts Co | 10 | 4 |
| 1989–90 | Notts Co | 40 | 18 |
| 1990–91 | Notts Co | 37 | 16 |
| 1991–92 | Notts Co | 31 | 9 |
| 1991–92 | Derby Co | 12 | 2 |
| 1992–93 | Derby Co | 35 | 8 |
| 1993–94 | Derby Co | 37 | 13 |
| 1994–95 | Derby Co | 14 | 7 |
| 1994–95 | Aston Villa | 14 | 4 |
| 1995–96 | Aston Villa | 23 | 5 |
| 1996–97 | Aston Villa | 20 | 4 |
| 1996–97 | Celtic | 4 | 1 |
| 1997–98 | Celtic | 2 | 0 |
| **Total:** | | **279** | **91** |

## JOHNSTON, Allan — Forward

H: 5 7 W: 9 07 b.Glasgow 14-12-73

*Source:* Tynecastle BC. *Honours:* Scotland Under-21, B.

| | | | |
|---|---|---|---|
| 1991–92 | Hearts | 0 | 0 |
| 1992–93 | Hearts | 2 | 1 |
| 1993–94 | Hearts | 28 | 1 |
| 1994–95 | Hearts | 21 | 1 |
| 1995–96 | Hearts | 33 | 9 |
| 1996–97 | Rennes | 23 | 2 |
| 1996–97 | Sunderland | 6 | 1 |
| 1997–98 | Sunderland | 40 | 11 |
| **Total:** | | **153** | **26** |

## JONES, Anthony — Midfield

b.London 28-1-79

*Source:* Trainee.

| | | | |
|---|---|---|---|
| 1997–98 | Leyton Orient | 0 | 0 |

## JONES, Barry — Defender

H: 6 0 W: 11 07 b.Prescot 20-6-70

*Source:* Prescot T.

| | | | |
|---|---|---|---|
| 1988–89 | Liverpool | 0 | 0 |
| 1989–90 | Liverpool | 0 | 0 |
| 1990–91 | Liverpool | 0 | 0 |
| 1991–92 | Liverpool | 0 | 0 |
| 1992–93 | Wrexham | 42 | 2 |
| 1993–94 | Wrexham | 33 | 2 |
| 1994–95 | Wrexham | 44 | 0 |
| 1995–96 | Wrexham | 40 | 0 |
| 1996–97 | Wrexham | 22 | 0 |
| 1997–98 | Wrexham | 14 | 1 |
| 1997–98 | York C | 23 | 2 |
| **Total:** | | **218** | **7** |

## JONES, David — Midfield

H: 5 7 W: 9 10 b.Goole 17-11-78

*Source:* Goole T.

| | | | |
|---|---|---|---|
| 1997–98 | Blackpool | 0 | 0 |

## JONES, Dean — Defender

H: 6 1 W: 12 05 b.Barnsley 12-10-77

*Source:* Trainee.

| | | | |
|---|---|---|---|
| 1996–97 | Barnsley | 0 | 0 |
| 1997–98 | Barnsley | 0 | 0 |

## JONES, Eifion — Defender

b.Llanrug 28-9-80

*Source:* Trainee.

| | | | |
|---|---|---|---|
| 1997–98 | Liverpool | 0 | 0 |

## JONES, Gary — Forward

H: 6 1 W: 12 09 b.Huddersfield 6-4-69

*Source:* Rossington Main.

| | | | |
|---|---|---|---|
| 1988–89 | Doncaster R | 17 | 2 |
| 1989–90 | Doncaster R | 3 | 0 |
| From Boston U. | | | |
| 1993–94 | Southend U | 22 | 3 |
| 1993–94 | Lincoln C (loan) | 4 | 2 |
| 1994–95 | Southend U | 25 | 11 |
| 1995–96 | Southend U | 23 | 2 |
| 1995–96 | Notts Co | 18 | 5 |
| 1996–97 | Notts Co | 27 | 3 |
| 1996–97 | Scunthorpe U (loan) | 11 | 5 |
| 1997–98 | Notts Co | 44 | 28 |
| **Total:** | | **194** | **61** |

## JONES, Gary — Forward

H: 6 3 W: 13 05 b.Chester 10-5-75

*Source:* Trainee.

| | | | |
|---|---|---|---|
| 1993–94 | Tranmere R | 6 | 2 |
| 1994–95 | Tranmere R | 19 | 3 |
| 1995–96 | Tranmere R | 23 | 1 |
| 1996–97 | Tranmere R | 30 | 6 |
| 1997–98 | Tranmere R | 43 | 8 |
| **Total:** | | **121** | **20** |

## JONES, Gary — Midfield

H: 5 9 W: 11 10 b.Birkenhead 3-6-77

| | | | |
|---|---|---|---|
| 1997–98 | Swansea C | 8 | 0 |
| 1997–98 | Rochdale | 17 | 2 |
| **Total:** | | **25** | **2** |

## JONES, Graeme — Forward

H: 6 0 W: 12 12 b.Gateshead 13-3-70

*Source:* Bridlington T.

| | | | |
|---|---|---|---|
| 1993–94 | Doncaster R | 28 | 4 |
| 1994–95 | Doncaster R | 32 | 12 |
| 1995–96 | Doncaster R | 32 | 10 |
| 1996–97 | Wigan Ath | 40 | 31 |
| 1997–98 | Wigan Ath | 33 | 9 |
| **Total:** | | **165** | **66** |

## JONES, Ian — Defender

H: 5 9 W: 11 13 b.Merthyr 18-11-78

*Source:* Trainee.

| | | | |
|---|---|---|---|
| 1997–98 | Luton T | 0 | 0 |

## JONES, Jason — Goalkeeper

b.Wrexham 10-5-79

*Source:* Liverpool Trainee.

| | | | |
|---|---|---|---|
| 1997–98 | Swansea C | 1 | 0 |
| **Total:** | | **1** | **0** |

## JONES, Jon — Forward

H: 5 9 W: 11 05 b.Wrexham 27-10-78

*Source:* Trainee.

| | | | |
|---|---|---|---|
| 1996–97 | Chester C | 17 | 1 |
| 1997–98 | Chester C | 7 | 1 |
| **Total:** | | **24** | **2** |

## JONES, Keith — Midfield

H: 5 7 W: 11 02 b.Dulwich 14-10-65

*Source:* Apprentice. *Honours:* England Schools, Youth.

| | | | |
|---|---|---|---|
| 1982–83 | Chelsea | 2 | 0 |
| 1983–84 | Chelsea | 0 | 0 |
| 1984–85 | Chelsea | 19 | 2 |
| 1985–86 | Chelsea | 14 | 2 |
| 1986–87 | Chelsea | 17 | 3 |
| 1987–88 | Chelsea | 0 | 0 |
| 1987–88 | Brentford | 36 | 1 |
| 1988–89 | Brentford | 40 | 3 |
| 1989–90 | Brentford | 42 | 2 |
| 1990–91 | Brentford | 45 | 6 |
| 1991–92 | Brentford | 6 | 1 |
| 1991–92 | Southend U | 34 | 5 |
| 1992–93 | Southend U | 29 | 1 |
| 1993–94 | Southend U | 20 | 5 |
| 1994–95 | Southend U | 7 | 0 |
| 1994–95 | Charlton Ath | 31 | 1 |
| 1995–96 | Charlton Ath | 25 | 0 |
| 1996–97 | Charlton Ath | 19 | 0 |
| 1997–98 | Charlton Ath | 44 | 3 |
| **Total:** | | **430** | **35** |

## JONES, Lea — Defender

H: 6 0 W: 14 06 b.Southport 25-9-77

*Source:* Trainee.

| | | | |
|---|---|---|---|
| 1996–97 | Stockport Co | 0 | 0 |
| 1997–98 | Stockport Co | 0 | 0 |

## JONES, Lee — Forward

H: 5 9 W: 10 06 b.Wrexham 29-5-73

*Source:* Trainee. *Honours:* Wales Under-21, 2 full caps.

| | | | |
|---|---|---|---|
| 1990–91 | Wrexham | 18 | 5 |
| 1991–92 | Wrexham | 21 | 5 |
| 1991–92 | Liverpool | 0 | 0 |
| 1992–93 | Liverpool | 0 | 0 |
| 1993–94 | Liverpool | 0 | 0 |
| 1993–94 | Crewe Alex (loan) | 8 | 1 |
| 1994–95 | Liverpool | 1 | 0 |
| 1995–96 | Liverpool | 0 | 0 |
| 1995–96 | Wrexham (loan) | 20 | 9 |
| 1996–97 | Liverpool | 2 | 0 |
| 1996–97 | Wrexham (loan) | 6 | 0 |
| 1996–97 | Tranmere R (loan) | 8 | 5 |
| 1997–98 | Tranmere R | 34 | 9 |
| **Total:** | | **118** | **34** |

## JONES, Lee — Goalkeeper

H: 6 3 W: 14 07 b.Pontypridd 9-8-70

*Source:* Porth.

| | | | |
|---|---|---|---|
| 1993–94 | Swansea C | 0 | 0 |
| 1994–95 | Swansea C | 2 | 0 |
| 1995–96 | Swansea C | 1 | 0 |
| 1995–96 | Crewe Alex (loan) | 0 | 0 |
| 1996–97 | Swansea C | 1 | 0 |
| 1997–98 | Swansea C | 2 | 0 |
| 1997–98 | Bristol R | 8 | 0 |
| **Total:** | | **14** | **0** |

## JONES, Mark — Midfield

b.Walsall 7-9-79

*Source:* Trainee. *Honours:* England Schools.

| | | | |
|---|---|---|---|
| 1996–97 | Wolverhampton W | 0 | 0 |
| 1997–98 | Wolverhampton W | 0 | 0 |

## JONES, Mark — Midfield

b.Havering 4-8-79

*Source:* Trainee.

| | | | |
|---|---|---|---|
| 1996–97 | Southend U | 1 | 0 |
| 1997–98 | Southend U | 0 | 0 |
| **Total:** | | **1** | **0** |

## JONES, Matthew — Midfield

H: 5 11 W: 11 05 b.Llanelli 1-9-80

*Source:* Trainee. *Honours:* Wales Youth, Under-21, B.

| | | | |
|---|---|---|---|
| 1997–98 | Leeds U | 0 | 0 |

## JONES, Nathan — Defender

H: 5 7 W: 10 12 b.Rhondda 28-5-73

*Source:* Cardiff C Trainee, Maesteg Park, Ton Pentre, Merthyr T.

| | | | |
|---|---|---|---|
| 1995–96 | Luton T | 0 | 0 |
| Badajoz, Numaicia | | | |
| 1997–98 | Southend U | 39 | 0 |
| **Total:** | | **39** | **0** |

## JONES, Paul — Goalkeeper

H: 6 2 W: 15 02 b.Chirk 18-4-67

*Source:* Bridgnorth, Kidderminster H. *Honours:* Wales 5 full caps.

| | | | |
|---|---|---|---|
| 1991–92 | Wolverhampton W | 0 | 0 |
| 1992–93 | Wolverhampton W | 16 | 0 |
| 1993–94 | Wolverhampton W | 0 | 0 |
| 1994–95 | Wolverhampton W | 9 | 0 |

| | | | |
|---|---|---|---|
| 1995–96 | Wolverhampton W | 8 | 0 |
| 1996–97 | Stockport Co | 46 | 0 |
| 1997–98 | Southampton | 38 | 0 |
| **Total:** | | **117** | **0** |

## JONES, Rob — Defender

H: 5 8 W: 11 00 b.Wrexham 5-11-71

*Source:* Trainee. *Honours:* England Under-21, 8 full caps.

| | | | |
|---|---|---|---|
| 1987–88 | Crewe Alex | 5 | 0 |
| 1988–89 | Crewe Alex | 19 | 1 |
| 1989–90 | Crewe Alex | 11 | 0 |
| 1990–91 | Crewe Alex | 32 | 1 |
| 1991–92 | Crewe Alex | 8 | 0 |
| 1991–92 | Liverpool | 28 | 0 |
| 1992–93 | Liverpool | 30 | 0 |
| 1993–94 | Liverpool | 38 | 0 |
| 1994–95 | Liverpool | 31 | 0 |
| 1995–96 | Liverpool | 33 | 0 |
| 1996–97 | Liverpool | 2 | 0 |
| 1997–98 | Liverpool | 21 | 0 |
| **Total:** | | **258** | **2** |

## JONES, Ryan — Midfield

H: 6 3 W: 14 00 b.Sheffield 23-7-73

*Source:* Trainee. *Honours:* Wales Under-21, 1 full cap.

| | | | |
|---|---|---|---|
| 1991–92 | Sheffield W | 0 | 0 |
| 1992–93 | Sheffield W | 9 | 0 |
| 1993–94 | Sheffield W | 27 | 6 |
| 1994–95 | Sheffield W | 5 | 0 |
| 1995–96 | Sheffield W | 0 | 0 |
| 1995–96 | Scunthorpe U (loan) | 11 | 3 |
| 1996–97 | Sheffield W | 0 | 0 |
| 1997–98 | Sheffield W | 0 | 0 |
| **Total:** | | **52** | **9** |

## JONES, Scott — Defender

H: 5 10 W: 12 08 b.Sheffield 1-5-75

*Source:* Trainee.

| | | | |
|---|---|---|---|
| 1993–94 | Barnsley | 0 | 0 |
| 1994–95 | Barnsley | 0 | 0 |
| 1995–96 | Barnsley | 4 | 0 |
| 1996–97 | Barnsley | 18 | 0 |
| 1997–98 | Barnsley | 12 | 1 |
| 1997–98 | Mansfield T (loan) | 6 | 0 |
| 1997–98 | Notts Co (loan) | 0 | 0 |
| **Total:** | | **40** | **1** |

## JONES, Steve — Forward

H: 6 1 W: 13 03 b.Cambridge 17-3-70

*Source:* Billericay T.

| | | | |
|---|---|---|---|
| 1992–93 | West Ham U | 6 | 2 |
| 1993–94 | West Ham U | 8 | 2 |
| 1994–95 | West Ham U | 2 | 0 |
| 1994–95 | Bournemouth | 30 | 9 |
| 1995–96 | Bournemouth | 44 | 17 |
| 1995–96 | West Ham U | 0 | 0 |
| 1996–97 | West Ham U | 8 | 0 |
| 1996–97 | Charlton Ath | 2 | 0 |
| 1997–98 | Charlton Ath | 23 | 7 |
| 1997–98 | Bournemouth (loan) | 5 | 4 |
| **Total:** | | **128** | **41** |

## JONES, Steve — Defender

H: 5 10 W: 12 02 b.Bristol 25-12-70

*Source:* Cheltenham T.

| | | | |
|---|---|---|---|
| 1995–96 | Swansea C | 17 | 0 |
| 1996–97 | Swansea C | 46 | 1 |
| 1997–98 | Swansea C | 0 | 0 |
| **Total:** | | **63** | **1** |

## JONES, Stuart — Goalkeeper

b.Bristol 24-10-77

*Source:* Weston-Super-Mare.

| | | | |
|---|---|---|---|
| 1997–98 | Sheffield W | 0 | 0 |

## JONES, Vinnie — Midfield

H: 6 0 W: 11 12 b.Watford 5-1-65

*Source:* Wealdstone. *Honours:* Wales 9 full caps.

| | | | |
|---|---|---|---|
| 1986–87 | Wimbledon | 22 | 4 |
| 1987–88 | Wimbledon | 24 | 2 |
| 1988–89 | Wimbledon | 31 | 3 |
| 1989–90 | Leeds U | 45 | 5 |
| 1990–91 | Leeds U | 1 | 0 |
| 1990–91 | Sheffield U | 31 | 2 |
| 1991–92 | Sheffield U | 4 | 0 |
| 1991–92 | Chelsea | 35 | 3 |
| 1992–93 | Chelsea | 7 | 1 |
| 1992–93 | Wimbledon | 27 | 1 |
| 1993–94 | Wimbledon | 33 | 2 |
| 1994–95 | Wimbledon | 33 | 3 |
| 1995–96 | Wimbledon | 31 | 3 |
| 1996–97 | Wimbledon | 29 | 3 |
| 1997–98 | Wimbledon | 24 | 0 |
| 1997–98 | QPR | 7 | 1 |
| **Total:** | | **384** | **33** |

## JONSSON, Gunnlauger — Midfield

b.Iceland 29-11-74

| | | | |
|---|---|---|---|
| 1994 | IA Akranes | 1 | 0 |
| 1995 | IA Akranes | 3 | 0 |
| 1996 | IA Akranes | 12 | 1 |
| 1997 | IA Akranes | 17 | 0 |
| 1997–98 | Motherwell | 2 | 0 |
| **Total:** | | **35** | **1** |

## JONSSON, Siggi — Defender

H: 5 11 W: 12 06 b.Akranes 26-9-66

*Source:* IA Akranes. *Honours:* Iceland 54 full caps, 2 goals.

| | | | |
|---|---|---|---|
| 1984–85 | Sheffield W | 3 | 0 |
| 1985–86 | Sheffield W | 10 | 2 |
| 1985–86 | Barnsley (loan) | 5 | 0 |
| 1986–87 | Sheffield W | 13 | 0 |
| 1987–88 | Sheffield W | 13 | 1 |
| 1988–89 | Sheffield W | 28 | 1 |
| 1989–90 | Arsenal | 6 | 1 |
| 1990–91 | Arsenal | 2 | 0 |
| 1991–92 | Arsenal | 0 | 0 |
| 1992 | IA Akranes | 11 | 0 |
| 1993 | IA Akranes | 16 | 1 |
| 1994 | IA Akranes | 13 | 3 |
| 1995 | IA Akranes | 16 | 2 |
| 1996 | Orebro | 20 | 0 |
| 1997 | Orebro | 22 | 2 |
| 1997–98 | Dundee U | 15 | 0 |
| **Total:** | | **193** | **13** |

## JORDAN, Andrew — Defender

b.Manchester 14-12-79

*Source:* Trainee.

| | | | |
|---|---|---|---|
| 1997–98 | Bristol C | 0 | 0 |

## JORDAN, Scott — Midfield

H: 5 9 W: 11 05 b.Newcastle 19-7-75

*Source:* Trainee.

| | | | |
|---|---|---|---|
| 1992–93 | York C | 1 | 0 |
| 1993–94 | York C | 0 | 0 |
| 1994–95 | York C | 37 | 3 |
| 1995–96 | York C | 26 | 1 |
| 1996–97 | York C | 15 | 1 |
| 1997–98 | York C | 16 | 0 |
| **Total:** | | **95** | **5** |

## JOSEPH, Marc — Defender

H: 6 1 W: 12 09 b.Leicester 10-11-76

*Source:* Trainee.

| | | | |
|---|---|---|---|
| 1995–96 | Cambridge U | 12 | 0 |
| 1996–97 | Cambridge U | 8 | 0 |
| 1997–98 | Cambridge U | 41 | 0 |
| **Total:** | | **61** | **0** |

## JOSEPH, Matt — Defender

H: 5 7 W: 10 02 b.Bethnal Green 30-9-72

*Source:* Trainee.

| | | | |
|---|---|---|---|
| 1991–92 | Arsenal | 0 | 0 |
| 1992–93 | Gillingham | 0 | 0 |
| 1993–94 | Cambridge U | 27 | 2 |
| 1994–95 | Cambridge U | 39 | 2 |
| 1995–96 | Cambridge U | 42 | 2 |
| 1996–97 | Cambridge U | 44 | 0 |
| 1997–98 | Cambridge U | 7 | 0 |
| 1997–98 | Leyton Orient | 14 | 1 |
| **Total:** | | **173** | **7** |

## JOSEPH, Roger — Defender

H: 5 11 W: 11 10 b.Paddington 24-12-65

*Source:* Juniors. *Honours:* England B.

| | | | |
|---|---|---|---|
| 1984–85 | Brentford | 1 | 0 |
| 1985–86 | Brentford | 28 | 1 |
| 1986–87 | Brentford | 32 | 1 |
| 1987–88 | Brentford | 43 | 0 |
| 1988–89 | Wimbledon | 31 | 0 |
| 1989–90 | Wimbledon | 19 | 0 |
| 1990–91 | Wimbledon | 38 | 0 |
| 1991–92 | Wimbledon | 26 | 0 |
| 1992–93 | Wimbledon | 32 | 0 |
| 1993–94 | Wimbledon | 13 | 0 |
| 1994–95 | Wimbledon | 3 | 0 |
| 1994–95 | Millwall (loan) | 5 | 0 |
| 1995–96 | Wimbledon | 0 | 0 |
| 1996–97 | Leyton Orient | 15 | 0 |
| 1996–97 | WBA | 2 | 0 |
| 1997–98 | Leyton Orient | 25 | 0 |
| **Total:** | | **313** | **2** |

## JOYCE, Joe — Defender

H: 5 9 W: 11 01 b.Consett 18-3-61

*Source:* School.

| | | | |
|---|---|---|---|
| 1979–80 | Barnsley | 8 | 0 |
| 1980–81 | Barnsley | 33 | 0 |
| 1981–82 | Barnsley | 20 | 0 |
| 1982–83 | Barnsley | 32 | 1 |
| 1983–84 | Barnsley | 40 | 1 |

| | | | |
|---|---|---|---|
| 1984–85 | Barnsley | 41 | 0 |
| 1985–86 | Barnsley | 40 | 0 |
| 1986–87 | Barnsley | 34 | 0 |
| 1987–88 | Barnsley | 38 | 2 |
| 1988–89 | Barnsley | 45 | 0 |
| 1989–90 | Barnsley | 0 | 0 |
| 1990–91 | Barnsley | 3 | 0 |
| 1990–91 | Scunthorpe U | 21 | 0 |
| 1991–92 | Scunthorpe U | 40 | 2 |
| 1992–93 | Scunthorpe U | 30 | 0 |
| 1993–94 | Carlisle U | 29 | 0 |
| 1993–94 | Darlington (loan) | 4 | 0 |
| 1994–95 | Carlisle U | 21 | 0 |
| 1995–96 | Carlisle U | 0 | 0 |
| 1996–97 | Carlisle U | 0 | 0 |
| 1997–98 | Carlisle U | 0 | 0 |
| **Total:** | | **479** | **6** |

## JOYCE, Warren — Midfield

H: 5 9 W: 12 00 b.Oldham 20-1-65

*Source:* School.

| | | | |
|---|---|---|---|
| 1982–83 | Bolton W | 8 | 0 |
| 1983–84 | Bolton W | 45 | 3 |
| 1984–85 | Bolton W | 45 | 5 |
| 1985–86 | Bolton W | 31 | 4 |
| 1986–87 | Bolton W | 44 | 5 |
| 1987–88 | Bolton W | 11 | 0 |
| 1987–88 | Preston NE | 22 | 0 |
| 1988–89 | Preston NE | 40 | 9 |
| 1989–90 | Preston NE | 44 | 11 |
| 1990–91 | Preston NE | 42 | 9 |
| 1991–92 | Preston NE | 29 | 5 |
| 1992–93 | Plymouth Arg | 30 | 3 |
| 1993–94 | Burnley | 22 | 4 |
| 1994–95 | Burnley | 5 | 0 |
| 1994–95 | Hull C (loan) | 9 | 3 |
| 1995–96 | Burnley | 43 | 5 |
| 1996–97 | Hull C | 45 | 5 |
| 1997–98 | Hull C | 45 | 4 |
| **Total:** | | **560** | **75** |

## JUKES, Nathan — Midfield

H: 5 11 W: 11 13 b.Worcester 10-4-79

*Source:* Trainee.

| | | | |
|---|---|---|---|
| 1997–98 | Portsmouth | 0 | 0 |

## JULES, Mark — Defender

H: 5 7 W: 10 09 b.Bradford 5-9-71

*Source:* Trainee.

| | | | |
|---|---|---|---|
| 1990–91 | Bradford C | 0 | 0 |
| 1991–92 | Scarborough | 41 | 8 |
| 1992–93 | Scarborough | 36 | 8 |
| 1993–94 | Chesterfield | 33 | 1 |
| 1994–95 | Chesterfield | 23 | 0 |
| 1995–96 | Chesterfield | 32 | 2 |
| 1996–97 | Chesterfield | 42 | 0 |
| 1997–98 | Chesterfield | 33 | 1 |
| **Total:** | | **240** | **20** |

## JUPP, Duncan — Defender

H: 6 0 W: 12 11 b.Guildford 25-1-75

*Source:* Trainee. *Honours:* Scotland Under-21.

| | | | |
|---|---|---|---|
| 1992–93 | Fulham | 3 | 0 |
| 1993–94 | Fulham | 30 | 0 |
| 1994–95 | Fulham | 36 | 2 |
| 1995–96 | Fulham | 36 | 0 |
| 1996–97 | Wimbledon | 6 | 0 |
| 1997–98 | Wimbledon | 3 | 0 |
| **Total:** | | **114** | **2** |

## KADI, Junior — Midfield

b.London 16-8-79

*Source:* Trainee.

| | | | |
|---|---|---|---|
| 1997-98 | Coventry C | 0 | 0 |

## KALOGERACUS, Vas — Forward

H: 5 7 W: 11 00 b.Perth 21-3-75

*Source:* Floreat Athena. *Honours:* Australia Under-21.

| | | | |
|---|---|---|---|
| 1993–94 | Birmingham C | 0 | 0 |
| From Floreat Athena. | | | |
| 1997–98 | Stockport Co | 2 | 0 |
| **Total:** | | **2** | **0** |

## KAMARK, Pontus — Defender

H: 5 11 W: 12 02 b.Fasteras 5-4-69

*Honours:* Sweden 35 full caps.

| | | | |
|---|---|---|---|
| 1990 | IFK Gothenburg | 8 | 0 |
| 1991 | IFK Gothenburg | 26 | 0 |
| 1992 | IFK Gothenburg | 24 | 0 |
| 1993 | IFK Gothenburg | 26 | 0 |
| 1994 | IFK Gothenburg | 22 | 0 |
| 1995 | IFK Gothenburg | 20 | 1 |
| 1995–96 | Leicester C | 1 | 0 |
| 1996–97 | Leicester C | 10 | 0 |
| 1997–98 | Leicester C | 35 | 0 |
| **Total:** | | **172** | **1** |

## KANE, Paul — Midfield

H: 5 8 W: 9 09 b.Edinburgh 20-6-65

*Source:* Salvesen BC. *Honours:* Scotland Youth.

| | | | |
|---|---|---|---|
| 1982–83 | Hibernian | 0 | 0 |
| 1983–84 | Hibernian | 13 | 1 |
| 1984–85 | Hibernian | 34 | 8 |
| 1985–86 | Hibernian | 32 | 5 |
| 1986–87 | Hibernian | 37 | 1 |
| 1987–88 | Hibernian | 44 | 10 |
| 1988–89 | Hibernian | 35 | 5 |
| 1989–90 | Hibernian | 31 | 3 |
| 1990–91 | Hibernian | 21 | 0 |
| 1990–91 | Oldham Ath | 17 | 0 |
| 1991–92 | Oldham Ath | 4 | 0 |
| 1991–92 | Aberdeen | 25 | 2 |
| 1992–93 | Aberdeen | 27 | 4 |
| 1993–94 | Aberdeen | 39 | 3 |
| 1994–95 | Aberdeen | 27 | 2 |
| 1995–96 | Barnsley (loan) | 4 | 0 |
| 1996 | Viking | 15 | 3 |
| 1997–98 | St Johnstone | 27 | 1 |
| **Total:** | | **432** | **48** |

## KARIMZADEH, Ashkan — Forward

H: 5 11 W: 11 07 b.Iran 12-10-78

*Source:* Trainee.

| | | | |
|---|---|---|---|
| 1997–98 | Portsmouth | 0 | 0 |

## KATCHURO, Petr — Forward

H: 6 0 W: 12 06 b.Minsk 2-8-72

*Honours:* Russia Youth, Belarus 19 full caps, 3 goals.

| | | | |
|---|---|---|---|
| 1993–94 | Dynamo 93 | 15 | 7 |
| 1993–94 | Dynamo Minsk | 13 | 14 |
| 1994–95 | Dynamo Minsk | 22 | 14 |
| 1995 | Dynamo Minsk | 15 | 15 |
| 1996 | Dynamo Minsk | 10 | 9 |
| 1996–97 | Sheffield U | 40 | 12 |
| 1997–98 | Sheffield U | 16 | 0 |
| **Total:** | | **131** | **71** |

## KAVANAGH, Graham — Midfield

H: 5 10 W: 12 06 b.Dublin 2-12-73

*Source:* Home Farm. *Honours:* Eire Under-21, 1 full cap.

| | | | |
|---|---|---|---|
| 1991–92 | Middlesbrough | 0 | 0 |
| 1992–93 | Middlesbrough | 10 | 0 |
| 1993–94 | Middlesbrough | 11 | 2 |
| 1993–94 | Darlington (loan) | 5 | 0 |
| 1994–95 | Middlesbrough | 7 | 0 |
| 1995–96 | Middlesbrough | 7 | 1 |
| 1996–97 | Middlesbrough | 0 | 0 |
| 1996–97 | Stoke C | 38 | 4 |
| 1997–98 | Stoke C | 44 | 5 |
| **Total:** | | **122** | **12** |

## KAVANAGH, Jason — Defender

H: 5 9 W: 12 01 b.Birmingham 23-11-71

*Source:* Birmingham C Schoolboy. *Honours:* England Schools, FA Schools, Youth.

| | | | |
|---|---|---|---|
| 1988–89 | Derby Co | 0 | 0 |
| 1989–90 | Derby Co | 0 | 0 |
| 1990–91 | Derby Co | 11 | 0 |
| 1991–92 | Derby Co | 25 | 0 |
| 1992–93 | Derby Co | 10 | 0 |
| 1993–94 | Derby Co | 19 | 0 |
| 1994–95 | Derby Co | 25 | 1 |
| 1995–96 | Derby Co | 9 | 0 |
| 1996–97 | Derby Co | 0 | 0 |
| 1996–97 | Wycombe W | 27 | 0 |
| 1997–98 | Wycombe W | 45 | 1 |
| **Total:** | | **171** | **2** |

## KAVELASHVILI, Mikhail — Midfield

H: 5 11 W: 12 01 b.Tbilisi 22-7-71

*Source:* Spartak Vladikavkaz. *Honours:* Georgia 20 full caps, 3 goals.

| | | | |
|---|---|---|---|
| 1995–96 | Manchester C | 4 | 1 |
| 1996–97 | Manchester C | 24 | 2 |
| 1997–98 | Manchester C | 0 | 0 |
| **Total:** | | **28** | **3** |

## KAY, John — Defender

H: 5 10 W: 11 08 b.Sunderland 29-1-64

*Source:* Apprentice.

| | | | |
|---|---|---|---|
| 1981–82 | Arsenal | 0 | 0 |
| 1982–83 | Arsenal | 7 | 0 |
| 1983–84 | Arsenal | 7 | 0 |
| 1984–85 | Wimbledon | 21 | 1 |
| 1984–85 | Middlesbrough (loan) | 8 | 0 |
| 1985–86 | Wimbledon | 26 | 1 |
| 1986–87 | Wimbledon | 16 | 0 |
| 1987–88 | Sunderland | 46 | 0 |
| 1988–89 | Sunderland | 11 | 0 |
| 1989–90 | Sunderland | 32 | 0 |
| 1990–91 | Sunderland | 30 | 0 |
| 1991–92 | Sunderland | 41 | 0 |
| 1992–93 | Sunderland | 36 | 0 |
| 1993–94 | Sunderland | 3 | 0 |
| 1994–95 | Sunderland | 0 | 0 |
| 1995–96 | Sunderland | 0 | 0 |
| 1995–96 | Shrewsbury T (loan) | 7 | 0 |
| 1996–97 | Preston NE | 7 | 0 |

| | | | |
|---|---|---|---|
| 1996–97 | Scarborough | 34 | 0 |
| 1997–98 | Scarborough | 40 | 0 |
| **Total:** | | **372** | **2** |

## KAYE, Peter — Forward

H: 5 7 W: 11 00 b.Huddersfield 30-7-75

*Source:* Trainee.

| | | | |
|---|---|---|---|
| 1996–97 | Huddersfield T | 1 | 0 |
| 1997–98 | Huddersfield T | 0 | 0 |
| **Total:** | | **1** | **0** |

## KEAN, Robert — Midfield

H: 5 7 W: 10 00 b.Luton 3-6-78

*Source:* Trainee.

| | | | |
|---|---|---|---|
| 1995–96 | Luton T | 0 | 0 |
| 1996–97 | Luton T | 0 | 0 |
| 1997–98 | Luton T | 1 | 0 |
| **Total:** | | **1** | **0** |

## KEANE, Robbie — Forward

H: 5 9 W: 11 07 b.Dublin 8-7-80

*Source:* Trainee. *Honours:* Eire 3 full caps.

| | | | |
|---|---|---|---|
| 1997–98 | Wolverhampton W | 38 | 11 |
| **Total:** | | **38** | **11** |

## KEANE, Roy — Midfield

H: 5 11 W: 12 01 b.Cork 10-8-71

*Source:* Cobh Ramb. *Honours:* Eire Youth, Under-21, 38 full caps, 3 goals.

| | | | |
|---|---|---|---|
| 1990–91 | Nottingham F | 35 | 8 |
| 1991–92 | Nottingham F | 39 | 8 |
| 1992–93 | Nottingham F | 40 | 6 |
| 1993–94 | Manchester U | 37 | 5 |
| 1994–95 | Manchester U | 25 | 2 |
| 1995–96 | Manchester U | 29 | 6 |
| 1996–97 | Manchester U | 21 | 2 |
| 1997–98 | Manchester U | 9 | 2 |
| **Total:** | | **235** | **39** |

## KEARLEY, Dean — Defender

b.Greenwich 11-10-77

*Source:* Trainee.

| | | | |
|---|---|---|---|
| 1996–97 | Charlton Ath | 0 | 0 |
| 1997–98 | Charlton Ath | 0 | 0 |

## KEARTON, Jason — Goalkeeper

H: 6 1 W: 12 03 b.Ipswich (Aus) 9-7-69

*Source:* Brisbane Lions.

| | | | |
|---|---|---|---|
| 1988–89 | Everton | 0 | 0 |
| 1989–90 | Everton | 0 | 0 |
| 1990–91 | Everton | 0 | 0 |
| 1991–92 | Everton | 0 | 0 |
| 1991–92 | Stoke C (loan) | 16 | 0 |
| 1991–92 | Blackpool (loan) | 14 | 0 |
| 1992–93 | Everton | 5 | 0 |
| 1993–94 | Everton | 0 | 0 |
| 1994–95 | Everton | 1 | 0 |
| 1994–95 | Notts Co (loan) | 10 | 0 |
| 1995–96 | Everton | 0 | 0 |
| 1995–96 | Preston NE (loan) | 0 | 0 |
| 1996–97 | Everton | 0 | 0 |
| 1996–97 | Crewe Alex | 30 | 0 |
| 1997–98 | Crewe Alex | 43 | 0 |
| **Total:** | | **119** | **0** |

## KEATES, Dean — Midfield

H: 5 6 W: 10 08 b.Walsall 30-6-78

*Source:* Trainee.

| | | | |
|---|---|---|---|
| 1996–97 | Walsall | 2 | 0 |
| 1997–98 | Walsall | 33 | 1 |
| **Total:** | | **35** | **1** |

## KEEBLE, Chris — Midfield

H: 5 10 W: 10 07 b.Colchester 17-9-78

*Source:* Trainee.

| | | | |
|---|---|---|---|
| 1997–98 | Ipswich T | 1 | 0 |
| **Total:** | | **1** | **0** |

## KEEN, Kevin — Midfield

H: 5 7 W: 10 09 b.Amersham 25-2-67

*Source:* Wycombe W and Apprentice. *Honours:* England Schools, Youth.

| | | | |
|---|---|---|---|
| 1983–84 | West Ham U | 0 | 0 |
| 1984–85 | West Ham U | 0 | 0 |
| 1985–86 | West Ham U | 0 | 0 |
| 1986–87 | West Ham U | 13 | 0 |
| 1987–88 | West Ham U | 23 | 1 |
| 1988–89 | West Ham U | 24 | 3 |
| 1989–90 | West Ham U | 44 | 10 |
| 1990–91 | West Ham U | 40 | 0 |
| 1991–92 | West Ham U | 29 | 0 |
| 1992–93 | West Ham U | 46 | 7 |
| 1993–94 | Wolverhampton W | 41 | 7 |
| 1994–95 | Wolverhampton W | 1 | 0 |
| 1994–95 | Stoke C | 21 | 2 |

| | | | |
|---|---|---|---|
| 1995–96 | Stoke C | 33 | 3 |
| 1996–97 | Stoke C | 16 | 1 |
| 1997–98 | Stoke C | 40 | 1 |
| **Total:** | | **371** | **35** |

## KEEN, Peter — Goalkeeper

H: 6 0 W: 11 10 b.Middlesbrough 16-11-76

*Source:* Trainee.

| | | | |
|---|---|---|---|
| 1995–96 | Newcastle U | 0 | 0 |
| 1996–97 | Newcastle U | 0 | 0 |
| 1997–98 | Newcastle U | 0 | 0 |

## KEIDAL, Ralf — Midfield

H: 5 8 W: 10 12 b.Wurzburg 6-3-77

*Source:* Schweinfurt.

| | | | |
|---|---|---|---|
| 1997–98 | Newcastle U | 0 | 0 |

## KEISTER, John — Midfield

H: 5 8 W: 10 10 b.Manchester 11-11-70

*Source:* Faweh FC.

| | | | |
|---|---|---|---|
| 1993–94 | Walsall | 22 | 1 |
| 1994–95 | Walsall | 11 | 0 |
| 1995–96 | Walsall | 21 | 0 |
| 1996–97 | Walsall | 36 | 1 |
| 1997–98 | Walsall | 13 | 0 |
| **Total:** | | **103** | **2** |

## KEITH, Joseph — Defender

b.London 1-10-78

*Source:* Trainee.

| | | | |
|---|---|---|---|
| 1997–98 | West Ham U | 0 | 0 |

## KELLER, Kasey — Goalkeeper

H: 6 2 W: 13 12 b.Washington 27-11-69

*Source:* Portland Univ. *Honours:* USA 35 full caps.

| | | | |
|---|---|---|---|
| 1991–92 | Millwall | 1 | 0 |
| 1992–93 | Millwall | 45 | 0 |
| 1993–94 | Millwall | 44 | 0 |
| 1994–95 | Millwall | 44 | 0 |
| 1995–96 | Millwall | 42 | 0 |
| 1996–97 | Leicester C | 31 | 0 |
| 1997–98 | Leicester C | 32 | 0 |
| **Total:** | | **239** | **0** |

## KELLY, Alan — Goalkeeper

H: 6 3 W: 14 02 b.Preston 11-8-68

*Source:* Trainee. *Honours:* Eire Youth, Under-21, Under-23, 20 full caps.

| | | | |
|---|---|---|---|
| 1985–86 | Preston NE | 13 | 0 |
| 1986–87 | Preston NE | 22 | 0 |
| 1987–88 | Preston NE | 19 | 0 |
| 1988–89 | Preston NE | 0 | 0 |
| 1989–90 | Preston NE | 42 | 0 |
| 1990–91 | Preston NE | 23 | 0 |
| 1991–92 | Preston NE | 23 | 0 |
| 1992–93 | Sheffield U | 33 | 0 |
| 1993–94 | Sheffield U | 30 | 0 |
| 1994–95 | Sheffield U | 38 | 0 |
| 1995–96 | Sheffield U | 35 | 0 |
| 1996–97 | Sheffield U | 39 | 0 |
| 1997–98 | Sheffield U | 19 | 0 |
| **Total:** | | **336** | **0** |

## KELLY, David — Forward

H: 5 11 W: 11 10 b.Birmingham 25-11-65

*Source:* Alvechurch. *Honours:* Eire Under-21, Under-23, B, 26 full caps, 9 goals.

| | | | |
|---|---|---|---|
| 1983–84 | Walsall | 6 | 3 |
| 1984–85 | Walsall | 32 | 7 |
| 1985–86 | Walsall | 28 | 10 |
| 1986–87 | Walsall | 42 | 23 |
| 1987–88 | Walsall | 39 | 20 |
| 1988–89 | West Ham U | 25 | 6 |
| 1989–90 | West Ham U | 16 | 1 |
| 1989–90 | Leicester C | 10 | 7 |
| 1990–91 | Leicester C | 44 | 14 |
| 1991–92 | Leicester C | 12 | 1 |
| 1991–92 | Newcastle U | 25 | 11 |
| 1992–93 | Newcastle U | 45 | 24 |
| 1993–94 | Wolverhampton W | 36 | 11 |
| 1994–95 | Wolverhampton W | 42 | 15 |
| 1995–96 | Wolverhampton W | 5 | 0 |
| 1995–96 | Sunderland | 10 | 2 |
| 1996–97 | Sunderland | 24 | 0 |
| 1997–98 | Tranmere R | 29 | 11 |
| **Total:** | | **470** | **166** |

## KELLY, Gary — Goalkeeper

H: 5 11 W: 12 06 b.Fulwood 3-8-66

*Source:* Apprentice. *Honours:* Eire Under-21, B.

| | | | |
|---|---|---|---|
| 1984–85 | Newcastle U | 0 | 0 |
| 1985–86 | Newcastle U | 0 | 0 |
| 1986–87 | Newcastle U | 3 | 0 |
| 1987–88 | Newcastle U | 37 | 0 |
| 1988–89 | Newcastle U | 9 | 0 |
| 1988–89 | Blackpool (loan) | 5 | 0 |

| | | | |
|---|---|---|---|
| 1989–90 | Newcastle U | 4 | 0 |
| 1989–90 | Bury | 38 | 0 |
| 1990–91 | Bury | 46 | 0 |
| 1991–92 | Bury | 46 | 0 |
| 1992–93 | Bury | 42 | 0 |
| 1993–94 | Bury | 1 | 0 |
| 1993–94 | West Ham U (loan) | 0 | 0 |
| 1994–95 | Bury | 38 | 0 |
| 1995–96 | Bury | 25 | 0 |
| 1996–97 | Oldham Ath | 42 | 0 |
| 1997–98 | Oldham Ath | 26 | 0 |
| **Total:** | | **362** | **0** |

## KELLY, Gary — Defender

H: 5 8 W: 13 03 b.Drogheda 9-7-74

*Source:* Home Farm. *Honours:* Eire Youth, 28 full caps, 1 goal.

| | | | |
|---|---|---|---|
| 1991–92 | Leeds U | 2 | 0 |
| 1992–93 | Leeds U | 0 | 0 |
| 1993–94 | Leeds U | 42 | 0 |
| 1994–95 | Leeds U | 42 | 0 |
| 1995–96 | Leeds U | 34 | 0 |
| 1996–97 | Leeds U | 36 | 2 |
| 1997–98 | Leeds U | 34 | 0 |
| **Total:** | | **190** | **2** |

## KELLY, Paddy — Defender

H: 6 0 W: 11 07 b.Kirkcaldy 26-4-78

*Source:* Celtic BC. *Honours:* Scotland Under-18.

| | | | |
|---|---|---|---|
| 1995–96 | Celtic | 0 | 0 |
| 1996–97 | Celtic | 1 | 0 |
| 1997–98 | Newcastle U | 0 | 0 |
| 1997–98 | Reading (loan) | 3 | 0 |
| **Total:** | | **4** | **0** |

## KELLY, Ray — Forward

H: 5 11 W: 12 00 b.Ballinasloe 29-12-76

*Source:* Athlone T.

| | | | |
|---|---|---|---|
| 1994–95 | Manchester C | 0 | 0 |
| 1995–96 | Manchester C | 0 | 0 |
| 1996–97 | Manchester C | 0 | 0 |
| 1997–98 | Manchester C | 1 | 0 |
| 1997–98 | Wrexham (loan) | 10 | 1 |
| **Total:** | | **11** | **1** |

## KELLY, Russell — Midfield

H: 5 10 W: 11 00 b.Ballymoney 10-8-76

*Source:* Trainee.

| | | | |
|---|---|---|---|
| 1995–96 | Leyton Orient (loan) | 6 | 0 |
| 1996–97 | Darlington | 23 | 2 |
| 1997–98 | Dundee | 19 | 2 |
| **Total:** | | **48** | **4** |

## KENDALL, Lee — Goalkeeper

b.Newport 8-1-81

*Source:* Trainee.

| | | | |
|---|---|---|---|
| 1997–98 | Crystal Palace | 0 | 0 |

## KENNA, Jeff — Defender

H: 5 11 W: 12 03 b.Dublin 28-8-70

*Source:* Trainee. *Honours:* Eire Youth, Under-21, B, 24 full caps.

| | | | |
|---|---|---|---|
| 1988–89 | Southampton | 0 | 0 |
| 1989–90 | Southampton | 0 | 0 |
| 1990–91 | Southampton | 2 | 0 |
| 1991–92 | Southampton | 14 | 0 |
| 1992–93 | Southampton | 29 | 2 |
| 1993–94 | Southampton | 41 | 2 |
| 1994–95 | Southampton | 28 | 0 |
| 1994–95 | Blackburn R | 9 | 1 |
| 1995–96 | Blackburn R | 32 | 0 |
| 1996–97 | Blackburn R | 37 | 0 |
| 1997–98 | Blackburn R | 37 | 0 |
| **Total:** | | **229** | **5** |

## KENNEDY, John — Defender

H: 5 9 W: 10 03 b.Cambridge 19-8-78

*Source:* Trainee.

| | | | |
|---|---|---|---|
| 1997–98 | Ipswich T | 1 | 0 |
| **Total:** | | **1** | **0** |

## KENNEDY, Mark — Forward

H: 5 11 W: 11 00 b.Dublin 15-5-76

*Source:* Belvedere, Trainee. *Honours:* Eire Under-21, 18 full caps.

| | | | |
|---|---|---|---|
| 1992–93 | Millwall | 1 | 0 |
| 1993–94 | Millwall | 12 | 4 |
| 1994–95 | Millwall | 30 | 5 |
| 1994–95 | Liverpool | 6 | 0 |
| 1995–96 | Liverpool | 4 | 0 |
| 1996–97 | Liverpool | 5 | 0 |
| 1997–98 | Liverpool | 1 | 0 |

| | | | |
|---|---|---|---|
| 1997–98 | QPR (loan) | 8 | 2 |
| 1997–98 | Wimbledon | 4 | 0 |
| **Total:** | | **71** | **11** |

## KENNEDY, Peter — Midfield

H: 5 8 W: 11 11 b.Lisburn 10-9-73

*Source:* Portadown.

| | | | |
|---|---|---|---|
| 1996–97 | Notts Co | 22 | 0 |
| 1997–98 | Watford | 34 | 11 |
| **Total:** | | **56** | **11** |

## KENNEDY, Richard — Midfield

H: 5 10 W: 10 05 b.Waterford 28-8-78

*Source:* Trainee.

| | | | |
|---|---|---|---|
| 1996–97 | Crystal Palace | 0 | 0 |
| 1997–98 | Crystal Palace | 0 | 0 |

## KENTON, Darren — Defender

H: 5 9 W: 11 02 b.Wandsworth 13-9-78

*Source:* Trainee.

| | | | |
|---|---|---|---|
| 1997–98 | Norwich C | 11 | 0 |
| **Total:** | | **11** | **0** |

## KEOWN, Martin — Defender

H: 6 1 W: 12 04 b.Oxford 24-7-66

*Source:* Apprentice. *Honours:* England Youth, Under-21, B, 18 full caps, 3 goals.

| | | | |
|---|---|---|---|
| 1983–84 | Arsenal | 0 | 0 |
| 1984–85 | Arsenal | 0 | 0 |
| 1984–85 | Brighton & HA (loan) | 16 | 0 |
| 1985–86 | Arsenal | 22 | 0 |
| 1985–86 | Brighton & HA (loan) | 7 | 1 |
| 1986–87 | Aston Villa | 36 | 0 |
| 1987–88 | Aston Villa | 42 | 3 |
| 1988–89 | Aston Villa | 34 | 0 |
| 1989–90 | Everton | 20 | 0 |
| 1990–91 | Everton | 24 | 0 |
| 1991–92 | Everton | 39 | 0 |
| 1992–93 | Everton | 13 | 0 |
| 1992–93 | Arsenal | 16 | 0 |
| 1993–94 | Arsenal | 33 | 0 |
| 1994–95 | Arsenal | 31 | 1 |
| 1995–96 | Arsenal | 34 | 0 |
| 1996–97 | Arsenal | 33 | 1 |
| 1997–98 | Arsenal | 18 | 0 |
| **Total:** | | **418** | **6** |

## KERNAGHAN, Alan — Defender

H: 6 2 W: 14 01 b.Otley 25-4-67

*Source:* Apprentice. *Honours:* Eire 22 full caps, 1 goal.

| | | | |
|---|---|---|---|
| 1984–85 | Middlesbrough | 8 | 1 |
| 1985–86 | Middlesbrough | 6 | 0 |
| 1986–87 | Middlesbrough | 13 | 0 |
| 1987–88 | Middlesbrough | 35 | 6 |
| 1988–89 | Middlesbrough | 23 | 0 |
| 1989–90 | Middlesbrough | 37 | 4 |
| 1990–91 | Middlesbrough | 24 | 0 |
| 1990–91 | Charlton Ath (loan) | 13 | 0 |
| 1991–92 | Middlesbrough | 38 | 2 |
| 1992–93 | Middlesbrough | 22 | 2 |
| 1993–94 | Middlesbrough | 6 | 1 |
| 1993–94 | Manchester C | 24 | 0 |
| 1994–95 | Manchester C | 22 | 1 |
| 1994–95 | Bolton W (loan) | 11 | 0 |
| 1995–96 | Manchester C | 6 | 0 |
| 1995–96 | Bradford C (loan) | 5 | 0 |
| 1996–97 | Manchester C | 10 | 0 |
| 1997–98 | Manchester C | 1 | 0 |
| 1997–98 | St Johnstone (loan) | 28 | 2 |
| **Total:** | | **332** | **19** |

## KERR, David — Midfield

H: 5 11 W: 12 01 b.Dumfries 6-9-74

*Source:* Trainee.

| | | | |
|---|---|---|---|
| 1991–92 | Manchester C | 0 | 0 |
| 1992–93 | Manchester C | 1 | 0 |
| 1993–94 | Manchester C | 2 | 0 |
| 1994–95 | Manchester C | 2 | 0 |
| 1995–96 | Manchester C | 1 | 0 |
| 1995–96 | Mansfield T (loan) | 5 | 0 |
| 1996–97 | Mansfield T | 9 | 0 |
| 1997–98 | Mansfield T | 18 | 2 |
| **Total:** | | **38** | **2** |

## KERR, Dylan — Defender

H: 5 9 W: 11 04 b.Valletta 14-1-67

*Source:* Arcadia Shepherds.

| | | | |
|---|---|---|---|
| 1988–89 | Leeds U | 3 | 0 |
| 1989–90 | Leeds U | 5 | 0 |
| 1990–91 | Leeds U | 0 | 0 |
| 1991–92 | Leeds U | 0 | 0 |
| 1991–92 | Doncaster R (loan) | 7 | 1 |
| 1991–92 | Blackpool (loan) | 12 | 1 |
| 1992–93 | Leeds U | 5 | 0 |
| 1993–94 | Reading | 45 | 2 |
| 1994–95 | Reading | 36 | 1 |
| 1995–96 | Reading | 8 | 2 |
| 1996–97 | Reading | 0 | 0 |
| 1996–97 | Carlisle U | 1 | 0 |

| | | | |
|---|---|---|---|
| 1996–97 | Kilmarnock | 27 | 0 |
| 1997–98 | Kilmarnock | 14 | 0 |
| **Total:** | | **163** | **7** |

## KERRIGAN, Steve — Forward

H: 6 1 W: 12 04 b.Bailleston 9-10-72

*Source:* Newmains J.

| | | | |
|---|---|---|---|
| 1992–93 | Albion R | 29 | 8 |
| 1993–94 | Albion R | 24 | 6 |
| 1993–94 | Clydebank | 15 | 0 |
| 1994–95 | Clydebank | 14 | 0 |
| 1995–96 | Clydebank | 1 | 0 |
| 1995–96 | Stranraer | 21 | 5 |
| 1996–97 | Ayr U | 27 | 14 |
| 1997–98 | Ayr U | 6 | 3 |
| 1997–98 | Shrewsbury T | 14 | 2 |
| **Total:** | | **151** | **38** |

## KERSEY, Lee — Midfield

b.Harlow 12-8-79

*Source:* Trainee.

| | | | |
|---|---|---|---|
| 1997–98 | Tottenham H | 0 | 0 |

## KERSLAKE, David — Defender

H: 5 9 W: 12 04 b.Stepney 19-6-66

*Source:* Apprentice. *Honours:* England Schools, Youth, Under-21. Football League.

| | | | |
|---|---|---|---|
| 1983–84 | QPR | 0 | 0 |
| 1984–85 | QPR | 1 | 0 |
| 1985–86 | QPR | 14 | 1 |
| 1986–87 | QPR | 3 | 0 |
| 1987–88 | QPR | 18 | 5 |
| 1988–89 | QPR | 21 | 0 |
| 1989–90 | QPR | 1 | 0 |
| 1989–90 | Swindon T | 28 | 0 |
| 1990–91 | Swindon T | 37 | 0 |
| 1991–92 | Swindon T | 39 | 1 |
| 1992–93 | Swindon T | 31 | 0 |
| 1992–93 | Leeds U | 8 | 0 |
| 1993–94 | Tottenham H | 17 | 0 |
| 1994–95 | Tottenham H | 18 | 0 |
| 1995–96 | Tottenham H | 2 | 0 |
| 1996–97 | Tottenham H | 0 | 0 |
| 1996–97 | Swindon T (loan) | 8 | 0 |
| 1997–98 | Ipswich T | 7 | 0 |
| 1997–98 | Wycombe W (loan) | 10 | 0 |
| 1997–98 | Swindon T | 10 | 0 |
| **Total:** | | **273** | **7** |

## KETSBAIA, Temuri — Midfield

H: 5 8 W: 10 12 b.Gale 18-3-68

*Source:* Dynamo Sukhumi. *Honours:* Georgia 25 full caps, 9 goals.

| | | | |
|---|---|---|---|
| 1987 | Dynamo Tbilisi | 14 | 4 |
| 1988 | Dynamo Tbilisi | 13 | 0 |
| 1989 | Dynamo Tbilisi | 27 | 4 |
| 1990 | Dynamo Tbilisi* | 0 | 0 |
| 1991–92 | Anorthosis | 26 | 13 |
| 1992–93 | Anorthosis | 24 | 4 |
| 1993–94 | Anorthosis | 26 | 19 |
| 1994–95 | AEK Athens | 22 | 5 |
| 1995–96 | AEK Athens | 32 | 14 |
| 1996–97 | AEK Athens | 30 | 5 |
| 1997–98 | Newcastle U | 31 | 3 |
| **Total:** | | **245** | **71** |

## KEWELL, Harry — Midfield

H: 5 11 W: 12 00 b.Sydney 22-9-78

*Source:* NSW Soccer Academy. *Honours:* Australia 6 full caps, 3 goals.

| | | | |
|---|---|---|---|
| 1995–96 | Leeds U | 2 | 0 |
| 1996–97 | Leeds U | 1 | 0 |
| 1997–98 | Leeds U | 29 | 5 |
| **Total:** | | **32** | **5** |

## KEY, Lance — Goalkeeper

H: 6 3 W: 15 00 b.Kettering 13-5-68

*Source:* Histon.

| | | | |
|---|---|---|---|
| 1991–92 | Sheffield W | 0 | 0 |
| 1991–92 | York C (loan) | 0 | 0 |
| 1992–93 | Sheffield W | 0 | 0 |
| 1993–94 | Sheffield W | 0 | 0 |
| 1993–94 | Oldham Ath (loan) | 2 | 0 |
| 1993–94 | Portsmouth (loan) | 0 | 0 |
| 1994–95 | Sheffield W | 0 | 0 |
| 1994–95 | Oxford U (loan) | 6 | 0 |
| 1995–96 | Sheffield W | 0 | 0 |
| 1995–96 | Lincoln C (loan) | 5 | 0 |
| 1995–96 | Hartlepool U (loan) | 1 | 0 |
| 1995–96 | Rochdale (loan) | 14 | 0 |
| 1996–97 | Dundee U | 4 | 0 |
| 1996–97 | Sheffield U | 0 | 0 |
| 1997–98 | Rochdale | 19 | 0 |
| **Total:** | | **51** | **0** |

## KHARINE, Dmitri — Goalkeeper

H: 6 2 W: 13 11 b.Moscow 16-8-68

*Honours:* USSR Youth, Under-21, 15 full caps, Russia 21 full caps.

| | | | |
|---|---|---|---|
| 1984 | Torpedo Moscow | 1 | 0 |
| 1985 | Torpedo Moscow | 10 | 0 |
| 1986 | Torpedo Moscow | 25 | 0 |
| 1987 | Torpedo Moscow | 27 | 0 |
| 1988 | Dynamo Moscow | 19 | 0 |
| 1989 | Dynamo Moscow | 20 | 0 |
| 1990 | Dynamo Moscow | 1 | 0 |
| 1991 | CSKA Moscow | 11 | 0 |
| 1992 | CSKA Moscow | 23 | 0 |
| 1992–93 | Chelsea | 5 | 0 |
| 1993–94 | Chelsea | 40 | 0 |
| 1994–95 | Chelsea | 31 | 0 |
| 1995–96 | Chelsea | 26 | 0 |
| 1996–97 | Chelsea | 5 | 0 |
| 1997–98 | Chelsea | 10 | 0 |
| **Total:** | | **254** | **0** |

## KIDD, Ryan — Defender

H: 5 11 W: 10 08 b.Radcliffe 16-10-71

*Source:* Trainee.

| | | | |
|---|---|---|---|
| 1990–91 | Port Vale | 0 | 0 |
| 1991–92 | Port Vale | 1 | 0 |
| 1992–93 | Preston NE | 15 | 0 |
| 1993–94 | Preston NE | 36 | 1 |
| 1994–95 | Preston NE | 32 | 3 |
| 1995–96 | Preston NE | 30 | 0 |
| 1996–97 | Preston NE | 35 | 0 |
| 1997–98 | Preston NE | 33 | 2 |
| **Total:** | | **182** | **6** |

## KIELY, Dean — Goalkeeper

H: 6 0 W: 12 13 b.Salford 10-10-70

*Source:* WBA School. *Honours:* England Schools, FA Schools, Youth.

| | | | |
|---|---|---|---|
| 1987–88 | Coventry C | 0 | 0 |
| 1988–89 | Coventry C | 0 | 0 |
| 1989–90 | Coventry C | 0 | 0 |
| 1989–90 | Ipswich T (loan) | 0 | 0 |
| 1989–90 | York C (loan) | 0 | 0 |
| 1990–91 | York C | 17 | 0 |
| 1991–92 | York C | 21 | 0 |
| 1992–93 | York C | 40 | 0 |
| 1993–94 | York C | 46 | 0 |
| 1994–95 | York C | 46 | 0 |
| 1995–96 | York C | 40 | 0 |
| 1996–97 | Bury | 46 | 0 |
| 1997–98 | Bury | 46 | 0 |
| **Total:** | | **302** | **0** |

## KIKO, Manuel — Forward

H: 5 10 W: 12 05 b.Portugal 24-10-76

*Source:* Belenenses.

| | | | |
|---|---|---|---|
| 1996–97 | Stockport Co | 3 | 0 |
| 1997–98 | Stockport Co | 0 | 0 |
| **Total:** | | **3** | **0** |

## KILBANE, Kevin — Forward

H: 6 0 W: 12 07 b.Preston 1-2-77

*Source:* Trainee. *Honours:* Eire 3 full caps.

| | | | |
|---|---|---|---|
| 1993–94 | Preston NE | 0 | 0 |
| 1994–95 | Preston NE | 0 | 0 |
| 1995–96 | Preston NE | 11 | 1 |
| 1996–97 | Preston NE | 36 | 2 |
| 1997–98 | WBA | 43 | 4 |
| **Total:** | | **90** | **7** |

## KILCLINE, Brian — Defender

H: 6 2 W: 14 13 b.Nottingham 7-5-62

*Source:* Apprentice. *Honours:* England Under-21.

| | | | |
|---|---|---|---|
| 1979–80 | Notts Co | 16 | 1 |
| 1980–81 | Notts Co | 42 | 1 |
| 1981–82 | Notts Co | 36 | 3 |
| 1982–83 | Notts Co | 40 | 3 |
| 1983–84 | Notts Co | 24 | 1 |
| 1984–85 | Coventry C | 26 | 2 |
| 1985–86 | Coventry C | 32 | 7 |
| 1986–87 | Coventry C | 29 | 3 |
| 1987–88 | Coventry C | 28 | 8 |
| 1988–89 | Coventry C | 33 | 4 |
| 1989–90 | Coventry C | 11 | 1 |
| 1990–91 | Coventry C | 14 | 3 |
| 1991–92 | Oldham Ath | 8 | 0 |
| 1991–92 | Newcastle U | 12 | 0 |
| 1992–93 | Newcastle U | 19 | 0 |
| 1993–94 | Newcastle U | 1 | 0 |
| 1993–94 | Swindon T | 10 | 0 |
| 1994–95 | Swindon T | 7 | 0 |
| 1995–96 | Swindon T | 0 | 0 |
| 1995–96 | Mansfield T | 19 | 0 |
| 1996–97 | Mansfield T | 31 | 3 |
| 1997–98 | Mansfield T | 0 | 0 |
| **Total:** | | **438** | **40** |

## KILDUFF, Danny
Defender

H: 6 1 W: 13 00 b.Stockport 27-12-78

*Source:* Trainee.

| | | | |
|---|---|---|---|
| 1997–98 | Stockport Co | 0 | 0 |

## KILFORD, Ian
Midfield

H: 5 10 W: 11 00 b.Bristol 6-10-73

*Source:* Trainee.

| | | | |
|---|---|---|---|
| 1991–92 | Nottingham F | 0 | 0 |
| 1992–93 | Nottingham F | 0 | 0 |
| 1993–94 | Nottingham F | 1 | 0 |
| 1993–94 | Wigan Ath (loan) | 8 | 3 |
| 1994–95 | Wigan Ath | 35 | 5 |
| 1995–96 | Wigan Ath | 25 | 3 |
| 1996–97 | Wigan Ath | 35 | 8 |
| 1997–98 | Wigan Ath | 30 | 10 |
| **Total:** | | **134** | **29** |

## KIMBLE, Alan
Defender

H: 5 10 W: 12 04 b.Poole 6-8-66

| | | | |
|---|---|---|---|
| 1984–85 | Charlton Ath | 6 | 0 |
| 1985–86 | Charlton Ath | 0 | 0 |
| 1985–86 | Exeter C (loan) | 1 | 0 |
| 1986–87 | Cambridge U | 35 | 0 |
| 1987–88 | Cambridge U | 41 | 2 |
| 1988–89 | Cambridge U | 45 | 6 |
| 1989–90 | Cambridge U | 44 | 8 |
| 1990–91 | Cambridge U | 43 | 4 |
| 1991–92 | Cambridge U | 45 | 0 |
| 1992–93 | Cambridge U | 46 | 4 |
| 1993–94 | Wimbledon | 14 | 0 |
| 1994–95 | Wimbledon | 26 | 0 |
| 1995–96 | Wimbledon | 31 | 0 |
| 1996–97 | Wimbledon | 31 | 0 |
| 1997–98 | Wimbledon | 25 | 0 |
| **Total:** | | **433** | **24** |

## KINDER, Vladimir
Defender

H: 5 8 W: 12 11 b.Bratislava 9-3-69

*Source:* Karlovy Vary. *Honours:* Czechoslovakia 1 full cap, Slovakia 34 full caps, 1 goal.

| | | | |
|---|---|---|---|
| 1990–91 | Slovan Bratislava | 10 | 2 |
| 1991–92 | Slovan Bratislava | 29 | 2 |
| 1992–93 | Slovan Bratislava | 29 | 5 |
| 1993–94 | Slovan Bratislava | 31 | 3 |
| 1994–95 | Slovan Bratislava | 26 | 4 |
| 1995–96 | Slovan Bratislava | 23 | 3 |
| 1996–97 | Slovan Bratislava | 13 | 3 |
| 1996–97 | Middlesbrough | 6 | 1 |
| 1997–98 | Middlesbrough | 26 | 2 |
| **Total:** | | **193** | **25** |

## KING, Phil
Defender

H: 5 11 W: 12 07 b.Bristol 28-12-67

*Source:* Apprentice. *Honours:* England B.

| | | | |
|---|---|---|---|
| 1984–85 | Exeter C | 16 | 0 |
| 1985–86 | Exeter C | 11 | 0 |
| 1986–87 | Torquay U | 24 | 3 |
| 1986–87 | Swindon T | 21 | 0 |
| 1987–88 | Swindon T | 44 | 1 |
| 1988–89 | Swindon T | 37 | 2 |
| 1989–90 | Swindon T | 14 | 1 |
| 1989–90 | Sheffield W | 25 | 0 |
| 1990–91 | Sheffield W | 43 | 0 |
| 1991–92 | Sheffield W | 39 | 1 |
| 1992–93 | Sheffield W | 12 | 1 |
| 1993–94 | Sheffield W | 10 | 0 |
| 1993–94 | Notts Co (loan) | 6 | 0 |
| 1994–95 | Aston Villa | 16 | 0 |
| 1995–96 | Aston Villa | 0 | 0 |
| 1995–96 | WBA (loan) | 4 | 0 |
| 1996–97 | Aston Villa | 0 | 0 |
| 1996–97 | Swindon T | 5 | 0 |
| 1997–98 | Swindon T | 0 | 0 |
| 1997–98 | Blackpool (loan) | 6 | 0 |
| **Total:** | | **333** | **9** |

## KING, Robert
Defender

H: 5 8 W: 10 06 b.Merthyr 2-9-77

*Source:* Trainee.

| | | | |
|---|---|---|---|
| 1996–97 | Swansea C | 2 | 0 |
| 1997–98 | Swansea C | 0 | 0 |
| **Total:** | | **2** | **0** |

## KINKLADZE, Georgiou
Midfield

H: 5 8 W: 10 09 b.Tbilisi 6-7-73

*Source:* Dynamo Tbilisi. *Honours:* Georgia 26 full caps, 5 goals.

| | | | |
|---|---|---|---|
| 1995–96 | Manchester C | 37 | 4 |
| 1996–97 | Manchester C | 39 | 12 |
| 1997–98 | Manchester C | 30 | 4 |
| **Total:** | | **106** | **20** |

## KINSELLA, Mark
Midfield

H: 5 8 W: 11 04 b.Dublin 12-8-72

*Source:* Home Farm. *Honours:* Eire 2 full caps.

| | | | |
|---|---|---|---|
| 1989–90 | Colchester U | 6 | 0 |
| 1990–91 | Colchester U | 0 | 0 |

| | | | |
|---|---|---|---|
| 1991–92 | Colchester U | 0 | 0 |
| 1992–93 | Colchester U | 38 | 6 |
| 1993–94 | Colchester U | 42 | 8 |
| 1994–95 | Colchester U | 42 | 6 |
| 1995–96 | Colchester U | 45 | 5 |
| 1996–97 | Colchester U | 7 | 2 |
| 1996–97 | Charlton Ath | 37 | 6 |
| 1997–98 | Charlton Ath | 46 | 6 |
| **Total:** | | **263** | **39** |

## KIRBY, Alan — Midfield

H: 5 7 W: 10 06 b.Waterford 8-9-77

*Source:* Trainee. *Honours:* Eire Youth.

| | | | |
|---|---|---|---|
| 1995–96 | Aston Villa | 0 | 0 |
| 1996–97 | Aston Villa | 0 | 0 |
| 1997–98 | Aston Villa | 0 | 0 |

## KIRIAKOV, Ilian — Midfield

H: 5 5 W: 11 09 b.Pavlikeni 4-8-67

*Source:* Etur. *Honours:* Bulgaria 57 full caps.

| | | | |
|---|---|---|---|
| 1991–92 | La Coruna | 36 | 3 |
| 1992–93 | La Coruna | 3 | 0 |
| From Merida. | | | |
| 1994–95 | CSKA Sofia | 18 | 0 |
| 1994–95 | Etur | 8 | 3 |
| 1995–96 | Anorthosis | 19 | 8 |
| 1996–97 | Aberdeen | 27 | 1 |
| 1997–98 | Aberdeen | 15 | 0 |
| **Total:** | | **126** | **15** |

## KIRKLAND, Christopher — Goalkeeper

H: 6 3 W: 11 07 b.Leicester 2-5-81

*Source:* Trainee.

| | | | |
|---|---|---|---|
| 1997–98 | Coventry C | 0 | 0 |

## KITE, Phil — Goalkeeper

H: 6 2 W: 15 04 b.Bristol 26-10-62

*Source:* Apprentice. *Honours:* England Youth.

| | | | |
|---|---|---|---|
| 1980–81 | Bristol R | 4 | 0 |
| 1981–82 | Bristol R | 27 | 0 |
| 1982–83 | Bristol R | 46 | 0 |
| 1983–84 | Bristol R | 19 | 0 |
| 1983–84 | Tottenham H (loan) | 0 | 0 |
| 1984–85 | Southampton | 1 | 0 |
| 1985–86 | Southampton | 3 | 0 |
| 1985–86 | Middlesbrough (loan) | 2 | 0 |
| 1986–87 | Gillingham | 17 | 0 |
| 1987–88 | Gillingham | 26 | 0 |
| 1988–89 | Gillingham | 27 | 0 |
| 1989–90 | Bournemouth | 7 | 0 |
| 1990–91 | Sheffield U | 7 | 0 |
| 1991–92 | Sheffield U | 4 | 0 |
| 1991–92 | Mansfield T (loan) | 11 | 0 |
| 1992–93 | Sheffield U | 0 | 0 |
| 1992–93 | Plymouth Arg (loan) | 2 | 0 |
| 1992–93 | Rotherham U (loan) | 1 | 0 |
| 1992–93 | Crewe Alex (loan) | 5 | 0 |
| 1992–93 | Stockport Co (loan) | 5 | 0 |
| 1993–94 | Cardiff C | 18 | 0 |
| 1994–95 | Bristol C | 2 | 0 |
| 1995–96 | Bristol C | 4 | 0 |
| 1996–97 | Bristol R | 0 | 0 |
| 1997–98 | Bristol R | 0 | 0 |
| **Total:** | | **238** | **0** |

## KITSON, Paul — Forward

H: 5 11 W: 10 12 b.Murton 9-1-71

*Source:* Trainee. *Honours:* England Under-21.

| | | | |
|---|---|---|---|
| 1988–89 | Leicester C | 0 | 0 |
| 1989–90 | Leicester C | 13 | 0 |
| 1990–91 | Leicester C | 7 | 0 |
| 1991–92 | Leicester C | 30 | 6 |
| 1991–92 | Derby Co | 12 | 4 |
| 1992–93 | Derby Co | 44 | 17 |
| 1993–94 | Derby Co | 41 | 13 |
| 1994–95 | Derby Co | 8 | 2 |
| 1994–95 | Newcastle U | 26 | 8 |
| 1995–96 | Newcastle U | 7 | 2 |
| 1996–97 | Newcastle U | 3 | 0 |
| 1996–97 | West Ham U | 14 | 8 |
| 1997–98 | West Ham U | 13 | 4 |
| **Total:** | | **218** | **64** |

## KIWOMYA, Andy — Forward

H: 5 10 W: 10 10 b.Huddersfield 1-10-67

*Source:* Trainee. *Honours:* England Youth.

| | | | |
|---|---|---|---|
| 1985–86 | Barnsley | 1 | 0 |
| 1986–87 | Sheffield W | 0 | 0 |
| 1987–88 | Sheffield W | 0 | 0 |
| 1988–89 | Sheffield W | 0 | 0 |
| Retired injury | | | |
| 1992–93 | Dundee | 21 | 1 |
| 1993–94 | Rotherham U | 7 | 0 |
| From Halifax T. | | | |
| 1994–95 | Scunthorpe U | 9 | 3 |
| 1995–96 | Bradford C | 16 | 2 |
| 1996–97 | Bradford C | 27 | 1 |
| 1996–97 | Luton T (loan) | 5 | 1 |
| 1997–98 | Bradford C | 0 | 0 |
| 1997–98 | Burnley (loan) | 3 | 0 |
| 1997–98 | Notts Co | 2 | 0 |
| **Total:** | | **91** | **8** |

## KIWOMYA, Chris — Forward

H: 5 9 W: 10 07 b.Huddersfield 2-12-69

*Source:* Trainee.

| | | | |
|---|---|---|---|
| 1986–87 | Ipswich T | 0 | 0 |
| 1987–88 | Ipswich T | 0 | 0 |
| 1988–89 | Ipswich T | 26 | 2 |
| 1989–90 | Ipswich T | 29 | 5 |
| 1990–91 | Ipswich T | 37 | 10 |
| 1991–92 | Ipswich T | 43 | 16 |
| 1992–93 | Ipswich T | 38 | 10 |
| 1993–94 | Ipswich T | 37 | 5 |
| 1994–95 | Ipswich T | 15 | 3 |
| 1994–95 | Arsenal | 14 | 3 |
| 1995–96 | Arsenal | 0 | 0 |
| 1996–97 | Arsenal | 0 | 0 |
| 1996–97 | Le Havre (loan) | 7 | 0 |
| 1997–98 | Arsenal | 0 | 0 |
| **Total:** | | **246** | **54** |

## KLINSMANN, Jurgen — Forward

H: 6 2 W: 12 13 b.Goppingen 30-7-64

*Source:* Geislingen, Gingen. *Honours:* Germany 108 full caps, 47 goals.

| | | | |
|---|---|---|---|
| 1981–82 | Stuttgart Kickers | 6 | 1 |
| 1982–83 | Stuttgart Kickers | 20 | 2 |
| 1983–84 | Stuttgart Kickers | 35 | 19 |
| 1984–85 | Stuttgart | 32 | 15 |
| 1985–86 | Stuttgart | 33 | 16 |
| 1986–87 | Stuttgart | 32 | 16 |
| 1987–88 | Stuttgart | 34 | 19 |
| 1988–89 | Stuttgart | 25 | 13 |
| 1989–90 | Internazionale | 31 | 13 |
| 1990–91 | Internazionale | 33 | 14 |
| 1991–92 | Internazionale | 31 | 7 |
| 1992–93 | Monaco | 35 | 19 |
| 1993–94 | Monaco | 30 | 10 |
| 1994–95 | Tottenham H | 41 | 20 |
| 1995–96 | Bayern Munich | 32 | 16 |
| 1996–97 | Bayern Munich | 33 | 15 |
| 1997–98 | Sampdoria | 8 | 2 |
| 1997–98 | Tottenham H | 15 | 9 |
| **Total:** | | **506** | **226** |

## KNARVIK, Tommy — Midfield

b.Bergen 1-11-79

*Source:* Skjerjard.

| | | | |
|---|---|---|---|
| 1996–97 | Leeds U | 0 | 0 |
| 1997–98 | Leeds U | 0 | 0 |

## KNIGHT, Alan — Goalkeeper

H: 6 1 W: 13 11 b.Balham 3-7-61

*Source:* Apprentice. *Honours:* England Youth, Under-21.

| | | | |
|---|---|---|---|
| 1977–78 | Portsmouth | 1 | 0 |
| 1978–79 | Portsmouth | 0 | 0 |
| 1979–80 | Portsmouth | 8 | 0 |
| 1980–81 | Portsmouth | 1 | 0 |
| 1981–82 | Portsmouth | 45 | 0 |
| 1982–83 | Portsmouth | 46 | 0 |
| 1983–84 | Portsmouth | 42 | 0 |
| 1984–85 | Portsmouth | 42 | 0 |
| 1985–86 | Portsmouth | 38 | 0 |
| 1986–87 | Portsmouth | 42 | 0 |
| 1987–88 | Portsmouth | 36 | 0 |
| 1988–89 | Portsmouth | 32 | 0 |
| 1989–90 | Portsmouth | 46 | 0 |
| 1990–91 | Portsmouth | 22 | 0 |
| 1991–92 | Portsmouth | 45 | 0 |
| 1992–93 | Portsmouth | 46 | 0 |
| 1993–94 | Portsmouth | 43 | 0 |
| 1994–95 | Portsmouth | 43 | 0 |
| 1995–96 | Portsmouth | 42 | 0 |
| 1996–97 | Portsmouth | 22 | 0 |
| 1997–98 | Portsmouth | 20 | 0 |
| **Total:** | | **662** | **0** |

## KNIGHT, Paul — Forward

H: 5 7 W: 10 07 b.Dublin 16-10-80

*Source:* Trainee.

| | | | |
|---|---|---|---|
| 1997–98 | Newcastle U | 0 | 0 |

## KNIGHT, Richard — Goalkeeper

H: 6 1 W: 14 00 b.Burton 3-8-79

*Source:* Burton Alb. *Honours:* England Youth.

| | | | |
|---|---|---|---|
| 1997–98 | Derby Co | 0 | 0 |

## KNILL, Alan — Defender

H: 6 4 W: 13 00 b.Slough 8-10-64

*Source:* Apprentice. *Honours:* Wales Youth, 1 full cap.

| | | | |
|---|---|---|---|
| 1982–83 | Southampton | 0 | 0 |
| 1983–84 | Southampton | 0 | 0 |
| 1984–85 | Halifax T | 44 | 1 |
| 1985–86 | Halifax T | 33 | 2 |
| 1986–87 | Halifax T | 41 | 3 |
| 1987–88 | Swansea C | 46 | 1 |
| 1988–89 | Swansea C | 43 | 2 |
| 1989–90 | Bury | 43 | 1 |
| 1990–91 | Bury | 20 | 1 |
| 1991–92 | Bury | 35 | 1 |
| 1992–93 | Bury | 38 | 5 |

| | | | |
|---|---|---|---|
| 1993–94 | Bury | 8 | 0 |
| 1993–94 | Cardiff C (loan) | 4 | 0 |
| 1993–94 | Scunthorpe U | 25 | 1 |
| 1994–95 | Scunthorpe U | 39 | 4 |
| 1995–96 | Scunthorpe U | 38 | 3 |
| 1996–97 | Scunthorpe U | 29 | 0 |
| 1997–98 | Rotherham U | 38 | 3 |
| **Total:** | | **524** | **28** |

## KNOWLES, Darren — Defender

H: 5 6 W: 11 05 b.Sheffield 8-10-70

*Source:* Trainee.

| | | | |
|---|---|---|---|
| 1989–90 | Sheffield U | 0 | 0 |
| 1989–90 | Stockport Co | 9 | 0 |
| 1990–91 | Stockport Co | 12 | 0 |
| 1991–92 | Stockport Co | 31 | 0 |
| 1992–93 | Stockport Co | 11 | 0 |
| 1993–94 | Scarborough | 42 | 1 |
| 1994–95 | Scarborough | 39 | 0 |
| 1995–96 | Scarborough | 46 | 1 |
| 1996–97 | Scarborough | 17 | 0 |
| 1996–97 | Hartlepool U | 7 | 0 |
| 1997–98 | Hartlepool U | 46 | 1 |
| **Total:** | | **260** | **3** |

## KOMBOUARE, Antoine — Defender

H: 6 1 W: 12 06 b.Noumba 16-11-63

*Source:* Nantes, Toulon.

| | | | |
|---|---|---|---|
| 1990–91 | Paris St Germain | 20 | 0 |
| 1991–92 | Paris St Germain | 32 | 2 |
| 1992–93 | Paris St Germain | 19 | 0 |
| 1993–94 | Paris St Germain | 9 | 0 |
| 1994–95 | Paris St Germain | 26 | 1 |
| 1995–96 | Sion | 25 | 7 |
| 1996–97 | Aberdeen | 30 | 3 |
| 1997–98 | Aberdeen | 12 | 0 |
| **Total:** | | **173** | **13** |

## KONCHESKY, Paul — Midfield

b.Barking 15-5-81

*Source:* Trainee. *Honours:* England Youth.

| | | | |
|---|---|---|---|
| 1997–98 | Charlton Ath | 3 | 0 |
| **Total:** | | **3** | **0** |

## KOOGI, Anders — Defender

H: 5 10 W: 11 01 b.Denmark 8-9-79

*Source:* Trainee.

| | | | |
|---|---|---|---|
| 1997–98 | Peterborough U | 0 | 0 |

## KOORDES, Rogier — Midfield

H: 6 1 W: 12 11 b.Holland 13-6-72

| | | | |
|---|---|---|---|
| 1996–97 | Telstar | 12 | 0 |
| 1996–97 | Port Vale | 13 | 0 |
| 1997–98 | Port Vale | 10 | 0 |
| **Total:** | | **35** | **0** |

## KOTYLO, Krystof — Midfield

H: 5 10 W: 11 02 b.Sheffield 28-9-77

*Source:* School.

| | | | |
|---|---|---|---|
| 1996–97 | Sheffield W | 0 | 0 |
| 1997–98 | Sheffield W | 0 | 0 |

## KOUMAS, Jason — Forward

H: 5 10 W: 11 00 b.Wrexham 25-9-79

*Source:* Trainee.

| | | | |
|---|---|---|---|
| 1997–98 | Tranmere R | 0 | 0 |

## KOZLUK, Robert — Defender

H: 5 7 W: 10 12 b.Sutton-in-Ashfield 5-8-77

*Source:* Trainee. *Honours:* England Under-21.

| | | | |
|---|---|---|---|
| 1995–96 | Derby Co | 0 | 0 |
| 1996–97 | Derby Co | 0 | 0 |
| 1997–98 | Derby Co | 9 | 0 |
| **Total:** | | **9** | **0** |

## KRIZAN, Ales — Defender

H: 5 8 W: 12 12 b.Maribor 25-7-71

*Source:* Slovenia 24 full caps.

| | | | |
|---|---|---|---|
| 1992–93 | Branik Maribor | 34 | 0 |
| 1993–94 | Branik Maribor | 28 | 0 |
| 1994–95 | Branik Maribor | 29 | 0 |
| 1995–96 | Branik Maribor | 33 | 0 |
| 1996–97 | Branik Maribor | 35 | 0 |
| 1997–98 | Barnsley | 12 | 0 |
| **Total:** | | **171** | **0** |

## KUBICKI, Dariusz — Defender

H: 5 10 W: 11 07 b.Kozuchow 6-6-63

*Source:* Mielec, Zastra, Legia Warsaw. *Honours:* Poland 46 full caps, 1 goal.

| | | | |
|---|---|---|---|
| 1991–92 | Aston Villa | 23 | 0 |
| 1992–93 | Aston Villa | 0 | 0 |
| 1993–94 | Aston Villa | 2 | 0 |
| 1993–94 | Sunderland (loan) | 15 | 0 |
| 1994–95 | Sunderland | 46 | 0 |
| 1995–96 | Sunderland | 46 | 0 |

| | | | |
|---|---|---|---|
| 1996–97 | Sunderland | 29 | 0 |
| 1997–98 | Wolverhampton W | 12 | 0 |
| 1997–98 | Tranmere R (loan) | 12 | 0 |
| **Total:** | | **185** | **0** |

## KULCSAR, George — Midfield

H: 6 1 W: 13 08 b.Budapest 12-8-67

*Honours:* Australia 1 full cap.

| | | | |
|---|---|---|---|
| 1992–93 | Antwerp | 4 | 0 |
| 1993–94 | Antwerp | 8 | 0 |
| 1994–95 | Antwerp | 25 | 1 |
| 1995–96 | Antwerp | 12 | 0 |
| 1996–97 | Antwerp | 17 | 0 |
| 1996–97 | Bradford C | 9 | 0 |
| 1997–98 | Bradford C | 17 | 1 |
| 1997–98 | QPR | 12 | 0 |
| **Total:** | | **104** | **2** |

## KVARME, Bjorn — Defender

H: 5 11 W: 12 04 b.Trondheim 17-6-72

*Honours:* Norway 1 full cap.

| | | | |
|---|---|---|---|
| 1991 | Rosenborg | 9 | 1 |
| 1992 | Rosenborg | 5 | 0 |
| 1993 | Rosenborg | 17 | 0 |
| 1994 | Rosenborg | 22 | 1 |
| 1995 | Rosenborg | 23 | 0 |
| 1996 | Rosenborg | 12 | 0 |
| 1996–97 | Liverpool | 15 | 0 |
| 1997–98 | Liverpool | 23 | 0 |
| **Total:** | | **126** | **2** |

## KYD, Michael — Forward

H: 5 9 W: 12 10 b.Hackney 21-5-77

*Source:* Trainee.

| | | | |
|---|---|---|---|
| 1994–95 | Cambridge U | 19 | 1 |
| 1995–96 | Cambridge U | 9 | 1 |
| 1996–97 | Cambridge U | 28 | 7 |
| 1997–98 | Cambridge U | 38 | 11 |
| **Total:** | | **94** | **20** |

## KYRATZOGLOU, Alex — Midfield

H: 5 10 W: 12 01 b.Armitale 27-8-74

| | | | |
|---|---|---|---|
| 1997–98 | Oldham Ath | 1 | 0 |
| **Total:** | | **1** | **0** |

## LACEY, Damien — Midfield

H: 5 9 W: 11 03 b.Bridgend 3-8-77

*Source:* Trainee.

| | | | |
|---|---|---|---|
| 1996–97 | Swansea C | 10 | 0 |
| 1997–98 | Swansea C | 22 | 1 |
| **Total:** | | **32** | **1** |

## LAGAN, Brian — Midfield

H: 5 5 W: 9 10 b.Northern Ireland 3-10-80

*Source:* Trainee.

| | | | |
|---|---|---|---|
| 1997–98 | Leeds U | 0 | 0 |

## LAMA, Bernard — Goalkeeper

H: 6 3 W: 12 05 b.St Symphoricu 7-4-63

*Honours:* France 37 full caps.

| | | | |
|---|---|---|---|
| 1985–86 | Lille | 2 | 0 |
| 1986–87 | Lille | 29 | 0 |
| 1987–88 | Lille | 36 | 0 |
| 1988–89 | Lille | 36 | 1 |
| 1989–90 | Metz | 38 | 0 |
| 1990–91 | Brest | 38 | 0 |
| 1991–92 | Lens | 36 | 1 |
| 1992–93 | Paris St Germain | 38 | 0 |
| 1993–94 | Paris St Germain | 37 | 0 |
| 1994–95 | Paris St Germain | 36 | 0 |
| 1995–96 | Paris St Germain | 34 | 0 |
| 1996–97 | Paris St Germain | 32 | 0 |
| 1997–98 | West Ham U | 12 | 0 |
| **Total:** | | **404** | **2** |

## LAMBERT, James — Forward

H: 5 7 W: 11 02 b.Henley 14-9-73

*Source:* School.

| | | | |
|---|---|---|---|
| 1992–93 | Reading | 27 | 3 |
| 1993–94 | Reading | 6 | 0 |
| 1994–95 | Reading | 11 | 1 |
| 1995–96 | Reading | 15 | 4 |
| 1996–97 | Reading | 31 | 5 |
| 1997–98 | Reading | 34 | 3 |
| **Total:** | | **124** | **16** |

## LAMBERT, Paul — Midfield

H: 5 11 W: 9 10 b.Glasgow 7-8-69

*Source:* Linwood Rangers BC. *Honours:* Scotland Under-21, 15 full caps.

| | | | |
|---|---|---|---|
| 1985–86 | St Mirren | 1 | 0 |
| 1986–87 | St Mirren | 36 | 2 |
| 1987–88 | St Mirren | 36 | 2 |

| | | | |
|---|---|---|---|
| 1988–89 | St Mirren | 16 | 2 |
| 1989–90 | St Mirren | 25 | 3 |
| 1990–91 | St Mirren | 31 | 2 |
| 1991–92 | St Mirren | 40 | 2 |
| 1992–93 | St Mirren | 39 | 1 |
| 1993–94 | St Mirren | 3 | 0 |
| 1993–94 | Motherwell | 32 | 3 |
| 1994–95 | Motherwell | 36 | 1 |
| 1995–96 | Motherwell | 35 | 2 |
| 1996–97 | Borussia Dortmund | 31 | 1 |
| 1997–98 | Borussia Dortmund | 13 | 0 |
| 1997–98 | Celtic | 26 | 2 |
| **Total:** | | **400** | **23** |

## LAMBOURDE, Bernard — Defender

H: 6 2 W: 12 02 b.Pointe-A-Pitre 11-5-71

*Source:* Cannes.

| | | | |
|---|---|---|---|
| 1996–97 | Bordeaux | 28 | 1 |
| 1997–98 | Chelsea | 7 | 0 |
| **Total:** | | **35** | **1** |

## LAMEY, Nathan — Forward

b.Leeds 14-10-80

*Source:* Trainee.

| | | | |
|---|---|---|---|
| 1997–98 | Wolverhampton W | 0 | 0 |

## LAMPARD, Frank — Midfield

H: 6 0 W: 11 12 b.Romford 20-6-78

*Source:* Trainee. *Honours:* England Youth, Under-21, B.

| | | | |
|---|---|---|---|
| 1994–95 | West Ham U | 0 | 0 |
| 1995–96 | West Ham U | 2 | 0 |
| 1995–96 | Swansea C (loan) | 9 | 1 |
| 1996–97 | West Ham U | 13 | 0 |
| 1997–98 | West Ham U | 31 | 4 |
| **Total:** | | **55** | **5** |

## LANCASHIRE, Graham — Forward

H: 5 10 W: 11 12 b.Blackpool 19-10-72

*Source:* Trainee.

| | | | |
|---|---|---|---|
| 1990–91 | Burnley | 1 | 0 |
| 1991–92 | Burnley | 25 | 8 |
| 1992–93 | Burnley | 3 | 0 |
| 1992–93 | Halifax T (loan) | 2 | 0 |
| 1993–94 | Burnley | 1 | 0 |
| 1993–94 | Chester C (loan) | 11 | 7 |
| 1994–95 | Burnley | 1 | 0 |
| 1994–95 | Preston NE | 17 | 0 |
| 1995–96 | Preston NE | 6 | 2 |
| 1995–96 | Wigan Ath | 5 | 3 |
| 1996–97 | Wigan Ath | 24 | 9 |
| 1997–98 | Wigan Ath | 1 | 0 |
| 1997–98 | Rochdale | 27 | 9 |
| **Total:** | | **124** | **38** |

## LANDON, Richard — Forward

H: 6 2 W: 13 10 b.Worthing 22-3-70

*Source:* Bedworth U.

| | | | |
|---|---|---|---|
| 1993–94 | Plymouth Arg | 6 | 5 |
| 1994–95 | Plymouth Arg | 24 | 7 |
| 1995–96 | Stockport Co | 11 | 5 |
| 1996–97 | Stockport Co | 2 | 0 |
| 1996–97 | Rotherham U (loan) | 8 | 0 |
| 1997–98 | Macclesfield T | 18 | 7 |
| **Total:** | | **69** | **24** |

## LANE, Christopher — Defender

b.Liverpool 24-5-79

*Source:* Trainee.

| | | | |
|---|---|---|---|
| 1997–98 | Everton | 0 | 0 |

## LANGAN, Kevin — Defender

H: 5 11 W: 11 02 b.Jersey 7-4-78

*Source:* Trainee.

| | | | |
|---|---|---|---|
| 1996–97 | Bristol C | 0 | 0 |
| 1997–98 | Bristol C | 3 | 0 |
| **Total:** | | **3** | **0** |

## LANGLEY, Richard — Midfield

H: 5 10 W: 11 04 b.London 27-12-79

*Source:* Trainee. *Honours:* England Youth.

| | | | |
|---|---|---|---|
| 1996–97 | QPR | 0 | 0 |
| 1997–98 | QPR | 0 | 0 |

## LAPPER, Mike — Defender

H: 6 0 W: 12 02 b.California 28-8-70

*Source:* USSF. *Honours:* USA full caps.

| | | | |
|---|---|---|---|
| 1995–96 | Southend U | 24 | 0 |
| 1996–97 | Southend U | 28 | 1 |
| 1997–98 | Southend U | 0 | 0 |
| **Total:** | | **52** | **1** |

## LARKIN, James — Goalkeeper

b.Canada 23-10-75

| | | | |
|---|---|---|---|
| 1997–98 | Cambridge U | 1 | 0 |
| 1997–98 | Walsall | 0 | 0 |
| **Total:** | | **1** | **0** |

## LARSEN, Stig — Forward

H: 6 1 W: 13 04 b.Bergen 29-9-73

*Source:* Fana.

| | | | |
|---|---|---|---|
| 1997–98 | Hartlepool U | 4 | 0 |
| **Total:** | | **4** | **0** |

## LARSSON, Henrik — Forward

H: 5 10 W: 11 11 b.Sweden 20-9-71

*Source:* Helsingborg. *Honours:* Sweden 28 full caps, 7 goals.

| | | | |
|---|---|---|---|
| 1993–94 | Feyenoord | 15 | 1 |
| 1994–95 | Feyenoord | 23 | 8 |
| 1995–96 | Feyenoord | 32 | 10 |
| 1996–97 | Feyenoord | 31 | 7 |
| 1997–98 | Celtic | 35 | 16 |
| **Total:** | | **136** | **42** |

## LARUSSON, Bjarnolfur — Midfield

b.Iceland 11-3-76

| | | | |
|---|---|---|---|
| 1993 | IBV | 4 | 0 |
| 1994 | IBV | 15 | 0 |
| 1995 | IBV | 13 | 1 |
| 1996 | IBV | 15 | 2 |
| 1997 | IBV | 13 | 2 |
| 1997–98 | Hibernian | 7 | 1 |
| **Total:** | | **67** | **6** |

## LAUCHLAN, James — Midfield

H: 6 1 W: 10 13 b.Glasgow 2-2-77

*Source:* Highbury BC. *Honours:* Scotland Under-21.

| | | | |
|---|---|---|---|
| 1993–94 | Kilmarnock | 1 | 0 |
| 1994–95 | Kilmarnock | 2 | 0 |
| 1995–96 | Kilmarnock | 5 | 0 |
| 1996–97 | Kilmarnock | 10 | 0 |
| 1997–98 | Kilmarnock | 22 | 0 |
| **Total:** | | **40** | **0** |

## LAUDRUP, Brian — Forward

H: 6 0 W: 13 02 b.Vienna 22-2-69

*Honours:* Denmark 82 full caps, 21 goals.

| | | | |
|---|---|---|---|
| 1986 | Brondby | 2 | 0 |
| 1987 | Brondby | 24 | 11 |
| 1988 | Brondby | 12 | 0 |
| 1989 | Brondby | 11 | 2 |
| 1989–90 | Uerdingen | 34 | 6 |
| 1990–91 | Bayern Munich | 33 | 9 |
| 1991–92 | Bayern Munich | 20 | 2 |
| 1992–93 | Fiorentina | 31 | 5 |
| 1993–94 | AC Milan | 9 | 1 |
| 1994–95 | Rangers | 33 | 10 |
| 1995–96 | Rangers | 22 | 2 |
| 1996–97 | Rangers | 33 | 16 |
| 1997–98 | Rangers | 28 | 5 |
| **Total:** | | **292** | **69** |

## LAURENT, Pierre — Midfield

H: 5 8 W: 10 10 b.Tulle 13-12-70

*Source:* Brive, Tulle.

| | | | |
|---|---|---|---|
| 1994–95 | Bastia | 23 | 4 |
| 1995–96 | Bastia | 26 | 6 |
| 1996–97 | Bastia | 24 | 3 |
| 1996–97 | Leeds U | 4 | 0 |
| 1997–98 | Leeds U | 0 | 0 |
| **Total:** | | **77** | **13** |

## LAURSEN, Jacob — Defender

H: 5 11 W: 12 01 b.Vejle 6-10-71

*Honours:* Denmark 22 full caps.

| | | | |
|---|---|---|---|
| 1992–93 | Silkeborg | 32 | 0 |
| 1993–94 | Silkeborg | 30 | 1 |
| 1994–95 | Silkeborg | 31 | 3 |
| 1995–96 | Silkeborg | 32 | 4 |
| 1996–97 | Derby Co | 36 | 1 |
| 1997–98 | Derby Co | 28 | 1 |
| **Total:** | | **189** | **10** |

## LAVETY, Barry — Forward

H: 6 0 W: 12 02 b.Johnstone 21-8-74

*Source:* Gleniffer Thistle. *Honours:* Scotland Under-21.

| | | | |
|---|---|---|---|
| 1991–92 | St Mirren | 5 | 2 |
| 1992–93 | St Mirren | 42 | 18 |
| 1993–94 | St Mirren | 42 | 10 |
| 1994–95 | St Mirren | 31 | 7 |
| 1995–96 | St Mirren | 29 | 11 |
| 1996–97 | Hibernian | 10 | 0 |
| 1997–98 | Hibernian | 26 | 7 |
| **Total:** | | **185** | **55** |

## LAVIN, Gerard — Defender

H: 5 10 W: 11 00 b.Corby 5-2-74

*Source:* Trainee. *Honours:* Scotland Under-21.

| | | | |
|---|---|---|---|
| 1991–92 | Watford | 1 | 0 |
| 1992–93 | Watford | 28 | 0 |
| 1993–94 | Watford | 46 | 3 |
| 1994–95 | Watford | 35 | 0 |
| 1995–96 | Watford | 16 | 0 |
| 1995–96 | Millwall | 20 | 0 |

| | | | |
|---|---|---|---|
| 1996–97 | Millwall | 9 | 0 |
| 1997–98 | Millwall | 7 | 0 |
| **Total:** | | **162** | **3** |

## LAW, Brian — Defender

H: 6 2 W: 11 12 b.Merthyr 1-1-70

*Source:* Apprentice. *Honours:* Wales Under-21, 1 full cap.

| | | | |
|---|---|---|---|
| 1987–88 | QPR | 1 | 0 |
| 1988–89 | QPR | 6 | 0 |
| 1989–90 | QPR | 10 | 0 |
| 1990–91 | QPR | 3 | 0 |
| 1991–92 | QPR | 0 | 0 |
| 1992–93 | QPR | 0 | 0 |
| 1993–94 | QPR | 0 | 0 |
| 1994–95 | Wolverhampton W | 17 | 0 |
| 1995–96 | Wolverhampton W | 7 | 1 |
| 1996–97 | Wolverhampton W | 7 | 0 |
| 1997–98 | Millwall | 40 | 4 |
| **Total:** | | **91** | **5** |

## LAWRENCE, Jamie — Midfield

H: 6 0 W: 12 06 b.Balham 8-3-70

*Source:* Cowes.

| | | | |
|---|---|---|---|
| 1993–94 | Sunderland | 4 | 0 |
| 1993–94 | Doncaster R | 9 | 1 |
| 1994–95 | Doncaster R | 16 | 2 |
| 1994–95 | Leicester C | 17 | 1 |
| 1995–96 | Leicester C | 15 | 0 |
| 1996–97 | Leicester C | 15 | 0 |
| 1997–98 | Bradford C | 43 | 3 |
| **Total:** | | **119** | **7** |

## LAWRENCE, Matthew — Defender

H: 6 1 W: 12 05 b.Northampton 19-6-74

*Source:* Grays Ath. *Honours:* England Schools.

| | | | |
|---|---|---|---|
| 1995–96 | Wycombe W | 3 | 0 |
| 1996–97 | Wycombe W | 13 | 1 |
| 1996–97 | Fulham | 15 | 0 |
| 1997–98 | Fulham | 43 | 0 |
| **Total:** | | **74** | **1** |

## LAWS, Brian — Defender

H: 5 9 W: 12 04 b.Wallsend 14-10-61

*Source:* Apprentice. *Honours:* England B.

| | | | |
|---|---|---|---|
| 1979–80 | Burnley | 1 | 0 |
| 1980–81 | Burnley | 42 | 2 |
| 1981–82 | Burnley | 44 | 6 |
| 1982–83 | Burnley | 38 | 4 |
| 1983–84 | Huddersfield T | 31 | 0 |
| 1984–85 | Huddersfield T | 25 | 1 |
| 1984–85 | Middlesbrough | 11 | 1 |
| 1985–86 | Middlesbrough | 42 | 2 |
| 1986–87 | Middlesbrough | 26 | 8 |
| 1987–88 | Middlesbrough | 28 | 1 |
| 1988–89 | Nottingham F | 22 | 1 |
| 1989–90 | Nottingham F | 38 | 3 |
| 1990–91 | Nottingham F | 32 | 0 |
| 1991–92 | Nottingham F | 15 | 0 |
| 1992–93 | Nottingham F | 33 | 0 |
| 1993–94 | Nottingham F | 7 | 0 |
| 1994–95 | Nottingham F | 0 | 0 |
| 1994–95 | Grimsby T | 16 | 1 |
| 1995–96 | Grimsby T | 27 | 1 |
| 1996–97 | Grimsby T | 3 | 0 |
| 1996–97 | Darlington | 10 | 0 |
| 1996–97 | Scunthorpe U | 4 | 0 |
| 1997–98 | Scunthorpe U | 14 | 0 |
| **Total:** | | **509** | **31** |

## LAWSON, Ian — Forward

H: 5 11 W: 11 00 b.Huddersfield 4-11-77

*Source:* Trainee.

| | | | |
|---|---|---|---|
| 1994–95 | Huddersfield T | 0 | 0 |
| 1995–96 | Huddersfield T | 0 | 0 |
| 1996–97 | Huddersfield T | 18 | 3 |
| 1997–98 | Huddersfield T | 18 | 0 |
| **Total:** | | **36** | **3** |

## LAZARIDIS, Stan — Defender

H: 5 9 W: 12 00 b.Perth 16-8-72

*Source:* West Adelaide. *Honours:* Australia 27 full caps, 4 goals.

| | | | |
|---|---|---|---|
| 1995–96 | West Ham U | 4 | 0 |
| 1996–97 | West Ham U | 22 | 1 |
| 1997–98 | West Ham U | 28 | 2 |
| **Total:** | | **54** | **3** |

## LE SAUX, Graeme — Defender

H: 5 10 W: 11 09 b.Jersey 17-10-68

*Source:* St Pauls. *Honours:* England Under-21, B, 29 full caps, 1 goal.

| | | | |
|---|---|---|---|
| 1987–88 | Chelsea | 0 | 0 |
| 1988–89 | Chelsea | 1 | 0 |
| 1989–90 | Chelsea | 7 | 1 |
| 1990–91 | Chelsea | 28 | 4 |
| 1991–92 | Chelsea | 40 | 3 |
| 1992–93 | Chelsea | 14 | 0 |
| 1992–93 | Blackburn R | 9 | 0 |
| 1993–94 | Blackburn R | 41 | 2 |
| 1994–95 | Blackburn R | 39 | 3 |

| 1995–96 | Blackburn R | 14 | 1 |
|---|---|---|---|
| 1996–97 | Blackburn R | 26 | 1 |
| 1997–98 | Chelsea | 26 | 1 |
| **Total:** | | **245** | **16** |

## LE TISSIER, Matthew — Forward

H: 6 0 W: 13 09 b.Guernsey 14-10-68

*Source:* Trainee. *Honours:* England Youth, B, 8 full caps.

| 1986–87 | Southampton | 24 | 6 |
|---|---|---|---|
| 1987–88 | Southampton | 19 | 0 |
| 1988–89 | Southampton | 28 | 9 |
| 1989–90 | Southampton | 35 | 20 |
| 1990–91 | Southampton | 35 | 19 |
| 1991–92 | Southampton | 32 | 6 |
| 1992–93 | Southampton | 40 | 15 |
| 1993–94 | Southampton | 38 | 25 |
| 1994–95 | Southampton | 41 | 20 |
| 1995–96 | Southampton | 34 | 7 |
| 1996–97 | Southampton | 31 | 13 |
| 1997–98 | Southampton | 26 | 11 |
| **Total:** | | **383** | **151** |

## LEABURN, Carl — Forward

H: 6 3 W: 13 00 b.Lewisham 30-3-69

*Source:* Apprentice. *Honours:* England Youth.

| 1986–87 | Charlton Ath | 3 | 1 |
|---|---|---|---|
| 1987–88 | Charlton Ath | 12 | 0 |
| 1988–89 | Charlton Ath | 32 | 2 |
| 1989–90 | Charlton Ath | 13 | 0 |
| 1989–90 | Northampton T (loan) | 9 | 0 |
| 1990–91 | Charlton Ath | 20 | 1 |
| 1991–92 | Charlton Ath | 39 | 11 |
| 1992–93 | Charlton Ath | 39 | 5 |
| 1993–94 | Charlton Ath | 39 | 10 |
| 1994–95 | Charlton Ath | 27 | 3 |
| 1995–96 | Charlton Ath | 40 | 9 |
| 1996–97 | Charlton Ath | 44 | 8 |
| 1997–98 | Charlton Ath | 14 | 3 |
| 1997–98 | Wimbledon | 16 | 4 |
| **Total:** | | **347** | **57** |

## LEADBEATER, Richard — Forward

H: 6 2 W: 12 06 b.Dudley 21-10-77

*Source:* Trainee.

| 1996–97 | Wolverhampton W | 1 | 0 |
|---|---|---|---|
| 1997–98 | Wolverhampton W | 0 | 0 |
| **Total:** | | **1** | **0** |

## LEADBITTER, Chris — Midfield

H: 5 9 W: 10 06 b.Middlesbrough 17-10-67

*Source:* Apprentice.

| 1985–86 | Grimsby T | 0 | 0 |
|---|---|---|---|
| 1986–87 | Hereford U | 6 | 0 |
| 1987–88 | Hereford U | 30 | 1 |
| 1988–89 | Cambridge U | 31 | 6 |
| 1989–90 | Cambridge U | 43 | 4 |
| 1990–91 | Cambridge U | 39 | 1 |
| 1991–92 | Cambridge U | 25 | 1 |
| 1992–93 | Cambridge U | 38 | 6 |
| 1993–94 | Bournemouth | 27 | 0 |
| 1994–95 | Bournemouth | 27 | 3 |
| 1995–96 | Plymouth Arg | 33 | 1 |
| 1996–97 | Plymouth Arg | 19 | 0 |
| 1997–98 | Torquay U | 26 | 1 |
| **Total:** | | **344** | **24** |

## LEANING, Andy — Goalkeeper

H: 6 2 W: 13 00 b.York 18-5-63

*Source:* Rowntree Mackintosh.

| 1984–85 | York C | 0 | 0 |
|---|---|---|---|
| 1985–86 | York C | 30 | 0 |
| 1986–87 | York C | 39 | 0 |
| 1987–88 | Sheffield U | 21 | 0 |
| 1988–89 | Sheffield U | 0 | 0 |
| 1988–89 | Bristol C | 6 | 0 |
| 1989–90 | Bristol C | 19 | 0 |
| 1990–91 | Bristol C | 29 | 0 |
| 1991–92 | Bristol C | 20 | 0 |
| 1992–93 | Bristol C | 1 | 0 |
| 1993–94 | Bristol C | 0 | 0 |
| 1993–94 | Lincoln C | 8 | 0 |
| 1994–95 | Lincoln C | 21 | 0 |
| 1995–96 | Lincoln C | 7 | 0 |
| 1996–97 | Lincoln C | 0 | 0 |
| 1996–97 | Chesterfield | 9 | 0 |
| 1997–98 | Chesterfield | 5 | 0 |
| **Total:** | | **215** | **0** |

## LEBOEUF, Franck — Defender

H: 6 0 W: 12 00 b.Marseille 22-1-68

*Source:* Hyeres, Meaux, Laval. *Honours:* France 16 full caps, 2 goals.

| 1991–92 | Strasbourg | 31 | 11 |
|---|---|---|---|
| 1992–93 | Strasbourg | 36 | 12 |
| 1993–94 | Strasbourg | 36 | 6 |
| 1994–95 | Strasbourg | 34 | 7 |
| 1995–96 | Strasbourg | 35 | 4 |

| | | | |
|---|---|---|---|
| 1996–97 | Chelsea | 26 | 6 |
| 1997–98 | Chelsea | 32 | 5 |
| **Total:** | | **230** | **51** |

## LECZYNSKI, Alex — Forward

H: 5 8 W: 11 02 b.London 7-6-79

*Source:* Trainee.

| | | | |
|---|---|---|---|
| 1997–98 | Northampton T | 0 | 0 |

## LEE, Alan — Forward

H: 6 2 W: 13 09 b.Galway 21-8-78

*Source:* Trainee.

| | | | |
|---|---|---|---|
| 1995–96 | Aston Villa | 0 | 0 |
| 1996–97 | Aston Villa | 0 | 0 |
| 1997–98 | Aston Villa | 0 | 0 |

## LEE, Christian — Forward

H: 6 2 W: 11 07 b.Aylesbury 8-10-76

*Source:* Doncaster R.

| | | | |
|---|---|---|---|
| 1995–96 | Northampton T | 5 | 0 |
| 1996–97 | Northampton T | 29 | 7 |
| 1997–98 | Northampton T | 6 | 0 |
| **Total:** | | **40** | **7** |

## LEE, David — Forward

H: 5 7 W: 11 00 b.Whitefield 5-11-67

*Source:* Blackburn Schools.

| | | | |
|---|---|---|---|
| 1984–85 | Bury | 0 | 0 |
| 1985–86 | Bury | 1 | 0 |
| 1986–87 | Bury | 30 | 4 |
| 1987–88 | Bury | 40 | 3 |
| 1988–89 | Bury | 45 | 4 |
| 1989–90 | Bury | 45 | 8 |
| 1990–91 | Bury | 45 | 15 |
| 1991–92 | Bury | 2 | 1 |
| 1991–92 | Southampton | 19 | 0 |
| 1992–93 | Southampton | 1 | 0 |
| 1992–93 | Bolton W | 32 | 5 |
| 1993–94 | Bolton W | 41 | 5 |
| 1994–95 | Bolton W | 39 | 4 |
| 1995–96 | Bolton W | 18 | 1 |
| 1996–97 | Bolton W | 25 | 2 |
| 1997–98 | Wigan Ath | 43 | 5 |
| **Total:** | | **426** | **57** |

## LEE, David — Defender

H: 6 3 W: 15 00 b.Kingswood 26-11-69

*Source:* Trainee. *Honours:* England Youth, Under-21.

| | | | |
|---|---|---|---|
| 1988–89 | Chelsea | 20 | 4 |
| 1989–90 | Chelsea | 30 | 1 |
| 1990–91 | Chelsea | 21 | 1 |
| 1991–92 | Chelsea | 1 | 0 |
| 1991–92 | Reading (loan) | 5 | 5 |
| 1991–92 | Plymouth Arg (loan) | 9 | 1 |
| 1992–93 | Chelsea | 25 | 2 |
| 1993–94 | Chelsea | 7 | 1 |
| 1994–95 | Chelsea | 14 | 0 |
| 1994–95 | Portsmouth (loan) | 5 | 0 |
| 1995–96 | Chelsea | 31 | 1 |
| 1996–97 | Chelsea | 1 | 1 |
| 1997–98 | Chelsea | 1 | 0 |
| 1997–98 | Sheffield U (loan) | 5 | 0 |
| **Total:** | | **175** | **17** |

## LEE, Graeme — Defender

H: 6 2 W: 13 07 b.Middlesbrough 31-5-78

*Source:* Trainee.

| | | | |
|---|---|---|---|
| 1995–96 | Hartlepool U | 6 | 0 |
| 1996–97 | Hartlepool U | 24 | 0 |
| 1997–98 | Hartlepool U | 37 | 3 |
| **Total:** | | **67** | **3** |

## LEE, Jason — Forward

H: 6 3 W: 13 03 b.Newham 9-5-71

*Source:* Trainee.

| | | | |
|---|---|---|---|
| 1989–90 | Charlton Ath | 1 | 0 |
| 1990–91 | Charlton Ath | 0 | 0 |
| 1990–91 | Stockport Co (loan) | 2 | 0 |
| 1990–91 | Lincoln C | 17 | 3 |
| 1991–92 | Lincoln C | 35 | 6 |
| 1992–93 | Lincoln C | 41 | 12 |
| 1993–94 | Southend U | 24 | 3 |
| 1993–94 | Nottingham F | 13 | 2 |
| 1994–95 | Nottingham F | 22 | 3 |
| 1995–96 | Nottingham F | 28 | 8 |
| 1996–97 | Nottingham F | 13 | 1 |
| 1996–97 | Charlton Ath (loan) | 8 | 3 |
| 1996–97 | Grimsby T (loan) | 7 | 1 |
| 1997–98 | Watford | 36 | 10 |
| **Total:** | | **247** | **52** |

## LEE, Mark — Midfield

H: 6 0 W: 13 00 b.Consett 31-5-79

*Source:* Trainee.

| | | | |
|---|---|---|---|
| 1997–98 | Scarborough | 0 | 0 |

## LEE, Matt
Defender

H: 5 11 W: 11 00 b.Farnborough 13-5-79

*Source:* Trainee.

| | | | |
|---|---|---|---|
| 1996–97 | Charlton Ath | 0 | 0 |
| 1997–98 | Charlton Ath | 0 | 0 |

## LEE, Robert
Midfield

H: 5 10 W: 11 03 b.West Ham 1-2-66

*Source:* Hornchurch. *Honours:* England Under-21, 18 full caps, 2 goals.

| | | | |
|---|---|---|---|
| 1983–84 | Charlton Ath | 11 | 4 |
| 1984–85 | Charlton Ath | 39 | 10 |
| 1985–86 | Charlton Ath | 35 | 8 |
| 1986–87 | Charlton Ath | 33 | 3 |
| 1987–88 | Charlton Ath | 23 | 2 |
| 1988–89 | Charlton Ath | 31 | 5 |
| 1989–90 | Charlton Ath | 37 | 1 |
| 1990–91 | Charlton Ath | 43 | 13 |
| 1991–92 | Charlton Ath | 39 | 12 |
| 1992–93 | Charlton Ath | 7 | 1 |
| 1992–93 | Newcastle U | 36 | 10 |
| 1993–94 | Newcastle U | 41 | 7 |
| 1994–95 | Newcastle U | 35 | 9 |
| 1995–96 | Newcastle U | 36 | 8 |
| 1996–97 | Newcastle U | 33 | 5 |
| 1997–98 | Newcastle U | 28 | 4 |
| **Total:** | | **507** | **102** |

## LEESE, Lars
Goalkeeper

H: 6 3 W: 14 07 b.Cologne 18-8-69

*Source:* Leverkusen.

| | | | |
|---|---|---|---|
| 1997–98 | Barnsley | 9 | 0 |
| **Total:** | | **9** | **0** |

## LEGG, Andy
Defender

H: 5 8 W: 10 07 b.Neath 28-7-66

*Source:* Briton Ferry. *Honours:* Wales 4 full caps.

| | | | |
|---|---|---|---|
| 1988–89 | Swansea C | 6 | 0 |
| 1989–90 | Swansea C | 26 | 3 |
| 1990–91 | Swansea C | 39 | 5 |
| 1991–92 | Swansea C | 46 | 9 |
| 1992–93 | Swansea C | 46 | 12 |
| 1993–94 | Notts Co | 30 | 2 |
| 1994–95 | Notts Co | 34 | 3 |
| 1995–96 | Notts Co | 25 | 4 |
| 1995–96 | Birmingham C | 12 | 1 |
| 1996–97 | Birmingham C | 33 | 4 |
| 1997–98 | Birmingham C | 0 | 0 |
| 1997–98 | Ipswich T (loan) | 6 | 1 |
| 1997–98 | Reading | 10 | 0 |
| **Total:** | | **313** | **44** |

## LEHTINEN, Ville
Midfield

H: 5 10 W: 11 07 b.Tampere 17-12-78

*Honours:* Finland Under-21.

| | | | |
|---|---|---|---|
| 1996 | JJK | 22 | 1 |
| 1997 | HJK Helsinki | 2 | 0 |
| 1997–98 | Sheffield U | 0 | 0 |
| **Total:** | | **24** | **1** |

## LEIGHTON, Jim
Goalkeeper

H: 6 1 W: 12 09 b.Johnstone 24-7-58

*Source:* Dalry Thistle. *Honours:* Scotland Under-21, 89 full caps.

| | | | |
|---|---|---|---|
| 1978–79 | Aberdeen | 11 | 0 |
| 1979–80 | Aberdeen | 1 | 0 |
| 1980–81 | Aberdeen | 35 | 0 |
| 1981–82 | Aberdeen | 36 | 0 |
| 1982–83 | Aberdeen | 35 | 0 |
| 1983–84 | Aberdeen | 36 | 0 |
| 1984–85 | Aberdeen | 34 | 0 |
| 1985–86 | Aberdeen | 26 | 0 |
| 1986–87 | Aberdeen | 42 | 0 |
| 1987–88 | Aberdeen | 44 | 0 |
| 1988–89 | Manchester U | 38 | 0 |
| 1989–90 | Manchester U | 35 | 0 |
| 1990–91 | Manchester U | 0 | 0 |
| 1990–91 | Arsenal (loan) | 0 | 0 |
| 1991–92 | Manchester U | 0 | 0 |
| 1991–92 | Reading (loan) | 8 | 0 |
| 1991–92 | Dundee | 13 | 0 |
| 1992–93 | Dundee | 8 | 0 |
| 1992–93 | Sheffield U (loan) | 0 | 0 |
| 1993–94 | Hibernian | 44 | 0 |
| 1994–95 | Hibernian | 36 | 0 |
| 1995–96 | Hibernian | 36 | 0 |
| 1996–97 | Hibernian | 35 | 0 |
| 1997–98 | Aberdeen | 34 | 0 |
| **Total:** | | **587** | **0** |

## LEITCH, Scott
Midfield

H: 5 10 W: 12 00 b.Motherwell 6-10-69

*Source:* Shettleston Jun.

| | | | |
|---|---|---|---|
| 1990–91 | Dunfermline Ath | 14 | 3 |
| 1991–92 | Dunfermline Ath | 33 | 4 |
| 1992–93 | Dunfermline Ath | 42 | 9 |
| 1993–94 | Hearts | 28 | 2 |
| 1994–95 | Hearts | 21 | 0 |
| 1995–96 | Hearts | 6 | 0 |
| 1995–96 | Swindon T | 7 | 0 |

| | | | |
|---|---|---|---|
| 1996–97 | Swindon T | 36 | 0 |
| 1997–98 | Swindon T | 26 | 1 |
| **Total:** | | **213** | **19** |

## LEKOVIC, Dragote — Goalkeeper

H: 6 2 W: 12 09 b.Sivac, Montenegro 21-11-67

*Source:* Buducnost Podogorica. *Honours:* Yugoslavia 8 full caps.

| | | | |
|---|---|---|---|
| 1994–95 | Kilmarnock | 20 | 0 |
| 1995–96 | Kilmarnock | 33 | 0 |
| 1996–97 | Kilmarnock | 30 | 0 |
| 1997–98 | Kilmarnock | 13 | 0 |
| **Total:** | | **96** | **0** |

## LENAGH, Steven — Defender

H: 5 11 W: 10 09 b.Durham 21-3-79

*Source:* Sheffield W Trainee.

| | | | |
|---|---|---|---|
| 1997–98 | Chesterfield | 3 | 0 |
| **Total:** | | **3** | **0** |

## LENNON, Neil — Midfield

H: 5 9 W: 13 02 b.Lurgan 25-6-71

*Source:* Trainee. *Honours:* Northern Ireland Under-21, 21 full caps, 1 goal.

| | | | |
|---|---|---|---|
| 1987–88 | Manchester C | 1 | 0 |
| 1988–89 | Manchester C | 0 | 0 |
| 1989–90 | Manchester C | 0 | 0 |
| 1990–91 | Crewe Alex | 34 | 3 |
| 1991–92 | Crewe Alex | 0 | 0 |
| 1992–93 | Crewe Alex | 24 | 0 |
| 1993–94 | Crewe Alex | 33 | 4 |
| 1994–95 | Crewe Alex | 31 | 6 |
| 1995–96 | Crewe Alex | 25 | 2 |
| 1995–96 | Leicester C | 15 | 1 |
| 1996–97 | Leicester C | 35 | 1 |
| 1997–98 | Leicester C | 37 | 2 |
| **Total:** | | **235** | **19** |

## LEONARD, Mark — Forward

H: 6 1 W: 13 02 b.St Helens 27-9-62

*Source:* Witton Alb. *Honours:* England Schools.

| | | | |
|---|---|---|---|
| 1981–82 | Everton | 0 | 0 |
| 1982–83 | Everton | 0 | 0 |
| 1982–83 | Tranmere R (loan) | 7 | 0 |
| 1983–84 | Crewe Alex | 38 | 10 |
| 1984–85 | Crewe Alex | 16 | 5 |
| 1984–85 | Stockport Co | 23 | 4 |
| 1985–86 | Stockport Co | 44 | 20 |
| 1986–87 | Stockport Co | 6 | 0 |
| 1986–87 | Bradford C | 24 | 3 |
| 1987–88 | Bradford C | 28 | 10 |
| 1988–89 | Bradford C | 44 | 7 |
| 1989–90 | Bradford C | 24 | 5 |
| 1990–91 | Bradford C | 18 | 4 |
| 1991–92 | Bradford C | 19 | 0 |
| 1991–92 | Rochdale | 9 | 1 |
| 1992–93 | Preston NE | 22 | 1 |
| 1993–94 | Chester C | 32 | 8 |
| 1994–95 | Chester C | 0 | 0 |
| 1994–95 | Wigan Ath | 29 | 5 |
| 1995–96 | Wigan Ath | 35 | 7 |
| 1996–97 | Rochdale | 39 | 4 |
| 1997–98 | Rochdale | 33 | 2 |
| **Total:** | | **490** | **96** |

## LEONHARDSEN, Oyvind — Midfield

H: 5 10 W: 11 02 b.Kristiansund 17-8-70

*Source:* Clausenengen. *Honours:* Norway 58 full caps, 13 goals.

| | | | |
|---|---|---|---|
| 1989 | Molde | 22 | 5 |
| 1990 | Molde | 21 | 2 |
| 1991 | Molde | 21 | 2 |
| 1992 | Rosenborg | 22 | 6 |
| 1993 | Rosenborg | 19 | 6 |
| 1994 | Rosenborg | 22 | 8 |
| 1994–95 | Wimbledon | 20 | 4 |
| 1995–96 | Wimbledon | 29 | 4 |
| 1996–97 | Wimbledon | 27 | 5 |
| 1997–98 | Liverpool | 28 | 6 |
| **Total:** | | **231** | **48** |

## LESCOTT, Aaron — Midfield

H: 5 8 W: 10 09 b.Birmingham 2-12-78

*Source:* Trainee. *Honours:* England Schools.

| | | | |
|---|---|---|---|
| 1996–97 | Aston Villa | 0 | 0 |
| 1997–98 | Aston Villa | 0 | 0 |

## LESTER, Jack — Forward

H: 5 10 W: 12 00 b.Sheffield 8-10-75

*Source:* Trainee. *Honours:* England Schools.

| | | | |
|---|---|---|---|
| 1994–95 | Grimsby T | 7 | 0 |
| 1995–96 | Grimsby T | 5 | 0 |
| 1996–97 | Grimsby T | 22 | 5 |
| 1996–97 | Doncaster R (loan) | 11 | 1 |
| 1997–98 | Grimsby T | 40 | 4 |
| **Total:** | | **85** | **10** |

## LEVENDIS, Andy — Midfield

H: 5 8 W: 10 12 b.Cheadle 4-7-78

*Source:* Oldham Ath.

| | | | |
|---|---|---|---|
| 1997–98 | Macclesfield T | 0 | 0 |

## LEVER, Mark — Defender

H: 6 3 W: 13 06 b.Beverley 29-3-70

*Source:* Trainee.

| | | | |
|---|---|---|---|
| 1987–88 | Grimsby T | 1 | 0 |
| 1988–89 | Grimsby T | 37 | 2 |
| 1989–90 | Grimsby T | 38 | 2 |
| 1990–91 | Grimsby T | 40 | 2 |
| 1991–92 | Grimsby T | 36 | 0 |
| 1992–93 | Grimsby T | 14 | 1 |
| 1993–94 | Grimsby T | 22 | 0 |
| 1994–95 | Grimsby T | 31 | 0 |
| 1995–96 | Grimsby T | 24 | 1 |
| 1996–97 | Grimsby T | 21 | 0 |
| 1997–98 | Grimsby T | 38 | 0 |
| **Total:** | | **302** | **8** |

## LEWIS, Ben — Defender

H: 6 0 W: 12 10 b.Chelmsford 22-6-77

*Source:* Trainee.

| | | | |
|---|---|---|---|
| 1995–96 | Colchester U | 2 | 0 |
| 1996–97 | Colchester U | 0 | 0 |
| 1997–98 | Southend U | 14 | 1 |
| **Total:** | | **16** | **1** |

## LEWIS, Gary — Forward

H: 5 9 W: 10 12 b.Bolton 5-10-78

*Source:* Trainee.

| | | | |
|---|---|---|---|
| 1997–98 | Stockport Co | 0 | 0 |

## LEWIS, Mickey — Midfield

H: 5 9 W: 12 10 b.Birmingham 15-2-65

*Source:* School. *Honours:* England Youth.

| | | | |
|---|---|---|---|
| 1981–82 | WBA | 4 | 0 |
| 1982–83 | WBA | 5 | 0 |
| 1983–84 | WBA | 14 | 0 |
| 1984–85 | WBA | 1 | 0 |
| 1984–85 | Derby Co | 22 | 0 |
| 1985–86 | Derby Co | 5 | 1 |
| 1986–87 | Derby Co | 0 | 0 |
| 1987–88 | Derby Co | 16 | 0 |
| 1988–89 | Oxford U | 36 | 0 |
| 1989–90 | Oxford U | 45 | 1 |
| 1990–91 | Oxford U | 34 | 1 |
| 1991–92 | Oxford U | 40 | 4 |
| 1992–93 | Oxford U | 41 | 0 |
| 1993–94 | Oxford U | 46 | 0 |
| 1994–95 | Oxford U | 39 | 1 |
| 1995–96 | Oxford U | 19 | 0 |
| 1996–97 | Oxford U | 0 | 0 |
| 1997–98 | Oxford U | 0 | 0 |
| **Total:** | | **367** | **8** |

## LEWIS, Neil — Defender

H: 5 8 W: 10 05 b.Wolverhampton 28-6-74

*Source:* Trainee.

| | | | |
|---|---|---|---|
| 1992–93 | Leicester C | 7 | 0 |
| 1993–94 | Leicester C | 24 | 0 |
| 1994–95 | Leicester C | 16 | 0 |
| 1995–96 | Leicester C | 14 | 1 |
| 1996–97 | Leicester C | 6 | 0 |
| 1997–98 | Peterborough U | 34 | 0 |
| **Total:** | | **101** | **1** |

## LIBURD, Richard — Defender

H: 5 9 W: 11 01 b.Nottingham 26-9-73

*Source:* Forest Ath.

| | | | |
|---|---|---|---|
| 1992–93 | Middlesbrough | 0 | 0 |
| 1993–94 | Middlesbrough | 41 | 1 |
| 1994–95 | Bradford C | 9 | 1 |
| 1995–96 | Bradford C | 33 | 1 |
| 1996–97 | Bradford C | 36 | 1 |
| 1997–98 | Bradford C | 0 | 0 |
| 1997–98 | Carlisle U | 9 | 0 |
| **Total:** | | **128** | **4** |

## LIDDELL, Andrew — Forward

H: 5 6 W: 11 06 b.Leeds 28-6-73

*Source:* Trainee. *Honours:* Scotland Under-21.

| | | | |
|---|---|---|---|
| 1990–91 | Barnsley | 0 | 0 |
| 1991–92 | Barnsley | 1 | 0 |
| 1992–93 | Barnsley | 21 | 2 |
| 1993–94 | Barnsley | 22 | 1 |
| 1994–95 | Barnsley | 39 | 13 |
| 1995–96 | Barnsley | 43 | 9 |
| 1996–97 | Barnsley | 38 | 8 |
| 1997–98 | Barnsley | 26 | 1 |
| **Total:** | | **190** | **34** |

## LIDDLE, Craig — Defender

H: 5 11 W: 12 03 b.Chester-le-Street 21-10-71

*Source:* Blyth Spartans.

| | | | |
|---|---|---|---|
| 1994–95 | Middlesbrough | 1 | 0 |
| 1995–96 | Middlesbrough | 13 | 0 |

| | | | |
|---|---|---|---|
| 1996–97 | Middlesbrough | 5 | 0 |
| 1997–98 | Middlesbrough | 6 | 0 |
| 1997–98 | Darlington (loan) | 15 | 0 |
| **Total:** | | **40** | **0** |

## LIGHTBOURNE, Kyle — Forward

H: 6 2  W: 12 00  b.Bermuda 29-9-68

*Honours:* Bermuda full caps.

| | | | |
|---|---|---|---|
| 1992–93 | Scarborough | 19 | 3 |
| 1993–94 | Scarborough | 0 | 0 |
| 1993–94 | Walsall | 35 | 7 |
| 1994–95 | Walsall | 42 | 23 |
| 1995–96 | Walsall | 43 | 15 |
| 1996–97 | Walsall | 45 | 20 |
| 1997–98 | Coventry C | 7 | 0 |
| 1997–98 | Fulham (loan) | 4 | 2 |
| 1997–98 | Stoke C | 13 | 2 |
| **Total:** | | **208** | **72** |

## LIGHTFOOT, Chris — Defender

H: 6 1  W: 12 00  b.Penketh 1-4-70

*Source:* Trainee.

| | | | |
|---|---|---|---|
| 1987–88 | Chester C | 16 | 1 |
| 1988–89 | Chester C | 36 | 7 |
| 1989–90 | Chester C | 40 | 1 |
| 1990–91 | Chester C | 37 | 2 |
| 1991–92 | Chester C | 44 | 5 |
| 1992–93 | Chester C | 39 | 2 |
| 1993–94 | Chester C | 37 | 11 |
| 1994–95 | Chester C | 28 | 3 |
| 1995–96 | Wigan Ath | 14 | 1 |
| 1995–96 | Crewe Alex | 6 | 0 |
| 1996–97 | Crewe Alex | 25 | 0 |
| 1997–98 | Crewe Alex | 13 | 1 |
| **Total:** | | **335** | **34** |

## LILLEY, Derek — Forward

H: 5 11  W: 12 07  b.Paisley 9-2-74

*Source:* Everton BC.

| | | | |
|---|---|---|---|
| 1991–92 | Morton | 25 | 3 |
| 1992–93 | Morton | 22 | 4 |
| 1993–94 | Morton | 38 | 5 |
| 1994–95 | Morton | 35 | 16 |
| 1995–96 | Morton | 35 | 14 |
| 1996–97 | Morton | 25 | 15 |
| 1996–97 | Leeds U | 6 | 0 |
| 1997–98 | Leeds U | 13 | 1 |
| **Total:** | | **199** | **58** |

## LINDQVIST, Stefan — Midfield

H: 5 11  W: 12 13  b.Halmstad 18-3-67

*Source:* Wanda.

| | | | |
|---|---|---|---|
| 1997–98 | Motherwell | 6 | 1 |
| **Total:** | | **6** | **1** |

## LING, Martin — Midfield

H: 5 7  W: 10 08  b.West Ham 15-7-66

*Source:* Apprentice.

| | | | |
|---|---|---|---|
| 1983–84 | Exeter C | 29 | 0 |
| 1984–85 | Exeter C | 42 | 6 |
| 1985–86 | Exeter C | 45 | 8 |
| 1986–87 | Swindon T | 2 | 0 |
| 1986–87 | Southend U | 24 | 8 |
| 1987–88 | Southend U | 42 | 7 |
| 1988–89 | Southend U | 44 | 6 |
| 1989–90 | Southend U | 25 | 10 |
| 1990–91 | Southend U | 3 | 0 |
| 1990–91 | Mansfield T (loan) | 3 | 0 |
| 1990–91 | Swindon T (loan) | 1 | 0 |
| 1991–92 | Swindon T | 21 | 3 |
| 1992–93 | Swindon T | 43 | 3 |
| 1993–94 | Swindon T | 33 | 1 |
| 1994–95 | Swindon T | 36 | 3 |
| 1995–96 | Swindon T | 16 | 0 |
| 1996–97 | Leyton Orient | 44 | 1 |
| 1997–98 | Leyton Orient | 46 | 2 |
| **Total:** | | **499** | **58** |

## LINGER, Paul — Midfield

H: 5 6  W: 10 03  b.Stepney 20-12-74

*Source:* Trainee.

| | | | |
|---|---|---|---|
| 1992–93 | Charlton Ath | 2 | 0 |
| 1993–94 | Charlton Ath | 5 | 0 |
| 1994–95 | Charlton Ath | 8 | 0 |
| 1995–96 | Charlton Ath | 8 | 1 |
| 1996–97 | Charlton Ath | 0 | 0 |
| 1997–98 | Leyton Orient | 3 | 0 |
| 1997–98 | Brighton & HA | 19 | 0 |
| **Total:** | | **45** | **1** |

## LINIGHAN, Andy — Defender

H: 6 4  W: 13 10  b.Hartlepool 18-6-62

*Source:* Smiths BC. *Honours:* England B.

| | | | |
|---|---|---|---|
| 1980–81 | Hartlepool U | 6 | 0 |
| 1981–82 | Hartlepool U | 17 | 0 |
| 1982–83 | Hartlepool U | 45 | 3 |
| 1983–84 | Hartlepool U | 42 | 1 |
| 1984–85 | Leeds U | 42 | 2 |
| 1985–86 | Leeds U | 24 | 1 |

| | | | |
|---|---|---|---|
| 1985–86 | Oldham Ath | 15 | 1 |
| 1986–87 | Oldham Ath | 40 | 3 |
| 1987–88 | Oldham Ath | 32 | 2 |
| 1987–88 | Norwich C | 12 | 2 |
| 1988–89 | Norwich C | 37 | 4 |
| 1989–90 | Norwich C | 37 | 2 |
| 1990–91 | Arsenal | 10 | 0 |
| 1991–92 | Arsenal | 17 | 0 |
| 1992–93 | Arsenal | 21 | 2 |
| 1993–94 | Arsenal | 21 | 0 |
| 1994–95 | Arsenal | 20 | 2 |
| 1995–96 | Arsenal | 18 | 0 |
| 1996–97 | Arsenal | 11 | 1 |
| 1996–97 | Crystal Palace | 19 | 2 |
| 1997–98 | Crystal Palace | 26 | 0 |
| **Total:** | | **512** | **28** |

## LINIGHAN, Brian — Defender

H: 6 4 W: 11 04 b.Hartlepool 2-11-73

*Source:* Trainee.

| | | | |
|---|---|---|---|
| 1992–93 | Sheffield W | 0 | 0 |
| 1993–94 | Sheffield W | 1 | 0 |
| 1994–95 | Sheffield W | 0 | 0 |
| 1995–96 | Sheffield W | 0 | 0 |
| 1996–97 | Sheffield W | 0 | 0 |
| 1997–98 | Bury | 0 | 0 |
| **Total:** | | **1** | **0** |

## LINIGHAN, David — Defender

H: 6 2 W: 12 06 b.Hartlepool 9-1-65

*Source:* Local.

| | | | |
|---|---|---|---|
| 1981–82 | Hartlepool U | 6 | 0 |
| 1982–83 | Hartlepool U | 6 | 1 |
| 1983–84 | Hartlepool U | 23 | 1 |
| 1984–85 | Hartlepool U | 17 | 2 |
| 1984–85 | Leeds U (loan) | 0 | 0 |
| 1985–86 | Hartlepool U | 39 | 1 |
| 1986–87 | Derby Co | 0 | 0 |
| 1986–87 | Shrewsbury T | 24 | 0 |
| 1987–88 | Shrewsbury T | 41 | 1 |
| 1988–89 | Ipswich T | 41 | 2 |
| 1989–90 | Ipswich T | 41 | 0 |
| 1990–91 | Ipswich T | 45 | 3 |
| 1991–92 | Ipswich T | 36 | 3 |
| 1992–93 | Ipswich T | 42 | 1 |
| 1993–94 | Ipswich T | 38 | 3 |
| 1994–95 | Ipswich T | 32 | 0 |
| 1995–96 | Ipswich T | 2 | 0 |
| 1995–96 | Blackpool | 29 | 4 |
| 1996–97 | Blackpool | 42 | 1 |
| 1997–98 | Blackpool | 29 | 0 |
| **Total:** | | **533** | **23** |

## LINTON, Des — Defender

H: 6 1 W: 13 10 b.Birmingham 5-9-71

*Source:* Trainee.

| | | | |
|---|---|---|---|
| 1989–90 | Leicester C | 2 | 0 |
| 1990–91 | Leicester C | 8 | 0 |
| 1991–92 | Leicester C | 1 | 0 |
| 1991–92 | Luton T | 3 | 0 |
| 1992–93 | Luton T | 20 | 1 |
| 1993–94 | Luton T | 33 | 0 |
| 1994–95 | Luton T | 10 | 0 |
| 1995–96 | Luton T | 10 | 0 |
| 1996–97 | Luton T | 7 | 0 |
| 1996–97 | Peterborough U | 8 | 0 |
| 1997–98 | Peterborough U | 30 | 0 |
| **Total:** | | **132** | **1** |

## LISBIE, Kevin — Forward

H: 5 8 W: 10 12 b.Hackney 17-10-78

*Source:* Trainee. *Honours:* England Youth.

| | | | |
|---|---|---|---|
| 1996–97 | Charlton Ath | 25 | 1 |
| 1997–98 | Charlton Ath | 17 | 1 |
| **Total:** | | **42** | **2** |

## LITTLE, Colin — Forward

H: 5 10 W: 11 00 b.Wythenshaw 4-11-72

*Source:* Hyde U.

| | | | |
|---|---|---|---|
| 1995–96 | Crewe Alex | 12 | 1 |
| 1996–97 | Crewe Alex | 17 | 0 |
| 1997–98 | Crewe Alex | 40 | 13 |
| **Total:** | | **69** | **14** |

## LITTLE, Glen — Midfield

H: 6 3 W: 13 00 b.Wimbledon 15-10-75

*Source:* Trainee.

| | | | |
|---|---|---|---|
| 1994–95 | Crystal Palace | 0 | 0 |
| 1995–96 | Crystal Palace | 0 | 0 |
| 1996–97 | Glentoran | 6 | 2 |
| 1996–97 | Burnley | 9 | 0 |
| 1997–98 | Burnley | 24 | 4 |
| **Total:** | | **39** | **6** |

## LITTLEJOHN, Adrian — Forward

H: 5 9 W: 10 07 b.Wolverhampton 26-9-70

*Source:* WBA Trainee.

| | | | |
|---|---|---|---|
| 1989–90 | Walsall | 11 | 0 |
| 1990–91 | Walsall | 33 | 1 |
| 1991–92 | Sheffield U | 7 | 0 |
| 1992–93 | Sheffield U | 27 | 8 |

## Livingstone, Steve

| | | | |
|---|---|---|---|
| 1993–94 | Sheffield U | 19 | 3 |
| 1994–95 | Sheffield U | 16 | 1 |
| 1995–96 | Plymouth Arg | 42 | 17 |
| 1996–97 | Plymouth Arg | 37 | 6 |
| 1997–98 | Plymouth Arg | 31 | 6 |
| 1997–98 | Oldham Ath | 5 | 3 |
| **Total:** | | **228** | **45** |

## LIVINGSTONE, Steve — Forward

H: 6 1 W: 13 07 b.Middlesbrough 8-9-68

*Source:* Trainee.

| | | | |
|---|---|---|---|
| 1986–87 | Coventry C | 3 | 0 |
| 1987–88 | Coventry C | 4 | 0 |
| 1988–89 | Coventry C | 1 | 0 |
| 1989–90 | Coventry C | 13 | 3 |
| 1990–91 | Coventry C | 10 | 2 |
| 1990–91 | Blackburn R | 18 | 9 |
| 1991–92 | Blackburn R | 10 | 1 |
| 1992–93 | Blackburn R | 2 | 0 |
| 1992–93 | Chelsea | 1 | 0 |
| 1993–94 | Chelsea | 0 | 0 |
| 1993–94 | Port Vale (loan) | 5 | 0 |
| 1993–94 | Grimsby T | 27 | 3 |
| 1994–95 | Grimsby T | 34 | 8 |
| 1995–96 | Grimsby T | 38 | 11 |
| 1996–97 | Grimsby T | 32 | 6 |
| 1997–98 | Grimsby T | 41 | 5 |
| **Total:** | | **239** | **48** |

## LJUNG, Per-Ola — Midfield

b.Almhult 7-11-67

*Source:* Helsingborg.

| | | | |
|---|---|---|---|
| 1997–98 | Watford | 0 | 0 |

## LLEWELLYN, Chris — Forward

H: 5 11 W: 11 06 b.Swansea 28-8-79

*Source:* Trainee. *Honours:* Wales B, 2 full caps.

| | | | |
|---|---|---|---|
| 1996–97 | Norwich C | 0 | 0 |
| 1997–98 | Norwich C | 15 | 4 |
| **Total:** | | **15** | **4** |

## LLOYD, Kevin — Defender

H: 6 0 W: 12 03 b.Llanidloes 26-9-70

*Source:* Caersws.

| | | | |
|---|---|---|---|
| 1994–95 | Hereford U | 24 | 3 |
| 1995–96 | Hereford U | 27 | 0 |
| 1996–97 | Cardiff C | 31 | 1 |
| 1997–98 | Cardiff C | 2 | 0 |
| **Total:** | | **84** | **4** |

## LOCK, Tony — Forward

H: 5 10 W: 12 08 b.Harlow 3-9-76

*Source:* Trainee.

| | | | |
|---|---|---|---|
| 1994–95 | Colchester U | 3 | 1 |
| 1995–96 | Colchester U | 0 | 0 |
| 1996–97 | Colchester U | 6 | 1 |
| 1997–98 | Colchester U | 32 | 6 |
| **Total:** | | **41** | **8** |

## LOCKE, Adam — Defender

H: 6 0 W: 12 07 b.Croydon 20-8-70

*Source:* Trainee.

| | | | |
|---|---|---|---|
| 1988–89 | Crystal Palace | 0 | 0 |
| 1989–90 | Crystal Palace | 0 | 0 |
| 1990–91 | Southend U | 28 | 4 |
| 1991–92 | Southend U | 10 | 0 |
| 1992–93 | Southend U | 27 | 0 |
| 1993–94 | Southend U | 8 | 0 |
| 1993–94 | Colchester U (loan) | 4 | 0 |
| 1994–95 | Colchester U | 22 | 1 |
| 1995–96 | Colchester U | 25 | 3 |
| 1996–97 | Colchester U | 32 | 4 |
| 1997–98 | Bristol C | 37 | 1 |
| **Total:** | | **193** | **13** |

## LOCKE, Gary — Midfield

H: 5 8 W: 10 07 b.Edinburgh 16-6-75

*Source:* Whitehill Welfare. *Honours:* Scotland Under-21.

| | | | |
|---|---|---|---|
| 1992–93 | Hearts | 1 | 0 |
| 1993–94 | Hearts | 33 | 0 |
| 1994–95 | Hearts | 9 | 0 |
| 1995–96 | Hearts | 29 | 4 |
| 1996–97 | Hearts | 11 | 0 |
| 1997–98 | Hearts | 21 | 0 |
| **Total:** | | **104** | **4** |

## LOCKWOOD, Matt — Midfield

H: 5 9 W: 10 12 b.Rochford 17-10-76

*Source:* Trainee.

| | | | |
|---|---|---|---|
| 1994–95 | QPR | 0 | 0 |
| 1995–96 | QPR | 0 | 0 |
| 1996–97 | Bristol R | 39 | 1 |
| 1997–98 | Bristol R | 24 | 0 |
| **Total:** | | **63** | **1** |

## LOGAN, Richard — Defender

H: 6 0 W: 13 03 b.Barnsley 24-5-69

*Source:* Gainsborough T.

| | | | |
|---|---|---|---|
| 1993–94 | Huddersfield T | 16 | 0 |
| 1994–95 | Huddersfield T | 27 | 1 |
| 1995–96 | Huddersfield T | 2 | 0 |
| 1995–96 | Plymouth Arg | 31 | 4 |
| 1996–97 | Plymouth Arg | 28 | 4 |
| 1997–98 | Plymouth Arg | 27 | 4 |
| **Total:** | | **131** | **13** |

## LOMAS, Jamie — Midfield

H: 5 11 W: 10 09 b.Chesterfield 18-10-77

*Source:* Trainee.

| | | | |
|---|---|---|---|
| 1996–97 | Chesterfield | 2 | 0 |
| 1997–98 | Chesterfield | 4 | 0 |
| **Total:** | | **6** | **0** |

## LOMAS, Steve — Midfield

H: 6 0 W: 12 08 b.Hanover 18-1-74

*Source:* Trainee. *Honours:* Northern Ireland 26 full caps, 2 goals.

| | | | |
|---|---|---|---|
| 1991–92 | Manchester C | 0 | 0 |
| 1992–93 | Manchester C | 0 | 0 |
| 1993–94 | Manchester C | 23 | 0 |
| 1994–95 | Manchester C | 20 | 2 |
| 1995–96 | Manchester C | 33 | 3 |
| 1996–97 | Manchester C | 35 | 3 |
| 1996–97 | West Ham U | 7 | 0 |
| 1997–98 | West Ham U | 33 | 2 |
| **Total:** | | **151** | **10** |

## LOMBARDO, Attilio — Midfield

H: 5 11 W: 11 07 b.St. Maria La Fossa 6-1-66

*Honours:* Italy 18 full caps, 3 goals.

| | | | |
|---|---|---|---|
| 1983–84 | Pergocrema | 7 | 2 |
| 1984–85 | Pergocrema | 31 | 7 |
| 1985–86 | Cremonese | 31 | 4 |
| 1986–87 | Cremonese | 36 | 3 |
| 1987–88 | Cremonese | 37 | 5 |
| 1988–89 | Cremonese | 37 | 5 |
| 1989–90 | Sampdoria | 34 | 7 |
| 1990–91 | Sampdoria | 32 | 3 |
| 1991–92 | Sampdoria | 34 | 4 |
| 1992–93 | Sampdoria | 34 | 6 |
| 1993–94 | Sampdoria | 34 | 8 |
| 1994–95 | Sampdoria | 33 | 6 |
| 1995–96 | Juventus | 13 | 2 |
| 1996–97 | Juventus | 22 | 0 |
| 1997–98 | Crystal Palace | 24 | 5 |
| **Total:** | | **439** | **67** |

## LONERGAN, Darren — Defender

H: 6 0 W: 13 01 b.Waterford 28-1-74

*Source:* Waterford.

| | | | |
|---|---|---|---|
| 1994–95 | Oldham Ath | 0 | 0 |
| 1995–96 | Oldham Ath | 2 | 0 |
| 1996–97 | Oldham Ath | 0 | 0 |
| 1997–98 | Bury | 0 | 0 |
| **Total:** | | **2** | **0** |

## LONGWORTH, Steve — Forward

H: 5 9 W: 11 00 b.Leyland 6-2-80

*Source:* Trainee.

| | | | |
|---|---|---|---|
| 1997–98 | Blackpool | 2 | 0 |
| **Total:** | | **2** | **0** |

## LOPEZ, Rik — Midfield

H: 5 10 W: 11 04 b.Northwick Park 25-12-79

*Source:* Arsenal Trainee.

| | | | |
|---|---|---|---|
| 1996–97 | QPR | 0 | 0 |
| 1997–98 | QPR | 0 | 0 |

## LORMOR, Tony — Forward

H: 6 1 W: 12 06 b.Ashington 29-10-70

*Source:* Trainee.

| | | | |
|---|---|---|---|
| 1987–88 | Newcastle U | 5 | 2 |
| 1988–89 | Newcastle U | 3 | 1 |
| 1988–89 | Norwich C (loan) | 0 | 0 |
| 1989–90 | Newcastle U | 0 | 0 |
| 1989–90 | Lincoln C | 21 | 8 |
| 1990–91 | Lincoln C | 34 | 12 |
| 1991–92 | Lincoln C | 35 | 9 |
| 1992–93 | Lincoln C | 0 | 0 |
| 1993–94 | Lincoln C | 10 | 1 |
| 1994–95 | Peterborough U | 5 | 0 |
| 1994–95 | Chesterfield | 23 | 10 |
| 1995–96 | Chesterfield | 41 | 13 |
| 1996–97 | Chesterfield | 36 | 8 |
| 1997–98 | Chesterfield | 13 | 4 |
| 1997–98 | Preston NE | 12 | 3 |
| 1997–98 | Notts Co (loan) | 7 | 0 |
| **Total:** | | **245** | **71** |

## LOVE, Andrew — Goalkeeper

H: 6 2 W: 13 10 b.Grimsby 28-3-79

*Source:* Trainee.

| | | | |
|---|---|---|---|
| 1996–97 | Grimsby T | 3 | 0 |
| 1997–98 | Grimsby T | 0 | 0 |
| **Total:** | | **3** | **0** |

## LOVELL, Stuart — Forward

H: 5 10 W: 12 03 b.Sydney 9-1-72

*Source:* Trainee.

| | | | |
|---|---|---|---|
| 1990–91 | Reading | 30 | 2 |
| 1991–92 | Reading | 24 | 4 |
| 1992–93 | Reading | 22 | 8 |
| 1993–94 | Reading | 45 | 20 |
| 1994–95 | Reading | 30 | 11 |
| 1995–96 | Reading | 35 | 7 |
| 1996–97 | Reading | 26 | 5 |
| 1997–98 | Reading | 15 | 1 |
| **Total:** | | **227** | **58** |

## LOW, Josh — Forward

H: 6 0 W: 11 12 b.Bristol 15-12-79

*Source:* Trainee.

| | | | |
|---|---|---|---|
| 1995–96 | Bristol R | 1 | 0 |
| 1996–97 | Bristol R | 3 | 0 |
| 1997–98 | Bristol R | 10 | 0 |
| **Total:** | | **14** | **0** |

## LOWE, David — Forward

H: 5 10 W: 11 04 b.Liverpool 30-8-65

*Source:* Apprentice. *Honours:* England Youth, Under-21.

| | | | |
|---|---|---|---|
| 1982–83 | Wigan Ath | 28 | 6 |
| 1983–84 | Wigan Ath | 40 | 8 |
| 1984–85 | Wigan Ath | 29 | 5 |
| 1985–86 | Wigan Ath | 46 | 5 |
| 1986–87 | Wigan Ath | 45 | 16 |
| 1987–88 | Ipswich T | 41 | 17 |
| 1988–89 | Ipswich T | 32 | 6 |
| 1989–90 | Ipswich T | 34 | 13 |
| 1990–91 | Ipswich T | 13 | 0 |
| 1991–92 | Ipswich T | 14 | 1 |
| 1991–92 | Port Vale (loan) | 9 | 2 |
| 1992–93 | Leicester C | 32 | 11 |
| 1993–94 | Leicester C | 5 | 0 |
| 1993–94 | Port Vale (loan) | 19 | 5 |
| 1994–95 | Leicester C | 29 | 8 |
| 1995–96 | Leicester C | 28 | 3 |
| 1995–96 | Wigan Ath | 7 | 3 |
| 1996–97 | Wigan Ath | 42 | 6 |
| 1997–98 | Wigan Ath | 43 | 16 |
| **Total:** | | **536** | **131** |

## LOWE, Kenny — Midfield

H: 6 1 W: 11 13 b.Sedgefield 6-11-64

*Source:* Apprentice.

| | | | |
|---|---|---|---|
| 1981–82 | Hartlepool U | 4 | 0 |
| 1982–83 | Hartlepool U | 22 | 1 |
| 1983–84 | Hartlepool U | 28 | 2 |
| From Barrow. | | | |
| 1987–88 | Scarborough | 4 | 0 |
| 1988–89 | Scarborough | 0 | 0 |
| From Barrow. | | | |
| 1991–92 | Barnet | 36 | 3 |
| 1992–93 | Barnet | 36 | 2 |
| 1993–94 | Stoke C | 9 | 0 |
| 1993–94 | Birmingham C | 12 | 1 |
| 1994–95 | Birmingham C | 7 | 2 |
| 1994–95 | Carlisle U (loan) | 2 | 0 |
| 1995–96 | Birmingham C | 2 | 0 |
| 1995–96 | Hartlepool U (loan) | 13 | 3 |
| 1996–97 | Darlington | 7 | 0 |
| 1997–98 | Darlington | 7 | 0 |
| **Total:** | | **189** | **14** |

## LOWNDES, Nathan — Forward

H: 5 11 W: 10 04 b.Salford 2-6-77

*Source:* Trainee.

| | | | |
|---|---|---|---|
| 1994–95 | Leeds U | 0 | 0 |
| 1995–96 | Leeds U | 0 | 0 |
| 1995–96 | Watford | 0 | 0 |
| 1996–97 | Watford | 3 | 0 |
| 1997–98 | Watford | 4 | 0 |
| **Total:** | | **7** | **0** |

## LOWTHORPE, Adam — Defender

H: 5 7 W: 11 03 b.Hull 7-8-75

*Source:* Trainee.

| | | | |
|---|---|---|---|
| 1993–94 | Hull C | 3 | 0 |
| 1994–95 | Hull C | 22 | 0 |
| 1995–96 | Hull C | 19 | 0 |
| 1996–97 | Hull C | 14 | 1 |
| 1997–98 | Hull C | 23 | 2 |
| **Total:** | | **81** | **3** |

## LUCAS, David — Goalkeeper

H: 6 1 W: 11 06 b.Preston 23-11-77

*Source:* Trainee. *Honours:* England Youth.

| | | | |
|---|---|---|---|
| 1995–96 | Preston NE | 1 | 0 |
| 1995–96 | Darlington (loan) | 6 | 0 |
| 1996–97 | Preston NE | 2 | 0 |
| 1996–97 | Darlington (loan) | 7 | 0 |
| 1996–97 | Scunthorpe U (loan) | 6 | 0 |
| 1997–98 | Preston NE | 6 | 0 |
| **Total:** | | **28** | **0** |

## LUCAS, Richard — Defender

H: 5 10 W: 12 10 b.Chapeltown 22-9-70

*Source:* Trainee.

| Season | Club | Apps | Goals |
|---|---|---|---|
| 1989–90 | Sheffield U | 0 | 0 |
| 1990–91 | Sheffield U | 9 | 0 |
| 1991–92 | Sheffield U | 1 | 0 |
| 1992–93 | Sheffield U | 0 | 0 |
| 1992–93 | Preston NE | 26 | 0 |
| 1993–94 | Preston NE | 24 | 0 |
| 1994–95 | Preston NE | 0 | 0 |
| 1994–95 | Lincoln C (loan) | 4 | 0 |
| 1994–95 | Preston NE | 0 | 0 |
| 1995–96 | Scarborough | 44 | 0 |
| 1996–97 | Scarborough | 28 | 0 |
| 1996–97 | Hartlepool U | 7 | 0 |
| 1997–98 | Hartlepool U | 42 | 2 |
| **Total:** | | **229** | **2** |

## LUCKETTI, Chris — Defender

H: 6 0 W: 13 06 b.Littleborough 28-9-71

*Source:* Trainee.

| Season | Club | Apps | Goals |
|---|---|---|---|
| 1988–89 | Rochdale | 1 | 0 |
| 1989–90 | Rochdale | 0 | 0 |
| 1990–91 | Stockport Co | 0 | 0 |
| 1991–92 | Halifax T | 36 | 0 |
| 1992–93 | Halifax T | 42 | 2 |
| 1993–94 | Bury | 27 | 1 |
| 1994–95 | Bury | 39 | 3 |
| 1995–96 | Bury | 42 | 1 |
| 1996–97 | Bury | 38 | 0 |
| 1997–98 | Bury | 46 | 2 |
| **Total:** | | **271** | **9** |

## LUDDEN, Dominic — Defender

H: 5 7 W: 10 09 b.Basildon 30-3-74

*Source:* Trainee. *Honours:* England Schools.

| Season | Club | Apps | Goals |
|---|---|---|---|
| 1992–93 | Leyton Orient | 24 | 1 |
| 1993–94 | Leyton Orient | 34 | 0 |
| 1994–95 | Watford | 1 | 0 |
| 1995–96 | Watford | 12 | 0 |
| 1996–97 | Watford | 20 | 0 |
| 1997–98 | Watford | 0 | 0 |
| **Total:** | | **91** | **1** |

## LUDLAM, Ryan — Midfield

H: 6 0 W: 12 06 b.Carlisle 12-5-79

*Source:* Trainee.

| Season | Club | Apps | Goals |
|---|---|---|---|
| 1997–98 | Sheffield U | 0 | 0 |

## LUKIC, John — Goalkeeper

H: 6 4 W: 13 07 b.Chesterfield 11-12-60

*Source:* Apprentice. *Honours:* England Youth, Under-21, B.

| Season | Club | Apps | Goals |
|---|---|---|---|
| 1978–79 | Leeds U | 0 | 0 |
| 1979–80 | Leeds U | 33 | 0 |
| 1980–81 | Leeds U | 42 | 0 |
| 1981–82 | Leeds U | 42 | 0 |
| 1982–83 | Leeds U | 29 | 0 |
| 1983–84 | Arsenal | 4 | 0 |
| 1984–85 | Arsenal | 27 | 0 |
| 1985–86 | Arsenal | 40 | 0 |
| 1986–87 | Arsenal | 36 | 0 |
| 1987–88 | Arsenal | 40 | 0 |
| 1988–89 | Arsenal | 38 | 0 |
| 1989–90 | Arsenal | 38 | 0 |
| 1990–91 | Leeds U | 38 | 0 |
| 1991–92 | Leeds U | 42 | 0 |
| 1992–93 | Leeds U | 39 | 0 |
| 1993–94 | Leeds U | 20 | 0 |
| 1994–95 | Leeds U | 42 | 0 |
| 1995–96 | Leeds U | 28 | 0 |
| 1996–97 | Arsenal | 15 | 0 |
| 1997–98 | Arsenal | 0 | 0 |
| **Total:** | | **593** | **0** |

## LUMSDON, Chris — Midfield

H: 5 7 W: 10 03 b.Newcastle 15-12-79

*Source:* Trainee.

| Season | Club | Apps | Goals |
|---|---|---|---|
| 1997–98 | Sunderland | 1 | 0 |
| **Total:** | | **1** | **0** |

## LUNDEKVAM, Claus — Defender

H: 6 3 W: 12 11 b.Norway 22-2-73

*Honours:* Norway 5 full caps.

| Season | Club | Apps | Goals |
|---|---|---|---|
| 1993 | Brann | 3 | 0 |
| 1994 | Brann | 20 | 0 |
| 1995 | Brann | 14 | 0 |
| 1996 | Brann | 16 | 0 |
| 1996–97 | Southampton | 29 | 0 |
| 1997–98 | Southampton | 31 | 0 |
| **Total:** | | **113** | **0** |

## LUNT, Kenny — Midfield

H: 5 10 W: 10 00 b.Runcorn 20-11-79

*Source:* Trainee. *Honours:* England Schools, Youth.

| Season | Club | Apps | Goals |
|---|---|---|---|
| 1997–98 | Crewe Alex | 41 | 2 |
| **Total:** | | **41** | **2** |

## LUSARDI, Mario — Forward

H: 5 9 W: 10 02 b.Islington 27-9-79

*Source:* Trainee.

| | | | |
|---|---|---|---|
| 1996–97 | QPR | 0 | 0 |
| 1997–98 | QPR | 0 | 0 |

## LYDIATE, Jason — Defender

H: 5 11 W: 12 03 b.Manchester 29-10-71

*Source:* Trainee.

| | | | |
|---|---|---|---|
| 1989–90 | Manchester U | 0 | 0 |
| 1990–91 | Manchester U | 0 | 0 |
| 1991–92 | Manchester U | 0 | 0 |
| 1991–92 | Bolton W | 1 | 0 |
| 1992–93 | Bolton W | 6 | 0 |
| 1993–94 | Bolton W | 5 | 0 |
| 1994–95 | Bolton W | 18 | 0 |
| 1994–95 | Blackpool | 11 | 0 |
| 1995–96 | Blackpool | 32 | 1 |
| 1996–97 | Blackpool | 20 | 0 |
| 1997–98 | Blackpool | 23 | 1 |
| **Total:** | | **116** | **2** |

## LYNCH, Damien — Defender

b.Dublin 31-7-79

| | | | |
|---|---|---|---|
| 1996–97 | Leeds U | 0 | 0 |
| 1997–98 | Leeds U | 0 | 0 |

## LYTTLE, Des — Defender

H: 5 8 W: 12 13 b.Wolverhampton 26-9-71

*Source:* Worcester C.

| | | | |
|---|---|---|---|
| 1992–93 | Swansea C | 46 | 1 |
| 1993–94 | Nottingham F | 37 | 1 |
| 1994–95 | Nottingham F | 38 | 0 |
| 1995–96 | Nottingham F | 33 | 1 |
| 1996–97 | Nottingham F | 32 | 1 |
| 1997–98 | Nottingham F | 35 | 0 |
| **Total:** | | **221** | **4** |

## MABBUTT, Gary — Defender

H: 5 10 W: 13 01 b.Bristol 23-8-61

*Source:* Apprentice. *Honours:* England Youth, Under-21, B, 16 full caps, 1 goal.

| | | | |
|---|---|---|---|
| 1978–79 | Bristol R | 11 | 0 |
| 1979–80 | Bristol R | 33 | 0 |
| 1980–81 | Bristol R | 42 | 5 |
| 1981–82 | Bristol R | 45 | 5 |
| 1982–83 | Tottenham H | 38 | 10 |
| 1983–84 | Tottenham H | 21 | 2 |
| 1984–85 | Tottenham H | 25 | 2 |
| 1985–86 | Tottenham H | 32 | 3 |
| 1986–87 | Tottenham H | 37 | 1 |
| 1987–88 | Tottenham H | 37 | 2 |
| 1988–89 | Tottenham H | 38 | 1 |
| 1989–90 | Tottenham H | 36 | 0 |
| 1990–91 | Tottenham H | 35 | 2 |
| 1991–92 | Tottenham H | 40 | 2 |
| 1992–93 | Tottenham H | 29 | 2 |
| 1993–94 | Tottenham H | 29 | 0 |
| 1994–95 | Tottenham H | 36 | 0 |
| 1995–96 | Tottenham H | 32 | 0 |
| 1996–97 | Tottenham H | 1 | 0 |
| 1997–98 | Tottenham H | 11 | 0 |
| **Total:** | | **608** | **37** |

## MACKAY, Malcolm — Defender

H: 6 1 W: 11 07 b.Bellshill 19-2-72

*Source:* Queen's Park Youth.

| | | | |
|---|---|---|---|
| 1990–91 | Queen's Park | 10 | 0 |
| 1991–92 | Queen's Park | 27 | 3 |
| 1992–93 | Queen's Park | 33 | 3 |
| 1993–94 | Celtic | 0 | 0 |
| 1994–95 | Celtic | 1 | 0 |
| 1995–96 | Celtic | 11 | 1 |
| 1996–97 | Celtic | 20 | 1 |
| 1997–98 | Celtic | 4 | 1 |
| **Total:** | | **106** | **9** |

## MACKENZIE, Chris — Goalkeeper

H: 6 0 W: 12 06 b.Northampton 14-5-72

*Source:* Corby T.

| | | | |
|---|---|---|---|
| 1994–95 | Hereford U | 22 | 0 |
| 1995–96 | Hereford U | 38 | 1 |
| 1996–97 | Hereford U | 0 | 0 |
| 1997–98 | Leyton Orient | 4 | 0 |
| **Total:** | | **64** | **1** |

## MACPHERSON, Angus — Defender

H: 5 11 W: 10 04 b.Glasgow 11-10-68

*Source:* 'S' Form.

| | | | |
|---|---|---|---|
| 1988–89 | Rangers | 0 | 0 |
| 1989–90 | Rangers | 0 | 0 |
| 1989–90 | Exeter C (loan) | 11 | 1 |
| 1990–91 | Kilmarnock | 11 | 0 |
| 1991–92 | Kilmarnock | 43 | 3 |
| 1992–93 | Kilmarnock | 40 | 5 |
| 1993–94 | Kilmarnock | 43 | 2 |
| 1994–95 | Kilmarnock | 33 | 1 |
| 1995–96 | Kilmarnock | 35 | 1 |
| 1996–97 | Kilmarnock | 33 | 1 |
| 1997–98 | Kilmarnock | 25 | 0 |
| **Total:** | | **274** | **14** |

## MACARI, Jon — Forward

H: 5 9 W: 11 04 b.Stoke 15-12-79

*Source:* Trainee.

| | | | |
|---|---|---|---|
| 1996–97 | Nottingham F | 0 | 0 |
| 1997–98 | Nottingham F | 0 | 0 |

## MACARI, Mike — Forward

H: 5 7 W: 11 05 b.Kilwinning 4-2-73

*Source:* Trainee.

| | | | |
|---|---|---|---|
| 1991–92 | West Ham U | 0 | 0 |
| 1991–92 | Stoke C | 0 | 0 |
| 1992–93 | Stoke C | 0 | 0 |
| 1993–94 | Stoke C | 0 | 0 |
| 1994–95 | Stoke C | 0 | 0 |
| 1995–96 | Stoke C | 0 | 0 |
| 1996–97 | Stoke C | 30 | 3 |
| 1997–98 | Stoke C | 0 | 0 |
| **Total:** | | **30** | **3** |

## MACARI, Paul — Forward

H: 5 8 W: 11 06 b.Manchester 23-8-76

*Source:* Trainee.

| | | | |
|---|---|---|---|
| 1993–94 | Stoke C | 0 | 0 |
| 1994–95 | Stoke C | 0 | 0 |
| 1995–96 | Stoke C | 0 | 0 |
| 1996–97 | Stoke C | 0 | 0 |
| 1997–98 | Stoke C | 3 | 0 |
| **Total:** | | **3** | **0** |

## MACAULEY, Steve — Defender

H: 6 1 W: 12 00 b.Lytham 4-3-69

*Source:* Fleetwood T.

| | | | |
|---|---|---|---|
| 1991–92 | Crewe Alex | 9 | 1 |
| 1992–93 | Crewe Alex | 25 | 3 |
| 1993–94 | Crewe Alex | 17 | 3 |
| 1994–95 | Crewe Alex | 43 | 4 |
| 1995–96 | Crewe Alex | 29 | 7 |
| 1996–97 | Crewe Alex | 42 | 2 |
| 1997–98 | Crewe Alex | 0 | 0 |
| **Total:** | | **165** | **20** |

## MACDONALD, James — Midfield

H: 6 0 W: 12 05 b.Inverness 21-2-79

*Source:* Trainee.

| | | | |
|---|---|---|---|
| 1995–96 | Arsenal | 0 | 0 |
| 1996–97 | Arsenal | 0 | 0 |
| 1997–98 | Arsenal | 0 | 0 |

## MACKEN, Jonathan — Forward

H: 5 10 W: 12 01 b.Manchester 7-9-77

*Source:* Trainee. *Honours:* England Youth.

| | | | |
|---|---|---|---|
| 1996–97 | Manchester U | 0 | 0 |
| 1997–98 | Preston NE | 29 | 6 |
| **Total:** | | **29** | **6** |

## MACKENZIE, Neil — Midfield

H: 6 2 W: 12 05 b.Birmingham 15-4-76

| | | | |
|---|---|---|---|
| 1996–97 | Stoke C | 22 | 1 |
| 1997–98 | Stoke C | 12 | 0 |
| **Total:** | | **34** | **1** |

## MACKLIN, Gareth — Defender

H: 5 8 W: 10 06 b.Belfast 27-8-80

*Source:* Trainee.

| | | | |
|---|---|---|---|
| 1997–98 | Newcastle U | 0 | 0 |

## MADAR, Mikael — Forward

H: 6 1 W: 12 06 b.Paris 8-5-68

*Source:* Paris FC, Laval. *Honours:* France 3 full caps, 1 goal.

| | | | |
|---|---|---|---|
| 1989–90 | Sochaux | 7 | 0 |
| 1990–91 | Sochaux | 18 | 4 |
| 1991–92 | Sochaux | 21 | 2 |
| 1992–93 | Cannes | 27 | 16 |
| 1993–94 | Cannes | 27 | 10 |
| 1994–95 | Monaco | 23 | 6 |
| 1995–96 | Monaco | 29 | 8 |
| 1996–97 | La Coruna | 17 | 3 |
| 1997–98 | La Coruna | 7 | 1 |
| 1997–98 | Everton | 17 | 6 |
| **Total:** | | **193** | **56** |

## MADDISON, Lee — Defender

H: 6 0 W: 12 10 b.Bristol 5-10-72

*Source:* Trainee.

| | | | |
|---|---|---|---|
| 1991–92 | Bristol R | 10 | 0 |
| 1992–93 | Bristol R | 12 | 0 |
| 1993–94 | Bristol R | 37 | 0 |
| 1994–95 | Bristol R | 14 | 0 |
| 1995–96 | Bristol R | 0 | 0 |
| 1995–96 | Northampton T | 21 | 0 |
| 1996–97 | Northampton T | 34 | 0 |
| 1997–98 | Dundee | 24 | 1 |
| **Total:** | | **152** | **1** |

## MADDISON, Neil — Midfield

H: 5 10 W: 12 00 b.Darlington 2-10-69

*Source:* Trainee.

| | | | |
|---|---|---|---|
| 1987–88 | Southampton | 0 | 0 |
| 1988–89 | Southampton | 5 | 2 |
| 1989–90 | Southampton | 2 | 0 |
| 1990–91 | Southampton | 4 | 0 |
| 1991–92 | Southampton | 6 | 0 |
| 1992–93 | Southampton | 37 | 4 |
| 1993–94 | Southampton | 41 | 7 |
| 1994–95 | Southampton | 35 | 3 |
| 1995–96 | Southampton | 15 | 1 |
| 1996–97 | Southampton | 18 | 1 |
| 1997–98 | Southampton | 6 | 1 |
| 1997–98 | Middlesbrough | 22 | 4 |
| **Total:** | | **191** | **23** |

## MADDIX, Danny — Defender

H: 5 11 W: 12 00 b.Ashford 11-10-67

*Source:* Apprentice.

| | | | |
|---|---|---|---|
| 1985–86 | Tottenham H | 0 | 0 |
| 1986–87 | Tottenham H | 0 | 0 |
| 1986–87 | Southend U (loan) | 2 | 0 |
| 1987–88 | QPR | 9 | 0 |
| 1988–89 | QPR | 33 | 2 |
| 1989–90 | QPR | 32 | 3 |
| 1990–91 | QPR | 32 | 1 |
| 1991–92 | QPR | 19 | 0 |
| 1992–93 | QPR | 14 | 0 |
| 1993–94 | QPR | 0 | 0 |
| 1994–95 | QPR | 27 | 1 |
| 1995–96 | QPR | 22 | 0 |
| 1996–97 | QPR | 25 | 0 |
| 1997–98 | QPR | 25 | 1 |
| **Total:** | | **240** | **8** |

## MAGEE, Darren — Midfield

H: 5 10 W: 12 00 b.Glasgow 14-4-77

*Source:* Milngavie W.

| | | | |
|---|---|---|---|
| 1997–98 | Dundee | 17 | 0 |
| **Total:** | | **17** | **0** |

## MAGILTON, Jim — Midfield

H: 6 0 W: 14 00 b.Belfast 6-5-69

*Source:* Apprentice. *Honours:* Northern Ireland Under-21, 39 full caps, 5 goals. Football League.

| | | | |
|---|---|---|---|
| 1986–87 | Liverpool | 0 | 0 |
| 1987–88 | Liverpool | 0 | 0 |
| 1988–89 | Liverpool | 0 | 0 |
| 1989–90 | Liverpool | 0 | 0 |
| 1990–91 | Liverpool | 0 | 0 |
| 1990–91 | Oxford U | 37 | 6 |
| 1991–92 | Oxford U | 44 | 12 |
| 1992–93 | Oxford U | 40 | 11 |
| 1993–94 | Oxford U | 29 | 5 |
| 1993–94 | Southampton | 15 | 0 |
| 1994–95 | Southampton | 42 | 6 |
| 1995–96 | Southampton | 31 | 3 |
| 1996–97 | Southampton | 37 | 4 |
| 1997–98 | Southampton | 5 | 0 |
| 1997–98 | Sheffield W | 21 | 1 |
| **Total:** | | **301** | **48** |

## MAHE, Stephane — Defender

H: 5 11 W: 11 11 b.Puteaux 23-9-68

| | | | |
|---|---|---|---|
| 1988–89 | Auxerre | 1 | 0 |
| 1989–90 | Auxerre | 0 | 0 |
| 1990–91 | Auxerre | 6 | 0 |
| 1991–92 | Auxerre | 34 | 1 |
| 1992–93 | Auxerre | 21 | 0 |
| 1993–94 | Auxerre | 32 | 2 |
| 1994–95 | Auxerre | 29 | 0 |
| 1995–96 | Paris St Germain | 23 | 0 |
| 1996–97 | Rennes | 33 | 0 |
| 1997–98 | Celtic | 23 | 0 |
| **Total:** | | **202** | **3** |

## MAHER, Kevin — Midfield

H: 5 11 W: 12 08 b.Ilford 17-10-76

*Source:* Trainee.

| | | | |
|---|---|---|---|
| 1995–96 | Tottenham H | 0 | 0 |
| 1996–97 | Tottenham H | 0 | 0 |
| 1997–98 | Tottenham H | 0 | 0 |
| 1997–98 | Southend U | 18 | 1 |
| **Total:** | | **18** | **1** |

## MAHER, Shaun — Defender

H: 6 2 W: 12 03 b.Dublin 10-6-78

*Source:* Bohemians.

| | | | |
|---|---|---|---|
| 1997–98 | Fulham | 0 | 0 |

## MAHON, Alan — Midfield

H: 5 10 W: 11 05 b.Dublin 4-4-78

*Source:* Crumplin U.

| | | | |
|---|---|---|---|
| 1994–95 | Tranmere R | 0 | 0 |
| 1995–96 | Tranmere R | 2 | 0 |
| 1996–97 | Tranmere R | 25 | 2 |
| 1997–98 | Tranmere R | 18 | 1 |
| **Total:** | | **45** | **3** |

## MAHONEY-JOHNSON, Michael

Midfield

H: 5 10 W: 12 10 b.Paddington 6-11-76

*Source:* Trainee.

| | | | |
|---|---|---|---|
| 1994–95 | QPR | 0 | 0 |
| 1995–96 | QPR | 0 | 0 |
| 1996–97 | QPR | 2 | 0 |
| 1996–97 | Wycombe W (loan) | 4 | 2 |
| 1997–98 | QPR | 1 | 0 |
| 1997–98 | Brighton & HA (loan) | 4 | 0 |
| **Total:** | | **11** | **2** |

## MAHORN, Paul

Forward

H: 5 10 W: 13 01 b.Whipps Cross 13-8-73

*Source:* Trainee.

| | | | |
|---|---|---|---|
| 1991–92 | Tottenham H | 0 | 0 |
| 1992–93 | Tottenham H | 0 | 0 |
| 1993–94 | Tottenham H | 1 | 0 |
| 1993–94 | Fulham (loan) | 3 | 0 |
| 1994–95 | Tottenham H | 0 | 0 |
| 1995–96 | Tottenham H | 0 | 0 |
| 1995–96 | Burnley (loan) | 8 | 1 |
| 1996–97 | Tottenham H | 0 | 0 |
| 1996–97 | Brentford (loan) | 0 | 0 |
| 1997–98 | Tottenham H | 2 | 0 |
| 1997–98 | Port Vale | 1 | 0 |
| **Total:** | | **15** | **1** |

## MAIN, Alan

Goalkeeper

H: 5 11 W: 12 03 b.Elgin 5-12-67

*Source:* Elgin City. *Honours:* Scotland Under-21, B.

| | | | |
|---|---|---|---|
| 1986–97 | Dundee U | 2 | 0 |
| 1987–88 | Dundee U | 8 | 0 |
| 1988–89 | Dundee U | 0 | 0 |
| 1988–89 | Cowdenbeath (loan) | 3 | 0 |
| 1988–89 | East Stirling (loan) | 2 | 0 |
| 1989–90 | Dundee U | 27 | 0 |
| 1990–91 | Dundee U | 31 | 0 |
| 1991–92 | Dundee U | 17 | 0 |
| 1992–93 | Dundee U | 43 | 0 |
| 1993–94 | Dundee U | 18 | 0 |
| 1994–95 | Dundee U | 6 | 0 |
| 1994–95 | St Johnstone | 17 | 0 |
| 1995–96 | St Johnstone | 34 | 0 |
| 1996–97 | St Johnstone | 34 | 0 |
| 1997–98 | St Johnstone | 34 | 0 |
| **Total:** | | **276** | **0** |

## MAINWARING, Carl

Forward

H: 5 11 W: 12 07 b.Swansea 15-3-80

*Source:* Trainee.

| | | | |
|---|---|---|---|
| 1997–98 | Swansea C | 3 | 0 |
| **Total:** | | **3** | **0** |

## MAKEL, Lee

Midfield

H: 5 9 W: 11 05 b.Sunderland 11-1-73

*Source:* Trainee.

| | | | |
|---|---|---|---|
| 1990–91 | Newcastle U | 3 | 0 |
| 1991–92 | Newcastle U | 9 | 1 |
| 1992–93 | Blackburn R | 1 | 0 |
| 1993–94 | Blackburn R | 2 | 0 |
| 1994–95 | Blackburn R | 0 | 0 |
| 1995–96 | Blackburn R | 3 | 0 |
| 1995–96 | Huddersfield T | 33 | 2 |
| 1996–97 | Huddersfield T | 19 | 3 |
| 1997–98 | Huddersfield T | 13 | 0 |
| 1997–98 | Hearts | 5 | 0 |
| **Total:** | | **88** | **6** |

## MAKIN, Chris

Defender

H: 5 10 W: 10 06 b.Manchester 8-5-73

*Source:* Trainee. *Honours:* England Schools, Under-21.

| | | | |
|---|---|---|---|
| 1991–92 | Oldham Ath | 0 | 0 |
| 1992–93 | Oldham Ath | 0 | 0 |
| 1992–93 | Wigan Ath (loan) | 15 | 2 |
| 1993–94 | Oldham Ath | 27 | 1 |
| 1994–95 | Oldham Ath | 28 | 1 |
| 1995–96 | Oldham Ath | 39 | 2 |
| 1996–97 | Marseille | 29 | 0 |
| 1997–98 | Sunderland | 25 | 0 |
| **Total:** | | **163** | **6** |

## MALEY, Mark

Defender

H: 5 9 W: 12 03 b.Newcastle 26-1-81

*Source:* Trainee. *Honours:* England Schools.

| | | | |
|---|---|---|---|
| 1997–98 | Sunderland | 0 | 0 |

## MALKIN, Chris

Forward

H: 6 3 W: 12 09 b.Hoylake 4-6-67

*Source:* Stork, Overpool.

| | | | |
|---|---|---|---|
| 1987–88 | Tranmere R | 5 | 0 |
| 1988–89 | Tranmere R | 20 | 4 |
| 1989–90 | Tranmere R | 40 | 18 |
| 1990–91 | Tranmere R | 25 | 4 |
| 1991–92 | Tranmere R | 35 | 3 |
| 1992–93 | Tranmere R | 36 | 7 |

| | | | |
|---|---|---|---|
| 1993–94 | Tranmere R | 28 | 8 |
| 1994–95 | Tranmere R | 43 | 16 |
| 1995–96 | Millwall | 43 | 11 |
| 1996–97 | Millwall | 9 | 3 |
| 1996–97 | Blackpool | 15 | 3 |
| 1997–98 | Blackpool | 20 | 2 |
| **Total:** | | **319** | **79** |

## MALPAS, Maurice — Defender

H: 5 8 W: 10 11 b.Dunfermline 3-8-62

*Source:* 'S' Form. *Honours:* Scotland Schools, Youth, Under-21, 55 full caps.

| | | | |
|---|---|---|---|
| 1979–80 | Dundee U | 0 | 0 |
| 1980–81 | Dundee U | 0 | 0 |
| 1981–82 | Dundee U | 19 | 0 |
| 1982–83 | Dundee U | 34 | 1 |
| 1983–84 | Dundee U | 34 | 2 |
| 1984–85 | Dundee U | 35 | 2 |
| 1985–86 | Dundee U | 36 | 2 |
| 1986–87 | Dundee U | 36 | 0 |
| 1987–88 | Dundee U | 44 | 0 |
| 1988–89 | Dundee U | 36 | 1 |
| 1989–90 | Dundee U | 30 | 2 |
| 1990–91 | Dundee U | 36 | 1 |
| 1991–92 | Dundee U | 44 | 3 |
| 1992–93 | Dundee U | 37 | 0 |
| 1993–94 | Dundee U | 35 | 0 |
| 1994–95 | Dundee U | 31 | 2 |
| 1995–96 | Dundee U | 30 | 2 |
| 1996–97 | Dundee U | 26 | 1 |
| 1997–98 | Dundee U | 31 | 1 |
| **Total:** | | **574** | **20** |

## MANN, Neil — Midfield

H: 5 10 W: 12 01 b.Nottingham 19-11-72

*Source:* Notts Co, Spalding U, Grantham T.

| | | | |
|---|---|---|---|
| 1993–94 | Hull C | 5 | 0 |
| 1994–95 | Hull C | 31 | 2 |
| 1995–96 | Hull C | 38 | 1 |
| 1996–97 | Hull C | 32 | 2 |
| 1997–98 | Hull C | 34 | 3 |
| **Total:** | | **140** | **8** |

## MANNINGER, Alex — Goalkeeper

H: 6 2 W: 13 03 b.Salzburg 4-6-77

*Honours:* Austria Under-21.

| | | | |
|---|---|---|---|
| 1995–96 | Vorwaerts Steyr | 5 | 0 |
| 1995–96 | Salzburg | 1 | 0 |
| 1996–97 | Graz | 23 | 0 |
| 1997–98 | Arsenal | 7 | 0 |
| **Total:** | | **36** | **0** |

## MANNION, Sean — Midfield

b.Dublin 3-3-80

*Source:* Stella Maris.

| | | | |
|---|---|---|---|
| 1997–98 | Stockport Co | 0 | 0 |

## MANUEL, Billy — Midfield

H: 5 9 W: 11 10 b.Hackney 28-6-69

*Source:* Apprentice.

| | | | |
|---|---|---|---|
| 1987–88 | Tottenham H | 0 | 0 |
| 1988–89 | Tottenham H | 0 | 0 |
| 1988–89 | Gillingham | 17 | 1 |
| 1989–90 | Gillingham | 32 | 4 |
| 1990–91 | Gillingham | 38 | 0 |
| 1991–92 | Brentford | 35 | 0 |
| 1992–93 | Brentford | 41 | 1 |
| 1993–94 | Brentford | 18 | 0 |
| 1994–95 | Cambridge U | 10 | 0 |
| 1994–95 | Peterborough U | 14 | 1 |
| 1995–96 | Peterborough U | 13 | 1 |
| 1995–96 | Gillingham | 10 | 0 |
| 1996–97 | Gillingham | 11 | 0 |
| 1997–98 | Barnet | 17 | 0 |
| **Total:** | | **256** | **8** |

## MARCELLE, Clint — Midfield

H: 5 4 W: 10 00 b.Port of Spain 9-11-68

*Honours:* Trinidad & Tobago 30 full caps.

| | | | |
|---|---|---|---|
| 1995–96 | Falgueiras | 21 | 0 |
| 1996–97 | Barnsley | 40 | 8 |
| 1997–98 | Barnsley | 20 | 0 |
| **Total:** | | **81** | **8** |

## MARCELLO — Forward

H: 6 0 W: 13 08 b.Niteroi 11-10-69

*Source:* Alaves.

| | | | |
|---|---|---|---|
| 1997–98 | Sheffield U | 21 | 6 |
| **Total:** | | **21** | **6** |

## MARDON, Paul — Defender

H: 6 0 W: 11 10 b.Bristol 14-9-69

*Source:* Trainee. *Honours:* Wales 1 full cap.

| | | | |
|---|---|---|---|
| 1987–88 | Bristol C | 8 | 0 |
| 1988–89 | Bristol C | 20 | 0 |
| 1989–90 | Bristol C | 7 | 0 |
| 1990–91 | Bristol C | 7 | 0 |
| 1990–91 | Doncaster R (loan) | 3 | 0 |
| 1991–92 | Birmingham C | 35 | 0 |
| 1992–93 | Birmingham C | 21 | 0 |

| | | | |
|---|---|---|---|
| 1993–94 | Birmingham C | 8 | 0 |
| 1993–94 | WBA | 22 | 1 |
| 1994–95 | WBA | 28 | 1 |
| 1995–96 | WBA | 39 | 0 |
| 1996–97 | WBA | 14 | 0 |
| 1997–98 | WBA | 18 | 1 |
| **Total:** | | **230** | **3** |

## MARGETSON, Martyn — Goalkeeper

H: 6 0 W: 14 00 b.West Neath 8-9-71

*Source:* Trainee. *Honours:* Wales Under-21.

| | | | |
|---|---|---|---|
| 1990–91 | Manchester C | 2 | 0 |
| 1991–92 | Manchester C | 3 | 0 |
| 1992–93 | Manchester C | 1 | 0 |
| 1993–94 | Manchester C | 0 | 0 |
| 1993–94 | Bristol R (loan) | 3 | 0 |
| 1993–94 | Bolton W (loan) | 0 | 0 |
| 1994–95 | Manchester C | 0 | 0 |
| 1994–95 | Luton T (loan) | 0 | 0 |
| 1995–96 | Manchester C | 0 | 0 |
| 1996–97 | Manchester C | 17 | 0 |
| 1997–98 | Manchester C | 28 | 0 |
| **Total:** | | **54** | **0** |

## MARKER, Nicky — Defender

H: 6 0 W: 13 00 b.Exeter 3-5-65

*Source:* Apprentice.

| | | | |
|---|---|---|---|
| 1981–82 | Exeter C | 14 | 1 |
| 1982–83 | Exeter C | 18 | 1 |
| 1983–84 | Exeter C | 31 | 0 |
| 1984–85 | Exeter C | 45 | 0 |
| 1985–86 | Exeter C | 40 | 0 |
| 1986–87 | Exeter C | 43 | 1 |
| 1987–88 | Exeter C | 11 | 0 |
| 1987–88 | Plymouth Arg | 26 | 1 |
| 1988–89 | Plymouth Arg | 43 | 6 |
| 1989–90 | Plymouth Arg | 43 | 1 |
| 1990–91 | Plymouth Arg | 39 | 2 |
| 1991–92 | Plymouth Arg | 44 | 1 |
| 1992–93 | Plymouth Arg | 7 | 2 |
| 1992–93 | Blackburn R | 15 | 0 |
| 1993–94 | Blackburn R | 23 | 0 |
| 1994–95 | Blackburn R | 0 | 0 |
| 1995–96 | Blackburn R | 9 | 1 |
| 1996–97 | Blackburn R | 7 | 0 |
| 1997–98 | Sheffield U | 43 | 2 |
| **Total:** | | **501** | **19** |

## MARKEY, Brendan — Forward

H: 5 10 W: 12 00 b.Dublin 19-5-76

*Source:* Bohemians.

| | | | |
|---|---|---|---|
| 1995–96 | Millwall | 0 | 0 |
| 1996–97 | Millwall | 0 | 0 |
| 1997–98 | Millwall | 0 | 0 |

## MARKLUND, Goran — Forward

H: 5 11 W: 11 08 b.Stockholm 2-10-75

| | | | |
|---|---|---|---|
| 1997 | Vasalund | 14 | 4 |
| 1997–98 | Dundee U | 3 | 0 |
| **Total:** | | **17** | **4** |

## MARKS, Jamie — Defender

H: 5 9 W: 10 13 b.Belfast 18-3-77

*Source:* Trainee.

| | | | |
|---|---|---|---|
| 1994–95 | Leeds U | 0 | 0 |
| 1995–96 | Leeds U | 0 | 0 |
| 1995–96 | Hull C | 5 | 0 |
| 1996–97 | Hull C | 10 | 0 |
| 1997–98 | Hull C | 0 | 0 |
| **Total:** | | **15** | **0** |

## MARKSTEDT, Peter — Defender

H: 5 9 W: 14 00 b.Vasteras 11-1-72

| | | | |
|---|---|---|---|
| 1997 | Vasteras | 23 | 4 |
| 1997–98 | Barnsley | 7 | 0 |
| **Total:** | | **30** | **4** |

## MARRIOTT, Alan — Midfield

b.Bedford 3-9-78

*Source:* Trainee.

| | | | |
|---|---|---|---|
| 1997–98 | Tottenham H | 0 | 0 |

## MARRIOTT, Andy — Goalkeeper

H: 6 1 W: 12 08 b.Sutton-in-Ashfield 11-10-70

*Source:* Trainee. *Honours:* England Schools, FA Schools, Youth, Under-21, Wales 5 full caps.

| | | | |
|---|---|---|---|
| 1988–89 | Arsenal | 0 | 0 |
| 1989–90 | Nottingham F | 0 | 0 |
| 1989–90 | WBA (loan) | 3 | 0 |
| 1989–90 | Blackburn R (loan) | 2 | 0 |
| 1989–90 | Colchester U (loan) | 10 | 0 |
| 1990–91 | Nottingham F | 0 | 0 |
| 1991–92 | Nottingham F | 6 | 0 |
| 1991–92 | Burnley (loan) | 15 | 0 |
| 1992–93 | Nottingham F | 5 | 0 |
| 1993–94 | Nottingham F | 0 | 0 |
| 1993–94 | Wrexham | 36 | 0 |
| 1994–95 | Wrexham | 46 | 0 |
| 1995–96 | Wrexham | 46 | 0 |
| 1996–97 | Wrexham | 43 | 0 |
| 1997–98 | Wrexham | 42 | 0 |
| **Total:** | | **254** | **0** |

## MARSDEN, Chris — Midfield

H: 5 11 W: 10 12 b.Sheffield 3-1-69

*Source:* Trainee.

| | | | |
|---|---|---|---|
| 1986–87 | Sheffield U | 0 | 0 |
| 1987–88 | Sheffield U | 16 | 1 |
| 1988–89 | Huddersfield T | 14 | 1 |
| 1989–90 | Huddersfield T | 32 | 2 |
| 1990–91 | Huddersfield T | 43 | 5 |
| 1991–92 | Huddersfield T | 23 | 1 |
| 1992–93 | Huddersfield T | 7 | 0 |
| 1993–94 | Huddersfield T | 2 | 0 |
| 1993–94 | Coventry C (loan) | 7 | 0 |
| 1993–94 | Wolverhampton W | 8 | 0 |
| 1994–95 | Wolverhampton W | 0 | 0 |
| 1994–95 | Notts Co | 7 | 0 |
| 1995–96 | Notts Co | 3 | 0 |
| 1995–96 | Stockport Co | 20 | 1 |
| 1996–97 | Stockport Co | 35 | 2 |
| 1997–98 | Stockport Co | 10 | 0 |
| 1997–98 | Birmingham C | 32 | 1 |
| **Total:** | | **259** | **14** |

## MARSH, Chris — Defender

H: 5 11 W: 13 05 b.Dudley 14-1-70

*Source:* Trainee.

| | | | |
|---|---|---|---|
| 1987–88 | Walsall | 3 | 0 |
| 1988–89 | Walsall | 13 | 0 |
| 1989–90 | Walsall | 9 | 0 |
| 1990–91 | Walsall | 23 | 2 |
| 1991–92 | Walsall | 37 | 1 |
| 1992–93 | Walsall | 33 | 3 |
| 1993–94 | Walsall | 39 | 4 |
| 1994–95 | Walsall | 38 | 9 |
| 1995–96 | Walsall | 41 | 2 |
| 1996–97 | Walsall | 30 | 0 |
| 1997–98 | Walsall | 36 | 0 |
| **Total:** | | **302** | **21** |

## MARSH, Mike — Midfield

H: 5 8 W: 11 00 b.Liverpool 21-7-69

*Source:* Kirkby T.

| | | | |
|---|---|---|---|
| 1987–88 | Liverpool | 0 | 0 |
| 1988–89 | Liverpool | 1 | 0 |
| 1989–90 | Liverpool | 2 | 0 |
| 1990–91 | Liverpool | 2 | 0 |
| 1991–92 | Liverpool | 34 | 0 |
| 1992–93 | Liverpool | 28 | 1 |
| 1993–94 | Liverpool | 2 | 1 |
| 1993–94 | West Ham U | 33 | 1 |
| 1994–95 | West Ham U | 16 | 0 |
| 1994–95 | Coventry C | 15 | 2 |
| 1995–96 | Galatasaray | 3 | 0 |
| 1995–96 | Southend U | 40 | 5 |
| 1996–97 | Southend U | 35 | 5 |
| 1997–98 | Southend U | 9 | 1 |
| **Total:** | | **220** | **16** |

## MARSH, Simon — Defender

H: 6 0 W: 12 00 b.Ealing 29-1-77

*Source:* Trainee. *Honours:* England Under-21.

| | | | |
|---|---|---|---|
| 1994–95 | Oxford U | 8 | 0 |
| 1995–96 | Oxford U | 5 | 0 |
| 1996–97 | Oxford U | 8 | 1 |
| 1997–98 | Oxford U | 14 | 0 |
| **Total:** | | **35** | **1** |

## MARSHALL, Andy — Goalkeeper

H: 6 2 W: 13 01 b.Bury 14-4-76

*Source:* Trainee. *Honours:* England Under-21.

| | | | |
|---|---|---|---|
| 1993–94 | Norwich C | 0 | 0 |
| 1994–95 | Norwich C | 21 | 0 |
| 1995–96 | Norwich C | 3 | 0 |
| 1996–97 | Norwich C | 7 | 0 |
| 1996–97 | Bournemouth (loan) | 11 | 0 |
| 1996–97 | Gillingham (loan) | 5 | 0 |
| 1997–98 | Norwich C | 42 | 0 |
| **Total:** | | **89** | **0** |

## MARSHALL, Ben — Midfield

H: 6 0 W: 12 00 b.Sutton 5-9-79

*Source:* Trainee.

| | | | |
|---|---|---|---|
| 1997–98 | Notts Co | 0 | 0 |

## MARSHALL, Dwight — Forward

H: 6 1 W: 11 02 b.Jamaica 3-10-65

*Source:* Grays Ath.

| | | | |
|---|---|---|---|
| 1991–92 | Plymouth Arg | 44 | 14 |
| 1992–93 | Plymouth Arg | 24 | 1 |
| 1992–93 | Middlesbrough (loan) | 3 | 0 |
| 1993–94 | Plymouth Arg | 31 | 12 |
| 1994–95 | Luton T | 45 | 11 |
| 1995–96 | Luton T | 26 | 9 |
| 1996–97 | Luton T | 24 | 4 |
| 1997–98 | Luton T | 29 | 3 |
| **Total:** | | **226** | **54** |

## MARSHALL, Gordon — Goalkeeper

H: 6 2 W: 12 00 b.Edinburgh 19-4-64

*Source:* School. *Honours:* Scotland 1 full cap.

| | | | |
|---|---|---|---|
| 1982–83 | East Stirling | 15 | 0 |

| | | | |
|---|---|---|---|
| 1982–83 | East Fife | 10 | 0 |
| 1983–84 | East Fife | 34 | 0 |
| 1984–85 | East Fife | 39 | 0 |
| 1985–86 | East Fife | 39 | 0 |
| 1986–87 | East Fife | 36 | 0 |
| 1986–87 | Falkirk | 10 | 0 |
| 1987–88 | Falkirk | 44 | 0 |
| 1988–89 | Falkirk | 39 | 0 |
| 1989–90 | Falkirk | 39 | 0 |
| 1990–91 | Falkirk | 39 | 0 |
| 1991–92 | Celtic | 25 | 0 |
| 1992–93 | Celtic | 11 | 0 |
| 1993–94 | Celtic | 1 | 0 |
| 1993–94 | Stoke C (loan) | 10 | 0 |
| 1994–95 | Celtic | 16 | 0 |
| 1995–96 | Celtic | 36 | 0 |
| 1996–97 | Celtic | 11 | 0 |
| 1997–98 | Celtic | 1 | 0 |
| 1997–98 | Kilmarnock | 12 | 0 |
| **Total:** | | **467** | **0** |

## MARSHALL, Ian — Forward

H: 6 2 W: 13 09 b.Liverpool 20-3-66

*Source:* Apprentice.

| | | | |
|---|---|---|---|
| 1983–84 | Everton | 0 | 0 |
| 1984–85 | Everton | 0 | 0 |
| 1985–86 | Everton | 9 | 0 |
| 1986–87 | Everton | 2 | 1 |
| 1987–88 | Everton | 4 | 0 |
| 1987–88 | Oldham Ath | 10 | 0 |
| 1988–89 | Oldham Ath | 41 | 4 |
| 1989–90 | Oldham Ath | 25 | 3 |
| 1990–91 | Oldham Ath | 26 | 17 |
| 1991–92 | Oldham Ath | 41 | 10 |
| 1992–93 | Oldham Ath | 27 | 2 |
| 1993–94 | Ipswich T | 29 | 10 |
| 1994–95 | Ipswich T | 18 | 3 |
| 1995–96 | Ipswich T | 35 | 19 |
| 1996–97 | Ipswich T | 2 | 0 |
| 1996–97 | Leicester C | 28 | 8 |
| 1997–98 | Leicester C | 24 | 7 |
| **Total:** | | **321** | **84** |

## MARSHALL, John — Defender

H: 5 10 W: 12 04 b.Surrey 18-8-64

*Source:* Apprentice.

| | | | |
|---|---|---|---|
| 1982–83 | Fulham | 0 | 0 |
| 1983–84 | Fulham | 25 | 0 |
| 1984–85 | Fulham | 32 | 1 |
| 1985–86 | Fulham | 42 | 3 |
| 1986–87 | Fulham | 29 | 4 |
| 1987–88 | Fulham | 25 | 2 |
| 1988–89 | Fulham | 41 | 7 |
| 1989–90 | Fulham | 36 | 4 |
| 1990–91 | Fulham | 35 | 2 |
| 1991–92 | Fulham | 41 | 0 |
| 1992–93 | Fulham | 41 | 2 |
| 1993–94 | Fulham | 21 | 1 |
| 1994–95 | Fulham | 27 | 2 |
| 1995–96 | Fulham | 16 | 0 |
| 1996–97 | Fulham | 0 | 0 |
| 1997–98 | Fulham | 0 | 0 |
| **Total:** | | **411** | **28** |

## MARSHALL, Lee — Midfield

H: 5 10 W: 10 08 b.Nottingham 1-8-75

*Source:* Trainee.

| | | | |
|---|---|---|---|
| 1992–93 | Nottingham F | 0 | 0 |
| 1993–94 | Nottingham F | 0 | 0 |
| From Grantham T. | | | |
| 1994–95 | Stockport Co | 1 | 0 |
| 1995–96 | Stockport Co | 0 | 0 |
| From Eastwood T. | | | |
| 1997–98 | Scunthorpe U | 21 | 1 |
| **Total:** | | **22** | **1** |

## MARSHALL, Lee — Defender

H: 6 0 W: 11 10 b.Islington 21-1-79

*Source:* Enfield.

| | | | |
|---|---|---|---|
| 1996–97 | Norwich C | 0 | 0 |
| 1997–98 | Norwich C | 4 | 0 |
| **Total:** | | **4** | **0** |

## MARSHALL, Scott — Defender

H: 6 1 W: 12 05 b.Edinburgh 1-5-73

*Source:* Trainee. *Honours:* Scotland Under-21.

| | | | |
|---|---|---|---|
| 1992–93 | Arsenal | 2 | 0 |
| 1993–94 | Arsenal | 0 | 0 |
| 1993–94 | Rotherham U (loan) | 10 | 1 |
| 1993–94 | Oxford U (loan) | 0 | 0 |
| 1994–95 | Arsenal | 0 | 0 |
| 1994–95 | Sheffield U (loan) | 17 | 0 |
| 1995–96 | Arsenal | 11 | 1 |
| 1996–97 | Arsenal | 8 | 0 |
| 1997–98 | Arsenal | 3 | 0 |
| **Total:** | | **51** | **2** |

## MARSHALL, Shaun — Goalkeeper

H: 6 1 W: 12 11 b.Fakenham 3-10-78

*Source:* Trainee.

| | | | |
|---|---|---|---|
| 1996–97 | Cambridge U | 1 | 0 |
| 1997–98 | Cambridge U | 2 | 0 |
| **Total:** | | **3** | **0** |

## MARTIN, Andrew — Forward

H: 6 0 W: 10 12 b.Cardiff 28-2-80

*Source:* Trainee.

| | | | |
|---|---|---|---|
| 1996–97 | Crystal Palace | 0 | 0 |
| 1997–98 | Crystal Palace | 0 | 0 |

## MARTIN, Brian — Midfield

H: 6 0 W: 13 00 b.Bellshill 24-2-63

*Source:* Shotts Bon-Accord. *Honours:* Scotland 2 full caps.

| | | | |
|---|---|---|---|
| 1985–86 | Falkirk | 25 | 1 |
| 1986–87 | Falkirk | 34 | 1 |
| 1986–87 | Hamilton A | 7 | 0 |
| 1987–88 | Hamilton A | 23 | 0 |
| 1987–88 | St Mirren | 12 | 1 |
| 1988–89 | St Mirren | 34 | 2 |
| 1989–90 | St Mirren | 35 | 2 |
| 1990–91 | St Mirren | 31 | 2 |
| 1991–92 | St Mirren | 17 | 2 |
| 1991–92 | Motherwell | 25 | 0 |
| 1992–93 | Motherwell | 44 | 3 |
| 1993–94 | Motherwell | 43 | 2 |
| 1994–95 | Motherwell | 32 | 2 |
| 1995–96 | Motherwell | 33 | 2 |
| 1996–97 | Motherwell | 34 | 0 |
| 1997–98 | Motherwell | 26 | 1 |
| **Total:** | | **455** | **21** |

## MARTIN, Dave — Midfield

H: 6 1 W: 13 01 b.East Ham 25-4-63

*Source:* Apprentice. *Honours:* England Youth.

| | | | |
|---|---|---|---|
| 1979–80 | Millwall | 3 | 0 |
| 1980–81 | Millwall | 33 | 1 |
| 1981–82 | Millwall | 38 | 1 |
| 1982–83 | Millwall | 33 | 1 |
| 1983–84 | Millwall | 31 | 3 |
| 1984–85 | Millwall | 2 | 0 |
| 1984–85 | Wimbledon | 20 | 2 |
| 1985–86 | Wimbledon | 15 | 1 |
| 1986–87 | Southend U | 32 | 2 |
| 1987–88 | Southend U | 41 | 0 |
| 1988–89 | Southend U | 37 | 1 |
| 1989–90 | Southend U | 39 | 3 |
| 1990–91 | Southend U | 41 | 11 |
| 1991–92 | Southend U | 5 | 1 |
| 1992–93 | Southend U | 26 | 1 |
| 1993–94 | Bristol C | 34 | 1 |
| 1994–95 | Bristol C | 4 | 0 |
| 1994–95 | Northampton T (loan) | 7 | 1 |
| 1995–96 | Gillingham | 31 | 1 |
| 1996–97 | Leyton Orient | 8 | 0 |
| 1996–97 | Northampton T | 12 | 0 |
| 1996–97 | Brighton & HA (loan) | 1 | 0 |
| 1997–98 | Northampton T | 0 | 0 |
| **Total:** | | **493** | **31** |

## MARTIN, Jae — Forward

H: 5 11 W: 11 00 b.London 5-2-76

*Source:* Trainee.

| | | | |
|---|---|---|---|
| 1992–93 | Southend U | 0 | 0 |
| 1993–94 | Southend U | 4 | 0 |
| 1994–95 | Southend U | 4 | 0 |
| 1994–95 | Leyton Orient (loan) | 4 | 0 |
| 1995–96 | Birmingham C | 7 | 0 |
| 1996–97 | Birmingham C | 0 | 0 |
| 1996–97 | Lincoln C | 34 | 4 |
| 1997–98 | Lincoln C | 7 | 1 |
| **Total:** | | **60** | **5** |

## MARTIN, John — Defender

b.London 15-7-81

| | | | |
|---|---|---|---|
| 1997–98 | Leyton Orient | 1 | 0 |
| **Total:** | | **1** | **0** |

## MARTIN, Kevin — Goalkeeper

H: 6 0 W: 12 09 b.Bromsgrove 26-6-76

*Source:* Trainee.

| | | | |
|---|---|---|---|
| 1994–95 | Scarborough | 3 | 0 |
| 1995–96 | Scarborough | 0 | 0 |
| 1996–97 | Scarborough | 3 | 0 |
| 1997–98 | Scarborough | 17 | 0 |
| **Total:** | | **23** | **0** |

## MARTIN, Lee — Defender

H: 6 0 W: 12 08 b.Hyde 5-2-68

| | | | |
|---|---|---|---|
| 1986–87 | Manchester U | 0 | 0 |
| 1987–88 | Manchester U | 1 | 0 |
| 1988–89 | Manchester U | 24 | 1 |
| 1989–90 | Manchester U | 32 | 0 |
| 1990–91 | Manchester U | 14 | 0 |
| 1991–92 | Manchester U | 1 | 0 |
| 1992–93 | Manchester U | 0 | 0 |
| 1993–94 | Manchester U | 1 | 0 |
| 1993–94 | Celtic | 15 | 0 |
| 1994–95 | Celtic | 4 | 0 |
| 1995–96 | Celtic | 0 | 0 |
| 1996–97 | Bristol R | 25 | 0 |
| 1997–98 | Bristol R | 0 | 0 |
| 1997–98 | Huddersfield T (loan) | 3 | 0 |
| **Total:** | | **120** | **1** |

## MARTINDALE, Gary — Forward

H: 6 1 W: 11 13 b.Liverpool 24-6-71

*Source:* Burscough.

| | | | |
|---|---|---|---|
| 1993–94 | Bolton W | 0 | 0 |
| 1994–95 | Bolton W | 0 | 0 |
| 1995–96 | Peterborough U | 31 | 15 |
| 1995–96 | Notts Co | 16 | 6 |
| 1996–97 | Notts Co | 28 | 6 |
| 1996–97 | Mansfield T (loan) | 5 | 2 |
| 1997–98 | Notts Co | 22 | 1 |
| 1997–98 | Rotherham U | 8 | 2 |
| **Total:** | | **110** | **32** |

## MARTINEZ, Roberto — Midfield

H: 5 11 W: 11 12 b.Balaguer 13-7-73

*Source:* Balaguer.

| | | | |
|---|---|---|---|
| 1995–96 | Wigan Ath | 42 | 9 |
| 1996–97 | Wigan Ath | 43 | 4 |
| 1997–98 | Wigan Ath | 33 | 1 |
| **Total:** | | **118** | **14** |

## MARTYN, Nigel — Goalkeeper

H: 6 1 W: 14 07 b.St Austell 11-8-66

*Source:* St Blazey. *Honours:* England Under-21, B, 7 full caps.

| | | | |
|---|---|---|---|
| 1987–88 | Bristol R | 39 | 0 |
| 1988–89 | Bristol R | 46 | 0 |
| 1989–90 | Bristol R | 16 | 0 |
| 1989–90 | Crystal Palace | 25 | 0 |
| 1990–91 | Crystal Palace | 38 | 0 |
| 1991–92 | Crystal Palace | 38 | 0 |
| 1992–93 | Crystal Palace | 42 | 0 |
| 1993–94 | Crystal Palace | 46 | 0 |
| 1994–95 | Crystal Palace | 37 | 0 |
| 1995–96 | Crystal Palace | 46 | 0 |
| 1996–97 | Leeds U | 37 | 0 |
| 1997–98 | Leeds U | 37 | 0 |
| **Total:** | | **447** | **0** |

## MASKELL, Craig — Forward

H: 5 10 W: 11 10 b.Aldershot 10-4-68

*Source:* Apprentice. *Honours:* Football League.

| | | | |
|---|---|---|---|
| 1985–86 | Southampton | 2 | 1 |
| 1986–87 | Southampton | 4 | 0 |
| 1986–87 | Swindon T (loan) | 0 | 0 |
| 1987–88 | Southampton | 0 | 0 |
| 1988–89 | Huddersfield T | 46 | 28 |
| 1989–90 | Huddersfield T | 41 | 15 |
| 1990–91 | Reading | 38 | 10 |
| 1991–92 | Reading | 34 | 16 |
| 1992–93 | Swindon T | 33 | 19 |
| 1993–94 | Swindon T | 14 | 3 |
| 1993–94 | Southampton | 10 | 1 |
| 1994–95 | Southampton | 6 | 0 |
| 1995–96 | Southampton | 1 | 0 |
| 1995–96 | Bristol C (loan) | 5 | 1 |
| 1995–96 | Brighton & HA | 15 | 4 |
| 1996–97 | Brighton & HA | 37 | 14 |
| 1997–98 | Brighton & HA | 17 | 2 |
| From Happy Valley. | | | |
| 1997–98 | Leyton Orient | 8 | 2 |
| **Total:** | | **311** | **116** |

## MASON, Andy — Forward

H: 6 0 W: 12 02 b.Bolton 22-11-74

*Source:* Trainee.

| | | | |
|---|---|---|---|
| 1993–94 | Bolton W | 0 | 0 |
| 1994–95 | Bolton W | 0 | 0 |
| 1995–96 | Hull C | 20 | 1 |
| 1996–97 | Hull C | 6 | 3 |
| 1996–97 | Chesterfield | 2 | 0 |
| 1997–98 | Macclesfield T | 12 | 0 |
| **Total:** | | **40** | **4** |

## MASON, Gary — Midfield

H: 5 8 W: 10 01 b.Edinburgh 15-10-79

*Source:* Trainee.

| | | | |
|---|---|---|---|
| 1996–97 | Manchester C | 0 | 0 |
| 1997–98 | Manchester C | 0 | 0 |

## MASON, Paul — Midfield

H: 5 9 W: 12 01 b.Liverpool 3-9-63

*Source:* Groningen.

| | | | |
|---|---|---|---|
| 1988–89 | Aberdeen | 28 | 4 |
| 1989–90 | Aberdeen | 34 | 9 |
| 1990–91 | Aberdeen | 26 | 3 |
| 1991–92 | Aberdeen | 31 | 7 |
| 1992–93 | Aberdeen | 39 | 4 |
| 1993–94 | Ipswich T | 22 | 3 |
| 1994–95 | Ipswich T | 21 | 3 |
| 1995–96 | Ipswich T | 26 | 7 |
| 1996–97 | Ipswich T | 43 | 12 |
| 1997–98 | Ipswich T | 1 | 0 |
| **Total:** | | **271** | **52** |

## MASSEY, Miles — Midfield

b.York 21-4-79

| | | | |
|---|---|---|---|
| 1997–98 | Barnsley | 0 | 0 |

## MASSEY, Stuart — Midfield

H: 5 10 W: 13 07 b.Crawley 17-11-64

*Source:* Sutton U.

| | | | |
|---|---|---|---|
| 1992–93 | Crystal Palace | 1 | 0 |
| 1993–94 | Crystal Palace | 1 | 0 |
| 1994–95 | Oxford U | 22 | 0 |
| 1995–96 | Oxford U | 35 | 4 |
| 1996–97 | Oxford U | 29 | 3 |
| 1997–98 | Oxford U | 17 | 1 |
| **Total:** | | **105** | **8** |

## MASTERS, Neil — Defender

H: 6 0 W: 13 05 b.Lisburn 25-5-72

*Source:* Trainee.

| | | | |
|---|---|---|---|
| 1992–93 | Bournemouth | 20 | 0 |
| 1993–94 | Bournemouth | 18 | 2 |
| 1993–94 | Wolverhampton W | 4 | 0 |
| 1994–95 | Wolverhampton W | 5 | 0 |
| 1995–96 | Wolverhampton W | 3 | 0 |
| 1996–97 | Wolverhampton W | 0 | 0 |
| 1996–97 | Gillingham | 0 | 0 |
| 1997–98 | Gillingham | 11 | 0 |
| **Total:** | | **61** | **2** |

## MATHIE, Alex — Forward

H: 5 10 W: 11 07 b.Bathgate 20-12-68

*Source:* Celtic BC.

| | | | |
|---|---|---|---|
| 1987–88 | Celtic | 0 | 0 |
| 1988–89 | Celtic | 1 | 0 |
| 1989–90 | Celtic | 6 | 0 |
| 1990–91 | Celtic | 4 | 0 |
| 1991–92 | Morton | 42 | 18 |
| 1992–93 | Morton | 32 | 13 |
| 1992–93 | Port Vale (loan) | 3 | 0 |
| 1993–94 | Newcastle U | 16 | 3 |
| 1994–95 | Newcastle U | 9 | 1 |
| 1994–95 | Ipswich T | 13 | 2 |
| 1995–96 | Ipswich T | 39 | 18 |
| 1996–97 | Ipswich T | 12 | 4 |
| 1997–98 | Ipswich T | 37 | 13 |
| **Total:** | | **214** | **72** |

## MATTEO, Dominic — Defender

H: 6 1 W: 11 10 b.Dumfries 24-4-74

*Source:* Trainee. *Honours:* England Youth, Under-21, B.

| | | | |
|---|---|---|---|
| 1992–93 | Liverpool | 0 | 0 |
| 1993–94 | Liverpool | 11 | 0 |
| 1994–95 | Liverpool | 7 | 0 |
| 1994–95 | Sunderland (loan) | 1 | 0 |
| 1995–96 | Liverpool | 5 | 0 |
| 1996–97 | Liverpool | 26 | 0 |
| 1997–98 | Liverpool | 26 | 0 |
| **Total:** | | **76** | **0** |

## MATTHEW, Damian — Midfield

H: 5 11 W: 10 10 b.Islington 23-9-70

*Source:* Trainee. *Honours:* England Under-21.

| | | | |
|---|---|---|---|
| 1989–90 | Chelsea | 2 | 0 |
| 1990–91 | Chelsea | 8 | 0 |
| 1991–92 | Chelsea | 7 | 0 |
| 1992–93 | Chelsea | 4 | 0 |
| 1992–93 | Luton T (loan) | 5 | 0 |
| 1993–94 | Chelsea | 0 | 0 |
| 1993–94 | Crystal Palace | 12 | 1 |
| 1994–95 | Crystal Palace | 4 | 0 |
| 1995–96 | Crystal Palace | 8 | 0 |
| 1995–96 | Bristol R (loan) | 8 | 0 |
| 1996–97 | Burnley | 32 | 6 |
| 1997–98 | Burnley | 27 | 1 |
| **Total:** | | **117** | **8** |

## MATTHEWS, Lee — Midfield

b.Middlesbrough 16-1-79

*Source:* Trainee. *Honours:* England Youth.

| | | | |
|---|---|---|---|
| 1995–96 | Leeds U | 0 | 0 |
| 1996–97 | Leeds U | 0 | 0 |
| 1997–98 | Leeds U | 3 | 0 |
| **Total:** | | **3** | **0** |

## MATTHEWS, Rob — Midfield

H: 6 0 W: 12 05 b.Slough 14-10-70

*Source:* Loughborough Univ. *Honours:* England Schools.

| | | | |
|---|---|---|---|
| 1991–92 | Notts Co | 5 | 3 |
| 1992–93 | Notts Co | 8 | 2 |
| 1993–94 | Notts Co | 12 | 3 |
| 1994–95 | Notts Co | 18 | 3 |
| 1994–95 | Luton T | 11 | 0 |
| 1995–96 | Luton T | 0 | 0 |
| 1995–96 | York C | 17 | 1 |
| 1995–96 | Bury | 16 | 4 |
| 1996–97 | Bury | 27 | 5 |
| 1997–98 | Bury | 15 | 0 |
| **Total:** | | **129** | **21** |

## MAUGE, Ronnie — Midfield

H: 5 10 W: 10 06 b.Islington 10-3-69

*Source:* Trainee.

| | | | |
|---|---|---|---|
| 1987–88 | Charlton Ath | 0 | 0 |
| 1988–89 | Fulham | 13 | 0 |
| 1989–90 | Fulham | 37 | 2 |

| | | | |
|---|---|---|---|
| 1990–91 | Bury | 29 | 6 |
| 1991–92 | Bury | 22 | 0 |
| 1991–92 | Manchester C (loan) | 0 | 0 |
| 1992–93 | Bury | 13 | 1 |
| 1993–94 | Bury | 26 | 3 |
| 1994–95 | Bury | 18 | 0 |
| 1995–96 | Plymouth Arg | 37 | 7 |
| 1996–97 | Plymouth Arg | 35 | 3 |
| 1997–98 | Plymouth Arg | 31 | 1 |
| **Total:** | | **261** | **23** |

## MAURO — Midfield

H: 6 1 W: 12 12 b.Portugal 16-6-76

*Source:* Casapia.

| | | | |
|---|---|---|---|
| 1997–98 | Tranmere R | 0 | 0 |

## MAUTONE, Steve — Goalkeeper

H: 6 2 W: 13 03 b.Myrtleford 10-8-70

*Source:* Canberra Cosmos.

| | | | |
|---|---|---|---|
| 1995–96 | West Ham U | 0 | 0 |
| 1996–97 | West Ham U | 1 | 0 |
| 1996–97 | Crewe Alex (loan) | 3 | 0 |
| 1996–97 | Reading | 15 | 0 |
| 1997–98 | Reading | 14 | 0 |
| **Total:** | | **33** | **0** |

## MAWSON, Craig — Goalkeeper

b.Keighley 16-5-79

*Source:* Trainee.

| | | | |
|---|---|---|---|
| 1997–98 | Burnley | 0 | 0 |

## MAXFIELD, Scott — Defender

H: 5 10 W: 11 05 b.Doncaster 13-7-76

*Source:* Trainee.

| | | | |
|---|---|---|---|
| 1994–95 | Doncaster R | 10 | 0 |
| 1995–96 | Doncaster R | 19 | 1 |
| 1995–96 | Hull C | 4 | 0 |
| 1996–97 | Hull C | 17 | 0 |
| 1997–98 | Hull C | 14 | 0 |
| **Total:** | | **64** | **1** |

## MAXWELL, Leyton — Midfield

H: 5 8 W: 11 00 b.St Asaph 3-10-79

*Source:* Trainee.

| | | | |
|---|---|---|---|
| 1997–98 | Liverpool | 0 | 0 |

## MAY, David — Defender

H: 6 0 W: 13 05 b.Oldham 24-6-70

*Source:* Trainee.

| | | | |
|---|---|---|---|
| 1988–89 | Blackburn R | 1 | 0 |
| 1989–90 | Blackburn R | 17 | 0 |
| 1990–91 | Blackburn R | 19 | 1 |
| 1991–92 | Blackburn R | 12 | 0 |
| 1992–93 | Blackburn R | 34 | 1 |
| 1993–94 | Blackburn R | 40 | 1 |
| 1994–95 | Manchester U | 19 | 2 |
| 1995–96 | Manchester U | 16 | 1 |
| 1996–97 | Manchester U | 29 | 3 |
| 1997–98 | Manchester U | 9 | 0 |
| **Total:** | | **196** | **9** |

## MAY, Edward — Forward

H: 5 7 W: 10 03 b.Edinburgh 30-8-67

*Source:* Hutchison Vale BC. *Honours:* Scotland Youth, Under-21.

| | | | |
|---|---|---|---|
| 1983–84 | Dundee U | 0 | 0 |
| 1984–85 | Dundee U | 0 | 0 |
| 1984–85 | Hibernian | 0 | 0 |
| 1985–86 | Hibernian | 19 | 1 |
| 1986–87 | Hibernian | 30 | 5 |
| 1987–88 | Hibernian | 35 | 2 |
| 1988–89 | Hibernian | 25 | 2 |
| 1989–90 | Brentford | 30 | 8 |
| 1990–91 | Brentford | 17 | 2 |
| 1990–91 | Falkirk | 13 | 6 |
| 1991–92 | Falkirk | 36 | 9 |
| 1992–93 | Falkirk | 42 | 6 |
| 1993–94 | Falkirk | 38 | 9 |
| 1994–95 | Falkirk | 24 | 2 |
| 1994–95 | Motherwell | 10 | 2 |
| 1995–96 | Motherwell | 28 | 1 |
| 1996–97 | Motherwell | 34 | 2 |
| 1997–98 | Motherwell | 25 | 0 |
| **Total:** | | **406** | **57** |

## MAYBURY, Alan — Midfield

b.Dublin 8-8-78

*Source:* Trainee. *Honours:* Eire 1 full cap.

| | | | |
|---|---|---|---|
| 1995–96 | Leeds U | 1 | 0 |
| 1996–97 | Leeds U | 0 | 0 |
| 1997–98 | Leeds U | 12 | 0 |
| **Total:** | | **13** | **0** |

## MAYO, Kerry — Midfield

H: 5 10 W: 13 02 b.Cuckfield 21-9-77

*Source:* Trainee.

| | | | |
|---|---|---|---|
| 1996–97 | Brighton & HA | 24 | 0 |
| 1997–98 | Brighton & HA | 44 | 6 |
| **Total:** | | **68** | **6** |

## MAYRLEB, Christian — Forward

H: 5 8 W: 11 13 b.Leonding 8-6-72

| | | | |
|---|---|---|---|
| 1994–95 | Admira Wacker | 34 | 7 |
| 1995–96 | Admira Wacker | 32 | 8 |
| 1996–97 | Tirol | 33 | 7 |
| 1997–98 | Tirol | 20 | 9 |
| 1997–98 | Sheffield W | 3 | 0 |
| **Total:** | | **122** | **31** |

## McALINDON, Gareth — Forward

H: 5 9 W: 11 10 b.Hexham 6-4-77

*Source:* Newcastle U Trainee.

| | | | |
|---|---|---|---|
| 1995–96 | Carlisle U | 3 | 0 |
| 1996–97 | Carlisle U | 12 | 2 |
| 1997–98 | Carlisle U | 28 | 3 |
| **Total:** | | **43** | **5** |

## McALLISTER, Brian — Defender

H: 5 11 W: 12 05 b.Glasgow 30-11-70

*Source:* Trainee. *Honours:* Scotland 3 full caps.

| | | | |
|---|---|---|---|
| 1988–89 | Wimbledon | 0 | 0 |
| 1989–90 | Wimbledon | 3 | 0 |
| 1990–91 | Wimbledon | 0 | 0 |
| 1990–91 | Plymouth Arg (loan) | 8 | 0 |
| 1991–92 | Wimbledon | 10 | 0 |
| 1992–93 | Wimbledon | 27 | 0 |
| 1993–94 | Wimbledon | 13 | 0 |
| 1994–95 | Wimbledon | 0 | 0 |
| 1995–96 | Wimbledon | 2 | 0 |
| 1995–96 | Crewe Alex (loan) | 13 | 1 |
| 1996–97 | Wimbledon | 23 | 0 |
| 1997–98 | Wimbledon | 7 | 0 |
| **Total:** | | **106** | **1** |

## McALLISTER, Gary — Midfield

H: 6 1 W: 11 11 b.Motherwell 25-12-64

*Source:* Fir Park BC. *Honours:* Scotland Under-21, B, 56 full caps, 5 goals.

| | | | |
|---|---|---|---|
| 1981–82 | Motherwell | 1 | 0 |
| 1982–83 | Motherwell | 1 | 0 |
| 1983–84 | Motherwell | 21 | 0 |
| 1984–85 | Motherwell | 35 | 6 |
| 1985–86 | Motherwell | 1 | 0 |
| 1985–86 | Leicester C | 31 | 7 |
| 1986–87 | Leicester C | 39 | 10 |
| 1987–88 | Leicester C | 42 | 9 |
| 1988–89 | Leicester C | 46 | 11 |
| 1989–90 | Leicester C | 43 | 10 |
| 1990–91 | Leeds U | 38 | 2 |
| 1991–92 | Leeds U | 42 | 5 |
| 1992–93 | Leeds U | 32 | 5 |
| 1993–94 | Leeds U | 42 | 8 |
| 1994–95 | Leeds U | 41 | 6 |
| 1995–96 | Leeds U | 36 | 5 |
| 1996–97 | Coventry C | 38 | 6 |
| 1997–98 | Coventry C | 14 | 0 |
| **Total:** | | **543** | **90** |

## McALPINE, Joseph — Defender

b.Glasgow 12-9-81

| | | | |
|---|---|---|---|
| 1997–98 | Everton | 0 | 0 |

## McANESPIE, Kieran — Forward

H: 5 8 W: 10 13 b.Gosport 11-9-79

*Source:* St Johnstone BC. *Honours:* Scotland Under-17, Under-21.

| | | | |
|---|---|---|---|
| 1995–96 | St Johnstone | 0 | 0 |
| 1996–97 | St Johnstone | 9 | 2 |
| 1997–98 | St Johnstone | 3 | 0 |
| **Total:** | | **12** | **2** |

## McANESPIE, Steve — Defender

H: 5 9 W: 10 08 b.Kilmarnock 1-2-72

*Source:* Vasterhauringe.

| | | | |
|---|---|---|---|
| 1993–94 | Raith R | 3 | 0 |
| 1994–95 | Raith R | 34 | 0 |
| 1995–96 | Raith R | 3 | 0 |
| 1995–96 | Bolton W | 9 | 0 |
| 1996–97 | Bolton W | 13 | 0 |
| 1997–98 | Bolton W | 2 | 0 |
| 1997–98 | Fulham | 4 | 0 |
| 1997–98 | Bradford C (loan) | 7 | 0 |
| **Total:** | | **75** | **0** |

## McAREAVEY, Paul — Midfield

b.Belfast 3-12-80

*Source:* Trainee.

| | | | |
|---|---|---|---|
| 1997–98 | Swindon T | 1 | 0 |
| **Total:** | | **1** | **0** |

## McAREE, Rod — Midfield

: 5 7 W: 11 00 b.Dungannon 10-8-74

*ource:* Trainee.

| | | | |
|---|---|---|---|
| 991–92 | Liverpool | 0 | 0 |
| 992–93 | Liverpool | 0 | 0 |
| 993–94 | Liverpool | 0 | 0 |
| 994–95 | Bristol C | 6 | 0 |
| 995–96 | Bristol C | 0 | 0 |
| 995–96 | Fulham | 17 | 2 |
| 996–97 | Fulham | 9 | 1 |
| 997–98 | Fulham | 2 | 0 |
| **otal:** | | **34** | **3** |

## McATEER, Jason — Midfield

: 5 11 W: 11 10 b.Birkenhead 18-6-71

*ource:* Marine. *Honours:* Eire B, 25 full caps, 1 goal.

| | | | |
|---|---|---|---|
| 991–92 | Bolton W | 0 | 0 |
| 992–93 | Bolton W | 21 | 0 |
| 993–94 | Bolton W | 46 | 3 |
| 994–95 | Bolton W | 43 | 5 |
| 995–96 | Bolton W | 4 | 0 |
| 995–96 | Liverpool | 29 | 0 |
| 996–97 | Liverpool | 37 | 1 |
| 997–98 | Liverpool | 21 | 2 |
| **otal:** | | **201** | **11** |

## McAULEY, Sean — Defender

: 5 11 W: 12 02 b.Sheffield 23-6-72

*ource:* Trainee. *Honours:* Scotland Under-21.

| | | | |
|---|---|---|---|
| 991–92 | Manchester U | 0 | 0 |
| 992–93 | St Johnstone | 26 | 0 |
| 993–94 | St Johnstone | 28 | 0 |
| 994–95 | St Johnstone | 8 | 0 |
| 994–95 | Chesterfield (loan) | 1 | 1 |
| 995–96 | Hartlepool U | 46 | 0 |
| 996–97 | Hartlepool U | 38 | 1 |
| 996–97 | Scunthorpe U | 9 | 0 |
| 997–98 | Scunthorpe U | 35 | 1 |
| **otal:** | | **191** | **3** |

## McAVOY, Andy — Midfield

: 6 0 W: 12 00 b.Middlesbrough 28-8-79

*ource:* Trainee.

| | | | |
|---|---|---|---|
| 997–98 | Blackburn R | 0 | 0 |

## McAVOY, Lawrence — Defender

b.Lambeth 7-9-79

*Source:* Trainee.

| | | | |
|---|---|---|---|
| 1997–98 | Cambridge U | 0 | 0 |

## McCAFFREY, Stuart — Defender

H: 5 11 W: 11 11 b.Glasgow 30-5-79

*Source:* Duntocher BC.

| | | | |
|---|---|---|---|
| 1996–97 | Hibernian | 0 | 0 |
| 1997–98 | Hibernian | 2 | 0 |
| **Total:** | | **2** | **0** |

## McCALL, Steve — Midfield

H: 5 11 W: 12 06 b.Carlisle 15-10-60

*Source:* Apprentice. *Honours:* England Youth, Under-21, B.

| | | | |
|---|---|---|---|
| 1978–79 | Ipswich T | 0 | 0 |
| 1979–80 | Ipswich T | 10 | 0 |
| 1980–81 | Ipswich T | 31 | 1 |
| 1981–82 | Ipswich T | 42 | 1 |
| 1982–83 | Ipswich T | 42 | 4 |
| 1983–84 | Ipswich T | 42 | 1 |
| 1984–85 | Ipswich T | 31 | 0 |
| 1985–86 | Ipswich T | 33 | 0 |
| 1986–87 | Ipswich T | 26 | 0 |
| 1987–88 | Sheffield W | 5 | 0 |
| 1988–89 | Sheffield W | 2 | 0 |
| 1989–90 | Sheffield W | 3 | 0 |
| 1989–90 | Carlisle U (loan) | 6 | 0 |
| 1990–91 | Sheffield W | 19 | 2 |
| 1991–92 | Sheffield W | 0 | 0 |
| 1991–92 | Plymouth Arg | 9 | 1 |
| 1992–93 | Plymouth Arg | 35 | 1 |
| 1993–94 | Plymouth Arg | 45 | 2 |
| 1994–95 | Plymouth Arg | 7 | 1 |
| 1995–96 | Plymouth Arg | 4 | 0 |
| 1996–97 | Torquay U | 24 | 1 |
| 1997–98 | Torquay U | 27 | 1 |
| **Total:** | | **443** | **16** |

## McCALL, Stuart — Midfield

H: 5 6 W: 10 01 b.Leeds 10-6-64

*Source:* Apprentice. *Honours:* Scotland Under-21, 40 full caps, 1 goal.

| | | | |
|---|---|---|---|
| 1982–83 | Bradford C | 28 | 4 |
| 1983–84 | Bradford C | 46 | 5 |
| 1984–85 | Bradford C | 46 | 8 |
| 1985–86 | Bradford C | 38 | 4 |
| 1986–87 | Bradford C | 36 | 7 |
| 1987–88 | Bradford C | 44 | 9 |
| 1988–89 | Everton | 33 | 0 |

| | | | |
|---|---|---|---|
| 1989–90 | Everton | 37 | 3 |
| 1990–91 | Everton | 33 | 3 |
| 1991–92 | Rangers | 36 | 1 |
| 1992–93 | Rangers | 36 | 5 |
| 1993–94 | Rangers | 34 | 3 |
| 1994–95 | Rangers | 30 | 2 |
| 1995–96 | Rangers | 21 | 3 |
| 1996–97 | Rangers | 7 | 0 |
| 1997–98 | Rangers | 30 | 0 |
| **Total:** | | **535** | **57** |

## McCALLION, Edward — Defender

b.Derry 25-1-79

| | | | |
|---|---|---|---|
| 1996–97 | Blackburn R | 0 | 0 |
| 1997–98 | Blackburn R | 0 | 0 |

## McCAMMON, Mark — Forward

b.Barnet 7-8-78

| | | | |
|---|---|---|---|
| 1997–98 | Cambridge U | 2 | 0 |
| **Total:** | | **2** | **0** |

## McCANN, Gavin — Midfield

H: 5 11 W: 11 00 b.Blackpool 10-1-78

*Source:* Trainee.

| | | | |
|---|---|---|---|
| 1995–96 | Everton | 0 | 0 |
| 1996–97 | Everton | 0 | 0 |
| 1997–98 | Everton | 11 | 0 |
| **Total:** | | **11** | **0** |

## McCANN, Neil — Forward

H: 5 10 W: 10 00 b.Greenock 11-8-74

*Source:* Port Glasgow BC. *Honours:* Scotland Under-21, B.

| | | | |
|---|---|---|---|
| 1992–93 | Dundee | 3 | 0 |
| 1993–94 | Dundee | 22 | 1 |
| 1994–95 | Dundee | 32 | 2 |
| 1995–96 | Dundee | 22 | 2 |
| 1996–97 | Hearts | 30 | 5 |
| 1997–98 | Hearts | 35 | 10 |
| **Total:** | | **144** | **20** |

## McCARTHY, Jon — Midfield

H: 5 9 W: 11 05 b.Middlesbrough 18-8-70

*Honours:* Northern Ireland 7 full caps.

| | | | |
|---|---|---|---|
| 1987–88 | Hartlepool U | 1 | 0 |
| From Shepshed. | | | |
| 1990–91 | York C | 27 | 2 |
| 1991–92 | York C | 42 | 6 |
| 1992–93 | York C | 42 | 7 |
| 1993–94 | York C | 44 | 7 |
| 1994–95 | York C | 44 | [illegible] |
| 1995–96 | Port Vale | 45 | [illegible] |
| 1996–97 | Port Vale | 45 | [illegible] |
| 1997–98 | Port Vale | 4 | [illegible] |
| 1997–98 | Birmingham C | 41 | [illegible] |
| **Total:** | | **335** | [illegible] |

## McCARTHY, Paul — Defende[illegible]

H: 5 10 W: 13 10 b.Cork 4-8-71

*Source:* Trainee. *Honours:* Eire Youth, Under-21.

| | | | |
|---|---|---|---|
| 1989–90 | Brighton & HA | 3 | [illegible] |
| 1990–91 | Brighton & HA | 21 | [illegible] |
| 1991–92 | Brighton & HA | 20 | [illegible] |
| 1992–93 | Brighton & HA | 30 | [illegible] |
| 1993–94 | Brighton & HA | 37 | [illegible] |
| 1994–95 | Brighton & HA | 37 | [illegible] |
| 1995–96 | Brighton & HA | 33 | [illegible] |
| 1996–97 | Wycombe W | 40 | [illegible] |
| 1997–98 | Wycombe W | 31 | [illegible] |
| **Total:** | | **252** | [illegible] |

## McCARTHY, Sean — Forwar[illegible]

H: 6 1 W: 11 07 b.Bridgend 12-9-67

*Source:* Bridgend. *Honours:* Wales B.

| | | | |
|---|---|---|---|
| 1985–86 | Swansea C | 22 | [illegible] |
| 1986–87 | Swansea C | 44 | [illegible] |
| 1987–88 | Swansea C | 25 | [illegible] |
| 1988–89 | Plymouth Arg | 38 | [illegible] |
| 1989–90 | Plymouth Arg | 32 | [illegible] |
| 1990–91 | Bradford C | 42 | [illegible] |
| 1991–92 | Bradford C | 29 | [illegible] |
| 1992–93 | Bradford C | 42 | [illegible] |
| 1993–94 | Bradford C | 18 | [illegible] |
| 1993–94 | Oldham Ath | 20 | [illegible] |
| 1994–95 | Oldham Ath | 39 | [illegible] |
| 1995–96 | Oldham Ath | 35 | [illegible] |
| 1996–97 | Oldham Ath | 21 | [illegible] |
| 1997–98 | Oldham Ath | 25 | [illegible] |
| 1997–98 | Bristol C (loan) | 7 | [illegible] |
| **Total:** | | **439** | **147** |

## McCLAIR, Brian — Forwar[illegible]

H: 5 10 W: 12 12 b.Airdrie 8-12-63

*Source:* Apprentice. *Honours:* Scotland Youth, Under-21, B, 30 full caps, 2 goals.

| | | | |
|---|---|---|---|
| 1980–81 | Aston Villa | 0 | [illegible] |
| 1981–82 | Motherwell | 11 | [illegible] |
| 1982–83 | Motherwell | 28 | [illegible] |
| 1983–84 | Celtic | 35 | [illegible] |
| 1984–85 | Celtic | 32 | [illegible] |
| 1985–86 | Celtic | 34 | [illegible] |
| 1986–87 | Celtic | 44 | [illegible] |

| | | | |
|---|---|---|---|
| 1987–88 | Manchester U | 40 | 24 |
| 1988–89 | Manchester U | 38 | 10 |
| 1989–90 | Manchester U | 37 | 5 |
| 1990–91 | Manchester U | 36 | 13 |
| 1991–92 | Manchester U | 42 | 18 |
| 1992–93 | Manchester U | 42 | 9 |
| 1993–94 | Manchester U | 26 | 1 |
| 1994–95 | Manchester U | 40 | 5 |
| 1995–96 | Manchester U | 22 | 3 |
| 1996–97 | Manchester U | 19 | 0 |
| 1997–98 | Manchester U | 13 | 0 |
| **Total:** | | **539** | **202** |

## McCLARE, Sean — Midfield

H: 5 9 W: 11 06 b.Rotherham 12-1-78

*Source:* Trainee.

| | | | |
|---|---|---|---|
| 1996–97 | Barnsley | 0 | 0 |
| 1997–98 | Barnsley | 0 | 0 |

## McCLEN, Jamie — Midfield

H: 5 8 W: 10 07 b.Newcastle 13-5-79

*Source:* Trainee.

| | | | |
|---|---|---|---|
| 1997–98 | Newcastle U | 0 | 0 |

## McCLUSKEY, Stuart — Defender

H: 5 11 W: 10 03 b.Bellshill 29-10-77

*Source:* 'S' Form. *Honours:* Scotland Under-18, Under-21.

| | | | |
|---|---|---|---|
| 1994–95 | St Johnstone | 2 | 0 |
| 1995–96 | St Johnstone | 2 | 0 |
| 1996–97 | St Johnstone | 10 | 1 |
| 1997–98 | St Johnstone | 18 | 1 |
| **Total:** | | **32** | **2** |

## McCOIST, Ally — Forward

H: 5 10 W: 12 00 b.Bellshill 24-9-62

*Source:* Fir Park BC. *Honours:* Scotland Youth, Under-21, 59 full caps, 19 goals.

| | | | |
|---|---|---|---|
| 1978–79 | St Johnstone | 4 | 0 |
| 1979–80 | St Johnstone | 15 | 0 |
| 1980–81 | St Johnstone | 38 | 22 |
| 1981–82 | Sunderland | 28 | 2 |
| 1982–83 | Sunderland | 28 | 6 |
| 1983–84 | Rangers | 30 | 9 |
| 1984–85 | Rangers | 25 | 12 |
| 1985–86 | Rangers | 33 | 24 |
| 1986–87 | Rangers | 44 | 33 |
| 1987–88 | Rangers | 40 | 31 |
| 1988–89 | Rangers | 19 | 9 |
| 1989–90 | Rangers | 34 | 14 |
| 1990–91 | Rangers | 26 | 11 |
| 1991–92 | Rangers | 38 | 34 |
| 1992–93 | Rangers | 34 | 34 |
| 1993–94 | Rangers | 21 | 7 |
| 1994–95 | Rangers | 9 | 1 |
| 1995–96 | Rangers | 25 | 16 |
| 1996–97 | Rangers | 25 | 10 |
| 1997–98 | Rangers | 15 | 5 |
| **Total:** | | **531** | **280** |

## McCONNELL, Barry — Forward

H: 5 11 W: 10 03 b.Exeter 1-1-77

*Source:* Trainee.

| | | | |
|---|---|---|---|
| 1995–96 | Exeter C | 8 | 0 |
| 1996–97 | Exeter C | 34 | 0 |
| 1997–98 | Exeter C | 16 | 6 |
| **Total:** | | **58** | **6** |

## McCORMICK, Stephen — Forward

H: 6 4 W: 11 04 b.Dumbarton 14-8-69

*Source:* Yoker Ath.

| | | | |
|---|---|---|---|
| 1993–94 | Queen's Park | 36 | 7 |
| 1994–95 | Queen's Park | 22 | 8 |
| 1995–96 | Stirling A | 33 | 25 |
| 1996–97 | Stirling A | 31 | 8 |
| 1997–98 | Stirling A | 8 | 0 |
| 1997–98 | Dundee | 14 | 5 |
| **Total:** | | **144** | **53** |

## McCULLOCH, Lee — Midfield

H: 5 11 W: 12 05 b.Bellshill 14-5-78

*Source:* Cumbernauld U. *Honours:* Scotland Under-18, Under-21.

| | | | |
|---|---|---|---|
| 1995–96 | Motherwell | 1 | 0 |
| 1996–97 | Motherwell | 15 | 0 |
| 1997–98 | Motherwell | 25 | 2 |
| **Total:** | | **41** | **2** |

## McCULLOCH, Scott — Defender

H: 6 0 W: 13 04 b.Cumnock 29-11-75

*Source:* Rangers BC.

| | | | |
|---|---|---|---|
| 1992–93 | Rangers | 0 | 0 |
| 1993–94 | Rangers | 0 | 0 |
| 1994–95 | Hamilton A | 8 | 1 |
| 1995–96 | Hamilton A | 10 | 1 |
| 1996–97 | Hamilton A | 24 | 1 |
| 1997–98 | Hamilton A | 15 | 1 |
| 1997–98 | Dunfermline Ath | 18 | 0 |
| **Total:** | | **75** | **4** |

## McCUTCHEON, Gary — Forward

H: 5 4 W: 9 11 b.Dumfries 8-10-78

*Source:* Kilmarnock BC.

| | | | |
|---|---|---|---|
| 1995–96 | Kilmarnock | 0 | 0 |
| 1996–97 | Kilmarnock | 0 | 0 |
| 1997–98 | Kilmarnock | 1 | 0 |
| **Total:** | | **1** | **0** |

## McDERMOTT, Andy — Defender

H: 5 9 W: 11 03 b.Sydney 24-3-77

*Source:* Australian Institute of Sport.

| | | | |
|---|---|---|---|
| 1995–96 | QPR | 0 | 0 |
| 1996–97 | QPR | 6 | 2 |
| 1996–97 | WBA | 6 | 0 |
| 1997–98 | WBA | 13 | 0 |
| **Total:** | | **25** | **2** |

## McDERMOTT, John — Defender

H: 5 7 W: 10 13 b.Middlesbrough 3-2-69

*Source:* Trainee.

| | | | |
|---|---|---|---|
| 1986–87 | Grimsby T | 13 | 0 |
| 1987–88 | Grimsby T | 28 | 0 |
| 1988–89 | Grimsby T | 38 | 1 |
| 1989–90 | Grimsby T | 39 | 0 |
| 1990–91 | Grimsby T | 43 | 0 |
| 1991–92 | Grimsby T | 39 | 1 |
| 1992–93 | Grimsby T | 38 | 2 |
| 1993–94 | Grimsby T | 26 | 0 |
| 1994–95 | Grimsby T | 12 | 0 |
| 1995–96 | Grimsby T | 28 | 1 |
| 1996–97 | Grimsby T | 29 | 1 |
| 1997–98 | Grimsby T | 41 | 1 |
| **Total:** | | **374** | **7** |

## McDONALD, Alan — Defender

H: 6 3 W: 13 10 b.Belfast 12-10-63

*Source:* Apprentice. *Honours:* Northern Ireland Youth, 52 full caps, 3 goals.

| | | | |
|---|---|---|---|
| 1981–82 | QPR | 0 | 0 |
| 1982–83 | QPR | 0 | 0 |
| 1982–83 | Charlton Ath (loan) | 9 | 0 |
| 1983–84 | QPR | 5 | 0 |
| 1984–85 | QPR | 16 | 1 |
| 1985–86 | QPR | 42 | 0 |
| 1986–87 | QPR | 39 | 4 |
| 1987–88 | QPR | 36 | 3 |
| 1988–89 | QPR | 30 | 0 |
| 1989–90 | QPR | 34 | 0 |
| 1990–91 | QPR | 17 | 0 |
| 1991–92 | QPR | 28 | 0 |
| 1992–93 | QPR | 39 | 0 |
| 1993–94 | QPR | 12 | 1 |
| 1994–95 | QPR | 39 | 1 |
| 1995–96 | QPR | 26 | 1 |
| 1996–97 | QPR | 39 | 2 |
| 1997–98 | Swindon T | 33 | 1 |
| **Total:** | | **444** | **14** |

## McDONALD, Chris — Defender

H: 6 0 W: 13 04 b.Edinburgh 14-10-75

*Source:* Trainee.

| | | | |
|---|---|---|---|
| 1993–94 | Arsenal | 0 | 0 |
| 1994–95 | Arsenal | 0 | 0 |
| 1995–96 | Arsenal | 0 | 0 |
| 1996–97 | Hartlepool U | 9 | 0 |
| 1997–98 | Hartlepool U | 6 | 0 |
| **Total:** | | **15** | **0** |

## McDONALD, David — Defender

H: 5 10 W: 12 11 b.Dublin 2-1-71

*Source:* Trainee. *Honours:* Eire Youth, Under-21, B.

| | | | |
|---|---|---|---|
| 1989–90 | Tottenham H | 0 | 0 |
| 1990–91 | Tottenham H | 0 | 0 |
| 1990–91 | Gillingham (loan) | 10 | 0 |
| 1991–92 | Tottenham H | 0 | 0 |
| 1992–93 | Tottenham H | 2 | 0 |
| 1992–93 | Bradford C (loan) | 7 | 0 |
| 1992–93 | Reading (loan) | 11 | 0 |
| 1993–94 | Peterborough U | 29 | 0 |
| 1993–94 | Barnet | 10 | 0 |
| 1994–95 | Barnet | 35 | 0 |
| 1995–96 | Barnet | 32 | 0 |
| 1996–97 | Barnet | 18 | 0 |
| 1997–98 | Barnet | 1 | 0 |
| **Total:** | | **155** | **0** |

## McDONALD, Jamie — Midfield

b.Luton 29-1-80

*Source:* Trainee.

| | | | |
|---|---|---|---|
| 1996–97 | Derby Co | 0 | 0 |
| 1997–98 | Derby Co | 0 | 0 |

## McDONALD, Martin — Midfield

H: 5 11 W: 11 12 b.Irvine 4-12-73

*Source:* Macclesfield T, Southport.

| | | | |
|---|---|---|---|
| 1996–97 | Doncaster R | 33 | 2 |
| 1997–98 | Doncaster R | 15 | 2 |
| 1997–98 | Macclesfield T | 22 | 1 |
| **Total:** | | **70** | **5** |

## McDONALD, Neil — Defender

H: 6 0 W: 13 10 b.Wallsend 2-11-65

*Source:* Wallsend BC. *Honours:* England Schools, Youth, Under-21.

| | | | |
|---|---|---|---|
| 1982–83 | Newcastle U | 24 | 4 |
| 1983–84 | Newcastle U | 12 | 0 |
| 1984–85 | Newcastle U | 36 | 6 |
| 1985–86 | Newcastle U | 28 | 4 |
| 1986–87 | Newcastle U | 40 | 7 |
| 1987–88 | Newcastle U | 40 | 3 |
| 1988–89 | Everton | 25 | 1 |
| 1989–90 | Everton | 31 | 1 |
| 1990–91 | Everton | 29 | 2 |
| 1991–92 | Everton | 5 | 0 |
| 1991–92 | Oldham Ath | 17 | 1 |
| 1992–93 | Oldham Ath | 4 | 0 |
| 1993–94 | Oldham Ath | 3 | 0 |
| 1994–95 | Bolton W | 4 | 0 |
| 1995–96 | Bolton W | 0 | 0 |
| 1995–96 | Preston NE | 11 | 0 |
| 1996–97 | Preston NE | 22 | 0 |
| 1997–98 | Preston NE | 0 | 0 |
| **Total:** | | **331** | **29** |

## McDONALD, Paul — Forward

H: 5 6 W: 10 00 b.Motherwell 20-4-68

*Source:* Merry Street BC.

| | | | |
|---|---|---|---|
| 1986–87 | Hamilton A | 5 | 0 |
| 1987–88 | Hamilton A | 18 | 0 |
| 1988–89 | Hamilton A | 34 | 0 |
| 1989–90 | Hamilton A | 38 | 3 |
| 1990–91 | Hamilton A | 38 | 7 |
| 1991–92 | Hamilton A | 38 | 5 |
| 1992–93 | Hamilton A | 44 | 11 |
| 1993–94 | Southampton | 0 | 0 |
| 1994–95 | Southampton | 2 | 0 |
| 1995–96 | Southampton | 1 | 0 |
| 1995–96 | Burnley (loan) | 9 | 1 |
| 1995–96 | Brighton & HA | 5 | 0 |
| 1996–97 | Brighton & HA | 45 | 4 |
| 1997–98 | Brighton & HA | 11 | 1 |
| 1997–98 | Dunfermline Ath | 3 | 0 |
| **Total:** | | **291** | **32** |

## McDONALD, Rod — Forward

H: 5 10 W: 12 06 b.London 20-3-67

*Source:* South Liverpool, Colne Dynamoes.

| | | | |
|---|---|---|---|
| 1990–91 | Walsall | 36 | 5 |
| 1991–92 | Walsall | 39 | 18 |
| 1992–93 | Walsall | 39 | 12 |
| 1993–94 | Walsall | 35 | 6 |
| 1994–95 | Partick T | 25 | 5 |
| 1995–96 | Partick T | 16 | 5 |
| 1996–97 | Chester C | 22 | 6 |
| 1997–98 | Chester C | 31 | 5 |
| **Total:** | | **243** | **62** |

## McDOUGALD, Junior — Forward

H: 5 9 W: 11 00 b.Big Spring 12-1-75

*Source:* Trainee.

| | | | |
|---|---|---|---|
| 1993–94 | Tottenham H | 0 | 0 |
| 1994–95 | Brighton & HA | 41 | 10 |
| 1995–96 | Brighton & HA | 37 | 4 |
| 1995–96 | Chesterfield (loan) | 9 | 3 |
| 1996–97 | Rotherham U | 18 | 2 |
| 1997–98 | Rotherham U | 0 | 0 |
| **Total:** | | **105** | **19** |

## McELHATTON, Mike — Midfield

H: 6 1 W: 12 08 b.Co. Kerry 16-4-75

*Source:* Trainee.

| | | | |
|---|---|---|---|
| 1992–93 | Bournemouth | 1 | 0 |
| 1993–94 | Bournemouth | 10 | 0 |
| 1994–95 | Bournemouth | 27 | 2 |
| 1995–96 | Bournemouth | 4 | 0 |
| 1996–97 | Bournemouth | 0 | 0 |
| 1996–97 | Scarborough | 28 | 1 |
| 1997–98 | Scarborough | 42 | 6 |
| **Total:** | | **112** | **9** |

## McFARLANE, Andy — Forward

H: 6 3 W: 13 08 b.Wolverhampton 30-11-66

*Source:* Cradley T.

| | | | |
|---|---|---|---|
| 1990–91 | Portsmouth | 0 | 0 |
| 1991–92 | Portsmouth | 2 | 0 |
| 1992–93 | Swansea C | 24 | 5 |
| 1993–94 | Swansea C | 28 | 3 |
| 1994–95 | Swansea C | 3 | 0 |
| 1995–96 | Scunthorpe U | 46 | 16 |
| 1996–97 | Scunthorpe U | 14 | 3 |
| 1996–97 | Torquay U | 19 | 3 |
| 1997–98 | Torquay U | 22 | 5 |
| **Total:** | | **158** | **35** |

## McFARLANE, Anthony — Midfield

b.London 24-3-79

*Source:* Trainee.

| | | | |
|---|---|---|---|
| 1997–98 | West Ham U | 0 | 0 |

## McFLYNN, Terry — Defender

b.Magherafelt 27-3-81

*Source:* Trainee.

| | | | |
|---|---|---|---|
| 1997–98 | QPR | 0 | 0 |

## McGAVIN, Steve — Forward

H: 5 8 W: 12 05 b.North Walsham 24-1-69

*Source:* Sudbury T.

| | | | |
|---|---|---|---|
| 1990–91 | Colchester U | 0 | 0 |
| 1991–92 | Colchester U | 0 | 0 |
| 1992–93 | Colchester U | 37 | 9 |
| 1993–94 | Colchester U | 21 | 8 |
| 1993–94 | Birmingham C | 8 | 1 |
| 1994–95 | Birmingham C | 15 | 1 |
| 1994–95 | Wycombe W | 12 | 2 |
| 1995–96 | Wycombe W | 31 | 2 |
| 1996–97 | Wycombe W | 35 | 8 |
| 1997–98 | Wycombe W | 37 | 2 |
| **Total:** | | **196** | **33** |

## McGHEE, David — Defender

H: 5 11 W: 12 05 b.Sussex 19-6-76

*Source:* Trainee.

| | | | |
|---|---|---|---|
| 1994–95 | Brentford | 7 | 1 |
| 1995–96 | Brentford | 36 | 5 |
| 1996–97 | Brentford | 45 | 1 |
| 1997–98 | Brentford | 29 | 1 |
| **Total:** | | **117** | **8** |

## McGIBBON, Pat — Defender

H: 6 1 W: 13 02 b.Lurgan 6-9-73

*Source:* Portadown. *Honours:* Northern Ireland Under-21, 6 full caps.

| | | | |
|---|---|---|---|
| 1992–93 | Manchester U | 0 | 0 |
| 1993–94 | Manchester U | 0 | 0 |
| 1994–95 | Manchester U | 0 | 0 |
| 1995–96 | Manchester U | 0 | 0 |
| 1996–97 | Manchester U | 0 | 0 |
| 1996–97 | Swansea C (loan) | 1 | 0 |
| 1996–97 | Wigan Ath (loan) | 10 | 1 |
| 1997–98 | Wigan Ath | 35 | 0 |
| **Total:** | | **46** | **1** |

## McGINLAY, John — Forward

H: 5 9 W: 11 04 b.Inverness 8-4-64

*Source:* Elgin C. *Honours:* Scotland 13 full caps, 4 goals.

| | | | |
|---|---|---|---|
| 1988–89 | Shrewsbury T | 16 | 5 |
| 1989–90 | Shrewsbury T | 44 | 22 |
| 1990–91 | Bury | 25 | 9 |
| 1990–91 | Millwall | 2 | 0 |
| 1991–92 | Millwall | 25 | 8 |
| 1992–93 | Millwall | 7 | 2 |
| 1992–93 | Bolton W | 34 | 16 |
| 1993–94 | Bolton W | 39 | 25 |
| 1994–95 | Bolton W | 37 | 16 |
| 1995–96 | Bolton W | 32 | 6 |
| 1996–97 | Bolton W | 43 | 24 |
| 1997–98 | Bolton W | 7 | 0 |
| 1997–98 | Bradford C | 17 | 3 |
| **Total:** | | **328** | **136** |

## McGINLAY, Pat — Midfield

H: 5 10 W: 10 10 b.Glasgow 30-5-67

*Source:* Scottish Junior.

| | | | |
|---|---|---|---|
| 1985–86 | Blackpool | 0 | 0 |
| 1986–87 | Blackpool | 12 | 1 |
| 1987–88 | Hibernian | 0 | 0 |
| 1988–89 | Hibernian | 2 | 0 |
| 1989–90 | Hibernian | 28 | 3 |
| 1990–91 | Hibernian | 32 | 1 |
| 1991–92 | Hibernian | 43 | 9 |
| 1992–93 | Hibernian | 40 | 10 |
| 1993–94 | Celtic | 41 | 10 |
| 1994–95 | Celtic | 8 | 1 |
| 1994–95 | Hibernian | 24 | 7 |
| 1995–96 | Hibernian | 31 | 5 |
| 1996–97 | Hibernian | 29 | 6 |
| 1997–98 | Hibernian | 33 | 4 |
| **Total:** | | **323** | **57** |

## McGINTY, Brian — Midfield

H: 6 1 W: 11 04 b.East Kilbride 10-12-76

*Source:* Rangers BC.

| | | | |
|---|---|---|---|
| 1993–94 | Rangers | 0 | 0 |
| 1994–95 | Rangers | 1 | 0 |
| 1995–96 | Rangers | 2 | 0 |
| 1996–97 | Rangers | 0 | 0 |
| 1997–98 | Rangers | 0 | 0 |
| 1997–98 | Hull C | 21 | 2 |
| **Total:** | | **24** | **2** |

## McGLASHAN, John — Midfield

H: 6 2 W: 13 00 b.Dundee 3-6-67

*Source:* Dundee Violet.

| | | | |
|---|---|---|---|
| 1988–89 | Montrose | 35 | 2 |
| 1989–90 | Montrose | 33 | 9 |
| 1990–91 | Millwall | 8 | 0 |
| 1991–92 | Millwall | 8 | 0 |
| 1992–93 | Millwall | 0 | 0 |
| 1992–93 | Cambridge U (loan) | 1 | 0 |

| | | | |
|---|---|---|---|
| 1992–93 | Fulham (loan) | 5 | 1 |
| 1992–93 | Peterborough U | 18 | 0 |
| 1993–94 | Peterborough U | 28 | 3 |
| 1994–95 | Peterborough U | 0 | 0 |
| 1994–95 | Rotherham U | 27 | 3 |
| 1995–96 | Rotherham U | 16 | 2 |
| 1996–97 | Rotherham U | 31 | 0 |
| 1997–98 | Dundee | 8 | 1 |
| **Total:** | | **218** | **21** |

## McGLEISH, Scott — Forward

H: 5 9 W: 11 00 b.Camden Town 10-2-74

*Source:* Edgware T.

| | | | |
|---|---|---|---|
| 1994–95 | Charlton Ath | 6 | 0 |
| 1994–95 | Leyton Orient (loan) | 6 | 1 |
| 1995–96 | Peterborough U | 12 | 0 |
| 1995–96 | Colchester U (loan) | 15 | 6 |
| 1996–97 | Peterborough U | 1 | 0 |
| 1996–97 | Cambridge U (loan) | 10 | 7 |
| 1996–97 | Leyton Orient | 28 | 7 |
| 1997–98 | Leyton Orient | 8 | 0 |
| 1997–98 | Barnet | 37 | 13 |
| **Total:** | | **123** | **34** |

## McGLINCHEY, Brian — Midfield

H: 5 7 W: 10 02 b.Derry 26-10-77

*Source:* Trainee. *Honours:* Northern Ireland Under-21.

| | | | |
|---|---|---|---|
| 1995–96 | Manchester C | 0 | 0 |
| 1996–97 | Manchester C | 0 | 0 |
| 1997–98 | Manchester C | 0 | 0 |

## McGOLDRICK, Eddie — Midfield

H: 5 10 W: 11 07 b.London 30-4-65

*Source:* Nuneaton Bor, Kettering T. *Honours:* Eire 15 full caps.

| | | | |
|---|---|---|---|
| 1986–87 | Northampton T | 39 | 5 |
| 1987–88 | Northampton T | 46 | 2 |
| 1988–89 | Northampton T | 22 | 2 |
| 1988–89 | Crystal Palace | 21 | 0 |
| 1989–90 | Crystal Palace | 22 | 0 |
| 1990–91 | Crystal Palace | 26 | 0 |
| 1991–92 | Crystal Palace | 36 | 3 |
| 1992–93 | Crystal Palace | 42 | 8 |
| 1993–94 | Arsenal | 26 | 0 |
| 1994–95 | Arsenal | 11 | 0 |
| 1995–96 | Arsenal | 1 | 0 |
| 1996–97 | Arsenal | 0 | 0 |
| 1996–97 | Manchester C | 33 | 0 |
| 1997–98 | Manchester C | 7 | 0 |
| 1997–98 | Stockport Co (loan) | 2 | 0 |
| **Total:** | | **334** | **20** |

## McGOVERN, Brian — Defender

b.Dublin 23-4-80

| | | | |
|---|---|---|---|
| 1997–98 | Arsenal | 0 | 0 |

## McGOWAN, Gavin — Defender

H: 5 8 W: 11 07 b.Blackheath 16-1-76

*Source:* Trainee. *Honours:* England Schools, Youth.

| | | | |
|---|---|---|---|
| 1992–93 | Arsenal | 2 | 0 |
| 1993–94 | Arsenal | 0 | 0 |
| 1994–95 | Arsenal | 1 | 0 |
| 1995–96 | Arsenal | 1 | 0 |
| 1996–97 | Arsenal | 1 | 0 |
| 1996–97 | Luton T (loan) | 2 | 0 |
| 1997–98 | Arsenal | 1 | 0 |
| 1997–98 | Luton T (loan) | 8 | 0 |
| **Total:** | | **16** | **0** |

## McGOWNE, Kevin — Defender

H: 6 0 W: 12 03 b.Kilmarnock 16-12-69

*Source:* Hurlford Utd.

| | | | |
|---|---|---|---|
| 1988–89 | St Mirren | 0 | 0 |
| 1989–90 | St Mirren | 2 | 0 |
| 1990–91 | St Mirren | 10 | 0 |
| 1991–92 | St Mirren | 36 | 0 |
| 1992–93 | St Johnstone | 26 | 0 |
| 1993–94 | St Johnstone | 41 | 0 |
| 1994–95 | St Johnstone | 30 | 1 |
| 1995–96 | St Johnstone | 23 | 2 |
| 1996–97 | St Johnstone | 2 | 0 |
| 1996–97 | Kilmarnock | 31 | 0 |
| 1997–98 | Kilmarnock | 26 | 0 |
| **Total:** | | **227** | **3** |

## McGRATH, Paul — Defender

H: 6 2 W: 14 03 b.Ealing 4-12-59

*Source:* St Patrick's Ath. *Honours:* Eire 83 full caps, 8 goals. Football League.

| | | | |
|---|---|---|---|
| 1981–82 | Manchester U | 0 | 0 |
| 1982–83 | Manchester U | 14 | 3 |
| 1983–84 | Manchester U | 9 | 1 |
| 1984–85 | Manchester U | 23 | 0 |
| 1985–86 | Manchester U | 40 | 3 |
| 1986–87 | Manchester U | 35 | 2 |
| 1987–88 | Manchester U | 22 | 2 |
| 1988–89 | Manchester U | 20 | 1 |
| 1989–90 | Aston Villa | 35 | 1 |
| 1990–91 | Aston Villa | 35 | 0 |
| 1991–92 | Aston Villa | 41 | 1 |
| 1992–93 | Aston Villa | 42 | 4 |
| 1993–94 | Aston Villa | 30 | 1 |

McGreal, John

| | | | |
|---|---|---|---|
| 1994–95 | Aston Villa | 40 | 0 |
| 1995–96 | Aston Villa | 30 | 2 |
| 1996–97 | Aston Villa | 0 | 0 |
| 1996–97 | Derby Co | 24 | 0 |
| 1997–98 | Sheffield U | 12 | 0 |
| **Total:** | | **452** | **21** |

## McGREAL, John — Defender

H: 5 11 W: 11 00 b.Birkenhead 2-6-72

*Source:* Trainee.

| | | | |
|---|---|---|---|
| 1990–91 | Tranmere R | 3 | 0 |
| 1991–92 | Tranmere R | 0 | 0 |
| 1992–93 | Tranmere R | 0 | 0 |
| 1993–94 | Tranmere R | 15 | 1 |
| 1994–95 | Tranmere R | 43 | 0 |
| 1995–96 | Tranmere R | 32 | 0 |
| 1996–97 | Tranmere R | 24 | 0 |
| 1997–98 | Tranmere R | 42 | 0 |
| **Total:** | | **159** | **1** |

## McGREGOR, Mark — Defender

H: 5 10 W: 11 05 b.Chester 16-2-77

*Source:* Trainee.

| | | | |
|---|---|---|---|
| 1994–95 | Wrexham | 1 | 0 |
| 1995–96 | Wrexham | 32 | 1 |
| 1996–97 | Wrexham | 38 | 1 |
| 1997–98 | Wrexham | 42 | 2 |
| **Total:** | | **113** | **4** |

## McGREGOR, Paul — Forward

H: 5 10 W: 11 06 b.Liverpool 17-12-74

*Source:* Trainee.

| | | | |
|---|---|---|---|
| 1991–92 | Nottingham F | 0 | 0 |
| 1992–93 | Nottingham F | 0 | 0 |
| 1993–94 | Nottingham F | 0 | 0 |
| 1994–95 | Nottingham F | 11 | 1 |
| 1995–96 | Nottingham F | 14 | 2 |
| 1996–97 | Nottingham F | 5 | 0 |
| 1997–98 | Nottingham F | 0 | 0 |
| **Total:** | | **30** | **3** |

## McGUCKIN, Ian — Defender

H: 6 2 W: 14 02 b.Middlesbrough 24-4-73

*Source:* Trainee.

| | | | |
|---|---|---|---|
| 1991–92 | Hartlepool U | 7 | 0 |
| 1992–93 | Hartlepool U | 14 | 1 |
| 1993–94 | Hartlepool U | 35 | 2 |
| 1994–95 | Hartlepool U | 34 | 3 |
| 1995–96 | Hartlepool U | 40 | 2 |
| 1996–97 | Hartlepool U | 22 | 0 |
| 1997–98 | Fulham | 0 | 0 |
| **Total:** | | **152** | **8** |

## McINALLY, Jim — Midfield

H: 6 0 W: 12 00 b.Glasgow 19-2-64

*Source:* Celtic BC. *Honours:* Scottish Youth, Under-21, 10 full caps.

| | | | |
|---|---|---|---|
| 1982–83 | Celtic | 1 | 0 |
| 1983–84 | Celtic | 0 | 0 |
| 1983–84 | Dundee (loan) | 11 | 2 |
| 1984–85 | Nottingham F | 24 | 0 |
| 1985–86 | Nottingham F | 12 | 0 |
| 1985–86 | Coventry C | 5 | 0 |
| 1986–87 | Dundee U | 32 | 1 |
| 1987–88 | Dundee U | 36 | 2 |
| 1988–89 | Dundee U | 29 | 1 |
| 1989–90 | Dundee U | 35 | 3 |
| 1990–91 | Dundee U | 33 | 1 |
| 1991–92 | Dundee U | 32 | 4 |
| 1992–93 | Dundee U | 32 | 0 |
| 1993–94 | Dundee U | 31 | 0 |
| 1994–95 | Dundee U | 24 | 0 |
| 1995–96 | Raith R | 25 | 0 |
| 1996–97 | Raith R | 4 | 0 |
| 1996–97 | Dundee U | 16 | 1 |
| 1997–98 | Dundee | 32 | 1 |
| **Total:** | | **414** | **16** |

## McINDOE, Michael — Midfield

H: 5 8 W: 11 00 b.Edinburgh 2-12-79

*Source:* Trainee.

| | | | |
|---|---|---|---|
| 1997–98 | Luton T | 0 | 0 |

## McINTOSH, Martin — Defender

H: 6 3 W: 12 05 b.East Kilbride 19-3-71

*Honours:* Scotland B.

| | | | |
|---|---|---|---|
| 1988–89 | St Mirren | 2 | 0 |
| 1989–90 | St Mirren | 2 | 0 |
| 1990–91 | St Mirren | 0 | 0 |
| 1991–92 | Clydebank | 28 | 5 |
| 1992–93 | Clydebank | 33 | 4 |
| 1993–94 | Clydebank | 4 | 1 |
| 1993–94 | Hamilton A | 13 | 2 |
| 1994–95 | Hamilton A | 30 | 2 |
| 1995–96 | Hamilton A | 23 | 1 |
| 1996–97 | Hamilton A | 33 | 7 |
| 1997–98 | Stockport Co | 38 | 2 |
| **Total:** | | **206** | **24** |

## McINTYRE, Jim — Forward

H: 5 11 W: 12 00 b.Alexandria 24-5-72

*Source:* Duntocher Boys. *Honours:* Scotland B.

| | | | |
|---|---|---|---|
| 1991–92 | Bristol C | 1 | 0 |
| 1992–93 | Bristol C | 0 | 0 |
| 1992–93 | Exeter C (loan) | 15 | 3 |
| 1993–94 | Airdrieonians | 13 | 0 |
| 1994–95 | Airdrieonians | 12 | 1 |
| 1995–96 | Airdrieonians | 29 | 9 |
| 1995–96 | Kilmarnock | 7 | 2 |
| 1996–97 | Kilmarnock | 31 | 6 |
| 1997–98 | Kilmarnock | 8 | 1 |
| 1997–98 | Reading | 6 | 0 |
| **Total:** | | **122** | **22** |

## McINTYRE, Kevin — Midfield

H: 5 10 W: 12 00 b.Liverpool 23-12-77

*Source:* Trainee.

| | | | |
|---|---|---|---|
| 1996–97 | Tranmere R | 0 | 0 |
| 1997–98 | Tranmere R | 2 | 0 |
| **Total:** | | **2** | **0** |

## McKAY, Matthew — Midfield

b.Warrington 21-1-81

*Source:* Trainee.

| | | | |
|---|---|---|---|
| 1997–98 | Chester C | 5 | 0 |
| 1997–98 | Everton | 0 | 0 |
| **Total:** | | **5** | **0** |

## McKECHNIE, Ewan — Defender

b.Paisley 27-8-79

*Source:* Trainee.

| | | | |
|---|---|---|---|
| 1997–98 | Oldham Ath | 0 | 0 |

## McKEEVER, Mark — Forward

H: 5 9 W: 11 08 b.Derry 16-11-78

*Source:* Trainee.

| | | | |
|---|---|---|---|
| 1996–97 | Peterborough U | 3 | 0 |
| 1996–97 | Sheffield W | 0 | 0 |
| 1997–98 | Sheffield W | 0 | 0 |
| **Total:** | | **3** | **0** |

## McKENNA, Paul — Midfield

H: 5 8 W: 11 11 b.Chorley 20-10-77

*Source:* Trainee.

| | | | |
|---|---|---|---|
| 1995–96 | Preston NE | 0 | 0 |
| 1996–97 | Preston NE | 5 | 1 |
| 1997–98 | Preston NE | 5 | 0 |
| **Total:** | | **10** | **1** |

## McKENZIE, Leon — Forward

H: 5 10 W: 10 03 b.Croydon 17-5-78

*Source:* Trainee.

| | | | |
|---|---|---|---|
| 1995–96 | Crystal Palace | 12 | 0 |
| 1996–97 | Crystal Palace | 21 | 2 |
| 1997–98 | Crystal Palace | 3 | 0 |
| 1997–98 | Fulham (loan) | 3 | 0 |
| **Total:** | | **39** | **2** |

## McKENZIE, Robert — Midfield

H: 5 10 W: 12 05 b.Hexham 22-3-79

*Source:* Trainee.

| | | | |
|---|---|---|---|
| 1996–97 | Rotherham U | 11 | 0 |
| 1997–98 | Rotherham U | 0 | 0 |
| **Total:** | | **11** | **0** |

## McKENZIE, Roderick — Goalkeeper

H: 6 0 W: 12 00 b.Bellshill 8-8-75

*Source:* Mill Utd. *Honours:* Scotland Under-21.

| | | | |
|---|---|---|---|
| 1993–94 | Hearts | 0 | 0 |
| 1994–95 | Hearts | 0 | 0 |
| 1995–96 | Stenhousemuir | 36 | 0 |
| 1996–97 | Hearts | 3 | 0 |
| 1997–98 | Hearts | 4 | 0 |
| **Total:** | | **43** | **0** |

## McKEOWN, Francis — Midfield

H: 5 9 W: 11 07 b.Belfast 11-2-81

*Source:* Trainee.

| | | | |
|---|---|---|---|
| 1997–98 | Sunderland | 0 | 0 |

## McKIMMIE, Stuart — Defender

H: 5 8 W: 10 07 b.Aberdeen 27-10-62

*Source:* Banks o' Dee. *Honours:* Scotland Under-21, 40 full caps, 1 goal.

| | | | |
|---|---|---|---|
| 1980–81 | Dundee | 17 | 0 |
| 1981–82 | Dundee | 16 | 0 |
| 1982–83 | Dundee | 31 | 0 |
| 1983–84 | Dundee | 16 | 0 |
| 1983–84 | Aberdeen | 18 | 1 |
| 1984–85 | Aberdeen | 34 | 3 |
| 1985–86 | Aberdeen | 34 | 3 |
| 1986–87 | Aberdeen | 37 | 0 |
| 1987–88 | Aberdeen | 42 | 0 |

## McKinlay, Billy

| | | | |
|---|---|---|---|
| 1988–89 | Aberdeen | 35 | 0 |
| 1989–90 | Aberdeen | 33 | 0 |
| 1990–91 | Aberdeen | 26 | 1 |
| 1991–92 | Aberdeen | 39 | 0 |
| 1992–93 | Aberdeen | 14 | 0 |
| 1993–94 | Aberdeen | 40 | 0 |
| 1994–95 | Aberdeen | 34 | 1 |
| 1995–96 | Aberdeen | 29 | 0 |
| 1996–97 | Aberdeen | 14 | 0 |
| 1996–97 | Dundee U | 6 | 0 |
| 1997–98 | Dundee U | 4 | 0 |
| **Total:** | | **519** | **9** |

## McKINLAY, Billy — Midfield

H: 5 8 W: 11 06 b.Glasgow 22-4-69

*Source:* Hamilton Th. *Honours:* Scotland Under-21, B, 27 full caps, 4 goals.

| | | | |
|---|---|---|---|
| 1986–87 | Dundee U | 3 | 0 |
| 1987–88 | Dundee U | 12 | 1 |
| 1988–89 | Dundee U | 30 | 1 |
| 1989–90 | Dundee U | 13 | 0 |
| 1990–91 | Dundee U | 34 | 2 |
| 1991–92 | Dundee U | 22 | 1 |
| 1992–93 | Dundee U | 37 | 1 |
| 1993–94 | Dundee U | 39 | 9 |
| 1994–95 | Dundee U | 27 | 4 |
| 1995–96 | Dundee U | 5 | 4 |
| 1995–96 | Blackburn R | 19 | 2 |
| 1996–97 | Blackburn R | 25 | 1 |
| 1997–98 | Blackburn R | 30 | 0 |
| **Total:** | | **296** | **26** |

## McKINLAY, Tosh — Defender

H: 5 7 W: 10 03 b.Glasgow 3-12-64

*Source:* Celtic BC. *Honours:* Scotland Youth, Under-21, B, 22 full caps.

| | | | |
|---|---|---|---|
| 1981–82 | Dundee | 0 | 0 |
| 1982–83 | Dundee | 1 | 0 |
| 1983–84 | Dundee | 36 | 3 |
| 1984–85 | Dundee | 34 | 3 |
| 1985–86 | Dundee | 22 | 0 |
| 1986–87 | Dundee | 32 | 2 |
| 1987–88 | Dundee | 19 | 0 |
| 1988–89 | Dundee | 18 | 0 |
| 1988–89 | Hearts | 17 | 1 |
| 1989–90 | Hearts | 29 | 1 |
| 1990–91 | Hearts | 33 | 2 |
| 1991–92 | Hearts | 39 | 2 |
| 1992–93 | Hearts | 34 | 0 |
| 1993–94 | Hearts | 43 | 0 |
| 1994–95 | Hearts | 11 | 0 |
| 1994–95 | Celtic | 17 | 0 |
| 1995–96 | Celtic | 32 | 0 |
| 1996–97 | Celtic | 27 | 0 |
| 1997–98 | Celtic | 5 | 0 |
| 1997–98 | Stoke C (loan) | 3 | 0 |
| **Total:** | | **452** | **14** |

## McKINNON, Ray — Defender

H: 5 8 W: 9 11 b.Dundee 5-8-70

*Source:* 'S' Form. *Honours:* Scotland Under-21.

| | | | |
|---|---|---|---|
| 1987–88 | Dundee U | 0 | 0 |
| 1988–89 | Dundee U | 1 | 0 |
| 1989–90 | Dundee U | 10 | 0 |
| 1990–91 | Dundee U | 17 | 2 |
| 1991–92 | Dundee U | 25 | 4 |
| 1992–93 | Nottingham F | 6 | 1 |
| 1993–94 | Nottingham F | 0 | 0 |
| 1993–94 | Aberdeen | 5 | 0 |
| 1994–95 | Aberdeen | 20 | 0 |
| 1995–96 | Aberdeen | 1 | 0 |
| 1995–96 | Dundee U | 9 | 0 |
| 1996–97 | Dundee U | 26 | 6 |
| 1997–98 | Dundee U | 9 | 0 |
| **Total:** | | **129** | **13** |

## McLAREN, Andrew — Forward

H: 5 10 W: 10 06 b.Glasgow 5-6-73

*Source:* Rangers Amateur BC. *Honours:* Scotland Under-21.

| | | | |
|---|---|---|---|
| 1989–90 | Dundee U | 0 | 0 |
| 1990–91 | Dundee U | 0 | 0 |
| 1991–92 | Dundee U | 13 | 0 |
| 1992–93 | Dundee U | 5 | 0 |
| 1993–94 | Dundee U | 27 | 1 |
| 1994–95 | Dundee U | 20 | 0 |
| 1995–96 | Dundee U | 31 | 3 |
| 1996–97 | Dundee U | 34 | 4 |
| 1997–98 | Dundee U | 27 | 4 |
| **Total:** | | **157** | **12** |

## McLAREN, Paul — Midfield

H: 6 1 W: 13 04 b.High Wycombe 17-11-76

*Source:* Trainee.

| | | | |
|---|---|---|---|
| 1993–94 | Luton T | 1 | 0 |
| 1994–95 | Luton T | 0 | 0 |
| 1995–96 | Luton T | 12 | 1 |
| 1996–97 | Luton T | 24 | 0 |
| 1997–98 | Luton T | 43 | 0 |
| **Total:** | | **80** | **1** |

## McLEAN, Ian — Defender

H: 5 10 W: 11 04 b.Leeds 13-9-78

*Source:* Trainee.

| | | | |
|---|---|---|---|
| 1997–98 | Bradford C | 0 | 0 |

## McLEARY, Alan — Defender

H: 6 0 W: 11 11 b.Lambeth 6-10-64

*Source:* Apprentice. *Honours:* England Youth, Under-21, B.

| | | | |
|---|---|---|---|
| 1981–82 | Millwall | 0 | 0 |
| 1982–83 | Millwall | 3 | 1 |
| 1983–84 | Millwall | 30 | 0 |
| 1984–85 | Millwall | 21 | 0 |
| 1985–86 | Millwall | 35 | 3 |
| 1986–87 | Millwall | 42 | 0 |
| 1987–88 | Millwall | 31 | 0 |
| 1988–89 | Millwall | 38 | 1 |
| 1989–90 | Millwall | 31 | 0 |
| 1990–91 | Millwall | 42 | 0 |
| 1991–92 | Millwall | 28 | 0 |
| 1992–93 | Millwall | 6 | 0 |
| 1992–93 | Sheffield U (loan) | 3 | 0 |
| 1992–93 | Wimbledon (loan) | 4 | 0 |
| 1993–94 | Charlton Ath | 44 | 3 |
| 1994–95 | Charlton Ath | 22 | 0 |
| 1995–96 | Bristol C | 31 | 0 |
| 1996–97 | Bristol C | 3 | 0 |
| 1996–97 | Millwall | 15 | 0 |
| 1997–98 | Millwall | 19 | 0 |
| **Total:** | | **448** | **8** |

## McLOUGHLIN, Alan — Midfield

H: 5 8 W: 10 10 b.Manchester 20-4-67

*Source:* Local. *Honours:* Eire B, 34 full caps, 2 goals.

| | | | |
|---|---|---|---|
| 1984–85 | Manchester U | 0 | 0 |
| 1985–86 | Manchester U | 0 | 0 |
| 1986–87 | Swindon T | 9 | 0 |
| 1986–87 | Torquay U | 16 | 1 |
| 1987–88 | Torquay U | 8 | 3 |
| 1987–88 | Swindon T | 8 | 0 |
| 1988–89 | Swindon T | 26 | 3 |
| 1989–90 | Swindon T | 46 | 12 |
| 1990–91 | Swindon T | 17 | 4 |
| 1990–91 | Southampton | 22 | 1 |
| 1991–92 | Southampton | 2 | 0 |
| 1991–92 | Aston Villa (loan) | 0 | 0 |
| 1991–92 | Portsmouth | 14 | 2 |
| 1992–93 | Portsmouth | 46 | 9 |
| 1993–94 | Portsmouth | 38 | 6 |
| 1994–95 | Portsmouth | 38 | 6 |
| 1995–96 | Portsmouth | 40 | 10 |
| 1996–97 | Portsmouth | 36 | 5 |
| 1997–98 | Portsmouth | 37 | 4 |
| **Total:** | | **403** | **66** |

## McMAHON, David — Forward

H: 6 1 W: 11 05 b.Dublin 17-1-81

*Source:* Trainee.

| | | | |
|---|---|---|---|
| 1997–98 | Newcastle U | 0 | 0 |

## McMAHON, Gerry — Forward

H: 5 11 W: 11 13 b.Belfast 29-12-73

*Source:* Glenavon. *Honours:* Northern Ireland Under-21, 17 full caps, 2 goals.

| | | | |
|---|---|---|---|
| 1992–93 | Tottenham H | 0 | 0 |
| 1993–94 | Tottenham H | 0 | 0 |
| 1994–95 | Tottenham H | 2 | 0 |
| 1994–95 | Barnet (loan) | 10 | 2 |
| 1995–96 | Tottenham H | 14 | 0 |
| 1996–97 | Tottenham H | 0 | 0 |
| 1996–97 | Stoke C | 35 | 3 |
| 1997–98 | Stoke C | 17 | 0 |
| 1997–98 | St Johnstone | 10 | 0 |
| **Total:** | | **88** | **5** |

## McMAHON, Sam — Midfield

H: 5 9 W: 11 09 b.Newark 10-2-76

*Source:* Trainee.

| | | | |
|---|---|---|---|
| 1994–95 | Leicester C | 1 | 0 |
| 1995–96 | Leicester C | 3 | 1 |
| 1996–97 | Leicester C | 0 | 0 |
| 1997–98 | Leicester C | 1 | 0 |
| **Total:** | | **5** | **1** |

## McMAHON, Steve — Midfield

H: 5 9 W: 11 08 b.Liverpool 20-8-61

*Source:* Apprentice. *Honours:* England Under-21, B, 17 full caps.

| | | | |
|---|---|---|---|
| 1979–80 | Everton | 0 | 0 |
| 1980–81 | Everton | 34 | 5 |
| 1981–82 | Everton | 32 | 2 |
| 1982–83 | Everton | 34 | 4 |
| 1983–84 | Aston Villa | 37 | 5 |
| 1984–85 | Aston Villa | 35 | 2 |
| 1985–86 | Aston Villa | 3 | 0 |
| 1985–86 | Liverpool | 23 | 6 |
| 1986–87 | Liverpool | 37 | 5 |
| 1987–88 | Liverpool | 40 | 9 |
| 1988–89 | Liverpool | 29 | 3 |
| 1989–90 | Liverpool | 38 | 5 |
| 1990–91 | Liverpool | 22 | 0 |
| 1991–92 | Liverpool | 15 | 1 |
| 1991–92 | Manchester C | 18 | 0 |
| 1992–93 | Manchester C | 27 | 1 |
| 1993–94 | Manchester C | 35 | 0 |

| | | | |
|---|---|---|---|
| 1994–95 | Manchester C | 7 | 0 |
| 1994–95 | Swindon T | 17 | 0 |
| 1995–96 | Swindon T | 21 | 0 |
| 1996–97 | Swindon T | 3 | 0 |
| 1997–98 | Swindon T | 1 | 0 |
| **Total:** | | **508** | **48** |

## McMANAMAN, Steve — Midfield

H: 6 0 W: 10 06 b.Liverpool 11-2-72

*Source:* School. *Honours:* England Youth, Under-21, 22 full caps.

| | | | |
|---|---|---|---|
| 1989–90 | Liverpool | 0 | 0 |
| 1990–91 | Liverpool | 2 | 0 |
| 1991–92 | Liverpool | 30 | 5 |
| 1992–93 | Liverpool | 31 | 4 |
| 1993–94 | Liverpool | 30 | 2 |
| 1994–95 | Liverpool | 40 | 7 |
| 1995–96 | Liverpool | 38 | 6 |
| 1996–97 | Liverpool | 37 | 7 |
| 1997–98 | Liverpool | 36 | 11 |
| **Total:** | | **244** | **42** |

## McMANUS, Allan — Defender

H: 6 0 W: 12 00 b.Paisley 17-11-74

*Source:* Links U.

| | | | |
|---|---|---|---|
| 1992–93 | Hearts | 0 | 0 |
| 1993–94 | Hearts | 0 | 0 |
| 1994–95 | Hearts | 0 | 0 |
| 1995–96 | Hearts | 18 | 2 |
| 1996–97 | Hearts | 15 | 1 |
| 1997–98 | Hearts | 12 | 0 |
| **Total:** | | **45** | **3** |

## McMENAMIN, Chris — Midfield

H: 5 10 W: 11 10 b.Donegal 27-12-73

*Source:* Hitchin T.

| | | | |
|---|---|---|---|
| 1996–97 | Coventry C | 0 | 0 |
| 1997–98 | Peterborough U | 28 | 0 |
| **Total:** | | **28** | **0** |

## McMENEMY, Tom — Midfield

H: 5 11 W: 11 01 b.Southampton 3-3-79

*Source:* Trainee.

| | | | |
|---|---|---|---|
| 1997–98 | Barnet | 0 | 0 |

## McMILLAN, Andy — Defender

H: 5 10 W: 11 09 b.Bloemfontein 22-6-68

| | | | |
|---|---|---|---|
| 1987–88 | York C | 22 | 0 |
| 1988–89 | York C | 2 | 0 |
| 1989–90 | York C | 25 | 0 |
| 1990–91 | York C | 45 | 1 |
| 1991–92 | York C | 41 | 1 |
| 1992–93 | York C | 42 | 0 |
| 1993–94 | York C | 46 | 0 |
| 1994–95 | York C | 43 | 1 |
| 1995–96 | York C | 46 | 1 |
| 1996–97 | York C | 46 | 0 |
| 1997–98 | York C | 30 | 1 |
| **Total:** | | **388** | **5** |

## McMILLAN, Stephen — Midfield

H: 5 10 W: 11 00 b.Edinburgh 19-1-76

*Source:* Troon Juniors. *Honours:* Scotland Under-21.

| | | | |
|---|---|---|---|
| 1993–94 | Motherwell | 1 | 0 |
| 1994–95 | Motherwell | 3 | 0 |
| 1995–96 | Motherwell | 12 | 0 |
| 1996–97 | Motherwell | 16 | 0 |
| 1997–98 | Motherwell | 34 | 1 |
| **Total:** | | **66** | **1** |

## McNALLY, Mark — Defender

H: 5 11 W: 12 02 b.Bellshill 10-3-71

*Source:* Celtic BC. *Honours:* Scotland Under-21.

| | | | |
|---|---|---|---|
| 1987–88 | Celtic | 0 | 0 |
| 1988–89 | Celtic | 0 | 0 |
| 1989–90 | Celtic | 0 | 0 |
| 1990–91 | Celtic | 19 | 0 |
| 1991–92 | Celtic | 25 | 1 |
| 1992–93 | Celtic | 27 | 0 |
| 1993–94 | Celtic | 32 | 2 |
| 1994–95 | Celtic | 20 | 0 |
| 1995–96 | Southend U | 20 | 2 |
| 1996–97 | Southend U | 34 | 0 |
| 1996–97 | Stoke C | 3 | 0 |
| 1997–98 | Stoke C | 4 | 0 |
| **Total:** | | **184** | **5** |

## McNALLY, Ross — Defender

H: 6 1 W: 12 05 b.Dublin 6-9-78

*Source:* Trainee.

| | | | |
|---|---|---|---|
| 1997–98 | Brighton & HA | 2 | 0 |
| **Total:** | | **2** | **0** |

## McNAMARA, Jackie — Midfield

H: 5 8 W: 9 07 b.Glasgow 24-10-73

*Source:* Gairdoch U. *Honours:* Scotland B, Under-21, 9 full caps.

| | | | |
|---|---|---|---|
| 1991–92 | Dunfermline Ath | 0 | 0 |
| 1992–93 | Dunfermline Ath | 3 | 0 |

| | | | |
|---|---|---|---|
| 1993–94 | Dunfermline Ath | 39 | 0 |
| 1994–95 | Dunfermline Ath | 30 | 2 |
| 1995–96 | Dunfermline Ath | 7 | 1 |
| 1995–96 | Celtic | 26 | 1 |
| 1996–97 | Celtic | 30 | 1 |
| 1997–98 | Celtic | 31 | 2 |
| **Total:** | | **166** | **7** |

## McNEVIN, Alan — Forward

b.Dublin 10-1-80

| | | | |
|---|---|---|---|
| 1997–98 | Arsenal | 0 | 0 |

## McNIVEN, David — Forward

H: 5 11 W: 12 00 b.Leeds 27-5-78

*Source:* Trainee.

| | | | |
|---|---|---|---|
| 1995–96 | Oldham Ath | 0 | 0 |
| 1996–97 | Oldham Ath | 8 | 0 |
| 1997–98 | Oldham Ath | 8 | 1 |
| **Total:** | | **16** | **1** |

## McNIVEN, Scott — Defender

H: 5 11 W: 12 01 b.Leeds 27-5-78

*Source:* Trainee. *Honours:* Scotland Under-21.

| | | | |
|---|---|---|---|
| 1994–95 | Oldham Ath | 1 | 0 |
| 1995–96 | Oldham Ath | 15 | 0 |
| 1996–97 | Oldham Ath | 12 | 0 |
| 1997–98 | Oldham Ath | 32 | 1 |
| **Total:** | | **60** | **1** |

## McPHAIL, Stephen — Midfield

b.London 9-12-79

*Source:* Trainee.

| | | | |
|---|---|---|---|
| 1996–97 | Leeds U | 0 | 0 |
| 1997–98 | Leeds U | 4 | 0 |
| **Total:** | | **4** | **0** |

## McPHERSON, David — Defender

H: 6 3 W: 11 11 b.Paisley 28-1-64

*Source:* Gartcosh United. *Honours:* Scotland Youth, Under-21 B, 27 full caps.

| | | | |
|---|---|---|---|
| 1980–81 | Rangers | 0 | 0 |
| 1981–82 | Rangers | 0 | 0 |
| 1982–83 | Rangers | 18 | 1 |
| 1983–84 | Rangers | 36 | 2 |
| 1984–85 | Rangers | 31 | 0 |
| 1985–86 | Rangers | 34 | 5 |
| 1986–87 | Rangers | 42 | 7 |
| 1987–88 | Rangers | 44 | 4 |
| 1988–89 | Hearts | 32 | 4 |
| 1989–90 | Hearts | 35 | 4 |
| 1990–91 | Hearts | 34 | 2 |
| 1991–92 | Hearts | 44 | 2 |
| 1992–93 | Rangers | 34 | 2 |
| 1993–94 | Rangers | 28 | 1 |
| 1994–95 | Rangers | 9 | 0 |
| 1994–95 | Hearts | 23 | 2 |
| 1995–96 | Hearts | 26 | 1 |
| 1996–97 | Hearts | 26 | 1 |
| 1997–98 | Hearts | 13 | 3 |
| **Total:** | | **509** | **41** |

## McPHERSON, Keith — Defender

H: 5 10 W: 12 00 b.Greenwich 11-9-63

*Source:* Apprentice.

| | | | |
|---|---|---|---|
| 1981–82 | West Ham U | 0 | 0 |
| 1982–83 | West Ham U | 0 | 0 |
| 1983–84 | West Ham U | 0 | 0 |
| 1984–85 | West Ham U | 1 | 0 |
| 1985–86 | West Ham U | 0 | 0 |
| 1985–86 | Cambridge U (loan) | 11 | 1 |
| 1985–86 | Northampton T | 20 | 0 |
| 1986–87 | Northampton T | 46 | 5 |
| 1987–88 | Northampton T | 32 | 0 |
| 1988–89 | Northampton T | 41 | 2 |
| 1989–90 | Northampton T | 43 | 1 |
| 1990–91 | Reading | 46 | 3 |
| 1991–92 | Reading | 44 | 1 |
| 1992–93 | Reading | 44 | 1 |
| 1993–94 | Reading | 20 | 1 |
| 1994–95 | Reading | 23 | 0 |
| 1995–96 | Reading | 16 | 0 |
| 1996–97 | Reading | 39 | 2 |
| 1997–98 | Reading | 24 | 0 |
| **Total:** | | **450** | **17** |

## McPHERSON, Malcolm — Forward

H: 6 1 W: 12 00 b.Glasgow 19-12-74

*Source:* Yeovil T.

| | | | |
|---|---|---|---|
| 1993–94 | West Ham U | 0 | 0 |
| 1994–95 | West Ham U | 0 | 0 |
| 1995–96 | West Ham U | 0 | 0 |
| 1996–97 | Brentford | 3 | 0 |
| 1997–98 | Brentford | 9 | 0 |
| **Total:** | | **12** | **0** |

## McQUILKEN, James — Defender

H: 5 9 W: 10 07 b.Glasgow 3-10-74

*Source:* Giffnock North.

| | | | |
|---|---|---|---|
| 1992–93 | Celtic | 1 | 0 |
| 1993–94 | Celtic | 0 | 0 |
| 1994–95 | Celtic | 0 | 0 |

## McQuillan, John

| | | | |
|---|---|---|---|
| 1995–96 | Celtic | 4 | 0 |
| 1995–96 | Dundee U | 9 | 0 |
| 1996–97 | Dundee U | 9 | 0 |
| 1996–97 | Hibernian | 9 | 0 |
| 1997–98 | Hibernian | 1 | 0 |
| **Total:** | | **33** | **0** |

## McQUILLAN, John — Defender

H: 5 10 W: 11 07 b.Stranraer 20-7-70

*Source:* Stranraer schools.

| | | | |
|---|---|---|---|
| 1986–87 | Stranraer | 0 | 0 |
| 1987–88 | Dundee | 0 | 0 |
| 1988–89 | Dundee | 0 | 0 |
| 1989–90 | Dundee | 2 | 0 |
| 1990–91 | Dundee | 14 | 1 |
| 1991–92 | Dundee | 40 | 3 |
| 1992–93 | Dundee | 29 | 0 |
| 1993–94 | Dundee | 34 | 0 |
| 1994–95 | Dundee | 32 | 0 |
| 1995–96 | St Johnstone | 25 | 2 |
| 1996–97 | St Johnstone | 32 | 0 |
| 1997–98 | St Johnstone | 34 | 1 |
| **Total:** | | **242** | **7** |

## McROBERT, Lee — Midfield

H: 5 9 W: 10 12 b.Bromley 4-10-72

*Source:* Sittingbourne.

| | | | |
|---|---|---|---|
| 1994–95 | Millwall | 7 | 1 |
| 1995–96 | Millwall | 7 | 0 |
| 1996–97 | Millwall | 4 | 0 |
| 1997–98 | Millwall | 5 | 0 |
| **Total:** | | **23** | **1** |

## McSHANE, Tony — Midfield

H: 5 9 W: 10 07 b.Belfast 29-9-78

*Source:* Trainee.

| | | | |
|---|---|---|---|
| 1997–98 | Port Vale | 0 | 0 |

## McSKIMMING, Shaun — Defender

H: 5 11 W: 10 08 b.Stranraer 29-5-70

*Source:* School.

| | | | |
|---|---|---|---|
| 1986–87 | Stranraer | 0 | 0 |
| 1987–88 | Dundee | 0 | 0 |
| 1988–89 | Dundee | 0 | 0 |
| 1989–90 | Dundee | 7 | 0 |
| 1990–91 | Dundee | 16 | 3 |
| 1991–92 | Kilmarnock | 30 | 1 |
| 1992–93 | Kilmarnock | 35 | 5 |
| 1993–94 | Kilmarnock | 40 | 3 |
| 1994–95 | Kilmarnock | 8 | 0 |
| 1994–95 | Motherwell | 14 | 2 |
| 1995–96 | Motherwell | 15 | 1 |
| 1996–97 | Motherwell | 23 | 4 |
| 1997–98 | Motherwell | 12 | 0 |
| **Total:** | | **200** | **19** |

## McSWEGAN, Gary — Forward

H: 5 8 W: 10 09 b.Glasgow 24-9-70

*Source:* Rangers Amateur BC.

| | | | |
|---|---|---|---|
| 1986–87 | Rangers | 0 | 0 |
| 1987–88 | Rangers | 1 | 0 |
| 1988–89 | Rangers | 1 | 0 |
| 1989–90 | Rangers | 0 | 0 |
| 1990–91 | Rangers | 3 | 0 |
| 1991–92 | Rangers | 4 | 0 |
| 1992–93 | Rangers | 9 | 4 |
| 1993–94 | Notts Co | 37 | 15 |
| 1994–95 | Notts Co | 22 | 6 |
| 1995–96 | Notts Co | 3 | 0 |
| 1995–96 | Dundee U | 25 | 17 |
| 1996–97 | Dundee U | 31 | 7 |
| 1997–98 | Dundee U | 31 | 5 |
| **Total:** | | **167** | **54** |

## McVEIGH, Paul — Forward

H: 5 6 W: 10 05 b.Belfast 6-12-77

*Source:* Trainee. *Honours:* Northern Ireland Under-21.

| | | | |
|---|---|---|---|
| 1995–96 | Tottenham H | 0 | 0 |
| 1996–97 | Tottenham H | 3 | 1 |
| 1997–98 | Tottenham H | 0 | 0 |
| **Total:** | | **3** | **1** |

## MEAKER, Michael — Midfield

H: 5 11 W: 12 00 b.Greenford 18-8-71

*Source:* Trainee. *Honours:* Wales Under-21.

| | | | |
|---|---|---|---|
| 1989–90 | QPR | 0 | 0 |
| 1990–91 | QPR | 8 | 0 |
| 1991–92 | QPR | 1 | 0 |
| 1991–92 | Plymouth Arg (loan) | 4 | 0 |
| 1992–93 | QPR | 3 | 0 |
| 1993–94 | QPR | 14 | 1 |
| 1994–95 | QPR | 8 | 0 |
| 1995–96 | Reading | 21 | 0 |
| 1996–97 | Reading | 25 | 1 |
| 1997–98 | Reading | 21 | 1 |
| **Total:** | | **105** | **3** |

## MEAN, Scott — Midfield

H: 5 11 W: 13 08 b.Crawley 13-12-73

*Source:* Trainee.

| | | | |
|---|---|---|---|
| 1992–93 | Bournemouth | 15 | 1 |
| 1993–94 | Bournemouth | 5 | 0 |
| 1994–95 | Bournemouth | 40 | 6 |
| 1995–96 | Bournemouth | 14 | 1 |
| 1996–97 | Bournemouth | 0 | 0 |
| 1996–97 | West Ham U | 0 | 0 |
| 1997–98 | West Ham U | 3 | 0 |
| **Total:** | | **77** | **8** |

## MEDLIN, Nicky — Midfield

H: 5 7 W: 10 01 b.Camborne 23-11-76

*Source:* Trainee.

| | | | |
|---|---|---|---|
| 1995–96 | Exeter C | 6 | 0 |
| 1996–97 | Exeter C | 11 | 1 |
| 1997–98 | Exeter C | 20 | 0 |
| **Total:** | | **37** | **1** |

## MEECHAN, Alex — Forward

b.Plymouth 29-1-80

*Source:* Trainee.

| | | | |
|---|---|---|---|
| 1997–98 | Swindon T | 1 | 0 |
| **Total:** | | **1** | **0** |

## MELDRUM, Colin — Goalkeeper

H: 5 10 W: 13 04 b.Kilmarnock 26-11-75

*Source:* Kilwinning Rangers. *Honours:* Scotland Under-21.

| | | | |
|---|---|---|---|
| 1993–94 | Kilmarnock | 0 | 0 |
| 1994–95 | Kilmarnock | 40 | 0 |
| 1995–96 | Kilmarnock | 1 | 0 |
| 1996–97 | Kilmarnock | 6 | 0 |
| 1997–98 | Kilmarnock | 11 | 0 |
| **Total:** | | **58** | **0** |

## MELLON, Micky — Midfield

H: 5 10 W: 12 11 b.Paisley 18-3-72

*Source:* Trainee.

| | | | |
|---|---|---|---|
| 1989–90 | Bristol C | 9 | 0 |
| 1990–91 | Bristol C | 0 | 0 |
| 1991–92 | Bristol C | 16 | 0 |
| 1992–93 | Bristol C | 10 | 1 |
| 1992–93 | WBA | 17 | 3 |
| 1993–94 | WBA | 21 | 2 |
| 1994–95 | WBA | 7 | 1 |
| 1994–95 | Blackpool | 26 | 4 |
| 1995–96 | Blackpool | 45 | 6 |
| 1996–97 | Blackpool | 43 | 4 |
| 1997–98 | Blackpool | 10 | 0 |
| 1997–98 | Tranmere R | 33 | 2 |
| **Total:** | | **237** | **23** |

## MELTON, Stephen — Midfield

H: 5 11 W: 10 11 b.Lincoln 3-10-78

*Source:* Trainee.

| | | | |
|---|---|---|---|
| 1995–96 | Nottingham F | 0 | 0 |
| 1996–97 | Nottingham F | 0 | 0 |
| 1997–98 | Nottingham F | 0 | 0 |

## MELVANG, Lars — Defender

H: 5 9 W: 11 06 b.Seattle 3-4-69

| | | | |
|---|---|---|---|
| 1990 | Silkeborg | 18 | 2 |
| 1991–92 | Silkeborg | 30 | 0 |
| 1992–93 | Silkeborg | 17 | 2 |
| 1993–94 | Silkeborg | 32 | 1 |
| 1994–95 | Silkeborg | 25 | 1 |
| 1995–96 | Silkeborg | 6 | 0 |
| 1996–97 | Silkeborg | 12 | 0 |
| 1997–98 | Watford | 4 | 1 |
| **Total:** | | **144** | **7** |

## MELVILLE, Andy — Defender

H: 6 1 W: 12 06 b.Swansea 29-11-68

*Source:* School. *Honours:* Wales Under-21, B, 32 full caps, 3 goals.

| | | | |
|---|---|---|---|
| 1985–86 | Swansea C | 5 | 0 |
| 1986–87 | Swansea C | 42 | 3 |
| 1987–88 | Swansea C | 37 | 4 |
| 1988–89 | Swansea C | 45 | 10 |
| 1989–90 | Swansea C | 46 | 5 |
| 1990–91 | Oxford U | 46 | 3 |
| 1991–92 | Oxford U | 45 | 4 |
| 1992–93 | Oxford U | 44 | 6 |
| 1993–94 | Sunderland | 44 | 2 |
| 1994–95 | Sunderland | 36 | 3 |
| 1995–96 | Sunderland | 40 | 4 |
| 1996–97 | Sunderland | 30 | 2 |
| 1997–98 | Sunderland | 10 | 1 |
| 1997–98 | Bradford C (loan) | 6 | 1 |
| **Total:** | | **476** | **48** |

## MENDEZ, Alberto — Midfield

H: 5 11 W: 11 09 b.Nuremberg 24-10-74

*Source:* FC Feucht.

| | | | |
|---|---|---|---|
| 1997–98 | Arsenal | 3 | 0 |
| **Total:** | | **3** | **0** |

## MENDONCA, Clive — Forward

H: 5 10 W: 12 05 b.Islington 9-9-68

*Source:* Apprentice.

| | | | |
|---|---|---|---|
| 1986–87 | Sheffield U | 2 | 0 |
| 1987–88 | Sheffield U | 11 | 4 |
| 1987–88 | Doncaster R (loan) | 2 | 0 |
| 1987–88 | Rotherham U | 8 | 2 |
| 1988–89 | Rotherham U | 10 | 1 |
| 1989–90 | Rotherham U | 32 | 14 |
| 1990–91 | Rotherham U | 34 | 10 |
| 1991–92 | Sheffield U | 10 | 1 |
| 1991–92 | Grimsby T (loan) | 10 | 3 |
| 1992–93 | Grimsby T | 42 | 10 |
| 1993–94 | Grimsby T | 39 | 14 |
| 1994–95 | Grimsby T | 22 | 11 |
| 1995–96 | Grimsby T | 8 | 4 |
| 1996–97 | Grimsby T | 45 | 17 |
| 1997–98 | Charlton Ath | 40 | 23 |
| **Total:** | | **315** | **114** |

## MERCER, Billy — Goalkeeper

H: 6 1 W: 11 00 b.Liverpool 22-5-69

*Source:* Trainee.

| | | | |
|---|---|---|---|
| 1987–88 | Liverpool | 0 | 0 |
| 1988–89 | Liverpool | 0 | 0 |
| 1988–89 | Rotherham U | 0 | 0 |
| 1989–90 | Rotherham U | 2 | 0 |
| 1990–91 | Rotherham U | 13 | 0 |
| 1991–92 | Rotherham U | 35 | 0 |
| 1992–93 | Rotherham U | 36 | 0 |
| 1993–94 | Rotherham U | 17 | 0 |
| 1994–95 | Rotherham U | 1 | 0 |
| 1994–95 | Sheffield U | 3 | 0 |
| 1994–95 | Nottingham F (loan) | 0 | 0 |
| 1995–96 | Sheffield U | 1 | 0 |
| 1995–96 | Chesterfield | 34 | 0 |
| 1996–97 | Chesterfield | 35 | 0 |
| 1997–98 | Chesterfield | 36 | 0 |
| **Total:** | | **213** | **0** |

## MERINO, Carlos — Midfield

H: 5 8 W: 10 00 b.Bilbao 15-3-80

*Source:* Urdaneta.

| | | | |
|---|---|---|---|
| 1997–98 | Nottingham F | 0 | 0 |

## MERSON, Paul — Forward

H: 6 0 W: 12 07 b.London 20-3-68

*Source:* Apprentice. *Honours:* England Youth, Under-21, B, 19 full caps, 2 goals.

| | | | |
|---|---|---|---|
| 1985–86 | Arsenal | 0 | 0 |
| 1986–87 | Arsenal | 7 | 3 |
| 1986–87 | Brentford (loan) | 7 | 0 |
| 1987–88 | Arsenal | 15 | 5 |
| 1988–89 | Arsenal | 37 | 10 |
| 1989–90 | Arsenal | 29 | 7 |
| 1990–91 | Arsenal | 37 | 13 |
| 1991–92 | Arsenal | 42 | 12 |
| 1992–93 | Arsenal | 33 | 6 |
| 1993–94 | Arsenal | 33 | 7 |
| 1994–95 | Arsenal | 24 | 4 |
| 1995–96 | Arsenal | 38 | 5 |
| 1996–97 | Arsenal | 32 | 6 |
| 1997–98 | Middlesbrough | 45 | 11 |
| **Total:** | | **379** | **89** |

## MESSER, Gary — Forward

H: 6 1 W: 13 00 b.Consett 22-9-79

*Source:* Trainee.

| | | | |
|---|---|---|---|
| 1996–97 | Doncaster R | 1 | 0 |
| 1997–98 | Doncaster R | 13 | 1 |
| **Total:** | | **14** | **1** |

## MIDDLETON, Craig — Midfield

H: 5 10 W: 11 10 b.Nuneaton 10-9-70

*Source:* Trainee.

| | | | |
|---|---|---|---|
| 1989–90 | Coventry C | 1 | 0 |
| 1990–91 | Coventry C | 0 | 0 |
| 1991–92 | Coventry C | 1 | 0 |
| 1992–93 | Coventry C | 1 | 0 |
| 1993–94 | Cambridge U | 19 | 2 |
| 1994–95 | Cambridge U | 0 | 0 |
| 1995–96 | Cambridge U | 40 | 8 |
| 1996–97 | Cardiff C | 41 | 4 |
| 1997–98 | Cardiff C | 33 | 0 |
| **Total:** | | **136** | **14** |

## MIDDLETON, Darren — Forward

H: 6 0 W: 11 05 b.Lichfield 28-12-78

*Source:* Trainee.

| | | | |
|---|---|---|---|
| 1995–96 | Aston Villa | 0 | 0 |
| 1996–97 | Aston Villa | 0 | 0 |
| 1997–98 | Aston Villa | 0 | 0 |

## MIDGLEY, Craig — Forward

H: 5 7 W: 11 07 b.Bradford 24-5-76

*Source:* Trainee.

| | | | |
|---|---|---|---|
| 1994–95 | Bradford C | 3 | 0 |
| 1995–96 | Bradford C | 5 | 1 |
| 1995–96 | Scarborough (loan) | 16 | 1 |
| 1996–97 | Bradford C | 1 | 0 |

| | | | |
|---|---|---|---|
| 1996–97 | Scarborough (loan) | 6 | 2 |
| 1997–98 | Bradford C | 2 | 0 |
| 1997–98 | Darlington (loan) | 1 | 0 |
| 1997–98 | Hartlepool U | 9 | 3 |
| **Total:** | | **43** | **7** |

## MIDGLEY, Neil — Forward

H: 5 11 W: 11 03 b.Cambridge 21-10-78

*Source:* Trainee.

| | | | |
|---|---|---|---|
| 1997–98 | Ipswich T | 0 | 0 |

## MIDWOOD, Michael — Forward

b.Huddersfield 19-4-76

*Source:* Trainee.

| | | | |
|---|---|---|---|
| 1994–95 | Huddersfield T | 0 | 0 |
| 1995–96 | Huddersfield T | 0 | 0 |
| 1996–97 | Huddersfield T | 0 | 0 |
| 1997–98 | Huddersfield T | 1 | 0 |
| **Total:** | | **1** | **0** |

## MIKE, Adie — Forward

H: 6 0 W: 12 10 b.Manchester 16-11-73

*Source:* Trainee. *Honours:* England Schools, Youth.

| | | | |
|---|---|---|---|
| 1991–92 | Manchester C | 2 | 1 |
| 1992–93 | Manchester C | 3 | 0 |
| 1992–93 | Bury (loan) | 7 | 1 |
| 1993–94 | Manchester C | 9 | 1 |
| 1994–95 | Manchester C | 2 | 0 |
| 1995–96 | Manchester C | 0 | 0 |
| 1995–96 | Stockport Co | 8 | 0 |
| 1996–97 | Stockport Co | 1 | 0 |
| 1996–97 | Hartlepool U (loan) | 7 | 1 |
| 1996–97 | Doncaster R (loan) | 5 | 1 |
| 1997–98 | Doncaster R | 42 | 4 |
| **Total:** | | **86** | **9** |

## MIKLOSKO, Ludek — Goalkeeper

H: 6 5 W: 14 00 b.Protesov 9-12-61

*Source:* Banik Ostrava. *Honours:* Czech Republic 42 full caps.

| | | | |
|---|---|---|---|
| 1989–90 | West Ham U | 18 | 0 |
| 1990–91 | West Ham U | 46 | 0 |
| 1991–92 | West Ham U | 36 | 0 |
| 1992–93 | West Ham U | 46 | 0 |
| 1993–94 | West Ham U | 42 | 0 |
| 1994–95 | West Ham U | 42 | 0 |
| 1995–96 | West Ham U | 36 | 0 |
| 1996–97 | West Ham U | 36 | 0 |
| 1997–98 | West Ham U | 13 | 0 |
| **Total:** | | **315** | **0** |

## MILBOURNE, Ian — Forward

H: 5 11 W: 11 02 b.Hexham 21-1-79

*Source:* Trainee.

| | | | |
|---|---|---|---|
| 1997–98 | Newcastle U | 0 | 0 |

## MILDENHALL, Steve — Goalkeeper

H: 6 4 W: 14 01 b.Swindon 13-5-78

*Source:* Trainee.

| | | | |
|---|---|---|---|
| 1996–97 | Swindon T | 1 | 0 |
| 1997–98 | Swindon T | 4 | 0 |
| **Total:** | | **5** | **0** |

## MILLAR, Marc — Forward

H: 5 9 W: 10 12 b.Dundee 10-4-69

*Source:* Riverside Ath.

| | | | |
|---|---|---|---|
| 1991–92 | Brechin C | 17 | 1 |
| 1992–93 | Brechin C | 31 | 11 |
| 1993–94 | Brechin C | 39 | 10 |
| 1994–95 | Brechin C | 8 | 1 |
| 1994–95 | Dunfermline Ath | 24 | 2 |
| 1995–96 | Dunfermline Ath | 24 | 5 |
| 1996–97 | Dunfermline Ath | 23 | 6 |
| 1997–98 | Dunfermline Ath | 12 | 2 |
| **Total:** | | **178** | **38** |

## MILLARD, Ross — Defender

b.Bristol 1-1-79

*Source:* Trainee.

| | | | |
|---|---|---|---|
| 1997–98 | Manchester U | 0 | 0 |

## MILLEN, Keith — Defender

H: 6 2 W: 12 04 b.Croydon 26-9-66

*Source:* Juniors.

| | | | |
|---|---|---|---|
| 1984–85 | Brentford | 17 | 0 |
| 1985–86 | Brentford | 32 | 2 |
| 1986–87 | Brentford | 39 | 2 |
| 1987–88 | Brentford | 40 | 3 |
| 1988–89 | Brentford | 36 | 3 |
| 1989–90 | Brentford | 32 | 0 |
| 1990–91 | Brentford | 32 | 2 |
| 1991–92 | Brentford | 34 | 1 |
| 1992–93 | Brentford | 43 | 4 |
| 1993–94 | Brentford | 0 | 0 |
| 1993–94 | Watford | 10 | 0 |
| 1994–95 | Watford | 31 | 1 |
| 1995–96 | Watford | 33 | 0 |
| 1996–97 | Watford | 42 | 2 |
| 1997–98 | Watford | 38 | 1 |
| **Total:** | | **459** | **21** |

## MILLER, Alan — Goalkeeper

H: 6 3 W: 14 06 b.Epping 29-3-70

*Source:* Trainee. *Honours:* England Schools, FA Schools, Under-21.

| | | | |
|---|---|---|---|
| 1987–88 | Arsenal | 0 | 0 |
| 1988–89 | Arsenal | 0 | 0 |
| 1988–89 | Plymouth Arg (loan) | 13 | 0 |
| 1989–90 | Arsenal | 0 | 0 |
| 1990–91 | Arsenal | 0 | 0 |
| 1991–92 | Arsenal | 0 | 0 |
| 1991–92 | WBA (loan) | 3 | 0 |
| 1991–92 | Birmingham C (loan) | 15 | 0 |
| 1992–93 | Arsenal | 4 | 0 |
| 1993–94 | Arsenal | 4 | 0 |
| 1994–95 | Middlesbrough | 41 | 0 |
| 1995–96 | Middlesbrough | 6 | 0 |
| 1996–97 | Middlesbrough | 10 | 0 |
| 1996–97 | Huddersfield T (loan) | 0 | 0 |
| 1996–97 | Grimsby T (loan) | 3 | 0 |
| 1996–97 | WBA | 12 | 0 |
| 1997–98 | WBA | 41 | 0 |
| **Total:** | | **152** | **0** |

## MILLER, Charles — Forward

H: 5 9 W: 10 08 b.Glasgow 18-3-76

*Source:* Rangers BC. *Honours:* Scotland Under-21.

| | | | |
|---|---|---|---|
| 1992–93 | Rangers | 0 | 0 |
| 1993–94 | Rangers | 3 | 0 |
| 1994–95 | Rangers | 21 | 3 |
| 1995–96 | Rangers | 23 | 3 |
| 1996–97 | Rangers | 13 | 1 |
| 1997–98 | Rangers | 7 | 0 |
| **Total:** | | **67** | **7** |

## MILLER, Colin — Defender

H: 5 7 W: 12 02 b.Lanark 4-10-64

*Source:* Toronto Blizzard. *Honours:* Canada 59 full caps.

| | | | |
|---|---|---|---|
| 1985–86 | Rangers | 2 | 0 |
| 1986–87 | Doncaster R | 20 | 2 |
| 1987–88 | Doncaster R | 41 | 1 |
| From Hamilton Steelers. | | | |
| 1988–89 | Hamilton A | 21 | 0 |
| 1989–90 | Hamilton A | 37 | 1 |
| 1990–91 | Hamilton A | 37 | 0 |
| 1991–92 | Hamilton A | 43 | 1 |
| 1992–93 | Hamilton A | 29 | 3 |
| 1993–94 | Hamilton A | 31 | 0 |
| 1993–94 | St Johnstone | 12 | 0 |
| 1994–95 | St Johnstone | 12 | 0 |
| 1994–95 | Hearts | 16 | 1 |
| 1995–96 | Hearts | 3 | 0 |
| 1995–96 | Dunfermline Ath | 25 | 0 |
| 1996–97 | Dunfermline Ath | 22 | 0 |
| 1997–98 | Dunfermline Ath | 15 | 0 |
| **Total:** | | **366** | **9** |

## MILLER, Greg — Midfield

H: 5 7 W: 10 00 b.Glasgow 1-4-76

*Source:* Hutcheson Vale BC.

| | | | |
|---|---|---|---|
| 1994–95 | Hibernian | 0 | 0 |
| 1995–96 | Hibernian | 3 | 0 |
| 1996–97 | Hibernian | 6 | 0 |
| 1997–98 | Hibernian | 3 | 0 |
| **Total:** | | **12** | **0** |

## MILLER, Joe — Forward

H: 5 8 W: 9 12 b.Glasgow 8-12-67

*Source:* 'S' Form. *Honours:* Scotland Schools, Youth, Under-21.

| | | | |
|---|---|---|---|
| 1984–85 | Aberdeen | 1 | 0 |
| 1985–86 | Aberdeen | 18 | 3 |
| 1986–87 | Aberdeen | 27 | 6 |
| 1987–88 | Aberdeen | 14 | 4 |
| 1987–88 | Celtic | 27 | 3 |
| 1988–89 | Celtic | 22 | 8 |
| 1989–90 | Celtic | 24 | 5 |
| 1990–91 | Celtic | 30 | 8 |
| 1991–92 | Celtic | 26 | 2 |
| 1992–93 | Celtic | 23 | 2 |
| 1993–94 | Aberdeen | 27 | 4 |
| 1994–95 | Aberdeen | 27 | 0 |
| 1995–96 | Aberdeen | 31 | 9 |
| 1996–97 | Aberdeen | 30 | 4 |
| 1997–98 | Aberdeen | 29 | 1 |
| **Total:** | | **356** | **59** |

## MILLER, Kenneth — Forward

H: 5 9 W: 10 09 b.Edinburgh 23-12-79

*Source:* Hutchison Vale.

| | | | |
|---|---|---|---|
| 1996–97 | Hibernian | 0 | 0 |
| 1997–98 | Hibernian | 7 | 0 |
| **Total:** | | **7** | **0** |

## MILLER, Kevin — Goalkeeper

H: 6 1 W: 13 00 b.Falmouth 15-3-69

*Source:* Newquay.

| | | | |
|---|---|---|---|
| 1988–89 | Exeter C | 3 | 0 |
| 1989–90 | Exeter C | 28 | 0 |
| 1990–91 | Exeter C | 46 | 0 |
| 1991–92 | Exeter C | 42 | 0 |
| 1992–93 | Exeter C | 44 | 0 |
| 1993–94 | Birmingham C | 24 | 0 |

| | | | |
|---|---|---|---|
| 1994–95 | Watford | 44 | 0 |
| 1995–96 | Watford | 42 | 0 |
| 1996–97 | Watford | 42 | 0 |
| 1997–98 | Crystal Palace | 38 | 0 |
| **Total:** | | **353** | **0** |

## MILLER, Paul — Forward

H: 6 0 W: 11 07 b.Bisley 31-1-68

*Source:* Trainee.

| | | | |
|---|---|---|---|
| 1987–88 | Wimbledon | 5 | 0 |
| 1987–88 | Newport Co (loan) | 6 | 2 |
| 1988–89 | Wimbledon | 18 | 5 |
| 1989–90 | Wimbledon | 15 | 2 |
| 1989–90 | Bristol C (loan) | 3 | 0 |
| 1990–91 | Wimbledon | 1 | 0 |
| 1991–92 | Wimbledon | 22 | 2 |
| 1992–93 | Wimbledon | 19 | 1 |
| 1993–94 | Wimbledon | 0 | 0 |
| 1994–95 | Bristol R | 42 | 16 |
| 1995–96 | Bristol R | 38 | 4 |
| 1996–97 | Bristol R | 25 | 2 |
| 1997–98 | Lincoln C | 24 | 2 |
| **Total:** | | **218** | **36** |

## MILLER, Thomas — Defender

H: 6 1 W: 11 12 b.Easington 8-1-79

*Source:* Trainee.

| | | | |
|---|---|---|---|
| 1997–98 | Hartlepool U | 13 | 1 |
| **Total:** | | **13** | **1** |

## MILLER, William — Defender

H: 5 8 W: 10 06 b.Edinburgh 1-11-69

*Source:* Edina Hibs BC. *Honours:* Scotland Under-21.

| | | | |
|---|---|---|---|
| 1989–90 | Hibernian | 11 | 0 |
| 1990–91 | Hibernian | 25 | 1 |
| 1991–92 | Hibernian | 30 | 0 |
| 1992–93 | Hibernian | 34 | 0 |
| 1993–94 | Hibernian | 37 | 0 |
| 1994–95 | Hibernian | 34 | 0 |
| 1995–96 | Hibernian | 13 | 0 |
| 1996–97 | Hibernian | 31 | 0 |
| 1997–98 | Hibernian | 31 | 1 |
| **Total:** | | **246** | **2** |

## MILLIGAN, Jamie — Forward

b.Blackpool 3-1-80

*Source:* Trainee. *Honours:* England Youth.

| | | | |
|---|---|---|---|
| 1997–98 | Everton | 0 | 0 |

## MILLIGAN, Mike — Midfield

H: 5 8 W: 11 00 b.Manchester 20-2-67

*Source:* Trainee. *Honours:* Eire Under-21, B, 1 full cap.

| | | | |
|---|---|---|---|
| 1984–85 | Oldham Ath | 0 | 0 |
| 1985–86 | Oldham Ath | 5 | 1 |
| 1986–87 | Oldham Ath | 38 | 2 |
| 1987–88 | Oldham Ath | 39 | 1 |
| 1988–89 | Oldham Ath | 39 | 6 |
| 1989–90 | Oldham Ath | 41 | 7 |
| 1990–91 | Everton | 17 | 1 |
| 1991–92 | Oldham Ath | 36 | 3 |
| 1992–93 | Oldham Ath | 42 | 3 |
| 1993–94 | Oldham Ath | 39 | 0 |
| 1994–95 | Norwich C | 26 | 2 |
| 1995–96 | Norwich C | 28 | 2 |
| 1996–97 | Norwich C | 37 | 1 |
| 1997–98 | Norwich C | 20 | 0 |
| **Total:** | | **407** | **29** |

## MILLIGAN, Ross — Defender

H: 5 11 W: 12 10 b.Dumfries 2-6-78

*Source:* Maxwelton T.

| | | | |
|---|---|---|---|
| 1996–97 | Rangers | 0 | 0 |
| 1997–98 | Carlisle U | 7 | 0 |
| **Total:** | | **7** | **0** |

## MILLS, Danny — Midfield

H: 5 11 W: 11 07 b.Sidcup 13-2-75

*Source:* Trainee.

| | | | |
|---|---|---|---|
| 1993–94 | Charlton Ath | 0 | 0 |
| 1994–95 | Charlton Ath | 0 | 0 |
| 1995–96 | Barnet | 19 | 0 |
| 1996–97 | Barnet | 2 | 0 |
| 1997–98 | Barnet | 6 | 0 |
| **Total:** | | **27** | **0** |

## MILLS, Danny — Defender

H: 5 10 W: 11 11 b.Norwich 18-5-77

*Source:* Trainee. *Honours:* England Youth.

| | | | |
|---|---|---|---|
| 1994–95 | Norwich C | 0 | 0 |
| 1995–96 | Norwich C | 14 | 0 |
| 1996–97 | Norwich C | 32 | 0 |
| 1997–98 | Norwich C | 20 | 0 |
| 1997–98 | Charlton Ath | 9 | 1 |
| **Total:** | | **75** | **1** |

## MILLS, Lee — Forward

H: 6 2 W: 12 09 b.Mexborough 10-7-70

*Source:* Stocksbridge PS.

| | | | |
|---|---|---|---|
| 1992–93 | Wolverhampton W | 0 | 0 |
| 1993–94 | Wolverhampton W | 14 | 1 |
| 1994–95 | Wolverhampton W | 11 | 1 |
| 1994–95 | Derby Co | 16 | 7 |
| 1995–96 | Port Vale | 32 | 8 |
| 1996–97 | Port Vale | 35 | 13 |
| 1997–98 | Port Vale | 42 | 14 |
| **Total:** | | **150** | **44** |

## MILNE, Steven — Forward

b.Dundee 5-5-80

*Source:* Downfield J.

| | | | |
|---|---|---|---|
| 1997–98 | Dundee | 2 | 0 |
| **Total:** | | **2** | **0** |

## MILNER, Andy — Forward

H: 6 0 W: 11 00 b.Kendal 10-2-67

*Source:* Netherfield.

| | | | |
|---|---|---|---|
| 1988–89 | Manchester C | 0 | 0 |
| 1989–90 | Manchester C | 0 | 0 |
| 1989–90 | Rochdale | 16 | 4 |
| 1990–91 | Rochdale | 35 | 5 |
| 1991–92 | Rochdale | 33 | 10 |
| 1992–93 | Rochdale | 18 | 4 |
| 1993–94 | Rochdale | 25 | 2 |
| 1994–95 | Chester C | 36 | 8 |
| 1995–96 | Chester C | 42 | 4 |
| 1996–97 | Chester C | 46 | 12 |
| 1997–98 | Chester C | 1 | 0 |
| **Total:** | | **252** | **49** |

## MILNER, Jonathan — Forward

H: 5 8 W: 11 07 b.Mansfield 30-3-81

*Source:* Trainee.

| | | | |
|---|---|---|---|
| 1997–98 | Mansfield T | 7 | 0 |
| **Total:** | | **7** | **0** |

## MILOSEVIC, Savo — Forward

H: 6 1 W: 13 08 b.Bijelina 2-9-73

*Honours:* Yugoslavia 28 full caps, 16 goals.

| | | | |
|---|---|---|---|
| 1992–93 | Partizan Belgrade | 31 | 14 |
| 1993–94 | Partizan Belgrade | 32 | 20 |
| 1994–95 | Partizan Belgrade | 35 | 30 |
| 1995–96 | Aston Villa | 37 | 12 |
| 1996–97 | Aston Villa | 30 | 9 |
| 1997–98 | Aston Villa | 23 | 7 |
| **Total:** | | **188** | **92** |

## MILTON, Simon — Midfield

H: 5 10 W: 11 05 b.Fulham 23-8-63

*Source:* Bury St Edmunds.

| | | | |
|---|---|---|---|
| 1987–88 | Ipswich T | 8 | 1 |
| 1987–88 | Exeter C (loan) | 2 | 3 |
| 1987–88 | Torquay U (loan) | 4 | 1 |
| 1988–89 | Ipswich T | 35 | 10 |
| 1989–90 | Ipswich T | 41 | 10 |
| 1990–91 | Ipswich T | 31 | 6 |
| 1991–92 | Ipswich T | 34 | 7 |
| 1992–93 | Ipswich T | 12 | 2 |
| 1993–94 | Ipswich T | 15 | 1 |
| 1994–95 | Ipswich T | 25 | 2 |
| 1995–96 | Ipswich T | 37 | 9 |
| 1996–97 | Ipswich T | 23 | 0 |
| 1997–98 | Ipswich T | 20 | 0 |
| **Total:** | | **287** | **52** |

## MIMMS, Bobby — Goalkeeper

H: 6 2 W: 14 01 b.York 12-10-63

*Source:* Halifax T Apprentice. *Honours:* England Under-21.

| | | | |
|---|---|---|---|
| 1981–82 | Rotherham U | 2 | 0 |
| 1982–83 | Rotherham U | 13 | 0 |
| 1983–84 | Rotherham U | 22 | 0 |
| 1984–85 | Rotherham U | 46 | 0 |
| 1985–86 | Everton | 10 | 0 |
| 1985–86 | Notts Co (loan) | 2 | 0 |
| 1986–87 | Everton | 11 | 0 |
| 1986–87 | Sunderland (loan) | 4 | 0 |
| 1986–87 | Blackburn R (loan) | 6 | 0 |
| 1987–88 | Everton | 8 | 0 |
| 1987–88 | Manchester C (loan) | 3 | 0 |
| 1987–88 | Tottenham H | 13 | 0 |
| 1988–89 | Tottenham H | 20 | 0 |
| 1989–90 | Tottenham H | 4 | 0 |
| 1989–90 | Aberdeen (loan) | 6 | 0 |
| 1990–91 | Tottenham H | 0 | 0 |
| 1990–91 | Blackburn R | 22 | 0 |
| 1991–92 | Blackburn R | 45 | 0 |
| 1992–93 | Blackburn R | 42 | 0 |
| 1993–94 | Blackburn R | 13 | 0 |
| 1994–95 | Blackburn R | 4 | 0 |
| 1995–96 | Blackburn R | 2 | 0 |
| 1996–97 | Crystal Palace | 1 | 0 |
| 1996–97 | Preston NE | 27 | 0 |
| 1997–98 | Rotherham U | 43 | 0 |
| **Total:** | | **369** | **0** |

## MINETT, Jason — Midfield

H: 5 9 W: 10 04 b.Peterborough 12-8-71

*Source:* Trainee.

| | | | |
|---|---|---|---|
| 1989–90 | Norwich C | 0 | 0 |
| 1990–91 | Norwich C | 2 | 0 |
| 1991–92 | Norwich C | 0 | 0 |
| 1992–93 | Norwich C | 1 | 0 |
| 1992–93 | Exeter C (loan) | 12 | 0 |
| 1993–94 | Exeter C | 38 | 1 |
| 1994–95 | Exeter C | 38 | 2 |
| 1995–96 | Lincoln C | 42 | 5 |
| 1996–97 | Lincoln C | 4 | 0 |
| 1996–97 | Exeter C | 13 | 0 |
| 1997–98 | Exeter C | 6 | 0 |
| **Total:** | | **156** | **8** |

## MINORS, Dwayne — Forward

b.Hackney 6-9-78

*Source:* Trainee.

| | | | |
|---|---|---|---|
| 1997–98 | Charlton Ath | 0 | 0 |

## MINTON, Jeffrey — Midfield

H: 5 6 W: 11 11 b.Hackney 28-12-73

*Source:* Trainee.

| | | | |
|---|---|---|---|
| 1991–92 | Tottenham H | 2 | 1 |
| 1992–93 | Tottenham H | 0 | 0 |
| 1993–94 | Tottenham H | 0 | 0 |
| 1994–95 | Brighton & HA | 39 | 5 |
| 1995–96 | Brighton & HA | 39 | 8 |
| 1996–97 | Brighton & HA | 25 | 3 |
| 1997–98 | Brighton & HA | 36 | 6 |
| **Total:** | | **141** | **23** |

## MISKELLY, David — Goalkeeper

b.Ards 3-9-79

*Source:* Trainee.

| | | | |
|---|---|---|---|
| 1997–98 | Oldham Ath | 0 | 0 |

## MISSE-MISSE, Jean-Jacques — Forward

H: 5 10 W: 11 00 b.Yaounde 7-8-68

*Honours:* Cameroon full caps.

| | | | |
|---|---|---|---|
| 1993–94 | Charleroi | 33 | 15 |
| 1994–95 | Charleroi | 31 | 10 |
| 1995–96 | Charleroi | 29 | 12 |
| 1996–97 | Sporting Lisbon | 4 | 0 |
| From Trabzonspor. | | | |
| 1997–98 | Dundee U | 4 | 0 |
| 1997–98 | Chesterfield | 1 | 0 |
| **Total:** | | **102** | **37** |

## MITCHELL, Alistair — Forward

H: 5 7 W: 11 00 b.Kirkcaldy 3-12-68

*Source:* Ballingry Rovers.

| | | | |
|---|---|---|---|
| 1988–89 | East Fife | 18 | 4 |
| 1989–90 | East Fife | 35 | 12 |
| 1990–91 | East Fife | 34 | 7 |
| 1991–92 | Kilmarnock | 42 | 10 |
| 1992–93 | Kilmarnock | 32 | 6 |
| 1993–94 | Kilmarnock | 34 | 5 |
| 1994–95 | Kilmarnock | 35 | 4 |
| 1995–96 | Kilmarnock | 30 | 3 |
| 1996–97 | Kilmarnock | 30 | 3 |
| 1997–98 | Kilmarnock | 33 | 4 |
| **Total:** | | **323** | **58** |

## MITCHELL, Jamie — Forward

H: 5 7 W: 9 10 b.Glasgow 6-11-76

*Source:* Trainee.

| | | | |
|---|---|---|---|
| 1995–96 | Norwich C | 0 | 0 |
| 1996–97 | Scarborough | 43 | 7 |
| 1997–98 | Scarborough | 35 | 3 |
| **Total:** | | **78** | **10** |

## MITCHELL, Neil — Forward

H: 5 7 W: 11 00 b.Lytham 7-11-74

*Source:* Trainee.

| | | | |
|---|---|---|---|
| 1991–92 | Blackpool | 1 | 0 |
| 1992–93 | Blackpool | 12 | 1 |
| 1993–94 | Blackpool | 24 | 3 |
| 1994–95 | Blackpool | 30 | 4 |
| 1995–96 | Blackpool | 0 | 0 |
| 1995–96 | Rochdale (loan) | 4 | 0 |
| 1996–97 | Blackpool | 0 | 0 |
| 1997–98 | Macclesfield T | 6 | 0 |
| **Total:** | | **77** | **8** |

## MITCHELL, Paul — Midfield

H: 5 10 W: 12 00 b.Bournemouth 20-10-71

*Source:* Trainee.

| | | | |
|---|---|---|---|
| 1990–91 | Bournemouth | 2 | 0 |
| 1991–92 | Bournemouth | 5 | 0 |
| 1992–93 | Bournemouth | 5 | 0 |
| 1993–94 | West Ham U | 1 | 0 |
| 1994–95 | West Ham U | 0 | 0 |
| 1995–96 | West Ham U | 0 | 0 |
| 1995–96 | Bournemouth | 4 | 0 |
| 1996–97 | Torquay U | 24 | 0 |
| 1997–98 | Torquay U | 14 | 1 |
| **Total:** | | **55** | **1** |

## MITCHELL, Paul — Defender

H: 5 9 W: 10 08 b.Nottingham 8-11-78

*Source:* Trainee.

| | | | |
|---|---|---|---|
| 1996–97 | Notts Co | 1 | 0 |
| 1997–98 | Notts Co | 1 | 0 |
| **Total:** | | **2** | **0** |

## MITCHELL, Ross — Midfield

H: 5 11 W: 10 13 b.Halifax 24-8-78

*Source:* Trainee.

| | | | |
|---|---|---|---|
| 1997–98 | Leicester C | 0 | 0 |

## MOHAN, Nicky — Defender

H: 6 1 W: 14 00 b.Middlesbrough 6-10-70

*Source:* Trainee.

| | | | |
|---|---|---|---|
| 1987–88 | Middlesbrough | 0 | 0 |
| 1988–89 | Middlesbrough | 6 | 0 |
| 1989–90 | Middlesbrough | 22 | 0 |
| 1990–91 | Middlesbrough | 0 | 0 |
| 1991–92 | Middlesbrough | 27 | 2 |
| 1992–93 | Middlesbrough | 18 | 2 |
| 1992–93 | Hull C (loan) | 5 | 1 |
| 1993–94 | Middlesbrough | 26 | 0 |
| 1994–95 | Leicester C | 23 | 0 |
| 1995–96 | Bradford C | 39 | 4 |
| 1996–97 | Bradford C | 44 | 0 |
| 1997–98 | Bradford C | 0 | 0 |
| 1997–98 | Wycombe W | 33 | 0 |
| **Total:** | | **243** | **9** |

## MOILANEN, Teuvo — Goalkeeper

H: 6 5 W: 12 06 b.Oulu 12-12-73

*Honours:* Iceland Under-21, full caps.

| | | | |
|---|---|---|---|
| 1990 | Ilves | 3 | 0 |
| 1991 | Ilves | 7 | 0 |
| 1992 | Ilves | 29 | 0 |
| 1993 | Ilves | 5 | 0 |
| 1994 | Ilves | 19 | 0 |
| 1995 | Jaro | 26 | 0 |
| 1995–96 | Preston NE | 2 | 0 |
| 1996–97 | Preston NE | 4 | 0 |
| 1996–97 | Scarborough (loan) | 4 | 0 |
| 1996–97 | Darlington (loan) | 16 | 0 |
| 1997–98 | Preston NE | 40 | 0 |
| **Total:** | | **155** | **0** |

## MOLBY, Jan — Midfield

H: 6 2 W: 15 10 b.Kolding 4-7-63

*Source:* Kolding, Ajax. *Honours:* Denmark Youth, Under-21, 33 full caps.

| | | | |
|---|---|---|---|
| 1984–85 | Liverpool | 22 | 1 |
| 1985–86 | Liverpool | 39 | 14 |
| 1986–87 | Liverpool | 34 | 7 |
| 1987–88 | Liverpool | 7 | 0 |
| 1988–89 | Liverpool | 13 | 2 |
| 1989–90 | Liverpool | 17 | 1 |
| 1990–91 | Liverpool | 25 | 9 |
| 1991–92 | Liverpool | 26 | 3 |
| 1992–93 | Liverpool | 10 | 3 |
| 1993–94 | Liverpool | 11 | 2 |
| 1994–95 | Liverpool | 14 | 2 |
| 1995–96 | Liverpool | 0 | 0 |
| 1995–96 | Barnsley (loan) | 5 | 0 |
| 1995–96 | Norwich C (loan) | 3 | 0 |
| 1995–96 | Swansea C | 12 | 2 |
| 1996–97 | Swansea C | 28 | 6 |
| 1997–98 | Swansea C | 1 | 0 |
| **Total:** | | **267** | **52** |

## MOLDOVAN, Viorel — Forward

H: 5 9 W: 11 08 b.Bistrita 8-7-72

*Honours:* Romania 27 full caps, 16 goals.

| | | | |
|---|---|---|---|
| 1990–91 | Gloria | 30 | 9 |
| 1991–92 | Gloria | 26 | 6 |
| 1992–93 | Gloria | 28 | 7 |
| 1993–94 | Dynamo Bucharest | 29 | 9 |
| 1994–95 | Dynamo Bucharest | 31 | 10 |
| 1995–96 | Neuchatel Xamax | 32 | 19 |
| 1996–97 | Grasshoppers | 32 | 27 |
| 1997–98 | Grasshoppers | 19 | 17 |
| 1997–98 | Coventry C | 10 | 1 |
| **Total:** | | **237** | **105** |

## MOLENAAR, Robert — Defender

H: 6 2 W: 14 04 b.Zaamdam 27-2-69

| | | | |
|---|---|---|---|
| 1992–93 | Volendam | 28 | 2 |
| 1993–94 | Volendam | 27 | 1 |
| 1994–95 | Volendam | 31 | 0 |
| 1995–96 | Volendam | 21 | 0 |
| 1996–97 | Volendam | 17 | 0 |
| 1996–97 | Leeds U | 12 | 1 |
| 1997–98 | Leeds U | 22 | 2 |
| **Total:** | | **158** | **6** |

## MONCRIEFFE, Prince — Forward

H: 5 9 W: 11 00 b.Manchester 27-2-77

*Source:* Hyde U.

| | | | |
|---|---|---|---|
| 1997–98 | Doncaster R | 38 | 8 |
| **Total:** | | **38** | **8** |

## MONCUR, John — Midfield

H: 5 7 W: 9 10 b.Stepney 22-9-66

*Source:* Apprentice.

| | | | |
|---|---|---|---|
| 1984–85 | Tottenham H | 0 | 0 |
| 1985–86 | Tottenham H | 0 | 0 |
| 1986–87 | Tottenham H | 1 | 0 |
| 1986–87 | Cambridge U (loan) | 4 | 0 |
| 1986–87 | Doncaster R (loan) | 4 | 0 |
| 1987–88 | Tottenham H | 5 | 0 |
| 1988–89 | Tottenham H | 1 | 0 |
| 1988–89 | Portsmouth (loan) | 7 | 0 |
| 1989–90 | Tottenham H | 5 | 1 |
| 1989–90 | Brentford (loan) | 5 | 1 |
| 1990–91 | Tottenham H | 9 | 0 |
| 1991–92 | Ipswich T (loan) | 6 | 0 |
| 1991–92 | Nottingham F (loan) | 0 | 0 |
| 1991–92 | Swindon T | 3 | 0 |
| 1992–93 | Swindon T | 14 | 1 |
| 1993–94 | Swindon T | 41 | 4 |
| 1994–95 | West Ham U | 30 | 2 |
| 1995–96 | West Ham U | 20 | 0 |
| 1996–97 | West Ham U | 27 | 2 |
| 1997–98 | West Ham U | 20 | 1 |
| **Total:** | | **202** | **12** |

## MONINGTON, Mark — Defender

H: 6 1 W: 14 02 b.Bilsthorpe 21-10-70

*Source:* School.

| | | | |
|---|---|---|---|
| 1988–89 | Burnley | 8 | 1 |
| 1989–90 | Burnley | 13 | 0 |
| 1990–91 | Burnley | 0 | 0 |
| 1991–92 | Burnley | 12 | 1 |
| 1992–93 | Burnley | 31 | 2 |
| 1993–94 | Burnley | 20 | 1 |
| 1994–95 | Burnley | 0 | 0 |
| 1994–95 | Rotherham U | 25 | 2 |
| 1995–96 | Rotherham U | 11 | 0 |
| 1996–97 | Rotherham U | 28 | 0 |
| 1997–98 | Rotherham U | 15 | 1 |
| **Total:** | | **163** | **8** |

## MONK, Gary — Defender

H: 6 0 W: 13 00 b.Bedford 6-3-79

*Source:* Trainee.

| | | | |
|---|---|---|---|
| 1995–96 | Torquay U | 5 | 0 |
| 1996–97 | Southampton | 0 | 0 |
| 1997–98 | Southampton | 0 | 0 |
| **Total:** | | **5** | **0** |

## MONKOU, Ken — Defender

H: 6 3 W: 14 07 b.Surinam 29-11-64

*Source:* Feyenoord. *Honours:* Holland Under-21.

| | | | |
|---|---|---|---|
| 1988–89 | Chelsea | 2 | 0 |
| 1989–90 | Chelsea | 34 | 1 |
| 1990–91 | Chelsea | 27 | 1 |
| 1991–92 | Chelsea | 31 | 0 |
| 1992–93 | Chelsea | 0 | 0 |
| 1992–93 | Southampton | 33 | 1 |
| 1993–94 | Southampton | 35 | 4 |
| 1994–95 | Southampton | 31 | 1 |
| 1995–96 | Southampton | 32 | 2 |
| 1996–97 | Southampton | 13 | 0 |
| 1997–98 | Southampton | 32 | 1 |
| **Total:** | | **270** | **11** |

## MONTGOMERIE, Ray — Defender

H: 5 8 W: 11 07 b.Irvine 17-4-61

*Source:* Saltcoats Vic.

| | | | |
|---|---|---|---|
| 1980–81 | Newcastle U | 0 | 0 |
| 1981–82 | Dumbarton | 20 | 5 |
| 1982–83 | Dumbarton | 25 | 2 |
| 1983–84 | Dumbarton | 39 | 1 |
| 1984–85 | Dumbarton | 6 | 0 |
| 1985–86 | Dumbarton | 24 | 0 |
| 1986–87 | Dumbarton | 35 | 0 |
| 1987–88 | Dumbarton | 31 | 0 |
| 1988–89 | Kilmarnock | 31 | 2 |
| 1989–90 | Kilmarnock | 35 | 3 |
| 1990–91 | Kilmarnock | 37 | 0 |
| 1991–92 | Kilmarnock | 30 | 1 |
| 1992–93 | Kilmarnock | 42 | 0 |
| 1993–94 | Kilmarnock | 42 | 0 |
| 1994–95 | Kilmarnock | 12 | 0 |
| 1995–96 | Kilmarnock | 14 | 0 |
| 1996–97 | Kilmarnock | 21 | 1 |
| 1997–98 | Kilmarnock | 27 | 0 |
| **Total:** | | **471** | **15** |

## MOODY, Paul
Forward

H: 6 3 W: 14 08 b.Portsmouth 13-6-67

*Source:* Waterlooville.

| | | | |
|---|---|---|---|
| 1991–92 | Southampton | 4 | 0 |
| 1992–93 | Southampton | 3 | 0 |
| 1992–93 | Reading (loan) | 5 | 1 |
| 1993–94 | Southampton | 5 | 0 |
| 1993–94 | Oxford U | 15 | 8 |
| 1994–95 | Oxford U | 41 | 20 |
| 1995–96 | Oxford U | 42 | 17 |
| 1996–97 | Oxford U | 38 | 4 |
| 1997–98 | Fulham | 33 | 15 |
| **Total:** | | **186** | **65** |

## MOONEY, Gerard
Defender

H: 5 9 W: 11 00 b.Glasgow 28-8-80

*Source:* Trainee.

| | | | |
|---|---|---|---|
| 1997–98 | Coventry C | 0 | 0 |

## MOONEY, Tommy
Defender

H: 5 9 W: 12 10 b.Teesside North 11-8-71

*Source:* Trainee.

| | | | |
|---|---|---|---|
| 1989–90 | Aston Villa | 0 | 0 |
| 1990–91 | Scarborough | 27 | 13 |
| 1991–92 | Scarborough | 40 | 8 |
| 1992–93 | Scarborough | 40 | 9 |
| 1993–94 | Southend U | 14 | 5 |
| 1993–94 | Watford (loan) | 10 | 2 |
| 1994–95 | Watford | 29 | 3 |
| 1995–96 | Watford | 42 | 6 |
| 1996–97 | Watford | 37 | 13 |
| 1997–98 | Watford | 45 | 6 |
| **Total:** | | **284** | **65** |

## MOORE, Alan
Midfield

H: 5 9 W: 11 06 b.Dublin 25-11-74

*Source:* Rivermount. *Honours:* Eire Under-21, 8 full caps.

| | | | |
|---|---|---|---|
| 1991–92 | Middlesbrough | 0 | 0 |
| 1992–93 | Middlesbrough | 2 | 0 |
| 1993–94 | Middlesbrough | 42 | 10 |
| 1994–95 | Middlesbrough | 37 | 4 |
| 1995–96 | Middlesbrough | 12 | 0 |
| 1996–97 | Middlesbrough | 17 | 0 |
| 1997–98 | Middlesbrough | 4 | 0 |
| **Total:** | | **114** | **14** |

## MOORE, Allan
Forward

H: 5 7 W: 10 00 b.Glasgow 25-12-64

*Source:* Possil YM.

| | | | |
|---|---|---|---|
| 1983–84 | Dumbarton | 4 | 0 |
| 1984–85 | Dumbarton | 4 | 0 |
| 1985–86 | Dumbarton | 33 | 4 |
| 1986–87 | Dumbarton | 18 | 3 |
| 1986–87 | Hearts | 10 | 0 |
| 1987–88 | Hearts | 7 | 1 |
| 1988–89 | Hearts | 12 | 2 |
| 1989–90 | St Johnstone | 33 | 13 |
| 1990–91 | St Johnstone | 31 | 5 |
| 1991–92 | St Johnstone | 21 | 1 |
| 1992–93 | St Johnstone | 26 | 3 |
| 1993–94 | St Johnstone | 13 | 1 |
| 1993–94 | Dunfermline Ath | 8 | 0 |
| 1994–95 | Dunfermline Ath | 12 | 1 |
| 1995–96 | Dunfermline Ath | 28 | 5 |
| 1996–97 | Dunfermline Ath | 26 | 3 |
| 1997–98 | Dunfermline Ath | 22 | 0 |
| **Total:** | | **308** | **42** |

## MOORE, Craig
Defender

H: 6 1 W: 12 00 b.Canterbury, Australia 12-12-75

*Source:* Australian Institute of Sport.

| | | | |
|---|---|---|---|
| 1993–94 | Rangers | 1 | 0 |
| 1994–95 | Rangers | 21 | 2 |
| 1995–96 | Rangers | 11 | 1 |
| 1996–97 | Rangers | 23 | 1 |
| 1997–98 | Rangers | 10 | 0 |
| **Total:** | | **66** | **4** |

## MOORE, Darren
Defender

H: 6 3 W: 15 08 b.Birmingham 22-4-74

*Source:* Trainee.

| | | | |
|---|---|---|---|
| 1991–92 | Torquay U | 5 | 1 |
| 1992–93 | Torquay U | 31 | 2 |
| 1993–94 | Torquay U | 37 | 2 |
| 1994–95 | Torquay U | 30 | 3 |
| 1995–96 | Doncaster R | 35 | 2 |
| 1996–97 | Doncaster R | 41 | 5 |
| 1997–98 | Bradford C | 18 | 0 |
| **Total:** | | **197** | **15** |

## MOORE, Ian
Forward

H: 5 11 W: 12 02 b.Birkenhead 26-8-76

*Source:* Trainee. *Honours:* England Youth, Under-21.

| | | | |
|---|---|---|---|
| 1994–95 | Tranmere R | 1 | 0 |
| 1995–96 | Tranmere R | 36 | 9 |
| 1996–97 | Tranmere R | 21 | 3 |

| | | | |
|---|---|---|---|
| 1996–97 | Bradford C (loan) | 6 | 0 |
| 1996–97 | Nottingham F | 5 | 0 |
| 1997–98 | Nottingham F | 10 | 1 |
| 1997–98 | West Ham U (loan) | 1 | 0 |
| **Total:** | | **80** | **13** |

## MOORE, Jason — Defender

H: 5 8 W: 11 04 b.Dover 16-2-79

*Source:* Trainee.

| | | | |
|---|---|---|---|
| 1995–96 | West Ham U | 0 | 0 |
| 1996–97 | West Ham U | 0 | 0 |
| 1997–98 | West Ham U | 0 | 0 |

## MOORE, Mark — Midfield

b.Bradford 9-7-72

| | | | |
|---|---|---|---|
| 1997–98 | Cambridge U | 1 | 0 |
| **Total:** | | **1** | **0** |

## MOORE, Neil — Defender

H: 6 1 W: 12 07 b.Liverpool 21-9-72

*Source:* Trainee.

| | | | |
|---|---|---|---|
| 1991–92 | Everton | 0 | 0 |
| 1992–93 | Everton | 1 | 0 |
| 1993–94 | Everton | 4 | 0 |
| 1994–95 | Everton | 0 | 0 |
| 1994–95 | Blackpool (loan) | 7 | 0 |
| 1994–95 | Oldham Ath (loan) | 5 | 0 |
| 1995–96 | Everton | 0 | 0 |
| 1995–96 | Carlisle U (loan) | 13 | 0 |
| 1995–96 | Rotherham U (loan) | 11 | 0 |
| 1996–97 | Everton | 0 | 0 |
| 1996–97 | Norwich C | 2 | 0 |
| 1997–98 | Burnley | 40 | 3 |
| **Total:** | | **83** | **3** |

## MOORE, Richard — Midfield

b.Scunthorpe 2-9-77

| | | | |
|---|---|---|---|
| 1997–98 | Birmingham C | 0 | 0 |

## MORALEE, Jamie — Forward

H: 5 11 W: 11 00 b.Wandsworth 2-12-71

*Source:* Trainee.

| | | | |
|---|---|---|---|
| 1989–90 | Crystal Palace | 0 | 0 |
| 1990–91 | Crystal Palace | 0 | 0 |
| 1991–92 | Crystal Palace | 6 | 0 |
| 1992–93 | Crystal Palace | 0 | 0 |
| 1992–93 | Millwall | 37 | 15 |
| 1993–94 | Millwall | 30 | 4 |
| 1994–95 | Watford | 24 | 4 |
| 1995–96 | Watford | 25 | 3 |
| 1996–97 | Crewe Alex | 7 | 0 |
| 1997–98 | Crewe Alex | 9 | 0 |
| **Total:** | | **138** | **26** |

## MORAN, Andy — Forward

H: 5 11 W: 11 03 b.Wigan 7-10-79

*Source:* Trainee.

| | | | |
|---|---|---|---|
| 1997–98 | Tranmere R | 0 | 0 |

## MOREIRA, Fabio — Defender

H: 5 10 W: 11 06 b.Rio 14-3-72

*Source:* Chaves.

| | | | |
|---|---|---|---|
| 1996–97 | Middlesbrough | 0 | 0 |
| 1997–98 | Middlesbrough | 1 | 0 |
| **Total:** | | **1** | **0** |

## MOREIRA, Joao — Defender

H: 6 2 W: 13 00 b.Angola 30-6-70

*Source:* Benfica.

| | | | |
|---|---|---|---|
| 1996–97 | Swansea C | 10 | 0 |
| 1997–98 | Swansea C | 5 | 0 |
| **Total:** | | **15** | **0** |

## MORENO, Jaime — Forward

H: 5 9 W: 11 09 b.Bolivia 19-1-74

*Source:* Blooming. *Honours:* Bolivia full caps.

| | | | |
|---|---|---|---|
| 1994–95 | Middlesbrough | 14 | 1 |
| 1995–96 | Middlesbrough | 7 | 0 |
| From Washington D. | | | |
| 1997–98 | Middlesbrough | 5 | 1 |
| **Total:** | | **26** | **2** |

## MORGAN, Alan — Defender

H: 5 10 W: 11 00 b.Aberystwyth 2-11-73

*Source:* Trainee. *Honours:* Wales Under-21.

| | | | |
|---|---|---|---|
| 1991–92 | Tranmere R | 0 | 0 |
| 1992–93 | Tranmere R | 0 | 0 |
| 1993–94 | Tranmere R | 0 | 0 |
| 1994–95 | Tranmere R | 0 | 0 |
| 1995–96 | Tranmere R | 4 | 1 |
| 1996–97 | Tranmere R | 1 | 0 |
| 1997–98 | Tranmere R | 19 | 0 |
| **Total:** | | **24** | **1** |

## MORGAN, Chris — Defender

H: 5 10 W: 12 09 b.Barnsley 9-11-77

*Source:* Trainee.

| | | | |
|---|---|---|---|
| 1996–97 | Barnsley | 0 | 0 |
| 1997–98 | Barnsley | 11 | 0 |
| **Total:** | | **11** | **0** |

## MORGAN, Paul — Forward

H: 6 0 W: 11 03 b.Belfast 23-10-78

*Source:* Trainee.

| | | | |
|---|---|---|---|
| 1997–98 | Preston NE | 0 | 0 |

## MORGAN, Phil — Goalkeeper

H: 6 2 W: 14 01 b.Stoke 18-12-74

*Source:* Trainee. *Honours:* England Schools.

| | | | |
|---|---|---|---|
| 1993–94 | Ipswich T | 0 | 0 |
| 1994–95 | Ipswich T | 1 | 0 |
| 1995–96 | Ipswich T | 0 | 0 |
| 1995–96 | Stoke C | 0 | 0 |
| 1996–97 | Stoke C | 0 | 0 |
| 1996–97 | Chesterfield (loan) | 2 | 0 |
| 1997–98 | Stoke C | 0 | 0 |
| **Total:** | | **3** | **0** |

## MORGAN, Ryan — Midfield

H: 6 1 W: 12 07 b.Bristol 12-7-78

*Source:* Trainee.

| | | | |
|---|---|---|---|
| 1996–97 | Bristol R | 1 | 0 |
| 1997–98 | Bristol R | 0 | 0 |
| **Total:** | | **1** | **0** |

## MORGAN, Simon — Defender

H: 5 10 W: 12 05 b.Birmingham 5-9-66

*Source:* Trainee. *Honours:* England Under-21.

| | | | |
|---|---|---|---|
| 1984–85 | Leicester C | 0 | 0 |
| 1985–86 | Leicester C | 30 | 0 |
| 1986–87 | Leicester C | 41 | 1 |
| 1987–88 | Leicester C | 40 | 0 |
| 1988–89 | Leicester C | 32 | 0 |
| 1989–90 | Leicester C | 17 | 2 |
| 1990–91 | Leicester C | 0 | 0 |
| 1990–91 | Fulham | 32 | 0 |
| 1991–92 | Fulham | 36 | 3 |
| 1992–93 | Fulham | 39 | 8 |
| 1993–94 | Fulham | 37 | 6 |
| 1994–95 | Fulham | 42 | 11 |
| 1995–96 | Fulham | 41 | 6 |
| 1996–97 | Fulham | 44 | 8 |
| 1997–98 | Fulham | 19 | 1 |
| **Total:** | | **450** | **46** |

## MORGAN, Steve — Defender

H: 6 0 W: 11 00 b.Oldham 19-9-68

*Source:* Apprentice. *Honours:* England Youth.

| | | | |
|---|---|---|---|
| 1985–86 | Blackpool | 5 | 0 |
| 1986–87 | Blackpool | 11 | 0 |
| 1987–88 | Blackpool | 46 | 6 |
| 1988–89 | Blackpool | 44 | 3 |
| 1989–90 | Blackpool | 38 | 1 |
| 1990–91 | Plymouth Arg | 40 | 3 |
| 1991–92 | Plymouth Arg | 45 | 2 |
| 1992–93 | Plymouth Arg | 36 | 1 |
| 1993–94 | Coventry C | 40 | 2 |
| 1994–95 | Coventry C | 28 | 0 |
| 1995–96 | Coventry C | 0 | 0 |
| 1995–96 | Bristol R (loan) | 5 | 0 |
| 1996–97 | Wigan Ath | 23 | 1 |
| 1997–98 | Wigan Ath | 13 | 1 |
| 1997–98 | Bury (loan) | 5 | 0 |
| **Total:** | | **379** | **20** |

## MORLEY, Ben — Defender

b.Hull 20-12-80

*Source:* Trainee.

| | | | |
|---|---|---|---|
| 1997–98 | Hull C | 8 | 0 |
| **Total:** | | **8** | **0** |

## MORLEY, David — Defender

b.St Helens 25-9-77

*Source:* Trainee.

| | | | |
|---|---|---|---|
| 1995–96 | Manchester C | 0 | 0 |
| 1996–97 | Manchester C | 0 | 0 |
| 1997–98 | Manchester C | 3 | 1 |
| 1997–98 | Ayr U (loan) | 4 | 0 |
| **Total:** | | **7** | **1** |

## MORLEY, Neil — Midfield

H: 5 8 W: 10 02 b.Warrington 16-11-78

*Source:* Trainee.

| | | | |
|---|---|---|---|
| 1996–97 | Manchester C | 0 | 0 |
| 1997–98 | Manchester C | 0 | 0 |

## MORLEY, Trevor — Forward

H: 5 11 W: 12 01 b.Nottingham 20-3-61

*Source:* Derby Co, Corby T, Nuneaton Bor.

| | | | |
|---|---|---|---|
| 1985–86 | Northampton T | 43 | 13 |
| 1986–87 | Northampton T | 37 | 16 |
| 1987–88 | Northampton T | 27 | 10 |
| 1987–88 | Manchester C | 15 | 4 |
| 1988–89 | Manchester C | 40 | 12 |
| 1989–90 | Manchester C | 17 | 2 |
| 1989–90 | West Ham U | 19 | 10 |
| 1990–91 | West Ham U | 38 | 12 |
| 1991–92 | West Ham U | 24 | 2 |
| 1992 | Brann | 8 | 4 |
| 1992–93 | West Ham U | 41 | 20 |
| 1993 | Brann | 6 | 1 |
| 1993–94 | West Ham U | 42 | 13 |
| 1994–95 | West Ham U | 14 | 0 |
| 1995 | Brann | 7 | 4 |
| 1995–96 | Reading | 17 | 4 |
| 1996–97 | Reading | 37 | 22 |
| 1997–98 | Reading | 23 | 5 |
| **Total:** | | **455** | **154** |

## MORRIS, Andy — Forward

H: 6 4 W: 14 07 b.Sheffield 17-11-67

*Source:* School.

| | | | |
|---|---|---|---|
| 1984–85 | Rotherham U | 1 | 0 |
| 1985–86 | Rotherham U | 0 | 0 |
| 1986–87 | Rotherham U | 6 | 0 |
| 1987–88 | Rotherham U | 0 | 0 |
| 1987–88 | Chesterfield | 10 | 0 |
| 1988–89 | Chesterfield | 42 | 9 |
| 1989–90 | Chesterfield | 43 | 4 |
| 1990–91 | Chesterfield | 15 | 4 |
| 1991–92 | Chesterfield | 8 | 2 |
| 1991–92 | Exeter C (loan) | 7 | 2 |
| 1992–93 | Chesterfield | 40 | 10 |
| 1993–94 | Chesterfield | 34 | 11 |
| 1994–95 | Chesterfield | 26 | 6 |
| 1995–96 | Chesterfield | 16 | 5 |
| 1996–97 | Chesterfield | 27 | 4 |
| 1997–98 | Chesterfield | 4 | 1 |
| **Total:** | | **279** | **58** |

## MORRIS, Jody — Midfield

H: 5 5 W: 10 11 b.Hammersmith 22-12-78

*Source:* Trainee. *Honours:* England Schools, Youth, Under-21.

| | | | |
|---|---|---|---|
| 1995–96 | Chelsea | 1 | 0 |
| 1996–97 | Chelsea | 12 | 0 |
| 1997–98 | Chelsea | 12 | 1 |
| **Total:** | | **25** | **1** |

## MORRIS, Lee — Midfield

H: 5 10 W: 10 07 b.Blackpool 30-4-80

*Source:* Trainee. *Honours:* England Youth.

| | | | |
|---|---|---|---|
| 1997–98 | Sheffield U | 5 | 0 |
| **Total:** | | **5** | **0** |

## MORRIS, Mark — Defender

H: 6 2 W: 14 00 b.Carshalton 26-9-62

*Source:* Apprentice.

| | | | |
|---|---|---|---|
| 1980–81 | Wimbledon | 0 | 0 |
| 1981–82 | Wimbledon | 33 | 1 |
| 1982–83 | Wimbledon | 26 | 3 |
| 1983–84 | Wimbledon | 39 | 3 |
| 1984–85 | Wimbledon | 29 | 1 |
| 1985–86 | Wimbledon | 20 | 1 |
| 1985–86 | Aldershot (loan) | 14 | 0 |
| 1986–87 | Wimbledon | 21 | 0 |
| 1987–88 | Watford | 39 | 1 |
| 1988–89 | Watford | 2 | 0 |
| 1989–90 | Sheffield U | 42 | 3 |
| 1990–91 | Sheffield U | 14 | 0 |
| 1991–92 | Bournemouth | 43 | 3 |
| 1992–93 | Bournemouth | 43 | 1 |
| 1993–94 | Bournemouth | 38 | 0 |
| 1994–95 | Bournemouth | 38 | 3 |
| 1995–96 | Bournemouth | 31 | 1 |
| 1996–97 | Bournemouth | 1 | 0 |
| 1996–97 | Gillingham (loan) | 6 | 0 |
| 1996–97 | Brighton & HA | 12 | 1 |
| 1997–98 | Brighton & HA | 19 | 1 |
| **Total:** | | **510** | **23** |

## MORRIS, Rob — Defender

H: 5 10 W: 11 12 b.Oswestry 4-9-78

*Source:* From Trainee.

| | | | |
|---|---|---|---|
| 1997–98 | Wrexham | 0 | 0 |

## MORRIS, Steve — Forward

H: 5 10 W: 12 00 b.Liverpool 13-5-76

*Source:* Liverpool Trainee.

| | | | |
|---|---|---|---|
| 1994–95 | Wrexham | 12 | 2 |
| 1995–96 | Wrexham | 13 | 3 |
| 1996–97 | Wrexham | 17 | 4 |
| 1997–98 | Wrexham | 0 | 0 |
| 1997–98 | Rochdale (loan) | 0 | 0 |
| **Total:** | | **42** | **9** |

## MORRISON, Andy — Defender

H: 5 11 W: 15 06 b.Inverness 30-7-70

*Source:* Trainee.

| | | | |
|---|---|---|---|
| 1987–88 | Plymouth Arg | 1 | 0 |
| 1988–89 | Plymouth Arg | 2 | 0 |
| 1989–90 | Plymouth Arg | 19 | 1 |
| 1990–91 | Plymouth Arg | 32 | 2 |
| 1991–92 | Plymouth Arg | 30 | 3 |
| 1992–93 | Plymouth Arg | 29 | 0 |
| 1993–94 | Blackburn R | 5 | 0 |
| 1994–95 | Blackburn R | 0 | 0 |
| 1994–95 | Blackpool | 18 | 0 |
| 1995–96 | Blackpool | 29 | 3 |
| 1996–97 | Huddersfield T | 10 | 1 |
| 1997–98 | Huddersfield T | 23 | 1 |
| **Total:** | | **198** | **11** |

## MORRISON, Clinton — Forward

H: 6 1 W: 11 02 b.Tooting 14-5-79

*Source:* Trainee.

| | | | |
|---|---|---|---|
| 1996–97 | Crystal Palace | 0 | 0 |
| 1997–98 | Crystal Palace | 1 | 1 |
| **Total:** | | **1** | **1** |

## MORRISON, Dave — Midfield

H: 5 11 W: 12 10 b.Waltham Forest 30-11-74

*Source:* Chelmsford C.

| | | | |
|---|---|---|---|
| 1993–94 | Peterborough U | 0 | 0 |
| 1994–95 | Peterborough U | 42 | 8 |
| 1995–96 | Peterborough U | 24 | 2 |
| 1996–97 | Peterborough U | 11 | 2 |
| 1996–97 | Leyton Orient | 8 | 0 |
| 1997–98 | Leyton Orient | 2 | 0 |
| **Total:** | | **87** | **12** |

## MORRISSEY, John — Forward

H: 5 8 W: 11 09 b.Liverpool 8-3-65

*Source:* Apprentice. *Honours:* England Youth.

| | | | |
|---|---|---|---|
| 1982–83 | Everton | 0 | 0 |
| 1983–84 | Everton | 0 | 0 |
| 1984–85 | Everton | 1 | 0 |
| 1985–86 | Wolverhampton W | 10 | 1 |
| 1985–86 | Tranmere R | 32 | 5 |
| 1986–87 | Tranmere R | 38 | 7 |
| 1987–88 | Tranmere R | 39 | 4 |
| 1988–89 | Tranmere R | 42 | 4 |
| 1989–90 | Tranmere R | 27 | 4 |
| 1990–91 | Tranmere R | 40 | 9 |
| 1991–92 | Tranmere R | 40 | 5 |
| 1992–93 | Tranmere R | 43 | 5 |
| 1993–94 | Tranmere R | 25 | 1 |
| 1994–95 | Tranmere R | 36 | 3 |
| 1995–96 | Tranmere R | 16 | 0 |
| 1996–97 | Tranmere R | 31 | 1 |
| 1997–98 | Tranmere R | 37 | 2 |
| **Total:** | | **457** | **51** |

## MORROW, Steve — Defender

H: 6 0 W: 11 03 b.Bangor 2-7-70

*Source:* Trainee. *Honours:* Northern Ireland Youth, Under-23, 32 full caps, 1 goal.

| | | | |
|---|---|---|---|
| 1987–88 | Arsenal | 0 | 0 |
| 1988–89 | Arsenal | 0 | 0 |
| 1989–90 | Arsenal | 0 | 0 |
| 1990–91 | Reading (loan) | 10 | 0 |
| 1991–92 | Arsenal | 2 | 0 |
| 1991–92 | Watford (loan) | 8 | 0 |
| 1991–92 | Reading (loan) | 3 | 0 |
| 1991–92 | Barnet (loan) | 1 | 0 |
| 1992–93 | Arsenal | 16 | 0 |
| 1993–94 | Arsenal | 11 | 0 |
| 1994–95 | Arsenal | 15 | 1 |
| 1995–96 | Arsenal | 4 | 0 |
| 1996–97 | Arsenal | 14 | 0 |
| 1996–97 | QPR | 5 | 1 |
| 1997–98 | QPR | 31 | 1 |
| **Total:** | | **120** | **3** |

## MORSE, Peter — Midfield

b.Stoke 5-3-79

*Source:* Trainee.

| | | | |
|---|---|---|---|
| 1997–98 | Crewe Alex | 0 | 0 |

## MORTIMER, Paul — Midfield

H: 5 11 W: 12 07 b.Kensington 8-5-68

*Source:* Fulham Apprentice. *Honours:* England Under-21.

| | | | |
|---|---|---|---|
| 1987–88 | Charlton Ath | 12 | 0 |
| 1988–89 | Charlton Ath | 33 | 5 |
| 1989–90 | Charlton Ath | 36 | 5 |
| 1990–91 | Charlton Ath | 32 | 7 |
| 1991–92 | Aston Villa | 12 | 1 |
| 1991–92 | Crystal Palace | 21 | 2 |
| 1992–93 | Crystal Palace | 1 | 0 |
| 1992–93 | Brentford (loan) | 6 | 0 |
| 1993–94 | Crystal Palace | 0 | 0 |
| 1994–95 | Charlton Ath | 26 | 4 |
| 1995–96 | Charlton Ath | 19 | 5 |
| 1996–97 | Charlton Ath | 11 | 1 |
| 1997–98 | Charlton Ath | 13 | 4 |
| **Total:** | | **222** | **34** |

## MOSES, Adrian — Defender

H: 5 10 W: 12 02 b.Doncaster 4-5-75

*Source:* School. *Honours:* England Under-21.

| Season | Club | | |
|---|---|---|---|
| 1993–94 | Barnsley | 0 | 0 |
| 1994–95 | Barnsley | 4 | 0 |
| 1995–96 | Barnsley | 24 | 1 |
| 1996–97 | Barnsley | 28 | 2 |
| 1997–98 | Barnsley | 35 | 0 |
| **Total:** | | **91** | **3** |

## MOSS, Neil — Goalkeeper

H: 6 2 W: 13 00 b.New Milton 10-5-75

*Source:* Trainee.

| Season | Club | | |
|---|---|---|---|
| 1992–93 | Bournemouth | 1 | 0 |
| 1993–94 | Bournemouth | 6 | 0 |
| 1994–95 | Bournemouth | 8 | 0 |
| 1995–96 | Bournemouth | 7 | 0 |
| 1995–96 | Southampton | 0 | 0 |
| 1996–97 | Southampton | 3 | 0 |
| 1997–98 | Southampton | 0 | 0 |
| 1997–98 | Gillingham (loan) | 10 | 0 |
| **Total:** | | **35** | **0** |

## MOUNTFIELD, Derek — Defender

H: 6 1 W: 13 08 b.Liverpool 2-11-62

*Source:* Apprentice. *Honours:* England Under-21, B.

| Season | Club | | |
|---|---|---|---|
| 1980–81 | Tranmere R | 5 | 0 |
| 1981–82 | Tranmere R | 21 | 1 |
| 1982–83 | Everton | 1 | 0 |
| 1983–84 | Everton | 31 | 3 |
| 1984–85 | Everton | 37 | 10 |
| 1985–86 | Everton | 15 | 3 |
| 1986–87 | Everton | 13 | 3 |
| 1987–88 | Everton | 9 | 0 |
| 1988–89 | Aston Villa | 24 | 1 |
| 1989–90 | Aston Villa | 32 | 4 |
| 1990–91 | Aston Villa | 32 | 4 |
| 1991–92 | Aston Villa | 2 | 0 |
| 1991–92 | Wolverhampton W | 28 | 1 |
| 1992–93 | Wolverhampton W | 36 | 2 |
| 1993–94 | Wolverhampton W | 19 | 1 |
| 1994–95 | Carlisle U | 31 | 3 |
| 1995–96 | Carlisle U | 0 | 0 |
| 1995–96 | Northampton T | 4 | 0 |
| 1995–96 | Walsall | 28 | 1 |
| 1996–97 | Walsall | 42 | 0 |
| 1997–98 | Walsall | 27 | 1 |
| **Total:** | | **437** | **38** |

## MOWBRAY, Tony — Defender

H: 6 1 W: 13 00 b.Saltburn 22-11-63

*Source:* Apprentice. *Honours:* England B.

| Season | Club | | |
|---|---|---|---|
| 1981–82 | Middlesbrough | 0 | 0 |
| 1982–83 | Middlesbrough | 26 | 0 |
| 1983–84 | Middlesbrough | 35 | 1 |
| 1984–85 | Middlesbrough | 40 | 2 |
| 1985–86 | Middlesbrough | 35 | 4 |
| 1986–87 | Middlesbrough | 46 | 7 |
| 1987–88 | Middlesbrough | 44 | 3 |
| 1988–89 | Middlesbrough | 37 | 3 |
| 1989–90 | Middlesbrough | 28 | 2 |
| 1990–91 | Middlesbrough | 40 | 3 |
| 1991–92 | Middlesbrough | 17 | 0 |
| 1991–92 | Celtic | 15 | 2 |
| 1992–93 | Celtic | 26 | 2 |
| 1993–94 | Celtic | 22 | 1 |
| 1994–95 | Celtic | 15 | 1 |
| 1995–96 | Ipswich T | 19 | 2 |
| 1996–97 | Ipswich T | 8 | 0 |
| 1997–98 | Ipswich T | 25 | 0 |
| **Total:** | | **478** | **33** |

## MOYES, David — Defender

H: 6 1 W: 12 12 b.Glasgow 25-4-63

*Source:* Drumchapel Amateur.

| Season | Club | | |
|---|---|---|---|
| 1980–81 | Celtic | 0 | 0 |
| 1981–82 | Celtic | 19 | 0 |
| 1982–83 | Celtic | 5 | 0 |
| 1983–84 | Celtic | 0 | 0 |
| 1983–84 | Cambridge U | 30 | 0 |
| 1984–85 | Cambridge U | 40 | 1 |
| 1985–86 | Cambridge U | 9 | 0 |
| 1985–86 | Bristol C | 27 | 2 |
| 1986–87 | Bristol C | 41 | 3 |
| 1987–88 | Bristol C | 15 | 1 |
| 1987–88 | Shrewsbury T | 17 | 2 |
| 1988–89 | Shrewsbury T | 33 | 1 |
| 1989–90 | Shrewsbury T | 46 | 8 |
| 1990–91 | Dunfermline Ath | 35 | 7 |
| 1991–92 | Dunfermline Ath | 39 | 5 |
| 1992–93 | Dunfermline Ath | 30 | 1 |
| 1993–94 | Dunfermline Ath | 1 | 0 |
| 1993–94 | Hamilton A | 5 | 0 |
| 1993–94 | Preston NE | 29 | 4 |
| 1994–95 | Preston NE | 38 | 4 |
| 1995–96 | Preston NE | 41 | 3 |
| 1996–97 | Preston NE | 26 | 4 |
| 1997–98 | Preston NE | 9 | 0 |
| **Total:** | | **535** | **46** |

## MUGGLETON, Carl — Goalkeeper

H: 6 2 W: 13 03 b.Leicester 13-9-68

*Source:* Apprentice. *Honours:* England Under-21.

| | | | |
|---|---|---|---|
| 1986–87 | Leicester C | 0 | 0 |
| 1987–88 | Leicester C | 0 | 0 |
| 1987–88 | Chesterfield (loan) | 17 | 0 |
| 1987–88 | Blackpool (loan) | 2 | 0 |
| 1988–89 | Leicester C | 3 | 0 |
| 1988–89 | Hartlepool U (loan) | 8 | 0 |
| 1989–90 | Leicester C | 0 | 0 |
| 1989–90 | Stockport Co (loan) | 4 | 0 |
| 1990–91 | Leicester C | 22 | 0 |
| 1990–91 | Liverpool (loan) | 0 | 0 |
| 1991–92 | Leicester C | 4 | 0 |
| 1992–93 | Leicester C | 17 | 0 |
| 1993–94 | Leicester C | 0 | 0 |
| 1993–94 | Stoke C (loan) | 6 | 0 |
| 1993–94 | Sheffield U (loan) | 0 | 0 |
| 1993–94 | Celtic | 12 | 0 |
| 1994–95 | Stoke C | 24 | 0 |
| 1995–96 | Stoke C | 6 | 0 |
| 1995–96 | Rotherham U (loan) | 6 | 0 |
| 1995–96 | Sheffield U (loan) | 1 | 0 |
| 1996–97 | Stoke C | 33 | 0 |
| 1997–98 | Stoke C | 34 | 0 |
| **Total:** | | **199** | **0** |

## MULLIN, John — Forward

H: 6 0 W: 11 05 b.Bury 11-8-75

*Source:* School.

| | | | |
|---|---|---|---|
| 1992–93 | Burnley | 0 | 0 |
| 1993–94 | Burnley | 6 | 1 |
| 1994–95 | Burnley | 12 | 1 |
| 1995–96 | Sunderland | 10 | 1 |
| 1996–97 | Sunderland | 10 | 1 |
| 1997–98 | Sunderland | 6 | 0 |
| 1997–98 | Preston NE (loan) | 7 | 0 |
| 1997–98 | Burnley (loan) | 6 | 0 |
| **Total:** | | **57** | **4** |

## MULLINS, Hayden — Defender

H: 6 0 W: 11 12 b.Reading 27-3-79

*Source:* Trainee.

| | | | |
|---|---|---|---|
| 1996–97 | Crystal Palace | 0 | 0 |
| 1997–98 | Crystal Palace | 0 | 0 |

## MULRYNE, Philip — Midfield

H: 5 7 W: 10 11 b.Belfast 1-6-78

*Source:* Trainee. *Honours:* Northern Ireland Under-21, 5 full caps, 1 goal.

| | | | |
|---|---|---|---|
| 1994–95 | Manchester U | 0 | 0 |
| 1995–96 | Manchester U | 0 | 0 |
| 1996–97 | Manchester U | 0 | 0 |
| 1997–98 | Manchester U | 1 | 0 |
| **Total:** | | **1** | **0** |

## MUNDEE, Denny — Midfield

H: 5 10 W: 13 00 b.Swindon 10-10-68

*Source:* Apprentice.

| | | | |
|---|---|---|---|
| 1986–87 | QPR | 0 | 0 |
| 1986–87 | Swindon T | 0 | 0 |
| 1987–88 | Bournemouth | 0 | 0 |
| 1988–89 | Bournemouth | 2 | 0 |
| 1989–90 | Bournemouth | 10 | 0 |
| 1989–90 | Torquay U (loan) | 9 | 0 |
| 1990–91 | Bournemouth | 21 | 2 |
| 1991–92 | Bournemouth | 41 | 2 |
| 1992–93 | Bournemouth | 26 | 2 |
| 1993–94 | Brentford | 39 | 11 |
| 1994–95 | Brentford | 39 | 5 |
| 1995–96 | Brentford | 6 | 0 |
| 1995–96 | Brighton & HA | 32 | 3 |
| 1996–97 | Brighton & HA | 29 | 4 |
| 1997–98 | Brighton & HA | 0 | 0 |
| **Total:** | | **254** | **29** |

## MUNROE, Karl — Midfield

b.Manchester 23-9-79

*Source:* Trainee.

| | | | |
|---|---|---|---|
| 1997–98 | Swansea C | 1 | 0 |
| **Total:** | | **1** | **0** |

## MUNTASSER, Jehad — Midfield

H: 5 11 W: 12 05 b.Tripoli 26-7-78

*Source:* Atalanta, Prosesto.

| | | | |
|---|---|---|---|
| 1997–98 | Arsenal | 0 | 0 |
| 1997–98 | Bristol C | 0 | 0 |

## MURDOCK, Colin — Defender

H: 6 1 W: 12 00 b.Ballymena 2-7-75

*Source:* Trainee.

| | | | |
|---|---|---|---|
| 1992–93 | Manchester U | 0 | 0 |
| 1993–94 | Manchester U | 0 | 0 |
| 1994–95 | Manchester U | 0 | 0 |

| | | | |
|---|---|---|---|
| 1995–96 | Manchester U | 0 | 0 |
| 1996–97 | Manchester U | 0 | 0 |
| 1997–98 | Preston NE | 27 | 1 |
| **Total:** | | **27** | **1** |

## MURIE, David — Defender

H: 5 8 W: 10 04 b.Edinburgh 2-8-76

*Source:* Tynecastle BC.

| | | | |
|---|---|---|---|
| 1992–93 | Hearts | 0 | 0 |
| 1993–94 | Hearts | 0 | 0 |
| 1994–95 | Hearts | 0 | 0 |
| 1995–96 | Hearts | 0 | 0 |
| 1996–97 | Hearts | 7 | 0 |
| 1997–98 | Hearts | 1 | 0 |
| **Total:** | | **8** | **0** |

## MURPHY, Brendan — Goalkeeper

H: 5 11 W: 11 12 b.Wexford 19-8-75

*Source:* Bradford C Trainee. *Honours:* Eire Under-21.

| | | | |
|---|---|---|---|
| 1994–95 | Wimbledon | 0 | 0 |
| 1995–96 | Wimbledon | 0 | 0 |
| 1996–97 | Wimbledon | 0 | 0 |
| 1997–98 | Wimbledon | 0 | 0 |

## MURPHY, Danny — Midfield

H: 5 9 W: 10 08 b.Chester 18-3-77

*Source:* Trainee. *Honours:* England Schools, Youth, Under-21.

| | | | |
|---|---|---|---|
| 1993–94 | Crewe Alex | 12 | 2 |
| 1994–95 | Crewe Alex | 35 | 5 |
| 1995–96 | Crewe Alex | 42 | 10 |
| 1996–97 | Crewe Alex | 45 | 10 |
| 1997–98 | Liverpool | 16 | 0 |
| **Total:** | | **150** | **27** |

## MURPHY, Gerard — Midfield

b.Manchester 19-12-78

*Source:* Trainee.

| | | | |
|---|---|---|---|
| 1996–97 | Oldham Ath | 0 | 0 |
| 1997–98 | Oldham Ath | 0 | 0 |

## MURPHY, Jamie — Defender

H: 6 1 W: 13 00 b.Manchester 25-2-73

*Source:* Trainee.

| | | | |
|---|---|---|---|
| 1991–92 | Blackpool | 0 | 0 |
| 1992–93 | Blackpool | 33 | 0 |
| 1993–94 | Blackpool | 16 | 0 |
| 1994–95 | Blackpool | 6 | 1 |
| 1995–96 | Blackpool | 0 | 0 |
| 1995–96 | Doncaster R | 23 | 0 |
| 1996–97 | Doncaster R | 31 | 0 |
| 1997–98 | Cambridge U | 0 | 0 |
| **Total:** | | **109** | **1** |

## MURPHY, John — Forward

H: 6 3 W: 14 00 b.Whiston 18-10-76

*Source:* Trainee.

| | | | |
|---|---|---|---|
| 1994–95 | Chester C | 5 | 0 |
| 1995–96 | Chester C | 18 | 3 |
| 1996–97 | Chester C | 11 | 1 |
| 1997–98 | Chester C | 27 | 4 |
| **Total:** | | **61** | **8** |

## MURPHY, Leroy — Midfield

b.Birmingham 26-12-78

*Source:* Trainee.

| | | | |
|---|---|---|---|
| 1997–98 | Derby Co | 0 | 0 |

## MURPHY, Matt — Forward

H: 6 0 W: 12 01 b.Northampton 20-8-71

*Source:* Corby T.

| | | | |
|---|---|---|---|
| 1992–93 | Oxford U | 2 | 0 |
| 1993–94 | Oxford U | 0 | 0 |
| 1994–95 | Oxford U | 22 | 7 |
| 1995–96 | Oxford U | 34 | 5 |
| 1996–97 | Oxford U | 30 | 3 |
| 1997–98 | Oxford U | 29 | 2 |
| 1997–98 | Scunthorpe U (loan) | 3 | 0 |
| **Total:** | | **120** | **17** |

## MURPHY, Neil — Defender

b.Liverpool 19-5-80

*Source:* Trainee.

| | | | |
|---|---|---|---|
| 1997–98 | Liverpool | 0 | 0 |

## MURPHY, Shaun — Defender

H: 6 1 W: 12 00 b.Sydney 5-11-70

*Source:* Perth Italia.

| | | | |
|---|---|---|---|
| 1992–93 | Notts Co | 8 | 1 |
| 1993–94 | Notts Co | 11 | 1 |
| 1994–95 | Notts Co | 35 | 0 |
| 1995–96 | Notts Co | 39 | 3 |
| 1996–97 | Notts Co | 16 | 0 |
| 1996–97 | WBA | 17 | 2 |
| 1997–98 | WBA | 17 | 1 |
| **Total:** | | **143** | **8** |

## MURPHY, Stephen — Midfield

H: 5 11 W: 11 06 b.Dublin 5-4-78

*Source:* Belvedere. *Honours:* Eire Youth.

| | | | |
|---|---|---|---|
| 1994–95 | Huddersfield T | 0 | 0 |
| 1995–96 | Huddersfield T | 0 | 0 |
| 1996–97 | Huddersfield T | 0 | 0 |
| 1997–98 | Huddersfield T | 0 | 0 |

## MURRAY, Frazer — Midfield

H: 5 8 W: 10 10 b.Paisley 24-9-79

*Source:* Trainee. *Honours:* England Under-21.

| | | | |
|---|---|---|---|
| 1996–97 | QPR | 0 | 0 |
| 1997–98 | QPR | 0 | 0 |

## MURRAY, Grant — Midfield

H: 5 10 W: 12 00 b.Edinburgh 29-8-75

*Source:* Bonnyrigg Rose.

| | | | |
|---|---|---|---|
| 1995–96 | Hearts | 0 | 0 |
| 1996–97 | Hearts | 4 | 0 |
| 1997–98 | Hearts | 10 | 0 |
| **Total:** | | **14** | **0** |

## MURRAY, Matthew — Midfield

b.Solihull 2-5-81

*Source:* Trainee.

| | | | |
|---|---|---|---|
| 1997–98 | Wolverhampton W | 0 | 0 |

## MURRAY, Paul — Midfield

H: 5 8 W: 10 05 b.Carlisle 31-8-76

*Source:* Trainee. *Honours:* England Youth, Under-21, B.

| | | | |
|---|---|---|---|
| 1993–94 | Carlisle U | 8 | 0 |
| 1994–95 | Carlisle U | 5 | 0 |
| 1995–96 | Carlisle U | 28 | 1 |
| 1995–96 | QPR | 1 | 0 |
| 1996–97 | QPR | 32 | 5 |
| 1997–98 | QPR | 32 | 1 |
| **Total:** | | **106** | **7** |

## MURRAY, Robert — Midfield

H: 5 11 W: 12 07 b.Hammersmith 31-10-74

*Source:* Trainee. *Honours:* Scotland Under-21.

| | | | |
|---|---|---|---|
| 1992–93 | Bournemouth | 25 | 4 |
| 1993–94 | Bournemouth | 20 | 4 |
| 1994–95 | Bournemouth | 31 | 0 |
| 1995–96 | Bournemouth | 35 | 2 |
| 1996–97 | Bournemouth | 32 | 2 |
| 1997–98 | Bournemouth | 4 | 0 |
| **Total:** | | **147** | **12** |

## MURRAY, Scott — Midfiel

H: 5 9 W: 11 00 b.Aberdeen 26-5-74

*Source:* Fraserburgh.

| | | | |
|---|---|---|---|
| 1993–94 | Aston Villa | 0 | [illegible] |
| 1994–95 | Aston Villa | 0 | [illegible] |
| 1995–96 | Aston Villa | 3 | [illegible] |
| 1996–97 | Aston Villa | 1 | [illegible] |
| 1997–98 | Aston Villa | 0 | [illegible] |
| 1997–98 | Bristol C | 23 | [illegible] |
| **Total:** | | **27** | [illegible] |

## MURRAY, Shaun — Midfiel

H: 5 7 W: 10 10 b.Newcastle 7-2-70

*Source:* Trainee. *Honours:* England Schools, Youth.

| | | | |
|---|---|---|---|
| 1987–88 | Tottenham H | 0 | [illegible] |
| 1988–89 | Tottenham H | 0 | [illegible] |
| 1989–90 | Portsmouth | 0 | [illegible] |
| 1990–91 | Portsmouth | 25 | [illegible] |
| 1991–92 | Portsmouth | 2 | [illegible] |
| 1992–93 | Portsmouth | 7 | [illegible] |
| 1993–94 | Portsmouth | 0 | [illegible] |
| 1993–94 | Millwall (loan) | 0 | [illegible] |
| 1993–94 | Scarborough | 29 | [illegible] |
| 1994–95 | Bradford C | 41 | [illegible] |
| 1995–96 | Bradford C | 34 | [illegible] |
| 1996–97 | Bradford C | 17 | [illegible] |
| 1997–98 | Bradford C | 38 | [illegible] |
| **Total:** | | **193** | **14** |

## MURTY, Graeme — Midfiel

H: 5 10 W: 11 12 b.Middlesbrough 13-11-74

*Source:* Trainee.

| | | | |
|---|---|---|---|
| 1992–93 | York C | 0 | [illegible] |
| 1993–94 | York C | 1 | [illegible] |
| 1994–95 | York C | 20 | [illegible] |
| 1995–96 | York C | 35 | [illegible] |
| 1996–97 | York C | 27 | [illegible] |
| 1997–98 | York C | 34 | [illegible] |
| **Total:** | | **117** | [illegible] |

## MUSCAT, Kevin — Defende

H: 5 11 W: 11 07 b.Crawley 7-8-73

*Source:* South Melbourne. *Honours:* Australia 13 full caps, 1 goal.

| | | | |
|---|---|---|---|
| 1996–97 | Crystal Palace | 44 | [illegible] |
| 1997–98 | Crystal Palace | 9 | [illegible] |
| 1997–98 | Wolverhampton W | 24 | [illegible] |
| **Total:** | | **77** | [illegible] |

## MUSSELWHITE, Paul — Goalkeeper

H: 6 2  W: 14 04  b.Portsmouth 22-12-68

| | | | |
|---|---|---|---|
| 1987–88 | Portsmouth | 0 | 0 |
| 1988–89 | Scunthorpe U | 41 | 0 |
| 1989–90 | Scunthorpe U | 29 | 0 |
| 1990–91 | Scunthorpe U | 38 | 0 |
| 1991–92 | Scunthorpe U | 24 | 0 |
| 1992–93 | Port Vale | 41 | 0 |
| 1993–94 | Port Vale | 46 | 0 |
| 1994–95 | Port Vale | 44 | 0 |
| 1995–96 | Port Vale | 39 | 0 |
| 1996–97 | Port Vale | 33 | 0 |
| 1997–98 | Port Vale | 41 | 0 |
| **Total:** | | **376** | **0** |

## MUSTAFA, Tarkan — Midfield

H: 5 10  W: 11 07  b.London 28-8-73

*Source:* Kettering T.

| | | | |
|---|---|---|---|
| 1997–98 | Barnet | 11 | 0 |
| **Total:** | | **11** | **0** |

## MUSTOE, Neil — Midfield

H: 5 8  W: 12 13  b.Gloucester 5-11-76

*Source:* Trainee.

| | | | |
|---|---|---|---|
| 1995–96 | Manchester U | 0 | 0 |
| 1996–97 | Manchester U | 0 | 0 |
| 1997–98 | Manchester U | 0 | 0 |

## MUSTOE, Robbie — Midfield

H: 5 10  W: 11 10  b.Oxford 28-8-68

| | | | |
|---|---|---|---|
| 1986–87 | Oxford U | 3 | 0 |
| 1987–88 | Oxford U | 17 | 0 |
| 1988–89 | Oxford U | 33 | 3 |
| 1989–90 | Oxford U | 38 | 7 |
| 1990–91 | Middlesbrough | 41 | 4 |
| 1991–92 | Middlesbrough | 30 | 2 |
| 1992–93 | Middlesbrough | 23 | 1 |
| 1993–94 | Middlesbrough | 38 | 2 |
| 1994–95 | Middlesbrough | 27 | 3 |
| 1995–96 | Middlesbrough | 21 | 1 |
| 1996–97 | Middlesbrough | 31 | 3 |
| 1997–98 | Middlesbrough | 32 | 3 |
| **Total:** | | **334** | **29** |

## MUTCH, Andy — Forward

H: 5 10  W: 11 00  b.Liverpool 28-12-63

*Source:* Southport. *Honours:* England Under-21, B.

| | | | |
|---|---|---|---|
| 1985–86 | Wolverhampton W | 15 | 7 |
| 1986–87 | Wolverhampton W | 41 | 11 |
| 1987–88 | Wolverhampton W | 46 | 19 |
| 1988–89 | Wolverhampton W | 45 | 21 |
| 1989–90 | Wolverhampton W | 37 | 11 |
| 1990–91 | Wolverhampton W | 29 | 8 |
| 1991–92 | Wolverhampton W | 37 | 10 |
| 1992–93 | Wolverhampton W | 39 | 9 |
| 1993–94 | Swindon T | 30 | 6 |
| 1994–95 | Swindon T | 20 | 0 |
| 1995–96 | Swindon T | 0 | 0 |
| 1995–96 | Wigan Ath (loan) | 7 | 1 |
| 1995–96 | Stockport Co | 11 | 4 |
| 1996–97 | Stockport Co | 33 | 4 |
| 1997–98 | Stockport Co | 20 | 2 |
| **Total:** | | **410** | **113** |

## MYALL, Stuart — Midfield

H: 5 10  W: 13 07  b.Eastbourne 12-11-74

*Source:* Trainee.

| | | | |
|---|---|---|---|
| 1992–93 | Brighton & HA | 7 | 0 |
| 1993–94 | Brighton & HA | 13 | 0 |
| 1994–95 | Brighton & HA | 27 | 2 |
| 1995–96 | Brighton & HA | 33 | 2 |
| 1996–97 | Brentford | 0 | 0 |
| 1997–98 | Brentford | 2 | 0 |
| **Total:** | | **82** | **4** |

## MYERS, Andy — Midfield

H: 5 10  W: 13 11  b.Isleworth 3-11-73

*Source:* Trainee. *Honours:* England Schools, Youth, Under-21.

| | | | |
|---|---|---|---|
| 1990–91 | Chelsea | 3 | 0 |
| 1991–92 | Chelsea | 11 | 1 |
| 1992–93 | Chelsea | 3 | 0 |
| 1993–94 | Chelsea | 6 | 0 |
| 1994–95 | Chelsea | 10 | 0 |
| 1995–96 | Chelsea | 20 | 0 |
| 1996–97 | Chelsea | 18 | 1 |
| 1997–98 | Chelsea | 12 | 0 |
| **Total:** | | **83** | **2** |

## MYHRE, Thomas — Goalkeeper

b.Sarpsborg 16-10-73

*Honours:* Norway 1 full cap.

| | | | |
|---|---|---|---|
| 1993 | Viking | 22 | 0 |
| 1994 | Viking | 22 | 0 |
| 1995 | Viking | 24 | 0 |
| 1996 | Viking | 0 | 0 |
| 1997 | Viking | 26 | 0 |
| 1997–98 | Everton | 22 | 0 |
| **Total:** | | **116** | **0** |

## N'DIAYE, Sada — Forward

H: 5 8 W: 11 01 b.Dakar 27-3-75

*Source:* Troyes.

| | | | |
|---|---|---|---|
| 1997–98 | Southend U | 17 | 2 |
| **Total:** | | **17** | **2** |

## NAISBETT, Philip — Goalkeeper

b.Easington 2-1-79

*Source:* Trainee.

| | | | |
|---|---|---|---|
| 1996–97 | Sunderland | 0 | 0 |
| 1997–98 | Sunderland | 0 | 0 |

## NAISBITT, Daniel — Goalkeeper

H: 6 1 W: 11 13 b.Bishop Auckland 21-11-78

*Source:* From Trainee.

| | | | |
|---|---|---|---|
| 1997–98 | Walsall | 0 | 0 |

## NASH, Carlo — Goalkeeper

H: 6 5 W: 14 01 b.Bolton 13-9-73

*Source:* Clitheroe.

| | | | |
|---|---|---|---|
| 1996–97 | Crystal Palace | 21 | 0 |
| 1997–98 | Crystal Palace | 0 | 0 |
| **Total:** | | **21** | **0** |

## NASH, Marc — Forward

H: 5 9 W: 11 07 b.Newcastle 13-5-78

*Source:* Benfield Park.

| | | | |
|---|---|---|---|
| 1997–98 | Hartlepool U | 1 | 0 |
| **Total:** | | **1** | **0** |

## NASH, Martin — Midfield

H: 5 11 W: 12 03 b.Regina 27-12-75

*Source:* Vancouver. *Honours:* Canada 2 full caps.

| | | | |
|---|---|---|---|
| 1996–97 | Stockport Co | 3 | 0 |
| 1997–98 | Stockport Co | 8 | 0 |
| **Total:** | | **11** | **0** |

## NAYLOR, Dominic — Defender

H: 5 9 W: 12 01 b.Watford 12-8-70

*Source:* Trainee.

| | | | |
|---|---|---|---|
| 1988–89 | Watford | 0 | 0 |
| 1989–90 | Watford | 0 | 0 |
| 1989–90 | Halifax T | 6 | 1 |
| From Barnet. | | | |
| 1991–92 | Barnet | 26 | 0 |
| 1992–93 | Barnet | 25 | [illegible] |
| 1993–94 | Plymouth Arg | 43 | [illegible] |
| 1994–95 | Plymouth Arg | 42 | [illegible] |
| 1995–96 | Gillingham | 31 | [illegible] |
| 1996–97 | Leyton Orient | 44 | [illegible] |
| 1997–98 | Leyton Orient | 43 | [illegible] |
| **Total:** | | **260** | [illegible] |

## NAYLOR, Gavin — Forwar

H: 5 7 W: 11 02 b.North Cleveland 30-5-79

*Source:* Trainee.

| | | | |
|---|---|---|---|
| 1997–98 | Manchester U | 0 | [illegible] |

## NAYLOR, Glenn — Forwar

H: 5 10 W: 11 10 b.York 11-8-72

*Source:* Trainee.

| | | | |
|---|---|---|---|
| 1989–90 | York C | 1 | [illegible] |
| 1990–91 | York C | 20 | [illegible] |
| 1991–92 | York C | 21 | [illegible] |
| 1992–93 | York C | 4 | [illegible] |
| 1993–94 | York C | 10 | [illegible] |
| 1994–95 | York C | 29 | [illegible] |
| 1995–96 | York C | 25 | [illegible] |
| 1995–96 | Darlington (loan) | 4 | [illegible] |
| 1996–97 | York C | 1 | [illegible] |
| 1996–97 | Darlington | 37 | [illegible] |
| 1997–98 | Darlington | 42 | [illegible] |
| **Total:** | | **194** | [illegible] |

## NAYLOR, Lee — Defende

H: 5 8 W: 11 08 b.Bloxwich 19-3-80

*Source:* Trainee.

| | | | |
|---|---|---|---|
| 1997–98 | Wolverhampton W | 16 | [illegible] |
| **Total:** | | **16** | [illegible] |

## NAYLOR, Martyn — Defende

H: 5 9 W: 10 02 b.Walsall 2-8-77

*Source:* Hereford U Trainee, Telford U.

| | | | |
|---|---|---|---|
| 1997–98 | Shrewsbury T | 2 | [illegible] |
| **Total:** | | **2** | [illegible] |

## NAYLOR, Richard — Forwar

H: 6 1 W: 13 07 b.Leeds 28-2-77

*Source:* Trainee.

| | | | |
|---|---|---|---|
| 1995–96 | Ipswich T | 0 | [illegible] |
| 1996–97 | Ipswich T | 27 | [illegible] |
| 1997–98 | Ipswich T | 5 | [illegible] |
| **Total:** | | **32** | [illegible] |

## NAYLOR, Roy — Goalkeeper

H: 6 0 W: 12 00 b.Liverpool 15-9-78

*Source:* Trainee.

| | | | |
|---|---|---|---|
| 1997–98 | Liverpool | 0 | 0 |

## NAYLOR, Stuart — Goalkeeper

H: 6 4 W: 11 03 b.Wetherby 6-12-62

*Source:* Yorkshire Amateur. *Honours:* England Youth, B.

| | | | |
|---|---|---|---|
| 1980–81 | Lincoln C | 0 | 0 |
| 1981–82 | Lincoln C | 3 | 0 |
| 1982–83 | Lincoln C | 1 | 0 |
| 1982–83 | Peterborough U (loan) | 8 | 0 |
| 1983–84 | Lincoln C | 0 | 0 |
| 1983–84 | Crewe Alex (loan) | 38 | 0 |
| 1984–85 | Crewe Alex (loan) | 17 | 0 |
| 1984–85 | Lincoln C | 25 | 0 |
| 1985–86 | Lincoln C | 20 | 0 |
| 1985–86 | WBA | 12 | 0 |
| 1986–87 | WBA | 42 | 0 |
| 1987–88 | WBA | 35 | 0 |
| 1988–89 | WBA | 44 | 0 |
| 1989–90 | WBA | 39 | 0 |
| 1990–91 | WBA | 28 | 0 |
| 1991–92 | WBA | 34 | 0 |
| 1992–93 | WBA | 32 | 0 |
| 1993–94 | WBA | 20 | 0 |
| 1994–95 | WBA | 42 | 0 |
| 1995–96 | WBA | 27 | 0 |
| 1996–97 | Bristol C | 35 | 0 |
| 1997–98 | Bristol C | 2 | 0 |
| **Total:** | | **504** | **0** |

## NAYLOR, Tony — Forward

H: 5 7 W: 10 06 b.Manchester 29-3-67

*Source:* Droylsden.

| | | | |
|---|---|---|---|
| 1989–90 | Crewe Alex | 2 | 0 |
| 1990–91 | Crewe Alex | 14 | 1 |
| 1991–92 | Crewe Alex | 34 | 15 |
| 1992–93 | Crewe Alex | 35 | 16 |
| 1993–94 | Crewe Alex | 37 | 13 |
| 1994–95 | Port Vale | 33 | 9 |
| 1995–96 | Port Vale | 39 | 11 |
| 1996–97 | Port Vale | 43 | 17 |
| 1997–98 | Port Vale | 38 | 10 |
| **Total:** | | **275** | **92** |

## NAYSMITH, Gary — Forward

H: 5 7 W: 11 08 b.Edinburgh 16-11-78

*Source:* Whitehill Welfare Colts. *Honours:* Scotland Under-18, Under-21.

| | | | |
|---|---|---|---|
| 1995–96 | Hearts | 1 | 0 |
| 1996–97 | Hearts | 10 | 0 |
| 1997–98 | Hearts | 16 | 2 |
| **Total:** | | **27** | **2** |

## NDAH, George — Forward

H: 6 1 W: 11 04 b.Camberwell 23-12-74

*Source:* Trainee.

| | | | |
|---|---|---|---|
| 1992–93 | Crystal Palace | 13 | 0 |
| 1993–94 | Crystal Palace | 1 | 0 |
| 1994–95 | Crystal Palace | 12 | 1 |
| 1995–96 | Crystal Palace | 23 | 4 |
| 1995–96 | Bournemouth (loan) | 12 | 2 |
| 1996–97 | Crystal Palace | 26 | 3 |
| 1997–98 | Crystal Palace | 3 | 0 |
| 1997–98 | Gillingham (loan) | 4 | 0 |
| 1997–98 | Swindon T | 14 | 2 |
| **Total:** | | **108** | **12** |

## NDLOVU, Peter — Forward

H: 5 8 W: 10 02 b.Zimbabwe 25-2-73

*Source:* Highlanders. *Honours:* Zimbabwe 37 full caps.

| | | | |
|---|---|---|---|
| 1991–92 | Coventry C | 23 | 2 |
| 1992–93 | Coventry C | 32 | 7 |
| 1993–94 | Coventry C | 40 | 11 |
| 1994–95 | Coventry C | 30 | 11 |
| 1995–96 | Coventry C | 32 | 5 |
| 1996–97 | Coventry C | 20 | 1 |
| 1997–98 | Birmingham C | 39 | 9 |
| **Total:** | | **216** | **46** |

## NEAL, Ashley — Defender

H: 6 1 W: 14 10 b.Northampton 16-12-74

*Source:* Trainee.

| | | | |
|---|---|---|---|
| 1992–93 | Liverpool | 0 | 0 |
| 1993–94 | Liverpool | 0 | 0 |
| 1994–95 | Liverpool | 0 | 0 |
| 1995–96 | Liverpool | 0 | 0 |
| 1996–97 | Liverpool | 0 | 0 |
| 1996–97 | Brighton & HA (loan) | 8 | 0 |
| 1996–97 | Huddersfield T | 0 | 0 |
| 1996–97 | Peterborough U | 4 | 0 |
| 1997–98 | Peterborough U | 4 | 0 |
| **Total:** | | **16** | **0** |

## NEGRI, Marco — Forward

H: 5 11 W: 12 10 b.Milan 27-10-70

| | | | |
|---|---|---|---|
| 1988–89 | Udinese | 3 | 0 |
| 1989–90 | Novara | 27 | 0 |
| 1990–91 | Udinese | 5 | 0 |
| 1991–92 | Udinese | 0 | 0 |
| 1991–92 | Ternana | 23 | 4 |
| 1992–93 | Ternana | 9 | 1 |
| 1992–93 | Cosenza | 25 | 4 |
| 1993–94 | Cosenza | 0 | 0 |
| 1993–94 | Bologna | 24 | 8 |
| 1994–95 | Cosenza | 34 | 19 |
| 1995–96 | Perugia | 33 | 18 |
| 1996–97 | Perugia | 27 | 15 |
| 1997–98 | Rangers | 29 | 32 |
| **Total:** | | **239** | **101** |

## NEIL, Gary — Forward

H: 6 0 W: 12 10 b.Glasgow 16-8-78

*Source:* Trainee.

| | | | |
|---|---|---|---|
| 1997–98 | Leicester C | 0 | 0 |

## NEIL, Jim — Defender

H: 5 8 W: 12 01 b.Bury St Edmunds 28-2-76

*Source:* Trainee.

| | | | |
|---|---|---|---|
| 1994–95 | Grimsby T | 0 | 0 |
| 1995–96 | Grimsby T | 1 | 0 |
| 1996–97 | Grimsby T | 1 | 0 |
| 1997–98 | Scunthorpe U | 7 | 0 |
| **Total:** | | **9** | **0** |

## NEILL, Lucas — Midfield

H: 6 1 W: 12 00 b.Sydney 9-3-78

*Source:* NSW Soccer Academy. *Honours:* Australia Youth, full caps.

| | | | |
|---|---|---|---|
| 1995–96 | Millwall | 13 | 0 |
| 1996–97 | Millwall | 39 | 3 |
| 1997–98 | Millwall | 6 | 0 |
| **Total:** | | **58** | **3** |

## NEILL, Warren — Midfield

H: 5 9 W: 11 05 b.Acton 21-11-62

*Source:* Apprentice. *Honours:* England Schools.

| | | | |
|---|---|---|---|
| 1980–81 | QPR | 4 | 0 |
| 1981–82 | QPR | 11 | 0 |
| 1982–83 | QPR | 39 | 2 |
| 1983–84 | QPR | 41 | 1 |
| 1984–85 | QPR | 18 | 0 |
| 1985–86 | QPR | 16 | 0 |
| 1986–87 | QPR | 29 | 0 |
| 1987–88 | QPR | 23 | 0 |
| 1988–89 | Portsmouth | 43 | 0 |
| 1989–90 | Portsmouth | 37 | 0 |
| 1990–91 | Portsmouth | 30 | 0 |
| 1991–92 | Portsmouth | 38 | 0 |
| 1992–93 | Portsmouth | 28 | 0 |
| 1993–94 | Portsmouth | 35 | 2 |
| 1994–95 | Portsmouth | 7 | 0 |
| 1995–96 | Watford | 1 | 0 |
| 1996–97 | Watford | 0 | 0 |
| 1997–98 | Watford | 0 | 0 |
| **Total:** | | **400** | **5** |

## NEILSON, Alan — Defender

H: 5 11 W: 12 08 b.Wegburg 26-9-72

*Source:* Trainee. *Honours:* Wales Under-21, 5 full caps.

| | | | |
|---|---|---|---|
| 1990–91 | Newcastle U | 3 | 0 |
| 1991–92 | Newcastle U | 16 | 1 |
| 1992–93 | Newcastle U | 3 | 0 |
| 1993–94 | Newcastle U | 14 | 0 |
| 1994–95 | Newcastle U | 6 | 0 |
| 1995–96 | Southampton | 18 | 0 |
| 1996–97 | Southampton | 29 | 0 |
| 1997–98 | Southampton | 8 | 0 |
| 1997–98 | Fulham | 17 | 0 |
| **Total:** | | **114** | **1** |

## NELSON, Fernando — Defender

H: 5 11 W: 11 08 b.Oporto 5-11-71

*Honours:* Portugal 6 full caps.

| | | | |
|---|---|---|---|
| 1991–92 | Sporting | 2 | 0 |
| 1992–93 | Sporting | 15 | 0 |
| 1993–94 | Sporting | 33 | 1 |
| 1994–95 | Sporting | 33 | 1 |
| 1995–96 | Sporting | 32 | 1 |
| 1996–97 | Aston Villa | 34 | 0 |
| 1997–98 | Aston Villa | 25 | 0 |
| **Total:** | | **174** | **3** |

## NETHERCOTT, Stuart — Defender

H: 6 1 W: 14 00 b.Chadwell Heath 21-3-73

*Source:* Trainee. *Honours:* England Under-21.

| | | | |
|---|---|---|---|
| 1991–92 | Tottenham H | 0 | 0 |
| 1991–92 | Maidstone U (loan) | 13 | 1 |
| 1991–92 | Barnet (loan) | 3 | 0 |
| 1992–93 | Tottenham H | 5 | 0 |
| 1993–94 | Tottenham H | 10 | 0 |
| 1994–95 | Tottenham H | 17 | 0 |
| 1995–96 | Tottenham H | 13 | 0 |

| | | | |
|---|---|---|---|
| 1996–97 | Tottenham H | 9 | 0 |
| 1997–98 | Tottenham H | 0 | 0 |
| 1997–98 | Millwall | 10 | 0 |
| **Total:** | | **80** | **1** |

## NEVILLE, Gary — Defender

H: 5 11 W: 12 07 b.Bury 18-2-75

*Source:* Trainee. *Honours:* England Youth, 30 full caps.

| | | | |
|---|---|---|---|
| 1992–93 | Manchester U | 0 | 0 |
| 1993–94 | Manchester U | 1 | 0 |
| 1994–95 | Manchester U | 18 | 0 |
| 1995–96 | Manchester U | 31 | 0 |
| 1996–97 | Manchester U | 31 | 1 |
| 1997–98 | Manchester U | 34 | 0 |
| **Total:** | | **115** | **1** |

## NEVILLE, Philip — Defender

H: 5 11 W: 11 11 b.Bury 21-1-77

*Source:* Trainee. *Honours:* England Schools, Youth, Under-21, 12 full caps.

| | | | |
|---|---|---|---|
| 1994–95 | Manchester U | 2 | 0 |
| 1995–96 | Manchester U | 24 | 0 |
| 1996–97 | Manchester U | 18 | 0 |
| 1997–98 | Manchester U | 30 | 1 |
| **Total:** | | **74** | **1** |

## NEVIN, Pat — Forward

H: 5 6 W: 11 09 b.Glasgow 6-9-63

*Source:* Gartcosh U. *Honours:* Scotland Youth, Under-21, B, 28 full caps, 5 goals.

| | | | |
|---|---|---|---|
| 1981–82 | Clyde | 34 | 12 |
| 1982–83 | Clyde | 39 | 5 |
| 1983–84 | Chelsea | 38 | 14 |
| 1984–85 | Chelsea | 41 | 4 |
| 1985–86 | Chelsea | 40 | 7 |
| 1986–87 | Chelsea | 37 | 5 |
| 1987–88 | Chelsea | 37 | 6 |
| 1988–89 | Everton | 25 | 2 |
| 1989–90 | Everton | 30 | 4 |
| 1990–91 | Everton | 37 | 8 |
| 1991–92 | Everton | 17 | 2 |
| 1991–92 | Tranmere R (loan) | 8 | 0 |
| 1992–93 | Tranmere R | 43 | 13 |
| 1993–94 | Tranmere R | 45 | 8 |
| 1994–95 | Tranmere R | 44 | 4 |
| 1995–96 | Tranmere R | 40 | 3 |
| 1996–97 | Tranmere R | 21 | 2 |
| 1997–98 | Kilmarnock | 31 | 5 |
| **Total:** | | **607** | **104** |

## NEVLAND, Erik — Forward

H: 5 10 W: 11 12 b.Stavanger 10-11-77

| | | | |
|---|---|---|---|
| 1996 | Viking | 1 | 0 |
| 1997 | Viking | 13 | 5 |
| 1997–98 | Manchester U | 1 | 0 |
| **Total:** | | **15** | **5** |

## NEWBY, John — Forward

H: 6 0 W: 12 00 b.Warrington 28-11-78

*Source:* Trainee.

| | | | |
|---|---|---|---|
| 1997–98 | Liverpool | 0 | 0 |

## NEWELL, Justin — Forward

H: 6 1 W: 10 07 b.Germany 8-2-80

*Source:* Trainee.

| | | | |
|---|---|---|---|
| 1997–98 | Torquay U | 1 | 0 |
| **Total:** | | **1** | **0** |

## NEWELL, Mike — Forward

H: 6 0 W: 13 00 b.Liverpool 27-1-65

*Source:* Liverpool Amateur. *Honours:* England Under-21, B.

| | | | |
|---|---|---|---|
| 1983–84 | Crewe Alex | 3 | 0 |
| 1983–84 | Wigan Ath | 9 | 0 |
| 1984–85 | Wigan Ath | 39 | 9 |
| 1985–86 | Wigan Ath | 24 | 16 |
| 1985–86 | Luton T | 16 | 6 |
| 1986–87 | Luton T | 42 | 12 |
| 1987–88 | Luton T | 5 | 0 |
| 1987–88 | Leicester C | 36 | 8 |
| 1988–89 | Leicester C | 45 | 13 |
| 1989–90 | Everton | 26 | 7 |
| 1990–91 | Everton | 29 | 7 |
| 1991–92 | Everton | 13 | 1 |
| 1991–92 | Blackburn R | 20 | 6 |
| 1992–93 | Blackburn R | 40 | 13 |
| 1993–94 | Blackburn R | 28 | 6 |
| 1994–95 | Blackburn R | 12 | 0 |
| 1995–96 | Blackburn R | 30 | 3 |
| 1996–97 | Birmingham C | 15 | 1 |
| 1996–97 | West Ham U (loan) | 7 | 0 |
| 1996–97 | Bradford C (loan) | 7 | 0 |
| 1997–98 | Aberdeen | 21 | 4 |
| **Total:** | | **467** | **112** |

## NEWELL, Paul — Goalkeeper

H: 6 1 W: 14 07 b.Woolwich 23-2-69

*Source:* Trainee.

| | | | |
|---|---|---|---|
| 1987–88 | Southend U | 13 | 0 |
| 1988–89 | Southend U | 2 | 0 |

| | | | |
|---|---|---|---|
| 1989–90 | Southend U | 0 | 0 |
| 1990–91 | Leyton Orient | 8 | 0 |
| 1991–92 | Leyton Orient | 10 | 0 |
| 1992–93 | Leyton Orient | 3 | 0 |
| 1992–93 | Colchester U (loan) | 14 | 0 |
| 1993–94 | Leyton Orient | 40 | 0 |
| 1994–95 | Barnet | 15 | 0 |
| 1995–96 | Barnet | 1 | 0 |
| 1995–96 | Darlington | 21 | 0 |
| 1996–97 | Darlington | 20 | 0 |
| 1997–98 | Colchester U | 0 | 0 |
| 1997–98 | Northampton T | 0 | 0 |
| **Total:** | | **147** | **0** |

## NEWHOUSE, Aidan — Forward

H: 6 2 W: 13 10 b.Wallasey 23-5-72

*Source:* Trainee. *Honours:* England Youth.

| | | | |
|---|---|---|---|
| 1987–88 | Chester C | 1 | 0 |
| 1988–89 | Chester C | 25 | 2 |
| 1989–90 | Chester C | 18 | 4 |
| 1989–90 | Wimbledon | 2 | 0 |
| 1990–91 | Wimbledon | 8 | 1 |
| 1991–92 | Wimbledon | 12 | 1 |
| 1992–93 | Wimbledon | 1 | 0 |
| 1993–94 | Wimbledon | 0 | 0 |
| 1993–94 | Tranmere R (loan) | 0 | 0 |
| 1993–94 | Port Vale (loan) | 2 | 0 |
| 1994–95 | Wimbledon | 0 | 0 |
| 1994–95 | Portsmouth (loan) | 6 | 1 |
| 1995–96 | Wimbledon | 0 | 0 |
| 1995–96 | Torquay U (loan) | 4 | 2 |
| 1996–97 | Wimbledon | 0 | 0 |
| 1997–98 | Fulham | 8 | 1 |
| 1997–98 | Swansea C | 8 | 0 |
| **Total:** | | **95** | **12** |

## NEWMAN, Ricky — Midfield

H: 5 10 W: 12 06 b.Guildford 5-8-70

*Source:* Trainee.

| | | | |
|---|---|---|---|
| 1987–88 | Crystal Palace | 0 | 0 |
| 1988–89 | Crystal Palace | 0 | 0 |
| 1989–90 | Crystal Palace | 0 | 0 |
| 1990–91 | Crystal Palace | 0 | 0 |
| 1991–92 | Crystal Palace | 0 | 0 |
| 1991–92 | Maidstone U (loan) | 10 | 1 |
| 1992–93 | Crystal Palace | 2 | 0 |
| 1993–94 | Crystal Palace | 11 | 0 |
| 1994–95 | Crystal Palace | 35 | 3 |
| 1995–96 | Millwall | 36 | 1 |
| 1996–97 | Millwall | 41 | 3 |
| 1997–98 | Millwall | 35 | 1 |
| **Total:** | | **170** | **9** |

## NEWMAN, Rob — Defender

H: 6 2 W: 13 00 b.Bradford-on-Avon 13-12-63

*Source:* Apprentice.

| | | | |
|---|---|---|---|
| 1981–82 | Bristol C | 21 | 3 |
| 1982–83 | Bristol C | 43 | 3 |
| 1983–84 | Bristol C | 30 | 1 |
| 1984–85 | Bristol C | 34 | 3 |
| 1985–86 | Bristol C | 39 | 3 |
| 1986–87 | Bristol C | 45 | 6 |
| 1987–88 | Bristol C | 44 | 11 |
| 1988–89 | Bristol C | 46 | 6 |
| 1989–90 | Bristol C | 46 | 8 |
| 1990–91 | Bristol C | 46 | 8 |
| 1991–92 | Norwich C | 41 | 7 |
| 1992–93 | Norwich C | 18 | 2 |
| 1993–94 | Norwich C | 32 | 2 |
| 1994–95 | Norwich C | 32 | 1 |
| 1995–96 | Norwich C | 23 | 1 |
| 1996–97 | Norwich C | 44 | 1 |
| 1997–98 | Norwich C | 15 | 0 |
| 1997–98 | Motherwell (loan) | 11 | 0 |
| 1997–98 | Wigan Ath (loan) | 8 | 0 |
| **Total:** | | **618** | **66** |

## NEWSOME, Jon — Defender

H: 6 3 W: 13 10 b.Sheffield 6-9-70

*Source:* Trainee.

| | | | |
|---|---|---|---|
| 1989–90 | Sheffield W | 6 | 0 |
| 1990–91 | Sheffield W | 1 | 0 |
| 1991–92 | Leeds U | 10 | 2 |
| 1992–93 | Leeds U | 37 | 0 |
| 1993–94 | Leeds U | 29 | 1 |
| 1994–95 | Norwich C | 35 | 3 |
| 1995–96 | Norwich C | 27 | 4 |
| 1995–96 | Sheffield W | 8 | 1 |
| 1996–97 | Sheffield W | 10 | 1 |
| 1997–98 | Sheffield W | 25 | 2 |
| **Total:** | | **188** | **14** |

## NEWTON, Eddie — Forward

H: 6 0 W: 12 11 b.Hammersmith 13-12-71

*Source:* Trainee. *Honours:* England Under-21.

| | | | |
|---|---|---|---|
| 1990–91 | Chelsea | 0 | 0 |
| 1991–92 | Chelsea | 1 | 1 |
| 1991–92 | Cardiff C (loan) | 18 | 4 |
| 1992–93 | Chelsea | 34 | 5 |
| 1993–94 | Chelsea | 36 | 0 |
| 1994–95 | Chelsea | 30 | 1 |
| 1995–96 | Chelsea | 24 | 1 |
| 1996–97 | Chelsea | 15 | 0 |
| 1997–98 | Chelsea | 18 | 0 |
| **Total:** | | **176** | **12** |

## NEWTON, Shaun — Midfield

H: 5 8 W: 11 07 b.Camberwell 20-8-75

*Source:* Trainee. *Honours:* England Under-21.

| | | | |
|---|---|---|---|
| 1992–93 | Charlton Ath | 2 | 0 |
| 1993–94 | Charlton Ath | 19 | 2 |
| 1994–95 | Charlton Ath | 26 | 0 |
| 1995–96 | Charlton Ath | 41 | 5 |
| 1996–97 | Charlton Ath | 43 | 3 |
| 1997–98 | Charlton Ath | 41 | 5 |
| **Total:** | | **172** | **15** |

## NICHOLLS, Kevin — Midfield

H: 6 0 W: 11 00 b.Newham 2-1-79

*Source:* Trainee. *Honours:* England Youth.

| | | | |
|---|---|---|---|
| 1995–96 | Charlton Ath | 0 | 0 |
| 1996–97 | Charlton Ath | 6 | 1 |
| 1997–98 | Charlton Ath | 6 | 0 |
| **Total:** | | **12** | **1** |

## NICHOLLS, Mark — Forward

H: 5 10 W: 10 04 b.Hillingdon 30-5-77

*Source:* Trainee.

| | | | |
|---|---|---|---|
| 1995–96 | Chelsea | 0 | 0 |
| 1996–97 | Chelsea | 8 | 0 |
| 1997–98 | Chelsea | 19 | 3 |
| **Total:** | | **27** | **3** |

## NICHOLSON, Kevin — Midfield

b.Derby 2-10-80

*Source:* Trainee.

| | | | |
|---|---|---|---|
| 1997–98 | Sheffield W | 0 | 0 |

## NICHOLSON, Shane — Defender

H: 5 10 W: 11 10 b.Newark 3-6-70

*Source:* Trainee.

| | | | |
|---|---|---|---|
| 1986–87 | Lincoln C | 7 | 0 |
| 1987–88 | Lincoln C | 0 | 0 |
| 1988–89 | Lincoln C | 34 | 1 |
| 1989–90 | Lincoln C | 23 | 0 |
| 1990–91 | Lincoln C | 40 | 4 |
| 1991–92 | Lincoln C | 29 | 1 |
| 1991–92 | Derby Co | 0 | 0 |
| 1992–93 | Derby Co | 17 | 0 |
| 1993–94 | Derby Co | 22 | 1 |
| 1994–95 | Derby Co | 15 | 0 |
| 1995–96 | Derby Co | 20 | 0 |
| 1995–96 | WBA | 18 | 0 |
| 1996–97 | WBA | 18 | 0 |
| 1997–98 | WBA | 16 | 0 |
| **Total:** | | **259** | **7** |

## NICOL, Steve — Defender

H: 5 10 W: 12 07 b.Irvine 11-12-61

*Source:* Ayr U BC. *Honours:* Scotland Under-21, 27 full caps.

| | | | |
|---|---|---|---|
| 1979–80 | Ayr U | 20 | 2 |
| 1980–81 | Ayr U | 39 | 3 |
| 1981–82 | Ayr U | 11 | 2 |
| 1981–82 | Liverpool | 0 | 0 |
| 1982–83 | Liverpool | 4 | 0 |
| 1983–84 | Liverpool | 23 | 5 |
| 1984–85 | Liverpool | 31 | 5 |
| 1985–86 | Liverpool | 34 | 4 |
| 1986–87 | Liverpool | 14 | 3 |
| 1987–88 | Liverpool | 40 | 6 |
| 1988–89 | Liverpool | 38 | 2 |
| 1989–90 | Liverpool | 23 | 6 |
| 1990–91 | Liverpool | 35 | 3 |
| 1991–92 | Liverpool | 34 | 1 |
| 1992–93 | Liverpool | 32 | 0 |
| 1993–94 | Liverpool | 31 | 1 |
| 1994–95 | Liverpool | 4 | 0 |
| 1994–95 | Notts Co | 19 | 0 |
| 1995–96 | Notts Co | 13 | 2 |
| 1995–96 | Sheffield W | 19 | 0 |
| 1996–97 | Sheffield W | 23 | 0 |
| 1997–98 | Sheffield W | 7 | 0 |
| 1997–98 | WBA (loan) | 9 | 0 |
| **Total:** | | **503** | **45** |

## NIELSEN, Allan — Midfield

H: 5 8 W: 11 02 b.Esbjerg 13-3-71

*Source:* Esbjerg. *Honours:* Denmark Under-21, 23 full caps, 6 goals.

| | | | |
|---|---|---|---|
| 1988–89 | Bayern Munich | 0 | 0 |
| 1989–90 | Bayern Munich | 0 | 0 |
| 1990–91 | Bayern Munich | 1 | 0 |
| 1991–92 | Sion | 0 | 0 |
| 1991–92 | Odense | 8 | 2 |
| 1992–93 | Odense | 30 | 4 |
| 1993–94 | Odense | 17 | 3 |
| 1993–94 | FC Copenhagen | 8 | 0 |
| 1994–95 | FC Copenhagen | 18 | 3 |
| 1994–95 | Brondby | 10 | 3 |
| 1995–96 | Brondby | 28 | 6 |
| 1996–97 | Brondby | 4 | 2 |
| 1996–97 | Tottenham H | 29 | 6 |
| 1997–98 | Tottenham H | 26 | 3 |
| **Total:** | | **179** | **32** |

## NIELSEN, John — Midfield

H: 5 9 W: 11 12 b.Aarhus 7-4-72

| | | | |
|---|---|---|---|
| 1995–96 | Ikast | 19 | 0 |
| 1996–97 | Southend U | 24 | 3 |
| 1997–98 | Southend U | 5 | 0 |
| **Total:** | | **48** | **3** |

## NIELSEN, Jorgen — Goalkeeper

H: 6 0 W: 13 00 b.Nykabing 6-5-71

| | | | |
|---|---|---|---|
| 1996–97 | Liverpool | 0 | 0 |
| 1997–98 | Liverpool | 0 | 0 |

## NIELSEN, Martin — Forward

b.Aarhus 24-3-73

| | | | |
|---|---|---|---|
| 1995–96 | FC Copenhagen | 26 | 4 |
| 1996–97 | FC Copenhagen | 25 | 0 |
| 1997–98 | FC Copenhagen | 8 | 0 |
| 1997–98 | Huddersfield T | 3 | 0 |
| **Total:** | | **62** | **4** |

## NIEMI, Antti — Goalkeeper

H: 6 1 W: 14 00 b.Oulu 31-5-72

*Honours:* Finland 25 full caps.

| | | | |
|---|---|---|---|
| 1991 | HJK Helsinki | 2 | 0 |
| 1992 | HJK Helsinki | 27 | 0 |
| 1993 | HJK Helsinki | 24 | 0 |
| 1994 | HJK Helsinki | 24 | 0 |
| 1995 | HJK Helsinki | 24 | 0 |
| 1995–96 | FC Copenhagen | 17 | 0 |
| 1996–97 | FC Copenhagen | 30 | 0 |
| 1997–98 | Rangers | 5 | 0 |
| **Total:** | | **153** | **0** |

## NILSEN, Roger — Defender

H: 5 11 W: 12 06 b.Tromso 8-8-69

*Source:* Viking Stavanger. *Honours:* Norway 31 full caps, 3 goals.

| | | | |
|---|---|---|---|
| 1993–94 | Sheffield U | 22 | 0 |
| 1994–95 | Sheffield U | 33 | 0 |
| 1995–96 | Sheffield U | 39 | 0 |
| 1996–97 | Sheffield U | 33 | 0 |
| 1997–98 | Sheffield U | 22 | 0 |
| **Total:** | | **149** | **0** |

## NILSSON, Roland — Defender

H: 5 10 W: 11 10 b.Helsingborg 27-11-63

*Source:* IFK Gothenburg. *Honours:* Sweden 94 full caps, 1 goal.

| | | | |
|---|---|---|---|
| 1989–90 | Sheffield W | 20 | 0 |
| 1990–91 | Sheffield W | 22 | 0 |
| 1991–92 | Sheffield W | 39 | 1 |
| 1992–93 | Sheffield W | 32 | 1 |
| 1993–94 | Sheffield W | 38 | 0 |
| 1994 | Helsingborg | 17 | 0 |
| 1995 | Helsingborg | 16 | 1 |
| 1996 | Helsingborg | 25 | 4 |
| 1997 | Helsingborg | 6 | 1 |
| 1997–98 | Coventry C | 32 | 0 |
| **Total:** | | **247** | **8** |

## NIVEN, Stuart — Midfield

H: 5 11 W: 12 08 b.Glasgow 24-12-78

*Source:* Trainee.

| | | | |
|---|---|---|---|
| 1996–97 | Ipswich T | 2 | 0 |
| 1997–98 | Ipswich T | 0 | 0 |
| **Total:** | | **2** | **0** |

## NIXON, Eric — Goalkeeper

H: 6 4 W: 14 00 b.Manchester 4-10-62

*Source:* Curzon Ashton.

| | | | |
|---|---|---|---|
| 1983–84 | Manchester C | 0 | 0 |
| 1984–85 | Manchester C | 0 | 0 |
| 1985–86 | Manchester C | 28 | 0 |
| 1986–87 | Manchester C | 5 | 0 |
| 1986–87 | Wolverhampton W (loan) | 16 | 0 |
| 1986–87 | Bradford C (loan) | 3 | 0 |
| 1986–87 | Southampton (loan) | 4 | 0 |
| 1986–87 | Carlisle U (loan) | 16 | 0 |
| 1987–88 | Manchester C | 25 | 0 |
| 1987–88 | Tranmere R (loan) | 8 | 0 |
| 1988–89 | Tranmere R | 45 | 0 |
| 1989–90 | Tranmere R | 46 | 0 |
| 1990–91 | Tranmere R | 43 | 0 |
| 1991–92 | Tranmere R | 46 | 0 |
| 1992–93 | Tranmere R | 45 | 0 |
| 1993–94 | Tranmere R | 42 | 0 |
| 1994–95 | Tranmere R | 41 | 0 |
| 1995–96 | Tranmere R | 0 | 0 |
| 1995–96 | Blackpool (loan) | 20 | 0 |
| 1996–97 | Tranmere R | 25 | 0 |
| 1996–97 | Bradford C (loan) | 12 | 0 |
| 1997–98 | Stockport Co | 43 | 0 |
| **Total:** | | **513** | **0** |

## NOEL-WILLIAMS, Gifton — Forward

H: 6 1 W: 14 06 b.Islington 21-1-80

*Source:* Trainee. *Honours:* England Youth.

| | | | |
|---|---|---|---|
| 1996–97 | Watford | 25 | 2 |
| 1997–98 | Watford | 38 | 7 |
| **Total:** | | **63** | **9** |

## NOGAN, Kurt — Forward

H: 5 10 W: 11 01 b.Cardiff 9-9-70

*Source:* Trainee. *Honours:* Wales Under-21.

| | | | |
|---|---|---|---|
| 1989–90 | Luton T | 10 | 2 |
| 1990–91 | Luton T | 9 | 0 |
| 1991–92 | Luton T | 14 | 1 |
| 1992–93 | Peterborough U | 0 | 0 |
| 1992–93 | Brighton & HA | 30 | 20 |
| 1993–94 | Brighton & HA | 41 | 22 |
| 1994–95 | Brighton & HA | 26 | 7 |
| 1994–95 | Burnley | 15 | 3 |
| 1995–96 | Burnley | 46 | 20 |
| 1996–97 | Burnley | 31 | 10 |
| 1996–97 | Preston NE | 7 | 0 |
| 1997–98 | Preston NE | 22 | 5 |
| **Total:** | | **251** | **90** |

## NOGAN, Lee — Forward

H: 5 8 W: 11 01 b.Cardiff 21-5-69

*Source:* Apprentice. *Honours:* Wales Under-21, B, 2 full caps.

| | | | |
|---|---|---|---|
| 1986–87 | Oxford U | 0 | 0 |
| 1986–87 | Brentford (loan) | 11 | 2 |
| 1987–88 | Oxford U | 3 | 0 |
| 1987–88 | Southend U (loan) | 6 | 1 |
| 1988–89 | Oxford U | 3 | 0 |
| 1989–90 | Oxford U | 4 | 0 |
| 1990–91 | Oxford U | 32 | 5 |
| 1991–92 | Oxford U | 22 | 5 |
| 1991–92 | Watford | 23 | 5 |
| 1992–93 | Watford | 42 | 11 |
| 1993–94 | Watford | 26 | 3 |
| 1993–94 | Southend U (loan) | 5 | 0 |
| 1994–95 | Watford | 14 | 7 |
| 1994–95 | Reading | 20 | 10 |
| 1995–96 | Reading | 39 | 10 |
| 1996–97 | Reading | 32 | 6 |
| 1996–97 | Notts Co (loan) | 6 | 0 |
| 1997–98 | Grimsby T | 36 | 8 |
| **Total:** | | **324** | **73** |

## NOLAN, Ian — Defender

H: 5 11 W: 12 02 b.Liverpool 9-7-70

*Source:* Preston NE Trainee, Northwich Vic, Marine. *Honours:* Northern Ireland 7 full caps.

| | | | |
|---|---|---|---|
| 1991–92 | Tranmere R | 34 | 1 |
| 1992–93 | Tranmere R | 14 | 0 |
| 1993–94 | Tranmere R | 40 | 0 |
| 1994–95 | Sheffield W | 42 | 3 |
| 1995–96 | Sheffield W | 29 | 0 |
| 1996–97 | Sheffield W | 38 | 1 |
| 1997–98 | Sheffield W | 27 | 0 |
| **Total:** | | **224** | **5** |

## NORMAN, Steven — Midfield

b.Harold Wood 30-1-79

*Source:* Trainee.

| | | | |
|---|---|---|---|
| 1997–98 | Gillingham | 0 | 0 |

## NORRIS, Richard — Midfield

b.Birkenhead 5-1-78

*Source:* Marine.

| | | | |
|---|---|---|---|
| 1996–97 | Crewe Alex | 0 | 0 |
| 1997–98 | Crewe Alex | 0 | 0 |

## NOTMAN, Alex — Forward

H: 5 7 W: 10 11 b.Edinburgh 10-12-79

*Source:* Trainee.

| | | | |
|---|---|---|---|
| 1996–97 | Manchester U | 0 | 0 |
| 1997–98 | Manchester U | 0 | 0 |

## NOTTINGHAM, Steve — Defender

b.Peterborough 21-2-80

*Source:* Trainee.

| | | | |
|---|---|---|---|
| 1997–98 | Scunthorpe U | 1 | 0 |
| **Total:** | | **1** | **0** |

## NOWLAND, Adam — Forward

H: 5 11 W: 11 06 b.Preston 6-7-81

*Source:* Trainee.

| | | | |
|---|---|---|---|
| 1997–98 | Blackpool | 1 | 0 |
| **Total:** | | **1** | **0** |

## NUGENT, Kevin — Forward

H: 6 2 W: 13 04 b.Edmonton 10-4-69

*Source:* Trainee. *Honours:* Eire Youth.

| | | | |
|---|---|---|---|
| 1987–88 | Leyton Orient | 11 | 3 |
| 1988–89 | Leyton Orient | 3 | 0 |
| 1989–90 | Leyton Orient | 11 | 0 |
| 1990–91 | Leyton Orient | 33 | 5 |
| 1991–92 | Leyton Orient | 36 | 12 |
| 1991–92 | Plymouth Arg | 4 | 0 |
| 1992–93 | Plymouth Arg | 45 | 11 |
| 1993–94 | Plymouth Arg | 39 | 14 |
| 1994–95 | Plymouth Arg | 37 | 7 |
| 1995–96 | Plymouth Arg | 6 | 0 |
| 1995–96 | Bristol C | 34 | 8 |
| 1996–97 | Bristol C | 36 | 6 |
| 1997–98 | Cardiff C | 4 | 0 |
| **Total:** | | **299** | **66** |

## NURSE, David — Goalkeeper

H: 6 4 W: 12 06 b.Kings Lynn 12-10-76

*Source:* Trainee.

| | | | |
|---|---|---|---|
| 1995–96 | Manchester C | 0 | 0 |
| 1996–97 | Millwall | 0 | 0 |
| 1997–98 | Millwall | 0 | 0 |
| 1997–98 | Brentford (loan) | 0 | 0 |

## NWADIKE, Emeka — Defender

H: 6 0 W: 13 00 b.Camberwell 9-8-78

*Source:* Trainee.

| | | | |
|---|---|---|---|
| 1996–97 | Wolverhampton W | 0 | 0 |
| 1996–97 | Shrewsbury T | 2 | 0 |
| 1997–98 | Shrewsbury T | 1 | 0 |
| **Total:** | | **3** | **0** |

## NYAMAH, Kofi — Defender

H: 5 10 W: 11 07 b.Islington 20-6-75

*Source:* Trainee.

| | | | |
|---|---|---|---|
| 1993–94 | Cambridge U | 14 | 2 |
| 1994–95 | Cambridge U | 9 | 0 |
| 1995–96 | Cambridge U | 0 | 0 |
| 1996–97 | Cambridge U | 0 | 0 |
| From Kettering T. | | | |
| 1996–97 | Stoke C | 7 | 0 |
| 1997–98 | Stoke C | 10 | 0 |
| **Total:** | | **40** | **2** |

## NZAMBA, Guy — Forward

b.Gabon 13-7-70

*Source:* Trieste.

| | | | |
|---|---|---|---|
| 1997–98 | Southend U | 1 | 0 |
| **Total:** | | **1** | **0** |

## O'BOYLE, George — Forward

H: 5 8 W: 11 09 b.Belfast 14-12-67

*Source:* Linfield. *Honours:* Northern Ireland 12 full caps, 1 goal.

| | | | |
|---|---|---|---|
| 1989–90 | Dunfermline Ath | 28 | 3 |
| 1990–91 | Dunfermline Ath | 16 | 6 |
| 1991–92 | Dunfermline Ath | 16 | 1 |
| 1992–93 | Dunfermline Ath | 3 | 2 |
| 1993–94 | Dunfermline Ath | 32 | 17 |
| 1994–95 | St Johnstone | 32 | 19 |
| 1995–96 | St Johnstone | 35 | 21 |
| 1996–97 | St Johnstone | 25 | 12 |
| 1997–98 | St Johnstone | 33 | 10 |
| **Total:** | | **220** | **91** |

## O'BRIEN, Andrew — Defender

H: 5 10 W: 10 06 b.Harrogate 29-6-79

*Source:* Trainee. *Honours:* England Youth.

| | | | |
|---|---|---|---|
| 1996–97 | Bradford C | 22 | 2 |
| 1997–98 | Bradford C | 26 | 0 |
| **Total:** | | **48** | **2** |

## O'BRIEN, Liam — Midfield

H: 6 1 W: 11 10 b.Dublin 5-9-64

*Source:* Shamrock R. *Honours:* Eire Youth, 16 full caps.

| | | | |
|---|---|---|---|
| 1986–87 | Manchester U | 11 | 0 |
| 1987–88 | Manchester U | 17 | 2 |
| 1988–89 | Manchester U | 3 | 0 |
| 1988–89 | Newcastle U | 20 | 4 |
| 1989–90 | Newcastle U | 19 | 2 |
| 1990–91 | Newcastle U | 33 | 3 |
| 1991–92 | Newcastle U | 40 | 4 |
| 1992–93 | Newcastle U | 33 | 6 |
| 1993–94 | Newcastle U | 6 | 0 |
| 1993–94 | Tranmere R | 17 | 1 |
| 1994–95 | Tranmere R | 38 | 1 |
| 1995–96 | Tranmere R | 22 | 4 |
| 1996–97 | Tranmere R | 41 | 1 |
| 1997–98 | Tranmere R | 40 | 3 |
| **Total:** | | **340** | **31** |

## O'BRIEN, Michael — Midfield

b.Liverpool 25-9-79

*Source:* Trainee. *Honours:* England Schools.

| | | | |
|---|---|---|---|
| 1997–98 | Everton | 0 | 0 |

## O'BRIEN, Ronnie — Midfield

b.Dublin 15-1-79

*Source:* St Joseph's BC.

| | | | |
|---|---|---|---|
| 1997–98 | Middlesbrough | 0 | 0 |

## O'CONNELL, Brendan — Midfield

H: 5 9 W: 12 01 b.London 12-11-66

| | | | |
|---|---|---|---|
| 1984–85 | Portsmouth | 0 | 0 |
| 1985–86 | Portsmouth | 0 | 0 |
| 1986–87 | Exeter C | 42 | 8 |
| 1987–88 | Exeter C | 39 | 11 |
| 1988–89 | Burnley | 43 | 13 |
| 1989–90 | Burnley | 21 | 4 |
| 1989–90 | Huddersfield T (loan) | 11 | 1 |
| 1989–90 | Barnsley | 11 | 2 |
| 1990–91 | Barnsley | 45 | 9 |
| 1991–92 | Barnsley | 36 | 4 |
| 1992–93 | Barnsley | 40 | 6 |
| 1993–94 | Barnsley | 38 | 6 |
| 1994–95 | Barnsley | 45 | 7 |
| 1995–96 | Barnsley | 25 | 1 |
| 1996–97 | Charlton Ath | 38 | 2 |
| 1997–98 | Wigan Ath | 17 | 5 |
| **Total:** | | **451** | **79** |

## O'CONNOR, Derek — Goalkeeper

H: 5 11 W: 12 06 b.Dublin 9-3-78

*Source:* Crumplin U. *Honours:* Eire Youth.

| | | | |
|---|---|---|---|
| 1994–95 | Huddersfield T | 0 | 0 |
| 1995–96 | Huddersfield T | 0 | 0 |
| 1996–97 | Huddersfield T | 0 | 0 |
| 1997–98 | Huddersfield T | 1 | 0 |
| **Total:** | | **1** | **0** |

## O'CONNOR, James — Midfield

H: 5 8 W: 11 00 b.Dublin 1-9-79

*Source:* Trainee.

| | | | |
|---|---|---|---|
| 1996–97 | Stoke C | 0 | 0 |
| 1997–98 | Stoke C | 0 | 0 |

## O'CONNOR, Jon — Defender

H: 6 0 W: 11 10 b.Darlington 29-10-76

*Source:* Trainee. *Honours:* England Youth, Under-21.

| | | | |
|---|---|---|---|
| 1993–94 | Everton | 0 | 0 |
| 1994–95 | Everton | 0 | 0 |
| 1995–96 | Everton | 4 | 0 |
| 1996–97 | Everton | 0 | 0 |
| 1997–98 | Everton | 1 | 0 |
| 1997–98 | Sheffield U | 2 | 0 |
| **Total:** | | **7** | **0** |

## O'CONNOR, Mark — Midfield

H: 5 8 W: 11 03 b.Rochdale 10-3-63

*Source:* Apprentice. *Honours:* Eire Under-21.

| | | | |
|---|---|---|---|
| 1980–81 | QPR | 0 | 0 |
| 1981–82 | QPR | 1 | 0 |
| 1982–83 | QPR | 2 | 0 |
| 1983–84 | QPR | 0 | 0 |
| 1983–84 | Exeter C (loan) | 38 | 1 |
| 1984–85 | Bristol R | 46 | 8 |
| 1985–86 | Bristol R | 34 | 2 |
| 1985–86 | Bournemouth | 9 | 1 |
| 1986–87 | Bournemouth | 43 | 7 |
| 1987–88 | Bournemouth | 37 | 2 |
| 1988–89 | Bournemouth | 33 | 2 |
| 1989–90 | Bournemouth | 6 | 0 |
| 1989–90 | Gillingham | 15 | 1 |
| 1990–91 | Gillingham | 41 | 3 |
| 1991–92 | Gillingham | 39 | 3 |
| 1992–93 | Gillingham | 21 | 1 |
| 1993–94 | Bournemouth | 45 | 3 |
| 1994–95 | Bournemouth | 13 | 0 |
| 1995–96 | Gillingham | 18 | 1 |
| 1996–97 | Gillingham | 22 | 0 |
| 1997–98 | Gillingham | 0 | 0 |
| **Total:** | | **463** | **35** |

## O'CONNOR, Martin — Midfield

H: 5 8 W: 10 08 b.Walsall 10-12-67

*Source:* Bromsgrove R.

| | | | |
|---|---|---|---|
| 1992–93 | Crystal Palace | 0 | 0 |
| 1992–93 | Walsall (loan) | 10 | 1 |
| 1993–94 | Crystal Palace | 2 | 0 |
| 1993–94 | Walsall | 14 | 2 |
| 1994–95 | Walsall | 39 | 10 |
| 1995–96 | Walsall | 41 | 9 |
| 1996–97 | Peterborough U | 18 | 3 |
| 1996–97 | Birmingham C | 24 | 4 |
| 1997–98 | Birmingham C | 33 | 1 |
| **Total:** | | **181** | **30** |

## O'CONNOR, Richard — Forward

H: 5 9 W: 10 07 b.Wandsworth 30-8-78

*Source:* Trainee.

| | | | |
|---|---|---|---|
| 1996–97 | Wimbledon | 0 | 0 |
| 1997–98 | Wimbledon | 0 | 0 |

## O'DONNELL, Phillip — Midfield

H: 5 10 W: 10 05 b.Bellshill 25-3-72

*Source:* X Form. *Honours:* Scotland Under-21, 1 full cap.

| | | | |
|---|---|---|---|
| 1990–91 | Motherwell | 12 | 0 |
| 1991–92 | Motherwell | 42 | 4 |
| 1992–93 | Motherwell | 32 | 4 |
| 1993–94 | Motherwell | 35 | 7 |
| 1994–95 | Motherwell | 3 | 0 |
| 1994–95 | Celtic | 27 | 6 |
| 1995–96 | Celtic | 15 | 3 |
| 1996–97 | Celtic | 19 | 2 |
| 1997–98 | Celtic | 14 | 2 |
| **Total:** | | **199** | **28** |

## O'DRISCOLL, Jerry — Forward

H: 6 0 W: 11 09 b.Aberdeen 4-4-78

*Source:* Crombie J.

| | | | |
|---|---|---|---|
| 1995–96 | Dundee | 5 | 1 |
| 1996–97 | Dundee | 21 | 10 |
| 1997–98 | Dundee | 13 | 1 |
| **Total:** | | **39** | **12** |

## O'GORMAN, Dave — Forward

H: 6 0 W: 13 00 b.Chester 20-6-72

*Source:* School.

| | | | |
|---|---|---|---|
| 1990–91 | Wrexham | 17 | 0 |
| Hyde U, Northwich V, Barry T | | | |
| 1997–98 | Swansea C | 34 | 5 |
| **Total:** | | **51** | **5** |

## O'HAGAN, Danny — Forward

H: 6 1 W: 13 08 b.Padstow 24-4-76

*Source:* Trainee.

| | | | |
|---|---|---|---|
| 1994–95 | Plymouth Arg | 3 | 1 |
| 1995–96 | Plymouth Arg | 6 | 0 |
| 1996–97 | Plymouth Arg | 0 | 0 |
| From Weston-s-Mare. | | | |
| 1997–98 | Plymouth Arg | 9 | 0 |
| **Total:** | | **18** | **1** |

## O'HALLORAN, Keith — Defender

H: 5 9 W: 11 06 b.Ireland 10-11-75

*Source:* Cherry Orchard.

| | | | |
|---|---|---|---|
| 1994–95 | Middlesbrough | 1 | 0 |
| 1995–96 | Middlesbrough | 3 | 0 |
| 1995–96 | Scunthorpe U (loan) | 7 | 0 |
| 1996–97 | Middlesbrough | 0 | 0 |
| 1996–97 | Cardiff C (loan) | 8 | 0 |
| 1996–97 | St Johnstone | 5 | 0 |
| 1997–98 | St Johnstone | 22 | 1 |
| **Total:** | | **46** | **1** |

## O'HANLON, Kelham — Goalkeeper

H: 6 1 W: 13 12 b.Saltburn 16-5-62

*Source:* Apprentice. *Honours:* Eire Under-21, 1 full cap.

| | | | |
|---|---|---|---|
| 1980–81 | Middlesbrough | 0 | 0 |
| 1981–82 | Middlesbrough | 0 | 0 |
| 1982–83 | Middlesbrough | 19 | 0 |
| 1983–84 | Middlesbrough | 30 | 0 |
| 1984–85 | Middlesbrough | 38 | 0 |
| 1985–86 | Rotherham U | 46 | 0 |
| 1986–87 | Rotherham U | 40 | 0 |
| 1987–88 | Rotherham U | 40 | 0 |
| 1988–89 | Rotherham U | 46 | 0 |
| 1989–90 | Rotherham U | 43 | 0 |
| 1990–91 | Rotherham U | 33 | 0 |
| 1991–92 | Carlisle U | 42 | 0 |
| 1992–93 | Carlisle U | 41 | 0 |
| 1993–94 | Preston NE | 23 | 0 |
| 1994–95 | Dundee U | 29 | 0 |
| 1995–96 | Dundee U | 1 | 0 |
| 1996–97 | Dundee U | 0 | 0 |
| 1996–97 | Preston NE | 13 | 0 |
| 1997–98 | Preston NE | 0 | 0 |
| **Total:** | | **484** | **0** |

## O'KANE, John — Defender

H: 5 10 W: 12 04 b.Nottingham 15-11-74

*Source:* Trainee.

| | | | |
|---|---|---|---|
| 1992–93 | Manchester U | 0 | 0 |
| 1993–94 | Manchester U | 0 | 0 |
| 1994–95 | Manchester U | 0 | 0 |
| 1994–95 | Wimbledon (loan) | 0 | 0 |
| 1995–96 | Manchester U | 1 | 0 |
| 1996–97 | Manchester U | 1 | 0 |
| 1996–97 | Bury (loan) | 13 | 3 |
| 1997–98 | Manchester U | 0 | 0 |
| 1997–98 | Bradford C (loan) | 7 | 0 |
| 1997–98 | Everton | 12 | 0 |
| **Total:** | | **34** | **3** |

## O'LEARY, Kristian — Defender

H: 6 0 W: 13 04 b.Port Talbot 30-8-77

*Source:* Trainee.

| | | | |
|---|---|---|---|
| 1995–96 | Swansea C | 1 | 0 |
| 1996–97 | Swansea C | 12 | 1 |
| 1997–98 | Swansea C | 29 | 0 |
| **Total:** | | **42** | **1** |

## O'LOUGHLIN, John — Midfield

b.Letterkenny 31-1-79

*Source:* Bruncrana Hearts. *Honours:*

| | | | |
|---|---|---|---|
| 1997–98 | Middlesbrough | 0 | 0 |

## O'MARA, Paul — Defender

b.Dublin 23-11-80

*Source:* Trainee.

| | | | |
|---|---|---|---|
| 1997–98 | Liverpool | 0 | 0 |

## O'NEIL, Brian — Midfield

H: 6 1 W: 12 04 b.Paisley 6-9-72

*Source:* X Form. *Honours:* Scotland Under-21, 1 full cap.

| | | | |
|---|---|---|---|
| 1991–92 | Celtic | 28 | 1 |
| 1992–93 | Celtic | 17 | 3 |
| 1993–94 | Celtic | 28 | 2 |
| 1994–95 | Celtic | 26 | 0 |
| 1995–96 | Celtic | 5 | 0 |
| 1996–97 | Celtic | 16 | 2 |
| 1996–97 | Nottingham F (loan) | 5 | 0 |
| 1997–98 | Aberdeen | 29 | 1 |
| **Total:** | | **154** | **9** |

## O'NEIL, John — Midfield

H: 5 7 W: 10 02 b.Bellshill 6-7-71

*Source:* Fir Park BC. *Honours:* Scotland Under-21.

| | | | |
|---|---|---|---|
| 1988–89 | Dundee U | 1 | 0 |
| 1989–90 | Dundee U | 10 | 0 |
| 1990–91 | Dundee U | 15 | 0 |
| 1991–92 | Dundee U | 12 | 0 |
| 1992–93 | Dundee U | 28 | 3 |
| 1993–94 | Dundee U | 12 | 1 |
| 1994–95 | St Johnstone | 27 | 3 |
| 1995–96 | St Johnstone | 34 | 6 |
| 1996–97 | St Johnstone | 29 | 3 |
| 1997–98 | St Johnstone | 30 | 5 |
| **Total:** | | **198** | **21** |

## O'NEILL, Jon — Forward

H: 5 11 W: 12 00 b.Glasgow 2-1-74

*Source:* Queen's Park BC.

| | | | |
|---|---|---|---|
| 1991–92 | Queen's Park | 25 | 6 |
| 1992–93 | Queen's Park | 27 | 6 |
| 1993–94 | Queen's Park | 39 | 18 |
| 1994–95 | Celtic | 1 | 0 |
| 1995–96 | Bournemouth | 6 | 0 |
| 1996–97 | Bournemouth | 18 | 1 |
| 1997–98 | Bournemouth | 43 | 3 |
| **Total:** | | **159** | **34** |

## O'NEILL, Keith — Forward

H: 6 1 W: 12 04 b.Dublin 16-2-76

*Source:* Trainee. *Honours:* Eire 9 full caps, 4 goals.

| | | | |
|---|---|---|---|
| 1994–95 | Norwich C | 1 | 0 |
| 1995–96 | Norwich C | 19 | 1 |
| 1996–97 | Norwich C | 26 | 6 |
| 1997–98 | Norwich C | 9 | 1 |
| **Total:** | | **55** | **8** |

## O'NEILL, Martin — Midfield

H: 5 7 W: 10 10 b.Glasgow 17-6-75

*Source:* Clyde BC.

| | | | |
|---|---|---|---|
| 1993–94 | Clyde | 9 | 1 |
| 1994–95 | Clyde | 21 | 2 |
| 1995–96 | Clyde | 23 | 2 |
| 1996–97 | Clyde | 29 | 4 |
| 1997–98 | Kilmarnock | 2 | 0 |
| **Total:** | | **84** | **9** |

## O'NEILL, Michael — Forward

H: 5 11 W: 10 10 b.Portadown 5-7-69

*Source:* Coleraine. *Honours:* Northern Ireland Under-21, 31 full caps, 4 goals.

| | | | |
|---|---|---|---|
| 1987–88 | Newcastle U | 21 | 12 |
| 1988–89 | Newcastle U | 27 | 3 |
| 1989–90 | Dundee U | 18 | 5 |
| 1990–91 | Dundee U | 13 | 0 |
| 1991–92 | Dundee U | 8 | 4 |
| 1992–93 | Dundee U | 25 | 2 |
| 1993–94 | Hibernian | 36 | 3 |
| 1994–95 | Hibernian | 33 | 10 |
| 1995–96 | Hibernian | 29 | 6 |
| 1996–97 | Coventry C | 1 | 0 |
| 1997–98 | Coventry C | 4 | 0 |
| 1997–98 | Reading (loan) | 9 | 1 |
| **Total:** | | **224** | **46** |

## O'REILLY, Justin — Forward

H: 6 0 W: 13 08 b.Derby 29-6-73

*Source:* Gresley R.

| | | | |
|---|---|---|---|
| 1995–96 | Port Vale | 0 | 0 |
| 1996–97 | Port Vale | 0 | 0 |
| 1997–98 | Port Vale | 0 | 0 |

## O'SULLIVAN, Wayne — Midfield

H: 5 8 W: 10 12 b.Akrotiri 25-2-74

*Source:* Trainee.

| | | | |
|---|---|---|---|
| 1992–93 | Swindon T | 0 | 0 |
| 1993–94 | Swindon T | 0 | 0 |
| 1994–95 | Swindon T | 30 | 0 |
| 1995–96 | Swindon T | 34 | 3 |
| 1996–97 | Swindon T | 25 | 0 |
| 1997–98 | Swindon T | 0 | 0 |
| 1997–98 | Cardiff C | 43 | 2 |
| **Total:** | | **132** | **5** |

## O'TOOLE, John — Goalkeeper

b.Merseyside 23-2-79

*Source:* Trainee. *Honours:* England Schools.

| | | | |
|---|---|---|---|
| 1996–97 | Everton | 0 | 0 |
| 1997–98 | Everton | 0 | 0 |

## OAKES, Michael — Goalkeeper

H: 6 2 W: 14 07 b.Northwich 30-10-73

*Source:* Trainee. *Honours:* England Under-21.

| | | | |
|---|---|---|---|
| 1991–92 | Aston Villa | 0 | 0 |
| 1992–93 | Aston Villa | 0 | 0 |
| 1993–94 | Aston Villa | 0 | 0 |
| 1993–94 | Scarborough (loan) | 1 | 0 |
| 1993–94 | Tranmere R (loan) | 0 | 0 |
| 1994–95 | Aston Villa | 0 | 0 |
| 1995–96 | Aston Villa | 0 | 0 |
| 1996–97 | Aston Villa | 20 | 0 |
| 1997–98 | Aston Villa | 8 | 0 |
| **Total:** | | **29** | **0** |

## OAKES, Scott — Midfield

H: 5 11 W: 11 12 b.Leicester 5-8-72

*Source:* Trainee.

| | | | |
|---|---|---|---|
| 1989–90 | Leicester C | 2 | 0 |
| 1990–91 | Leicester C | 0 | 0 |
| 1991–92 | Leicester C | 1 | 0 |
| 1991–92 | Luton T | 21 | 2 |
| 1992–93 | Luton T | 44 | 5 |
| 1993–94 | Luton T | 36 | 8 |
| 1994–95 | Luton T | 43 | 9 |
| 1995–96 | Luton T | 29 | 3 |
| 1996–97 | Sheffield W | 19 | 1 |
| 1997–98 | Sheffield W | 4 | 0 |
| **Total:** | | **199** | **28** |

## OAKES, Stefan — Midfield

H: 5 11 W: 12 04 b.Leicester 6-9-78

*Source:* Trainee.

| | | | |
|---|---|---|---|
| 1997–98 | Leicester C | 0 | 0 |

## OAKLEY, Matthew — Midfield

H: 5 10 W: 12 02 b.Peterborough 17-8-77

*Source:* Trainee. *Honours:* England Under-21.

| | | | |
|---|---|---|---|
| 1994–95 | Southampton | 1 | 0 |
| 1995–96 | Southampton | 10 | 0 |
| 1996–97 | Southampton | 28 | 3 |
| 1997–98 | Southampton | 33 | 1 |
| **Total:** | | **72** | **4** |

## OATWAY, Charlie — Midfield

H: 5 7 W: 10 10 b.Hammersmith 28-11-73

*Source:* Yeading.

| | | | |
|---|---|---|---|
| 1994–95 | Cardiff C | 30 | 0 |
| 1995–96 | Cardiff C | 2 | 0 |
| 1995–96 | Torquay U | 24 | 0 |
| 1996–97 | Torquay U | 41 | 1 |
| 1997–98 | Torquay U | 2 | 0 |
| 1997–98 | Brentford | 33 | 0 |
| **Total:** | | **132** | **1** |

## ODLUM, Gary — Defender

H: 5 11 W: 11 04 b.Beckenham 19-10-78

*Source:* Trainee.

| | | | |
|---|---|---|---|
| 1996–97 | Wimbledon | 0 | 0 |
| 1997–98 | Wimbledon | 0 | 0 |

## OGRIZOVIC, Steve — Goalkeeper

H: 6 3 W: 15 00 b.Mansfield 12-9-57

*Source:* ONRYC.

| | | | |
|---|---|---|---|
| 1977–78 | Chesterfield | 16 | 0 |
| 1977–78 | Liverpool | 2 | 0 |
| 1978–79 | Liverpool | 0 | 0 |
| 1979–80 | Liverpool | 1 | 0 |
| 1980–81 | Liverpool | 1 | 0 |
| 1981–82 | Liverpool | 0 | 0 |
| 1982–83 | Shrewsbury T | 42 | 0 |
| 1983–84 | Shrewsbury T | 42 | 0 |

| | | | |
|---|---|---|---|
| 1984–85 | Coventry C | 42 | 0 |
| 1985–86 | Coventry C | 42 | 0 |
| 1986–87 | Coventry C | 42 | 1 |
| 1987–88 | Coventry C | 40 | 0 |
| 1988–89 | Coventry C | 38 | 0 |
| 1989–90 | Coventry C | 37 | 0 |
| 1990–91 | Coventry C | 37 | 0 |
| 1991–92 | Coventry C | 38 | 0 |
| 1992–93 | Coventry C | 33 | 0 |
| 1993–94 | Coventry C | 33 | 0 |
| 1994–95 | Coventry C | 33 | 0 |
| 1995–96 | Coventry C | 25 | 0 |
| 1996–97 | Coventry C | 38 | 0 |
| 1997–98 | Coventry C | 24 | 0 |
| **Total:** | | **606** | **1** |

## OHANDJANIAN, Dmis — Forward

b.Manchester 1-5-78

*Source:* Curzon Ashton.

| | | | |
|---|---|---|---|
| 1996–97 | Doncaster R | 1 | 0 |
| 1997–98 | Doncaster R | 0 | 0 |
| **Total:** | | **1** | **0** |

## OLDFIELD, David — Forward

H: 6 0 W: 13 04 b.Perth (Aus) 30-5-68

*Source:* Apprentice. *Honours:* England Under-21.

| | | | |
|---|---|---|---|
| 1986–87 | Luton T | 0 | 0 |
| 1987–88 | Luton T | 8 | 3 |
| 1988–89 | Luton T | 21 | 1 |
| 1988–89 | Manchester C | 11 | 3 |
| 1989–90 | Manchester C | 15 | 3 |
| 1989–90 | Leicester C | 20 | 5 |
| 1990–91 | Leicester C | 42 | 7 |
| 1991–92 | Leicester C | 41 | 4 |
| 1992–93 | Leicester C | 44 | 5 |
| 1993–94 | Leicester C | 27 | 4 |
| 1994–95 | Leicester C | 14 | 1 |
| 1994–95 | Millwall (loan) | 17 | 6 |
| 1995–96 | Luton T | 34 | 2 |
| 1996–97 | Luton T | 38 | 6 |
| 1997–98 | Luton T | 45 | 10 |
| **Total:** | | **377** | **60** |

## OLDHAM, Gavin — Midfield

b.Manchester 25-12-78

*Source:* Trainee.

| | | | |
|---|---|---|---|
| 1997–98 | Oldham Ath | 0 | 0 |

## OLIVER, Michael — Midfield

H: 5 10 W: 11 04 b.Middlesbrough 2-8-75

*Source:* Trainee.

| | | | |
|---|---|---|---|
| 1992–93 | Middlesbrough | 0 | 0 |
| 1993–94 | Middlesbrough | 0 | 0 |
| 1994–95 | Stockport Co | 13 | 0 |
| 1995–96 | Stockport Co | 9 | 1 |
| 1996–97 | Darlington | 39 | 9 |
| 1997–98 | Darlington | 39 | 2 |
| **Total:** | | **100** | **12** |

## OLOFSSON, Kjell — Forward

H: 6 2 W: 13 08 b.Gothenburg 23-7-65

| | | | |
|---|---|---|---|
| 1996 | Moss | 25 | 9 |
| 1996–97 | Dundee U | 25 | 12 |
| 1997–98 | Dundee U | 32 | 18 |
| **Total:** | | **82** | **39** |

## OMIGIE, Joe — Forward

H: 6 2 W: 13 00 b.Hammersmith 13-6-72

*Source:* Donna.

| | | | |
|---|---|---|---|
| 1994–95 | Brentford | 0 | 0 |
| 1995–96 | Brentford | 10 | 0 |
| 1996–97 | Brentford | 13 | 1 |
| 1997–98 | Brentford | 1 | 0 |
| **Total:** | | **24** | **1** |

## OMOGBEHIN, Colin — Defender

b.Croydon 10-9-74

| | | | |
|---|---|---|---|
| 1997–98 | Luton T | 0 | 0 |

## OMOYIMNI, Emmanuel — Forward

H: 5 6 W: 10 07 b.Nigeria 28-12-77

*Source:* Trainee. *Honours:* England Schools.

| | | | |
|---|---|---|---|
| 1994–95 | West Ham U | 0 | 0 |
| 1995–96 | West Ham U | 0 | 0 |
| 1996–97 | West Ham U | 1 | 0 |
| 1996–97 | Bournemouth (loan) | 7 | 0 |
| 1997–98 | West Ham U | 5 | 2 |
| 1997–98 | Dundee U (loan) | 4 | 0 |
| **Total:** | | **17** | **2** |

## ONUORA, Iffy — Forward

H: 6 0 W: 13 01 b.Glasgow 28-7-67

*Source:* British Univ.

| | | | |
|---|---|---|---|
| 1989–90 | Huddersfield T | 20 | 3 |
| 1990–91 | Huddersfield T | 43 | 7 |

| | | | |
|---|---|---|---|
| 1991–92 | Huddersfield T | 41 | 8 |
| 1992–93 | Huddersfield T | 39 | 6 |
| 1993–94 | Huddersfield T | 22 | 6 |
| 1994–95 | Mansfield T | 14 | 7 |
| 1995–96 | Mansfield T | 14 | 1 |
| 1996–97 | Gillingham | 40 | 21 |
| 1997–98 | Gillingham | 22 | 2 |
| 1997–98 | Swindon T | 6 | 1 |
| **Total:** | | **261** | **62** |

## ONWERE, Udo — Midfield

H: 6 0 W: 11 07 b.Hammersmith 9-11-72

*Source:* Trainee.

| | | | |
|---|---|---|---|
| 1990–91 | Fulham | 7 | 1 |
| 1991–92 | Fulham | 27 | 3 |
| 1992–93 | Fulham | 29 | 3 |
| 1993–94 | Fulham | 22 | 0 |
| 1994–95 | Lincoln C | 8 | 0 |
| 1995–96 | Lincoln C | 35 | 4 |
| 1996–97 | Lincoln C | 0 | 0 |
| 1996–97 | Blackpool | 9 | 0 |
| 1997–98 | Barnet | 17 | 0 |
| **Total:** | | **154** | **11** |

## ORD, Richard — Defender

H: 6 2 W: 12 08 b.Murton 3-3-70

*Source:* Trainee. *Honours:* England Under-21.

| | | | |
|---|---|---|---|
| 1987–88 | Sunderland | 8 | 0 |
| 1988–89 | Sunderland | 34 | 1 |
| 1989–90 | Sunderland | 7 | 1 |
| 1989–90 | York C (loan) | 3 | 0 |
| 1990–91 | Sunderland | 14 | 0 |
| 1991–92 | Sunderland | 6 | 0 |
| 1992–93 | Sunderland | 24 | 0 |
| 1993–94 | Sunderland | 28 | 2 |
| 1994–95 | Sunderland | 33 | 0 |
| 1995–96 | Sunderland | 42 | 1 |
| 1996–97 | Sunderland | 33 | 2 |
| 1997–98 | Sunderland | 14 | 0 |
| **Total:** | | **246** | **7** |

## ORLYGSSON, Toddy — Midfield

H: 5 11 W: 11 07 b.Odense 2-8-66

*Source:* FC Akureyi. *Honours:* Iceland 41 full caps, 7 goals.

| | | | |
|---|---|---|---|
| 1989–90 | Nottingham F | 12 | 1 |
| 1990–91 | Nottingham F | 0 | 0 |
| 1991–92 | Nottingham F | 5 | 0 |
| 1992–93 | Nottingham F | 20 | 1 |
| 1993–94 | Stoke C | 45 | 9 |
| 1994–95 | Stoke C | 38 | 7 |
| 1995–96 | Stoke C | 7 | 0 |
| 1995–96 | Oldham Ath | 16 | 0 |
| 1996–97 | Oldham Ath | 27 | 1 |
| 1997–98 | Oldham Ath | 11 | 0 |
| **Total:** | | **181** | **19** |

## ORMEROD, Anthony — Midfield

H: 5 10 W: 11 08 b.Middlesbrough 31-3-79

*Source:* Trainee. *Honours:* England Youth.

| | | | |
|---|---|---|---|
| 1995–96 | Middlesbrough | 0 | 0 |
| 1996–97 | Middlesbrough | 0 | 0 |
| 1997–98 | Middlesbrough | 18 | 3 |
| **Total:** | | **18** | **3** |

## ORMEROD, Brett — Forward

H: 5 11 W: 11 04 b.Blackburn 18-10-76

*Source:* Blackburn R Trainee, Accrington S.

| | | | |
|---|---|---|---|
| 1996–97 | Blackpool | 4 | 0 |
| 1997–98 | Blackpool | 9 | 2 |
| **Total:** | | **13** | **2** |

## ORMEROD, Mark — Goalkeeper

H: 6 0 W: 12 08 b.Bournemouth 5-2-76

*Source:* Trainee.

| | | | |
|---|---|---|---|
| 1994–95 | Brighton & HA | 0 | 0 |
| 1995–96 | Brighton & HA | 0 | 0 |
| 1996–97 | Brighton & HA | 21 | 0 |
| 1997–98 | Brighton & HA | 30 | 0 |
| **Total:** | | **51** | **0** |

## ORMONDROYD, Ian — Forward

H: 6 5 W: 13 09 b.Bradford 22-9-64

*Source:* Thackley.

| | | | |
|---|---|---|---|
| 1985–86 | Bradford C | 12 | 3 |
| 1986–87 | Bradford C | 13 | 4 |
| 1986–87 | Oldham Ath (loan) | 10 | 1 |
| 1987–88 | Bradford C | 37 | 9 |
| 1988–89 | Bradford C | 25 | 4 |
| 1988–89 | Aston Villa | 12 | 1 |
| 1989–90 | Aston Villa | 25 | 4 |
| 1990–91 | Aston Villa | 18 | 1 |
| 1991–92 | Aston Villa | 1 | 0 |
| 1991–92 | Derby Co | 25 | 8 |
| 1991–92 | Leicester C | 14 | 1 |
| 1992–93 | Leicester C | 26 | 2 |
| 1993–94 | Leicester C | 31 | 4 |
| 1994–95 | Leicester C | 6 | 0 |
| 1994–95 | Hull C (loan) | 10 | 6 |
| 1995–96 | Bradford C | 37 | 6 |
| 1996–97 | Bradford C | 1 | 0 |
| 1996–97 | Oldham Ath | 30 | 8 |

| | | | |
|---|---|---|---|
| 1997–98 | Oldham Ath | 1 | 0 |
| 1997–98 | Scunthorpe U | 20 | 0 |
| **Total:** | | **354** | **62** |

## ORMSHAW, Gareth — Goalkeeper

H: 6 0 W: 12 10 b.Durban 8-7-79

*Source:* Ramblers.

| | | | |
|---|---|---|---|
| 1996–97 | Crystal Palace | 0 | 0 |
| 1997–98 | Crystal Palace | 0 | 0 |

## OSBORN, Simon — Midfield

H: 5 10 W: 11 04 b.New Addington 19-1-72

*Source:* Apprentice.

| | | | |
|---|---|---|---|
| 1989–90 | Crystal Palace | 0 | 0 |
| 1990–91 | Crystal Palace | 4 | 0 |
| 1991–92 | Crystal Palace | 14 | 2 |
| 1992–93 | Crystal Palace | 31 | 2 |
| 1993–94 | Crystal Palace | 6 | 1 |
| 1994–95 | Reading | 32 | 5 |
| 1995–96 | QPR | 9 | 1 |
| 1995–96 | Wolverhampton W | 21 | 2 |
| 1996–97 | Wolverhampton W | 35 | 5 |
| 1997–98 | Wolverhampton W | 24 | 2 |
| **Total:** | | **176** | **20** |

## OSMAN, Russell — Defender

H: 5 11 W: 12 01 b.Repton 14-2-59

*Source:* Apprentice. *Honours:* England Under-21, B, 11 full caps.

| | | | |
|---|---|---|---|
| 1975–76 | Ipswich T | 0 | 0 |
| 1976–77 | Ipswich T | 0 | 0 |
| 1977–78 | Ipswich T | 28 | 0 |
| 1978–79 | Ipswich T | 39 | 2 |
| 1979–80 | Ipswich T | 42 | 2 |
| 1980–81 | Ipswich T | 42 | 1 |
| 1981–82 | Ipswich T | 39 | 2 |
| 1982–83 | Ipswich T | 38 | 4 |
| 1983–84 | Ipswich T | 37 | 3 |
| 1984–85 | Ipswich T | 29 | 3 |
| 1985–86 | Leicester C | 40 | 0 |
| 1986–87 | Leicester C | 31 | 3 |
| 1987–88 | Leicester C | 37 | 5 |
| 1988–89 | Southampton | 36 | 0 |
| 1989–90 | Southampton | 35 | 5 |
| 1990–91 | Southampton | 20 | 1 |
| 1991–92 | Southampton | 5 | 0 |
| 1991–92 | Bristol C | 31 | 2 |
| 1992–93 | Bristol C | 34 | 0 |
| 1993–94 | Bristol C | 5 | 1 |
| 1994–95 | Bristol C | 0 | 0 |
| 1994–95 | Plymouth Arg | 0 | 0 |
| 1995–96 | Plymouth Arg | 0 | 0 |
| 1995–96 | Brighton & HA | 12 | 0 |
| 1995–96 | Cardiff C | 15 | 0 |
| 1996–97 | Cardiff C | 0 | 0 |
| 1997–98 | Cardiff C | 0 | 0 |
| **Total:** | | **595** | **34** |

## OSTENSTAD, Egil — Forward

H: 5 11 W: 13 01 b.Haugesund 2-1-72

*Honours:* Norway 15 full caps, 6 goals.

| | | | |
|---|---|---|---|
| 1990 | Viking | 10 | 1 |
| 1991 | Viking | 10 | 1 |
| 1992 | Viking | 20 | 1 |
| 1993 | Viking | 22 | 10 |
| 1994 | Viking | 21 | 6 |
| 1995 | Viking | 21 | 12 |
| 1996 | Viking | 24 | 23 |
| 1996–97 | Southampton | 30 | 9 |
| 1997–98 | Southampton | 29 | 11 |
| **Total:** | | **187** | **74** |

## OSTER, John — Forward

H: 5 8 W: 10 08 b.Boston 8-12-78

*Source:* Trainee. *Honours:* Wales Under-21, 2 full caps.

| | | | |
|---|---|---|---|
| 1996–97 | Grimsby T | 24 | 3 |
| 1997–98 | Everton | 31 | 1 |
| **Total:** | | **55** | **4** |

## OTTO, Ricky — Midfield

H: 5 10 W: 11 00 b.Hackney 9-11-67

*Source:* Dartford.

| | | | |
|---|---|---|---|
| 1990–91 | Leyton Orient | 1 | 0 |
| 1991–92 | Leyton Orient | 32 | 5 |
| 1992–93 | Leyton Orient | 23 | 8 |
| 1993–94 | Southend U | 45 | 13 |
| 1994–95 | Southend U | 19 | 4 |
| 1994–95 | Birmingham C | 24 | 4 |
| 1995–96 | Birmingham C | 18 | 2 |
| 1996–97 | Birmingham C | 4 | 0 |
| 1996–97 | Charlton Ath (loan) | 7 | 0 |
| 1996–97 | Peterborough U (loan) | 15 | 4 |
| 1997–98 | Birmingham C | 0 | 0 |
| 1997–98 | Notts Co (loan) | 4 | 0 |
| **Total:** | | **192** | **40** |

## OVENDALE, Mark — Goalkeeper

H: 6 2 W: 13 02 b.Leicester 22-11-73

*Source:* Wisbech T.

| | | | |
|---|---|---|---|
| 1994–95 | Northampton T | 6 | 0 |
| From Barry T. | | | |
| 1997–98 | Bournemouth | 0 | 0 |
| **Total:** | | **6** | **0** |

## OVERMARS, Marc — Forward

H: 5 8 W: 11 04 b.Emst 29-3-73

*Honours:* Holland 46 full caps, 10 goals.

| | | | |
|---|---|---|---|
| 1990–91 | Go Ahead | 11 | 1 |
| 1991–92 | Willem II | 31 | 1 |
| 1992–93 | Ajax | 34 | 3 |
| 1993–94 | Ajax | 34 | 12 |
| 1994–95 | Ajax | 27 | 8 |
| 1995–96 | Ajax | 15 | 11 |
| 1996–97 | Ajax | 25 | 2 |
| 1997–98 | Arsenal | 32 | 12 |
| **Total:** | | **209** | **50** |

## OVERSON, Vince — Defender

H: 6 2 W: 14 13 b.Kettering 15-5-62

*Source:* Apprentice.

| | | | |
|---|---|---|---|
| 1979–80 | Burnley | 22 | 0 |
| 1980–81 | Burnley | 39 | 1 |
| 1981–82 | Burnley | 36 | 4 |
| 1982–83 | Burnley | 6 | 0 |
| 1983–84 | Burnley | 38 | 0 |
| 1984–85 | Burnley | 42 | 1 |
| 1985–86 | Burnley | 28 | 0 |
| 1986–87 | Birmingham C | 34 | 1 |
| 1987–88 | Birmingham C | 37 | 0 |
| 1988–89 | Birmingham C | 41 | 0 |
| 1989–90 | Birmingham C | 30 | 0 |
| 1990–91 | Birmingham C | 40 | 2 |
| 1991–92 | Stoke C | 35 | 3 |
| 1992–93 | Stoke C | 43 | 1 |
| 1993–94 | Stoke C | 39 | 2 |
| 1994–95 | Stoke C | 35 | 0 |
| 1995–96 | Stoke C | 18 | 0 |
| 1996–97 | Burnley | 8 | 0 |
| 1997–98 | Burnley | 0 | 0 |
| 1997–98 | Shrewsbury T (loan) | 2 | 0 |
| **Total:** | | **573** | **15** |

## OWEN, Gareth — Midfield

H: 5 7 W: 12 00 b.Chester 21-10-71

*Source:* Trainee. *Honours:* Wales Under-21.

| | | | |
|---|---|---|---|
| 1989–90 | Wrexham | 13 | 0 |
| 1990–91 | Wrexham | 27 | 2 |
| 1991–92 | Wrexham | 36 | 7 |
| 1992–93 | Wrexham | 41 | 3 |
| 1993–94 | Wrexham | 27 | 3 |
| 1994–95 | Wrexham | 28 | 3 |
| 1995–96 | Wrexham | 19 | 2 |
| 1996–97 | Wrexham | 23 | 1 |
| 1997–98 | Wrexham | 40 | 7 |
| **Total:** | | **254** | **28** |

## OWEN, Karl — Defender

H: 5 11 W: 12 06 b.Coventry 12-10-79

*Source:* Trainee.

| | | | |
|---|---|---|---|
| 1996–97 | QPR | 0 | 0 |
| 1997–98 | QPR | 0 | 0 |

## OWEN, Michael — Forward

H: 5 8 W: 11 00 b.Chester 14-12-79

*Source:* Trainee. *Honours:* England Schools, Youth, Under-21, 9 full caps, 3 goals.

| | | | |
|---|---|---|---|
| 1996–97 | Liverpool | 2 | 1 |
| 1997–98 | Liverpool | 36 | 18 |
| **Total:** | | **38** | **19** |

## OWERS, Gary — Midfield

H: 5 11 W: 11 01 b.Newcastle 3-10-68

*Source:* Apprentice.

| | | | |
|---|---|---|---|
| 1986–87 | Sunderland | 0 | 0 |
| 1987–88 | Sunderland | 37 | 4 |
| 1988–89 | Sunderland | 38 | 3 |
| 1989–90 | Sunderland | 43 | 9 |
| 1990–91 | Sunderland | 38 | 1 |
| 1991–92 | Sunderland | 30 | 4 |
| 1992–93 | Sunderland | 33 | 1 |
| 1993–94 | Sunderland | 30 | 2 |
| 1994–95 | Sunderland | 19 | 1 |
| 1994–95 | Bristol C | 21 | 2 |
| 1995–96 | Bristol C | 37 | 2 |
| 1996–97 | Bristol C | 46 | 4 |
| 1997–98 | Bristol C | 22 | 1 |
| **Total:** | | **394** | **34** |

## PAATELAINEN, Mixu — Forward

H: 6 0 W: 13 10 b.Helsinki 3-2-67

*Source:* Valkeakosken Haka. *Honours:* Finland 54 full caps, 14 goals.

| | | | |
|---|---|---|---|
| 1987–88 | Dundee U | 19 | 9 |
| 1988–89 | Dundee U | 33 | 10 |
| 1989–90 | Dundee U | 31 | 7 |
| 1990–91 | Dundee U | 20 | 1 |
| 1991–92 | Dundee U | 30 | 6 |
| 1991–92 | Aberdeen | 6 | 1 |
| 1992–93 | Aberdeen | 33 | 16 |
| 1993–94 | Aberdeen | 36 | 6 |
| 1994–95 | Bolton W | 44 | 12 |
| 1995–96 | Bolton W | 15 | 1 |
| 1996–97 | Bolton W | 10 | 2 |
| 1997–98 | Wolverhampton W | 23 | 0 |
| **Total:** | | **300** | **71** |

## PADOVANO, Michele — Forward

H: 5 10 W: 11 00 b.Turin 28-8-66

*Honours:* Italy 1 full cap.

| | | | |
|---|---|---|---|
| 1985–86 | Asti | 22 | 5 |
| 1986–87 | Asti | 2 | 0 |
| 1986–87 | Cosenza | 21 | 2 |
| 1987–88 | Cosenza | 21 | 7 |
| 1988–89 | Cosenza | 30 | 5 |
| 1989–90 | Cosenza | 31 | 11 |
| 1990–91 | Pisa | 30 | 11 |
| 1991–92 | Napoli | 27 | 7 |
| 1992–93 | Genoa | 27 | 9 |
| 1993–94 | Reggiana | 29 | 10 |
| 1994–95 | Genoa | 2 | 0 |
| 1994–95 | Reggiana | 19 | 7 |
| 1995–96 | Juventus | 21 | 4 |
| 1996–97 | Juventus | 20 | 8 |
| 1997–98 | Juventus | 1 | 0 |
| 1997–98 | Crystal Palace | 10 | 1 |
| **Total:** | | **313** | **87** |

## PAGAL, John — Defender

H: 5 11 W: 12 04 b.Cameroon 15-9-64

| | | | |
|---|---|---|---|
| 1997–98 | Carlisle U | 1 | 0 |
| **Total:** | | **1** | **0** |

## PAGE, Robert — Defender

H: 6 0 W: 12 05 b.Llwynipia 3-9-74

*Source:* Trainee. *Honours:* Wales Under-21, 6 full caps.

| | | | |
|---|---|---|---|
| 1992–93 | Watford | 0 | 0 |
| 1993–94 | Watford | 4 | 0 |
| 1994–95 | Watford | 5 | 0 |
| 1995–96 | Watford | 19 | 0 |
| 1996–97 | Watford | 36 | 0 |
| 1997–98 | Watford | 41 | 0 |
| **Total:** | | **105** | **0** |

## PAINTER, Robbie — Forward

H: 5 10 W: 12 02 b.Ince 26-1-71

*Source:* Trainee.

| | | | |
|---|---|---|---|
| 1987–88 | Chester C | 2 | 0 |
| 1988–89 | Chester C | 8 | 1 |
| 1989–90 | Chester C | 32 | 4 |
| 1990–91 | Chester C | 42 | 3 |
| 1991–92 | Maidstone U | 30 | 5 |
| 1991–92 | Burnley | 9 | 2 |
| 1992–93 | Burnley | 17 | 0 |
| 1993–94 | Burnley | 0 | 0 |
| 1993–94 | Darlington | 36 | 11 |
| 1994–95 | Darlington | 38 | 9 |
| 1995–96 | Darlington | 35 | 8 |
| 1996–97 | Darlington | 6 | 0 |
| 1996–97 | Rochdale | 27 | 7 |
| 1997–98 | Rochdale | 45 | 17 |
| **Total:** | | **327** | **67** |

## PALLISTER, Gary — Defender

H: 6 4 W: 14 12 b.Ramsgate 30-6-65

*Source:* Billingham T. *Honours:* England B, 22 full caps.

| | | | |
|---|---|---|---|
| 1984–85 | Middlesbrough | 0 | 0 |
| 1985–86 | Middlesbrough | 28 | 0 |
| 1985–86 | Darlington (loan) | 7 | 0 |
| 1986–87 | Middlesbrough | 44 | 1 |
| 1987–88 | Middlesbrough | 44 | 3 |
| 1988–89 | Middlesbrough | 37 | 1 |
| 1989–90 | Middlesbrough | 3 | 0 |
| 1989–90 | Manchester U | 35 | 3 |
| 1990–91 | Manchester U | 36 | 0 |
| 1991–92 | Manchester U | 40 | 1 |
| 1992–93 | Manchester U | 42 | 1 |
| 1993–94 | Manchester U | 41 | 1 |
| 1994–95 | Manchester U | 42 | 2 |
| 1995–96 | Manchester U | 21 | 1 |
| 1996–97 | Manchester U | 27 | 3 |
| 1997–98 | Manchester U | 33 | 0 |
| **Total:** | | **480** | **17** |

## PALMER, Carlton — Defender

H: 6 2 W: 13 03 b.Oldbury 5-12-65

*Source:* Trainee. *Honours:* England Under-21, B, 18 full caps, 1 goal.

| | | | |
|---|---|---|---|
| 1984–85 | WBA | 0 | 0 |
| 1985–86 | WBA | 20 | 0 |
| 1986–87 | WBA | 37 | 1 |
| 1987–88 | WBA | 38 | 3 |
| 1988–89 | WBA | 26 | 0 |
| 1988–89 | Sheffield W | 13 | 1 |
| 1989–90 | Sheffield W | 34 | 0 |
| 1990–91 | Sheffield W | 45 | 2 |
| 1991–92 | Sheffield W | 42 | 5 |
| 1992–93 | Sheffield W | 34 | 1 |
| 1993–94 | Sheffield W | 37 | 5 |
| 1994–95 | Leeds U | 39 | 3 |
| 1995–96 | Leeds U | 35 | 2 |
| 1996–97 | Leeds U | 28 | 0 |
| 1997–98 | Leeds U | 0 | 0 |
| 1997–98 | Southampton | 26 | 3 |
| **Total:** | | **454** | **26** |

## PALMER, Steve — Defender

H: 6 1 W: 12 13 b.Brighton 31-3-68

*Source:* Cambridge Univ. *Honours:* England Schools.

| | | | |
|---|---|---|---|
| 1989–90 | Ipswich T | 5 | 0 |
| 1990–91 | Ipswich T | 23 | 1 |
| 1991–92 | Ipswich T | 23 | 0 |
| 1992–93 | Ipswich T | 7 | 0 |
| 1993–94 | Ipswich T | 36 | 1 |
| 1994–95 | Ipswich T | 12 | 0 |
| 1995–96 | Ipswich T | 5 | 0 |
| 1995–96 | Watford | 35 | 1 |
| 1996–97 | Watford | 41 | 2 |
| 1997–98 | Watford | 41 | 2 |
| **Total:** | | **228** | **7** |

## PAPACONSTANTINOU, Loukas — Goalkeeper

H: 6 4 W: 14 00 b.Toronto 10-5-74

*Source:* Toronto, B, Alabama Saints.

| | | | |
|---|---|---|---|
| 1997–98 | Darlington | 1 | 0 |
| **Total:** | | **1** | **0** |

## PARKER, Garry — Midfield

H: 6 0 W: 13 03 b.Oxford 7-9-65

*Source:* Apprentice. *Honours:* England Youth, Under-21, B.

| | | | |
|---|---|---|---|
| 1982–83 | Luton T | 1 | 0 |
| 1983–84 | Luton T | 13 | 2 |
| 1984–85 | Luton T | 20 | 1 |
| 1985–86 | Luton T | 8 | 0 |
| 1985–86 | Hull C | 12 | 0 |
| 1986–87 | Hull C | 38 | 0 |
| 1987–88 | Hull C | 34 | 8 |
| 1987–88 | Nottingham F | 2 | 0 |
| 1988–89 | Nottingham F | 22 | 7 |
| 1989–90 | Nottingham F | 37 | 6 |
| 1990–91 | Nottingham F | 36 | 3 |
| 1991–92 | Nottingham F | 6 | 1 |
| 1991–92 | Aston Villa | 25 | 1 |
| 1992–93 | Aston Villa | 37 | 9 |
| 1993–94 | Aston Villa | 19 | 2 |
| 1994–95 | Aston Villa | 14 | 1 |
| 1994–95 | Leicester C | 14 | 2 |
| 1995–96 | Leicester C | 40 | 3 |
| 1996–97 | Leicester C | 31 | 2 |
| 1997–98 | Leicester C | 22 | 3 |
| **Total:** | | **431** | **51** |

## PARKER, Scott — Midfield

H: 5 9 W: 11 00 b.Lambeth 13-10-80

*Source:* Trainee. *Honours:* England Schools.

| | | | |
|---|---|---|---|
| 1997–98 | Charlton Ath | 3 | 0 |
| **Total:** | | **3** | **0** |

## PARKIN, Brian — Goalkeeper

H: 6 4 W: 14 02 b.Birkenhead 12-10-65

*Source:* Local.

| | | | |
|---|---|---|---|
| 1982–83 | Oldham Ath | 0 | 0 |
| 1983–84 | Oldham Ath | 5 | 0 |
| 1984–85 | Oldham Ath | 1 | 0 |
| 1984–85 | Crewe Alex (loan) | 12 | 0 |
| 1985–86 | Crewe Alex | 39 | 0 |
| 1986–87 | Crewe Alex | 44 | 0 |
| 1987–88 | Crewe Alex | 3 | 0 |
| 1987–88 | Crystal Palace (loan) | 0 | 0 |
| 1988–89 | Crystal Palace | 19 | 0 |
| 1989–90 | Crystal Palace | 1 | 0 |
| 1989–90 | Bristol R | 30 | 0 |
| 1990–91 | Bristol R | 39 | 0 |
| 1991–92 | Bristol R | 43 | 0 |
| 1992–93 | Bristol R | 26 | 0 |
| 1993–94 | Bristol R | 43 | 0 |
| 1994–95 | Bristol R | 40 | 0 |
| 1995–96 | Bristol R | 20 | 0 |
| 1996–97 | Wycombe W | 24 | 0 |
| 1997–98 | Wycombe W | 1 | 0 |
| **Total:** | | **390** | **0** |

## PARKIN, Steve — Defender

H: 5 6 W: 11 01 b.Mansfield 7-11-65

*Source:* Apprentice. *Honours:* England Schools, Youth, Under-21.

| | | | |
|---|---|---|---|
| 1982–83 | Stoke C | 2 | 0 |
| 1983–84 | Stoke C | 1 | 0 |
| 1984–85 | Stoke C | 13 | 1 |
| 1985–86 | Stoke C | 12 | 1 |
| 1986–87 | Stoke C | 38 | 0 |
| 1987–88 | Stoke C | 43 | 3 |
| 1988–89 | Stoke C | 4 | 0 |
| 1989–90 | WBA | 14 | 1 |
| 1990–91 | WBA | 25 | 1 |
| 1991–92 | WBA | 9 | 0 |
| 1992–93 | Mansfield T | 16 | 0 |
| 1993–94 | Mansfield T | 23 | 1 |
| 1994–95 | Mansfield T | 22 | 1 |
| 1995–96 | Mansfield T | 26 | 1 |
| 1996–97 | Mansfield T | 0 | 0 |
| 1997–98 | Mansfield T | 0 | 0 |
| **Total:** | | **248** | **10** |

## PARKINSON, Andy — Forward

H: 5 8 W: 10 12 b.Liverpool 27-6-79

*Source:* Liverpool Trainee.

| | | | |
|---|---|---|---|
| 1996–97 | Tranmere R | 0 | 0 |
| 1997–98 | Tranmere R | 18 | 1 |
| **Total:** | | **18** | **1** |

## PARKINSON, Gary — Defender

H: 5 10 W: 11 06 b.Middlesbrough 10-1-68

*Source:* Everton Amateur.

| | | | |
|---|---|---|---|
| 1985–86 | Middlesbrough | 0 | 0 |
| 1986–87 | Middlesbrough | 46 | 0 |
| 1987–88 | Middlesbrough | 38 | 0 |
| 1988–89 | Middlesbrough | 36 | 2 |
| 1989–90 | Middlesbrough | 41 | 2 |
| 1990–91 | Middlesbrough | 10 | 1 |
| 1991–92 | Middlesbrough | 27 | 0 |
| 1992–93 | Middlesbrough | 4 | 0 |
| 1992–93 | Southend U (loan) | 6 | 0 |
| 1992–93 | Bolton W | 2 | 0 |
| 1993–94 | Bolton W | 1 | 0 |
| 1993–94 | Burnley | 20 | 1 |
| 1994–95 | Burnley | 43 | 2 |
| 1995–96 | Burnley | 29 | 0 |
| 1996–97 | Burnley | 43 | 1 |
| 1997–98 | Preston NE | 45 | 5 |
| **Total:** | | **391** | **14** |

## PARKINSON, Joe — Midfield

H: 5 8 W: 12 02 b.Eccles 11-6-71

*Source:* Trainee.

| | | | |
|---|---|---|---|
| 1988–89 | Wigan Ath | 12 | 1 |
| 1989–90 | Wigan Ath | 33 | 2 |
| 1990–91 | Wigan Ath | 25 | 0 |
| 1991–92 | Wigan Ath | 36 | 3 |
| 1992–93 | Wigan Ath | 13 | 0 |
| 1993–94 | Bournemouth | 30 | 1 |
| 1993–94 | Everton | 0 | 0 |
| 1994–95 | Everton | 34 | 0 |
| 1995–96 | Everton | 28 | 3 |
| 1996–97 | Everton | 28 | 0 |
| 1997–98 | Everton | 0 | 0 |
| **Total:** | | **239** | **10** |

## PARKINSON, Phil — Midfield

H: 6 0 W: 12 09 b.Chorley 1-12-67

*Source:* Apprentice.

| | | | |
|---|---|---|---|
| 1985–86 | Southampton | 0 | 0 |
| 1986–87 | Southampton | 0 | 0 |
| 1987–88 | Southampton | 0 | 0 |
| 1987–88 | Bury | 8 | 1 |
| 1988–89 | Bury | 39 | 0 |
| 1989–90 | Bury | 22 | 2 |
| 1990–91 | Bury | 44 | 2 |
| 1991–92 | Bury | 32 | 0 |
| 1992–93 | Reading | 39 | 4 |
| 1993–94 | Reading | 42 | 3 |
| 1994–95 | Reading | 31 | 0 |
| 1995–96 | Reading | 42 | 0 |
| 1996–97 | Reading | 24 | 1 |
| 1997–98 | Reading | 37 | 0 |
| **Total:** | | **360** | **13** |

## PARKS, Tony — Goalkeeper

H: 5 10 W: 11 05 b.Hackney 28-1-63

*Source:* Apprentice.

| | | | |
|---|---|---|---|
| 1980–81 | Tottenham H | 0 | 0 |
| 1981–82 | Tottenham H | 2 | 0 |
| 1982–83 | Tottenham H | 1 | 0 |
| 1983–84 | Tottenham H | 16 | 0 |
| 1984–85 | Tottenham H | 0 | 0 |
| 1985–86 | Tottenham H | 0 | 0 |
| 1986–87 | Tottenham H | 2 | 0 |
| 1986–87 | Oxford U (loan) | 5 | 0 |
| 1987–88 | Tottenham H | 16 | 0 |
| 1987–88 | Gillingham (loan) | 2 | 0 |
| 1988–89 | Brentford | 33 | 0 |
| 1989–90 | Brentford | 37 | 0 |
| 1990–91 | Brentford | 1 | 0 |
| 1990–91 | QPR (loan) | 0 | 0 |
| 1990–91 | Fulham | 2 | 0 |
| 1991–92 | West Ham U | 6 | 0 |
| 1992–93 | Stoke C | 2 | 0 |
| 1992–93 | Falkirk | 15 | 0 |
| 1993–94 | Falkirk | 41 | 0 |
| 1994–95 | Falkirk | 28 | 0 |
| 1995–96 | Falkirk | 28 | 0 |
| 1996–97 | Blackpool | 0 | 0 |
| 1997–98 | Burnley | 0 | 0 |
| 1997–98 | Doncaster R (loan) | 6 | 0 |
| **Total:** | | **243** | **0** |

## PARLOUR, Ray — Midfield

H: 5 10 W: 11 12 b.Romford 7-3-73

*Source:* Trainee. *Honours:* England Under-21, B.

| | | | |
|---|---|---|---|
| 1990–91 | Arsenal | 0 | 0 |
| 1991–92 | Arsenal | 6 | 1 |
| 1992–93 | Arsenal | 21 | 1 |
| 1993–94 | Arsenal | 27 | 2 |
| 1994–95 | Arsenal | 30 | 0 |
| 1995–96 | Arsenal | 22 | 0 |
| 1996–97 | Arsenal | 30 | 2 |
| 1997–98 | Arsenal | 34 | 5 |
| **Total:** | | **170** | **11** |

## PARMENTER, Steve — Forward

H: 5 9 W: 11 00 b.Chelmsford 22-1-77

*Source:* Trainee.

| | | | |
|---|---|---|---|
| 1994–95 | QPR | 0 | 0 |
| 1995–96 | QPR | 0 | 0 |
| 1996–97 | Bristol R | 14 | 2 |
| 1997–98 | Bristol R | 4 | 0 |
| **Total:** | | **18** | **2** |

## PARRIS, George — Midfield

H: 5 9 W: 12 10 b.Barking 11-9-64

*Source:* Apprentice. *Honours:* England Schools.

| | | | |
|---|---|---|---|
| 1982–83 | West Ham U | 0 | 0 |
| 1983–84 | West Ham U | 0 | 0 |
| 1984–85 | West Ham U | 1 | 0 |
| 1985–86 | West Ham U | 26 | 1 |
| 1986–87 | West Ham U | 36 | 2 |
| 1987–88 | West Ham U | 30 | 1 |
| 1988–89 | West Ham U | 27 | 1 |
| 1989–90 | West Ham U | 38 | 2 |
| 1990–91 | West Ham U | 44 | 5 |
| 1991–92 | West Ham U | 21 | 0 |
| 1992–93 | West Ham U | 16 | 0 |
| 1992–93 | Birmingham C | 13 | 0 |
| 1993–94 | Birmingham C | 24 | 0 |
| 1994–95 | Birmingham C | 2 | 1 |
| 1994–95 | Brentford (loan) | 5 | 0 |
| 1994–95 | Bristol C (loan) | 6 | 0 |
| 1994–95 | Brighton & HA (loan) | 18 | 2 |
| 1995 | Norrkoping | 4 | 0 |
| 1995–96 | Brighton & HA | 38 | 2 |
| 1996–97 | Brighton & HA | 18 | 1 |
| 1997–98 | Southend U | 1 | 0 |
| **Total:** | | **368** | **18** |

## PARRISH, Sean — Midfield

H: 5 10 W: 11 10 b.Wrexham 14-3-72

*Source:* Trainee.

| | | | |
|---|---|---|---|
| 1989–90 | Shrewsbury T | 2 | 0 |
| 1990–91 | Shrewsbury T | 1 | 0 |
| From Telford U. | | | |
| 1994–95 | Doncaster R | 25 | 3 |
| 1995–96 | Doncaster R | 41 | 5 |
| 1996–97 | Northampton T | 39 | 8 |
| 1997–98 | Northampton T | 12 | 1 |
| **Total:** | | **120** | **17** |

## PARTRIDGE, David — Midfield

b.Westminster 26-11-78

*Source:* Trainee.

| | | | |
|---|---|---|---|
| 1997–98 | West Ham U | 0 | 0 |

## PARTRIDGE, Richie — Midfield

b.Dublin 12-9-80

*Source:* Trainee.

| | | | |
|---|---|---|---|
| 1997–98 | Liverpool | 0 | 0 |

## PARTRIDGE, Scott — Midfield

H: 5 9 W: 11 02 b.Leicester 13-10-74

*Source:* Trainee.

| | | | |
|---|---|---|---|
| 1992–93 | Bradford C | 4 | 0 |
| 1993–94 | Bradford C | 1 | 0 |
| 1993–94 | Bristol C | 9 | 4 |
| 1994–95 | Bristol C | 33 | 2 |
| 1995–96 | Bristol C | 9 | 1 |
| 1995–96 | Torquay U (loan) | 5 | 2 |
| 1995–96 | Plymouth Arg (loan) | 7 | 2 |
| 1995–96 | Scarborough (loan) | 7 | 0 |
| 1996–97 | Bristol C | 6 | 0 |
| 1996–97 | Cardiff C | 15 | 0 |
| 1997–98 | Cardiff C | 22 | 2 |
| 1997–98 | Torquay U | 5 | 0 |
| **Total:** | | **123** | **13** |

## PASCOLO, Marco — Goalkeeper

H: 6 2 W: 14 04 b.Sion 9-5-66

*Honours:* Switzerland 43 full caps.

| | | | |
|---|---|---|---|
| 1986–87 | Sion | 1 | 0 |
| 1987–88 | Sion | 13 | 0 |
| 1988–89 | Sion | 3 | 1 |
| 1989–90 | Neuchatel Xamax | 18 | 0 |
| 1990–91 | Neuchatel Xamax | 34 | 0 |
| 1991–92 | Servette | 35 | 0 |
| 1992–93 | Servette | 36 | 0 |
| 1993–94 | Servette | 35 | 0 |
| 1994–95 | Servette | 22 | 0 |
| 1995–96 | Servette | 35 | 0 |
| 1996–97 | Cagliari | 14 | 0 |
| 1997–98 | Nottingham F | 5 | 0 |
| **Total:** | | **251** | **1** |

## PATERSON, Jamie — Forward

H: 5 3 W: 10 02 b.Dumfries 26-4-73

*Source:* Trainee.

| | | | |
|---|---|---|---|
| 1990–91 | Halifax T | 6 | 1 |

| | | | |
|---|---|---|---|
| 1991–92 | Halifax T | 15 | 2 |
| 1992–93 | Halifax T | 23 | 2 |
| 1993–94 | Halifax T | 42 | 13 |
| 1994–95 | Falkirk | 4 | 0 |
| 1995–96 | Scunthorpe U | 26 | 2 |
| 1996–97 | Scunthorpe U | 29 | 0 |
| 1997–98 | Scunthorpe U | 0 | 0 |
| **Total:** | | **145** | **20** |

## PATERSON, Scott — Defender

H: 5 11 W: 11 09 b.Aberdeen 13-5-72

*Source:* Cove Rangers.

| | | | |
|---|---|---|---|
| 1991–92 | Liverpool | 0 | 0 |
| 1992–93 | Liverpool | 0 | 0 |
| 1993–94 | Liverpool | 0 | 0 |
| 1994–95 | Bristol C | 3 | 0 |
| 1995–96 | Bristol C | 18 | 1 |
| 1996–97 | Bristol C | 19 | 0 |
| 1997–98 | Bristol C | 10 | 0 |
| 1997–98 | Cardiff C (loan) | 5 | 0 |
| **Total:** | | **55** | **1** |

## PATTERSON, Andrew — Midfield

b.Kirkaldy 26-11-80

| | | | |
|---|---|---|---|
| 1997–98 | Bradford C | 0 | 0 |

## PATTERSON, Darren — Defender

H: 6 1 W: 12 10 b.Belfast 15-10-69

*Source:* Trainee. *Honours:* Northern Ireland Under-21, 12 full caps, 1 goal.

| | | | |
|---|---|---|---|
| 1988–89 | WBA | 0 | 0 |
| 1989–90 | Wigan Ath | 29 | 1 |
| 1990–91 | Wigan Ath | 28 | 4 |
| 1991–92 | Wigan Ath | 40 | 1 |
| 1992–93 | Crystal Palace | 0 | 0 |
| 1993–94 | Crystal Palace | 0 | 0 |
| 1994–95 | Crystal Palace | 22 | 1 |
| 1995–96 | Luton T | 23 | 0 |
| 1996–97 | Luton T | 10 | 0 |
| 1996–97 | Preston NE (loan) | 2 | 0 |
| 1997–98 | Luton T | 23 | 0 |
| **Total:** | | **177** | **7** |

## PATTERSON, Mark — Forward

H: 5 8 W: 11 12 b.Darwen 24-5-65

*Source:* Apprentice.

| | | | |
|---|---|---|---|
| 1983–84 | Blackburn R | 29 | 7 |
| 1984–85 | Blackburn R | 9 | 0 |
| 1985–86 | Blackburn R | 26 | 10 |
| 1986–87 | Blackburn R | 24 | 1 |
| 1987–88 | Blackburn R | 13 | 2 |
| 1988–89 | Preston NE | 42 | 15 |
| 1989–90 | Preston NE | 13 | 4 |
| 1989–90 | Bury | 20 | 4 |
| 1990–91 | Bury | 22 | 6 |
| 1990–91 | Bolton W | 19 | 2 |
| 1991–92 | Bolton W | 36 | 2 |
| 1992–93 | Bolton W | 37 | 2 |
| 1993–94 | Bolton W | 35 | 1 |
| 1994–95 | Bolton W | 26 | 3 |
| 1995–96 | Bolton W | 16 | 1 |
| 1995–96 | Sheffield U | 21 | 2 |
| 1996–97 | Sheffield U | 35 | 1 |
| 1996–97 | Southend U (loan) | 4 | 0 |
| 1997–98 | Sheffield U | 18 | 1 |
| 1997–98 | Bury | 18 | 2 |
| **Total:** | | **463** | **66** |

## PATTERSON, Mark — Defender

H: 5 9 W: 11 10 b.Leeds 13-9-68

*Source:* Trainee.

| | | | |
|---|---|---|---|
| 1986–87 | Carlisle U | 6 | 0 |
| 1987–88 | Carlisle U | 16 | 0 |
| 1987–88 | Derby Co | 0 | 0 |
| 1988–89 | Derby Co | 1 | 0 |
| 1989–90 | Derby Co | 9 | 0 |
| 1990–91 | Derby Co | 11 | 1 |
| 1991–92 | Derby Co | 12 | 2 |
| 1992–93 | Derby Co | 18 | 0 |
| 1993–94 | Plymouth Arg | 41 | 0 |
| 1994–95 | Plymouth Arg | 38 | 3 |
| 1995–96 | Plymouth Arg | 43 | 0 |
| 1996–97 | Plymouth Arg | 12 | 0 |
| 1997–98 | Plymouth Arg | 0 | 0 |
| 1997–98 | Gillingham | 23 | 0 |
| **Total:** | | **230** | **6** |

## PATTIMORE, Michael — Defender

H: 5 9 W: 11 02 b.Newport 15-3-79

*Source:* Trainee.

| | | | |
|---|---|---|---|
| 1996–97 | Swindon T | 1 | 0 |
| 1997–98 | Swindon T | 2 | 0 |
| **Total:** | | **3** | **0** |

## PATTON, Aaron — Midfield

H: 5 6 W: 12 01 b.London 27-2-79

*Source:* Trainee.

| | | | |
|---|---|---|---|
| 1997–98 | Wycombe W | 1 | 0 |
| **Total:** | | **1** | **0** |

## PAXTON, Graeme — Defender

H: 6 0 W: 11 05 b.Paisley 11-9-77

*Source:* Spennymoor U.

| | | | |
|---|---|---|---|
| 1997–98 | Newcastle U | 0 | 0 |

## PAYNE, Derek — Midfield

H: 5 6 W: 10 08 b.Edgware 26-4-67

*Source:* Kingsbury T, Burnham, Hayes.

| | | | |
|---|---|---|---|
| 1991–92 | Barnet | 14 | 1 |
| 1992–93 | Barnet | 37 | 5 |
| 1993–94 | Southend U | 35 | 0 |
| 1994–95 | Watford | 24 | 0 |
| 1995–96 | Watford | 12 | 1 |
| 1996–97 | Peterborough U | 36 | 2 |
| 1997–98 | Peterborough U | 37 | 2 |
| **Total:** | | **195** | **11** |

## PAYNE, Steve — Defender

H: 5 11 W: 12 05 b.Castleford 1-8-75

*Source:* Trainee.

| | | | |
|---|---|---|---|
| 1993–94 | Huddersfield T | 0 | 0 |
| 1994–95 | Huddersfield T | 0 | 0 |
| 1995–96 | Huddersfield T | 0 | 0 |
| 1996–97 | Huddersfield T | 0 | 0 |
| 1997–98 | Macclesfield T | 39 | 0 |
| **Total:** | | **39** | **0** |

## PAYTON, Andy — Forward

H: 5 9 W: 11 13 b.Burnley 23-10-67

*Source:* Apprentice.

| | | | |
|---|---|---|---|
| 1985–86 | Hull C | 0 | 0 |
| 1986–87 | Hull C | 2 | 0 |
| 1987–88 | Hull C | 22 | 2 |
| 1988–89 | Hull C | 28 | 4 |
| 1989–90 | Hull C | 39 | 17 |
| 1990–91 | Hull C | 43 | 25 |
| 1991–92 | Hull C | 10 | 7 |
| 1991–92 | Middlesbrough | 19 | 3 |
| 1992–93 | Celtic | 29 | 13 |
| 1993–94 | Celtic | 7 | 2 |
| 1993–94 | Barnsley | 25 | 12 |
| 1994–95 | Barnsley | 43 | 12 |
| 1995–96 | Barnsley | 40 | 17 |
| 1996–97 | Huddersfield T | 38 | 17 |
| 1997–98 | Huddersfield T | 5 | 0 |
| 1997–98 | Burnley | 19 | 9 |
| **Total:** | | **369** | **140** |

## PEACOCK, Darren — Defender

H: 6 2 W: 12 12 b.Bristol 3-2-68

*Source:* Apprentice.

| | | | |
|---|---|---|---|
| 1984–85 | Newport Co | 0 | 0 |
| 1985–86 | Newport Co | 18 | 0 |
| 1986–87 | Newport Co | 5 | 0 |
| 1987–88 | Newport Co | 5 | 0 |
| 1988–89 | Hereford U | 8 | 0 |
| 1989–90 | Hereford U | 36 | 3 |
| 1990–91 | Hereford U | 15 | 1 |
| 1990–91 | QPR | 19 | 0 |
| 1991–92 | QPR | 39 | 1 |
| 1992–93 | QPR | 38 | 2 |
| 1993–94 | QPR | 30 | 3 |
| 1993–94 | Newcastle U | 9 | 0 |
| 1994–95 | Newcastle U | 35 | 1 |
| 1995–96 | Newcastle U | 34 | 0 |
| 1996–97 | Newcastle U | 35 | 1 |
| 1997–98 | Newcastle U | 20 | 0 |
| **Total:** | | **346** | **12** |

## PEACOCK, Gavin — Midfield

H: 5 8 W: 11 08 b.Eltham 18-11-67

*Source:* Apprentice. *Honours:* England Schools, Youth, Football League.

| | | | |
|---|---|---|---|
| 1984–85 | QPR | 0 | 0 |
| 1985–86 | QPR | 0 | 0 |
| 1986–87 | QPR | 12 | 1 |
| 1987–88 | QPR | 5 | 0 |
| 1987–88 | Gillingham | 26 | 2 |
| 1988–89 | Gillingham | 44 | 9 |
| 1989–90 | Bournemouth | 41 | 4 |
| 1990–91 | Bournemouth | 15 | 4 |
| 1990–91 | Newcastle U | 27 | 7 |
| 1991–92 | Newcastle U | 46 | 16 |
| 1992–93 | Newcastle U | 32 | 12 |
| 1993–94 | Chelsea | 37 | 8 |
| 1994–95 | Chelsea | 38 | 4 |
| 1995–96 | Chelsea | 28 | 5 |
| 1996–97 | Chelsea | 0 | 0 |
| 1996–97 | QPR | 27 | 5 |
| 1997–98 | QPR | 39 | 9 |
| **Total:** | | **417** | **86** |

## PEACOCK, Lee — Forward

H: 6 0 W: 12 08 b.Paisley 9-10-76

*Source:* Trainee.

| | | | |
|---|---|---|---|
| 1993–94 | Carlisle U | 1 | 0 |
| 1994–95 | Carlisle U | 7 | 0 |
| 1995–96 | Carlisle U | 22 | 2 |
| 1996–97 | Carlisle U | 44 | 9 |

| | | | |
|---|---|---|---|
| 1997–98 | Carlisle U | 2 | 0 |
| 1997–98 | Mansfield T | 32 | 5 |
| **Total:** | | **108** | **16** |

## PEACOCK, Richard — Forward

H: 5 10 W: 11 05 b.Sheffield 29-10-72

*Source:* Sheffield FC.

| | | | |
|---|---|---|---|
| 1993–94 | Hull C | 11 | 1 |
| 1994–95 | Hull C | 37 | 5 |
| 1995–96 | Hull C | 45 | 7 |
| 1996–97 | Hull C | 40 | 4 |
| 1997–98 | Hull C | 27 | 2 |
| **Total:** | | **160** | **19** |

## PEAKE, Jason — Midfield

H: 5 10 W: 13 00 b.Leicester 29-9-71

*Source:* Trainee. *Honours:* England Schools, Youth.

| | | | |
|---|---|---|---|
| 1989–90 | Leicester C | 0 | 0 |
| 1990–91 | Leicester C | 8 | 1 |
| 1991–92 | Leicester C | 0 | 0 |
| 1991–92 | Hartlepool U (loan) | 6 | 1 |
| 1992–93 | Halifax T | 33 | 1 |
| 1993–94 | Rochdale | 10 | 0 |
| 1994–95 | Rochdale | 39 | 2 |
| 1995–96 | Rochdale | 46 | 4 |
| 1996–97 | Brighton & HA | 30 | 1 |
| 1997–98 | Brighton & HA | 0 | 0 |
| 1997–98 | Bury | 6 | 0 |
| **Total:** | | **178** | **10** |

## PEAKE, Trevor — Defender

H: 6 0 W: 12 09 b.Nuneaton 10-2-57

*Source:* Nuneaton Bor.

| | | | |
|---|---|---|---|
| 1979–80 | Lincoln C | 45 | 1 |
| 1980–81 | Lincoln C | 43 | 1 |
| 1981–82 | Lincoln C | 37 | 4 |
| 1982–83 | Lincoln C | 46 | 1 |
| 1983–84 | Coventry C | 33 | 3 |
| 1984–85 | Coventry C | 35 | 1 |
| 1985–86 | Coventry C | 37 | 1 |
| 1986–87 | Coventry C | 39 | 0 |
| 1987–88 | Coventry C | 31 | 0 |
| 1988–89 | Coventry C | 32 | 0 |
| 1989–90 | Coventry C | 33 | 0 |
| 1990–91 | Coventry C | 36 | 1 |
| 1991–92 | Coventry C | 2 | 0 |
| 1991–92 | Luton T | 38 | 0 |
| 1992–93 | Luton T | 40 | 0 |
| 1993–94 | Luton T | 36 | 0 |
| 1994–95 | Luton T | 46 | 0 |
| 1995–96 | Luton T | 18 | 0 |
| 1996–97 | Luton T | 0 | 0 |
| 1997–98 | Luton T | 1 | 0 |
| **Total:** | | **628** | **13** |

## PEARCE, Andy — Defender

H: 6 4 W: 14 11 b.Bradford-on-Avon 20-4-66

*Source:* Halesowen T.

| | | | |
|---|---|---|---|
| 1990–91 | Coventry C | 11 | 1 |
| 1991–92 | Coventry C | 36 | 2 |
| 1992–93 | Coventry C | 24 | 1 |
| 1993–94 | Sheffield W | 32 | 3 |
| 1994–95 | Sheffield W | 34 | 0 |
| 1995–96 | Sheffield W | 3 | 0 |
| 1995–96 | Wimbledon | 7 | 0 |
| 1996–97 | Wimbledon | 0 | 0 |
| 1997–98 | Wimbledon | 0 | 0 |
| **Total:** | | **147** | **7** |

## PEARCE, Dennis — Defender

H: 5 10 W: 11 02 b.Wolverhampton 10-9-74

*Source:* Trainee.

| | | | |
|---|---|---|---|
| 1993–94 | Aston Villa | 0 | 0 |
| 1994–95 | Aston Villa | 0 | 0 |
| 1995–96 | Wolverhampton W | 5 | 0 |
| 1996–97 | Wolverhampton W | 4 | 0 |
| 1997–98 | Notts Co | 38 | 2 |
| **Total:** | | **47** | **2** |

## PEARCE, Greg — Midfield

H: 5 9 W: 10 09 b.Bolton 26-5-80

*Source:* Trainee.

| | | | |
|---|---|---|---|
| 1997–98 | Chesterfield | 0 | 0 |

## PEARCE, Ian — Defender

H: 6 4 W: 14 04 b.Bury St Edmunds 7-5-74

*Source:* School. *Honours:* England Youth, Under-21.

| | | | |
|---|---|---|---|
| 1990–91 | Chelsea | 1 | 0 |
| 1991–92 | Chelsea | 2 | 0 |
| 1992–93 | Chelsea | 1 | 0 |
| 1993–94 | Chelsea | 0 | 0 |
| 1993–94 | Blackburn R | 5 | 1 |
| 1994–95 | Blackburn R | 28 | 0 |
| 1995–96 | Blackburn R | 12 | 1 |
| 1996–97 | Blackburn R | 12 | 0 |
| 1997–98 | Blackburn R | 5 | 0 |
| 1997–98 | West Ham U | 30 | 1 |
| **Total:** | | **96** | **3** |

## PEARCE, Stuart — Defender

H: 5 10 W: 12 06 b.Shepherds Bush 24-4-62

*Source:* Wealdstone. *Honours:* England Under-21, 76 full caps, 4 goals.

| | | | |
|---|---|---|---|
| 1983–84 | Coventry C | 23 | 0 |
| 1984–85 | Coventry C | 28 | 4 |
| 1985–86 | Nottingham F | 30 | 1 |
| 1986–87 | Nottingham F | 39 | 6 |
| 1987–88 | Nottingham F | 34 | 5 |
| 1988–89 | Nottingham F | 36 | 6 |
| 1989–90 | Nottingham F | 34 | 5 |
| 1990–91 | Nottingham F | 33 | 11 |
| 1991–92 | Nottingham F | 30 | 5 |
| 1992–93 | Nottingham F | 23 | 2 |
| 1993–94 | Nottingham F | 42 | 6 |
| 1994–95 | Nottingham F | 36 | 8 |
| 1995–96 | Nottingham F | 31 | 3 |
| 1996–97 | Nottingham F | 33 | 5 |
| 1997–98 | Newcastle U | 25 | 0 |
| **Total:** | | **477** | **67** |

## PEARCEY, Jason — Goalkeeper

H: 6 1 W: 14 00 b.Leamington Spa 23-7-71

*Source:* Trainee.

| | | | |
|---|---|---|---|
| 1988–89 | Mansfield T | 1 | 0 |
| 1989–90 | Mansfield T | 5 | 0 |
| 1990–91 | Mansfield T | 4 | 0 |
| 1991–92 | Mansfield T | 22 | 0 |
| 1992–93 | Mansfield T | 33 | 0 |
| 1993–94 | Mansfield T | 9 | 0 |
| 1994–95 | Mansfield T | 3 | 0 |
| 1994–95 | Grimsby T | 3 | 0 |
| 1995–96 | Grimsby T | 2 | 0 |
| 1996–97 | Grimsby T | 40 | 0 |
| 1997–98 | Grimsby T | 4 | 0 |
| **Total:** | | **126** | **0** |

## PEARS, Steve — Goalkeeper

H: 6 0 W: 14 09 b.Brandon 22-1-62

*Source:* Apprentice.

| | | | |
|---|---|---|---|
| 1978–79 | Manchester U | 0 | 0 |
| 1979–80 | Manchester U | 0 | 0 |
| 1980–81 | Manchester U | 0 | 0 |
| 1981–82 | Manchester U | 0 | 0 |
| 1982–83 | Manchester U | 0 | 0 |
| 1983–84 | Manchester U | 0 | 0 |
| 1983–84 | Middlesbrough (loan) | 12 | 0 |
| 1984–85 | Manchester U | 4 | 0 |
| 1985–86 | Middlesbrough | 38 | 0 |
| 1986–87 | Middlesbrough | 46 | 0 |
| 1987–88 | Middlesbrough | 43 | 0 |
| 1988–89 | Middlesbrough | 26 | 0 |
| 1989–90 | Middlesbrough | 25 | 0 |
| 1990–91 | Middlesbrough | 27 | 0 |
| 1991–92 | Middlesbrough | 45 | 0 |
| 1992–93 | Middlesbrough | 26 | 0 |
| 1993–94 | Middlesbrough | 46 | 0 |
| 1994–95 | Middlesbrough | 5 | 0 |
| 1995–96 | Liverpool | 0 | 0 |
| 1996–97 | Hartlepool U | 16 | 0 |
| 1997–98 | Hartlepool U | 0 | 0 |
| **Total:** | | **359** | **0** |

## PEARSON, Nigel — Defender

H: 6 1 W: 14 01 b.Nottingham 21-8-63

*Source:* Heanor T.

| | | | |
|---|---|---|---|
| 1981–82 | Shrewsbury T | 0 | 0 |
| 1982–83 | Shrewsbury T | 39 | 1 |
| 1983–84 | Shrewsbury T | 26 | 0 |
| 1984–85 | Shrewsbury T | 0 | 0 |
| 1985–86 | Shrewsbury T | 35 | 1 |
| 1986–87 | Shrewsbury T | 42 | 3 |
| 1987–88 | Shrewsbury T | 11 | 0 |
| 1987–88 | Sheffield W | 19 | 2 |
| 1988–89 | Sheffield W | 37 | 2 |
| 1989–90 | Sheffield W | 33 | 1 |
| 1990–91 | Sheffield W | 39 | 6 |
| 1991–92 | Sheffield W | 31 | 2 |
| 1992–93 | Sheffield W | 16 | 1 |
| 1993–94 | Sheffield W | 5 | 0 |
| 1994–95 | Middlesbrough | 33 | 3 |
| 1995–96 | Middlesbrough | 36 | 0 |
| 1996–97 | Middlesbrough | 18 | 0 |
| 1997–98 | Middlesbrough | 29 | 2 |
| **Total:** | | **449** | **24** |

## PEDERSEN, Erik — Defender

b.Porsgrunn Norway 11-10-67

| | | | |
|---|---|---|---|
| 1995 | Viking | 23 | 2 |
| 1996 | Viking | 23 | 3 |
| 1996–97 | Dundee U | 25 | 0 |
| 1997–98 | Dundee U | 32 | 0 |
| **Total:** | | **103** | **5** |

## PEDERSEN, Jan Ove — Midfield

H: 5 8 W: 11 13 b.Oslo 12-11-68

| | | | |
|---|---|---|---|
| 1988 | Lillestrom | 21 | 1 |
| 1989 | Lillestrom | 20 | 0 |
| 1990 | Lillestrom | 21 | 1 |
| 1991 | Lillestrom | 16 | 4 |
| 1992 | Lillestrom | 21 | 2 |
| 1993 | Lillestrom | 21 | 2 |
| 1994 | Lillestrom | 20 | 4 |
| 1995 | Lillestrom | 26 | 1 |

| | | | |
|---|---|---|---|
| 1996 | Brann | 25 | 2 |
| 1997 | Brann | 21 | 2 |
| 1997–98 | Hartlepool U | 17 | 1 |
| **Total:** | | **229** | **20** |

## PEDERSEN, Per — Forward

H: 5 11 W: 13 00 b.Aalborg 30-3-69

*Honours:* Denmark 6 full caps, 2 goals.

| | | | |
|---|---|---|---|
| 1987 | Odense | 8 | 0 |
| 1988 | Odense | 11 | 7 |
| 1989 | Odense | 3 | 1 |
| 1990 | Odense | 22 | 8 |
| 1991 | Lyngby | 18 | 9 |
| 1991–92 | Lyngby | 22 | 10 |
| 1992–93 | Lyngby | 14 | 6 |
| 1993–94 | Lyngby | 17 | 3 |
| 1994–95 | Lyngby | 25 | 10 |
| 1995–96 | Odense | 32 | 16 |
| 1996–97 | Odense | 17 | 11 |
| 1996–97 | Blackburn R | 11 | 1 |
| 1997–98 | Blackburn R | 0 | 0 |
| **Total:** | | **200** | **82** |

## PEDERSEN, Tore — Defender

b.Fredrikstad 29-9-69

*Honours:* Norway 41 full caps.

| | | | |
|---|---|---|---|
| 1990 | IFK Gothenburg | 18 | 0 |
| 1991 | IFK Gothenburg | 25 | 0 |
| 1992 | IFK Gothenburg | 21 | 0 |
| 1993 | Brann | 22 | 0 |
| 1993–94 | Oldham Ath | 10 | 0 |
| 1994 | Brann | 1 | 0 |
| Sanfrecce | | | |
| 1995–96 | St Pauli | 12 | 0 |
| 1996–97 | St Pauli | 25 | 0 |
| 1997–98 | Blackburn R | 5 | 0 |
| **Total:** | | **139** | **0** |

## PEEL, Nathan — Forward

H: 6 1 W: 13 04 b.Blackburn 17-5-72

*Source:* Trainee.

| | | | |
|---|---|---|---|
| 1990–91 | Preston NE | 10 | 1 |
| 1991–92 | Sheffield U | 1 | 0 |
| 1992–93 | Sheffield U | 0 | 0 |
| 1992–93 | Halifax T (loan) | 3 | 0 |
| 1993–94 | Sheffield U | 0 | 0 |
| 1993–94 | Burnley | 13 | 2 |
| 1994–95 | Burnley | 3 | 0 |
| 1994–95 | Rotherham U (loan) | 9 | 4 |
| 1995–96 | Burnley | 0 | 0 |
| 1995–96 | Mansfield T (loan) | 2 | 0 |
| 1995–96 | Doncaster R (loan) | 2 | 0 |
| 1996–97 | Rotherham U | 0 | 0 |
| 1997–98 | Macclesfield T | 14 | 3 |
| **Total:** | | **57** | **10** |

## PEER, Dean — Midfield

H: 6 2 W: 12 04 b.Stourbridge 8-8-69

*Source:* Trainee.

| | | | |
|---|---|---|---|
| 1986–87 | Birmingham C | 2 | 0 |
| 1987–88 | Birmingham C | 0 | 0 |
| 1988–89 | Birmingham C | 17 | 1 |
| 1989–90 | Birmingham C | 27 | 3 |
| 1990–91 | Birmingham C | 40 | 2 |
| 1991–92 | Birmingham C | 21 | 1 |
| 1992–93 | Birmingham C | 13 | 1 |
| 1992–93 | Mansfield T (loan) | 10 | 0 |
| 1993–94 | Birmingham C | 0 | 0 |
| 1993–94 | Walsall | 33 | 8 |
| 1994–95 | Walsall | 12 | 0 |
| 1995–96 | Northampton T | 42 | 1 |
| 1996–97 | Northampton T | 21 | 1 |
| 1997–98 | Northampton T | 30 | 2 |
| **Total:** | | **268** | **20** |

## PELL, Robert — Defender

H: 6 1 W: 12 10 b.Leeds 5-2-79

*Source:* Trainee.

| | | | |
|---|---|---|---|
| 1996–97 | Rotherham U | 2 | 0 |
| 1997–98 | Rotherham U | 0 | 0 |
| 1997–98 | Doncaster R (loan) | 10 | 1 |
| **Total:** | | **12** | **1** |

## PEMBERTON, John — Defender

H: 5 11 W: 11 09 b.Oldham 18-11-64

*Source:* Chadderton.

| | | | |
|---|---|---|---|
| 1984–85 | Rochdale | 1 | 0 |
| 1984–85 | Crewe Alex | 6 | 0 |
| 1985–86 | Crewe Alex | 41 | 0 |
| 1986–87 | Crewe Alex | 43 | 0 |
| 1987–88 | Crewe Alex | 31 | 1 |
| 1987–88 | Crystal Palace | 2 | 0 |
| 1988–89 | Crystal Palace | 42 | 1 |
| 1989–90 | Crystal Palace | 34 | 1 |
| 1990–91 | Sheffield U | 21 | 0 |
| 1991–92 | Sheffield U | 20 | 0 |
| 1992–93 | Sheffield U | 19 | 0 |
| 1993–94 | Sheffield U | 8 | 0 |
| 1993–94 | Leeds U | 9 | 0 |
| 1994–95 | Leeds U | 27 | 0 |
| 1995–96 | Leeds U | 17 | 0 |
| 1996–97 | Leeds U | 0 | 0 |
| 1997–98 | Crewe Alex | 1 | 0 |
| **Total:** | | **322** | **3** |

## PEMBERTON, Martin — Forward

H: 5 9 W: 11 07 b.Bradford 1-2-76

*Source:* Trainee.

| | | | |
|---|---|---|---|
| 1994–95 | Oldham Ath | 0 | 0 |
| 1995–96 | Oldham Ath | 2 | 0 |
| 1996–97 | Oldham Ath | 3 | 0 |
| 1996–97 | Doncaster R | 9 | 1 |
| 1997–98 | Doncaster R | 26 | 1 |
| 1997–98 | Scunthorpe U | 6 | 0 |
| **Total:** | | **46** | **2** |

## PEMBRIDGE, Mark — Midfield

H: 5 7 W: 12 03 b.Merthyr Tydfil 28-11-70

*Source:* Trainee. *Honours:* Wales Under-21, B, 28 full caps, 5 goals.

| | | | |
|---|---|---|---|
| 1989–90 | Luton T | 0 | 0 |
| 1990–91 | Luton T | 18 | 1 |
| 1991–92 | Luton T | 42 | 5 |
| 1992–93 | Derby Co | 42 | 8 |
| 1993–94 | Derby Co | 41 | 11 |
| 1994–95 | Derby Co | 27 | 9 |
| 1995–96 | Sheffield W | 25 | 1 |
| 1996–97 | Sheffield W | 34 | 6 |
| 1997–98 | Sheffield W | 34 | 4 |
| **Total:** | | **263** | **45** |

## PENDER, John — Defender

H: 6 2 W: 13 05 b.Luton 19-11-63

*Source:* Apprentice. *Honours:* Eire Youth, Under-21.

| | | | |
|---|---|---|---|
| 1981–82 | Wolverhampton W | 8 | 0 |
| 1982–83 | Wolverhampton W | 39 | 1 |
| 1983–84 | Wolverhampton W | 34 | 1 |
| 1984–85 | Wolverhampton W | 36 | 1 |
| 1985–86 | Charlton Ath | 38 | 0 |
| 1986–87 | Charlton Ath | 1 | 0 |
| 1987–88 | Charlton Ath | 2 | 0 |
| 1987–88 | Bristol C | 28 | 2 |
| 1988–89 | Bristol C | 45 | 1 |
| 1989–90 | Bristol C | 10 | 0 |
| 1990–91 | Bristol C | 0 | 0 |
| 1990–91 | Burnley | 40 | 0 |
| 1991–92 | Burnley | 39 | 3 |
| 1992–93 | Burnley | 44 | 4 |
| 1993–94 | Burnley | 42 | 1 |
| 1994–95 | Burnley | 5 | 0 |
| 1995–96 | Burnley | 1 | 0 |
| 1995–96 | Wigan Ath | 41 | 1 |
| 1996–97 | Wigan Ath | 29 | 0 |
| 1997–98 | Rochdale | 14 | 0 |
| **Total:** | | **496** | **15** |

## PENNEY, David — Midfield

H: 5 9 W: 12 04 b.Wakefield 17-8-64

*Source:* Pontefract.

| | | | |
|---|---|---|---|
| 1985–86 | Derby Co | 0 | 0 |
| 1986–87 | Derby Co | 1 | 0 |
| 1987–88 | Derby Co | 9 | 0 |
| 1988–89 | Derby Co | 9 | 0 |
| 1989–90 | Oxford U | 29 | 2 |
| 1990–91 | Oxford U | 9 | 1 |
| 1990–91 | Swansea C (loan) | 12 | 3 |
| 1991–92 | Oxford U | 23 | 4 |
| 1992–93 | Oxford U | 33 | 6 |
| 1993–94 | Oxford U | 16 | 2 |
| 1993–94 | Swansea C (loan) | 11 | 2 |
| 1994–95 | Swansea C | 35 | 5 |
| 1995–96 | Swansea C | 29 | 0 |
| 1996–97 | Swansea C | 44 | 13 |
| 1997–98 | Cardiff C | 34 | 5 |
| **Total:** | | **294** | **43** |

## PENNOCK, Adrian — Midfield

H: 6 0 W: 12 12 b.Ipswich 27-3-71

*Source:* Trainee.

| | | | |
|---|---|---|---|
| 1989–90 | Norwich C | 1 | 0 |
| 1990–91 | Norwich C | 0 | 0 |
| 1991–92 | Norwich C | 0 | 0 |
| 1992–93 | Bournemouth | 43 | 1 |
| 1993–94 | Bournemouth | 40 | 3 |
| 1994–95 | Bournemouth | 31 | 5 |
| 1995–96 | Bournemouth | 17 | 0 |
| 1996–97 | Bournemouth | 0 | 0 |
| 1996–97 | Gillingham | 26 | 2 |
| 1997–98 | Gillingham | 20 | 0 |
| **Total:** | | **178** | **11** |

## PENRICE, Gary — Midfield

H: 5 8 W: 11 07 b.Bristol 23-3-64

*Source:* Bristol C Apprentice.

| | | | |
|---|---|---|---|
| 1984–85 | Bristol R | 5 | 1 |
| 1985–86 | Bristol R | 39 | 5 |
| 1986–87 | Bristol R | 43 | 7 |
| 1987–88 | Bristol R | 46 | 18 |
| 1988–89 | Bristol R | 43 | 20 |
| 1989–90 | Bristol R | 12 | 3 |
| 1989–90 | Watford | 29 | 13 |
| 1990–91 | Watford | 14 | 5 |
| 1990–91 | Aston Villa | 12 | 0 |
| 1991–92 | Aston Villa | 8 | 1 |
| 1991–92 | QPR | 19 | 3 |
| 1992–93 | QPR | 15 | 6 |
| 1993–94 | QPR | 26 | 8 |
| 1994–95 | QPR | 19 | 3 |

| | | | |
|---|---|---|---|
| 1995–96 | QPR | 3 | 0 |
| 1995–96 | Watford | 7 | 1 |
| 1996–97 | Watford | 32 | 1 |
| 1997–98 | Bristol R | 40 | 5 |
| **Total:** | | **412** | **100** |

## PEPPER, Nigel — Midfield

H: 5 10 W: 11 13 b.Rotherham 25-4-68

*Source:* Apprentice.

| | | | |
|---|---|---|---|
| 1985–86 | Rotherham U | 7 | 0 |
| 1986–87 | Rotherham U | 2 | 0 |
| 1987–88 | Rotherham U | 15 | 0 |
| 1988–89 | Rotherham U | 2 | 0 |
| 1989–90 | Rotherham U | 19 | 1 |
| 1990–91 | York C | 39 | 3 |
| 1991–92 | York C | 35 | 4 |
| 1992–93 | York C | 34 | 8 |
| 1993–94 | York C | 23 | 0 |
| 1994–95 | York C | 35 | 4 |
| 1995–96 | York C | 40 | 8 |
| 1996–97 | York C | 29 | 12 |
| 1996–97 | Bradford C | 11 | 5 |
| 1997–98 | Bradford C | 32 | 5 |
| **Total:** | | **323** | **50** |

## PEREZ, Lionel — Goalkeeper

H: 6 0 W: 13 05 b.Bagnois Ceze 24-4-67

| | | | |
|---|---|---|---|
| 1991–92 | Nimes | 38 | 0 |
| 1992–93 | Nimes | 36 | 0 |
| 1993–94 | Bordeaux | 9 | 0 |
| 1994–95 | Bordeaux | 7 | 0 |
| 1995–96 | Bordeaux | 0 | 0 |
| 1996–97 | Sunderland | 29 | 0 |
| 1997–98 | Sunderland | 46 | 0 |
| **Total:** | | **165** | **0** |

## PERKINS, Chris — Midfield

H: 5 11 W: 10 09 b.Nottingham 9-1-74

*Source:* Trainee.

| | | | |
|---|---|---|---|
| 1992–93 | Mansfield T | 5 | 0 |
| 1993–94 | Mansfield T | 3 | 0 |
| 1994–95 | Chesterfield | 18 | 0 |
| 1995–96 | Chesterfield | 22 | 0 |
| 1996–97 | Chesterfield | 30 | 0 |
| 1997–98 | Chesterfield | 43 | 2 |
| **Total:** | | **121** | **2** |

## PERKINS, Chris — Defender

b.Stepney 1-3-80

*Source:* Trainee.

| | | | |
|---|---|---|---|
| 1997–98 | Southend U | 5 | 0 |
| **Total:** | | **5** | **0** |

## PERON, Jean-Francois — Midfield

H: 5 8 W: 10 10 b.France 11-10-65

| | | | |
|---|---|---|---|
| 1997–98 | Walsall | 38 | 1 |
| **Total:** | | **38** | **1** |

## PERPETUINI, David — Midfield

H: 5 8 W: 10 00 b.Hitchin 26-9-79

*Source:* Trainee.

| | | | |
|---|---|---|---|
| 1997–98 | Watford | 0 | 0 |

## PERRETT, Russell — Defender

H: 6 2 W: 13 00 b.Barton-on-Sea 18-6-73

*Source:* AFC Lymington.

| | | | |
|---|---|---|---|
| 1995–96 | Portsmouth | 9 | 0 |
| 1996–97 | Portsmouth | 32 | 1 |
| 1997–98 | Portsmouth | 16 | 1 |
| **Total:** | | **57** | **2** |

## PERRY, Chris — Defender

H: 5 8 W: 10 08 b.Carshalton 26-4-73

*Source:* Trainee.

| | | | |
|---|---|---|---|
| 1991–92 | Wimbledon | 0 | 0 |
| 1992–93 | Wimbledon | 0 | 0 |
| 1993–94 | Wimbledon | 2 | 0 |
| 1994–95 | Wimbledon | 22 | 0 |
| 1995–96 | Wimbledon | 37 | 0 |
| 1996–97 | Wimbledon | 37 | 1 |
| 1997–98 | Wimbledon | 35 | 1 |
| **Total:** | | **133** | **2** |

## PERRY, Jason — Defender

H: 6 1 W: 11 12 b.Caerphilly 2-4-70

*Source:* Trainee. *Honours:* Wales Under-21, B, 1 full cap.

| | | | |
|---|---|---|---|
| 1986–87 | Cardiff C | 1 | 0 |
| 1987–88 | Cardiff C | 3 | 0 |
| 1988–89 | Cardiff C | 0 | 0 |
| 1989–90 | Cardiff C | 36 | 0 |
| 1990–91 | Cardiff C | 43 | 0 |
| 1991–92 | Cardiff C | 36 | 0 |
| 1992–93 | Cardiff C | 39 | 3 |
| 1993–94 | Cardiff C | 40 | 1 |
| 1994–95 | Cardiff C | 34 | 1 |
| 1995–96 | Cardiff C | 14 | 0 |
| 1996–97 | Cardiff C | 35 | 0 |
| 1997–98 | Bristol R | 25 | 0 |
| **Total:** | | **306** | **5** |

## PERRY, Jonathan — Defender

H: 6 0 W: 12 06 b.Hamilton 22-11-76

*Source:* Trainee.

| | | | |
|---|---|---|---|
| 1995–96 | Barnsley | 0 | 0 |
| 1996–97 | Barnsley | 0 | 0 |
| 1997–98 | Barnsley | 0 | 0 |

## PERRY, Mark — Defender

H: 5 10 W: 12 09 b.Perivale 19-10-78

*Source:* Trainee. *Honours:* England Schools, Youth.

| | | | |
|---|---|---|---|
| 1995–96 | QPR | 0 | 0 |
| 1996–97 | QPR | 2 | 1 |
| 1997–98 | QPR | 8 | 0 |
| **Total:** | | **10** | **1** |

## PERRY, Mark — Defender

H: 6 1 W: 11 00 b.Aberdeen 7-2-71

*Source:* Cove Rangers.

| | | | |
|---|---|---|---|
| 1988–89 | Dundee U | 0 | 0 |
| 1989–90 | Dundee U | 0 | 0 |
| 1990–91 | Dundee U | 0 | 0 |
| 1991–92 | Dundee U | 0 | 0 |
| 1992–93 | Dundee U | 18 | 1 |
| 1993–94 | Dundee U | 9 | 0 |
| 1994–95 | Dundee U | 9 | 0 |
| 1995–96 | Dundee U | 20 | 2 |
| 1996–97 | Dundee U | 35 | 0 |
| 1997–98 | Dundee U | 32 | 1 |
| **Total:** | | **123** | **4** |

## PERRY, Richard — Midfield

H: 5 11 W: 11 04 b.Darlington 24-8-78

*Source:* Trainee. *Honours:* Wales Youth.

| | | | |
|---|---|---|---|
| 1996–97 | Bristol C | 0 | 0 |
| 1997–98 | Bristol R | 0 | 0 |

## PESCHISOLIDO, Paul — Forward

H: 5 7 W: 11 02 b.Canada 25-5-71

*Source:* Toronto Blizzard. *Honours:* Canada full caps.

| | | | |
|---|---|---|---|
| 1992–93 | Birmingham C | 19 | 7 |
| 1993–94 | Birmingham C | 24 | 9 |
| 1994–95 | Stoke C | 40 | 13 |
| 1995–96 | Stoke C | 26 | 6 |
| 1995–96 | Birmingham C | 9 | 1 |
| 1996–97 | WBA | 37 | 15 |
| 1997–98 | WBA | 8 | 3 |
| 1997–98 | Fulham | 32 | 13 |
| **Total:** | | **195** | **67** |

## PETERS, Mark — Defender

H: 6 0 W: 11 03 b.St Asaph 6-7-72

*Source:* Trainee. *Honours:* Wales Under-21.

| | | | |
|---|---|---|---|
| 1991–92 | Manchester C | 0 | 0 |
| 1992–93 | Norwich C | 0 | 0 |
| 1993–94 | Peterborough U | 19 | 0 |
| 1994–95 | Peterborough U | 0 | 0 |
| 1994–95 | Mansfield T | 26 | 4 |
| 1995–96 | Mansfield T | 21 | 2 |
| 1996–97 | Mansfield T | 0 | 0 |
| 1997–98 | Mansfield T | 24 | 2 |
| **Total:** | | **90** | **8** |

## PETHICK, Robbie — Defender

H: 5 10 W: 11 11 b.Weymouth 8-9-70

*Source:* Weymouth.

| | | | |
|---|---|---|---|
| 1993–94 | Portsmouth | 18 | 0 |
| 1994–95 | Portsmouth | 44 | 1 |
| 1995–96 | Portsmouth | 38 | 0 |
| 1996–97 | Portsmouth | 35 | 0 |
| 1997–98 | Portsmouth | 44 | 2 |
| **Total:** | | **179** | **3** |

## PETIT, Emmanuel — Midfield

H: 6 1 W: 12 07 b.Dieppe 22-9-70

*Source:* ES Arques. *Honours:* France 26 full caps, 2 goals.

| | | | |
|---|---|---|---|
| 1988–89 | Monaco | 9 | 0 |
| 1989–90 | Monaco | 28 | 0 |
| 1990–91 | Monaco | 27 | 1 |
| 1991–92 | Monaco | 28 | 0 |
| 1992–93 | Monaco | 25 | 1 |
| 1993–94 | Monaco | 28 | 0 |
| 1994–95 | Monaco | 25 | 1 |
| 1995–96 | Monaco | 23 | 1 |
| 1996–97 | Monaco | 29 | 0 |
| 1997–98 | Arsenal | 32 | 2 |
| **Total:** | | **254** | **6** |

## PETRESCU, Dan — Midfield

H: 5 10 W: 11 07 b.Bucharest 22-12-67

*Honours:* Romania 71 full caps, 11 goals.

| | | | |
|---|---|---|---|
| 1985–86 | Steaua | 2 | 0 |
| 1986–87 | FC Olt (loan) | 24 | 0 |
| 1987–88 | Steaua | 11 | 0 |
| 1988–89 | Steaua | 28 | 4 |
| 1989–90 | Steaua | 23 | 9 |
| 1990–91 | Steaua | 31 | 13 |
| 1991–92 | Foggia | 25 | 4 |
| 1992–93 | Foggia | 30 | 3 |
| 1993–94 | Genoa | 24 | 1 |

| | | | |
|---|---|---|---|
| 1994–95 | Sheffield W | 29 | 3 |
| 1995–96 | Sheffield W | 8 | 0 |
| 1995–96 | Chelsea | 24 | 2 |
| 1996–97 | Chelsea | 34 | 3 |
| 1997–98 | Chelsea | 31 | 5 |
| **Total:** | | **324** | **47** |

## PETRIC, Gordan — Defender

H: 6 2 W: 13 09 b.Belgrade 30-7-69

*Source:* Partizan Belgrade. *Honours:* Yugoslavia full caps.

| | | | |
|---|---|---|---|
| 1993–94 | Dundee U | 27 | 1 |
| 1994–95 | Dundee U | 33 | 2 |
| 1995–96 | Rangers | 33 | 1 |
| 1996–97 | Rangers | 26 | 2 |
| 1997–98 | Rangers | 6 | 0 |
| **Total:** | | **125** | **6** |

## PETRIE, Stewart — Forward

H: 5 10 W: 11 11 b.Dundee 27-2-70

*Source:* East Craigie.

| | | | |
|---|---|---|---|
| 1988–89 | Forfar Ath | 0 | 0 |
| 1989–90 | Forfar Ath | 0 | 0 |
| 1990–91 | Forfar Ath | 36 | 6 |
| 1991–92 | Forfar Ath | 41 | 7 |
| 1992–93 | Forfar Ath | 37 | 21 |
| 1993–94 | Forfar Ath | 3 | 0 |
| 1993–94 | Dunfermline Ath | 37 | 6 |
| 1994–95 | Dunfermline Ath | 33 | 14 |
| 1995–96 | Dunfermline Ath | 34 | 13 |
| 1996–97 | Dunfermline Ath | 28 | 3 |
| 1997–98 | Dunfermline Ath | 27 | 2 |
| **Total:** | | **276** | **72** |

## PETROVIC, Timotije — Midfield

b.Essex 6-12-78

*Source:* Trainee.

| | | | |
|---|---|---|---|
| 1997–98 | Wimbledon | 0 | 0 |

## PETTA, Bobby — Midfield

H: 5 7 W: 11 03 b.Rotterdam 6-8-74

| | | | |
|---|---|---|---|
| 1996–97 | Ipswich T | 6 | 0 |
| 1997–98 | Ipswich T | 32 | 7 |
| **Total:** | | **38** | **7** |

## PETTERSON, Andy — Goalkeeper

H: 6 2 W: 14 07 b.Fremantle 26-9-69

| | | | |
|---|---|---|---|
| 1988–89 | Luton T | 0 | 0 |
| 1988–89 | Swindon T (loan) | 0 | 0 |
| 1989–90 | Luton T | 0 | 0 |
| 1990–91 | Luton T | 0 | 0 |
| 1991–92 | Luton T | 0 | 0 |
| 1991–92 | Ipswich T (loan) | 0 | 0 |
| 1992–93 | Luton T | 14 | 0 |
| 1992–93 | Ipswich T (loan) | 1 | 0 |
| 1993–94 | Luton T | 5 | 0 |
| 1994–95 | Charlton Ath | 9 | 0 |
| 1994–95 | Bradford C (loan) | 3 | 0 |
| 1995–96 | Charlton Ath | 9 | 0 |
| 1995–96 | Ipswich T (loan) | 1 | 0 |
| 1995–96 | Plymouth Arg (loan) | 6 | 0 |
| 1995–96 | Colchester U (loan) | 5 | 0 |
| 1996–97 | Charlton Ath | 21 | 0 |
| 1997–98 | Charlton Ath | 23 | 0 |
| **Total:** | | **97** | **0** |

## PETTINGER, Paul — Goalkeeper

H: 6 0 W: 13 00 b.Sheffield 1-10-75

*Source:* Barnsley. *Honours:* England Schools, Youth.

| | | | |
|---|---|---|---|
| 1992–93 | Leeds U | 0 | 0 |
| 1993–94 | Leeds U | 0 | 0 |
| 1994–95 | Leeds U | 0 | 0 |
| 1994–95 | Torquay U (loan) | 3 | 0 |
| 1995–96 | Leeds U | 0 | 0 |
| 1995–96 | Rotherham U (loan) | 1 | 0 |
| 1995–96 | Gillingham | 0 | 0 |
| 1996–97 | Carlisle U | 0 | 0 |
| 1997–98 | Rotherham U | 3 | 0 |
| **Total:** | | **7** | **0** |

## PETTY, Ben — Defender

H: 6 0 W: 12 05 b.Solihull 22-3-77

*Source:* Trainee.

| | | | |
|---|---|---|---|
| 1994–95 | Aston Villa | 0 | 0 |
| 1995–96 | Aston Villa | 0 | 0 |
| 1996–97 | Aston Villa | 0 | 0 |
| 1997–98 | Aston Villa | 0 | 0 |

## PHELAN, Mike — Defender

H: 5 11 W: 11 01 b.Nelson 24-9-62

*Source:* Apprentice. *Honours:* England Youth, 1 full cap.

| | | | |
|---|---|---|---|
| 1980–81 | Burnley | 16 | 2 |
| 1981–82 | Burnley | 23 | 1 |
| 1982–83 | Burnley | 42 | 3 |
| 1983–84 | Burnley | 44 | 2 |
| 1984–85 | Burnley | 43 | 1 |
| 1985–86 | Norwich C | 42 | 3 |
| 1986–87 | Norwich C | 40 | 4 |
| 1987–88 | Norwich C | 37 | 0 |
| 1988–89 | Norwich C | 37 | 2 |
| 1989–90 | Manchester U | 38 | 1 |
| 1990–91 | Manchester U | 33 | 1 |

| | | | |
|---|---|---|---|
| 1991–92 | Manchester U | 18 | 0 |
| 1992–93 | Manchester U | 11 | 0 |
| 1993–94 | Manchester U | 2 | 0 |
| 1994–95 | WBA | 20 | 0 |
| 1995–96 | WBA | 1 | 0 |
| 1996–97 | Blackpool | 0 | 0 |
| 1997–98 | Blackpool | 0 | 0 |
| 1997–98 | Stockport Co | 0 | 0 |
| **Total:** | | **447** | **20** |

## PHELAN, Terry — Defender

H: 5 8 W: 10 00 b.Manchester 16-3-67

*Source:* Trainee. *Honours:* Eire Youth, Under-21, Under-23, B, 38 full caps.

| | | | |
|---|---|---|---|
| 1984–85 | Leeds U | 0 | 0 |
| 1985–86 | Leeds U | 14 | 0 |
| 1986–87 | Swansea C | 45 | 0 |
| 1987–88 | Wimbledon | 30 | 0 |
| 1988–89 | Wimbledon | 29 | 0 |
| 1989–90 | Wimbledon | 34 | 0 |
| 1990–91 | Wimbledon | 29 | 0 |
| 1991–92 | Wimbledon | 37 | 1 |
| 1992–93 | Wimbledon | 0 | 0 |
| 1992–93 | Manchester C | 37 | 0 |
| 1993–94 | Manchester C | 30 | 1 |
| 1994–95 | Manchester C | 27 | 0 |
| 1995–96 | Manchester C | 9 | 0 |
| 1995–96 | Chelsea | 12 | 0 |
| 1996–97 | Chelsea | 3 | 0 |
| 1996–97 | Everton | 15 | 0 |
| 1997–98 | Everton | 9 | 0 |
| **Total:** | | **360** | **2** |

## PHILLIBEN, John — Defender

H: 5 10 W: 11 00 b.Stirling 14-3-64

*Source:* Gairdoch U. *Honours:* Scotland Youth.

| | | | |
|---|---|---|---|
| 1980–81 | Stirling Albion | 15 | 0 |
| 1981–82 | Stirling A | 37 | 1 |
| 1982–83 | Stirling A | 34 | 0 |
| 1983–84 | Stirling A | 23 | 0 |
| 1983–84 | Doncaster R | 12 | 0 |
| 1984–85 | Doncaster R | 36 | 1 |
| 1985–86 | Doncaster R | 22 | 0 |
| 1985–86 | Cambridge U (loan) | 6 | 0 |
| 1986–87 | Doncaster R | 1 | 0 |
| 1986–87 | Motherwell | 37 | 0 |
| 1987–88 | Motherwell | 35 | 2 |
| 1988–89 | Motherwell | 19 | 0 |
| 1989–90 | Motherwell | 24 | 0 |
| 1990–91 | Motherwell | 11 | 1 |
| 1991–92 | Motherwell | 32 | 1 |
| 1992–93 | Motherwell | 31 | 0 |
| 1993–94 | Motherwell | 28 | 2 |
| 1994–95 | Motherwell | 31 | 0 |
| 1995–96 | Motherwell | 24 | 0 |
| 1996–97 | Motherwell | 17 | 1 |
| 1997–98 | Motherwell | 13 | 0 |
| **Total:** | | **488** | **9** |

## PHILLIPS, Dave — Defender

H: 5 9 W: 12 03 b.Wegberg 29-7-63

*Source:* Apprentice. *Honours:* Wales Under-21, 62 full caps, 2 goals.

| | | | |
|---|---|---|---|
| 1981–82 | Plymouth Arg | 8 | 1 |
| 1982–83 | Plymouth Arg | 23 | 8 |
| 1983–84 | Plymouth Arg | 42 | 6 |
| 1984–85 | Manchester C | 42 | 12 |
| 1985–86 | Manchester C | 39 | 1 |
| 1986–87 | Coventry C | 39 | 4 |
| 1987–88 | Coventry C | 35 | 2 |
| 1988–89 | Coventry C | 26 | 2 |
| 1989–90 | Norwich C | 38 | 4 |
| 1990–91 | Norwich C | 38 | 4 |
| 1991–92 | Norwich C | 34 | 1 |
| 1992–93 | Norwich C | 42 | 9 |
| 1993–94 | Nottingham F | 43 | 4 |
| 1994–95 | Nottingham F | 38 | 1 |
| 1995–96 | Nottingham F | 18 | 0 |
| 1996–97 | Nottingham F | 27 | 0 |
| 1997–98 | Nottingham F | 0 | 0 |
| 1997–98 | Huddersfield T | 29 | 2 |
| **Total:** | | **561** | **61** |

## PHILLIPS, Gareth — Midfield

H: 5 8 W: 9 08 b.Porth 19-7-79

*Source:* Trainee.

| | | | |
|---|---|---|---|
| 1996–97 | Swansea C | 1 | 0 |
| 1997–98 | Swansea C | 6 | 0 |
| **Total:** | | **7** | **0** |

## PHILLIPS, Jimmy — Defender

H: 6 0 W: 12 07 b.Bolton 8-2-66

*Source:* Apprentice.

| | | | |
|---|---|---|---|
| 1983–84 | Bolton W | 1 | 0 |
| 1984–85 | Bolton W | 40 | 1 |
| 1985–86 | Bolton W | 33 | 1 |
| 1986–87 | Bolton W | 34 | 0 |
| 1986–87 | Rangers | 6 | 0 |
| 1987–88 | Rangers | 19 | 0 |
| 1988–89 | Oxford U | 45 | 5 |
| 1989–90 | Oxford U | 34 | 3 |
| 1989–90 | Middlesbrough | 12 | 0 |
| 1990–91 | Middlesbrough | 44 | 2 |
| 1991–92 | Middlesbrough | 43 | 2 |
| 1992–93 | Middlesbrough | 40 | 2 |

| | | | |
|---|---|---|---|
| 1993–94 | Bolton W | 42 | 0 |
| 1994–95 | Bolton W | 46 | 1 |
| 1995–96 | Bolton W | 37 | 0 |
| 1996–97 | Bolton W | 36 | 0 |
| 1997–98 | Bolton W | 22 | 1 |
| **Total:** | | **534** | **18** |

## PHILLIPS, Kevin — Forward

H: 5 7 W: 11 00 b.Hitchin 25-7-73

*Source:* Baldock T. *Honours:* England B.

| | | | |
|---|---|---|---|
| 1994–95 | Watford | 16 | 9 |
| 1995–96 | Watford | 27 | 11 |
| 1996–97 | Watford | 16 | 4 |
| 1997–98 | Sunderland | 43 | 29 |
| **Total:** | | **102** | **53** |

## PHILLIPS, Lee — Forward

H: 5 10 W: 12 00 b.Penzance 16-9-80

*Source:* School.

| | | | |
|---|---|---|---|
| 1996–97 | Plymouth Arg | 2 | 0 |
| 1997–98 | Plymouth Arg | 10 | 0 |
| **Total:** | | **12** | **0** |

## PHILLIPS, Lee — Defender

H: 6 1 W: 12 03 b.Aberdare 18-3-79

*Source:* Trainee.

| | | | |
|---|---|---|---|
| 1996–97 | Cardiff C | 3 | 0 |
| 1997–98 | Cardiff C | 8 | 0 |
| **Total:** | | **11** | **0** |

## PHILLIPS, Martin — Forward

H: 5 9 W: 10 03 b.Exeter 13-3-76

*Source:* Trainee.

| | | | |
|---|---|---|---|
| 1992–93 | Exeter C | 6 | 0 |
| 1993–94 | Exeter C | 9 | 0 |
| 1994–95 | Exeter C | 24 | 2 |
| 1995–96 | Exeter C | 13 | 3 |
| 1995–96 | Manchester C | 11 | 0 |
| 1996–97 | Manchester C | 4 | 0 |
| 1997–98 | Manchester C | 0 | 0 |
| 1997–98 | Scunthorpe U (loan) | 3 | 0 |
| 1997–98 | Exeter C (loan) | 8 | 0 |
| **Total:** | | **78** | **5** |

## PHILLIPS, Paul — Goalkeeper

H: 5 8 W: 12 01 b.Manchester 15-11-78

*Source:* Trainee.

| | | | |
|---|---|---|---|
| 1997–98 | Bury | 0 | 0 |

## PHILLIPS, Steve — Goalkeeper

H: 6 1 W: 11 10 b.Bath 6-5-78

*Source:* Paulton R.

| | | | |
|---|---|---|---|
| 1996–97 | Bristol C | 0 | 0 |
| 1997–98 | Bristol C | 0 | 0 |

## PHILLIPS, Wayne — Midfield

H: 5 10 W: 11 00 b.Bangor 15-12-70

*Source:* Trainee. *Honours:* Wales B.

| | | | |
|---|---|---|---|
| 1989–90 | Wrexham | 5 | 0 |
| 1990–91 | Wrexham | 28 | 0 |
| 1991–92 | Wrexham | 30 | 3 |
| 1992–93 | Wrexham | 15 | 0 |
| 1993–94 | Wrexham | 21 | 1 |
| 1994–95 | Wrexham | 18 | 1 |
| 1995–96 | Wrexham | 44 | 5 |
| 1996–97 | Wrexham | 26 | 5 |
| 1997–98 | Wrexham | 20 | 1 |
| 1997–98 | Stockport Co | 13 | 0 |
| **Total:** | | **220** | **16** |

## PHILLISKIRK, Tony — Forward

H: 6 2 W: 12 12 b.Sunderland 10-2-65

*Source:* Amateur. *Honours:* England Schools.

| | | | |
|---|---|---|---|
| 1983–84 | Sheffield U | 21 | 8 |
| 1984–85 | Sheffield U | 23 | 2 |
| 1985–86 | Sheffield U | 4 | 0 |
| 1986–87 | Sheffield U | 6 | 1 |
| 1986–87 | Rotherham U (loan) | 6 | 1 |
| 1987–88 | Sheffield U | 26 | 9 |
| 1988–89 | Oldham Ath | 10 | 1 |
| 1988–89 | Preston NE | 14 | 6 |
| 1989–90 | Bolton W | 45 | 18 |
| 1990–91 | Bolton W | 43 | 19 |
| 1991–92 | Bolton W | 43 | 12 |
| 1992–93 | Bolton W | 10 | 2 |
| 1992–93 | Peterborough U | 32 | 11 |
| 1993–94 | Peterborough U | 11 | 4 |
| 1993–94 | Burnley | 19 | 7 |
| 1994–95 | Burnley | 13 | 1 |
| 1995–96 | Burnley | 8 | 1 |
| 1995–96 | Carlisle U (loan) | 3 | 1 |
| 1995–96 | Cardiff C | 28 | 4 |
| 1996–97 | Cardiff C | 33 | 1 |
| 1997–98 | Cardiff C | 0 | 0 |
| 1997–98 | Macclesfield T (loan) | 10 | 1 |
| **Total:** | | **408** | **110** |

## PHILPOTT, Lee — Midfield

H: 5 9 W: 11 08 b.Barnet 21-2-70

*Source:* Trainee.

| | | | |
|---|---|---|---|
| 1987–88 | Peterborough U | 1 | 0 |
| 1988–89 | Peterborough U | 3 | 0 |
| 1989–90 | Cambridge U | 42 | 5 |
| 1990–91 | Cambridge U | 45 | 5 |
| 1991–92 | Cambridge U | 31 | 5 |
| 1992–93 | Cambridge U | 16 | 2 |
| 1992–93 | Leicester C | 27 | 3 |
| 1993–94 | Leicester C | 19 | 0 |
| 1994–95 | Leicester C | 23 | 0 |
| 1995–96 | Leicester C | 6 | 0 |
| 1995–96 | Blackpool | 10 | 0 |
| 1996–97 | Blackpool | 26 | 3 |
| 1997–98 | Blackpool | 35 | 2 |
| **Total:** | | **284** | **25** |

## PHILSON, Graeme — Defender

H: 5 10 W: 11 00 b.Ireland 24-3-75

*Source:* Coleraine.

| | | | |
|---|---|---|---|
| 1995–96 | West Ham U | 0 | 0 |
| 1996–97 | West Ham U | 0 | 0 |
| 1997–98 | West Ham U | 0 | 0 |

## PICKERING, Ally — Defender

H: 5 9 W: 11 05 b.Manchester 22-6-67

*Source:* Buxton.

| | | | |
|---|---|---|---|
| 1989–90 | Rotherham U | 10 | 0 |
| 1990–91 | Rotherham U | 1 | 0 |
| 1991–92 | Rotherham U | 27 | 0 |
| 1992–93 | Rotherham U | 38 | 1 |
| 1993–94 | Rotherham U | 12 | 1 |
| 1993–94 | Coventry C | 4 | 0 |
| 1994–95 | Coventry C | 31 | 0 |
| 1995–96 | Coventry C | 30 | 0 |
| 1996–97 | Stoke C | 40 | 0 |
| 1997–98 | Stoke C | 42 | 1 |
| **Total:** | | **235** | **3** |

## PILKINGTON, Kevin — Goalkeeper

H: 6 1 W: 13 01 b.Hitchin 8-3-74

*Source:* Trainee. *Honours:* England Schools.

| | | | |
|---|---|---|---|
| 1992–93 | Manchester U | 0 | 0 |
| 1993–94 | Manchester U | 0 | 0 |
| 1994–95 | Manchester U | 1 | 0 |
| 1995–96 | Manchester U | 3 | 0 |
| 1995–96 | Rochdale (loan) | 6 | 0 |
| 1996–97 | Manchester U | 0 | 0 |
| 1996–97 | Rotherham U (loan) | 17 | 0 |
| 1997–98 | Manchester U | 2 | 0 |
| **Total:** | | **29** | **0** |

## PINAS, Brian — Midfield

H: 5 8 W: 10 12 b.Rotterdam 29-12-78

*Source:* Feyenoord.

| | | | |
|---|---|---|---|
| 1997–98 | Newcastle U | 0 | 0 |

## PINNOCK, James — Forward

H: 5 8 W: 11 11 b.Dartford 1-8-78

*Source:* Trainee.

| | | | |
|---|---|---|---|
| 1996–97 | Gillingham | 2 | 0 |
| 1997–98 | Gillingham | 1 | 0 |
| **Total:** | | **3** | **0** |

## PIPER, David — Defender

H: 5 8 W: 10 00 b.Bournemouth 31-10-77

*Source:* Trainee.

| | | | |
|---|---|---|---|
| 1996–97 | Southampton | 0 | 0 |
| 1997–98 | Southampton | 0 | 0 |

## PIPER, Lennie — Forward

H: 5 8 W: 11 06 b.London 8-8-77

*Source:* Trainee. *Honours:* England Youth.

| | | | |
|---|---|---|---|
| 1995–96 | Wimbledon | 0 | 0 |
| 1996–97 | Gillingham | 19 | 1 |
| 1997–98 | Gillingham | 1 | 0 |
| **Total:** | | **20** | **1** |

## PISTONE, Alessandro — Defender

H: 5 11 W: 11 05 b.Milan 27-7-75

| | | | |
|---|---|---|---|
| 1992–93 | Vicenza | 0 | 0 |
| 1993–94 | Solbiatese | 20 | 1 |
| 1994–95 | Crevalcore | 29 | 4 |
| 1995–96 | Vicenza | 6 | 0 |
| 1995–96 | Internazionale | 19 | 1 |
| 1996–97 | Internazionale | 26 | 0 |
| 1997–98 | Newcastle U | 28 | 0 |
| **Total:** | | **128** | **6** |

## PITCHER, Darren — Midfield

H: 5 9 W: 12 02 b.London 12-10-69

*Source:* Trainee.

| | | | |
|---|---|---|---|
| 1987–88 | Charlton Ath | 0 | 0 |
| 1988–89 | Charlton Ath | 0 | 0 |
| 1989–90 | Charlton Ath | 0 | 0 |

| | | | |
|---|---|---|---|
| 1990–91 | Charlton Ath | 44 | 3 |
| 1991–92 | Charlton Ath | 46 | 2 |
| 1992–93 | Charlton Ath | 41 | 2 |
| 1993–94 | Charlton Ath | 42 | 1 |
| 1994–95 | Crystal Palace | 25 | 0 |
| 1995–96 | Crystal Palace | 36 | 0 |
| 1996–97 | Crystal Palace | 3 | 0 |
| 1997–98 | Crystal Palace | 0 | 0 |
| 1997–98 | Leyton Orient (loan) | 1 | 0 |
| **Total:** | | **238** | **8** |

## PITWOOD, Adam — Midfield

b.Crawley 24-1-80

*Source:* School.

| | | | |
|---|---|---|---|
| 1996–97 | Millwall | 0 | 0 |
| 1997–98 | Millwall | 0 | 0 |

## PLATT, Clive — Forward

H: 6 4 W: 13 00 b.Wolverhampton 27-10-77

*Source:* Trainee.

| | | | |
|---|---|---|---|
| 1995–96 | Walsall | 4 | 2 |
| 1996–97 | Walsall | 1 | 0 |
| 1997–98 | Walsall | 20 | 1 |
| **Total:** | | **25** | **3** |

## PLATT, David — Midfield

H: 5 10 W: 11 12 b.Chadderton 10-6-66

*Source:* Chadderton. *Honours:* England Under-21, B, 62 full caps, 27 goals.

| | | | |
|---|---|---|---|
| 1984–85 | Manchester U | 0 | 0 |
| 1984–85 | Crewe Alex | 22 | 5 |
| 1985–86 | Crewe Alex | 43 | 8 |
| 1986–87 | Crewe Alex | 43 | 23 |
| 1987–88 | Crewe Alex | 26 | 19 |
| 1987–88 | Aston Villa | 11 | 5 |
| 1988–89 | Aston Villa | 38 | 7 |
| 1989–90 | Aston Villa | 37 | 19 |
| 1990–91 | Aston Villa | 35 | 19 |
| 1991–92 | Bari | 29 | 11 |
| 1992–93 | Juventus | 16 | 3 |
| 1993–94 | Sampdoria | 29 | 9 |
| 1994–95 | Sampdoria | 26 | 8 |
| 1995–96 | Arsenal | 29 | 6 |
| 1996–97 | Arsenal | 28 | 4 |
| 1997–98 | Arsenal | 31 | 3 |
| **Total:** | | **443** | **149** |

## PLATTS, Mark — Forward

H: 5 8 W: 11 12 b.Sheffield 23-5-79

*Source:* Trainee. *Honours:* England Schools, Youth.

| | | | |
|---|---|---|---|
| 1995–96 | Sheffield W | 2 | 0 |
| 1996–97 | Sheffield W | 0 | 0 |
| 1997–98 | Sheffield W | 0 | 0 |
| **Total:** | | **2** | **0** |

## PLUCK, Colin — Defender

H: 6 0 W: 12 10 b.London 6-9-78

*Source:* Trainee.

| | | | |
|---|---|---|---|
| 1996–97 | Watford | 0 | 0 |
| 1997–98 | Watford | 1 | 0 |
| **Total:** | | **1** | **0** |

## PLUMMER, Chris — Defender

H: 6 2 W: 12 12 b.Isleworth 12-10-76

*Source:* Trainee. *Honours:* England Youth, Under-21.

| | | | |
|---|---|---|---|
| 1994–95 | QPR | 0 | 0 |
| 1995–96 | QPR | 1 | 0 |
| 1996–97 | QPR | 5 | 0 |
| 1997–98 | QPR | 0 | 0 |
| **Total:** | | **6** | **0** |

## PLUMMER, Dwayne — Forward

H: 5 9 W: 11 06 b.Bristol 12-10-76

*Source:* Trainee.

| | | | |
|---|---|---|---|
| 1995–96 | Bristol C | 11 | 0 |
| 1996–97 | Bristol C | 2 | 0 |
| 1997–98 | Bristol C | 1 | 0 |
| **Total:** | | **14** | **0** |

## POBORSKY, Karel — Forward

H: 5 9 W: 11 05 b.Jindinchuv-Hradec 30-3-72

*Honours:* Czech Republic 34 full caps, 1 goal.

| | | | |
|---|---|---|---|
| 1991–92 | Ceske Budejovice | 26 | 0 |
| 1992–93 | Ceske Budejovice | 29 | 7 |
| 1993–94 | Ceske Budejovice | 27 | 8 |
| 1994–95 | Viktoria Zizkov | 27 | 10 |
| 1995–96 | Viktoria Zizkov | 1 | 0 |
| 1995–96 | Slavia Prague | 26 | 11 |
| 1996–97 | Manchester U | 22 | 3 |
| 1997–98 | Manchester U | 10 | 2 |
| **Total:** | | **168** | **41** |

## POINTON, Neil — Defender

H: 5 10 W: 12 10 b.Church Warsop 28-11-64

*Source:* Apprentice.

| | | | |
|---|---|---|---|
| 1981–82 | Scunthorpe U | 5 | 0 |
| 1982–83 | Scunthorpe U | 46 | 1 |
| 1983–84 | Scunthorpe U | 45 | 1 |
| 1984–85 | Scunthorpe U | 46 | 0 |
| 1985–86 | Scunthorpe U | 17 | 0 |
| 1985–86 | Everton | 15 | 0 |
| 1986–87 | Everton | 12 | 1 |
| 1987–88 | Everton | 33 | 3 |
| 1988–89 | Everton | 23 | 0 |
| 1989–90 | Everton | 19 | 1 |
| 1990–91 | Manchester C | 35 | 1 |
| 1991–92 | Manchester C | 39 | 1 |
| 1992–93 | Oldham Ath | 34 | 3 |
| 1993–94 | Oldham Ath | 24 | 0 |
| 1994–95 | Oldham Ath | 32 | 0 |
| 1995–96 | Oldham Ath | 4 | 0 |
| 1995–96 | Hearts | 22 | 3 |
| 1996–97 | Hearts | 25 | 0 |
| 1997–98 | Hearts | 20 | 0 |
| **Total:** | | **496** | **15** |

## POLLITT, Michael — Goalkeeper

H: 6 4 W: 14 00 b.Farnworth 29-2-72

*Source:* Trainee.

| | | | |
|---|---|---|---|
| 1990–91 | Manchester U | 0 | 0 |
| 1990–91 | Oldham Ath (loan) | 0 | 0 |
| 1991–92 | Bury | 0 | 0 |
| 1992–93 | Lincoln C | 27 | 0 |
| 1993–94 | Lincoln C | 30 | 0 |
| 1994–95 | Darlington | 40 | 0 |
| 1995–96 | Darlington | 15 | 0 |
| 1995–96 | Notts Co | 0 | 0 |
| 1996–97 | Notts Co | 8 | 0 |
| 1997–98 | Notts Co | 2 | 0 |
| 1997–98 | Oldham Ath (loan) | 16 | 0 |
| 1997–98 | Gillingham (loan) | 6 | 0 |
| 1997–98 | Brentford (loan) | 5 | 0 |
| 1997–98 | Sunderland | 0 | 0 |
| **Total:** | | **149** | **0** |

## POLLOCK, Jamie — Midfield

H: 5 10 W: 14 01 b.Stockton 16-2-74

*Source:* Trainee. *Honours:* England Youth, Under-21.

| | | | |
|---|---|---|---|
| 1990–91 | Middlesbrough | 1 | 0 |
| 1991–92 | Middlesbrough | 26 | 1 |
| 1992–93 | Middlesbrough | 22 | 1 |
| 1993–94 | Middlesbrough | 34 | 9 |
| 1994–95 | Middlesbrough | 41 | 5 |
| 1995–96 | Middlesbrough | 31 | 1 |
| 1996–97 | Osasuna | 0 | 0 |
| 1996–97 | Bolton W | 20 | 4 |
| 1997–98 | Bolton W | 26 | 1 |
| 1997–98 | Manchester C | 8 | 1 |
| **Total:** | | **209** | **23** |

## POLSTON, John — Defender

H: 5 11 W: 11 12 b.Walthamstow 10-6-68

*Source:* Apprentice. *Honours:* England Youth.

| | | | |
|---|---|---|---|
| 1985–86 | Tottenham H | 0 | 0 |
| 1986–87 | Tottenham H | 6 | 0 |
| 1987–88 | Tottenham H | 2 | 0 |
| 1988–89 | Tottenham H | 3 | 0 |
| 1989–90 | Tottenham H | 13 | 1 |
| 1990–91 | Norwich C | 27 | 4 |
| 1991–92 | Norwich C | 19 | 1 |
| 1992–93 | Norwich C | 34 | 1 |
| 1993–94 | Norwich C | 24 | 0 |
| 1994–95 | Norwich C | 38 | 0 |
| 1995–96 | Norwich C | 30 | 0 |
| 1996–97 | Norwich C | 31 | 2 |
| 1997–98 | Norwich C | 12 | 0 |
| **Total:** | | **239** | **9** |

## POOLE, Gary — Defender

H: 6 0 W: 12 08 b.Stratford 11-9-67

*Source:* Arsenal Schoolboys.

| | | | |
|---|---|---|---|
| 1984–85 | Tottenham H | 0 | 0 |
| 1985–86 | Tottenham H | 0 | 0 |
| 1986–87 | Tottenham H | 0 | 0 |
| 1987–88 | Cambridge U | 42 | 0 |
| 1988–89 | Cambridge U | 1 | 0 |
| From Barnet. | | | |
| 1991–92 | Barnet | 40 | 2 |
| 1992–93 | Plymouth Arg | 39 | 5 |
| 1993–94 | Southend U | 38 | 2 |
| 1994–95 | Southend U | 6 | 0 |
| 1994–95 | Birmingham C | 34 | 0 |
| 1995–96 | Birmingham C | 28 | 0 |
| 1996–97 | Birmingham C | 10 | 0 |
| 1996–97 | Charlton Ath | 16 | 1 |
| 1997–98 | Charlton Ath | 0 | 0 |
| **Total:** | | **254** | **10** |

## POOLE, Kevin — Goalkeeper

H: 5 10 W: 11 11 b.Bromsgrove 21-7-63

*Source:* Apprentice.

| | | | |
|---|---|---|---|
| 1981–82 | Aston Villa | 0 | 0 |
| 1982–83 | Aston Villa | 0 | 0 |
| 1983–84 | Aston Villa | 0 | 0 |
| 1984–85 | Aston Villa | 7 | 0 |
| 1984–85 | Northampton T (loan) | 3 | 0 |

| | | | |
|---|---|---|---|
| 1985–86 | Aston Villa | 11 | 0 |
| 1986–87 | Aston Villa | 10 | 0 |
| 1987–88 | Middlesbrough | 1 | 0 |
| 1988–89 | Middlesbrough | 12 | 0 |
| 1989–90 | Middlesbrough | 21 | 0 |
| 1990–91 | Middlesbrough | 0 | 0 |
| 1990–91 | Hartlepool U (loan) | 12 | 0 |
| 1991–92 | Leicester C | 42 | 0 |
| 1992–93 | Leicester C | 19 | 0 |
| 1993–94 | Leicester C | 14 | 0 |
| 1994–95 | Leicester C | 36 | 0 |
| 1995–96 | Leicester C | 45 | 0 |
| 1996–97 | Leicester C | 7 | 0 |
| 1997–98 | Birmingham C | 1 | 0 |
| **Total:** | | **241** | **0** |

## POOM, Mart — Goalkeeper

H: 6 5 W: 13 05 b.Tallinn 3-2-72

*Source:* FC Wil. *Honours:* Estonia 57 full caps.

| | | | |
|---|---|---|---|
| 1994–95 | Portsmouth | 0 | 0 |
| 1995–96 | Portsmouth | 4 | 0 |
| 1996–97 | Portsmouth | 0 | 0 |
| From Flora Tallinn. | | | |
| 1996–97 | Derby Co | 4 | 0 |
| 1997–98 | Derby Co | 36 | 0 |
| **Total:** | | **44** | **0** |

## POPE, Steven — Defender

H: 5 11 W: 11 00 b.Stoke 8-9-76

*Source:* Trainee.

| | | | |
|---|---|---|---|
| 1995–96 | Crewe Alex | 0 | 0 |
| 1996–97 | Crewe Alex | 0 | 0 |
| 1997–98 | Crewe Alex | 6 | 0 |
| **Total:** | | **6** | **0** |

## POPPLETON, David — Midfield

b.Doncaster 19-12-79

*Source:* Trainee.

| | | | |
|---|---|---|---|
| 1997–98 | Everton | 0 | 0 |

## PORIC, Adem — Midfield

H: 5 8 W: 12 05 b.London 22-4-73

*Source:* St George's Budapest. *Honours:* Australia full caps.

| | | | |
|---|---|---|---|
| 1993–94 | Sheffield W | 6 | 0 |
| 1994–95 | Sheffield W | 4 | 0 |
| 1995–96 | Sheffield W | 0 | 0 |
| 1996–97 | Sheffield W | 0 | 0 |
| 1996–97 | Southend U (loan) | 7 | 0 |
| 1997–98 | Sheffield W | 4 | 0 |
| 1997–98 | Rotherham U | 4 | 0 |
| 1997–98 | Notts Co | 4 | 0 |
| **Total:** | | **29** | **0** |

## PORRINI, Sergio — Defender

H: 5 11 W: 12 04 b.Milan 8-11-68

| | | | |
|---|---|---|---|
| 1988–89 | AC Milan | 0 | 0 |
| 1989–90 | Atalanta | 8 | 1 |
| 1990–91 | Atalanta | 29 | 0 |
| 1991–92 | Atalanta | 30 | 0 |
| 1992–93 | Atalanta | 33 | 2 |
| 1993–94 | Juventus | 30 | 0 |
| 1994–95 | Juventus | 19 | 0 |
| 1995–96 | Juventus | 15 | 0 |
| 1996–97 | Juventus | 23 | 1 |
| 1997–98 | Rangers | 26 | 4 |
| **Total:** | | **213** | **8** |

## PORTEOUS, Andrew — Midfield

H: 5 11 W: 10 11 b.Edinburgh 13-9-79

*Source:* Trainee.

| | | | |
|---|---|---|---|
| 1996–97 | Nottingham F | 0 | 0 |
| 1997–98 | Nottingham F | 0 | 0 |
| 1997–98 | Manchester C | 0 | 0 |

## PORTER, Andy — Midfield

H: 5 9 W: 12 00 b.Holmes Chapel 17-9-68

*Source:* Trainee.

| | | | |
|---|---|---|---|
| 1986–87 | Port Vale | 1 | 0 |
| 1987–88 | Port Vale | 6 | 0 |
| 1988–89 | Port Vale | 14 | 1 |
| 1989–90 | Port Vale | 36 | 1 |
| 1990–91 | Port Vale | 40 | 0 |
| 1991–92 | Port Vale | 32 | 1 |
| 1992–93 | Port Vale | 17 | 1 |
| 1993–94 | Port Vale | 37 | 0 |
| 1994–95 | Port Vale | 44 | 3 |
| 1995–96 | Port Vale | 45 | 10 |
| 1996–97 | Port Vale | 44 | 4 |
| 1997–98 | Port Vale | 41 | 1 |
| **Total:** | | **357** | **22** |

## PORTER, Daniel — Midfield

b.Portsmouth 23-1-79

| | | | |
|---|---|---|---|
| 1997–98 | Derby Co | 0 | 0 |

## PORTER, Gary — Midfield

H: 5 7 W: 11 00 b.Sunderland 6-3-66

*Source:* Apprentice. *Honours:* England Youth, Under-21.

| | | | |
|---|---|---|---|
| 1983–84 | Watford | 2 | 0 |
| 1984–85 | Watford | 9 | 0 |
| 1985–86 | Watford | 8 | 1 |
| 1986–87 | Watford | 26 | 4 |
| 1987–88 | Watford | 40 | 3 |
| 1988–89 | Watford | 42 | 10 |
| 1989–90 | Watford | 32 | 4 |
| 1990–91 | Watford | 45 | 4 |
| 1991–92 | Watford | 44 | 8 |
| 1992–93 | Watford | 33 | 0 |
| 1993–94 | Watford | 43 | 9 |
| 1994–95 | Watford | 41 | 3 |
| 1995–96 | Watford | 29 | 1 |
| 1996–97 | Watford | 6 | 0 |
| 1997–98 | Walsall | 29 | 1 |
| **Total:** | | **429** | **48** |

## POTTER, Daniel — Goalkeeper

b.Ipswich 18-3-79

*Source:* Chelsea Trainee.

| | | | |
|---|---|---|---|
| 1997–98 | Colchester U | 0 | 0 |

## POTTER, Graham — Defender

H: 6 1 W: 11 12 b.Solihull 20-5-75

*Source:* Trainee. *Honours:* England Youth, Under-21.

| | | | |
|---|---|---|---|
| 1992–93 | Birmingham C | 18 | 2 |
| 1993–94 | Birmingham C | 7 | 0 |
| 1993–94 | Wycombe W (loan) | 3 | 0 |
| 1993–94 | Stoke C | 3 | 0 |
| 1994–95 | Stoke C | 1 | 0 |
| 1995–96 | Stoke C | 41 | 1 |
| 1996–97 | Southampton | 8 | 0 |
| 1996–97 | WBA | 6 | 0 |
| 1997–98 | WBA | 5 | 0 |
| 1997–98 | Northampton T (loan) | 4 | 0 |
| **Total:** | | **96** | **3** |

## POTTER, Lee — Forward

H: 5 11 W: 12 10 b.Salford 3-9-78

*Source:* Trainee.

| | | | |
|---|---|---|---|
| 1997–98 | Bolton W | 0 | 0 |

## POTTS, Steve — Defender

H: 5 7 W: 10 11 b.Hartford (USA) 7-5-67

*Source:* Apprentice. *Honours:* England Youth.

| | | | |
|---|---|---|---|
| 1984–85 | West Ham U | 1 | 0 |
| 1985–86 | West Ham U | 1 | 0 |
| 1986–87 | West Ham U | 8 | 0 |
| 1987–88 | West Ham U | 8 | 0 |
| 1988–89 | West Ham U | 28 | 0 |
| 1989–90 | West Ham U | 32 | 0 |
| 1990–91 | West Ham U | 37 | 1 |
| 1991–92 | West Ham U | 34 | 0 |
| 1992–93 | West Ham U | 46 | 0 |
| 1993–94 | West Ham U | 41 | 0 |
| 1994–95 | West Ham U | 42 | 0 |
| 1995–96 | West Ham U | 34 | 0 |
| 1996–97 | West Ham U | 20 | 0 |
| 1997–98 | West Ham U | 23 | 0 |
| **Total:** | | **355** | **1** |

## POUNEWATCHY, Stephane — Defender

H: 6 0 W: 15 00 b.Paris 10-2-68

| | | | |
|---|---|---|---|
| 1993–94 | Martigues | 29 | 1 |
| 1994–95 | Martigues | 15 | 1 |
| 1995–96 | Gueugnon | 30 | 0 |
| 1996–97 | Carlisle U | 42 | 1 |
| 1997–98 | Carlisle U | 39 | 2 |
| **Total:** | | **155** | **5** |

## POUNTNEY, Craig — Forward

H: 5 6 W: 9 07 b.Bromsgrove 23-11-79

*Source:* Trainee.

| | | | |
|---|---|---|---|
| 1997–98 | Shrewsbury T | 1 | 0 |
| **Total:** | | **1** | **0** |

## POUTON, Alan — Midfield

H: 6 0 W: 12 02 b.Newcastle 1-2-77

*Source:* Newcastle U Trainee.

| | | | |
|---|---|---|---|
| 1995–96 | Oxford U | 0 | 0 |
| 1995–96 | York C | 0 | 0 |
| 1996–97 | York C | 22 | 1 |
| 1997–98 | York C | 41 | 5 |
| **Total:** | | **63** | **6** |

## POWELL, Chris — Defender

H: 5 10 W: 11 07 b.Lambeth 8-6-69

*Source:* Trainee.

| | | | |
|---|---|---|---|
| 1987–88 | Crystal Palace | 0 | 0 |
| 1988–89 | Crystal Palace | 3 | 0 |
| 1989–90 | Crystal Palace | 0 | 0 |

| | | | |
|---|---|---|---|
| 1989–90 | Aldershot (loan) | 11 | 0 |
| 1990–91 | Southend U | 45 | 1 |
| 1991–92 | Southend U | 44 | 0 |
| 1992–93 | Southend U | 42 | 2 |
| 1993–94 | Southend U | 46 | 0 |
| 1994–95 | Southend U | 44 | 0 |
| 1995–96 | Southend U | 27 | 0 |
| 1995–96 | Derby Co | 19 | 0 |
| 1996–97 | Derby Co | 35 | 0 |
| 1997–98 | Derby Co | 37 | 1 |
| **Total:** | | **353** | **4** |

## POWELL, Darryl — Midfield

H: 6 0 W: 13 00 b.Lambeth 15-11-71

*Source:* Trainee. *Honours:* Jamaica 4 full caps, 1 goal.

| | | | |
|---|---|---|---|
| 1988–89 | Portsmouth | 3 | 0 |
| 1989–90 | Portsmouth | 0 | 0 |
| 1990–91 | Portsmouth | 8 | 0 |
| 1991–92 | Portsmouth | 36 | 6 |
| 1992–93 | Portsmouth | 23 | 0 |
| 1993–94 | Portsmouth | 28 | 5 |
| 1994–95 | Portsmouth | 34 | 5 |
| 1995–96 | Derby Co | 37 | 5 |
| 1996–97 | Derby Co | 33 | 1 |
| 1997–98 | Derby Co | 23 | 0 |
| **Total:** | | **225** | **22** |

## POWELL, Paul — Midfield

H: 5 8 W: 11 03 b.Wallingford 30-6-78

*Source:* Trainee.

| | | | |
|---|---|---|---|
| 1995–96 | Oxford U | 3 | 0 |
| 1996–97 | Oxford U | 0 | 0 |
| 1997–98 | Oxford U | 21 | 1 |
| **Total:** | | **24** | **1** |

## POWER, Graeme — Defender

H: 5 11 W: 10 10 b.Northwick Park 7-3-77

*Source:* Trainee. *Honours:* England Schools, Youth.

| | | | |
|---|---|---|---|
| 1994–95 | QPR | 0 | 0 |
| 1995–96 | QPR | 0 | 0 |
| 1996–97 | Bristol R | 16 | 0 |
| 1997–98 | Bristol R | 10 | 0 |
| **Total:** | | **26** | **0** |

## POWER, Lee — Forward

H: 5 10 W: 12 00 b.Lewisham 30-6-72

*Source:* Trainee. *Honours:* Eire Youth, Under-21, B.

| | | | |
|---|---|---|---|
| 1989–90 | Norwich C | 1 | 0 |
| 1990–91 | Norwich C | 16 | 3 |
| 1991–92 | Norwich C | 4 | 1 |
| 1992–93 | Norwich C | 18 | 6 |
| 1992–93 | Charlton Ath (loan) | 5 | 0 |
| 1993–94 | Norwich C | 5 | 0 |
| 1993–94 | Sunderland (loan) | 3 | 0 |
| 1993–94 | Portsmouth (loan) | 2 | 0 |
| 1993–94 | Bradford C | 3 | 2 |
| 1994–95 | Bradford C | 27 | 3 |
| 1994–95 | Millwall (loan) | 0 | 0 |
| 1995–96 | Peterborough U | 38 | 6 |
| 1996–97 | Hibernian | 6 | 1 |
| 1997–98 | Hibernian | 5 | 1 |
| **Total:** | | **133** | **23** |

## POWER, Phil — Forward

H: 5 7 W: 11 00 b.Salford 25-7-67

*Source:* Northwich V, Witton A.

| | | | |
|---|---|---|---|
| 1985–86 | Crewe Alex | 11 | 2 |
| From Stalybridge C. | | | |
| 1997–98 | Macclesfield T | 38 | 7 |
| **Total:** | | **49** | **9** |

## POYET, Gustavo — Midfield

H: 6 1 W: 13 01 b.Montevideo 15-11-67

*Source:* Bella Vista. *Honours:* Uruguay 13 full caps.

| | | | |
|---|---|---|---|
| 1990–91 | Zaragoza | 31 | 7 |
| 1991–92 | Zaragoza | 33 | 3 |
| 1992–93 | Zaragoza | 33 | 6 |
| 1993–94 | Zaragoza | 34 | 11 |
| 1994–95 | Zaragoza | 34 | 11 |
| 1995–96 | Zaragoza | 36 | 11 |
| 1996–97 | Zaragoza | 38 | 14 |
| 1997–98 | Chelsea | 14 | 4 |
| **Total:** | | **253** | **67** |

## PREECE, Andy — Forward

H: 6 1 W: 12 00 b.Evesham 27-3-67

*Source:* Evesham U.

| | | | |
|---|---|---|---|
| 1988–89 | Northampton T | 1 | 0 |
| From Worcester C. | | | |
| 1989–90 | Wrexham | 7 | 1 |
| 1990–91 | Wrexham | 34 | 4 |
| 1991–92 | Wrexham | 10 | 2 |
| 1991–92 | Stockport Co | 25 | 13 |
| 1992–93 | Stockport Co | 29 | 8 |
| 1993–94 | Stockport Co | 43 | 21 |
| 1994–95 | Crystal Palace | 20 | 4 |
| 1995–96 | Blackpool | 41 | 14 |
| 1996–97 | Blackpool | 41 | 10 |
| 1997–98 | Blackpool | 44 | 11 |
| **Total:** | | **295** | **88** |

## PREECE, David — Midfield

H: 5 6 W: 10 12 b.Bridgnorth 28-5-63

*Source:* Apprentice. *Honours:* England B.

| | | | |
|---|---|---|---|
| 1980–81 | Walsall | 8 | 0 |
| 1981–82 | Walsall | 8 | 0 |
| 1982–83 | Walsall | 42 | 2 |
| 1983–84 | Walsall | 41 | 3 |
| 1984–85 | Walsall | 12 | 0 |
| 1984–85 | Luton T | 21 | 2 |
| 1985–86 | Luton T | 41 | 2 |
| 1986–87 | Luton T | 14 | 0 |
| 1987–88 | Luton T | 13 | 0 |
| 1988–89 | Luton T | 26 | 0 |
| 1989–90 | Luton T | 32 | 1 |
| 1990–91 | Luton T | 37 | 1 |
| 1991–92 | Luton T | 38 | 3 |
| 1992–93 | Luton T | 43 | 3 |
| 1993–94 | Luton T | 29 | 5 |
| 1994–95 | Luton T | 42 | 4 |
| 1995–96 | Derby Co | 13 | 1 |
| 1995–96 | Birmingham C (loan) | 6 | 0 |
| 1995–96 | Swindon T (loan) | 7 | 1 |
| 1996–97 | Cambridge U | 25 | 0 |
| 1997–98 | Cambridge U | 22 | 0 |
| **Total:** | | **520** | **28** |

## PREECE, David — Goalkeeper

H: 6 2 W: 11 11 b.Sunderland 26-8-76

*Source:* Trainee. *Honours:* England Under-18.

| | | | |
|---|---|---|---|
| 1994–95 | Sunderland | 0 | 0 |
| 1995–96 | Sunderland | 0 | 0 |
| 1996–97 | Sunderland | 0 | 0 |
| 1997–98 | Darlington | 45 | 0 |
| **Total:** | | **45** | **0** |

## PREECE, Roger — Midfield

H: 5 8 W: 10 13 b.Much Wenlock 9-6-69

*Source:* Coventry C Apprentice.

| | | | |
|---|---|---|---|
| 1986–87 | Wrexham | 7 | 2 |
| 1987–88 | Wrexham | 40 | 4 |
| 1988–89 | Wrexham | 31 | 5 |
| 1989–90 | Wrexham | 32 | 1 |
| 1990–91 | Chester C | 35 | 0 |
| 1991–92 | Chester C | 29 | 0 |
| 1992–93 | Chester C | 23 | 0 |
| 1993–94 | Chester C | 39 | 2 |
| 1994–95 | Chester C | 43 | 2 |
| 1995–96 | Chester C | 1 | 0 |
| 1996–97 | Chester C | 0 | 0 |
| 1997–98 | Shrewsbury T | 27 | 1 |
| **Total:** | | **307** | **17** |

## PRENDERGAST, Rory — Midfield

H: 5 8 W: 11 13 b.Pontefract 6-4-78

*Source:* Rochdale.

| | | | |
|---|---|---|---|
| 1995–96 | Barnsley | 0 | 0 |
| 1996–97 | Barnsley | 0 | 0 |
| 1997–98 | Barnsley | 0 | 0 |

## PRENDERVILLE, Barry — Defender

H: 6 0 W: 12 08 b.Dublin 16-10-76

*Source:* Trainee.

| | | | |
|---|---|---|---|
| 1994–95 | Coventry C | 0 | 0 |
| 1995–96 | Coventry C | 0 | 0 |
| 1996–97 | Coventry C | 0 | 0 |
| 1997–98 | Coventry C | 0 | 0 |

## PRESSLEY, Steven — Defender

H: 6 0 W: 11 00 b.Elgin 11-10-73

| | | | |
|---|---|---|---|
| 1991–92 | Rangers | 1 | 0 |
| 1992–93 | Rangers | 8 | 0 |
| 1993–94 | Rangers | 23 | 0 |
| 1994–95 | Rangers | 2 | 1 |
| 1994–95 | Coventry C | 19 | 1 |
| 1995–96 | Coventry C | 0 | 0 |
| 1995–96 | Dundee U | 35 | 2 |
| 1996–97 | Dundee U | 36 | 2 |
| 1997–98 | Dundee U | 29 | 2 |
| **Total:** | | **153** | **8** |

## PRESSMAN, Kevin — Goalkeeper

H: 6 1 W: 15 05 b.Fareham 6-11-67

*Source:* Apprentice. *Honours:* England Schools, Youth, Under-21, B.

| | | | |
|---|---|---|---|
| 1985–86 | Sheffield W | 0 | 0 |
| 1986–87 | Sheffield W | 0 | 0 |
| 1987–88 | Sheffield W | 11 | 0 |
| 1988–89 | Sheffield W | 9 | 0 |
| 1989–90 | Sheffield W | 15 | 0 |
| 1990–91 | Sheffield W | 23 | 0 |
| 1991–92 | Sheffield W | 1 | 0 |
| 1991–92 | Stoke C (loan) | 4 | 0 |
| 1992–93 | Sheffield W | 3 | 0 |
| 1993–94 | Sheffield W | 32 | 0 |
| 1994–95 | Sheffield W | 34 | 0 |
| 1995–96 | Sheffield W | 30 | 0 |
| 1996–97 | Sheffield W | 38 | 0 |
| 1997–98 | Sheffield W | 36 | 0 |
| **Total:** | | **236** | **0** |

## PRESTON, Allan — Defender

H: 5 10 W: 11 04 b.Edinburgh 6-8-69

*Source:* Hutcheson Vale BC.

| | | | |
|---|---|---|---|
| 1985–86 | Dundee U | 0 | 0 |
| 1986–87 | Dundee U | 0 | 0 |
| 1987–88 | Dundee U | 2 | 0 |
| 1988–89 | Dundee U | 9 | 1 |
| 1989–90 | Dundee U | 8 | 0 |
| 1990–91 | Dundee U | 3 | 0 |
| 1991–92 | Dundee U | 2 | 0 |
| 1992–93 | Hearts | 21 | 2 |
| 1993–94 | St Johnstone | 9 | 0 |
| 1994–95 | St Johnstone | 26 | 2 |
| 1995–96 | St Johnstone | 27 | 2 |
| 1996–97 | St Johnstone | 32 | 1 |
| 1997–98 | St Johnstone | 35 | 1 |
| **Total:** | | **174** | **9** |

## PRESTON, Michael — Midfield

H: 5 7 W: 11 00 b.Plymouth 22-11-77

*Source:* Trainee.

| | | | |
|---|---|---|---|
| 1995–96 | Torquay U | 8 | 0 |
| 1996–97 | Torquay U | 2 | 0 |
| 1997–98 | Torquay U | 0 | 0 |
| **Total:** | | **10** | **0** |

## PRICE, Jason — Midfield

H: 6 2 W: 11 05 b.Aberdare 12-4-77

*Source:* Aberaman Ath. *Honours:* Wales Under-21.

| | | | |
|---|---|---|---|
| 1995–96 | Swansea C | 0 | 0 |
| 1996–97 | Swansea C | 2 | 0 |
| 1997–98 | Swansea C | 34 | 3 |
| **Total:** | | **36** | **3** |

## PRICE, Ryan — Goalkeeper

H: 6 6 W: 14 00 b.Wolverhampton 13-3-70

*Source:* Stafford R.

| | | | |
|---|---|---|---|
| 1994–95 | Birmingham C | 0 | 0 |
| 1995–96 | Birmingham C | 0 | 0 |
| From Macclesfield T. | | | |
| 1997–98 | Macclesfield T | 46 | 0 |
| **Total:** | | **46** | **0** |

## PRIDHAM, Christopher — Midfield

b.Neath 11-8-78

*Source:* Trainee.

| | | | |
|---|---|---|---|
| 1997–98 | Manchester C | 0 | 0 |

## PRIEST, Chris — Midfield

H: 5 8 W: 10 10 b.Leigh 18-10-73

*Source:* Trainee.

| | | | |
|---|---|---|---|
| 1992–93 | Everton | 0 | 0 |
| 1993–94 | Everton | 0 | 0 |
| 1994–95 | Everton | 0 | 0 |
| 1994–95 | Chester C | 24 | 1 |
| 1995–96 | Chester C | 39 | 13 |
| 1996–97 | Chester C | 32 | 2 |
| 1997–98 | Chester C | 37 | 6 |
| **Total:** | | **132** | **22** |

## PRIMUS, Linvoy — Defender

H: 6 0 W: 13 07 b.Stratford 14-9-73

*Source:* Trainee.

| | | | |
|---|---|---|---|
| 1992–93 | Charlton Ath | 4 | 0 |
| 1993–94 | Charlton Ath | 0 | 0 |
| 1994–95 | Barnet | 39 | 0 |
| 1995–96 | Barnet | 42 | 4 |
| 1996–97 | Barnet | 46 | 3 |
| 1997–98 | Reading | 36 | 1 |
| **Total:** | | **167** | **8** |

## PRINGLE, Alan — Midfield

b.Sunderland 8-3-78

*Source:* Trainee.

| | | | |
|---|---|---|---|
| 1996–97 | Sheffield W | 0 | 0 |
| 1997–98 | Sheffield W | 0 | 0 |

## PRIOR, Spencer — Defender

H: 6 3 W: 13 04 b.Rochford 22-4-71

*Source:* Trainee.

| | | | |
|---|---|---|---|
| 1988–89 | Southend U | 14 | 1 |
| 1989–90 | Southend U | 15 | 1 |
| 1990–91 | Southend U | 19 | 0 |
| 1991–92 | Southend U | 42 | 1 |
| 1992–93 | Southend U | 45 | 0 |
| 1993–94 | Norwich C | 13 | 0 |
| 1994–95 | Norwich C | 17 | 0 |
| 1995–96 | Norwich C | 44 | 1 |
| 1996–97 | Leicester C | 34 | 0 |
| 1997–98 | Leicester C | 30 | 0 |
| **Total:** | | **273** | **4** |

## PRITCHARD, David — Defender

H: 5 7 W: 11 04 b.Wolverhampton 27-5-72

*Source:* Telford U. *Honours:* Wales B.

| | | | |
|---|---|---|---|
| 1990–91 | WBA | 0 | 0 |

| | | | |
|---|---|---|---|
| 1991–92 | WBA | 5 | 0 |
| 1993–94 | Bristol R | 11 | 0 |
| 1994–95 | Bristol R | 43 | 0 |
| 1995–96 | Bristol R | 12 | 0 |
| 1996–97 | Bristol R | 26 | 0 |
| 1997–98 | Bristol R | 33 | 0 |
| **Total:** | | **130** | **0** |

## PROCTOR, Michael — Forward

H: 5 11 W: 12 07 b.Sunderland 3-10-80

*Source:* Trainee.

| | | | |
|---|---|---|---|
| 1997–98 | Sunderland | 0 | 0 |

## PROKAS, Richard — Midfield

H: 5 8 W: 11 04 b.Penrith 22-1-76

*Source:* Trainee.

| | | | |
|---|---|---|---|
| 1994–95 | Carlisle U | 39 | 1 |
| 1995–96 | Carlisle U | 20 | 0 |
| 1996–97 | Carlisle U | 13 | 1 |
| 1997–98 | Carlisle U | 34 | 0 |
| **Total:** | | **106** | **2** |

## PRUDHOE, Mark — Goalkeeper

H: 6 0 W: 14 00 b.Washington 8-11-63

*Source:* Apprentice.

| | | | |
|---|---|---|---|
| 1981–82 | Sunderland | 0 | 0 |
| 1982–83 | Sunderland | 7 | 0 |
| 1983–84 | Sunderland | 0 | 0 |
| 1983–84 | Hartlepool U (loan) | 3 | 0 |
| 1984–85 | Sunderland | 0 | 0 |
| 1984–85 | Birmingham C | 1 | 0 |
| 1985–86 | Walsall | 16 | 0 |
| 1986–87 | Walsall | 10 | 0 |
| 1986–87 | Doncaster R (loan) | 5 | 0 |
| 1986–87 | Sheffield W (loan) | 0 | 0 |
| 1986–87 | Grimsby T (loan) | 8 | 0 |
| 1987–88 | Walsall | 0 | 0 |
| 1987–88 | Hartlepool U (loan) | 13 | 0 |
| 1987–88 | Bristol C (loan) | 3 | 0 |
| 1987–88 | Carlisle U | 22 | 0 |
| 1988–89 | Carlisle U | 12 | 0 |
| 1988–89 | Darlington | 12 | 0 |
| 1989–90 | Darlington | 0 | 0 |
| 1990–91 | Darlington | 46 | 0 |
| 1991–92 | Darlington | 46 | 0 |
| 1992–93 | Darlington | 42 | 0 |
| 1993–94 | Stoke C | 30 | 0 |
| 1994–95 | Stoke C | 0 | 0 |
| 1994–95 | Peterborough U (loan) | 6 | 0 |
| 1994–95 | Liverpool (loan) | 0 | 0 |
| 1995–96 | Stoke C | 39 | 0 |
| 1996–97 | Stoke C | 13 | 0 |
| 1996–97 | York C (loan) | 2 | 0 |
| 1997–98 | Bradford C | 8 | 0 |
| **Total:** | | **344** | **0** |

## PUGH, David — Forward

H: 6 2 W: 13 00 b.Liverpool 19-9-64

*Source:* Runcorn.

| | | | |
|---|---|---|---|
| 1989–90 | Chester C | 35 | 3 |
| 1990–91 | Chester C | 37 | 3 |
| 1991–92 | Chester C | 35 | 0 |
| 1992–93 | Chester C | 35 | 5 |
| 1993–94 | Chester C | 37 | 12 |
| 1994–95 | Bury | 42 | 16 |
| 1995–96 | Bury | 42 | 10 |
| 1996–97 | Bury | 18 | 2 |
| 1997–98 | Bury | 1 | 0 |
| **Total:** | | **282** | **51** |

## PURSE, Darren — Defender

H: 6 2 W: 12 08 b.Stepney 14-2-77

*Source:* Trainee. *Honours:* England Under-21.

| | | | |
|---|---|---|---|
| 1993–94 | Leyton Orient | 5 | 0 |
| 1994–95 | Leyton Orient | 38 | 3 |
| 1995–96 | Leyton Orient | 12 | 0 |
| 1996–97 | Oxford U | 31 | 1 |
| 1997–98 | Oxford U | 28 | 4 |
| 1997–98 | Birmingham C | 8 | 0 |
| **Total:** | | **122** | **8** |

## PURSER, Wayne — Forward

H: 5 9 W: 11 04 b.Basildon 13-4-80

*Source:* Trainee.

| | | | |
|---|---|---|---|
| 1996–97 | QPR | 0 | 0 |
| 1997–98 | QPR | 0 | 0 |

## PUTTNAM, Dave — Midfield

H: 5 10 W: 11 12 b.Leicester 3-2-67

*Source:* Leicester U.

| | | | |
|---|---|---|---|
| 1988–89 | Leicester C | 3 | 0 |
| 1989–90 | Leicester C | 4 | 0 |
| 1989–90 | Lincoln C | 23 | 1 |
| 1990–91 | Lincoln C | 43 | 6 |
| 1991–92 | Lincoln C | 39 | 6 |
| 1992–93 | Lincoln C | 37 | 2 |
| 1993–94 | Lincoln C | 13 | 1 |
| 1994–95 | Lincoln C | 17 | 4 |
| 1995–96 | Lincoln C | 5 | 1 |
| 1995–96 | Gillingham | 26 | 1 |
| 1996–97 | Gillingham | 14 | 1 |
| 1997–98 | Swansea C | 4 | 0 |
| **Total:** | | **228** | **23** |

## QUAILEY, Brian — Forward

H: 6 0 W: 12 10 b.Leicester 21-3-78

*Source:* Nuneaton B.

| | | | |
|---|---|---|---|
| 1997–98 | WBA | 5 | 0 |
| **Total:** | | **5** | **0** |

## QUASHIE, Nigel — Midfield

H: 6 0 W: 12 04 b.Nunhead 20-7-78

*Source:* Trainee. *Honours:* England Youth, Under-21, B.

| | | | |
|---|---|---|---|
| 1995–96 | QPR | 11 | 0 |
| 1996–97 | QPR | 13 | 0 |
| 1997–98 | QPR | 33 | 3 |
| **Total:** | | **57** | **3** |

## QUAYLE, Mark — Forward

H: 5 9 W: 10 02 b.Liverpool 2-10-78

*Source:* Trainee.

| | | | |
|---|---|---|---|
| 1995–96 | Everton | 0 | 0 |
| 1996–97 | Everton | 0 | 0 |
| 1997–98 | Everton | 0 | 0 |

## QUIGLEY, Michael — Midfield

H: 5 7 W: 11 04 b.Manchester 2-10-70

*Source:* Trainee.

| | | | |
|---|---|---|---|
| 1990–91 | Manchester C | 0 | 0 |
| 1991–92 | Manchester C | 5 | 0 |
| 1992–93 | Manchester C | 5 | 0 |
| 1993–94 | Manchester C | 2 | 0 |
| 1994–95 | Manchester C | 0 | 0 |
| 1994–95 | Wrexham (loan) | 4 | 0 |
| 1995–96 | Hull C | 13 | 1 |
| 1996–97 | Hull C | 29 | 1 |
| 1997–98 | Hull C | 9 | 1 |
| **Total:** | | **67** | **3** |

## QUINN, Alan — Forward

b.Dublin 13-6-79

| | | | |
|---|---|---|---|
| 1997–98 | Sheffield W | 1 | 0 |
| **Total:** | | **1** | **0** |

## QUINN, Andrew — Midfield

b.Halifax 1-9-79

| | | | |
|---|---|---|---|
| 1996–97 | Leeds U | 0 | 0 |
| 1997–98 | Leeds U | 0 | 0 |

## QUINN, Barry — Midfield

H: 6 0 W: 12 02 b.Dublin 9-5-79

*Source:* Trainee.

| | | | |
|---|---|---|---|
| 1996–97 | Coventry C | 0 | 0 |
| 1997–98 | Coventry C | 0 | 0 |

## QUINN, James — Forward

H: 6 1 W: 12 10 b.Coventry 15-12-74

*Source:* Trainee. *Honours:* Northern Ireland Under-21, 12 full caps, 1 goal.

| | | | |
|---|---|---|---|
| 1992–93 | Birmingham C | 4 | 0 |
| 1993–94 | Blackpool | 14 | 2 |
| 1993–94 | Stockport Co (loan) | 1 | 0 |
| 1994–95 | Blackpool | 41 | 9 |
| 1995–96 | Blackpool | 44 | 9 |
| 1996–97 | Blackpool | 38 | 13 |
| 1997–98 | Blackpool | 14 | 4 |
| 1997–98 | WBA | 13 | 2 |
| **Total:** | | **169** | **39** |

## QUINN, Jimmy — Forward

H: 6 1 W: 13 10 b.Belfast 18-11-59

*Source:* Oswestry T. *Honours:* Northern Ireland 46 full caps, 12 goals.

| | | | |
|---|---|---|---|
| 1981–82 | Swindon T | 4 | 0 |
| 1982–83 | Swindon T | 13 | 3 |
| 1983–84 | Swindon T | 32 | 7 |
| 1984–85 | Blackburn R | 25 | 10 |
| 1985–86 | Blackburn R | 31 | 4 |
| 1986–87 | Blackburn R | 15 | 3 |
| 1986–87 | Swindon T | 22 | 9 |
| 1987–88 | Swindon T | 42 | 21 |
| 1988–89 | Leicester C | 31 | 6 |
| 1988–89 | Bradford C | 12 | 8 |
| 1989–90 | Bradford C | 23 | 6 |
| 1989–90 | West Ham U | 21 | 12 |
| 1990–91 | West Ham U | 26 | 6 |
| 1991–92 | Bournemouth | 43 | 19 |
| 1992–93 | Reading | 42 | 17 |
| 1993–94 | Reading | 46 | 35 |
| 1994–95 | Reading | 35 | 5 |
| 1995–96 | Reading | 35 | 11 |
| 1996–97 | Reading | 24 | 3 |
| 1997–98 | Peterborough U | 42 | 20 |
| **Total:** | | **564** | **205** |

## QUINN, Niall — Forward

H: 6 4 W: 12 04 b.Dublin 6-10-66

*Honours:* Eire Youth, Under-21, Under-23, B, 63 full caps, 16 goals.

| | | | |
|---|---|---|---|
| 1983–84 | Arsenal | 0 | 0 |
| 1984–85 | Arsenal | 0 | 0 |
| 1985–86 | Arsenal | 12 | 1 |
| 1986–87 | Arsenal | 35 | 8 |
| 1987–88 | Arsenal | 11 | 2 |
| 1988–89 | Arsenal | 3 | 1 |
| 1989–90 | Arsenal | 6 | 2 |
| 1989–90 | Manchester C | 9 | 4 |
| 1990–91 | Manchester C | 38 | 20 |
| 1991–92 | Manchester C | 35 | 12 |
| 1992–93 | Manchester C | 39 | 9 |
| 1993–94 | Manchester C | 15 | 5 |
| 1994–95 | Manchester C | 35 | 8 |
| 1995–96 | Manchester C | 32 | 8 |
| 1996–97 | Sunderland | 12 | 2 |
| 1997–98 | Sunderland | 35 | 14 |
| **Total:** | | **317** | **96** |

## QUINN, Robert — Defender

H: 5 11 W: 11 02 b.Sidcup 8-11-76

*Source:* Trainee.

| | | | |
|---|---|---|---|
| 1994–95 | Crystal Palace | 0 | 0 |
| 1995–96 | Crystal Palace | 1 | 0 |
| 1996–97 | Crystal Palace | 21 | 1 |
| 1997–98 | Crystal Palace | 1 | 0 |
| **Total:** | | **23** | **1** |

## QUINN, Wayne — Midfield

H: 5 10 W: 11 11 b.Truro 19-11-76

*Honours:* England Under-21, B.

| | | | |
|---|---|---|---|
| 1994–95 | Sheffield U | 0 | 0 |
| 1995–96 | Sheffield U | 0 | 0 |
| 1996–97 | Sheffield U | 0 | 0 |
| 1997–98 | Sheffield U | 28 | 2 |
| **Total:** | | **28** | **2** |

## QUITONGO, Jose — Forward

H: 5 7 W: 10 07 b.Luanda 18-11-74

| | | | |
|---|---|---|---|
| 1995–96 | Darlington | 1 | 0 |
| 1995–96 | Hamilton A | 22 | 4 |
| 1996–97 | Hamilton A | 34 | 3 |
| 1997–98 | Hamilton A | 6 | 2 |
| 1997–98 | Hearts | 17 | 3 |
| **Total:** | | **80** | **12** |

## RACHEL, Adam — Goalkeeper

H: 5 11 W: 12 08 b.Birmingham 10-12-76

*Source:* Trainee.

| | | | |
|---|---|---|---|
| 1994–95 | Aston Villa | 0 | 0 |
| 1995–96 | Aston Villa | 0 | 0 |
| 1996–97 | Aston Villa | 0 | 0 |
| 1997–98 | Aston Villa | 0 | 0 |

## RADEBE, Lucas — Defender

H: 6 1 W: 11 09 b.Johannesburg 12-4-69

*Source:* Kaiser Chiefs. *Honours:* South Africa 46 full caps, 1 goal.

| | | | |
|---|---|---|---|
| 1994–95 | Leeds U | 12 | 0 |
| 1995–96 | Leeds U | 13 | 0 |
| 1996–97 | Leeds U | 32 | 0 |
| 1997–98 | Leeds U | 27 | 0 |
| **Total:** | | **84** | **0** |

## RADZKI, Lee — Midfield

b.Mansfield 14-11-78

*Source:* Trainee.

| | | | |
|---|---|---|---|
| 1995–96 | Derby Co | 0 | 0 |
| 1996–97 | Derby Co | 0 | 0 |
| 1997–98 | Derby Co | 0 | 0 |

## RAE, Alex — Midfield

H: 5 8 W: 11 08 b.Glasgow 30-9-69

*Source:* Bishopbriggs. *Honours:* Scotland Under-21, B.

| | | | |
|---|---|---|---|
| 1987–88 | Falkirk | 12 | 0 |
| 1988–89 | Falkirk | 37 | 12 |
| 1989–90 | Falkirk | 34 | 8 |
| 1990–91 | Millwall | 39 | 10 |
| 1991–92 | Millwall | 38 | 11 |
| 1992–93 | Millwall | 30 | 6 |
| 1993–94 | Millwall | 36 | 13 |
| 1994–95 | Millwall | 38 | 10 |
| 1995–96 | Millwall | 37 | 13 |
| 1996–97 | Sunderland | 23 | 2 |
| 1997–98 | Sunderland | 29 | 3 |
| **Total:** | | **353** | **88** |

## RAE, Gavin — Defender

H: 5 11 W: 10 04 b.Aberdeen 28-11-77

*Source:* Hermes J.

| | | | |
|---|---|---|---|
| 1995–96 | Dundee | 6 | 0 |
| 1996–97 | Dundee | 17 | 2 |
| 1997–98 | Dundee | 6 | 0 |
| **Total:** | | **29** | **2** |

## RAESIDE, Robert — Defender

H: 6 0 W: 11 10 b.South Africa 7-7-72

*Source:* From St Andrews University.

| | | | |
|---|---|---|---|
| 1990–91 | Raith R | 14 | 0 |
| 1991–92 | Raith R | 13 | 0 |
| 1992–93 | Raith R | 10 | 0 |
| 1993–94 | Raith R | 0 | 0 |
| 1994–95 | Raith R | 10 | 0 |
| 1995–96 | Raith R | 8 | 1 |
| 1996–97 | Dundee | 34 | 4 |
| 1997–98 | Dundee | 11 | 0 |
| **Total:** | | **100** | **5** |

## RAINFORD, David — Midfield

H: 6 0 W: 11 11 b.Stepney 21-4-79

*Source:* Trainee.

| | | | |
|---|---|---|---|
| 1997–98 | Colchester U | 0 | 0 |

## RAMAGE, Craig — Midfield

H: 5 9 W: 11 08 b.Derby 30-3-70

*Source:* Trainee. *Honours:* England Under-21.

| | | | |
|---|---|---|---|
| 1988–89 | Derby Co | 0 | 0 |
| 1988–89 | Wigan Ath (loan) | 10 | 2 |
| 1989–90 | Derby Co | 12 | 1 |
| 1990–91 | Derby Co | 17 | 1 |
| 1991–92 | Derby Co | 7 | 2 |
| 1992–93 | Derby Co | 1 | 0 |
| 1993–94 | Derby Co | 5 | 0 |
| 1993–94 | Watford | 13 | 0 |
| 1994–95 | Watford | 44 | 9 |
| 1995–96 | Watford | 36 | 15 |
| 1996–97 | Watford | 11 | 3 |
| 1996–97 | Peterborough U (loan) | 7 | 0 |
| 1997–98 | Bradford C | 32 | 1 |
| **Total:** | | **195** | **34** |

## RAMASUT, Tom — Midfield

H: 5 10 W: 11 00 b.Cardiff 30-8-77

*Honours:* Wales Under-21, B.

| | | | |
|---|---|---|---|
| 1995–96 | Norwich C | 0 | 0 |
| 1996–97 | Bristol R | 11 | 0 |
| 1997–98 | Bristol R | 31 | 6 |
| **Total:** | | **42** | **6** |

## RAMMELL, Andy — Forward

H: 6 2 W: 13 10 b.Nuneaton 10-2-67

*Source:* Atherstone U.

| | | | |
|---|---|---|---|
| 1989–90 | Manchester U | 0 | 0 |
| 1990–91 | Barnsley | 40 | 12 |
| 1991–92 | Barnsley | 37 | 8 |
| 1992–93 | Barnsley | 30 | 7 |
| 1993–94 | Barnsley | 34 | 6 |
| 1994–95 | Barnsley | 24 | 7 |
| 1995–96 | Barnsley | 20 | 4 |
| 1995–96 | Southend U | 7 | 2 |
| 1996–97 | Southend U | 36 | 9 |
| 1997–98 | Southend U | 26 | 2 |
| **Total:** | | **254** | **57** |

## RAMPLIN, Jamie — Midfield

b.Manchester 14-10-79

*Source:* Trainee.

| | | | |
|---|---|---|---|
| 1996–97 | Oldham Ath | 0 | 0 |
| 1997–98 | Oldham Ath | 0 | 0 |

## RAMSAY, John — Midfield

H: 5 8 W: 9 10 b.Sunderland 25-1-79

*Source:* Trainee.

| | | | |
|---|---|---|---|
| 1997–98 | Doncaster R | 10 | 0 |
| **Total:** | | **10** | **0** |

## RANDALL, Adrian — Midfield

H: 5 11 W: 12 04 b.Salisbury 10-11-68

*Source:* Apprentice. *Honours:* England Youth.

| | | | |
|---|---|---|---|
| 1985–86 | Bournemouth | 2 | 0 |
| 1986–87 | Bournemouth | 0 | 0 |
| 1987–88 | Bournemouth | 1 | 0 |
| 1988–89 | Bournemouth | 0 | 0 |
| 1988–89 | Aldershot | 37 | 2 |
| 1989–90 | Aldershot | 34 | 2 |
| 1990–91 | Aldershot | 36 | 8 |
| 1991–92 | Aldershot | 0 | 0 |
| 1991–92 | Burnley | 18 | 2 |
| 1992–93 | Burnley | 23 | 1 |
| 1993–94 | Burnley | 37 | 4 |
| 1994–95 | Burnley | 32 | 1 |
| 1995–96 | Burnley | 15 | 0 |
| 1995–96 | York C | 16 | 0 |
| 1996–97 | York C | 16 | 2 |
| 1996–97 | Bury | 19 | 3 |
| 1997–98 | Bury | 15 | 0 |
| **Total:** | | **301** | **25** |

## RANDALL, Dean — Defender

H: 6 1 W: 12 00 b.Nottingham 15-5-79

*Source:* Trainee.

| | | | |
|---|---|---|---|
| 1997–98 | Notts Co | 0 | 0 |

## RANKIN, Isiah — Forward

H: 5 10 W: 11 00 b.London 22-5-78

*Source:* Trainee.

| | | | |
|---|---|---|---|
| 1995–96 | Arsenal | 0 | 0 |
| 1996–97 | Arsenal | 0 | 0 |
| 1997–98 | Arsenal | 1 | 0 |
| 1997–98 | Colchester U (loan) | 11 | 5 |
| **Total:** | | **12** | **5** |

## RANKINE, Mark — Midfield

H: 5 10 W: 11 08 b.Doncaster 30-9-69

*Source:* Trainee.

| | | | |
|---|---|---|---|
| 1987–88 | Doncaster R | 18 | 2 |
| 1988–89 | Doncaster R | 46 | 11 |
| 1989–90 | Doncaster R | 36 | 2 |
| 1990–91 | Doncaster R | 40 | 2 |
| 1991–92 | Doncaster R | 24 | 3 |
| 1991–92 | Wolverhampton W | 15 | 1 |
| 1992–93 | Wolverhampton W | 27 | 0 |
| 1993–94 | Wolverhampton W | 31 | 0 |
| 1994–95 | Wolverhampton W | 27 | 0 |
| 1995–96 | Wolverhampton W | 32 | 0 |
| 1996–97 | Wolverhampton W | 0 | 0 |
| 1996–97 | Preston NE | 23 | 0 |
| 1997–98 | Preston NE | 35 | 1 |
| **Total:** | | **354** | **22** |

## RAPLEY, Kevin — Forward

H: 5 9 W: 10 08 b.Reading 21-9-77

*Source:* Trainee.

| | | | |
|---|---|---|---|
| 1996–97 | Brentford | 2 | 0 |
| 1997–98 | Brentford | 37 | 9 |
| **Total:** | | **39** | **9** |

## RATCLIFFE, Kevin — Defender

H: 6 1 W: 13 06 b.Mancot 12-11-60

*Source:* Apprentice. *Honours:* Wales Schools, Youth, Under-21, 59 full caps.

| | | | |
|---|---|---|---|
| 1978–79 | Everton | 0 | 0 |
| 1979–80 | Everton | 2 | 0 |
| 1980–81 | Everton | 21 | 0 |
| 1981–82 | Everton | 25 | 0 |
| 1982–83 | Everton | 29 | 1 |
| 1983–84 | Everton | 38 | 0 |
| 1984–85 | Everton | 40 | 0 |
| 1985–86 | Everton | 39 | 1 |
| 1986–87 | Everton | 42 | 0 |
| 1987–88 | Everton | 24 | 0 |
| 1988–89 | Everton | 30 | 0 |
| 1989–90 | Everton | 24 | 0 |
| 1990–91 | Everton | 36 | 0 |
| 1991–92 | Everton | 9 | 0 |
| 1992–93 | Dundee | 4 | 0 |
| 1992–93 | Everton | 0 | 0 |
| 1992–93 | Cardiff C | 19 | 1 |
| 1993–94 | Cardiff C | 6 | 0 |
| 1993–94 | Nottingham F | 0 | 0 |
| 1993–94 | Derby Co | 6 | 0 |
| 1994–95 | Chester C | 23 | 0 |
| 1995–96 | Chester C | 0 | 0 |
| 1996–97 | Chester C | 0 | 0 |
| 1997–98 | Chester C | 0 | 0 |
| **Total:** | | **417** | **3** |

## RATCLIFFE, Simon — Midfield

H: 6 0 W: 12 13 b.Davyhulme 6-2-67

*Source:* Apprentice. *Honours:* England Schools, Youth.

| | | | |
|---|---|---|---|
| 1984–85 | Manchester U | 0 | 0 |
| 1985–86 | Manchester U | 0 | 0 |
| 1986–87 | Manchester U | 0 | 0 |
| 1987–88 | Norwich C | 9 | 0 |
| 1988–89 | Norwich C | 0 | 0 |
| 1988–89 | Brentford | 9 | 1 |
| 1989–90 | Brentford | 35 | 2 |
| 1990–91 | Brentford | 38 | 2 |
| 1991–92 | Brentford | 34 | 2 |
| 1992–93 | Brentford | 30 | 2 |
| 1993–94 | Brentford | 43 | 4 |
| 1994–95 | Brentford | 25 | 1 |
| 1995–96 | Gillingham | 41 | 3 |
| 1996–97 | Gillingham | 43 | 6 |
| 1997–98 | Gillingham | 21 | 1 |
| **Total:** | | **328** | **24** |

## RATTRAY, Kevin — Midfield

H: 5 11 W: 11 02 b.London 6-10-68

*Source:* Woking.

| | | | |
|---|---|---|---|
| 1995–96 | Gillingham | 26 | 3 |
| 1996–97 | Gillingham | 0 | 0 |
| 1996–97 | Barnet | 9 | 0 |
| 1997–98 | Barnet | 0 | 0 |
| **Total:** | | **35** | **3** |

## RAVANELLI, Fabrizio — Forward

H: 6 2 W: 13 04 b.Perugia 11-12-68

*Honours:* Italy 21 full caps, 9 goals.

| | | | |
|---|---|---|---|
| 1986–87 | Perugia | 26 | 5 |
| 1987–88 | Perugia | 32 | 23 |
| 1988–89 | Perugia | 32 | 13 |
| 1989–90 | Avellino | 7 | 0 |
| 1989–90 | Casertana (loan) | 27 | 12 |
| 1990–91 | Avellino | 0 | 0 |

| | | | |
|---|---|---|---|
| 1990–91 | Reggiana | 34 | 16 |
| 1991–92 | Reggiana | 32 | 8 |
| 1992–93 | Juventus | 22 | 5 |
| 1993–94 | Juventus | 30 | 9 |
| 1994–95 | Juventus | 33 | 15 |
| 1995–96 | Juventus | 26 | 12 |
| 1996–97 | Middlesbrough | 33 | 16 |
| 1997–98 | Middlesbrough | 2 | 1 |
| **Total:** | | **336** | **135** |

## RAVEN, Paul — Defender

H: 6 1 W: 12 11 b.Salisbury 28-7-70

*Source:* School. *Honours:* England Schools, Youth.

| | | | |
|---|---|---|---|
| 1987–88 | Doncaster R | 17 | 3 |
| 1988–89 | Doncaster R | 35 | 1 |
| 1988–89 | WBA | 3 | 0 |
| 1989–90 | WBA | 7 | 0 |
| 1990–91 | WBA | 13 | 0 |
| 1991–92 | WBA | 7 | 1 |
| 1991–92 | Doncaster R (loan) | 7 | 0 |
| 1992–93 | WBA | 44 | 7 |
| 1993–94 | WBA | 34 | 1 |
| 1994–95 | WBA | 31 | 0 |
| 1995–96 | WBA | 40 | 4 |
| 1996–97 | WBA | 33 | 1 |
| 1997–98 | WBA | 8 | 0 |
| **Total:** | | **279** | **18** |

## RAWLINSON, Mark — Midfield

H: 5 10 W: 11 04 b.Bolton 9-6-75

*Source:* Trainee.

| | | | |
|---|---|---|---|
| 1993–94 | Manchester U | 0 | 0 |
| 1994–95 | Manchester U | 0 | 0 |
| 1995–96 | Bournemouth | 19 | 0 |
| 1996–97 | Bournemouth | 25 | 2 |
| 1997–98 | Bournemouth | 25 | 0 |
| **Total:** | | **69** | **2** |

## RAYNOR, Paul — Midfield

H: 5 11 W: 13 03 b.Nottingham 29-4-66

*Source:* Apprentice.

| | | | |
|---|---|---|---|
| 1983–84 | Nottingham F | 0 | 0 |
| 1984–85 | Nottingham F | 3 | 0 |
| 1984–85 | Bristol R (loan) | 8 | 0 |
| 1985–86 | Huddersfield T | 30 | 5 |
| 1986–87 | Huddersfield T | 20 | 4 |
| 1986–87 | Swansea C | 12 | 1 |
| 1987–88 | Swansea C | 44 | 8 |
| 1988–89 | Swansea C | 26 | 5 |
| 1988–89 | Wrexham (loan) | 6 | 0 |
| 1989–90 | Swansea C | 40 | 6 |
| 1990–91 | Swansea C | 43 | 5 |
| 1991–92 | Swansea C | 26 | 2 |
| 1991–92 | Cambridge U | 8 | 0 |
| 1992–93 | Cambridge U | 41 | 2 |
| 1993–94 | Preston NE | 39 | 6 |
| 1994–95 | Preston NE | 38 | 3 |
| 1995–96 | Preston NE | 3 | 0 |
| 1995–96 | Cambridge U | 35 | 3 |
| 1996–97 | Cambridge U | 44 | 4 |
| 1997–98 | Cambridge U | 0 | 0 |
| Guang Deong | | | |
| 1997–98 | Leyton Orient | 10 | 0 |
| **Total:** | | **476** | **54** |

## REA, Simon — Defender

H: 6 1 W: 13 00 b.Coventry 20-9-76

*Source:* Trainee.

| | | | |
|---|---|---|---|
| 1994–95 | Birmingham C | 0 | 0 |
| 1995–96 | Birmingham C | 1 | 0 |
| 1996–97 | Birmingham C | 0 | 0 |
| 1997–98 | Birmingham C | 0 | 0 |
| **Total:** | | **1** | **0** |

## READ, Paul — Forward

H: 5 8 W: 12 06 b.Harlow 25-9-73

*Source:* Trainee. *Honours:* England Schools.

| | | | |
|---|---|---|---|
| 1991–92 | Arsenal | 0 | 0 |
| 1992–93 | Arsenal | 0 | 0 |
| 1993–94 | Arsenal | 0 | 0 |
| 1994–95 | Arsenal | 0 | 0 |
| 1994–95 | Leyton Orient (loan) | 11 | 0 |
| 1995–96 | Arsenal | 0 | 0 |
| 1995–96 | Southend U (loan) | 4 | 1 |
| 1996–97 | Arsenal | 0 | 0 |
| 1996–97 | Wycombe W | 13 | 4 |
| 1997–98 | Wycombe W | 28 | 4 |
| **Total:** | | **56** | **9** |

## READY, Karl — Defender

H: 6 1 W: 12 10 b.Neath 14-8-72

*Source:* Trainee. *Honours:* Wales Under-21, B, 5 full caps.

| | | | |
|---|---|---|---|
| 1990–91 | QPR | 0 | 0 |
| 1991–92 | QPR | 1 | 0 |
| 1992–93 | QPR | 3 | 0 |
| 1993–94 | QPR | 22 | 1 |
| 1994–95 | QPR | 13 | 1 |
| 1995–96 | QPR | 22 | 1 |
| 1996–97 | QPR | 29 | 0 |
| 1997–98 | QPR | 39 | 3 |
| **Total:** | | **129** | **6** |

## REDFEARN, Neil — Midfield

H: 5 8 W: 13 07 b.Bradford 20-6-65

*Source:* Nottingham F Apprentice.

| | | | |
|---|---|---|---|
| 1982–83 | Bolton W | 10 | 0 |
| 1983–84 | Bolton W | 25 | 1 |
| 1983–84 | Lincoln C (loan) | 10 | 1 |
| 1984–85 | Lincoln C | 45 | 4 |
| 1985–86 | Lincoln C | 45 | 8 |
| 1986–87 | Doncaster R | 46 | 14 |
| 1987–88 | Crystal Palace | 42 | 8 |
| 1988–89 | Crystal Palace | 15 | 2 |
| 1988–89 | Watford | 12 | 2 |
| 1989–90 | Watford | 12 | 1 |
| 1989–90 | Oldham Ath | 17 | 2 |
| 1990–91 | Oldham Ath | 45 | 14 |
| 1991–92 | Barnsley | 36 | 4 |
| 1992–93 | Barnsley | 46 | 3 |
| 1993–94 | Barnsley | 46 | 12 |
| 1994–95 | Barnsley | 39 | 11 |
| 1995–96 | Barnsley | 45 | 14 |
| 1996–97 | Barnsley | 43 | 17 |
| 1997–98 | Barnsley | 37 | 10 |
| **Total:** | | **616** | **128** |

## REDKNAPP, Jamie — Midfield

H: 6 0 W: 12 10 b.Barton-on-Sea 25-6-73

*Source:* Tottenham H Schoolboy, Bournemouth Trainee. *Honours:* England Schools, Youth, B, Under-21, 8 full caps.

| | | | |
|---|---|---|---|
| 1989–90 | Bournemouth | 4 | 0 |
| 1990–91 | Bournemouth | 9 | 0 |
| 1990–91 | Liverpool | 0 | 0 |
| 1991–92 | Liverpool | 6 | 1 |
| 1992–93 | Liverpool | 29 | 2 |
| 1993–94 | Liverpool | 35 | 4 |
| 1994–95 | Liverpool | 41 | 3 |
| 1995–96 | Liverpool | 23 | 3 |
| 1996–97 | Liverpool | 23 | 2 |
| 1997–98 | Liverpool | 20 | 3 |
| **Total:** | | **190** | **18** |

## REDMILE, Matthew — Defender

H: 6 4 W: 12 11 b.Nottingham 12-11-76

*Source:* Trainee.

| | | | |
|---|---|---|---|
| 1995–96 | Notts Co | 0 | 0 |
| 1996–97 | Notts Co | 23 | 2 |
| 1997–98 | Notts Co | 34 | 3 |
| **Total:** | | **57** | **5** |

## REDMOND, Steve — Defender

H: 5 10 W: 11 07 b.Liverpool 2-11-67

*Source:* Apprentice. *Honours:* England Youth, Under-21.

| | | | |
|---|---|---|---|
| 1984–85 | Manchester C | 0 | 0 |
| 1985–86 | Manchester C | 9 | 0 |
| 1986–87 | Manchester C | 30 | 2 |
| 1987–88 | Manchester C | 44 | 0 |
| 1988–89 | Manchester C | 46 | 1 |
| 1989–90 | Manchester C | 38 | 0 |
| 1990–91 | Manchester C | 37 | 3 |
| 1991–92 | Manchester C | 31 | 1 |
| 1992–93 | Oldham Ath | 31 | 0 |
| 1993–94 | Oldham Ath | 33 | 1 |
| 1994–95 | Oldham Ath | 43 | 0 |
| 1995–96 | Oldham Ath | 40 | 1 |
| 1996–97 | Oldham Ath | 24 | 2 |
| 1997–98 | Oldham Ath | 34 | 0 |
| **Total:** | | **440** | **11** |

## REED, Adam — Defender

H: 6 2 W: 11 00 b.Bishop Auckland 18-2-75

*Source:* Trainee.

| | | | |
|---|---|---|---|
| 1991–92 | Darlington | 1 | 0 |
| 1992–93 | Darlington | 0 | 0 |
| 1993–94 | Darlington | 13 | 0 |
| 1994–95 | Darlington | 38 | 1 |
| 1995–96 | Blackburn R | 0 | 0 |
| 1996–97 | Blackburn R | 0 | 0 |
| 1996–97 | Darlington (loan) | 14 | 0 |
| 1997–98 | Blackburn R | 0 | 0 |
| 1997–98 | Rochdale (loan) | 10 | 0 |
| **Total:** | | **76** | **1** |

## REED, Ian — Midfield

H: 5 8 W: 10 13 b.Lichfield 4-9-75

*Source:* Trainee.

| | | | |
|---|---|---|---|
| 1994–95 | Shrewsbury T | 4 | 0 |
| 1995–96 | Shrewsbury T | 11 | 2 |
| 1996–97 | Shrewsbury T | 3 | 0 |
| 1997–98 | Shrewsbury T | 0 | 0 |
| **Total:** | | **18** | **2** |

## REED, John — Midfield

H: 5 10 W: 10 11 b.Rotherham 27-8-72

*Source:* Trainee.

| | | | |
|---|---|---|---|
| 1990–91 | Sheffield U | 0 | 0 |
| 1990–91 | Scarborough (loan) | 14 | 6 |
| 1991–92 | Sheffield U | 1 | 0 |
| 1991–92 | Scarborough (loan) | 6 | 0 |
| 1992–93 | Sheffield U | 0 | 0 |

| | | | |
|---|---|---|---|
| 1992–93 | Darlington (loan) | 10 | 2 |
| 1993–94 | Sheffield U | 0 | 0 |
| 1993–94 | Mansfield T (loan) | 13 | 2 |
| 1994–95 | Sheffield U | 12 | 2 |
| 1995–96 | Sheffield U | 2 | 0 |
| 1996–97 | Sheffield U | 0 | 0 |
| 1997–98 | Sheffield U | 0 | 0 |
| 1997–98 | Blackpool | 3 | 0 |
| **Total:** | | **61** | **12** |

## REED, Martin — Defender

H: 6 1 W: 11 07 b.Scarborough 10-1-78

*Source:* Trainee.

| | | | |
|---|---|---|---|
| 1996–97 | York C | 2 | 0 |
| 1997–98 | York C | 22 | 0 |
| **Total:** | | **24** | **0** |

## REED, Matthew — Goalkeeper

H: 5 10 W: 11 10 b.Stanford-Le-Hope 7-4-80

*Source:* Trainee.

| | | | |
|---|---|---|---|
| 1997–98 | Newcastle U | 0 | 0 |

## REES, Gavin — Defender

H: 6 1 W: 12 08 b.Pembroke 1-11-78

*Source:* Trainee.

| | | | |
|---|---|---|---|
| 1997–98 | Portsmouth | 0 | 0 |

## REES, Jason — Forward

H: 5 5 W: 10 00 b.Aberdare 22-12-69

*Source:* Trainee. *Honours:* Wales Schools, Youth, Under-21, B, 1 full cap.

| | | | |
|---|---|---|---|
| 1988–89 | Luton T | 0 | 0 |
| 1989–90 | Luton T | 14 | 0 |
| 1990–91 | Luton T | 21 | 0 |
| 1991–92 | Luton T | 5 | 0 |
| 1992–93 | Luton T | 32 | 0 |
| 1993–94 | Luton T | 10 | 0 |
| 1993–94 | Mansfield T (loan) | 15 | 1 |
| 1994–95 | Portsmouth | 19 | 1 |
| 1995–96 | Portsmouth | 21 | 1 |
| 1996–97 | Portsmouth | 3 | 1 |
| 1996–97 | Exeter C (loan) | 7 | 0 |
| 1997–98 | Cambridge U | 20 | 0 |
| **Total:** | | **167** | **4** |

## REESON, Nicholas — Midfield

b.Boston 5-5-80

*Source:* Trainee.

| | | | |
|---|---|---|---|
| 1997–98 | Lincoln C | 0 | 0 |

## REEVE, Chris — Forward

b.Darlington 1-10-79

*Source:* Trainee.

| | | | |
|---|---|---|---|
| 1997–98 | Middlesbrough | 0 | 0 |

## REEVES, Alan — Defender

H: 6 0 W: 12 00 b.Birkenhead 19-11-67

*Source:* Heswall.

| | | | |
|---|---|---|---|
| 1988–89 | Norwich C | 0 | 0 |
| 1988–89 | Gillingham (loan) | 18 | 0 |
| 1989–90 | Chester C | 30 | 2 |
| 1990–91 | Chester C | 10 | 0 |
| 1991–92 | Rochdale | 34 | 3 |
| 1992–93 | Rochdale | 41 | 3 |
| 1993–94 | Rochdale | 41 | 3 |
| 1994–95 | Rochdale | 5 | 0 |
| 1994–95 | Wimbledon | 31 | 3 |
| 1995–96 | Wimbledon | 24 | 1 |
| 1996–97 | Wimbledon | 2 | 0 |
| 1997–98 | Wimbledon | 0 | 0 |
| **Total:** | | **236** | **15** |

## REEVES, David — Forward

H: 6 0 W: 12 06 b.Birkenhead 19-11-67

*Source:* Heswall.

| | | | |
|---|---|---|---|
| 1986–87 | Sheffield W | 0 | 0 |
| 1986–87 | Scunthorpe U (loan) | 4 | 2 |
| 1987–88 | Sheffield W | 0 | 0 |
| 1987–88 | Scunthorpe U (loan) | 6 | 4 |
| 1987–88 | Burnley (loan) | 16 | 8 |
| 1988–89 | Sheffield W | 17 | 2 |
| 1989–90 | Bolton W | 41 | 10 |
| 1990–91 | Bolton W | 44 | 10 |
| 1991–92 | Bolton W | 35 | 8 |
| 1992–93 | Bolton W | 14 | 1 |
| 1992–93 | Notts Co | 9 | 2 |
| 1993–94 | Notts Co | 4 | 0 |
| 1993–94 | Carlisle U | 34 | 11 |
| 1994–95 | Carlisle U | 42 | 21 |
| 1995–96 | Carlisle U | 43 | 13 |
| 1996–97 | Carlisle U | 8 | 3 |
| 1996–97 | Preston NE | 34 | 11 |
| 1997–98 | Preston NE | 13 | 1 |
| 1997–98 | Chesterfield | 26 | 5 |
| **Total:** | | **390** | **112** |

## REGAN, Carl — Defender

b.Liverpool 9-9-80

*Source:* Trainee.

| | | | |
|---|---|---|---|
| 1997–98 | Everton | 0 | 0 |

## REGIS, Dave — Forward

H: 6 0 W: 13 08 b.Paddington 3-3-64

*Source:* Barnet.

| | | | |
|---|---|---|---|
| 1990–91 | Notts Co | 37 | 15 |
| 1991–92 | Notts Co | 9 | 0 |
| 1991–92 | Plymouth Arg | 24 | 2 |
| 1992–93 | Plymouth Arg | 7 | 2 |
| 1992–93 | Bournemouth (loan) | 6 | 2 |
| 1992–93 | Stoke C | 25 | 5 |
| 1993–94 | Stoke C | 38 | 10 |
| 1994–95 | Birmingham C | 6 | 2 |
| 1994–95 | Southend U | 9 | 1 |
| 1995–96 | Southend U | 29 | 8 |
| 1995–96 | Barnsley | 12 | 1 |
| 1996–97 | Barnsley | 4 | 0 |
| 1996–97 | Peterborough U (loan) | 7 | 1 |
| 1996–97 | Notts Co (loan) | 10 | 2 |
| 1997–98 | Barnsley | 0 | 0 |
| 1997–98 | Leyton Orient | 4 | 0 |
| 1997–98 | Lincoln C | 1 | 0 |
| 1997–98 | Scunthorpe U | 9 | 2 |
| **Total:** | | **237** | **53** |

## REID, Christopher — Goalkeeper

H: 5 11 W: 13 10 b.Edinburgh 4-11-71

*Source:* Hutcheson Vale BC. *Honours:* Scotland Under-21.

| | | | |
|---|---|---|---|
| 1989–90 | Hibernian | 2 | 0 |
| 1990–91 | Hibernian | 1 | 0 |
| 1991–92 | Hibernian | 9 | 0 |
| 1992–93 | Hibernian | 14 | 0 |
| 1993–94 | Hibernian | 0 | 0 |
| 1994–95 | Hibernian | 0 | 0 |
| 1995–96 | Hibernian | 0 | 0 |
| 1996–97 | Hibernian | 1 | 0 |
| 1997–98 | Hibernian | 8 | 0 |
| **Total:** | | **35** | **0** |

## REID, Paul — Midfield

H: 5 9 W: 10 07 b.Oldbury 19-1-68

*Source:* Apprentice.

| | | | |
|---|---|---|---|
| 1985–86 | Leicester C | 0 | 0 |
| 1986–87 | Leicester C | 6 | 0 |
| 1987–88 | Leicester C | 26 | 5 |
| 1988–89 | Leicester C | 45 | 6 |
| 1989–90 | Leicester C | 40 | 8 |
| 1990–91 | Leicester C | 33 | 2 |
| 1991–92 | Leicester C | 12 | 0 |
| 1991–92 | Bradford C (loan) | 7 | 0 |
| 1992–93 | Bradford C | 44 | 6 |
| 1993–94 | Bradford C | 38 | 9 |
| 1994–95 | Huddersfield T | 42 | 6 |
| 1995–96 | Huddersfield T | 13 | 0 |
| 1996–97 | Huddersfield T | 22 | 0 |
| 1996–97 | Oldham Ath | 9 | 1 |
| 1997–98 | Oldham Ath | 44 | 4 |
| **Total:** | | **381** | **47** |

## REID, Shaun — Midfield

H: 5 8 W: 12 10 b.Huyton 13-10-65

*Source:* Local.

| | | | |
|---|---|---|---|
| 1983–84 | Rochdale | 17 | 0 |
| 1984–85 | Rochdale | 21 | 1 |
| 1985–86 | Rochdale | 8 | 0 |
| 1985–86 | Preston NE (loan) | 3 | 0 |
| 1986–87 | Rochdale | 41 | 1 |
| 1987–88 | Rochdale | 28 | 0 |
| 1988–89 | Rochdale | 18 | 2 |
| 1988–89 | York C | 24 | 2 |
| 1989–90 | York C | 25 | 4 |
| 1990–91 | York C | 29 | 0 |
| 1991–92 | York C | 28 | 1 |
| 1992–93 | Rochdale | 40 | 4 |
| 1993–94 | Rochdale | 39 | 3 |
| 1994–95 | Rochdale | 28 | 3 |
| 1995–96 | Bury | 21 | 0 |
| 1996–97 | Bury | 0 | 0 |
| 1996–97 | Chester C | 27 | 1 |
| 1997–98 | Chester C | 0 | 0 |
| **Total:** | | **397** | **22** |

## REID, Steven — Midfield

H: 5 11 W: 11 10 b.Kingston 10-3-81

*Source:* Trainee.

| | | | |
|---|---|---|---|
| 1997–98 | Millwall | 1 | 0 |
| **Total:** | | **1** | **0** |

## REILLY, Mark — Defender

H: 5 8 W: 10 00 b.Bellshill 30-3-69

*Source:* Wishaw Jun. *Honours:* Scotland B.

| | | | |
|---|---|---|---|
| 1988–89 | Motherwell | 0 | 0 |
| 1989–90 | Motherwell | 4 | 0 |
| 1990–91 | Motherwell | 0 | 0 |
| 1991–92 | Kilmarnock | 19 | 0 |
| 1992–93 | Kilmarnock | 19 | 3 |
| 1993–94 | Kilmarnock | 38 | 0 |
| 1994–95 | Kilmarnock | 32 | 0 |
| 1995–96 | Kilmarnock | 28 | 0 |

| | | | |
|---|---|---|---|
| 1996–97 | Kilmarnock | 33 | 2 |
| 1997–98 | Kilmarnock | 36 | 3 |
| **Total:** | | **209** | **8** |

## REINA, Ricky — Forward

H: 6 0 W: 13 05 b.Folkestone 2-10-71

*Source:* Dover Ath.

| | | | |
|---|---|---|---|
| 1997–98 | Brentford | 6 | 1 |
| **Total:** | | **6** | **1** |

## REINELT, Robbie — Forward

H: 5 11 W: 11 11 b.Epping 11-3-74

*Source:* Trainee.

| | | | |
|---|---|---|---|
| 1990–91 | Aldershot | 5 | 0 |
| 1991–92 | Aldershot | 0 | 0 |
| 1992–93 | Gillingham | 0 | 0 |
| 1993–94 | Gillingham | 25 | 1 |
| 1994–95 | Gillingham | 27 | 4 |
| 1994–95 | Colchester U | 5 | 0 |
| 1995–96 | Colchester U | 22 | 7 |
| 1996–97 | Colchester U | 21 | 3 |
| 1996–97 | Brighton & HA | 12 | 3 |
| 1997–98 | Brighton & HA | 32 | 4 |
| **Total:** | | **149** | **22** |

## REMY, Christophe — Defender

H: 5 9 W: 12 01 b.Besancon 6-8-71

| | | | |
|---|---|---|---|
| 1992–93 | Auxerre | 1 | 0 |
| 1993–94 | Auxerre | 0 | 0 |
| 1994–95 | Auxerre | 8 | 0 |
| 1995–96 | Auxerre | 13 | 0 |
| 1996–97 | Derby Co | 0 | 0 |
| 1997–98 | Oxford U | 16 | 0 |
| **Total:** | | **38** | **0** |

## RENDELL, John — Midfield

H: 6 1 W: 12 00 b.Bristol 8-8-78

*Source:* Trainee.

| | | | |
|---|---|---|---|
| 1997–98 | Cardiff C | 0 | 0 |

## RENNER, Victor — Forward

H: 6 0 W: 11 02 b.Sierra Leone 18-4-79

*Source:* Trainee.

| | | | |
|---|---|---|---|
| 1996–97 | Wimbledon | 0 | 0 |
| 1997–98 | Wimbledon | 0 | 0 |

## RENNIE, David — Defender

H: 6 0 W: 13 00 b.Edinburgh 29-8-64

*Source:* Apprentice. *Honours:* Scotland Youth.

| | | | |
|---|---|---|---|
| 1982–83 | Leicester C | 0 | 0 |
| 1983–84 | Leicester C | 15 | 0 |
| 1984–85 | Leicester C | 3 | 1 |
| 1985–86 | Leicester C | 3 | 0 |
| 1985–86 | Leeds U | 16 | 2 |
| 1986–87 | Leeds U | 24 | 0 |
| 1987–88 | Leeds U | 28 | 2 |
| 1988–89 | Leeds U | 33 | 1 |
| 1989–90 | Bristol C | 45 | 4 |
| 1990–91 | Bristol C | 32 | 2 |
| 1991–92 | Bristol C | 27 | 2 |
| 1991–92 | Birmingham C | 17 | 2 |
| 1992–93 | Birmingham C | 18 | 2 |
| 1992–93 | Coventry C | 9 | 0 |
| 1993–94 | Coventry C | 34 | 1 |
| 1994–95 | Coventry C | 28 | 0 |
| 1995–96 | Coventry C | 11 | 2 |
| 1996–97 | Northampton T | 43 | 3 |
| 1997–98 | Northampton T | 5 | 0 |
| 1997–98 | Peterborough U | 18 | 0 |
| **Total:** | | **409** | **24** |

## RENNISON, Graham

b.Northallerton 2-10-78

*Source:* Trainee.

| | | | |
|---|---|---|---|
| 1997–98 | York C | 1 | 0 |
| **Total:** | | **1** | **0** |

## RENWICK, Michael — Defender

H: 5 9 W: 11 00 b.Edinburgh 29-2-76

*Source:* Hutchison Vale BC.

| | | | |
|---|---|---|---|
| 1994–95 | Hibernian | 1 | 0 |
| 1995–96 | Hibernian | 2 | 0 |
| 1996–97 | Hibernian | 9 | 0 |
| 1997–98 | Hibernian | 6 | 0 |
| **Total:** | | **18** | **0** |

## RESCH, Franz — Midfield

H: 6 0 W: 12 00 b.Vienna 4-5-69

*Source:* Rapid Vienna, Modling. *Honours:* Austria 4 full caps.

| | | | |
|---|---|---|---|
| 1997–98 | Motherwell | 3 | 0 |
| 1997–98 | Darlington | 17 | 1 |
| **Total:** | | **20** | **1** |

## REYNOLDS, Paul — Defender

H: 6 1 W: 11 04 b.Widnes 13-9-78

*Source:* Trainee.

| | | | |
|---|---|---|---|
| 1996–97 | Wimbledon | 0 | 0 |
| 1997–98 | Wimbledon | 0 | 0 |

## RHODES, Andy — Goalkeeper

H: 6 0 W: 13 06 b.Doncaster 23-8-64

*Source:* Apprentice.

| | | | |
|---|---|---|---|
| 1982–83 | Barnsley | 0 | 0 |
| 1983–84 | Barnsley | 31 | 0 |
| 1984–85 | Barnsley | 5 | 0 |
| 1985–86 | Barnsley | 0 | 0 |
| 1985–86 | Doncaster R | 30 | 0 |
| 1986–87 | Doncaster R | 41 | 0 |
| 1987–88 | Doncaster R | 35 | 0 |
| 1987–88 | Oldham Ath | 11 | 0 |
| 1988–89 | Oldham Ath | 27 | 0 |
| 1989–90 | Oldham Ath | 31 | 0 |
| 1990–91 | Dunfermline Ath | 35 | 0 |
| 1991–92 | Dunfermline Ath | 44 | 0 |
| 1992–93 | St Johnstone | 44 | 0 |
| 1993–94 | St Johnstone | 44 | 0 |
| 1994–95 | St Johnstone | 19 | 0 |
| 1994–95 | Bolton W (loan) | 0 | 0 |
| 1995–96 | Airdrieonians | 16 | 0 |
| 1996–97 | Airdrieonians | 9 | 0 |
| 1997–98 | Airdrieonians | 4 | 0 |
| 1997–98 | Scarborough | 11 | 0 |
| **Total:** | | **437** | **0** |

## RIBEIRO, Bruno — Midfield

H: 5 9 W: 12 03 b.Setubal 22-10-75

*Honours:* Portugal Under-21.

| | | | |
|---|---|---|---|
| 1994–95 | Setubal | 11 | 1 |
| 1995–96 | Setubal* | 0 | 0 |
| 1996–97 | Setubal | 20 | 1 |
| 1997–98 | Leeds U | 29 | 3 |
| **Total:** | | **60** | **5** |

## RICARD, Hamilton — Forward

H: 6 2 W: 14 05 b.Colombia 12-1-74

*Source:* Deportivo Cali. *Honours:* Colombia 19 caps, 4 goals.

| | | | |
|---|---|---|---|
| 1997–98 | Middlesbrough | 9 | 2 |
| **Total:** | | **9** | **2** |

## RICE, Gary — Defender

H: 5 9 W: 11 10 b.Zambia 29-9-75

*Source:* Trainee.

| | | | |
|---|---|---|---|
| 1994–95 | Exeter C | 10 | 0 |
| 1995–96 | Exeter C | 19 | 0 |
| 1996–97 | Exeter C | 15 | 0 |
| 1997–98 | Exeter C | 0 | 0 |
| **Total:** | | **44** | **0** |

## RICHARDS, Dean — Defender

H: 6 2 W: 13 07 b.Bradford 9-6-74

*Source:* Trainee. *Honours:* England Under-21.

| | | | |
|---|---|---|---|
| 1991–92 | Bradford C | 7 | 1 |
| 1992–93 | Bradford C | 3 | 0 |
| 1993–94 | Bradford C | 46 | 2 |
| 1994–95 | Bradford C | 30 | 1 |
| 1994–95 | Wolverhampton W (loan) | 10 | 2 |
| 1995–96 | Wolverhampton W | 37 | 1 |
| 1996–97 | Wolverhampton W | 21 | 1 |
| 1997–98 | Wolverhampton W | 13 | 0 |
| **Total:** | | **167** | **8** |

## RICHARDS, Ian — Defender

H: 5 8 W: 11 04 b.Barnsley 5-10-79

*Source:* Trainee.

| | | | |
|---|---|---|---|
| 1997–98 | Blackburn R | 0 | 0 |

## RICHARDS, Tony — Forward

H: 5 10 W: 13 06 b.Newham 17-9-73

*Source:* West Ham U Trainee, Sudbury T.

| | | | |
|---|---|---|---|
| 1995–96 | Cambridge U | 19 | 1 |
| 1996–97 | Cambridge U | 23 | 4 |
| 1997–98 | Leyton Orient | 17 | 2 |
| **Total:** | | **59** | **7** |

## RICHARDSON, Barry — Goalkeeper

H: 6 1 W: 12 01 b.Wallsend 5-8-69

*Source:* Trainee.

| | | | |
|---|---|---|---|
| 1987–88 | Sunderland | 0 | 0 |
| 1988–89 | Scunthorpe U | 0 | 0 |
| 1989–90 | Scarborough | 24 | 0 |
| 1990–91 | Scarborough | 6 | 0 |
| 1991–92 | Northampton T | 27 | 0 |
| 1992–93 | Northampton T | 42 | 0 |
| 1993–94 | Northampton T | 27 | 0 |
| 1994–95 | Preston NE | 17 | 0 |
| 1995–96 | Preston NE | 3 | 0 |
| 1995–96 | Lincoln C | 34 | 0 |

| | | | |
|---|---|---|---|
| 1996–97 | Lincoln C | 36 | 0 |
| 1997–98 | Lincoln C | 26 | 0 |
| **Total:** | | **242** | **0** |

## RICHARDSON, Craig — Defender

b.Newham 8-10-79

*Source:* Trainee.

| | | | |
|---|---|---|---|
| 1997–98 | Leyton Orient | 1 | 0 |
| **Total:** | | **1** | **0** |

## RICHARDSON, Ian — Midfield

H: 5 10 W: 11 01 b.Barking 22-10-70

*Source:* Dagenham & Redbridge.

| | | | |
|---|---|---|---|
| 1995–96 | Birmingham C | 7 | 0 |
| 1995–96 | Notts Co | 15 | 0 |
| 1996–97 | Notts Co | 19 | 1 |
| 1997–98 | Notts Co | 30 | 2 |
| **Total:** | | **71** | **3** |

## RICHARDSON, Jay — Midfield

b.Keston 14-11-79

*Source:* Trainee.

| | | | |
|---|---|---|---|
| 1997–98 | Chelsea | 0 | 0 |

## RICHARDSON, Jon — Defender

H: 6 1 W: 12 05 b.Nottingham 29-8-75

*Source:* Trainee.

| | | | |
|---|---|---|---|
| 1993–94 | Exeter C | 7 | 0 |
| 1994–95 | Exeter C | 38 | 1 |
| 1995–96 | Exeter C | 43 | 1 |
| 1996–97 | Exeter C | 43 | 1 |
| 1997–98 | Exeter C | 41 | 2 |
| **Total:** | | **172** | **5** |

## RICHARDSON, Kevin — Midfield

H: 5 10 W: 12 00 b.Newcastle 4-12-62

*Source:* Apprentice. *Honours:* England 1 full cap.

| | | | |
|---|---|---|---|
| 1980–81 | Everton | 0 | 0 |
| 1981–82 | Everton | 18 | 2 |
| 1982–83 | Everton | 29 | 3 |
| 1983–84 | Everton | 28 | 4 |
| 1984–85 | Everton | 15 | 4 |
| 1985–86 | Everton | 18 | 3 |
| 1986–87 | Everton | 1 | 0 |
| 1986–87 | Watford | 39 | 2 |
| 1987–88 | Arsenal | 29 | 4 |
| 1988–89 | Arsenal | 34 | 1 |
| 1989–90 | Arsenal | 33 | 0 |
| 1990–91 | Real Sociedad | 37 | 0 |
| 1991–92 | Aston Villa | 42 | 6 |
| 1992–93 | Aston Villa | 42 | 2 |
| 1993–94 | Aston Villa | 40 | 5 |
| 1994–95 | Aston Villa | 19 | 0 |
| 1994–95 | Coventry C | 14 | 0 |
| 1995–96 | Coventry C | 33 | 0 |
| 1996–97 | Coventry C | 28 | 0 |
| 1997–98 | Coventry C | 3 | 0 |
| 1997–98 | Southampton | 28 | 0 |
| **Total:** | | **530** | **36** |

## RICHARDSON, Leam — Defender

b.Leeds 19-11-79

*Source:* Trainee.

| | | | |
|---|---|---|---|
| 1997–98 | Blackburn R | 0 | 0 |

## RICHARDSON, Lee J — Midfield

H: 5 11 W: 11 00 b.Halifax 12-3-69

| | | | |
|---|---|---|---|
| 1986–87 | Halifax T | 1 | 0 |
| 1987–88 | Halifax T | 30 | 1 |
| 1988–89 | Halifax T | 25 | 1 |
| 1988–89 | Watford | 9 | 0 |
| 1989–90 | Watford | 32 | 1 |
| 1990–91 | Blackburn R | 38 | 2 |
| 1991–92 | Blackburn R | 24 | 1 |
| 1992–93 | Blackburn R | 0 | 0 |
| 1992–93 | Aberdeen | 29 | 2 |
| 1993–94 | Aberdeen | 35 | 4 |
| 1994–95 | Oldham Ath | 30 | 6 |
| 1995–96 | Oldham Ath | 27 | 11 |
| 1996–97 | Oldham Ath | 31 | 4 |
| 1997–98 | Oldham Ath | 0 | 0 |
| 1997–98 | Stockport Co (loan) | 6 | 0 |
| 1997–98 | Huddersfield T | 21 | 3 |
| **Total:** | | **338** | **36** |

## RICHARDSON, Lloyd M — Midfield

H: 5 11 W: 12 02 b.Dewsbury 7-10-77

*Source:* Trainee. *Honours:* England Youth.

| | | | |
|---|---|---|---|
| 1994–95 | Oldham Ath | 0 | 0 |
| 1995–96 | Oldham Ath | 0 | 0 |
| 1996–97 | Oldham Ath | 1 | 0 |
| 1997–98 | Oldham Ath | 0 | 0 |
| **Total:** | | **1** | **0** |

## RICHARDSON, Neil — Defender

H: 6 0 W: 13 00 b.Sunderland 3-3-68

*Source:* Brandon U.

| | | | |
|---|---|---|---|
| 1989–90 | Rotherham U | 2 | 0 |

## Richardson, Nick

| | | | |
|---|---|---|---|
| 1990–91 | Rotherham U | 16 | 2 |
| 1991–92 | Rotherham U | 18 | 2 |
| 1992–93 | Rotherham U | 14 | 0 |
| 1993–94 | Rotherham U | 27 | 0 |
| 1994–95 | Rotherham U | 25 | 0 |
| 1995–96 | Rotherham U | 25 | 2 |
| 1996–97 | Rotherham U | 14 | 1 |
| 1996–97 | Exeter C (loan) | 14 | 0 |
| 1997–98 | Rotherham U | 38 | 2 |
| **Total:** | | **193** | **9** |

## RICHARDSON, Nick — Midfield

H: 6 0 W: 12 06 b.Halifax 11-4-67

*Source:* Local.

| | | | |
|---|---|---|---|
| 1988–89 | Halifax T | 7 | 0 |
| 1989–90 | Halifax T | 27 | 6 |
| 1990–91 | Halifax T | 26 | 3 |
| 1991–92 | Halifax T | 41 | 8 |
| 1992–93 | Cardiff C | 39 | 4 |
| 1993–94 | Cardiff C | 39 | 5 |
| 1994–95 | Cardiff C | 33 | 4 |
| 1994–95 | Wrexham (loan) | 4 | 2 |
| 1994–95 | Chester C (loan) | 6 | 1 |
| 1995–96 | Bury | 5 | 0 |
| 1995–96 | Chester C | 37 | 4 |
| 1996–97 | Chester C | 9 | 0 |
| 1997–98 | Chester C | 44 | 2 |
| **Total:** | | **317** | **39** |

## RICHARDSON, Paul — Midfield

b.Oldham 7-12-78

*Source:* Trainee.

| | | | |
|---|---|---|---|
| 1997–98 | Crewe Alex | 0 | 0 |

## RICKERS, Paul — Midfield

H: 5 10 W: 11 02 b.Leeds 9-5-75

*Source:* Trainee.

| | | | |
|---|---|---|---|
| 1993–94 | Oldham Ath | 0 | 0 |
| 1994–95 | Oldham Ath | 4 | 1 |
| 1995–96 | Oldham Ath | 23 | 0 |
| 1996–97 | Oldham Ath | 46 | 4 |
| 1997–98 | Oldham Ath | 40 | 4 |
| **Total:** | | **113** | **9** |

## RICKETTS, Michael — Forward

H: 6 3 W: 13 01 b.Birmingham 4-12-78

*Source:* Trainee.

| | | | |
|---|---|---|---|
| 1995–96 | Walsall | 1 | 1 |
| 1996–97 | Walsall | 11 | 1 |
| 1997–98 | Walsall | 24 | 1 |
| **Total:** | | **36** | **3** |

## RIDLER, Dave — Defender

H: 6 0 W: 12 02 b.Liverpool 12-3-76

*Source:* Prescot T.

| | | | |
|---|---|---|---|
| 1996–97 | Wrexham | 11 | 0 |
| 1997–98 | Wrexham | 20 | 0 |
| **Total:** | | **31** | **0** |

## RIDLEY, Martin — Defender

b.Leicester 30-3-80

*Source:* Trainee.

| | | | |
|---|---|---|---|
| 1997–98 | Aston Villa | 0 | 0 |

## RIEDLE, Karlheinz — Forward

H: 5 11 W: 12 00 b.Weiler 16-9-65

*Source:* Augsburg. *Honours:* Germany 42 full caps, 16 goals.

| | | | |
|---|---|---|---|
| 1986–87 | Blau-Weiss 90 | 34 | 10 |
| 1987–88 | Werder Bremen | 33 | 17 |
| 1988–89 | Werder Bremen | 33 | 13 |
| 1989–90 | Werder Bremen | 20 | 8 |
| 1990–91 | Lazio | 33 | 9 |
| 1991–92 | Lazio | 29 | 13 |
| 1992–93 | Lazio | 22 | 8 |
| 1993–94 | Borussia Dortmund | 22 | 4 |
| 1994–95 | Borussia Dortmund | 29 | 6 |
| 1995–96 | Borussia Dortmund | 18 | 7 |
| 1996–97 | Borussia Dortmund | 18 | 7 |
| 1997–98 | Liverpool | 25 | 6 |
| **Total:** | | **316** | **108** |

## RIEPER, Marc — Defender

H: 6 3 W: 13 10 b.Denmark 5-6-68

*Source:* Aarhus. *Honours:* Denmark 58 full caps, 2 goal.

| | | | |
|---|---|---|---|
| 1992–93 | Brondby | 32 | 2 |
| 1993–94 | Brondby | 31 | 0 |
| 1994–95 | Brondby | 18 | 1 |
| 1994–95 | West Ham U | 21 | 1 |
| 1995–96 | West Ham U | 36 | 2 |
| 1996–97 | West Ham U | 28 | 1 |
| 1997–98 | West Ham U | 5 | 1 |
| 1997–98 | Celtic | 30 | 2 |
| **Total:** | | **201** | **10** |

## RIGBY, Tony — Midfield

H: 5 10 W: 12 12 b.Ormskirk 10-8-72

*Source:* Barrow.

| | | | |
|---|---|---|---|
| 1992–93 | Bury | 21 | 2 |
| 1993–94 | Bury | 33 | 7 |

| | | | |
|---|---|---|---|
| 1994–95 | Bury | 30 | 2 |
| 1995–96 | Bury | 41 | 7 |
| 1996–97 | Bury | 15 | 0 |
| 1996–97 | Scarborough (loan) | 5 | 1 |
| 1997–98 | Bury | 24 | 1 |
| **Total:** | | **169** | **20** |

## RIMMER, Stephen — Defender

H: 6 3 W: 13 02 b.Liverpool 23-5-79

*Source:* Trainee.

| | | | |
|---|---|---|---|
| 1996–97 | Manchester C | 0 | 0 |
| 1997–98 | Manchester C | 0 | 0 |

## RIMMER, Stuart — Forward

H: 5 7 W: 11 00 b.Southport 12-10-64

*Source:* Apprentice. *Honours:* England Youth.

| | | | |
|---|---|---|---|
| 1981–82 | Everton | 2 | 0 |
| 1982–83 | Everton | 0 | 0 |
| 1983–84 | Everton | 1 | 0 |
| 1984–85 | Everton | 0 | 0 |
| 1984–85 | Chester C | 24 | 14 |
| 1985–86 | Chester C | 18 | 16 |
| 1986–87 | Chester C | 38 | 13 |
| 1987–88 | Chester C | 34 | 24 |
| 1987–88 | Watford | 9 | 1 |
| 1988–89 | Watford | 1 | 0 |
| 1988–89 | Notts Co | 4 | 2 |
| 1988–89 | Walsall | 20 | 8 |
| 1989–90 | Walsall | 41 | 10 |
| 1990–91 | Walsall | 27 | 13 |
| 1990–91 | Barnsley | 15 | 1 |
| 1991–92 | Chester C | 44 | 13 |
| 1992–93 | Chester C | 43 | 20 |
| 1993–94 | Chester C | 35 | 8 |
| 1994–95 | Chester C | 25 | 2 |
| 1994–95 | Rochdale (loan) | 3 | 0 |
| 1994–95 | Preston NE (loan) | 2 | 0 |
| 1995–96 | Chester C | 41 | 13 |
| 1996–97 | Chester C | 25 | 4 |
| 1997–98 | Chester C | 34 | 8 |
| **Total:** | | **486** | **170** |

## RIOCH, Greg — Defender

H: 5 11 W: 12 10 b.Sutton Coldfield 24-6-75

*Source:* Trainee.

| | | | |
|---|---|---|---|
| 1993–94 | Luton T | 0 | 0 |
| 1993–94 | Barnet (loan) | 3 | 0 |
| 1994–95 | Luton T | 0 | 0 |
| 1995–96 | Peterborough U | 18 | 0 |
| 1996–97 | Hull C | 39 | 1 |
| 1997–98 | Hull C | 39 | 5 |
| **Total:** | | **99** | **6** |

## RIPLEY, Stuart — Forward

H: 6 0 W: 13 00 b.Middlesbrough 20-11-67

*Source:* Apprentice. *Honours:* England Youth, Under-21, 2 full caps.

| | | | |
|---|---|---|---|
| 1984–85 | Middlesbrough | 1 | 0 |
| 1985–86 | Middlesbrough | 8 | 0 |
| 1985–86 | Bolton W (loan) | 5 | 1 |
| 1986–87 | Middlesbrough | 44 | 4 |
| 1987–88 | Middlesbrough | 43 | 8 |
| 1988–89 | Middlesbrough | 36 | 4 |
| 1989–90 | Middlesbrough | 39 | 1 |
| 1990–91 | Middlesbrough | 39 | 6 |
| 1991–92 | Middlesbrough | 39 | 3 |
| 1992–93 | Blackburn R | 40 | 7 |
| 1993–94 | Blackburn R | 40 | 4 |
| 1994–95 | Blackburn R | 37 | 0 |
| 1995–96 | Blackburn R | 28 | 0 |
| 1996–97 | Blackburn R | 13 | 0 |
| 1997–98 | Blackburn R | 29 | 2 |
| **Total:** | | **441** | **40** |

## RITCHIE, Andy — Forward

H: 5 11 W: 11 10 b.Manchester 28-11-60

*Source:* Apprentice. *Honours:* England Schools, Youth, Under-21.

| | | | |
|---|---|---|---|
| 1977–78 | Manchester U | 4 | 0 |
| 1978–79 | Manchester U | 17 | 10 |
| 1979–80 | Manchester U | 8 | 3 |
| 1980–81 | Manchester U | 4 | 0 |
| 1980–81 | Brighton & HA | 26 | 5 |
| 1981–82 | Brighton & HA | 39 | 13 |
| 1982–83 | Brighton & HA | 24 | 5 |
| 1982–83 | Leeds U | 10 | 3 |
| 1983–84 | Leeds U | 38 | 7 |
| 1984–85 | Leeds U | 28 | 12 |
| 1985–86 | Leeds U | 29 | 11 |
| 1986–87 | Leeds U | 31 | 7 |
| 1987–88 | Oldham Ath | 36 | 19 |
| 1988–89 | Oldham Ath | 31 | 14 |
| 1989–90 | Oldham Ath | 38 | 15 |
| 1990–91 | Oldham Ath | 31 | 15 |
| 1991–92 | Oldham Ath | 14 | 3 |
| 1992–93 | Oldham Ath | 12 | 3 |
| 1993–94 | Oldham Ath | 22 | 1 |
| 1994–95 | Oldham Ath | 33 | 12 |
| 1995–96 | Scarborough | 37 | 8 |
| 1996–97 | Scarborough | 31 | 9 |
| 1996–97 | Oldham Ath | 10 | 0 |
| 1997–98 | Oldham Ath | 15 | 2 |
| **Total:** | | **568** | **177** |

## RITCHIE, Paul — Defender

H: 5 11 W: 12 00 b.Kirkcaldy 21-8-75

*Source:* Links U. *Honours:* Scotland Under-21, B.

| | | | |
|---|---|---|---|
| 1992–93 | Hearts | 0 | 0 |
| 1993–94 | Hearts | 0 | 0 |
| 1994–95 | Hearts | 0 | 0 |
| 1995–96 | Hearts | 28 | 1 |
| 1996–97 | Hearts | 28 | 1 |
| 1997–98 | Hearts | 34 | 0 |
| **Total:** | | **90** | **2** |

## RIVERS, Mark — Forward

H: 5 10 W: 11 00 b.Crewe 26-11-75

*Source:* Trainee.

| | | | |
|---|---|---|---|
| 1993–94 | Crewe Alex | 0 | 0 |
| 1994–95 | Crewe Alex | 0 | 0 |
| 1995–96 | Crewe Alex | 33 | 10 |
| 1996–97 | Crewe Alex | 27 | 6 |
| 1997–98 | Crewe Alex | 35 | 6 |
| **Total:** | | **95** | **22** |

## RIX, Graham — Forward

H: 5 9 W: 11 00 b.Doncaster 23-10-57

*Source:* Apprentice. *Honours:* England Under-21, 17 full caps.

| | | | |
|---|---|---|---|
| 1974–75 | Arsenal | 0 | 0 |
| 1975–76 | Arsenal | 0 | 0 |
| 1976–77 | Arsenal | 7 | 1 |
| 1977–78 | Arsenal | 39 | 2 |
| 1978–79 | Arsenal | 39 | 3 |
| 1979–80 | Arsenal | 38 | 4 |
| 1980–81 | Arsenal | 35 | 5 |
| 1981–82 | Arsenal | 39 | 9 |
| 1982–83 | Arsenal | 36 | 6 |
| 1983–84 | Arsenal | 34 | 4 |
| 1984–85 | Arsenal | 18 | 2 |
| 1985–86 | Arsenal | 38 | 3 |
| 1986–87 | Arsenal | 18 | 2 |
| 1987–88 | Arsenal | 10 | 0 |
| 1987–88 | Brentford (loan) | 6 | 0 |
| From Caen, Le Havre. | | | |
| 1992–93 | Dundee | 14 | 2 |
| 1993–94 | Chelsea | 0 | 0 |
| 1994–95 | Chelsea | 1 | 0 |
| 1995–96 | Chelsea | 0 | 0 |
| 1996–97 | Chelsea | 0 | 0 |
| 1997–98 | Chelsea | 0 | 0 |
| **Total:** | | **372** | **43** |

## RIZZO, Nicky — Midfield

H: 5 10 W: 12 00 b.Sydney 9-6-79

*Source:* Sydney Olympic.

| | | | |
|---|---|---|---|
| 1996–97 | Liverpool | 0 | 0 |
| 1997–98 | Liverpool | 0 | 0 |

## ROACH, Neville — Forward

H: 5 10 W: 11 00 b.Reading 29-9-78

*Source:* Trainee.

| | | | |
|---|---|---|---|
| 1996–97 | Reading | 3 | 1 |
| 1997–98 | Reading | 8 | 0 |
| **Total:** | | **11** | **1** |

## ROBERTS, Andy — Midfield

H: 5 10 W: 13 00 b.Dartford 20-3-74

*Source:* Trainee. *Honours:* England Under-21.

| | | | |
|---|---|---|---|
| 1991–92 | Millwall | 7 | 0 |
| 1992–93 | Millwall | 45 | 0 |
| 1993–94 | Millwall | 42 | 2 |
| 1994–95 | Millwall | 44 | 3 |
| 1995–96 | Crystal Palace | 38 | 0 |
| 1996–97 | Crystal Palace | 45 | 2 |
| 1997–98 | Crystal Palace | 25 | 0 |
| 1997–98 | Wimbledon | 12 | 1 |
| **Total:** | | **258** | **8** |

## ROBERTS, Ben — Goalkeeper

H: 6 1 W: 13 03 b.Bishop Auckland 22-6-75

*Source:* Trainee. *Honours:* England Under-21.

| | | | |
|---|---|---|---|
| 1992–93 | Middlesbrough | 0 | 0 |
| 1993–94 | Middlesbrough | 0 | 0 |
| 1994–95 | Middlesbrough | 0 | 0 |
| 1995–96 | Middlesbrough | 0 | 0 |
| 1995–96 | Hartlepool U (loan) | 4 | 0 |
| 1995–96 | Wycombe W (loan) | 15 | 0 |
| 1996–97 | Middlesbrough | 10 | 0 |
| 1996–97 | Bradford C (loan) | 2 | 0 |
| 1997–98 | Middlesbrough | 6 | 0 |
| **Total:** | | **37** | **0** |

## ROBERTS, Chris — Forward

H: 5 11 W: 11 12 b.Cardiff 22-10-79

*Source:* Trainee.

| | | | |
|---|---|---|---|
| 1997–98 | Cardiff C | 11 | 3 |
| **Total:** | | **11** | **3** |

## ROBERTS, Darren — Forward

H: 6 0 W: 12 04 b.Birmingham 12-10-69

*Source:* Burton Alb.

| | | | |
|---|---|---|---|
| 1991–92 | Wolverhampton W | 0 | 0 |
| 1992–93 | Wolverhampton W | 21 | 5 |
| 1993–94 | Wolverhampton W | 0 | 0 |
| 1993–94 | Hereford U (loan) | 6 | 5 |
| 1994–95 | Doncaster R | 0 | 0 |
| 1994–95 | Chesterfield | 11 | 1 |
| 1995–96 | Chesterfield | 14 | 0 |
| 1996–97 | Darlington | 44 | 16 |
| 1997–98 | Darlington | 28 | 12 |
| 1997–98 | Peterborough U (loan) | 3 | 0 |
| **Total:** | | **127** | **39** |

## ROBERTS, Gareth — Defender

H: 5 8 W: 11 00 b.Wrexham 6-2-78

*Source:* Trainee. *Honours:* Wales Under-21, B.

| | | | |
|---|---|---|---|
| 1995–96 | Liverpool | 0 | 0 |
| 1996–97 | Liverpool | 0 | 0 |
| 1997–98 | Liverpool | 0 | 0 |

## ROBERTS, Iwan — Forward

H: 6 3 W: 14 00 b.Bangor 26-6-68

*Source:* Trainee. *Honours:* Wales Youth, 7 full caps.

| | | | |
|---|---|---|---|
| 1985–86 | Watford | 4 | 0 |
| 1986–87 | Watford | 3 | 1 |
| 1987–88 | Watford | 25 | 2 |
| 1988–89 | Watford | 22 | 6 |
| 1989–90 | Watford | 9 | 0 |
| 1990–91 | Huddersfield T | 44 | 13 |
| 1991–92 | Huddersfield T | 46 | 24 |
| 1992–93 | Huddersfield T | 37 | 9 |
| 1993–94 | Huddersfield T | 15 | 4 |
| 1993–94 | Leicester C | 26 | 13 |
| 1994–95 | Leicester C | 37 | 9 |
| 1995–96 | Leicester C | 37 | 19 |
| 1996–97 | Wolverhampton W | 33 | 12 |
| 1997–98 | Norwich C | 31 | 5 |
| **Total:** | | **369** | **117** |

## ROBERTS, Jason — Forward

b.Middlesex 25-1-78

*Source:* Hayes.

| | | | |
|---|---|---|---|
| 1997–98 | Wolverhampton W | 0 | 0 |
| 1997–98 | Torquay U (loan) | 14 | 6 |
| 1997–98 | Bristol C (loan) | 3 | 1 |
| **Total:** | | **17** | **7** |

## ROBERTS, Mark — Forward

H: 5 9 W: 9 10 b.Irvine 29-10-75

*Source:* Bellfield BC.

| | | | |
|---|---|---|---|
| 1991–92 | Kilmarnock | 1 | 0 |
| 1992–93 | Kilmarnock | 5 | 0 |
| 1993–94 | Kilmarnock | 13 | 2 |
| 1994–95 | Kilmarnock | 4 | 1 |
| 1995–96 | Kilmarnock | 11 | 0 |
| 1996–97 | Kilmarnock | 10 | 2 |
| 1997–98 | Kilmarnock | 31 | 7 |
| **Total:** | | **75** | **12** |

## ROBERTS, Neil — Forward

H: 5 10 W: 11 01 b.Wrexham 7-4-78

*Source:* Trainee.

| | | | |
|---|---|---|---|
| 1996–97 | Wrexham | 0 | 0 |
| 1997–98 | Wrexham | 34 | 8 |
| **Total:** | | **34** | **8** |

## ROBERTS, Paul — Forward

H: 5 11 W: 11 09 b.Bangor 29-7-77

*Source:* Porthmadog.

| | | | |
|---|---|---|---|
| 1996–97 | Wrexham | 1 | 0 |
| 1997–98 | Wrexham | 0 | 0 |
| **Total:** | | **1** | **0** |

## ROBERTS, Stephen — Midfield

b.Wrexham 24-2-80

*Source:* Trainee.

| | | | |
|---|---|---|---|
| 1997–98 | Wrexham | 0 | 0 |

## ROBERTS, Tony — Goalkeeper

H: 6 0 W: 13 07 b.Bangor 4-8-69

*Source:* Trainee. *Honours:* Wales Under-21, 2 full caps.

| | | | |
|---|---|---|---|
| 1987–88 | QPR | 1 | 0 |
| 1988–89 | QPR | 0 | 0 |
| 1989–90 | QPR | 5 | 0 |
| 1990–91 | QPR | 12 | 0 |
| 1991–92 | QPR | 1 | 0 |
| 1992–93 | QPR | 28 | 0 |
| 1993–94 | QPR | 16 | 0 |
| 1994–95 | QPR | 31 | 0 |
| 1995–96 | QPR | 5 | 0 |
| 1996–97 | QPR | 13 | 0 |
| 1997–98 | QPR | 10 | 0 |
| **Total:** | | **122** | **0** |

## ROBERTSON, Craig — Midfield

H: 5 10 W: 12 00 b.Dunfermline 22-4-63

*Source:* 'S' Form.

| | | | |
|---|---|---|---|
| 1979–80 | Hearts | 0 | 0 |
| 1980–81 | Raith R | 0 | 0 |
| 1981–82 | Raith R | 11 | 0 |
| 1982–83 | Raith R | 22 | 0 |
| 1983–84 | Raith R | 38 | 3 |
| 1984–85 | Raith R | 39 | 11 |
| 1985–86 | Raith R | 25 | 2 |
| 1986–87 | Raith R | 35 | 3 |
| 1987–88 | Dunfermline Ath | 42 | 13 |
| 1988–89 | Dunfermline Ath | 13 | 5 |
| 1988–89 | Aberdeen | 4 | 1 |
| 1989–90 | Aberdeen | 22 | 2 |
| 1990–91 | Aberdeen | 8 | 1 |
| 1991–92 | Dunfermline Ath | 33 | 1 |
| 1992–93 | Dunfermline Ath | 34 | 3 |
| 1993–94 | Dunfermline Ath | 40 | 3 |
| 1994–95 | Dunfermline Ath | 35 | 6 |
| 1995–96 | Dunfermline Ath | 28 | 5 |
| 1996–97 | Dunfermline Ath | 31 | 0 |
| 1997–98 | Dunfermline Ath | 21 | 0 |
| **Total:** | | **481** | **59** |

## ROBERTSON, David — Defender

H: 5 11 W: 12 10 b.Aberdeen 17-10-68

*Source:* Deeside BC. *Honours:* Scotland Under-21, 3 full caps.

| | | | |
|---|---|---|---|
| 1986–87 | Aberdeen | 34 | 0 |
| 1987–88 | Aberdeen | 23 | 0 |
| 1988–89 | Aberdeen | 23 | 0 |
| 1989–90 | Aberdeen | 20 | 1 |
| 1990–91 | Aberdeen | 35 | 1 |
| 1991–92 | Rangers | 42 | 1 |
| 1992–93 | Rangers | 39 | 3 |
| 1993–94 | Rangers | 32 | 1 |
| 1994–95 | Rangers | 23 | 3 |
| 1995–96 | Rangers | 25 | 3 |
| 1996–97 | Rangers | 22 | 4 |
| 1997–98 | Leeds U | 26 | 0 |
| **Total:** | | **344** | **17** |

## ROBERTSON, Graham — Midfield

H: 5 10 W: 11 11 b.Edinburgh 12-11-76

*Source:* Balgorie Colts.

| | | | |
|---|---|---|---|
| 1993–94 | Raith R | 0 | 0 |
| 1994–95 | Raith R | 0 | 0 |
| 1995–96 | Raith R | 0 | 0 |
| 1996–97 | Millwall | 1 | 0 |
| 1997–98 | Millwall | 1 | 0 |
| **Total:** | | **2** | **0** |

## ROBERTSON, John — Defender

H: 6 2 W: 12 08 b.Liverpool 8-1-74

*Source:* Trainee.

| | | | |
|---|---|---|---|
| 1992–93 | Wigan Ath | 24 | 1 |
| 1993–94 | Wigan Ath | 34 | 1 |
| 1994–95 | Wigan Ath | 40 | 1 |
| 1995–96 | Wigan Ath | 14 | 1 |
| 1995–96 | Lincoln C | 22 | 0 |
| 1996–97 | Lincoln C | 16 | 1 |
| 1997–98 | Lincoln C | 2 | 0 |
| **Total:** | | **152** | **5** |

## ROBERTSON, John — Forward

H: 5 7 W: 11 06 b.Edinburgh 2-10-64

*Source:* Edina Hibs. *Honours:* Scotland, Under-21 B, 16 full caps, 2 goals.

| | | | |
|---|---|---|---|
| 1980–81 | Hearts | 0 | 0 |
| 1981–82 | Hearts | 1 | 0 |
| 1982–83 | Hearts | 23 | 19 |
| 1983–84 | Hearts | 35 | 15 |
| 1984–85 | Hearts | 33 | 8 |
| 1985–86 | Hearts | 35 | 20 |
| 1986–87 | Hearts | 37 | 16 |
| 1987–88 | Hearts | 39 | 26 |
| 1987–88 | Newcastle U | 0 | 0 |
| 1988–89 | Newcastle U | 12 | 0 |
| 1988–89 | Hearts | 15 | 4 |
| 1989–90 | Hearts | 32 | 17 |
| 1990–91 | Hearts | 31 | 12 |
| 1991–92 | Hearts | 42 | 14 |
| 1992–93 | Hearts | 42 | 11 |
| 1993–94 | Hearts | 36 | 10 |
| 1994–95 | Hearts | 31 | 10 |
| 1995–96 | Hearts | 33 | 11 |
| 1996–97 | Hearts | 28 | 15 |
| 1997–98 | Hearts | 21 | 6 |
| 1997–98 | Dundee (loan) | 4 | 1 |
| **Total:** | | **530** | **215** |

## ROBERTSON, Mark — Midfield

b.Sydney 6-4-77

*Source:* Marconi.

| | | | |
|---|---|---|---|
| 1997–98 | Burnley | 11 | 0 |
| **Total:** | | **11** | **0** |

## ROBERTSON, Stephen — Goalkeeper

H: 5 10 W: 11 13 b.Glasgow 16-3-77

*Source:* Ashfield J.

| | | | |
|---|---|---|---|
| 1994–95 | St Johnstone | 0 | 0 |
| 1995–96 | St Johnstone | 2 | 0 |

| | | | |
|---|---|---|---|
| 1996–97 | St Johnstone | 2 | 0 |
| 1997–98 | St Johnstone | 2 | 0 |
| **Total:** | | **6** | **0** |

## ROBINS, Mark — Forward

H: 5 8 W: 11 11 b.Ashton-under-Lyne 22-12-69

*Source:* Apprentice. *Honours:* England Under-21.

| | | | |
|---|---|---|---|
| 1986–87 | Manchester U | 0 | 0 |
| 1987–88 | Manchester U | 0 | 0 |
| 1988–89 | Manchester U | 10 | 0 |
| 1989–90 | Manchester U | 17 | 7 |
| 1990–91 | Manchester U | 19 | 4 |
| 1991–92 | Manchester U | 2 | 0 |
| 1992–93 | Norwich C | 37 | 15 |
| 1993–94 | Norwich C | 13 | 1 |
| 1994–95 | Norwich C | 17 | 4 |
| 1994–95 | Leicester C | 17 | 5 |
| 1995–96 | Leicester C | 31 | 6 |
| 1996–97 | Leicester C | 8 | 1 |
| 1997–98 | Leicester C | 0 | 0 |
| 1997–98 | Reading (loan) | 5 | 0 |
| **Total:** | | **176** | **43** |

## ROBINSON, Carl — Midfield

H: 5 10 W: 11 11 b.Llandrindod Wells 13-10-76

*Source:* Trainee. *Honours:* Wales Under-21, B.

| | | | |
|---|---|---|---|
| 1995–96 | Wolverhampton W | 0 | 0 |
| 1995–96 | Shrewsbury T (loan) | 4 | 0 |
| 1996–97 | Wolverhampton W | 2 | 0 |
| 1997–98 | Wolverhampton W | 32 | 3 |
| **Total:** | | **38** | **3** |

## ROBINSON, Jamie — Defender

H: 6 1 W: 12 08 b.Liverpool 26-2-72

*Source:* Trainee.

| | | | |
|---|---|---|---|
| 1991–92 | Liverpool | 0 | 0 |
| 1992–93 | Barnsley | 8 | 0 |
| 1993–94 | Barnsley | 1 | 0 |
| 1993–94 | Carlisle U | 16 | 1 |
| 1994–95 | Carlisle U | 14 | 1 |
| 1995–96 | Carlisle U | 20 | 2 |
| 1996–97 | Carlisle U | 7 | 0 |
| 1997–98 | Torquay U | 46 | 0 |
| **Total:** | | **112** | **4** |

## ROBINSON, John — Midfield

H: 5 10 W: 11 07 b.Bulawayo 29-8-71

*Source:* Apprentice. *Honours:* Wales Under-21, 10 full caps, 1 goal.

| | | | |
|---|---|---|---|
| 1989–90 | Brighton & HA | 5 | 0 |
| 1990–91 | Brighton & HA | 15 | 0 |
| 1991–92 | Brighton & HA | 36 | 6 |
| 1992–93 | Brighton & HA | 6 | 0 |
| 1992–93 | Charlton Ath | 15 | 2 |
| 1993–94 | Charlton Ath | 27 | 1 |
| 1994–95 | Charlton Ath | 21 | 3 |
| 1995–96 | Charlton Ath | 44 | 6 |
| 1996–97 | Charlton Ath | 42 | 3 |
| 1997–98 | Charlton Ath | 38 | 8 |
| **Total:** | | **249** | **29** |

## ROBINSON, Les — Defender

H: 5 9 W: 12 08 b.Shirerook 1-3-67

*Source:* Local.

| | | | |
|---|---|---|---|
| 1984–85 | Mansfield T | 6 | 0 |
| 1985–86 | Mansfield T | 7 | 0 |
| 1986–87 | Mansfield T | 2 | 0 |
| 1986–87 | Stockport Co | 30 | 1 |
| 1987–88 | Stockport Co | 37 | 2 |
| 1987–88 | Doncaster R | 7 | 1 |
| 1988–89 | Doncaster R | 43 | 3 |
| 1989–90 | Doncaster R | 32 | 8 |
| 1989–90 | Oxford U | 1 | 0 |
| 1990–91 | Oxford U | 43 | 0 |
| 1991–92 | Oxford U | 27 | 0 |
| 1992–93 | Oxford U | 16 | 0 |
| 1993–94 | Oxford U | 36 | 2 |
| 1994–95 | Oxford U | 46 | 0 |
| 1995–96 | Oxford U | 41 | 0 |
| 1996–97 | Oxford U | 38 | 0 |
| 1997–98 | Oxford U | 46 | 1 |
| **Total:** | | **458** | **18** |

## ROBINSON, Liam — Forward

H: 5 8 W: 12 07 b.Bradford 26-12-65

*Source:* Nottingham F Schoolboy.

| | | | |
|---|---|---|---|
| 1983–84 | Huddersfield T | 5 | 1 |
| 1984–85 | Huddersfield T | 15 | 1 |
| 1985–86 | Huddersfield T | 1 | 0 |
| 1985–86 | Tranmere R (loan) | 4 | 3 |
| 1986–87 | Bury | 33 | 13 |
| 1987–88 | Bury | 43 | 19 |
| 1988–89 | Bury | 43 | 20 |
| 1989–90 | Bury | 45 | 17 |
| 1990–91 | Bury | 43 | 4 |
| 1991–92 | Bury | 41 | 10 |
| 1992–93 | Bury | 14 | 6 |
| 1993–94 | Bristol C | 41 | 4 |
| 1994–95 | Burnley | 39 | 7 |
| 1995–96 | Burnley | 16 | 2 |
| 1996–97 | Burnley | 8 | 0 |
| 1997–98 | Scarborough | 36 | 4 |
| **Total:** | | **427** | **111** |

## ROBINSON, Mark — Defender

H: 5 9 W: 12 04 b.Rochdale 21-11-68

*Source:* Trainee.

| | | | |
|---|---|---|---|
| 1985–86 | WBA | 1 | 0 |
| 1986–87 | WBA | 1 | 0 |
| 1987–88 | Barnsley | 3 | 0 |
| 1988–89 | Barnsley | 18 | 2 |
| 1989–90 | Barnsley | 24 | 0 |
| 1990–91 | Barnsley | 22 | 1 |
| 1991–92 | Barnsley | 41 | 2 |
| 1992–93 | Barnsley | 29 | 1 |
| 1992–93 | Newcastle U | 9 | 0 |
| 1993–94 | Newcastle U | 16 | 0 |
| 1994–95 | Swindon T | 40 | 0 |
| 1995–96 | Swindon T | 46 | 1 |
| 1996–97 | Swindon T | 43 | 1 |
| 1997–98 | Swindon T | 27 | 1 |
| **Total:** | | **320** | **9** |

## ROBINSON, Matthew — Defender

H: 5 11 W: 11 10 b.Exeter 23-12-74

*Source:* Trainee.

| | | | |
|---|---|---|---|
| 1993–94 | Southampton | 0 | 0 |
| 1994–95 | Southampton | 1 | 0 |
| 1995–96 | Southampton | 5 | 0 |
| 1996–97 | Southampton | 7 | 0 |
| 1997–98 | Southampton | 1 | 0 |
| 1997–98 | Portsmouth | 15 | 0 |
| **Total:** | | **29** | **0** |

## ROBINSON, Paul — Forward

H: 5 10 W: 10 12 b.Sunderland 20-11-78

*Source:* Trainee.

| | | | |
|---|---|---|---|
| 1995–96 | Darlington | 4 | 0 |
| 1996–97 | Darlington | 3 | 0 |
| 1997–98 | Darlington | 19 | 3 |
| 1997–98 | Newcastle U | 0 | 0 |
| **Total:** | | **26** | **3** |

## ROBINSON, Paul — Midfield

H: 5 9 W: 12 11 b.Watford 14-12-78

*Source:* Trainee.

| | | | |
|---|---|---|---|
| 1996–97 | Watford | 12 | 0 |
| 1997–98 | Watford | 22 | 2 |
| **Total:** | | **34** | **2** |

## ROBINSON, Paul — Goalkeeper

b.Beverley 15-10-79

*Source:* Trainee.

| | | | |
|---|---|---|---|
| 1996–97 | Leeds U | 0 | 0 |
| 1997–98 | Leeds U | 0 | 0 |

## ROBINSON, Phil — Midfield

H: 5 10 W: 11 07 b.Stafford 6-1-67

*Source:* Apprentice.

| | | | |
|---|---|---|---|
| 1984–85 | Aston Villa | 0 | 0 |
| 1985–86 | Aston Villa | 0 | 0 |
| 1986–87 | Aston Villa | 3 | 1 |
| 1987–88 | Wolverhampton W | 41 | 5 |
| 1988–89 | Wolverhampton W | 30 | 3 |
| 1989–90 | Notts Co | 46 | 2 |
| 1990–91 | Notts Co | 19 | 3 |
| 1990–91 | Birmingham C (loan) | 9 | 0 |
| 1991–92 | Notts Co | 1 | 0 |
| 1992–93 | Notts Co | 0 | 0 |
| 1992–93 | Huddersfield T | 36 | 4 |
| 1993–94 | Huddersfield T | 39 | 1 |
| 1994–95 | Huddersfield T | 0 | 0 |
| 1994–95 | Northampton T (loan) | 14 | 0 |
| 1994–95 | Chesterfield | 22 | 8 |
| 1995–96 | Chesterfield | 39 | 9 |
| 1996–97 | Notts Co | 37 | 2 |
| 1997–98 | Notts Co | 40 | 3 |
| **Total:** | | **376** | **41** |

## ROBINSON, Steve — Forward

H: 5 9 W: 11 02 b.Lisburn 10-12-74

*Source:* Trainee. *Honours:* Northern Ireland Under-21, 1 full cap.

| | | | |
|---|---|---|---|
| 1992–93 | Tottenham H | 0 | 0 |
| 1993–94 | Tottenham H | 2 | 0 |
| 1994–95 | Tottenham H | 0 | 0 |
| 1994–95 | Leyton Orient (loan) | 0 | 0 |
| 1994–95 | Bournemouth | 32 | 5 |
| 1995–96 | Bournemouth | 41 | 7 |
| 1996–97 | Bournemouth | 40 | 7 |
| 1997–98 | Bournemouth | 45 | 10 |
| **Total:** | | **160** | **29** |

## ROBINSON, Steve — Midfield

H: 5 9 W: 11 00 b.Nottingham 17-10-75

*Source:* Trainee.

| | | | |
|---|---|---|---|
| 1993–94 | Birmingham C | 0 | 0 |
| 1994–95 | Birmingham C | 6 | 0 |
| 1995–96 | Birmingham C | 0 | 0 |
| 1995–96 | Peterborough U (loan) | 5 | 0 |

| | | | |
|---|---|---|---|
| 1996–97 | Birmingham C | 9 | 0 |
| 1997–98 | Birmingham C | 25 | 0 |
| **Total:** | | **45** | **0** |

## ROBSON, Bryan — Midfield

H: 5 9 W: 12 05 b.Witton Gilbert 11-1-57

*Source:* Apprentice. *Honours:* England Youth, Under-21, B, 90 full caps, 26 goals.

| | | | |
|---|---|---|---|
| 1974–75 | WBA | 3 | 2 |
| 1975–76 | WBA | 16 | 1 |
| 1976–77 | WBA | 23 | 8 |
| 1977–78 | WBA | 35 | 3 |
| 1978–79 | WBA | 41 | 7 |
| 1979–80 | WBA | 34 | 8 |
| 1980–81 | WBA | 40 | 10 |
| 1981–82 | WBA | 5 | 0 |
| 1981–82 | Manchester U | 32 | 5 |
| 1982–83 | Manchester U | 33 | 10 |
| 1983–84 | Manchester U | 33 | 12 |
| 1984–85 | Manchester U | 33 | 9 |
| 1985–86 | Manchester U | 21 | 7 |
| 1986–87 | Manchester U | 30 | 7 |
| 1987–88 | Manchester U | 36 | 11 |
| 1988–89 | Manchester U | 34 | 4 |
| 1989–90 | Manchester U | 20 | 2 |
| 1990–91 | Manchester U | 17 | 1 |
| 1991–92 | Manchester U | 27 | 4 |
| 1992–93 | Manchester U | 14 | 1 |
| 1993–94 | Manchester U | 15 | 1 |
| 1994–95 | Middlesbrough | 22 | 1 |
| 1995–96 | Middlesbrough | 2 | 0 |
| 1996–97 | Middlesbrough | 1 | 0 |
| 1997–98 | Middlesbrough | 0 | 0 |
| **Total:** | | **567** | **114** |

## ROBSON, Glen — Forward

H: 5 10 W: 10 10 b.Sunderland 25-9-77

*Source:* Murton.

| | | | |
|---|---|---|---|
| 1996–97 | Rochdale | 3 | 0 |
| 1997–98 | Rochdale | 7 | 0 |
| **Total:** | | **10** | **0** |

## ROBSON, Mark — Midfield

H: 5 7 W: 10 02 b.Newham 22-5-69

*Source:* Trainee.

| | | | |
|---|---|---|---|
| 1986–87 | Exeter C | 26 | 7 |
| 1987–88 | Tottenham H | 0 | 0 |
| 1987–88 | Reading (loan) | 7 | 0 |
| 1988–89 | Tottenham H | 5 | 0 |
| 1989–90 | Tottenham H | 3 | 0 |
| 1989–90 | Watford (loan) | 1 | 0 |
| 1989–90 | Plymouth Arg (loan) | 7 | 0 |
| 1990–91 | Tottenham H | 0 | 0 |
| 1991–92 | Tottenham H | 0 | 0 |
| 1991–92 | Exeter C (loan) | 8 | 1 |
| 1992–93 | West Ham U | 44 | 8 |
| 1993–94 | West Ham U | 3 | 0 |
| 1993–94 | Charlton Ath | 23 | 2 |
| 1994–95 | Charlton Ath | 40 | 3 |
| 1995–96 | Charlton Ath | 27 | 1 |
| 1996–97 | Charlton Ath | 15 | 3 |
| 1997–98 | Notts Co | 28 | 4 |
| **Total:** | | **237** | **29** |

## ROCASTLE, David — Forward

H: 5 9 W: 12 07 b.Lewisham 2-5-67

*Source:* Apprentice. *Honours:* England Under-21, B, 14 full caps.

| | | | |
|---|---|---|---|
| 1984–85 | Arsenal | 0 | 0 |
| 1985–86 | Arsenal | 16 | 1 |
| 1986–87 | Arsenal | 36 | 2 |
| 1987–88 | Arsenal | 40 | 7 |
| 1988–89 | Arsenal | 38 | 6 |
| 1989–90 | Arsenal | 33 | 2 |
| 1990–91 | Arsenal | 16 | 2 |
| 1991–92 | Arsenal | 39 | 4 |
| 1992–93 | Leeds U | 18 | 1 |
| 1993–94 | Leeds U | 7 | 1 |
| 1993–94 | Manchester C | 21 | 2 |
| 1994–95 | Chelsea | 28 | 0 |
| 1995–96 | Chelsea | 1 | 0 |
| 1996–97 | Chelsea | 0 | 0 |
| 1996–97 | Norwich C (loan) | 11 | 0 |
| 1997–98 | Chelsea | 0 | 0 |
| 1997–98 | Hull C (loan) | 10 | 1 |
| **Total:** | | **314** | **29** |

## ROCHE, Stephen — Midfield

H: 6 1 W: 11 05 b.Dublin 2-10-78

*Source:* Belvedere.

| | | | |
|---|---|---|---|
| 1995–96 | Millwall | 0 | 0 |
| 1996–97 | Millwall | 7 | 0 |
| 1997–98 | Millwall | 1 | 0 |
| **Total:** | | **8** | **0** |

## ROCKETT, Jason — Defender

H: 6 1 W: 13 04 b.London 26-9-69

| | | | |
|---|---|---|---|
| 1992–93 | Rotherham U | 0 | 0 |
| 1993–94 | Scarborough | 34 | 0 |
| 1994–95 | Scarborough | 27 | 0 |
| 1995–96 | Scarborough | 39 | 4 |
| 1996–97 | Scarborough | 40 | 5 |
| 1997–98 | Scarborough | 32 | 2 |
| **Total:** | | **172** | **11** |

## RODGER, Graham — Defender

H: 6 2 W: 13 08 b.Glasgow 1-4-67

*Source:* Apprentice. *Honours:* England Under-21.

| | | | |
|---|---|---|---|
| 1983–84 | Wolverhampton W | 1 | 0 |
| 1984–85 | Coventry C | 0 | 0 |
| 1985–86 | Coventry C | 10 | 0 |
| 1986–87 | Coventry C | 6 | 0 |
| 1987–88 | Coventry C | 12 | 1 |
| 1988–89 | Coventry C | 8 | 1 |
| 1989–90 | Luton T | 2 | 0 |
| 1990–91 | Luton T | 14 | 2 |
| 1991–92 | Luton T | 12 | 0 |
| 1991–92 | Grimsby T | 16 | 0 |
| 1992–93 | Grimsby T | 30 | 7 |
| 1993–94 | Grimsby T | 24 | 1 |
| 1994–95 | Grimsby T | 21 | 1 |
| 1995–96 | Grimsby T | 16 | 0 |
| 1996–97 | Grimsby T | 28 | 2 |
| 1997–98 | Grimsby T | 11 | 0 |
| **Total:** | | **211** | **15** |

## RODGER, Simon — Midfield

H: 5 9 W: 11 09 b.Shoreham 3-10-71

*Source:* Trainee.

| | | | |
|---|---|---|---|
| 1989–90 | Crystal Palace | 0 | 0 |
| 1990–91 | Crystal Palace | 0 | 0 |
| 1991–92 | Crystal Palace | 22 | 0 |
| 1992–93 | Crystal Palace | 23 | 2 |
| 1993–94 | Crystal Palace | 42 | 3 |
| 1994–95 | Crystal Palace | 4 | 0 |
| 1995–96 | Crystal Palace | 24 | 0 |
| 1996–97 | Crystal Palace | 11 | 0 |
| 1996–97 | Manchester C (loan) | 8 | 1 |
| 1996–97 | Stoke C (loan) | 5 | 0 |
| 1997–98 | Crystal Palace | 29 | 2 |
| **Total:** | | **168** | **8** |

## RODOSTHENOUS, Michael — Forward

H: 5 11 W: 11 02 b.Islington 25-8-76

*Source:* Trainee.

| | | | |
|---|---|---|---|
| 1995–96 | WBA | 0 | 0 |
| 1996–97 | WBA | 1 | 0 |
| 1997–98 | WBA | 0 | 0 |
| 1997–98 | Cambridge U | 2 | 0 |
| **Total:** | | **3** | **0** |

## ROGAN, Anton — Defender

H: 6 0 W: 13 00 b.Belfast 25-3-66

*Source:* Distillery. *Honours:* Northern Ireland 18 full caps.

| | | | |
|---|---|---|---|
| 1986–87 | Celtic | 10 | 1 |
| 1987–88 | Celtic | 33 | |
| 1988–89 | Celtic | 34 | |
| 1989–90 | Celtic | 18 | |
| 1990–91 | Celtic | 27 | |
| 1991–92 | Celtic | 5 | |
| 1991–92 | Sunderland | 33 | |
| 1992–93 | Sunderland | 13 | |
| 1993–94 | Oxford U | 29 | |
| 1994–95 | Oxford U | 29 | |
| 1995–96 | Millwall | 8 | |
| 1996–97 | Millwall | 28 | |
| 1997–98 | Blackpool | 1 | |
| **Total:** | | **268** | |

## ROGERS, Alan — Defender

H: 5 7 W: 12 07 b.Liverpool 3-1-77

*Source:* Trainee.

| | | | |
|---|---|---|---|
| 1995–96 | Tranmere R | 26 | |
| 1996–97 | Tranmere R | 31 | |
| 1997–98 | Nottingham F | 46 | |
| **Total:** | | **103** | |

## ROGERS, Darren — Defender

H: 5 11 W: 13 02 b.Birmingham 9-4-70

*Source:* Trainee.

| | | | |
|---|---|---|---|
| 1988–89 | WBA | 0 | |
| 1989–90 | WBA | 0 | |
| 1990–91 | WBA | 4 | |
| 1991–92 | WBA | 10 | |
| 1992–93 | Birmingham C | 17 | |
| 1993–94 | Birmingham C | 1 | |
| 1993–94 | Wycombe W (loan) | 1 | |
| 1994–95 | Walsall | 27 | |
| 1995–96 | Walsall | 25 | |
| 1996–97 | Walsall | 2 | |
| 1997–98 | Walsall | 4 | |
| **Total:** | | **91** | |

## ROGERS, Dave — Defender

H: 6 1 W: 12 00 b.Liverpool 25-8-75

*Source:* Trainee.

| | | | |
|---|---|---|---|
| 1994–95 | Tranmere R | 0 | |
| 1995–96 | Chester C | 20 | |
| 1996–97 | Chester C | 5 | |
| From Southport. | | | |
| 1997–98 | Dundee | 32 | |
| **Total:** | | **57** | |

## ROGERS, Lee — Defender

H: 5 11 W: 12 01 b.Doncaster 28-10-66

*Source:* Doncaster R.

| | | | |
|---|---|---|---|
| 1986–87 | Chesterfield | 36 | 0 |
| 1987–88 | Chesterfield | 43 | 0 |
| 1988–89 | Chesterfield | 24 | 0 |
| 1989–90 | Chesterfield | 32 | 0 |
| 1990–91 | Chesterfield | 34 | 0 |
| 1991–92 | Chesterfield | 18 | 0 |
| 1992–93 | Chesterfield | 35 | 1 |
| 1993–94 | Chesterfield | 32 | 0 |
| 1994–95 | Chesterfield | 39 | 0 |
| 1995–96 | Chesterfield | 21 | 0 |
| 1996–97 | Chesterfield | 17 | 0 |
| 1997–98 | Chesterfield | 3 | 0 |
| **Total:** | | **334** | **1** |

## ROGERS, Paul — Midfield

H: 6 0 W: 11 13 b.Portsmouth 21-3-65

*Source:* Sutton U.

| | | | |
|---|---|---|---|
| 1991–92 | Sheffield U | 13 | 0 |
| 1992–93 | Sheffield U | 27 | 3 |
| 1993–94 | Sheffield U | 25 | 3 |
| 1994–95 | Sheffield U | 44 | 4 |
| 1995–96 | Sheffield U | 16 | 0 |
| 1995–96 | Notts Co | 21 | 2 |
| 1996–97 | Notts Co | 1 | 0 |
| 1996–97 | Wigan Ath | 20 | 3 |
| 1997–98 | Wigan Ath | 38 | 0 |
| **Total:** | | **205** | **15** |

## ROGET, Leo — Defender

H: 6 1 W: 12 02 b.Ilford 1-8-77

*Source:* Trainee.

| | | | |
|---|---|---|---|
| 1995–96 | Southend U | 8 | 1 |
| 1996–97 | Southend U | 25 | 0 |
| 1997–98 | Southend U | 11 | 0 |
| **Total:** | | **44** | **1** |

## ROLLING, Frank — Defender

H: 6 2 W: 13 00 b.Colmar 23-8-68

*Source:* FC Pau.

| | | | |
|---|---|---|---|
| 1994–95 | Ayr U | 33 | 2 |
| 1995–96 | Ayr U | 2 | 0 |
| 1995–96 | Leicester C | 17 | 0 |
| 1996–97 | Leicester C | 1 | 0 |
| 1997–98 | Bournemouth | 30 | 4 |
| **Total:** | | **83** | **6** |

## ROLLO, Jimmy — Midfield

H: 6 0 W: 11 00 b.Wisbech 22-5-76

*Source:* Trainee.

| | | | |
|---|---|---|---|
| 1995–96 | Walsall | 0 | 0 |
| 1996–97 | Walsall | 0 | 0 |
| 1996–97 | Cardiff C | 10 | 0 |
| 1997–98 | Cardiff C | 5 | 0 |
| **Total:** | | **15** | **0** |

## ROONEY, Mark — Defender

H: 5 10 W: 10 10 b.Lambeth 19-5-78

*Source:* Trainee.

| | | | |
|---|---|---|---|
| 1996–97 | Watford | 0 | 0 |
| 1997–98 | Watford | 0 | 0 |

## ROPER, Ian — Defender

H: 6 3 W: 13 04 b.Nuneaton 20-6-77

*Source:* Trainee.

| | | | |
|---|---|---|---|
| 1994–95 | Walsall | 0 | 0 |
| 1995–96 | Walsall | 5 | 0 |
| 1996–97 | Walsall | 11 | 0 |
| 1997–98 | Walsall | 21 | 0 |
| **Total:** | | **37** | **0** |

## ROSCOE, Andy — Midfield

H: 5 10 W: 11 08 b.Liverpool 4-6-73

*Source:* Trainee.

| | | | |
|---|---|---|---|
| 1991–92 | Liverpool | 0 | 0 |
| 1992–93 | Bolton W | 0 | 0 |
| 1993–94 | Bolton W | 3 | 0 |
| 1994–95 | Bolton W | 0 | 0 |
| 1994–95 | Rotherham U | 31 | 4 |
| 1995–96 | Rotherham U | 45 | 2 |
| 1996–97 | Rotherham U | 43 | 0 |
| 1997–98 | Rotherham U | 45 | 7 |
| **Total:** | | **167** | **13** |

## ROSE, Andrew — Defender

H: 5 9 W: 10 03 b.Ascot 9-8-78

*Source:* Trainee.

| | | | |
|---|---|---|---|
| 1997–98 | Oxford U | 1 | 0 |
| **Total:** | | **1** | **0** |

## ROSE, Colin — Midfield

H: 5 8 W: 11 00 b.Winsford 22-1-72

*Source:* Trainee.

| | | | |
|---|---|---|---|
| 1990–91 | Crewe Alex | 17 | 1 |

| | | | |
|---|---|---|---|
| 1991–92 | Crewe Alex | 5 | 0 |
| From Witton A. | | | |
| 1997–98 | Macclesfield T | 19 | 0 |
| **Total:** | | **41** | **1** |

## ROSE, Karl — Forward

H: 5 8 W: 11 04 b.Barnsley 12-10-78

| | | | |
|---|---|---|---|
| 1995–96 | Barnsley | 0 | 0 |
| 1996–97 | Barnsley | 0 | 0 |
| 1997–98 | Barnsley | 0 | 0 |

## ROSE, Matthew — Defender

H: 5 11 W: 11 01 b.Dartford 24-9-75

*Source:* Trainee. *Honours:* England Under-21.

| | | | |
|---|---|---|---|
| 1994–95 | Arsenal | 0 | 0 |
| 1995–96 | Arsenal | 4 | 0 |
| 1996–97 | Arsenal | 1 | 0 |
| 1997–98 | QPR | 16 | 0 |
| **Total:** | | **21** | **0** |

## ROSENTHAL, Ronny — Forward

H: 5 11 W: 12 13 b.Haifa 4-10-63

*Source:* Maccabi Haifa, FC Brugge, Standard Liege. *Honours:* Israel 60 full caps, 11 goals.

| | | | |
|---|---|---|---|
| 1989–90 | Luton T (loan) | 0 | 0 |
| 1989–90 | Liverpool (loan) | 8 | 7 |
| 1990–91 | Liverpool | 16 | 5 |
| 1991–92 | Liverpool | 20 | 3 |
| 1992–93 | Liverpool | 27 | 6 |
| 1993–94 | Liverpool | 3 | 0 |
| 1993–94 | Tottenham H | 15 | 2 |
| 1994–95 | Tottenham H | 20 | 0 |
| 1995–96 | Tottenham H | 33 | 1 |
| 1996–97 | Tottenham H | 20 | 1 |
| 1997–98 | Watford | 25 | 8 |
| **Total:** | | **187** | **33** |

## ROSLER, Uwe — Forward

H: 6 0 W: 12 06 b.Attenburg 15-11-68

*Source:* Chemie Leipzig. *Honours:* East Germany 5 full caps.

| | | | |
|---|---|---|---|
| 1988–89 | Magdeburg | 12 | 3 |
| 1989–90 | Magdeburg | 24 | 10 |
| 1990–91 | Magdeburg | 26 | 9 |
| 1991–92 | Dynamo Dresden | 33 | 4 |
| 1992–93 | Nuremberg | 28 | 0 |
| 1993–94 | Dynamo Dresden | 7 | 0 |
| 1993–94 | Manchester C | 12 | 5 |
| 1994–95 | Manchester C | 31 | 15 |
| 1995–96 | Manchester C | 36 | 9 |
| 1996–97 | Manchester C | 44 | [illegible] |
| 1997–98 | Manchester C | 29 | [illegible] |
| **Total:** | | **282** | **[illegible]** |

## ROSS, Ian — Midfiel

H: 5 10 W: 10 07 b.Broxburn 27-8-74

*Source:* Bathgate Th.

| | | | |
|---|---|---|---|
| 1993–94 | Motherwell | 0 | [illegible] |
| 1994–95 | Motherwell | 0 | [illegible] |
| 1995–96 | Motherwell | 1 | [illegible] |
| 1996–97 | Motherwell | 30 | [illegible] |
| 1997–98 | Motherwell | 22 | [illegible] |
| **Total:** | | **53** | **[illegible]** |

## ROUGIER, Anthony — Midfiel

H: 6 00 W: 14 01 b.Trinidad & Tobago 17-7-71

*Source:* Trinity Pros.

| | | | |
|---|---|---|---|
| 1994–95 | Raith R | 4 | [illegible] |
| 1995–96 | Raith R | 22 | [illegible] |
| 1996–97 | Raith R | 30 | [illegible] |
| 1997–98 | Hibernian | 20 | [illegible] |
| **Total:** | | **76** | **[illegible]** |

## ROUSSET, Gilles — Goalkeepe

H: 6 5 W: 14 07 b.Hyeres 22-8-63

*Source:* Sochaux, Lyon, Marseille, Rennes. *Honours:* France 2 full caps.

| | | | |
|---|---|---|---|
| 1995–96 | Hearts | 25 | [illegible] |
| 1996–97 | Hearts | 33 | [illegible] |
| 1997–98 | Hearts | 32 | [illegible] |
| **Total:** | | **90** | **[illegible]** |

## ROWBOTHAM, Darren — Forwar

H: 5 10 W: 12 13 b.Cardiff 22-10-66

*Source:* Trainee.

| | | | |
|---|---|---|---|
| 1984–85 | Plymouth Arg | 7 | [illegible] |
| 1985–86 | Plymouth Arg | 14 | [illegible] |
| 1986–87 | Plymouth Arg | 16 | [illegible] |
| 1987–88 | Plymouth Arg | 9 | [illegible] |
| 1987–88 | Exeter C | 23 | [illegible] |
| 1988–89 | Exeter C | 45 | [illegible] |
| 1989–90 | Exeter C | 32 | [illegible] |
| 1990–91 | Exeter C | 13 | [illegible] |
| 1991–92 | Exeter C | 5 | [illegible] |
| 1991–92 | Torquay U | 14 | [illegible] |
| 1991–92 | Birmingham C | 22 | [illegible] |
| 1992–93 | Birmingham C | 14 | [illegible] |
| 1992–93 | Hereford U (loan) | 8 | [illegible] |
| 1992–93 | Mansfield T (loan) | 4 | [illegible] |
| 1993–94 | Crewe Alex | 40 | [illegible] |

| | | | |
|---|---|---|---|
| 994–95 | Crewe Alex | 21 | 6 |
| 995–96 | Shrewsbury T | 26 | 8 |
| 996–97 | Shrewsbury T | 14 | 1 |
| 996–97 | Exeter C | 25 | 9 |
| 997–98 | Exeter C | 43 | 20 |
| **otal:** | | **395** | **119** |

## OWBOTHAM, Jason — Defender

: 5 9 W: 11 09 b.Cardiff 3-1-69

*ource:* Trainee.

| | | | |
|---|---|---|---|
| 987–88 | Plymouth Arg | 4 | 0 |
| 988–89 | Plymouth Arg | 5 | 0 |
| 989–90 | Plymouth Arg | 0 | 0 |
| 990–91 | Plymouth Arg | 0 | 0 |
| 991–92 | Shrewsbury T | 0 | 0 |
| 992–93 | Hereford U | 5 | 1 |
| 993–94 | Raith R | 36 | 1 |
| 994–95 | Raith R | 20 | 0 |
| 995–96 | Wycombe W | 27 | 0 |
| 996–97 | Wycombe W | 0 | 0 |
| 996–97 | Plymouth Arg | 15 | 0 |
| 997–98 | Plymouth Arg | 25 | 0 |
| **otal:** | | **137** | **2** |

## OWE, Rodney — Forward

5 8 W: 12 08 b.Plymouth 30-7-75

*ource:* Trainee.

| | | | |
|---|---|---|---|
| 993–94 | Huddersfield T | 13 | 1 |
| 994–95 | Huddersfield T | 0 | 0 |
| 994–95 | Scarborough (loan) | 14 | 1 |
| 994–95 | Bury (loan) | 3 | 0 |
| 995–96 | Huddersfield T | 14 | 1 |
| 996–97 | Huddersfield T | 7 | 0 |
| 996–97 | York C | 10 | 3 |
| 997–98 | York C | 41 | 10 |
| **otal:** | | **102** | **16** |

## OWE, Zeke — Forward

5 10 W: 11 08 b.Stoke Newington 30-10-73

*ource:* Trainee.

| | | | |
|---|---|---|---|
| 992–93 | Chelsea | 0 | 0 |
| 993–94 | Chelsea | 0 | 0 |
| 993–94 | Barnet (loan) | 10 | 2 |
| 994–95 | Chelsea | 0 | 0 |
| 995–96 | Chelsea | 0 | 0 |
| 995–96 | Brighton & HA (loan) | 9 | 3 |
| 996–97 | Peterborough U | 22 | 3 |
| 997–98 | Peterborough U | 6 | 0 |
| 997–98 | Doncaster R (loan) | 6 | 2 |
| **otal:** | | **53** | **10** |

## ROWETT, Gary — Defender

H: 6 0 W: 12 07 b.Bromsgrove 6-3-74

*Source:* Trainee.

| | | | |
|---|---|---|---|
| 1991–92 | Cambridge U | 13 | 2 |
| 1992–93 | Cambridge U | 21 | 2 |
| 1993–94 | Cambridge U | 29 | 5 |
| 1993–94 | Everton | 2 | 0 |
| 1994–95 | Everton | 2 | 0 |
| 1994–95 | Blackpool (loan) | 17 | 0 |
| 1995–96 | Derby Co | 35 | 0 |
| 1996–97 | Derby Co | 35 | 1 |
| 1997–98 | Derby Co | 35 | 1 |
| **Total:** | | **189** | **11** |

## ROWLAND, Keith — Midfield

H: 5 10 W: 10 00 b.Portadown 1-9-71

*Source:* Trainee. *Honours:* Northern Ireland 13 full caps.

| | | | |
|---|---|---|---|
| 1990–91 | Bournemouth | 0 | 0 |
| 1991–92 | Bournemouth | 37 | 0 |
| 1992–93 | Bournemouth | 35 | 2 |
| 1992–93 | Coventry C (loan) | 2 | 0 |
| 1993–94 | West Ham U | 23 | 0 |
| 1994–95 | West Ham U | 12 | 0 |
| 1995–96 | West Ham U | 23 | 0 |
| 1996–97 | West Ham U | 15 | 1 |
| 1997–98 | West Ham U | 7 | 0 |
| 1997–98 | QPR | 7 | 0 |
| **Total:** | | **161** | **3** |

## ROWLANDS, Aled — Forward

H: 5 6 W: 10 00 b.Bangor 9-6-78

*Source:* Trainee. *Honours:* Wales Under-21.

| | | | |
|---|---|---|---|
| 1995–96 | Manchester C | 0 | 0 |
| 1996–97 | Manchester C | 0 | 0 |
| 1997–98 | Manchester C | 0 | 0 |

## ROWLANDS, James — Forward

H: 5 9 W: 10 07 b.Aberdare 31-5-79

*Source:* Trainee.

| | | | |
|---|---|---|---|
| 1997–98 | Brighton & HA | 0 | 0 |

## ROWSON, David — Midfield

H: 5 10 W: 11 10 b.Aberdeen 14-9-76

*Source:* FC Stoneywood. *Honours:* Scotland Under-21.

| | | | |
|---|---|---|---|
| 1994–95 | Aberdeen | 0 | 0 |
| 1995–96 | Aberdeen | 9 | 0 |

## Royce, Simon

| | | | |
|---|---|---|---|
| 1996–97 | Aberdeen | 34 | 2 |
| 1997–98 | Aberdeen | 30 | 5 |
| **Total:** | | **73** | **7** |

## ROYCE, Simon — Goalkeeper

H: 6 2 W: 12 10 b.Forest Gate 9-9-71

*Source:* Heybridge Swifts. *Honours:*

| | | | |
|---|---|---|---|
| 1991–92 | Southend U | 1 | 0 |
| 1992–93 | Southend U | 3 | 0 |
| 1993–94 | Southend U | 6 | 0 |
| 1994–95 | Southend U | 13 | 0 |
| 1995–96 | Southend U | 46 | 0 |
| 1996–97 | Southend U | 43 | 0 |
| 1997–98 | Southend U | 37 | 0 |
| **Total:** | | **149** | **0** |

## ROZENTAL, Sebastian — Forward

H: 5 10 W: 12 13 b.Santiago 1-9-76

*Source:* Univ Catolica, Chile. *Honours:* Chile full caps.

| | | | |
|---|---|---|---|
| 1996–97 | Rangers | 1 | 0 |
| 1997–98 | Rangers | 2 | 0 |
| **Total:** | | **3** | **0** |

## RUDDOCK, Neil — Defender

H: 6 2 W: 12 12 b.London 9-5-68

*Source:* Apprentice. *Honours:* England Youth, Under-21, B, 1 full cap.

| | | | |
|---|---|---|---|
| 1985–86 | Millwall | 0 | 0 |
| 1985–86 | Tottenham H | 0 | 0 |
| 1986–87 | Tottenham H | 4 | 0 |
| 1987–88 | Tottenham H | 5 | 0 |
| 1988–89 | Millwall | 2 | 1 |
| 1988–89 | Southampton | 13 | 3 |
| 1989–90 | Southampton | 29 | 3 |
| 1990–91 | Southampton | 35 | 3 |
| 1991–92 | Southampton | 30 | 0 |
| 1992–93 | Tottenham H | 38 | 3 |
| 1993–94 | Liverpool | 39 | 3 |
| 1994–95 | Liverpool | 37 | 2 |
| 1995–96 | Liverpool | 20 | 5 |
| 1996–97 | Liverpool | 17 | 1 |
| 1997–98 | Liverpool | 2 | 0 |
| 1997–98 | QPR (loan) | 7 | 0 |
| **Total:** | | **278** | **24** |

## RUDI, Petter — Defender

b.Kristiansund 17-9-73

*Honours:* Norway 16 full caps, 2 goals.

| | | | |
|---|---|---|---|
| 1991 | Molde | 12 | 0 |
| 1992 | Molde | 20 | 2 |
| 1993 | Molde | 22 | |
| 1994 | Molde* | 0 | |
| 1995 | Molde | 25 | |
| 1996 | Molde | 26 | |
| 1997 | Molde | 11 | |
| 1997–98 | Sheffield W | 22 | |
| **Total:** | | **138** | |

## RUFUS, Richard — Defend

H: 6 1 W: 11 10 b.Lewisham 12-1-75

*Source:* Trainee. *Honours:* England Under-21.

| | | |
|---|---|---|
| 1993–94 | Charlton Ath | 0 |
| 1994–95 | Charlton Ath | 28 |
| 1995–96 | Charlton Ath | 41 |
| 1996–97 | Charlton Ath | 34 |
| 1997–98 | Charlton Ath | 42 |
| **Total:** | | **145** |

## RUSH, David — Forwa

H: 5 11 W: 10 10 b.Sunderland 15-5-71

*Source:* Trainee.

| | | | |
|---|---|---|---|
| 1989–90 | Sunderland | 0 | |
| 1990–91 | Sunderland | 11 | |
| 1991–92 | Sunderland | 25 | |
| 1991–92 | Hartlepool U (loan) | 8 | |
| 1992–93 | Sunderland | 18 | |
| 1993–94 | Sunderland | 5 | |
| 1993–94 | Peterborough U (loan) | 4 | |
| 1994–95 | Sunderland | 0 | |
| 1994–95 | Cambridge U (loan) | 2 | |
| 1994–95 | Oxford U | 34 | |
| 1995–96 | Oxford U | 43 | |
| 1996–97 | Oxford U | 15 | |
| 1996–97 | York C | 2 | |
| 1997–98 | York C | 3 | |
| **Total:** | | **170** | **3** |

## RUSH, Ian — Forwa

H: 6 0 W: 12 06 b.St Asaph 20-10-61

*Source:* Apprentice. *Honours:* Wales Schools, Under-21, 73 full caps, 28 goals.

| | | |
|---|---|---|
| 1978–79 | Chester C | 1 |
| 1979–80 | Chester C | 33 |
| 1979–80 | Liverpool | 0 |
| 1980–81 | Liverpool | 7 |
| 1981–82 | Liverpool | 32 |
| 1982–83 | Liverpool | 34 |
| 1983–84 | Liverpool | 41 |
| 1984–85 | Liverpool | 28 |
| 1985–86 | Liverpool | 40 |
| 1986–87 | Liverpool | 42 |
| 1987–88 | Juventus | 29 |

| | | | |
|---|---|---|---|
| 988–89 | Liverpool | 24 | 7 |
| 989–90 | Liverpool | 36 | 18 |
| 990–91 | Liverpool | 37 | 16 |
| 991–92 | Liverpool | 18 | 4 |
| 992–93 | Liverpool | 32 | 14 |
| 993–94 | Liverpool | 42 | 14 |
| 994–95 | Liverpool | 36 | 12 |
| 995–96 | Liverpool | 20 | 5 |
| 995–96 | Leeds U | 0 | 0 |
| 996–97 | Leeds U | 36 | 3 |
| 997–98 | Leeds U | 0 | 0 |
| 997–98 | Newcastle U | 10 | 0 |
| 997–98 | Sheffield U (loan) | 4 | 0 |
| **otal:** | | **582** | **253** |

## USH, Matthew — Forward

511 W: 12 05 b.Dalston 6-8-71

*ource:* Trainee. *Honours:* Eire Under-21.

| | | | |
|---|---|---|---|
| 990–91 | West Ham U | 5 | 0 |
| 991–92 | West Ham U | 10 | 2 |
| 992–93 | West Ham U | 0 | 0 |
| 992–93 | Cambridge U (loan) | 10 | 0 |
| 993–94 | West Ham U | 10 | 1 |
| 993–94 | Swansea C (loan) | 13 | 0 |
| 994–95 | West Ham U | 23 | 2 |
| 995–96 | Norwich C | 1 | 0 |
| 996–97 | Norwich C | 2 | 0 |
| 996–97 | Northampton T (loan) | 14 | 3 |
| 996–97 | Oldham Ath | 8 | 2 |
| 997–98 | Oldham Ath | 16 | 1 |
| **otal:** | | **112** | **11** |

## USSELL, Alex — Midfield

510 W: 11 00 b.Crosby 17-3-73

*ource:* Burscough.

| | | | |
|---|---|---|---|
| 994–95 | Rochdale | 7 | 1 |
| 995–96 | Rochdale | 25 | 0 |
| 996–97 | Rochdale | 39 | 9 |
| 997–98 | Rochdale | 31 | 4 |
| **otal:** | | **102** | **14** |

## USSELL, Craig — Forward

59 W: 12 00 b.Jarrow 4-2-74

*ource:* Trainee.

| | | | |
|---|---|---|---|
| 991–92 | Sunderland | 4 | 0 |
| 992–93 | Sunderland | 0 | 0 |
| 993–94 | Sunderland | 35 | 9 |
| 994–95 | Sunderland | 38 | 5 |
| 995–96 | Sunderland | 41 | 13 |
| 996–97 | Sunderland | 29 | 4 |
| 1997–98 | Sunderland | 3 | 0 |
| 1997–98 | Manchester C | 24 | 1 |
| **Total:** | | **174** | **32** |

## RUSSELL, Darel — Midfield

H: 5 10 W: 11 01 b.London 22-10-80

*Source:* Trainee.

| | | | |
|---|---|---|---|
| 1997–98 | Norwich C | 1 | 0 |
| **Total:** | | **1** | **0** |

## RUSSELL, Keith — Midfield

H: 5 10 W: 12 00 b.Aldridge 31-1-74

*Source:* Hednesford T.

| | | | |
|---|---|---|---|
| 1996–97 | Blackpool | 1 | 0 |
| 1997–98 | Blackpool | 0 | 0 |
| **Total:** | | **1** | **0** |

## RUSSELL, Kevin — Forward

H: 5 9 W: 10 12 b.Portsmouth 6-12-66

*Source:* Brighton & HA Apprentice. *Honours:* England Youth.

| | | | |
|---|---|---|---|
| 1984–85 | Portsmouth | 0 | 0 |
| 1985–86 | Portsmouth | 1 | 0 |
| 1986–87 | Portsmouth | 3 | 1 |
| 1987–88 | Wrexham | 38 | 21 |
| 1988–89 | Wrexham | 46 | 22 |
| 1989–90 | Leicester C | 10 | 0 |
| 1990–91 | Leicester C | 13 | 5 |
| 1990–91 | Peterborough U (loan) | 7 | 3 |
| 1990–91 | Cardiff C (loan) | 3 | 0 |
| 1991–92 | Leicester C | 20 | 5 |
| 1991–92 | Hereford U (loan) | 3 | 1 |
| 1991–92 | Stoke C (loan) | 5 | 1 |
| 1992–93 | Stoke C | 40 | 5 |
| 1993–94 | Burnley | 28 | 6 |
| 1993–94 | Bournemouth | 17 | 1 |
| 1994–95 | Bournemouth | 13 | 0 |
| 1994–95 | Notts Co | 11 | 0 |
| 1995–96 | Wrexham | 40 | 7 |
| 1996–97 | Wrexham | 41 | 0 |
| 1997–98 | Wrexham | 16 | 0 |
| **Total:** | | **355** | **78** |

## RUSSELL, Lee — Defender

H: 5 10 W: 11 09 b.Southampton 3-9-69

*Source:* Trainee.

| | | | |
|---|---|---|---|
| 1988–89 | Portsmouth | 2 | 0 |
| 1989–90 | Portsmouth | 3 | 0 |
| 1990–91 | Portsmouth | 19 | 1 |
| 1991–92 | Portsmouth | 9 | 0 |

## Russell, Matthew

| | | | |
|---|---|---|---|
| 1992–93 | Portsmouth | 14 | 0 |
| 1993–94 | Portsmouth | 10 | 0 |
| 1994–95 | Portsmouth | 19 | 0 |
| 1994–95 | Bournemouth (loan) | 3 | 0 |
| 1995–96 | Portsmouth | 19 | 0 |
| 1996–97 | Portsmouth | 20 | 2 |
| 1997–98 | Portsmouth | 8 | 0 |
| **Total:** | | **126** | **3** |

## RUSSELL, Matthew — Forward

H: 5 11 W: 11 05 b.Dewsbury 17-1-78

*Source:* Trainee.

| | | | |
|---|---|---|---|
| 1996–97 | Scarborough | 5 | 0 |
| 1997–98 | Scarborough | 2 | 0 |
| 1997–98 | Doncaster R (loan) | 5 | 0 |
| **Total:** | | **12** | **0** |

## RUST, Nicky — Goalkeeper

H: 6 0 W: 13 02 b.Ely 25-9-74

*Source:* Arsenal Trainee.

| | | | |
|---|---|---|---|
| 1993–94 | Brighton & HA | 46 | 0 |
| 1994–95 | Brighton & HA | 44 | 0 |
| 1995–96 | Brighton & HA | 46 | 0 |
| 1996–97 | Brighton & HA | 25 | 0 |
| 1997–98 | Brighton & HA | 16 | 0 |
| **Total:** | | **177** | **0** |

## RYAN, Ciaran — Defender

H: 5 8 W: 11 00 b.Dublin 3-9-79

*Source:* Trainee.

| | | | |
|---|---|---|---|
| 1996–97 | Blackburn R | 0 | 0 |
| 1997–98 | Blackburn R | 0 | 0 |

## RYAN, Darragh — Forward

H: 5 10 W: 10 10 b.Cuckfield 21-5-80

*Source:* Trainee.

| | | | |
|---|---|---|---|
| 1997–98 | Brighton & HA | 4 | 1 |
| **Total:** | | **4** | **1** |

## RYAN, Keith — Midfield

H: 5 11 W: 12 05 b.Northampton 25-6-70

*Source:* Berkhamsted T.

| | | | |
|---|---|---|---|
| 1993–94 | Wycombe W | 42 | 1 |
| 1994–95 | Wycombe W | 24 | 4 |
| 1995–96 | Wycombe W | 23 | 4 |
| 1996–97 | Wycombe W | 0 | 0 |
| 1997–98 | Wycombe W | 40 | 3 |
| **Total:** | | **129** | **12** |

## RYAN, Robbie — Defende

H: 5 10 W: 11 06 b.Dublin 16-5-77

*Source:* Belvedere. *Honours:* Eire Youth.

| | | |
|---|---|---|
| 1994–95 | Huddersfield T | 0 |
| 1995–96 | Huddersfield T | 0 |
| 1996–97 | Huddersfield T | 5 |
| 1997–98 | Huddersfield T | 10 |
| 1997–98 | Millwall | 16 |
| **Total:** | | **31** |

## RYDER, Stuart — Defende

H: 6 1 W: 12 09 b.Sutton Coldfield 6-11-73

*Source:* Trainee. *Honours:* England Under-21.

| | | |
|---|---|---|
| 1992–93 | Walsall | 22 |
| 1993–94 | Walsall | 26 |
| 1994–95 | Walsall | 36 |
| 1995–96 | Walsall | 3 |
| 1996–97 | Walsall | 1 |
| 1997–98 | Walsall | 13 |
| **Total:** | | **101** |

## SADLIER, Richard — Forwar

H: 6 2 W: 12 10 b.Dublin 14-1-79

*Source:* Belvedere. *Honours:* Eire Youth.

| | | |
|---|---|---|
| 1996–97 | Millwall | 10 |
| 1997–98 | Millwall | 4 |
| **Total:** | | **14** |

## SAIB, Moussa — Midfiel

H: 5 9 W: 11 08 b.Theniet-El-Had 5-3-69

| | | | |
|---|---|---|---|
| 1992–93 | Auxerre | 9 | |
| 1993–94 | Auxerre | 33 | |
| 1994–95 | Auxerre | 26 | |
| 1995–96 | Auxerre | 33 | |
| 1996–97 | Auxerre | 33 | |
| 1997–98 | Valencia | 14 | |
| 1997–98 | Tottenham H | 9 | |
| **Total:** | | **157** | **2** |

## SALAKO, John — Midfiel

H: 5 9 W: 12 03 b.Nigeria 11-2-69

*Source:* Trainee. *Honours:* England 5 full caps.

| | | |
|---|---|---|
| 1986–87 | Crystal Palace | 4 |
| 1987–88 | Crystal Palace | 31 |
| 1988–89 | Crystal Palace | 28 |
| 1989–90 | Crystal Palace | 17 |
| 1989–90 | Swansea C (loan) | 13 |
| 1990–91 | Crystal Palace | 35 |
| 1991–92 | Crystal Palace | 10 |

| | | | |
|---|---|---|---|
| 1992–93 | Crystal Palace | 13 | 0 |
| 1993–94 | Crystal Palace | 38 | 8 |
| 1994–95 | Crystal Palace | 39 | 4 |
| 1995–96 | Coventry C | 37 | 3 |
| 1996–97 | Coventry C | 24 | 1 |
| 1997–98 | Coventry C | 11 | 0 |
| 1997–98 | Bolton W | 7 | 0 |
| **Total:** | | **307** | **29** |

## SALE, Mark — Forward

H: 6 5 W: 14 07 b.Burton-on-Trent 27-2-72

*Source:* Trainee.

| | | | |
|---|---|---|---|
| 1989–90 | Stoke C | 2 | 0 |
| 1990–91 | Stoke C | 0 | 0 |
| 1991–92 | Cambridge U | 0 | 0 |
| 1991–92 | Birmingham C | 6 | 0 |
| 1992–93 | Birmingham C | 15 | 0 |
| 1992–93 | Torquay U | 11 | 2 |
| 1993–94 | Torquay U | 33 | 6 |
| 1994–95 | Preston NE | 13 | 7 |
| 1995–96 | Mansfield T | 27 | 7 |
| 1996–97 | Mansfield T | 18 | 5 |
| 1996–97 | Colchester U | 10 | 3 |
| 1997–98 | Colchester U | 39 | 7 |
| **Total:** | | **174** | **37** |

## SALMON, Mike — Goalkeeper

H: 6 2 W: 14 00 b.Leyland 14-7-64

*Source:* Local.

| | | | |
|---|---|---|---|
| 1981–82 | Blackburn R | 1 | 0 |
| 1982–83 | Blackburn R | 0 | 0 |
| 1982–83 | Chester C (loan) | 16 | 0 |
| 1983–84 | Stockport Co | 46 | 0 |
| 1984–85 | Stockport Co | 46 | 0 |
| 1985–86 | Stockport Co | 26 | 0 |
| 1986–87 | Bolton W | 26 | 0 |
| 1986–87 | Wrexham (loan) | 17 | 0 |
| 1987–88 | Wrexham | 40 | 0 |
| 1988–89 | Wrexham | 43 | 0 |
| 1989–90 | Charlton Ath | 0 | 0 |
| 1990–91 | Charlton Ath | 7 | 0 |
| 1991–92 | Charlton Ath | 0 | 0 |
| 1992–93 | Charlton Ath | 19 | 0 |
| 1993–94 | Charlton Ath | 41 | 0 |
| 1994–95 | Charlton Ath | 20 | 0 |
| 1995–96 | Charlton Ath | 27 | 0 |
| 1996–97 | Charlton Ath | 25 | 0 |
| 1997–98 | Charlton Ath | 9 | 0 |
| **Total:** | | **409** | **0** |

## SALT, Philip — Defender

H: 5 11 W: 11 09 b.Huddersfield 2-3-79

*Source:* Trainee.

| | | | |
|---|---|---|---|
| 1997–98 | Oldham Ath | 2 | 0 |
| **Total:** | | **2** | **0** |

## SALVATORI, Stefano — Midfield

H: 5 10 W: 12 03 b.Rome 29-12-67

| | | | |
|---|---|---|---|
| 1986–87 | AC Milan | 0 | 0 |
| 1987–88 | Virescit | 32 | 0 |
| 1988–89 | Parma | 7 | 0 |
| 1988–89 | Fiorentina | 23 | 1 |
| 1989–90 | AC Milan | 10 | 0 |
| 1990–91 | AC Milan | 0 | 0 |
| 1990–91 | Fiorentina | 18 | 1 |
| 1991–92 | Fiorentina | 27 | 0 |
| 1992–93 | Fiorentina | 0 | 0 |
| 1992–93 | Spal | 22 | 0 |
| 1993–94 | Spal | 8 | 0 |
| 1994–95 | Atalanta | 23 | 0 |
| 1995–96 | Atalanta | 22 | 0 |
| 1996–97 | Hearts | 14 | 0 |
| 1997–98 | Hearts | 32 | 1 |
| **Total:** | | **238** | **3** |

## SAMBROOK, Andrew — Midfield

b.Chatham 13-7-79

*Source:* Trainee. *Honours:* England Schools.

| | | | |
|---|---|---|---|
| 1996–97 | Gillingham | 1 | 0 |
| 1997–98 | Gillingham | 0 | 0 |
| **Total:** | | **1** | **0** |

## SAMPSON, Ian — Defender

H: 6 2 W: 13 03 b.Wakefield 14-11-68

*Source:* Goole T.

| | | | |
|---|---|---|---|
| 1990–91 | Sunderland | 0 | 0 |
| 1991–92 | Sunderland | 8 | 0 |
| 1992–93 | Sunderland | 5 | 1 |
| 1993–94 | Sunderland | 4 | 0 |
| 1993–94 | Northampton T (loan) | 8 | 0 |
| 1994–95 | Northampton T | 42 | 2 |
| 1995–96 | Northampton T | 33 | 4 |
| 1996–97 | Northampton T | 43 | 5 |
| 1997–98 | Northampton T | 39 | 3 |
| **Total:** | | **182** | **15** |

## SAMUELS, Dean — Forward

H: 5 10 W: 12 06 b.Hackney 29-3-73

*Source:* Boreham Wood.

| | | | |
|---|---|---|---|
| 1996–97 | Barnet | 17 | 1 |
| 1997–98 | Barnet | 22 | 3 |
| **Total:** | | **39** | **4** |

## SAMWAYS, Mark — Goalkeeper

H: 6 2 W: 14 01 b.Doncaster 11-11-68

*Source:* Trainee.

| | | | |
|---|---|---|---|
| 1987–88 | Doncaster R | 11 | 0 |
| 1988–89 | Doncaster R | 12 | 0 |
| 1989–90 | Doncaster R | 46 | 0 |
| 1990–91 | Doncaster R | 26 | 0 |
| 1991–92 | Doncaster R | 26 | 0 |
| 1991–92 | Scunthorpe U (loan) | 8 | 0 |
| 1992–93 | Scunthorpe U | 31 | 0 |
| 1993–94 | Scunthorpe U | 41 | 0 |
| 1994–95 | Scunthorpe U | 42 | 0 |
| 1995–96 | Scunthorpe U | 33 | 0 |
| 1996–97 | Scunthorpe U | 25 | 0 |
| 1996–97 | York C (loan) | 0 | 0 |
| 1997–98 | York C | 29 | 0 |
| **Total:** | | **330** | **0** |

## SANDERS, Steve — Defender

H: 5 9 W: 11 02 b.Halifax 2-6-78

*Source:* Trainee.

| | | | |
|---|---|---|---|
| 1996–97 | Huddersfield T | 0 | 0 |
| 1997–98 | Doncaster R | 25 | 0 |
| 1997–98 | Lincoln C | 0 | 0 |
| **Total:** | | **25** | **0** |

## SANDFORD, Lee — Defender

H: 6 0 W: 13 07 b.Basingstoke 22-4-68

*Source:* Apprentice. *Honours:* England Youth.

| | | | |
|---|---|---|---|
| 1985–86 | Portsmouth | 7 | 0 |
| 1986–87 | Portsmouth | 0 | 0 |
| 1987–88 | Portsmouth | 21 | 1 |
| 1988–89 | Portsmouth | 31 | 0 |
| 1989–90 | Portsmouth | 13 | 0 |
| 1989–90 | Stoke C | 23 | 2 |
| 1990–91 | Stoke C | 32 | 2 |
| 1991–92 | Stoke C | 38 | 0 |
| 1992–93 | Stoke C | 42 | 2 |
| 1993–94 | Stoke C | 42 | 1 |
| 1994–95 | Stoke C | 35 | 1 |
| 1995–96 | Stoke C | 46 | 0 |
| 1996–97 | Sheffield U | 30 | 2 |
| 1997–98 | Sheffield U | 15 | 0 |
| 1997–98 | Reading (loan) | 5 | 0 |
| **Total:** | | **380** | **11** |

## SANDWITH, Kevin — Defender

H: 5 11 W: 12 05 b.Workington 30-4-78

*Source:* Trainee.

| | | | |
|---|---|---|---|
| 1996–97 | Carlisle U | 0 | 0 |
| 1997–98 | Carlisle U | 3 | 0 |
| **Total:** | | **3** | **0** |

## SANETTI, Francesco — Forward

b.Rome 11-1-79

*Source:* Genoa.

| | | | |
|---|---|---|---|
| 1997–98 | Sheffield W | 2 | 1 |
| **Total:** | | **2** | **1** |

## SARLI, Cosimo — Midfield

b.Italy 13-3-79

| | | | |
|---|---|---|---|
| 1997–98 | Southampton | 0 | 0 |

## SAUL, Eric — Defender

H: 5 7 W: 10 10 b.Dublin 28-10-78

*Source:* Trainee.

| | | | |
|---|---|---|---|
| 1997–98 | Brighton & HA | 4 | 0 |
| **Total:** | | **4** | **0** |

## SAUNDERS, Dean — Forward

H: 5 8 W: 10 06 b.Swansea 21-6-64

*Source:* Apprentice. *Honours:* Wales 63 full caps, 21 goals.

| | | | |
|---|---|---|---|
| 1982–83 | Swansea C | 0 | 0 |
| 1983–84 | Swansea C | 19 | 3 |
| 1984–85 | Swansea C | 30 | 9 |
| 1984–85 | Cardiff C (loan) | 4 | 0 |
| 1985–86 | Brighton & HA | 42 | 15 |
| 1986–87 | Brighton & HA | 30 | 6 |
| 1986–87 | Oxford U | 12 | 6 |
| 1987–88 | Oxford U | 37 | 12 |
| 1988–89 | Oxford U | 10 | 4 |
| 1988–89 | Derby Co | 30 | 14 |
| 1989–90 | Derby Co | 38 | 11 |
| 1990–91 | Derby Co | 38 | 17 |
| 1991–92 | Liverpool | 36 | 10 |
| 1992–93 | Liverpool | 6 | 1 |
| 1992–93 | Aston Villa | 35 | 12 |
| 1993–94 | Aston Villa | 38 | 10 |
| 1994–95 | Aston Villa | 39 | 15 |
| 1995–96 | Galatasaray | 27 | 15 |

| | | | |
|---|---|---|---|
| 1996–97 | Nottingham F | 34 | 3 |
| 1997–98 | Nottingham F | 9 | 2 |
| 1997–98 | Sheffield U | 24 | 10 |
| **Total:** | | **538** | **175** |

## SAUNDERS, Mark — Midfield

H: 5 10 W: 11 06 b.Reading 23-7-71

*Source:* Tiverton.

| | | | |
|---|---|---|---|
| 1995–96 | Plymouth Arg | 10 | 1 |
| 1996–97 | Plymouth Arg | 25 | 3 |
| 1997–98 | Plymouth Arg | 37 | 7 |
| **Total:** | | **72** | **11** |

## SAVAGE, Dave — Midfield

H: 6 2 W: 12 07 b.Dublin 30-7-73

*Source:* Longford T. *Honours:* Eire Under-21, 5 full caps.

| | | | |
|---|---|---|---|
| 1994–95 | Millwall | 37 | 2 |
| 1995–96 | Millwall | 27 | 0 |
| 1996–97 | Millwall | 35 | 3 |
| 1997–98 | Millwall | 31 | 1 |
| **Total:** | | **130** | **6** |

## SAVAGE, Robbie — Forward

H: 6 2 W: 11 11 b.Wrexham 18-10-74

*Source:* Trainee. *Honours:* Wales Under-21, 9 full caps, 1 goal.

| | | | |
|---|---|---|---|
| 1993–94 | Manchester U | 0 | 0 |
| 1994–95 | Crewe Alex | 6 | 2 |
| 1995–96 | Crewe Alex | 30 | 7 |
| 1996–97 | Crewe Alex | 41 | 1 |
| 1997–98 | Leicester C | 35 | 2 |
| **Total:** | | **112** | **12** |

## SAVILLE, Andy — Forward

H: 6 1 W: 12 10 b.Hull 12-12-64

*Source:* Local.

| | | | |
|---|---|---|---|
| 1983–84 | Hull C | 1 | 0 |
| 1984–85 | Hull C | 4 | 1 |
| 1985–86 | Hull C | 9 | 1 |
| 1986–87 | Hull C | 35 | 9 |
| 1987–88 | Hull C | 31 | 6 |
| 1988–89 | Hull C | 20 | 1 |
| 1988–89 | Walsall | 12 | 4 |
| 1989–90 | Walsall | 26 | 1 |
| 1989–90 | Barnsley | 15 | 3 |
| 1990–91 | Barnsley | 45 | 12 |
| 1991–92 | Barnsley | 22 | 6 |
| 1991–92 | Hartlepool U | 1 | 0 |
| 1992–93 | Hartlepool U | 36 | 13 |
| 1992–93 | Birmingham C | 10 | 7 |
| 1993–94 | Birmingham C | 39 | 10 |
| 1994–95 | Birmingham C | 10 | 0 |
| 1994–95 | Burnley (loan) | 4 | 1 |
| 1995–96 | Preston NE | 44 | 29 |
| 1996–97 | Preston NE | 12 | 1 |
| 1996–97 | Wigan Ath | 20 | 4 |
| 1997–98 | Wigan Ath | 5 | 0 |
| 1997–98 | Cardiff C | 33 | 11 |
| **Total:** | | **434** | **120** |

## SAWYERS, Robert — Defender

H: 5 10 W: 11 03 b.Dudley 20-11-78

*Source:* Wolverhampton W Trainee.

| | | | |
|---|---|---|---|
| 1997–98 | Barnet | 1 | 0 |
| **Total:** | | **1** | **0** |

## SCALES, John — Defender

H: 6 2 W: 13 05 b.Harrogate 4-7-66

*Honours:* England B, 3 full caps.

| | | | |
|---|---|---|---|
| 1984–85 | Leeds U | 0 | 0 |
| 1985–86 | Bristol R | 29 | 1 |
| 1986–87 | Bristol R | 43 | 1 |
| 1987–88 | Wimbledon | 25 | 1 |
| 1988–89 | Wimbledon | 38 | 5 |
| 1989–90 | Wimbledon | 28 | 2 |
| 1990–91 | Wimbledon | 36 | 2 |
| 1991–92 | Wimbledon | 41 | 0 |
| 1992–93 | Wimbledon | 32 | 1 |
| 1993–94 | Wimbledon | 37 | 0 |
| 1994–95 | Wimbledon | 3 | 0 |
| 1994–95 | Liverpool | 35 | 2 |
| 1995–96 | Liverpool | 27 | 0 |
| 1996–97 | Liverpool | 3 | 0 |
| 1996–97 | Tottenham H | 12 | 0 |
| 1997–98 | Tottenham H | 10 | 0 |
| **Total:** | | **399** | **15** |

## SCARGILL, Jon — Goalkeeper

H: 6 1 W: 14 10 b.Dewsbury 9-4-77

*Source:* Trainee.

| | | | |
|---|---|---|---|
| 1994–95 | Sheffield W | 0 | 0 |
| 1995–96 | Sheffield W | 0 | 0 |
| 1996–97 | Sheffield W | 0 | 0 |
| 1997–98 | Sheffield W | 0 | 0 |
| 1997–98 | Chesterfield | 0 | 0 |
| 1997–98 | Oldham Ath | 0 | 0 |

## SCATES, Garth — Midfield

b.Dundonald 27-8-79

*Source:* Trainee.

| | | | |
|---|---|---|---|
| 1997–98 | Blackburn R | 0 | 0 |

## SCHEUBER, Stuart — Midfield

b.Rhuddlan 3-4-81

*Source:* Trainee.

| | | | |
|---|---|---|---|
| 1997–98 | Stoke C | 0 | 0 |

## SCHMEICHEL, Peter — Goalkeeper

H: 6 4 W: 16 00 b.Gladsaxe 18-11-63

*Honours:* Denmark 105 full caps.

| | | | |
|---|---|---|---|
| 1984 | Hvidovre | 30 | 0 |
| 1985 | Hvidovre | 28 | 6 |
| 1986 | Hvidovre | 30 | 0 |
| 1987 | Brondby | 23 | 2 |
| 1988 | Brondby | 26 | 0 |
| 1989 | Brondby | 26 | 0 |
| 1990 | Brondby | 26 | 0 |
| 1991 | Brondby | 18 | 0 |
| 1991–92 | Manchester U | 40 | 0 |
| 1992–93 | Manchester U | 42 | 0 |
| 1993–94 | Manchester U | 40 | 0 |
| 1994–95 | Manchester U | 32 | 0 |
| 1995–96 | Manchester U | 36 | 0 |
| 1996–97 | Manchester U | 36 | 0 |
| 1997–98 | Manchester U | 32 | 0 |
| **Total:** | | **465** | **8** |

## SCHOFIELD, Jon — Forward

H: 5 11 W: 11 03 b.Barnsley 16-5-65

*Source:* Gainsborough T.

| | | | |
|---|---|---|---|
| 1988–89 | Lincoln C | 29 | 2 |
| 1989–90 | Lincoln C | 29 | 2 |
| 1990–91 | Lincoln C | 42 | 3 |
| 1991–92 | Lincoln C | 39 | 1 |
| 1992–93 | Lincoln C | 40 | 0 |
| 1993–94 | Lincoln C | 40 | 2 |
| 1994–95 | Lincoln C | 12 | 1 |
| 1994–95 | Doncaster R | 27 | 1 |
| 1995–96 | Doncaster R | 41 | 4 |
| 1996–97 | Doncaster R | 42 | 7 |
| 1997–98 | Mansfield T | 44 | 0 |
| **Total:** | | **385** | **23** |

## SCHOLES, Paul — Midfield

H: 5 7 W: 11 08 b.Salford 16-11-74

*Source:* Trainee. *Honours:* England Youth, 11 full caps, 4 goals.

| | | | |
|---|---|---|---|
| 1992–93 | Manchester U | 0 | 0 |
| 1993–94 | Manchester U | 0 | 0 |
| 1994–95 | Manchester U | 17 | 5 |
| 1995–96 | Manchester U | 26 | 10 |
| 1996–97 | Manchester U | 24 | 3 |
| 1997–98 | Manchester U | 31 | 8 |
| **Total:** | | **98** | **26** |

## SCHREUDER, Jan-Dirk — Midfield

b.Barneveld 2-8-71

| | | | |
|---|---|---|---|
| 1991–92 | PSV Eindhoven | 4 | 0 |
| 1992–93 | PSV Eindhoven | 3 | 0 |
| 1993–94 | Sparta | 14 | 0 |
| 1994–95 | Groningen | 29 | 4 |
| 1995–96 | RKC | 24 | 1 |
| 1996–97 | RKC | 18 | 1 |
| 1997–98 | Stoke C | 0 | 0 |
| **Total:** | | **92** | **6** |

## SCHWARZER, Mark — Goalkeeper

H: 6 5 W: 13 08 b.Sydney 6-10-72

*Source:* Blacktown Assoc, Marconi Sydney, Dynamo Dresden. *Honours:* Australia 5 full caps, 1 goal.

| | | | |
|---|---|---|---|
| 1995–96 | Kaiserslautern | 4 | 0 |
| 1996–97 | Kaiserslautern | 0 | 0 |
| 1996–97 | Bradford C | 13 | 0 |
| 1996–97 | Middlesbrough | 7 | 0 |
| 1997–98 | Middlesbrough | 35 | 0 |
| **Total:** | | **59** | **0** |

## SCIMECA, Riccardo — Defender

H: 6 0 W: 13 03 b.Leamington Spa 13-6-75

*Source:* Trainee. *Honours:* England Under-21, B.

| | | | |
|---|---|---|---|
| 1993–94 | Aston Villa | 0 | 0 |
| 1994–95 | Aston Villa | 0 | 0 |
| 1995–96 | Aston Villa | 17 | 0 |
| 1996–97 | Aston Villa | 17 | 0 |
| 1997–98 | Aston Villa | 21 | 0 |
| **Total:** | | **55** | **0** |

## SCOPE, Tynan — Goalkeeper

H: 6 2 W: 13 09 b.Sydney 30-7-79

| | | | |
|---|---|---|---|
| 1997–98 | Coventry C | 0 | 0 |

## SCOTT, Andy — Defender

H: 6 1 W: 11 05 b.Manchester 27-6-75

*Source:* Trainee.

| | | | |
|---|---|---|---|
| 1992–93 | Blackburn R | 0 | 0 |
| 1993–94 | Blackburn R | 0 | 0 |
| 1994–95 | Cardiff C | 13 | 1 |
| 1995–96 | Cardiff C | 1 | 0 |
| 1996–97 | Cardiff C | 2 | 0 |
| 1997–98 | Rochdale | 3 | 0 |
| **Total:** | | **19** | **1** |

## SCOTT, Andy — Forward

H: 6 1 W: 11 05 b.Epsom 2-8-72

*Source:* Sutton U.

| | | | |
|---|---|---|---|
| 1992–93 | Sheffield U | 2 | 1 |
| 1993–94 | Sheffield U | 15 | 0 |
| 1994–95 | Sheffield U | 37 | 4 |
| 1995–96 | Sheffield U | 7 | 0 |
| 1996–97 | Sheffield U | 8 | 1 |
| 1996–97 | Chesterfield (loan) | 5 | 3 |
| 1996–97 | Bury (loan) | 8 | 0 |
| 1997–98 | Sheffield U | 6 | 0 |
| 1997–98 | Brentford | 26 | 5 |
| **Total:** | | **114** | **14** |

## SCOTT, Gary — Defender

H: 5 8 W: 10 09 b.Liverpool 2-3-78

*Source:* Trainee.

| | | | |
|---|---|---|---|
| 1995–96 | Tranmere R | 0 | 0 |
| 1996–97 | Tranmere R | 0 | 0 |
| 1997–98 | Rotherham U | 7 | 0 |
| **Total:** | | **7** | **0** |

## SCOTT, Keith — Forward

H: 6 2 W: 14 07 b.Westminster 9-6-67

*Source:* Leicester U.

| | | | |
|---|---|---|---|
| 1989–90 | Lincoln C | 10 | 2 |
| 1990–91 | Lincoln C | 6 | 0 |
| From Wycombe W. | | | |
| 1993–94 | Wycombe W | 15 | 10 |
| 1993–94 | Swindon T | 27 | 4 |
| 1994–95 | Swindon T | 24 | 8 |
| 1994–95 | Stoke C | 18 | 3 |
| 1995–96 | Stoke C | 7 | 0 |
| 1995–96 | Norwich C | 12 | 2 |
| 1995–96 | Bournemouth (loan) | 8 | 1 |
| 1996–97 | Norwich C | 13 | 3 |
| 1996–97 | Watford (loan) | 6 | 2 |
| 1996–97 | Wycombe W (loan) | 9 | 3 |
| 1997–98 | Wycombe W | 29 | 11 |
| **Total:** | | **184** | **49** |

## SCOTT, Kevin — Defender

H: 6 2 W: 14 01 b.Easington 17-12-66

*Source:* Middlesbrough.

| | | | |
|---|---|---|---|
| 1984–85 | Newcastle U | 0 | 0 |
| 1985–86 | Newcastle U | 0 | 0 |
| 1986–87 | Newcastle U | 3 | 1 |
| 1987–88 | Newcastle U | 4 | 1 |
| 1988–89 | Newcastle U | 29 | 0 |
| 1989–90 | Newcastle U | 42 | 3 |
| 1990–91 | Newcastle U | 42 | 0 |
| 1991–92 | Newcastle U | 44 | 1 |
| 1992–93 | Newcastle U | 45 | 2 |
| 1993–94 | Newcastle U | 18 | 0 |
| 1993–94 | Tottenham H | 12 | 1 |
| 1994–95 | Tottenham H | 4 | 0 |
| 1994–95 | Port Vale (loan) | 17 | 1 |
| 1995–96 | Tottenham H | 2 | 0 |
| 1996–97 | Tottenham H | 0 | 0 |
| 1996–97 | Charlton Ath (loan) | 4 | 0 |
| 1996–97 | Norwich C | 9 | 0 |
| 1997–98 | Norwich C | 24 | 0 |
| **Total:** | | **299** | **10** |

## SCOTT, Martin — Defender

H: 5 9 W: 11 00 b.Sheffield 7-1-68

*Source:* Apprentice.

| | | | |
|---|---|---|---|
| 1984–85 | Rotherham U | 3 | 0 |
| 1985–86 | Rotherham U | 0 | 0 |
| 1986–87 | Rotherham U | 12 | 0 |
| 1987–88 | Rotherham U | 19 | 0 |
| 1987–88 | Nottingham F (loan) | 0 | 0 |
| 1988–89 | Rotherham U | 19 | 1 |
| 1989–90 | Rotherham U | 28 | 1 |
| 1990–91 | Rotherham U | 13 | 1 |
| 1990–91 | Bristol C | 27 | 1 |
| 1991–92 | Bristol C | 46 | 3 |
| 1992–93 | Bristol C | 35 | 3 |
| 1993–94 | Bristol C | 45 | 5 |
| 1994–95 | Bristol C | 18 | 2 |
| 1994–95 | Sunderland | 24 | 0 |
| 1995–96 | Sunderland | 43 | 6 |
| 1996–97 | Sunderland | 15 | 1 |
| 1997–98 | Sunderland | 8 | 0 |
| **Total:** | | **355** | **24** |

## SCOTT, Philip — Midfield

H: 5 9 W: 11 01 b.Perth 14-11-74

*Source:* Scone Thistle. *Honours:* Scotland Under-21.

| | | | |
|---|---|---|---|
| 1991–92 | St Johnstone | 0 | 0 |
| 1992–93 | St Johnstone | 3 | 0 |
| 1993–94 | St Johnstone | 24 | 3 |
| 1994–95 | St Johnstone | 12 | 1 |
| 1995–96 | St Johnstone | 28 | 8 |
| 1996–97 | St Johnstone | 29 | 12 |
| 1997–98 | St Johnstone | 22 | 1 |
| **Total:** | | **118** | **25** |

## SCOTT, Richard — Midfield

H: 5 9 W: 10 10 b.Dudley 29-9-74

*Source:* Trainee.

| | | | |
|---|---|---|---|
| 1992–93 | Birmingham C | 1 | 0 |
| 1993–94 | Birmingham C | 6 | 0 |
| 1994–95 | Birmingham C | 5 | 0 |
| 1994–95 | Shrewsbury T | 8 | 1 |
| 1995–96 | Shrewsbury T | 36 | 6 |
| 1996–97 | Shrewsbury T | 27 | 1 |
| 1997–98 | Shrewsbury T | 34 | 10 |
| **Total:** | | **117** | **18** |

## SCOTT, Rob — Forward

H: 6 1 W: 12 02 b.Epsom 15-8-73

*Source:* Sutton U.

| | | | |
|---|---|---|---|
| 1993–94 | Sheffield U | 0 | 0 |
| 1994–95 | Sheffield U | 1 | 0 |
| 1994–95 | Scarborough (loan) | 8 | 3 |
| 1995–96 | Sheffield U | 5 | 1 |
| 1995–96 | Northampton T (loan) | 5 | 0 |
| 1995–96 | Fulham | 21 | 5 |
| 1996–97 | Fulham | 43 | 9 |
| 1997–98 | Fulham | 17 | 3 |
| **Total:** | | **100** | **21** |

## SCOWCROFT, James — Forward

H: 6 1 W: 12 02 b.Bury St Edmunds 15-11-75

*Source:* Trainee. *Honours:* England Under-21.

| | | | |
|---|---|---|---|
| 1994–95 | Ipswich T | 0 | 0 |
| 1995–96 | Ipswich T | 23 | 2 |
| 1996–97 | Ipswich T | 41 | 9 |
| 1997–98 | Ipswich T | 31 | 6 |
| **Total:** | | **95** | **17** |

## SCULLY, Tony — Midfield

H: 5 7 W: 11 05 b.Dublin 12-6-76

*Source:* Trainee. *Honours:* Eire Under-21.

| | | | |
|---|---|---|---|
| 1993–94 | Crystal Palace | 0 | 0 |
| 1994–95 | Crystal Palace | 0 | 0 |
| 1994–95 | Bournemouth (loan) | 10 | 0 |
| 1995–96 | Crystal Palace | 2 | 0 |
| 1995–96 | Cardiff C (loan) | 14 | 0 |
| 1996–97 | Crystal Palace | 1 | 0 |
| 1997–98 | Crystal Palace | 0 | 0 |
| 1997–98 | Manchester C | 9 | 0 |
| 1997–98 | Stoke C (loan) | 7 | 0 |
| 1997–98 | QPR | 7 | 0 |
| **Total:** | | **50** | **0** |

## SEABURY, Kevin — Defender

H: 5 10 W: 11 06 b.Shrewsbury 24-11-73

*Source:* Trainee.

| | | | |
|---|---|---|---|
| 1992–93 | Shrewsbury T | 1 | 0 |
| 1993–94 | Shrewsbury T | 0 | 0 |
| 1994–95 | Shrewsbury T | 30 | 0 |
| 1995–96 | Shrewsbury T | 34 | 0 |
| 1996–97 | Shrewsbury T | 38 | 0 |
| 1997–98 | Shrewsbury T | 39 | 2 |
| **Total:** | | **142** | **2** |

## SEAGRAVES, Mark — Defender

H: 6 0 W: 12 10 b.Bootle 22-10-66

*Source:* Apprentice. *Honours:* England Schools, Youth.

| | | | |
|---|---|---|---|
| 1983–84 | Liverpool | 0 | 0 |
| 1984–85 | Liverpool | 0 | 0 |
| 1985–86 | Liverpool | 0 | 0 |
| 1986–87 | Liverpool | 0 | 0 |
| 1986–87 | Norwich C (loan) | 3 | 0 |
| 1987–88 | Liverpool | 0 | 0 |
| 1987–88 | Manchester C | 17 | 0 |
| 1988–89 | Manchester C | 23 | 0 |
| 1989–90 | Manchester C | 2 | 0 |
| 1990–91 | Bolton W | 32 | 0 |
| 1991–92 | Bolton W | 40 | 1 |
| 1992–93 | Bolton W | 37 | 5 |
| 1993–94 | Bolton W | 35 | 1 |
| 1994–95 | Bolton W | 13 | 0 |
| 1995–96 | Swindon T | 28 | 0 |
| 1996–97 | Swindon T | 28 | 0 |
| 1997–98 | Swindon T | 5 | 0 |
| **Total:** | | **263** | **7** |

## SEAL, David — Forward

H: 5 11 W: 12 04 b.Penrith 26-1-72

*Source:* Aalst.

| | | | |
|---|---|---|---|
| 1994–95 | Bristol C | 9 | 0 |
| 1995–96 | Bristol C | 30 | 10 |
| 1996–97 | Bristol C | 12 | 0 |
| 1997–98 | Northampton T | 37 | 12 |
| **Total:** | | **88** | **22** |

## SEALEY, Les — Goalkeeper

H: 6 1 W: 13 06 b.Bethnal Green 29-9-57

*Source:* Apprentice.

| | | | |
|---|---|---|---|
| 1975–76 | Coventry C | 0 | 0 |
| 1976–77 | Coventry C | 11 | 0 |
| 1977–78 | Coventry C | 2 | 0 |
| 1978–79 | Coventry C | 36 | 0 |
| 1979–80 | Coventry C | 20 | 0 |
| 1980–81 | Coventry C | 35 | 0 |
| 1981–82 | Coventry C | 15 | 0 |
| 1982–83 | Coventry C | 39 | 0 |
| 1983–84 | Luton T | 42 | 0 |
| 1984–85 | Luton T | 26 | 0 |
| 1984–85 | Plymouth Arg (loan) | 6 | 0 |
| 1985–86 | Luton T | 35 | 0 |
| 1986–87 | Luton T | 41 | 0 |
| 1987–88 | Luton T | 31 | 0 |
| 1988–89 | Luton T | 32 | 0 |
| 1989–90 | Luton T | 0 | 0 |
| 1989–90 | Manchester U (loan) | 2 | 0 |
| 1990–91 | Manchester U | 31 | 0 |
| 1991–92 | Aston Villa | 18 | 0 |
| 1991–92 | Coventry C (loan) | 2 | 0 |
| 1992–93 | Aston Villa | 0 | 0 |
| 1992–93 | Birmingham C (loan) | 12 | 0 |
| 1992–93 | Manchester U | 0 | 0 |
| 1993–94 | Manchester U | 0 | 0 |
| 1994–95 | Blackpool | 7 | 0 |
| 1994–95 | West Ham U | 0 | 0 |
| 1995–96 | West Ham U | 2 | 0 |
| 1996–97 | Leyton Orient | 12 | 0 |
| 1996–97 | West Ham U | 2 | 0 |
| 1997–98 | West Ham U | 0 | 0 |
| 1997–98 | Bury (loan) | 0 | 0 |
| **Total:** | | **459** | **0** |

## SEAMAN, David — Goalkeeper

H: 6 4 W: 14 10 b.Rotherham 19-9-63

*Source:* Apprentice. *Honours:* England Under-21, B, 44 full caps.

| | | | |
|---|---|---|---|
| 1981–82 | Leeds U | 0 | 0 |
| 1982–83 | Peterborough U | 38 | 0 |
| 1983–84 | Peterborough U | 45 | 0 |
| 1984–85 | Peterborough U | 8 | 0 |
| 1984–85 | Birmingham C | 33 | 0 |
| 1985–86 | Birmingham C | 42 | 0 |
| 1986–87 | QPR | 41 | 0 |
| 1987–88 | QPR | 32 | 0 |
| 1988–89 | QPR | 35 | 0 |
| 1989–90 | QPR | 33 | 0 |
| 1990–91 | Arsenal | 38 | 0 |
| 1991–92 | Arsenal | 42 | 0 |
| 1992–93 | Arsenal | 39 | 0 |
| 1993–94 | Arsenal | 39 | 0 |
| 1994–95 | Arsenal | 31 | 0 |
| 1995–96 | Arsenal | 38 | 0 |
| 1996–97 | Arsenal | 22 | 0 |
| 1997–98 | Arsenal | 31 | 0 |
| **Total:** | | **587** | **0** |

## SEARLE, Damon — Defender

H: 5 11 W: 10 04 b.Cardiff 26-10-71

*Source:* Trainee. *Honours:* Wales Schools, Youth, Under-21.

| | | | |
|---|---|---|---|
| 1990–91 | Cardiff C | 35 | 0 |
| 1991–92 | Cardiff C | 42 | 1 |
| 1992–93 | Cardiff C | 42 | 1 |
| 1993–94 | Cardiff C | 42 | 0 |
| 1994–95 | Cardiff C | 32 | 0 |
| 1995–96 | Cardiff C | 41 | 1 |
| 1996–97 | Stockport Co | 10 | 0 |
| 1997–98 | Stockport Co | 31 | 0 |
| **Total:** | | **275** | **3** |

## SEARLE, Stevie — Midfield

H: 5 10 W: 11 02 b.Lambeth 7-3-77

*Source:* Sittingbourne.

| | | | |
|---|---|---|---|
| 1997–98 | Barnet | 30 | 2 |
| **Total:** | | **30** | **2** |

## SEDGEMORE, Ben — Midfield

H: 6 0 W: 12 08 b.Wolverhampton 5-8-75

*Source:* Trainee. *Honours:* England Schools.

| | | | |
|---|---|---|---|
| 1993–94 | Birmingham C | 0 | 0 |
| 1994–95 | Birmingham C | 0 | 0 |
| 1994–95 | Northampton T (loan) | 1 | 0 |
| 1995–96 | Birmingham C | 0 | 0 |
| 1995–96 | Mansfield T (loan) | 9 | 0 |
| 1995–96 | Peterborough U | 17 | 0 |
| 1996–97 | Peterborough U | 0 | 0 |
| 1996–97 | Mansfield T | 39 | 4 |
| 1997–98 | Mansfield T | 28 | 2 |
| 1997–98 | Macclesfield T | 5 | 0 |
| **Total:** | | **99** | **6** |

## SEDGLEY, Steve — Defender

H: 6 1 W: 13 13 b.Enfield 26-5-68

*Source:* Apprentice. *Honours:* England Under-21.

| | | | |
|---|---|---|---|
| 1986–87 | Coventry C | 26 | 0 |
| 1987–88 | Coventry C | 27 | 2 |
| 1988–89 | Coventry C | 31 | 1 |
| 1989–90 | Tottenham H | 32 | 0 |
| 1990–91 | Tottenham H | 34 | 0 |
| 1991–92 | Tottenham H | 34 | 0 |
| 1992–93 | Tottenham H | 22 | 3 |
| 1993–94 | Tottenham H | 42 | 5 |
| 1994–95 | Ipswich T | 26 | 4 |
| 1995–96 | Ipswich T | 40 | 4 |
| 1996–97 | Ipswich T | 39 | 7 |
| 1997–98 | Wolverhampton W | 19 | 0 |
| **Total:** | | **372** | **26** |

## SEDGWICK, Chris — Forward

H: 5 11 W: 10 10 b.Sheffield 28-4-80

*Source:* Trainee.

| | | | |
|---|---|---|---|
| 1997–98 | Rotherham U | 4 | 0 |
| **Total:** | | **4** | **0** |

## SEDLAN, Jason — Midfield

b.Peterborough 5-8-79

*Source:* Trainee.

| | | | |
|---|---|---|---|
| 1997–98 | Mansfield T | 1 | 0 |
| **Total:** | | **1** | **0** |

## SEDLOSKI, Goce — Defender

H: 6 2 W: 13 00 b.Golemo Konjari 10-4-74

*Source:* Hajduk Split. *Honours:* Macedonia 10 full caps.

| | | | |
|---|---|---|---|
| 1997–98 | Sheffield W | 4 | 0 |
| **Total:** | | **4** | **0** |

## SEGERS, Hans — Goalkeeper

H: 5 11 W: 12 12 b.Eindhoven 30-10-61

*Source:* PSV Eindhoven.

| | | | |
|---|---|---|---|
| 1984–85 | Nottingham F | 28 | 0 |
| 1985–86 | Nottingham F | 11 | 0 |
| 1986–87 | Nottingham F | 14 | 0 |
| 1986–87 | Stoke C (loan) | 1 | 0 |
| 1987–88 | Nottingham F | 5 | 0 |
| 1987–88 | Sheffield U (loan) | 10 | 0 |
| 1987–88 | Dunfermline Ath (loan) | 4 | 0 |
| 1988–89 | Nottingham F | 0 | 0 |
| 1988–89 | Wimbledon | 33 | 0 |
| 1989–90 | Wimbledon | 38 | 0 |
| 1990–91 | Wimbledon | 37 | 0 |
| 1991–92 | Wimbledon | 41 | 0 |
| 1992–93 | Wimbledon | 41 | 0 |
| 1993–94 | Wimbledon | 41 | 0 |
| 1994–95 | Wimbledon | 32 | 0 |
| 1995–96 | Wimbledon | 4 | 0 |
| 1996–97 | Wolverhampton W | 0 | 0 |
| 1997–98 | Wolverhampton W | 11 | 0 |
| **Total:** | | **351** | **0** |

## SEGURA, Victor — Defender

H: 5 11 W: 11 09 b.Zaragoza 13-3-73

*Source:* Lleida.

| | | | |
|---|---|---|---|
| 1997–98 | Norwich C | 25 | 0 |
| **Total:** | | **25** | **0** |

## SEKERLIOGLU, Attila — Midfield

H: 6 1 W: 12 07 b.Linz 27-1-65

| | | | |
|---|---|---|---|
| 1988–89 | FK Austria | 28 | 0 |
| 1989–90 | FK Austria | 21 | 0 |
| 1990–91 | FK Austria | 24 | 0 |
| 1991–92 | FK Austria | 34 | 1 |
| 1992–93 | FK Austria | 24 | 3 |
| 1993–94 | FK Austria | 23 | 1 |
| 1994–95 | FK Austria | 20 | 2 |
| 1995–96 | Tirol | 16 | 0 |
| 1995–96 | St Johnstone | 17 | 2 |
| 1996–97 | St Johnstone | 24 | 6 |
| 1997–98 | St Johnstone | 17 | 1 |
| **Total:** | | **248** | **16** |

## SELFE, Oliver — Defender

b.Warrington 1-10-79

*Source:* Trainee.

| | | | |
|---|---|---|---|
| 1997–98 | Oldham Ath | 0 | 0 |

## SELLARS, Scott — Midfield

H: 5 8 W: 10 00 b.Sheffield 27-11-65

*Source:* Apprentice. *Honours:* England Under-21.

| | | | |
|---|---|---|---|
| 1982–83 | Leeds U | 1 | 0 |
| 1983–84 | Leeds U | 19 | 3 |
| 1984–85 | Leeds U | 39 | 7 |
| 1985–86 | Leeds U | 17 | 2 |
| 1986–87 | Blackburn R | 32 | 4 |
| 1987–88 | Blackburn R | 42 | 7 |
| 1988–89 | Blackburn R | 46 | 2 |
| 1989–90 | Blackburn R | 43 | 14 |
| 1990–91 | Blackburn R | 9 | 1 |
| 1991–92 | Blackburn R | 30 | 7 |
| 1992–93 | Leeds U | 7 | 0 |

| | | | |
|---|---|---|---|
| 1992–93 | Newcastle U | 13 | 2 |
| 1993–94 | Newcastle U | 30 | 3 |
| 1994–95 | Newcastle U | 12 | 0 |
| 1995–96 | Newcastle U | 6 | 0 |
| 1995–96 | Bolton W | 22 | 3 |
| 1996–97 | Bolton W | 42 | 8 |
| 1997–98 | Bolton W | 22 | 2 |
| **Total:** | | **432** | **65** |

## SELLEY, Ian — Midfield

H: 5 9 W: 11 05 b.Chertsey 14-6-74

*Source:* Trainee. *Honours:* England Youth, Under-21.

| | | | |
|---|---|---|---|
| 1992–93 | Arsenal | 9 | 0 |
| 1993–94 | Arsenal | 18 | 0 |
| 1994–95 | Arsenal | 13 | 0 |
| 1995–96 | Arsenal | 0 | 0 |
| 1996–97 | Arsenal | 1 | 0 |
| 1996–97 | Southend U (loan) | 4 | 0 |
| 1997–98 | Arsenal | 0 | 0 |
| 1997–98 | Fulham | 3 | 0 |
| **Total:** | | **48** | **0** |

## SEPP, Dennis — Forward

H: 5 9 W: 11 04 b.Apeldoorn 5-6-73

*Source:* HSC 21.

| | | | |
|---|---|---|---|
| 1997–98 | Bradford C | 3 | 0 |
| **Total:** | | **3** | **0** |

## SERRANT, Carl — Defender

H: 6 0 W: 11 02 b.Bradford 12-9-75

*Source:* Trainee. *Honours:* England Under-21, B.

| | | | |
|---|---|---|---|
| 1994–95 | Oldham Ath | 0 | 0 |
| 1995–96 | Oldham Ath | 20 | 1 |
| 1996–97 | Oldham Ath | 40 | 0 |
| 1997–98 | Oldham Ath | 30 | 0 |
| **Total:** | | **90** | **1** |

## SERTORI, Mark — Defender

H: 6 1 W: 14 07 b.Manchester 1-9-67

| | | | |
|---|---|---|---|
| 1986–87 | Stockport Co | 3 | 0 |
| 1987–88 | Stockport Co | 1 | 0 |
| 1987–88 | Lincoln C | 0 | 0 |
| 1988–89 | Lincoln C | 26 | 4 |
| 1989–90 | Lincoln C | 24 | 5 |
| 1989–90 | Wrexham | 18 | 2 |
| 1990–91 | Wrexham | 29 | 0 |
| 1991–92 | Wrexham | 36 | 0 |
| 1992–93 | Wrexham | 12 | 0 |
| 1993–94 | Wrexham | 15 | 1 |
| 1994–95 | Bury | 2 | 0 |
| 1995–96 | Bury | 11 | 1 |
| 1996–97 | Scunthorpe U | 42 | 1 |
| 1997–98 | Scunthorpe U | 41 | 1 |
| **Total:** | | **260** | **15** |

## SHAIL, Mark — Defender

H: 6 1 W: 13 03 b.Sweden 15-10-66

*Source:* Yeovil T.

| | | | |
|---|---|---|---|
| 1992–93 | Bristol C | 4 | 0 |
| 1993–94 | Bristol C | 36 | 2 |
| 1994–95 | Bristol C | 38 | 2 |
| 1995–96 | Bristol C | 12 | 0 |
| 1996–97 | Bristol C | 11 | 0 |
| 1997–98 | Bristol C | 2 | 0 |
| **Total:** | | **103** | **4** |

## SHAKESPEARE, Craig — Midfield

H: 5 10 W: 13 06 b.Birmingham 26-10-63

*Source:* Apprentice.

| | | | |
|---|---|---|---|
| 1981–82 | Walsall | 0 | 0 |
| 1982–83 | Walsall | 31 | 4 |
| 1983–84 | Walsall | 46 | 6 |
| 1984–85 | Walsall | 41 | 9 |
| 1985–86 | Walsall | 32 | 4 |
| 1986–87 | Walsall | 44 | 11 |
| 1987–88 | Walsall | 45 | 8 |
| 1988–89 | Walsall | 45 | 3 |
| 1989–90 | Sheffield W | 17 | 0 |
| 1989–90 | WBA | 18 | 1 |
| 1990–91 | WBA | 36 | 1 |
| 1991–92 | WBA | 44 | 8 |
| 1992–93 | WBA | 14 | 2 |
| 1993–94 | Grimsby T | 33 | 3 |
| 1994–95 | Grimsby T | 19 | 3 |
| 1995–96 | Grimsby T | 28 | 2 |
| 1996–97 | Grimsby T | 26 | 2 |
| 1997–98 | Scunthorpe U | 4 | 0 |
| **Total:** | | **523** | **67** |

## SHANNON, Greg — Goalkeeper

H: 6 1 W: 11 04 b.Maghreafelt 15-2-81

*Source:* Trainee.

| | | | |
|---|---|---|---|
| 1997–98 | Sunderland | 0 | 0 |

## SHARMAN, Sam — Defender

H: 5 10 W: 12 01 b.Hull 7-11-77

*Source:* Sheffield W Trainee.

| | | | |
|---|---|---|---|
| 1996–97 | Hull C | 4 | 0 |
| 1997–98 | Hull C | 0 | 0 |
| **Total:** | | **4** | **0** |

## SHARP, Kevin — Defender

H: 5 9 W: 10 07 b.Ontario 19-9-74

*Source:* Auxerre. *Honours:* England Schools, Youth.

| | | | |
|---|---|---|---|
| 1992–93 | Leeds U | 4 | 0 |
| 1993–94 | Leeds U | 10 | 0 |
| 1994–95 | Leeds U | 2 | 0 |
| 1995–96 | Leeds U | 1 | 0 |
| 1995–96 | Wigan Ath | 20 | 6 |
| 1996–97 | Wigan Ath | 35 | 2 |
| 1997–98 | Wigan Ath | 38 | 0 |
| **Total:** | | **110** | **8** |

## SHARP, Ray — Defender

H: 5 11 W: 12 06 b.Stirling 16-11-69

*Source:* Gairdoch U. *Honours:* Scotland Under-21.

| | | | |
|---|---|---|---|
| 1986–87 | Dunfermline Ath | 0 | 0 |
| 1987–88 | Dunfermline Ath | 0 | 0 |
| 1988–89 | Stenhousemuir (loan) | 5 | 0 |
| 1988–89 | Dunfermline Ath | 9 | 0 |
| 1989–90 | Dunfermline Ath | 27 | 0 |
| 1990–91 | Dunfermline Ath | 31 | 0 |
| 1991–92 | Dunfermline Ath | 25 | 0 |
| 1992–93 | Dunfermline Ath | 27 | 0 |
| 1993–94 | Dunfermline Ath | 30 | 1 |
| 1994–95 | Dunfermline Ath | 2 | 0 |
| 1994–95 | Preston NE | 21 | 0 |
| 1995–96 | Preston NE | 1 | 0 |
| 1996–97 | Dunfermline Ath | 15 | 0 |
| 1997–98 | Dunfermline Ath | 3 | 0 |
| **Total:** | | **196** | **1** |

## SHARPE, Lee — Midfield

H: 6 0 W: 12 06 b.Halesowen 27-5-71

*Source:* Trainee. *Honours:* England Under-21, B, 8 full caps.

| | | | |
|---|---|---|---|
| 1987–88 | Torquay U | 14 | 3 |
| 1988–89 | Manchester U | 22 | 0 |
| 1989–90 | Manchester U | 18 | 1 |
| 1990–91 | Manchester U | 23 | 2 |
| 1991–92 | Manchester U | 14 | 1 |
| 1992–93 | Manchester U | 27 | 1 |
| 1993–94 | Manchester U | 30 | 9 |
| 1994–95 | Manchester U | 28 | 3 |
| 1995–96 | Manchester U | 31 | 4 |
| 1996–97 | Leeds U | 26 | 5 |
| 1997–98 | Leeds U | 0 | 0 |
| **Total:** | | **233** | **29** |

## SHARPLES, John — Defender

H: 6 0 W: 11 03 b.Bury 26-1-73

*Source:* Manchester U Trainee.

| | | | |
|---|---|---|---|
| 1991–92 | Hearts | 0 | 0 |
| 1992–93 | Hearts | 0 | 0 |
| 1993–94 | Hearts | 0 | 0 |
| 1994–95 | Ayr U | 27 | 0 |
| 1995–96 | Ayr U | 26 | 4 |
| 1995–96 | York C | 10 | 0 |
| 1996–97 | York C | 28 | 1 |
| 1997–98 | York C | 0 | 0 |
| **Total:** | | **91** | **5** |

## SHAW, George — Forward

H: 5 7 W: 10 09 b.Glasgow 10-2-69

*Source:* Ayresome N.

| | | | |
|---|---|---|---|
| 1987–88 | St Mirren | 2 | 0 |
| 1988–89 | St Mirren | 10 | 1 |
| 1989–90 | St Mirren | 23 | 2 |
| 1990–91 | St Mirren | 33 | 1 |
| 1991–92 | Partick T | 43 | 9 |
| 1992–93 | Partick T | 31 | 10 |
| 1993–94 | Partick T | 17 | 2 |
| 1993–94 | Dundee | 17 | 6 |
| 1994–95 | Dundee | 34 | 16 |
| 1995–96 | Dundee | 36 | 7 |
| 1996–97 | Dundee | 8 | 3 |
| From Home Farm. | | | |
| 1996–97 | Dundee | 13 | 2 |
| 1997–98 | Dunfermline Ath | 23 | 2 |
| **Total:** | | **290** | **61** |

## SHAW, Paul — Forward

H: 5 11 W: 12 02 b.Burnham 4-9-73

*Source:* Trainee.

| | | | |
|---|---|---|---|
| 1991–92 | Arsenal | 0 | 0 |
| 1992–93 | Arsenal | 0 | 0 |
| 1993–94 | Arsenal | 0 | 0 |
| 1994–95 | Arsenal | 1 | 0 |
| 1994–95 | Burnley (loan) | 9 | 4 |
| 1995–96 | Arsenal | 3 | 0 |
| 1995–96 | Cardiff C (loan) | 6 | 0 |
| 1995–96 | Peterborough U (loan) | 12 | 5 |
| 1996–97 | Arsenal | 8 | 2 |
| 1997–98 | Arsenal | 0 | 0 |
| 1997–98 | Millwall | 40 | 11 |
| **Total:** | | **79** | **22** |

## SHAW, Richard — Defender

H: 5 9 W: 12 08 b.Brentford 11-9-68

*Source:* Apprentice.

| | | | |
|---|---|---|---|
| 1986–87 | Crystal Palace | 0 | 0 |
| 1987–88 | Crystal Palace | 3 | 0 |
| 1988–89 | Crystal Palace | 14 | 0 |
| 1989–90 | Crystal Palace | 21 | 0 |
| 1989–90 | Hull C (loan) | 4 | 0 |
| 1990–91 | Crystal Palace | 36 | 1 |
| 1991–92 | Crystal Palace | 10 | 0 |
| 1992–93 | Crystal Palace | 33 | 0 |
| 1993–94 | Crystal Palace | 34 | 2 |
| 1994–95 | Crystal Palace | 41 | 0 |
| 1995–96 | Crystal Palace | 15 | 0 |
| 1995–96 | Coventry C | 21 | 0 |
| 1996–97 | Coventry C | 35 | 0 |
| 1997–98 | Coventry C | 33 | 0 |
| **Total:** | | **300** | **3** |

## SHAW, Simon — Midfield

H: 6 0 W: 12 00 b.Middlesbrough 21-9-73

*Source:* Trainee.

| | | | |
|---|---|---|---|
| 1991–92 | Darlington | 1 | 0 |
| 1992–93 | Darlington | 23 | 4 |
| 1993–94 | Darlington | 30 | 1 |
| 1994–95 | Darlington | 12 | 1 |
| 1995–96 | Darlington | 41 | 1 |
| 1996–97 | Darlington | 38 | 3 |
| 1997–98 | Darlington | 31 | 2 |
| **Total:** | | **176** | **12** |

## SHEARER, Alan — Forward

H: 5 11 W: 12 06 b.Newcastle 13-8-70

*Source:* Trainee. *Honours:* England Youth, Under-21, B, 43 full caps, 20 goals.

| | | | |
|---|---|---|---|
| 1987–88 | Southampton | 5 | 3 |
| 1988–89 | Southampton | 10 | 0 |
| 1989–90 | Southampton | 26 | 3 |
| 1990–91 | Southampton | 36 | 4 |
| 1991–92 | Southampton | 41 | 13 |
| 1992–93 | Blackburn R | 21 | 16 |
| 1993–94 | Blackburn R | 40 | 31 |
| 1994–95 | Blackburn R | 42 | 34 |
| 1995–96 | Blackburn R | 35 | 31 |
| 1996–97 | Newcastle U | 31 | 25 |
| 1997–98 | Newcastle U | 17 | 2 |
| **Total:** | | **304** | **162** |

## SHEARER, Lee — Defender

H: 6 4 W: 12 01 b.Rochford 23-10-77

*Source:* Trainee.

| | | | |
|---|---|---|---|
| 1994–95 | Leyton Orient | 2 | 0 |
| 1995–96 | Leyton Orient | 8 | 1 |
| 1996–97 | Leyton Orient | 8 | 0 |
| 1997–98 | Leyton Orient | 0 | 0 |
| **Total:** | | **18** | **1** |

## SHEARER, Lee — Forward

H: 5 9 W: 11 00 b.Clackmannan 30-9-78

*Source:* Trainee.

| | | | |
|---|---|---|---|
| 1997–98 | Stockport Co | 0 | 0 |

## SHEARER, Peter — Midfield

H: 6 0 W: 11 00 b.Birmingham 4-2-67

*Source:* Apprentice.

| | | | |
|---|---|---|---|
| 1984–85 | Birmingham C | 4 | 0 |
| 1985–86 | Birmingham C | 0 | 0 |
| 1986–87 | Rochdale | 1 | 0 |
| From Cheltenham T. | | | |
| 1988–89 | Bournemouth | 4 | 1 |
| 1989–90 | Bournemouth | 34 | 4 |
| 1990–91 | Bournemouth | 5 | 0 |
| 1991–92 | Bournemouth | 8 | 1 |
| 1992–93 | Bournemouth | 34 | 4 |
| 1993–94 | Bournemouth | 0 | 0 |
| 1993–94 | Birmingham C | 2 | 0 |
| 1994–95 | Birmingham C | 23 | 7 |
| 1995–96 | Birmingham C | 0 | 0 |
| 1996–97 | Birmingham C | 0 | 0 |
| 1997–98 | Peterborough U | 0 | 0 |
| **Total:** | | **115** | **17** |

## SHEERIN, Joe — Forward

H: 6 1 W: 13 09 b.Hammersmith 1-2-79

*Source:* Trainee.

| | | | |
|---|---|---|---|
| 1996–97 | Chelsea | 1 | 0 |
| 1997–98 | Chelsea | 0 | 0 |
| **Total:** | | **1** | **0** |

## SHEFFIELD, Jon — Goalkeeper

H: 6 0 W: 12 08 b.Bedworth 1-2-69

*Source:* Apprentice.

| | | | |
|---|---|---|---|
| 1986–87 | Norwich C | 0 | 0 |
| 1987–88 | Norwich C | 0 | 0 |
| 1988–89 | Norwich C | 1 | 0 |
| 1989–90 | Norwich C | 0 | 0 |

## Sheldon, Gareth

| | | | |
|---|---|---|---|
| 1989–90 | Aldershot (loan) | 11 | 0 |
| 1989–90 | Ipswich T (loan) | 0 | 0 |
| 1990–91 | Norwich C | 0 | 0 |
| 1990–91 | Aldershot (loan) | 15 | 0 |
| 1990–91 | Cambridge U (loan) | 2 | 0 |
| 1991–92 | Cambridge U | 13 | 0 |
| 1992–93 | Cambridge U | 13 | 0 |
| 1993–94 | Cambridge U | 0 | 0 |
| 1993–94 | Colchester U (loan) | 6 | 0 |
| 1993–94 | Swindon T (loan) | 2 | 0 |
| 1994–95 | Cambridge U | 28 | 0 |
| 1994–95 | Hereford U (loan) | 8 | 0 |
| 1995–96 | Peterborough U | 46 | 0 |
| 1996–97 | Peterborough U | 16 | 0 |
| 1996–97 | Watford (loan) | 0 | 0 |
| 1996–97 | Oldham Ath (loan) | 0 | 0 |
| 1997–98 | Plymouth Arg | 46 | 0 |
| **Total:** | | **207** | **0** |

### SHELDON, Gareth — Forward

b.Birmingham 31-1-80

*Source:* Trainee.

| | | | |
|---|---|---|---|
| 1997–98 | Scunthorpe U | 1 | 0 |
| **Total:** | | **1** | **0** |

### SHELIA, Murtaz — Defender

H: 6 1 W: 13 00 b.Georgia 25-3-69

*Honours:* Georgia 25 full caps.

| | | | |
|---|---|---|---|
| 1994–95 | Dynamo Tbilisi | 10 | 2 |
| 1995 | Alania | 22 | 4 |
| 1996 | Alania | 27 | 5 |
| 1997 | Alania | 13 | 0 |
| 1997–98 | Manchester C | 12 | 2 |
| **Total:** | | **84** | **13** |

### SHELTON, Andrew — Midfield

H: 6 0 W: 12 00 b.Sutton Coldfield 19-6-80

*Source:* Trainee.

| | | | |
|---|---|---|---|
| 1997–98 | Chester C | 2 | 0 |
| **Total:** | | **2** | **0** |

### SHELTON, Gary — Midfield

H: 5 7 W: 10 12 b.Nottingham 21-3-58

*Source:* Apprentice. *Honours:* England Under-21.

| | | | |
|---|---|---|---|
| 1975–76 | Walsall | 2 | 0 |
| 1976–77 | Walsall | 10 | 0 |
| 1977–78 | Walsall | 12 | 0 |
| 1977–78 | Aston Villa | 0 | 0 |
| 1978–79 | Aston Villa | 19 | 7 |
| 1979–80 | Aston Villa | 4 | 0 |
| 1979–80 | Notts Co (loan) | 8 | 0 |
| 1980–81 | Aston Villa | 0 | 0 |
| 1981–82 | Aston Villa | 1 | 0 |
| 1981–82 | Sheffield W | 9 | 1 |
| 1982–83 | Sheffield W | 40 | 4 |
| 1983–84 | Sheffield W | 40 | 5 |
| 1984–85 | Sheffield W | 41 | 4 |
| 1985–86 | Sheffield W | 31 | 1 |
| 1986–87 | Sheffield W | 37 | 3 |
| 1987–88 | Oxford U | 32 | 0 |
| 1988–89 | Oxford U | 33 | 1 |
| 1989–90 | Bristol C | 43 | 9 |
| 1990–91 | Bristol C | 43 | 8 |
| 1991–92 | Bristol C | 19 | 3 |
| 1992–93 | Bristol C | 42 | 4 |
| 1993–94 | Bristol C | 3 | 0 |
| 1993–94 | Rochdale (loan) | 3 | 0 |
| 1994–95 | Chester C | 33 | 2 |
| 1995–96 | Chester C | 11 | 1 |
| 1996–97 | Chester C | 22 | 2 |
| 1997–98 | Chester C | 3 | 0 |
| **Total:** | | **541** | **55** |

### SHENTON, Daniel — Midfield

H: 5 11 W: 12 07 b.Sheffield 29-9-78

*Source:* Trainee.

| | | | |
|---|---|---|---|
| 1997–98 | Barnsley | 0 | 0 |

### SHEPHERD, Paul — Forward

b.Leeds 17-11-77

*Source:* Trainee. *Honours:* England Youth.

| | | | |
|---|---|---|---|
| 1995–96 | Leeds U | 0 | 0 |
| 1996–97 | Leeds U | 1 | 0 |
| 1997–98 | Leeds U | 0 | 0 |
| 1997–98 | Ayr U (loan) | 6 | 1 |
| **Total:** | | **7** | **1** |

### SHERIDAN, Darragh — Midfield

H: 5 11 W: 11 01 b.Galway 11-1-79

*Source:* Trainee.

| | | | |
|---|---|---|---|
| 1997–98 | Aston Villa | 0 | 0 |

### SHERIDAN, Darren — Midfield

H: 5 4 W: 11 05 b.Manchester 8-12-67

*Source:* Winsford U.

| | | | |
|---|---|---|---|
| 1993–94 | Barnsley | 3 | 0 |
| 1994–95 | Barnsley | 35 | 2 |
| 1995–96 | Barnsley | 41 | 0 |
| 1996–97 | Barnsley | 41 | 2 |
| 1997–98 | Barnsley | 26 | 0 |
| **Total:** | | **146** | **4** |

## SHERIDAN, John — Midfield

H: 5 10 W: 12 01 b.Stretford 1-10-64

*Source:* Local. *Honours:* Eire Youth, Under-21, Under-23, B, 34 full caps, 5 goals.

| | | | |
|---|---|---|---|
| 1981–82 | Leeds U | 0 | 0 |
| 1982–83 | Leeds U | 27 | 2 |
| 1983–84 | Leeds U | 11 | 1 |
| 1984–85 | Leeds U | 42 | 6 |
| 1985–86 | Leeds U | 32 | 4 |
| 1986–87 | Leeds U | 40 | 15 |
| 1987–88 | Leeds U | 38 | 12 |
| 1988–89 | Leeds U | 40 | 7 |
| 1989–90 | Nottingham F | 0 | 0 |
| 1989–90 | Sheffield W | 27 | 2 |
| 1990–91 | Sheffield W | 46 | 10 |
| 1991–92 | Sheffield W | 24 | 6 |
| 1992–93 | Sheffield W | 25 | 3 |
| 1993–94 | Sheffield W | 20 | 3 |
| 1994–95 | Sheffield W | 36 | 1 |
| 1995–96 | Sheffield W | 17 | 0 |
| 1995–96 | Birmingham C (loan) | 2 | 0 |
| 1996–97 | Sheffield W | 2 | 0 |
| 1996–97 | Bolton W | 20 | 2 |
| 1997–98 | Bolton W | 12 | 0 |
| **Total:** | | **461** | **74** |

## SHERINGHAM, Teddy — Forward

H: 6 0 W: 13 00 b.Highams Park 2-4-66

*Source:* Apprentice. *Honours:* England Youth, 35 full caps, 9 goals.

| | | | |
|---|---|---|---|
| 1983–84 | Millwall | 7 | 1 |
| 1984–85 | Millwall | 0 | 0 |
| 1984–85 | Aldershot (loan) | 5 | 0 |
| 1985–86 | Millwall | 18 | 4 |
| 1986–87 | Millwall | 42 | 13 |
| 1987–88 | Millwall | 43 | 22 |
| 1988–89 | Millwall | 33 | 11 |
| 1989–90 | Millwall | 31 | 9 |
| 1990–91 | Millwall | 46 | 33 |
| 1991–92 | Nottingham F | 39 | 13 |
| 1992–93 | Nottingham F | 3 | 1 |
| 1992–93 | Tottenham H | 38 | 21 |
| 1993–94 | Tottenham H | 19 | 14 |
| 1994–95 | Tottenham H | 42 | 18 |
| 1995–96 | Tottenham H | 38 | 16 |
| 1996–97 | Tottenham H | 29 | 7 |
| 1997–98 | Manchester U | 31 | 9 |
| **Total:** | | **464** | **192** |

## SHERON, Mike — Forward

H: 5 9 W: 11 06 b.Liverpool 11-1-72

*Source:* Trainee. *Honours:* England Under-21.

| | | | |
|---|---|---|---|
| 1990–91 | Manchester C | 0 | 0 |
| 1990–91 | Bury (loan) | 5 | 1 |
| 1991–92 | Manchester C | 29 | 7 |
| 1992–93 | Manchester C | 38 | 11 |
| 1993–94 | Manchester C | 33 | 6 |
| 1994–95 | Norwich C | 21 | 1 |
| 1995–96 | Norwich C | 7 | 1 |
| 1995–96 | Stoke C | 28 | 15 |
| 1996–97 | Stoke C | 41 | 19 |
| 1997–98 | QPR | 40 | 11 |
| **Total:** | | **242** | **72** |

## SHERWOOD, Tim — Midfield

H: 6 1 W: 12 09 b.St Albans 2-2-69

*Source:* Trainee. *Honours:* England Under-21, B.

| | | | |
|---|---|---|---|
| 1986–87 | Watford | 0 | 0 |
| 1987–88 | Watford | 13 | 0 |
| 1988–89 | Watford | 19 | 2 |
| 1989–90 | Norwich C | 27 | 3 |
| 1990–91 | Norwich C | 37 | 7 |
| 1991–92 | Norwich C | 7 | 0 |
| 1991–92 | Blackburn R | 11 | 0 |
| 1992–93 | Blackburn R | 39 | 3 |
| 1993–94 | Blackburn R | 38 | 2 |
| 1994–95 | Blackburn R | 38 | 6 |
| 1995–96 | Blackburn R | 33 | 3 |
| 1996–97 | Blackburn R | 37 | 3 |
| 1997–98 | Blackburn R | 31 | 5 |
| **Total:** | | **330** | **34** |

## SHIELDS, Anthony — Defender

b.Derry 4-6-80

*Source:* Trainee.

| | | | |
|---|---|---|---|
| 1997–98 | Peterborough U | 1 | 0 |
| **Total:** | | **1** | **0** |

## SHIELDS, Greg — Defender

H: 5 9 W: 10 10 b.Falkirk 21-8-76

*Source:* Rangers BC. *Honours:* Scotland Under-21.

| | | | |
|---|---|---|---|
| 1994–95 | Rangers | 0 | 0 |
| 1995–96 | Rangers | 1 | 0 |
| 1996–97 | Rangers | 6 | 0 |
| 1997–98 | Dunfermline Ath | 36 | 0 |
| **Total:** | | **43** | **0** |

## SHILTON, Peter — Goalkeeper

H: 6 1 W: 14 02 b.Leicester 18-9-49

*Source:* Apprentice. *Honours:* England Schools, Youth, Under-23, 125 full caps. Football League.

| | | | |
|---|---|---|---|
| 1965–66 | Leicester C | 1 | 0 |
| 1966–67 | Leicester C | 4 | 0 |
| 1967–68 | Leicester C | 35 | 1 |
| 1968–69 | Leicester C | 42 | 0 |
| 1969–70 | Leicester C | 39 | 0 |
| 1970–71 | Leicester C | 40 | 0 |
| 1971–72 | Leicester C | 37 | 0 |
| 1972–73 | Leicester C | 41 | 0 |
| 1973–74 | Leicester C | 42 | 0 |
| 1974–75 | Leicester C | 5 | 0 |
| 1974–75 | Stoke C | 25 | 0 |
| 1975–76 | Stoke C | 42 | 0 |
| 1976–77 | Stoke C | 40 | 0 |
| 1977–78 | Stoke C | 3 | 0 |
| 1977–78 | Nottingham F | 37 | 0 |
| 1978–79 | Nottingham F | 42 | 0 |
| 1979–80 | Nottingham F | 42 | 0 |
| 1980–81 | Nottingham F | 40 | 0 |
| 1981–82 | Nottingham F | 41 | 0 |
| 1982–83 | Southampton | 39 | 0 |
| 1983–84 | Southampton | 42 | 0 |
| 1984–85 | Southampton | 41 | 0 |
| 1985–86 | Southampton | 37 | 0 |
| 1986–87 | Southampton | 29 | 0 |
| 1987–88 | Derby Co | 40 | 0 |
| 1988–89 | Derby Co | 38 | 0 |
| 1989–90 | Derby Co | 35 | 0 |
| 1990–91 | Derby Co | 31 | 0 |
| 1991–92 | Derby Co | 31 | 0 |
| 1991–92 | Plymouth Arg | 7 | 0 |
| 1992–93 | Plymouth Arg | 23 | 0 |
| 1993–94 | Plymouth Arg | 4 | 0 |
| 1994–95 | Plymouth Arg | 0 | 0 |
| 1994–95 | Wimbledon | 0 | 0 |
| 1994–95 | Bolton W | 1 | 0 |
| 1995–96 | Coventry C | 0 | 0 |
| 1995–96 | West Ham U | 0 | 0 |
| 1996–97 | West Ham U | 0 | 0 |
| 1996–97 | Leyton Orient | 9 | 0 |
| 1997–98 | Middlesbrough | 0 | 0 |
| **Total:** | | **1005** | **1** |

## SHILTON, Sam — Midfield

H: 5 11 W: 11 06 b.Nottingham 21-7-78

*Source:* School.

| | | | |
|---|---|---|---|
| 1994–95 | Plymouth Arg | 2 | 0 |
| 1995–96 | Plymouth Arg | 1 | 0 |
| 1995–96 | Coventry C | 0 | 0 |
| 1996–97 | Coventry C | 0 | 0 |
| 1997–98 | Coventry C | 2 | 0 |
| **Total:** | | **5** | **0** |

## SHIPPERLEY, Neil — Forward

H: 6 1 W: 13 11 b.Chatham 30-10-74

*Source:* Trainee. *Honours:* England Under-21.

| | | | |
|---|---|---|---|
| 1992–93 | Chelsea | 3 | 1 |
| 1993–94 | Chelsea | 24 | 4 |
| 1994–95 | Chelsea | 10 | 2 |
| 1994–95 | Watford (loan) | 6 | 1 |
| 1994–95 | Southampton | 19 | 4 |
| 1995–96 | Southampton | 37 | 7 |
| 1996–97 | Southampton | 10 | 1 |
| 1996–97 | Crystal Palace | 32 | 12 |
| 1997–98 | Crystal Palace | 26 | 7 |
| **Total:** | | **167** | **39** |

## SHIRTLIFF, Peter — Defender

H: 6 1 W: 12 02 b.Sheffield 6-4-61

*Source:* Apprentice.

| | | | |
|---|---|---|---|
| 1978–79 | Sheffield W | 26 | 1 |
| 1979–80 | Sheffield W | 3 | 0 |
| 1980–81 | Sheffield W | 28 | 0 |
| 1981–82 | Sheffield W | 31 | 2 |
| 1982–83 | Sheffield W | 8 | 0 |
| 1983–84 | Sheffield W | 36 | 1 |
| 1984–85 | Sheffield W | 35 | 0 |
| 1985–86 | Sheffield W | 21 | 0 |
| 1986–87 | Charlton Ath | 33 | 3 |
| 1987–88 | Charlton Ath | 36 | 2 |
| 1988–89 | Charlton Ath | 34 | 2 |
| 1989–90 | Sheffield W | 33 | 2 |
| 1990–91 | Sheffield W | 39 | 2 |
| 1991–92 | Sheffield W | 12 | 0 |
| 1992–93 | Sheffield W | 20 | 0 |
| 1993–94 | Wolverhampton W | 39 | 0 |
| 1994–95 | Wolverhampton W | 28 | 0 |
| 1995–96 | Wolverhampton W | 2 | 0 |
| 1995–96 | Barnsley | 32 | 0 |
| 1996–97 | Barnsley | 13 | 0 |
| 1996–97 | Carlisle U (loan) | 5 | 0 |
| 1997–98 | Barnsley | 4 | 0 |
| **Total:** | | **518** | **15** |

## SHIVUTE, Eliphas — Forward

H: 5 11 W: 11 04 b.Windhoek 27-9-74

*Source:* Eleven Arrows.

| | | | |
|---|---|---|---|
| 1997–98 | Motherwell | 23 | 3 |
| **Total:** | | **23** | **3** |

## SHONE, Gareth — Defender

H: 6 0 W: 13 00 b.Aldershot 5-1-79

*Source:* Trainee.

| | | | |
|---|---|---|---|
| 1997–98 | Wrexham | 0 | 0 |

## SHORE, Jamie — Midfield

H: 5 9 W: 11 00 b.Bristol 1-9-77

*Source:* Trainee. *Honours:* England Youth.

| | | | |
|---|---|---|---|
| 1994–95 | Norwich C | 0 | 0 |
| 1995–96 | Norwich C | 0 | 0 |
| 1996–97 | Norwich C | 0 | 0 |
| 1997–98 | Norwich C | 0 | 0 |

## SHORT, Chris — Defender

H: 5 10 W: 12 04 b.Munster 9-5-70

*Source:* Pickering T.

| | | | |
|---|---|---|---|
| 1988–89 | Scarborough | 2 | 0 |
| 1989–90 | Scarborough | 41 | 1 |
| 1990–91 | Scarborough | 0 | 0 |
| 1990–91 | Manchester U (loan) | 0 | 0 |
| 1990–91 | Notts Co | 15 | 1 |
| 1991–92 | Notts Co | 27 | 0 |
| 1992–93 | Notts Co | 31 | 1 |
| 1993–94 | Notts Co | 6 | 0 |
| 1994–95 | Notts Co | 13 | 0 |
| 1994–95 | Huddersfield T (loan) | 6 | 0 |
| 1995–96 | Notts Co | 2 | 0 |
| 1995–96 | Sheffield U | 15 | 0 |
| 1996–97 | Sheffield U | 24 | 0 |
| 1997–98 | Sheffield U | 5 | 0 |
| **Total:** | | **187** | **3** |

## SHORT, Craig — Defender

H: 6 0 W: 11 04 b.Bridlington 25-6-68

*Source:* Pickering T. *Honours:* England Schools.

| | | | |
|---|---|---|---|
| 1987–88 | Scarborough | 21 | 2 |
| 1988–89 | Scarborough | 42 | 5 |
| 1989–90 | Notts Co | 44 | 2 |
| 1990–91 | Notts Co | 0 | 0 |
| 1990–91 | Notts Co | 43 | 0 |
| 1991–92 | Notts Co | 38 | 3 |
| 1992–93 | Notts Co | 3 | 1 |
| 1992–93 | Derby Co | 38 | 3 |
| 1993–94 | Derby Co | 43 | 3 |
| 1994–95 | Derby Co | 37 | 3 |
| 1995–96 | Everton | 23 | 2 |
| 1996–97 | Everton | 23 | 2 |
| 1997–98 | Everton | 31 | 0 |
| **Total:** | | **386** | **26** |

## SHOWLER, Paul — Midfield

H: 5 7 W: 11 00 b.Doncaster 10-10-66

*Source:* Sheffield W, Sunderland, Colne Dynamoes, Altrincham.

| | | | |
|---|---|---|---|
| 1991–92 | Barnet | 39 | 7 |
| 1992–93 | Barnet | 32 | 5 |
| 1993–94 | Bradford C | 32 | 5 |
| 1994–95 | Bradford C | 23 | 2 |
| 1995–96 | Bradford C | 33 | 8 |
| 1996–97 | Luton T | 23 | 6 |
| 1997–98 | Luton T | 1 | 0 |
| **Total:** | | **183** | **33** |

## SHUTT, Carl — Forward

H: 5 10 W: 12 10 b.Sheffield 10-10-61

*Source:* Spalding U.

| | | | |
|---|---|---|---|
| 1984–85 | Sheffield W | 0 | 0 |
| 1985–86 | Sheffield W | 19 | 9 |
| 1986–87 | Sheffield W | 20 | 7 |
| 1987–88 | Sheffield W | 1 | 0 |
| 1987–88 | Bristol C | 22 | 9 |
| 1988–89 | Bristol C | 24 | 1 |
| 1988–89 | Leeds U | 3 | 4 |
| 1989–90 | Leeds U | 20 | 2 |
| 1990–91 | Leeds U | 28 | 10 |
| 1991–92 | Leeds U | 14 | 1 |
| 1992–93 | Leeds U | 14 | 0 |
| 1993–94 | Leeds U | 0 | 0 |
| 1993–94 | Birmingham C | 26 | 4 |
| 1993–94 | Manchester C (loan) | 6 | 0 |
| 1994–95 | Bradford C | 32 | 4 |
| 1995–96 | Bradford C | 34 | 8 |
| 1996–97 | Bradford C | 22 | 3 |
| 1996–97 | Darlington | 6 | 2 |
| 1997–98 | Darlington | 33 | 5 |
| **Total:** | | **324** | **69** |

## SHUTTLEWORTH, Barry — Defender

H: 5 8 W: 10 00 b.Accrington 9-7-77

*Source:* Trainee.

| | | | |
|---|---|---|---|
| 1995–96 | Bury | 0 | 0 |
| 1996–97 | Bury | 0 | 0 |
| 1997–98 | Rotherham U | 0 | 0 |

## SIGURDSSON, Kris — Defender

H: 5 11 W: 11 11 b.Akureyri 7-10-80

| | | | |
|---|---|---|---|
| 1997 | KA | 15 | 0 |
| 1997–98 | Stoke C | 0 | 0 |
| **Total:** | | **15** | **0** |

### SIGURDSSON, Larus — Defender

H: 6 0 W: 13 11 b.Akureyri 4-6-73

*Source:* Thor. *Honours:* Iceland 15 full caps.

| | | | |
|---|---|---|---|
| 1994–95 | Stoke C | 23 | 1 |
| 1995–96 | Stoke C | 46 | 0 |
| 1996–97 | Stoke C | 45 | 0 |
| 1997–98 | Stoke C | 43 | 1 |
| **Total:** | | **157** | **2** |

### SILENZI, Andrea — Forward

H: 6 3 W: 11 13 b.Rome 10-2-66

*Honours:* Italy 1 full cap.

| | | | |
|---|---|---|---|
| 1984–85 | Lodigiani | 15 | 0 |
| 1985–86 | Lodigiani | 4 | 0 |
| 1986–87 | Lodigiani | 30 | 18 |
| 1987–88 | Arezzo | 19 | 0 |
| 1988–89 | Reggiana | 31 | 9 |
| 1989–90 | Reggiana | 36 | 23 |
| 1990–91 | Napoli | 19 | 2 |
| 1991–92 | Napoli | 20 | 4 |
| 1992–93 | Torino | 25 | 3 |
| 1993–94 | Torino | 31 | 17 |
| 1994–95 | Torino | 26 | 4 |
| 1995–96 | Nottingham F | 10 | 0 |
| 1996–97 | Nottingham F | 2 | 0 |
| 1997–98 | Nottingham F | 0 | 0 |
| **Total:** | | **268** | **80** |

### SIMMS, Gordon — Midfield

b.Larne 23-3-81

*Source:* Trainee.

| | | | |
|---|---|---|---|
| 1997–98 | Wolverhampton W | 0 | 0 |

### SIMONSEN, Steve — Goalkeeper

H: 6 3 W: 13 02 b.South Shields 3-4-79

*Source:* Trainee. *Honours:* England Youth, Under-21.

| | | | |
|---|---|---|---|
| 1996–97 | Tranmere R | 0 | 0 |
| 1997–98 | Tranmere R | 30 | 0 |
| **Total:** | | **30** | **0** |

### SIMPKINS, James — Midfield

b.Sheffield 28-11-78

*Source:* Trainee.

| | | | |
|---|---|---|---|
| 1997–98 | Sheffield W | 0 | 0 |
| 1997–98 | Chesterfield | 0 | 0 |

### SIMPKINS, Michael — Defender

H: 6 0 W: 11 11 b.Sheffield 28-11-78

*Source:* Trainee.

| | | | |
|---|---|---|---|
| 1997–98 | Sheffield W | 0 | 0 |
| 1997–98 | Chesterfield | 0 | 0 |

### SIMPSON, Colin — Forward

H: 6 1 W: 11 05 b.Oxford 30-4-76

*Source:* Trainee.

| | | | |
|---|---|---|---|
| 1994–95 | Watford | 0 | 0 |
| 1995–96 | Watford | 1 | 0 |
| 1996–97 | Watford | 0 | 0 |
| 1997–98 | Watford | 0 | 0 |
| From Hendon. | | | |
| 1997–98 | Leyton Orient | 14 | 3 |
| **Total:** | | **15** | **3** |

### SIMPSON, Fitzroy — Midfield

H: 5 8 W: 12 00 b.Trowbridge 26-2-70

*Source:* Trainee. *Honours:* Jamaica 25 full caps, 1 goal.

| | | | |
|---|---|---|---|
| 1988–89 | Swindon T | 7 | 0 |
| 1989–90 | Swindon T | 30 | 2 |
| 1990–91 | Swindon T | 38 | 3 |
| 1991–92 | Swindon T | 30 | 4 |
| 1991–92 | Manchester C | 11 | 1 |
| 1992–93 | Manchester C | 29 | 1 |
| 1993–94 | Manchester C | 15 | 0 |
| 1994–95 | Manchester C | 16 | 2 |
| 1994–95 | Bristol C (loan) | 4 | 0 |
| 1995–96 | Manchester C | 0 | 0 |
| 1995–96 | Portsmouth | 30 | 5 |
| 1996–97 | Portsmouth | 41 | 4 |
| 1997–98 | Portsmouth | 19 | 0 |
| **Total:** | | **270** | **22** |

### SIMPSON, Karl — Midfield

H: 5 11 W: 11 06 b.Newmarket 14-10-76

*Source:* Trainee.

| | | | |
|---|---|---|---|
| 1994–95 | Norwich C | 0 | 0 |
| 1995–96 | Norwich C | 1 | 0 |
| 1996–97 | Norwich C | 3 | 0 |
| 1997–98 | Norwich C | 6 | 0 |
| **Total:** | | **10** | **0** |

### SIMPSON, Michael — Midfield

H: 5 6 W: 11 07 b.Nottingham 28-2-74

*Source:* Trainee.

| | | | |
|---|---|---|---|
| 1992–93 | Notts Co | 0 | 0 |

| | | | |
|---|---|---|---|
| 1993–94 | Notts Co | 6 | 1 |
| 1994–95 | Notts Co | 19 | 2 |
| 1995–96 | Notts Co | 23 | 0 |
| 1996–97 | Notts Co | 1 | 0 |
| 1996–97 | Plymouth Arg (loan) | 12 | 0 |
| 1996–97 | Wycombe W | 20 | 1 |
| 1997–98 | Wycombe W | 21 | 0 |
| **Total:** | | **102** | **4** |

## SIMPSON, Paul — Midfield

H: 5 8  W: 11 11  b.Carlisle 26-7-66

*Source:* Apprentice. *Honours:* England Youth, Under-21.

| | | | |
|---|---|---|---|
| 1982–83 | Manchester C | 3 | 0 |
| 1983–84 | Manchester C | 0 | 0 |
| 1984–85 | Manchester C | 10 | 6 |
| 1985–86 | Manchester C | 37 | 8 |
| 1986–87 | Manchester C | 32 | 3 |
| 1987–88 | Manchester C | 38 | 1 |
| 1988–89 | Manchester C | 1 | 0 |
| 1988–89 | Oxford U | 25 | 8 |
| 1989–90 | Oxford U | 42 | 9 |
| 1990–91 | Oxford U | 46 | 17 |
| 1991–92 | Oxford U | 31 | 9 |
| 1991–92 | Derby Co | 16 | 7 |
| 1992–93 | Derby Co | 35 | 12 |
| 1993–94 | Derby Co | 34 | 9 |
| 1994–95 | Derby Co | 42 | 8 |
| 1995–96 | Derby Co | 39 | 10 |
| 1996–97 | Derby Co | 19 | 2 |
| 1996–97 | Sheffield U (loan) | 6 | 0 |
| 1997–98 | Derby Co | 1 | 0 |
| 1997–98 | Wolverhampton W | 28 | 4 |
| **Total:** | | **485** | **113** |

## SIMPSON, Phil — Midfield

H: 5 9  W: 11 01  b.London 18-10-69

*Source:* Stevenage Bor.

| | | | |
|---|---|---|---|
| 1995–96 | Barnet | 24 | 1 |
| 1996–97 | Barnet | 32 | 2 |
| 1997–98 | Barnet | 31 | 4 |
| **Total:** | | **87** | **7** |

## SIMPSON, Robbie — Forward

H: 5 10  W: 11 06  b.Luton 3-3-76

*Source:* Trainee. *Honours:* England Youth.

| | | | |
|---|---|---|---|
| 1993–94 | Tottenham H | 0 | 0 |
| 1994–95 | Tottenham H | 0 | 0 |
| 1995–96 | Tottenham H | 0 | 0 |
| 1996–97 | Portsmouth | 0 | 0 |
| 1997–98 | Portsmouth | 2 | 0 |
| **Total:** | | **2** | **0** |

## SINCLAIR, David — Defender

H: 5 11  W: 12 10  b.Dunfermline 6-10-69

*Source:* Kelty Under-21.

| | | | |
|---|---|---|---|
| 1990–91 | Raith R | 23 | 1 |
| 1991–92 | Raith R | 22 | 1 |
| 1992–93 | Raith R | 32 | 0 |
| 1993–94 | Raith R | 36 | 2 |
| 1994–95 | Raith R | 32 | 3 |
| 1995–96 | Raith R | 32 | 3 |
| 1996–97 | Millwall | 8 | 0 |
| 1996–97 | Dundee U | 6 | 0 |
| 1997–98 | Dundee U | 4 | 0 |
| **Total:** | | **195** | **10** |

## SINCLAIR, Frank — Defender

H: 5 9  W: 12 07  b.Lambeth 3-12-71

*Source:* Trainee. *Honours:* Jamaica 8 full caps.

| | | | |
|---|---|---|---|
| 1989–90 | Chelsea | 0 | 0 |
| 1990–91 | Chelsea | 4 | 0 |
| 1991–92 | Chelsea | 8 | 1 |
| 1991–92 | WBA (loan) | 6 | 1 |
| 1992–93 | Chelsea | 32 | 0 |
| 1993–94 | Chelsea | 35 | 0 |
| 1994–95 | Chelsea | 35 | 3 |
| 1995–96 | Chelsea | 13 | 1 |
| 1996–97 | Chelsea | 20 | 1 |
| 1997–98 | Chelsea | 22 | 1 |
| **Total:** | | **175** | **8** |

## SINCLAIR, Ronnie — Goalkeeper

H: 5 11  W: 12 09  b.Stirling 19-11-64

*Source:* Apprentice. *Honours:* Scotland Schools, Youth.

| | | | |
|---|---|---|---|
| 1982–83 | Nottingham F | 0 | 0 |
| 1983–84 | Nottingham F | 0 | 0 |
| 1983–84 | Wrexham (loan) | 11 | 0 |
| 1984–85 | Nottingham F | 0 | 0 |
| 1984–85 | Derby Co (loan) | 0 | 0 |
| 1985–86 | Nottingham F | 0 | 0 |
| 1985–86 | Sheffield U (loan) | 0 | 0 |
| 1985–86 | Leeds U (loan) | 0 | 0 |
| 1986–87 | Leeds U | 8 | 0 |
| 1986–87 | Halifax T (loan) | 4 | 0 |
| 1987–88 | Leeds U | 0 | 0 |
| 1988–89 | Leeds U | 0 | 0 |
| 1988–89 | Halifax T (loan) | 10 | 0 |
| 1989–90 | Leeds U | 0 | 0 |
| 1989–90 | Bristol C | 27 | 0 |
| 1990–91 | Bristol C | 17 | 0 |
| 1991–92 | Bristol C | 0 | 0 |
| 1991–92 | Walsall (loan) | 10 | 0 |
| 1991–92 | Stoke C | 26 | 0 |
| 1992–93 | Stoke C | 29 | 0 |

| | | | |
|---|---|---|---|
| 1993–94 | Stoke C | 0 | 0 |
| 1994–95 | Stoke C | 24 | 0 |
| 1994–95 | Bradford C (loan) | 0 | 0 |
| 1995–96 | Stoke C | 1 | 0 |
| 1996–97 | Chester C | 37 | 0 |
| 1997–98 | Chester C | 33 | 0 |
| **Total:** | | **237** | **0** |

## SINCLAIR, Trevor — Forward

H: 5 10 W: 12 10 b.Dulwich 2-3-73

*Source:* Trainee. *Honours:* England Youth, Under-21, B.

| | | | |
|---|---|---|---|
| 1989–90 | Blackpool | 9 | 0 |
| 1990–91 | Blackpool | 31 | 1 |
| 1991–92 | Blackpool | 27 | 3 |
| 1992–93 | Blackpool | 45 | 11 |
| 1993–94 | QPR | 32 | 4 |
| 1994–95 | QPR | 33 | 4 |
| 1995–96 | QPR | 37 | 2 |
| 1996–97 | QPR | 39 | 3 |
| 1997–98 | QPR | 26 | 3 |
| 1997–98 | West Ham U | 14 | 7 |
| **Total:** | | **293** | **38** |

## SINNOTT, Lee — Defender

H: 6 2 W: 12 10 b.Pelsall 12-7-65

*Source:* Apprentice. *Honours:* England Youth, Under-21.

| | | | |
|---|---|---|---|
| 1981–82 | Walsall | 4 | 0 |
| 1982–83 | Walsall | 32 | 2 |
| 1983–84 | Walsall | 4 | 0 |
| 1983–84 | Watford | 20 | 0 |
| 1984–85 | Watford | 30 | 0 |
| 1985–86 | Watford | 18 | 2 |
| 1986–87 | Watford | 10 | 0 |
| 1987–88 | Bradford C | 42 | 1 |
| 1988–89 | Bradford C | 42 | 2 |
| 1989–90 | Bradford C | 45 | 2 |
| 1990–91 | Bradford C | 44 | 1 |
| 1991–92 | Crystal Palace | 36 | 0 |
| 1992–93 | Crystal Palace | 19 | 0 |
| 1993–94 | Crystal Palace | 0 | 0 |
| 1993–94 | Bradford C | 18 | 0 |
| 1994–95 | Bradford C | 16 | 1 |
| 1994–95 | Huddersfield T | 25 | 1 |
| 1995–96 | Huddersfield T | 32 | 0 |
| 1996–97 | Huddersfield T | 30 | 0 |
| 1997–98 | Oldham Ath | 13 | 0 |
| 1997–98 | Bradford C (loan) | 7 | 0 |
| **Total:** | | **487** | **12** |

## SINTON, Andy — Midfield

H: 5 8 W: 11 01 b.Newcastle 19-3-66

*Source:* Apprentice. *Honours:* England Schools, B, 12 full caps.

| | | | |
|---|---|---|---|
| 1982–83 | Cambridge U | 13 | 5 |
| 1983–84 | Cambridge U | 34 | 6 |
| 1984–85 | Cambridge U | 26 | 2 |
| 1985–86 | Cambridge U | 20 | 0 |
| 1985–86 | Brentford | 26 | 3 |
| 1986–87 | Brentford | 46 | 5 |
| 1987–88 | Brentford | 46 | 11 |
| 1988–89 | Brentford | 31 | 9 |
| 1988–89 | QPR | 10 | 3 |
| 1989–90 | QPR | 38 | 6 |
| 1990–91 | QPR | 38 | 3 |
| 1991–92 | QPR | 38 | 3 |
| 1992–93 | QPR | 36 | 7 |
| 1993–94 | Sheffield W | 25 | 3 |
| 1994–95 | Sheffield W | 25 | 0 |
| 1995–96 | Sheffield W | 10 | 0 |
| 1995–96 | Tottenham H | 9 | 0 |
| 1996–97 | Tottenham H | 33 | 6 |
| 1997–98 | Tottenham H | 19 | 0 |
| **Total:** | | **523** | **72** |

## SISSOKO, Habib — Forward

b.Juvisy Orge 24-5-71

*Source:* Louhans-C.

| | | | |
|---|---|---|---|
| 1997–98 | Preston NE | 7 | 0 |
| **Total:** | | **7** | **0** |

## SISSON, Michael — Midfield

H: 5 8 W: 10 06 b.Mansfield 24-11-78

*Source:* Trainee.

| | | | |
|---|---|---|---|
| 1997–98 | Mansfield T | 1 | 0 |
| **Total:** | | **1** | **0** |

## SKEDD, Anthony — Midfield

H: 5 5 W: 10 01 b.Hartlepool 19-5-75

*Source:* Trainee.

| | | | |
|---|---|---|---|
| 1992–93 | Hartlepool U | 1 | 0 |
| 1993–94 | Hartlepool U | 22 | 0 |
| 1994–95 | Hartlepool U | 23 | 0 |
| 1995–96 | Hartlepool U | 0 | 0 |
| 1996–97 | Hartlepool U | 0 | 0 |
| 1997–98 | Hartlepool U | 0 | 0 |
| **Total:** | | **46** | **0** |

## SKELDON, Kevin — Forward

H: 5 11 W: 11 05 b.Edinburgh 27-4-78

*Source:* Trainee.

| | | | |
|---|---|---|---|
| 1996–97 | Leicester C | 0 | 0 |
| 1997–98 | Leicester C | 0 | 0 |

## SKELTON, Aaron — Defender

H: 6 0 W: 12 01 b.Welwyn 22-11-74

*Source:* Trainee.

| | | | |
|---|---|---|---|
| 1992–93 | Luton T | 0 | 0 |
| 1993–94 | Luton T | 0 | 0 |
| 1994–95 | Luton T | 5 | 0 |
| 1995–96 | Luton T | 0 | 0 |
| 1996–97 | Luton T | 3 | 0 |
| 1997–98 | Colchester U | 39 | 7 |
| **Total:** | | **47** | **7** |

## SKINNER, Craig — Midfield

H: 5 8 W: 11 00 b.Bury 21-10-70

*Source:* Trainee.

| | | | |
|---|---|---|---|
| 1989–90 | Blackburn R | 0 | 0 |
| 1990–91 | Blackburn R | 7 | 0 |
| 1991–92 | Blackburn R | 9 | 0 |
| 1992–93 | Plymouth Arg | 13 | 1 |
| 1993–94 | Plymouth Arg | 16 | 0 |
| 1994–95 | Plymouth Arg | 24 | 3 |
| 1995–96 | Wrexham | 23 | 3 |
| 1996–97 | Wrexham | 27 | 4 |
| 1997–98 | Wrexham | 25 | 1 |
| **Total:** | | **144** | **12** |

## SKINNER, Justin — Midfield

H: 6 0 W: 11 03 b.Hounslow 30-1-69

*Source:* Apprentice.

| | | | |
|---|---|---|---|
| 1986–87 | Fulham | 3 | 0 |
| 1987–88 | Fulham | 32 | 6 |
| 1988–89 | Fulham | 38 | 8 |
| 1989–90 | Fulham | 30 | 4 |
| 1990–91 | Fulham | 32 | 5 |
| 1991–92 | Bristol R | 42 | 3 |
| 1992–93 | Bristol R | 12 | 0 |
| 1993–94 | Bristol R | 29 | 5 |
| 1994–95 | Bristol R | 38 | 2 |
| 1995–96 | Bristol R | 28 | 0 |
| 1996–97 | Bristol R | 34 | 2 |
| 1997–98 | Bristol R | 4 | 0 |
| 1997–98 | Walsall (loan) | 10 | 0 |
| 1997–98 | Hibernian | 6 | 0 |
| **Total:** | | **338** | **35** |

## SKOLDMARK, Magnus — Defender

H: 6 1 W: 12 00 b.Langsele 22-9-68

*Source:* Dalian Wanda.

| | | | |
|---|---|---|---|
| 1997–98 | Dundee U | 19 | 0 |
| **Total:** | | **19** | **0** |

## SLADE, Steve — Forward

H: 6 0 W: 10 13 b.Hackney 6-10-75

*Source:* Trainee. *Honours:* England Under-21.

| | | | |
|---|---|---|---|
| 1994–95 | Tottenham H | 0 | 0 |
| 1995–96 | Tottenham H | 5 | 0 |
| 1996–97 | QPR | 17 | 4 |
| 1996–97 | Brentford (loan) | 4 | 0 |
| 1997–98 | QPR | 22 | 0 |
| **Total:** | | **48** | **4** |

## SLATER, Robbie — Defender

H: 5 10 W: 13 03 b.Ormskirk 22-11-64

*Source:* Anderlecht. *Honours:* Australia 29 full caps, 1 goal.

| | | | |
|---|---|---|---|
| 1991–92 | Lens | 34 | 2 |
| 1992–93 | Lens | 25 | 0 |
| 1993–94 | Lens | 22 | 2 |
| 1994–95 | Blackburn R | 18 | 0 |
| 1995–96 | West Ham U | 22 | 2 |
| 1996–97 | West Ham U | 3 | 0 |
| 1996–97 | Southampton | 30 | 2 |
| 1997–98 | Southampton | 11 | 0 |
| 1997–98 | Wolverhampton W | 6 | 0 |
| **Total:** | | **171** | **8** |

## SLATER, Stuart — Midfield

H: 5 8 W: 10 05 b.Sudbury 27-3-69

*Source:* Apprentice. *Honours:* England Under-21, B.

| | | | |
|---|---|---|---|
| 1986–87 | West Ham U | 0 | 0 |
| 1987–88 | West Ham U | 2 | 0 |
| 1988–89 | West Ham U | 18 | 1 |
| 1989–90 | West Ham U | 40 | 7 |
| 1990–91 | West Ham U | 40 | 3 |
| 1991–92 | West Ham U | 41 | 0 |
| 1992–93 | Celtic | 39 | 2 |
| 1993–94 | Celtic | 4 | 1 |
| 1993–94 | Ipswich T | 28 | 1 |
| 1994–95 | Ipswich T | 27 | 1 |
| 1995–96 | Ipswich T | 17 | 2 |
| 1996–97 | Ipswich T | 0 | 0 |
| 1996–97 | Leicester C | 0 | 0 |
| 1996–97 | Watford | 16 | 1 |
| 1997–98 | Watford | 14 | 0 |
| **Total:** | | **286** | **19** |

## SLATTER, Danny — Midfield

b.Cardiff 15-11-80

*Source:* Trainee.

| | | | |
|---|---|---|---|
| 1997–98 | Chelsea | 0 | 0 |

## SMALL, Bryan — Defender

H: 5 9 W: 11 09 b.Birmingham 15-11-71

*Source:* Trainee. *Honours:* England Under-21.

| | | | |
|---|---|---|---|
| 1989–90 | Aston Villa | 0 | 0 |
| 1990–91 | Aston Villa | 0 | 0 |
| 1991–92 | Aston Villa | 8 | 0 |
| 1992–93 | Aston Villa | 14 | 0 |
| 1993–94 | Aston Villa | 9 | 0 |
| 1994–95 | Aston Villa | 5 | 0 |
| 1994–95 | Birmingham C (loan) | 3 | 0 |
| 1995–96 | Aston Villa | 0 | 0 |
| 1995–96 | Bolton W | 1 | 0 |
| 1996–97 | Bolton W | 11 | 0 |
| 1997–98 | Bolton W | 0 | 0 |
| 1997–98 | Luton T (loan) | 15 | 0 |
| 1997–98 | Bradford C (loan) | 5 | 0 |
| 1997–98 | Bury | 18 | 1 |
| **Total:** | | **89** | **1** |

## SMART, Allan — Forward

H: 6 2 W: 12 07 b.Perth 8-7-74

| | | | |
|---|---|---|---|
| 1994–95 | Caledonian Th | 4 | 0 |
| 1994–95 | Preston NE | 19 | 6 |
| 1995–96 | Preston NE | 2 | 0 |
| 1995–96 | Carlisle U (loan) | 4 | 0 |
| 1996–97 | Preston NE | 0 | 0 |
| 1996–97 | Northampton T (loan) | 1 | 0 |
| 1996–97 | Carlisle U | 28 | 10 |
| 1997–98 | Carlisle U | 16 | 6 |
| **Total:** | | **74** | **22** |

## SMEETS, Jorg — Forward

b.Bussum 5-11-70

| | | | |
|---|---|---|---|
| 1997–98 | Heracles | 8 | 2 |
| 1997–98 | Wigan Ath | 23 | 3 |
| **Total:** | | **31** | **5** |

## SMITH, Alan — Forward

H: 5 9 W: 10 06 b.Wakefield 28-10-80

*Source:* Trainee. *Honours:* England Youth.

| | | | |
|---|---|---|---|
| 1997–98 | Leeds U | 0 | 0 |

## SMITH, Alex — Defender

H: 5 6 W: 11 10 b.Liverpool 15-2-76

*Source:* Trainee.

| | | | |
|---|---|---|---|
| 1994–95 | Everton | 0 | 0 |
| 1995–96 | Everton | 0 | 0 |
| 1995–96 | Swindon T | 8 | 0 |
| 1996–97 | Swindon T | 18 | 1 |
| 1997–98 | Swindon T | 5 | 0 |
| 1997–98 | Huddersfield T | 0 | 0 |
| **Total:** | | **31** | **1** |

## SMITH, Andy — Forward

H: 6 1 W: 12 07 b.Aberdeen 22-11-68

*Source:* Peterhead. *Honours:* Scotland B.

| | | | |
|---|---|---|---|
| 1990–91 | Airdrieonians | 28 | 3 |
| 1991–92 | Airdrieonians | 29 | 4 |
| 1992–93 | Airdrieonians | 34 | 4 |
| 1993–94 | Airdrieonians | 38 | 7 |
| 1994–95 | Airdrieonians | 36 | 12 |
| 1995–96 | Dunfermline Ath | 19 | 9 |
| 1996–97 | Dunfermline Ath | 35 | 10 |
| 1997–98 | Dunfermline Ath | 33 | 16 |
| **Total:** | | **252** | **65** |

## SMITH, Barry — Defender

H: 5 10 W: 12 00 b.Paisley 19-2-74

*Source:* Giffnock N. *Honours:* Scotland Under-21.

| | | | |
|---|---|---|---|
| 1991–92 | Celtic | 3 | 0 |
| 1992–93 | Celtic | 6 | 0 |
| 1993–94 | Celtic | 7 | 0 |
| 1994–95 | Celtic | 3 | 0 |
| 1995–96 | Celtic | 0 | 0 |
| 1995–96 | Dundee | 20 | 0 |
| 1996–97 | Dundee | 36 | 0 |
| 1997–98 | Dundee | 34 | 1 |
| **Total:** | | **109** | **1** |

## SMITH, Ben — Midfield

H: 5 9 W: 11 09 b.Chelmsford 23-11-78

*Source:* Arsenal Trainee.

| | | | |
|---|---|---|---|
| 1996–97 | Reading | 1 | 0 |
| 1997–98 | Reading | 0 | 0 |
| **Total:** | | **1** | **0** |

## SMITH, Carl — Midfield

H: 5 8 W: 11 00 b.Sheffield 15-1-79

*Source:* Trainee.

| | | | |
|---|---|---|---|
| 1997–98 | Burnley | 1 | 0 |
| **Total:** | | **1** | **0** |

## SMITH, Craig — Defender

H: 6 1 W: 13 07 b.Mansfield 2-8-76

*Source:* Trainee.

| | | | |
|---|---|---|---|
| 1995–96 | Derby Co | 0 | 0 |
| 1996–97 | Derby Co | 0 | 0 |
| 1997–98 | Derby Co | 0 | 0 |
| 1997–98 | Rochdale (loan) | 3 | 0 |
| **Total:** | | **3** | **0** |

## SMITH, David — Midfield

H: 5 10 W: 12 11 b.Liverpool 26-12-70

*Source:* Trainee.

| | | | |
|---|---|---|---|
| 1989–90 | Norwich C | 1 | 0 |
| 1990–91 | Norwich C | 3 | 0 |
| 1991–92 | Norwich C | 1 | 0 |
| 1992–93 | Norwich C | 6 | 0 |
| 1993–94 | Norwich C | 7 | 0 |
| 1994–95 | Oxford U | 42 | 0 |
| 1995–96 | Oxford U | 45 | 1 |
| 1996–97 | Oxford U | 45 | 0 |
| 1997–98 | Oxford U | 44 | 1 |
| **Total:** | | **194** | **2** |

## SMITH, David — Midfield

H: 5 8 W: 10 08 b.Stonehouse 29-3-68

*Honours:* England Under-21.

| | | | |
|---|---|---|---|
| 1986–87 | Coventry C | 0 | 0 |
| 1987–88 | Coventry C | 16 | 4 |
| 1988–89 | Coventry C | 35 | 3 |
| 1989–90 | Coventry C | 37 | 6 |
| 1990–91 | Coventry C | 36 | 1 |
| 1991–92 | Coventry C | 24 | 4 |
| 1992–93 | Coventry C | 6 | 1 |
| 1992–93 | Bournemouth (loan) | 1 | 0 |
| 1992–93 | Birmingham C | 13 | 1 |
| 1993–94 | Birmingham C | 25 | 2 |
| 1993–94 | WBA | 18 | 0 |
| 1994–95 | WBA | 22 | 0 |
| 1995–96 | WBA | 16 | 0 |
| 1996–97 | WBA | 24 | 2 |
| 1997–98 | WBA | 22 | 0 |
| 1997–98 | Grimsby T | 17 | 1 |
| **Total:** | | **312** | **25** |

## SMITH, David — Goalkeeper

H: 6 0 W: 14 07 b.Stockport 2-5-73

*Source:* Bramhall.

| | | | |
|---|---|---|---|
| 1997–98 | Doncaster R | 1 | 0 |
| **Total:** | | **1** | **0** |

## SMITH, Dean — Defender

H: 6 0 W: 13 00 b.West Bromwich 19-3-71

*Source:* Trainee.

| | | | |
|---|---|---|---|
| 1988–89 | Walsall | 15 | 0 |
| 1989–90 | Walsall | 7 | 0 |
| 1990–91 | Walsall | 33 | 0 |
| 1991–92 | Walsall | 9 | 0 |
| 1992–93 | Walsall | 42 | 1 |
| 1993–94 | Walsall | 36 | 1 |
| 1994–95 | Hereford U | 35 | 3 |
| 1995–96 | Hereford U | 40 | 8 |
| 1996–97 | Hereford U | 42 | 8 |
| 1997–98 | Leyton Orient | 43 | 9 |
| **Total:** | | **302** | **30** |

## SMITH, Gary — Defender

H: 6 0 W: 12 03 b.Glasgow 25-3-71

*Source:* Duntocher BC.

| | | | |
|---|---|---|---|
| 1988–89 | Falkirk | 3 | 0 |
| 1989–90 | Falkirk | 36 | 0 |
| 1990–91 | Falkirk | 31 | 0 |
| 1991–92 | Aberdeen | 16 | 1 |
| 1992–93 | Aberdeen | 40 | 0 |
| 1993–94 | Aberdeen | 21 | 0 |
| 1994–95 | Aberdeen | 31 | 0 |
| 1995–96 | Aberdeen | 33 | 0 |
| 1996–97 | Rennes | 14 | 0 |
| 1997–98 | Aberdeen | 31 | 1 |
| **Total:** | | **256** | **2** |

## SMITH, Gavin — Forward

H: 5 10 W: 10 09 b.Sheffield 24-9-77

*Source:* Trainee.

| | | | |
|---|---|---|---|
| 1994–95 | Sheffield W | 0 | 0 |
| 1995–96 | Sheffield W | 0 | 0 |
| 1996–97 | Sheffield W | 0 | 0 |
| 1997–98 | Sheffield W | 0 | 0 |

## SMITH, Gordon — Midfield

b.Glasgow 18-12-80

*Source:* Trainee.

| | | | |
|---|---|---|---|
| 1997–98 | Bolton W | 0 | 0 |

## SMITH, Jamie — Defender

H: 5 8 W: 11 02 b.Birmingham 17-9-74

*Source:* Trainee.

| | | | |
|---|---|---|---|
| 1993–94 | Wolverhampton W | 0 | 0 |
| 1994–95 | Wolverhampton W | 25 | 0 |
| 1995–96 | Wolverhampton W | 13 | 0 |
| 1996–97 | Wolverhampton W | 38 | 0 |
| 1997–98 | Wolverhampton W | 11 | 0 |
| 1997–98 | Crystal Palace | 18 | 0 |
| **Total:** | | **105** | **0** |

## SMITH, Mark — Goalkeeper

H: 6 1 W: 13 09 b.Birmingham 2-1-73

*Source:* Trainee.

| | | | |
|---|---|---|---|
| 1991–92 | Nottingham F | 0 | 0 |
| 1992–93 | Nottingham F | 0 | 0 |
| 1992–93 | Crewe Alex | 7 | 0 |
| 1993–94 | Crewe Alex | 32 | 0 |
| 1994–95 | Crewe Alex | 24 | 0 |
| 1995–96 | Crewe Alex | 0 | 0 |
| 1996–97 | Walsall | 0 | 0 |
| 1997–98 | Walsall | 0 | 0 |
| **Total:** | | **63** | **0** |

## SMITH, Martin — Forward

H: 5 11 W: 12 00 b.Sunderland 13-11-74

*Source:* Trainee. *Honours:* England Schools, Under-21.

| | | | |
|---|---|---|---|
| 1992–93 | Sunderland | 0 | 0 |
| 1993–94 | Sunderland | 29 | 8 |
| 1994–95 | Sunderland | 35 | 10 |
| 1995–96 | Sunderland | 20 | 2 |
| 1996–97 | Sunderland | 11 | 0 |
| 1997–98 | Sunderland | 16 | 2 |
| **Total:** | | **111** | **22** |

## SMITH, Mike — Forward

H: 5 9 W: 11 01 b.Liverpool 28-9-73

*Source:* Runcorn.

| | | | |
|---|---|---|---|
| 1995–96 | Doncaster R | 13 | 0 |
| 1996–97 | Doncaster R | 18 | 2 |
| 1997–98 | Doncaster R | 19 | 3 |
| **Total:** | | **50** | **5** |

## SMITH, Neil — Midfield

H: 5 8 W: 12 02 b.Lambeth 30-9-71

*Source:* Trainee.

| | | | |
|---|---|---|---|
| 1990–91 | Tottenham H | 0 | 0 |
| 1991–92 | Tottenham H | 0 | 0 |
| 1991–92 | Gillingham | 26 | 2 |
| 1992–93 | Gillingham | 39 | 3 |
| 1993–94 | Gillingham | 35 | 2 |
| 1994–95 | Gillingham | 33 | 1 |
| 1995–96 | Gillingham | 37 | 1 |
| 1996–97 | Gillingham | 42 | 1 |
| 1997–98 | Fulham | 44 | 0 |
| **Total:** | | **256** | **10** |

## SMITH, Paul — Midfield

H: 5 10 W: 12 05 b.East Ham 18-9-71

*Source:* Trainee.

| | | | |
|---|---|---|---|
| 1989–90 | Southend U | 10 | 1 |
| 1990–91 | Southend U | 2 | 0 |
| 1991–92 | Southend U | 0 | 0 |
| 1992–93 | Southend U | 8 | 0 |
| 1993–94 | Brentford | 32 | 3 |
| 1994–95 | Brentford | 35 | 3 |
| 1995–96 | Brentford | 46 | 4 |
| 1996–97 | Brentford | 46 | 1 |
| 1997–98 | Gillingham | 46 | 3 |
| **Total:** | | **225** | **15** |

## SMITH, Paul — Midfield

H: 5 11 W: 11 07 b.Hastings 25-1-76

*Source:* Hastings T.

| | | | |
|---|---|---|---|
| 1994–95 | Nottingham F | 0 | 0 |
| 1995–96 | Nottingham F | 0 | 0 |
| 1996–97 | Nottingham F | 0 | 0 |
| 1997–98 | Nottingham F | 0 | 0 |
| 1997–98 | Lincoln C (loan) | 17 | 3 |
| **Total:** | | **17** | **3** |

## SMITH, Paul — Forward

H: 6 0 W: 13 03 b.Leeds 22-1-76

*Source:* Trainee.

| | | | |
|---|---|---|---|
| 1993–94 | Burnley | 1 | 0 |
| 1994–95 | Burnley | 0 | 0 |
| 1995–96 | Burnley | 10 | 0 |
| 1996–97 | Burnley | 37 | 4 |
| 1997–98 | Burnley | 14 | 0 |
| **Total:** | | **62** | **4** |

## SMITH, Peter — Defender

H: 6 2 W: 12 10 b.Stone 12-7-69

*Source:* Alma Swanley.

| | | | |
|---|---|---|---|
| 1994–95 | Brighton & HA | 38 | 1 |
| 1995–96 | Brighton & HA | 31 | 1 |
| 1996–97 | Brighton & HA | 30 | 1 |
| 1997–98 | Brighton & HA | 27 | 2 |
| **Total:** | | **126** | **5** |

## SMITH, Peter — Forward

H: 5 10 W: 10 00 b.Rhuddlan 15-9-78

*Source:* Trainee.

| | | | |
|---|---|---|---|
| 1996–97 | Crewe Alex | 1 | 0 |
| 1997–98 | Crewe Alex | 6 | 0 |
| **Total:** | | **7** | **0** |

## SMITH, Phil — Goalkeeper

b.Wembley 14-12-79

*Source:* Trainee.

| | | | |
|---|---|---|---|
| 1997–98 | Millwall | 0 | 0 |

## SMITH, Richard — Defender

H: 6 0 W: 13 05 b.Lutterworth 3-10-70

*Source:* Trainee.

| | | | |
|---|---|---|---|
| 1988–89 | Leicester C | 0 | 0 |
| 1989–90 | Leicester C | 4 | 0 |
| 1989–90 | Cambridge U (loan) | 4 | 0 |
| 1990–91 | Leicester C | 4 | 0 |
| 1991–92 | Leicester C | 25 | 1 |
| 1992–93 | Leicester C | 44 | 0 |
| 1993–94 | Leicester C | 8 | 0 |
| 1994–95 | Leicester C | 12 | 0 |
| 1995–96 | Leicester C | 1 | 0 |
| 1995–96 | Grimsby T | 18 | 0 |
| 1996–97 | Grimsby T | 14 | 0 |
| 1997–98 | Grimsby T | 0 | 0 |
| **Total:** | | **134** | **1** |

## SMITH, Shaun — Defender

H: 5 10 W: 11 00 b.Leeds 9-4-71

*Source:* Trainee.

| | | | |
|---|---|---|---|
| 1988–89 | Halifax T | 1 | 0 |
| 1989–90 | Halifax T | 6 | 0 |
| 1990–91 | Halifax T | 0 | 0 |
| 1991–92 | Crewe Alex | 10 | 0 |
| 1992–93 | Crewe Alex | 36 | 4 |
| 1993–94 | Crewe Alex | 37 | 7 |
| 1994–95 | Crewe Alex | 45 | 8 |
| 1995–96 | Crewe Alex | 29 | 1 |
| 1996–97 | Crewe Alex | 38 | 4 |
| 1997–98 | Crewe Alex | 43 | 6 |
| **Total:** | | **245** | **30** |

## SMITH, Steve — Midfield

b.Huddersfield 13-10-78

*Source:* Trainee.

| | | | |
|---|---|---|---|
| 1997–98 | Huddersfield T | 6 | 0 |
| **Total:** | | **6** | **0** |

## SMITH, Tommy — Midfield

H: 5 9 W: 13 00 b.Northampton 25-11-77

*Source:* Trainee.

| | | | |
|---|---|---|---|
| 1994–95 | Manchester U | 0 | 0 |
| 1995–96 | Manchester U | 0 | 0 |
| 1996–97 | Manchester U | 0 | 0 |
| 1997–98 | Manchester U | 0 | 0 |
| 1997–98 | Cambridge U | 1 | 0 |
| **Total:** | | **1** | **0** |

## SMITH, Tommy — Midfield

H: 5 8 W: 10 00 b.Hemel Hempsted 22-5-80

*Source:* Trainee. *Honours:* England Youth.

| | | | |
|---|---|---|---|
| 1997–98 | Watford | 1 | 0 |
| **Total:** | | **1** | **0** |

## SMYTH, Gary — Midfield

b.Dublin 21-3-79

*Source:* St Joseph's BC.

| | | | |
|---|---|---|---|
| 1997–98 | Sunderland | 0 | 0 |

## SNEEKES, Richard — Midfield

H: 5 11 W: 12 03 b.Amsterdam 30-10-68

*Honours:* Holland Under-21.

| | | | |
|---|---|---|---|
| 1985–86 | Ajax | 1 | 0 |
| 1986–87 | Ajax | 1 | 0 |
| 1987–88 | Ajax | 1 | 0 |
| 1988–89 | Volendam | 31 | 7 |
| 1989–90 | Fortuna Sittard | 32 | 2 |
| 1990–91 | Fortuna Sittard | 32 | 7 |
| 1991–92 | Fortuna Sittard | 33 | 5 |
| 1992–93 | Fortuna Sittard | 29 | 6 |
| From Locarno, Fortuna Sittard. | | | |
| 1994–95 | Bolton W | 38 | 6 |
| 1995–96 | Bolton W | 17 | 1 |
| 1995–96 | WBA | 13 | 10 |
| 1996–97 | WBA | 45 | 8 |
| 1997–98 | WBA | 42 | 3 |
| **Total:** | | **315** | **55** |

## SNELDERS, Theo — Goalkeeper

H: 6 2 W: 14 02 b.Westervoort 7-12-63

*Source:* Twente. *Honours:* Holland full caps.

| | | | |
|---|---|---|---|
| 1988–89 | Aberdeen | 36 | 0 |
| 1989–90 | Aberdeen | 23 | 0 |
| 1990–91 | Aberdeen | 21 | 0 |
| 1991–92 | Aberdeen | 42 | 0 |
| 1992–93 | Aberdeen | 41 | 0 |

| | | | |
|---|---|---|---|
| 1993–94 | Aberdeen | 33 | 0 |
| 1994–95 | Aberdeen | 24 | 0 |
| 1995–96 | Aberdeen | 7 | 0 |
| 1995–96 | Rangers | 2 | 0 |
| 1996–97 | Rangers | 4 | 0 |
| 1997–98 | Rangers | 7 | 0 |
| **Total:** | | **240** | **0** |

## SNIJDERS, Mark — Defender

H: 6 1 W: 13 12 b.Alkmaar 12-3-72

| | | | |
|---|---|---|---|
| 1997–98 | Port Vale | 24 | 2 |
| **Total:** | | **24** | **2** |

## SNODIN, Glynn — Defender

H: 5 6 W: 11 00 b.Rotherham 14-2-60

*Source:* Apprentice.

| | | | |
|---|---|---|---|
| 1976–77 | Doncaster R | 4 | 0 |
| 1977–78 | Doncaster R | 22 | 2 |
| 1978–79 | Doncaster R | 34 | 3 |
| 1979–80 | Doncaster R | 41 | 1 |
| 1980–81 | Doncaster R | 44 | 3 |
| 1981–82 | Doncaster R | 40 | 7 |
| 1982–83 | Doncaster R | 38 | 14 |
| 1983–84 | Doncaster R | 43 | 13 |
| 1984–85 | Doncaster R | 43 | 18 |
| 1985–86 | Sheffield W | 28 | 1 |
| 1986–87 | Sheffield W | 31 | 0 |
| 1987–88 | Leeds U | 35 | 7 |
| 1988–89 | Leeds U | 35 | 3 |
| 1989–90 | Leeds U | 4 | 0 |
| 1990–91 | Leeds U | 20 | 0 |
| 1991–92 | Leeds U | 0 | 0 |
| 1991–92 | Oldham Ath (loan) | 8 | 1 |
| 1991–92 | Rotherham U | 3 | 0 |
| 1991–92 | Hearts | 7 | 0 |
| 1992–93 | Hearts | 27 | 0 |
| 1993–94 | Barnsley | 11 | 0 |
| 1994–95 | Barnsley | 14 | 0 |
| 1995–96 | Barnsley | 0 | 0 |
| 1995–96 | Carlisle U | 0 | 0 |
| 1996–97 | Carlisle U | 0 | 0 |
| 1997–98 | Scarborough | 0 | 0 |
| **Total:** | | **532** | **73** |

## SNODIN, Ian — Midfield

H: 5 9 W: 11 03 b.Rotherham 15-8-63

*Source:* Apprentice. *Honours:* England Youth, Under-21.

| | | | |
|---|---|---|---|
| 1979–80 | Doncaster R | 9 | 1 |
| 1980–81 | Doncaster R | 32 | 2 |
| 1981–82 | Doncaster R | 33 | 2 |
| 1982–83 | Doncaster R | 34 | 3 |
| 1983–84 | Doncaster R | 39 | 9 |
| 1984–85 | Doncaster R | 41 | 8 |
| 1985–86 | Leeds U | 37 | 5 |
| 1986–87 | Leeds U | 14 | 1 |
| 1986–87 | Everton | 16 | 0 |
| 1987–88 | Everton | 31 | 2 |
| 1988–89 | Everton | 23 | 0 |
| 1989–90 | Everton | 25 | 0 |
| 1990–91 | Everton | 1 | 0 |
| 1991–92 | Everton | 0 | 0 |
| 1992–93 | Everton | 20 | 1 |
| 1993–94 | Everton | 29 | 0 |
| 1994–95 | Everton | 3 | 0 |
| 1994–95 | Sunderland (loan) | 6 | 0 |
| 1994–95 | Oldham Ath | 17 | 0 |
| 1995–96 | Oldham Ath | 26 | 0 |
| 1996–97 | Oldham Ath | 14 | 0 |
| 1997–98 | Scarborough | 35 | 0 |
| **Total:** | | **485** | **34** |

## SOBIECH, Jorg — Defender

b.Gelsenkirchen 15-1-69

*Source:* Schalke, Wattenscheid, Stuttgart Kickers, Wattenscheid.

| | | | |
|---|---|---|---|
| 1996–97 | NEC | 32 | 0 |
| 1997–98 | NEC | 12 | 2 |
| 1997–98 | Stoke C | 3 | 0 |
| **Total:** | | **47** | **2** |

## SODJE, Efetobar — Defender

H: 6 1 W: 12 00 b.Greenwich 5-10-72

*Source:* Delta Steel Pioneer, Stevenage Bor.

| | | | |
|---|---|---|---|
| 1997–98 | Macclesfield T | 41 | 3 |
| **Total:** | | **41** | **3** |

## SOLBAKKEN, Stale — Midfield

b.Norway 27-2-68

*Honours:* Norway 37 full caps, 6 goals.

| | | | |
|---|---|---|---|
| 1992 | Hamark | 21 | 6 |
| 1993 | Hamark | 18 | 3 |
| 1994 | Lillestrom | 22 | 9 |
| 1995 | Lillestrom | 26 | 13 |
| 1996 | Lillestrom | 26 | 8 |
| 1997 | Lillestrom | 25 | 5 |
| 1997–98 | Wimbledon | 6 | 1 |
| **Total:** | | **144** | **45** |

## SOLIS, Mauricio — Midfield

H: 5 8 W: 12 00 b.Costa Rica 13-12-72

*Source:* Herediano. *Honours:* Costa Rica full caps.

| | | | |
|---|---|---|---|
| 1996–97 | Derby Co | 2 | 0 |
| 1997–98 | Derby Co | 9 | 0 |
| **Total:** | | **11** | **0** |

## SOLSKJAER, Ole Gunnar — Forward

H: 5 10 W: 11 06 b.Kristiansund 26-2-73

*Honours:* Norway Under-21, 16 full caps, 8 goals.

| | | | |
|---|---|---|---|
| 1995 | Molde | 26 | 20 |
| 1996 | Molde | 16 | 11 |
| 1996–97 | Manchester U | 33 | 17 |
| 1997–98 | Manchester U | 22 | 6 |
| **Total:** | | **97** | **54** |

## SOLTVEDT, Trond Egil — Midfield

H: 6 1 W: 12 08 b.Voss 15-2-67

*Honours:* Norway 4 full caps.

| | | | |
|---|---|---|---|
| 1990 | Viking | 20 | 3 |
| 1991 | Viking | 13 | 1 |
| 1992 | Brann | 22 | 6 |
| 1993 | Brann | 21 | 16 |
| 1994 | Brann | 21 | 12 |
| 1995 | Rosenborg | 25 | 4 |
| 1996 | Rosenborg | 26 | 10 |
| 1997 | Rosenborg | 9 | 4 |
| 1997–98 | Coventry C | 30 | 1 |
| **Total:** | | **187** | **57** |

## SOMMER, Jurgen — Goalkeeper

H: 6 5 W: 15 07 b.New York 27-2-69

*Honours:* USA full caps.

| | | | |
|---|---|---|---|
| 1991–92 | Luton T | 0 | 0 |
| 1991–92 | Brighton & HA (loan) | 1 | 0 |
| 1992–93 | Luton T | 0 | 0 |
| 1992–93 | Torquay U (loan) | 10 | 0 |
| 1993–94 | Luton T | 43 | 0 |
| 1994–95 | Luton T | 37 | 0 |
| 1995–96 | Luton T | 2 | 0 |
| 1995–96 | QPR | 33 | 0 |
| 1996–97 | QPR | 33 | 0 |
| 1997–98 | QPR | 0 | 0 |
| **Total:** | | **159** | **0** |

## SONNER, Danny — Midfield

H: 5 11 W: 12 08 b.Wigan 9-1-72

*Source:* Wigan Ath. *Honours:* Northern Ireland B, 1 full cap.

| | | | |
|---|---|---|---|
| 1990–91 | Burnley | 2 | 0 |
| 1991–92 | Burnley | 3 | 0 |
| 1992–93 | Burnley | 1 | 0 |
| 1992–93 | Bury (loan) | 5 | 3 |
| From Erzgebirge Aue. | | | |
| 1996–97 | Ipswich T | 29 | 2 |
| 1997–98 | Ipswich T | 23 | 1 |
| **Total:** | | **63** | **6** |

## SORVEL, Neil — Midfield

H: 6 0 W: 12 09 b.Whiston 2-3-73

*Source:* Trainee.

| | | | |
|---|---|---|---|
| 1991–92 | Crewe Alex | 9 | 0 |
| 1992–93 | Crewe Alex | 0 | 0 |
| From Macclesfield T. | | | |
| 1997–98 | Macclesfield T | 45 | 3 |
| **Total:** | | **54** | **3** |

## SOUTHALL, Neville — Goalkeeper

H: 6 1 W: 13 00 b.Llandudno 16-9-58

*Source:* Winsford U. *Honours:* Wales Under-21, 92 full caps.

| | | | |
|---|---|---|---|
| 1980–81 | Bury | 39 | 0 |
| 1981–82 | Everton | 26 | 0 |
| 1982–83 | Everton | 17 | 0 |
| 1982–83 | Port Vale (loan) | 9 | 0 |
| 1983–84 | Everton | 35 | 0 |
| 1984–85 | Everton | 42 | 0 |
| 1985–86 | Everton | 32 | 0 |
| 1986–87 | Everton | 31 | 0 |
| 1987–88 | Everton | 32 | 0 |
| 1988–89 | Everton | 38 | 0 |
| 1989–90 | Everton | 38 | 0 |
| 1990–91 | Everton | 38 | 0 |
| 1991–92 | Everton | 42 | 0 |
| 1992–93 | Everton | 40 | 0 |
| 1993–94 | Everton | 42 | 0 |
| 1994–95 | Everton | 41 | 0 |
| 1995–96 | Everton | 38 | 0 |
| 1996–97 | Everton | 34 | 0 |
| 1997–98 | Everton | 12 | 0 |
| 1997–98 | Southend U (loan) | 9 | 0 |
| 1997–98 | Stoke C | 12 | 0 |
| **Total:** | | **647** | **0** |

## SOUTHALL, Nicky — Midfield

H: 5 9 W: 12 00 b.Middlesbrough 28-1-72

*Source:* Trainee.

| | | | |
|---|---|---|---|
| 1990–91 | Hartlepool U | 0 | 0 |
| 1991–92 | Hartlepool U | 22 | 3 |
| 1992–93 | Hartlepool U | 39 | 6 |
| 1993–94 | Hartlepool U | 40 | 9 |
| 1994–95 | Hartlepool U | 37 | 6 |
| 1995–96 | Grimsby T | 33 | 2 |
| 1996–97 | Grimsby T | 34 | 3 |
| 1997–98 | Grimsby T | 5 | 0 |
| 1997–98 | Gillingham | 23 | 2 |
| **Total:** | | **233** | **31** |

## SOUTHGATE, Gareth — Defender

H: 6 0 W: 12 03 b.Watford 3-9-70

*Source:* Trainee. *Honours:* England 27 full caps.

| | | | |
|---|---|---|---|
| 1988–89 | Crystal Palace | 0 | 0 |
| 1989–90 | Crystal Palace | 0 | 0 |
| 1990–91 | Crystal Palace | 1 | 0 |
| 1991–92 | Crystal Palace | 30 | 0 |
| 1992–93 | Crystal Palace | 33 | 3 |
| 1993–94 | Crystal Palace | 46 | 9 |
| 1994–95 | Crystal Palace | 42 | 3 |
| 1995–96 | Aston Villa | 31 | 1 |
| 1996–97 | Aston Villa | 28 | 1 |
| 1997–98 | Aston Villa | 32 | 0 |
| **Total:** | | **243** | **17** |

## SPACKMAN, Nigel — Midfield

H: 6 1 W: 13 02 b.Romsey 2-12-60

*Source:* Andover.

| | | | |
|---|---|---|---|
| 1980–81 | Bournemouth | 44 | 3 |
| 1981–82 | Bournemouth | 35 | 3 |
| 1982–83 | Bournemouth | 40 | 4 |
| 1983–84 | Chelsea | 40 | 3 |
| 1984–85 | Chelsea | 42 | 1 |
| 1985–86 | Chelsea | 39 | 7 |
| 1986–87 | Chelsea | 20 | 1 |
| 1986–87 | Liverpool | 12 | 0 |
| 1987–88 | Liverpool | 27 | 0 |
| 1988–89 | Liverpool | 12 | 0 |
| 1988–89 | QPR | 16 | 1 |
| 1989–90 | QPR | 13 | 0 |
| 1989–90 | Rangers | 21 | 1 |
| 1990–91 | Rangers | 35 | 0 |
| 1991–92 | Rangers | 42 | 0 |
| 1992–93 | Rangers | 2 | 0 |
| 1992–93 | Chelsea | 6 | 0 |
| 1993–94 | Chelsea | 9 | 0 |
| 1994–95 | Chelsea | 36 | 0 |
| 1995–96 | Chelsea | 16 | 0 |
| 1996–97 | Sheffield U | 23 | 0 |
| 1997–98 | Sheffield U | 0 | 0 |
| **Total:** | | **530** | **24** |

## SPARROW, Paul — Defender

H: 6 0 W: 11 00 b.London 24-3-75

*Source:* Trainee.

| | | | |
|---|---|---|---|
| 1993–94 | Crystal Palace | 0 | 0 |
| 1994–95 | Crystal Palace | 0 | 0 |
| 1995–96 | Crystal Palace | 1 | 0 |
| 1995–96 | Preston NE | 13 | 0 |
| 1996–97 | Preston NE | 6 | 0 |
| 1997–98 | Preston NE | 1 | 0 |
| **Total:** | | **21** | **0** |

## SPEDDING, Duncan — Defender

H: 6 1 W: 11 03 b.Camberley 7-9-77

*Source:* Trainee.

| | | | |
|---|---|---|---|
| 1996–97 | Southampton | 0 | 0 |
| 1997–98 | Southampton | 7 | 0 |
| **Total:** | | **7** | **0** |

## SPEED, Gary — Midfield

H: 5 11 W: 10 12 b.Mancot 8-9-69

*Source:* Trainee. *Honours:* Wales Under-21, 47 full caps, 3 goals.

| | | | |
|---|---|---|---|
| 1988–89 | Leeds U | 1 | 0 |
| 1989–90 | Leeds U | 25 | 3 |
| 1990–91 | Leeds U | 38 | 7 |
| 1991–92 | Leeds U | 41 | 7 |
| 1992–93 | Leeds U | 39 | 7 |
| 1993–94 | Leeds U | 36 | 10 |
| 1994–95 | Leeds U | 39 | 3 |
| 1995–96 | Leeds U | 29 | 2 |
| 1996–97 | Everton | 37 | 9 |
| 1997–98 | Everton | 21 | 7 |
| 1997–98 | Newcastle U | 13 | 1 |
| **Total:** | | **319** | **56** |

## SPENCER, John — Forward

H: 5 7 W: 11 05 b.Glasgow 11-9-70

*Source:* Rangers BC. *Honours:* Scotland Under-21, 14 full caps.

| | | | |
|---|---|---|---|
| 1986–87 | Rangers | 0 | 0 |
| 1987–88 | Rangers | 0 | 0 |
| 1988–89 | Rangers | 0 | 0 |
| 1988–89 | Morton (loan) | 4 | 1 |
| From Lai Sun. | | | |
| 1990–91 | Rangers | 5 | 1 |
| 1991–92 | Rangers | 8 | 1 |
| 1992–93 | Chelsea | 23 | 7 |
| 1993–94 | Chelsea | 19 | 5 |
| 1994–95 | Chelsea | 29 | 11 |
| 1995–96 | Chelsea | 28 | 13 |
| 1996–97 | Chelsea | 4 | 0 |
| 1996–97 | QPR | 25 | 17 |
| 1997–98 | QPR | 23 | 5 |
| 1997–98 | Everton | 6 | 0 |
| **Total:** | | **174** | **61** |

## SPENCER, Ryan — Midfield

b.Harrow 3-1-79

*Source:* Trainee.

| | | | |
|---|---|---|---|
| 1997–98 | Tottenham H | 0 | 0 |

## SPENCER, Simon — Midfield

H: 5 9 W: 10 04 b.Islington 10-9-76

*Source:* Trainee. *Honours:* England Youth.

| | | | |
|---|---|---|---|
| 1995–96 | Tottenham H | 0 | 0 |
| 1996–97 | Tottenham H | 0 | 0 |
| 1997–98 | Brentford | 1 | 0 |
| **Total:** | | **1** | **0** |

## SPINK, Dean — Forward

H: 6 1 W: 14 00 b.Halesowen 22-1-67

*Source:* Halesowen T.

| | | | |
|---|---|---|---|
| 1989–90 | Aston Villa | 0 | 0 |
| 1989–90 | Scarborough (loan) | 3 | 2 |
| 1989–90 | Bury (loan) | 6 | 1 |
| 1989–90 | Shrewsbury T | 13 | 5 |
| 1990–91 | Shrewsbury T | 43 | 6 |
| 1991–92 | Shrewsbury T | 40 | 1 |
| 1992–93 | Shrewsbury T | 23 | 1 |
| 1993–94 | Shrewsbury T | 40 | 18 |
| 1994–95 | Shrewsbury T | 39 | 11 |
| 1995–96 | Shrewsbury T | 34 | 6 |
| 1996–97 | Shrewsbury T | 41 | 4 |
| 1997–98 | Wrexham | 36 | 6 |
| **Total:** | | **318** | **61** |

## SPINK, Nigel — Goalkeeper

H: 6 2 W: 14 06 b.Chelmsford 8-8-58

*Source:* Chelmsford C. *Honours:* England B, 1 full cap.

| | | | |
|---|---|---|---|
| 1976–77 | Aston Villa | 0 | 0 |
| 1977–78 | Aston Villa | 0 | 0 |
| 1978–79 | Aston Villa | 0 | 0 |
| 1979–80 | Aston Villa | 1 | 0 |
| 1980–81 | Aston Villa | 0 | 0 |
| 1981–82 | Aston Villa | 0 | 0 |
| 1982–83 | Aston Villa | 22 | 0 |
| 1983–84 | Aston Villa | 28 | 0 |
| 1984–85 | Aston Villa | 19 | 0 |
| 1985–86 | Aston Villa | 31 | 0 |
| 1986–87 | Aston Villa | 32 | 0 |
| 1987–88 | Aston Villa | 44 | 0 |
| 1988–89 | Aston Villa | 34 | 0 |
| 1989–90 | Aston Villa | 38 | 0 |
| 1990–91 | Aston Villa | 34 | 0 |
| 1991–92 | Aston Villa | 23 | 0 |
| 1992–93 | Aston Villa | 25 | 0 |
| 1993–94 | Aston Villa | 15 | 0 |
| 1994–95 | Aston Villa | 13 | 0 |
| 1995–96 | Aston Villa | 2 | 0 |
| 1995–96 | WBA | 15 | 0 |
| 1996–97 | WBA | 4 | 0 |
| 1997–98 | WBA | 0 | 0 |
| 1997–98 | Millwall | 21 | 0 |
| **Total:** | | **401** | **0** |

## SPOONER, Nicky — Defender

H: 5 10 W: 11 09 b.Manchester 5-6-71

*Source:* Trainee.

| | | | |
|---|---|---|---|
| 1990–91 | Bolton W | 0 | 0 |
| 1991–92 | Bolton W | 15 | 1 |
| 1992–93 | Bolton W | 6 | 1 |
| 1993–94 | Bolton W | 1 | 0 |
| 1994–95 | Bolton W | 1 | 0 |
| 1995–96 | Bolton W | 0 | 0 |
| 1996–97 | Bolton W | 0 | 0 |
| 1997–98 | Bolton W | 0 | 0 |
| **Total:** | | **23** | **2** |

## SPRING, Matthew — Midfield

H: 5 11 W: 11 07 b.Harlow 17-11-79

*Source:* Trainee.

| | | | |
|---|---|---|---|
| 1997–98 | Luton T | 12 | 0 |
| **Total:** | | **12** | **0** |

## SQUIRES, Jamie — Defender

H: 6 2 W: 13 03 b.Preston 15-11-75

*Source:* Trainee.

| | | | |
|---|---|---|---|
| 1993–94 | Preston NE | 4 | 0 |
| 1994–95 | Preston NE | 11 | 0 |
| 1995–96 | Preston NE | 7 | 0 |
| 1996–97 | Preston NE | 9 | 0 |
| 1997–98 | Preston NE | 0 | 0 |
| 1997–98 | Mansfield T (loan) | 1 | 0 |
| 1997–98 | Dunfermline Ath | 5 | 0 |
| **Total:** | | **37** | **0** |

## SQUIRES, Oliver — Midfield

H: 5 11 W: 12 03 b.Harrow 15-9-80

*Source:* Trainee.

| | | | |
|---|---|---|---|
| 1997–98 | Watford | 0 | 0 |

## SRNICEK, Pavel — Goalkeeper

H: 6 2 W: 14 07 b.Ostrava 10-3-68

*Source:* Banik Ostrava. *Honours:* Czech Republic 18 full caps.

| | | | |
|---|---|---|---|
| 1990–91 | Newcastle U | 7 | 0 |
| 1991–92 | Newcastle U | 13 | 0 |
| 1992–93 | Newcastle U | 32 | 0 |
| 1993–94 | Newcastle U | 21 | 0 |
| 1994–95 | Newcastle U | 38 | 0 |
| 1995–96 | Newcastle U | 15 | 0 |
| 1996–97 | Newcastle U | 22 | 0 |
| 1997–98 | Newcastle U | 1 | 0 |
| **Total:** | | **149** | **0** |

## STALLARD, Mark — Forward

H: 5 11 W: 13 08 b.Derby 24-10-74

*Source:* Trainee.

| | | | |
|---|---|---|---|
| 1991–92 | Derby Co | 3 | 0 |
| 1992–93 | Derby Co | 5 | 0 |
| 1993–94 | Derby Co | 0 | 0 |
| 1994–95 | Derby Co | 16 | 2 |
| 1994–95 | Fulham (loan) | 4 | 3 |
| 1995–96 | Derby Co | 3 | 0 |
| 1995–96 | Bradford C | 21 | 9 |
| 1996–97 | Bradford C | 22 | 1 |
| 1996–97 | Preston NE (loan) | 4 | 1 |
| 1996–97 | Wycombe W | 12 | 4 |
| 1997–98 | Wycombe W | 43 | 17 |
| **Total:** | | **133** | **37** |

## STAMP, Darryn — Forward

H: 6 1 W: 11 10 b.Beverley 21-9-78

| | | | |
|---|---|---|---|
| 1997–98 | Scunthorpe U | 10 | 1 |
| **Total:** | | **10** | **1** |

## STAMP, Phil — Midfield

H: 5 10 W: 13 10 b.Middlesbrough 12-12-75

*Source:* Trainee. *Honours:* England Youth.

| | | | |
|---|---|---|---|
| 1992–93 | Middlesbrough | 0 | 0 |
| 1993–94 | Middlesbrough | 10 | 0 |
| 1994–95 | Middlesbrough | 3 | 0 |
| 1995–96 | Middlesbrough | 12 | 2 |
| 1996–97 | Middlesbrough | 24 | 1 |
| 1997–98 | Middlesbrough | 10 | 0 |
| **Total:** | | **59** | **3** |

## STAMPS, Scott — Defender

H: 5 9 W: 11 07 b.Edgbaston 20-3-75

*Source:* Trainee.

| | | | |
|---|---|---|---|
| 1992–93 | Torquay U | 2 | 0 |
| 1993–94 | Torquay U | 6 | 0 |
| 1994–95 | Torquay U | 25 | 1 |
| 1995–96 | Torquay U | 23 | 1 |
| 1996–97 | Torquay U | 30 | 3 |
| 1996–97 | Colchester U | 8 | 0 |
| 1997–98 | Colchester U | 27 | 1 |
| **Total:** | | **121** | **6** |

## STANDING, Michael — Midfield

b.Shoreham 20-3-81

*Source:* Trainee. *Honours:* England Schools.

| | | | |
|---|---|---|---|
| 1997–98 | Aston Villa | 0 | 0 |

## STANNARD, Jim — Goalkeeper

H: 6 2 W: 16 07 b.London 16-10-62

*Source:* Local.

| | | | |
|---|---|---|---|
| 1980–81 | Fulham | 17 | 0 |
| 1981–82 | Fulham | 2 | 0 |
| 1982–83 | Fulham | 0 | 0 |
| 1983–84 | Fulham | 15 | 0 |
| 1984–85 | Fulham | 7 | 0 |
| 1984–85 | Charlton Ath (loan) | 1 | 0 |
| 1984–85 | Southend U (loan) | 17 | 0 |
| 1985–86 | Southend U | 46 | 0 |
| 1986–87 | Southend U | 46 | 0 |
| 1987–88 | Fulham | 46 | 0 |
| 1988–89 | Fulham | 45 | 0 |
| 1989–90 | Fulham | 44 | 1 |
| 1990–91 | Fulham | 42 | 0 |
| 1991–92 | Fulham | 46 | 0 |
| 1992–93 | Fulham | 43 | 0 |
| 1993–94 | Fulham | 46 | 0 |
| 1994–95 | Fulham | 36 | 0 |
| 1995–96 | Gillingham | 46 | 0 |
| 1996–97 | Gillingham | 38 | 0 |
| 1997–98 | Gillingham | 20 | 0 |
| **Total:** | | **603** | **1** |

## STANSFIELD, James — Defender

b.Dewsbury 18-9-78

*Source:* Trainee.

| | | | |
|---|---|---|---|
| 1997–98 | Huddersfield T | 0 | 0 |

## STANT, Phil — Forward

H: 6 1 W: 12 07 b.Bolton 13-10-62

*Source:* Camberley.

| | | | |
|---|---|---|---|
| 1982–83 | Reading | 4 | 2 |
| From Army. | | | |
| 1986–87 | Hereford U | 9 | 1 |
| 1987–88 | Hereford U | 39 | 9 |
| 1988–89 | Hereford U | 41 | 28 |
| 1989–90 | Notts Co | 22 | 6 |
| 1990–91 | Notts Co | 0 | 0 |
| 1990–91 | Blackpool (loan) | 12 | 5 |
| 1990–91 | Lincoln C (loan) | 4 | 0 |
| 1990–91 | Huddersfield T (loan) | 5 | 1 |
| 1990–91 | Fulham | 19 | 5 |
| 1991–92 | Mansfield T | 40 | 26 |
| 1992–93 | Mansfield T | 17 | 6 |
| 1992–93 | Cardiff C | 24 | 11 |
| 1993–94 | Cardiff C | 36 | 10 |
| 1993–94 | Mansfield T (loan) | 4 | 1 |
| 1994–95 | Cardiff C | 19 | 13 |
| 1994–95 | Bury | 20 | 13 |
| 1995–96 | Bury | 34 | 9 |

| | | | |
|---|---|---|---|
| 1996–97 | Bury | 8 | 1 |
| 1996–97 | Northampton T (loan) | 5 | 2 |
| 1996–97 | Lincoln C | 22 | 15 |
| 1997–98 | Lincoln C | 21 | 2 |
| **Total:** | | **405** | **166** |

## STANTON, Nathan — Defender

b.Nottingham 6-5-81

*Source:* Trainee.

| | | | |
|---|---|---|---|
| 1997–98 | Scunthorpe U | 1 | 0 |
| **Total:** | | **1** | **0** |

## STARBUCK, Phil — Midfield

H: 5 10 W: 10 13 b.Nottingham 24-11-68

*Source:* Apprentice.

| | | | |
|---|---|---|---|
| 1986–87 | Nottingham F | 5 | 2 |
| 1987–88 | Nottingham F | 10 | 0 |
| 1987–88 | Birmingham C (loan) | 3 | 0 |
| 1988–89 | Nottingham F | 7 | 0 |
| 1989–90 | Nottingham F | 2 | 0 |
| 1989–90 | Hereford U (loan) | 6 | 0 |
| 1990–91 | Nottingham F | 12 | 0 |
| 1990–91 | Blackburn R (loan) | 6 | 1 |
| 1991–92 | Huddersfield T | 44 | 14 |
| 1992–93 | Huddersfield T | 38 | 9 |
| 1993–94 | Huddersfield T | 46 | 12 |
| 1994–95 | Huddersfield T | 9 | 1 |
| 1994–95 | Sheffield U | 23 | 1 |
| 1995–96 | Sheffield U | 11 | 1 |
| 1995–96 | Bristol C (loan) | 5 | 1 |
| 1996–97 | Sheffield U | 2 | 0 |
| 1997–98 | Oldham Ath | 9 | 1 |
| 1997–98 | Plymouth Arg | 7 | 0 |
| **Total:** | | **245** | **43** |

## STATHAM, Brian — Defender

H: 5 7 W: 11 06 b.Zimbabwe 21-5-69

*Source:* Apprentice. *Honours:* England Youth, Under-21.

| | | | |
|---|---|---|---|
| 1987–88 | Tottenham H | 18 | 0 |
| 1988–89 | Tottenham H | 6 | 0 |
| 1989–90 | Tottenham H | 0 | 0 |
| 1990–91 | Tottenham H | 0 | 0 |
| 1990–91 | Reading (loan) | 8 | 0 |
| 1991–92 | Tottenham H | 0 | 0 |
| 1991–92 | Bournemouth (loan) | 2 | 0 |
| 1991–92 | Brentford (loan) | 18 | 0 |
| 1992–93 | Brentford | 45 | 0 |
| 1993–94 | Brentford | 31 | 1 |
| 1994–95 | Brentford | 36 | 0 |
| 1995–96 | Brentford | 17 | 0 |
| 1996–97 | Brentford | 19 | 0 |
| 1997–98 | Gillingham | 20 | 0 |
| **Total:** | | **220** | **1** |

## STATON, Luke — Midfield

H: 5 7 W: 10 07 b.Doncaster 10-3-79

*Source:* Trainee. *Honours:* England Schools, Youth.

| | | | |
|---|---|---|---|
| 1995–96 | Blackburn R | 0 | 0 |
| 1996–97 | Blackburn R | 0 | 0 |
| 1997–98 | Blackburn R | 0 | 0 |

## STAUNTON, Steve — Defender

H: 6 1 W: 12 11 b.Drogheda 19-1-69

*Source:* Dundalk. *Honours:* Eire Under-21, 74 full caps, 5 goals.

| | | | |
|---|---|---|---|
| 1986–87 | Liverpool | 0 | 0 |
| 1987–88 | Liverpool | 0 | 0 |
| 1987–88 | Bradford C (loan) | 8 | 0 |
| 1988–89 | Liverpool | 21 | 0 |
| 1989–90 | Liverpool | 20 | 0 |
| 1990–91 | Liverpool | 24 | 0 |
| 1991–92 | Aston Villa | 37 | 4 |
| 1992–93 | Aston Villa | 42 | 2 |
| 1993–94 | Aston Villa | 24 | 2 |
| 1994–95 | Aston Villa | 35 | 5 |
| 1995–96 | Aston Villa | 13 | 0 |
| 1996–97 | Aston Villa | 30 | 2 |
| 1997–98 | Aston Villa | 27 | 1 |
| **Total:** | | **281** | **16** |

## STEELE, Lee — Forward

H: 5 8 W: 12 05 b.Liverpool 2-12-73

*Source:* Bootle, Northwich V.

| | | | |
|---|---|---|---|
| 1997–98 | Shrewsbury T | 38 | 13 |
| **Total:** | | **38** | **13** |

## STEFANOVIC, Dejan — Defender

H: 6 2 W: 13 00 b.Yugoslavia 28-10-74

*Honours:* Yugoslavia 10 full caps.

| | | | |
|---|---|---|---|
| 1995–96 | Sheffield W | 6 | 0 |
| 1996–97 | Sheffield W | 29 | 2 |
| 1997–98 | Sheffield W | 20 | 2 |
| **Total:** | | **55** | **4** |

## STEIN, Mark — Forward

H: 5 6 W: 11 07 b.S. Africa 29-1-66

*Honours:* England Youth.

| | | | |
|---|---|---|---|
| 1983–84 | Luton T | 1 | 0 |
| 1984–85 | Luton T | 1 | 0 |

| | | | |
|---|---|---|---|
| 1985–86 | Luton T | 6 | 0 |
| 1985–86 | Aldershot (loan) | 2 | 1 |
| 1986–87 | Luton T | 21 | 8 |
| 1987–88 | Luton T | 25 | 11 |
| 1988–89 | QPR | 31 | 4 |
| 1989–90 | QPR | 2 | 0 |
| 1989–90 | Oxford U | 41 | 9 |
| 1990–91 | Oxford U | 34 | 8 |
| 1991–92 | Oxford U | 7 | 1 |
| 1991–92 | Stoke C | 36 | 16 |
| 1992–93 | Stoke C | 46 | 26 |
| 1993–94 | Stoke C | 12 | 8 |
| 1993–94 | Chelsea | 18 | 13 |
| 1994–95 | Chelsea | 24 | 8 |
| 1995–96 | Chelsea | 8 | 0 |
| 1996–97 | Chelsea | 0 | 0 |
| 1996–97 | Stoke C (loan) | 11 | 4 |
| 1997–98 | Chelsea | 0 | 0 |
| 1997–98 | Ipswich T (loan) | 7 | 2 |
| 1997–98 | Bournemouth (loan) | 11 | 4 |
| **Total:** | | **344** | **123** |

## STEINER, Rob — Forward

H: 6 2 W: 13 00 b.Finsprong 20-6-73

*Honours:* Sweden 4 full caps, 1 goal.

| | | | |
|---|---|---|---|
| 1995 | Norrkoping | 16 | 2 |
| 1996 | Norrkoping | 25 | 12 |
| 1996–97 | Bradford C | 15 | 4 |
| 1997 | Norrkoping | 6 | 1 |
| 1997–98 | Bradford C | 37 | 10 |
| **Total:** | | **99** | **29** |

## STENSAAS, Stale — Defender

H: 5 11 W: 12 01 b.Trondheim 7-7-71

| | | | |
|---|---|---|---|
| 1992 | Rosenborg | 1 | 0 |
| 1993 | Rosenborg | 6 | 0 |
| 1994 | Rosenborg | 20 | 0 |
| 1995 | Rosenborg | 24 | 1 |
| 1996 | Rosenborg | 25 | 1 |
| 1997 | Rosenborg | 9 | 0 |
| 1997–98 | Rangers | 20 | 1 |
| **Total:** | | **105** | **3** |

## STEPHENSON, Ashlyn — Goalkeeper

H: 6 2 W: 11 05 b.Manchester 6-7-74

| | | | |
|---|---|---|---|
| 1995–96 | Birmingham C | 0 | 0 |
| 1995–96 | Darlington | 1 | 0 |
| 1996–97 | Darlington | 0 | 0 |
| From Kilkenny. | | | |
| 1997–98 | Darlington | 0 | 0 |
| **Total:** | | **1** | **0** |

## STEPHENSON, Lee — Forward

H: 5 11 W: 13 00 b.Grimsby 18-8-78

*Source:* Trainee.

| | | | |
|---|---|---|---|
| 1997–98 | Grimsby T | 0 | 0 |

## STEPHENSON, Paul — Forward

H: 5 10 W: 12 07 b.Wallsend 2-1-68

*Source:* Apprentice. *Honours:* England Youth.

| | | | |
|---|---|---|---|
| 1985–86 | Newcastle U | 22 | 1 |
| 1986–87 | Newcastle U | 24 | 0 |
| 1987–88 | Newcastle U | 7 | 0 |
| 1988–89 | Newcastle U | 8 | 0 |
| 1989–90 | Millwall | 12 | 1 |
| 1989–90 | Millwall | 23 | 2 |
| 1990–91 | Millwall | 30 | 1 |
| 1991–92 | Millwall | 28 | 2 |
| 1992–93 | Millwall | 5 | 0 |
| 1992–93 | Gillingham (loan) | 12 | 2 |
| 1992–93 | Brentford | 11 | 0 |
| 1993–94 | Brentford | 25 | 0 |
| 1994–95 | Brentford | 34 | 2 |
| 1995–96 | York C | 27 | 2 |
| 1996–97 | York C | 35 | 1 |
| 1997–98 | York C | 35 | 5 |
| 1997–98 | Hartlepool U | 3 | 0 |
| **Total:** | | **341** | **19** |

## STEVENS, David — Forward

H: 5 10 W: 11 04 b.Ashford 29-4-79

*Source:* Trainee.

| | | | |
|---|---|---|---|
| 1996–97 | Crystal Palace | 0 | 0 |
| 1997–98 | Crystal Palace | 0 | 0 |

## STEVENS, Gary — Defender

H: 5 11 W: 11 02 b.Barrow 27-3-63

*Source:* Apprentice. *Honours:* England 46 full caps.

| | | | |
|---|---|---|---|
| 1980–81 | Everton | 0 | 0 |
| 1981–82 | Everton | 19 | 1 |
| 1982–83 | Everton | 28 | 0 |
| 1983–84 | Everton | 27 | 1 |
| 1984–85 | Everton | 37 | 3 |
| 1985–86 | Everton | 41 | 1 |
| 1986–87 | Everton | 25 | 2 |
| 1987–88 | Everton | 31 | 0 |
| 1988–89 | Rangers | 35 | 1 |
| 1989–90 | Rangers | 35 | 1 |
| 1990–91 | Rangers | 36 | 4 |
| 1991–92 | Rangers | 43 | 2 |
| 1992–93 | Rangers | 9 | 0 |
| 1993–94 | Rangers | 29 | 0 |

| | | | |
|---|---|---|---|
| 1994–95 | Tranmere R | 37 | 1 |
| 1995–96 | Tranmere R | 34 | 0 |
| 1996–97 | Tranmere R | 31 | 0 |
| 1997–98 | Tranmere R | 25 | 1 |
| **Total:** | | **522** | **18** |

## STEVENS, Ian — Forward

H: 5 10 W: 12 07 b.Malta 21-10-66

*Source:* Trainee.

| | | | |
|---|---|---|---|
| 1984–85 | Preston NE | 4 | 1 |
| 1985–86 | Preston NE | 7 | 1 |
| 1986–87 | Stockport Co | 2 | 0 |
| From Lancaster C. | | | |
| 1986–87 | Bolton W | 8 | 2 |
| 1987–88 | Bolton W | 9 | 0 |
| 1988–89 | Bolton W | 21 | 5 |
| 1989–90 | Bolton W | 4 | 0 |
| 1990–91 | Bolton W | 5 | 0 |
| 1991–92 | Bury | 45 | 17 |
| 1992–93 | Bury | 32 | 14 |
| 1993–94 | Bury | 33 | 7 |
| 1994–95 | Shrewsbury T | 38 | 8 |
| 1995–96 | Shrewsbury T | 32 | 12 |
| 1996–97 | Shrewsbury T | 41 | 17 |
| 1996–97 | Carlisle U | 0 | 0 |
| 1997–98 | Carlisle U | 37 | 17 |
| **Total:** | | **318** | **101** |

## STEVENS, Keith — Defender

H: 6 0 W: 12 12 b.Merton 21-6-64

*Source:* Apprentice.

| | | | |
|---|---|---|---|
| 1980–81 | Millwall | 1 | 0 |
| 1981–82 | Millwall | 7 | 0 |
| 1982–83 | Millwall | 26 | 0 |
| 1983–84 | Millwall | 17 | 0 |
| 1984–85 | Millwall | 41 | 0 |
| 1985–86 | Millwall | 33 | 1 |
| 1986–87 | Millwall | 35 | 1 |
| 1987–88 | Millwall | 35 | 1 |
| 1988–89 | Millwall | 23 | 0 |
| 1989–90 | Millwall | 28 | 0 |
| 1990–91 | Millwall | 42 | 1 |
| 1991–92 | Millwall | 27 | 0 |
| 1992–93 | Millwall | 31 | 2 |
| 1993–94 | Millwall | 44 | 1 |
| 1994–95 | Millwall | 20 | 0 |
| 1995–96 | Millwall | 39 | 2 |
| 1996–97 | Millwall | 6 | 0 |
| 1997–98 | Millwall | 4 | 0 |
| **Total:** | | **459** | **9** |

## STEVENS, Mark — Forward

H: 6 5 W: 12 07 b.Swindon 3-12-77

*Source:* School. *Honours:* England Schools.

| | | | |
|---|---|---|---|
| 1996–97 | Oxford U | 0 | 0 |
| 1997–98 | Oxford U | 1 | 0 |
| **Total:** | | **1** | **0** |

## STEVENS, Shaun — Defender

H: 5 10 W: 11 07 b.Chertsey 8-3-76

| | | | |
|---|---|---|---|
| 1994–95 | Wycombe W | 0 | 0 |
| 1995–96 | Wycombe W | 0 | 0 |
| 1996–97 | Wycombe W | 0 | 0 |
| 1997–98 | Millwall | 0 | 0 |

## STEWART, Gareth — Goalkeeper

H: 6 0 W: 12 08 b.Preston 3-2-80

*Source:* Trainee. *Honours:* England Schools, Youth.

| | | | |
|---|---|---|---|
| 1996–97 | Blackburn R | 0 | 0 |
| 1997–98 | Blackburn R | 0 | 0 |

## STEWART, Marcus — Forward

H: 5 10 W: 11 00 b.Bristol 7-11-72

*Source:* Trainee. *Honours:* England Schools, Football League.

| | | | |
|---|---|---|---|
| 1991–92 | Bristol R | 33 | 5 |
| 1992–93 | Bristol R | 38 | 11 |
| 1993–94 | Bristol R | 29 | 5 |
| 1994–95 | Bristol R | 27 | 15 |
| 1995–96 | Bristol R | 44 | 21 |
| 1996–97 | Huddersfield T | 20 | 7 |
| 1997–98 | Huddersfield T | 41 | 15 |
| **Total:** | | **232** | **79** |

## STEWART, Michael — Midfield

b.Edinburgh 26-2-81

*Source:* Trainee.

| | | | |
|---|---|---|---|
| 1997–98 | Manchester U | 0 | 0 |

## STEWART, Paul — Forward

H: 6 0 W: 13 10 b.Manchester 7-10-64

*Source:* Apprentice. *Honours:* England Youth, Under-21, B, 3 full caps.

| | | | |
|---|---|---|---|
| 1981–82 | Blackpool | 14 | 3 |
| 1982–83 | Blackpool | 38 | 7 |
| 1983–84 | Blackpool | 44 | 10 |
| 1984–85 | Blackpool | 31 | 7 |
| 1985–86 | Blackpool | 42 | 8 |

## Stewart, Simon

| | | | |
|---|---|---|---|
| 1986–87 | Blackpool | 32 | 21 |
| 1986–87 | Manchester C | 11 | 2 |
| 1987–88 | Manchester C | 40 | 24 |
| 1988–89 | Tottenham H | 30 | 12 |
| 1989–90 | Tottenham H | 28 | 8 |
| 1990–91 | Tottenham H | 35 | 3 |
| 1991–92 | Tottenham H | 38 | 5 |
| 1992–93 | Liverpool | 24 | 1 |
| 1993–94 | Liverpool | 8 | 0 |
| 1993–94 | Crystal Palace (loan) | 18 | 3 |
| 1994–95 | Liverpool | 0 | 0 |
| 1994–95 | Wolverhampton W (loan) | 8 | 2 |
| 1994–95 | Burnley (loan) | 6 | 0 |
| 1995–96 | Liverpool | 0 | 0 |
| 1995–96 | Sunderland | 12 | 1 |
| 1996–97 | Sunderland | 24 | 4 |
| 1997–98 | Stoke C | 22 | 3 |
| **Total:** | | **505** | **124** |

## STEWART, Simon — Defender

H: 6 2 W: 13 09 b.Leeds 1-11-73

*Source:* Trainee.

| | | | |
|---|---|---|---|
| 1992–93 | Sheffield W | 6 | 0 |
| 1993–94 | Sheffield W | 0 | 0 |
| 1994–95 | Sheffield W | 0 | 0 |
| 1995–96 | Sheffield W | 0 | 0 |
| 1995–96 | Shrewsbury T (loan) | 4 | 0 |
| 1996–97 | Fulham | 3 | 0 |
| 1997–98 | Fulham | 0 | 0 |
| **Total:** | | **13** | **0** |

## STILLIE, Derek — Goalkeeper

H: 6 0 W: 12 00 b.Irvine 3-12-73

*Source:* Notts Co. *Honours:* Scotland Under-21.

| | | | |
|---|---|---|---|
| 1991–92 | Aberdeen | 0 | 0 |
| 1992–93 | Aberdeen | 0 | 0 |
| 1993–94 | Aberdeen | 5 | 0 |
| 1994–95 | Aberdeen | 0 | 0 |
| 1995–96 | Aberdeen | 0 | 0 |
| 1996–97 | Aberdeen | 8 | 0 |
| 1997–98 | Aberdeen | 2 | 0 |
| **Total:** | | **15** | **0** |

## STIMAC, Igor — Defender

H: 6 2 W: 13 00 b.Metkovic 6-9-67

*Source:* Cibalia Vinkovci, Hajduk Split. *Honours:* Yugoslavia Youth. Croatia 36 full caps, 2 goals.

| | | | |
|---|---|---|---|
| 1992–93 | Cadiz | 32 | 0 |
| 1993–94 | Cadiz | 30 | 4 |
| 1994–95 | Hajduk Split | 21 | 2 |
| 1995–96 | Derby Co | 27 | 1 |
| 1996–97 | Derby Co | 21 | 1 |
| 1997–98 | Derby Co | 22 | 1 |
| **Total:** | | **153** | **9** |

## STIMSON, Mark — Defender

H: 5 10 W: 12 06 b.Plaistow 27-12-67

*Source:* Trainee.

| | | | |
|---|---|---|---|
| 1984–85 | Tottenham H | 0 | 0 |
| 1985–86 | Tottenham H | 0 | 0 |
| 1986–87 | Tottenham H | 1 | 0 |
| 1987–88 | Tottenham H | 0 | 0 |
| 1987–88 | Leyton Orient (loan) | 10 | 0 |
| 1988–89 | Tottenham H | 1 | 0 |
| 1988–89 | Gillingham (loan) | 18 | 0 |
| 1989–90 | Newcastle U | 37 | 1 |
| 1990–91 | Newcastle U | 23 | 1 |
| 1991–92 | Newcastle U | 24 | 0 |
| 1992–93 | Newcastle U | 2 | 0 |
| 1992–93 | Portsmouth (loan) | 4 | 0 |
| 1993–94 | Portsmouth | 29 | 1 |
| 1994–95 | Portsmouth | 15 | 0 |
| 1995–96 | Portsmouth | 14 | 1 |
| 1995–96 | Barnet (loan) | 5 | 0 |
| 1995–96 | Southend U | 10 | 0 |
| 1996–97 | Southend U | 9 | 0 |
| 1997–98 | Southend U | 20 | 0 |
| **Total:** | | **222** | **4** |

## STOCKDALE, Robert — Defender

b.Redcar 30-11-79

*Source:* Trainee.

| | | | |
|---|---|---|---|
| 1997–98 | Middlesbrough | 1 | 0 |
| **Total:** | | **1** | **0** |

## STOCKLEY, Sam — Defender

H: 5 8 W: 11 00 b.Tiverton 5-9-77

*Source:* Trainee.

| | | | |
|---|---|---|---|
| 1996–97 | Southampton | 0 | 0 |
| 1996–97 | Barnet | 21 | 0 |
| 1997–98 | Barnet | 41 | 0 |
| **Total:** | | **62** | **0** |

## STOCKWELL, Mick — Midfield

H: 5 9 W: 11 04 b.Chelmsford 14-2-65

*Source:* Apprentice.

| | | | |
|---|---|---|---|
| 1982–83 | Ipswich T | 0 | 0 |
| 1983–84 | Ipswich T | 0 | 0 |
| 1984–85 | Ipswich T | 0 | 0 |
| 1985–86 | Ipswich T | 8 | 0 |

| | | | |
|---|---|---|---|
| 1986–87 | Ipswich T | 21 | 1 |
| 1987–88 | Ipswich T | 43 | 1 |
| 1988–89 | Ipswich T | 23 | 2 |
| 1989–90 | Ipswich T | 34 | 3 |
| 1990–91 | Ipswich T | 44 | 6 |
| 1991–92 | Ipswich T | 46 | 2 |
| 1992–93 | Ipswich T | 39 | 4 |
| 1993–94 | Ipswich T | 42 | 1 |
| 1994–95 | Ipswich T | 15 | 0 |
| 1995–96 | Ipswich T | 37 | 1 |
| 1996–97 | Ipswich T | 43 | 7 |
| 1997–98 | Ipswich T | 46 | 3 |
| **Total:** | | **441** | **31** |

## STOKER, Gareth — Midfield

H: 5 9 W: 11 04 b.Bishop Auckland 22-2-73

*Source:* Leeds U Trainee.

| | | | |
|---|---|---|---|
| 1991–92 | Hull C | 24 | 2 |
| 1992–93 | Hull C | 6 | 0 |
| 1993–94 | Hull C | 0 | 0 |
| 1994–95 | Hereford U | 10 | 0 |
| 1995–96 | Hereford U | 33 | 3 |
| 1996–97 | Hereford U | 27 | 3 |
| 1996–97 | Cardiff C | 17 | 3 |
| 1997–98 | Cardiff C | 20 | 1 |
| **Total:** | | **137** | **12** |

## STOKES, Dean — Defender

H: 5 8 W: 11 02 b.Birmingham 23-5-70

*Source:* Halesowen T.

| | | | |
|---|---|---|---|
| 1992–93 | Port Vale | 0 | 0 |
| 1993–94 | Port Vale | 21 | 0 |
| 1994–95 | Port Vale | 3 | 0 |
| 1995–96 | Port Vale | 18 | 0 |
| 1996–97 | Port Vale | 10 | 0 |
| 1997–98 | Port Vale | 8 | 0 |
| **Total:** | | **60** | **0** |

## STOKOE, Graham — Midfield

H: 6 1 W: 12 13 b.Newcastle 17-12-75

*Source:* Birmingham C.

| | | | |
|---|---|---|---|
| 1994–95 | Stoke C | 0 | 0 |
| 1995–96 | Stoke C | 0 | 0 |
| 1995–96 | Hartlepool U (loan) | 8 | 0 |
| 1996–97 | Stoke C | 2 | 0 |
| 1997–98 | Stoke C | 0 | 0 |
| **Total:** | | **10** | **0** |

## STONE, Steve — Midfield

H: 5 8 W: 12 05 b.Gateshead 20-8-71

*Source:* Trainee. *Honours:* England 9 full caps, 2 goals.

| | | | |
|---|---|---|---|
| 1989–90 | Nottingham F | 0 | 0 |
| 1990–91 | Nottingham F | 0 | 0 |
| 1991–92 | Nottingham F | 1 | 0 |
| 1992–93 | Nottingham F | 12 | 1 |
| 1993–94 | Nottingham F | 45 | 5 |
| 1994–95 | Nottingham F | 41 | 5 |
| 1995–96 | Nottingham F | 34 | 7 |
| 1996–97 | Nottingham F | 5 | 0 |
| 1997–98 | Nottingham F | 29 | 2 |
| **Total:** | | **167** | **20** |

## STONES, Craig — Midfield

b.Scunthorpe 31-5-80

*Source:* Trainee.

| | | | |
|---|---|---|---|
| 1996–97 | Lincoln C | 2 | 0 |
| 1997–98 | Lincoln C | 15 | 0 |
| **Total:** | | **17** | **0** |

## STORER, Stuart — Forward

H: 5 11 W: 12 12 b.Rugby 16-1-67

*Source:* Local.

| | | | |
|---|---|---|---|
| 1983–84 | Mansfield T | 1 | 0 |
| 1984–85 | Birmingham C | 0 | 0 |
| 1985–86 | Birmingham C | 2 | 0 |
| 1986–87 | Birmingham C | 6 | 0 |
| 1986–87 | Everton | 0 | 0 |
| 1987–88 | Everton | 0 | 0 |
| 1987–88 | Wigan Ath (loan) | 12 | 0 |
| 1987–88 | Bolton W | 15 | 1 |
| 1988–89 | Bolton W | 23 | 2 |
| 1989–90 | Bolton W | 38 | 4 |
| 1990–91 | Bolton W | 35 | 5 |
| 1991–92 | Bolton W | 9 | 0 |
| 1992–93 | Bolton W | 3 | 0 |
| 1992–93 | Exeter C | 10 | 4 |
| 1993–94 | Exeter C | 44 | 2 |
| 1994–95 | Exeter C | 23 | 2 |
| 1994–95 | Brighton & HA | 2 | 1 |
| 1995–96 | Brighton & HA | 38 | 2 |
| 1996–97 | Brighton & HA | 42 | 6 |
| 1997–98 | Brighton & HA | 37 | 2 |
| **Total:** | | **340** | **31** |

## STOWELL, Mike — Goalkeeper

H: 6 2 W: 13 10 b.Portsmouth 19-4-65

*Source:* Leyland Motors.

| | | | |
|---|---|---|---|
| 1984–85 | Preston NE | 0 | 0 |

| | | | |
|---|---|---|---|
| 1985–86 | Preston NE | 0 | 0 |
| 1985–86 | Everton | 0 | 0 |
| 1986–87 | Everton | 0 | 0 |
| 1987–88 | Chester C (loan) | 14 | 0 |
| 1987–88 | York C (loan) | 6 | 0 |
| 1987–88 | Manchester C (loan) | 14 | 0 |
| 1988–89 | Everton | 0 | 0 |
| 1988–89 | Port Vale (loan) | 7 | 0 |
| 1988–89 | Wolverhampton W (loan) | 7 | 0 |
| 1989–90 | Everton | 0 | 0 |
| 1989–90 | Preston NE (loan) | 2 | 0 |
| 1990–91 | Wolverhampton W | 39 | 0 |
| 1991–92 | Wolverhampton W | 46 | 0 |
| 1992–93 | Wolverhampton W | 26 | 0 |
| 1993–94 | Wolverhampton W | 46 | 0 |
| 1994–95 | Wolverhampton W | 37 | 0 |
| 1995–96 | Wolverhampton W | 38 | 0 |
| 1996–97 | Wolverhampton W | 46 | 0 |
| 1997–98 | Wolverhampton W | 35 | 0 |
| **Total:** | | **363** | **0** |

## STRACHAN, Gavin — Midfield

H: 5 10 W: 11 07 b.Aberdeen 23-12-78

*Source:* Trainee. *Honours:* Scotland Under-21.

| | | | |
|---|---|---|---|
| 1996–97 | Coventry C | 0 | 0 |
| 1997–98 | Coventry C | 9 | 0 |
| **Total:** | | **9** | **0** |

## STRACHAN, Gordon — Midfield

H: 5 6 W: 10 06 b.Edinburgh 9-2-57

| | | | |
|---|---|---|---|
| 1974–75 | Dundee | 1 | 0 |
| 1975–76 | Dundee | 23 | 6 |
| 1976–77 | Dundee | 36 | 7 |
| 1977–78 | Aberdeen | 12 | 2 |
| 1978–79 | Aberdeen | 31 | 5 |
| 1979–80 | Aberdeen | 33 | 10 |
| 1980–81 | Aberdeen | 20 | 6 |
| 1981–82 | Aberdeen | 30 | 7 |
| 1982–83 | Aberdeen | 32 | 12 |
| 1983–84 | Aberdeen | 25 | 13 |
| 1984–85 | Manchester U | 41 | 15 |
| 1985–86 | Manchester U | 28 | 5 |
| 1986–87 | Manchester U | 34 | 4 |
| 1987–88 | Manchester U | 36 | 8 |
| 1988–89 | Manchester U | 21 | 1 |
| 1988–89 | Leeds U | 11 | 3 |
| 1989–90 | Leeds U | 46 | 16 |
| 1990–91 | Leeds U | 34 | 7 |
| 1991–92 | Leeds U | 36 | 4 |
| 1992–93 | Leeds U | 31 | 4 |
| 1993–94 | Leeds U | 33 | 3 |
| 1994–95 | Leeds U | 6 | 0 |
| 1994–95 | Coventry C | 5 | 0 |
| 1995–96 | Coventry C | 12 | 0 |
| 1996–97 | Coventry C | 9 | 0 |
| 1997–98 | Coventry C | 0 | 0 |
| **Total:** | | **626** | **138** |

## STREET, Kevin — Forward

H: 5 10 W: 10 08 b.Crewe 25-11-77

*Source:* Trainee.

| | | | |
|---|---|---|---|
| 1996–97 | Crewe Alex | 0 | 0 |
| 1997–98 | Crewe Alex | 32 | 4 |
| **Total:** | | **32** | **4** |

## STREETER, Terry — Midfield

b.Brighton 26-10-79

*Source:* Trainee.

| | | | |
|---|---|---|---|
| 1997–98 | Brighton & HA | 2 | 0 |
| **Total:** | | **2** | **0** |

## STRODDER, Gary — Defender

H: 6 1 W: 13 03 b.Cleckheaton 1-4-65

*Source:* Apprentice.

| | | | |
|---|---|---|---|
| 1982–83 | Lincoln C | 8 | 0 |
| 1983–84 | Lincoln C | 22 | 1 |
| 1984–85 | Lincoln C | 26 | 2 |
| 1985–86 | Lincoln C | 43 | 1 |
| 1986–87 | Lincoln C | 33 | 2 |
| 1986–87 | West Ham U | 12 | 0 |
| 1987–88 | West Ham U | 30 | 1 |
| 1988–89 | West Ham U | 7 | 0 |
| 1989–90 | West Ham U | 16 | 1 |
| 1990–91 | WBA | 34 | 1 |
| 1991–92 | WBA | 37 | 3 |
| 1992–93 | WBA | 29 | 1 |
| 1993–94 | WBA | 21 | 2 |
| 1994–95 | WBA | 19 | 1 |
| 1995–96 | Notts Co | 43 | 3 |
| 1996–97 | Notts Co | 28 | 2 |
| 1997–98 | Notts Co | 39 | 4 |
| **Total:** | | **447** | **25** |

## STRONG, Greg — Defender

H: 6 2 W: 11 12 b.Bolton 5-9-75

*Source:* Trainee. *Honours:* England Schools, Youth.

| | | | |
|---|---|---|---|
| 1992–93 | Wigan Ath | 0 | 0 |
| 1993–94 | Wigan Ath | 18 | 1 |
| 1994–95 | Wigan Ath | 17 | 2 |
| 1995–96 | Bolton W | 1 | 0 |
| 1996–97 | Bolton W | 0 | 0 |

| | | | |
|---|---|---|---|
| 1997–98 | Bolton W | 0 | 0 |
| 1997–98 | Blackpool (loan) | 11 | 1 |
| **Total:** | | **47** | **4** |

## STUART, Graham — Midfield

H: 5 8 W: 11 11 b.Tooting 24-10-70

*Source:* Trainee. *Honours:* FA Schools, England Under-21.

| | | | |
|---|---|---|---|
| 1989–90 | Chelsea | 2 | 1 |
| 1990–91 | Chelsea | 19 | 4 |
| 1991–92 | Chelsea | 27 | 0 |
| 1992–93 | Chelsea | 39 | 9 |
| 1993–94 | Everton | 30 | 3 |
| 1994–95 | Everton | 28 | 3 |
| 1995–96 | Everton | 29 | 9 |
| 1996–97 | Everton | 35 | 5 |
| 1997–98 | Everton | 14 | 2 |
| 1997–98 | Sheffield U | 28 | 5 |
| **Total:** | | **251** | **41** |

## STUART, Jamie — Defender

H: 5 10 W: 11 00 b.Southwark 15-10-76

*Source:* Trainee. *Honours:* England Youth, Under-21.

| | | | |
|---|---|---|---|
| 1994–95 | Charlton Ath | 12 | 0 |
| 1995–96 | Charlton Ath | 27 | 2 |
| 1996–97 | Charlton Ath | 10 | 1 |
| 1997–98 | Charlton Ath | 1 | 0 |
| **Total:** | | **50** | **3** |

## STUART, Mark — Midfield

H: 5 9 W: 11 09 b.Hammersmith 15-12-66

*Source:* QPR Schoolboy.

| | | | |
|---|---|---|---|
| 1984–85 | Charlton Ath | 6 | 1 |
| 1985–86 | Charlton Ath | 30 | 12 |
| 1986–87 | Charlton Ath | 36 | 9 |
| 1987–88 | Charlton Ath | 31 | 6 |
| 1988–89 | Charlton Ath | 4 | 0 |
| 1988–89 | Plymouth Arg | 32 | 5 |
| 1989–90 | Plymouth Arg | 25 | 6 |
| 1989–90 | Ipswich T (loan) | 5 | 2 |
| 1990–91 | Bradford C | 13 | 2 |
| 1991–92 | Bradford C | 16 | 3 |
| 1992–93 | Bradford C | 0 | 0 |
| 1992–93 | Huddersfield T | 15 | 3 |
| 1993–94 | Rochdale | 42 | 13 |
| 1994–95 | Rochdale | 31 | 2 |
| 1995–96 | Rochdale | 34 | 13 |
| 1996–97 | Rochdale | 31 | 7 |
| 1997–98 | Rochdale | 45 | 6 |
| **Total:** | | **396** | **90** |

## STUBBS, Alan — Defender

H: 6 2 W: 13 10 b.Kirkby 6-10-71

*Source:* Trainee.

| | | | |
|---|---|---|---|
| 1990–91 | Bolton W | 23 | 0 |
| 1991–92 | Bolton W | 32 | 1 |
| 1992–93 | Bolton W | 42 | 2 |
| 1993–94 | Bolton W | 41 | 1 |
| 1994–95 | Bolton W | 39 | 1 |
| 1995–96 | Bolton W | 25 | 4 |
| 1996–97 | Celtic | 20 | 0 |
| 1997–98 | Celtic | 29 | 1 |
| **Total:** | | **251** | **10** |

## STURGESS, Paul — Defender

H: 5 11 W: 12 05 b.Dartford 4-8-75

*Source:* Trainee.

| | | | |
|---|---|---|---|
| 1992–93 | Charlton Ath | 4 | 0 |
| 1993–94 | Charlton Ath | 8 | 0 |
| 1994–95 | Charlton Ath | 23 | 0 |
| 1995–96 | Charlton Ath | 13 | 0 |
| 1996–97 | Charlton Ath | 3 | 0 |
| 1997–98 | Millwall | 14 | 0 |
| **Total:** | | **65** | **0** |

## STURRIDGE, Dean — Forward

H: 5 8 W: 12 06 b.Birmingham 27-7-73

*Source:* Trainee.

| | | | |
|---|---|---|---|
| 1991–92 | Derby Co | 1 | 0 |
| 1992–93 | Derby Co | 10 | 0 |
| 1993–94 | Derby Co | 0 | 0 |
| 1994–95 | Derby Co | 12 | 1 |
| 1994–95 | Torquay U (loan) | 10 | 5 |
| 1995–96 | Derby Co | 39 | 20 |
| 1996–97 | Derby Co | 30 | 11 |
| 1997–98 | Derby Co | 30 | 9 |
| **Total:** | | **132** | **46** |

## STURRIDGE, Simon — Forward

H: 5 6 W: 11 10 b.Birmingham 9-12-69

*Source:* Trainee.

| | | | |
|---|---|---|---|
| 1988–89 | Birmingham C | 21 | 3 |
| 1989–90 | Birmingham C | 31 | 10 |
| 1990–91 | Birmingham C | 38 | 6 |
| 1991–92 | Birmingham C | 40 | 10 |
| 1992–93 | Birmingham C | 20 | 1 |
| 1993–94 | Birmingham C | 0 | 0 |
| 1993–94 | Stoke C | 13 | 0 |
| 1994–95 | Stoke C | 8 | 1 |
| 1995–96 | Stoke C | 41 | 13 |

Sullivan, Neil

| | | | |
|---|---|---|---|
| 1996–97 | Stoke C | 5 | 0 |
| 1997–98 | Stoke C | 1 | 0 |
| **Total:** | | **218** | **44** |

## SULLIVAN, Neil — Goalkeeper

H: 6 0 W: 12 01 b.Sutton 24-2-70

*Source:* Trainee. *Honours:* Scotland 3 full caps.

| | | | |
|---|---|---|---|
| 1988–89 | Wimbledon | 0 | 0 |
| 1989–90 | Wimbledon | 0 | 0 |
| 1990–91 | Wimbledon | 1 | 0 |
| 1991–92 | Wimbledon | 1 | 0 |
| 1991–92 | Crystal Palace (loan) | 1 | 0 |
| 1992–93 | Wimbledon | 1 | 0 |
| 1993–94 | Wimbledon | 2 | 0 |
| 1994–95 | Wimbledon | 11 | 0 |
| 1995–96 | Wimbledon | 16 | 0 |
| 1996–97 | Wimbledon | 36 | 0 |
| 1997–98 | Wimbledon | 38 | 0 |
| **Total:** | | **107** | **0** |

## SUMMERBEE, Nicky — Forward

H: 5 8 W: 11 08 b.Altrincham 26-8-71

*Source:* Trainee. *Honours:* England Under-21.

| | | | |
|---|---|---|---|
| 1989–90 | Swindon T | 1 | 0 |
| 1990–91 | Swindon T | 7 | 0 |
| 1991–92 | Swindon T | 27 | 0 |
| 1992–93 | Swindon T | 39 | 3 |
| 1993–94 | Swindon T | 38 | 3 |
| 1994–95 | Manchester C | 41 | 1 |
| 1995–96 | Manchester C | 37 | 1 |
| 1996–97 | Manchester C | 44 | 4 |
| 1997–98 | Manchester C | 9 | 0 |
| 1997–98 | Sunderland | 25 | 3 |
| **Total:** | | **268** | **15** |

## SUMMERBELL, Mark — Midfield

H: 5 8 W: 10 06 b.Durham 30-10-76

*Source:* Trainee.

| | | | |
|---|---|---|---|
| 1995–96 | Middlesbrough | 1 | 0 |
| 1996–97 | Middlesbrough | 2 | 0 |
| 1997–98 | Middlesbrough | 11 | 0 |
| **Total:** | | **14** | **0** |

## SUMNER, Jed — Goalkeeper

b.Basildon 1-8-79

*Source:* Coventry C Trainee.

| | | | |
|---|---|---|---|
| 1997–98 | Cambridge U | 0 | 0 |

## SUNDGOT, Ole — Forward

H: 6 1 W: 11 04 b.Olsumd 21-3-72

*Source:* Molde.

| | | | |
|---|---|---|---|
| 1991 | Molde | 17 | 3 |
| 1992 | Molde | 22 | 12 |
| 1993 | Molde | 4 | 2 |
| 1994 | Molde | 0 | 0 |
| 1995 | Molde | 26 | 13 |
| 1995–96 | Oldham Ath | 0 | 0 |
| 1996–97 | Bradford C | 20 | 6 |
| 1997–98 | Bradford C | 5 | 0 |
| **Total:** | | **94** | **36** |

## SUTCH, Daryl — Defender

H: 6 0 W: 11 10 b.Lowestoft 11-9-71

*Source:* Trainee. *Honours:* England Youth, Under-21.

| | | | |
|---|---|---|---|
| 1989–90 | Norwich C | 0 | 0 |
| 1990–91 | Norwich C | 4 | 0 |
| 1991–92 | Norwich C | 9 | 0 |
| 1992–93 | Norwich C | 22 | 2 |
| 1993–94 | Norwich C | 3 | 0 |
| 1994–95 | Norwich C | 30 | 1 |
| 1995–96 | Norwich C | 13 | 0 |
| 1996–97 | Norwich C | 44 | 3 |
| 1997–98 | Norwich C | 40 | 1 |
| **Total:** | | **165** | **7** |

## SUTHERLAND, Colin — Defender

H: 6 0 W: 11 10 b.Glasgow 15-3-75

| | | | |
|---|---|---|---|
| 1994–95 | Clydebank | 9 | 0 |
| 1995–96 | Clydebank | 26 | 2 |
| 1996–97 | Scarborough | 21 | 0 |
| 1997–98 | Scarborough | 22 | 0 |
| **Total:** | | **78** | **2** |

## SUTTON, Chris — Forward

H: 6 3 W: 13 07 b.Nottingham 10-3-73

*Source:* Trainee. *Honours:* England Under-21, B, 1 full cap.

| | | | |
|---|---|---|---|
| 1990–91 | Norwich C | 2 | 0 |
| 1991–92 | Norwich C | 21 | 2 |
| 1992–93 | Norwich C | 38 | 8 |
| 1993–94 | Norwich C | 41 | 25 |
| 1994–95 | Blackburn R | 40 | 15 |
| 1995–96 | Blackburn R | 13 | 0 |
| 1996–97 | Blackburn R | 25 | 11 |
| 1997–98 | Blackburn R | 35 | 18 |
| **Total:** | | **215** | **79** |

## SUTTON, Wayne — Defender

H: 6 0 W: 13 09 b.Derby 1-10-75

*Source:* Trainee.

| | | | |
|---|---|---|---|
| 1992–93 | Derby Co | 0 | 0 |
| 1993–94 | Derby Co | 0 | 0 |
| 1994–95 | Derby Co | 6 | 0 |
| 1995–96 | Derby Co | 1 | 0 |
| 1996–97 | Derby Co | 0 | 0 |
| 1996–97 | Hereford U (loan) | 4 | 0 |
| 1997–98 | Derby Co | 0 | 0 |
| **Total:** | | **11** | **0** |

## SVENSSON, Mathias — Forward

H: 6 0 W: 12 06 b.Boras 24-9-74

*Honours:* Sweden 2 full caps.

| | | | |
|---|---|---|---|
| 1996 | Elfsborg | 22 | 15 |
| 1996–97 | Portsmouth | 19 | 6 |
| 1997–98 | Portsmouth | 26 | 4 |
| **Total:** | | **67** | **25** |

## SWAILES, Chris — Defender

H: 6 2 W: 12 07 b.Gateshead 19-10-70

*Source:* Ipswich T Trainee, Peterborough U, Boston U, Birmingham C, Bridlington T.

| | | | |
|---|---|---|---|
| 1993–94 | Doncaster R | 17 | 0 |
| 1994–95 | Doncaster R | 32 | 0 |
| 1995–96 | Ipswich T | 5 | 0 |
| 1996–97 | Ipswich T | 23 | 1 |
| 1997–98 | Ipswich T | 5 | 0 |
| 1997–98 | Bury | 13 | 1 |
| **Total:** | | **95** | **2** |

## SWAILES, Daniel — Defender

H: 6 3 W: 12 06 b.Bolton 1-4-79

*Source:* Trainee.

| | | | |
|---|---|---|---|
| 1997–98 | Bury | 0 | 0 |

## SWALES, Steve — Defender

H: 5 8 W: 10 03 b.Whitby 26-12-73

*Source:* Trainee.

| | | | |
|---|---|---|---|
| 1991–92 | Scarborough | 4 | 0 |
| 1992–93 | Scarborough | 3 | 0 |
| 1993–94 | Scarborough | 26 | 0 |
| 1994–95 | Scarborough | 21 | 1 |
| 1995–96 | Reading | 9 | 0 |
| 1996–97 | Reading | 3 | 0 |
| 1997–98 | Reading | 31 | 1 |
| **Total:** | | **97** | **2** |

## SWALWELL, Andrew — Midfield

b.Middlesbrough 29-3-79

*Source:* Trainee.

| | | | |
|---|---|---|---|
| 1995–96 | Middlesbrough | 0 | 0 |
| 1996–97 | Middlesbrough | 0 | 0 |
| 1997–98 | Middlesbrough | 0 | 0 |

## SWAN, Iain — Midfield

b.Glasgow 16-10-79

*Source:* Trainee.

| | | | |
|---|---|---|---|
| 1996–97 | Oldham Ath | 0 | 0 |
| 1997–98 | Oldham Ath | 0 | 0 |

## SWAN, Peter — Forward

H: 6 2 W: 14 12 b.Leeds 28-9-66

*Source:* Local.

| | | | |
|---|---|---|---|
| 1984–85 | Leeds U | 0 | 0 |
| 1985–86 | Leeds U | 16 | 3 |
| 1986–87 | Leeds U | 7 | 0 |
| 1987–88 | Leeds U | 25 | 8 |
| 1988–89 | Leeds U | 1 | 0 |
| 1988–89 | Hull C | 11 | 1 |
| 1989–90 | Hull C | 31 | 11 |
| 1990–91 | Hull C | 38 | 12 |
| 1991–92 | Port Vale | 33 | 3 |
| 1992–93 | Port Vale | 38 | 2 |
| 1993–94 | Port Vale | 40 | 0 |
| 1994–95 | Plymouth Arg | 27 | 2 |
| 1995–96 | Plymouth Arg | 0 | 0 |
| 1995–96 | Burnley | 32 | 5 |
| 1996–97 | Burnley | 17 | 2 |
| 1997–98 | Bury | 37 | 6 |
| **Total:** | | **353** | **55** |

## SWEENEY, Terry — Forward

H: 5 6 W: 10 10 b.Paisley 26-1-79

*Source:* Trainee.

| | | | |
|---|---|---|---|
| 1996–97 | Luton T | 0 | 0 |
| 1997–98 | Luton T | 0 | 0 |

## SYMONS, Kit — Defender

H: 6 1 W: 13 07 b.Basingstoke 8-3-71

*Source:* Trainee. *Honours:* Wales Under-21, 27 full caps, 1 goal.

| | | | |
|---|---|---|---|
| 1988–89 | Portsmouth | 2 | 0 |
| 1989–90 | Portsmouth | 1 | 0 |
| 1990–91 | Portsmouth | 1 | 0 |
| 1991–92 | Portsmouth | 46 | 1 |

| | | | |
|---|---|---|---|
| 1992–93 | Portsmouth | 41 | 2 |
| 1993–94 | Portsmouth | 29 | 3 |
| 1994–95 | Portsmouth | 40 | 4 |
| 1995–96 | Portsmouth | 1 | 0 |
| 1995–96 | Manchester C | 38 | 2 |
| 1996–97 | Manchester C | 44 | 0 |
| 1997–98 | Manchester C | 42 | 2 |
| **Total:** | | **285** | **14** |

## TAAFFE, Steven — Forward

H: 5 7 W: 9 0 b.Stoke 10-9-79

*Source:* Trainee.

| | | | |
|---|---|---|---|
| 1996–97 | Stoke C | 0 | 0 |
| 1997–98 | Stoke C | 3 | 0 |
| **Total:** | | **3** | **0** |

## TAGGART, Gerry — Defender

H: 6 1 W: 12 00 b.Belfast 18-10-70

*Source:* Trainee. *Honours:* Northern Ireland Under-23, 45 full caps, 7 goals.

| | | | |
|---|---|---|---|
| 1988–89 | Manchester C | 11 | 1 |
| 1989–90 | Manchester C | 1 | 0 |
| 1989–90 | Barnsley | 21 | 2 |
| 1990–91 | Barnsley | 30 | 2 |
| 1991–92 | Barnsley | 38 | 3 |
| 1992–93 | Barnsley | 44 | 4 |
| 1993–94 | Barnsley | 38 | 2 |
| 1994–95 | Barnsley | 41 | 3 |
| 1995–96 | Bolton W | 11 | 1 |
| 1996–97 | Bolton W | 43 | 3 |
| 1997–98 | Bolton W | 15 | 0 |
| **Total:** | | **293** | **21** |

## TAIT, Mick — Defender

H: 5 11 W: 14 05 b.Wallsend 30-9-56

*Source:* Apprentice.

| | | | |
|---|---|---|---|
| 1974–75 | Oxford U | 4 | 0 |
| 1975–76 | Oxford U | 37 | 12 |
| 1976–77 | Oxford U | 23 | 11 |
| 1976–77 | Carlisle U | 13 | 3 |
| 1977–78 | Carlisle U | 43 | 10 |
| 1978–79 | Carlisle U | 46 | 7 |
| 1979–80 | Carlisle U | 4 | 0 |
| 1979–80 | Hull C | 33 | 3 |
| 1980–81 | Portsmouth | 38 | 8 |
| 1981–82 | Portsmouth | 35 | 9 |
| 1982–83 | Portsmouth | 44 | 6 |
| 1983–84 | Portsmouth | 36 | 3 |
| 1984–85 | Portsmouth | 33 | 1 |
| 1985–86 | Portsmouth | 26 | 2 |
| 1986–87 | Portsmouth | 28 | 1 |
| 1987–88 | Portsmouth | 0 | 0 |
| 1987–88 | Reading | 35 | 2 |
| 1988–89 | Reading | 36 | 4 |
| 1989–90 | Reading | 28 | 3 |
| 1990–91 | Darlington | 45 | 2 |
| 1991–92 | Darlington | 34 | 0 |
| 1992–93 | Hartlepool U | 35 | 1 |
| 1993–94 | Hartlepool U | 26 | 0 |

From Gretna.

| | | | |
|---|---|---|---|
| 1994–95 | Hartlepool U | 20 | 0 |
| 1995–96 | Hartlepool U | 39 | 2 |
| 1996–97 | Hartlepool U | 19 | 0 |
| 1997–98 | Hartlepool U | 0 | 0 |
| **Total:** | | **760** | **90** |

## TAIT, Paul — Midfield

H: 6 1 W: 10 07 b.Sutton Coldfield 31-7-71

*Source:* Trainee.

| | | | |
|---|---|---|---|
| 1987–88 | Birmingham C | 1 | 0 |
| 1988–89 | Birmingham C | 10 | 0 |
| 1989–90 | Birmingham C | 14 | 2 |
| 1990–91 | Birmingham C | 17 | 3 |
| 1991–92 | Birmingham C | 12 | 0 |
| 1992–93 | Birmingham C | 28 | 2 |
| 1993–94 | Birmingham C | 10 | 0 |
| 1993–94 | Millwall (loan) | 0 | 0 |
| 1994–95 | Birmingham C | 25 | 4 |
| 1995–96 | Birmingham C | 27 | 3 |
| 1996–97 | Birmingham C | 26 | 0 |
| 1997–98 | Birmingham C | 0 | 0 |
| 1997–98 | Northampton T (loan) | 3 | 0 |
| **Total:** | | **173** | **14** |

## TALBOT, Paul — Defender

H: 5 10 W: 10 09 b.Gateshead 11-8-79

*Source:* Trainee.

| | | | |
|---|---|---|---|
| 1997–98 | Newcastle U | 0 | 0 |

## TALBOT, Stuart — Midfield

H: 6 0 W: 13 07 b.Birmingham 14-6-73

*Source:* Doncaster R, Moor Green.

| | | | |
|---|---|---|---|
| 1994–95 | Port Vale | 2 | 0 |
| 1995–96 | Port Vale | 20 | 0 |
| 1996–97 | Port Vale | 34 | 4 |
| 1997–98 | Port Vale | 42 | 6 |
| **Total:** | | **98** | **10** |

## TALBOYS, Steve — Midfield

H: 5 11 W: 11 10 b.Bristol 18-9-66

*Source:* Gloucester C.

| | | | |
|---|---|---|---|
| 1991–92 | Wimbledon | 0 | 0 |

| | | | |
|---|---|---|---|
| 1992–93 | Wimbledon | 7 | 0 |
| 1993–94 | Wimbledon | 7 | 0 |
| 1994–95 | Wimbledon | 7 | 1 |
| 1995–96 | Wimbledon | 5 | 0 |
| 1996–97 | Watford | 3 | 0 |
| 1997–98 | Watford | 2 | 0 |
| **Total:** | | **31** | **1** |

## TALIA, Frank
Goalkeeper

H: 6 1 W: 13 06 b.Melbourne 20-7-72

*Source:* Sunshine GC.

| | | | |
|---|---|---|---|
| 1992–93 | Blackburn R | 0 | 0 |
| 1992–93 | Hartlepool U (loan) | 14 | 0 |
| 1993–94 | Blackburn R | 0 | 0 |
| 1994–95 | Blackburn R | 0 | 0 |
| 1995–96 | Blackburn R | 0 | 0 |
| 1995–96 | Swindon T | 16 | 0 |
| 1996–97 | Swindon T | 15 | 0 |
| 1997–98 | Swindon T | 2 | 0 |
| **Total:** | | **47** | **0** |

## TALLON, Gary
Midfield

H: 5 7 W: 11 07 b.Drogheda 5-9-73

*Honours:* Trainee.

| | | | |
|---|---|---|---|
| 1991–92 | Blackburn R | 0 | 0 |
| 1992–93 | Blackburn R | 0 | 0 |
| 1993–94 | Blackburn R | 0 | 0 |
| 1994–95 | Blackburn R | 0 | 0 |
| 1995–96 | Blackburn R | 0 | 0 |
| 1996–97 | Kilmarnock | 4 | 0 |
| 1996–97 | Chester C (loan) | 1 | 0 |
| 1997–98 | Kilmarnock | 0 | 0 |
| 1997–98 | Mansfield T | 26 | 1 |
| **Total:** | | **31** | **1** |

## TANKARD, Allen
Defender

H: 5 10 W: 12 10 b.Islington 21-5-69

*Source:* Trainee. *Honours:* England Youth.

| | | | |
|---|---|---|---|
| 1985–86 | Southampton | 3 | 0 |
| 1986–87 | Southampton | 2 | 0 |
| 1987–88 | Southampton | 0 | 0 |
| 1988–89 | Wigan Ath | 33 | 1 |
| 1989–90 | Wigan Ath | 45 | 1 |
| 1990–91 | Wigan Ath | 46 | 1 |
| 1991–92 | Wigan Ath | 44 | 0 |
| 1992–93 | Wigan Ath | 41 | 1 |
| 1993–94 | Port Vale | 26 | 0 |
| 1994–95 | Port Vale | 39 | 1 |
| 1995–96 | Port Vale | 29 | 0 |
| 1996–97 | Port Vale | 37 | 1 |
| 1997–98 | Port Vale | 39 | 0 |
| **Total:** | | **384** | **6** |

## TANNER, Adam
Midfield

H: 6 0 W: 12 01 b.Maldon 25-10-73

*Source:* Trainee.

| | | | |
|---|---|---|---|
| 1992–93 | Ipswich T | 0 | 0 |
| 1993–94 | Ipswich T | 0 | 0 |
| 1994–95 | Ipswich T | 10 | 2 |
| 1995–96 | Ipswich T | 10 | 0 |
| 1996–97 | Ipswich T | 16 | 4 |
| 1997–98 | Ipswich T | 18 | 1 |
| **Total:** | | **54** | **7** |

## TARICCO, Mauricio
Defender

H: 5 8 W: 11 05 b.Buenos Aires 10-3-73

*Source:* Argentinos Juniors. *Honours:* Argentina Under-23.

| | | | |
|---|---|---|---|
| 1994–95 | Ipswich T | 0 | 0 |
| 1995–96 | Ipswich T | 39 | 0 |
| 1996–97 | Ipswich T | 41 | 3 |
| 1997–98 | Ipswich T | 41 | 0 |
| **Total:** | | **121** | **3** |

## TARRANT, Neil
Midfield

H: 6 0 W: 12 00 b.Darlington 24-6-79

| | | | |
|---|---|---|---|
| 1997–98 | Darlington | 0 | 0 |

## TATE, Chris
Forward

H: 6 0 W: 12 00 b.York 27-12-77

*Source:* York C Trainee.

| | | | |
|---|---|---|---|
| 1996–97 | Sunderland | 0 | 0 |
| 1997–98 | Scarborough | 24 | 1 |
| **Total:** | | **24** | **1** |

## TAYLOR, Bob
Forward

H: 5 10 W: 12 12 b.Easington 3-2-67

*Source:* Horden CW.

| | | | |
|---|---|---|---|
| 1985–86 | Leeds U | 2 | 0 |
| 1986–87 | Leeds U | 2 | 0 |
| 1987–88 | Leeds U | 32 | 9 |
| 1988–89 | Leeds U | 6 | 0 |
| 1988–89 | Bristol C | 12 | 8 |
| 1989–90 | Bristol C | 37 | 27 |
| 1990–91 | Bristol C | 39 | 11 |
| 1991–92 | Bristol C | 18 | 4 |
| 1991–92 | WBA | 19 | 8 |
| 1992–93 | WBA | 46 | 30 |
| 1993–94 | WBA | 42 | 18 |

| | | | |
|---|---|---|---|
| 1994–95 | WBA | 42 | 11 |
| 1995–96 | WBA | 42 | 17 |
| 1996–97 | WBA | 32 | 10 |
| 1997–98 | WBA | 15 | 2 |
| 1997–98 | Bolton W (loan) | 12 | 3 |
| **Total:** | | **398** | **158** |

## TAYLOR, Craig — Defender

H: 6 1 W: 12 03 b.Plymouth 24-1-74

| | | | |
|---|---|---|---|
| 1992–93 | Exeter C | 5 | 0 |
| From Dorchester T. | | | |
| 1996–97 | Swindon T | 0 | 0 |
| 1997–98 | Swindon T | 32 | 2 |
| **Total:** | | **37** | **2** |

## TAYLOR, Gareth — Forward

H: 6 2 W: 13 08 b.Weston-Super-Mare 25-2-73

*Source:* Southampton Trainee. *Honours:* Wales Under-21, 8 full caps.

| | | | |
|---|---|---|---|
| 1991–92 | Bristol R | 1 | 0 |
| 1992–93 | Bristol R | 0 | 0 |
| 1993–94 | Bristol R | 0 | 0 |
| 1994–95 | Bristol R | 39 | 12 |
| 1995–96 | Bristol R | 7 | 4 |
| 1995–96 | Crystal Palace | 20 | 1 |
| 1995–96 | Sheffield U | 10 | 2 |
| 1996–97 | Sheffield U | 34 | 12 |
| 1997–98 | Sheffield U | 28 | 10 |
| **Total:** | | **139** | **41** |

## TAYLOR, Ian — Midfield

H: 6 1 W: 12 00 b.Birmingham 4-6-68

*Source:* Moor Green.

| | | | |
|---|---|---|---|
| 1992–93 | Port Vale | 41 | 15 |
| 1993–94 | Port Vale | 42 | 13 |
| 1994–95 | Sheffield W | 14 | 1 |
| 1994–95 | Aston Villa | 22 | 1 |
| 1995–96 | Aston Villa | 25 | 3 |
| 1996–97 | Aston Villa | 34 | 2 |
| 1997–98 | Aston Villa | 32 | 6 |
| **Total:** | | **210** | **41** |

## TAYLOR, John — Forward

H: 6 1 W: 14 00 b.Norwich 24-10-64

*Source:* Local.

| | | | |
|---|---|---|---|
| 1982–83 | Colchester U | 0 | 0 |
| 1983–84 | Colchester U | 0 | 0 |
| 1984–85 | Colchester U | 0 | 0 |
| From Sudbury T. | | | |
| 1988–89 | Cambridge U | 40 | 12 |
| 1989–90 | Cambridge U | 45 | 15 |
| 1990–91 | Cambridge U | 40 | 14 |
| 1991–92 | Cambridge U | 35 | 5 |
| 1991–92 | Bristol R | 8 | 7 |
| 1992–93 | Bristol R | 42 | 14 |
| 1993–94 | Bristol R | 45 | 23 |
| 1994–95 | Bradford C | 36 | 11 |
| 1994–95 | Luton T | 9 | 3 |
| 1995–96 | Luton T | 28 | 0 |
| 1996–97 | Luton T | 0 | 0 |
| 1996–97 | Lincoln C (loan) | 5 | 2 |
| 1996–97 | Colchester U (loan) | 8 | 5 |
| 1996–97 | Cambridge U | 21 | 4 |
| 1997–98 | Cambridge U | 34 | 10 |
| **Total:** | | **396** | **125** |

## TAYLOR, John — Midfield

H: 5 8 W: 11 09 b.Liverpool 4-12-78

*Source:* Tranmere R Trainee.

| | | | |
|---|---|---|---|
| 1997–98 | Rotherham U | 0 | 0 |

## TAYLOR, Lee — Defender

H: 6 0 W: 11 05 b.Hammersmith 24-2-76

*Source:* Faweh.

| | | | |
|---|---|---|---|
| 1996–97 | Shrewsbury T | 16 | 0 |
| 1997–98 | Shrewsbury T | 1 | 0 |
| **Total:** | | **17** | **0** |

## TAYLOR, Lee — Defender

H: 6 0 W: 12 13 b.Whitehaven 12-9-77

*Source:* Trainee.

| | | | |
|---|---|---|---|
| 1996–97 | Carlisle U | 0 | 0 |
| 1997–98 | Carlisle U | 0 | 0 |

## TAYLOR, Maik — Goalkeeper

H: 6 3 W: 13 09 b.Hildeshein 4-9-71

*Source:* Farnborough T. *Honours:* Northern Ireland Under-21.

| | | | |
|---|---|---|---|
| 1995–96 | Barnet | 45 | 0 |
| 1996–97 | Barnet | 25 | 0 |
| 1996–97 | Southampton | 18 | 0 |
| 1997–98 | Southampton | 0 | 0 |
| 1997–98 | Fulham | 28 | 0 |
| **Total:** | | **116** | **0** |

## TAYLOR, Mark — Midfield

H: 5 9 W: 11 08 b.Walsall 22-2-66

*Source:* Local.

| | | | |
|---|---|---|---|
| 1984–85 | Walsall | 4 | 0 |

| | | | |
|---|---|---|---|
| 1985–86 | Walsall | 18 | 2 |
| 1986–87 | Walsall | 17 | 0 |
| 1987–88 | Walsall | 40 | 1 |
| 1988–89 | Walsall | 34 | 1 |
| 1989–90 | Sheffield W | 9 | 0 |
| 1990–91 | Shrewsbury T (loan) | 19 | 2 |
| 1991–92 | Shrewsbury T | 29 | 2 |
| 1992–93 | Shrewsbury T | 42 | 5 |
| 1993–94 | Shrewsbury T | 41 | 2 |
| 1994–95 | Shrewsbury T | 44 | 2 |
| 1995–96 | Shrewsbury T | 38 | 1 |
| 1996–97 | Shrewsbury T | 37 | 1 |
| 1997–98 | Shrewsbury T | 18 | 0 |
| **Total:** | | **390** | **19** |

## TAYLOR, Martin — Goalkeeper

H: 5 11 W: 14 07 b.Tamworth 9-12-66

*Source:* Mile Oak R.

| | | | |
|---|---|---|---|
| 1986–87 | Derby Co | 0 | 0 |
| 1987–88 | Derby Co | 0 | 0 |
| 1987–88 | Carlisle U (loan) | 10 | 0 |
| 1987–88 | Scunthorpe U (loan) | 8 | 0 |
| 1988–89 | Derby Co | 0 | 0 |
| 1989–90 | Derby Co | 3 | 0 |
| 1990–91 | Derby Co | 7 | 0 |
| 1991–92 | Derby Co | 5 | 0 |
| 1992–93 | Derby Co | 21 | 0 |
| 1993–94 | Derby Co | 46 | 0 |
| 1994–95 | Derby Co | 12 | 0 |
| 1995–96 | Derby Co | 0 | 0 |
| 1996–97 | Derby Co | 3 | 0 |
| 1996–97 | Crewe Alex (loan) | 6 | 0 |
| 1996–97 | Wycombe W (loan) | 4 | 0 |
| 1997–98 | Wycombe W | 45 | 0 |
| **Total:** | | **170** | **0** |

## TAYLOR, Martin — Defender

b.Northumberland 9-11-79

*Source:* Trainee. *Honours:* England Youth.

| | | | |
|---|---|---|---|
| 1997–98 | Blackburn R | 0 | 0 |

## TAYLOR, Paul — Midfield

b.Basildon 30-9-78

*Source:* Trainee.

| | | | |
|---|---|---|---|
| 1997–98 | Southend U | 0 | 0 |

## TAYLOR, Robert — Forward

H: 6 1 W: 13 06 b.Norwich 30-4-71

*Source:* Trainee.

| | | | |
|---|---|---|---|
| 1989–90 | Norwich C | 0 | 0 |
| 1990–91 | Norwich C | 0 | 0 |
| 1990–91 | Leyton Orient (loan) | 3 | 1 |
| 1991–92 | Birmingham C | 0 | 0 |
| 1991–92 | Leyton Orient | 11 | 1 |
| 1992–93 | Leyton Orient | 39 | 18 |
| 1993–94 | Leyton Orient | 23 | 1 |
| 1993–94 | Brentford | 5 | 2 |
| 1994–95 | Brentford | 43 | 23 |
| 1995–96 | Brentford | 42 | 11 |
| 1996–97 | Brentford | 43 | 7 |
| 1997–98 | Brentford | 40 | 13 |
| **Total:** | | **249** | **77** |

## TAYLOR, Ross — Defender

H: 5 10 W: 11 12 b.Southend 14-1-77

*Source:* Trainee. *Honours:* England Schools, Youth.

| | | | |
|---|---|---|---|
| 1995–96 | Arsenal | 0 | 0 |
| 1996–97 | Arsenal | 0 | 0 |
| 1997–98 | Arsenal | 0 | 0 |

## TAYLOR, Scott — Forward

H: 5 10 W: 11 04 b.Chertsey 5-5-76

*Source:* Staines T.

| | | | |
|---|---|---|---|
| 1994–95 | Millwall | 6 | 0 |
| 1995–96 | Millwall | 22 | 0 |
| 1995–96 | Bolton W | 1 | 0 |
| 1996–97 | Bolton W | 11 | 1 |
| 1997–98 | Bolton W | 0 | 0 |
| 1997–98 | Rotherham U (loan) | 10 | 3 |
| 1997–98 | Blackpool (loan) | 5 | 1 |
| **Total:** | | **55** | **5** |

## TAYLOR, Scott — Midfield

H: 5 9 W: 11 05 b.Portsmouth 23-11-70

*Source:* Trainee.

| | | | |
|---|---|---|---|
| 1988–89 | Reading | 3 | 0 |
| 1989–90 | Reading | 29 | 2 |
| 1990–91 | Reading | 32 | 1 |
| 1991–92 | Reading | 29 | 2 |
| 1992–93 | Reading | 32 | 5 |
| 1993–94 | Reading | 38 | 6 |
| 1994–95 | Reading | 44 | 8 |
| 1995–96 | Leicester C | 39 | 6 |
| 1996–97 | Leicester C | 25 | 0 |
| 1997–98 | Leicester C | 0 | 0 |
| **Total:** | | **271** | **30** |

## TAYLOR, Shaun — Defender

H: 6 1 W: 12 08 b.Plymouth 26-2-63

*Source:* Bideford.

| | | | |
|---|---|---|---|
| 1986–87 | Exeter C | 23 | 0 |
| 1987–88 | Exeter C | 41 | 1 |
| 1988–89 | Exeter C | 46 | 6 |
| 1989–90 | Exeter C | 45 | 5 |
| 1990–91 | Exeter C | 45 | 4 |
| 1991–92 | Swindon T | 42 | 4 |
| 1992–93 | Swindon T | 46 | 11 |
| 1993–94 | Swindon T | 42 | 4 |
| 1994–95 | Swindon T | 37 | 4 |
| 1995–96 | Swindon T | 43 | 7 |
| 1996–97 | Swindon T | 2 | 0 |
| 1996–97 | Bristol C | 29 | 1 |
| 1997–98 | Bristol C | 43 | 2 |
| **Total:** | | **484** | **49** |

## TEAGUE, Simon — Forward

H: 5 6 W: 10 00 b.Henley 23-2-79

*Source:* Trainee.

| | | | |
|---|---|---|---|
| 1997–98 | Bristol R | 0 | 0 |

## TEALE, Shaun — Defender

H: 6 0 W: 13 07 b.Southport 10-3-64

*Source:* Southport, Northwich Vic, Weymouth.

| | | | |
|---|---|---|---|
| 1988–89 | Bournemouth | 20 | 0 |
| 1989–90 | Bournemouth | 34 | 0 |
| 1990–91 | Bournemouth | 46 | 4 |
| 1991–92 | Aston Villa | 42 | 0 |
| 1992–93 | Aston Villa | 39 | 1 |
| 1993–94 | Aston Villa | 38 | 1 |
| 1994–95 | Aston Villa | 28 | 0 |
| 1995–96 | Tranmere R | 29 | 0 |
| 1996–97 | Tranmere R | 25 | 0 |
| 1996–97 | Preston NE (loan) | 5 | 0 |
| 1997–98 | Tranmere R | 0 | 0 |
| **Total:** | | **306** | **6** |

## TEATHER, Paul — Defender

H: 6 0 W: 11 08 b.Rotherham 28-12-77

*Source:* Trainee. *Honours:* England Schools, Youth.

| | | | |
|---|---|---|---|
| 1994–95 | Manchester U | 0 | 0 |
| 1995–96 | Manchester U | 0 | 0 |
| 1996–97 | Manchester U | 0 | 0 |
| 1997–98 | Manchester U | 0 | 0 |
| 1997–98 | Bournemouth (loan) | 10 | 0 |
| **Total:** | | **10** | **0** |

## TEDALDI, Dino — Forward

H: 5 11 W: 11 10 b.Aberystwyth 12-8-80

*Source:* Trainee.

| | | | |
|---|---|---|---|
| 1997–98 | Doncaster R | 2 | 1 |
| **Total:** | | **2** | **1** |

## TELFER, Paul — Midfield

H: 5 9 W: 11 06 b.Edinburgh 21-10-71

*Source:* Trainee. *Honours:* Scotland Under-21.

| | | | |
|---|---|---|---|
| 1988–89 | Luton T | 0 | 0 |
| 1989–90 | Luton T | 0 | 0 |
| 1990–91 | Luton T | 1 | 0 |
| 1991–92 | Luton T | 20 | 1 |
| 1992–93 | Luton T | 32 | 2 |
| 1993–94 | Luton T | 45 | 7 |
| 1994–95 | Luton T | 46 | 9 |
| 1995–96 | Coventry C | 31 | 1 |
| 1996–97 | Coventry C | 34 | 0 |
| 1997–98 | Coventry C | 33 | 3 |
| **Total:** | | **242** | **23** |

## TEN HEUVEL, Laurens — Forward

H: 6 0 W: 12 01 b.Duivendrecht 6-6-76

*Source:* Den Bosch.

| | | | |
|---|---|---|---|
| 1995–96 | Barnsley | 3 | 0 |
| 1996–97 | Barnsley | 3 | 0 |
| 1997–98 | Barnsley | 2 | 0 |
| 1997–98 | Northampton (loan) | 0 | 0 |
| **Total:** | | **8** | **0** |

## TERRIER, David — Defender

H: 5 11 W: 11 03 b.Verdun 4-8-73

| | | | |
|---|---|---|---|
| 1992–93 | Metz | 20 | 0 |
| 1993–94 | Metz | 30 | 0 |
| 1994–95 | Metz | 26 | 0 |
| 1995–96 | Metz | 20 | 0 |
| 1996–97 | Metz | 31 | 0 |
| 1997–98 | West Ham U | 1 | 0 |
| 1997–98 | Newcastle U | 0 | 0 |
| **Total:** | | **128** | **0** |

## TERRY, John — Defender

b.London 7-12-80

*Source:* Trainee.

| | | | |
|---|---|---|---|
| 1997–98 | Chelsea | 0 | 0 |

## THATCHER, Ben — Defender

H: 5 11 W: 12 07 b.Swindon 30-11-75

*Source:* Trainee. *Honours:* England Youth, Under-21.

| | | | |
|---|---|---|---|
| 1992–93 | Millwall | 0 | 0 |
| 1993–94 | Millwall | 8 | 0 |
| 1994–95 | Millwall | 40 | 1 |
| 1995–96 | Millwall | 42 | 0 |
| 1996–97 | Wimbledon | 9 | 0 |
| 1997–98 | Wimbledon | 26 | 0 |
| **Total:** | | **125** | **1** |

## THEOBALD, David — Defender

H: 6 2 W: 11 06 b.Cambridge 15-12-78

*Source:* Trainee.

| | | | |
|---|---|---|---|
| 1997–98 | Ipswich T | 0 | 0 |

## THERN, Jonas — Midfield

H: 5 11 W: 13 03 b.Falkoping 20-3-67

*Honours:* Sweden 75 full caps, 6 goals.

| | | | |
|---|---|---|---|
| 1985 | Malmo | 1 | 0 |
| 1986 | Malmo | 16 | 2 |
| 1987 | Malmo | 20 | 3 |
| 1987–88 | Zurich | 0 | 0 |
| 1988 | Malmo | 22 | 4 |
| 1989 | Malmo | 13 | 1 |
| 1989–90 | Benfica | 21 | 2 |
| 1990–91 | Benfica | 24 | 4 |
| 1991–92 | Benfica | 27 | 2 |
| 1992–93 | Napoli | 27 | 0 |
| 1993–94 | Napoli | 21 | 1 |
| 1994–95 | Roma | 12 | 0 |
| 1995–96 | Roma | 22 | 1 |
| 1996–97 | Roma | 25 | 2 |
| 1997–98 | Rangers | 22 | 5 |
| **Total:** | | **273** | **27** |

## THIRLWELL, Paul — Midfield

H: 5 11 W: 11 04 b.Newcastle 13-2-79

*Source:* Trainee.

| | | | |
|---|---|---|---|
| 1996–97 | Sunderland | 0 | 0 |
| 1997–98 | Sunderland | 0 | 0 |

## THOLOT, Didier — Forward

b.Feurs 2-4-64

*Source:* INF Vichy, Toulon, Niort, Reims, St Etienne, Martigues, Bordeaux, Sion.

| | | | |
|---|---|---|---|
| 1997–98 | Walsall | 14 | 4 |
| **Total:** | | **14** | **4** |

## THOM, Andreas — Forward

H: 5 8 W: 11 10 b.Rudersdorf 7-9-65

*Source:* TSV Bayer 04 Leverkusen. *Honours:* East Germany 51 full caps, 16 goals; Germany 10 full caps, 2 goals.

| | | | |
|---|---|---|---|
| 1995–96 | Celtic | 32 | 5 |
| 1996–97 | Celtic | 23 | 7 |
| 1997–98 | Celtic | 15 | 3 |
| **Total:** | | **70** | **15** |

## THOM, Stuart — Defender

H: 6 2 W: 11 12 b.Dewsbury 27-12-76

*Source:* Trainee.

| | | | |
|---|---|---|---|
| 1993–94 | Nottingham F | 0 | 0 |
| 1994–95 | Nottingham F | 0 | 0 |
| 1995–96 | Nottingham F | 0 | 0 |
| 1996–97 | Nottingham F | 0 | 0 |
| 1997–98 | Nottingham F | 0 | 0 |
| 1997–98 | Mansfield T (loan) | 5 | 0 |
| **Total:** | | **5** | **0** |

## THOMAS, Danny — Midfield

b.Leamington Spa 1-5-81

*Source:* Trainee.

| | | | |
|---|---|---|---|
| 1997–98 | Nottingham F | 0 | 0 |
| 1997–98 | Leicester C | 0 | 0 |

## THOMAS, David — Forward

H: 5 11 W: 12 07 b.Caerphilly 26-9-75

*Source:* Trainee. *Honours:* Wales Under-21.

| | | | |
|---|---|---|---|
| 1994–95 | Swansea C | 4 | 0 |
| 1995–96 | Swansea C | 16 | 1 |
| 1996–97 | Swansea C | 36 | 9 |
| 1997–98 | Watford | 16 | 3 |
| **Total:** | | **72** | **13** |

## THOMAS, Geoff — Midfield

H: 6 1 W: 13 02 b.Manchester 5-8-64

*Source:* Local. *Honours:* England B, 9 full caps.

| | | | |
|---|---|---|---|
| 1981–82 | Rochdale | 0 | 0 |
| 1982–83 | Rochdale | 1 | 0 |
| 1983–84 | Rochdale | 10 | 1 |
| 1983–84 | Crewe Alex | 8 | 1 |
| 1984–85 | Crewe Alex | 40 | 4 |
| 1985–86 | Crewe Alex | 37 | 6 |
| 1986–87 | Crewe Alex | 40 | 9 |
| 1987–88 | Crystal Palace | 41 | 6 |
| 1988–89 | Crystal Palace | 22 | 5 |
| 1989–90 | Crystal Palace | 35 | 1 |

| | | | |
|---|---|---|---|
| 1990–91 | Crystal Palace | 38 | 6 |
| 1991–92 | Crystal Palace | 30 | 6 |
| 1992–93 | Crystal Palace | 29 | 2 |
| 1993–94 | Wolverhampton W | 8 | 4 |
| 1994–95 | Wolverhampton W | 14 | 1 |
| 1995–96 | Wolverhampton W | 2 | 0 |
| 1996–97 | Wolverhampton W | 22 | 3 |
| 1997–98 | Nottingham F | 20 | 3 |
| **Total:** | | **397** | **58** |

## THOMAS, Glen — Defender

H: 6 0 W: 14 00 b.Hackney 6-10-67

*Source:* Apprentice.

| | | | |
|---|---|---|---|
| 1985–86 | Fulham | 0 | 0 |
| 1986–87 | Fulham | 1 | 0 |
| 1987–88 | Fulham | 27 | 0 |
| 1988–89 | Fulham | 40 | 1 |
| 1989–90 | Fulham | 17 | 1 |
| 1990–91 | Fulham | 34 | 1 |
| 1991–92 | Fulham | 45 | 3 |
| 1992–93 | Fulham | 43 | 0 |
| 1993–94 | Fulham | 37 | 0 |
| 1994–95 | Fulham | 7 | 0 |
| 1994–95 | Peterborough U | 8 | 0 |
| 1994–95 | Barnet | 7 | 0 |
| 1995–96 | Barnet | 16 | 0 |
| 1995–96 | Gillingham | 15 | 0 |
| 1996–97 | Gillingham | 10 | 0 |
| 1997–98 | Gillingham | 3 | 0 |
| **Total:** | | **310** | **6** |

## THOMAS, James — Forward

b.Swansea 16-1-79

*Source:* Trainee. *Honours:* Wales Under-21.

| | | | |
|---|---|---|---|
| 1996–97 | Blackburn R | 0 | 0 |
| 1997–98 | Blackburn R | 0 | 0 |
| 1997–98 | WBA (loan) | 3 | 0 |
| **Total:** | | **3** | **0** |

## THOMAS, Kevin — Forward

H: 5 8 W: 12 00 b.Edinburgh 25-4-75

*Source:* Links U. *Honours:* Scotland Under-21.

| | | | |
|---|---|---|---|
| 1992–93 | Hearts | 4 | 2 |
| 1993–94 | Hearts | 12 | 0 |
| 1994–95 | Hearts | 18 | 5 |
| 1995–96 | Hearts | 3 | 0 |
| 1996–97 | Hearts | 13 | 0 |
| 1997–98 | Hearts | 1 | 0 |
| 1997–98 | Stirling A | 6 | 0 |
| **Total:** | | **57** | **7** |

## THOMAS, Martin — Midfield

H: 5 8 W: 12 04 b.Lyndhurst 12-9-73

*Source:* Trainee.

| | | | |
|---|---|---|---|
| 1992–93 | Southampton | 0 | 0 |
| 1993–94 | Southampton | 0 | 0 |
| 1993–94 | Leyton Orient | 5 | 2 |
| 1994–95 | Fulham | 23 | 3 |
| 1995–96 | Fulham | 37 | 5 |
| 1996–97 | Fulham | 26 | 0 |
| 1997–98 | Fulham | 4 | 0 |
| **Total:** | | **95** | **10** |

## THOMAS, Michael — Midfield

H: 5 9 W: 12 06 b.Lambeth 24-8-67

*Source:* Apprentice. *Honours:* England Schools, Youth, Under-21, B, 2 full caps.

| | | | |
|---|---|---|---|
| 1985–86 | Arsenal | 0 | 0 |
| 1986–87 | Arsenal | 12 | 0 |
| 1986–87 | Portsmouth (loan) | 3 | 0 |
| 1987–88 | Arsenal | 37 | 9 |
| 1988–89 | Arsenal | 37 | 7 |
| 1989–90 | Arsenal | 36 | 5 |
| 1990–91 | Arsenal | 31 | 2 |
| 1991–92 | Arsenal | 10 | 1 |
| 1991–92 | Liverpool | 17 | 3 |
| 1992–93 | Liverpool | 8 | 1 |
| 1993–94 | Liverpool | 7 | 0 |
| 1994–95 | Liverpool | 23 | 0 |
| 1995–96 | Liverpool | 27 | 1 |
| 1996–97 | Liverpool | 31 | 3 |
| 1997–98 | Liverpool | 11 | 1 |
| 1997–98 | Middlesbrough (loan) | 10 | 0 |
| **Total:** | | **300** | **33** |

## THOMAS, Mitchell — Defender

H: 6 2 W: 13 00 b.Luton 2-10-64

*Source:* Apprentice. *Honours:* England Youth, Under-21, B.

| | | | |
|---|---|---|---|
| 1982–83 | Luton T | 4 | 0 |
| 1983–84 | Luton T | 26 | 0 |
| 1984–85 | Luton T | 36 | 0 |
| 1985–86 | Luton T | 41 | 1 |
| 1986–87 | Tottenham H | 39 | 4 |
| 1987–88 | Tottenham H | 36 | 0 |
| 1988–89 | Tottenham H | 25 | 1 |
| 1989–90 | Tottenham H | 26 | 1 |
| 1990–91 | Tottenham H | 31 | 0 |
| 1991–92 | West Ham U | 35 | 3 |
| 1992–93 | West Ham U | 3 | 0 |
| 1993–94 | West Ham U | 0 | 0 |
| 1993–94 | Luton T | 20 | 1 |
| 1994–95 | Luton T | 36 | 0 |
| 1995–96 | Luton T | 27 | 0 |

| 1996–97 | Luton T | 42 | 3 |
|---|---|---|---|
| 1997–98 | Luton T | 28 | 1 |
| **Total:** | | **455** | **15** |

## THOMAS, Rod — Forward

H: 5 4 W: 11 02 b.London 10-10-70

*Source:* Trainee. *Honours:* England Schools, Youth, Under-21.

| 1987–88 | Watford | 4 | 0 |
|---|---|---|---|
| 1988–89 | Watford | 18 | 2 |
| 1989–90 | Watford | 32 | 6 |
| 1990–91 | Watford | 24 | 1 |
| 1991–92 | Watford | 5 | 0 |
| 1991–92 | Gillingham (loan) | 8 | 1 |
| 1992–93 | Watford | 1 | 0 |
| 1993–94 | Carlisle U | 38 | 9 |
| 1994–95 | Carlisle U | 36 | 6 |
| 1995–96 | Carlisle U | 36 | 1 |
| 1996–97 | Carlisle U | 36 | 0 |
| 1997–98 | Chester C | 38 | 4 |
| **Total:** | | **276** | **30** |

## THOMAS, Scott — Midfield

H: 5 9 W: 11 02 b.Bury 30-10-74

*Source:* Trainee.

| 1991–92 | Manchester C | 0 | 0 |
|---|---|---|---|
| 1992–93 | Manchester C | 0 | 0 |
| 1993–94 | Manchester C | 0 | 0 |
| 1994–95 | Manchester C | 2 | 0 |
| 1995–96 | Manchester C | 0 | 0 |
| 1996–97 | Manchester C | 0 | 0 |
| 1997–98 | Manchester C | 0 | 0 |
| 1997–98 | Brighton & HA (loan) | 7 | 0 |
| **Total:** | | **9** | **0** |

## THOMAS, Steve — Midfield

H: 5 10 W: 11 12 b.Hartlepool 23-6-79

*Source:* Trainee.

| 1997–98 | Wrexham | 0 | 0 |
|---|---|---|---|

## THOMAS, Tony — Defender

H: 5 11 W: 12 05 b.Liverpool 12-7-71

*Source:* Trainee.

| 1988–89 | Tranmere R | 9 | 2 |
|---|---|---|---|
| 1989–90 | Tranmere R | 42 | 2 |
| 1990–91 | Tranmere R | 33 | 3 |
| 1991–92 | Tranmere R | 30 | 3 |
| 1992–93 | Tranmere R | 16 | 0 |
| 1993–94 | Tranmere R | 40 | 2 |
| 1994–95 | Tranmere R | 26 | 0 |
| 1995–96 | Tranmere R | 31 | 0 |
| 1996–97 | Tranmere R | 30 | 0 |
| 1997–98 | Everton | 7 | 0 |
| **Total:** | | **264** | **12** |

## THOMAS, Wayne — Defender

H: 5 11 W: 11 12 b.Gloucester 17-5-79

*Source:* Trainee.

| 1995–96 | Torquay U | 6 | 0 |
|---|---|---|---|
| 1996–97 | Torquay U | 12 | 0 |
| 1997–98 | Torquay U | 21 | 1 |
| **Total:** | | **39** | **1** |

## THOMAS, Wayne — Midfield

H: 5 9 W: 12 07 b.Manchester 28-8-78

*Source:* Trainee.

| 1996–97 | Walsall | 20 | 0 |
|---|---|---|---|
| 1997–98 | Walsall | 5 | 0 |
| **Total:** | | **25** | **0** |

## THOMPSON, Alan — Midfield

H: 6 0 W: 12 08 b.Newcastle 22-12-73

*Source:* Trainee. *Honours:* England Youth, Under-21.

| 1990–91 | Newcastle U | 0 | 0 |
|---|---|---|---|
| 1991–92 | Newcastle U | 14 | 0 |
| 1992–93 | Newcastle U | 2 | 0 |
| 1993–94 | Bolton W | 27 | 6 |
| 1994–95 | Bolton W | 37 | 7 |
| 1995–96 | Bolton W | 26 | 1 |
| 1996–97 | Bolton W | 34 | 10 |
| 1997–98 | Bolton W | 33 | 9 |
| **Total:** | | **173** | **33** |

## THOMPSON, Andy — Defender

H: 5 4 W: 10 06 b.Cannock 9-11-67

*Source:* Apprentice.

| 1985–86 | WBA | 15 | 1 |
|---|---|---|---|
| 1986–87 | WBA | 9 | 0 |
| 1986–87 | Wolverhampton W | 29 | 8 |
| 1987–88 | Wolverhampton W | 42 | 2 |
| 1988–89 | Wolverhampton W | 46 | 6 |
| 1989–90 | Wolverhampton W | 33 | 4 |
| 1990–91 | Wolverhampton W | 44 | 3 |
| 1991–92 | Wolverhampton W | 17 | 0 |
| 1992–93 | Wolverhampton W | 20 | 0 |
| 1993–94 | Wolverhampton W | 37 | 3 |
| 1994–95 | Wolverhampton W | 31 | 9 |
| 1995–96 | Wolverhampton W | 45 | 6 |

| | | | |
|---|---|---|---|
| 1996–97 | Wolverhampton W | 32 | 2 |
| 1997–98 | Tranmere R | 44 | 3 |
| **Total:** | | **444** | **47** |

## THOMPSON, David — Defender

H: 6 2 W: 12 11 b.Ashington 20-11-68

*Source:* Trainee.

| | | | |
|---|---|---|---|
| 1986–87 | Millwall | 0 | 0 |
| 1987–88 | Millwall | 0 | 0 |
| 1988–89 | Millwall | 15 | 1 |
| 1989–90 | Millwall | 27 | 2 |
| 1990–91 | Millwall | 17 | 3 |
| 1991–92 | Millwall | 33 | 0 |
| 1992–93 | Bristol C | 17 | 0 |
| 1993–94 | Bristol C | 0 | 0 |
| 1993–94 | Brentford | 10 | 1 |
| 1994–95 | Brentford | 0 | 0 |
| 1994–95 | Blackpool | 17 | 0 |
| 1994–95 | Cambridge U | 7 | 0 |
| 1995–96 | Cambridge U | 15 | 0 |
| 1996–97 | Cambridge U | 22 | 2 |
| 1997–98 | Cambridge U | 0 | 0 |
| **Total:** | | **180** | **9** |

## THOMPSON, David — Midfield

H: 5 7 W: 10 00 b.Birkenhead 12-9-77

*Source:* Trainee. *Honours:* England Youth, Under-21.

| | | | |
|---|---|---|---|
| 1994–95 | Liverpool | 0 | 0 |
| 1995–96 | Liverpool | 0 | 0 |
| 1996–97 | Liverpool | 2 | 0 |
| 1997–98 | Liverpool | 5 | 1 |
| 1997–98 | Swindon T (loan) | 10 | 0 |
| **Total:** | | **17** | **1** |

## THOMPSON, Garry — Forward

H: 6 1 W: 14 07 b.Birmingham 7-10-59

*Source:* Apprentice. *Honours:* England Under-21.

| | | | |
|---|---|---|---|
| 1977–78 | Coventry C | 6 | 2 |
| 1978–79 | Coventry C | 20 | 8 |
| 1979–80 | Coventry C | 17 | 6 |
| 1980–81 | Coventry C | 35 | 8 |
| 1981–82 | Coventry C | 36 | 10 |
| 1982–83 | Coventry C | 20 | 4 |
| 1982–83 | WBA | 12 | 7 |
| 1983–84 | WBA | 37 | 13 |
| 1984–85 | WBA | 42 | 19 |
| 1985–86 | Sheffield W | 36 | 7 |
| 1986–87 | Aston Villa | 31 | 6 |
| 1987–88 | Aston Villa | 24 | 11 |
| 1988–89 | Aston Villa | 5 | 0 |
| 1988–89 | Watford | 21 | 7 |
| 1989–90 | Watford | 13 | 1 |
| 1989–90 | Crystal Palace | 9 | 2 |
| 1990–91 | Crystal Palace | 11 | 1 |
| 1991–92 | QPR | 15 | 1 |
| 1992–93 | QPR | 4 | 0 |
| 1993–94 | Cardiff C | 30 | 5 |
| 1994–95 | Cardiff C | 13 | 0 |
| 1994–95 | Northampton T | 15 | 4 |
| 1995–96 | Northampton T | 34 | 2 |
| 1996–97 | Northampton T | 1 | 0 |
| 1997–98 | Northampton T | 0 | 0 |
| **Total:** | | **487** | **124** |

## THOMPSON, Mark — Midfield

H: 6 1 W: 11 10 b.Southampton 17-9-77

*Source:* Trainee.

| | | | |
|---|---|---|---|
| 1996–97 | Portsmouth | 0 | 0 |
| 1997–98 | Portsmouth | 0 | 0 |

## THOMPSON, Neil — Defender

H: 5 11 W: 13 08 b.Beverley 2-10-63

*Source:* Nottingham F Apprentice.

| | | | |
|---|---|---|---|
| 1981–82 | Hull C | 23 | 0 |
| 1982–83 | Hull C | 8 | 0 |
| From Scarborough. | | | |
| 1987–88 | Scarborough | 41 | 6 |
| 1988–89 | Scarborough | 46 | 9 |
| 1989–90 | Ipswich T | 45 | 3 |
| 1990–91 | Ipswich T | 38 | 6 |
| 1991–92 | Ipswich T | 45 | 6 |
| 1992–93 | Ipswich T | 31 | 3 |
| 1993–94 | Ipswich T | 32 | 0 |
| 1994–95 | Ipswich T | 10 | 0 |
| 1995–96 | Ipswich T | 5 | 1 |
| 1996–97 | Barnsley | 24 | 5 |
| 1997–98 | Barnsley | 3 | 0 |
| 1997–98 | Oldham Ath (loan) | 8 | 0 |
| 1997–98 | York C | 12 | 2 |
| **Total:** | | **371** | **41** |

## THOMPSON, Niall — Forward

H: 5 11 W: 11 00 b.Birmingham 16-4-74

*Source:* Trainee.

| | | | |
|---|---|---|---|
| 1992–93 | Crystal Palace | 0 | 0 |
| 1993–94 | Crystal Palace | 0 | 0 |
| 1994–95 | Colchester U | 13 | 5 |
| From Zulte VV. | | | |
| 1997–98 | Brentford | 8 | 0 |
| **Total:** | | **21** | **5** |

## THOMPSON, Phil — Defender

H: 5 11 W: 12 00 b.Blackpool 1-4-81

*Source:* Trainee.

| | | | |
|---|---|---|---|
| 1997–98 | Blackpool | 1 | 0 |
| **Total:** | | **1** | **0** |

## THOMPSON, Steve — Midfield

H: 5 11 W: 13 00 b.Oldham 2-11-64

*Source:* Apprentice.

| | | | |
|---|---|---|---|
| 1982–83 | Bolton W | 3 | 0 |
| 1983–84 | Bolton W | 40 | 3 |
| 1984–85 | Bolton W | 34 | 4 |
| 1985–86 | Bolton W | 35 | 8 |
| 1986–87 | Bolton W | 44 | 7 |
| 1987–88 | Bolton W | 44 | 7 |
| 1988–89 | Bolton W | 43 | 9 |
| 1989–90 | Bolton W | 45 | 6 |
| 1990–91 | Bolton W | 45 | 5 |
| 1991–92 | Bolton W | 2 | 0 |
| 1991–92 | Luton T | 5 | 0 |
| 1991–92 | Leicester C | 34 | 3 |
| 1992–93 | Leicester C | 44 | 8 |
| 1993–94 | Leicester C | 30 | 7 |
| 1994–95 | Leicester C | 19 | 0 |
| 1994–95 | Burnley | 12 | 0 |
| 1995–96 | Burnley | 18 | 0 |
| 1996–97 | Burnley | 19 | 1 |
| 1997–98 | Rotherham U | 39 | 3 |
| **Total:** | | **555** | **71** |

## THOMPSON, Steven — Forward

H: 6 2 W: 12 05 b.Paisley 14-10-78

*Source:* Dundee U BC. *Honours:* Scotland Under-21.

| | | | |
|---|---|---|---|
| 1996–97 | Dundee U | 1 | 0 |
| 1997–98 | Dundee U | 8 | 0 |
| **Total:** | | **9** | **0** |

## THOMSEN, Claus — Midfield

H: 6 3 W: 11 06 b.Aarhus 31-5-70

*Source:* Aarhus. *Honours:* Denmark Under-21, 16 full caps.

| | | | |
|---|---|---|---|
| 1994–95 | Ipswich T | 33 | 5 |
| 1995–96 | Ipswich T | 37 | 2 |
| 1996–97 | Ipswich T | 11 | 0 |
| 1996–97 | Everton | 16 | 0 |
| 1997–98 | Everton | 8 | 1 |
| **Total:** | | **105** | **8** |

## THOMSON, Andy — Defender

H: 6 3 W: 14 00 b.Swindon 28-3-74

*Source:* Trainee.

| | | | |
|---|---|---|---|
| 1992–93 | Swindon T | 0 | 0 |
| 1993–94 | Swindon T | 1 | 0 |
| 1994–95 | Swindon T | 21 | 0 |
| 1995–96 | Swindon T | 0 | 0 |
| 1995–96 | Portsmouth | 16 | 0 |
| 1996–97 | Portsmouth | 28 | 1 |
| 1997–98 | Portsmouth | 35 | 2 |
| **Total:** | | **101** | **3** |

## THOMSON, Andy — Forward

H: 5 10 W: 10 12 b.Motherwell 1-4-71

*Source:* Jerviston BC.

| | | | |
|---|---|---|---|
| 1989–90 | Q of S | 26 | 6 |
| 1990–91 | Q of S | 37 | 11 |
| 1991–92 | Q of S | 39 | 26 |
| 1992–93 | Q of S | 38 | 21 |
| 1993–94 | Q of S | 35 | 29 |
| 1994–95 | Southend U | 39 | 11 |
| 1995–96 | Southend U | 33 | 6 |
| 1996–97 | Southend U | 17 | 5 |
| 1997–98 | Southend U | 33 | 6 |
| **Total:** | | **297** | **121** |

## THOMSON, Scott M — Midfield

H: 5 10 W: 11 10 b.Aberdeen 29-1-72

*Source:* Shrewsbury T Trainee.

| | | | |
|---|---|---|---|
| 1990–91 | Brechin C | 30 | 3 |
| 1991–92 | Brechin C | 11 | 3 |
| 1991–92 | Aberdeen | 0 | 0 |
| 1992–93 | Aberdeen | 2 | 0 |
| 1993–94 | Aberdeen | 3 | 0 |
| 1994–95 | Aberdeen | 10 | 1 |
| 1995–96 | Aberdeen | 4 | 0 |
| 1995–96 | Raith R | 9 | 1 |
| 1996–97 | Raith R | 22 | 2 |
| 1997–98 | Raith R | 0 | 0 |
| **Total:** | | **91** | **10** |

## THOMSON, Scott Y — Goalkeeper

H: 6 0 W: 11 09 b.Edinburgh 8-11-66

*Source:* Hutchison Vale BC.

| | | | |
|---|---|---|---|
| 1986–87 | Dundee U | 3 | 0 |
| 1987–88 | Dundee U | 0 | 0 |
| 1988–89 | Dundee U | 1 | 0 |
| 1989–90 | Dundee U | 2 | 0 |
| 1990–91 | Dundee U | 0 | 0 |
| 1991–92 | Forfar Ath | 44 | 0 |

| | | | |
|---|---|---|---|
| 1992–93 | Forfar Ath | 39 | 0 |
| 1993–94 | Forfar Ath | 5 | 0 |
| 1993–94 | Raith R | 34 | 0 |
| 1994–95 | Raith R | 35 | 0 |
| 1995–96 | Raith R | 26 | 0 |
| 1996–97 | Raith R | 28 | 0 |
| 1997–98 | Hull C | 9 | 0 |
| 1997–98 | Motherwell | 1 | 0 |
| **Total:** | | **227** | **0** |

## THOMSON, Steve — Midfield

H: 5 8 W: 10 04 b.Glasgow 23-1-78

*Source:* Trainee.

| | | | |
|---|---|---|---|
| 1995–96 | Crystal Palace | 0 | 0 |
| 1996–97 | Crystal Palace | 0 | 0 |
| 1997–98 | Crystal Palace | 0 | 0 |

## THORN, Andy — Defender

H: 6 0 W: 11 06 b.Carshalton 12-11-66

*Source:* Apprentice. *Honours:* England Under-21.

| | | | |
|---|---|---|---|
| 1984–85 | Wimbledon | 10 | 0 |
| 1985–86 | Wimbledon | 28 | 0 |
| 1986–87 | Wimbledon | 34 | 2 |
| 1987–88 | Wimbledon | 35 | 0 |
| 1988–89 | Newcastle U | 26 | 1 |
| 1989–90 | Newcastle U | 10 | 1 |
| 1989–90 | Crystal Palace | 17 | 1 |
| 1990–91 | Crystal Palace | 34 | 1 |
| 1991–92 | Crystal Palace | 33 | 0 |
| 1992–93 | Crystal Palace | 34 | 1 |
| 1993–94 | Crystal Palace | 10 | 0 |
| 1994–95 | Crystal Palace | 0 | 0 |
| 1994–95 | Wimbledon | 23 | 1 |
| 1995–96 | Wimbledon | 14 | 0 |
| 1996–97 | Wimbledon | 0 | 0 |
| 1996–97 | Hearts | 1 | 0 |
| 1996–97 | Tranmere R | 19 | 1 |
| 1997–98 | Tranmere R | 17 | 0 |
| **Total:** | | **345** | **9** |

## THORNE, Peter — Forward

H: 6 0 W: 13 07 b.Manchester 21-6-73

*Source:* Trainee.

| | | | |
|---|---|---|---|
| 1991–92 | Blackburn R | 0 | 0 |
| 1992–93 | Blackburn R | 0 | 0 |
| 1993–94 | Blackburn R | 0 | 0 |
| 1993–94 | Wigan Ath (loan) | 11 | 0 |
| 1994–95 | Blackburn R | 0 | 0 |
| 1994–95 | Swindon T | 20 | 9 |
| 1995–96 | Swindon T | 26 | 10 |
| 1996–97 | Swindon T | 31 | 8 |
| 1997–98 | Stoke C | 36 | 12 |
| **Total:** | | **124** | **39** |

## THORNLEY, Ben — Forward

H: 5 9 W: 11 07 b.Bury 21-4-75

*Source:* Trainee. *Honours:* England Schools, Under-21.

| | | | |
|---|---|---|---|
| 1992–93 | Manchester U | 0 | 0 |
| 1993–94 | Manchester U | 1 | 0 |
| 1994–95 | Manchester U | 0 | 0 |
| 1995–96 | Manchester U | 1 | 0 |
| 1995–96 | Stockport Co (loan) | 10 | 1 |
| 1995–96 | Huddersfield T (loan) | 12 | 2 |
| 1996–97 | Manchester U | 2 | 0 |
| 1997–98 | Manchester U | 5 | 0 |
| **Total:** | | **31** | **3** |

## THORNLEY, Rob — Forward

H: 5 9 W: 11 05 b.Bury 2-8-77

*Source:* Warrington T.

| | | | |
|---|---|---|---|
| 1997–98 | Doncaster R | 1 | 0 |
| **Total:** | | **1** | **0** |

## THOROGOOD, Marc — Forward

b.Waltham Abbey 13-1-79

*Source:* Trainee.

| | | | |
|---|---|---|---|
| 1997–98 | Arsenal | 0 | 0 |

## THORP, Hamilton — Forward

H: 6 3 W: 13 10 b.Australia 21-8-73

*Source:* West Adelaide.

| | | | |
|---|---|---|---|
| 1997–98 | Portsmouth | 7 | 0 |
| **Total:** | | **7** | **0** |

## THORP, Michael — Defender

H: 6 0 W: 11 07 b.Wallington 5-12-75

*Source:* Trainee.

| | | | |
|---|---|---|---|
| 1994–95 | Reading | 0 | 0 |
| 1995–96 | Reading | 2 | 0 |
| 1996–97 | Reading | 0 | 0 |
| 1997–98 | Reading | 3 | 0 |
| **Total:** | | **5** | **0** |

## THORPE, Andy — Defender

H: 5 11 W: 12 02 b.Stockport 15-9-60

*Source:* Amateur.

| | | | |
|---|---|---|---|
| 1977–78 | Stockport Co | 4 | 0 |

| | | | |
|---|---|---|---|
| 1978–79 | Stockport Co | 38 | 0 |
| 1979–80 | Stockport Co | 36 | 1 |
| 1980–81 | Stockport Co | 38 | 1 |
| 1981–82 | Stockport Co | 46 | 0 |
| 1982–83 | Stockport Co | 46 | 0 |
| 1983–84 | Stockport Co | 45 | 1 |
| 1984–85 | Stockport Co | 31 | 0 |
| 1985–86 | Stockport Co | 30 | 0 |
| 1986–87 | Tranmere R | 39 | 0 |
| 1987–88 | Tranmere R | 14 | 0 |
| 1987–88 | Stockport Co | 20 | 0 |
| 1988–89 | Stockport Co | 41 | 0 |
| 1989–90 | Stockport Co | 40 | 0 |
| 1990–91 | Stockport Co | 40 | 0 |
| 1991–92 | Stockport Co | 34 | 0 |
| From Chorley. | | | |
| 1997–98 | Doncaster R | 2 | 0 |
| **Total:** | | **544** | **3** |

## THORPE, Jeff — Defender

H: 5 11 W: 12 08 b.Cockermouth 17-11-72

*Source:* Trainee.

| | | | |
|---|---|---|---|
| 1990–91 | Carlisle U | 13 | 0 |
| 1991–92 | Carlisle U | 28 | 1 |
| 1992–93 | Carlisle U | 28 | 0 |
| 1993–94 | Carlisle U | 0 | 0 |
| 1994–95 | Carlisle U | 28 | 4 |
| 1995–96 | Carlisle U | 34 | 1 |
| 1996–97 | Carlisle U | 5 | 0 |
| 1997–98 | Carlisle U | 14 | 0 |
| **Total:** | | **150** | **6** |

## THORPE, Lee — Forward

H: 6 0 W: 11 06 b.Wolverhampton 14-12-75

*Source:* Trainee.

| | | | |
|---|---|---|---|
| 1993–94 | Blackpool | 1 | 0 |
| 1994–95 | Blackpool | 1 | 0 |
| 1995–96 | Blackpool | 1 | 0 |
| 1996–97 | Blackpool | 9 | 0 |
| 1997–98 | Lincoln C | 44 | 14 |
| **Total:** | | **56** | **14** |

## THORPE, Tony — Forward

H: 5 9 W: 12 03 b.Leicester 10-4-74

*Source:* Leicester C.

| | | | |
|---|---|---|---|
| 1992–93 | Luton T | 0 | 0 |
| 1993–94 | Luton T | 14 | 1 |
| 1994–95 | Luton T | 4 | 0 |
| 1995–96 | Luton T | 33 | 7 |
| 1996–97 | Luton T | 41 | 28 |
| 1997–98 | Luton T | 28 | 14 |
| 1997–98 | Fulham | 13 | 3 |
| **Total:** | | **133** | **53** |

## THORRINGTON, John — Forward

H: 5 7 W: 10 05 b.Johannesburg 17-10-79

*Source:* US College.

| | | | |
|---|---|---|---|
| 1997–98 | Manchester U | 0 | 0 |

## TIATTO, Danny

b.Melbourne 22-5-73

*Source:* Baden.

| | | | |
|---|---|---|---|
| 1997–98 | Stoke C | 15 | 1 |
| **Total:** | | **15** | **1** |

## TIERNEY, Fran — Forward

H: 5 10 W: 11 00 b.Liverpool 10-9-75

*Source:* Trainee.

| | | | |
|---|---|---|---|
| 1992–93 | Crewe Alex | 1 | 0 |
| 1993–94 | Crewe Alex | 8 | 1 |
| 1994–95 | Crewe Alex | 20 | 4 |
| 1995–96 | Crewe Alex | 22 | 2 |
| 1996–97 | Crewe Alex | 32 | 3 |
| 1997–98 | Crewe Alex | 4 | 0 |
| **Total:** | | **87** | **10** |

## TILER, Carl — Defender

H: 6 2 W: 13 10 b.Sheffield 11-2-70

*Source:* Trainee. *Honours:* England Under-21.

| | | | |
|---|---|---|---|
| 1987–88 | Barnsley | 1 | 0 |
| 1988–89 | Barnsley | 4 | 0 |
| 1989–90 | Barnsley | 21 | 1 |
| 1990–91 | Barnsley | 45 | 2 |
| 1991–92 | Nottingham F | 26 | 1 |
| 1992–93 | Nottingham F | 37 | 0 |
| 1993–94 | Nottingham F | 3 | 0 |
| 1994–95 | Nottingham F | 3 | 0 |
| 1994–95 | Swindon T (loan) | 2 | 0 |
| 1995–96 | Nottingham F | 0 | 0 |
| 1995–96 | Aston Villa | 1 | 0 |
| 1996–97 | Aston Villa | 11 | 1 |
| 1996–97 | Sheffield U | 6 | 1 |
| 1997–98 | Sheffield U | 17 | 1 |
| 1997–98 | Everton | 19 | 1 |
| **Total:** | | **196** | **8** |

## TILLSON, Andrew — Defender

H: 6 2 W: 12 10 b.Huntingdon 30-6-66

*Source:* Kettering T.

| | | | |
|---|---|---|---|
| 1988–89 | Grimsby T | 45 | 2 |
| 1989–90 | Grimsby T | 42 | 3 |
| 1990–91 | Grimsby T | 18 | 0 |
| 1990–91 | QPR | 19 | 2 |
| 1991–92 | QPR | 10 | 0 |
| 1992–93 | QPR | 0 | 0 |
| 1992–93 | Grimsby T (loan) | 4 | 0 |
| 1992–93 | Bristol R | 29 | 0 |
| 1993–94 | Bristol R | 13 | 0 |
| 1994–95 | Bristol R | 40 | 2 |
| 1995–96 | Bristol R | 38 | 1 |
| 1996–97 | Bristol R | 38 | 2 |
| 1997–98 | Bristol R | 33 | 3 |
| **Total:** | | **329** | **15** |

## TIMONS, Chris — Defender

H: 6 1 W: 12 07 b.Longworth 8-12-74

*Source:* Clipstone Welfare.

| | | | |
|---|---|---|---|
| 1993–94 | Mansfield T | 16 | 1 |
| 1994–95 | Mansfield T | 6 | 0 |
| 1995–96 | Mansfield T | 17 | 1 |
| 1996–97 | Chesterfield | 0 | 0 |
| 1996–97 | Leyton Orient | 6 | 2 |
| 1997–98 | Leyton Orient | 0 | 0 |
| **Total:** | | **45** | **4** |

## TINDALL, Jason — Defender

H: 6 1 W: 11 10 b.Mile End 15-11-77

*Source:* Trainee.

| | | | |
|---|---|---|---|
| 1996–97 | Charlton Ath | 0 | 0 |
| 1997–98 | Charlton Ath | 0 | 0 |

## TINKLER, Eric — Midfield

H: 6 2 W: 12 03 b.Roodepoort 30-7-70

*Honours:* South Africa 5 full caps.

| | | | |
|---|---|---|---|
| 1993–94 | Vitoria Setubal | 21 | 0 |
| 1994–95 | Vitoria Setubal | 17 | 1 |
| 1995–96 | Vitoria Setubal | 19 | 0 |
| 1996–97 | Cagliari | 20 | 0 |
| 1997–98 | Barnsley | 25 | 2 |
| **Total:** | | **102** | **3** |

## TINKLER, Mark — Midfield

H: 5 11 W: 13 03 b.Bishop Auckland 24-10-74

*Source:* Trainee. *Honours:* England Schools, Youth.

| | | | |
|---|---|---|---|
| 1991–92 | Leeds U | 0 | 0 |
| 1992–93 | Leeds U | 7 | 0 |
| 1993–94 | Leeds U | 3 | 0 |
| 1994–95 | Leeds U | 3 | 0 |
| 1995–96 | Leeds U | 9 | 0 |
| 1996–97 | Leeds U | 3 | 0 |
| 1996–97 | York C | 9 | 1 |
| 1997–98 | York C | 44 | 5 |
| **Total:** | | **78** | **6** |

## TINNION, Brian — Midfield

H: 5 11 W: 11 05 b.Stanley 23-2-68

*Source:* Apprentice.

| | | | |
|---|---|---|---|
| 1985–86 | Newcastle U | 0 | 0 |
| 1986–87 | Newcastle U | 3 | 0 |
| 1987–88 | Newcastle U | 16 | 1 |
| 1988–89 | Newcastle U | 13 | 1 |
| 1988–89 | Bradford C | 14 | 1 |
| 1989–90 | Bradford C | 37 | 5 |
| 1990–91 | Bradford C | 41 | 5 |
| 1991–92 | Bradford C | 26 | 8 |
| 1992–93 | Bradford C | 27 | 3 |
| 1992–93 | Bristol C | 11 | 2 |
| 1993–94 | Bristol C | 41 | 5 |
| 1994–95 | Bristol C | 35 | 2 |
| 1995–96 | Bristol C | 30 | 3 |
| 1996–97 | Bristol C | 32 | 1 |
| 1997–98 | Bristol C | 44 | 3 |
| **Total:** | | **370** | **40** |

## TINSON, Darren — Defender

H: 6 0 W: 14 04 b.Birmingham 15-11-69

*Source:* Northwich V.

| | | | |
|---|---|---|---|
| 1997–98 | Macclesfield T | 44 | 0 |
| **Total:** | | **44** | **0** |

## TIPPLE, Gaven — Midfield

H: 5 9 W: 11 00 b.Welwyn 9-2-79

*Source:* Trainee.

| | | | |
|---|---|---|---|
| 1997–98 | Norwich C | 0 | 0 |

## TIPTON, Matthew — Forward

H: 5 10 W: 10 07 b.Bangor 29-6-80

*Source:* Trainee. *Honours:* Wales Under-21.

| | | | |
|---|---|---|---|
| 1997–98 | Oldham Ath | 3 | 0 |
| **Total:** | | **3** | **0** |

## TISDALE, Paul — Midfield

H: 5 9 W: 10 09 b.Malta 14-1-73

*Source:* School. *Honours:* England Schools.

| | | | |
|---|---|---|---|
| 1991–92 | Southampton | 0 | 0 |
| 1992–93 | Southampton | 0 | 0 |
| 1992–93 | Northampton T (loan) | 5 | 0 |
| 1993–94 | Southampton | 0 | 0 |
| 1994–95 | Southampton | 7 | 0 |
| 1995–96 | Southampton | 9 | 1 |
| 1996–97 | Southampton | 0 | 0 |
| 1996–97 | Huddersfield T (loan) | 2 | 0 |
| 1997–98 | Bristol C | 5 | 0 |
| 1997–98 | Exeter C (loan) | 10 | 1 |
| **Total:** | | **38** | **2** |

## TOD, Andrew — Defender

H: 6 3 W: 12 00 b.Dunfermline 4-11-71

*Source:* Kelty Hearts.

| | | | |
|---|---|---|---|
| 1993–94 | Dunfermline Ath | 22 | 11 |
| 1994–95 | Dunfermline Ath | 35 | 6 |
| 1995–96 | Dunfermline Ath | 36 | 5 |
| 1996–97 | Dunfermline Ath | 35 | 4 |
| 1997–98 | Dunfermline Ath | 35 | 6 |
| **Total:** | | **163** | **32** |

## TODD, Andrew — Midfield

H: 6 0 W: 11 03 b.Nottingham 22-2-79

*Source:* Eastwood T.

| | | | |
|---|---|---|---|
| 1995–96 | Nottingham F | 0 | 0 |
| 1996–97 | Nottingham F | 0 | 0 |
| 1997–98 | Nottingham F | 0 | 0 |

## TODD, Andy — Defender

H: 5 10 W: 10 11 b.Derby 21-9-74

*Source:* Trainee.

| | | | |
|---|---|---|---|
| 1991–92 | Middlesbrough | 0 | 0 |
| 1992–93 | Middlesbrough | 0 | 0 |
| 1993–94 | Middlesbrough | 3 | 0 |
| 1994–95 | Middlesbrough | 5 | 0 |
| 1994–95 | Swindon T (loan) | 13 | 0 |
| 1995–96 | Bolton W | 12 | 2 |
| 1996–97 | Bolton W | 15 | 0 |
| 1997–98 | Bolton W | 25 | 0 |
| **Total:** | | **73** | **2** |

## TODD, Lee — Defender

H: 5 7 W: 11 00 b.Hartlepool 7-3-72

*Source:* Hartlepool U Trainee.

| | | | |
|---|---|---|---|
| 1990–91 | Stockport Co | 14 | 0 |
| 1991–92 | Stockport Co | 19 | 0 |
| 1992–93 | Stockport Co | 39 | 0 |
| 1993–94 | Stockport Co | 33 | 0 |
| 1994–95 | Stockport Co | 37 | 2 |
| 1995–96 | Stockport Co | 42 | 0 |
| 1996–97 | Stockport Co | 41 | 0 |
| 1997–98 | Southampton | 10 | 0 |
| **Total:** | | **235** | **2** |

## TODD, Luke — Midfield

b.Doncaster 26-12-78

*Source:* Sheffield W Trainee.

| | | | |
|---|---|---|---|
| 1997–98 | Chesterfield | 0 | 0 |

## TOLSON, Neil — Forward

H: 6 3 W: 11 05 b.Wordley 25-10-73

*Source:* Trainee.

| | | | |
|---|---|---|---|
| 1991–92 | Walsall | 9 | 1 |
| 1991–92 | Oldham Ath | 0 | 0 |
| 1992–93 | Oldham Ath | 3 | 0 |
| 1993–94 | Oldham Ath | 0 | 0 |
| 1993–94 | Bradford C | 22 | 2 |
| 1994–95 | Bradford C | 10 | 2 |
| 1994–95 | Chester C (loan) | 4 | 0 |
| 1995–96 | Bradford C | 31 | 8 |
| 1996–97 | York C | 40 | 12 |
| 1997–98 | York C | 16 | 3 |
| **Total:** | | **135** | **28** |

## TOMASSON, Jon Dahl — Forward

H: 6 0 W: 11 02 b.Copenhagen 29-8-76

*Source:* Koge. *Honours:* Denmark 4 full caps.

| | | | |
|---|---|---|---|
| 1994–95 | Heerenveen | 16 | 5 |
| 1995–96 | Heerenveen | 30 | 14 |
| 1996–97 | Heerenveen | 32 | 18 |
| 1997–98 | Newcastle U | 23 | 3 |
| **Total:** | | **101** | **40** |

## TOMLINSON, Graeme — Forward

H: 5 10 W: 12 07 b.Watford 10-12-75

*Source:* Trainee.

| | | | |
|---|---|---|---|
| 1993–94 | Bradford C | 17 | 6 |
| 1994–95 | Manchester U | 0 | 0 |
| 1995–96 | Manchester U | 0 | 0 |

## Tomlinson, Micky

| | | | |
|---|---|---|---|
| 1995–96 | Luton T (loan) | 7 | 0 |
| 1996–97 | Manchester U | 0 | 0 |
| 1997–98 | Manchester U | 0 | 0 |
| 1997–98 | Bournemouth (loan) | 7 | 1 |
| 1997–98 | Millwall (loan) | 3 | 1 |
| **Total:** | | **34** | **8** |

## TOMLINSON, Micky — Forward

H: 5 8 W: 11 00 b.Lambeth 15-9-72

*Source:* Trainee.

| | | | |
|---|---|---|---|
| 1990–91 | Leyton Orient | 1 | 1 |
| 1991–92 | Leyton Orient | 1 | 0 |
| 1992–93 | Leyton Orient | 8 | 0 |
| 1993–94 | Leyton Orient | 4 | 0 |
| 1993–94 | Barnet | 11 | 0 |
| 1994–95 | Barnet | 27 | 1 |
| 1995–96 | Barnet | 25 | 2 |
| 1996–97 | Barnet | 30 | 1 |
| 1997–98 | Barnet | 0 | 0 |
| **Total:** | | **107** | **5** |

## TOPLEY, Jonathan — Forward

b.Craigavon 12-7-80

*Source:* Trainee.

| | | | |
|---|---|---|---|
| 1997–98 | Blackburn R | 0 | 0 |

## TORPEY, Steve — Forward

H: 6 3 W: 13 03 b.Islington 8-12-70

*Source:* Trainee.

| | | | |
|---|---|---|---|
| 1988–89 | Millwall | 0 | 0 |
| 1989–90 | Millwall | 7 | 0 |
| 1990–91 | Millwall | 0 | 0 |
| 1990–91 | Bradford C | 29 | 7 |
| 1991–92 | Bradford C | 43 | 10 |
| 1992–93 | Bradford C | 24 | 5 |
| 1993–94 | Swansea C | 40 | 9 |
| 1994–95 | Swansea C | 41 | 11 |
| 1995–96 | Swansea C | 42 | 15 |
| 1996–97 | Swansea C | 39 | 9 |
| 1997–98 | Bristol C | 29 | 8 |
| **Total:** | | **294** | **74** |

## TOSH, Paul — Forward

H: 6 0 W: 11 10 b.Arbroath 18-10-73

*Source:* Arbroath Lads.

| | | | |
|---|---|---|---|
| 1991–92 | Arbroath | 8 | 1 |
| 1992–93 | Arbroath | 34 | 12 |
| 1993–94 | Dundee | 26 | 1 |
| 1994–95 | Dundee | 27 | 5 |
| 1995–96 | Dundee | 30 | 9 |
| 1996–97 | Dundee | 23 | 4 |
| 1996–97 | Hibernian | 6 | 1 |
| 1997–98 | Hibernain | 15 | 1 |
| **Total:** | | **169** | **34** |

## TOSH, Steven — Midfield

H: 5 9 W: 10 02 b.Kirkcaldy 27-4-73

*Source:* Glenrothes Juniors.

| | | | |
|---|---|---|---|
| 1993–94 | Arbroath | 7 | 1 |
| 1994–95 | Arbroath | 31 | 11 |
| 1995–96 | St Johnstone | 9 | 1 |
| 1996–97 | St Johnstone | 27 | 3 |
| 1997–98 | St Johnstone | 8 | 1 |
| 1997–98 | Raith R | 6 | 0 |
| **Total:** | | **88** | **17** |

## TOWN, David — Forward

H: 5 7 W: 11 13 b.Bournemouth 9-12-76

*Source:* Trainee.

| | | | |
|---|---|---|---|
| 1993–94 | Bournemouth | 1 | 0 |
| 1994–95 | Bournemouth | 5 | 0 |
| 1995–96 | Bournemouth | 7 | 0 |
| 1996–97 | Bournemouth | 26 | 2 |
| 1997–98 | Bournemouth | 7 | 0 |
| **Total:** | | **46** | **2** |

## TOWNLEY, Leon — Defender

H: 6 2 W: 13 11 b.Loughton 16-2-76

*Source:* Trainee.

| | | | |
|---|---|---|---|
| 1994–95 | Tottenham H | 0 | 0 |
| 1995–96 | Tottenham H | 0 | 0 |
| 1996–97 | Tottenham H | 0 | 0 |
| 1997–98 | Tottenham H | 0 | 0 |
| 1997–98 | Brentford | 16 | 2 |
| **Total:** | | **16** | **2** |

## TOWNSEND, Andy — Midfield

H: 5 11 W: 13 06 b.Maidstone 27-7-63

*Source:* Welling U, Weymouth. *Honours:* Eire B, 70 full caps, 7 goals.

| | | | |
|---|---|---|---|
| 1984–85 | Southampton | 5 | 0 |
| 1985–86 | Southampton | 27 | 1 |
| 1986–87 | Southampton | 14 | 1 |
| 1987–88 | Southampton | 37 | 3 |
| 1988–89 | Norwich C | 36 | 5 |
| 1989–90 | Norwich C | 35 | 3 |
| 1990–91 | Chelsea | 34 | 2 |
| 1991–92 | Chelsea | 35 | 6 |
| 1992–93 | Chelsea | 41 | 4 |
| 1993–94 | Aston Villa | 32 | 3 |

| | | | |
|---|---|---|---|
| 1994–95 | Aston Villa | 32 | 1 |
| 1995–96 | Aston Villa | 33 | 2 |
| 1996–97 | Aston Villa | 34 | 2 |
| 1997–98 | Aston Villa | 3 | 0 |
| 1997–98 | Middlesbrough | 37 | 2 |
| **Total:** | | **435** | **35** |

## TRACEY, Richard — Midfield

H: 5 11 W: 10 12 b.Dewsbury 9-7-79

*Source:* Trainee.

| | | | |
|---|---|---|---|
| 1997–98 | Sheffield U | 0 | 0 |
| 1997–98 | Rotherham U | 0 | 0 |

## TRACEY, Simon — Goalkeeper

H: 6 0 W: 13 12 b.Woolwich 9-12-67

*Source:* Apprentice.

| | | | |
|---|---|---|---|
| 1985–86 | Wimbledon | 0 | 0 |
| 1986–87 | Wimbledon | 0 | 0 |
| 1987–88 | Wimbledon | 0 | 0 |
| 1988–89 | Wimbledon | 1 | 0 |
| 1988–89 | Sheffield U | 7 | 0 |
| 1989–90 | Sheffield U | 46 | 0 |
| 1990–91 | Sheffield U | 31 | 0 |
| 1991–92 | Sheffield U | 29 | 0 |
| 1992–93 | Sheffield U | 10 | 0 |
| 1993–94 | Sheffield U | 15 | 0 |
| 1994–95 | Sheffield U | 5 | 0 |
| 1994–95 | Manchester C (loan) | 3 | 0 |
| 1994–95 | Norwich C (loan) | 1 | 0 |
| 1995–96 | Sheffield U | 11 | 0 |
| 1995–96 | Wimbledon (loan) | 1 | 0 |
| 1996–97 | Sheffield U | 7 | 0 |
| 1997–98 | Sheffield U | 27 | 0 |
| **Total:** | | **194** | **0** |

## TRAVIS, Simon — Midfield

H: 5 7 W: 10 00 b.Preston 22-3-77

*Source:* Trainee.

| | | | |
|---|---|---|---|
| 1995–96 | Torquay U | 8 | 0 |
| 1996–97 | Torquay U | 0 | 0 |
| From Holywell T. | | | |
| 1997–98 | Stockport Co | 13 | 2 |
| **Total:** | | **21** | **2** |

## TRETTON, Andrew — Defender

H: 6 0 W: 12 08 b.Derby 9-10-76

*Source:* Trainee.

| | | | |
|---|---|---|---|
| 1993–94 | Derby Co | 0 | 0 |
| 1994–95 | Derby Co | 0 | 0 |
| 1995–96 | Derby Co | 0 | 0 |
| 1996–97 | Derby Co | 0 | 0 |
| 1997–98 | Chesterfield | 0 | 0 |
| 1997–98 | Shrewsbury T | 14 | 1 |
| **Total:** | | **14** | **1** |

## TREVITT, Simon — Defender

H: 5 11 W: 12 09 b.Dewsbury 20-12-67

*Source:* Apprentice.

| | | | |
|---|---|---|---|
| 1986–87 | Huddersfield T | 11 | 0 |
| 1987–88 | Huddersfield T | 37 | 1 |
| 1988–89 | Huddersfield T | 39 | 0 |
| 1989–90 | Huddersfield T | 7 | 0 |
| 1990–91 | Huddersfield T | 38 | 0 |
| 1991–92 | Huddersfield T | 41 | 1 |
| 1992–93 | Huddersfield T | 0 | 0 |
| 1993–94 | Huddersfield T | 31 | 1 |
| 1994–95 | Huddersfield T | 21 | 0 |
| 1995–96 | Huddersfield T | 4 | 0 |
| 1995–96 | Hull C | 25 | 0 |
| 1996–97 | Hull C | 22 | 1 |
| 1997–98 | Hull C | 4 | 0 |
| 1997–98 | Swansea C (loan) | 1 | 0 |
| **Total:** | | **281** | **4** |

## TREVOR, Kris — Forward

b.South Shields 15-5-79

*Source:* Trainee.

| | | | |
|---|---|---|---|
| 1997–98 | Middlesbrough | 0 | 0 |

## TROLLOPE, Paul — Midfield

H: 6 0 W: 12 01 b.Swindon 3-6-72

*Source:* Trainee. *Honours:* Wales 5 full caps.

| | | | |
|---|---|---|---|
| 1989–90 | Swindon T | 0 | 0 |
| 1990–91 | Swindon T | 0 | 0 |
| 1991–92 | Swindon T | 0 | 0 |
| 1991–92 | Torquay U (loan) | 10 | 0 |
| 1992–93 | Torquay U | 36 | 2 |
| 1993–94 | Torquay U | 42 | 10 |
| 1994–95 | Torquay U | 18 | 4 |
| 1994–95 | Derby Co | 24 | 4 |
| 1995–96 | Derby Co | 17 | 0 |
| 1996–97 | Derby Co | 14 | 1 |
| 1996–97 | Grimsby T (loan) | 7 | 1 |
| 1996–97 | Crystal Palace (loan) | 9 | 0 |
| 1997–98 | Derby Co | 10 | 0 |
| 1997–98 | Fulham | 24 | 3 |
| **Total:** | | **211** | **25** |

## TSKHADADZE, Kakhabor — Defender

b.Rustavi 7-9-68

*Honours:* Georgia 23 full caps, 1 goal.

| | | | |
|---|---|---|---|
| 1988 | Dynamo Tbilisi | 14 | 1 |
| 1989 | Dynamo Tbilisi | 27 | 0 |
| 1990 | Sundsvall* | 0 | 0 |
| 1991 | Sundsvall | 4 | 0 |
| 1992 | Spartak Moscow | 7 | 0 |
| 1992–93 | Eintracht Frankfurt | 17 | 0 |
| 1993–94 | Eintracht Frankfurt | 29 | 0 |
| 1994–95 | Eintracht Frankfurt | 15 | 1 |
| 1995–96 | Eintracht Frankfurt | 3 | 0 |
| 1996–97 | Eintracht Frankfurt* | 0 | 0 |
| 1997 | Alania | 17 | 1 |
| 1997–98 | Manchester C | 10 | 1 |
| **Total:** | | **143** | **4** |

## TUCK, Stuart — Defender

H: 5 10 W: 11 10 b.Brighton 1-10-74

*Source:* Trainee.

| | | | |
|---|---|---|---|
| 1993–94 | Brighton & HA | 11 | 0 |
| 1994–95 | Brighton & HA | 23 | 0 |
| 1995–96 | Brighton & HA | 8 | 0 |
| 1996–97 | Brighton & HA | 27 | 0 |
| 1997–98 | Brighton & HA | 22 | 1 |
| **Total:** | | **91** | **1** |

## TUCKER, Dexter — Midfield

b.Pontefract 22-9-79

*Source:* Trainee.

| | | | |
|---|---|---|---|
| 1997–98 | Hull C | 7 | 0 |
| **Total:** | | **7** | **0** |

## TULLY, Craig — Defender

H: 5 11 W: 11 00 b.Stirling 7-1-76

*Source:* Victoria Juv.

| | | | |
|---|---|---|---|
| 1993–94 | Dundee | 1 | 0 |
| 1994–95 | Dundee | 0 | 0 |
| 1995–96 | Dundee | 2 | 0 |
| 1996–97 | Dundee | 21 | 0 |
| 1997–98 | Dundee | 14 | 0 |
| **Total:** | | **38** | **0** |

## TULLY, Stephen — Defender

H: 5 9 W: 11 00 b.Paignton 10-2-80

*Source:* Trainee.

| | | | |
|---|---|---|---|
| 1997–98 | Torquay U | 9 | 0 |
| **Total:** | | **9** | **0** |

## TURKINGTON, Eddie — Midfield

H: 6 1 W: 13 00 b.Merseyside 15-5-78

*Source:* Trainee.

| | | | |
|---|---|---|---|
| 1995–96 | Liverpool | 0 | 0 |
| 1996–97 | Liverpool | 0 | 0 |
| 1997–98 | Liverpool | 0 | 0 |

## TURLEY, Billy — Goalkeeper

H: 6 4 W: 14 10 b.Wolverhampton 15-7-73

*Source:* Evesham U.

| | | | |
|---|---|---|---|
| 1995–96 | Northampton T | 2 | 0 |
| 1996–97 | Northampton T | 1 | 0 |
| 1997–98 | Northampton T | 0 | 0 |
| 1997–98 | Leyton Orient (loan) | 14 | 0 |
| **Total:** | | **17** | **0** |

## TURNBULL, Lee — Defender

H: 6 0 W: 13 04 b.Stockton 27-9-67

*Source:* Local.

| | | | |
|---|---|---|---|
| 1985–86 | Middlesbrough | 2 | 0 |
| 1986–87 | Middlesbrough | 14 | 4 |
| 1987–88 | Middlesbrough | 0 | 0 |
| 1987–88 | Aston Villa | 0 | 0 |
| 1987–88 | Doncaster R | 30 | 1 |
| 1988–89 | Doncaster R | 32 | 4 |
| 1989–90 | Doncaster R | 42 | 10 |
| 1990–91 | Doncaster R | 19 | 6 |
| 1990–91 | Chesterfield | 19 | 9 |
| 1991–92 | Chesterfield | 27 | 7 |
| 1992–93 | Chesterfield | 33 | 8 |
| 1993–94 | Chesterfield | 8 | 2 |
| 1993–94 | Doncaster R | 11 | 1 |
| 1993–94 | Wycombe W | 6 | 0 |
| 1994–95 | Wycombe W | 5 | 1 |
| 1994–95 | Scunthorpe U (loan) | 10 | 3 |
| 1995–96 | Scunthorpe U | 23 | 3 |
| 1996–97 | Scunthorpe U | 14 | 1 |
| 1997–98 | Darlington | 9 | 0 |
| **Total:** | | **304** | **60** |

## TURNER, Andy — Forward

H: 5 10 W: 11 10 b.Woolwich 23-3-75

*Source:* Trainee. *Honours:* England Schools, Eire Under-21.

| | | | |
|---|---|---|---|
| 1991–92 | Tottenham H | 0 | 0 |
| 1992–93 | Tottenham H | 18 | 3 |
| 1993–94 | Tottenham H | 1 | 0 |
| 1994–95 | Tottenham H | 1 | 0 |
| 1994–95 | Wycombe W (loan) | 4 | 0 |
| 1994–95 | Doncaster R (loan) | 4 | 1 |
| 1995–96 | Tottenham H | 0 | 0 |

| | | | |
|---|---|---|---|
| 1995–96 | Huddersfield T (loan) | 5 | 1 |
| 1995–96 | Southend U (loan) | 6 | 0 |
| 1996–97 | Tottenham H | 0 | 0 |
| 1996–97 | Portsmouth | 24 | 2 |
| 1997–98 | Portsmouth | 16 | 1 |
| **Total:** | | **79** | **8** |

## TURNER, Barry — Midfield

H: 5 9 W: 10 01 b.Nottingham 1-12-78

*Source:* Trainee.

| | | | |
|---|---|---|---|
| 1995–96 | Nottingham F | 0 | 0 |
| 1996–97 | Nottingham F | 0 | 0 |
| 1997–98 | Nottingham F | 0 | 0 |

## TUTILL, Steve — Defender

H: 5 10 W: 12 06 b.Derwent 1-10-69

*Source:* Trainee. *Honours:* England Schools.

| | | | |
|---|---|---|---|
| 1987–88 | York C | 21 | 0 |
| 1988–89 | York C | 22 | 1 |
| 1989–90 | York C | 42 | 0 |
| 1990–91 | York C | 42 | 0 |
| 1991–92 | York C | 39 | 1 |
| 1992–93 | York C | 8 | 0 |
| 1993–94 | York C | 46 | 4 |
| 1994–95 | York C | 39 | 0 |
| 1995–96 | York C | 25 | 0 |
| 1996–97 | York C | 15 | 0 |
| 1997–98 | York C | 2 | 0 |
| 1997–98 | Darlington | 7 | 0 |
| **Total:** | | **308** | **6** |

## TUTTLE, David — Defender

H: 6 2 W: 12 10 b.Reading 6-2-72

*Source:* Trainee. *Honours:* England Youth.

| | | | |
|---|---|---|---|
| 1989–90 | Tottenham H | 0 | 0 |
| 1990–91 | Tottenham H | 6 | 0 |
| 1991–92 | Tottenham H | 2 | 0 |
| 1992–93 | Tottenham H | 5 | 0 |
| 1992–93 | Peterborough U (loan) | 7 | 0 |
| 1993–94 | Sheffield U | 31 | 0 |
| 1994–95 | Sheffield U | 6 | 0 |
| 1995–96 | Sheffield U | 26 | 1 |
| 1995–96 | Crystal Palace | 10 | 1 |
| 1996–97 | Crystal Palace | 39 | 2 |
| 1997–98 | Crystal Palace | 9 | 0 |
| **Total:** | | **141** | **4** |

## TWEED, Steven — Defender

H: 6 3 W: 14 07 b.Edinburgh 8-8-72

*Source:* Hutchison Vale. *Honours:* Scotland Under-21.

| | | | |
|---|---|---|---|
| 1991–92 | Hibernian | 1 | 0 |
| 1992–93 | Hibernian | 14 | 0 |
| 1993–94 | Hibernian | 29 | 3 |
| 1994–95 | Hibernian | 33 | 0 |
| 1995–96 | Hibernian | 31 | 0 |
| 1996–97 | Ionikos | 2 | 0 |
| 1997–98 | Stoke C | 38 | 0 |
| **Total:** | | **148** | **3** |

## TWISS, Michael — Midfield

H: 5 11 W: 12 08 b.Salford 26-12-77

*Source:* Trainee.

| | | | |
|---|---|---|---|
| 1996–97 | Manchester U | 0 | 0 |
| 1997–98 | Manchester U | 0 | 0 |

## TYDEMAN, Sam — Midfield

H: 5 11 W: 11 05 b.Chatham 14-12-78

*Source:* Trainee.

| | | | |
|---|---|---|---|
| 1997–98 | Gillingham | 0 | 0 |

## TYLER, Mark — Goalkeeper

H: 5 11 W: 12 00 b.Norwich 2-4-77

*Source:* Trainee. *Honours:* England Youth.

| | | | |
|---|---|---|---|
| 1994–95 | Peterborough U | 5 | 0 |
| 1995–96 | Peterborough U | 0 | 0 |
| 1996–97 | Peterborough U | 3 | 0 |
| 1997–98 | Peterborough U | 46 | 0 |
| **Total:** | | **54** | **0** |

## TZVETANOV, Tzanko — Defender

H: 5 9 W: 12 07 b.Svichtov 6-1-70

*Source:* SV Waldorf-Mannheim. *Honours:* Bulgaria 40 full caps.

| | | | |
|---|---|---|---|
| 1996–97 | Aberdeen | 27 | 0 |
| 1997–98 | Aberdeen | 11 | 0 |
| **Total:** | | **38** | **0** |

## UHLENBEEK, Gus — Midfield

H: 5 10 W: 12 06 b.Paramaribo 20-8-70

| | | | |
|---|---|---|---|
| 1990–91 | Ajax | 2 | 0 |
| 1991–92 | Ajax | 0 | 0 |
| 1992–93 | Cambuur | 24 | 0 |
| 1993–94 | Cambuur | 15 | 0 |
| 1994–95 | TOPS SV | 22 | 3 |

| | | | |
|---|---|---|---|
| 1995–96 | Ipswich T | 40 | 4 |
| 1996–97 | Ipswich T | 38 | 0 |
| 1997–98 | Ipswich T | 11 | 0 |
| **Total:** | | **152** | **7** |

## ULLATHORNE, Robert — Midfield

H: 5 8 W: 10 10 b.Wakefield 11-10-71

*Source:* Trainee.

| | | | |
|---|---|---|---|
| 1989–90 | Norwich C | 0 | 0 |
| 1990–91 | Norwich C | 2 | 0 |
| 1991–92 | Norwich C | 20 | 3 |
| 1992–93 | Norwich C | 0 | 0 |
| 1993–94 | Norwich C | 16 | 2 |
| 1994–95 | Norwich C | 27 | 2 |
| 1995–96 | Norwich C | 29 | 0 |
| 1996–97 | Osasuna | 18 | 0 |
| 1996–97 | Leicester C | 0 | 0 |
| 1997–98 | Leicester C | 6 | 1 |
| **Total:** | | **118** | **8** |

## UNSWORTH, David — Defender

H: 6 0 W: 14 00 b.Chorley 16-10-73

*Source:* Trainee. *Honours:* England Youth, Under-21, 1 full cap.

| | | | |
|---|---|---|---|
| 1991–92 | Everton | 2 | 1 |
| 1992–93 | Everton | 3 | 0 |
| 1993–94 | Everton | 8 | 0 |
| 1994–95 | Everton | 38 | 3 |
| 1995–96 | Everton | 31 | 2 |
| 1996–97 | Everton | 34 | 5 |
| 1997–98 | West Ham U | 32 | 2 |
| **Total:** | | **148** | **13** |

## UNSWORTH, Lee — Defender

H: 5 11 W: 11 02 b.Eccles 25-2-73

*Source:* Ashton U.

| | | | |
|---|---|---|---|
| 1994–95 | Crewe Alex | 0 | 0 |
| 1995–96 | Crewe Alex | 29 | 0 |
| 1996–97 | Crewe Alex | 29 | 0 |
| 1997–98 | Crewe Alex | 36 | 0 |
| **Total:** | | **94** | **0** |

## UPSON, Matthew — Defender

H: 6 1 W: 11 05 b.Eye 18-4-79

*Source:* Trainee. *Honours:* England Youth.

| | | | |
|---|---|---|---|
| 1995–96 | Luton T | 0 | 0 |
| 1996–97 | Luton T | 1 | 0 |
| 1996–97 | Arsenal | 0 | 0 |
| 1997–98 | Arsenal | 5 | 0 |
| **Total:** | | **6** | **0** |

## UTLEY, Darren — Defender

H: 6 1 W: 12 11 b.Barnsley 28-9-77

*Source:* Trainee.

| | | | |
|---|---|---|---|
| 1995–96 | Doncaster R | 1 | 0 |
| 1996–97 | Doncaster R | 23 | 1 |
| 1997–98 | Doncaster R | 4 | 0 |
| **Total:** | | **28** | **1** |

## VALAKARI, Simo — Midfield

H: 5 10 W: 11 11 b.Helsinki 28-4-73

*Honours:* Finland 3 full caps.

| | | | |
|---|---|---|---|
| 1995 | Finn PA | 22 | 3 |
| 1996 | Finn PA | 26 | 2 |
| 1996–97 | Motherwell | 11 | 0 |
| 1997–98 | Motherwell | 28 | 0 |
| **Total:** | | **87** | **5** |

## VALERY, Patrick — Defender

H: 5 8 W: 13 04 b.Brignoles 3-7-69

*Source:* AS Brignoles.

| | | | |
|---|---|---|---|
| 1988–89 | Monaco | 28 | 0 |
| 1989–90 | Monaco | 19 | 0 |
| 1990–91 | Monaco | 32 | 0 |
| 1991–92 | Monaco | 14 | 0 |
| 1992–93 | Monaco | 29 | 0 |
| 1993–94 | Monaco | 32 | 0 |
| 1994–95 | Monaco | 23 | 0 |
| 1995–96 | Monaco | 3 | 0 |
| 1996–97 | Monaco | 30 | 0 |
| 1997–98 | Blackburn R | 15 | 0 |
| **Total:** | | **225** | **0** |

## VALLE, Oscar — Forward

H: 5 10 W: 10 13 b.Madrid 11-2-73

*Source:* Villareal.

| | | | |
|---|---|---|---|
| 1997–98 | Walsall | 0 | 0 |
| 1997–98 | Dundee U | 1 | 0 |
| **Total:** | | **1** | **0** |

## VAN BLERK, Jason — Defender

H: 6 1 W: 13 00 b.Sydney 16-3-68

*Source:* Go Ahead. *Honours:* Australia 23 full caps, 1 goal.

| | | | |
|---|---|---|---|
| 1994–95 | Millwall | 27 | 1 |
| 1995–96 | Millwall | 42 | 1 |
| 1996–97 | Millwall | 4 | 0 |
| 1997–98 | Manchester C | 19 | 0 |
| 1997–98 | WBA | 8 | 0 |
| **Total:** | | **100** | **2** |

### VAN DULLEMEN, Raymond — Forward

H: 6 2 W: 14 00 b.Gravenhag 6-5-73

| | | | |
|---|---|---|---|
| 1997–98 | Northampton T | 1 | 0 |
| **Total:** | | **1** | **0** |

### VAN GOBBEL, Ulrich — Defender

H: 6 0 W: 15 00 b.Surinam 16-1-71

*Honours:* Holland Under-21, 8 full caps.

| | | | |
|---|---|---|---|
| 1988–89 | Willem II | 16 | 3 |
| 1989–90 | Willem II | 18 | 0 |
| 1989–90 | Feyenoord | 2 | 0 |
| 1990–91 | Feyenoord | 19 | 0 |
| 1991–92 | Feyenoord | 20 | 1 |
| 1992–93 | Feyenoord | 22 | 0 |
| 1993–94 | Feyenoord | 22 | 1 |
| 1994–95 | Feyenoord | 20 | 0 |
| 1995–96 | Feyenoord | 17 | 0 |
| 1995–96 | Galatasaray | 16 | 2 |
| 1996–97 | Galatasaray | 8 | 0 |
| 1996–97 | Southampton | 25 | 1 |
| 1997–98 | Southampton | 2 | 0 |
| **Total:** | | **207** | **8** |

### VAN HEUSDEN, Arjan — Goalkeeper

H: 6 0 W: 13 12 b.Alphen 11-12-72

*Source:* Noordwijk.

| | | | |
|---|---|---|---|
| 1994–95 | Port Vale | 2 | 0 |
| 1995–96 | Port Vale | 7 | 0 |
| 1996–97 | Port Vale | 13 | 0 |
| 1997–98 | Port Vale | 5 | 0 |
| 1997–98 | Oxford U (loan) | 11 | 0 |
| **Total:** | | **38** | **0** |

### VAN HOOIJDONK, Pierre — Forward

H: 6 4 W: 13 13 b.Steenbergen 29-11-69

*Source:* NAC Breda. *Honours:* Holland Under-21, 15 full caps, 6 goals.

| | | | |
|---|---|---|---|
| 1989–90 | RBC | 32 | 6 |
| 1990–91 | RBC | 37 | 27 |
| 1991–92 | NAC | 35 | 20 |
| 1992–93 | NAC | 33 | 26 |
| 1993–94 | NAC | 31 | 25 |
| 1994–95 | Celtic | 14 | 4 |
| 1995–96 | Celtic | 34 | 26 |
| 1996–97 | Celtic | 21 | 14 |
| 1996–97 | Nottingham F | 8 | 1 |
| 1997–98 | Nottingham F | 42 | 29 |
| **Total:** | | **287** | **178** |

### VAN VOSSEN, Peter — Forward

H: 6 0 W: 12 02 b.Zieriksee 21-4-68

*Honours:* Holland 18 full caps, 7 goals.

| | | | |
|---|---|---|---|
| 1991–92 | Beveren | 29 | 13 |
| 1992–93 | Anderlecht | 28 | 6 |
| 1993–94 | Ajax | 15 | 1 |
| 1994–95 | Ajax | 25 | 5 |
| 1995–96 | Istanbul | 16 | 5 |
| 1995–96 | Rangers | 7 | 0 |
| 1996–97 | Rangers | 14 | 5 |
| 1997–98 | Rangers | 1 | 0 |
| **Total:** | | **135** | **35** |

### VAN DER GOUW, Raimond — Goalkeeper

H: 6 3 W: 13 07 b.Oldenzaal 24-3-63

| | | | |
|---|---|---|---|
| 1985–86 | Go Ahead | 28 | 0 |
| 1986–87 | Go Ahead | 34 | 0 |
| 1987–88 | Go Ahead | 35 | 0 |
| 1988–89 | Vitesse | 36 | 0 |
| 1989–90 | Vitesse | 34 | 0 |
| 1990–91 | Vitesse | 31 | 0 |
| 1991–92 | Vitesse | 34 | 0 |
| 1992–93 | Vitesse | 34 | 0 |
| 1993–94 | Vitesse | 34 | 0 |
| 1994–95 | Vitesse | 34 | 0 |
| 1995–96 | Vitesse | 21 | 0 |
| 1996–97 | Manchester U | 2 | 0 |
| 1997–98 | Manchester U | 5 | 0 |
| **Total:** | | **362** | **0** |

### VAN DER LAAN, Robin — Midfield

H: 6 0 W: 13 08 b.Schiedam 5-9-68

*Source:* Wageningen.

| | | | |
|---|---|---|---|
| 1990–91 | Port Vale | 18 | 4 |
| 1991–92 | Port Vale | 43 | 5 |
| 1992–93 | Port Vale | 38 | 6 |
| 1993–94 | Port Vale | 33 | 4 |
| 1994–95 | Port Vale | 44 | 5 |
| 1995–96 | Derby Co | 39 | 6 |
| 1996–97 | Derby Co | 16 | 2 |
| 1996–97 | Wolverhampton W (loan) | 7 | 0 |
| 1997–98 | Derby Co | 10 | 0 |
| **Total:** | | **248** | **32** |

### VAN DER VELDEN, Carel — Midfield

H: 6 0 W: 13 08 b.Arnheim 3-8-72

*Source:* Den Bosch.

| | | | |
|---|---|---|---|
| 1995–96 | Barnsley | 7 | 0 |
| 1996–97 | Barnsley | 2 | 0 |
| 1997–98 | Scarborough | 8 | 1 |
| **Total:** | | **17** | **1** |

## VANES, Michael — Midfield

H: 5 6 W: 10 00 b.Cayman Islands 16-3-79

*Source:* Trainee.

| | | | |
|---|---|---|---|
| 1997–98 | Bristol C | 0 | 0 |

## VAREILLE, Jerome — Forward

H: 5 11 W: 12 12 b.Vernoux 1-6-74

*Source:* Mulhouse.

| | | | |
|---|---|---|---|
| 1997–98 | Kilmarnock | 34 | 4 |
| **Total:** | | **34** | **4** |

## VARTY, Will — Defender

H: 6 0 W: 12 04 b.Workington 1-10-76

*Source:* Trainee.

| | | | |
|---|---|---|---|
| 1995–96 | Carlisle U | 0 | 0 |
| 1996–97 | Carlisle U | 32 | 0 |
| 1997–98 | Carlisle U | 44 | 1 |
| **Total:** | | **76** | **1** |

## VASSELL, Darius — Forward

b.Birmingham 13-6-80

*Source:* Trainee.

| | | | |
|---|---|---|---|
| 1997–98 | Aston Villa | 0 | 0 |

## VAUGHAN, Francis — Midfield

b.Salford 8-9-79

*Source:* Trainee.

| | | | |
|---|---|---|---|
| 1997–98 | Stockport Co | 0 | 0 |

## VAUGHAN, John — Goalkeeper

H: 5 10 W: 13 01 b.Isleworth 26-6-64

*Source:* Apprentice.

| | | | |
|---|---|---|---|
| 1981–82 | West Ham U | 0 | 0 |
| 1982–83 | West Ham U | 0 | 0 |
| 1983–84 | West Ham U | 0 | 0 |
| 1984–85 | West Ham U | 0 | 0 |
| 1984–85 | Charlton Ath (loan) | 6 | 0 |
| 1985–86 | West Ham U | 0 | 0 |
| 1985–86 | Bristol R (loan) | 6 | 0 |
| 1985–86 | Wrexham (loan) | 4 | 0 |
| 1985–86 | Bristol C (loan) | 2 | 0 |
| 1986–87 | Fulham | 44 | 0 |
| 1987–88 | Fulham | 0 | 0 |
| 1987–88 | Bristol C (loan) | 3 | 0 |
| 1988–89 | Cambridge U | 29 | 0 |
| 1989–90 | Cambridge U | 46 | 0 |
| 1990–91 | Cambridge U | 43 | 0 |
| 1991–92 | Cambridge U | 33 | |
| 1992–93 | Cambridge U | 27 | |
| 1993–94 | Charlton Ath | 6 | |
| 1994–95 | Preston NE | 26 | |
| 1995–96 | Preston NE | 40 | |
| 1996–97 | Lincoln C | 10 | |
| 1996–97 | Colchester U (loan) | 5 | |
| 1997–98 | Lincoln C | 19 | |
| **Total:** | | **349** | |

## VAUGHAN, Tony — Defend

H: 6 0 W: 11 02 b.Manchester 11-10-75

*Source:* Trainee. *Honours:* England Schools.

| | | | |
|---|---|---|---|
| 1994–95 | Ipswich T | 10 | |
| 1995–96 | Ipswich T | 25 | |
| 1996–97 | Ipswich T | 32 | |
| 1997–98 | Manchester C | 19 | |
| **Total:** | | **86** | |

## VAUGHAN, Wayne — Midfie

b.Barking 18-2-80

*Source:* Trainee.

| | | | |
|---|---|---|---|
| 1997–98 | Tottenham H | 0 | |

## VEART, Carl — Midfie

H: 5 10 W: 11 05 b.Whyalla 21-5-70

*Source:* Adelaide C. *Honours:* Australia 14 full caps.

| | | | |
|---|---|---|---|
| 1994–95 | Sheffield U | 39 | |
| 1995–96 | Sheffield U | 27 | |
| 1995–96 | Crystal Palace | 12 | |
| 1996–97 | Crystal Palace | 39 | |
| 1997–98 | Crystal Palace | 6 | |
| 1997–98 | Millwall | 8 | |
| **Total:** | | **131** | **2** |

## VEGA, Ramon — Defend

H: 6 3 W: 13 00 b.Olten 14-6-71

*Source:* Trimbach. *Honours:* Switzerland 19 full caps, 2 goals.

| | | | |
|---|---|---|---|
| 1990–91 | Grasshoppers | 3 | |
| 1991–92 | Grasshoppers | 34 | |
| 1992–93 | Grasshoppers | 20 | |
| 1993–94 | Grasshoppers | 36 | |
| 1994–95 | Grasshoppers | 33 | |
| 1995–96 | Grasshoppers | 30 | |
| 1996–97 | Cagliari | 14 | |
| 1996–97 | Tottenham H | 8 | |
| 1997–98 | Tottenham H | 25 | |
| **Total:** | | **203** | **1** |

## VENISON, Barry — Midfield

H: 5 10 W: 11 12 b.Consett 16-8-64

*Source:* Apprentice. *Honours:* England Youth, Under-21, 2 full caps.

| | | | |
|---|---|---|---|
| 1981–82 | Sunderland | 20 | 1 |
| 1982–83 | Sunderland | 37 | 0 |
| 1983–84 | Sunderland | 41 | 0 |
| 1984–85 | Sunderland | 39 | 1 |
| 1985–86 | Sunderland | 36 | 0 |
| 1986–87 | Liverpool | 33 | 0 |
| 1987–88 | Liverpool | 18 | 0 |
| 1988–89 | Liverpool | 15 | 0 |
| 1989–90 | Liverpool | 25 | 0 |
| 1990–91 | Liverpool | 6 | 0 |
| 1991–92 | Liverpool | 13 | 1 |
| 1992–93 | Newcastle U | 44 | 0 |
| 1993–94 | Newcastle U | 37 | 0 |
| 1994–95 | Newcastle U | 28 | 1 |
| 1995–96 | Galatasaray | 8 | 0 |
| 1995–96 | Southampton | 22 | 0 |
| 1996–97 | Southampton | 2 | 0 |
| 1997–98 | Southampton | 0 | 0 |
| **Total:** | | **424** | **4** |

## VENUS, Mark — Defender

H: 6 0 W: 12 12 b.Hartlepool 6-4-67

| | | | |
|---|---|---|---|
| 1984–85 | Hartlepool U | 4 | 0 |
| 1985–86 | Leicester C | 1 | 0 |
| 1986–87 | Leicester C | 39 | 0 |
| 1987–88 | Leicester C | 21 | 1 |
| 1987–88 | Wolverhampton W | 4 | 0 |
| 1988–89 | Wolverhampton W | 35 | 0 |
| 1989–90 | Wolverhampton W | 44 | 2 |
| 1990–91 | Wolverhampton W | 6 | 0 |
| 1991–92 | Wolverhampton W | 46 | 1 |
| 1992–93 | Wolverhampton W | 12 | 0 |
| 1993–94 | Wolverhampton W | 39 | 1 |
| 1994–95 | Wolverhampton W | 39 | 3 |
| 1995–96 | Wolverhampton W | 22 | 0 |
| 1996–97 | Wolverhampton W | 40 | 0 |
| 1997–98 | Ipswich T | 14 | 1 |
| **Total:** | | **366** | **9** |

## VERITY, Daniel — Defender

H: 5 11 W: 10 12 b.Bradford 19-4-80

*Source:* Trainee.

| | | | |
|---|---|---|---|
| 1997–98 | Bradford C | 1 | 0 |
| **Total:** | | **1** | **0** |

## VERNAZZA, Paulo — Midfield

b.Islington 1-11-79

*Source:* Trainee. *Honours:* England Youth.

| | | | |
|---|---|---|---|
| 1997–98 | Arsenal | 1 | 0 |
| **Total:** | | **1** | **0** |

## VEYSEY, Kenneth — Goalkeeper

H: 5 10 W: 12 07 b.Hackney 8-6-67

From Dorchester T.

| | | | |
|---|---|---|---|
| 1997–98 | Torquay U | 27 | 0 |
| **Total:** | | **27** | **0** |

## VIALLI, Gianluca — Forward

H: 5 10 W: 13 06 b.Cremona 9-7-64

*Honours:* Italy Youth, Under-21, 59 full caps, 16 goals.

| | | | |
|---|---|---|---|
| 1980–81 | Cremonese | 2 | 0 |
| 1981–82 | Cremonese | 31 | 5 |
| 1982–83 | Cremonese | 35 | 8 |
| 1983–84 | Cremonese | 37 | 10 |
| 1984–85 | Sampdoria | 28 | 3 |
| 1985–86 | Sampdoria | 28 | 6 |
| 1986–87 | Sampdoria | 28 | 12 |
| 1987–88 | Sampdoria | 30 | 10 |
| 1988–89 | Sampdoria | 30 | 14 |
| 1989–90 | Sampdoria | 22 | 10 |
| 1990–91 | Sampdoria | 26 | 19 |
| 1991–92 | Sampdoria | 31 | 11 |
| 1992–93 | Juventus | 32 | 6 |
| 1993–94 | Juventus | 10 | 4 |
| 1994–95 | Juventus | 30 | 17 |
| 1995–96 | Juventus | 30 | 11 |
| 1996–97 | Chelsea | 28 | 9 |
| 1997–98 | Chelsea | 21 | 11 |
| **Total:** | | **479** | **166** |

## VICKERS, Ashley — Defender

H: 6 3 W: 13 10 b.Sheffield 14-6-72

*Source:* Heybridge S.

| | | | |
|---|---|---|---|
| 1997–98 | Peterborough U | 1 | 0 |
| **Total:** | | **1** | **0** |

## VICKERS, Steve — Defender

H: 6 1 W: 13 02 b.Bishop Auckland 13-10-67

*Source:* Spennymoor U.

| | | | |
|---|---|---|---|
| 1985–86 | Tranmere R | 3 | 0 |
| 1986–87 | Tranmere R | 36 | 2 |
| 1987–88 | Tranmere R | 46 | 1 |
| 1988–89 | Tranmere R | 46 | 3 |
| 1989–90 | Tranmere R | 42 | 3 |

| | | | |
|---|---|---|---|
| 1990–91 | Tranmere R | 42 | 1 |
| 1991–92 | Tranmere R | 43 | 1 |
| 1992–93 | Tranmere R | 42 | 0 |
| 1993–94 | Tranmere R | 11 | 0 |
| 1993–94 | Middlesbrough | 26 | 3 |
| 1994–95 | Middlesbrough | 44 | 3 |
| 1995–96 | Middlesbrough | 32 | 1 |
| 1996–97 | Middlesbrough | 29 | 0 |
| 1997–98 | Middlesbrough | 33 | 0 |
| **Total:** | | **475** | **18** |

### VIDMAR, Tony — Defender

H: 6 1 W: 12 13 b.Adelaide 4-7-70

*Source:* Adelaide C. *Honours:* Australia 8 full caps.

| | | | |
|---|---|---|---|
| 1992–93 | Ekeren | 9 | 1 |
| From Adelaide C. | | | |
| 1995–96 | NAC | 30 | 2 |
| 1996–97 | NAC | 31 | 2 |
| 1997–97 | Rangers | 12 | 0 |
| **Total:** | | **82** | **5** |

### VIEIRA, Patrick — Midfield

H: 6 4 W: 13 00 b.Dakar 23-6-76

*Honours:* France Under-21, 9 full caps.

| | | | |
|---|---|---|---|
| 1993–94 | Cannes | 5 | 0 |
| 1994–95 | Cannes | 31 | 2 |
| 1995–96 | Cannes | 13 | 0 |
| 1995–96 | AC Milan | 2 | 0 |
| 1996–97 | Arsenal | 31 | 2 |
| 1997–98 | Arsenal | 33 | 2 |
| **Total:** | | **115** | **6** |

### VINCENT, Jamie — Defender

H: 5 10 W: 11 09 b.London 18-6-75

*Source:* Trainee.

| | | | |
|---|---|---|---|
| 1993–94 | Crystal Palace | 0 | 0 |
| 1994–95 | Crystal Palace | 0 | 0 |
| 1994–95 | Bournemouth (loan) | 8 | 0 |
| 1995–96 | Crystal Palace | 25 | 0 |
| 1996–97 | Crystal Palace | 0 | 0 |
| 1996–97 | Bournemouth | 29 | 0 |
| 1997–98 | Bournemouth | 44 | 3 |
| **Total:** | | **106** | **3** |

### VINCENT, Robert — Midfield

H: 5 6 W: 10 01 b.Glasgow 13-11-77

*Source:* Kilmarnock Youth.

| | | | |
|---|---|---|---|
| 1996–97 | Kilmarnock | 0 | 0 |
| 1997–98 | Kilmarnock | 2 | 0 |
| **Total:** | | **2** | **0** |

### VINNICOMBE, Chris — Defende

H: 5 8 W: 10 12 b.Exeter 20-10-70

*Honours:* England Under-21.

| | | | |
|---|---|---|---|
| 1988–89 | Exeter C | 25 | [illegible] |
| 1989–90 | Exeter C | 14 | [illegible] |
| 1989–90 | Rangers | 7 | [illegible] |
| 1990–91 | Rangers | 10 | [illegible] |
| 1991–92 | Rangers | 2 | [illegible] |
| 1992–93 | Rangers | 0 | [illegible] |
| 1993–94 | Rangers | 4 | [illegible] |
| 1994–95 | Burnley | 29 | [illegible] |
| 1995–96 | Burnley | 35 | [illegible] |
| 1996–97 | Burnley | 8 | [illegible] |
| 1997–98 | Burnley | 23 | [illegible] |
| **Total:** | | **157** | [illegible] |

### VIVEASH, Adrian — Defende

H: 6 2 W: 12 12 b.Swindon 30-9-69

*Source:* Trainee.

| | | | |
|---|---|---|---|
| 1988–89 | Swindon T | 0 | [illegible] |
| 1989–90 | Swindon T | 0 | [illegible] |
| 1990–91 | Swindon T | 25 | [illegible] |
| 1991–92 | Swindon T | 10 | [illegible] |
| 1992–93 | Swindon T | 5 | [illegible] |
| 1992–93 | Reading (loan) | 5 | [illegible] |
| 1993–94 | Swindon T | 0 | [illegible] |
| 1994–95 | Swindon T | 14 | [illegible] |
| 1994–95 | Reading (loan) | 6 | [illegible] |
| 1995–96 | Swindon T | 0 | [illegible] |
| 1995–96 | Barnsley (loan) | 2 | [illegible] |
| 1995–96 | Walsall | 31 | [illegible] |
| 1996–97 | Walsall | 46 | [illegible] |
| 1997–98 | Walsall | 42 | [illegible] |
| **Total:** | | **186** | [illegible] |

### VLACHOS, Michalis — Midfiel

H: 5 10 W: 12 00 b.Athens 20-9-67

*Honours:* Greece 10 full caps.

| | | | |
|---|---|---|---|
| 1988–89 | Apollon | 22 | [illegible] |
| 1989–90 | Apollon | 29 | [illegible] |
| 1990–91 | Apollon | 29 | [illegible] |
| 1991–92 | Olympiakos | 27 | [illegible] |
| 1992–93 | Olympiakos | 20 | [illegible] |
| 1993–94 | AEK Athens | 26 | [illegible] |
| 1994–95 | AEK Athens | 20 | [illegible] |
| 1995–96 | AEK Athens | 24 | [illegible] |
| 1996–97 | AEK Athens | 25 | [illegible] |
| 1997–98 | AEK Athens | 10 | [illegible] |
| 1997–98 | Portsmouth | 15 | [illegible] |
| **Total:** | | **247** | [illegible] |

## VONK, Michael — Defender

H: 6 3 W: 13 03 b.Alkmaar 28-10-68

| | | | |
|---|---|---|---|
| 1986–87 | AZ | 19 | 3 |
| 1987–88 | AZ | 25 | 1 |
| 1988–89 | AZ | 35 | 4 |
| 1989–90 | AZ | 33 | 0 |
| 1990–91 | SVV/Dordrecht | 29 | 1 |
| 1991–92 | Manchester C | 9 | 0 |
| 1992–93 | Manchester C | 26 | 2 |
| 1993–94 | Manchester C | 35 | 1 |
| 1994–95 | Manchester C | 21 | 0 |
| 1995–96 | Manchester C | 0 | 0 |
| 1995–96 | Oldham Ath (loan) | 5 | 1 |
| 1995–96 | Sheffield U | 17 | 0 |
| 1996–97 | Sheffield U | 17 | 2 |
| 1997–98 | Sheffield U | 3 | 0 |
| **Total:** | | **274** | **15** |

## WADDLE, Chris — Forward

H: 6 1 W: 13 03 b.Hedworth 14-12-60

*Source:* Tow Law T. *Honours:* England Under-21, 62 full caps, 6 goals. Football League.

| | | | |
|---|---|---|---|
| 1980–81 | Newcastle U | 13 | 1 |
| 1981–82 | Newcastle U | 42 | 7 |
| 1982–83 | Newcastle U | 37 | 7 |
| 1983–84 | Newcastle U | 42 | 18 |
| 1984–85 | Newcastle U | 36 | 13 |
| 1985–86 | Tottenham H | 39 | 11 |
| 1986–87 | Tottenham H | 39 | 6 |
| 1987–88 | Tottenham H | 22 | 2 |
| 1988–89 | Tottenham H | 38 | 14 |
| 1989–90 | Marseille | 37 | 9 |
| 1990–91 | Marseille | 35 | 6 |
| 1991–92 | Marseille | 35 | 7 |
| 1992–93 | Sheffield W | 33 | 1 |
| 1993–94 | Sheffield W | 19 | 3 |
| 1994–95 | Sheffield W | 25 | 4 |
| 1995–96 | Sheffield W | 32 | 2 |
| 1996–97 | Sheffield W | 0 | 0 |
| 1996–97 | Falkirk | 4 | 1 |
| 1996–97 | Bradford C | 25 | 5 |
| 1996–97 | Sunderland | 7 | 1 |
| 1997–98 | Burnley | 31 | 1 |
| **Total:** | | **591** | **119** |

## WADDOCK, Gary — Midfield

H: 5 10 W: 12 05 b.Alperton 17-3-62

*Source:* Apprentice. *Honours:* Eire Youth, Under-21, Under-23, B, 21 full caps, 3 goals.

| | | | |
|---|---|---|---|
| 1979–80 | QPR | 16 | 1 |
| 1980–81 | QPR | 33 | 3 |
| 1981–82 | QPR | 35 | 0 |
| 1982–83 | QPR | 33 | 0 |
| 1983–84 | QPR | 36 | 3 |
| 1984–85 | QPR | 31 | 1 |
| 1985–86 | QPR | 15 | 0 |
| 1986–87 | QPR | 4 | 0 |
| 1987–88 | QPR | 0 | 0 |
| From Charleroi. | | | |
| 1989–90 | Millwall | 18 | 0 |
| 1990–91 | Millwall | 40 | 2 |
| 1991–92 | QPR | 0 | 0 |
| 1991–92 | Swindon T (loan) | 6 | 0 |
| 1992–93 | QPR | 0 | 0 |
| 1992–93 | Bristol R | 31 | 0 |
| 1993–94 | Bristol R | 39 | 1 |
| 1994–95 | Bristol R | 1 | 0 |
| 1994–95 | Luton T | 40 | 1 |
| 1995–96 | Luton T | 36 | 0 |
| 1996–97 | Luton T | 39 | 2 |
| 1997–98 | Luton T | 38 | 0 |
| **Total:** | | **491** | **14** |

## WAINWRIGHT, Neil — Midfield

H: 5 11 W: 10 02 b.Warrington 4-11-77

*Source:* Trainee.

| | | | |
|---|---|---|---|
| 1996–97 | Wrexham | 0 | 0 |
| 1997–98 | Wrexham | 11 | 3 |
| **Total:** | | **11** | **3** |

## WALKER, Andy — Forward

H: 5 8 W: 11 05 b.Glasgow 6-4-65

*Source:* Baillieston Jun. *Honours:* Scotland Under-21, 3 full caps.

| | | | |
|---|---|---|---|
| 1984–85 | Motherwell | 11 | 3 |
| 1985–86 | Motherwell | 22 | 4 |
| 1986–87 | Motherwell | 43 | 10 |
| 1987–88 | Celtic | 42 | 16 |
| 1988–89 | Celtic | 22 | 8 |
| 1989–90 | Celtic | 32 | 6 |
| 1990–91 | Celtic | 11 | 0 |
| 1991–92 | Celtic | 1 | 0 |
| 1991–92 | Newcastle U (loan) | 2 | 0 |
| 1991–92 | Bolton W | 24 | 15 |
| 1992–93 | Bolton W | 32 | 26 |
| 1993–94 | Bolton W | 11 | 3 |
| 1994–95 | Celtic | 26 | 6 |
| 1995–96 | Celtic | 16 | 3 |
| 1995–96 | Sheffield U | 14 | 8 |
| 1996–97 | Sheffield U | 37 | 12 |
| 1997–98 | Sheffield U | 1 | 0 |
| 1997–98 | Hibernian (loan) | 8 | 3 |
| 1997–98 | Raith R (loan) | 7 | 2 |
| **Total:** | | **362** | **125** |

## WALKER, Des — Defender

H: 5 11 W: 11 12 b.Hackney 26-11-65

*Source:* Apprentice. *Honours:* England Under-21, 59 full caps.

| | | | |
|---|---|---|---|
| 1983–84 | Nottingham F | 4 | 0 |
| 1984–85 | Nottingham F | 3 | 0 |
| 1985–86 | Nottingham F | 39 | 0 |
| 1986–87 | Nottingham F | 41 | 0 |
| 1987–88 | Nottingham F | 35 | 0 |
| 1988–89 | Nottingham F | 34 | 0 |
| 1989–90 | Nottingham F | 38 | 0 |
| 1990–91 | Nottingham F | 37 | 0 |
| 1991–92 | Nottingham F | 33 | 1 |
| 1992–93 | Sampdoria | 30 | 0 |
| 1993–94 | Sheffield W | 42 | 0 |
| 1994–95 | Sheffield W | 38 | 0 |
| 1995–96 | Sheffield W | 36 | 0 |
| 1996–97 | Sheffield W | 36 | 0 |
| 1997–98 | Sheffield W | 38 | 0 |
| **Total:** | | **484** | **1** |

## WALKER, Ian — Goalkeeper

H: 6 2 W: 13 01 b.Watford 31-10-71

*Source:* Trainee. *Honours:* England Youth, Under-21, B, 3 full caps.

| | | | |
|---|---|---|---|
| 1989–90 | Tottenham H | 0 | 0 |
| 1990–91 | Tottenham H | 1 | 0 |
| 1990–91 | Oxford U (loan) | 2 | 0 |
| 1990–91 | Ipswich T (loan) | 0 | 0 |
| 1991–92 | Tottenham H | 18 | 0 |
| 1992–93 | Tottenham H | 17 | 0 |
| 1993–94 | Tottenham H | 11 | 0 |
| 1994–95 | Tottenham H | 41 | 0 |
| 1995–96 | Tottenham H | 38 | 0 |
| 1996–97 | Tottenham H | 37 | 0 |
| 1997–98 | Tottenham H | 29 | 0 |
| **Total:** | | **194** | **0** |

## WALKER, James — Goalkeeper

H: 5 11 W: 13 02 b.Nottingham 9-7-73

*Source:* Trainee.

| | | | |
|---|---|---|---|
| 1991–92 | Notts Co | 0 | 0 |
| 1992–93 | Notts Co | 0 | 0 |
| 1993–94 | Walsall | 31 | 0 |
| 1994–95 | Walsall | 4 | 0 |
| 1995–96 | Walsall | 26 | 0 |
| 1996–97 | Walsall | 36 | 0 |
| 1997–98 | Walsall | 46 | 0 |
| **Total:** | | **143** | **0** |

## WALKER, John — Midfiel

H: 5 9 W: 11 00 b.Glasgow 12-12-73

*Source:* Clydebank BC.

| | | |
|---|---|---|
| 1990–91 | Rangers | 0 |
| 1991–92 | Rangers | 0 |
| 1992–93 | Rangers | 0 |
| 1993–94 | Clydebank | 6 |
| 1994–95 | Clydebank | 21 |
| 1995–96 | Clydebank | 0 |
| 1995–96 | Grimsby T | 2 |
| 1996–97 | Grimsby T | 1 |
| 1996–97 | Mansfield T | 36 |
| 1997–98 | Mansfield T | 1 |
| **Total:** | | **67** |

## WALKER, Justin — Midfiel

H: 6 0 W: 13 03 b.Nottingham 6-9-75

*Source:* Trainee. *Honours:* England Schools, Youth.

| | | |
|---|---|---|
| 1992–93 | Nottingham F | 0 |
| 1993–94 | Nottingham F | 0 |
| 1994–95 | Nottingham F | 0 |
| 1995–96 | Nottingham F | 0 |
| 1996–97 | Nottingham F | 0 |
| 1996–97 | Scunthorpe U | 9 |
| 1997–98 | Scunthorpe U | 40 |
| **Total:** | | **49** |

## WALKER, Kashka — Midfiel

H: 5 9 W: 10 10 b.Toronto 10-11-78

*Source:* Canadian Soccer Academy.

| | | |
|---|---|---|
| 1996–97 | Newcastle U | 0 |
| 1997–98 | Newcastle U | 0 |

## WALKER, Keith — Defende

H: 6 0 W: 12 08 b.Edinburgh 17-4-66

*Source:* ICI Juveniles.

| | | |
|---|---|---|
| 1984–85 | Stirling Albion | 38 |
| 1985–86 | Stirling Albion | 32 |
| 1986–87 | Stirling Albion | 21 |
| 1987–88 | St Mirren | 19 |
| 1988–89 | St Mirren | 14 |
| 1989–90 | St Mirren | 10 |
| 1989–90 | Swansea C | 13 |
| 1990–91 | Swansea C | 24 |
| 1991–92 | Swansea C | 32 |
| 1992–93 | Swansea C | 42 |
| 1993–94 | Swansea C | 27 |
| 1994–95 | Swansea C | 28 |
| 1995–96 | Swansea C | 33 |

| | | | |
|---|---|---|---|
| 1996–97 | Swansea C | 31 | 1 |
| 1997–98 | Swansea C | 39 | 3 |
| **Total:** | | **403** | **32** |

## WALKER, Paul — Midfield

H: 5 5 W: 9 07 b.Kilwinning 20-8-77

*Source:* Dundee U BC.

| | | | |
|---|---|---|---|
| 1994–95 | Dundee U | 0 | 0 |
| 1995–96 | Dundee U | 2 | 0 |
| 1996–97 | Dundee U | 3 | 0 |
| 1997–98 | Dundee U | 1 | 0 |
| **Total:** | | **6** | **0** |

## WALKER, Richard — Forward

H: 6 0 W: 12 00 b.Sutton Coldfield 8-11-77

*Source:* Trainee.

| | | | |
|---|---|---|---|
| 1995–96 | Aston Villa | 0 | 0 |
| 1996–97 | Aston Villa | 0 | 0 |
| 1997–98 | Aston Villa | 1 | 0 |
| **Total:** | | **1** | **0** |

## WALLACE, Ray — Midfield

H: 5 7 W: 11 02 b.Lewisham 2-10-69

*Source:* Trainee. *Honours:* England Under-21.

| | | | |
|---|---|---|---|
| 1987–88 | Southampton | 0 | 0 |
| 1988–89 | Southampton | 26 | 0 |
| 1989–90 | Southampton | 9 | 0 |
| 1990–91 | Southampton | 0 | 0 |
| 1991–92 | Leeds U | 0 | 0 |
| 1991–92 | Swansea C (loan) | 2 | 0 |
| 1992–93 | Leeds U | 6 | 0 |
| 1993–94 | Leeds U | 1 | 0 |
| 1993–94 | Reading (loan) | 3 | 0 |
| 1994–95 | Stoke C | 20 | 1 |
| 1994–95 | Hull C (loan) | 7 | 0 |
| 1995–96 | Stoke C | 44 | 6 |
| 1996–97 | Stoke C | 45 | 2 |
| 1997–98 | Stoke C | 39 | 3 |
| **Total:** | | **202** | **12** |

## WALLACE, Rod — Forward

H: 5 7 W: 11 03 b.Lewisham 2-10-69

*Source:* Trainee. *Honours:* England Under-21, B.

| | | | |
|---|---|---|---|
| 1987–88 | Southampton | 15 | 1 |
| 1988–89 | Southampton | 38 | 12 |
| 1989–90 | Southampton | 38 | 18 |
| 1990–91 | Southampton | 37 | 14 |
| 1991–92 | Leeds U | 34 | 11 |
| 1992–93 | Leeds U | 32 | 7 |
| 1993–94 | Leeds U | 37 | 17 |
| 1994–95 | Leeds U | 32 | 4 |
| 1995–96 | Leeds U | 24 | 1 |
| 1996–97 | Leeds U | 22 | 3 |
| 1997–98 | Leeds U | 31 | 10 |
| **Total:** | | **340** | **98** |

## WALLING, Dean — Defender

H: 6 0 W: 10 08 b.Leeds 17-4-69

*Source:* Apprentice.

| | | | |
|---|---|---|---|
| 1986–87 | Leeds U | 0 | 0 |
| 1987–88 | Rochdale | 12 | 2 |
| 1988–89 | Rochdale | 34 | 3 |
| 1989–90 | Rochdale | 19 | 3 |
| From Guiseley. | | | |
| 1991–92 | Carlisle U | 37 | 5 |
| 1992–93 | Carlisle U | 23 | 0 |
| 1993–94 | Carlisle U | 40 | 5 |
| 1994–95 | Carlisle U | 41 | 7 |
| 1995–96 | Carlisle U | 43 | 2 |
| 1996–97 | Carlisle U | 46 | 3 |
| 1997–98 | Carlisle U | 6 | 0 |
| 1997–98 | Lincoln C | 35 | 5 |
| **Total:** | | **336** | **35** |

## WALLWORK, Ronnie — Defender

H: 5 10 W: 12 12 b.Manchester 10-9-77

*Source:* Trainee. *Honours:* England Youth.

| | | | |
|---|---|---|---|
| 1994–95 | Manchester U | 0 | 0 |
| 1995–96 | Manchester U | 0 | 0 |
| 1996–97 | Manchester U | 0 | 0 |
| 1997–98 | Manchester U | 1 | 0 |
| 1997–98 | Carlisle U (loan) | 10 | 1 |
| 1997–98 | Stockport Co (loan) | 7 | 0 |
| **Total:** | | **18** | **1** |

## WALSH, Dave — Goalkeeper

H: 6 1 W: 12 00 b.Wrexham 29-4-79

*Source:* Trainee.

| | | | |
|---|---|---|---|
| 1997–98 | Wrexham | 0 | 0 |

## WALSH, Gary — Goalkeeper

H: 6 3 W: 14 11 b.Wigan 21-3-68

*Source:* Apprentice. *Honours:* England Under-21.

| | | | |
|---|---|---|---|
| 1984–85 | Manchester U | 0 | 0 |
| 1985–86 | Manchester U | 0 | 0 |
| 1986–87 | Manchester U | 14 | 0 |
| 1987–88 | Manchester U | 16 | 0 |
| 1988–89 | Manchester U | 0 | 0 |
| 1988–89 | Airdrieonians (loan) | 3 | 0 |
| 1989–90 | Manchester U | 0 | 0 |

## Walsh, Michael

| | | | |
|---|---|---|---|
| 1990–91 | Manchester U | 5 | 0 |
| 1991–92 | Manchester U | 2 | 0 |
| 1992–93 | Manchester U | 0 | 0 |
| 1993–94 | Manchester U | 3 | 0 |
| 1993–94 | Oldham Ath (loan) | 6 | 0 |
| 1994–95 | Manchester U | 10 | 0 |
| 1995–96 | Middlesbrough | 32 | 0 |
| 1996–97 | Middlesbrough | 12 | 0 |
| 1997–98 | Middlesbrough | 0 | 0 |
| 1997–98 | Bradford C | 35 | 0 |
| **Total:** | | **138** | **0** |

## WALSH, Michael — Defender

H: 6 0 W: 13 01 b.Rotherham 5-8-77

*Source:* Trainee.

| | | | |
|---|---|---|---|
| 1994–95 | Scunthorpe U | 3 | 0 |
| 1995–96 | Scunthorpe U | 25 | 0 |
| 1996–97 | Scunthorpe U | 36 | 0 |
| 1997–98 | Scunthorpe U | 39 | 1 |
| **Total:** | | **103** | **1** |

## WALSH, Paul — Forward

H: 5 8 W: 10 04 b.Plumstead 1-10-62

*Source:* Apprentice. *Honours:* England Youth, Under-21, 5 full caps, 1 goal.

| | | | |
|---|---|---|---|
| 1979–80 | Charlton Ath | 9 | 0 |
| 1980–81 | Charlton Ath | 40 | 11 |
| 1981–82 | Charlton Ath | 38 | 13 |
| 1982–83 | Luton T | 41 | 13 |
| 1983–84 | Luton T | 39 | 11 |
| 1984–85 | Liverpool | 26 | 8 |
| 1985–86 | Liverpool | 20 | 11 |
| 1986–87 | Liverpool | 23 | 6 |
| 1987–88 | Liverpool | 8 | 0 |
| 1987–88 | Tottenham H | 11 | 1 |
| 1988–89 | Tottenham H | 33 | 6 |
| 1989–90 | Tottenham H | 26 | 2 |
| 1990–91 | Tottenham H | 29 | 7 |
| 1991–92 | Tottenham H | 29 | 3 |
| 1991–92 | QPR (loan) | 2 | 0 |
| 1992–93 | Portsmouth | 43 | 9 |
| 1993–94 | Portsmouth | 30 | 5 |
| 1993–94 | Manchester C | 11 | 4 |
| 1994–95 | Manchester C | 39 | 12 |
| 1995–96 | Manchester C | 3 | 0 |
| 1995–96 | Portsmouth | 21 | 5 |
| 1996–97 | Portsmouth | 0 | 0 |
| 1997–98 | Portsmouth | 0 | 0 |
| **Total:** | | **521** | **127** |

## WALSH, Steve — Defender

H: 6 3 W: 14 09 b.Fulwood 3-11-64

*Source:* Local.

| | | | |
|---|---|---|---|
| 1982–83 | Wigan Ath | 31 | [illegible] |
| 1983–84 | Wigan Ath | 42 | [illegible] |
| 1984–85 | Wigan Ath | 40 | [illegible] |
| 1985–86 | Wigan Ath | 13 | [illegible] |
| 1986–87 | Leicester C | 21 | [illegible] |
| 1987–88 | Leicester C | 32 | [illegible] |
| 1988–89 | Leicester C | 30 | [illegible] |
| 1989–90 | Leicester C | 34 | [illegible] |
| 1990–91 | Leicester C | 35 | [illegible] |
| 1991–92 | Leicester C | 43 | [illegible] |
| 1992–93 | Leicester C | 40 | [illegible] |
| 1993–94 | Leicester C | 10 | [illegible] |
| 1994–95 | Leicester C | 5 | [illegible] |
| 1995–96 | Leicester C | 37 | [illegible] |
| 1996–97 | Leicester C | 22 | [illegible] |
| 1997–98 | Leicester C | 26 | [illegible] |
| **Total:** | | **461** | **54** |

## WALTERS, Mark — Midfielder

H: 5 9 W: 11 05 b.Birmingham 2-6-64

*Source:* Apprentice. *Honours:* England Schools, Youth, Under-21, B, 1 full cap.

| | | | |
|---|---|---|---|
| 1981–82 | Aston Villa | 1 | [illegible] |
| 1982–83 | Aston Villa | 22 | [illegible] |
| 1983–84 | Aston Villa | 37 | [illegible] |
| 1984–85 | Aston Villa | 36 | [illegible] |
| 1985–86 | Aston Villa | 40 | [illegible] |
| 1986–87 | Aston Villa | 21 | [illegible] |
| 1987–88 | Aston Villa | 24 | [illegible] |
| 1987–88 | Rangers | 18 | [illegible] |
| 1988–89 | Rangers | 31 | [illegible] |
| 1989–90 | Rangers | 27 | [illegible] |
| 1990–91 | Rangers | 30 | [illegible] |
| 1991–92 | Liverpool | 25 | [illegible] |
| 1992–93 | Liverpool | 34 | [illegible] |
| 1993–94 | Liverpool | 17 | [illegible] |
| 1993–94 | Stoke C (loan) | 9 | [illegible] |
| 1994–95 | Liverpool | 18 | [illegible] |
| 1994–95 | Wolverhampton W (loan) | 11 | [illegible] |
| 1995–96 | Liverpool | 0 | [illegible] |
| 1995–96 | Southampton | 5 | [illegible] |
| 1996–97 | Swindon T | 27 | [illegible] |
| 1997–98 | Swindon T | 34 | [illegible] |
| **Total:** | | **467** | **103** |

## WALTON, David — Defender

H: 6 2 W: 14 07 b.Bedlingham 10-4-73

*Source:* Trainee.

| | | | |
|---|---|---|---|
| 1991–92 | Sheffield U | 0 | [illegible] |

| | | | |
|---|---|---|---|
| 1992–93 | Sheffield U | 0 | 0 |
| 1993–94 | Sheffield U | 0 | 0 |
| 1993–94 | Shrewsbury T | 27 | 5 |
| 1994–95 | Shrewsbury T | 36 | 3 |
| 1995–96 | Shrewsbury T | 35 | 0 |
| 1996–97 | Shrewsbury T | 24 | 1 |
| 1997–98 | Shrewsbury T | 6 | 1 |
| 1997–98 | Crewe Alex | 27 | 0 |
| **Total:** | | **155** | **10** |

## WALTON, Mark — Goalkeeper

H: 6 4 W: 16 00 b.Merthyr 1-6-69

*Source:* Swansea C. *Honours:* Wales Under-21.

| | | | |
|---|---|---|---|
| 1986–87 | Luton T | 0 | 0 |
| 1987–88 | Luton T | 0 | 0 |
| 1987–88 | Colchester U | 17 | 0 |
| 1988–89 | Colchester U | 23 | 0 |
| 1989–90 | Norwich C | 1 | 0 |
| 1990–91 | Norwich C | 4 | 0 |
| 1991–92 | Norwich C | 17 | 0 |
| 1992–93 | Norwich C | 0 | 0 |
| 1993–94 | Norwich C | 0 | 0 |
| 1993–94 | Wrexham (loan) | 6 | 0 |
| 1993–94 | Dundee | 0 | 0 |
| 1993–94 | Bolton W | 3 | 0 |
| From Fakenham T. | | | |
| 1996–97 | Fulham | 28 | 0 |
| 1997–98 | Fulham | 12 | 0 |
| 1997–98 | Gillingham (loan) | 1 | 0 |
| 1997–98 | Norwich C (loan) | 0 | 0 |
| **Total:** | | **112** | **0** |

## WALTON, Paul — Defender

H: 5 9 W: 11 04 b.Sunderland 2-7-79

*Source:* Trainee.

| | | | |
|---|---|---|---|
| 1995–96 | Hartlepool U | 6 | 0 |
| 1996–97 | Hartlepool U | 4 | 0 |
| 1997–98 | Hartlepool U | 0 | 0 |
| **Total:** | | **10** | **0** |

## WANCHOPE, Paulo — Forward

H: 6 4 W: 12 05 b.Costa Rica 31-7-76

*Source:* Herediano. *Honours:* Costa Rica full caps.

| | | | |
|---|---|---|---|
| 1996–97 | Derby Co | 5 | 1 |
| 1997–98 | Derby Co | 32 | 13 |
| **Total:** | | **37** | **14** |

## WANLESS, Paul — Midfield

H: 6 1 W: 13 11 b.Banbury 14-12-73

*Source:* Trainee.

| | | | |
|---|---|---|---|
| 1991–92 | Oxford U | 6 | 0 |
| 1992–93 | Oxford U | 7 | 0 |
| 1993–94 | Oxford U | 9 | 0 |
| 1994–95 | Oxford U | 10 | 0 |
| 1995–96 | Lincoln C | 8 | 0 |
| 1995–96 | Cambridge U (loan) | 14 | 1 |
| 1996–97 | Cambridge U | 30 | 3 |
| 1997–98 | Cambridge U | 42 | 8 |
| **Total:** | | **126** | **12** |

## WARBURTON, Ray — Defender

H: 6 0 W: 12 13 b.Rotherham 7-10-67

*Source:* Apprentice.

| | | | |
|---|---|---|---|
| 1984–85 | Rotherham U | 1 | 0 |
| 1985–86 | Rotherham U | 0 | 0 |
| 1986–87 | Rotherham U | 3 | 0 |
| 1987–88 | Rotherham U | 0 | 0 |
| 1988–89 | Rotherham U | 0 | 0 |
| 1989–90 | York C | 43 | 2 |
| 1990–91 | York C | 22 | 4 |
| 1991–92 | York C | 9 | 0 |
| 1992–93 | York C | 10 | 3 |
| 1993–94 | York C | 6 | 0 |
| 1993–94 | Northampton T (loan) | 17 | 1 |
| 1994–95 | Northampton T | 39 | 3 |
| 1995–96 | Northampton T | 44 | 3 |
| 1996–97 | Northampton T | 35 | 4 |
| 1997–98 | Northampton T | 39 | 0 |
| **Total:** | | **268** | **20** |

## WARD, Ashley — Forward

H: 6 2 W: 13 09 b.Manchester 24-11-70

*Source:* Trainee.

| | | | |
|---|---|---|---|
| 1989–90 | Manchester C | 1 | 0 |
| 1990–91 | Manchester C | 0 | 0 |
| 1990–91 | Wrexham (loan) | 4 | 2 |
| 1991–92 | Leicester C | 10 | 0 |
| 1992–93 | Leicester C | 0 | 0 |
| 1992–93 | Blackpool (loan) | 2 | 1 |
| 1992–93 | Crewe Alex | 20 | 4 |
| 1993–94 | Crewe Alex | 25 | 13 |
| 1994–95 | Crewe Alex | 16 | 8 |
| 1994–95 | Norwich C | 25 | 8 |
| 1995–96 | Norwich C | 28 | 10 |
| 1995–96 | Derby Co | 7 | 1 |
| 1996–97 | Derby Co | 30 | 8 |
| 1997–98 | Derby Co | 3 | 0 |

| | | | |
|---|---|---|---|
| 1997–98 | Barnsley | 29 | 8 |
| **Total:** | | **200** | **63** |

## WARD, Darran — Defender

H: 6 3 W: 12 10 b.Kenton 13-9-78

*Source:* Trainee.

| | | | |
|---|---|---|---|
| 1995–96 | Watford | 1 | 0 |
| 1996–97 | Watford | 7 | 0 |
| 1997–98 | Watford | 0 | 0 |
| **Total:** | | **8** | **0** |

## WARD, Darren — Goalkeeper

H: 5 11 W: 12 09 b.Worksop 11-5-74

*Source:* Trainee. *Honours:* Wales Under-21.

| | | | |
|---|---|---|---|
| 1992–93 | Mansfield T | 13 | 0 |
| 1993–94 | Mansfield T | 33 | 0 |
| 1994–95 | Mansfield T | 35 | 0 |
| 1995–96 | Notts Co | 46 | 0 |
| 1996–97 | Notts Co | 38 | 0 |
| 1997–98 | Notts Co | 44 | 0 |
| **Total:** | | **209** | **0** |

## WARD, Gavin — Goalkeeper

H: 6 2 W: 12 12 b.Sutton Coldfield 30-6-70

*Source:* Aston Villa Trainee.

| | | | |
|---|---|---|---|
| 1988–89 | Shrewsbury T | 0 | 0 |
| 1989–90 | WBA | 0 | 0 |
| 1989–90 | Cardiff C | 2 | 0 |
| 1990–91 | Cardiff C | 1 | 0 |
| 1991–92 | Cardiff C | 24 | 0 |
| 1992–93 | Cardiff C | 32 | 0 |
| 1993–94 | Leicester C | 32 | 0 |
| 1994–95 | Leicester C | 6 | 0 |
| 1995–96 | Bradford C | 36 | 0 |
| 1995–96 | Bolton W | 5 | 0 |
| 1996–97 | Bolton W | 11 | 0 |
| 1997–98 | Bolton W | 6 | 0 |
| **Total:** | | **155** | **0** |

## WARD, Mitch — Midfield

H: 5 9 W: 11 07 b.Sheffield 19-6-71

*Source:* Trainee.

| | | | |
|---|---|---|---|
| 1989–90 | Sheffield U | 0 | 0 |
| 1990–91 | Sheffield U | 4 | 0 |
| 1990–91 | Crewe Alex (loan) | 4 | 1 |
| 1991–92 | Sheffield U | 6 | 2 |
| 1992–93 | Sheffield U | 26 | 0 |
| 1993–94 | Sheffield U | 22 | 1 |
| 1994–95 | Sheffield U | 14 | 2 |
| 1995–96 | Sheffield U | 42 | 1 |
| 1996–97 | Sheffield U | 34 | 4 |
| 1997–98 | Sheffield U | 6 | 1 |
| 1997–98 | Everton | 8 | 0 |
| **Total:** | | **166** | **12** |

## WARD, Nick — Forward

H: 5 10 W: 10 09 b.Wrexham 30-11-77

*Source:* Trainee.

| | | | |
|---|---|---|---|
| 1996–97 | Shrewsbury T | 14 | 1 |
| 1997–98 | Shrewsbury T | 6 | 0 |
| **Total:** | | **20** | **1** |

## WARD, Peter — Midfield

H: 6 0 W: 11 07 b.Durham 15-10-64

*Source:* Chester-le-Street.

| | | | |
|---|---|---|---|
| 1986–87 | Huddersfield T | 7 | 0 |
| 1987–88 | Huddersfield T | 26 | 2 |
| 1988–89 | Huddersfield T | 4 | 0 |
| 1989–90 | Rochdale | 40 | 5 |
| 1990–91 | Rochdale | 44 | 5 |
| 1991–92 | Stockport Co | 44 | 1 |
| 1992–93 | Stockport Co | 35 | 3 |
| 1993–94 | Stockport Co | 35 | 3 |
| 1994–95 | Stockport Co | 28 | 3 |
| 1995–96 | Wrexham | 34 | 5 |
| 1996–97 | Wrexham | 24 | 1 |
| 1997–98 | Wrexham | 37 | 6 |
| **Total:** | | **358** | **34** |

## WARHURST, Paul — Defender

H: 6 1 W: 13 08 b.Stockport 26-6-69

*Source:* Trainee. *Honours:* England Under-21.

| | | | |
|---|---|---|---|
| 1987–88 | Manchester C | 0 | 0 |
| 1988–89 | Oldham Ath | 4 | 0 |
| 1989–90 | Oldham Ath | 30 | 1 |
| 1990–91 | Oldham Ath | 33 | 1 |
| 1991–92 | Sheffield W | 33 | 0 |
| 1992–93 | Sheffield W | 29 | 6 |
| 1993–94 | Sheffield W | 4 | 0 |
| 1993–94 | Blackburn R | 9 | 0 |
| 1994–95 | Blackburn R | 27 | 2 |
| 1995–96 | Blackburn R | 10 | 0 |
| 1996–97 | Blackburn R | 11 | 2 |
| 1997–98 | Crystal Palace | 22 | 3 |
| **Total:** | | **212** | **15** |

## WARNE, Paul — Forward

H: 5 9 W: 11 02 b.Norwich 8-5-73

*Source:* Wroxham.

| | | | |
|---|---|---|---|
| 1997–98 | Wigan Ath | 25 | 2 |
| **Total:** | | **25** | **2** |

## WARNER, Michael — Midfield

H: 5 9 W: 10 10 b.Harrogate 17-1-74

*Source:* Tamworth.

| | | | |
|---|---|---|---|
| 1995–96 | Northampton T | 0 | 0 |
| 1996–97 | Northampton T | 9 | 0 |
| 1997–98 | Northampton T | 10 | 0 |
| **Total:** | | **19** | **0** |

## WARNER, Phil — Defender

H: 5 10 W: 11 07 b.Southampton 2-2-79

*Source:* Trainee.

| | | | |
|---|---|---|---|
| 1997–98 | Southampton | 1 | 0 |
| **Total:** | | **1** | **0** |

## WARNER, Tony — Goalkeeper

H: 6 4 W: 13 09 b.Liverpool 11-5-74

*Source:* School.

| | | | |
|---|---|---|---|
| 1993–94 | Liverpool | 0 | 0 |
| 1994–95 | Liverpool | 0 | 0 |
| 1995–96 | Liverpool | 0 | 0 |
| 1996–97 | Liverpool | 0 | 0 |
| 1997–98 | Liverpool | 0 | 0 |
| 1997–98 | Swindon T (loan) | 2 | 0 |
| **Total:** | | **2** | **0** |

## WARNER, Vance — Defender

H: 6 0 W: 13 04 b.Leeds 3-9-74

*Source:* Trainee.

| | | | |
|---|---|---|---|
| 1991–92 | Nottingham F | 0 | 0 |
| 1992–93 | Nottingham F | 0 | 0 |
| 1993–94 | Nottingham F | 1 | 0 |
| 1994–95 | Nottingham F | 1 | 0 |
| 1995–96 | Nottingham F | 0 | 0 |
| 1995–96 | Grimsby T (loan) | 3 | 0 |
| 1996–97 | Nottingham F | 3 | 0 |
| 1997–98 | Nottingham F | 0 | 0 |
| 1997–98 | Rotherham U | 21 | 0 |
| **Total:** | | **29** | **0** |

## WARREN, Christer — Forward

H: 5 10 W: 11 12 b.Poole 10-10-74

*Source:* Cheltenham T.

| | | | |
|---|---|---|---|
| 1994–95 | Southampton | 0 | 0 |
| 1995–96 | Southampton | 7 | 0 |
| 1996–97 | Southampton | 1 | 0 |
| 1996–97 | Brighton & HA (loan) | 3 | 0 |
| 1996–97 | Fulham (loan) | 11 | 1 |
| 1997–98 | Southampton | 0 | 0 |
| 1997–98 | Bournemouth | 30 | 6 |
| **Total:** | | **52** | **7** |

## WARREN, Lee — Midfield

H: 6 1 W: 12 11 b.Manchester 28-2-69

*Source:* Trainee.

| | | | |
|---|---|---|---|
| 1987–88 | Leeds U | 0 | 0 |
| 1987–88 | Rochdale | 31 | 1 |
| 1988–89 | Hull C | 28 | 0 |
| 1989–90 | Hull C | 10 | 0 |
| 1990–91 | Hull C | 15 | 0 |
| 1990–91 | Lincoln C (loan) | 3 | 1 |
| 1991–92 | Hull C | 31 | 1 |
| 1992–93 | Hull C | 36 | 0 |
| 1993–94 | Hull C | 33 | 0 |
| 1994–95 | Doncaster R | 14 | 2 |
| 1995–96 | Doncaster R | 42 | 0 |
| 1996–97 | Doncaster R | 25 | 0 |
| 1997–98 | Doncaster R | 44 | 1 |
| **Total:** | | **312** | **6** |

## WARREN, Mark — Defender

H: 6 0 W: 12 02 b.Hackney 12-11-74

*Source:* Trainee.

| | | | |
|---|---|---|---|
| 1991–92 | Leyton Orient | 1 | 0 |
| 1992–93 | Leyton Orient | 14 | 0 |
| 1993–94 | Leyton Orient | 6 | 0 |
| 1993–94 | West Ham U (loan) | 0 | 0 |
| 1994–95 | Leyton Orient | 31 | 3 |
| 1995–96 | Leyton Orient | 22 | 1 |
| 1996–97 | Leyton Orient | 27 | 1 |
| 1997–98 | Leyton Orient | 41 | 0 |
| **Total:** | | **142** | **5** |

## WARRINGTON, Andy — Goalkeeper

H: 6 3 W: 12 11 b.Sheffield 10-6-76

*Source:* Trainee.

| | | | |
|---|---|---|---|
| 1994–95 | York C | 0 | 0 |
| 1995–96 | York C | 6 | 0 |
| 1996–97 | York C | 27 | 0 |
| 1997–98 | York C | 17 | 0 |
| **Total:** | | **50** | **0** |

## WARRINGTON, Craig — Midfield

b.Chester 20-6-79

*Source:* Trainee.

| | | | |
|---|---|---|---|
| 1997–98 | Chester C | 0 | 0 |

## WASSALL, Darren — Defender

H: 6 0 W: 12 07 b.Edgbaston 27-6-68

| | | | |
|---|---|---|---|
| 1987–88 | Nottingham F | 3 | 0 |
| 1987–88 | Hereford U (loan) | 5 | 0 |
| 1988–89 | Nottingham F | 0 | 0 |
| 1988–89 | Bury (loan) | 7 | 1 |
| 1989–90 | Nottingham F | 3 | 0 |
| 1990–91 | Nottingham F | 7 | 0 |
| 1991–92 | Nottingham F | 14 | 0 |
| 1992–93 | Derby Co | 24 | 0 |
| 1993–94 | Derby Co | 25 | 0 |
| 1994–95 | Derby Co | 32 | 0 |
| 1995–96 | Derby Co | 17 | 0 |
| 1996–97 | Derby Co | 0 | 0 |
| 1996–97 | Manchester C (loan) | 15 | 0 |
| 1996–97 | Birmingham C (loan) | 8 | 0 |
| 1997–98 | Birmingham C | 14 | 0 |
| **Total:** | | **174** | **1** |

## WATERMAN, David — Defender

H: 5 10 W: 13 02 b.Guernsey 16-5-77

*Source:* Trainee. *Honours:* Northern Ireland Under-21.

| | | | |
|---|---|---|---|
| 1995–96 | Portsmouth | 0 | 0 |
| 1996–97 | Portsmouth | 4 | 0 |
| 1997–98 | Portsmouth | 15 | 0 |
| **Total:** | | **19** | **0** |

## WATKIN, Steve — Forward

H: 5 10 W: 11 10 b.Wrexham 16-6-71

*Source:* School.

| | | | |
|---|---|---|---|
| 1989–90 | Wrexham | 0 | 0 |
| 1990–91 | Wrexham | 9 | 1 |
| 1991–92 | Wrexham | 28 | 8 |
| 1992–93 | Wrexham | 33 | 18 |
| 1993–94 | Wrexham | 40 | 9 |
| 1994–95 | Wrexham | 32 | 4 |
| 1995–96 | Wrexham | 29 | 7 |
| 1996–97 | Wrexham | 26 | 7 |
| 1997–98 | Wrexham | 3 | 1 |
| 1997–98 | Swansea C | 32 | 3 |
| **Total:** | | **232** | **58** |

## WATKINSON, Russ — Forward

H: 6 0 W: 12 00 b.Epsom 3-12-77

*Source:* Woking.

| | | | |
|---|---|---|---|
| 1996–97 | Southampton | 2 | 0 |
| 1997–98 | Southampton | 0 | 0 |
| 1997–98 | Bristol C | 0 | 0 |
| 1997–98 | Millwall | 0 | 0 |
| **Total:** | | **2** | **0** |

## WATKISS, Stuart — Defender

H: 6 2 W: 13 06 b.Wolverhampton 8-5-66

*Source:* Apprentice.

| | | | |
|---|---|---|---|
| 1983–84 | Wolverhampton W | 2 | 0 |
| From Rushall Olympic. | | | |
| 1993–94 | Walsall | 39 | 2 |
| 1994–95 | Walsall | 8 | 0 |
| 1995–96 | Walsall | 15 | 0 |
| 1995–96 | Hereford U | 19 | 0 |
| 1996–97 | Mansfield T | 31 | 1 |
| 1997–98 | Mansfield T | 10 | 0 |
| **Total:** | | **124** | **3** |

## WATSON, Alex — Defender

H: 6 1 W: 13 00 b.Liverpool 5-4-68

*Source:* Apprentice. *Honours:* England Youth.

| | | | |
|---|---|---|---|
| 1984–85 | Liverpool | 0 | 0 |
| 1985–86 | Liverpool | 0 | 0 |
| 1986–87 | Liverpool | 0 | 0 |
| 1987–88 | Liverpool | 2 | 0 |
| 1988–89 | Liverpool | 2 | 0 |
| 1989–90 | Liverpool | 0 | 0 |
| 1990–91 | Liverpool | 0 | 0 |
| 1990–91 | Derby Co (loan) | 5 | 0 |
| 1990–91 | Bournemouth | 23 | 3 |
| 1991–92 | Bournemouth | 15 | 0 |
| 1992–93 | Bournemouth | 46 | 1 |
| 1993–94 | Bournemouth | 45 | 1 |
| 1994–95 | Bournemouth | 22 | 0 |
| 1995–96 | Bournemouth | 0 | 0 |
| 1995–96 | Gillingham (loan) | 10 | 1 |
| 1995–96 | Torquay U | 29 | 2 |
| 1996–97 | Torquay U | 46 | 1 |
| 1997–98 | Torquay U | 46 | 1 |
| **Total:** | | **291** | **10** |

## WATSON, Andy — Forward

H: 5 9 W: 12 06 b.Leeds 1-4-67

*Source:* Harrogate T.

| | | | |
|---|---|---|---|
| 1988–89 | Halifax T | 45 | 5 |
| 1989–90 | Halifax T | 38 | 10 |
| 1990–91 | Swansea C | 14 | 1 |
| 1991–92 | Swansea C | 0 | 0 |
| 1991–92 | Carlisle U | 35 | 14 |
| 1992–93 | Carlisle U | 21 | 8 |
| 1992–93 | Blackpool | 15 | 2 |
| 1993–94 | Blackpool | 40 | 20 |
| 1994–95 | Blackpool | 33 | 15 |
| 1995–96 | Blackpool | 27 | 6 |
| 1996–97 | Blackpool | 0 | 0 |
| 1996–97 | Walsall | 36 | 5 |
| 1997–98 | Walsall | 27 | 7 |
| **Total:** | | **331** | **93** |

## WATSON, Dave — Defender

H: 5 11 W: 11 12 b.Liverpool 20-11-61

*Source:* Amateur. *Honours:* England Under-21, 12 full caps.

| | | | |
|---|---|---|---|
| 1979–80 | Liverpool | 0 | 0 |
| 1980–81 | Liverpool | 0 | 0 |
| 1980–81 | Norwich C | 18 | 3 |
| 1981–82 | Norwich C | 38 | 3 |
| 1982–83 | Norwich C | 35 | 1 |
| 1983–84 | Norwich C | 40 | 1 |
| 1984–85 | Norwich C | 39 | 0 |
| 1985–86 | Norwich C | 42 | 3 |
| 1986–87 | Everton | 35 | 4 |
| 1987–88 | Everton | 37 | 4 |
| 1988–89 | Everton | 32 | 3 |
| 1989–90 | Everton | 29 | 1 |
| 1990–91 | Everton | 32 | 2 |
| 1991–92 | Everton | 35 | 3 |
| 1992–93 | Everton | 40 | 1 |
| 1993–94 | Everton | 28 | 1 |
| 1994–95 | Everton | 38 | 2 |
| 1995–96 | Everton | 34 | 1 |
| 1996–97 | Everton | 29 | 1 |
| 1997–98 | Everton | 26 | 0 |
| **Total:** | | **607** | **34** |

## WATSON, David — Goalkeeper

H: 5 11 W: 12 12 b.Barnsley 10-11-73

*Source:* Trainee. *Honours:* England Youth, Under-21.

| | | | |
|---|---|---|---|
| 1992–93 | Barnsley | 5 | 0 |
| 1993–94 | Barnsley | 9 | 0 |
| 1994–95 | Barnsley | 37 | 0 |
| 1995–96 | Barnsley | 45 | 0 |
| 1996–97 | Barnsley | 46 | 0 |
| 1997–98 | Barnsley | 30 | 0 |
| **Total:** | | **172** | **0** |

## WATSON, Gordon — Forward

H: 5 10 W: 12 08 b.Sidcup 20-3-71

*Source:* Trainee. *Honours:* England Under-21.

| | | | |
|---|---|---|---|
| 1988–89 | Charlton Ath | 0 | 0 |
| 1989–90 | Charlton Ath | 9 | 0 |
| 1990–91 | Charlton Ath | 22 | 7 |
| 1990–91 | Sheffield W | 5 | 0 |
| 1991–92 | Sheffield W | 4 | 0 |
| 1992–93 | Sheffield W | 11 | 1 |
| 1993–94 | Sheffield W | 23 | 12 |
| 1994–95 | Sheffield W | 23 | 2 |
| 1994–95 | Southampton | 12 | 3 |
| 1995–96 | Southampton | 25 | 3 |
| 1996–97 | Southampton | 15 | 2 |
| 1996–97 | Bradford C | 3 | 1 |
| 1997–98 | Bradford C | 0 | 0 |
| **Total:** | | **152** | **31** |

## WATSON, Kevin — Midfield

H: 5 9 W: 12 08 b.Hackney 3-1-74

*Source:* Trainee.

| | | | |
|---|---|---|---|
| 1991–92 | Tottenham H | 0 | 0 |
| 1992–93 | Tottenham H | 5 | 0 |
| 1993–94 | Tottenham H | 0 | 0 |
| 1993–94 | Brentford (loan) | 3 | 0 |
| 1994–95 | Tottenham H | 0 | 0 |
| 1994–95 | Bristol C (loan) | 2 | 0 |
| 1994–95 | Barnet (loan) | 13 | 0 |
| 1995–96 | Tottenham H | 0 | 0 |
| 1996–97 | Swindon T | 27 | 1 |
| 1997–98 | Swindon T | 18 | 0 |
| **Total:** | | **68** | **1** |

## WATSON, Paul — Defender

H: 5 8 W: 10 09 b.Hastings 4-1-75

*Source:* Trainee.

| | | | |
|---|---|---|---|
| 1992–93 | Gillingham | 1 | 0 |
| 1993–94 | Gillingham | 14 | 0 |
| 1994–95 | Gillingham | 39 | 2 |
| 1995–96 | Gillingham | 8 | 0 |
| 1996–97 | Fulham | 44 | 3 |
| 1997–98 | Fulham | 6 | 1 |
| 1997–98 | Brentford (loan) | 25 | 0 |
| **Total:** | | **137** | **6** |

## WATSON, Richard — Midfield

H: 5 10 W: 11 10 b.Salford 2-11-78

*Source:* Trainee.

| | | | |
|---|---|---|---|
| 1997–98 | Bury | 0 | 0 |

## WATSON, Simon — Midfield

H: 5 10 W: 12 10 b.Strabane 22-9-80

*Source:* Trainee.

| | | | |
|---|---|---|---|
| 1997–98 | Leeds U | 0 | 0 |

## WATSON, Steve — Defender

H: 6 1 W: 12 07 b.North Shields 1-4-74

*Source:* Trainee. *Honours:* England Youth, Under-21, B.

| | | | |
|---|---|---|---|
| 1990–91 | Newcastle U | 24 | 0 |
| 1991–92 | Newcastle U | 28 | 1 |
| 1992–93 | Newcastle U | 2 | 0 |
| 1993–94 | Newcastle U | 32 | 2 |

| | | | |
|---|---|---|---|
| 1994–95 | Newcastle U | 27 | 4 |
| 1995–96 | Newcastle U | 23 | 3 |
| 1996–97 | Newcastle U | 36 | 1 |
| 1997–98 | Newcastle U | 29 | 1 |
| **Total:** | | **201** | **12** |

## WATT, Michael — Goalkeeper

H: 6 1 W: 11 10 b.Aberdeen 27-11-70

*Source:* Cove Rangers. *Honours:* Scotland Under-21.

| | | | |
|---|---|---|---|
| 1989–90 | Aberdeen | 7 | 0 |
| 1990–91 | Aberdeen | 10 | 0 |
| 1991–92 | Aberdeen | 2 | 0 |
| 1992–93 | Aberdeen | 3 | 0 |
| 1993–94 | Aberdeen | 4 | 0 |
| 1994–95 | Aberdeen | 14 | 0 |
| 1995–96 | Aberdeen | 30 | 0 |
| 1996–97 | Aberdeen | 9 | 0 |
| 1997–98 | Blackburn R | 0 | 0 |
| **Total:** | | **79** | **0** |

## WATTS, Julian — Defender

H: 6 2 W: 13 07 b.Sheffield 17-3-71

*Source:* Trainee.

| | | | |
|---|---|---|---|
| 1990–91 | Rotherham U | 10 | 0 |
| 1991–92 | Rotherham U | 10 | 1 |
| 1991–92 | Sheffield W | 0 | 0 |
| 1992–93 | Sheffield W | 4 | 0 |
| 1992–93 | Shrewsbury T (loan) | 9 | 0 |
| 1993–94 | Sheffield W | 1 | 0 |
| 1994–95 | Sheffield W | 0 | 0 |
| 1995–96 | Sheffield W | 11 | 1 |
| 1995–96 | Leicester C | 9 | 0 |
| 1996–97 | Leicester C | 26 | 1 |
| 1997–98 | Leicester C | 3 | 0 |
| 1997–98 | Crewe Alex (loan) | 5 | 0 |
| 1997–98 | Huddersfield T (loan) | 8 | 0 |
| **Total:** | | **96** | **3** |

## WDOWCZYK, Dariusz — Defender

H: 5 11 W: 11 11 b.Warsaw 21-9-62

*Source:* Legia Warsaw. *Honours:* Poland full caps.

| | | | |
|---|---|---|---|
| 1989–90 | Celtic | 23 | 1 |
| 1990–91 | Celtic | 24 | 0 |
| 1991–92 | Celtic | 19 | 0 |
| 1992–93 | Celtic | 25 | 3 |
| 1993–94 | Celtic | 25 | 0 |
| 1994–95 | Reading | 38 | 0 |
| 1995–96 | Reading | 30 | 0 |
| 1996–97 | Reading | 8 | 0 |
| 1997–98 | Reading | 6 | 0 |
| **Total:** | | **198** | **4** |

## WEATHERSTONE, Simon — Forward

H: 5 10 W: 12 01 b.Reading 26-1-80

*Source:* Trainee.

| | | | |
|---|---|---|---|
| 1996–97 | Oxford U | 1 | 0 |
| 1997–98 | Oxford U | 11 | 1 |
| **Total:** | | **12** | **1** |

## WEAVER, Luke — Goalkeeper

H: 6 2 W: 13 02 b.Woolwich 26-6-79

*Source:* Trainee. *Honours:* England Schools, Youth.

| | | | |
|---|---|---|---|
| 1996–97 | Leyton Orient | 9 | 0 |
| 1996–97 | West Ham U (loan) | 0 | 0 |
| 1997–98 | Leyton Orient | 0 | 0 |
| 1997–98 | Sunderland | 0 | 0 |
| **Total:** | | **9** | **0** |

## WEAVER, Nick — Goalkeeper

H: 6 3 W: 13 01 b.Sheffield 2-3-79

*Source:* Trainee.

| | | | |
|---|---|---|---|
| 1995–96 | Mansfield T | 1 | 0 |
| 1996–97 | Mansfield T | 0 | 0 |
| 1996–97 | Manchester C | 0 | 0 |
| 1997–98 | Manchester C | 0 | 0 |
| **Total:** | | **1** | **0** |

## WEAVER, Simon — Defender

H: 6 1 W: 10 07 b.Doncaster 20-12-77

*Source:* Trainee.

| | | | |
|---|---|---|---|
| 1996–97 | Sheffield W | 0 | 0 |
| 1996–97 | Doncaster R (loan) | 2 | 0 |
| 1997–98 | Sheffield W | 0 | 0 |
| **Total:** | | **2** | **0** |

## WEBB, Darren — Midfield

b.Brighton 24-10-79

*Source:* Trainee.

| | | | |
|---|---|---|---|
| 1997–98 | Cambridge U | 0 | 0 |

## WEBB, Nicholas — Goalkeeper

H: 6 1 W: 12 13 b.Hitchin 23-2-79

*Source:* Trainee.

| | | | |
|---|---|---|---|
| 1997–98 | Luton T | 0 | 0 |

## WEBB, Simon — Midfield

H: 5 11 W: 12 03 b.Castle Bar 19-1-78

*Source:* Trainee.

| | | | |
|---|---|---|---|
| 1994–95 | Tottenham H | 0 | 0 |
| 1995–96 | Tottenham H | 0 | 0 |
| 1996–97 | Tottenham H | 0 | 0 |
| 1997–98 | Tottenham H | 0 | 0 |

## WEBBER, Damien — Defender

H: 6 4 W: 14 00 b.Rustington 8-10-68

*Source:* Bognor Regis T.

| | | | |
|---|---|---|---|
| 1994–95 | Millwall | 22 | 2 |
| 1995–96 | Millwall | 16 | 0 |
| 1996–97 | Millwall | 26 | 2 |
| 1997–98 | Millwall | 1 | 0 |
| **Total:** | | **65** | **4** |

## WEIR, David — Defender

H: 6 2 W: 13 07 b.Falkirk 10-5-70

*Source:* Celtic BC. *Honours:* Scotland 7 full caps.

| | | | |
|---|---|---|---|
| 1992–93 | Falkirk | 30 | 1 |
| 1993–94 | Falkirk | 37 | 3 |
| 1994–95 | Falkirk | 32 | 1 |
| 1995–96 | Falkirk | 34 | 3 |
| 1996–97 | Hearts | 34 | 6 |
| 1997–98 | Hearts | 35 | 1 |
| **Total:** | | **202** | **15** |

## WEIR, James — Defender

H: 6 1 W: 12 05 b.Motherwell 15-6-69

*Source:* Motherwell Orbiston BC.

| | | | |
|---|---|---|---|
| 1987–88 | Hamilton A | 6 | 0 |
| 1988–89 | Hamilton A | 29 | 0 |
| 1989–90 | Hamilton A | 30 | 1 |
| 1990–91 | Hamilton A | 39 | 2 |
| 1991–92 | Hamilton A | 40 | 1 |
| 1992–93 | Hamilton A | 37 | 1 |
| 1993–94 | Hamilton A | 2 | 0 |
| 1993–94 | Hearts | 26 | 0 |
| 1994–95 | Hearts | 2 | 0 |
| 1994–95 | St Johnstone | 17 | 0 |
| 1995–96 | St Johnstone | 29 | 0 |
| 1996–97 | St Johnstone | 32 | 3 |
| 1997–98 | St Johnstone | 25 | 0 |
| **Total:** | | **314** | **8** |

## WEIR, Micky — Midfield

H: 5 4 W: 10 03 b.Edinburgh 16-1-66

*Source:* Portobello T.

| | | | |
|---|---|---|---|
| 1982–83 | Hibernian | 0 | 0 |
| 1983–84 | Hibernian | 0 | 0 |
| 1984–85 | Hibernian | 12 | 0 |
| 1985–86 | Hibernian | 7 | 0 |
| 1986–87 | Hibernian | 24 | 4 |
| 1987–88 | Hibernian | 5 | 1 |
| 1987–88 | Luton T | 8 | 0 |
| 1987–88 | Hibernian | 13 | 2 |
| 1988–89 | Hibernian | 7 | 0 |
| 1989–90 | Hibernian | 18 | 3 |
| 1990–91 | Hibernian | 20 | 1 |
| 1991–92 | Hibernian | 31 | 11 |
| 1992–93 | Hibernian | 33 | 5 |
| 1993–94 | Hibernian | 0 | 0 |
| 1994–95 | Hibernian | 19 | 1 |
| 1995–96 | Hibernian | 9 | 1 |
| 1995–96 | Millwall | 8 | 0 |
| 1996–97 | Hibernian | 8 | 1 |
| 1996–97 | Motherwell | 5 | 2 |
| 1997–98 | Motherwell | 18 | 4 |
| **Total:** | | **245** | **36** |

## WELCH, Keith — Goalkeeper

H: 6 2 W: 12 05 b.Bolton 3-10-68

*Source:* Trainee.

| | | | |
|---|---|---|---|
| 1986–87 | Bolton W | 0 | 0 |
| 1986–87 | Rochdale | 24 | 0 |
| 1987–88 | Rochdale | 46 | 0 |
| 1988–89 | Rochdale | 46 | 0 |
| 1989–90 | Rochdale | 46 | 0 |
| 1990–91 | Rochdale | 43 | 0 |
| 1991–92 | Bristol C | 26 | 0 |
| 1992–93 | Bristol C | 45 | 0 |
| 1993–94 | Bristol C | 45 | 0 |
| 1994–95 | Bristol C | 44 | 0 |
| 1995–96 | Bristol C | 35 | 0 |
| 1996–97 | Bristol C | 11 | 0 |
| 1997–98 | Bristol C | 44 | 0 |
| **Total:** | | **455** | **0** |

## WELLENS, Richard — Midfield

H: 5 9 W: 11 05 b.Manchester 26-3-80

*Source:* Trainee. *Honours:* England Youth.

| | | | |
|---|---|---|---|
| 1996–97 | Manchester U | 0 | 0 |
| 1997–98 | Manchester U | 0 | 0 |

## WELLER, Paul — Midfield

H: 5 8 W: 11 02 b.Brighton 6-3-75

*Source:* Trainee.

| | | | |
|---|---|---|---|
| 1993–94 | Burnley | 0 | 0 |
| 1994–95 | Burnley | 0 | 0 |
| 1995–96 | Burnley | 25 | 1 |
| 1996–97 | Burnley | 31 | 2 |
| 1997–98 | Burnley | 39 | 2 |
| **Total:** | | **95** | **5** |

## WELLS, David — Goalkeeper

H: 6 2 W: 12 07 b.Portsmouth 29-12-77

*Source:* Trainee.

| | | | |
|---|---|---|---|
| 1994–95 | Bournemouth | 1 | 0 |
| 1995–96 | Bournemouth | 0 | 0 |
| 1996–97 | Bournemouth | 0 | 0 |
| 1997–98 | Bournemouth | 0 | 0 |
| **Total:** | | **1** | **0** |

## WELSH, Brian — Defender

H: 6 2 W: 12 01 b.Edinburgh 23-2-69

*Source:* Tynecastle BC.

| | | | |
|---|---|---|---|
| 1986–87 | Dundee U | 1 | 0 |
| 1987–88 | Dundee U | 1 | 1 |
| 1988–89 | Dundee U | 1 | 0 |
| 1989–90 | Dundee U | 5 | 0 |
| 1990–91 | Dundee U | 17 | 0 |
| 1991–92 | Dundee U | 11 | 1 |
| 1992–93 | Dundee U | 15 | 1 |
| 1993–94 | Dundee U | 37 | 1 |
| 1994–95 | Dundee U | 27 | 4 |
| 1995–96 | Dundee U | 23 | 1 |
| 1996–97 | Hibernian | 17 | 0 |
| 1996–97 | Dunfermline Ath | 20 | 1 |
| 1997–98 | Hibernian | 17 | 1 |
| **Total:** | | **192** | **11** |

## WELSH, Steve — Defender

H: 6 1 W: 12 03 b.Glasgow 19-4-68

*Source:* Army.

| | | | |
|---|---|---|---|
| 1989–90 | Cambridge U | 0 | 0 |
| 1990–91 | Cambridge U | 1 | 0 |
| 1991–92 | Peterborough U | 42 | 0 |
| 1992–93 | Peterborough U | 45 | 1 |
| 1993–94 | Peterborough U | 45 | 1 |
| 1994–95 | Peterborough U | 14 | 0 |
| 1994–95 | Preston NE (loan) | 0 | 0 |
| 1994–95 | Partick T | 20 | 0 |
| 1995–96 | Partick T | 35 | 0 |
| 1996–97 | Peterborough U | 6 | 0 |
| 1997–98 | Dunfermline Ath | 6 | 0 |
| **Total:** | | **214** | **2** |

## WENLOCK, Stephen — Defender

H: 5 7 W: 11 01 b.Peterborough 11-3-78

*Source:* Trainee.

| | | | |
|---|---|---|---|
| 1996–97 | Leicester C | 0 | 0 |
| 1997–98 | Leicester C | 0 | 0 |

## WEST, Colin — Forward

H: 6 1 W: 13 09 b.Wallsend 13-11-62

*Source:* Apprentice.

| | | | |
|---|---|---|---|
| 1980–81 | Sunderland | 0 | 0 |
| 1981–82 | Sunderland | 18 | 6 |
| 1982–83 | Sunderland | 23 | 3 |
| 1983–84 | Sunderland | 38 | 9 |
| 1984–85 | Sunderland | 23 | 3 |
| 1984–85 | Watford | 12 | 7 |
| 1985–86 | Watford | 33 | 13 |
| 1986–87 | Rangers | 9 | 2 |
| 1987–88 | Rangers | 1 | 0 |
| 1987–88 | Sheffield W | 25 | 7 |
| 1988–89 | Sheffield W | 20 | 1 |
| 1988–89 | WBA | 17 | 8 |
| 1989–90 | WBA | 21 | 4 |
| 1990–91 | WBA | 28 | 8 |
| 1991–92 | WBA | 7 | 2 |
| 1991–92 | Port Vale (loan) | 5 | 1 |
| 1992–93 | Swansea C | 33 | 12 |
| 1993–94 | Leyton Orient | 43 | 14 |
| 1994–95 | Leyton Orient | 30 | 9 |
| 1995–96 | Leyton Orient | 39 | 16 |
| 1996–97 | Leyton Orient | 23 | 3 |
| 1997–98 | Leyton Orient | 7 | 0 |
| 1997–98 | Northampton T (loan) | 2 | 0 |
| **Total:** | | **457** | **128** |

## WEST, Dean — Defender

H: 5 10 W: 11 07 b.Wakefield 5-12-72

*Source:* Leeds U Schoolboy.

| | | | |
|---|---|---|---|
| 1990–91 | Lincoln C | 1 | 1 |
| 1991–92 | Lincoln C | 32 | 3 |
| 1992–93 | Lincoln C | 19 | 3 |
| 1993–94 | Lincoln C | 18 | 6 |
| 1994–95 | Lincoln C | 41 | 6 |
| 1995–96 | Lincoln C | 8 | 1 |
| 1995–96 | Bury | 37 | 1 |
| 1996–97 | Bury | 46 | 4 |
| 1997–98 | Bury | 4 | 0 |
| **Total:** | | **206** | **25** |

## WEST, Gareth — Defender

H: 6 1 W: 11 10 b.Oldham 1-8-78

*Source:* Trainee.

| | | | |
|---|---|---|---|
| 1996–97 | Burnley | 0 | 0 |
| 1997–98 | Burnley | 0 | 0 |

## WESTCOTT, John — Forward

H: 5 6 W: 10 04 b.Eastbourne 31-5-79

*Source:* Trainee.

| | | | |
|---|---|---|---|
| 1997–98 | Brighton & HA | 34 | 0 |
| **Total:** | | **34** | **0** |

## WESTLEY, Shane — Defender

H: 6 2 W: 13 01 b.Canterbury 16-6-65

*Source:* Apprentice.

| | | | |
|---|---|---|---|
| 1983–84 | Charlton Ath | 8 | 0 |
| 1984–85 | Charlton Ath | 0 | 0 |
| 1984–85 | Southend U | 12 | 0 |
| 1985–86 | Southend U | 36 | 5 |
| 1986–87 | Southend U | 32 | 0 |
| 1986–87 | Norwich C (loan) | 0 | 0 |
| 1987–88 | Southend U | 36 | 5 |
| 1988–89 | Southend U | 28 | 0 |
| 1989–90 | Wolverhampton W | 37 | 0 |
| 1990–91 | Wolverhampton W | 5 | 1 |
| 1991–92 | Wolverhampton W | 0 | 0 |
| 1992–93 | Wolverhampton W | 8 | 1 |
| 1992–93 | Brentford | 17 | 1 |
| 1993–94 | Brentford | 31 | 0 |
| 1994–95 | Brentford | 16 | 0 |
| 1994–95 | Southend U (loan) | 5 | 0 |
| 1995–96 | Cambridge U | 3 | 0 |
| 1995–96 | Lincoln C | 9 | 1 |
| 1996–97 | Lincoln C | 0 | 0 |
| 1997–98 | Lincoln C | 0 | 0 |
| **Total:** | | **283** | **14** |

## WESTWATER, Ian — Goalkeeper

H: 6 0 W: 13 00 b.Loughborough 8-11-63

*Source:* Salvesen BC.

| | | | |
|---|---|---|---|
| 1980–81 | Hearts | 2 | 0 |
| 1981–82 | Hearts | 0 | 0 |
| 1982–83 | Hearts | 0 | 0 |
| 1983–84 | Hearts | 0 | 0 |
| 1984–85 | Dunfermline Ath | 8 | 0 |
| 1985–86 | Dunfermline Ath | 38 | 0 |
| 1986–87 | Dunfermline Ath | 42 | 0 |
| 1987–88 | Dunfermline Ath | 28 | 0 |
| 1988–89 | Dunfermline Ath | 39 | 0 |
| 1989–90 | Dunfermline Ath | 36 | 0 |
| 1990–91 | Dunfermline Ath | 1 | 0 |
| 1991–92 | Falkirk | 40 | 0 |
| 1992–93 | Falkirk | 24 | 0 |
| 1993–94 | Falkirk | 3 | 0 |
| 1993–94 | Dunfermline Ath | 9 | 0 |
| 1994–95 | Dunfermline Ath | 17 | 0 |
| 1995–96 | Dunfermline Ath | 11 | 0 |
| 1996–97 | Dunfermline Ath | 29 | 0 |
| 1997–98 | Dunfermline Ath | 36 | 0 |
| **Total:** | | **363** | **0** |

## WESTWOOD, Ashley — Defender

H: 5 11 W: 11 02 b.Bridgnorth 31-8-76

*Source:* Trainee. *Honours:* England Youth.

| | | | |
|---|---|---|---|
| 1994–95 | Manchester U | 0 | 0 |
| 1995–96 | Crewe Alex | 33 | 4 |
| 1996–97 | Crewe Alex | 44 | 2 |
| 1997–98 | Crewe Alex | 21 | 3 |
| **Total:** | | **98** | **9** |

## WESTWOOD, Chris — Defender

H: 6 0 W: 12 02 b.Dudley 13-2-77

*Source:* Trainee.

| | | | |
|---|---|---|---|
| 1995–96 | Wolverhampton W | 0 | 0 |
| 1996–97 | Wolverhampton W | 0 | 0 |
| 1997–98 | Wolverhampton W | 4 | 1 |
| **Total:** | | **4** | **1** |

## WETHERALL, David — Defender

H: 6 2 W: 13 12 b.Sheffield 14-3-71

*Source:* School. *Honours:* England Schools.

| | | | |
|---|---|---|---|
| 1989–90 | Sheffield W | 0 | 0 |
| 1990–91 | Sheffield W | 0 | 0 |
| 1991–92 | Leeds U | 1 | 0 |
| 1992–93 | Leeds U | 13 | 1 |
| 1993–94 | Leeds U | 32 | 1 |
| 1994–95 | Leeds U | 38 | 3 |
| 1995–96 | Leeds U | 34 | 4 |
| 1996–97 | Leeds U | 29 | 0 |
| 1997–98 | Leeds U | 34 | 3 |
| **Total:** | | **181** | **12** |

## WHALLEY, Gareth — Midfield

H: 5 10 W: 11 06 b.Manchester 19-12-73

*Source:* Trainee.

| | | | |
|---|---|---|---|
| 1992–93 | Crewe Alex | 25 | 1 |
| 1993–94 | Crewe Alex | 15 | 1 |
| 1994–95 | Crewe Alex | 40 | 1 |
| 1995–96 | Crewe Alex | 44 | 2 |

## Wharton, Paul

| | | | |
|---|---|---|---|
| 1996–97 | Crewe Alex | 38 | 3 |
| 1997–98 | Crewe Alex | 18 | 1 |
| **Total:** | | **180** | **9** |

## WHARTON, Paul — Midfield

H: 5 4 W: 10 00 b.Newcastle 26-6-77

*Source:* Trainee.

| | | | |
|---|---|---|---|
| 1994–95 | Leeds U | 0 | 0 |
| 1995–96 | Leeds U | 0 | 0 |
| 1995–96 | Hull C | 9 | 0 |
| 1996–97 | Hull C | 1 | 0 |
| 1997–98 | Hull C | 1 | 0 |
| **Total:** | | **11** | **0** |

## WHEALING, Anthony — Defender

H: 5 9 W: 10 02 b.Manchester 3-9-76

*Source:* Trainee.

| | | | |
|---|---|---|---|
| 1995–96 | Blackburn R | 0 | 0 |
| 1996–97 | Blackburn R | 0 | 0 |
| 1997–98 | Blackburn R | 0 | 0 |

## WHELAN, Noel — Forward

H: 6 2 W: 12 03 b.Leeds 30-12-74

*Source:* Trainee. *Honours:* England Under-21.

| | | | |
|---|---|---|---|
| 1992–93 | Leeds U | 1 | 0 |
| 1993–94 | Leeds U | 16 | 0 |
| 1994–95 | Leeds U | 23 | 7 |
| 1995–96 | Leeds U | 8 | 0 |
| 1995–96 | Coventry C | 21 | 8 |
| 1996–97 | Coventry C | 35 | 6 |
| 1997–98 | Coventry C | 21 | 6 |
| **Total:** | | **125** | **27** |

## WHELAN, Phil — Defender

H: 6 4 W: 14 03 b.Stockport 7-3-72

*Honours:* England Under-21.

| | | | |
|---|---|---|---|
| 1989–90 | Ipswich T | 0 | 0 |
| 1990–91 | Ipswich T | 0 | 0 |
| 1991–92 | Ipswich T | 8 | 2 |
| 1992–93 | Ipswich T | 32 | 0 |
| 1993–94 | Ipswich T | 29 | 0 |
| 1994–95 | Ipswich T | 13 | 0 |
| 1994–95 | Middlesbrough | 0 | 0 |
| 1995–96 | Middlesbrough | 13 | 1 |
| 1996–97 | Middlesbrough | 9 | 0 |
| 1997–98 | Oxford U | 8 | 0 |
| **Total:** | | **112** | **3** |

## WHELAN, Spencer — Defender

H: 6 2 W: 11 00 b.Liverpool 17-9-71

*Source:* Liverpool.

| | | | |
|---|---|---|---|
| 1990–91 | Chester C | 11 | 0 |
| 1991–92 | Chester C | 32 | 0 |
| 1992–93 | Chester C | 28 | 0 |
| 1993–94 | Chester C | 22 | 0 |
| 1994–95 | Chester C | 23 | 1 |
| 1995–96 | Chester C | 39 | 2 |
| 1996–97 | Chester C | 25 | 1 |
| 1997–98 | Chester C | 35 | 4 |
| **Total:** | | **215** | **8** |

## WHITBREAD, Adrian — Defender

H: 6 1 W: 13 00 b.Epping 22-10-71

*Source:* Trainee.

| | | | |
|---|---|---|---|
| 1989–90 | Leyton Orient | 8 | 0 |
| 1990–91 | Leyton Orient | 38 | 0 |
| 1991–92 | Leyton Orient | 43 | 1 |
| 1992–93 | Leyton Orient | 36 | 1 |
| 1993–94 | Swindon T | 35 | 1 |
| 1994–95 | Swindon T | 1 | 0 |
| 1994–95 | West Ham U | 8 | 0 |
| 1995–96 | West Ham U | 2 | 0 |
| 1995–96 | Portsmouth (loan) | 13 | 0 |
| 1996–97 | West Ham U | 0 | 0 |
| 1996–97 | Portsmouth | 24 | 0 |
| 1997–98 | Portsmouth | 38 | 1 |
| **Total:** | | **246** | **4** |

## WHITE, Alan — Defender

H: 6 0 W: 13 04 b.Darlington 22-3-76

*Source:* Derby Co Schoolboy.

| | | | |
|---|---|---|---|
| 1994–95 | Middlesbrough | 0 | 0 |
| 1995–96 | Middlesbrough | 0 | 0 |
| 1996–97 | Middlesbrough | 0 | 0 |
| 1997–98 | Middlesbrough | 0 | 0 |
| 1997–98 | Luton T | 28 | 1 |
| **Total:** | | **28** | **1** |

## WHITE, Darren — Defender

b.Easington 13-1-79

*Source:* Trainee.

| | | | |
|---|---|---|---|
| 1995–96 | Middlesbrough | 0 | 0 |
| 1996–97 | Middlesbrough | 0 | 0 |
| 1997–98 | Middlesbrough | 0 | 0 |

## WHITE, David — Midfield

H: 6 1 W: 13 09 b.Manchester 30-10-67

*Honours:* England Youth, Under-21, B, 1 full cap.

| | | | |
|---|---|---|---|
| 1985–86 | Manchester C | 0 | 0 |
| 1986–87 | Manchester C | 24 | 1 |
| 1987–88 | Manchester C | 44 | 13 |
| 1988–89 | Manchester C | 45 | 6 |
| 1989–90 | Manchester C | 37 | 8 |
| 1990–91 | Manchester C | 38 | 16 |
| 1991–92 | Manchester C | 39 | 18 |
| 1992–93 | Manchester C | 42 | 16 |
| 1993–94 | Manchester C | 16 | 1 |
| 1993–94 | Leeds U | 15 | 5 |
| 1994–95 | Leeds U | 23 | 3 |
| 1995–96 | Leeds U | 4 | 1 |
| 1995–96 | Sheffield U | 28 | 7 |
| 1996–97 | Sheffield U | 37 | 6 |
| 1997–98 | Sheffield U | 1 | 0 |
| **Total:** | | **393** | **101** |

## WHITE, Devon — Forward

H: 6 3 W: 14 00 b.Nottingham 2-3-64

*Source:* Arnold T.

| | | | |
|---|---|---|---|
| 1984–85 | Lincoln C | 7 | 1 |
| 1985–86 | Lincoln C | 22 | 3 |
| 1986–87 | Lincoln C | 0 | 0 |
| From Boston U. | | | |
| 1987–88 | Bristol R | 39 | 15 |
| 1988–89 | Bristol R | 40 | 5 |
| 1989–90 | Bristol R | 43 | 12 |
| 1990–91 | Bristol R | 45 | 11 |
| 1991–92 | Bristol R | 35 | 10 |
| 1991–92 | Cambridge U | 2 | 0 |
| 1992–93 | Cambridge U | 20 | 4 |
| 1992–93 | QPR | 7 | 2 |
| 1993–94 | QPR | 18 | 7 |
| 1994–95 | QPR | 1 | 0 |
| 1994–95 | Notts Co | 20 | 7 |
| 1995–96 | Notts Co | 20 | 8 |
| 1995–96 | Watford | 16 | 5 |
| 1996–97 | Watford | 22 | 2 |
| 1996–97 | Notts Co | 9 | 2 |
| 1997–98 | Notts Co | 6 | 2 |
| 1997–98 | Shrewsbury T | 32 | 10 |
| **Total:** | | **404** | **106** |

## WHITE, Jason — Forward

H: 6 1 W: 12 12 b.Meriden 19-10-71

*Source:* Derby Co Trainee. *Honours:*

| | | | |
|---|---|---|---|
| 1991–92 | Scunthorpe U | 22 | 11 |
| 1992–93 | Scunthorpe U | 37 | 5 |
| 1993–94 | Scunthorpe U | 9 | 0 |
| 1993–94 | Darlington (loan) | 4 | 1 |
| 1993–94 | Scarborough | 24 | 9 |
| 1994–95 | Scarborough | 39 | 11 |
| 1995–96 | Northampton T | 45 | 16 |
| 1996–97 | Northampton T | 32 | 2 |
| 1997–98 | Northampton T | 0 | 0 |
| 1997–98 | Rotherham U | 27 | 13 |
| **Total:** | | **239** | **68** |

## WHITE, Steve — Forward

H: 5 10 W: 12 08 b.Chipping Sodbury 2-1-59

*Source:* Mangotsfield U. *Honours:* England Schools.

| | | | |
|---|---|---|---|
| 1977–78 | Bristol R | 8 | 4 |
| 1978–79 | Bristol R | 27 | 10 |
| 1979–80 | Bristol R | 15 | 6 |
| 1979–80 | Luton T | 9 | 0 |
| 1980–81 | Luton T | 21 | 7 |
| 1981–82 | Luton T | 42 | 18 |
| 1982–83 | Charlton Ath | 29 | 12 |
| 1982–83 | Lincoln C (loan) | 3 | 0 |
| 1982–83 | Luton T (loan) | 4 | 0 |
| 1983–84 | Bristol R | 43 | 9 |
| 1984–85 | Bristol R | 18 | 3 |
| 1985–86 | Bristol R | 40 | 12 |
| 1986–87 | Swindon T | 35 | 15 |
| 1987–88 | Swindon T | 25 | 11 |
| 1988–89 | Swindon T | 43 | 13 |
| 1989–90 | Swindon T | 43 | 18 |
| 1990–91 | Swindon T | 35 | 9 |
| 1991–92 | Swindon T | 23 | 10 |
| 1992–93 | Swindon T | 34 | 7 |
| 1993–94 | Swindon T | 6 | 0 |
| 1994–95 | Hereford U | 36 | 15 |
| 1995–96 | Hereford U | 40 | 29 |
| 1996–97 | Cardiff C | 38 | 13 |
| 1997–98 | Cardiff C | 29 | 2 |
| **Total:** | | **646** | **223** |

## WHITE, Tom — Defender

H: 5 11 W: 12 02 b.Bristol 26-1-76

*Source:* Trainee.

| | | | |
|---|---|---|---|
| 1994–95 | Bristol R | 4 | 0 |
| 1995–96 | Bristol R | 2 | 0 |
| 1996–97 | Bristol R | 21 | 0 |
| 1997–98 | Bristol R | 24 | 1 |
| **Total:** | | **51** | **1** |

## WHITEFORD, Andrew — Defender

H: 5 10 W: 11 04 b.Bellshill 22-8-77

*Source:* Possil YMcA. *Honours:* Scotland Under-21, Under-18.

| | | | |
|---|---|---|---|
| 1994–95 | St Johnstone | 0 | 0 |

| | | | |
|---|---|---|---|
| 1995–96 | St Johnstone | 4 | 0 |
| 1996–97 | St Johnstone | 11 | 0 |
| 1997–98 | St Johnstone | 1 | 0 |
| **Total:** | | **16** | **0** |

## WHITEHALL, Steve — Forward

H: 5 10 W: 11 00 b.Bromborough 8-12-66

*Source:* Southport.

| | | | |
|---|---|---|---|
| 1991–92 | Rochdale | 34 | 8 |
| 1992–93 | Rochdale | 42 | 14 |
| 1993–94 | Rochdale | 39 | 14 |
| 1994–95 | Rochdale | 42 | 10 |
| 1995–96 | Rochdale | 46 | 20 |
| 1996–97 | Rochdale | 35 | 9 |
| 1997–98 | Mansfield T | 43 | 24 |
| **Total:** | | **281** | **99** |

## WHITEHEAD, Phil — Goalkeeper

H: 6 3 W: 15 11 b.Halifax 17-12-69

*Source:* Trainee.

| | | | |
|---|---|---|---|
| 1986–87 | Halifax T | 12 | 0 |
| 1987–88 | Halifax T | 0 | 0 |
| 1988–89 | Halifax T | 11 | 0 |
| 1989–90 | Halifax T | 19 | 0 |
| 1989–90 | Barnsley | 0 | 0 |
| 1990–91 | Barnsley | 0 | 0 |
| 1990–91 | Halifax T (loan) | 9 | 0 |
| 1991–92 | Barnsley | 3 | 0 |
| 1991–92 | Scunthorpe U (loan) | 8 | 0 |
| 1992–93 | Barnsley | 13 | 0 |
| 1992–93 | Scunthorpe U (loan) | 8 | 0 |
| 1992–93 | Bradford C (loan) | 6 | 0 |
| 1993–94 | Barnsley | 0 | 0 |
| 1993–94 | Oxford U | 39 | 0 |
| 1994–95 | Oxford U | 38 | 0 |
| 1995–96 | Oxford U | 34 | 0 |
| 1996–97 | Oxford U | 43 | 0 |
| 1997–98 | Oxford U | 32 | 0 |
| **Total:** | | **275** | **0** |

## WHITEHEAD, Stuart — Midfield

H: 5 11 W: 12 04 b.Bromsgrove 17-7-76

*Source:* Bromsgrove R.

| | | | |
|---|---|---|---|
| 1995–96 | Bolton W | 0 | 0 |
| 1996–97 | Bolton W | 0 | 0 |
| 1997–98 | Bolton W | 0 | 0 |

## WHITEHOUSE, Dane — Midfield

H: 5 10 W: 12 08 b.Sheffield 14-10-70

*Source:* Trainee.

| | | | |
|---|---|---|---|
| 1988–89 | Sheffield U | 5 | 0 |
| 1989–90 | Sheffield U | 12 | 1 |
| 1990–91 | Sheffield U | 4 | 0 |
| 1991–92 | Sheffield U | 34 | 7 |
| 1992–93 | Sheffield U | 14 | 5 |
| 1993–94 | Sheffield U | 38 | 5 |
| 1994–95 | Sheffield U | 39 | 8 |
| 1995–96 | Sheffield U | 38 | 4 |
| 1996–97 | Sheffield U | 30 | 6 |
| 1997–98 | Sheffield U | 17 | 3 |
| **Total:** | | **231** | **39** |

## WHITLEY, Jeff — Midfield

H: 5 9 W: 11 00 b.Zambia 28-1-79

*Source:* Trainee. *Honours:* Northern Ireland Under-21, 3 full caps.

| | | | |
|---|---|---|---|
| 1995–96 | Manchester C | 0 | 0 |
| 1996–97 | Manchester C | 23 | 1 |
| 1997–98 | Manchester C | 17 | 1 |
| **Total:** | | **40** | **2** |

## WHITLEY, Jim — Midfield

H: 5 9 W: 11 00 b.Zambia 14-4-75

*Source:* Trainee. *Honours:* Northern Ireland 1 full cap.

| | | | |
|---|---|---|---|
| 1993–94 | Manchester C | 0 | 0 |
| 1994–95 | Manchester C | 0 | 0 |
| 1995–96 | Manchester C | 0 | 0 |
| 1996–97 | Manchester C | 0 | 0 |
| 1997–98 | Manchester C | 19 | 0 |
| **Total:** | | **19** | **0** |

## WHITLOW, Mike — Defender

H: 6 0 W: 13 03 b.Northwich 13-1-68

*Source:* Witton Alb.

| | | | |
|---|---|---|---|
| 1988–89 | Leeds U | 20 | 1 |
| 1989–90 | Leeds U | 29 | 1 |
| 1990–91 | Leeds U | 18 | 1 |
| 1991–92 | Leeds U | 10 | 1 |
| 1991–92 | Leicester C | 5 | 0 |
| 1992–93 | Leicester C | 24 | 1 |
| 1993–94 | Leicester C | 31 | 2 |
| 1994–95 | Leicester C | 28 | 2 |
| 1995–96 | Leicester C | 42 | 3 |
| 1996–97 | Leicester C | 17 | 0 |
| 1997–98 | Leicester C | 0 | 0 |
| 1997–98 | Bolton W | 13 | 0 |
| **Total:** | | **237** | **12** |

## WHITNEY, Jon — Defender

H: 5 11 W: 13 08 b.Nantwich 23-12-70

*Source:* Winsford U.

| | | | |
|---|---|---|---|
| 1993–94 | Huddersfield T | 14 | 0 |
| 1994–95 | Huddersfield T | 0 | 0 |
| 1994–95 | Wigan Ath (loan) | 12 | 0 |
| 1995–96 | Huddersfield T | 4 | 0 |
| 1995–96 | Lincoln C | 26 | 2 |
| 1996–97 | Lincoln C | 18 | 3 |
| 1997–98 | Lincoln C | 44 | 1 |
| **Total:** | | **118** | **6** |

## WHITTAKER, David — Midfield

b.Stockport 13-8-78

*Source:* Trainee.

| | | | |
|---|---|---|---|
| 1997–98 | Crewe Alex | 0 | 0 |

## WHITTAKER, Stuart — Midfield

H: 5 7 W: 10 00 b.Liverpool 2-1-75

*Source:* Liverpool Trainee.

| | | | |
|---|---|---|---|
| 1993–94 | Bolton W | 2 | 0 |
| 1994–95 | Bolton W | 1 | 0 |
| 1995–96 | Bolton W | 0 | 0 |
| 1996–97 | Bolton W | 0 | 0 |
| 1996–97 | Wigan Ath (loan) | 3 | 0 |
| 1997–98 | Macclesfield T | 31 | 4 |
| **Total:** | | **37** | **4** |

## WHITTINGHAM, Guy — Forward

H: 5 8 W: 12 02 b.Evesham 10-11-64

*Source:* Yeovil T, Army.

| | | | |
|---|---|---|---|
| 1989–90 | Portsmouth | 42 | 23 |
| 1990–91 | Portsmouth | 37 | 12 |
| 1991–92 | Portsmouth | 35 | 11 |
| 1992–93 | Portsmouth | 46 | 42 |
| 1993–94 | Aston Villa | 18 | 3 |
| 1993–94 | Wolverhampton W (loan) | 13 | 8 |
| 1994–95 | Aston Villa | 7 | 2 |
| 1994–95 | Sheffield W | 21 | 9 |
| 1995–96 | Sheffield W | 29 | 6 |
| 1996–97 | Sheffield W | 33 | 3 |
| 1997–98 | Sheffield W | 28 | 4 |
| **Total:** | | **309** | **123** |

## WHITTLE, David — Defender

H: 5 10 W: 12 07 b.Waterford 2-12-78

*Source:* Trainee.

| | | | |
|---|---|---|---|
| 1996–97 | QPR | 0 | 0 |
| 1997–98 | QPR | 0 | 0 |

## WHITTLE, Justin — Defender

H: 6 1 W: 12 13 b.Derby 18-3-71

*Source:* Celtic.

| | | | |
|---|---|---|---|
| 1994–95 | Stoke C | 0 | 0 |
| 1995–96 | Stoke C | 8 | 0 |
| 1996–97 | Stoke C | 37 | 0 |
| 1997–98 | Stoke C | 20 | 0 |
| **Total:** | | **65** | **0** |

## WHITTON, Steve — Forward

H: 6 0 W: 11 08 b.East Ham 4-12-60

*Source:* Apprentice.

| | | | |
|---|---|---|---|
| 1978–79 | Coventry C | 0 | 0 |
| 1979–80 | Coventry C | 7 | 0 |
| 1980–81 | Coventry C | 1 | 0 |
| 1981–82 | Coventry C | 28 | 9 |
| 1982–83 | Coventry C | 38 | 12 |
| 1983–84 | West Ham U | 22 | 5 |
| 1984–85 | West Ham U | 17 | 1 |
| 1985–86 | West Ham U | 0 | 0 |
| 1985–86 | Birmingham C (loan) | 8 | 2 |
| 1986–87 | Birmingham C | 39 | 9 |
| 1987–88 | Birmingham C | 33 | 14 |
| 1988–89 | Birmingham C | 23 | 5 |
| 1988–89 | Sheffield W | 12 | 3 |
| 1989–90 | Sheffield W | 19 | 1 |
| 1990–91 | Sheffield W | 1 | 0 |
| 1990–91 | Ipswich T | 10 | 2 |
| 1991–92 | Ipswich T | 43 | 9 |
| 1992–93 | Ipswich T | 24 | 3 |
| 1993–94 | Ipswich T | 11 | 1 |
| 1993–94 | Colchester U | 8 | 2 |
| 1994–95 | Colchester U | 36 | 10 |
| 1995–96 | Colchester U | 12 | 2 |
| 1996–97 | Colchester U | 39 | 6 |
| 1997–98 | Colchester U | 21 | 1 |
| **Total:** | | **452** | **97** |

## WHITWORTH, Neil — Defender

H: 6 2 W: 12 06 b.Wigan 12-4-72

*Source:* Trainee. *Honours:* England Youth.

| | | | |
|---|---|---|---|
| 1989–90 | Wigan Ath | 2 | 0 |
| 1990–91 | Manchester U | 1 | 0 |
| 1991–92 | Manchester U | 0 | 0 |
| 1991–92 | Preston NE (loan) | 6 | 0 |
| 1991–92 | Barnsley (loan) | 11 | 0 |
| 1992–93 | Manchester U | 0 | 0 |
| 1993–94 | Manchester U | 0 | 0 |
| 1993–94 | Rotherham U (loan) | 8 | 1 |
| 1993–94 | Blackpool (loan) | 3 | 0 |
| 1994–95 | Kilmarnock | 30 | 3 |
| 1995–96 | Kilmarnock | 28 | 0 |

## Whyte, David

| | | | |
|---|---|---|---|
| 1996–97 | Kilmarnock | 7 | 0 |
| 1997–98 | Kilmarnock | 11 | 0 |
| 1997–98 | Wigan Ath | 4 | 0 |
| **Total:** | | **111** | **4** |

## WHYTE, David — Forward

H: 5 8 W: 12 00 b.Greenwich 20-4-71

*Source:* Greenwich Bor.

| | | | |
|---|---|---|---|
| 1988–89 | Crystal Palace | 0 | 0 |
| 1989–90 | Crystal Palace | 0 | 0 |
| 1990–91 | Crystal Palace | 0 | 0 |
| 1991–92 | Crystal Palace | 11 | 1 |
| 1991–92 | Charlton Ath (loan) | 8 | 2 |
| 1992–93 | Crystal Palace | 0 | 0 |
| 1993–94 | Crystal Palace | 16 | 3 |
| 1994–95 | Charlton Ath | 38 | 19 |
| 1995–96 | Charlton Ath | 25 | 2 |
| 1996–97 | Charlton Ath | 22 | 7 |
| 1997–98 | Ipswich T | 2 | 0 |
| 1997–98 | Bristol R | 4 | 0 |
| 1997–98 | Southend U | 8 | 1 |
| **Total:** | | **134** | **35** |

## WHYTE, Derek — Defender

H: 5 11 W: 12 13 b.Glasgow 31-8-68

*Source:* Celtic BC. *Honours:* Scotland Schools, Youth, Under-21, B, 11 full caps.

| | | | |
|---|---|---|---|
| 1985–86 | Celtic | 11 | 0 |
| 1986–87 | Celtic | 42 | 0 |
| 1987–88 | Celtic | 41 | 3 |
| 1988–89 | Celtic | 22 | 0 |
| 1989–90 | Celtic | 35 | 1 |
| 1990–91 | Celtic | 24 | 2 |
| 1991–92 | Celtic | 40 | 1 |
| 1992–93 | Celtic | 1 | 0 |
| 1992–93 | Middlesbrough | 35 | 0 |
| 1993–94 | Middlesbrough | 42 | 1 |
| 1994–95 | Middlesbrough | 36 | 1 |
| 1995–96 | Middlesbrough | 25 | 0 |
| 1996–97 | Middlesbrough | 21 | 0 |
| 1997–98 | Middlesbrough | 8 | 0 |
| 1997–98 | Aberdeen | 19 | 0 |
| **Total:** | | **402** | **9** |

## WICKS, Matthew — Defender

H: 6 2 W: 13 05 b.Reading 8-9-78

*Source:* Manchester U Trainee. *Honours:* England Youth.

| | | | |
|---|---|---|---|
| 1995–96 | Arsenal | 0 | 0 |
| 1996–97 | Arsenal | 0 | 0 |
| 1997–98 | Arsenal | 0 | 0 |

## WIDDRINGTON, Tommy — Midfield

H: 5 8 W: 11 01 b.Newcastle 1-10-71

*Source:* Trainee.

| | | | |
|---|---|---|---|
| 1989–90 | Southampton | 0 | 0 |
| 1990–91 | Southampton | 0 | 0 |
| 1991–92 | Southampton | 3 | 0 |
| 1991–92 | Wigan Ath (loan) | 6 | 0 |
| 1992–93 | Southampton | 12 | 0 |
| 1993–94 | Southampton | 11 | 1 |
| 1994–95 | Southampton | 28 | 0 |
| 1995–96 | Southampton | 21 | 2 |
| 1996–97 | Grimsby T | 42 | 4 |
| 1997–98 | Grimsby T | 21 | 3 |
| **Total:** | | **144** | **10** |

## WIEGHORST, Morten — Midfield

H: 6 3 W: 14 00 b.Glostrup 25-2-71

*Source:* Lyngby. *Honours:* Denmark 14 full caps, 2 goals.

| | | | |
|---|---|---|---|
| 1992–93 | Dundee | 23 | 2 |
| 1993–94 | Dundee | 24 | 2 |
| 1994–95 | Dundee | 29 | 3 |
| 1995–96 | Dundee | 14 | 4 |
| 1995–96 | Celtic | 11 | 1 |
| 1996–97 | Celtic | 17 | 2 |
| 1997–98 | Celtic | 31 | 4 |
| **Total:** | | **149** | **18** |

## WIEKENS, Gerard — Defender

H: 6 1 W: 13 00 b.Tolhuiswyk 25-2-73

| | | | |
|---|---|---|---|
| 1996–97 | Veendam | 33 | 1 |
| 1997–98 | Manchester C | 37 | 5 |
| **Total:** | | **70** | **6** |

## WILBRAHAM, Aaron — Forward

H: 6 3 W: 12 04 b.Knutsford 21-10-79

*Source:* Trainee.

| | | | |
|---|---|---|---|
| 1997–98 | Stockport Co | 7 | 1 |
| **Total:** | | **7** | **1** |

## WILCOX, Jason — Forward

H: 6 0 W: 11 00 b.Bolton 15-7-71

*Source:* Trainee. *Honours:* England B, 1 full cap.

| | | | |
|---|---|---|---|
| 1989–90 | Blackburn R | 1 | 0 |
| 1990–91 | Blackburn R | 18 | 0 |
| 1991–92 | Blackburn R | 38 | 4 |
| 1992–93 | Blackburn R | 33 | 4 |
| 1993–94 | Blackburn R | 33 | 6 |
| 1994–95 | Blackburn R | 27 | 5 |
| 1995–96 | Blackburn R | 10 | 3 |

| | | | |
|---|---|---|---|
| 1996–97 | Blackburn R | 28 | 2 |
| 1997–98 | Blackburn R | 31 | 4 |
| **Total:** | | **219** | **28** |

## WILCOX, Russ — Defender

H: 6 0 W: 12 13 b.Hemsworth 25-3-64

*Source:* Apprentice.

| | | | |
|---|---|---|---|
| 1980–81 | Doncaster R | 1 | 0 |
| From Cambridge U, Frickley Ath. | | | |
| 1986–87 | Northampton T | 35 | 1 |
| 1987–88 | Northampton T | 46 | 4 |
| 1988–89 | Northampton T | 11 | 1 |
| 1989–90 | Northampton T | 46 | 3 |
| 1990–91 | Hull C | 31 | 1 |
| 1991–92 | Hull C | 40 | 4 |
| 1992–93 | Hull C | 29 | 2 |
| 1993–94 | Doncaster R | 40 | 2 |
| 1994–95 | Doncaster R | 37 | 4 |
| 1995–96 | Doncaster R | 4 | 0 |
| 1995–96 | Preston NE | 27 | 1 |
| 1996–97 | Preston NE | 35 | 0 |
| 1997–98 | Scunthorpe U | 31 | 2 |
| **Total:** | | **413** | **25** |

## WILDE, Adam — Defender

H: 5 10 W: 11 09 b.Southampton 22-5-79

*Source:* Trainee.

| | | | |
|---|---|---|---|
| 1996–97 | Cambridge U | 1 | 0 |
| 1997–98 | Cambridge U | 2 | 0 |
| **Total:** | | **3** | **0** |

## WILDER, Chris — Defender

H: 5 11 W: 12 07 b.Stocksbridge 23-9-67

*Source:* Apprentice.

| | | | |
|---|---|---|---|
| 1985–86 | Southampton | 0 | 0 |
| 1986–87 | Sheffield U | 11 | 0 |
| 1987–88 | Sheffield U | 25 | 0 |
| 1988–89 | Sheffield U | 29 | 1 |
| 1989–90 | Sheffield U | 8 | 0 |
| 1989–90 | Walsall (loan) | 4 | 0 |
| 1990–91 | Sheffield U | 16 | 0 |
| 1990–91 | Charlton Ath (loan) | 1 | 0 |
| 1991–92 | Sheffield U | 4 | 0 |
| 1991–92 | Charlton Ath (loan) | 2 | 0 |
| 1991–92 | Leyton Orient (loan) | 16 | 1 |
| 1992–93 | Rotherham U | 32 | 8 |
| 1993–94 | Rotherham U | 37 | 2 |
| 1994–95 | Rotherham U | 45 | 1 |
| 1995–96 | Rotherham U | 18 | 0 |
| 1995–96 | Notts Co | 9 | 0 |
| 1996–97 | Notts Co | 37 | 0 |
| 1996–97 | Bradford C | 7 | 0 |
| 1997–98 | Bradford C | 35 | 0 |
| 1997–98 | Sheffield U | 8 | 0 |
| **Total:** | | **344** | **13** |

## WILDING, Peter — Defender

H: 6 1 W: 12 09 b.Shrewsbury 28-11-68

*Source:* Telford U.

| | | | |
|---|---|---|---|
| 1997–98 | Shrewsbury T | 34 | 1 |
| **Total:** | | **34** | **1** |

## WILKINS, Ian — Defender

b.Lincoln 3-4-80

*Source:* Trainee.

| | | | |
|---|---|---|---|
| 1997–98 | Lincoln C | 2 | 0 |
| **Total:** | | **2** | **0** |

## WILKINS, Richard — Midfield

H: 6 0 W: 11 08 b.Streatham 28-5-65

*Source:* Haverhill R.

| | | | |
|---|---|---|---|
| 1986–87 | Colchester U | 23 | 2 |
| 1987–88 | Colchester U | 46 | 9 |
| 1988–89 | Colchester U | 40 | 7 |
| 1989–90 | Colchester U | 43 | 4 |
| 1990–91 | Cambridge U | 41 | 3 |
| 1991–92 | Cambridge U | 32 | 4 |
| 1992–93 | Cambridge U | 1 | 0 |
| 1993–94 | Cambridge U | 7 | 0 |
| 1994–95 | Hereford U | 35 | 2 |
| 1995–96 | Hereford U | 42 | 3 |
| 1996–97 | Colchester U | 40 | 2 |
| 1997–98 | Colchester U | 37 | 5 |
| **Total:** | | **387** | **41** |

## WILKINSON, Ian — Defender

H: 6 2 W: 13 00 b.Ferriby 19-9-77

*Source:* Trainee.

| | | | |
|---|---|---|---|
| 1995–96 | Hull C | 8 | 1 |
| 1996–97 | Hull C | 0 | 0 |
| 1997–98 | Hull C | 0 | 0 |
| **Total:** | | **8** | **1** |

## WILKINSON, John — Midfield

b.Exeter 24-8-79

*Source:* Trainee.

| | | | |
|---|---|---|---|
| 1997–98 | Exeter C | 1 | 0 |
| **Total:** | | **1** | **0** |

## WILKINSON, Mark — Midfield

H: 5 6 W: 10 08 b.Nuneaton 16-3-79

*Source:* Trainee.

| | | | |
|---|---|---|---|
| 1996–97 | Derby Co | 0 | 0 |
| 1997–98 | Derby Co | 0 | 0 |

## WILKINSON, Paul — Forward

H: 6 1 W: 12 06 b.Louth 30-10-64

*Source:* Apprentice. *Honours:* England Under-21.

| | | | |
|---|---|---|---|
| 1982–83 | Grimsby T | 4 | 1 |
| 1983–84 | Grimsby T | 37 | 12 |
| 1984–85 | Grimsby T | 30 | 14 |
| 1984–85 | Everton | 5 | 2 |
| 1985–86 | Everton | 4 | 1 |
| 1986–87 | Everton | 22 | 4 |
| 1986–87 | Nottingham F | 8 | 0 |
| 1987–88 | Nottingham F | 26 | 5 |
| 1988–89 | Watford | 45 | 19 |
| 1989–90 | Watford | 43 | 15 |
| 1990–91 | Watford | 46 | 18 |
| 1991–92 | Middlesbrough | 46 | 15 |
| 1992–93 | Middlesbrough | 41 | 13 |
| 1993–94 | Middlesbrough | 45 | 15 |
| 1994–95 | Middlesbrough | 31 | 6 |
| 1995–96 | Middlesbrough | 3 | 0 |
| 1995–96 | Oldham Ath (loan) | 4 | 1 |
| 1995–96 | Watford (loan) | 4 | 0 |
| 1995–96 | Luton T (loan) | 3 | 0 |
| 1996–97 | Barnsley | 45 | 9 |
| 1997–98 | Barnsley | 4 | 0 |
| 1997–98 | Millwall | 30 | 3 |
| **Total:** | | **526** | **153** |

## WILKINSON, Steve — Forward

H: 5 11 W: 11 11 b.Lincoln 1-9-68

*Source:* Apprentice.

| | | | |
|---|---|---|---|
| 1986–87 | Leicester C | 1 | 0 |
| 1987–88 | Leicester C | 5 | 1 |
| 1988–89 | Leicester C | 1 | 0 |
| 1988–89 | Rochdale (loan) | 0 | 0 |
| 1988–89 | Crewe Alex (loan) | 5 | 2 |
| 1989–90 | Leicester C | 2 | 0 |
| 1989–90 | Mansfield T | 37 | 15 |
| 1990–91 | Mansfield T | 39 | 11 |
| 1991–92 | Mansfield T | 30 | 14 |
| 1992–93 | Mansfield T | 43 | 11 |
| 1993–94 | Mansfield T | 42 | 10 |
| 1994–95 | Mansfield T | 41 | 22 |
| 1995–96 | Preston NE | 42 | 10 |
| 1996–97 | Preston NE | 10 | 3 |
| 1997–98 | Chesterfield | 30 | 6 |
| **Total:** | | **328** | **105** |

## WILLEMS, Ron — Forward

H: 6 1 W: 12 05 b.Epe 20-9-66

| | | | |
|---|---|---|---|
| 1983–84 | PEC Zwolle | 14 | 1 |
| 1984–85 | PEC Zwolle | 29 | 6 |
| 1985–86 | Twente | 22 | 0 |
| 1986–87 | Twente | 31 | 5 |
| 1987–88 | Twente | 32 | 11 |
| 1988–89 | Ajax | 1 | 0 |
| 1989–90 | Ajax | 19 | 7 |
| 1990–91 | Ajax | 22 | 6 |
| 1991–92 | Ajax | 3 | 0 |
| 1992–93 | Ajax | 2 | 2 |
| 1993–94 | Grasshoppers | 27 | 9 |
| 1994–95 | Grasshoppers | 29 | 9 |
| 1995–96 | Derby Co | 33 | 11 |
| 1996–97 | Derby Co | 16 | 2 |
| 1997–98 | Derby Co | 10 | 0 |
| **Total:** | | **290** | **69** |

## WILLIAMS, Adrian — Defender

H: 6 2 W: 12 06 b.Reading 16-8-71

*Source:* Trainee. *Honours:* Wales 9 full caps.

| | | | |
|---|---|---|---|
| 1988–89 | Reading | 8 | 0 |
| 1989–90 | Reading | 16 | 2 |
| 1990–91 | Reading | 7 | 0 |
| 1991–92 | Reading | 40 | 4 |
| 1992–93 | Reading | 31 | 4 |
| 1993–94 | Reading | 41 | 0 |
| 1994–95 | Reading | 22 | 1 |
| 1995–96 | Reading | 31 | 3 |
| 1996–97 | Wolverhampton W | 6 | 0 |
| 1997–98 | Wolverhampton W | 20 | 0 |
| **Total:** | | **222** | **14** |

## WILLIAMS, Andy — Forward

H: 5 9 W: 10 07 b.Bristol 8-10-77

*Source:* Trainee. *Honours:* Wales Under-21, 2 full caps.

| | | | |
|---|---|---|---|
| 1996–97 | Southampton | 0 | 0 |
| 1997–98 | Southampton | 20 | 0 |
| **Total:** | | **20** | **0** |

## WILLIAMS, Anthony — Goalkeeper

b.Ogwr 20-9-77

*Source:* Trainee. *Honours:* Wales Under-21.

| | | | |
|---|---|---|---|
| 1996–97 | Blackburn R | 0 | 0 |
| 1997–98 | Blackburn R | 0 | 0 |
| 1997–98 | QPR (loan) | 0 | 0 |

## WILLIAMS, Danny — Midfield

H: 6 1 W: 13 00 b.Wrexham 12-7-79

*Source:* Trainee. *Honours:* Wales Under-21.

| | | | |
|---|---|---|---|
| 1996–97 | Liverpool | 0 | 0 |
| 1997–98 | Liverpool | 0 | 0 |

## WILLIAMS, Darren — Defender

H: 5 11 W: 11 11 b.Middlebrough 28-4-77

*Source:* Trainee. *Honours:* England Under-21, B.

| | | | |
|---|---|---|---|
| 1994–95 | York C | 1 | 0 |
| 1995–96 | York C | 18 | 0 |
| 1996–97 | York C | 1 | 0 |
| 1996–97 | Sunderland | 11 | 2 |
| 1997–98 | Sunderland | 36 | 2 |
| **Total:** | | **67** | **4** |

## WILLIAMS, Dean — Goalkeeper

H: 6 0 W: 12 07 b.Lichfield 5-1-72

*Source:* Tamworth.

| | | | |
|---|---|---|---|
| 1993–94 | Brentford | 7 | 0 |
| 1994–95 | Doncaster R | 35 | 0 |
| 1995–96 | Doncaster R | 17 | 0 |
| 1996–97 | Doncaster R | 27 | 0 |
| 1997–98 | Doncaster R | 6 | 0 |
| 1997–98 | Huddersfield T (loan) | 0 | 0 |
| **Total:** | | **92** | **0** |

## WILLIAMS, Gareth — Forward

H: 5 10 W: 12 02 b.Newport 12-3-67

*Source:* Gosport Bor.

| | | | |
|---|---|---|---|
| 1987–88 | Aston Villa | 1 | 0 |
| 1988–89 | Aston Villa | 1 | 0 |
| 1989–90 | Aston Villa | 10 | 0 |
| 1990–91 | Aston Villa | 0 | 0 |
| 1991–92 | Barnsley | 17 | 0 |
| 1992–93 | Barnsley | 8 | 5 |
| 1992–93 | Hull C (loan) | 4 | 0 |
| 1993–94 | Barnsley | 9 | 1 |
| 1993–94 | Hull C (loan) | 16 | 2 |
| 1994–95 | Barnsley | 0 | 0 |
| 1994–95 | Bournemouth | 1 | 0 |
| 1994–95 | Northampton T | 15 | 0 |
| 1995–96 | Northampton T | 35 | 1 |
| 1996–97 | Scarborough | 45 | 10 |
| 1997–98 | Scarborough | 43 | 15 |
| **Total:** | | **205** | **34** |

## WILLIAMS, Geraint — Midfield

H: 5 7 W: 12 06 b.Cwmpare 5-1-62

*Source:* Apprentice. *Honours:* Wales Youth, Under-21, 13 full caps.

| | | | |
|---|---|---|---|
| 1979–80 | Bristol R | 0 | 0 |
| 1980–81 | Bristol R | 28 | 1 |
| 1981–82 | Bristol R | 16 | 0 |
| 1982–83 | Bristol R | 35 | 3 |
| 1983–84 | Bristol R | 34 | 4 |
| 1984–85 | Bristol R | 28 | 0 |
| 1984–85 | Derby Co | 12 | 0 |
| 1985–86 | Derby Co | 40 | 4 |
| 1986–87 | Derby Co | 40 | 1 |
| 1987–88 | Derby Co | 40 | 1 |
| 1988–89 | Derby Co | 37 | 1 |
| 1989–90 | Derby Co | 38 | 0 |
| 1990–91 | Derby Co | 31 | 0 |
| 1991–92 | Derby Co | 39 | 2 |
| 1992–93 | Ipswich T | 37 | 0 |
| 1993–94 | Ipswich T | 34 | 0 |
| 1994–95 | Ipswich T | 38 | 1 |
| 1995–96 | Ipswich T | 42 | 1 |
| 1996–97 | Ipswich T | 43 | 1 |
| 1997–98 | Ipswich T | 23 | 0 |
| **Total:** | | **635** | **20** |

## WILLIAMS, Jamie — Defender

H: 5 9 W: 12 00 b.Bedworth 3-1-80

*Source:* Trainee.

| | | | |
|---|---|---|---|
| 1997–98 | Coventry C | 0 | 0 |

## WILLIAMS, John — Midfield

H: 6 1 W: 13 12 b.Birmingham 11-5-68

*Source:* Cradley T.

| | | | |
|---|---|---|---|
| 1991–92 | Swansea C | 39 | 11 |
| 1992–93 | Coventry C | 41 | 8 |
| 1993–94 | Coventry C | 32 | 3 |
| 1994–95 | Coventry C | 7 | 0 |
| 1994–95 | Notts Co (loan) | 5 | 2 |
| 1994–95 | Stoke C (loan) | 4 | 0 |
| 1994–95 | Swansea C (loan) | 7 | 2 |
| 1995–96 | Coventry C | 0 | 0 |
| 1995–96 | Wycombe W | 29 | 7 |
| 1996–97 | Wycombe W | 19 | 1 |
| 1996–97 | Hereford U | 11 | 3 |
| 1997–98 | Walsall | 1 | 0 |
| 1997–98 | Exeter C (loan) | 36 | 4 |
| **Total:** | | **231** | **41** |

## WILLIAMS, Lee — Defender

H: 5 7 W: 12 00 b.Edgbaston 3-2-73

*Source:* Trainee.

| | | | |
|---|---|---|---|
| 1991–92 | Aston Villa | 0 | 0 |
| 1992–93 | Aston Villa | 0 | 0 |
| 1992–93 | Shrewsbury T (loan) | 3 | 0 |
| 1993–94 | Aston Villa | 0 | 0 |
| 1993–94 | Peterborough U | 18 | 0 |
| 1994–95 | Peterborough U | 40 | 1 |
| 1995–96 | Peterborough U | 33 | 0 |
| 1996–97 | Tranmere R | 0 | 0 |
| 1996–97 | Mansfield T | 6 | 0 |
| 1997–98 | Mansfield T | 38 | 3 |
| **Total:** | | **138** | **4** |

## WILLIAMS, Mark — Defender

H: 6 0 W: 12 04 b.Stalybridge 28-9-70

*Source:* Newtown.

| | | | |
|---|---|---|---|
| 1991–92 | Shrewsbury T | 3 | 0 |
| 1992–93 | Shrewsbury T | 28 | 1 |
| 1993–94 | Shrewsbury T | 36 | 1 |
| 1994–95 | Shrewsbury T | 35 | 1 |
| 1995–96 | Chesterfield | 42 | 3 |
| 1996–97 | Chesterfield | 42 | 3 |
| 1997–98 | Chesterfield | 44 | 3 |
| **Total:** | | **230** | **12** |

## WILLIAMS, Mark — Forward

H: 5 11 W: 12 07 b.Bangor 10-12-73

| | | | |
|---|---|---|---|
| 1991–92 | Shrewsbury T | 1 | 0 |
| 1992–93 | Shrewsbury T | 2 | 0 |
| 1997–98 | Shrewsbury T | 5 | 0 |
| **Total:** | | **8** | **0** |

## WILLIAMS, Martin — Forward

H: 5 9 W: 11 12 b.Luton 12-7-73

*Source:* Leicester C Trainee.

| | | | |
|---|---|---|---|
| 1991–92 | Luton T | 1 | 0 |
| 1992–93 | Luton T | 22 | 1 |
| 1993–94 | Luton T | 15 | 1 |
| 1994–95 | Luton T | 2 | 0 |
| 1994–95 | Colchester U (loan) | 3 | 0 |
| 1995–96 | Reading | 15 | 1 |
| 1996–97 | Reading | 29 | 3 |
| 1997–98 | Reading | 29 | 6 |
| **Total:** | | **116** | **12** |

## WILLIAMS, Michael — Forward

H: 5 11 W: 11 04 b.Bradford 21-11-69

*Source:* Maltby MW.

| | | | |
|---|---|---|---|
| 1991–92 | Sheffield W | 0 | 0 |
| 1992–93 | Sheffield W | 3 | 0 |
| 1992–93 | Halifax T (loan) | 9 | 1 |
| 1993–94 | Sheffield W | 4 | 0 |
| 1994–95 | Sheffield W | 10 | 1 |
| 1995–96 | Sheffield W | 5 | 0 |
| 1996–97 | Sheffield W | 1 | 0 |
| 1996–97 | Huddersfield T (loan) | 2 | 0 |
| 1996–97 | Peterborough U (loan) | 6 | 0 |
| 1997–98 | Burnley | 14 | 1 |
| **Total:** | | **54** | **3** |

## WILLIAMS, Michael — Midfield

b.Stepney 9-10-78

*Source:* Trainee.

| | | | |
|---|---|---|---|
| 1997–98 | Leyton Orient | 1 | 0 |
| **Total:** | | **1** | **0** |

## WILLIAMS, Paul — Defender

H: 5 10 W: 11 00 b.Leicester 11-9-69

*Source:* Trainee.

| | | | |
|---|---|---|---|
| 1988–89 | Leicester C | 0 | 0 |
| 1989–90 | Stockport Co | 7 | 0 |
| 1990–91 | Stockport Co | 24 | 2 |
| 1991–92 | Stockport Co | 13 | 1 |
| 1992–93 | Stockport Co | 26 | 1 |
| 1993–94 | Coventry C | 9 | 0 |
| 1993–94 | WBA (loan) | 5 | 0 |
| 1994–95 | Coventry C | 5 | 0 |
| 1994–95 | Huddersfield T (loan) | 9 | 0 |
| 1995–96 | Plymouth Arg | 46 | 2 |
| 1996–97 | Plymouth Arg | 46 | 2 |
| 1997–98 | Plymouth Arg | 39 | 0 |
| **Total:** | | **229** | **8** |

## WILLIAMS, Paul — Forward

H: 5 7 W: 10 09 b.London 16-8-65

*Source:* Woodford T. *Honours:* England Under-21, B.

| | | | |
|---|---|---|---|
| 1986–87 | Charlton Ath | 0 | 0 |
| 1987–88 | Charlton Ath | 12 | 0 |
| 1987–88 | Brentford (loan) | 7 | 3 |
| 1988–89 | Charlton Ath | 32 | 13 |
| 1989–90 | Charlton Ath | 38 | 10 |
| 1990–91 | Sheffield W | 46 | 15 |
| 1991–92 | Sheffield W | 40 | 9 |
| 1992–93 | Sheffield W | 7 | 1 |
| 1992–93 | Crystal Palace | 18 | 0 |

| | | | |
|---|---|---|---|
| 1993–94 | Crystal Palace | 24 | 7 |
| 1994–95 | Crystal Palace | 4 | 0 |
| 1994–95 | Sunderland (loan) | 3 | 0 |
| 1994–95 | Birmingham C (loan) | 11 | 0 |
| 1995–96 | Charlton Ath | 9 | 0 |
| 1995–96 | Torquay U (loan) | 9 | 0 |
| 1996–97 | Southend U | 33 | 6 |
| 1997–98 | Southend U | 6 | 1 |
| **Total:** | | **299** | **65** |

## WILLIAMS, Paul — Defender

H: 5 11 W: 12 10 b.Burton 26-3-71

*Source:* Trainee. *Honours:* England Under-21.

| | | | |
|---|---|---|---|
| 1989–90 | Derby Co | 10 | 1 |
| 1989–90 | Lincoln C (loan) | 3 | 0 |
| 1990–91 | Derby Co | 19 | 4 |
| 1991–92 | Derby Co | 41 | 13 |
| 1992–93 | Derby Co | 19 | 4 |
| 1993–94 | Derby Co | 34 | 1 |
| 1994–95 | Derby Co | 37 | 3 |
| 1995–96 | Coventry C | 32 | 2 |
| 1996–97 | Coventry C | 32 | 2 |
| 1997–98 | Coventry C | 20 | 0 |
| **Total:** | | **247** | **30** |

## WILLIAMS, Ryan — Midfield

H: 5 5 W: 11 02 b.Chesterfield 31-8-78

*Source:* Trainee. *Honours:* England Youth.

| | | | |
|---|---|---|---|
| 1995–96 | Mansfield T | 10 | 3 |
| 1996–97 | Mansfield T | 16 | 0 |
| 1997–98 | Tranmere R | 0 | 0 |
| **Total:** | | **26** | **3** |

## WILLIAMS, Scott — Midfield

H: 6 0 W: 12 00 b.Bangor 7-8-74

*Source:* Trainee. *Honours:* Wales Under-21.

| | | | |
|---|---|---|---|
| 1992–93 | Wrexham | 1 | 0 |
| 1993–94 | Wrexham | 14 | 0 |
| 1994–95 | Wrexham | 10 | 0 |
| 1995–96 | Wrexham | 0 | 0 |
| 1996–97 | Wrexham | 4 | 0 |
| 1997–98 | Wrexham | 3 | 0 |
| **Total:** | | **32** | **0** |

## WILLIAMS, Steve — Forward

H: 6 2 W: 14 05 b.Liverpool 25-9-78

*Source:* Trainee.

| | | | |
|---|---|---|---|
| 1997–98 | Port Vale | 0 | 0 |

## WILLIAMSON, Danny — Midfield

H: 5 10 W: 11 06 b.West Ham 5-12-73

*Source:* Trainee.

| | | | |
|---|---|---|---|
| 1992–93 | West Ham U | 0 | 0 |
| 1993–94 | West Ham U | 3 | 1 |
| 1993–94 | Doncaster R (loan) | 13 | 1 |
| 1994–95 | West Ham U | 4 | 0 |
| 1995–96 | West Ham U | 29 | 4 |
| 1996–97 | West Ham U | 15 | 0 |
| 1997–98 | West Ham U | 0 | 0 |
| 1997–98 | Everton | 15 | 0 |
| **Total:** | | **79** | **6** |

## WILLIAMSON, Davey — Defender

H: 5 6 W: 10 06 b.Hong Kong 15-12-75

*Source:* Irvine Vics.

| | | | |
|---|---|---|---|
| 1995–96 | Motherwell | 0 | 0 |
| 1996–97 | Cambridge U | 0 | 0 |
| 1997–98 | Cambridge U | 6 | 0 |
| **Total:** | | **6** | **0** |

## WILLIAMSON, Michael — Midfield

b.Liverpool 29-12-78

| | | | |
|---|---|---|---|
| 1997–98 | Crewe Alex | 0 | 0 |

## WILLIS, Adam — Defender

H: 6 1 W: 12 02 b.Nuneaton 21-9-76

*Source:* Trainee.

| | | | |
|---|---|---|---|
| 1995–96 | Coventry C | 0 | 0 |
| 1996–97 | Coventry C | 0 | 0 |
| 1997–98 | Coventry C | 0 | 0 |
| 1997–98 | Swindon T | 0 | 0 |

## WILLIS, Roger — Midfield

H: 6 0 W: 12 00 b.Islington 17-6-67

| | | | |
|---|---|---|---|
| 1989–90 | Grimsby T | 9 | 0 |
| From Barnet. | | | |
| 1991–92 | Barnet | 38 | 12 |
| 1992–93 | Barnet | 6 | 1 |
| 1992–93 | Watford | 32 | 2 |
| 1993–94 | Watford | 4 | 0 |
| 1993–94 | Birmingham C | 16 | 5 |
| 1994–95 | Birmingham C | 3 | 0 |
| 1994–95 | Southend U | 21 | 4 |
| 1995–96 | Southend U | 10 | 3 |
| 1996–97 | Peterborough U | 40 | 6 |
| 1997–98 | Chesterfield | 34 | 8 |
| **Total:** | | **213** | **41** |

## WILLMOTT, Chris — Defender

H: 6 2 W: 11 05 b.Bedford 30-9-77

*Source:* Trainee.

| | | | |
|---|---|---|---|
| 1995–96 | Luton T | 0 | 0 |
| 1996–97 | Luton T | 0 | 0 |
| 1997–98 | Luton T | 0 | 0 |

## WILLS, David — Forward

H: 5 5 W: 9 04 b.Manchester 9-3-79

*Source:* Trainee.

| | | | |
|---|---|---|---|
| 1996–97 | Manchester C | 0 | 0 |
| 1997–98 | Manchester C | 0 | 0 |

## WILSON, Che — Midfield

H: 5 9 W: 11 03 b.Ely 17-1-79

*Source:* Trainee.

| | | | |
|---|---|---|---|
| 1997–98 | Norwich C | 0 | 0 |

## WILSON, Clive — Defender

H: 5 7 W: 11 04 b.Manchester 13-11-61

*Source:* Local.

| | | | |
|---|---|---|---|
| 1979–80 | Manchester C | 0 | 0 |
| 1980–81 | Manchester C | 0 | 0 |
| 1981–82 | Manchester C | 4 | 0 |
| 1982–83 | Manchester C | 0 | 0 |
| 1982–83 | Chester (loan) | 21 | 2 |
| 1983–84 | Manchester C | 11 | 0 |
| 1984–85 | Manchester C | 27 | 4 |
| 1985–86 | Manchester C | 25 | 5 |
| 1986–87 | Manchester C | 31 | 0 |
| 1986–87 | Chelsea | 0 | 0 |
| 1986–87 | Manchester C (loan) | 11 | 0 |
| 1987–88 | Chelsea | 31 | 2 |
| 1988–89 | Chelsea | 32 | 3 |
| 1989–90 | Chelsea | 18 | 0 |
| 1990–91 | QPR | 13 | 1 |
| 1991–92 | QPR | 40 | 3 |
| 1992–93 | QPR | 41 | 3 |
| 1993–94 | QPR | 42 | 3 |
| 1994–95 | QPR | 36 | 2 |
| 1995–96 | Tottenham H | 28 | 0 |
| 1996–97 | Tottenham H | 26 | 1 |
| 1997–98 | Tottenham H | 16 | 0 |
| **Total:** | | **453** | **29** |

## WILSON, Kevin — Forward

H: 5 8 W: 11 04 b.Banbury 18-4-61

*Source:* Banbury U. *Honours:* Northern Ireland 42 full caps, 6 goals.

| | | | |
|---|---|---|---|
| 1979–80 | Derby Co | 4 | 0 |
| 1980–81 | Derby Co | 27 | 7 |
| 1981–82 | Derby Co | 24 | 9 |
| 1982–83 | Derby Co | 22 | 4 |
| 1983–84 | Derby Co | 32 | 2 |
| 1984–85 | Derby Co | 13 | 8 |
| 1984–85 | Ipswich T | 17 | 7 |
| 1985–86 | Ipswich T | 39 | 7 |
| 1986–87 | Ipswich T | 42 | 20 |
| 1987–88 | Chelsea | 25 | 5 |
| 1988–89 | Chelsea | 46 | 13 |
| 1989–90 | Chelsea | 37 | 14 |
| 1990–91 | Chelsea | 22 | 7 |
| 1991–92 | Chelsea | 22 | 3 |
| 1991–92 | Notts Co | 8 | 1 |
| 1992–93 | Notts Co | 32 | 1 |
| 1993–94 | Notts Co | 29 | 1 |
| 1993–94 | Bradford C (loan) | 5 | 0 |
| 1994–95 | Walsall | 42 | 16 |
| 1995–96 | Walsall | 46 | 15 |
| 1996–97 | Walsall | 37 | 7 |
| 1997–98 | Northampton T | 9 | 0 |
| **Total:** | | **580** | **147** |

## WILSON, Mark — Midfield

H: 6 0 W: 13 02 b.Scunthorpe 9-2-79

*Source:* Trainee. *Honours:* England Schools.

| | | | |
|---|---|---|---|
| 1995–96 | Manchester U | 0 | 0 |
| 1996–97 | Manchester U | 0 | 0 |
| 1997–98 | Manchester U | 0 | 0 |
| 1997–98 | Wrexham (loan) | 13 | 4 |
| **Total:** | | **13** | **4** |

## WILSON, Padi — Midfield

H: 5 8 W: 10 10 b.Manchester 9-11-71

*Source:* Ashton U.

| | | | |
|---|---|---|---|
| 1997–98 | Plymouth Arg | 11 | 1 |
| 1997–98 | Doncaster R | 10 | 1 |
| **Total:** | | **21** | **2** |

## WILSON, Paul — Midfield

H: 5 10 W: 11 02 b.London 26-9-64

*Source:* West Ham U, Billericay, Barking.

| | | | |
|---|---|---|---|
| 1991–92 | Barnet | 25 | 1 |
| 1992–93 | Barnet | 9 | 0 |
| 1993–94 | Barnet | 34 | 3 |

| | | | |
|---|---|---|---|
| 1994–95 | Barnet | 36 | 3 |
| 1995–96 | Barnet | 33 | 4 |
| 1996–97 | Barnet | 37 | 5 |
| 1997–98 | Barnet | 39 | 5 |
| **Total:** | | **213** | **21** |

## WILSON, Paul — Defender

H: 5 11 W: 11 10 b.Bradford 2-8-68

*Source:* Trainee.

| | | | |
|---|---|---|---|
| 1985–86 | Huddersfield T | 7 | 0 |
| 1986–87 | Huddersfield T | 8 | 0 |
| 1987–88 | Norwich C | 0 | 0 |
| 1987–88 | Northampton T | 15 | 1 |
| 1988–89 | Northampton T | 39 | 1 |
| 1989–90 | Northampton T | 27 | 0 |
| 1990–91 | Northampton T | 44 | 3 |
| 1991–92 | Northampton T | 16 | 1 |
| 1991–92 | Halifax T | 23 | 5 |
| 1992–93 | Halifax T | 22 | 2 |
| 1992–93 | Burnley | 20 | 0 |
| 1993–94 | Burnley | 11 | 0 |
| 1994–95 | Burnley | 0 | 0 |
| 1994–95 | York C | 22 | 0 |
| 1995–96 | Scunthorpe U | 40 | 1 |
| 1996–97 | Scunthorpe U | 37 | 1 |
| 1996–97 | Cambridge U (loan) | 7 | 0 |
| 1997–98 | Cambridge U | 31 | 5 |
| **Total:** | | **369** | **20** |

## WILSON, Steve — Goalkeeper

H: 5 10 W: 10 12 b.Hull 24-4-74

*Source:* Trainee.

| | | | |
|---|---|---|---|
| 1990–91 | Hull C | 2 | 0 |
| 1991–92 | Hull C | 3 | 0 |
| 1992–93 | Hull C | 26 | 0 |
| 1993–94 | Hull C | 9 | 0 |
| 1994–95 | Hull C | 20 | 0 |
| 1995–96 | Hull C | 19 | 0 |
| 1996–97 | Hull C | 15 | 0 |
| 1997–98 | Hull C | 37 | 0 |
| **Total:** | | **131** | **0** |

## WILSON, Stevie — Goalkeeper

H: 6 0 W: 12 07 b.Leicester 28-11-78

*Source:* Trainee.

| | | | |
|---|---|---|---|
| 1997–98 | Leicester C | 0 | 0 |

## WILSON, Stuart — Midfield

H: 5 8 W: 9 12 b.Leicester 16-9-77

*Source:* Trainee.

| | | | |
|---|---|---|---|
| 1996–97 | Leicester C | 2 | 1 |
| 1997–98 | Leicester C | 11 | 2 |
| **Total:** | | **13** | **3** |

## WILSTERMAN, Brian — Defender

H: 6 1 W: 13 09 b.Surinam 19-11-66

*Source:* Beerschot.

| | | | |
|---|---|---|---|
| 1996–97 | Oxford U | 1 | 0 |
| 1997–98 | Oxford U | 24 | 0 |
| **Total:** | | **25** | **0** |

## WINDASS, Dean — Forward

H: 5 9 W: 12 03 b.Hull 1-4-69

*Source:* N Ferriby U.

| | | | |
|---|---|---|---|
| 1991–92 | Hull C | 32 | 6 |
| 1992–93 | Hull C | 41 | 7 |
| 1993–94 | Hull C | 43 | 23 |
| 1994–95 | Hull C | 44 | 17 |
| 1995–96 | Hull C | 16 | 4 |
| 1995–96 | Aberdeen | 20 | 6 |
| 1996–97 | Aberdeen | 29 | 10 |
| 1997–98 | Aberdeen | 24 | 5 |
| **Total:** | | **249** | **78** |

## WINROW, Brian — Defender

H: 5 9 W: 10 00 b.Oldham 19-5-79

*Source:* Trainee.

| | | | |
|---|---|---|---|
| 1997–98 | Bury | 0 | 0 |

## WINSTANLEY, Mark — Defender

H: 6 1 W: 12 08 b.St Helens 22-1-68

*Source:* Trainee.

| | | | |
|---|---|---|---|
| 1984–85 | Bolton W | 0 | 0 |
| 1985–86 | Bolton W | 3 | 0 |
| 1986–87 | Bolton W | 13 | 0 |
| 1987–88 | Bolton W | 8 | 1 |
| 1988–89 | Bolton W | 44 | 0 |
| 1989–90 | Bolton W | 43 | 1 |
| 1990–91 | Bolton W | 32 | 0 |
| 1991–92 | Bolton W | 27 | 0 |
| 1992–93 | Bolton W | 29 | 1 |
| 1993–94 | Bolton W | 21 | 0 |
| 1994–95 | Burnley | 44 | 2 |
| 1995–96 | Burnley | 45 | 3 |

## Winston, Sam

| | | | |
|---|---|---|---|
| 1996–97 | Burnley | 35 | 0 |
| 1997–98 | Burnley | 27 | 0 |
| **Total:** | | **371** | **8** |

## WINSTON, Sam — Forward

b.London 6-8-78

*Source:* Norwich C Trainee.

| | | | |
|---|---|---|---|
| 1996–97 | Leyton Orient | 11 | 1 |
| 1997–98 | Leyton Orient | 0 | 0 |
| **Total:** | | **11** | **1** |

## WINTERBURN, Nigel — Defender

H: 5 8 W: 11 04 b.Coventry 11-12-63

*Source:* Local. *Honours:* England Youth, Under-21, B, 2 full caps.

| | | | |
|---|---|---|---|
| 1981–82 | Birmingham C | 0 | 0 |
| 1982–83 | Birmingham C | 0 | 0 |
| 1983–84 | Oxford U | 0 | 0 |
| 1983–84 | Wimbledon | 43 | 1 |
| 1984–85 | Wimbledon | 41 | 4 |
| 1985–86 | Wimbledon | 39 | 1 |
| 1986–87 | Wimbledon | 42 | 2 |
| 1987–88 | Arsenal | 17 | 0 |
| 1988–89 | Arsenal | 38 | 3 |
| 1989–90 | Arsenal | 36 | 0 |
| 1990–91 | Arsenal | 38 | 0 |
| 1991–92 | Arsenal | 41 | 1 |
| 1992–93 | Arsenal | 29 | 1 |
| 1993–94 | Arsenal | 34 | 0 |
| 1994–95 | Arsenal | 39 | 0 |
| 1995–96 | Arsenal | 36 | 2 |
| 1996–97 | Arsenal | 38 | 0 |
| 1997–98 | Arsenal | 36 | 1 |
| **Total:** | | **547** | **16** |

## WINTERS, Kris — Midfield

b.Dundalk 28-8-79

*Source:* Trainee.

| | | | |
|---|---|---|---|
| 1996–97 | Nottingham F | 0 | 0 |
| 1997–98 | Nottingham F | 0 | 0 |
| 1997–98 | Manchester C | 0 | 0 |

## WINTERS, Robert — Forward

H: 5 10 W: 11 06 b.East Kilbride 4-11-74

*Source:* Muirend Amateur.

| | | | |
|---|---|---|---|
| 1993–94 | Dundee U | 0 | 0 |
| 1994–95 | Dundee U | 13 | 2 |
| 1995–96 | Dundee U | 35 | 7 |
| 1996–97 | Dundee U | 36 | 8 |
| 1997–98 | Dundee U | 30 | 8 |
| **Total:** | | **114** | **25** |

## WISE, Dennis — Forward

H: 5 6 W: 10 11 b.Kensington 16-12-66

*Source:* Southampton Apprentice. *Honours:* England Under-21, B, 12 full caps, 1 goal.

| | | | |
|---|---|---|---|
| 1984–85 | Wimbledon | 1 | 0 |
| 1985–86 | Wimbledon | 4 | 0 |
| 1986–87 | Wimbledon | 28 | 4 |
| 1987–88 | Wimbledon | 30 | 10 |
| 1988–89 | Wimbledon | 37 | 5 |
| 1989–90 | Wimbledon | 35 | 8 |
| 1990–91 | Chelsea | 33 | 10 |
| 1991–92 | Chelsea | 38 | 10 |
| 1992–93 | Chelsea | 27 | 3 |
| 1993–94 | Chelsea | 35 | 4 |
| 1994–95 | Chelsea | 19 | 6 |
| 1995–96 | Chelsea | 35 | 7 |
| 1996–97 | Chelsea | 31 | 3 |
| 1997–98 | Chelsea | 26 | 3 |
| **Total:** | | **379** | **73** |

## WITTER, Tony — Defender

H: 6 2 W: 13 02 b.London 12-8-65

*Source:* Grays Ath.

| | | | |
|---|---|---|---|
| 1990–91 | Crystal Palace | 0 | 0 |
| 1991–92 | QPR | 0 | 0 |
| 1991–92 | Millwall (loan) | 0 | 0 |
| 1991–92 | Plymouth Arg (loan) | 3 | 1 |
| 1992–93 | QPR | 0 | 0 |
| 1993–94 | QPR | 1 | 0 |
| 1993–94 | Reading (loan) | 4 | 0 |
| 1994–95 | QPR | 0 | 0 |
| 1994–95 | Millwall | 27 | 1 |
| 1995–96 | Millwall | 31 | 1 |
| 1996–97 | Millwall | 33 | 0 |
| 1997–98 | Millwall | 11 | 0 |
| **Total:** | | **110** | **3** |

## WOAN, Ian — Midfield

H: 5 10 W: 12 02 b.Wirrall 14-12-67

*Source:* Runcorn.

| | | | |
|---|---|---|---|
| 1989–90 | Nottingham F | 0 | 0 |
| 1990–91 | Nottingham F | 12 | 3 |
| 1991–92 | Nottingham F | 21 | 5 |
| 1992–93 | Nottingham F | 28 | 3 |
| 1993–94 | Nottingham F | 24 | 5 |
| 1994–95 | Nottingham F | 37 | 5 |
| 1995–96 | Nottingham F | 33 | 8 |
| 1996–97 | Nottingham F | 32 | 1 |
| 1997–98 | Nottingham F | 21 | 1 |
| **Total:** | | **208** | **31** |

## WOOD, Jamie — Forward

H: 5 10 W: 12 11 b.Salford 21-9-78

*Source:* Trainee.

| | | | |
|---|---|---|---|
| 1997–98 | Manchester U | 0 | 0 |

## WOOD, Scott — Midfield

H: 5 10 W: 11 11 b.Nottingham 16-11-79

*Source:* Trainee.

| | | | |
|---|---|---|---|
| 1996–97 | Nottingham F | 0 | 0 |
| 1997–98 | Nottingham F | 0 | 0 |

## WOOD, Steve — Midfield

H: 5 9 W: 10 10 b.Oldham 23-6-63

*Source:* Ashton U.

| | | | |
|---|---|---|---|
| 1997–98 | Macclesfield T | 43 | 13 |
| **Total:** | | **43** | **13** |

## WOODCOCK, Chris — Forward

H: 5 7 W: 10 08 b.Bradford 7-5-80

*Source:* Trainee.

| | | | |
|---|---|---|---|
| 1997–98 | Newcastle U | 0 | 0 |

## WOODFIELD, Craig — Midfield

b.Coventry 4-9-79

*Source:* Trainee.

| | | | |
|---|---|---|---|
| 1997–98 | Blackburn R | 0 | 0 |

## WOODGATE, Jonathan — Defender

b.Middlesbrough 22-1-80

*Source:* Trainee. *Honours:* England Youth.

| | | | |
|---|---|---|---|
| 1996–97 | Leeds U | 0 | 0 |
| 1997–98 | Leeds U | 0 | 0 |

## WOODHOUSE, Curtis — Midfield

H: 5 8 W: 11 00 b.Driffield 17-4-80

*Source:* Trainee.

| | | | |
|---|---|---|---|
| 1997–98 | Sheffield U | 9 | 0 |
| **Total:** | | **9** | **0** |

## WOODMAN, Andy — Goalkeeper

H: 6 3 W: 13 07 b.Camberwell 11-8-71

*Source:* Apprentice.

| | | | |
|---|---|---|---|
| 1989–90 | Crystal Palace | 0 | 0 |
| 1990–91 | Crystal Palace | 0 | 0 |
| 1991–92 | Crystal Palace | 0 | 0 |
| 1992–93 | Crystal Palace | 0 | 0 |
| 1993–94 | Crystal Palace | 0 | 0 |
| 1994–95 | Exeter C | 6 | 0 |
| 1994–95 | Northampton T | 10 | 0 |
| 1995–96 | Northampton T | 44 | 0 |
| 1996–97 | Northampton T | 45 | 0 |
| 1997–98 | Northampton T | 46 | 0 |
| **Total:** | | **151** | **0** |

## WOODS, Chris — Goalkeeper

H: 6 2 W: 14 12 b.Boston 14-11-59

*Source:* Apprentice. *Honours:* England Under-21, B, 43 full caps.

| | | | |
|---|---|---|---|
| 1976–77 | Nottingham F | 0 | 0 |
| 1977–78 | Nottingham F | 0 | 0 |
| 1978–79 | Nottingham F | 0 | 0 |
| 1979–80 | QPR | 41 | 0 |
| 1980–81 | QPR | 22 | 0 |
| 1980–81 | Norwich C (loan) | 10 | 0 |
| 1981–82 | Norwich C | 42 | 0 |
| 1982–83 | Norwich C | 42 | 0 |
| 1983–84 | Norwich C | 42 | 0 |
| 1984–85 | Norwich C | 38 | 0 |
| 1985–86 | Norwich C | 42 | 0 |
| 1986–87 | Rangers | 42 | 0 |
| 1987–88 | Rangers | 39 | 0 |
| 1988–89 | Rangers | 24 | 0 |
| 1989–90 | Rangers | 32 | 0 |
| 1990–91 | Rangers | 36 | 0 |
| 1991–92 | Sheffield W | 41 | 0 |
| 1992–93 | Sheffield W | 39 | 0 |
| 1993–94 | Sheffield W | 10 | 0 |
| 1994–95 | Sheffield W | 9 | 0 |
| 1995–96 | Sheffield W | 8 | 0 |
| 1995–96 | Reading (loan) | 5 | 0 |
| From Colorado Rapids. | | | |
| 1996–97 | Southampton | 4 | 0 |
| From USSF. | | | |
| 1996–97 | Sunderland | 0 | 0 |
| 1997–98 | Burnley | 12 | 0 |
| **Total:** | | **580** | **0** |

## WOODS, Mattie — Defender

H: 6 0 W: 12 13 b.Gosport 9-9-76

*Source:* Trainee.

| | | | |
|---|---|---|---|
| 1995–96 | Everton | 0 | 0 |
| 1996–97 | Chester C | 21 | 1 |
| 1997–98 | Chester C | 29 | 2 |
| **Total:** | | **50** | **3** |

## WOODS, Neil — Forward

H: 6 0 W: 13 00 b.York 30-7-66

*Source:* Apprentice.

| | | | |
|---|---|---|---|
| 1982–83 | Doncaster R | 4 | 0 |
| 1983–84 | Doncaster R | 7 | 1 |
| 1984–85 | Doncaster R | 6 | 2 |
| 1985–86 | Doncaster R | 30 | 7 |
| 1986–87 | Doncaster R | 18 | 6 |
| 1986–87 | Rangers | 3 | 0 |
| 1987–88 | Ipswich T | 19 | 4 |
| 1988–89 | Ipswich T | 1 | 0 |
| 1989–90 | Ipswich T | 7 | 1 |
| 1989–90 | Bradford C | 14 | 2 |
| 1990–91 | Bradford C | 0 | 0 |
| 1990–91 | Grimsby T | 44 | 12 |
| 1991–92 | Grimsby T | 37 | 8 |
| 1992–93 | Grimsby T | 30 | 4 |
| 1993–94 | Grimsby T | 11 | 0 |
| 1994–95 | Grimsby T | 37 | 14 |
| 1995–96 | Grimsby T | 33 | 3 |
| 1996–97 | Grimsby T | 24 | 1 |
| 1997–98 | Grimsby T | 10 | 0 |
| 1997–98 | Wigan Ath (loan) | 1 | 0 |
| 1997–98 | Scunthorpe U (loan) | 2 | 0 |
| 1997–98 | Mansfield T (loan) | 6 | 0 |
| **Total:** | | **344** | **65** |

## WOODS, Stephen — Defender

H: 5 11 W: 11 13 b.Davenham 15-12-76

*Source:* Trainee.

| | | | |
|---|---|---|---|
| 1995–96 | Stoke C | 0 | 0 |
| 1996–97 | Stoke C | 0 | 0 |
| 1997–98 | Stoke C | 1 | 0 |
| 1997–98 | Plymouth Arg (loan) | 5 | 0 |
| **Total:** | | **6** | **0** |

## WOODS, Stephen — Goalkeeper

H: 6 2 W: 12 00 b.Glasgow 23-2-70

*Source:* Kilpatrick BC.

| | | | |
|---|---|---|---|
| 1989–90 | Hibernian | 0 | 0 |
| 1990–91 | Hibernian | 0 | 0 |
| 1991–92 | Hibernian | 0 | 0 |
| 1991–92 | Clydebank | 5 | 0 |
| 1992–93 | Clydebank | 42 | 0 |
| 1993–94 | Preston NE | 20 | 0 |
| 1994–95 | Motherwell | 33 | 0 |
| 1995–96 | Motherwell | 0 | 0 |
| 1996–97 | Motherwell | 6 | 0 |
| 1997–98 | Motherwell | 35 | 0 |
| **Total:** | | **141** | **0** |

## WOODTHORPE, Colin — Defender

H: 5 11 W: 11 08 b.Ellesmere Pt 13-1-69

*Source:* Apprentice.

| | | | |
|---|---|---|---|
| 1986–87 | Chester C | 30 | 2 |
| 1987–88 | Chester C | 35 | 0 |
| 1988–89 | Chester C | 44 | 3 |
| 1989–90 | Chester C | 46 | 1 |
| 1990–91 | Norwich C | 1 | 0 |
| 1991–92 | Norwich C | 15 | 1 |
| 1992–93 | Norwich C | 7 | 0 |
| 1993–94 | Norwich C | 20 | 0 |
| 1994–95 | Aberdeen | 14 | 0 |
| 1995–96 | Aberdeen | 15 | 1 |
| 1996–97 | Aberdeen | 19 | 0 |
| 1997–98 | Stockport Co | 32 | 1 |
| **Total:** | | **278** | **9** |

## WOODWARD, Andy — Defender

H: 5 10 W: 10 12 b.Stockport 23-9-73

*Source:* Trainee.

| | | | |
|---|---|---|---|
| 1992–93 | Crewe Alex | 6 | 0 |
| 1993–94 | Crewe Alex | 12 | 0 |
| 1994–95 | Crewe Alex | 2 | 0 |
| 1994–95 | Bury | 8 | 0 |
| 1995–96 | Bury | 1 | 0 |
| 1996–97 | Bury | 23 | 0 |
| 1997–98 | Bury | 32 | 0 |
| **Total:** | | **84** | **0** |

## WOODWARD, Jonathan — Goalkeeper

b.Sheffield 16-6-79

*Source:* Trainee.

| | | | |
|---|---|---|---|
| 1997–98 | Sheffield W | 0 | 0 |

## WOOLISCROFT, Ashley — Defender

H: 5 10 W: 11 02 b.Stoke 28-12-79

*Source:* Trainee.

| | | | |
|---|---|---|---|
| 1996–97 | Stoke C | 0 | 0 |
| 1997–98 | Stoke C | 0 | 0 |

## WOOLSEY, Jeff — Defender

H: 5 11 W: 12 03 b.Upminster 8-11-77

*Source:* Trainee.

| | | | |
|---|---|---|---|
| 1995–96 | Arsenal | 0 | 0 |
| 1996–97 | Arsenal | 0 | 0 |
| 1997–98 | QPR | 0 | 0 |
| 1997–98 | Brighton & HA | 3 | 0 |
| **Total:** | | **3** | **0** |

## WOOZLEY, David — Defender

H: 6 0 W: 12 10 b.Berkshire 6-12-79

*Source:* Trainee.

| | | | |
|---|---|---|---|
| 1997–98 | Crystal Palace | 0 | 0 |

## WORDSWORTH, Dean — Forward

H: 6 2 W: 13 00 b.London 2-7-72

*Source:* Bromley.

| | | | |
|---|---|---|---|
| 1996–97 | Crystal Palace | 0 | 0 |
| 1997–98 | Crystal Palace | 0 | 0 |

## WORMULL, Simon — Midfield

H: 5 10 W: 12 03 b.Crawley 1-12-76

*Source:* Trainee.

| | | | |
|---|---|---|---|
| 1995–96 | Tottenham H | 0 | 0 |
| 1996–97 | Tottenham H | 0 | 0 |
| 1997–98 | Brentford | 5 | 0 |
| 1997–98 | Brighton & HA | 0 | 0 |
| **Total:** | | **5** | **0** |

## WORRALL, Ben — Midfield

H: 5 6 W: 11 06 b.Swindon 7-12-75

*Source:* Trainee. *Honours:* England Youth.

| | | | |
|---|---|---|---|
| 1994–95 | Swindon T | 3 | 0 |
| 1995–96 | Swindon T | 0 | 0 |
| 1996–97 | Scarborough | 15 | 1 |
| 1997–98 | Scarborough | 21 | 2 |
| **Total:** | | **39** | **3** |

## WORRELL, David — Defender

H: 6 0 W: 12 04 b.Dublin 12-1-78

*Source:* Trainee. *Honours:* Eire Youth.

| | | | |
|---|---|---|---|
| 1994–95 | Blackburn R | 0 | 0 |
| 1995–96 | Blackburn R | 0 | 0 |
| 1996–97 | Blackburn R | 0 | 0 |
| 1997–98 | Blackburn R | 0 | 0 |

## WORTHINGTON, Nigel — Defender

H: 5 11 W: 12 06 b.Ballymena 4-11-61

*Source:* Ballymena U. *Honours:* Northern Ireland Youth, 66 full caps.

| | | | |
|---|---|---|---|
| 1981–82 | Notts Co | 2 | 0 |
| 1982–83 | Notts Co | 41 | 3 |
| 1983–84 | Notts Co | 24 | 1 |
| 1983–84 | Sheffield W | 14 | 1 |
| 1984–85 | Sheffield W | 38 | 1 |
| 1985–86 | Sheffield W | 15 | 0 |
| 1986–87 | Sheffield W | 35 | 0 |
| 1987–88 | Sheffield W | 38 | 0 |
| 1988–89 | Sheffield W | 28 | 0 |
| 1989–90 | Sheffield W | 32 | 2 |
| 1990–91 | Sheffield W | 33 | 1 |
| 1991–92 | Sheffield W | 34 | 5 |
| 1992–93 | Sheffield W | 40 | 1 |
| 1993–94 | Sheffield W | 31 | 1 |
| 1994–95 | Leeds U | 27 | 1 |
| 1995–96 | Leeds U | 16 | 0 |
| 1996–97 | Stoke C | 12 | 0 |
| 1997–98 | Blackpool | 9 | 0 |
| **Total:** | | **469** | **17** |

## WOTTON, Paul — Midfield

H: 5 11 W: 11 08 b.Plymouth 17-8-77

*Source:* Trainee.

| | | | |
|---|---|---|---|
| 1994–95 | Plymouth Arg | 7 | 0 |
| 1995–96 | Plymouth Arg | 1 | 0 |
| 1996–97 | Plymouth Arg | 9 | 1 |
| 1997–98 | Plymouth Arg | 34 | 1 |
| **Total:** | | **51** | **2** |

## WRACK, Darren — Forward

H: 5 9 W: 12 07 b.Cleethorpes 5-5-76

*Source:* Trainee.

| | | | |
|---|---|---|---|
| 1994–95 | Derby Co | 16 | 1 |
| 1995–96 | Derby Co | 10 | 0 |
| 1996–97 | Grimsby T | 12 | 1 |
| 1996–97 | Shrewsbury T (loan) | 4 | 0 |
| 1997–98 | Grimsby T | 1 | 0 |
| **Total:** | | **43** | **2** |

## WRAIGHT, Gary — Midfield

H: 5 6 W: 11 07 b.Epping 5-3-79

*Source:* Trainee.

| | | | |
|---|---|---|---|
| 1997–98 | Wycombe W | 1 | 0 |
| **Total:** | | **1** | **0** |

## WRAY, Shaun — Forward

H: 6 1 W: 12 10 b.Dudley 14-3-78

*Source:* Trainee.

| | | | |
|---|---|---|---|
| 1995–96 | Shrewsbury T | 3 | 0 |
| 1996–97 | Shrewsbury T | 1 | 0 |
| 1997–98 | Shrewsbury T | 0 | 0 |
| **Total:** | | **4** | **0** |

## WREH, Christopher — Forward

H: 5 8 W: 11 13 b.Liberia 14-5-75

| | | | |
|---|---|---|---|
| 1995–96 | Monaco | 13 | 3 |
| 1996–97 | Guincamp | 33 | 10 |
| 1997–98 | Arsenal | 16 | 3 |
| **Total:** | | **62** | **16** |

## WRIGHT, Alan — Defender

H: 5 4 W: 9 09 b.Ashton-under-Lyme 28-9-71

*Source:* Trainee. *Honours:* England Schools, Youth, Under-21.

| | | | |
|---|---|---|---|
| 1987–88 | Blackpool | 1 | 0 |
| 1988–89 | Blackpool | 16 | 0 |
| 1989–90 | Blackpool | 24 | 0 |
| 1990–91 | Blackpool | 45 | 0 |
| 1991–92 | Blackpool | 12 | 0 |
| 1991–92 | Blackburn R | 33 | 1 |
| 1992–93 | Blackburn R | 24 | 0 |
| 1993–94 | Blackburn R | 12 | 0 |
| 1994–95 | Blackburn R | 5 | 0 |
| 1994–95 | Aston Villa | 8 | 0 |
| 1995–96 | Aston Villa | 38 | 2 |
| 1996–97 | Aston Villa | 38 | 1 |
| 1997–98 | Aston Villa | 37 | 0 |
| **Total:** | | **293** | **4** |

## WRIGHT, Andrew — Midfield

b.Leeds 21-10-78

*Source:* Trainee.

| | | | |
|---|---|---|---|
| 1995–96 | Leeds U | 0 | 0 |
| 1996–97 | Leeds U | 0 | 0 |
| 1997–98 | Leeds U | 0 | 0 |

## WRIGHT, Darren — Forward

H: 5 8 W: 11 00 b.Warrington 7-9-79

*Source:* Trainee.

| | | | |
|---|---|---|---|
| 1997–98 | Chester C | 5 | 0 |
| **Total:** | | **5** | **0** |

## WRIGHT, David — Defender

H: 5 11 W: 10 08 b.Warrington 1-5-80

*Source:* Trainee.

| | | | |
|---|---|---|---|
| 1997–98 | Crewe Alex | 3 | 0 |
| **Total:** | | **3** | **0** |

## WRIGHT, Ian — Forward

H: 5 9 W: 11 08 b.Woolwich 3-11-63

*Source:* Greenwich Bor. *Honours:* England B, 31 full caps, 9 goals.

| | | | |
|---|---|---|---|
| 1985–86 | Crystal Palace | 32 | 9 |
| 1986–87 | Crystal Palace | 38 | 8 |
| 1987–88 | Crystal Palace | 41 | 20 |
| 1988–89 | Crystal Palace | 42 | 24 |
| 1989–90 | Crystal Palace | 26 | 8 |
| 1990–91 | Crystal Palace | 38 | 15 |
| 1991–92 | Crystal Palace | 8 | 5 |
| 1991–92 | Arsenal | 30 | 24 |
| 1992–93 | Arsenal | 31 | 15 |
| 1993–94 | Arsenal | 39 | 23 |
| 1994–95 | Arsenal | 31 | 18 |
| 1995–96 | Arsenal | 31 | 15 |
| 1996–97 | Arsenal | 35 | 23 |
| 1997–98 | Arsenal | 24 | 10 |
| **Total:** | | **446** | **217** |

## WRIGHT, Ian — Defender

H: 6 1 W: 13 04 b.Lichfield 10-3-72

*Source:* Trainee.

| | | | |
|---|---|---|---|
| 1989–90 | Stoke C | 1 | 0 |
| 1990–91 | Stoke C | 1 | 0 |
| 1991–92 | Stoke C | 3 | 0 |
| 1992–93 | Stoke C | 1 | 0 |
| 1993–94 | Stoke C | 0 | 0 |
| 1993–94 | Bristol R | 29 | 0 |
| 1994–95 | Bristol R | 7 | 1 |
| 1995–96 | Bristol R | 18 | 0 |
| 1996–97 | Hull C | 40 | 0 |
| 1997–98 | Hull C | 33 | 2 |
| **Total:** | | **133** | **3** |

## WRIGHT, Jermaine — Midfield

H: 5 10 W: 11 09 b.Greenwich 21-10-75

*Source:* Trainee. *Honours:* England Youth.

| | | | |
|---|---|---|---|
| 1992–93 | Millwall | 0 | 0 |
| 1993–94 | Millwall | 0 | 0 |
| 1994–95 | Millwall | 0 | 0 |
| 1994–95 | Wolverhampton W | 6 | 0 |
| 1995–96 | Wolverhampton W | 7 | 0 |
| 1995–96 | Doncaster R (loan) | 13 | 0 |
| 1996–97 | Wolverhampton W | 3 | 0 |
| 1997–98 | Wolverhampton W | 4 | 0 |
| 1997–98 | Crewe Alex | 5 | 0 |
| **Total:** | | **38** | **0** |

## WRIGHT, Keith — Forward

H: 5 11 W: 11 00 b.Edinburgh 17-5-65

*Source:* Melbourne Th. *Honours:* Scotland 1 full cap.

| | | | |
|---|---|---|---|
| 1983–84 | Raith R | 37 | 5 |
| 1984–85 | Raith R | 38 | 22 |
| 1985–86 | Raith R | 39 | 21 |
| 1986–87 | Raith R | 17 | 13 |
| 1986–87 | Dundee | 20 | 10 |
| 1987–88 | Dundee | 42 | 15 |
| 1988–89 | Dundee | 35 | 8 |
| 1989–90 | Dundee | 34 | 11 |
| 1990–91 | Dundee | 36 | 18 |
| 1991–92 | Hibernian | 40 | 9 |
| 1992–93 | Hibernian | 42 | 11 |
| 1993–94 | Hibernian | 42 | 16 |
| 1994–95 | Hibernian | 19 | 10 |
| 1995–96 | Hibernian | 28 | 9 |
| 1996–97 | Hibernian | 26 | 4 |
| 1997–98 | Hibernian | 0 | 0 |
| **Total:** | | **495** | **182** |

## WRIGHT, Mark — Defender

H: 6 2 W: 13 03 b.Dorchester 1-8-63

*Source:* Amateur. *Honours:* England Under-21, 45 full caps, 1 goal.

| | | | |
|---|---|---|---|
| 1980–81 | Oxford U | 0 | 0 |
| 1981–82 | Oxford U | 10 | 0 |
| 1981–82 | Southampton | 3 | 0 |
| 1982–83 | Southampton | 39 | 2 |
| 1983–84 | Southampton | 29 | 1 |
| 1984–85 | Southampton | 36 | 0 |
| 1985–86 | Southampton | 33 | 3 |
| 1986–87 | Southampton | 30 | 1 |
| 1987–88 | Southampton | 0 | 0 |
| 1987–88 | Derby Co | 38 | 3 |
| 1988–89 | Derby Co | 33 | 1 |
| 1989–90 | Derby Co | 36 | 6 |
| 1990–91 | Derby Co | 37 | 0 |
| 1991–92 | Liverpool | 21 | 0 |
| 1992–93 | Liverpool | 33 | 2 |
| 1993–94 | Liverpool | 31 | 1 |
| 1994–95 | Liverpool | 6 | 0 |
| 1995–96 | Liverpool | 28 | 2 |
| 1996–97 | Liverpool | 33 | 0 |
| 1997–98 | Liverpool | 6 | 0 |
| **Total:** | | **482** | **22** |

## WRIGHT, Nick — Forward

H: 5 11 W: 11 02 b.Derby 15-10-75

*Source:* Trainee.

| | | | |
|---|---|---|---|
| 1994–95 | Derby Co | 0 | 0 |
| 1995–96 | Derby Co | 0 | 0 |
| 1996–97 | Derby Co | 0 | 0 |
| 1997–98 | Derby Co | 0 | 0 |
| 1997–98 | Carlisle U | 25 | 5 |
| **Total:** | | **25** | **5** |

## WRIGHT, Paul — Forward

H: 5 8 W: 10 08 b.East Kilbride 17-8-67

*Source:* 'S' Form. *Honours:* Scotland Youth, Under-21, B.

| | | | |
|---|---|---|---|
| 1983–84 | Aberdeen | 1 | 0 |
| 1984–85 | Aberdeen | 0 | 0 |
| 1985–86 | Aberdeen | 10 | 2 |
| 1986–87 | Aberdeen | 25 | 4 |
| 1987–88 | Aberdeen | 9 | 4 |
| 1988–89 | Aberdeen | 23 | 6 |
| 1989–90 | QPR | 15 | 5 |
| 1989–90 | Hibernian | 3 | 1 |
| 1990–91 | Hibernian | 33 | 6 |
| 1991–92 | St Johnstone | 41 | 18 |
| 1992–93 | St Johnstone | 42 | 14 |
| 1993–94 | St Johnstone | 17 | 7 |
| 1994–95 | St Johnstone | 12 | 1 |
| 1994–95 | Kilmarnock | 7 | 1 |
| 1995–96 | Kilmarnock | 36 | 13 |
| 1996–97 | Kilmarnock | 31 | 14 |
| 1997–98 | Kilmarnock | 28 | 10 |
| **Total:** | | **333** | **106** |

## WRIGHT, Richard — Goalkeeper

H: 6 2 W: 13 00 b.Ipswich 5-11-77

*Source:* Trainee. *Honours:* England Schools, Youth, Under-21.

| | | | |
|---|---|---|---|
| 1994–95 | Ipswich T | 3 | 0 |
| 1995–96 | Ipswich T | 23 | 0 |
| 1996–97 | Ipswich T | 40 | 0 |
| 1997–98 | Ipswich T | 46 | 0 |
| **Total:** | | **112** | **0** |

## WRIGHT, Stephen — Defender

H: 5 8 W: 12 02 b.Bellshill 27-8-71

*Source:* Aberdeen Lads. *Honours:* Scotland Under-21, 2 full caps.

| | | | |
|---|---|---|---|
| 1987–88 | Aberdeen | 0 | 0 |
| 1988–89 | Aberdeen | 0 | 0 |
| 1989–90 | Aberdeen | 1 | 0 |
| 1990–91 | Aberdeen | 17 | 1 |
| 1991–92 | Aberdeen | 23 | 0 |
| 1992–93 | Aberdeen | 36 | 0 |
| 1993–94 | Aberdeen | 36 | 0 |
| 1994–95 | Aberdeen | 34 | 1 |
| 1995–96 | Rangers | 6 | 0 |

| | | | |
|---|---|---|---|
| 1996–97 | Rangers | 1 | 0 |
| 1997–98 | Rangers | 0 | 0 |
| 1997–98 | Wolverhampton W (loan) | 3 | 0 |
| **Total:** | | **157** | **2** |

## WRIGHT, Stephen — Defender

b.Liverpool 8-2-80

*Source:* Trainee.

| | | | |
|---|---|---|---|
| 1997–98 | Liverpool | 0 | 0 |

## WRIGHT, Tommy — Forward

H: 5 7 W: 11 05 b.Dunfermline 10-1-66

*Source:* Apprentice. *Honours:* Scotland Under-21.

| | | | |
|---|---|---|---|
| 1982–83 | Leeds U | 4 | 1 |
| 1983–84 | Leeds U | 25 | 8 |
| 1984–85 | Leeds U | 42 | 14 |
| 1985–86 | Leeds U | 10 | 1 |
| 1986–87 | Leeds U | 0 | 0 |
| 1986–87 | Oldham Ath | 28 | 7 |
| 1987–88 | Oldham Ath | 41 | 9 |
| 1988–89 | Oldham Ath | 43 | 7 |
| 1989–90 | Leicester C | 41 | 3 |
| 1990–91 | Leicester C | 44 | 7 |
| 1991–92 | Leicester C | 44 | 12 |
| 1992–93 | Middlesbrough | 36 | 5 |
| 1993–94 | Middlesbrough | 16 | 0 |
| 1994–95 | Middlesbrough | 1 | 0 |
| 1995–96 | Bradford C | 34 | 4 |
| 1996–97 | Bradford C | 11 | 1 |
| 1997–98 | Oldham Ath | 12 | 2 |
| 1997–98 | St Johnstone | 5 | 0 |
| **Total:** | | **437** | **81** |

## WRIGHT, Tommy — Goalkeeper

H: 6 1 W: 14 05 b.Belfast 29-8-63

*Source:* Linfield. *Honours:* Northern Ireland 29 full caps. Football League.

| | | | |
|---|---|---|---|
| 1987–88 | Newcastle U | 0 | 0 |
| 1988–89 | Newcastle U | 9 | 0 |
| 1989–90 | Newcastle U | 14 | 0 |
| 1990–91 | Newcastle U | 0 | 0 |
| 1990–91 | Hull C (loan) | 6 | 0 |
| 1991–92 | Newcastle U | 33 | 0 |
| 1992–93 | Newcastle U | 14 | 0 |
| 1993–94 | Newcastle U | 3 | 0 |
| 1993–94 | Nottingham F | 10 | 0 |
| 1994–95 | Nottingham F | 0 | 0 |
| 1995–96 | Nottingham F | 0 | 0 |
| 1996–97 | Nottingham F | 1 | 0 |
| 1996–97 | Reading (loan) | 17 | 0 |
| 1996–97 | Manchester C | 13 | 0 |
| 1997–98 | Manchester C | 18 | 0 |
| **Total:** | | **138** | **0** |

## WRIGHT, Tony — Midfield

H: 5 7 W: 10 11 b.Swansea 1-9-79

*Source:* Trainee. *Honours:* Wales Under-21.

| | | | |
|---|---|---|---|
| 1997–98 | Oxford U | 1 | 0 |
| **Total:** | | **1** | **0** |

## XAUSA, Davide — Forward

b.Vancouver 10-3-76

*Source:* Univ of Portland. *Honours:*

| | | | |
|---|---|---|---|
| 1997–98 | Port Vale | 0 | 0 |
| 1997–98 | Stoke C | 1 | 0 |
| 1997–98 | St Johnstone | 1 | 0 |
| **Total:** | | **2** | **0** |

## XIOUROUPPA, Costas — Forward

b.Dudley 11-9-79

*Source:* Trainee.

| | | | |
|---|---|---|---|
| 1996–97 | Bolton W | 0 | 0 |
| 1997–98 | Bolton W | 0 | 0 |

## YATES, Dean — Defender

H: 6 1 W: 12 08 b.Leicester 26-10-67

*Source:* Apprentice. *Honours:* England Under-21.

| | | | |
|---|---|---|---|
| 1984–85 | Notts Co | 8 | 0 |
| 1985–86 | Notts Co | 44 | 4 |
| 1986–87 | Notts Co | 42 | 9 |
| 1987–88 | Notts Co | 46 | 2 |
| 1988–89 | Notts Co | 41 | 6 |
| 1989–90 | Notts Co | 45 | 6 |
| 1990–91 | Notts Co | 41 | 4 |
| 1991–92 | Notts Co | 25 | 2 |
| 1992–93 | Notts Co | 0 | 0 |
| 1993–94 | Notts Co | 1 | 0 |
| 1994–95 | Notts Co | 21 | 0 |
| 1994–95 | Derby Co | 11 | 1 |
| 1995–96 | Derby Co | 38 | 2 |
| 1996–97 | Derby Co | 10 | 0 |
| 1997–98 | Derby Co | 9 | 0 |
| **Total:** | | **382** | **36** |

## YATES, Steve — Defender

H: 5 10 W: 12 02 b.Bristol 29-1-70

*Source:* Trainee.

| | | | |
|---|---|---|---|
| 1986–87 | Bristol R | 2 | 0 |
| 1987–88 | Bristol R | 0 | 0 |
| 1988–89 | Bristol R | 35 | 0 |
| 1989–90 | Bristol R | 42 | 0 |
| 1990–91 | Bristol R | 34 | 0 |
| 1991–92 | Bristol R | 39 | 0 |
| 1992–93 | Bristol R | 44 | 0 |

| | | | |
|---|---|---|---|
| 1993–94 | Bristol R | 1 | 0 |
| 1993–94 | QPR | 29 | 0 |
| 1994–95 | QPR | 23 | 1 |
| 1995–96 | QPR | 30 | 0 |
| 1996–97 | QPR | 16 | 1 |
| 1997–98 | QPR | 30 | 0 |
| **Total:** | | **325** | **2** |

## YEBOAH, Tony — Forward

H: 5 11 W: 13 13 b.Kumasi 6-6-66

*Source:* Corner Stores, Okwawu U. *Honours:* Ghana 25 full caps.

| | | | |
|---|---|---|---|
| 1988–89 | Saarbrucken | 28 | 9 |
| 1989–90 | Saarbrucken | 37 | 17 |
| 1990–91 | Eintracht Frankfurt | 26 | 8 |
| 1991–92 | Eintracht Frankfurt | 34 | 15 |
| 1992–93 | Eintracht Frankfurt | 27 | 20 |
| 1993–94 | Eintracht Frankfurt | 22 | 18 |
| 1994–95 | Eintracht Frankfurt | 14 | 7 |
| 1994–95 | Leeds U | 18 | 12 |
| 1995–96 | Leeds U | 22 | 12 |
| 1996–97 | Leeds U | 7 | 0 |
| 1997–98 | Leeds U | 0 | 0 |
| **Total:** | | **235** | **118** |

## YORKE-ROBINSON, David — Forward

b.Ratcliffe 21-12-79

*Source:* Trainee.

| | | | |
|---|---|---|---|
| 1997–98 | Oldham Ath | 0 | 0 |

## YORKE, Dwight — Forward

H: 5 9 W: 12 03 b.Tobago 3-11-71

*Source:* St Clair's, Tobago. *Honours:* Trinidad & Tobago 10 full caps.

| | | | |
|---|---|---|---|
| 1989–90 | Aston Villa | 2 | 0 |
| 1990–91 | Aston Villa | 18 | 2 |
| 1991–92 | Aston Villa | 32 | 11 |
| 1992–93 | Aston Villa | 27 | 6 |
| 1993–94 | Aston Villa | 12 | 2 |
| 1994–95 | Aston Villa | 37 | 6 |
| 1995–96 | Aston Villa | 35 | 17 |
| 1996–97 | Aston Villa | 37 | 17 |
| 1997–98 | Aston Villa | 30 | 12 |
| **Total:** | | **230** | **73** |

## YOUDS, Eddie — Defender

H: 6 3 W: 14 00 b.Liverpool 3-5-70

*Source:* Trainee.

| | | | |
|---|---|---|---|
| 1988–89 | Everton | 0 | 0 |
| 1989–90 | Everton | 0 | 0 |
| 1989–90 | Cardiff C (loan) | 1 | 0 |
| 1989–90 | Wrexham (loan) | 20 | 2 |
| 1990–91 | Everton | 8 | 0 |
| 1991–92 | Everton | 0 | 0 |
| 1991–92 | Ipswich T | 1 | 0 |
| 1992–93 | Ipswich T | 16 | 0 |
| 1993–94 | Ipswich T | 23 | 1 |
| 1994–95 | Ipswich T | 10 | 0 |
| 1994–95 | Bradford C | 17 | 3 |
| 1995–96 | Bradford C | 30 | 4 |
| 1996–97 | Bradford C | 0 | 0 |
| 1997–98 | Bradford C | 38 | 1 |
| 1997–98 | Charlton Ath | 8 | 0 |
| **Total:** | | **172** | **11** |

## YOUNG, Darren — Forward

H: 5 8 W: 10 03 b.Glasgow 13-10-78

*Source:* Crombie Sports. *Honours:* Scotland Under-17, Under-21.

| | | | |
|---|---|---|---|
| 1995–96 | Aberdeen | 0 | 0 |
| 1996–97 | Aberdeen | 26 | 1 |
| 1997–98 | Aberdeen | 5 | 0 |
| **Total:** | | **31** | **1** |

## YOUNG, Luke — Midfield

b.Harlow 19-7-79

*Source:* Trainee. *Honours:* England Youth.

| | | | |
|---|---|---|---|
| 1997–98 | Tottenham H | 0 | 0 |

## YOUNG, Neil — Defender

H: 5 9 W: 12 00 b.Harlow 31-8-73

*Source:* Trainee.

| | | | |
|---|---|---|---|
| 1991–92 | Tottenham H | 0 | 0 |
| 1992–93 | Tottenham H | 0 | 0 |
| 1993–94 | Tottenham H | 0 | 0 |
| 1994–95 | Bournemouth | 32 | 0 |
| 1995–96 | Bournemouth | 41 | 0 |
| 1996–97 | Bournemouth | 44 | 0 |
| 1997–98 | Bournemouth | 44 | 2 |
| **Total:** | | **161** | **2** |

## YOUNG, Scott — Midfield

H: 6 1 W: 12 00 b.Tonypandy 14-1-76

*Source:* Trainee. *Honours:* Wales Under-21.

| | | | |
|---|---|---|---|
| 1993–94 | Cardiff C | 6 | 0 |
| 1994–95 | Cardiff C | 22 | 0 |
| 1995–96 | Cardiff C | 41 | 0 |
| 1996–97 | Cardiff C | 32 | 1 |
| 1997–98 | Cardiff C | 31 | 3 |
| **Total:** | | **132** | **4** |

## YOUNGS, Tom — Forward

H: 5 8 W: 10 08 b.Bury St Edmunds 31-8-79

*Source:* Trainee.

| | | | |
|---|---|---|---|
| 1997–98 | Cambridge U | 4 | 0 |
| **Total:** | | **4** | **0** |

## ZABEK, Lee — Midfield

H: 6 0 W: 12 00 b.Bristol 13-10-78

*Source:* Trainee.

| | | | |
|---|---|---|---|
| 1996–97 | Bristol R | 1 | 0 |
| 1997–98 | Bristol R | 13 | 1 |
| **Total:** | | **14** | **1** |

## ZABICA, Robert — Goalkeeper

H: 6 2 W: 13 01 b.Perth 9-4-64

*Source:* Spearwood.

| | | | |
|---|---|---|---|
| 1997–98 | Bradford C | 3 | 0 |
| **Total:** | | **3** | **0** |

## ZAGORAKIS, Theo — Midfield

H: 5 9 W: 11 08 b.Kavala 27-10-71

*Source:* PAOK Salonika. *Honours:* Greece 33 full caps.

| | | | |
|---|---|---|---|
| 1997–98 | Leicester C | 14 | 1 |
| **Total:** | | **14** | **1** |

## ZETTERLUND, Lars — Midfield

H: 6 2 W: 11 13 b.HÑrnîsand, Sweden 11-2-64

| | | | |
|---|---|---|---|
| 1987 | IFK Gothenburg | 18 | 1 |
| 1988 | IFK Gothenburg | 22 | 5 |
| 1989 | IFK Gothenburg | 13 | 1 |
| 1990 | Orebro | 24 | 2 |
| 1991 | Orebro | 10 | 0 |
| 1992 | Orebro | 1 | 0 |
| 1993 | Orebro | 26 | 1 |
| 1994 | Orebro | 26 | 2 |
| 1995 | Orebro | 24 | 2 |
| 1996 | Orebro | 26 | 4 |
| 1996–97 | Dundee U | 25 | 1 |
| 1997–98 | Dundee U | 33 | 2 |
| **Total:** | | **248** | **21** |

## ZOETEBIER, Edwin — Goalkeeper

b.Purnerend 7-5-70

| | | | |
|---|---|---|---|
| 1997–98 | Sunderland | 0 | 0 |

## ZOHAR, Itzhak — Midfield

H: 6 1 W: 12 08 b.Tel Aviv 31-10-70

*Source:* Antwerp. *Honours:* Israel 29 full caps, 9 goals.

| | | | |
|---|---|---|---|
| 1997–98 | Crystal Palace | 6 | 0 |
| **Total:** | | **6** | **0** |

## ZOIS, Peter — Goalkeeper

b.Australia 21-4-78

| | | | |
|---|---|---|---|
| 1997–98 | Cardiff C | 1 | 0 |
| **Total:** | | **1** | **0** |

## ZOLA, Gianfranco — Forward

H: 5 6 W: 10 10 b.Oliena 5-7-66

*Honours:* Italy 34 full caps, 9 goals.

| | | | |
|---|---|---|---|
| 1984–85 | Nuorese | 4 | 0 |
| 1985–86 | Nuorese | 27 | 10 |
| 1986–87 | Torres | 30 | 8 |
| 1987–88 | Torres | 24 | 2 |
| 1988–89 | Torres | 34 | 11 |
| 1989–90 | Napoli | 18 | 2 |
| 1990–91 | Napoli | 20 | 6 |
| 1991–92 | Napoli | 34 | 12 |
| 1992–93 | Napoli | 33 | 12 |
| 1993–94 | Parma | 33 | 18 |
| 1994–95 | Parma | 32 | 19 |
| 1995–96 | Parma | 29 | 10 |
| 1996–97 | Parma | 8 | 2 |
| 1996–97 | Chelsea | 23 | 8 |
| 1997–98 | Chelsea | 27 | 8 |
| **Total:** | | **376** | **128** |

## STOP PRESS

Summer transfers included the following:
Ade Akinbiyi, Gillingham to Bristol C; David Amsalem, Beitar Jerusalem to Crystal Palace; Dean Austin, Tottenham H to Crystal Palace; Ian Brightwell, Manchester C to Coventry C; Mohamed Berthe, West Ham to Bournemouth; Ademola Bankole, Crewe Alex to QPR; James Beattie, Blackburn R to Southampton; Mark Blake, Fulham to Cannes; Gary Brady, Tottenham H to Newcastle U; David Bardsley, QPR to Blackpool; Roger Boli, Walsall to Dundee U; Paul Butler, Bury to Sunderland; Pierluigi Casiraghi, Lazio to Chelsea; Laurent Charvet, Cannes to Newcastle U; Horacio Angel Carbonari, Rosario Central to Derby Co; Jim Corbett, Gillingham to Blackburn R; Jean-Claude Darcheville, Rennes to Nottingham F; Kevin Davies, Southampton to Blackburn R; Sean Dundee, Karlsruhe to Liverpool; Marcel Desailly, AC Milan to Chelsea; Dwayne Darby, Hull C to Notts Co; Tony Daley, Wolverhampton W to Watford; Albert Ferrer, Barcelona to Chelsea; Stephane Guivarc'h, Auxerre to Newcastle U; Jimmy Glass, Bournemouth to Swindon T; Danny Granville, Chelsea to Leeds U; Dean Gordon, Crystal Palace to Middlesbrough; Ricardo Gardener, Harbour View to Bolton W; Danny Hill, Tottenham H to Oxford U; Shaka Hislop, Newcastle U to West Ham U; David Howells, Tottenham H to Southampton; Mark Hughes, Chelsea to Southampton; Carl Hutchings, Brentford to Bristol C; Rodney Jack, Torquay U to Crewe Alex; Claus Jensen, Lyngby to Bolton W; Georgi Kinkladze, Manchester C to Ajax; Nikos Kyzeridis, Paniliakos to Portsmouth; Andrei Kanchelskis, Fiorentina to Rangers; Brian Laudrup, Rangers to Chelsea; Stuart McCall, Rangers to Bradford C; Scott Marshall, Arsenal to Southampton; Graeme Murty, York C to Reading; Marco Materazzi, Perugia to Everton; Viorel Moldovan, Coventry C to Fenerbahce; Brian McClair, Manchester U to Motherwell; Lionel Perez, Sunderland to Newcastle U; Chris

Powell, Derby Co to Charlton Ath; Sebastien Perez, Bastia to Blackburn R; Darren Peacock, Newcastle U to Blackburn R; Gary Pallister, Manchester U to Middlesbrough; Martin Paul, Kings Lynn to Southampton; Mark Pembridge, Sheffield W to Benfica; Neil Redfearn, Barnsley to Charlton Ath; Stuart Ripley, Blackburn R to Southampton; Mark Reilly, Kilmarnock to Reading; Japp Stam, Ajax to Manchester U; John Salako, Bolton W to Fulham; Steve Staunton, Aston Villa to Liverpool; Thomas Sorensen, Odense to Sunderland; Masa Sarr, Hajduk Split to Reading; Liazid Sandjak, Neuchatel Xamax to Portsmouth; Mathias Svensson, Portsmouth to Innsbruck; Carl Serrant, Oldham Ath to Newcastle U; Bob Taylor, WBA to Bolton W; Paolo Tramezzani, Piacenza to Tottenham H; Alan Thompson, Bolton W to Aston Villa; Tony Thorpe, Fulham to Bristol C; Gerry Taggart, Bolton W to Leicester C; John Dahl Tomasson, Newcastle U to Feyenoord; Michael Thomas, Liverpool to Benfica; Nico Vasen, Aalst to Huddersfield T; Robin Van der Laan, Derby Co to Barnsley; Ian Wright, Arsenal to West Ham U; Rod Wallace, Leeds U to Rangers; Dean Windass, Aberdeen to Oxford U; Clyde Wijnhard, Willem II to Leeds U.

---

The Football League welcome Halifax Town, whose appearances and goals in the Vauxhall Conference for the 1997–98 season were as follows:–

**Conference Appearances:** Boardman, C. 4; Bradshaw, M. 42; Brook, G. 18(4); Brown, J. 37; Griffiths, W. 0(2); Hanson, D. 6(5); Horner, N. 10(8); Horsfield, G. 40; Hulme, K. 30; Hurst, C. 2(1); Jackson, P. 8; Kilcline, B. 23(1); Kiwomya, A. 0(5); Lyons, D. 13(11); Martin, L. 32; Midwood, M. 5; Morgan, P. 1; Murphy, J. 27(1); O'Regan, K. 36(1); Paterson, J. 36; Philliskirk, T. 4; Place, D. 0(1); Rhodes, A. 8; Stoneman, P. 38; Thackeray, A. 41; Woods, A. 1.

**Goals (74):** Bradshaw 5, Brook 3, Hanson 2, Horsfield 30, Hulme 7, Kilcline 2, Lyons 3, O'Regan 1, Paterson 14, Philliskirk 2, Stoneman 2, Thackeray 2, OG 1.